Visser's Annotated European Patent Convention

Visser's Annotated European Patent Convention

2018 Edition

updated till 15.11.2018

Derk Visser
Laurence Lai
Peter de Lange
Kaisa Suominen

Wolters Kluwer

Published by:
Kluwer Law International B.V.
PO Box 316
2400 AH Alphen aan den Rijn
The Netherlands
E-mail: international-sales@wolterskluwer.com
Website: lrus.wolterskluwer.com

Sold and distributed in North, Central and South America by:
Wolters Kluwer Legal & Regulatory U.S.
7201 McKinney Circle
Frederick, MD 21704
United States of America
Email: customer.service@wolterskluwer.com

Sold and distributed in all other countries by:
Air Business Subscriptions
Rockwood House
Haywards Heath
West Sussex
RH16 3DH
United Kingdom
Email: international-customerservice@wolterskluwer.com

Printed on acid-free paper.

ISBN 978-94-035-0674-6

e-Book: ISBN 978-94-035-0675-3
web-PDF: ISBN 978-94-035-0680-7

Printed in The Netherlands.

Introduction

The *Annotated European Patent Convention* reproduces the complete text of the European Patent Convention, the Implementing Regulations, two Protocols and the Rules relating to Fees in the form in which they are in force on 15 November 2018.

The notes to each individual article and rule of the Convention provide a commentary on the text of the law, explaining the interpretation of each paragraph. The notes give a short indication of important issues having a bearing on the interpretation of the law. They include references to case law up to 15 November 2018 and the Guidelines for Examination in the European Patent Office, edition November 2018. The notes give the transitional provisions from the EPC 1973 to the EPC 2000 where they are still relevant. The reader is referred to the 14th edition of this book for provisions of the EPC 1973 which may still be applicable to specific cases; the EPC 1973 is not included in this book.

The book is intended as a reference book, providing a quick grasp of the essentials of the law both for the patent attorney and the trainee. The detail in the notes reflects the detail required for daily practice and for answering questions posed in the European Qualifying Examinations of the last few years. Note, that the complete text of the Arrangement for Deposit Accounts and the Arrangements for Automatic Debiting is not included in the book; however, the notes to Rfees 5 give a summary. Trainees preparing for the examinations should note, that they must know the law and its interpretation on 31 October of the year prior to the examination (OJ 2017 A88).

Cross-references in the notes to articles and rules aim at giving an insight into the structure of the Convention. The abbreviation 'EPC' is only added to a reference where its absence could cause confusion. Cross-references from provisions in the EPC 2000 to the EPC 1973 provide quick access to the text of the old provisions. A cross-reference table links the EPC 1973 provisions to those of the EPC 2000.

Numerous references to case law and the November 2018 edition of the Guidelines allow the user to consult the sources of the information contained in the notes and give a quick access to important case law. The notes do not provide all possible references to the Guidelines but mainly those where the Guidelines are the main or only source of information and where they emphasise that case law is being followed by the departments of first instance. References in the notes to the EPC and case law have been highlighted to facilitate looking up the references.

The book includes a separate chapter on the PCT, which gives an overview of the PCT procedure as in force on 15 November 2018. The relation between the PCT and the EPC is given by numerous references.

The closing sections of the Annotated EPC consist of summaries of articles and rules of various law texts relevant for the EPC, included for easy reference.

A case law table provides a cross-reference between decisions of the boards of appeal and paragraphs of the book.

In spite of all due care taken during the compilation of the notes, the authors do not accept any responsibility for errors. The publisher wishes to express its gratitude to readers who provided comments, in particular Anette Hegner, Cees Mulder, Marko Prah and Wouter Rogiest. Any comments on inaccuracies or suggestions for improvement are welcomed. Please send them to Mrs A. Kramer at anja.kramer@wolterskluwer.com.

Haarlem, 15 November 2018

Contributors

The Annotated European Patent Convention was founded by Derk Visser, who updated the work annually up to and including the 25th edition, published in 2017. The title for the new, present edition is Visser's Annotated European Patent Convention 2018 Edition.

Contributors to the 2018 edition

Derk Visser, MSc, PhD, European and Dutch patent attorney at Visser-Tel Consultancy	Art. 1-51, 75-86, 113-118, 124-141, 164-178 and general editor
Laurence Lai, MEng, European and British patent attorney at Simmons & Simmons LLP	Art. 52-57
Peter de Lange, LLM, MSc, European and Dutch patent attorney at V.O. Patents & Trademarks	Art. 99-112a, 142-153, Rfees, Notes to PCT
Kaisa Suominen, MSc, European and Finnish patent attorney at Moosedog Oy	Art. 58-74, 87-98, 119-123

Revision note

A vertical line in the right-hand margin of a page indicates text amended or newly introduced on account of publications in the Official Journal of the EPO and on the EPO website as from November 2017.

The following important amendments have been made since November 2017:

- Safeguard against outages of electronic communication (R.134(1):2, 3)
- Decision G1/16 of the Enlarged Board of Appeal on undisclosed disclaimers (Art.123(2):2.4.4)
- New referral G1/18 to the Enlarged Board of Appeal on appeal deemed not filed or inadmissible (Art.108:4)
- Patentability of presentation of information, mathematical methods, mental acts, and rules for playing games (Art.52(2):3, 5, 7, 9)
- Unity of invention (R.44(1):1, 2)
- Amendments in the November 2018 edition of the Guidelines for Examination in the EPO

Note for EQE candidates

The legal status cut-off date for the European Qualifying Examination is 31 October of the year preceding the examination (OJ 2017 A88). Accordingly, the legal cut-off date for the 2019 pre-examination and main examination is 31.10.2018.

The 2018 Guidelines for Examination in the EPO came into force on 01.11.2018, meaning that candidates of the EQE 2019 are expected to refer to the 2017 Guidelines, which were in force at 31.10.2018.

In this book, references to the current Guidelines are in the form "C-IX,1.6" to denote part C, chapter IX, paragraph 1.6. Where paragraphs of the Guidelines have been re-numbered, the notation is given as "F-V,2.2.2.2; GL2017 F-V,5", providing both the current and former numbering. A reference to a completely new paragraph of the Guidelines has the format "G-II,3.3.1; not in GL2017".

Notation

The book uses the following abbreviations for terms and references. A reference placed before a full stop at the end of a sentence refers only to that sentence; a reference placed after the last full stop of a paragraph refers to the entire paragraph.

AAD.4	Point 4 of the Arrangements for the Automatic Debiting procedure; see Rfees5(2):3
Art.14(2):3 EPC	Article 14, paragraph 2 of the EPC, note 3
ADA.6	Point 6 of the Arrangements for Deposit Accounts; see Rfees5(2):2
AG-IP §243	PCT Applicant's Guide, International phase, paragraph 243
AG-IP Annex X(YY)	PCT Applicant's Guide, X= B: general information on PCT offices C: receiving offices D: international searching authorities E: international preliminary examining authorities YY= two-letter code of country or of intergovernmental organization
AG-NP §15	PCT Applicant's Guide, National phase, paragraph 15
Art.2 PCT	Article 2 of the PCT
A-X,7.5.5	Guidelines for Examination in the European Patent Office, part A, chapter X, paragraph 7.5.5
CA/65/17	Document 65 of 2017 of the Administrative Council; see EPO website
CA/PL 17/06	Explanatory remarks of the EPO to amendments of the Implementing Regulations EPC 2000, dated 07.08.2006
CA/PL 29/06	Explanatory remarks of the EPO to amendments of the Implementing Regulations EPC 2000, document Add. 1 dated 27.10.2006
Case Law of the BoA	Case Law of the Boards of Appeal of the EPO, 7th edition
Dec. of Pres.	Decision of the President of the EPO
D1/92	Decision of the Disciplinary Board of Appeal
Empel	The Granting of European Patents, M. van Empel (Sijthoff, Leiden 1975)
EPC 2000	European Patent Convention as revised by the diplomatic conference of November 2000
G1/93 hn1, r.16	Decision of the Enlarged Board of Appeal number 1 of the year 1993, Headnote 1 and point 16 of the Reasons for the Decision
Euro-PCT Guide §513	EPO publication: 'Euro-PCT Guide' (11th ed.), §513. Previously 'How to get, part 2'.
J27/94	Decision of the Legal Board of appeal
MR/2/00	Explanatory remarks of the EPO to amendments of the Articles of the Convention as proposed to the Diplomatic Conference, document dated 13.10.2000
MR/24/00	Discussion of the Diplomatic Conference of 20 to 29 November 2000, document of 15.07.2003

NatLaw	National law relating to the EPC, information brochure of the EPO
Not. of EPO	Notice of the EPO
OJ 1995, 9	Official Journal of the European Patent Office, year 1995, page 9 (until December 2013)
OJ 2007 se4	Official Journal of the European Patent Office, year 2007, special edition 4
OJ 2014 A12	Official Journal of the European Patent Office, year 2014, article 12 (as from January 2014)
OJ 2014 sp4	Official Journal of the European Patent Office, year 2014, Supplementary Publication 4
P:4.2	Preamble of the EPC, note 4.2
PCT §2.1	Paragraph 2.1 of the Chapter on PCT in this book
RPBoA	Rules of Procedure of the Boards of Appeal (see R.12c(2))
RPEBoA	Rules of Procedure of the Enlarged Board of Appeal (see R.13(2))
R1/08	Decision of the Enlarged Board of Appeal on a request for Revision under Art.112a
Rfees2	Article 2 of the Rules relating to Fees
R.88 EPC	Rule 88 of the EPC
Singer	The European Patent Convention, M. Singer und D. Stauder, 5. Edition (Heymanns, 2010)
Suppl. to OJ 1/2011, 82	Page 82 of the Supplement to issue 1 of the Official Journal, year 2011
T54/89	Decision of technical board of appeal
Trans. Pract.	Notice of the EPO on transitional practice of the EPC 2000, available via the link in the last paragraph of Not.EPO OJ 2007, 504

List of Contents

Convention on the Grant of European Patents

(EUROPEAN PATENT CONVENTION)

of 5 October 1973
as revised by the Act revising Article 63 EPC of 17 December 1991
and the Act revising the EPC of 29 November 2000

text as adopted by decision of
the Administrative Council of 28 June 2001

Part XI
TRANSITIONAL PROVISIONS (DELETED)

Part XII
FINAL PROVISIONS

PREAMBLE

The Contracting States,

DESIRING to strengthen co-operation between the States of Europe in respect of the protection of inventions,

DESIRING that such protection may be obtained in those States by a single procedure for the grant of patents and by the establishment of certain standard rules governing patents so granted,

DESIRING, for this purpose, to conclude a Convention which establishes a European Patent Organisation and which constitutes a special agreement within the meaning of Article 19 of the Convention for the Protection of Industrial Property, signed in Paris on 20 March 1883 and last revised on 14 July 1967, and a regional patent treaty within the meaning of Article 45, paragraph 1, of the Patent Co-operation Treaty of 19 June 1970,

HAVE AGREED on the following provisions:

1 General

The deliberations in the Preamble should be considered as a compulsory guideline for interpreting and expanding the EPC by the executive institutions, in the first place those of the EPO.

The EPC consists of the Preamble, Articles, Rules, and five protocols. The Rules relating to Fees are not part of the EPC and were included later. See **Art.164**.

2 Interpretation of the EPC

2.1 RULES FOR INTERPRETATION IN THE EPC

The following rules of interpretation of the provisions of the EPC are given in the EPC itself:

Preamble: relation with Paris Convention and PCT
Protocol on the interpretation of **Art.69**
Art.125: Reference to general principles of national law
Art.150: Application of the provisions of the PCT
Art.164: Order of prevalence between treaties, protocols and rules
Art.177: Three equally authoritative texts
R.26(1): Interpretation of **Art.53**.

2.2 THE VIENNA CONVENTION

The EPC is an international treaty and must be interpreted according to the rules of international law, which are equally applicable to both treaties between states, and lawmaking treaties binding persons. Basic rules for interpretation of treaties are given in the Vienna Convention. The Vienna Convention entered into force on 27 January 1980, whereas the EPC entered into force 7 October 1977 (see **Art.169**). In spite of the fact that the Vienna Convention does not have retroactive effect (**Art.4** Vienna Convention), the EPO has decided that the rules for interpretation in the Vienna Convention are also applicable to the EPC. It is well recognized that what the Vienna Convention says in **Art.31** and **32** about interpretation of treaties does nothing more than codify already-existing public international law. (**G5/83** r.1-4)

2.2.1 *Good faith*

Art.31(1) of the Vienna Convention, which states that a treaty must be interpreted in good faith, forms the basis of the principle of good faith as applied by the EPO. The application is set out in **Art.125:2.**

2.2.2 *Meaning of terms*

If the contracting states have not given a special meaning to a term in a treaty, the term shall have the ordinary meaning in its context and in the light of the object and purpose of the treaty (**Art.31(1)**, (4) Vienna Convention). This applies to the EPC and the agreements of the same date or later (e.g. Protocol on **Art.69**).

2.2.3 *Additional matter to be regarded*

Later agreements between the contracting states can also be taken into account in the interpretation of the EPC according to **Art.31(3)** of the Vienna Convention, e.g. clauses on subordination and superordination of rules in subsequent treaties. Also preparatory work and circumstances at the time of drafting the treaty can be used to confirm an interpretation (**Art.32** Vienna Convention, see e.g. **G5/83, G1/86, T128/82, J15/80, J20/84**), or to determine the interpretation, if the above rules have given ambiguous or conflicting results (**J6/83**).

2.3 HARMONISATION

The interpretation of the EPC must take into account the goal of harmonisation of national and international patent law, an aspect not dealt with by the Vienna Convention. The harmonisation requires a consistent interpretation of the EPC and the national provisions, many of which have been adopted from the EPC. Therefore, the Boards of Appeal must take into account national interpretation of the provisions of the EPC. (**G5/83** r.6)

3 Paris Convention

The Paris Convention is mentioned twice in the EPC, once in the Preamble and once in **Art.87(1)**. According to the Preamble the EPC constitutes a special agreement within the meaning of Article 19 of the Paris Convention. Article 19 states that the agreement may not contravene the provisions of the Paris Convention.

The provisions of the EPC contain no cross-references to articles of the Paris Convention to avoid that provisions would apply which were subject to differences of interpretation. In line with this policy, the priority provision of the Paris Convention (**Art.4A(1)**), which contains an obscurity, has not been adopted in the EPC. Rather, the EPC has adopted its own complete, self-contained code of rules on priority (**Art.87-89, R.52, 53**). This code of rules agrees with the general understanding of the priority rules of the Paris Convention in the contracting states of the EPC. Thus, the EPC does not contravene the provisions of the Paris Convention in the sense of Article 19 of the Paris Convention, to which the EPC is bound by its Preamble. (**J15/80**)

4 Amendments and revisions of the EPC

The Convention may only be revised by a diplomatic conference according to **Art.172**. The Administrative Council has a limited competence to amend the Convention and to amend the Implementing Regulations (**Art.33(1)**). The notes to the cited articles give an overview of the revisions and amendments.

See the EPO website www.epo.org/patents/law.html for legislative initiatives and documentation of the EPC 2000 and the London Agreement (OJ 2005, 325).

4.1 EFFECT OF AMENDMENT AND REVISION

New legislation, introduced by amendment or revision, normally does apply to pending cases unless its non-application is expressly provided for in the transitional provisions of the new legislation. As a corollary, new legislation normally does not apply retrospectively and, in order to safeguard interests based on the former state of the law, an express provision for retrospective effect is necessary before it will be judicially acknowledged. (**T315/03** r.5.9)

The principle of legitimate expectations does not apply in case of changes in legislation (**T315/03** r.5.11). Most amendments and revisions of the EPC contain detailed transitional provisions to provide some legal certainty for pending cases. See for example OJ 1994, 891.

4.2 DEVELOPMENT OF COMMON EU PATENT SYSTEM

On 17.12.2012 the member states of the European Union and the European Parliament laid the grounds for unitary patent protection in the EU by signing two Regulations, one setting up a unitary patent and the other establishing a translation regimen. The unitary patent is a European patent, granted by the EPO under the rules and procedures of the EPC, which has a unitary effect for the participating member states. The applicant may choose between either a national patent, a European patent with unitary effect, a European patent taking effect in one or more of the EPC contracting states or a European patent with unitary effect validated in addition in one or more other EPC contracting states not being participating member states. The Regulations were adopted by all EU member states except Spain because of the language hurdle. The Regulation setting up a unitary patent is a special agreement within the meaning of **Art.142**.

The third element of the unitary patent protection, the Agreement on a Unified Patent Court (UPC Agreement), sets up a single patent jurisdiction. The Agreement is presently (November 2018) open for ratification and accession. Once 13 states have done so, including France, Germany and the United Kingdom, the Agreement will enter into force and the two Regulations will apply as of that date (OJ 2013, 110). The ratification progress can be found on http://www.epo.org/law-practice/unitary.html.

The text of the Regulations is reproduced in OJ 2013, 111 and 132 and the text of the Agreement and the statute of the court in OJ 2013, 286 and 345. The rules governing the EPO when carrying out its tasks under the Regulations are published in OJ 2016 A39-A41.

At present (November 2018), it is uncertain when the system will enter into force. Germany has not yet ratified because of a complaint pending before the German Federal Constitutional Court. The United Kingdom ratified the UPC Agreement on 26.04.2018, when it was still member of the European Union. It is not clear what happens to the signatory status of the UK when it leaves the European Union.

PART I GENERAL AND INSTITUTIONAL PROVISIONS

1 **General**
The four principles of the European Patent Convention are: a common law for granting patents (**Art.1**) - called European patents (**Art.2(1)**) - designating one or more states (**Art.3**) - having the effect of a national patent in each state (**Art.2(2)**).

The EPC is self-executing and is independent of national laws for its implementation (J15/80).

Chapter I *General Provisions*

Art. 1 European law for the grant of patents

A system of law, common to the Contracting States, for the grant of patents for invention is established by this Convention.

Art. 2 European patent

Art. 2(1) Patents granted under this Convention shall be called European patents.

Art. 2(2) The European patent shall, in each of the Contracting States for which it is granted, have the effect of and be subject to the same conditions as a national patent granted by that State, unless this Convention provides otherwise.

1 **Effect of European patent**
A European patent does not completely fall apart in a bundle of national patents. It retains its special character after the grant: the EPC overrules national law if EPC provisions relating to European patents are at variance with national law. The desire for the harmonization of rules governing patents has been expressed in the Preamble. The main EPC provisions relating to European patents are:
- The protection of a process patent extends to the direct products of the process (**Art.64(2)**).
- The term of the patent is 20 years (**Art.63(1)**), possibly extended on the grounds of **Art.63(2)**.
- The text of the European patent in the language of the proceedings is the authentic text (**Art.70(1)**).

- A European patent may only be revoked in a national procedure on the grounds given in **Art.138.**
- The scope of protection is determined by the claims; the description and the drawings may be used for interpreting the claims (**Art.69** and protocol).
- The bundle of national patents is subject to the centralised opposition procedure of the EPC (**Art.99**) and the centralised limitation and revocation procedure of **Art.105a-c.**
- Revocation in an opposition procedure has retroactive effect (**Art.68**).
- A review of a board of appeal decision under **Art.112a** may affect a European patent.
- The minimum period for first payment of the renewal fees for a granted patent to a national patent office is set by **Art.141.**

The EPC allows a wide interpretation of patentability, including, for instance, pharmaceuticals and chemical products.

Art. 3 Territorial effect

The grant of a European patent may be requested for one or more of the Contracting States.

1 **Patent for one or more contracting states**
It was the intention of the drafters of the EPC 1973 to introduce a community patent. As this turned out to be impossible, the scope was reduced to a system for grant of patents for one or more states (see **J7/90** r.6.1). A list of contracting states is given in **Art.169:1.**

Under **Art.79** EPC 1973 contracting states could be designated when filing the patent application. The EPC2000 changed the designation system and all contracting states are designated on filing (**Art.79(1)**). The selection of contracting states where protection is desired is now made after grant by validating the patent only for the selected states; validation requires filing of any translation required under **Art.65** and payment of renewal fees under **Art.141** and any special fee and (see NatLaw table IV).

Art. 4 European Patent Organisation

Art. 4(1) A European Patent Organisation, hereinafter referred to as the Organisation, is established by this Convention. It shall have administrative and financial autonomy.

Art. 4(2) The organs of the Organisation shall be:
(a) the European Patent Office;
(b) the Administrative Council.

1 **Organisation versus Office**
The 'European Patent Office' is abbreviated as 'EPO' in the notes of this book, whereas the 'European Patent Organisation' is written in full. The EPO is the executive body of the European Patent Organisation.

2 **Academy of the European Patent Organisation**
By a decision of 17.06.2004 the Administrative Council has set up a European Patent Academy for education and training in the field of European and international patent law, including the preparation of candidates for the European qualifying examination. The Academy is an institution of the European Patent Organisation and is managed by the European Patent Office. The Regulations of the Academy have been published in OJ 2004, 362.

Art. 4(3) The task of the Organisation shall be to grant European patents. This shall be carried out by the European Patent Office supervised by the Administrative Council.

Art. 4a Conference of ministers of the Contracting States

A conference of ministers of the Contracting States responsible for patent matters shall meet at least every five years to discuss issues pertaining to the Organisation and to the European patent system.

1 **General**
This provision sets up a Conference of ministers of the contracting states responsible for patents matters. The conference is a permanent body within the framework of the EPC but is not an organ of the Organisation. The Conference cannot take decisions which have legally binding effects on the Organisation. The function of the Conference is of a purely political nature; it can set objectives for the Organisation and initiate co-operation between contracting states extending beyond the scope of the EPC. (Spec. Ed. 4 of OJ 2007)

The Conference cannot amend the EPC. An example of a conference of ministers is the London Intergovernmental Conference of October 2000, in which the London Agreement was set up (see **Art.65(1):2**).

Chapter II *The European Patent Organisation*

Art. 5 Legal status

Art. 5(1) The Organisation shall have legal personality.

Art. 5(2) In each of the Contracting States, the Organisation shall enjoy the most extensive legal capacity accorded to legal persons under the national law of that State; it may in particular acquire or dispose of movable and immovable property and may be a party to legal proceedings.

1 **Legal capacity of the European Patent Organisation**
The Organisation can take part in legal actions and in economic transactions because it has legal personality.

Art. 5(3) The President of the European Patent Office shall represent the Organisation.

1 **Representation of the Organisation**
The President may, according to this provision, represent the European Patent Organisation. This is one of his functions but not one of his powers. The President may only represent the Organisation by performing a legal act, such as the signing of an agreement, if he has the power to perform that act. His powers are governed by the EPC in articles other than **Art.5(3)**, such as **Art.10** and **Art.33(4)**. (**G5/88** hn.I, r.2.2-4, see also **Art.10:1**)

Art. 6 Headquarters

Art. 6(1) The Organisation shall have its headquarters in Munich.

Art. 6(2) The European Patent Office shall be located in Munich. It shall have a branch at The Hague.

1 **Branch of the EPO in The Hague**
The EPO has set up a branch at The Hague to avail itself of the search facilities of the Institut International des Brevets (IIB) in The Hague, which had an excellent search department (OJ 1978, 202). When the Netherlands started to provide protection for inventions in 1912, they could avoid the deficiencies of the search systems already set up in France and Germany. They devised a new system and had sufficient funds to copy the entire French and German patent documentation. Before the institution of the EPO, France already cooperated with the Netherlands in the IIB, because of the disorganized system in France. The IIB was incorporated into the EPO in 1978.

It should be noted that in 1973, at the time of drafting the Convention, the offices of the IIB that were to become the EPO branch were located in The Hague. When the EPO started its activities in 1978, the offices had been set up in Rijswijk, a city neighbouring The Hague. There has never been any EPO office in The Hague.

The revision of the EPC in 2000 did not change the location of the branch. The legislator held in an oral clarification that any geographical location in the EPC should be interpreted broadly, e.g. The Hague should mean the province of South Holland and Munich the country of Bavaria. Any geographical allocation would at some point restrict the reallocation of offices.

2 **Sub-office of the EPO in Berlin**

Under the Protocol on Centralisation, Section I(3)(a), a sub-office was created in Berlin in 1978 for searching European patent applications under the direction of The Hague (OJ 1978, 195, 245). The Protocol is part of the EPC according to **Art.164(1)**. The Berlin sub-office was set up to give West Berlin, at that time an exclave in East Germany, more ties to West Germany. Although the ties are no longer necessary after the reunification of East and West Germany in 1990, the relatively small sub-office is maintained because of its low operational costs.

Since 1989 the Berlin sub-office is also a filing office in the sense of **Art.75(1)(a)** (Dec. of Pres., based on his power acc. to **Art.10(2)(a)**, OJ 1989, 218).

3 **Location of the EPO in Haar**

On 09.10.2017 the Boards of Appeal Unit was relocated from the EPO headquarters in Munich to Haar, a municipality neighbouring Munich. The relocation is part of the reform of the boards of appeal to strengthen the perception of their independence (see **R.12a:1**). The office in Haar is not a filing office.

4 **Filing with incorrect office**

In Munich and Berlin the EPO and the German Patent Office are located in neighbouring buildings. The filing date of documents intended for the EPO but received by the German Patent Office and forwarded to the EPO will be the date of their actual receipt at the EPO (OJ 2005, 444).

Art. 7 Sub-offices of the European Patent Office

By decision of the Administrative Council, sub-offices of the European Patent Office may be created, if need be, for the purpose of information and liaison, in the Contracting States and with intergovernmental organisations in the field of industrial property, subject to the approval of the Contracting State or organisation concerned.

1 **Sub-offices**

Following a decision by the Administrative Council taken in 1992, a sub-office was opened in Brussels for liaison with the European Union to support industry and ensure competitiveness of the European economy (OJ 1993, 404; 2004, 88).

In 1990 the International Patent Documentation Centre (INPADOC) in Vienna was integrated into the EPO as a sub-office (Not. of Pres. OJ 1990, 492). The sub-office is in charge of the EPO's bibliographic data bases and has as its task to provide public access to patent information. Note that the Vienna sub-office is not a filing office of the EPO (Dec. Pres., Spec. Ed. 3 of OJ 2007, A.1 Art.1(2)).

Art. 8 Privileges and immunities

The Protocol on Privileges and Immunities annexed to this Convention shall define the conditions under which the Organisation, the members of the Administrative Council, the employees of the European Patent Office, and such other persons specified in that Protocol as take part in the work of the Organisation, shall enjoy, in each Contracting State, the privileges and immunities necessary for the performance of their duties.

1 **Protocol on Privileges and Immunities**

The Protocol on Privileges and Immunities is an integral part of the EPC (Art.164(1)). The Protocol defines the inviolability of the premises of the Organisation and the immunity of the people working in the Organisation. It ensures that the Organisation is not restricted in the execution of its tasks by national laws. The protocol also applies to members of the epi having specific duties (OJ 2009, 28). The text of the Protocol has not been reproduced in this book.

Art. 9 Liability

Art. 9(1) The contractual liability of the Organisation shall be governed by the law applicable to the contract in question.

The will of the parties as laid down in contracts is, in principle, decisive.

Art. 9(2) The non-contractual liability of the Organisation in respect of any damage caused by it or by the employees of the European Patent Office in the performance of their duties shall be governed by the law of the Federal Republic of Germany. Where the damage is caused by the branch at The Hague or a sub-office or employees attached thereto, the law of the Contracting State in which such branch or sub-office is located shall apply.

1 **Indemnities**

The board of appeal is not competent to decide on indemnities for loss or damage allegedly caused by the EPO in the course of proceedings (J14/87). A Board of Appeal has no power to make an order against the EPO to pay costs incurred by parties due to proceedings unjustifiably delayed by the EPO (T315/03 r.15.8; ten years to dispose of first instance opposition proceedings).

Employees of the EPO cannot be tried for neglect of duty (Art.14(a) Protocol on privileges and immunities); any claim must be made against the EPO.

Art. 9(3) The personal liability of the employees of the European Patent Office towards the Organisation shall be governed by their Service Regulations or conditions of employment.

1 **Personal liability of employees of the EPO**

The EPO can recover damages in whole or in part from an employee when such damages have been caused wilfully by him or her or result from serious negligence. No recovery is possible of damages caused by a decision of the board of appeal or the Enlarged Board of Appeal.

Art. 9(4) The courts with jurisdiction to settle disputes under paragraphs 1 and 2 shall be:

(a) for disputes under paragraph 1, the courts of the Federal Republic of Germany, unless the contract concluded between the parties designates a court of another State;

(b) for disputes under paragraph 2, the courts of the Federal Republic of Germany, or of the State in which the branch or sub-office is located.

Chapter III *The European Patent Office*

Chapter III deals with the management of the Office, the use of languages and the organisation of some departments. The EPO has approximately six thousand employees, who remain citizens of their contracting state of origin. An EPO salary is only subject to a low, internally levied tax.

Art. 10 Management

1 **Powers of the President**
The President directs the EPO according to **Art.10(1)**, which is to be interpreted in its context, in particular having regard to **Art.10(2)** and **Art.5(3)**. **Art.10(2)** contains a list of functions and powers of the President essentially concerned with internal matters of the EPO. It is not clear to what extent the President can direct the EPO in any external activity not directly related to one of the powers and functions listed in **Art.10(2)** without the supervision of the Administrative Council. However, it is clear that concluding an agreement with another patent office which has no connection with the functioning of the EPO and merely serves to satisfy political interests of that office is not within the President's power. Such an agreement requires authorisation and approval from the Administrative Council under **Art.33(4)**. Hence, an agreement of the President with the German patent office on mail intended for the EPO but erroneously addressed to the German patent office in Berlin at a time the EPO did not yet have a filing office in Berlin (OJ 1981, 381) was beyond the powers of the President. See also **Art.23(1):2**. (**G5/88** hn.II, r.2, **G7/88** and **G8/88**)

Art. 10(1) The European Patent Office shall be managed by the President, who shall be responsible for its activities to the Administrative Council.

Art. 10(2) To this end, the President shall have in particular the following functions and powers:
- **(a) he shall take all necessary steps to ensure the functioning of the European Patent Office, including the adoption of internal administrative instructions and information to the public;**
- **(b) unless this Convention provides otherwise, he shall prescribe which acts are to be performed at the European Patent Office in Munich and its branch at The Hague respectively;**
- **(c) he may submit to the Administrative Council any proposal for amending this Convention, for general regulations, or for decisions which come within the competence of the Administrative Council;**
- **(d) he shall prepare and implement the budget and any amending or supplementary budget;**
- **(e) he shall submit a management report to the Administrative Council each year;**
- **(f) he shall exercise supervisory authority over the staff;**
- **(g) subject to Article 11, he shall appoint the employees and decide on their promotion;**
- **(h) he shall exercise disciplinary authority over the employees other than those referred to in Article 11, and may propose disciplinary action to the Administrative Council with regard to employees referred to in Article 11, paragraphs 2 and 3;**
- **(i) he may delegate his functions and powers.**

1 **Guidelines for Examination in the EPO (Art.10(2)(a))**
The President has issued under sub-paragraph (a) the *Guidelines for Examination in the European Patent Office* to ensure a proper functioning of the EPO. The EPO has a policy of annually revising the Guidelines to keep them in line with legal and procedural developments.

The functions and powers specified in sub-paragraphs (b) to (i) are essentially concerned with the internal operations of the EPO (**G5/88** r.1.2).

Art. 10(3) The President shall be assisted by a number of Vice-Presidents. If the President is absent or indisposed, one of the Vice-Presidents shall take his place in accordance with the procedure laid down by the Administrative Council.

1 **Vice-Presidents**
There are three Vice-Presidents, one for each Directorate-General. See the decision of the Administrative Council on deputisation for the President of the EPO (OJ 1978, 326).

Art. 11 Appointment of senior employees

This article sets out the appointment of the President and higher personnel and lays down the powers of the President in the latter.

Art. 11(1) The President of the European Patent Office shall be appointed by the Administrative Council.

Art. 11(2) The Vice-Presidents shall be appointed by the Administrative Council after the President of the European Patent Office has been consulted.

Art. 11(3) The members, including the Chairmen, of the Boards of Appeal and of the Enlarged Board of Appeal shall be appointed by the Administrative Council on a proposal from the President of the European Patent Office. They may be re-appointed by the Administrative Council after the President of the European Patent Office has been consulted.

1 **Appointment of members of boards of appeal**
The powers of the president of the EPO under **Art.11(3)** have been delegated to the president of the Boards of Appeal under **R.12d(2)**. The persons to be appointed as members of boards of appeal are proposed by the president of the BoA on merit and appointed by the Administrative Council under **Art.11(3)**. Once appointed, a member cannot be removed by a decision of the president of the BoA alone.

The board members are appointed for a term of five years according to **Art.23(1)**, after which they may be re-appointed by the Administrative Council after consultation of the president of the BoA.

Art. 11(4) The Administrative Council shall exercise disciplinary authority over the employees referred to in paragraphs 1 to 3.

Art. 11(5) The Administrative Council, after consulting the President of the European Patent Office, may also appoint as members of the Enlarged Board of Appeal legally qualified members of the national courts or quasi-judicial authorities of the Contracting States, who may continue their judicial activities at the national level. They shall be appointed for a term of three years and may be re-appointed.

1 **External legally and technically qualified members**
The participation of external legally qualified members from the EPC contracting states in proceedings before the Enlarged Board of Appeal has proved to be a success. It is expected that the involvement of national judges will further the harmonisation of patent case law in Europe. (Spec. Ed. 4 of OJ 2007)

The EPC 2000 does no longer allow the appointment of external technically and legally qualified members for the technical and legal boards of appeal, because since the early days of the Office sufficient knowledge has become available in house. (Spec. Ed. 4 of OJ2007)

Art. 12 Duties of office

Employees of the European Patent Office shall be bound, even after the termination of their employment, neither to disclose nor to make use of information which by its nature is a professional secret.

Art. 13 Disputes between the Organisation and the employees of the European Patent Office

Art. 13(1) Employees and former employees of the European Patent Office or their successors in title may apply to the Administrative Tribunal of the International Labour Organization in the case of disputes with the European Patent Organisation, in accordance with the Statute of the Tribunal and within the limits and subject to the conditions laid down in the Service Regulations for permanent employees or the Pension Scheme Regulations or arising from the conditions of employment of other employees.

Art. 13(2) An appeal shall only be admissible if the person concerned has exhausted such other means of appeal as are available to him under the Service Regulations, the Pension Scheme Regulations or the conditions of employment.

Art. 14 Languages of the European Patent Office, European patent applications and other documents

See for the implementation:
R.3 Language in written proceedings
R.4 Language in oral proceedings
R.5 Certification of translations
R.6 Filing of translations and reduction of fees
R.7 Legal authenticity of the translation of the European patent application
R.36(2) Language of divisional application

1 **Transitional provision EPC 2000**
The revised **Art.14(1)** and (2) shall apply to European patent applications filed after entry into force of the EPC 2000 (Art.7(1) Revision Act, Spec. ED. no. 4, OJ 2007, p. 217). Hence, a filing date will be accorded for a European application filed in any language only if the application has a filing date on or after date of entry into force of the EPC 2000.

The revised **Art.14(3)** to (6) shall apply to European patent applications pending at the time of entry into force of the EPC 2000 and to European patents already granted at that time (Art.1(1) Dec. Adm. Council, Spec. Ed. no. 4, OJ 2007, page 219).

2 **Language restrictions**
The framework of language restrictions in the EPC is based on three categories of languages:

1 the three official languages of the EPO, i.e. English, French and German (**Art.14(1)**, first sentence)
2 the official languages of the EPC contracting states other than English, French or German (**Art.14(4)**, first sentence). These languages are also called 'admissible non-EPO languages'.
3 all other languages.

For the purpose of according a date of filing, a European patent application may be filed in any language (see **R.40**), thereby implementing Art.5(2) PLT. For the prosecution of an application by the EPO, the application must be available in one of the official EPO languages (**Art.14(2)**, first sentence). If the application was initially filed in an another language, it must be translated into one of the official EPO languages (**Art.14(2)**, first sentence), the choice of the official EPO language being at the option of the applicant. The official EPO language of filing or translation becomes the language of the proceedings (**Art.14(3)**). In all proceedings before the EPO a party must use the language of the proceedings. However, another official EPO language may be used in written and oral proceedings, provided a translation or interpretation is provided where required by **R.3** and **R.4**.

R.6(3) provides a reduction of fees where an admissible non-EPO language is used for filing patent applications to compensate for the burden of providing a translation into an official EPO language. **Art.14(4)** and **R.6(4)** restrict the fee reduction to certain persons.

Art. 14(1) The official languages of the European Patent Office shall be English, French and German.

Art. 14(2) A European patent application shall be filed in one of the official languages or, if filed in any other language, translated into one of the official languages in accordance with the Implementing Regulations. Throughout the proceedings before the European Patent Office, such translation may be brought into conformity with the application as filed. If a required translation is not filed in due time, the application shall be deemed to be withdrawn.

1 **Language of the patent application**
The requirements for obtaining a date of filing for a European patent application in **R.40(1)** do not contain a restriction on language. Hence, the application may be filed in any language, such as Chinese, Dutch or Latin. This is supported by the words 'any other language' in **Art.14(2)**. The documents of the application need not all be in the same language (A-VII,1.1; EPO practice changed in 2014, see Guidelines edition November 2014).

Art.14(2) imposes requirements to be met after accordance of a date of filing, to be examined during the formalities examination under **Art.90(3)** and **R.57(a)**. Hence, compliance with the requirements is not necessary for according a date of filing.

A European patent application may be filed with a national authority according to **Art.75(1)(b)** and **(2)**. Some national authorities restrict the freedom of language. The languages admitted by national authorities are given in NatLaw table II, column 3 and further requirements in column 5. At present (November 2018) all contracting states except Bulgaria, Cyprus, Macedonia, Norway and Spain allow all languages pursuant to **Art.14(1)** and **Art.14(2)** for applications filed with their national authorities.

Note that the choice of filing office may be restricted by national security requirements as set out in **Art.75(2):1** (see NatLaw table II, column 2).

Use of an admissible non-EPO language (see **Art.14(4):2**) for the application may entitle the applicant to a reduction of the filing fee (**G6/91** r.18-21). See **R.6(3)** and notes thereto for entitlement requirements, also for a reduction of the examination fee.

2 Translation of the patent application

If the application is filed in any other language than one of the official EPO languages English, French or German, a translation into one of the official languages must be filed according to **Art.14(2)**, first sentence. A translation in more than one language, e.g. partly in German and partly in English, does not comply with the 'into one of the official languages' of **Art.14(2)**.

The meaning of 'any other language' in **Art.14(2)** is ambiguous. It could mean any language other than the three official EPO languages or any language other than one of the official languages. The latter meaning is preferred, because it covers all cases other than a patent application filed in one of the official languages. It therefore covers the case of an application filed in two languages. Such an application is not in 'one of the official languages' but in two; since the case of two languages can be regarded as covered by 'any other language', the application must be translated into one of the official languages.

When an application is filed by reference to a previously filed application as permitted by **R.40(1)(c)**, this previously filed application must also be translated into an official EPO language if it is not in an official EPO language according to the parallel provision **R.40(3)**. For divisional applications see **R.36(2):2**.

Where an application filed in an official EPO language is a translation of an earlier application not in an EPO language from which it claims priority, **Art.14(2)**, second sentence, cannot be used to correct the translation. It might be possible to include translated parts of the earlier application under **R.56(3)** as missing parts for correcting the translation. The EPO has not yet confirmed that this is permitted.

3 Filing the translation

Any translation of the patent application must be filed within two months of filing the application (**R.6(1)**). When the application was filed by reference to a previously filed application, any translation must also be filed within two months of filing (**R.40(3)**). The translation must be presented in the same form as application documents (**R.49(1)**).

The procedure for examination of the filing of the translation is set out in A-III,14. The filing of a translation will not be examined when according a date of filing, because the language of the patent application is not a requirement for according a date of filing (**R.40(1)**). The EPO will check the filing of the translation only during the examination as to formal requirements under **R.57(a)** and, if not filed within the two-month period of **R.6(1)**, **R.36(2)** or **R.40(3)**, invite the applicant to correct this deficiency under **R.58** within two months from invitation. Thus, the applicant has at least four months to file the translation (CA/PL29/06 Add.1). During this relatively long period the EPO cannot carry out the examination as to formal requirements under **R.57** preparing the application for publication and the search, which makes it difficult to publish in time an application using the full 12 month priority period.

Failure to file the translation within the period of **R.58** results in the application being deemed withdrawn according to **Art.14(2)**, last sentence, which will be notified under **R.112(1)**. If applicable, the applicant can prove within two months of the notification that he did file the translation in due time (**R.112(2)**). The two-month periods of **R.6(1)**, **R.36(2)** and **R.58** are excluded from further processing (**R.135(2)**) but re-establishment according to **Art.122** and **R.136(3)** in these periods is possible if 'all due care' can be proven.

Some contracting states allow conversion of the deemed withdrawn European application to a national application under **Art.135**.

4 Correction of translation

An applicant or proprietor may correct the translation to bring it into conformity with the original text throughout any proceedings before the EPO (**Art.14(2)**, second sentence; **Art.70(2):1** and A-VII,7). A correction of the translation in opposition or limitation proceedings is not allowable if it offends against **Art.123(3)** (A-VII,7, last sentence). It is irrelevant whether the applicant or proprietor is a national or resident of an EPC contracting state or of any other state.

The correction possibility applies both to an application filed in a non-EPO language, to a divisional application filed in a non-EPO language where the parent was filed in this language (**R.36(2)**), and to an application filed by reference to a previously filed application in a non-EPO language under **R.40(1)(c)**. In all cases the translation may subsequently be brought into conformity with the original, earlier or previous application. (A-VII,7)

See **R.159(1)(a):2** for correction of the translation of a Euro-PCT application.

When assessing whether an amendment complies with **Art.123(2)**, the EPO assumes that the originally filed translation is in conformity with the text in the original language (A-VII,7). However, the basis for the assessment of an amendment is the text in the original language (**Art.70(2)**). An applicant should inform the EPO of any translation error.

5 Relevance of the translation

The text of the application in an official EPO language, either as filed directly or as translated, is the authentic text in any proceedings before the EPO (**Art.70(1)**). However, when the application is not filed in an official EPO language, the original text will be the 'application as filed' (**Art.70(2)**) for the purpose of a.o. determining extension of subject-matter in the sense of **Art.123(2)**. The EPO assumes for this purpose that the translation conforms to the original text of the application (**R.7**). If there is doubt about the accuracy of the translation, the EPO may request the filing of a certificate that the translation corresponds to the original text (**R.5**).

The content of a European prior right, i.e. a prior art document under **Art.54(3)**, is determined by the original text as filed, not by any translation into an official EPO language (A-VII,7).

It is in principle possible to file a computer translation if there is not sufficient time to prepare a proper translation within the time limit of **R.58** and to correct the translation subsequently. However, this may cause the search to be based on an incorrect translation or the issue of a declaration of an incomplete search, affecting the following proceedings. The EPO may ask a certificate of translation under **R.5** if it has doubts as to the accuracy of the translation.

Art. 14(3) The official language of the European Patent Office in which the European patent application is filed or into which it is translated shall be used as the language of the proceedings in all proceedings before the European Patent Office, unless the Implementing Regulations provide otherwise.

1 **Language of the proceedings**

The official EPO language in which the application is filed or translated becomes the language of the proceedings. The language of the proceedings cannot be changed during the proceedings concerning an application or the resulting patent, because this is not provided for in the EPC.

The language of the proceedings must be used in all proceedings before the EPO (**Art.14(3)**). Hence, in written proceedings all documents should be filed in the language of the proceedings. Derogations for written proceedings are provided in **R.3**, which allows that documents may be filed in any official EPO language (**R.3(1)**), except for amendments of the application or patent, which must be in the language of the proceedings (**R.3(2)**). Documents to be filed within a time limit may also be submitted in an admissible non-EPO language and subsequently translated into an official EPO language (**Art.14(4)**). Documentary evidence may be filed in any language (**R.3(3)**).

In oral proceedings the default language is the language of the proceedings (**Art.14(3)**), but any official language of the EPO or a contracting state may be used, provided the provisions for interpretation in **R.4** are observed.

Art. 14(4) Natural or legal persons having their residence or principal place of business within a Contracting State having a language other than English, French or German as an official language, and nationals of that State who are resident abroad, may file documents which have to be filed within a time limit in an official language of that State. They shall, however, file a translation in an official language of the European Patent Office in accordance with the Implementing Regulations. If any document, other than those documents making up the European patent application, is not filed in the prescribed language, or if any required translation is not filed in due time, the document shall be deemed not to have been filed.

1 **Language of further documents and translation**

Further documents, i.e. documents other than those making up the European patent application, must be filed in the language of the proceedings (**Art.14(3)**). By way of exception, a further document may also be filed in another official EPO language (**R.3(1)**). When the document concerns amendments of the patent application, it must be filed in the language of the proceedings (**R.3(2)**).

Art.14(4), first sentence, allows a restricted class of persons to file further documents in an official language of an EPC contracting state. These documents must subsequently be translated into an official EPO language (**Art.14(4)**, second sentence) in accordance with **R.3**: for most documents into any official EPO language (**R.3(1)**) and, where the documents concern amendments, into the language of the proceedings (**R.3(2)**).

Art.14(4) defines the persons that may file those further documents that have to be filed within a time limit in an official language of a contracting state. A translation in any official EPO language must normally be filed within one month of filing the document (**R.6(2)**).

Whereas a mistake in the translation of a patent application can be corrected using **Art.14(2)** second sentence, the translation of a further document can only be corrected as an error under **R.139** (**G6/91** r.10).

2 Admissible non-EPO language

The official languages of contracting states in which further documents in the meaning of **Art.14(4)** may be filed with the EPO are referred to in this book as 'admissible non-EPO languages', or 'admissible languages' if the latter does not cause confusion (see A-X,9.2.1(ii)). The terms 'authorised language' and 'allowed language' sometimes occur in case law.

The official languages of the contracting states are listed in NatLaw table II, column 4. A few special cases of official languages:

Belgium	Dutch, French and German
Finland	Finnish and Swedish
Ireland	Irish and English
Liechtenstein	German
Luxembourg	French, German and Luxembourgish
Switzerland	German, French, and Italian.

Where a contracting state has several official languages, the choice of language is up to the party. A party who has several nationalities may choose between the official languages of the contracting states of which he is a national and the contracting state where he has his residence (Münchner Gemeinschaftskommentar, K. Haertel (Heymanns) Art. 14, p. 15, Randnummer 18 und 22). For example, a Swiss party may choose Italian as language for the fee reduction of **R.6(3)**, even though his own language is German or French.

3 Entitled persons

Under **Art.14(4)**, first sentence, a person is entitled to use an admissible non-EPO language if:

- he has his residence within the territory of the state,
- he has his place of business within the territory of the state, *or*
- he is a national of the state and is resident abroad, inside or outside a contracting state.

Neither the EPC nor the Guidelines indicate how to apply **Art.14(4)** in the case of several applicants or proprietors having different nationalities. On the ground of the liberal interpretation of the language provisions of the EPC use of an official language of a contracting state other than an official EPO language should be admissible if at least one of the applicants is entitled to use this language. (Münchner Gemeinschaftskommentar, K. Haertel (Heymanns) Art. 14, p. 15, Randnummer 23)

If the admissible language is used by a natural person, his residence and nationality determine the admissible languages. If the admissible language is used by a legal person, the place of business of the company determines the admissible languages (**T149/85**). The nationality or residence of the applicant is decisive, not that of his representative (**T149/85**). See **Art.133(2):1** for the interpretation of 'principal' in the first sentence of **Art.14(4)**.

Note that the admissible language depends on nationality, residence or place of business, whereas compulsory representation before the EPO (**Art.133(2)**) depends on the residence or place of business only: the EPO needs a postal address within Europe for acts performed after filing.

4 Further documents to be filed within a time limit

Art.14(4) restricts the use of an admissible non-EPO language to documents to be filed within a time limit. An example of such a document is the response to a communication of the EPO under **Art.94(3)**, inviting the applicant to correct deficiencies in the application and usually specifying a period of four months. Other examples are a request for examination and a notice of opposition.

An observation by a third person under **Art.115** is an example of a document which need not be filed within a time limit. Hence, the provision of **Art.14(4)** does not apply and the observation must be filed in one of the official languages of the EPO according to **Art.14(1)**, as explicitly provided in **R.114(1)**. Note that **R.3(1)**, first sentence is not applicable, because the third person is not a party to the proceedings.

Although the filing of a request for revocation or limitation under **Art.105a** is not subject to any time limit, the request may nonetheless be filed in an admissible non-EPO language (D-X,2.1(iv)), because **R.6(2)** referring to the request acts as a lex specialis.

5 Period for filing translation

The period for filing the translation is fixed by **R.6(2)**. The period is normally one month of filing the document. If the translation is not filed in due time, the document will be deemed not to have been filed (**Art.14(4)**, third sentence) or disregarded (**R.3(3)**). This sanction applies not only to non-filed translations of documents filed in an admissible non-EPO language but also to non-filed translations in the language of proceedings of amendments of the patent application that had been filed in another official EPO language (consequence of 'any document' in **Art.14(4)**, third sentence). The fate of the document is set out in the next section.

Non-observance of the period may be remedied using further processing (**Art.121** and **R.135(2)**) by paying the further processing fee and filing the translation within two months from notification of the loss of rights. Re-establishment is ruled out by **R.136(3)**.

6 Wrong language of further document

A document filed in a wrong language or a document filed in an admissible non-EPO language for which no translation is filed in due time will be deemed not to have been filed (**Art.14(4)**, last sentence). The EPO notifies the person who filed the document. Such documents are put in the file and are open to public inspection according to **Art.128(4)**; observations and notices of opposition in a wrong language are communicated to the applicant or proprietor. (A-VII,5)

Examples of documents filed in a wrong language are: a reply to an invitation under **Art.94(3)** in Russian, a request for re-establishment in Italian by a Greek living in Greece, an observation under **Art.115** filed in Polish, an opposition filed in Dutch by a Dutch representative of a German opponent who has his residence in Germany, a notice of appeal filed in Japanese.

As an exception to **Art.14(4)**, an order for payment in a wrong language is validly filed, as far as the numbers make it clear what the amount and purpose of the payment are (**Rfees6**, **T170/83**, Dutch money order, **Rfees5(2):2.1.1**).

An accompanying document, such as a cover letter, relating to the performance of a procedural act within a time limit and filed in a wrong language, is put in the file and the procedural act is regarded as being performed, but any other content of the accompanying document is ignored. Examples of procedural acts are filing the designation of the inventor (**R.19**), a certified copy of an earlier application from which priority is claimed (**R.53(1)**), the translation of the earlier application (**R.53(3)**). (A-VII,5)

Art. 14(5) European patent applications shall be published in the language of the proceedings.

See **Art.93** for the publication of the application and **Art.14(3)** for the language of the proceedings.

Art. 14(6) Specifications of European patents shall be published in the language of the proceedings and shall include a translation of the claims in the other two official languages of the European Patent Office.

1 **Language of publication of the specification**

See **Art.98** for the publication of the specification of the patent.

The translations of the claims must be filed on invitation by the EPO under **R.71(3)**. The EPO does not check the correctness of the translations.

Art. 14(7) The following shall be published in the three official languages of the European Patent Office:

(a) the European Patent Bulletin;

(b) the Official Journal of the European Patent Office.

See **Art.129** for the publication of the Bulletin and the OJ.

Art. 14(8) Entries in the European Patent Register shall be made in the three official languages of the European Patent Office. In cases of doubt, the entry in the language of the proceedings shall be authentic.

Art.14(3) Language of the proceedings
Art.127 Register of European patents

Art. 15 The departments entrusted with the procedure

To carry out the procedures laid down in this Convention, the following shall be set up within the European Patent Office:

(a) a Receiving Section;

(b) Search Divisions;

(c) Examining Divisions;

(d) **Opposition Divisions;**
(e) **a Legal Division;**
(f) **Boards of Appeal;**
(g) **an Enlarged Board of Appeal.**

See for the implementation:
Art.16 Receiving Section
Art.17 Search Divisions
Art.18 Examining Divisions
Art.19 Opposition Divisions
Art.20 Legal Division
Art.21 Boards of Appeal
Art.22 Enlarged Board of Appeal
Art.23 Independence of the members of the boards
Art.24 Exclusion and objection
R.9-13 Organisation of the European Patent Office

1 **Reorganisations of the EPO**
The departments of the EPO mentioned in **Art.15** were grouped in Directorates-General (**R.9(1)**). Three reorganisations have changed the grouping from five Directorates-General to three and changed locations of the departments.

In 1990 the EPO started the BEST project (Bringing Examination and Search Together), which aims at improving quality and efficiency of search and examination. Before Best, the search and the examination were performed by two different persons, a searcher in the Hague and an examiner in Munich. Under BEST both the search and the examination are performed by the same examiner, who may be located in the Hague, Berlin or Munich (OJ 1990, 333 and EPO Annual Reports). The search examiner is also the primary examiner in the examining division (Not. Pres. OJ 2003, 206 §1; B-I,2). The BEST project was completed in 2006. The distinction between search divisions and examining divisions has not yet been removed from **Art.15**, because there was insufficient preparation time for the diplomatic conference to include such a change into the EPC 2000; it should be part of a next Diplomatic Conference.

In 2016 the departments of second instance, the Boards of Appeal and the Enlarged Board of Appeal, formerly Directorate-General 3, became part of the Boards of Appeal Unit as of 01.07.2016, a separate organisational unit to emphasise their perceived independence. The Boards of Appeal Unit has moved from the city of Munich to Haar. See **R.12a** and CA/43/16 Rev. 1.

In 2017 a further reorganisation combined the former Directorates-General DG1 (search, examination and opposition) and DG2 (patent administration) to have the entire patent granting process in one Directorate-General (CA/65/17). The proposed renumbering of DG4 and DG5 to DG2 and DG3 has not yet been implemented (situation 01.11.2018; see e.g. the vacancy notices for vice-presidents DG4 and DG5 in OJ 2018 A59 and A60).

2 **Administrative structure of the EPO**
Since 2017 the EPO is divided administratively into three Directorates-General, to which the departments of **Art.15(a) - (e)** are assigned (**R.9(1)**), and a Board of Appeal Unit to which the departments **(f)** and **(g)** are assigned.

The examiners, forming the search, examining and opposition divisions, are part of Directorate-General 1 (DG1), which is divided into three principal directorates according to technology. About the same number of examiners should be located in Munich and in the Hague (see the Protocol on the Staff Complement of the EPC 2000, reproduced in OJ 2001, Special Edition no. 1, p. 45). The examiners are assigned to a separate search division and examining division set up for each patent application filed; similarly, they are assigned to a separate opposition division set up for each patent for which a notice of opposition has been filed. The Receiving Section is also part of DG1.

Each principal directorate of DG1 includes formalities officers, which are responsible for examination on filing and examination as to formal requirements, tasks the EPC has allocated to the Receiving Section (**Art.16** and **R.10(1)**).

Directorate-General 4 (DG4) is Corporate Services, comprising human resources, general administration, central procurement and finance.

Directorate-General 5 (DG5) comprises the Legal Division and legal and international affairs, located in Munich.

Departments (a) till (e) are departments of first instance, departments (f) and (g) departments of second instance.

Although the EPC distinguishes the Receiving Section, search divisions, examining divisions, opposition divisions and the Legal Division as departments of the EPO, they are no longer indicated as separate organisational units in the Organisational Structure of the EPO. To ensure greater flexibility in allocating specific tasks, the EPC 2000 has removed several references to the Receiving Section and search divisions and replaced wording such as 'the Receiving Section shall ...' by 'the EPO shall ...' (compare **Art.90(1), 92, 93(1)**).

A case is transferred from one department to another at the moment of receipt of the appropriate message and a possible payment, e.g. the request for examination (see e.g. **R.10**). The department to which the case is transferred becomes competent to handle the case.

Art. 16 Receiving Section

The Receiving Section shall be responsible for the examination on filing and the examination as to formal requirements of European patent applications.

See for the implementation:
R.10(1) Limitation in time of responsibility of Receiving Section

1 **Responsibilities of the Receiving Section**

According to **Art.16** the Receiving Section is responsible for the examination on filing, i.e. whether a filed application can be accorded a filing date (**Art.90(1), R.55**) and the examination as to formal requirements (**Art.90(3), R.56-60**); according to A-VI,2.1, it also takes care of the publication of the application (**Art.93, R.67-69**). The Receiving Section is composed entirely of formalities officers (**G1/02**, r.6.1)

The Receiving Section is not competent to decide on a request for an amendment or correction of an application that requires a technical examination; the decision on such a matter must wait until the case has been transferred to the examining division, because the latter is competent in such matters (**J4/85**).

The transfer of responsibility of the Receiving Section to an examining division is governed by **R.10(1)**. The search division carries out the search while the case lies with the Receiving Section (consequence of **R.10(1)**; B-IV,1.2).

The Receiving Section of the EPO should not be confused with the receiving Office according to the PCT (**Art.151**).

Art. 17 Search Divisions

The Search Divisions shall be responsible for drawing up European search reports.

1 **Responsibilities of the search divisions**

According to **Art.17** the search division is responsible for carrying out the search and drawing up of the European search report for an application (**Art.92, R.61-65**). The 'European search report' should be interpreted as 'extended European search report' in the meaning of **R.62**, including the search report proper and the search opinion on patentability (B-II,4). The drawing up of any supplementary search report under **Art.153(7)** for a Euro-PCT application is also the responsibility of the search division (**J6/83**). The search division determines the definitive content of the abstract (**R.66**; F-II,2.2). A search division normally consists of one search examiner (B-I,2.2).

The search division starts the prior art search for a patent application after the application has been accorded a date of filing, the filing fee and search fee have been paid, claims have been filed and any translation of the application has been filed. The search is carried out in parallel with the formalities examination (B-IV,1.2).

The search division uses the international patent classification (**R.8**, B-V,1). A decision of the President on a classification of an application is not appealable (**Art.106(1)**).

The search report and the abstract will be published (A-VI,1.3) and transmitted to the applicant (B-X,12; F-II,2.6) and the examining division (B-X,11.1).

2 **Composition of a search division**

The search division to which the search of an application is entrusted consists usually of one examiner, who is also the first member of the examining division for that application. The search division may consist of more than one examiner where the invention covers widely dispersed specialised fields. (B-I,2)

Art. 18 Examining Divisions

Art. 18(1) The Examining Divisions shall be responsible for the examination of any European patent applications.

See for the implementation:
R.10(2)-(4) Start of responsibility of examining division
R.91 Responsibility for limitation and revocation proceedings

1 **Responsibilities of the examining divisions**

At the time the Receiving Section ceases to be responsible for a European patent application, an examining division becomes responsible according to **R.10**. The passing of competence has been laid down in the Implementing Regulations to ensure flexibility.

The examining division is responsible for the substantive examination of the application (**Art.18(1)**) using the procedure prescribed in **Art.94(3)**, for the grant of the patent or the refusal of the application (**Art.97**) and the publication of the patent under **Art.98**. The examining division is also responsible for issuing technical opinions under **Art.25**. The 'any' in **Art.18(1)** emphasizes that the responsibilities include the examination of both direct European patent applications and Euro-PCT patent applications.

The responsibility of the examining division ends with the notification that the application is regarded as withdrawn under **Art.94(4)** or with the notification of the decision to grant the patent or refuse the application (**Art.97**).

According to **R.91** the examining division is also responsible for decisions on requests for limitation or revocation under **Art.105a**.

Art. 18(2) An Examining Division shall consist of three technically qualified examiners. However, before a decision is taken on a European patent application, its examination shall, as a general rule, be entrusted to one member of the Examining Division. Oral proceedings shall be before the Examining Division itself. If the Examining Division considers that the nature of the decision so requires, it shall be enlarged by the addition of a legally qualified examiner. In the event of parity of votes, the vote of the Chairman of the Examining Division shall be decisive.

1 **Composition of an examining division**

An examining division consists of a chairman, a first member and a second member, who are all technically qualified examiners. In exceptional cases a legally qualified member is added.

The major part of the work of the examining division is, as a general rule, carried out by the first member, the primary examiner. However, oral proceedings are before the entire examining division of three or four examiners. Likewise, decisions are taken by the entire examining division. The chairman of the division checks the substance of the decision and the second member carries out formal checks. **Art.18(2)** clarifies that each decision, whether final or not, is taken by the entire examining division.

The EPC has opted for the relatively costly principle of collegiate decision taking to increase the quality of the decisions, thereby reducing the number of appeals against the decisions of the examining divisions. Another reason for collegiate decision taking was to avoid that in the early days, when the EPC was still a new law, a decision taken by a single examiner could be influenced by his national background. (Empel no. 443)

Art.33(3) provides flexibility in the number of examiners in an examining division. The Administrative Council may decide that, in the light of experience, in certain categories of cases, e.g. certain technical fields, an examining division consist of only one technical examiner.

The examiners must be impartial. If an examiner is suspected of partiality, he may be objected to as set out in **Art.24:2**.

Art. 19 Opposition Divisions

Art. 19(1) The Opposition Divisions shall be responsible for the examination of oppositions against any European patent.

Art. 19(2) An Opposition Division shall consist of three technically qualified examiners, at least two of whom shall not have taken part in the proceedings for grant of the patent to which the opposition relates. An examiner who has taken part in the proceedings for the grant of the European patent may not be the Chairman. Before a decision is taken on the opposition, the Opposition Division may entrust the examination of the opposition to one of its members. Oral proceedings shall be before the Opposition Division itself. If the Opposition Division considers that the nature of the decision so requires, it shall be enlarged by the addition of a legally qualified examiner who shall not have taken part in the proceedings for grant of the patent. In the event of parity of votes, the vote of the Chairman of the Opposition Division shall be decisive.

1 **Composition of opposition division**
Art.19(2) establishes the collegiate nature of opposition divisions. The presence of one member who may have taken part in the grant proceedings is a compromise. On the one hand the purpose of an opposition is the examination of new facts and/or arguments added to the proceedings, for which examination there is no reason to deprive the opposition division of the available knowledge of the case, and on the other hand the members of the opposition division should be unbiassed as in appeal proceedings. The possibly biased member is always in a minority position. (Empel no. 465)

A composition of an opposition division not complying with **Art.19(2)** is a substantial procedural violation in the sense of **R.103(1)(a)** (**T251/88**; **T382/92**; **G5/91** r.5).

The examiners must be impartial. If an examiner is suspected of partiality, he may be objected to as set out in **Art.24:2**.

Art. 20 Legal Division

Art. 20(1) The Legal Division shall be responsible for decisions in respect of entries in the Register of European Patents and in respect of registration on, and deletion from, the list of professional representatives.

1 **Duties of Legal Division**
The Legal Division has the sole responsibility for the following duties regarding the Register of Patents (**Art.127**): entitlement procedure (**Art.61(1)** and **Art.99(4)**), interruption of proceedings, registration of licences and other rights, registration of transfers of rights and changes of name, and rectification of the designation of the inventor (Dec. Pres. OJ 2013, 600).

The duty of registration of transfers of rights and changes of name and rectification of the designation of the inventor is entrusted to formalities officers of examining divisions and opposition divisions under **R.11(3)** if the request can be granted directly (Dec. Pres. OJ 2013, 601).

The Legal Division has also the sole responsibility for entries, registrations and deletions in the Register of Representatives (**Art.134(1)**) and for assessment of the legal incapacity of a professional representative (**J901/86** hn3) (OJ 2013, 600).

Art. 20(2) Decisions of the Legal Division shall be taken by one legally qualified member.

1 **Decisions of the Legal Division**
Decisions of the Legal Division can be appealed before the Legal Board of Appeal (**Art.106(1)** and **Art.21(2)**, see **J1/78** as an example).

Art. 21 Boards of Appeal

See for the implementation:
R.12a Boards of Appeal Unit and President of Boards of Appeal
R.12b Presidium of the Boards of Appeal
R.12c Boards of Appeal Committee and Rules of Procedure
R.12d (Re-)appointment of members of boards

1 **Competence of boards of appeal**
Art.21 governs the competence of the boards of appeal. The boards are responsible for the examination of appeals from decisions of first instance departments and have jurisdiction to interpret the EPC. The boards have also jurisdiction to refuse enforcement of legislation which has been defectively enacted, for example if passed by an insufficient number of contracting states or delegations of the Administrative Council, or enforcement of a Rule which conflicts with an Article in the sense of **Art.164(2)** (**T315/03** r.5.8).

A board of appeal has the status of an internationally recognized judicial authority, because its members are only bound by the EPC (**Art.23(3)**), they are appointed for a fixed term (**Art.23(1)**), their impartiality is safeguarded (**Art.24**), at least one of the members is legally qualified (**Art.21**), they have their own rules of procedure (**R.12c(2)**) and they issue written, reasoned decisions (**R.102**) (**G1/97** r.5(c)).

Duties are allocated to the departments of second instance by the Presidium of **R.12b(4)**, and not by the President. The Administrative Council can delegate disciplinary matters against a professional representative to an existing board of appeal (**R.12b(6)**). However, until now these matters have been dealt with by a separate board. The Rules of Procedure for the Boards of Appeal are adopted by the Boards of Appeal Committee (**R.12c(2)**).

Cases from examining divisions not handled by technical boards of appeal as specified in paragraphs (3a) and (3b) of **Art.21** are normally handled by the Legal Board of Appeal (paragraph (3c)), e.g. a decision from an examining division consisting of fewer than four members and not relating to the refusal of a patent application, the grant, limitation or revocation of a patent, but for example to re-establishment (**G2/90** r.3.2, adapted to the revised wording of **Art.21(3)(a)**). See **Art.21(3):1.2** for an exception.

Art. 21(1) The Boards of Appeal shall be responsible for the examination of appeals from decisions of the Receiving Section, the Examining Divisions and Opposition Divisions, and the Legal Division.

1 **Competence to examine appeals**
The search division does not issue decisions. Hence, an opinion of the search division, e.g. on lack of unity of invention, cannot be appealed. There is also no possibility to appeal a decision of the President or a decision of a board of appeal, because these decisions are not comprised in the exhaustive list of **Art.106(1)**.

Art. 21(2) For appeals from decisions of the Receiving Section or the Legal Division, a Board of Appeal shall consist of three legally qualified members.

Art. 21(3) For appeals from a decision of an Examining Division, a Board of Appeal shall consist of:

(a) **two technically qualified members and one legally qualified member, when the decision concerns the refusal of a European patent application or the grant, limitation or revocation of a European patent, and was taken by an Examining Division consisting of less than four members;**

(b) **three technically and two legally qualified members, when the decision was taken by an Examining Division consisting of four members, or when the Board of Appeal considers that the nature of the appeal so requires;**

(c) **three legally qualified members in all other cases.**

1 **Board competent to decide on appeal from decision of Ex. Div.**

The intention of the **Art.21(3)** is that appeal cases in which the emphasis is on technical problems are dealt with by the technical boards of appeal (**Art.21(3)(a)**) and appeal cases in which the emphasis is on legal questions are dealt with by the Legal Board of Appeal (**Art.21(3)(c)**) (**T850/95a** r.3.3; **G1/11** r.9). The formulation of **Art.21(3)** in terms of procedure instead of expertise of the boards has resulted in a complicated provision including gaps (**G1/11** r.13), the interpretation of which has required a large number of decisions of boards of appeal.

Appeals from a decision of an opposition division are always dealt with by a technical board of appeal, independent of the emphasis of the case (**Art.21(4)**).

1.1 DECISIONS BY TECHNICAL BOARD OF APPEAL (ART.21(3)(A) AND (B))

The decisions under paragraphs (a) and (b) are taken by a technical board of appeal and indicated by a T number. The composition of the technical board depends on the composition of the examining division as set out in **Art.18(2)**. A technical board includes at least one legally qualified member to ensure that expertise on legal matters is always available (**J21/09** r.21).

The criterion set out in paragraph (a) does not require that the decision to grant as such is appealed. It is sufficient for the decision to 'concern' the grant. This is necessarily the case if the subject of the decision is the text in which the patent is to be granted or has been granted. (**G8/95** r.4)

The examining division usually consists of three technical members and may be enlarged by a legal member if the case requires so (**Art.18(2)**). **Art.21(3)(b)** refers to such a four member division.

1.2 DECISIONS BY LEGAL BOARD OF APPEAL (ART.21(3)(C))

The decisions mentioned under paragraph (c) are taken by the Legal Board of Appeal and indicated by a J number (from the German 'Juristische Beschwerdekammer').

The Legal Board of Appeal is competent to hear appeals against decisions taken by an examining division consisting of fewer than four members when the decision does not concern the refusal of an application or the grant of a patent, but e.g. the refund of an examination fee under **Rfees11** (**J9/10**). In all other cases, i.e. those covered by **Art.21(3)(a), (3)(b)** and (4), the technical board of appeal is competent. (**G2/90** hn.I)

Since **Art.21(3)(a)** does not apply to an interlocutory decision of the examining division which only refuses a request for refund of a search fee under **R.64(2)**, the case should be handled by a Legal Board according to **Art.21(3)(c)**. However, that is inappropriate because of the technical character of the case. The EBoA decided that there is a hole in **Art.21(3)** and, in view of the objective of the provision, that such a case must be decided by a Technical Board. (G1/11 hn)

2 **Decisions concerning refusal or grant**

When appealing a decision of an examining division refusing a request for correction, the subject of the correction determines which board is competent.

A decision of an examining division refusing a correction of the decision to grant (**R.140**) concerns the grant within the meaning of **Art.21(3)(a)**, in that it relates to the text in which the patent has to be granted or has been granted. An appeal from such a decision is to be decided by a technical board of appeal. (**G8/95** hn r.4)

A decision refusing a request for correcting a designation of a contracting state under **R.139** and allowing a separate appeal is prejudicial to the territorial scope for which the patent may be granted later on. Such a decision does not terminate the proceedings. It therefore does not concern the grant and the Legal Board of Appeal is responsible for an appeal, unless the decision has been taken by an examining division of four members (see **Art.21(3)(b)**). (**G8/95** r.5)

3 **Decisions concerning request for limitation or revocation**

Requests for limitation or revocation of European patents under **Art.105a - 105c** will entail ex parte proceedings requiring a decision by an examining division. Since limitation proceedings will focus in particular on compliance with **Art.84** (clarity of the claims) and **Art.123(2)** and (3) (added subject-matter, extended scope), appeals against the resulting decisions should be heard by the technical boards, as set out in **Art.21(3)(a)**. (Spec. Ed. 4, OJ 2007)

Art. 21(4) For appeals from a decision of an Opposition Division, a Board of Appeal shall consist of:

(a) two technically qualified members and one legally qualified member, when the decision was taken by an Opposition Division consisting of three members;

(b) three technically and two legally qualified members, when the decision was taken by an Opposition Division consisting of four members, or when the Board of Appeal considers that the nature of the appeal so requires.

1 **Board competent to decide on appeal from decision of opp. div.**

Paragraph (4) does not include the phrase 'three legally qualified members in all other cases' of paragraph (3)(c). Therefore, the technical board of appeal is exclusively competent to hear all appeals against decisions of an opposition division. The Legal Board of Appeal is not competent to handle appeals against decisions from the opposition division.

Hence, an appeal against a decision issued by a formalities officer in opposition proceedings, e.g. revoking a patent for nonpayment of the fee for publishing under **R.82(3)**, must also be heard by a technical board of appeal. Since a formalities officer may only take decisions involving no legal difficulties, there is no reason why the three-member Legal Board should be competent to hear the proceedings. (**G2/90**)

If the Legal Division has taken an adverse decision during opposition proceedings, e.g. relating to a transfer, the Legal Board of appeal is competent to hear the appeal against this decision (see for example **T553/90** r.2.2).

Art. 22 Enlarged Board of Appeal

See for the implementation:
R.13 Business distribution scheme for the Enlarged Board of Appeal and adoption of its Rules of Procedure

1 **General**
The Enlarged Board of Appeal is in general not a further instance, but a special department ensuring the uniform application of the EPC and for deciding on petitions for review. However, it is a further instance for review of decisions of the boards of appeal under **Art.112a**. Its decisions and opinions obtain a G number (from the German 'Grosse Beschwerdekammer'), its decisions on a request for review an R number.

Art. 22(1) The Enlarged Board of Appeal shall be responsible for:
(a) deciding on points of law referred to it by Boards of Appeal under Article 112;
(b) giving opinions on points of law referred to it by the President of the European Patent Office under Article 112.
(c) deciding on petitions for review of decisions of the Boards of Appeal under Article 112a.

Art.112 Referral to the Enlarged Board of Appeal.
Art.112a Petition for review

Art. 22(2) In proceedings under paragraph 1(a) and (b), the Enlarged Board of Appeal shall consist of five legally and two technically qualified members. In proceedings under paragraph 1(c), the Enlarged Board of Appeal shall consist of three or five members as laid down in the Implementing Regulations. In all proceedings, a legally qualified member shall be the Chairman.

See for the implementation:
R.109(2) Composition EBoA for examining petitions for review

1 **Composition for petitions for review**
The measures laid down in **Art.22(2)** and **R.109(2)** have been laid down to avoid the work of the EBoA being blocked by petitions for review. First, a three-member panel filters out the clearly inadmissible and clearly ill-founded petitions for review. Second, admitted petitions will be examined by a five-member Enlarged Board of Appeal. The composition of the EBoA in proceedings relating to petitions for review is laid down in the Implementing Regulations to be able to react to future experience with the legal remedy introduced in the EPC 2000. (Spec. Ed. 4, OJ 2007)

Art. 23 Independence of the members of the Boards

Art. 23(1) The members of the Enlarged Board of Appeal and of the Boards of Appeal shall be appointed for a term of five years and may not be removed from office during this term, except if there are serious grounds for such removal and if the Administrative Council, on a proposal from the Enlarged Board of Appeal, takes a decision to this effect. Notwithstanding sentence 1, the term of office of members of the Boards shall end if they resign or are retired in accordance with the Service Regulations for permanent employees of the European Patent Office.

1 **Term of appointment**

A board member is appointed for a term of five years according to **Art.23(1)** with the possibility of re-appointment for a subsequent term (**Art.11(3)**). The legislator limited the term to five years, because the workload of the boards was not foreseeable when drafting the EPC. The finite term would allow the EPO to move board members with a low workload to another position in the office. (Singer, Art.11, rdn 3)

Independence of members of boards of appeal requires that the executive authorities cannot exert pressure on the members and that they do not have to fear for their position if they take decisions disagreeable to the authorities. For that reason, it is of vital importance that the members cannot be dismissed. The five-year term of **Art.23(1)** conflicts with the independence, because it gives the AC a possibility to dismiss a member by denying him a re-appointment. See also **R.12a:2.**

2 **Removal of board member**

A member of the EBoA or a BoA may be removed from office only on serious grounds. The Administrative Council (AC) must request the EBoA to make a proposal to remove the board member and then take a decision to this effect based on the proposal. The procedure before the EBoA is laid down in RPE-BoA Art.12a and Art.2(2) and (5).

In a disciplinary case against a board member the judicial independence of the Enlarged Board of Appeal according to **Art.23(3)** was fundamentally denied. In December 2014 the President ordered a house ban on a member of the boards of appeal because of alleged misconduct. Note, that according to **Art.10(2)(h)**, the President may only propose disciplinary actions to the AC with regard to board members (situation prior to the reform of the BoA in 2016, see **R.12a:1**) and that the AC has disciplinary power over these members under **Art.11(4)**. Nevertheless, the AC confirmed the suspension and requested the EBoA to make a proposal to remove the member from office.

During the proceedings dealing with the request in June 2016, the president of the EPO, who was not a party to the proceedings, intervened and instructed the EBoA not to carry out an investigation of the alleged facts and not to conduct the oral proceedings in public, contrary to the order of the EBoA, and threatened the members of the EBoA with disciplinary measures (Art.23 1/16, r.40). See the following section for the disciplinary measures. Since the intervention of the president violated the judicial independence of the EBoA and the AC as party to the proceedings did not distance itself sufficiently from the president's position, the board decided not to make the requested proposal.

The order of the EBoA to publish decision Art.23 1/16 has not yet been executed by the EPO. Therefore, reference is to be made to Wikipedia, English version, search for 'Art. 23', where the text of the decision can be found.

3 **Term and disciplinary measure**
Since 2015, the finite term has become an actual threat to the independence of the board members. A removal of a board member from office on serious grounds is normally preceded by a suspension until the AC has received a proposal from the EBoA and takes a decision to remove the member. The internal Service Regulations of the EPO, amended and approved by the AC in 2015, allow the AC to suspend a member to the end of his five year term under **Art.23(1)**. Upon expiry of the five-year term, the AC can deny re-appointment without a proper **Art.23(1)** proposal from the EBoA. Hence, any board member can be suspended indefinitely by a mere decision of the AC, which affects the independence of the members. (decision EBoA Art.23 1/16 r.9-13)

The board member who was given a house ban was removed from the boards of appeal at the end of December 2017, the expiry of his five-year term, without a proposal from the EBoA and without any reasons being published.

Art. 23(2) The members of the Boards may not be members of the Receiving Section, Examining Divisions, Opposition Divisions or Legal Division.

1 **Exclusions of membership**
The search divisions are not mentioned in this provision, because they cannot take appealable decisions and, hence, a conflict with the separation of instances is not possible.

Art. 23(3) In their decisions the members of the Boards shall not be bound by any instructions and shall comply only with the provisions of this Convention.

1 **Binding of board of appeal**
The boards are not bound by instructions such as those referred to in **Art.10(2)(a)**, i.e. the Guidelines (followed by **T162/82** hn.1) and by decisions of national courts (see e.g. **T885/02** r.3.3). Decisions of the Administrative Council on interpretation of provisions of the Convention do neither bind the boards; such decisions may nevertheless be taken into account for purposes of interpretation (**J16/96** r.2).

Art. 23(4) The Rules of Procedure of the Boards of Appeal and the Enlarged Board of Appeal shall be adopted in accordance with the Implementing Regulations. They shall be subject to the approval of the Administrative Council.

1 **Rules of Procedure of the boards of appeal**
See **R.12c(2)** for Rules of Procedure of the Boards of Appeal and of the Enlarged Board of Appeal. The Rules of Procedure are binding on the Boards of Appeal and the Enlarged Board of Appeal (**Art.23** R. Proc. BoA and **Art.19** R. Proc. EBoA).

Art.23(4) is directed to the process by which the Rules of Procedure are adopted; it does not require that the Rules of Procedure should always comply with the current version of the Implementing Regulations. The Implementing Regulations of the EPC may not be amended so as to cause a conflict with an already existing Rule of Procedure. Hence, **R.116(1)**, relating to the contents of the summons for oral proceedings, adopted by the Administrative Council although it is in conflict with **Art.11(2)** (since 12.12.2002 **Art.11(1)**) of the R. Proc. BoA, is not applicable to the Boards of Appeal. (**G6/95**)

Art. 24 Exclusion and objection

1 **General**

Any party is entitled to have his case decided in an objective way by unprejudiced, impartial judges. This legal principle is laid down in the EPC in **Art.24**, which allows members of boards of appeal and the Enlarged Board of Appeal to be objected to and excluded from proceedings. There are no comparable provisions for members of the departments of first instance; case law has provided corresponding rules (see below).

Specific grounds for objection are given in **Art.24(1)**. A member of a board may ask to be excluded from an appeal for any reason (**Art.24(2)**); a party may also request the exclusion of a member of a board for a reason stated in the law (**Art.24(3)**). **Art.24(4)** relates to the procedure to decide on the objection.

2 **Partiality in departments of first instance**

The EPC has no provisions for exclusion of a member of a department of first instance from participation because of suspected partiality, in contrast with the provision for the members of second instance departments (**Art.24**). The Enlarged Board of Appeal has decided that the basic requirement of impartiality also applies to employees of the departments of first instance, albeit less strictly than stipulated in **Art.24(1)** (**G5/91**). For instance, one member of an opposition division may have taken part in the proceedings for grant of the patent to which the opposition relates (**Art.19(2)**, in contrast with **Art.24(1)**). Different views of an examiner and a party held on issues of the case are in themselves not disqualifying, and can be remedied in appeal (**T261/88**). An examiner may be suspected of partiality if he is a former employee of a party. The length of time between the examiner's last action for his former employer and his first action as examiner in a case to which this employer is a party may be important when assessing partiality, since any residual bias due to this employment would gradually fade away with time; 21 months is regarded as sufficiently long (**T261/88**).

Any challenge to impartiality must be submitted to the division, which will forward it to the responsible superior of the members of the division, usually a Director of a department of first instance. A decision of the superior rejecting an objection to a member cannot be appealed separately. However, the decision regarding the objection may be challenged in an appeal against the final decision of the division or against an interlocutory decision allowing appeal. The opposition division itself may also decide on the objection by means of an appealable interlocutory decision. (**G5/91**; E-XI)

Partiality of a member of the first instance constitutes a substantial procedural violation in the sense of **R.103(1)(a)** (**T261/88** r.2.1). Where a decision by a first-instance department is set aside because of a substantial procedural violation, and a party has reasonable grounds to suspect that the same composition of the department would be tainted by the previous decision and therefore partial, the case will be reheard before a different composition of the department at the request of the party (**T433/93** hn.II).

Participation of a member in a decision of a board of appeal in breach of **Art.24(1)** or despite being excluded by a decision under **Art.24(4)** is a ground for review (**Art.112a(2)(a)**). Suspicion of partiality under **Art.24(3)** is only a ground for review if proven and decided by the board (**G2/08a** r.1.3).

Art. 24(1) Members of the Boards of Appeal or of the Enlarged Board of Appeal may not take part in a case in which they have any personal interest, or if they have previously been involved as representatives of one of the parties, or if they participated in the decision under appeal.

1 **Partiality in departments of second instance**
Members of a board of appeal may be objected to if there is a suspicion of partiality, so the members are prevented from being influenced in their decision-making by extraneous considerations, i.e. considerations other than the arguments that are factually and legally relevant for the case (**G1/05a**).

Partiality for objective reasons is a prejudice or apparent bias, i.e. a preconceived judgment regarding substantive issues on how a case should be decided. A preconceived judgment of a member of a board may be caused by participation in a previous decision on the case; such a judgment may result from the laudable desire of the member to be logical and coherent in his successive decisions (**T1028/96** r.6.1).

Partiality for subjective reasons is to willingly favour a party by granting it rights to which it is not entitled or by intentionally disregarding the rights of another party (**T843/91** hn.IV). Partiality for subjective reasons is related to persons, whereas partiality for objective reasons is related to subject-matter (see also E-X).

Art.24(1) contains three specific reasons for objection to members of the boards of appeal to safeguard parties from prejudice and partiality.

1 A member may not have a personal interest in the appeal.
2 A member may not have been involved previously as representative of one of the parties. The German and French version of the provision make clear that the exclusion must be limited to members that have previously been involved as representatives of one of the parties in this particular case; otherwise, a former representative of a company would be excluded from all cases of this company.
3 A member of a board of appeal or the Enlarged Board of Appeal may not have participated in the decision under appeal. The 'decision under appeal' is the decision of a department of first instance, not the decision of the board of appeal referring to the Enlarged Board of Appeal.

The first two reasons relate mainly to partiality for subjective reasons (see e.g. **T843/91** r.6.3), the third reason to partiality for objective reasons.

The exclusion does not apply to a member of a board deciding on a patent in opposition appeal who was also a member of a board deciding on the grant of the same patent, because the latter decision is not 'the decision under appeal'. However, his participation in the opposition appeal may be objected to under **Art.24(3)** on the ground of prejudice if the opposition appeal concerns the same or comparable crucial issue as the decision in grant, e.g. sufficiency of disclosure (**T1028/96** hn.I, r.6.2, 6.5).

2 **Partiality in Enlarged Board of Appeal**
Participation of members of the Enlarged Board of Appeal in the referring decision of the board of appeal is not governed by **Art.24(2)** but by the Rules of Procedure of the Enlarged Board of Appeal. **Art.2(4)** of these Rules requires that at least four of the members of the Enlarged Board shall not have taken part in the proceedings referring the point of law (even stricter in **G1/05a** r.26).

Art. 24(2) If, for one of the reasons mentioned in paragraph 1, or for any other reason, a member of a Board of Appeal or of the Enlarged Board of Appeal considers that he should not take part in any appeal, he shall inform the Board accordingly.

1 **Withdrawal of member**
If a member of a board of appeal or the Enlarged Board of Appeal considers, for a reason mentioned in paragraph 1 or for any other reason, that he should not take part in an appeal, he must inform the board accordingly (**Art.24(2)**). An example of any other reason is a close family relationship with a party, e.g. a party being represented by a law firm in which the EBoA member's husband and son were partners (**G1/05a** r.3, 4).

The requirement of impartiality in proceedings before the boards of appeal and the Enlarged Board of Appeal must be very strictly observed in view of their judicial functions at supreme level within the European system of patent law (**G5/91** r.3). **Art.24(2)** serves to safeguard this principle by obliging a member to inform the board if he considers that he should not take part in the appeal for any reason. This avoids that such reason comes up later and affects the proceedings. Hence, a ground put forward in a notice of withdrawal of a member should normally be respected by the decision on replacement. (**G1/05a** r.5-7)

However, a member cannot withdraw from the proceedings at will, i.e. for reasons not related to protection of a party from possible partiality of the member. On the other hand it should also be avoided that a board member has to sit in a case where he or she is convinced or fears that he or she might not be able to be impartial. If no party raises an objection to the withdrawal, the board will decide to replace the member. (**G1/05a** r.8-11)

Art. 24(3) Members of a Board of Appeal or of the Enlarged Board of Appeal may be objected to by any party for one of the reasons mentioned in paragraph 1, or if suspected of partiality. An objection shall not be admissible if, while being aware of a reason for objection, the party has taken a procedural step. An objection may not be based upon the nationality of members.

1 **Objections to members of board of appeal**
Members of a board of appeal may be objected to (**Art.24(3)**):
- for taking part in a case in which they have any personal interest, or
- if they have previously been involved in this case as representatives of one of the parties, or
- if they participated in the decision under appeal, or
- if suspected of partiality.

Nationality of a member cannot be used as a reason for objection.

In the first two cases partiality is presumed, in the fourth case partiality is suspected. For example, a former representative of a party that did not act in the case in suit is not presumed to be partial under **Art.24(1)** but may be suspected of partiality under **Art.24(3)**.

Participation of a member of the Enlarged Board of Appeal in a technical or legal board of appeal is not a ground for exclusion or objection, because the legislator has deliberately provided this structure. Otherwise, this fact would have been a ground for exclusion or objection. (**R19/12** r.13.3)

An objection of partiality cannot be based alone on the participation of a member of the Enlarged Board of Appeal in a decision referred to the Enlarged Board of Appeal. There may be a ground for objection if there was a reason to believe that the prior decision was the result of a preconceived attitude, or if the member had expressed himself in outspoken, extreme or unbalanced terms on the matter. (**G1/05a** r.20-27)

The vice-president of DG3, who is chairman of the Enlarged Board of Appeal by force of habit, has resigned part of his management functions in response to a partiality objection in order to avoid a possible conflict of interests as manager and chairman (**R19/12**).

A suspicion may be based on views expressed on other occasions. However, the suspicion must be substantiated in mentioning the member involved, stating concrete remarks and circumstances and the relation to the present case. A view on the issue to be decided expressed by a member on a previous occasion is insufficient to suspect partiality. There may be partiality if a member had expressed that he would never change his mind on a certain question. (**G3/08a** r.2)

When a party becomes aware of a reason for objection, he must raise the objection before he takes a procedural step. Raising an objection is not regarded as a procedural step in the sense of **Art.24(3)**.

Whereas the reasons for exclusion in **Art.24(1)** may be put forward by anyone (**G2/08a** r.1.2), a suspicion of partiality may only be put forward by a party to the proceedings under **Art.24(3)**. However, a suspicion of partiality raised by a third person, not party to the proceedings, may be taken into account under Art.4(1) RPEBoA (and, similarly, under Art. 3(1) RPBoA) (**G3/08a** r.1). When a third person files objections, the board should assess whether they amount to abuse of procedure (**G2/08a** r.2.3).

Art. 24(4) The Boards of Appeal and the Enlarged Board of Appeal shall decide as to the action to be taken in the cases specified in paragraphs 2 and 3, without the participation of the member concerned. For the purposes of taking this decision the member objected to shall be replaced by his alternate.

1 **Procedure**

An objection to one or more members of a board of appeal can only be made in the course of an appeal pending before that board of appeal (**T843/91**). The procedure to assess objections under **Art.24(1)** and (3) comprises a first step of determining the admissibility of the objection and a second step of examining the objection substantively. The first step prevents abuse to delay the proceedings.

The admissibility is assessed by the board in its original composition (**T1028/96** hn.II). The three formal conditions for admissibility are:

1 the party may not have taken a procedural step while being aware of a reason for objection (**Art.24(3)**); hence, the request should be filed as soon as there is a suspicion of partiality;
2 the objection may not be based upon the nationality of the members (**Art.24(3)**); and
3 the objection must be reasoned, indicating facts and arguments to support the objection (**T1028/96** r.2).

The first condition reduces the chances that a party makes the objection only because an adverse decision is expected. The membership of the boards of appeal as designated according to **R.12b(4)** is published annually in the first issue of the OJ and the actual composition of the board competent for a specific case is given in the summons to the oral proceedings.

If the objection is admissible, the second step in the assessment of the objection, i.e. the examination, starts with the appointment of the alternate(s) of the member(s) objected to. In its new composition the board decides on the objection and as to the action to be taken according to **Art.24(4)**. The issue is not whether the member was in fact partial but whether reasons exist to suspect the member of partiality (**T1028/96** r.6.1).

Proceedings in the case may only continue after the decision on objection has been taken (Art.3(3) RPBoA). Documents in a file relating to the exclusion of or objections to members of the boards of appeal or of the Enlarged Board of Appeal are excluded from public inspection (**R.144(a)**).

Art. 25 Technical opinion

At the request of the competent national court hearing an infringement or revocation action, the European Patent Office shall be obliged, on payment of an appropriate fee, to give a technical opinion concerning the European patent which is the subject of the action. The Examining Division shall be responsible for issuing such opinions.

1 **Formal and substantive issues**

The fee for a technical opinion is fixed in **Rfees2(1)20**. If the request for an opinion is withdrawn before the EPO has done any substantive work, 75% of the fee will be refunded (**Rfees10**).

The responsible examining division will give a technical opinion on any question which is similar to those normally dealt with in substantive examination work; it does not give an opinion on the scope of protection and does not make specific statements on the question whether or not a patent is valid or is infringed, because these matters are for the national courts to decide (E-XIII,2). An individual cannot obtain a technical opinion from the EPO, only national courts can (**Art.25**).

Chapter IV *The Administrative Council*

1 **General**
The Administrative Council is an organ of the European Patent Organisation (**Art.4(2)**). Its task is the supervision of the European Patent Office (**Art.4(3)**). The competence of the Administrative Council is given in **Art.33**.

Art. 26 Membership

Art. 26(1) The Administrative Council shall be composed of the Representatives and the alternate Representatives of the Contracting States. Each Contracting State shall be entitled to appoint one Representative and one alternate Representative to the Administrative Council.

1 **Representative in Administrative Council**
The appointed Representative of a contracting state in the Administrative Council is usually the president of the national patent office. The composition of the Administrative Council is published regularly in the Official Journal (see e.g. OJ 2008, 389).

Art. 26(2) The members of the Administrative Council may, in accordance with the Rules of Procedure of the Administrative Council, be assisted by advisers or experts.

Art. 27 Chairmanship

Art. 27(1) The Administrative Council shall elect a Chairman and a Deputy Chairman from among the Representatives and alternate Representatives of the Contracting States. The Deputy Chairman shall ex officio replace the Chairman if he is prevented from carrying out his duties.

Art. 27(2) The terms of office of the Chairman and the Deputy Chairman shall be three years. They may be re-elected.

Art. 28 Board

1 **Setting up of the Board**
By decision of the Administrative Council of 05.06.2003, which entered into force on 01.07.2003, a Board of the Administrative Council has been set up to assist the Chairman in preparing and ensuring the continuity of the work of the Council (OJ 2003, 333, 579).

Art. 28(1) When there are at least eight Contracting States, the Administrative Council may set up a Board composed of five of its members.

Art. 28(2) The Chairman and the Deputy Chairman of the Administrative Council shall be members of the Board ex officio; the other three members shall be elected by the Administrative Council.

Art. 28(3) The term of office of the members elected by the Administrative Council shall be three years. They may not be re-elected.

Art. 28(4) The Board shall perform the duties assigned to it by the Administrative Council in accordance with the Rules of Procedure.

Art. 29 Meetings

Art. 29(1) Meetings of the Administrative Council shall be convened by its Chairman.

Art. 29(2) The President of the European Patent Office shall take part in the deliberations of the Administrative Council.

Art. 29(3) The Administrative Council shall hold an ordinary meeting once each year. In addition, it shall meet on the initiative of its Chairman or at the request of one-third of the Contracting States.

Art. 29(4) The deliberations of the Administrative Council shall be based on an agenda, and shall be held in accordance with its Rules of Procedure.

Art. 29(5) The provisional agenda shall contain any question whose inclusion is requested by any Contracting State in accordance with the Rules of Procedure.

Art. 30 Attendance of observers

Art. 30(1) The World Intellectual Property Organization shall be represented at the meetings of the Administrative Council, in accordance with an agreement between the Organisation and the World Intellectual Property Organization.

Art. 30(2) Other intergovernmental organisations entrusted with carrying out international procedures in the field of patents, with which the Organisation has concluded an agreement, shall be represented at the meetings of the Administrative Council, in accordance with such agreement.

Art. 30(3) Any other intergovernmental and international non-governmental organisations carrying out an activity of interest to the Organisation may be invited by the Administrative Council to be represented at its meetings during any discussion of matters of mutual interest.

Art. 31 Languages of the Administrative Council

Art. 31(1) The languages used in the deliberations of the Administrative Council shall be English, French and German.

Art. 31(2) Documents submitted to the Administrative Council, and the minutes of its deliberations, shall be drawn up in the three languages specified in paragraph 1.

Art. 32 Staff, premises and equipment

The European Patent Office shall place at the disposal of the Administrative Council, and of any committee established by it, such staff, premises and equipment as may be necessary for the performance of their duties.

Art. 33 Competence of the Administrative Council in certain cases

Fields of competence of the Administrative Council as provided in some other articles of the EPC: **Art.4(3), 11(3), 23(1)** and the articles mentioned in **Art.35(2)**.

Art. 33(1) The Administrative Council shall be competent to amend:
(a) the time limits laid down in this Convention;
(b) Parts II to VIII and Part X of this Convention, to bring them into line with an international treaty relating to patents or European Community legislation relating to patents;
(c) the Implementing Regulations.

Part II-VII Art.52-141
Part X Art.150-153

1 **Amendment of the EPC**
The Convention can in principle only be amended by a Revision Conference (**Art.172**). **Art.33(1)** is an exception intended to allow the Organisation to respond quickly to changing circumstances. The Implementing regulations can be amended by the Administrative Council (Art.33(1)(c). Amendments are prepared by DG1 and DG5 in consultation with a.o. the epi (Art.134a(1)(a)). Since 2012 users of the patent system are consulted on the EPO website (OJ 2012, 643).

2 **Amendment of time limits in the Convention (Art.33(1)(a))**
Paragraph 1(a) allows the Administrative Council to amend the time limits in the Convention. These time limits are, in the sense of **Art.120**, periods within which a party has to perform an act before the EPO. Six such time limits have been amended in the EPC 1973 over about 30 years. Since the term of the patent in **Art.63** is not such a time limit, a revision of the term requires an amendment under **Art.33(1)(b)** or a Revision Conference according to **Art.172** (see **Art.63(2):1**).

3 **Amendment of the Convention in view of international treaties (Art.33(1)(b))**
The Administrative Council may bring the parts of the Convention relating to patent law and procedural law in line with international treaties or European Community legislation relating to patents under **Art.33(1)(b)**. It is understood that the Administrative Council can exercise this competence in the case of any treaty, convention or Community text containing provisions relating to patent law (for example, the provisions of Part II, Section 5 of Annex 1C (the TRIPs Agreement) to the Agreement Establishing the World Trade Organization of 15 April 1994). Any consensus already achieved at EU, WIPO or WTO level can be directly echoed in the EPC, avoiding having to hold a revision conference and without national ratification procedures of uncertain duration and outcome. (Spec. Ed. 4, OJ 2007)

It may only do so once an international treaty or EU legislation has entered into force or after expiry of the period for implementation if such period has been laid down in the EU legislation (**Art.33(5)**). A decision on amendment requires unanimity of the contracting states and representation of all of them (**Art.35(3)**). A decision on amendment will not take effect if a contracting state declares within 12 months of the date of the decision that it does not wish to be bound by that decision (**Art.35(3)**).

The conditions, introduced to accommodate misgivings of contracting states about a transfer of sovereign rights to the European Patent Organisation, have made the provision so restrictive that it will be barely applicable in practice.

4 **Amendment of the Implementing Regulations** (**Art.33(1)(c)**)

The Implementing Regulations can be amended under **Art.33(1)(c)** by a decision of the Administrative Council. Over the past years the Implementing Regulations were amended approximately twice a year.

The amendments may relate to procedural and substantive issues and are only limited by **Art.164(2)** (**G2/07** r.2.2, distinguishing **J11/91** r.2.3.4).

Art. 33(2) The Administrative Council shall be competent, in conformity with this Convention, to adopt or amend:

(a) the Financial Regulations;

(b) the Service Regulations for permanent employees and the conditions of employment of other employees of the European Patent Office, the salary scales of the said permanent and other employees, and also the nature of any supplementary benefits and the rules for granting them;

(c) the Pension Scheme Regulations and any appropriate increases in existing pensions to correspond to increases in salaries;

(d) the Rules relating to Fees;

(e) its Rules of Procedure.

1 **Service Regulations**

The Service Regulations are available on the EPO website; search for 'EPO' and 'Service Regulations'.

Art. 33(3) Notwithstanding Article 18, paragraph 2, the Administrative Council shall be competent to decide, in the light of experience, that in certain categories of cases Examining Divisions shall consist of one technically qualified examiner only. Such decision may be rescinded.

Art.18(2) Composition of examining divisions

No use has been made of this possibility.

Art. 33(4) The Administrative Council shall be competent to authorise the President of the European Patent Office to negotiate and, subject to its approval, to conclude agreements on behalf of the European Patent Organisation with States, with intergovernmental organisations and with documentation centres set up on the basis of agreements with such organisations.

1 **Agreements concluded by the President**
Examples of such agreements are: agreements regarding the seat of the EPO in Munich and the branch in The Hague, integration of the IIB and INPADOC into the EPO (see **Art.6(2)**), agreement between EPO and WIPO regarding PCT (**Art.152**).

Art. 33(5) The Administrative Council may not take a decision under paragraph 1(b):
- **concerning an international treaty, before its entry into force;**
- **concerning European Community legislation, before its entry into force or, where that legislation lays down a period for its implementation, before the expiry of that period.**

Art.33(1)(b) Amendment to align EPC with international treaties

Art. 34 Voting rights

Art. 34(1) The right to vote in the Administrative Council shall be restricted to the Contracting States.

Art. 34(2) Each Contracting State shall have one vote, except where Article 36 applies.

Art.36 Weighting of votes

Art. 35 Voting rules

Art. 35(1) The Administrative Council shall take its decisions, other than those referred to in paragraphs 2 and 3, by a simple majority of the Contracting States represented and voting.

Art. 35(2) A majority of three-quarters of the votes of the Contracting States represented and voting shall be required for the decisions which the Administrative Council is empowered to take under Article 7, Article 11, paragraph 1, Article 33, paragraphs 1(a) and (c), and 2 to 4, Article 39, paragraph 1, Article 40, paragraphs 2 and 4, Article 46, Article 134a, Article 149a, paragraph 2, Article 152, Article 153, paragraph 7, Article 166 and Article 172.

Art.7 Sub-offices of the EPO
Art.11(1) Appointment of senior employees
Art.33(1)(a) Amendment of Convention time limits
Art.33(1)(c) Amendment of the Implementing Regulations
Art.33(2) Amendment to the Financial Regulations, Service Regulations, Pension Scheme Regulations, Rules relating to Fees and Rules of Procedure of the Administrative Council
Art.33(3) Composition of Examining Divisions
Art.33(4) Authorisation of the President to conclude agreements
Art.39(1) Payment of proportion of renewal fees for a patent to the EPO
Art.40(2) Contribution by contracting states if EPO has insufficient income
Art.40(4) Decision on scale position of contracting state
Art.46 Preparation and adoption of the budget

Art.134a Provisions governing epi, admission to and conduct of the European qualifying examination, disciplinary power over representatives, obligation of confidentiality and non-disclosure privilege
Art.149a(2) Serving of members of the (E)BoA on a European patent court
Art.152 The EPO as ISA or IPEA
Art.153(7) Dispensing with supplementary search report or reduction of the search fee there for
Art.166 Accession to the Convention
Art.172 Revision of the Convention

Art. 35(3) Unanimity of the Contracting States voting shall be required for the decisions which the Administrative Council is empowered to take under Article 33, paragraph 1(b). The Administrative Council shall take such decisions only if all the Contracting States are represented. A decision taken on the basis of Article 33, paragraph 1(b), shall not take effect if a Contracting State declares, within twelve months of the date of the decision, that it does not wish to be bound by that decision.

Art.33(1)(b) Amendment to align EPC with international treaties

1 **Conditions for amending EPC in view of international treaties**
Art.35(3) is introduced in response to the need to lay down a special provision governing the adoption and entry into force of a decision of the Administrative Council under **Art.33(1)(b)** modifying the EPC.

Three guarantees are laid down in **Art.35(3)**:

- an Administrative Council decision under **Art.33(1)(b)** requires unanimity among the voting Contracting States (**Art.35(3)**, first sentence);
- all the Contracting States must be represented when votes are being cast (**Art.35(3)**, second sentence);
- each Contracting State has a period of 12 months from the time the decision is adopted by the Administrative Council in which to declare that it does not wish to be bound by the decision, thus preventing the decision's entry into force. This period allows representatives of the Contracting States on the Administrative Council to confer with the national legislative bodies to ensure that the change is acceptable (**Art.35(3)**, third sentence).

However, the guarantees offered by **Art.35(3)** differ from those in **Art.172** in one fundamental respect: whereas **Art.172(4)** obliges a Contracting State to cease to be a party to the EPC if it has not ratified a revised text of the EPC in due time, a state exercising its right to declare its opposition to the entry into force of an Administrative Council decision under **Art.33(1)(b)** would not of course incur any sanction. The alternative under **Art.172(4)** - between ratifying in due time and ceasing to be a party to the EPC - is therefore supplemented by a genuine possibility of intervention by national legislative bodies. (Spec. Ed. 4, OJ 2007)

Art. 35(4) Abstentions shall not be considered as votes.

Art. 36 Weighting of votes

Art. 36(1) **In respect of the adoption or amendment of the Rules relating to Fees and, if the financial contribution to be made by the Contracting States would thereby be increased, the adoption of the budget of the Organisation and of any amending or supplementary budget, any Contracting State may require, following a first ballot in which each Contracting State shall have one vote, and whatever the result of this ballot, that a second ballot be taken immediately, in which votes shall be given to the States in accordance with paragraph 2. The decision shall be determined by the result of this second ballot.**

Art. 36(2) **The number of votes that each Contracting State shall have in the second ballot shall be calculated as follows:**

(a) **the percentage obtained for each Contracting State in respect of the scale for the special financial contributions, pursuant to Article 40, paragraphs 3 and 4, shall be multiplied by the number of Contracting States and divided by five;**

(b) **the number of votes thus given shall be rounded upwards to the next whole number;**

(c) **five additional votes shall be added to this number;**

(d) **nevertheless, no Contracting State shall have more than 30 votes.**

Art.40(3), (4) Level of fees and payments - Special financial contributions

Chapter V *Financial provisions*

Art. 37 Budgetary funding

The budget of the Organisation shall be financed:

(a) by the Organisation's own resources;
(b) by payments made by the Contracting States in respect of renewal fees for European patents levied in these States;
(c) where necessary, by special financial contributions made by the Contracting States;
(d) where appropriate, by the revenue provided for in Article 146;
(e) where appropriate, and for tangible assets only, by third-party borrowings secured on land or buildings;
(f) where appropriate, by third-party funding for specific projects.

Art.146 Cover for expenditure for carrying out special tasks

Art. 38 The Organisation's own resources

The Organisation's own resources shall comprise:

(a) all income from fees and other sources and also the reserves of the Organisation;
(b) the resources of the Pension Reserve Fund, which shall be treated as a special class of asset of the Organisation, designed to support the Organisation's pension scheme by providing the appropriate reserves.

Art. 39 Payments by the Contracting States in respect of renewal fees for European patents

Art. 39(1) Each Contracting State shall pay to the Organisation in respect of each renewal fee received for a European patent in that State an amount equal to a proportion of that fee, to be fixed by the Administrative Council; the proportion shall not exceed 75% and shall be the same for all Contracting States. However, if the said proportion corresponds to an amount which is less than a uniform minimum amount fixed by the Administrative Council, the Contracting State shall pay that minimum to the Organisation.

1 **Renewal fee payment of contracting states**
At present a contracting state remits 50% of the renewal fee it has received for a European patent to the EPO (Dec. of Adm. Council of 08.06.1984, OJ 1984, 296). See Art.147:2 for the distribution of the renewal fee payments for European patents with unitary effect.

Art. 39(2) Each Contracting State shall communicate to the Organisation such information as the Administrative Council considers to be necessary to determine the amount of these payments.

Art. 39(3) The due dates for these payments shall be determined by the Administrative Council.

Art. 39(4) If a payment is not remitted fully by the due date, the Contracting State shall pay interest from the due date on the amount remaining unpaid.

Art. 40 Level of fees and payments – Special financial contributions

Art. 40(1) The amounts of the fees referred to in Article 38 and the proportion referred to in Article 39 shall be fixed at such a level as to ensure that the revenue in respect thereof is sufficient for the budget of the Organisation to be balanced.

Art.38 The organisation's own resources
Art.39 Payments by the Contracting States in respect of renewal fees for European patents

Art. 40(2) However, if the Organisation is unable to balance its budget under the conditions laid down in paragraph 1, the Contracting States shall remit to the Organisation special financial contributions, the amount of which shall be determined by the Administrative Council for the accounting period in question.

Art. 40(3) These special financial contributions shall be determined in respect of any Contracting State on the basis of the number of patent applications filed in the last year but one prior to that of entry into force of this Convention, and calculated in the following manner:

(a) one half in proportion to the number of patent applications filed in that Contracting State;

(b) one half in proportion to the second highest number of patent applications filed in the other Contracting States by natural or legal persons having their residence or principal place of business in that Contracting State.

However, the amounts to be contributed by States in which the number of patent applications filed exceeds 25 000 shall then be taken as a whole and a new scale drawn up in proportion to the total number of patent applications filed in these States.

Art. 40(4) Where the scale position of any Contracting State cannot be established in accordance with paragraph 3, the Administrative Council shall, with the consent of that State, decide its scale position.

Art. 40(5) Article 39, paragraphs 3 and 4, shall apply mutatis mutandis to the special financial contributions.

Art.39(3), (4) Payments by the Contracting States in respect of renewal fees for European patents

Art. 40(6) The special financial contributions shall be repaid with interest at a rate which shall be the same for all Contracting States. Repayments shall be made in so far as it is possible to provide for this purpose in the budget; the amount thus provided shall be distributed among the Contracting States in accordance with the scale referred to in paragraphs 3 and 4.

Art. 40(7) The special financial contributions remitted in any accounting period shall be repaid in full before any such contributions or parts thereof remitted in any subsequent accounting period are repaid.

Art. 41 Advances

Art. 41(1) At the request of the President of the European Patent Office, the Contracting States shall grant advances to the Organisation, on account of their payments and contributions, within the limit of the amount fixed by the Administrative Council. The amount of such advances shall be determined in proportion to the amounts due from the Contracting States for the accounting period in question.

Art. 41(2) Article 39, paragraphs 3 and 4, shall apply mutatis mutandis to the advances.

Art.39(3), (4) Payments by the Contracting States in respect of renewal fees for European patents

Art. 42 Budget

Art. 42(1) The budget of the Organisation shall be balanced. It shall be drawn up in accordance with the generally accepted accounting principles laid down in the Financial Regulations. If necessary, there may be amending or supplementary budgets.

Art. 42(2) The budget shall be drawn up in the unit of account fixed in the Financial Regulations.

Art. 43 Authorisation for expenditure

Art. 43(1) The expenditure entered in the budget shall be authorised for the duration of one accounting period, unless the Financial Regulations provide otherwise.

Art. 43(2) In accordance with the Financial Regulations, any appropriations, other than those relating to staff costs, which are unexpended at the end of the accounting period may be carried forward, but not beyond the end of the following accounting period.

Art. 43(3) Appropriations shall be set out under different headings according to type and purpose of the expenditure and subdivided, as far as necessary, in accordance with the Financial Regulations.

Art. 44 Appropriations for unforeseeable expenditure

Art. 44(1) The budget of the Organisation may contain appropriations for unforeseeable expenditure.

Art. 44(2) The employment of these appropriations by the Organisation shall be subject to the prior approval of the Administrative Council.

Art. 45 Accounting period

The accounting period shall commence on 1 January and end on 31 December.

Art. 46 Preparation and adoption of the budget

Art. 46(1) The President of the European Patent Office shall submit the draft budget to the Administrative Council no later than the date prescribed in the Financial Regulations.

Art. 46(2) The budget and any amending or supplementary budget shall be adopted by the Administrative Council.

Art. 47 Provisional budget

Art. 47(1) If, at the beginning of the accounting period, the budget has not been adopted by the Administrative Council, expenditures may be effected on a monthly basis per heading or other division of the budget, in accordance with the Financial Regulations, up to one-twelfth of the budget appropriations for the preceding accounting period, provided that the appropriations thus made available to the President of the European Patent Office shall not exceed one-twelfth of those provided for in the draft budget.

Art. 47(2) The Administrative Council may, subject to the observance of the other provisions laid down in paragraph 1, authorise expenditure in excess of one-twelfth of the appropriations.

Art. 47(3) The payments referred to in Article 37(b), shall continue to be made, on a provisional basis, under the conditions determined under Article 39 for the year preceding that to which the draft budget relates.

Art.37(b) Financing of budget by renewal fee payments by contracting states

Art.39 Payments by the contracting states in respect of renewal fees for European patents

Art. 47(4) The Contracting States shall pay each month, on a provisional basis and in accordance with the scale referred to in Article 40, paragraphs 3 and 4, any special financial contributions necessary to ensure implementation of paragraphs 1 and 2. Article 39, paragraph 4, shall apply mutatis mutandis to these contributions.

Art.40(3), (4) Level of fees and payments, special financial contributions

Art.39(4) Interest on payments

Art. 48 Budget implementation

Art. 48(1) The President of the European Patent Office shall implement the budget and any amending or supplementary budget on his own responsibility and within the limits of the allocated appropriations.

Art. 48(2) Within the budget, the President of the European Patent Office may, in accordance with the Financial Regulations, transfer funds between the various headings or sub-headings.

Art. 49 Auditing of accounts

Art. 49(1) The income and expenditure account and a balance sheet of the Organisation shall be examined by auditors whose independence is beyond doubt, appointed by the Administrative Council for a period of five years, which shall be renewable or extensible.

Art. 49(2) The audit shall be based on vouchers and shall take place, if necessary, in situ. The audit shall ascertain whether all income has been received and all expenditure effected in a lawful and proper manner and whether the financial management is sound. The auditors shall draw up a report containing a signed audit opinion after the end of each accounting period.

Art. 49(3) The President of the European Patent Office shall annually submit to the Administrative Council the accounts of the preceding accounting period in respect of the budget and the balance sheet showing the assets and liabilities of the Organisation together with the report of the auditors.

Art. 49(4) The Administrative Council shall approve the annual accounts together with the report of the auditors and shall discharge the President of the European Patent Office in respect of the implementation of the budget.

Art. 50 Financial Regulations

The Financial Regulations shall lay down in particular:

- **(a) the arrangements relating to the establishment and implementation of the budget and for the rendering and auditing of accounts;**
- **(b) the method and procedure whereby the payments and contributions provided for in Article 37 and the advances provided for in Article 41 are to be made available to the Organisation by the Contracting States;**
- **(c) the rules concerning the responsibilities of authorising and accounting officers and the arrangements for their supervision;**
- **(d) the rates of interest provided for in Articles 39, 40 and 47;**
- **(e) the method of calculating the contributions payable by virtue of Article 146;**
- **(f) the composition of and duties to be assigned to a Budget and Finance Committee which should be set up by the Administrative Council;**

(g) **the generally accepted accounting principles on which the budget and the annual financial statements shall be based.**

Art.37 Budgetary funding
Art.39 Payments by the contracting states in respect of renewal fees for European patents
Art.40 Level of fees and payments-Special financial contributions
Art.41 Advances to the Organisation
Art.47 Provisional budget
Art.146 Cover for expenditure for carrying out special tasks

Art. 51 Fees

1 **General**
The provision is the basis of a coherent and systematic fee system.

- **Art.51(1)** provides a general clause enabling the EPO to levy fees.
- There are two types of fees: those provided for in the Convention itself, in which case the legal consequences of failure to pay in due time are mentioned in the Convention; and those provided for in the Implementing Regulations, in which case the Implementing Regulations also lay down the consequences of failure to pay (new **Art.51(3)**). As an exception, the designation fee is provided in **Art.79(2)** and the consequences of failure to pay in **R.39(2)**, allowing easy amendment of the law when replacing the designation fee for each contracting state by a flat designation fee for all contracting states.
- The time limits for payment are given in the Implementing Regulations with three exceptions: the time limits for payment of the opposition and appeal fees (**Art.99** and **108**) and the time limit for payment of the first renewal fee for a European patent (**Art.141(2)**) are in the Convention.
- The amounts of the fees and the manner of payment are provided in the Rules relating to Fees (**Art.51(4)**).

(Spec. Ed. 4, OJ 2007)

2 **Right of Organisation to payment**
Rfees1 defines what fees are: fees to be paid to the EPO and provided for in the Articles and Rules, and fees fixed by the President for special services.

The EPO is not entitled to most of these fees; a party is free to pay them. The procedural fees prescribed under the EPC are generally due before the EPO performs the act for which the fee is charged. The sanction for failure to pay is generally either total or partial loss of rights. If the procedural act is not performed, the fee ceases to be due to the EPO. If a party does not pay, certain intended procedural acts will not be carried out, e.g. the request for examination (**Art.94(1)**), the opposition (**Art.99(1)**), the appeal (**Art.108**). In other cases the application will be regarded as withdrawn, e.g. when the filing fee or the search is not paid timely (**Art.78(2)**).

The Organisation is entitled to the fees fixed by the President in accordance with **Rfees3** for services rendered and charged after performance of the service, such as delivery of periodicals. The termination of financial obligations relating to these fees is laid down in **Rfees13**.

3 **Right of party to refund**
A party is entitled to refund of a fee if the payment lacks a legal basis (see **Rfees9**).

An example is the reimbursement of the fee for further processing or re-establishment when the request for further processing or re-establishment appeared to be necessary at one time, but later it turned out that no loss of rights had occurred. Another example is renewal fees paid during an appeal procedure about whether or not the application is correctly deemed to be withdrawn; if correct, these fees are refunded. Another example is the reimbursement of the appeal fee according to **R.103(1)**.

A refusal by a department of the EPO to reimburse may be appealed. A refusal by the President can only be opposed by filing grievances against the EPO under **Art.9**. See **Art.104(3)** for a provision for payment of costs in an opposition procedure through a civil court in a contracting state.

Art. 51(1) The European Patent Office may levy fees for any official task or procedure carried out under this Convention.

Art. 51(2) Time limits for the payment of fees other than those fixed by this Convention shall be laid down in the Implementing Regulations.

1 **Legal basis for payments**

The legal basis for payment of most fees is provided in the Convention, i.e. the Articles, whereas the time limit for payment is usually fixed in the Implementing Regulations. The obligation to pay a fee within a specified period is therefore usually governed by both an article and a rule; e.g. **Art.94(1)** and **R.70(1)** for the examination fee.

Exceptionally, the time limits for paying the opposition fee (**Art.99**) and the appeal fee (**Art.108**) are fixed in the Convention.

Art. 51(3) Where the Implementing Regulations provide that a fee shall be paid, they shall also lay down the legal consequences of failure to pay such fee in due time.

Art. 51(4) The Rules relating to Fees shall determine in particular the amounts of the fees and the ways in which they are to be paid.

1 **Rules relating to Fees**

Whereas the Convention lays down what fees are to be paid for and when, the Rules relating to Fees (Rfees) fix the amounts and the method of payment. The Rfees do not form part of the Convention (see **Art.164(1)**).

PART II SUBSTANTIVE PATENT LAW

Chapter I *Patentability*

1 Requirements for patentability

The EPC has two objectives: first to grant patents in a wide field (including chemical products, food, pharmaceuticals), second to provide clear rules for the grant, leading to a strong patent (absolute novelty, inventive step and industrial applicability). These objectives have been met, partly, by using the Harmonization Treaty of Strasbourg of 1963, taken effect in 1980, as a basis for the substantive requirements for a patent in the EPC. The Treaty of Strasbourg is part of the framework of the Council of Europe.

The peculiar order of the provisions in this chapter of the EPC is a result of the amendments in the subsequent drafts of the EPC. The relations between the provisions may be clarified by arranging them in a different order. In the scheme below the text of each provision is only a short-hand for the actual provision of the EPC it refers to.

The scheme indicates four essential requirements for patentability (§2.1.1(a) - (d)), which are expanded in §2.2 - 2.6. The first requirement, being an invention, is different from the third requirement, involving an inventive step. An invention is regarded as only the result of a mental activity and need not necessarily imply the presence of novelty and inventive step (**T384/91** r.5 §4). The definition of the state of the art in §2.3 below has been separated from the EPC provision on novelty (**Art.54**), as the definition relates not only to novelty but also to inventive step.

2 Overview of requirements

2.1 PATENTABLE INVENTIONS

1 European patents shall be granted for
   a) any inventions, in all fields of technology, provided they are
   b) new,
   c) involve an inventive step and
   d) are susceptible of industrial application. (**Art.52(1)**)

2 An invention is not patentable if
   a) it is contrary to morality (**Art.53(a)**);
   b) it relates to a plant or animal variety or a biological process for the production of plants or animals (**Art.53(b)**); or
   c) it relates to a method of medical treatment or a medical diagnostic method practised on the body (**Art.53(c)**).

2.2 INVENTIONS

1 An invention is not
   a) a discovery, scientific theory or mathematical method;
   b) an aesthetic creation;
   c) a scheme, rule or method for performing a mental act, playing a game or doing business, or a computer program; or

d) a presentation of information. (**Art.52(2)**)

2 Subject-matter or activities referred to in paragraph 1 are not patentable to the extent to which a European patent application or European patent relates to such subject-matter or activities as such. (**Art.52(3)**)

2.3 STATE OF THE ART

1 The state of the art of a European patent application comprises everything made available to the public before the date of filing of the European patent application. (**Art.54(2)**)

2 The state of the art also comprises European prior rights. (**Art.54(3)**)

3 The state of the art does not comprise a publication made not earlier than six months before the date of filing of the European patent application and due to

a) an evident abuse in relation to the applicant (**Art.55(1)(a)**), or

b) a display by the applicant at an international exhibition. (**Art.55(1)(b)**)

4 A substance, forming part of the state of the art, is not excluded from patentability if for use in a medical treatment or a medical diagnostic method, provided its use for any medical treatment or medical diagnostic method is not comprised in the state of the art. (**Art.54(4)**)

5 A substance is also patentable if for a specific use in a medical treatment or medical diagnostic method, provided that such specific use does not form part of the state of the art. (**Art.54(5)**)

2.4 NOVELTY

An invention is new if it does not form part of the state of the art. (**Art.54(1)**)

2.5 INVENTIVE STEP

An invention involves an inventive step if it is not obvious to a person skilled in the art having regard to the state of the art. Prior rights are not to be considered in deciding on inventive step. (**Art.56**)

2.6 INDUSTRIAL APPLICATION

An invention is susceptible of industrial application if it can be made or used in industry. (**Art.57**)

Art. 52 Patentable inventions

Art. 52(1) European patents shall be granted for any inventions, in all fields of technology, provided that they are new, involve an inventive step and are susceptible of industrial application.

1 **Requirements for patentability**

Art.52(1) indicates four essential requirements for patentability: (1) it must be an invention, (2) which is new, (3) involves an inventive step and (4) is susceptible of industrial application.

The wording of **Art.52(1)** plainly expresses that patent protection is reserved for creations in all fields of technology. In order to be patentable, the subject-matter claimed must therefore have a 'technical character' or - to be more precise - involve a 'technical teaching', i.e. an instruction addressed to a skilled person as to how to solve a particular technical problem using particular technical means. It is on this understanding of the term 'invention' that the patent granting practice of the EPO and the jurisprudence of the boards of appeal are based. The same considerations apply to the assessment of computer programs. (OJ 2007 se4)

Thus, it will remain incumbent on EPO practice and case law to determine whether subject-matter claimed as an invention has a technical character and to develop further the concept of invention in an appropriate manner, in light of technical developments and the state of knowledge at the time (OJ 2007 se4).

T748/03 held that the case law of the EPO has not provided a closed definition of 'technical character'; however in certain cases the criterion of a purposive exploitation of the effect of objectively identifiable and measurable natural forces is a condition for technical character of an invention relating to forces.

Human intervention, to bring about a result by utilising the forces of nature, pertains to the core of what an invention is understood to be. A definition, which still holds good today and is in conformity with the concept of 'invention' within the meaning of the EPC, taken from established national German case law, is: an invention is a technical teaching, i.e. a teaching to methodically utilize controllable natural forces to achieve a causal, perceivable result. (**G2/07** r.6.4.2.1)

The 'causal, perceivable' provides the causal link between the characterising features of an invention and the technical effect of the invention, necessary for an inventive step under **Art.56**.

An invention must relate to a physical entity or a physical activity (**G2/88**). An invention need not be tangible; hence, an electrical signal is not barred from patentability (**T533/09** hn).

Inventions which are contrary to morality, which relate to plant and animal varieties, or which relate to medical treatments or medical diagnostic methods are excluded from patentability according to **Art.53**.

In principle any invention is patentable; hence, an exception to this rule, such as given in **Art.52(2)**, must be interpreted narrowly (**G5/83**).

All technical fields are encompassed in **Art.52**, e.g. also biochemical and genetic technology. The EPC has the absolute protection of substances, thus not restricted to certain fields of industrial application. To be technical, an invention must have a technical character, or involve a technical teaching. An invention as claimed must encompass aspects that impart technical character to essentially all ways of performing the invention. If the claims encompass entirely non-technical embodiments, the invention is not technical (**T619/02** r.2.2). The phrase 'in all fields of technology' excludes non-technical subject-matter from patentability.

The industrial applicability need not be specified in the application - other than in the special case of gene sequences (**R.29**) - but advantages of the invention with respect to the state of the art, to be mentioned according to **R.42(1)(c)**, make industrial applicability likely.

Art. 52(2) The following in particular shall not be regarded as inventions within the meaning of paragraph 1:

(a) discoveries, scientific theories and mathematical methods;
(b) aesthetic creations;
(c) schemes, rules and methods for performing mental acts, playing games or doing business, and programs for computers;
(d) presentations of information.

1 Definition of invention

When drafting the EPC, there was no agreement on a positive definition of an invention; therefore, the negative definition of **Art.52(2)** was given. The following two positive requirements on inventions are implicitly contained in the EPC:

1 The invention must be such that it can be carried out by a skilled person (**Art.83**).
2 The invention must be of both a concrete and a technical character (G-II,1; **T854/90** hn1), and must not merely provide a direction for the human mind.

According to **Art.52(1)** an invention must lie in a field of technology, which results in the requirement of **R.42(1)(a)** that the description must state the technical field to which the invention relates. The invention must concern a technical problem (**R.42(1)(c)**) and it must have technical features in terms of which the matter for which protection is sought can be defined in the claim (**R.43(1)**) (G-I,2(ii)). If there is no technical means or technical effect, there is no patentability (**T51/84** hn.II Marking objects). See **Art.52(1):1** for the definition of the term 'technical'.

A 'technical character' is essential for there to be an invention; the determination of whether an invention exists is separate from the other requirements of **Art.52** (**T154/04**).

The EPC does not require that the invention must entail technical progress or any useful effect. However, any advantageous effects should be stated in the description (**R.42(1)(c)**); advantageous effects are often important in determining inventive step (G-I,3).

According to **Art.52(2)** subject-matter (including the 'activities' mentioned in **Art.52(3)**) which is abstract (e.g. discoveries, scientific theories) or non-technical (e.g. aesthetic creations or presentations of information) shall not be regarded as an invention. An application is not patentable only to the extent that it relates to such excluded subject-matter as such (**Art.52(3)**). Hence, an application relating to both technical subject-matter and abstract or non-technical subject-matter is not excluded from patentability; however, if the claims encompass entirely non-technical embodiments, the invention is not patentable (**T619/02**).

The limitations of **Art.52(2)** must be interpreted narrowly, as they restrict the patentability. However, in view of the phrase 'in particular' in **Art.52(2)**, the list of subject-matter excluded from patentability is not exhaustive, and the exclusion might arguably be generalised to subject-matter which is essentially abstract in character, which is non-physical and therefore not characterised by technical features in the sense of **R.43(1)**. (**T163/85** r.2)

Case law, in particular **T931/95** and **T258/03** (see also **Art.52(2):1**), has interpreted **Art.52(2)** such that a claim is not excluded from patentability if it comprises at least one technical feature. Since most claims containing non-technical features have at least one technical feature, exclusion will be more the exception than the rule. The determination of patentability of such claims has been moved from **Art.52(2)** to the assessment of inventive step under **Art.56** (**T258/03** r.4.6), where the requirement of technical character is not directly based on law but merely on the Guidelines (e.g. G-II,1 and 3.6) and case law.

Even if an invention does have technical character, a finding of inventive step cannot be based solely on excluded subject matter (**T336/07**).

2 **Discoveries (Art.52(2)(a))**

Finding a new property of a known product is a mere discovery and unpatentable. If that property is put to practical use, it may involve a patentable invention. For example, a gene discovered to exist in nature may be patentable if a technical effect is revealed, e.g. its use in making a certain polypeptide or in gene therapy (G-II,3.1). However, the explanation of a property of a known substance occurring in a known use in terms of a new technical effect is a mere discovery and will not make a claim directed to the use of the compound based on this effect novel (**T892/94** hn.II).

To find a substance freely occurring in nature is a mere discovery. However, if the substance found in nature has first to be isolated from its surroundings and a process for obtaining it is developed, that process is patentable. Moreover, if the substance can be properly characterised by either its structure, by the process by which it is obtained or by other parameters and it is new in the absolute sense of having no previously recognised existence, then the substance per se may be patentable. (Decision of the opposition division **V8/94** hn.II: Isolation of a DNA fragment encoding a human protein, published in OJ 1995, 388)

The recognition or discovery of a previously unknown property of a known compound, such property providing a new technical effect, can clearly involve a valuable and inventive contribution to the art. The fact that the idea or concept underlying claimed subject-matter resides in a discovery does not necessarily mean that the claimed subject-matter is a discovery 'as such'. A claim defining a new use of the known compound based on the unknown property may be allowable, because, on proper interpretation of the claim, the attaining of the new technical effect which underlies the new use is a technical feature of the claimed invention. (**G2/88** r.2.3, 8, 9)

3 **Mathematical methods (Art.52(2)(a))**

The exclusion to mathematical methods is applied narrowly. For example, the exclusion applies if a claim is directed to a method of performing a specific algorithm on abstract data and the claim does not require any technical means. However, if a claim specifies technical means such as a computer for carrying out the method, then it has technical character and so is not excluded under Art.52(2)(a).

A mathematical method performed on technical data without technical means may still be excluded from patentability as a method for performing mental acts (see **Art.52(2):5**). A mathematical method that is algorithmically more efficient than prior art methods does not contribute to technical character (G-II,3.3; not in GL2017).

Once technical character has been established, the claim is assessed for novelty and inventive step. In particular, in analysis of inventive step, a mathematical method may contribute to producing a technical effect that serves a technical purpose through its application to a field of technology and/or by being adapted to a specific technical implementation.

A technical purpose through application to a field of technology must be a specific one, for example controlling a specific technical system such as a car braking system, or encoding data for efficient storage such as image compression. Additional examples are given in G-II,3.3 (not in GL2017).

A generic purpose such as 'controlling a technical system' does not confer technical character to a mathematical method. Further, a claim involving a mathematical method needs to be functionally limited to a technical purpose, rather than merely being suitable for application to the technical purpose. This can be achieved by establishing a sufficient link between the technical purpose and the mathematical method steps; a detailed example is given in G-VII,5.4.2.4.

A claim to a mathematical method may also contribute to the technical character of an invention if the claim is directed to a specific technical implementation of the mathematical method and the mathematical method is particularly adapted for that implementation in that its design is motivated by technical considerations of the internal functioning of the computer (**T1358/09** r5.5). For example, the adaptation of a polynomial reduction algorithm to exploit word size shifts matched to the word size of a computer processor can contribute to producing a technical effect of an efficient hardware implementation of the algorithm.

4 **Aesthetic creations (Art.52(2)(b))**
The attribute 'aesthetic' refers normally to visual appearances and artistic creations. However, it refers more generally to entities having - as opposed to a technical character - an appearance intended to evoke or provoke impressions or to satisfy feeling requirements or taste expectations as apprehended or perceived by the human senses, including the sense of smell. (**T619/02** r.2.4.1)

An aesthetic creation relates to an article having aspects other than technical and the appreciation of which is mainly subjective. Such an article defined solely in terms of the aesthetic effect is not patentable. If an aesthetic effect is obtained by a technical structure or other technical means, although the aesthetic effect itself is not patentable, the means of obtaining it may be. A process for producing an aesthetic creation may comprise a technical innovation and may thus be patentable. (G-II,3.4)

An example of a feature excluded from patentability is the colour of an object which does not have a technical effect on the object, but merely provides an aesthetic effect by making fingerprints less visible or facilitates classification of the object, the latter being a form of presentation of information (**T119/88**). See G-II,3.4 for more examples.

Under the contribution approach applied previously, a claim was excluded from patentability if the features of the claim that distinguish the invention from the prior art are in a field excluded under **Art.52(2)** (see **Art.52(3):1**). Under current practice a claim containing at least one technical feature will not be excluded under **Art.52(2)**; in the examination of inventive step any non-technical features will be disregarded. For example, a painting having a known frame and a picture in Impressionist style will not be excluded under **Art.52(2)**, but regarded as lacking inventive step.

5 **Mental acts (Art.52(2)(c))**
A subconscious process which takes place in the human mind (such as perception of odours) is not to be considered a mental act (**T619/02**, r.2.1). From this it is implied that a mental act must be a conscious process.

The complexity of a method does not exclude it from being considered a mental act (T914/02). However, a claim to a method is not excluded as a mental act under Art.52(2)(c) if it comprises technical means, such as a computer, to carry out at least one of its steps or if it provides a physical entity as the resulting product. Such a claim may also include steps which are to be carried out mentally by the user of the method. These mental steps contribute to the technical character of the method only if, in the context of the invention, they contribute to producing a technical effect serving a technical purpose. (G-II,3.5.1; not in GL2017).

6 Computer programs (Art.52(2)(c))

The Diplomatic Conference for revision of the EPC in 2000 had debated the removal of computer programs from **Art.52(2)(c)**, with the argument being put forward that this exclusion was obsolete in view of existing EPO practice (MR/2/00). However, the removal of the exclusion could have had unforeseen consequences with regard to potential change of practice. Moreover, the Conference did not want to anticipate the forthcoming EU directive on computer programs, which, however, failed. It was therefore agreed to leave the exclusion as it stood, and to defer any consideration of amendment to a future conference.

Computer programs are only patentable in connection with a technical effect, which in itself must have an inventive step (**T38/86**; G-II,3.6).

A claimed process including a computer program is not patentable, if (i) the process does not affect the physical or technical functioning of a device; (ii) the data to be processed are not operating parameters of a device; and (iii) the process does not solve a technical problem (**T158/88** Arabic characters on display). Having a technical effect on a physical entity is sufficient for avoiding exclusion from patentability; it is not a necessary condition (**G3/08b** r.12.3).

A mathematical method is in general carried out on numbers and provides a result in numerical form. No direct technical result is produced by the method as such. In contrast thereto, if a mathematical method is used in a technical process, that process is carried out on a physical entity (which may be a material object but equally an image stored as an electric signal) by some technical means implementing the method and provides as its result a certain change in that entity. The technical means might include a computer comprising suitable hardware or an appropriately programmed general purpose computer. (**T208/84** r.5, Vicom, video processing in a known computer)

Information not having a technical character itself, such as linguistic information, may assume technical character by its use in a technical system, e.g. by being formatted or processed in a specific way (**T1177/97** r.3).

An allowable claim including a computer program does not make the program itself allowable. (i) A claim on a process based on a mathematical method does not protect the mathematical method. (ii) A technical change in a computer making it possible to run a new program makes the computer new. (iii) A claim on a technical process controlled by a computer program is not regarded as a claim on a computer program. (iv) The same applies to a computer adapted to run a special program. A new operating system makes a computer new. (**T208/84** Vicom).

A subsequent decision has extended the patentability of software beyond the line drawn by Vicom. An invention comprising functional features implemented by computer programs is not excluded from patentability if technical considerations concerning the solution of the problem solved by the invention are required to carry out the same invention (**T769/92** hn.I). Note that in this case no technical *means* are required any more but only technical *considerations*. These technical considerations lend a technical nature to the invention in that they imply a technical problem to be solved by (implicit) technical features (**T769/92** hn.II). In this particular case the teaching to provide, in a known computer memory, five files intended for different purposes and to cause the computer processing unit to perform five specified functions is assumed to require technical considerations (**T769/92** r.3.6).

Printer control characters in a text in the form of digital data are a characteristic of the technical internal working of a text-processing system. Consequently, transforming such control characters from one system to another one is a method having technical character. If such a transformation is carried out by a computer, the steps of the transformation are rather an algorithm on which a computer program is based than a computer program as such; the program must be considered to be the technical means for carrying out the method. (**T110/90**, following **T208/84**)

Even if the basic idea underlying an invention may be considered to reside in a computer program, a claim directed to its use in the solution of a technical problem cannot be regarded as seeking protection for the program as such (**T115/85**). When the functioning of an apparatus is improved by a computer program improving the internal communication, then the apparatus controlled by the program is patentable (**T6/83**).

Decision **T1173/97** hn. has changed the interpretation of **Art.52(2)(c)**. According to the combination of **Art.52(2)** and (3), not all computer programs are excluded from patentability but only 'computer programs as such'. A 'computer program as such' is considered to be solely the fundamental program content as yet devoid of any technical function, i.e. a mere abstract creation, lacking in technical character. Hence, a computer program will be patentable if it has a technical character. The technical character may be derived from a further technical effect, produced by the program when run on a computer, which effect goes beyond the 'normal' physical interactions between program and computer. The further technical effect may be known.

Examples of such a further technical effect are the control of an industrial process, the processing of data that represent physical entities, or the control of the internal functioning of a computer. Although the program itself does not disclose the effect in reality, it possesses the potential to produce the effect. Such a computer program may be claimed as a computer program by itself or as a record on medium. Additional examples of further technical effects are given in G-II,3.6.1 (not in GL2017).

In **T424/03** r.5.1 a distinction was made between a computer-implemented method and a computer program. The former was described as sequence of steps that are actually performed on a computer and achieving an effect. The latter was described as a sequence of computer-executable instructions which just have the potential of achieving such an effect when loaded into and run on a computer. The computer-implemented method can never be a computer program as such. Hence, a claim formulated as a computer-implemented method will not be excluded by **Art.52(2)(c)**.

Whereas a claim relating to a computer program may be excluded under **Art.52(2)(c)** and (3) as being a mere computer program as such, a program on a computer-readable storage medium or a method of operating a computer according to a certain program are technical because of the presence of the storage medium and computer and are therefore not excluded, whether or not the technical features are essential for the invention. Note, that a non-essential feature such as the storage medium can never support inventive step. (**G3/08b** r.10; following **T424/03** and overruling **T1173/97** r.13)

Programming a computer, i.e. the intellectual activity of working out what are the steps to be included in a computer program, may involve technical considerations since it is concerned with defining a method which can be carried out by a machine. However, such technical considerations are not enough to give a technical character to the program; the programmer must have had technical considerations beyond 'merely' finding a computer algorithm to carry out some procedure. (**G3/08b** r.13.5)

An extensive discussion of the examination procedure of computer-implemented inventions has been given in **T154/04** r.5-17, including a comparison with current practice in the UK.

The present practice of the EPO for examining computer-implemented inventions, with particular attention to business methods, has been set out in an article of the EPO published in OJ 2007, 594. Examples of sets of claims defining a computer implemented invention are given in F-IV,3.9. The Guidelines give in an annex a list of its sections relevant for computer-implemented inventions.

7 Rules for playing games (Art.52(2)(c))

The exclusion of rules and methods for playing games covers games including table-top games and video games. Generally, rules for table-top games, such as the dealing of cards and ranking of hands in poker, are perceived by players and are only meaningful in the context of the game. Hence game rules are of an abstract, purely mental nature and therefore excluded from patentability (**T336/07**). Video games may include interactive elements and storylines in a virtual game world. As these elements are conceptual in nature, they are considered to relate to abstract, non-technical schemes (**T12/08**).

A claim that includes technical means for implementing game rules has technical character and so is not excluded under **Art.52(2)(c)**. For example, if a game is won by matching two random numbers, the use of a pair of dice or a computer to generate the two random numbers imparts technical character. (G-II,3.5.2; not in GL2017)

Video games such as virtual reality games typically involve technical means for sensing user input, processing the game state and outputting visual, audio and haptic feedback. Such features may be assessed as presentation of information (see **Art.52(2):9**). For example, displaying the current score in a game is regarded as presentation of non-technical information.

Rules for games may have a psychological effect of amusing, surprising and entertaining players. In some cases, game rules lead to balanced or rewarding gameplay, e.g. matching gamers in a competitive video game based on each player's skill level. However, such effects do not qualify as technical effects. (G-II,3.5.2; not in GL2017)

8 Methods of doing business (Art.52(2)(c))

A method of doing business is any subject-matter which is of financial, commercial, administrative or organizational nature (G-II,3.5.3; not in GL2017).

Its patentability is assessed in the same way as the patentability of computer programs as set out in the previous section: the method must be an invention and, therefore, must have technical character to be patentable. The technical character may be imparted by steps solving a technical problem or achieving a technical effect (see e.g. **T38/86** hn.4).

According to **T854/90** hn.2, **T931/95** hn.2 (Pension benefit systems) the mere use of technical means in a method claim does not necessarily confer a technical character on such a claim. Examples of such mere use are the step of using data processing means for a purely non-technical purpose, e.g. for controlling a pension benefits system, and amounting to no more than the general teaching to use data processing means and the step of processing and producing information having purely administrative, actuarial and/or financial character (**T931/95** r.3). A technical character may be conferred if a step solves a technical problem or achieves a technical effect, the use of the data processing means requires technical considerations, or the information being processed relates to a physical entity. **T258/03** (Dutch auction) criticises **T931/95** in that the latter requires qualification of the relevance of technical features to determine the technical character of a method, which involves remnants of the contribution approach by implying an evaluation in the light of the available prior art or common general knowledge (r.4.3). According to **T258/03** a method involving technical means is an invention within the meaning of **Art.52(1)**.

In contrast with a method of doing business, an apparatus for carrying out a method of doing business is not excluded from patentability. Whereas the exclusion of the method is justified by the wording of **Art.52(2)(c)**, an apparatus in the sense of a physical entity or concrete product is not mentioned in **Art.52(2)**. The implied physical features of such an apparatus give it a technical character; hence, the apparatus is an invention in the sense of **Art.52(1)** (**T931/95** r.5, confirmed by **T258/03** r.3.7). However, the implied use of unspecified technical means to carry out a claimed method does not in itself provide technical character and does not take the claims beyond a business method as such; rather, only specified technical means will provide technical character to the method (**T388/04**, r.3).

A few examples of methods of doing business. A traffic control system for a city is not patentable, because it is a business-like ruling activity (**T16/83**). A method relating to the activity of checking authorisations of people by using cards and a card reader is essentially a business operation; it does not have technical character and is therefore not patentable (**T854/90** hn.2). A computer system for controlling an improved pension benefit system is not patentable if the only improvement is in a field excluded by **Art.52(2)** (**T931/95**). Similarly, a method of doing business is not excluded from patentability if the invention does not reside in an abstract method as such but relates to technical means such as computer networks to carry out the method and the invention solves a technical problem in a non-obvious way. For example, the rules as such of an automatic auction method using a computer network are excluded, but an auction system as a whole implementing those rules has technical character (**T688/05**).

The mere aim of financial gain or commercial success does not mean that an invention is inevitably a method of doing business (**T619/02** r.2.1).

A claim on a business method which includes technical features is not excluded from patentability under **Art.52(2)**; the presence of an inventive step will be assessed under **Art.56**, in which all non-technical features will be disregarded as non-contributing features (see **Art.56:8.2**).

9 Presentation of information (Art.52(2)(d))

Presentation of information is the conveying of information, e.g. visual, audio or haptic information, directly to a human user and concerns both the cognitive content of the information and the manner of its presentation (**T1194/97** r.3.7.3; **T1143/06**; **T1741/08**; G-II,3.7). Patentability under **Art.52(2)(d)** of information presented directly to a user is assessed differently from data conveyed to a technical system.

Data conveyed to a technical system that are defined in terms which inherently comprise the technical features of the system are considered to be 'functional data'. Functional data cover, for example, data encoding schemes, data structures and electronic communication protocols. Functional data are not regarded as presentations of information in the sense of **Art.52(2)(d)**.

For example, a claim to a television signal adapted to generate a picture is allowed if it is defined in terms of the technical features of the television system such as aspect ratio and active-video portion (**T163/85**). Likewise, a claim to a record carrier on which data is recorded in a specified data structure, e.g. including picture line synchronisations, line numbers and addresses, is allowed if the data structure is defined in terms of technical features of the system that the record carrier is used in (**T1194/97** r.3.4).

A claim relating to the presentation of information to a user and containing at least one technical feature for presenting the information, e.g. a computer display or a speaker, has technical character and will not be excluded from patentability under **Art.52(2)(d)** (see **Art.52(3):1**).

Once technical character has been established, the claim is assessed for novelty and inventive step. In particular in examination of inventive step, features relating to the presentation of information are disregarded if they do not contribute to producing a technical effect (see inventive step assessment of mixed inventions in **Art.56:8.2**). The technical effect is determined by considering what information is presented, why it is presented and how it is presented.

9.1 WHAT INFORMATION IS PRESENTED AND WHY

Information that is presented to a user may contribute to a technical effect if the information credibly assists the user in performing a technical task (**T336/14; T1802/13**). For example, **T1214/09** holds that searching and retrieval of an image by a user from a set of images presented on a display is not a technical task, and therefore the layout of the images has no technical effect.

Similarly, display of data in a colour-coded format to make it easier for a user to understand is not considered a credible technical effect because this choice is only concerned with the way in which information is processed by a human mind (**T1567/05**). Likewise, providing a predictive text input which may lower the cognitive burden on the user is not considered as making a technical contribution (**T1741/08**).

If what is presented to the user relates to static or predetermined information about an internal state of a device that assists the user with a non-technical task using the device, it does not make a technical contribution even though the device is technical. For example, displaying a button sequence that enables a user to configure a device without needing to learn the sequence of buttons is not a credible technical effect (**T1073/13**). On the other hand, information about an internal state of a device that may dynamically change and is automatically detected has a technical effect if it enables a user to properly operate the device. For example, the presentation of information that prompts a user to interact with a device to prevent a technical malfunction has a technical effect.

Information presented to a user for his subjective evaluation or non-technical decision making is not considered technical (**T756/06** r.13). For example, the state of a casino computer game is not considered technical information and so cannot contribute to a technical effect.

If information is presented to a viewer to cause a physiological reaction which can be measured when assessing a medical condition, that presentation of information may be considered to produce a technical effect. An example is an audio stimulus for assessing hearing impairment. However, the choice of where to put a notification on a display depending on its urgency, thereby minimising information overload for the user is not considered to qualify as a technical effect because it is not a physiological reaction (**T862/10**).

9.2 HOW THE INFORMATION IS PRESENTED

How information is presented generally relates to the form or arrangement in which, or the timing at which, information is conveyed to the user (G-II,3.7). How the information is presented to a viewer may contribute to a technical effect if it facilitates a continued human-machine interaction or enables the user to perform a technical task.

For example, facilitating a continued human-machine interaction was found in a football video game due to how the location of the nearest off-screen teammate was indicated by dynamically displaying a guide mark on the edge of the screen. This was found to resolve the conflicting technical requirements of displaying a zoomed-in area when the limited display area may be too small to show a complete area of interest. (**T928/03** KONAMI)

A technical effect may also arise if information is presented in a proactive and timely manner to enable the user to perform a technical task in a more efficient or precise manner. For example, in a visual aid for a surgeon, displaying the orientation of a ball joint implant which enables the surgeon to position the implant accurately is considered to provide a technical effect.

In **T643/00** the search and retrieval action of images by a user was facilitated by changing resolution of displayed images on selection of an image by the user, leading to a continued human-machine interaction.

However, the display of a diagram or layout is considered non-technical, even if the diagram or layout conveys information in a way that is appealing, lucid or logical to a viewer (**T125/04**).

9.3 USER INPUT

Features of a user interface that provide a mechanism for user input, e.g. entering text, making a selection or submitting a command, are usually considered to make a technical contribution because input requires compatibility with a predetermined protocol of a machine (G-II,3.7.1).

Methods of enabling user input, e.g. gestures or key strokes, could be considered to make a technical contribution if a physical ergonomic advantage can objectively be established. Performance-oriented improvements to the detection of input, such as allowing faster or more accurate gesture recognition or reducing the processing load of the device when performing recognition, can also make a technical contribution (G-II,3.7.1).

Features concerning the graphic design of a menu, such as its look and feel, that are determined by aesthetic considerations, subjective user preferences or administrative rules, do not contribute to the technical character of a menu-based user interface.

Art. 52(3) Paragraph 2 shall exclude the patentability of the subject-matter or activities referred to therein only to the extent to which a European patent application or European patent relates to such subject-matter or activities as such.

1 Exclusion of subject-matter 'as such'

An application is not patentable only to the extent that it relates to subject-matter not regarded as an invention according to **Art.52(2)** as such. An application relating to both technical subject-matter and abstract or non-technical subject-matter is not excluded from patentability, because the mix of subject-matter is regarded as an invention in the sense of the EPC.

The mix must involve technical means to solve a technical problem to be patentable (**T603/89**). Whereas the discovery of steam power is not patentable because of **Art.52(2)(a)**, technical means in the form of a steam engine using steam power is not excluded from patentability. The test to be met is whether the invention relates to excluded subject matter as such, and not whether the invention has practical utility (**T388/04**, r.4).

The test of whether there is an invention is separate and distinct from the questions whether the subject-matter is susceptible of industrial application, is new and involves an inventive step. The EPO is free to consider whether a claimed invention is excluded from patentability before examination of inventive step (**T388/04**, hn I). It is irrelevant whether the feature or features giving a claim a technical character are new or known from the prior art. The formerly applied contribution approach, stating that there is no invention if the contribution to the prior art, i.e. the one or more new, characterizing features, does not have a technical character, has no basis in the EPC. (**T931/95** r.6; G-II,2).

Art. 53 Exceptions to patentability

European patents shall not be granted in respect of:

(a) **inventions the commercial exploitation of which would be contrary to "ordre public" or morality; such exploitation shall not be deemed to be so contrary merely because it is prohibited by law or regulation in some or all of the Contracting States;**

(b) **plant or animal varieties or essentially biological processes for the production of plants or animals; this provision shall not apply to microbiological processes or the products thereof;**

(c) **methods for treatment of the human or animal body by surgery or therapy and diagnostic methods practised on the human or animal body; this provision shall not apply to products, in particular substances or compositions, for use in any of these methods.**

See for the implementation:

(a) **R.28** Exceptions to patentability
R.29 The body and its elements

(b) **R.26** General and definitions
R.27 Patentable biotechnological inventions
R.29 The body and its elements

1 **Exclusion based on ordre public and morality (Art.53(a))**

Art.53(a) excludes from patentability inventions the commercial exploitation of which would be contrary to 'ordre public' or morality. The provision is in line with both Article 27.2 of the TRIPs agreement and with Article 6.1 of Directive 98/44/EC relating to the legal protection of biotechnology inventions. The TRIPs agreement and the EC-Directive exclude from patentability only those inventions that must be barred from 'commercial exploitation' to protect public order or morality. (OJ 2007 se4)

1.1 ORDRE PUBLIC AND MORALITY

The concept of 'ordre public' covers the protection of public security and the physical integrity of individuals as part of society. It also encompasses the protection of the environment. In general, 'Ordre public' is formed by the ethically based constitutional or other rules, usually backed up by penal provisions, that reflect the basic values prevailing in society and trade (**T866/01** r.6.9). Accordingly, inventions the commercial exploitation of which is likely to breach public peace or social order or to prejudice the environment seriously are to be excluded from patentability as being contrary to 'ordre public' (**T356/93** r.5).

The concept of morality is related to the belief that some behaviour is right and acceptable whereas other behaviour is wrong; this belief is founded on the totality of the accepted norms which are deeply rooted in a particular culture. For the purposes of the EPC, the culture in question is the culture inherent in European society and civilisation. Accordingly, inventions the exploitation of which is not in conformity with the conventionally accepted standards of conduct pertaining to this culture are to be excluded from patentability as being contrary to morality. (**T356/93** r.6; **T866/01** r.6.12)

Since **Art.53(a)** raises only the question of whether the commercial exploitation of an invention is contrary to 'ordre public' or morality, any other questions of 'ordre public' and morality, such as the morality of patenting animals or genetically manipulating a mouse, cannot be considered under **Art.53(a)** (**T315/03** r.4.2). The provision refers only to commercial exploitation of the invention, not of the patent; so the EPO are not obliged to consider the effect of granting patent rights on ordre public as distinct from the effect of the invention. Where the invention was derived by the use of biological samples from patients, demonstration of informed consent for use of such samples is not required for ordre public to be satisfied (**T1213/05**).

In **R.28(1)** the EPC explicitly excludes the patentability of processes for cloning or modifying the genetic identity of human beings, industrial or commercial use of human embryos and genetic modification of animals causing them suffering without any substantial medical benefit to man or animal. The human body and the simple discovery of any of its elements, including the (partial) sequence of a gene, is not patentable according to **R.29(1)**. However, an element isolated from the human body or produced by a technical process is patentable, even if the structure of that element is identical to that of a natural element (**R.29(2)**).

Enlarged Board of Appeal case **G2/06** held that inventions (here, human embryonic stem cell cultures) which, at the time of filing the application, require the destruction of human embryos for their performance are excluded from patentability under **R.28(1)(c)**, which relates to uses of human embryos for commercial purposes, and which rule is within the scope of **Art.53(a)**. For further details, see the discussion at **R.28(1)(c)**.

1.2 TESTS FOR EXCLUSION UNDER ART.53(A)

The qualification in the second half-sentence of **Art.53(a)** clarifies that the assessment of whether or not particular subject-matter is to be considered contrary to 'ordre public' or morality is not dependent upon any national laws or regulations. Conversely, particular subject-matter is not automatically regarded as complying with the requirements of **Art.53(a)** merely because its exploitation is permitted in some or all of the contracting states. (**T356/93** r.7)

T356/93 r.8 derives from the Preparatory Documents of the EPC that **Art.53(a)** must be narrowly construed, in particular in respect of plant and animal varieties.

A fair test for raising an objection under **Art.53(a)** is to consider whether it is probable that the public in general would regard the invention as so abhorrent that the grant of patent rights would be inconceivable (G-II,4.1). Note however that **T1213/05** makes clear that the effect of the patent as such is not relevant, only the commercial exploitation of the invention must be considered. Further, the commercial exploitation of the invention may go beyond solely what is recited in the claims (**G2/06**, relating to human embryonic stem cells). A possible use of the invention is not decisive, but instead the use of the invention indicated in the application: an anti-personnel mine is excluded; a method to blow a safe is not excluded. Note that the previous example of a letter bomb as excluded under the previous version of **Art.53(a)** is no longer considered applicable, since there is no commercial market in letter bombs, such that there can be no commercial exploitation. In decision **T866/01** r.6 and 9 a composition for euthanasia of lower mammals was not considered to be excluded under the morality provisions of **Art.53(a)**, since euthanasia of mammals is a conventional part of the veterinary practitioner's professional work. This was in spite of the argument made that the composition was not solely useful for euthanasia of lower mammals, but could be used to euthanase higher mammals and humans.

'Ordre public' and morality may be two separate objections to patentability either or both of which can be raised in a particular case (**T315/03** r.10.2).

Decision **T315/03** has developed a three-step test for exclusion of a claim relating to genetically manipulated animals from patentability under **Art.53(a)** (see r.10 and its application to two requests in r.12 and 13). The first step is the test of **R.28(1)(d)** whether the manipulation process is likely to cause the animals suffering, the likelihood of a substantial medical benefit to man or animal and the correspondence between the suffering and benefit. A claim to a process of manipulation of an animal causing suffering without corresponding benefit fails the balancing test of **R.28(1)(d)** and must be excluded under **Art.53(a)**. Details of the test are given in **R.28(1)(d):3**; an example can be found in **T315/03** r.13.2.1-4.

A claim that has passed the first test must be subjected to the second test, formulated in decision **T19/90** r.5: the suffering of animals and possible risks to the environment must be balanced against the usefulness to mankind. This test can be used in 'ordre public' and morality cases (**T315/03** r.10.5). It is broader than the first test and allows criteria different from the first test to be taken into account (**T315/03** hn.VI.2). They may include the possible use of non-animal alternatives to obtain the benefit (**T315/03** r.10.6 and 13.2.7) and threats to the environment (r.13.2.8-9). Although the degree of suffering may be used as criterion in the second test, it is regarded as effectively impossible to make a distinction between acceptable and unacceptable suffering; accordingly, the degree of suffering is of no assistance in making the test (**T315/03** r.13.2.6). An example of the application of the test to a mouse genetically manipulated by insertion of an activated oncogene can be found in **T19/90** r.6 and **T315/03** r.13.2.5-9. In decision **T606/03** a claim to a transgenic mouse was rejected on the basis that only some of the mutant animals would be of medical benefit to humans, regardless of the potential suffering of the animals. However, claims were allowed to transgenic mice of a particular category which would not be expected to suffer.

A claim that has passed the second test must be subjected to the third test in which arguments can be considered relating to morality or 'ordre public' under **Art.53(a)** other than those regarded in the second test (**T315/03** r.10.7). Morality objections may include a possible threat to evolution or use of the genetically manipulated animals in research being morally unacceptable to the public (see the example in **T315/03** r.13.2.10). In decision **T315/03** nothing before the board was regarded to suggest that the use of animals for medical research has the status of moral disapproval in European culture (r.13.2.21).

The arguments put forward in the three tests can only be considered when supported by evidence (**T315/03** r.10.10). However, the EPO may give allegations without evidence weight if they are well-known and/or easily checked (**T315/03** r.13.2.14). Opinion poll evidence is of very limited value for establishing that subject-matter is contrary to 'ordre public' or morality (**T356/93** r.15; **T315/03** r.10.4). Since the **Art.53(a)** objection is made as of the effective date of the claim, evidence arising after that date may be taken into account provided it is directed to the position at the effective date (**T315/03** r.10.10). However, technical developments of the invention becoming available after the filing date and having a potential bearing on the issue of ordre public should not be considered; a later provided innocuous way to carry out the invention is not relevant for the issue. (**G2/06** r.33).

2 Exclusion of plant and animal varieties and biological processes (Art.53(b))

2.1 PLANT AND ANIMAL VARIETIES

In principle, plants and animals are patentable under the EPC, with the exception of plant and animal varieties, as provided in **Art.53(b)** (see also **T315/03** r.4.3 - 4.5). Methods of producing plants and animals are also patentable, except, according to **Art.53(b)**, where such methods are essentially biological. However, microbiological processes and their products are not excluded from patentability under **Art.53(b)**. Methods for treating plants and animals are in general patentable, but methods for treating animals with a therapeutic purpose are excluded under **Art.53(c)**.

The inconsistency between the three language versions of the provision in the EPC 1973 has been corrected in the EPC 2000. The previous German term 'Tierarten' (species), has been replaced by 'Tierrassen' which is in line with the English 'animal varieties' or the French 'races animales', which are sub-units of a species.

Several of the EPC contracting states have developed special legal protection for plant breeding at national and international level, specially adapted to meet the interests of plant breeders and farmers. The protection available under the 'International Union for the Protection Of new Varieties of plants' (UPOV = Union Internationale pour la Protection des Obtentions Végétales) is limited to plant varieties, i.e. the specific products which are used in farming and gardening. To avoid double protection by plant breeder's rights and patents, the EPC could have excluded from patent protection those plants already covered by the plant breeder's rights. However, to take the difference of these rights between the contracting states into account for a European patent application would have been contrary to the principle of uniform patent protection in all contracting states (**Art.118**). Therefore, the EPC has excluded all plant varieties from patent protection. (**G1/98** r.3.4-3.7)

A plant variety is a multiplicity of plants which are largely the same in their characteristics (i.e. homogeneous) and remain substantially the same after every propagation cycle (i.e. stable). The definition of a plant variety is given in **R.26(4)**, which follows the wording of the concept of variety in the UPOV Convention (see also **T320/87** r.12 and **T356/93** r.23). Plants that are not stable cannot be classified as plant varieties and, therefore, are patentable (**T320/87** r.14). A plant variety is excluded from patentability under **Art.53(b)** irrespective of the way in which it is produced, for example by customary breeding techniques or by recombinant gene technology (**G1/98** hn.III).

Seeds chemically treated to make them resistant to herbicides are patentable. The treatment does not cause genetic modification of the seed, and the effect of the treatment is not transmissible to future generations. (**T49/83**)

In **T356/93** it was held that a claim defining a distinctive feature common to all plants falling under its scope is not allowable, because the claim encompasses genetically transformed plant varieties, excluded from patentability under **Art.53(b)**. **G3/95** decided that decision **T356/93** is not in conflict with decisions **T49/83** and **T19/90**.

However, **G1/98** decided that a claim wherein specific plant varieties are not individually claimed, is not excluded from patentability under **Art.53(b)** even though it may embrace plant varieties. Hence, a distinction must be made between a claim in respect of or encompassing plant varieties, which is not excluded, and a claim directed to one or more specific plant varieties, which is excluded from patentability (**G1/98** r.3.10). Two steps can be distinguished in the development of a genetically modified plant variety: a first step in which a genetic engineer provides tools to bestow a desired property on plants by inserting a gene into the genome of those plants, and a second step in which the breeder develops a plant variety having not only the desired property, but also homogeneity and stability by inserting the gene into a specific plant. The first, more technical step cannot be protected by breeder's rights as it is not directed to a plant variety but can be implemented in an indefinite number of plant varieties, and should be protected by a patent. The second, more biological step should be protected by breeder's rights (**G1/98** r.3.8, 3.10).

Whether or not a plant is a plant variety and therefore excluded from patentability depends only on whether or not it meets the criteria set out in **R.26(4)**. It is irrelevant for the exclusion whether the method for its production is recombinant gene technology or a classical plant breeding process (**T1854/07** r.10.4; **G2/12** hn.1; G-II,5.4.1).

The principle of **G1/98** should also be followed in the case of animals: a patent should not be granted for a single animal variety but can be granted if varieties may fall within the scope of its claims, which is certainly true for a scope covering a taxonomic category of animals higher than species. (**T315/03** hn.VII.1, r.11.4).

The decision **G1/98** is in agreement with **R.27(b)**, according to which plants or animals are patentable if the technical feasibility of the invention is not confined to a particular plant or animal variety (see also Dec. Oppo. Div. Onco mouse, OJ 2003, 473, r.8.2). The development of **G1/98** has been taken into account in section G-II,5 of the Guidelines on biotechnological inventions (OJ 2001, 115). In the Onco mouse case the Ex. Div. allowed claims relating to genetically modified rodents and non-human mammals, which are not animal varieties but a higher-ranking taxonomic classification than varieties (OJ 1992, 588 and **T19/90**).

2.2 BIOLOGICAL PROCESSES AND PRODUCTS

The EPC has been adapted to the Directive of the European Union relating to the legal protection of biotechnological inventions by **R.26** to **29**. The text of the Directive is reproduced in OJ 1999, 101.

Art.53(b) excludes essentially biological processes for the production of plants or animals from patentability. Since **R.26(5)** does not provide a useful definition of 'essentially biological', the EBoA has determined its meaning in the case of plants, based on the legislative history, context and purpose of **Art.53(b)**. An exclusion of plant breeding processes from patentability was introduced to avoid dual protection by the EPC and the UPOV Convention. The processes were conventional methods for breeding of plant varieties at the time of drafting the law (~1961), which included in particular sexual crossing of plants, i.e. of their whole genomes, and subsequent selection of the plants having the desired trait(s). The traits were determined by the natural phenomenon of meiosis, a special type of cell division in which genes are mixed and which occurs in sexual reproduction. Conventional methods may also include steps to assist the breeding. However, processes changing the genome by technical means, such as irradiation, should be patentable. (**G2/07** = **G1/08** r.6.4.2.2-3)

The EBoA has excluded the conventional methods from patentability by interpreting 'essentially biological' in a process for the production of plants in **Art.53(b)** as relating to sexual crossing and selection where changes in the genes are only caused by meiosis. The EBoA has defined the extent of the exclusion for plant breeding as follows. The Guidelines have extended the definition to animals (G-II,5.4.2).

- A non-microbiological process for the production of plants relating to sexually crossing the whole genomes of plants and subsequently selecting plants is in principle excluded from patentability as being 'essentially biological' within the meaning of **Art.53(b)** (**G2/07** hn.1; **T315/03** distinguished). Hence, a method of breeding plants or animals by crossing specific plants and selecting the offspring with the desired traits is excluded from patentability. On the other hand, a process for treating plants or animals to improve properties such as yield or growth, e.g. a method of pruning a tree or treating soil to promote growth, is not excluded because the process does not include the steps of sexual crossing and selection.
- Any technical step to enable or assist the process, as a further step or as part of the steps of crossing or selection, does not make the process patentable (**G2/07** hn.2). It is irrelevant whether such a technical step is new or known, whether or not it occurs in nature or whether the essence of the invention lies in it (**G2/07** hn.4; **T320/87** and **T356/93** overruled). The technical step may be patentable per se. For example, the technical step of using a special greenhouse or genetic molecular markers to assist the breeding does not make the breeding process patentable; the greenhouse, markers and their use may be patentable per se.
- However, the process is not excluded from patentability if it includes in the crossing and selection steps an additional technical step of introducing a trait into the genome or modifies a trait in the genome of the plant produced, the introduction or modification not being the result of the mixing of genes of the plants chosen for sexual crossing (**G2/07** hn.3). The additional step in such a rare process must modify the crossing and selection steps.

  An additional step changing the genes which is not part of the crossing and selection steps but is applied before or after the sexual crossing and selection steps is to be ignored for assessment of the exclusion. Such a step can be patented per se under **R.27(c)**, without including explicitly or implicitly a sexual crossing and selection process. (**G2/07** r.6.4.2.3)

Inventions relating to plants and animals are patentable if the application of the invention is not technically confined to a single plant or animal variety (G-II,5.2(ii)). However, in line with the exclusion of an essentially biological process, plants and animals exclusively obtained by an essentially biological process are excluded from patentability (**R.28(2)**).

A biotechnological invention is patentable if it concerns biological material isolated from its natural environment or produced by a technical process, even if it previously occurred in nature (**R.27(a)**). Such material is new, because it was previously not technically available to the public. **R.27** gives the demarcation between invention and discovery under patent law for biotechnological inventions. (OJ 1999, 573)

2.3 MICROBIOLOGICAL PROCESSES AND PRODUCTS

Microbiological processes and the products thereof other than a plant or animal variety are patentable (**R.27(c)**). A microbiological process is a process involving or performed upon or resulting in microbiological material (**R.26(6)**). Neither the EPC nor the Directive define 'microbiological material'. **T356/93** r.34 and 35 defines 'microbiological' as relating to technical activities in which direct use is made of micro-organisms and 'micro-organisms' as generally unicellular organisms with dimensions beneath the limits of vision which can be propagated and manipulated in a laboratory. The EPC defines biological material as material containing genetic information and capable of reproducing itself or being reproduced in a biological system (**R.26(3)**). A microbiological process refers to a process in which micro-organisms are used to make or to modify products or in which new micro-organisms are developed for specific uses. Consequently, the products thereof encompass products which are made or modified by micro-organisms as well as new micro-organisms as such (**T356/93** hn.V). An application for a biological process or its product may require the deposition of a sample of biological material with a depositary institution under **R.31(1)**.

Propagation of a micro-organism is regarded as a microbiological process (G-II,5.5.1). Micro-organisms, including moulds, bacteria, actinomycetes, yeasts, viruses, plasmids and genes are also patentable (**T162/86, T281/86, T292/85**, G-II,5.5.1). Plant cells as such are not considered to be plants but microbiological products (**T356/93** hn.III).

3 **Exclusion of medical treatment (Art.53(c))**

Although therapeutic, surgical and diagnostic methods constitute inventions, they are in general not patentable under the EPC. The exclusion from patentability under **Art.53(c)** is based on socio-ethical and public health considerations, according to the Travaux Préparatoires of EPC 1973 and EPC 2000 (**T385/86** r.3.1; **T24/91** r.2.4; OJ 2007 se4). The exclusion is allowed by Article 27(3)(a) TRIPs. The intention underlying this article is to ensure that nobody who wants to use the methods specified in this article as part of the medical treatment of humans or animals should be prevented from this by patents (see **T116/85** r.3.7 and **T24/91** r.2.4). In other words, the exclusion of **Art.53(c)** intends to protect patients.

In the Travaux Préparatoires of the EPC 2000 the EPO admitted that the purpose of the provision, to keep medical practice free from patent law restrictions, was not in fact achieved in practice (CA/PL/PV9 §30; see also **T1020/03** r.46).

In EPC 1973, methods of medical treatment were not to be regarded as inventions which are susceptible of industrial application by way of legal fiction. Such methods therefore did not comply with the requirements of **Art.52(1)** and were not patentable. EPC 2000 removes this fiction and instead merely excludes such methods from patentability; the exclusion is moved from previous **Art.52(4)** EPC 1973 to **Art.53(c)** EPC 2000, to group it with the other public policy exclusions, and to bring the law into line with TRIPS Art.27.3(a). The intention of the exclusion is not clear from the text of the law, which makes it difficult to arrive at a coherent and adequate judicial policy on this subject. From a patent law point of view it is not clear why the application of a method in a cosmetic salon is regarded to be an industrial application but the application of the same method in a commercial private clinic for the treatment of obesity is not (see also Empel no. 118; **T144/83** r.5; **T116/85** r.4.1).

The statement of the Enlarged Board of Appeal in **G5/83** r. 22 that 'the intention of **Art.52(4)** EPC [1973] is only to free from restraint non-commercial and non-industrial medical and veterinary activities', based on the legal fiction of the EPC 1973 that medical methods are regarded as not industrially applicable, is too restrictive. Instead, any medical and veterinary activity should be free from restraint, whether or not the activity is commercial or industrial. The statement has led to an a contrario argument: a medical treatment that is industrially applicable is regarded as not falling within the exclusion of **Art.53(c)**, even when applied in a diagnostic method. The revision of the EPC in 2000 has changed the provision by removing the fiction of non-industrial applicability of medical methods, making the a contrario argument invalid. As a result, under the EPC 2000 more methods may be regarded as excluded from patentability. In contrast, **G1/04** r.10, 11 holds that the scope of the exclusion for diagnostic methods will remain valid when the EPC 2000 enters into force.

Art.53(c) distinguishes three different methods of medical treatment which are excluded from patentability: methods for treatment by surgery, methods for treatment by therapy and diagnostic methods. The interpretation of each group is given in the following sections. The interpretation must take into account the intention of the exclusion, i.e. it must provide sufficient freedom from patent legislation for anyone practising medicine. On the other hand, **Art.53(c)** must be construed narrowly, as must any exclusion to patentability (**G5/83** r.22; **T385/86** r.3.1, 3.2). The narrow interpretation may infringe on the freedom of the person practising medicine. Case law has not yet shown a consistent interpretation on all issues.

The exception under **Art.53(c)** does not extend to new products, particularly substances or compositions, for use in any of these three different types of treatment or diagnosis. Novelty for a substance or composition that is already known may be found from a new medical use in accordance with **Art.54(4)-(5)** (see **Art.54(4):2** and **Art.54(5):2**).

3.1 TREATMENT

The treatments mentioned in **Art.53(c)** are by their nature medical treatments, which include curative and non-curative treatments. A curative treatment has a therapeutic purpose. A non-curative treatment is not directed to the health of the body; it includes e.g. cosmetic treatment, the termination of pregnancy, castration, sterilisation, artificial insemination, embryo transplants, treatments for experimental and research purposes, removal of organs, skin or bone marrow from a living donor. (**T182/90** r. 2.2)

Since the Preparatory Documents state that the aim of **Art.53(c)** is merely to exclude curative treatments, the treatments in the provision should be restricted to those suitable or potentially suitable for maintaining or restoring the health, the physical integrity and the physical well-being of a human being or an animal and to prevent diseases (**T383/03** r.3.2 - 3.4, following **T144/83** r.3 and **T329/94** r.5; see **T182/90** r.2.4, 2.5.2 for an opposite opinion). Hence, cosmetic treatments do not fall within the exclusion (**T383/03** r.4.2).

Rearing of livestock is a part of agriculture and therefore an industrial activity according to **Art.57**. Hence, treatment of animals for improved growth, meat quality (G-II,4.2.1), wool or milk production (**T774/89**) should be patentable, as also expressed by the Munich Diplomatic Conference of 1973 (Empel no. 120). However, essentially biological processes for the production of animals are not patentable according to **Art.53(b)**. The medical treatment of animals, being part of rearing, may also be regarded as an industrial activity. Hence, a treatment to cure or immunize one or more animals is both a therapeutic treatment and an industrial activity. Such a treatment is excluded from patentability under **Art.53(c)** in spite of its industrial applicability, because **Art.53(c)** takes precedence over **Art.57** (**T116/85** r.3.5, 4.1). See below for methods having both therapeutic and non-therapeutic effects.

The exclusion from patentability of **Art.53(c)** applies to three types of method, irrespective of the person carrying out the method. This has been confirmed by several decisions. It is impossible to draw a distinction between a therapeutic treatment of an animal carried out by a farmer and the same treatment as carried out by a veterinarian (**T116/85** r.4.3). A medical treatment need not necessarily be carried out by a physician (**T182/90** r.2.2; **T329/94** r.5). The medical competence of the person carrying out a step of a method or under whose supervision the step is carried out may be, at first sight, a useful indication for objection to the method under **Art.53(c)**; however the purpose and inevitable effect of the step are much more important (**T329/94** r.5).

The opinion **G1/04** held that the qualification of an activity as having a diagnostic character may not depend on who is involved. The wording of **Art.53(c)** is unequivocal in that the exclusion relates only to the method and not to the person carrying out the method (**G1/04** r.6.3). When this is applied mutatis mutandis to treatments, the person carrying out a method of treatment is irrelevant for the exclusion of a method of treatment from patentability. Previous decisions **T24/91** and **T385/86** (holding that a diagnostic or therapeutic method is one which has to be carried out by a specialist medical practitioner) are overruled as far as the relevance of the person carrying out the method is concerned.

3.2 TREATMENT BY SURGERY

The term 'surgery', defined as a physical intervention on the body, includes manual and instrumental procedures on the structure of the living body, both non-invasive and invasive. A non-invasive procedure is a manipulation of a part, organ or tissue without making a skin incision. Surgery includes endoscopy, puncture, injection, excision, opening of the bodily cavities and catheter insertion. (**T182/90** r.2.3)

'Treatment by surgery' is the use of surgery in any method of treatment of a human or animal body. Treatment by surgery can be defined as a physical intervention on the human or animal body which, whatever its specific purpose, gives priority to maintaining the life or health of the body on which they are performed (**T35/99** r.4.1, following **T182/90**). **T383/03** restricted the meaning of 'treatment by surgery' to curative treatments, this being the intention of **Art.53(c)**. It regarded a method of removing excess hair, although being a surgical method on account of its invasive character, as not excluded from patentability because it is not potentially suitable for a curative treatment.

However, the earlier decision **T182/90** held that treatment by surgery included non-curative treatments (r.2.4). Hence, a method of cosmetic treatment, which is in principle patentable, will be excluded if one of its steps is a surgical treatment (G-II,4.2.1; **T290/86**). Further, **T1172/03** held that restricting a claim to cosmetic treatments did not avoid the exclusion from patentability if the method in substance was therapeutic, and the restriction did not reflect any technical features of the method.

The statement in the Guidelines G-II,4.2.1.1 'surgery defines the nature of the treatment rather than its purpose' is too broad, in that it includes destructive methods, e.g. those that end in a laboratory animal's death. Such methods are not in their nature methods of treatment, even if some of the steps they involve may have a surgical character (**T182/90** r.2.5.2). A treatment sacrificing an animal or a treatment of a dead body is in principle patentable, albeit subject to ethical consideration (**Art.53**(a)) and legal restrictions such as criminal penalties (**T35/99** r.4.2).

A method of treatment including at least one step of treatment by surgery is excluded from patentability (**T182/90** r.2.5.1; **T820/92** r.5.5; **T82/93** r.1.4). A patient could not receive the only available treatment without infringement if even a single step of the treatment were covered by patent protection (**T35/99** r.7, 8).

G1/07 hn.1 defines a method of treatment of the body by surgery as a method in which, when carried out, maintaining the life and health of the subject is important and which comprises or encompasses an invasive step representing a substantial physical intervention on the body which requires professional medical expertise to be carried out and which entails a substantial health risk even when carried out with the required professional care and expertise. The boundaries of the concept of treatment by surgery are to be defined by the departments of first instance and the boards of appeal (r.3.4.2.4). An injection into the heart represents such a treatment by surgery (r.3.4.2.7).

A claim which comprises a step encompassing an embodiment which is a method for treatment of the body by surgery cannot be left to encompass that embodiment. The embodiment may be disclaimed, provided the disclaimer complies with the requirements of **G1/03** and **G2/03**. (**G1/07** hn.2)

The surgical step may only be omitted from the claim if the omission is compatible with **Art.84** in that the step is not an essential feature defining the invention (see **G1/07** hn.2). Omission is possible for a method relating to operating a device without any functional link between the claimed method and the effects of the device on the body (**G1/07** r.4.3.2).

The health risk of a surgical method may be assessed using a risk matrix combining levels of likelihood and health impact of a complication of a medical act (**T663/02** hn.II).

See decisions **T836/08** and **T923/08** for the effect of claim category on the exclusion.

3.3 TREATMENT BY THERAPY

3.3.1 *Therapy*

The meaning of the term 'treatment' is explained in the above section. 'Therapy' is concerned with bringing a body from a pathological state back to its normal, healthy state and with preventing a pathological state (**T774/89** r.2.3.4). Treatment by therapy is defined as any treatment which is designed to cure, alleviate, remove or lessen the symptoms of, or prevent or reduce the possibility of contracting any disorder or malfunction of the human or animal body (**T24/91** r.2.27).

The concept of therapy should not be confined narrowly. As an example, the relief of pain, discomfort or incapacity is to be construed as therapy in the sense of **Art.53**(c), irrespective of its origin. The symptoms caused by natural circumstances (e.g. menstruation, pregnancy or age), or by reaction to the environment (e.g. atmospheric conditions provoking tiredness, headaches) overlap with and are often indistinguishable from symptoms of a disease or an injury. Moreover, the biochemical effects and mechanisms which medicaments generate in order to restore the normal, capable and painless state for the body are often very similar or identical in these instances, irrespective of the nature of the real cause. It would be impossible and undesirable to distinguish between causal and symptomatic therapy, i.e. healing or cure and mere relief. Therefore, a method for relieving menstrual discomfort by administering a chemical composition is a therapy excluded under **Art.53**(c) and a first medical use of the composition should be pursued if the composition is not yet known as medicament. (**T81/84** r.3, 4)

In contrast, the use of a compound for reducing the perception of fatigue before or after a physical exercise was regarded as a non-therapeutic treatment. Since the manifestations of fatigue induced by the natural circumstance of exercises do not overlap with symptoms of a disease or injury, this case must be distinguished from **T81/84**. The condition of fatigue is not comparable to a pathological state. Whereas a therapeutic treatment starts from a pathological state, a non-therapeutic treatment starts from a normal, healthy state. (**T469/94** r.4.2 and **T774/89** r.2.3.4)

Art.53(c) does not mention prophylactic treatment. The Munich Diplomatic Conference preferred to leave it to case law to include the treatment or not, because the industrial nature of the treatment, particularly when applied to animals, might justify the grant of a patent (Empel no. 119). Case law has established that prophylactic treatment is therapeutic in nature, because prophylactic and curative treatments are directed to the same objective, i.e. the maintenance or restoration of health (**T19/86** r.7; **T182/90** r.2.2; **T820/92** r.5.2).

The prevention of pregnancy is not in general a therapy according to **Art.53(c)**, because pregnancy is not an illness (**T74/93** r.2.2.3). Such a method may be susceptible of industrial application, provided the requirements of **Art.57** have been fulfilled. These are not fulfilled for a method of contraception which is to be applied by a woman herself in the private and personal sphere (**T74/93** r.2.2.4).

Recently, **T1635/09** held that use of a composition as a contraceptive in which concentrations of substances were selected to avoid side-effects is a medical method because such prevention is therapeutic; the use is therefore excluded from patentability (r.3.1). Note, that this reasoning makes a cosmetic use of any composition a therapeutic treatment because all cosmetic products try to prevent side-effects. 'Prevention of a side-effect' should not be regarded as therapeutic treatment, as prevention is not a treatment of the side-effect. For the same reason, 'prevention' can neither be regarded as prophylaxis, the latter being a preventive treatment of a disease.

The removal of the symptoms of myopia, hyperopia and astigmatism of an eye is a therapeutic treatment (**T24/91** r.2.7).

The treatment of an implant secured to the body is regarded as treatment of the body in the sense of **Art.53(c)** if the treatment has a direct therapeutic effect, e.g. laser ablation of an implanted cornea in a patient's eye, which directly changes the refractive power of the patient's eye (**T24/91** r.2.6). The manufacture of prostheses, e.g. limbs or teeth, outside the body as well as taking measurements therefor on the body is patentable; however, making a prosthetic tooth inside the mouth is excluded under **Art.53(c)** (G-II,4.2; **T775/97** r.2.6).

A claim is not allowable if it includes at least one feature defining a physical activity or action which constitutes a method for treatment of the human body by therapy, for instance the measurement of a pressure value in the body which has a functional link with the therapeutic treatment applied (**T82/93** r.1.4, following **T820/92**). A claim containing nothing but technical features directed to a technical operation performed on a technical object and a subsequent technical operation performed on a body is not allowable under **Art.53(c)** if it defines a method for treatment of the body by therapy or surgery (**T82/93** r.1.1, method for operating a cardiac pacer).

A method of measuring the flow of small quantities of liquid in an implanted drug dosimeter providing a reading characterising the capacity of the pump of the dosimeter is not a treatment under **Art.53(c)** if there is no functional link and hence no physical causality between the steps of the method and the therapeutic effect produced on the body by the dosimeter, i.e. determining when a certain volume of drug is administered. Such a method does not hinder the doctor in carrying out a therapeutic or surgical treatment. (T245/87 r.3.2.2, 3.2.3)

3.3.2 *Combination of therapeutic and non-therapeutic indications*

A method may have both a therapeutic and a non-therapeutic effect. Its patentability depends on the wording of the claim and the disclosure of the effects in the description of the application.

If the non-therapeutic effect and the therapeutic effect of a step in a method of treatment are inextricably linked, a claim including the non-therapeutic effect would necessarily include the therapeutic effect and would be excluded. It is not relevant for the purpose of **Art.53(c)** whether the main or even the only reason for carrying out the claimed method is non-therapeutic. Even the addition of a non-therapeutic purpose to the claim is of no avail. In the present case the method concerned the administering of two substances for preventing pregnancy. Whereas the first substance produced the preventive effect, which is non-therapeutic, the second substance had a prophylactic effect avoiding the ill consequences of the use of the first substance. Hence, if one step of the method has a therapeutic effect, the method claim will fall under the prohibition of **Art.53(c)**. (**T820/92** r.5.2; **T82/93** hn.I)

A method of incurring loss of body weight by administering a certain compound can have a therapeutic and a non-therapeutic effect. The two effects are not inseparably linked but are distinguishable because they involve two distinct groups of people. Application of the method to a person not suffering from obesity would not be beneficial to the health of that person but improve his bodily appearance (cosmetic treatment). However, application of the method to a person suffering from obesity is beneficial to the health (therapeutic treatment). The cosmetic treatment is not rendered unpatentable by the fact that the compound has both a cosmetic and therapeutic effect, however difficult it might be to distinguish between the two effects. Hence, a claim is not excluded from patentability if its wording is chosen to cover the cosmetic treatment only (**T144/83** r.3, 4, see also **T464/94**). This does not apply to surgery (**T1172/03**).

A method of removing plaque from teeth has the cosmetic effect of improving the appearance of the teeth and inevitably the therapeutic effect of preventing caries, as acknowledged in the description of the patent application. The two effects of the method are inseparably linked. The method is therefore excluded under **Art.53(c)**. (**T290/86** r.3.2)

If the patent disclosure reveals that it is the intention to obtain both a therapeutic effect (remedying scours in animals) and a linked non-therapeutic effect (weight increase of the animal being bred) at the same time, a claim directed to the non-therapeutic effect is excluded (**T438/91**). A method to increase the production of meat is not patentable when the increase is a consequence of the improvement of the animal's health due to therapeutic treatment; the increase is a secondary effect of a therapeutic treatment (**T780/89**).

A claim directed to thenoyl peroxide for use in a method of therapeutic treatment of the human or animal body (first medical indication) and a claim directed to the use of thenoyl peroxide as a cosmetic product were both allowed. Thenoyl peroxide in the same preparation can be used in the treatment of acne and in the cleansing of the skin. Hence, the cosmetic treatment may also incidentally involve a medical treatment. The term 'cosmetic' in the claim is regarded as a sufficient exclusion of the therapy. (**T36/83** r. 6)

The term 'non-therapeutic' in a claim relating to the use of a medication to increase milk production in cows served as a disclaimer of therapeutic effects of the medication. In this case the non-therapeutic treatment was independent of the state of health of the animal. (**T774/89** r.2.3.4)

3.4 DIAGNOSTIC METHODS

3.4.1 Diagnosis and diagnostic methods

Diagnosis is the determination of the nature of a medical or veterinary medicinal condition intended to identify or uncover a pathology (**G1/04** r.5.1).

According to opinion **G1/04** a claim relating to a diagnostic method is excluded from patentability under **Art.53(c)** if it includes all of the following phases:

1 the examination phase, involving the collection of data,
2 the comparison of these data with standard values,
3 the finding of any significant deviation, i.e. a symptom, during the comparison, and
4 the attribution of the deviation to a particular clinical picture, i.e. the deductive medical or veterinary decision phase (diagnosis for curative purposes *stricto sensu*)

The above four phases are an interpretation in G-II,4.2.1.3 of the less-intelligible three steps in the headnote 1 of **G1/04**.

Hence, a claim relates to a diagnostic method only if it includes all steps necessary to make a diagnosis. If one step is omitted, there is no diagnostic method but merely an intermediate finding of diagnostic relevance (**G1/04** r.6.2.2, 6.2.3). Further, for the diagnostic method to be 'practised on the human or animal body' each of the technical method steps must be so performed. The presence or otherwise of a medical practitioner is not relevant.

The Enlarged Board of Appeal follows the established case law based on **T385/86** and overrules **T964/99** concerning the scope of the exclusion. This narrow interpretation of diagnostic methods is based on the principle that exclusion clauses from patentability in the EPC are to be construed in a restrictive manner (**G1/04** r.6) and on the fact that a narrow interpretation gives more legal certainty. In the opinion the importance of legal certainty has outweighed that of the purpose of **Art.53(c)**, i.e. the protection of medical and veterinary practitioners. According to the Enlarged Board of Appeal protection of medical practitioners can be achieved on a national level by introducing a right to use the methods in question (**G1/04** r.6.1, 6.3). It should be noted, however, that the TRIPS Agreement does not allow immunity as an exception to the rights conferred by a patent (all EPC contracting states except Monaco are bound by TRIPS).

The exclusion cannot be circumvented by omitting one of the above features from a claim if its essentialness is unambiguously inferable from the patent application or patent as a whole, because such a claim does not comply with the requirements of **Art.84**. The clarity requirement of **Art.84** signifies that an independent claim in the meaning of **R.43** should explicitly specify all of the essential features needed to define the invention. Hence, a claim that contains only one single feature relating to a particular step out of several preceding steps and serving diagnostic purposes or being related to diagnosis for curative purposes (cf. **T965/99**) does not meet the requirement of **Art.84**. (**G1/04** r.6.2, 6.2.3)

Preparatory or intermediate steps in addition to the steps describing phases 1-4 are irrelevant for determining the diagnostic character of a method claim (G-II,4.2.1.3).

Although the EBoA held that phases 1-3 should comply with the criterion 'practised on the human or animal body', in most cases only phase 1 must comply with the criterion. The criterion involves an interaction with the human or animal body, in which direct physical contact is not necessary. The criterion is fulfilled if the method step requires the presence of the body. (G-II,4.2.1.3)

The clinical picture in phase 4 need not be an underlying disease; a pathology suffices (**T125/02**).

In the assessment of the diagnostic character of a method no distinction is to be made between essential method steps having diagnostic character and non-essential method steps lacking it (**G1/04** hn2).

In **T330/03** a method for measuring a parameter of a biological sample using illumination with light was regarded patentable, because the method did not enable a decision to be made on the treatment necessary and was therefore not a diagnostic method in the sense of **Art.53(c)**. Similarly, in **T504/03** a data processing method for an X-ray tomography device was not excluded from patentability.

An imaging method is not excluded as a treatment by surgery merely because the image data obtained by the method during a surgical intervention immediately allows a surgeon to decide on the course of action to be taken during the surgical intervention. (**G1/07** hn.3, r.5)

3.4.2 *Method practised 'on the body'*

Art.53(c) specifies that excluded diagnostic methods must be 'practised on the human or animal body'. The qualification was added to the draft EPC after interested circles had objected to the exclusion of diagnostic methods as such, which would cover diagnostic methods which were not of a specifically medical nature, such as the use of equipment to determine the blood group of a patient (Empel no.121). It appears that the legislator has intended to exclude from patent protection only methods practised on the body, whereas for instance extra-corporal laboratory tests would be patentable (**T964/99** r.4.3). The undesirable consequence of the qualification is that a doctor carrying out a diagnosis that includes an essential laboratory test may be inhibited by a patent on the test, which is contrary to the intention of **Art.53(c)**. As an example, a quick, reliable laboratory blood test for the diagnosis of colon cancer, where an early detection is of immense importance for the chances of curing, was regarded patentable (**T435/88** r.3).

Opinion **G1/04** ruled that in a diagnostic method under **Art.53(c)** all method steps of a technical nature belonging to the preceding steps which are constitutive for making the diagnosis for curative purposes stricto sensu must satisfy the criterion 'practised on the human or animal body'. The article does not require a specific type and intensity of interaction; a preceding step of a technical nature thus satisfies the criterion if its performance implies any interaction with the human or animal body, necessitating the presence of the latter. (**G1/04** hn3, 4)

The criterion is to be considered only in respect of method steps of a technical nature. Hence, it does not apply to the deductive phase and to method steps of a non-technical nature, such as comparing data collected in the examination phase with standard values (**G1/04** r.6.4.1). Only those steps identified above are to be considered when determining whether a method is a diagnostic method. Additional steps are not relevant, even if these are practised on the body (**T1197/02**). Data processing steps are typically neither part of the data collection phase, nor of the comparison phase (**T143/04** hn). This overrules **T385/86**, **T400/87** and **T964/99** as far as the criterion is concerned.

This narrow interpretation of 'on the body' makes a claim relating to a diagnostic method patentable if it comprises at least one technical method step without interaction with the body, such as processing or displaying data.

A diagnostic method having a step in which an object is inserted into the body may also be excluded from patentability on the ground of the surgical character of the step. For example, a method for blood extraction used in a diagnostic method was regarded not patentable in **T329/94** r.4 (see also **T964/99** r.6.1). However, in view of the more recent decision **G1/07** hn.1, the insertion of an object into the body need not be regarded as a surgical step in all situations.

3.4.3 *Method carried out by medical or technical staff*

Art.53(c) does not specify which persons have to carry out a diagnostic method for it to be excluded from patentability. It accords with the socio-ethical and public health considerations on which **Art.53(c)** is based: the provision protects a patient such that he can be diagnosed and receive the necessary treatment without infringing a patent, whether the necessary methods are carried out by a medical professional, a technician or a layman. The provision does not primarily intend to protect a medical professional in the exercise of his profession.

Since **Art.53(c)** relates only to the method and not to the person carrying out the method, whether a method is a diagnostic method cannot depend on the participation of a medical or veterinary practitioner, by being present or by bearing the responsibility, or on the fact that all method steps can also, or only, be practised by medical or technical support staff, the patient himself or herself or an automated system (opinion **G1/04** hn2). The opinion confirms **T116/85**, **T182/90**, **T329/94** and **T964/99** and overrules **T385/86** r.3.5, **T24/91** r.2.4, **T655/92** r.5.3, **T964/99** r.6.2 as far as the decisions relate to the relevance of the person carrying out the method.

3.4.4 *Diagnostic purpose and actual steps*

A method may derive a diagnostic character from its purpose or from its actual steps. A diagnostic method must contain a reference to the diagnosis to be established; without such a purpose, the method is not diagnostic (**T61/83** r.2.1; **T208/83** r.3.2). A blood extraction method per se, i.e. without stating its purpose, must be refused protection, since otherwise a large part of medical activities would be hampered (**T329/94** r.4).

3.5 PRODUCTS FOR USE IN MEDICAL METHODS

Art.53(c), second sentence, states that products, in particular substances or compositions, for use in any of the medical methods excluded from patentability, are in principle patentable. This second sentence is on equal legal ranking with **Art.54(4)** and **(5)**: either a method is not a treatment by therapy and is not excluded from patentability under **Art.53(c)**, first sentence; or the method is a treatment by therapy excluded from patentability under **Art.53(c)**, first sentence, but a substance or composition for use in the method may be patented for an unspecified or specified therapy under **Art.54(4)** or **(5)**, respectively (**G2/08b** r.5.9.1.2 and 5.10.9).

The manufacture of a product, irrespective of whether that product can be used in a medical method, represents an industrial activity that does not interfere with the practice of any such method (**T775/97** r.2.4). A second reason not to exclude products used in medical methods from patentability is the effect of patent inhibition on decisions taken by medical staff in view of the products. A doctor can take a decision on a method of treatment or diagnosis to be carried out without time-consuming considerations about patent infringement. All necessary products such as medicaments and equipment are usually available. Their use should not be covered by patents. The decision to purchase the products has been taken long before their actual use, at a moment when due consideration could be given to the medical methods to be made available, the financial resources and licence fees. The patentability of the products gives industry an impetus for further development in this field (Benkard Europäisches Patentübereinkommen (Beck, 2002), Art.52 no. 270).

Products used in medical methods include among others medicines for use in methods of therapy, tools for use in methods of surgery and devices for performing measurements in diagnostic methods. The patentability of medicines is underscored by the explicit mention of substances and compositions in **Art.53(c)**, second sentence. If a therapeutic use of a known substance is discovered, the substance can be patented for use as a medicament. The substance, known as such, derives its novelty from the new use according to **Art.54(4)**. See **Art.54(4)** and **(5)** for the so-called first and further medical indications of compounds and substances.

The features of a device are often defined in functional terms, i.e. in terms of operation of the device. A claim relating to a method of operating the device may be excluded from patentability under **Art.53(c)**, first sentence if a step of the method could be regarded as treatment by therapy or surgery or as a diagnostic method. For example, a claim relating to a method for controlling pulse energy in a pacemaker to prolong battery life is allowable if none of the steps of the computer program controlling the pulses has a therapeutic effect (**T789/96** hn). A claim relating to a method for operating a pacemaker for arresting tachycardia was rejected, whereas the amended claim relating to a pacemaker programmed for arresting tachycardia was regarded allowable (**T426/89** r.2, 3). In drafting a patent application on such a device, it is recommended to include not only method claims but also device claims, because otherwise an amendment of a method claim to a device claim may contravene **Art.123(3)** by extending the protection conferred. If a granted patent contains claims defining a method for treatment by therapy or surgery using a device is opposed on the ground that the claimed subject-matter is not patentable having regard to **Art.53(c)**, the patent cannot be amended so as to contain claims defining the device for use in such a method because the protection is extended from a device when in use to a device both when in use and not in use (**T82/93** r.2.7).

Art. 54 Novelty

Art. 54(1) An invention shall be considered to be new if it does not form part of the state of the art.

1 **Novelty**

Art.54(1) expresses the principle of novelty: an invention can be patented only if it is new, i.e. it does not form part of the state of the art (**T12/81**). The state of the art is defined in **Art.54(2)** as everything that has been made available to the public (see **Art.54(2):1**). The examination of the novelty of a claim requires first the determination of the effective date of the claim (see **Art.88(3):2**), second identifying the state of the art, i.e. relevant subject-matter published before the effective date and, third comparing the features of the claim with the contents of the state of the art.

Any element of subjectivity must be excluded in applying the concept of novelty (**G1/92** r.2.1). Lack of novelty can only be established by citing references; personal knowledge cannot be used as proof (**T21/83**). Moreover, citing documents is essential to the substantiated reasoning required by **R.71(2)** and B-XI,3.2.

For assessing novelty, previously published prior art must be evaluated as of the date it became available to the public; prior rights under **Art.54(3)** must be considered as of the date of filing or, where appropriate, the priority date (G-VI,3). This is to avoid wrongly taking into account any knowledge the skilled person may have of developments of the subject-matter of the prior art or prior rights after those dates. Such knowledge is to be taken into account in the assessment of inventive step.

The following sections set out important issues relating to novelty.

2 Single disclosure

The disclosure of a document must generally be considered in isolation from that of other documents when assessing novelty (**T153/85** hn.III Amorphous thermoplastic polymer). (See note 3 below for exceptions).

If several elements are disclosed in one document but not as a combination, that combination is new. It is not permissible to pull together features separately disclosed in a single document, e.g. a catalogue, and thus assemble an object not referred to in the document. (**T305/87** Shear catalogue)

The disclosure made by a prior art patent does not consist only of the invention claimed in that patent but also its statements on the prior art. The disclosure made may therefore include a combination of the invention and a statement of the prior art, provided the statement is unambiguously disclosed as forming part of the invention (**T333/02** r.6). However, when a statement is a no more than a general description of the state of the art, care must be taken in combining the statement with the teaching of the invention (**T291/85** r.9).

3 Cross-reference in document

Although a document must be considered in isolation in the assessment of novelty, the disclosure of a document may under certain limited circumstances be supplemented by incorporating part or all of the disclosure of a second prior art document.

The incorporation is allowed if the first document contains a specific reference to the second document for detailed information on certain features, for example where the first document discloses a chemical compound that can be prepared using a specific method disclosed in a second document (**T153/85** hn.4, r.4.2; G-IV,8). Only the features of the second document that are specifically referred to are incorporated; other features are not regarded as incorporated in the first document (**T422/92** r.2.3.1). A mere statement 'incorporated by reference' and nothing more is not a specific reference.

When interpreting a prior art document, it is necessary to read it having the common general knowledge of the skilled person in mind. For this purpose it is permitted to look at representative technical literature as an aid to the correct interpretation of any particular term in the prior art document. For example, a prior art disclosure of use of rubber where its elastic properties are used, even if not explicitly stated, takes away the novelty of the use of an elastic material. (G-VI,2; **T288/90** r.4.4)

For the effect of references in a patent application on sufficiency of disclosure, see **Art.83:2.1.2**. With regard to the content of the application as filed for assessing extension of subject matter, see **Art.123(2):1.1**.

4 **Conformance of all features**

An invention lacks novelty if and only if there is a complete conformance of features of the invention and one prejudicial disclosure (**T177/83**).

Products can be new because of their properties, structure, construction or method of manufacture. A product defined by a new parameter is only new if it is apparent that the product is different from known products, i.e. when clear differences in properties are shown (**T248/85** r.6.4). The spatial configuration of a chemical compound may be such a property (**T296/87** Enantiomers).

A prior art document is taken to disclose, and therefore take away the novelty of, subject-matter which is derivable directly and unambiguously from that document. However, there is an important distinction between information which can be derived directly and unambiguously from a document, and generally known equivalents of the subject-matter of the document not mentioned in it. The latter may not be taken into account when assessing novelty (G-VI,2), although they may be used when considering obviousness) (**T167/84**). This strict approach to novelty is justified in order to reduce the risk of self-collision (**T167/84**; see also **Art.54(3):1**).

5 **Extent of conformance**

Conformance between a prior art document and an alleged invention does not require equivalent wording; for an invention to lack novelty, the state of the art must disclose the basic idea, the content of the teaching (**T114/86** hn2, **T198/84** r.4).

A substance claimed in a prior art patent is prejudicial to the novelty of a patent application claiming the same substance in a better-defined form (**T12/81** Diastereomers).

If a production process for a class of compounds is known where the class is defined by values in certain ranges, and a skilled person can prepare all members of the class, then all members belong to the state of the art. A claim defining a class overlapping a known class is not novel. (**T124/87** hn.II Copolymers)

Disclosure of the production process of a chemical substance makes a claim to the substance non-novel, even though the substance has not been named or has not yet been manufactured (**T181/82**). The novelty of a chemical compound is not taken away merely because its name or formula is known, but only when its preparation and/or separation is known (G-VI,4).

5.1 INTENDED USE FEATURE

In the assessment of the novelty of a claim, a particular intended use ('An object X for use in application Y...') in the claim must be disregarded, unless the use referred to implies that the product has a particular form or property which distinguishes it from its known form. Thus a product which otherwise possesses all of the features specified in a claim, but which would be unsuitable for the stated purpose or which would require modification to enable it to be so used, should not normally be considered as prejudicial for the claim. For example, a plastic ice cube tray is not prejudicial for a claim referring to 'mould for molten steel', because the low melting point of the tray makes it unsuitable for the purpose of the mould. But a tray possessing all the features of the mould and having the necessary high melting point is prejudicial, even if such use of the tray as a mould has never been disclosed. (F-IV,4.13)

There are exceptions to the general rule that intended purpose is irrelevant to novelty. Some are expressly provided for by **Art.54** (see note 5.2 below) and others are the creation of EPO case law (see note 7.2 below).

See **Art.84:1.9** for the effect of use features on the clarity of a claim.

5.2 MEDICAL USES

Claims may be granted relating to a known substance or composition when it is for use in a new surgical, therapeutic or diagnostic method of the nature referred to in **Art.53(c)** (G-II,4.2). The novelty of such a claim, which takes the form: 'substance X for use as a medicament', is permitted under **Art.54(4)**. These claims are known as claims to a 'first medical use'.

In addition, even where the first medical use is known, a claim for a second (or further) medical use of the known product may be patentable under **Art.54(5)**, i.e. another use in a method of the type referred to in **Art.53(c)**, provided that this other use is new and includes an inventive step.

Examples of claims for first and second medical uses are given in **Art.54(4):2** and **(5):2** and **3**.

A different application method (administration) of a pharmaceutical substance makes a claim directed to the substance adapted for the method novel, because the method gives the substance distinctive characteristics (**T289/84** r.3.4).

6 Selection inventions

A selection invention is the identification of a sub-range of subject-matter from a larger known range, where the sub-range has an improved technical effect. The patentability of a selection invention is based on the rule that a disclosure of a genus does not take away the novelty of a species falling within that genus, whereas the disclosure of a species takes away the novelty of a genus. Hence, the prior disclosure of copper takes away the novelty of metal whereas metal does not take away the novelty of copper (G-VI,5); in other words, the novelty of a range is destroyed if prior art discloses an example which falls within the range (**T188/83** hn.I).

6.1 SELECTION OF INDIVIDUAL ENTITIES FROM A GROUP

An individual entity or a sub-group selected from a known group of elements is novel if the selected entity is not disclosed in an individualised form in the prior art (**T12/81**). An entity selected from a known single list of specifically disclosed entities is not novel. A selection from two or more known lists of a certain length to arrive at a specific combination of features is novel, provided this selection is not specifically disclosed in the prior art. An example of the two-list principle is the selection of an individual chemical compound of which specific substituents are selected from two or more lists of substituents given in the form of a known generic formula. (G-VI,8(i))

6.2 SELECTION OF SUB-RANGE FROM A NUMERICAL RANGE

Decision **T279/89** summarizes case law on selection inventions, and states that each of the following three requirements must be fulfilled:

1 the selected sub-range is narrow;
2 the selected sub-range is sufficiently far removed from the preferred embodiments of the known range; and
3 the selected sub-range is not an arbitrary specimen of the prior art, but another invention (purposive selection).

The 'other invention' in the third requirement may be a technical effect occurring in the sub-range, but not in the whole of the known range (G-VI,8(ii)). If the sub-range has the same technical effect, namely the same properties and capabilities, as the known range, the sub-range is an arbitrary selection and is not novel (**T198/84**). **T230/07** hn. questions the use of a technical effect to establish novelty of a sub-range; requirements 1 and 2 are necessary and sufficient.

The effect in the sub-range may be the improvement of a known property; i.e. the effect in the sub-range may be the same as the effect occurring in the known range but to a greater extent (G-VI,8(ii)). Note that for novelty the third requirement concerns a different technical effect, not necessarily a surprising technical effect. The latter is an issue in the assessment of inventive step.

A new effect on its own cannot confer novelty on a sub-range, the first two requirements must also be complied with (G-VI,8(ii)).

The meaning of 'narrow' and 'sufficiently far removed' has to be decided on a case-by-case basis (G-VI,8(ii)). It depends inter alia on the degree of difference in the technical effect of the sub-range relative to the known range as a whole; a minor difference is likely to require a greater distance from the disclosed embodiments of the known range.

The following is an example of what is novel and what not. The prior art discloses a temperature range from 20 to 90°C for a chemical reaction and a specific example at 30°C. The sub-range from 20 to 40°C is not novel, because it covers the specific example. The sub-range from 70 to 80°C having the same properties as the known range is not novel, as it is not a selection with a different technical effect. The sub-range from 80 to 90°C giving an increased yield is not novel, because it is not far removed from the known value of 90°C. The sub-range from 60 to 70°C, if it provides a higher purity, is novel.

A disclosure of a narrow range within a broad range may allow disclosure of the remaining ranges within the broad range but outside the narrow range, provided that the remaining ranges are disclosed in the application as filed, e.g. by showing that the effect of the invention is also obtained in the remaining ranges **T1170/02** r.4; H-IV,2.5). The decision distinguishes the so-called rules of logic reasoning, according to which a disclosure of the broad and narrow range also discloses the remaining ranges, i.e. the logical complement of the narrow range. The rules of logic reasoning on its own, without applying the disclosure test, is insufficient to establish disclosure of the remaining ranges from the narrow and broad ranges (see **G2/10** r.4.5.3).

6.3 OVERLAP OF RANGES

When a claimed range and a known range overlap, the novelty of the claimed range depends on the whole content of the prior art document. A single disclosed value in the range of overlap, e.g. the end point of the known range or a specifically disclosed value, takes away the novelty of the claimed range (G-VI,8(iii)).

A claimed range partly overlapping a range in a prior art document is not novel if the examples in the document lie close to the claimed range and the skilled person can learn from the document that its teaching can be applied all through the range (**T17/85**). If a claimed range overlaps with a known range and the skilled person, taking into account the general knowledge of the field, would seriously contemplate applying the prior art teaching in the overlap range, then the range is not novel (**T26/85** hn.I; **T666/89**; G-VI,1; see **Art.56:4.5**). A class of compounds overlapping a known class, all members of which a skilled person can prepare from the known teaching, is not novel (**T124/87** hn.II). If a prior art document contains a reasoned statement dissuading the use of a part of the claimed range, that part remains novel (**T26/85** hn.II).

A selection invention can be distinguished from the prior art by a disclaimer if that provides the shortest and most accurate formulation (**T4/80**). The disclaimer can only be used to make an invention novel, not inventive (**T170/87**). However, a disclaimer of specific novelty destroying values known from the prior art range will not confer novelty on a claimed range overlapping the prior art range if in view of the prior art the skilled person would seriously contemplate applying the prior art teaching in the range of overlap (G-VI,8(iii)). See **Art.84:1.7** and **Art.123(2):2.4** for the allowability of a disclaimer in the application as filed and added by way of amendment.

7 Use claims

7.1 USE VS. PROCESS CLAIMS

A claim directed to a product, i.e. a physical entity, confers protection upon such product, i.e. wherever it exists and whatever its context (and therefore for all uses of such product, whether known or unknown). If such a product is known, then a claim to it as such lacks novelty. On the other hand, a claim to a particular use of a product is in effect a claim to that product only when it is being used in the particular manner claimed, this being an additional technical feature of the claim. Such a claim therefore confers less protection than a claim to the product per se. A use claim relates to the use of a particular physical entity to achieve an effect, not to a use to produce a product. In general, a use claim is not a process claim within the meaning of **Art.64(2)**, extending protection to products produced by the use. (**G2/88** r.5)

If in a use invention defined by a claim in the form: 'Use of substance X in the application Y...' the use itself is the subject of the patent, then the use determines the novelty, even if the applied substance is known (**T30/86**).

7.2 USE CLAIMS

A claim relating to a new non-medical use of a known product to attain a new technical effect is novel. This is true even if the means to realise the new technical effect is identical to a known use of the product. In such a case the novelty of the use resides only in the new purpose, based on the technical effect. The attaining of the technical effect must be considered as a novel functional technical feature of the claim (**G2/88**, Friction reducing additive, second non-medical use). Hence, the intentional and purposive application of a known substance for a new use is novel. For example, a claim directed to the use of a known substance as an additive in oil for reducing friction based on the newly discovered friction-reducing effects of the substance is novel in spite of the known use of the same substance in oil for inhibiting rust (**T59/87**). Similarly, the new purpose of controlling fungi on plants makes the use of a substance for that purpose new despite its known use as growth regulator, even if both uses require the same treatment of spraying the plants (**T231/85**, Use of growth-regulator as fungicide). The two uses relate to the application of the substance in distinctly different situations, depending on the desired effect.

Thus the technical effect may be new, although both the technical realisation and the compound are known. The new effect may even have occurred inherently when the prior art use was employed, but remained unrecognized, and therefore hidden and unavailable to the public (**G6/88**, Plant growth regulating agent). Also, if the technical realisation is known, the new effect is nonetheless not available to the public if it is not revealed so clearly during execution of the prior art use as to disclose the invention's essential character to an unlimited number of skilled persons (**T208/88** hn; **T59/87** hn).

A claim directed to the use of a known substance for a *known* non-medical purpose to attain a new technical effect related to the known use is not novel. The mere explanation of an effect obtained when using a known substance in a known way does not confer novelty to a known use if the skilled person was aware of the occurrence of the desired effect. (**T892/94** hn.II)

A second non-medical use claim is restricted in **G2/88** and **G6/88** to 'use of a known compound' and cannot be expanded to 'use of a process' (**T684/02** hn).

The determination of infringement of a claim having only a purpose as the characterizing feature is difficult as the performance of the invention does not, in general, indicate the purpose; the purpose is merely in the mind of the user. The Enlarged Board has adopted the easy way out from its own point of view by leaving the problem of determining infringement to the national courts.

Art. 54(2) The state of the art shall be held to comprise everything made available to the public by means of a written or oral description, by use, or in any other way, before the date of filing of the European patent application.

1 Absolute state of the art

The novelty and inventive step of a claim are assessed in view of the state of the art as defined in **Art.54(2)** and (3). The EPC uses the so-called 'absolute state of the art' criterion, codified in **Art.54(2)**. This is sometimes called 'absolute novelty', but since the state of the art is relevant for both novelty and inventive step, it is more appropriate to use the term 'absolute state of the art' (see e.g. **T107/82** r.11). The absolute character of the state of the art is reflected in the fact that the EPC contains no restriction as to the means of disclosure, no restriction in time, no geographical restriction and no restriction as to the public to whom the art has been made available (Empel no. 76-82). There are only two exceptions to the absolute state of the art. First, a European prior right, although not available before the date of filing, is deemed to be part of the state of the art (**Art.54(3)**. Secondly, non-prejudicial disclosures, although available, are deemed not to have been made available to the public (**Art.55**).

The term 'state of the art' in **Art.54(2)** must be interpreted as 'state of technology', in compliance with the French and German text of the EPC, and does not include the state of the art in commerce and business methods. The term 'everything' in the provision must be understood as concerning such kind of information which is relevant to some field of technology. Hence, anything which is not related to any technological field or any field from which a skilled person would expect to derive technically relevant information, does not belong to the state of the art to be considered in the context of **Art.54** and **56**, even if it had been made available before the relevant priority date. (**T172/03** r.8-10)

The following sections deal with the issues of availability, means of disclosure and extent of disclosure. See also Guidelines G-IV.

2 Availability

2.1 GENERAL

Availability of information to the public for the purpose of **Art.54(2)** requires only the possibility that the public had access to the information; it is not necessary that a person has actually accessed it (**T444/88, T381/87**). The language of the information is irrelevant, because the skilled person is considered to be proficient in all languages (**T920/92** r.2.4). The EPO provides machine translation on its website. A machine translation of a document may be used in proceedings unless the quality of the translation is questioned with substantiated reasoning (**T991/01**; G-IV,4.1).

Subject-matter is available to the public if one person could have gained knowledge of it without a breach of confidentiality (G-IV,7.2.1; **T482/89** hn3). If a product is sold unconditionally, its full structure and contents are disclosed from the time of availability, even though knowledge of those would require destruction of the product and/or time consuming investigation (see section 2.4 below).

A mailed document is available to the public not at the time of posting it, but at the time of delivery. A document is available in a library if a member of the public could have looked at the document, it need not yet be entered in a catalogue. A doctoral thesis is not public if not entered in a catalogue and still in a publicly inaccessible archive of the library. On the other hand, the latest edition of a periodical which has not yet been entered in a catalogue and which may be requested is available to the public. (**T381/87** Document in library; see also **T1057/09**)

The issue of accessibility of information is frequently encountered in the assessment of public prior use. In particular, examination of a component or property of a device or compound may require a significant effort or advanced analysis. Accessibility in this context is discussed in the section below on public use.

2.2 DATE

According to **Art.54(2)** the state of the art comprises everything made available before the date of filing of the European patent application, the date of priority counting as the date of filing where priority has been claimed (**Art.89**). This defines a day as the minimum unit of time. The EPC does not take into account time zones, which may affect the date on which information becomes available. For example, a document published in Amsterdam at 00h30 and immediately transmitted to London is available in London the previous day at 23h30. Whereas in times past the location of publication was important, the present means of communication, such as fax and internet, allow a nearly instantaneous world-wide publication. There is no case law on this issue yet.

The date of filing in **Art.54(2)** for determining the state of the art is replaced by the priority date when priority has been claimed validly (**Art.89**).

A document with a vague publication date ('ca 1960') will still qualify as prior art if the date is sufficiently far earlier than the date of filing of the patent in suit (**T267/03** hn.1).

Instructions for use and installation of kitchen appliances are usually made available together with the product to be installed and therefore require proof of availability as for public use; a printing date in the instructions is not an adequate indication of the date of availability (**T511/02** r.4). However, a copyright notice in a manual of a television stating a year creates a presumption that the manual was published in that year; facts in a copyright notice are presumed to be correct (**T861/04** r.2.5).

A document published before the filing date is direct evidence of the state of the art, being an instance of what has been made available to the public before the filing date. Its status as part of the state of the art can only be challenged by reference to its authenticity. A post-published document is self-evidently not part of the state of the art but can be used to draw an inference about the state of the art or common general knowledge as of the relevant date. Such an inference is subject to challenge as to its plausibility, but an automatic rejection of such a document as evidence of prior art by the EPO is not justified. (**T1110/03** r.2)

2.3 PUBLIC

Art.54(2) requires that the information must have been made available to the public. The use of the term 'public' emphasises that the qualifications of the recipient of the information are irrelevant to the question whether the information forms part of the state of the art (Empel no. 82). Information need not have been made available to a skilled person to be regarded as state of the art.

At least one member of the public must have had access to the information. The sale of an article to one person not bound by confidentiality makes the article available to the public (**T482/89**). The public need not have a certain level of education (**T165/96** r.1.1.1.3). Where the disclosure is given orally, it has been held that the public must be a skilled person because he can understand the information and is able to distribute it further (see e.g. obiter dictum in **T877/90** r.2.1.6).

2.4 SECRECY

The availability of information implies the absence of an obligation to maintain its secrecy. Information bound by an obligation of confidentiality is not available in the sense of **Art.54(2)**. The content of a meeting understood by the parties to be secret, even tacitly and without a written contract, is not publicly disclosed (**T830/90**).

If something is disclosed in spite of a non-disclosure agreement, the matter is part of the state of the art, unless the exception of **Art.55(1)** applies.

Something does not automatically become public because of a demonstration on factory premises (G-IV,7.2.1 and 7.2.3).

A secret document, e.g. a document for licensees only, is not public, even if the distribution is large in comparison with the total number of people skilled in the art, since part of the public is excluded from access (**T300/86** r.2).

A document the contents of which may not be disseminated to third parties may still be available to the public, provided the third parties can in reality buy the document themselves to obtain the knowledge of its contents. Such a restriction may serve merely to protect the interests of the content provider. (**T50/02** r.2.4, 2.5)

The contents of an EPO file of a patent application are secret before publication of the application and public thereafter (**Art.128(4)**).

There is a prima facie assumption that any person involved in a medical process is obliged to maintain confidentiality where there is a need for patient confidentiality or a need to protect the development and testing of prototype devices (**T152/03** r.3.4).

3 Means of disclosure

3.1 WRITTEN DISCLOSURE

Written disclosure of technical information is usually in the form of patent documents and articles in scientific or technical papers. However, a written disclosure may be in any accessible form, even in a minor small-ad in a newspaper (**T165/96**). Technical documents from companies should be carefully checked to see whether they are typical secret company papers or publicly available documents (**T37/96**). The same applies to correspondence between companies and between companies and clients. The price of a document is not relevant to its availability; the price of technical information is usually adapted to the market (**T50/02** r.2.3.5, document of $ 6000).

Something can also be made public by advertising or otherwise showing it on television.

3.2 DRAWINGS

The drawings form part of the disclosure of a patent application and have the same ranking in disclosure as the description (**T169/83** r.3.2). Features only shown in drawings may be used in the amendment of claims, provided the features are clearly, unmistakably and fully derivable from the drawings in terms of structure and function by a person skilled in the art and so understood in relation to the content of the description as a whole as to be manifestly part of the invention (**T169/83** hn). It must be clear that the feature is the deliberate result of technical considerations directed to the solution of the technical problem involved (**T398/00** r.3.4).

A feature solely shown in a drawing belongs to the state of the art only if a skilled person can derive a teaching from it in the absence of any other description (**T204/83**). Dimensions which can only be obtained from a measurement in a schematic drawing are not part of the disclosure unless it is a construction drawing drawn to scale (**T204/83**). On the other hand, a photo is also a reproduction of an object and thus will normally be regarded as an exact representation of the object from which dimensions may be taken (**T857/91** r.3.2).

A document must be assessed in its entirety by the skilled person. A comparison of a patent with arbitrary parts taken out of a document is not allowed. A coincidental agreement between figures is not prejudicial to novelty (**T56/87** Electrodes in X-ray apparatus).

3.3 ORAL DISCLOSURE

An oral disclosure, such as a lecture or an account of a prior use, is valid prior art if the date and content of the disclosure and its availability to the public can be ascertained (**T406/92** r.6, 7). It may be difficult to prove what was actually disclosed during a lecture, as was the case in **T86/95** r.3 and **T1212/97** r.1-11. The standard of proof for ascertaining the contents of an oral disclosure is a high one (G-IV,7.3.4).

An oral disclosure is not part of the state of the art if the lecture was only accessible to persons bound by confidentiality or if the disclosure was an evident abuse in the sense of **Art.55(1)(a)** (G-IV,7.3.2).

When an oral disclosure is cited as prior art in grant proceedings and a document published on or after the relevant date reproduces the lecture or gives an account of the prior use, the examiner should start with the assumption that the written disclosure gives a true account of the oral disclosure. If the applicant provides good reason to the contrary, the oral disclosure should not be used as prior art and the examiner should not pursue the matter further. (G-IV,7.4)

As in grant proceedings, in opposition proceedings such a document is also assumed to give a true account of the oral disclosure, unless the proprietor provides proof to the contrary. The opponent may refute the proof. (G-IV,7.4)

3.4 DISPLAY

Where an object is only shown to the public in a display, e.g. at an exhibition, only its visible features are made available to the public (**T1085/92**). However, non-visible features may be disclosed in oral or written explanations provided with the display. When a device is displayed in operation, the visible changes may implicitly disclose internal features of the device. However an applicant may benefit from the exclusion of the object from the prior art when it is displayed at a recognized international exhibition under **Art.55(1)(b)** and the applicant complies with the requirements of **Art.55(2)**.

3.5 INTERNET DISCLOSURE

The more ephemeral character of an internet disclosure compared to a traditional publication on paper has led the EPO to require a stricter standard of proof when establishing the state of the art. The following practice of the EPO for internet documents both in the EPC and PCT procedure is set out in G-IV,7.5. Although the practice focusses on grant proceedings, the same principles are applied in opposition proceedings, taking into account the timing of the submission and the interests of the submitting party (G-IV,7.5.2).

3.5.1 *Content and date of internet publication*

Internet publications are in principle part of the state of the art according to **Art.54(2)**. In some technical fields, such as information and software technology, the internet often yields the most relevant prior art. Certain information, for example online manuals, tutorials for software products and other products with a short life cycle, are only available from the internet.

The EPO assumes that the content of web pages has not been manipulated, unless there are specific indications to the contrary. The relevant web pages must in principle be available without any bar to confidentiality. A requirement to pay for access (analogous to purchasing a book) or access to a limited circle of people (e.g. by password protection) is no bar to availability. (G-IV,7.5.1)

Note, that many websites, such as confidential, employee-only accessible company web pages, fall within the above definition of the access-limited web pages. Since such pages should not be included in the prior art, it is expected that the EPO will refine its definition of availability of web pages.

3.5.2 *Standard and burden of proof*

For each disclosure the date of publication and the content published must be established. The EPO uses the principle of free evaluation of evidence for establishing the facts of internet publications, as for any other piece of evidence, applying the balance of probabilities for assessing the circumstances of each case. Hence, it is not sufficient that an alleged fact is merely probable; it must be convincing; proof beyond reasonable doubt, i.e. up to the hilt, is not required. (G-IV,7.5.2)

When an objection is based on an internet publication, the examiner must reason (**R.71(2)**) why the publication is relevant and show on the balance of probabilities that the objection is well-founded. If this is done, the burden shifts to the applicant. If the applicant convincingly questions the publication date, the examiner will either have to provide further evidence to maintain the disputed publication date or not use the publication as prior art. Questioning a publication date without reasons or merely with generic statements about the reliability of internet disclosures will carry minimal weight. (G-IV,7.5.3)

The EPO generally considers an explicit publication date in an internet disclosure as reliable. The burden of proof is on the applicant to show otherwise; the more reliable a disclosure, the harder it will be for the applicant to prove that the publication date is incorrect. (G-IV,7.5.3)

Note, that the board of appeal in decision **T1134/06** r.4.1, taken before publication of the Notice of the EPO, applies the criteria for prior use and prior oral disclosure to internet disclosures and requires a proof 'beyond any reasonable doubt' of the date of publication of an internet disclosure and the circumstances under which it was made available. First instance requires as standard of proof for internet disclosures the 'free evaluation of evidence' (G-IV,7.5.2), which is easier to comply with as the standard 'beyond any reasonable doubt'.

3.5.3 Types of internet disclosures

i) The reliability of online technical journals from scientific publishers is the same as that of traditional paper journals, i.e. very high. (G-IV,7.5.3.1)

Some publishers make the internet version of a publication earlier available than the paper version. They sometimes pre-publish submitted but not yet approved manuscripts on the internet; if not approved, the manuscript may be the only disclosure of its content. The EPO treats a pre-published manuscript and the final version of the publication as separate documents having their own publication dates, because of possible differences between the two documents. (G-IV,7.5.3.1)

ii) Publishers of newspapers or periodicals, television or radio stations, academic institutions, international organisations, public organisations and standardisation bodies are generally deemed to provide reliable publication dates. (G-IV,7.5.3.2); **T1469/10** hn)

The EPO has signed agreements with many standardisation organisations, such as IEC, ISO, ITU, ETSI and IEEE-SA, and has full-text search access to their documents. Since the content of standards vary in time, they should be referred to by their version number and publication date. See also G-IV,7.6.

E-print archives of universities to which authors submit reports on research results before publication by a conference or journal often contain documents never published anywhere else. The date on documents on the internet that have previously been published on paper, such as manuals for software, handbooks for products, and white papers on products, can be taken as a date of publication. (G-IV,7.5.3.2))

iii) Documents from new internet information interchange services, such as discussion groups, blogs, e-mail archives of mailing lists or wiki pages, constitute prior art, although it may be more involved to establish their publication date and reliability. (G-IV,7.5.3.3)

The content of a transmitted e-mail is not regarded to be public merely because it could have been intercepted (**T2/09**; G-IV,7.5.3.3).

Computer-generated timestamps, such as the 'last modified' date, are considered as reliable publication dates, in the absence of indications to the contrary. (G-IV,7.5.4)

A 'last modified' date which was not updated when uploading new information may suggest an earlier date of publication than the actual date. The date on a document may be the date of production of the document rather than the publication date.

iv) Where a relevant internet disclosure does not give a date or a given date is shown to be unreliable, further evidence may be obtained from internet archiving services, such as at www.archive.org, or from indexing dates given to the web page by search engines (**T1961/13**). (G-IV,7.5.4)

The affidavit of the manager of www.archive.org, annexed to the EPO communication of 19.06.2008 for application EP 01305949.8, was accepted by the examining division as evidence of the validity of the publication date of a document retrieved from the internet archive.

If no date can be obtained, the disclosure cannot be used as prior art. The disclosure may be cited as L document in the search report. The disclosure is citable against future applications using the date of retrieval by the EPO as the date of publication. (G-IV,7.5.4)

3.5.4 *Hidden internet publications*

Decision **T1553/06** held that an internet publication is available in the sense of **Art.54(2)** if it remained accessible for three weeks; a document only accessible through a non-public URL is not available; a document that can only be found with a search engine using keywords not related to the content of the document is neither available. Such hidden publications may be used to question the validity of a patent at a moment that can be chosen only by the rare person having knowledge of the publication. **T1553/06** held that it should be a public policy of the EPO to prevent them as they jeopardise legal certainty (r.6.5.4).

It should be noted, that documents in the EPO files are public according to **Art.128(4)**, even though they cannot be found by search engines. Hence, a document filed as anonymous observation under **Art.115** in a technically unrelated case is a hidden publication that is public by force of the EPC.

T1553/06 has not been included in the Guidelines, because the policy to prevent hidden or defensive publications conflicts with the criterion of absolute state of the art used by the EPC, according to which there are no restrictions as to means of disclosure (**Art.54(2):1**). Further case law should clarify the matter.

3.6 PUBLIC USE

3.6.1 *General*

Public prior use is the term used to refer to the availability of an actual product or method to the public (as opposed to a description in a document) before the date of filing of the application. Disclosure by means of public use of the product or process imposes more demands on the evidence of availability and the assessment of the contents than the more usual written disclosure and commonly requires extensive evidence. The assessment of the content of a written disclosure is a matter of interpretation of text, while that of public prior use often requires analysis of a product (G-IV,7.2.1). Public prior use in opposition proceedings is normally complicated by the facts and evidence in general being only available to the opponent and not to the proprietor, influencing the desired degree of proof (see **Art.117(1):2**).

A product or method disclosed by prior public use is regarded as part of the state of the art if the following matters in relation to the alleged use are proved: When, What, How, Where and by Whom (G-IV,7.2; **T93/89** r.8.1, **T194/86**). In those public prior use cases where practically all evidence in support of the public prior use lies within the power and knowledge of the opponent, i.e. in the majority of cases, he has to prove his case up to the hilt (**T472/92** hn.I). A single sale is sufficient to render the article sold available to the public, provided the buyer is not bound by an obligation to maintain confidentiality (**T482/89**).) The opposition division may request a list of clients and dates of sale to prove availability of the product.

3.6.2 *Accessibility and analysability*

Decision **G1/92** deals with various aspects of public prior use. The composition or internal structure of a product, whether chemical or other, forms part of the state of the art when the product as such is available to the public and can be analysed and reproduced by the skilled person, irrespective of whether or not particular reasons can be identified for such analysis. This is based on **Art.54(2)**, which does not make any distinction between different means for making available information (r.1.2) and on the fact that the possibility of access to information makes it public, irrespective of whether there is any reason to search for it (r.2). Characteristics which are only revealed when the product is exposed to interaction with specific outside conditions, e.g. reactants or the like, in order to prove a particular effect or result or to discover potential results or capabilities, go beyond what is disclosed by the product per se as they are dependent on deliberate choices being made. Typical examples are the application of a known substance as pharmaceutical and the use of a known compound for a particular purpose based on a new technical effect (**G2/88**). Thus, such characteristics cannot be considered as having already been made available to the public (r.3). (**G1/92**, overruling **T93/89** (adhesive on paper; only available if there is reason for analysis) and **T461/88** r.6.3 (program on microchip too expensive to analyse), broadening **T406/86** (available only if analysis is simple).

Opinion **G1/92** must be read together with the later decision **T952/92**, because several passages of **G1/92** not relating to the question referred to the Enlarged Board of Appeal are contrary to established case law and, when read in isolation, would lead the reader astray. Some issues have been put right in **T952/92**.

The degree of burden involved in analysing a prior sold product is in principle irrelevant to the determination of what constitutes the state of the art (**T952/92** r.2.2, contrary to **G1/92** r.1.4). The possibility of a complete analysis of a prior sold product so as to enable an exact reproduction of such product is not necessary for destroying the novelty of a claimed product (**T952/92** r.2.3 last par., contrary to the requirement of complete analysis following from **G1/92** r.1.4). Information as to the composition and internal structure of a prior sold product is made available if direct and unambiguous access to such information is possible by means of known analytical techniques which were available for use by a skilled person before the relevant filing date (**T952/92** r.4.3).

G1/92 shifts the emphasis in the assessment of public prior use from the existence of the product to the technical teaching that may be directly and unambiguously derived from the product. Teaching that is not available by such deriving does not form state of the art. Hence, it is possible for an existing, publicly available product to be patented (as a product claim) based on a new teaching relating to the product. For example, an available polymer without an available method of manufacture is not part of the state of the art if an analysis of the polymer does not reveal the chemical process by which it was made. Similarly, a microbiological product does not belong to the state of the art if there is a high probability of variation upon reproduction of such microbes and a skilled person cannot establish the identity of the reproduced product or the prior art product because intrinsic or extrinsic features of those products are not accessible (**T977/93**).

4 Extent of disclosure

4.1 GENERAL

The contents of a document are what a skilled person would have read in it at the time of its publication or, where **Art.54(3)** applies, the date of filing, or priority where appropriate (G-VI,3). The knowledge of the skilled person must not be supplemented by knowledge which might have been obtained between the date of deemed assessment of the prior art and the filing or priority date of the patent in issue.

A document disclosing a chemical compound and its manufacture makes this compound available to the public in all desired grades of purity provided the required purification methods are known. Hence, the feature of a certain purity does not make a claim related to a known compound novel. Purity is an important issue in pharmaceuticals, for example where a compound is a racemate, i.e. a mixture of two isomers, one of the isomers producing the therapeutic effect and the other isomer causing only side-effects. (**T990/96** hn.I)

4.2 IMPLICIT DISCLOSURE

A document discloses not only subject-matter derivable directly and unambiguously from that document but also any features implicit to a person skilled in the art from what is expressly mentioned in the document. For example, a disclosure of the use of rubber in circumstances where its elastic properties are used, even if this is not explicitly stated, takes away the novelty of the use of an elastic material. (G-VI,2)

Other examples are: e.g. mains electricity implicitly discloses 230V @ 50 Hz; copper implicitly discloses a non-ferrous metal.

Also part of the state of the art is any feature implicit in a document in the sense that, in carrying out the teaching of the document, the skilled person would inevitably arrive at that feature. A document describing a process, which would inevitably result in a product not referred to, when carried out, implicitly discloses that product (**T666/89**). A claim defining a product by an unusual parameter lacks novelty if the same product results when carrying out a known process (G-VI,6; **T12/81**).

A document does not make available well-known equivalents not disclosed in the document; equivalents are a matter of obviousness (G-VI,2).

4.3 SUFFICIENCY OF DISCLOSURE

Knowledge from prior art is made available only if the disclosure is sufficient to enable a skilled person to practise the teaching, taking into account the general knowledge in the field. A document that does not provide an enabling disclosure, i.e. a disclosure which is insufficient in the sense of **Art.83**, does not form part of the state of the art (**T206/83** r.12, **T26/85** hn.I Thickness of magnetic layers). Hence, care must be taken not to include in an application elements which are not made sufficiently available; it might make the application useless for destroying the novelty of later applications.

The disclosure of a compound and the process steps for its manufacture without sufficient information or common general knowledge as to how to obtain necessary starting or intermediate materials is not an effective disclosure of either the compound or the process and hence neither is part of the state of the art. On the other hand, this would not be the case where the search and experimentation required to find such materials does not require an undue effort. Also, common general knowledge includes basic handbooks and textbooks on the subject and references therein, though not documents which can only be obtained after a comprehensive search, such as patents, abstracts or even review articles. (**T206/83** r.4, 5, 11 Herbicide; see also **Art.56:3.6** for common general knowledge)

4.4 EXCLUDED SUBJECT-MATTER

The disclosure contained in a document includes explicitly disclaimed subject-matter with the exception of disclaimers for unworkable embodiments (G-IV,5.1(i) and G-VI,1). A prior art document disclosing a range of values of a parameter and containing a reasoned statement dissuading a skilled person from using the range under a certain value does not disclose the part of the range under that value (**T26/85** hn.II). A claimed range of a selection invention overlapping the range disclosed in the prior art will not be novel if the skilled person would seriously contemplate applying the teachings of the document in the range of overlap (**T26/85** hn.I).

4.5 ERRONEOUS DISCLOSURE

Where the literal disclosure of a document is erroneous and does not represent the intended technical result, such an erroneous disclosure should not be considered as part of the state of the art (**T77/87** hn1). Similarly, published matter may be excluded from the state of the art if it is so implausible in the eyes of the skilled reader that he would reject it as erroneous (**T412/91** r.4.6).

An abstract, e.g. of a Japanese patent application or in a chemical journal, intended to reflect the contents of the original document, should be interpreted in the light of that original document if the latter is available. If the abstract diverges from the content of the original document, its contents should not be considered as part of the state of the art (**T77/87** hn II; **T1080/99** r.4).

A wrong number in a disclosure does not affect the validity of the disclosure if the skilled person could have easily corrected it with his general knowledge without extensive research (**T171/84**).

Art. 54(3) Additionally, the content of European patent applications as filed, the dates of filing of which are prior to the date referred to in paragraph 2 and which were published on or after that date, shall be considered as comprised in the state of the art.

1 **Prior rights**

In most patent systems, including the European one, a patent application is kept secret during the period between filing and publication. Therefore the contents of an application before publication do not belong to the state of the art by virtue of being 'made available to the public'. This raises the potential for a conflict with a later application for the same or a similar invention. In the case of such conflict, the earlier application is often referred to as a prior right. Double patenting - i.e. allowing two successive patents for the same invention - is avoided by taking the earlier application into account when assessing the patentability of the later application. How this is done depends on the patent system. There are two common approaches: the 'prior claim' approach and the 'whole contents' approach. In the 'prior claim' approach only the claims of the prior right are taken into account. The claims of the later application may not overlap the granted claims of the earlier application. In the 'whole contents' approach the whole contents of the earlier application, i.e. not only the subject-matter as claimed, is regarded as state of the art for the later application. Switzerland and Liechtenstein used the 'prior claim' approach for national applications until 2008 and made it a basis for conversion of a European application to a national application under **Art.135**.

The EPC has chosen the whole contents approach, whereby the entire disclosure of the prior right becomes part of the state of the art from the date of filing or, where applicable, the priority date of the prior right (**Art.54(3)** and **Art.89**). The otherwise harsh effect of the whole contents approach is mitigated by confining its application to novelty and disregarding prior rights in relation to inventive step (**Art.56**, last sentence).

It follows that for the purposes of novelty an applicant's own earlier application may form relevant prior art for his later application. This is sometimes known as 'self collision'. However the risk of this is reduced by the EPO's strict approach to novelty. When considering novelty, the teaching of a document is not interpreted to embrace well-known equivalents not disclosed in the document; such equivalents are relevant only to obviousness (**T167/84** r.6 and G-VI,2).

The content of the prior right includes neither a priority document (G-IV,5.1) nor the abstract (**Art.85** and G-IV,5.1). It is the content of the earlier application as filed which is relevant in case of **Art.54(3)**; errors in a subsequent translation of the earlier application have no effect (G-IV,5.1). If an application specifically refers to a document, the relevant part of the document referred to is to be considered as forming part of the content of the application for the purpose of citing the application under **Art.54(3)** (F-III,8).

The content of a prior right filed in a language admitted under **Art.14(2)** is that of the application in this language. If subject-matter is erroneously omitted from the translation in the language of proceedings and not published under **Art.93**, the content for the purpose of **Art.54(3)** is still determined by the original application in the non-official language. (G-IV,5.1)

If an applicant files two applications on the same day with nearly the same contents, he must withdraw one of them or amend the scope of the claims to make them distinct. Two patents may not be granted to one applicant for one invention. In the rare case that two applications from different applicants have the same priority date for the same invention, each application must be allowed to proceed as though the other did not exist. (see **Art.60(2)**; G-IV,5.4)

National prior rights do not form part of the state of the art within the meaning of **Art.54(3)** (**T550/88** hn1). However, they may be taken into account during grant and opposition proceedings before the EPO following **R.138** and during national revocation proceedings following **Art.138(1)** and **139**.

The prior right effect in an extension state to which a European application has been extended is dealt with in **Art.139:1**.

2 **Requirements for prior rights**

Art.54(3) recognizes only European applications as prior rights. National applications are excluded for the simple reason that they are not timely available at the EPO for searching.

The date of filing of the application must be before the date of filing of the application under examination. Where the earlier application claims priority, the filing date is replaced by the priority date (**Art.89**) for that subject-matter contained in the priority application. If the priority claim is abandoned or lost before publication of the earlier application, the date of filing will again be relevant. The priority date will also count as date of filing for the application under examination where it claims priority (**Art.89**).

The earlier application must be published on or after the filing date of the application under examination (**Art.54(3)**). It must still be pending on the publication date (**J5/81**). Changes taking effect before the publication date could affect the prior right effect. If the published application is not a valid publication under **Art.93** due to withdrawal of the application after completion of the technical preparations for publishing (**R.48** EPC 1973) but before the publication date, there will be no prior right, and the application will be a normal publication under **Art.54(2)** (**J5/81**). An abandonment or loss of priority taking effect before the publication date results in the filing date and not the priority date of the earlier application being relevant. (G-IV,5.1.1)

The prior right effect of an application is not affected by changes taking effect after the publication date of the application, e.g. withdrawal of a designation, non-payment of the designation fee, withdrawal of the priority claim or loss of the priority right for other reasons. (G-IV,5.1.1)

As an example, if the translation of the priority document or the declaration as required under **R.53(3)** is not filed in due time, the right to priority is lost. However, for reasons of legal certainty, the right of priority remains effective for determining the state of the art for the purposes of **Art.54(3)** in respect of any other European patent application (F-VI,3.4). The same applies if a copy of the priority document as required under **R.53(1)** is not provided in due time and the priority right is lost under **Art.90(5)** after publication of the application. This provision of the Guidelines appears to be in conflict with **Art.60(2)**.

A PCT prior right designating the EPO belongs to the state of the art only if the national fee has been paid and, if the international application is not published in an official EPO language, an English, French or German translation has been filed (**Art.153(5)**).

3 Establishment of prior right

Under the EPC 1973, a European patent application can be a valid prior right only for contracting states commonly designated in both the earlier application and the application under examination (**Art.54(4)** EPC 1973). A valid designation of a contracting state requires payment of a designation fee for each state (for applications filed before 01.04.2009). Originally, designation fees were due well before the publication of the application; the publication of the application showed the validly designated contracting states, so that prior rights could be identified for each contracting state by the time of publication.

The fee reform of 1997 allowed payment of the designation fees within 6 months of the mention of the publication of the search report. After the fee reform, the publication, now mentioning all contracting states, could no longer be used for establishing the contracting states where the prior right was valid and only the Register showed the validly designated contracting states.

The postponement of the time for establishing the **Art.54(3)** prior art till 6 months of the mention of publication of the search report caused legal uncertainty and logistic problems, as an application may be ready for grant before it is possible to ascertain the relevant prior rights. The ceiling in the number of designation fees to be paid, introduced in 1999, made most applicants designate all contracting states, thereby significantly reducing the number of cases in which an applicant could benefit from not commonly designated states. The legislator has changed the prior right system in the EPC 2000 in view of the diminished advantage of **Art.54(4)** EPC 1973 for applicants and the desire to reduce the legal uncertainty.

Under the EPC 2000 valid designations are no longer relevant for a prior right: the prior right has effect for all contracting states. As a consequence, **R.87** EPC 1973 has been amended and no longer covers European rights with non-overlapping designations but only national prior rights (**R.138** EPC 2000).

The following sections show the different systems under the EPC 1973 and the EPC 2000.

3.1 PRIOR RIGHTS UNDER ART.54(3) AND (4) EPC 1973

Under the EPC 1973 a prior right is valid prior art only for those contracting states commonly designated in the prior right as published and in the application under examination (**Art.54(4)** EPC 1973).

The prior right is established only if the prior application is properly published under **Art.93** EPC 1973 (see **Art.54(3)** EPC 1973) *and* the designation fees have duly been paid (see also **R.23a** EPC 1973 for the period after the fee reform). The Register has a record of payment of the designation fees (**R.143(1)(e)**). The publication of an application is not a good source for determining the valid designations. When filed before 1996, the publication shows the contracting states for which designation fees have been paid; when filed after 1997 the publication shows all contracting states, irrespective of payment of the designation fees; see **Art.79(2):3** for the transitional period.

When, during prosecution, an applicant is confronted with a European or national prior right, he can drop the designations of his own application in common with the prior right, or he may file different claims, description and drawings for the overlapping and non-overlapping states. Only the examining division decides on the need for different description and drawings (**R.87** EPC 1973, see also **R.138:1**).

3.2 PRIOR RIGHTS UNDER ART.54(3) EPC 2000

Under the EPC 2000 the prior right effect has effect for all contracting states and is independent of payment of a designation fee or withdrawal of designations. The prior right effect is restricted to the contracting states for which the EPC was in force at the date of filing of the application under examination. The contracting states for which the EPC was in force at the date of filing of the prior art application are irrelevant for the extent of the prior right effect.

4 Transitional provisions EPC 2000

The revised **Art.54(3)** applies to European patent applications filed on or after the time of EPC 2000 entry into force (OJ 2007 se4). The revision makes no practical difference since the amendments to the provision in EPC 2000 were made for clarity and were not intended to alter its effect.

The deleted **Art.54(4)** EPC 1973 is still applicable to European patents already granted at the time of EPC 2000 entry into force and to European patent applications pending at the time of EPC 2000 entry into force (OJ 2007 se4). Since the transitional provision determines the extent of the prior art for the term of the patent filed under the EPC 1973, **Art.54(4)** EPC 1973 and **R.87** EPC 1973 will have effect up to twenty years from entry into force of the EPC 2000, i.e. up to December 2027. Whether deleted **Art.54(4)** EPC 1973 is still applicable depends solely on the date of filing of the application or granted patent under examination; the priority date of the application or granted patent under examination is not relevant (Trans. Pract. §10.1). The details of the transitional provision are provided below for three different types of applications.

4.1 EUROPEAN APPLICATIONS

The date of filing of the application or granted patent under examination determines whether deleted **Art.54(4)** EPC 1973 still applies. The priority date of the application or granted patent under examination is not relevant. (Trans. Pract. §10.1)

For applications under examination pending at the time of entry into force, i.e. 13.12.2007, and for patents under examination granted before that time, **Art.54(4)** EPC 1973 in conjunction with **R.23a** EPC 1973 still applies. The prior art for such applications and patents includes European prior rights only for the commonly designated states for which the designation fees have been paid for the application or patent under examination and the conflicting application.

Art.54(4) EPC 1973 is no longer applicable for applications under examination filed on or after EPC 2000 entry into force and patents granted thereon. The prior art for such applications includes European prior rights for all designated states where the EPC was in force on the date of filing of the application under examination.

For example, a European application filed on 30.03.2008 designating only the Netherlands and claiming priority from an application having a filing date of 31.03.2007 is a prior right with effect for the Netherlands only for an application under examination filed on 12.12.2007 and claiming a priority from 21.06.2007. However, the same prior right is effective for all contracting states for an application under examination filed on 13.12.2007 and claiming priority from 21.06.2007.

4.2 DIVISIONAL APPLICATIONS

According to the EPO, the relevant date whether or not to apply **Art.54**(4) and **R.23a** EPC 1973 is the date of receipt of the divisional application at the EPO and not the date of filing of the parent application attributed to the divisional application. This means that a parent and divisional application may have different prior art. (Trans. Pract. §10.1)

For example, a parent application has 22.11.2006 as date of filing and two claims directed to non-unitary subject-matter A and B. Prior art is a European patent application having 20.06.2006 as filing date and 26.12.2007 as publication date, validly designating Germany and Luxembourg and disclosing only subject-matter B. The parent can claim A for all contracting states or B for all contracting states other than Germany and Luxembourg. A divisional filed on 12.12.2007 can claim B for all states other than Germany and Luxembourg or A for all contracting states. However, a divisional filed on 13.12.2007 can only claim A for all contracting states, because the prior right is effective against B for all contracting states.

The fact that the applicant does not have the right to the patent based on the divisional application for subject-matter B in the contracting states other than Germany and Luxembourg appears to be a violation of **Art.60(2)**.

It should be noted that according to **Art.76**(1) 'the divisional application shall be deemed to have been filed on the date of filing of the earlier application'. Hence, the application documents of the divisional application are deemed to have been received on the date of filing of the parent application. This might form a basis for applying **Art.54**(4) EPC 1973 also for the later-filed divisional application of the example.

4.3 EURO-PCT APPLICATIONS

The relevant date of a Euro-PCT application for the application of the EPC 2000 is the international filing date, not the date of entry into the European phase. Hence, **Art.54**(4) and **R.23a** EPC 1973 do not apply to a Euro-PCT application under examination when its international filing date is on or after 13.12.2007.

A Euro-PCT application can only be regarded as a European prior right if the conditions of **R.165** are met: the filing fee must have been paid and the international application or its translation must have been published.

Art. 54(4) Paragraphs 2 and 3 shall not exclude the patentability of any substance or composition, comprised in the state of the art, for use in a method referred to in Article 53(c), provided that its use for any such method is not comprised in the state of the art.

Art.53(c) Methods of treatment of the human or animal body by surgery or therapy and diagnostic methods

1 **Transitional provision EPC 2000**

The revised **Art.54(4)** is applicable to European patents already granted at the time of EPC 2000 entry into force and to European patent applications pending at, or filed on or after that time. (OJ 2007 se4)

2 **First medical use**

The invention of a new use of a known product can be protected in the form of a use claim: 'a new use of a known product'; a product claim in the form: 'a known product for a new use' is in general not novel under **Art.54(1)**, because a use feature usually cannot impart novelty to a known product (see e.g. F-IV,4.13). When the invention is a new use of a substance or composition X in a specific treatment by surgery or therapy or in an in vivo diagnostic method, protection cannot be obtained in the form of a use claim, because a claim in the form 'use of substance X in a specific medical method' will be a medical method, which is excluded from patentability under **Art.53(c)**, first sentence.

By way of compensation for the exclusion, **Art.54(4)** deems known substances or compositions to be new, provided they are used for the first time in such a medical method (OJ 2007 se4). The notional novelty and following it the non-obviousness, if any, is not derived from the substance or composition as such but from the claimed purpose, namely from its intended use (**G2/08b** r.5.10.9).

The EPO, following the case law of the boards of appeal, allows a broad claim for the first medical use, even if only one specific purpose is disclosed in the application (see **T128/82; T36/83**). Based on this practice, the inventor of a first use of a substance or composition in a medical method should receive broad protection covering any use in a medical method. This corresponds to the contribution to the art, namely opening the field of medical use for the substance or composition. (OJ 2007 se4)

A claim to a known substance or composition for the first use in a medical method provides such a broad protection if drafted in a form such as: 'Substance or composition X' followed by the indication of the use, e.g. 'for use as a medicament' or 'for use in therapy / in vivo diagnostics / surgery' (G-II,4.2). The use feature is regarded as a technical feature that, by way of exception for this type of claim, makes the claim novel (**T9/81** r.7).

This broad purpose-limited product protection for the first medical use by a generic claim is confirmed by the Enlarged Board of Appeal in **G5/83** r.15 and **G2/08b** r.5.8. The claim may have the form: 'a substance X for use in therapy (as a medicine)', even though the disclosed range of medical applications is very limited. See **Art.54(5):3** for an example of a set of claims protecting the medical use of a substance.

The novelty of a first medical use claim is not only destroyed by a previous disclosure of the same specific therapeutic effect, but also by a previous disclosure of any other specific therapeutic application (**T128/82** r.13).

Art.54(4) and (5) distinguish two different products: 'substance' and 'composition'. A substance is a species of matter of a definite chemical composition. A composition is a condition consisting in the combination or union of several things; a combination, aggregate, mixture. A composition thus covers two substances presented side-by-side (**T9/81** r.9). Note, that a compound is a substance composed chemically of two or more elements in definite proportions (as opposed to a mixture). (definitions from the Oxford English Dictionary)

Art. 54(5) Paragraphs 2 and 3 shall also not exclude the patentability of any substance or composition referred to in paragraph 4 for any specific use in a method referred to in Article 53(c), provided that such use is not comprised in the state of the art.

Art.53(c) Methods of treatment of the human or animal body by surgery or therapy and diagnostic methods

1 **Transitional provision EPC 2000**

The revised **Art.54(5)** is applicable to European patent applications pending at the time of EPC 2000 entry into force, in so far as a decision on the grant of the patent has not yet been taken and to European patent applications filed on or after the time of EPC 2000 entry into force. (OJ 2007 se4)

The relevant date for the decision to grant is the date of handing over the decision to the EPO postal service (Trans. Pract. §10.2). As a consequence, in opposition proceedings after 13.12.2007 relating to a patent granted before 13.12.2007, a Swiss-type claim may not be changed to a further medical use product claim.

A Swiss-type claim may not be used anymore in applications having a filing date or, if priority has been claimed, a priority date of 29.01.2011 or later (**G2/08b** r.7.1.4 and Not. EPO OJ 2010, 514).

2 **Second medical use**

A second medical use is a new medical use of a substance or composition where a first medical use is already known. Whereas **Art.54(4)** provides notional novelty of a known substance or composition for a first medical use, it does not provide novelty of a known substance or composition for a further medical use when a first medical use is already known, because **Art.54(4)** requires that 'its use for any such method is not comprised in the state of the art'.

Art.54(5) confers notional novelty on a known substance or composition for such a further new medical use. It permits purpose-related product protection for each further new medical use. A second medical use claim can be formulated as a substance or composition for a specific new medical use. (**G2/08b** r.5.9-10)

The form of a second medical use claim should be 'Substance or composition X' followed by the specific therapeutical / in vivo diagnostic / surgical use, e.g. 'for use in treating disease Y' (G-II,4.2).

2.1 SPECIFIC USE

Since **Art.54(5)** does not define the nature of 'any specific use', the Enlarged Board of Appeal has given the following interpretation, interpreting the law in its context and using the legislative history and the development of the case law of the boards of appeal. 'Any specific use' may be a new indication in the sense of a disease not yet treated by the claimed substance or composition or a new treatment of a particular disease where the use of the substance or composition for treatment of that disease is known. 'Any specific use' may also be one or more steps pertaining by their nature to a therapeutic method which may not be claimed as such. (**G2/08b** r.5.10)

The Board approved the following examples of specific uses of known substances and compositions directed to a new treatment of the same illness (**G2/08b** r.5.10.7):

- treatment of a novel group of subjects; **T19/86**: treatment of sero-positive pigs where treatment of sero-negative pigs is known; **T893/90**: controlling bleeding in non-haemophilic mammals whereas controlling haemophilic bleeding in haemophilic mammals is known; **T233/96** r.8.7: treatment of a novel group of subjects not overlapping with a group previously treated, the novel group not being an arbitrary choice.
- a new route or mode of administration; **T51/93** r.3.1: subcutaneous injection where intramuscular injection is known; **T138/95**: intrapulmonary adsorption where aerosol delivery is known.
- a different technical effect and leading to a truly new application as set out in **T1020/03**; **T290/86**: use of a salt solution for removing plaque from teeth where use of the salt solution for depressing the solubility of tooth enamel in organic acids is known; **T254/93** hn.II: a mere explanation of a known technical effect does not confer novelty on a known method.

Hence, a product claim having a specific use in the form of a new dosage regimen as only novel feature is not excluded from patenting (**G2/08b** hn, r. 6.1; confirming **T1020/03**: intermittent administration where continuous administration is known; overruling **T317/95**, **T56/97**, **T584/97**, **T4/98** and **T485/99**). Note, that some contracting states do not accept dosage regimen claims in European patents, even after issue of **G2/08b**.

2.2 PATENTABILITY ISSUES

The EPO will apply the whole body of jurisprudence relating to the assessment of novelty and inventive step to avoid any undue prolongation of patent rights using second medical use claims. The claimed second medical use must reflect a different technical teaching from the known medical uses. For example a claimed dosage regime within a broader prior art teaching must fulfill the requirements for selection inventions to avoid arbitrary selections. (**G2/08b** r.6.3)

The following decisions clarify when a technical effect of a claimed therapeutic application not previously described can be recognised as conferring novelty on said application: **T290/86**; **T1020/03**; **T836/01**; **T1074/06**. Any new technical effect of the distinguishing feature of a second medical use claim must be considered when examining inventive step under **Art.56**. (**G2/08b** r.6.3)

Infringement of a second medical use claim can usually be proven by the use and dosage stated in the product information leaflet manufacturers have to provide for prescription medicines.

2.3 SWISS-TYPE CLAIM AND PURPOSE-RELATED PRODUCT CLAIM

The above purpose-related product protection for a second medical use was not available before the entry into force of the EPC 2000. The EPC 1973 only had a provision for the patentability of a first medical use in the form of a purpose-related product claim (**Art.54(5)** EPC 1973). A product claim for a second medical use was not patentable. The Enlarged Board of Appeal allowed protection in the form of a claim directed to the manufacture of an known substance for a new medical use, thereby avoiding the lack of novelty of the substance and the prohibition of claiming a method of treatment. The basis of the decision was that exceptions to **Art.53(c)** should be interpreted narrowly (**G5/83** r.22).

The manufacture of the medicament derives its novelty from the new therapeutic use. Hence, the claim should preferably be directed to the 'use of a substance or composition for the manufacture of a medicament for a specified new and inventive therapeutic application' (**G5/83**, 'Second medical indication/EISAI'; **G1/83** and **G6/83** deal with the same issues but with different parties; see also OJ 1984, 581). This form of claim is called a Swiss-type claim, because of its Swiss origin.

Decision **G5/83** was not followed by the courts of all contracting states. To eliminate any legal uncertainty on the patentability of further medical uses, the EPC 2000 introduced new **Art.54(5)**, binding on all contracting states, which allows a purpose-related product claim for each further new medical use of a substance or composition already known as a medicine. (OJ 2007 se4)

Since the introduction of the EPC 2000 removed the cause of the Swiss-type claim approach, the use of this type of claim should cease. Hence, a claim deriving its novelty only from a new therapeutic use of a medicament may no longer have the format of a Swiss-type claim. (**G2/08b** r.7, overruling **T406/06** r.2-6)

The prohibition on Swiss-type claims applies to applications having a filing date or, if priority has been claimed, earliest priority date of 29.01.2011 or later. The relevant date for a divisional application is the filing or priority date of the parent application. Pending applications are not affected by the ruling. (**G2/08b** r.7 and Not. EPO OJ 2010, 514)

It should be noted that the Swiss-type claim provides protection only for the direct product of the manufacturing method claimed (**Art.64(2)**). In contrast, a product claim under the new **Art.54(5)** provides full product protection. Hence, the amendment of the EPC 2000 likely broadens the scope for infringement. A possible restriction of the freedom of medical practitioners should be addressed at a national level. (**G2/08b** r.6.5; contrary to OJ 2007 se4, Art.54 §4; see also **Art.53:3.4.1** for the restrictions imposed by TRIPs on national law; **T1780/12**)

As a consequence, an amendment during opposition of a Swiss-type claim to a product claim is likely to raise an objection under **Art.123(3)** as extending the scope of protection.

3 Medical use claims and unity

The following independent claims are possible for a novel substance X having a therapeutic application for diseases Y and Z:

1 Substance X;
2 Substance X for use as a medicament;
3 Substance X for use in treatment of Y;
4 Substance X for use in treatment of Z.

An application disclosing for the first time several medical uses for a known substance may have independent claims for the uses. As a general rule, no a priori objection will be raised against lack of unity. (G-VI,7.1)

If substance X per se turns out to be known, claim 2 in the form of a first medical indication forms the broadest possible fallback position.

If a therapeutic application of substance X turns out to be known, claims 3 and 4 in the form of a second and further medical indication may be patentable. However, the treatments of these claims must have a single general inventive concept in order to avoid a non-unity objection (G-VI,7.1).

4 **Special medical claims**
A composition may also be a kit of parts, provided the parts form a true combination through a purpose-directed, even sequential, application (**T9/81** Cytostatic combination of cytostatic and mucolytic suppressing side-effects). If the features of a claim do not form a 'true combination', but a 'mere juxtaposition of features', then the features can be attacked separately in an opposition, using different documents, which may be combined without incentive (used often in the qualifying examination, always quote the phrase in quotation marks).

Art. 55 Non-prejudicial disclosures

1 **General**
Art.55 defines two types of rare disclosure that are excluded from the prior art, although they are available to the public. They are the only non-prejudicial disclosures recognized by the EPC (G-V). The EPC does not provide for a grace period prior to filing a patent application, during which period the inventor may disclose his invention without that disclosure becoming state of the art. Arguments in favour of and against a grace period in the present discussion about its introduction in the EPC are given in OJ 1999, 155.

Art. 55(1) For the application of Article 54, a disclosure of the invention shall not be taken into consideration if it occurred no earlier than six months preceding the filing of the European patent application and if it was due to, or in consequence of:
(a) an evident abuse in relation to the applicant or his legal predecessor, or
(b) the fact that the applicant or his legal predecessor has displayed the invention at an official, or officially recognised, international exhibition falling within the terms of the Convention on international exhibitions signed at Paris on 22 November 1928 and last revised on 30 November 1972.

Art.54 Novelty

1 **Time limit and nature of disclosure**
The intention of **Art.55** is to protect an applicant against prior disclosure of his invention caused either by abuse or by display at an international exhibition. For an effective protection, any such prior disclosure must be removed from the prior art of the application, whether the disclosure is prejudicial to novelty or to inventive step or whether the disclosure is the publication of a prior right. The choice of the words 'no earlier than' instead of 'within' in **Art.55(1)** is meant to cover not only abusive publications before the date of filing of the application, but also European prior rights filed before the date of filing and published on or after the date of filing.

Neither the EPC nor the EPO clarifies whether the disclosure of **Art.55(1)** in the case of a European prior right relates to any priority date, filing date or date of publication of the prior right. Equating the date of disclosure with the date of publication of the prior right is in line with the purpose of **Art.55**, i.e. to give the applicant a limited period of time to file his own application after he has noticed the abusive publication of the invention. The interpretation is also in line with the Strasbourg Convention (see last paragraph of this section).

The relevant date for the calculation of the six-month period referred to in **Art.55(1)** is the date of the actual filing of the European patent application; the date of priority is not to be taken account of in calculating this period (**G3/98** hn). See also **R.38(1):1** on the difference between 'filing of the application' and 'date of filing'.

An abusive disclosure or a disclosure at an international exhibition will not be regarded as state of the art, if the applicant files the application with the EPO within 6 months from the disclosure and, in case of an exhibition, complies with the requirements of **Art.55(2)**. A later filing will make the disclosure prejudicial. If a national first filing is made, the subsequent priority claiming European application must be filed within 6 months from the disclosure. Alternatively, an international application designating the EPO may be filed within the 6 month period, because an international application for which the EPO acts as designated Office is deemed to be a European application (**Art.153(2)**). Note, that the 6-month period of **Art.55(1)** is not a time limit in the sense of **Art.120**. Hence, the extension of **R.134** is not applicable to the 6 months.

Note, that the term 'disclosure' in the provision is probably used in the meaning of 'publication', i.e. making available to the public in the sense of **Art.54(2)**. This interpretation of 'disclosure' is supported by Article 4(4) of the Strasbourg Convention (1963), to which **Art.55(1)** should correspond according to the Travaux Préparatoires EPC 1973. The article states '... the invention was made public, within six months preceding the filing of the application, if the disclosure was due to ...'. In contrast, the common, restricted meaning of 'disclosure' in the EPC does not relate to publication of a document but to content of a document, what a document reveals to a reader; see e.g. **Art.83** and H-IV,2.3.

2 Abusive publication (Art.55(1)(a))

The meaning of 'abusive' in the provision has been determined by **T585/92** r.6, followed in G-V,3, which holds that 'abuse' requires actual intent to harm or actual knowledge that harm would or could be expected. The decision does not regard a disclosure due to inadvertence or mistake as 'abuse'. An erroneous publication by the Brazilian patent office is inadvertent but not abusive because of lack of a personal or contractual relationship with the applicant. The decision does not give a legal basis for its arbitrary finding. **T436/92** r.5.2 follows this decision and holds that mere negligence or breach of confidentiality without intention to harm is not evident abuse.

Another decision, **T173/83** r.6, not followed by the Guidelines, holds that 'abuse' does not require the intention to harm; a disclosure due to negligence or mistake is regarded as abuse. Important is that the applicant experiences damages. The disclosure is not only non-prejudicial when the applicant told the invention himself to the discloser, but also if a third person is involved who happens to get to know the invention. This meaning of 'abuse' is more in line with the intention of the drafters of the EPC.

The legal predecessor of the applicant mentioned in **Art.55(1)** is often the inventor.

An agreement on secrecy is often tacit and derived from a relationship of good faith or trust. A parent company-subsidiary relationship, a joint venture, or delivery of test specimens may also be indicative of a tacit agreement. There is no disclosure of subject-matter to the public by use or in any other way, if there is an express or tacit agreement on secrecy which has not been broken. (G-IV,7.2.2; **T830/90** r.3.2.2)

In the case of a tacit understanding of preserving secrecy between parties, a piece of correspondence between the parties is not bound by this secrecy if nothing in the piece points to this secrecy, e.g. the piece is a brochure intended for advertising. In these circumstances the publication of the brochure by the receiving party is no evident abuse in relation to the sending party (**T173/83**).

To determine whether subject-matter was made available without an express or tacit agreement, the EPO applies the 'balance of probabilities' standard, unless practically all evidence lies within the power of the party bearing the burden of proof, in which case, the facts must be proven beyond reasonable doubt (G-IV,7.2.2; not in GL2017). However, the Board of Appeal takes the view in an old decision that the adjective 'evident' in the provision indicates that the standard of proof is a high one (**T291/97** r.13).

3 **Procedure in the case of abusive publication**

If an applicant notices an abusive publication of his invention, he has a period of six months from the date of the abusive publication to file his own patent application. If he has already filed a first application, he may file a subsequent application claiming priority from the first application within the six-month period or the twelve-month priority period, whichever expires first.

The applicant can raise the abusive character of the publication in his first substantive response to the EPO. The examining division will investigate the matter (B-VI,5.5) and if it regards the proof that the publication is abusive as sufficient, it will not take the abusive publication into consideration.

If the abusive publication relates to a patent application, the applicant can start an **Art.61** procedure against the non-entitled person that filed the application.

4 **Exhibition (Art.55(1)(b))**

The few exhibitions to which this provision applies are listed each year in OJ issue 4 under *International Treaties*. Currently, the upcoming international exhibitions are (OJ 2018 A44):

29.04.2019 to 07.10.2019	Expo 2019	Beijing, China
20.10.2020 to 10.04.2021	Expo 2020	Dubai, United Arab Emirates
28.04.2022 to 23.10.2022	Floriade 2022	Almere, The Netherlands

Art. 55(2) In the case of paragraph 1(b), paragraph 1 shall apply only if the applicant states, when filing the European patent application, that the invention has been so displayed and files a supporting certificate within the time limit and under the conditions laid down in the Implementing Regulations.

See for the implementation:
R.25 Certificate of exhibition

1 **Procedure in the case of display at an international exhibition**

An applicant who wants protection for an invention displayed at an international exhibition must file his patent application within six months from the first day of the display. The application may claim priority from an earlier filed first application, provided the European patent application is filed within said six months.

To exclude the display from the prior art under **Art.55(1)(b)** he must also file the statement of **Art.55(2)** and the certificate and identification of the invention according to **R.25**. The statement of **Art.55(2)** must be filed on the filing date (A-IV,3.1). If the statement is erroneously not filed, the only remedy available is refiling the patent application with statement.

The certificate and identification must be filed within 4 months of the filing date (**R.25**). The Receiving Section acknowledges receipt of the certificate and identification. It draws the applicant's attention to any manifest defects in the certificate and identification if rectification is still possible within the four-month period (A-IV,3.2).

If the statement has been filed on filing of the application and the EPO finds that the certificate and/or the identification has not been filed in due time, it notifies the applicant of the loss of rights (**R.112(1)** & **Art.55(1)**). If the applicant did file in time, he can, in response to this notice, prove within two months from the notice that he was in time (**R.112(2)**). Alternatively, he can request further processing under **Art.121** and **R.135** within the two month period. (A-IV,3.2)

The procedure for a Euro-PCT application is set out in **R.159(1):9**.

The examining division will investigate the identity between the claimed invention and the displayed invention as stated in the identification (B-VI,5.5).

A filing of the application after the six-month period, an omitted statement, an invalid or missing certificate or identification have the consequence that the disclosure at the exhibition is prejudicial to the application, and, hence, the application has often lost its novelty (unless one can argue that the display was non-enabling) and had better be withdrawn. The EPC does not recognise a priority claim based on the disclosure at the exhibition, but national law may do so (**T382/07** r.8.2).

Art. 56 Inventive step

An invention shall be considered as involving an inventive step if, having regard to the state of the art, it is not obvious to a person skilled in the art. If the state of the art also includes documents within the meaning of Article 54, paragraph 3, these documents shall not be considered in deciding whether there has been an inventive step.

Art.54(3) European prior rights

1 General

The four requirements of **Art.52(1)** for patentability are that the subject-matter of a claim must relate to an invention, which is industrially applicable, which is new and which involves an inventive step. An invention is new if it does not form part of the state of the art (**Art.54(1)**), i.e. if there is a difference between the invention and the state of the art. The extent of this difference determines whether there is an inventive step. The question of inventive step arises only if there is novelty (G-VII,1).

Whereas in the assessment of novelty the items of prior art are evaluated individually, inventive step requires evaluation of a combination of prior art items, often referred to as a 'mosaic' of prior art, to assess whether combining the prior art items is an obvious development of the state of the art a skilled person would deduce from the prior art. An inventive step is present if the invention lies beyond the contemplation or capability of the skilled person.

Art.56 defines in general terms what constitutes an inventive step by reference to the difference between the invention and the prior art. The few words of the article itself do not give much guidance. This is intentional, leaving its interpretation, and therewith the standard of inventive step required, largely a matter of EPO policy. The words indicate however, that the EPC contracting states have nonetheless chosen a relatively strict requirement so that applicants may not avoid national requirements for inventive step by obtaining a 'soft' European patent which would have effect in the territory of the state concerned. (Empel §92)

According to **Art.56**, an inventive step is present only if the invention is not obvious to a person skilled in the art having regard to the state of the art. The term 'obvious', which is usually a subjective notion involving a matter of degree, has been made objective and more predictable by the EPO's Guidelines and case law. Crucial to this are the characteristics of the skilled person.

In addition, the EPO has developed a well-defined procedure, the so-called problem-solution approach, for assessing the invention and following which, using the perspective of the skilled person, the question whether an inventive step is present is answered.

The guidance provides the objective criteria for the consideration of inventive step in accordance with the strict standard referred to above.

The following sections deal with the definition of the person skilled in the art, the state of the art, the moment in time at which inventive step is assessed, the use of these definitions in the assessment of inventive step and some special types of invention.

2 Person skilled in the art

The knowledge and abilities of the hypothetical person skilled in the art, also called the 'skilled person', are critical to the standard of obviousness: if a combination of prior art items leading to the invention is regarded by the skilled person as an obvious development of the prior art, there is no inventive step. Therefore, it is essential for the assessment of inventive step to characterise accurately the skilled person to know which developments he regards obvious. Relevant issues are his knowledge, capabilities and impediments, and to determine what he would have done in the relevant circumstances; all other matters tend to be of subordinate importance.

The skilled person neither has the level of knowledge of the average member of the public at large (Empel §95), nor that of an advanced senior scientist (**T500/91** r.2.2). The skilled person resembles an ordinary practitioner possessing the common general knowledge in his specific technical field at the relevant date. He has access to all items of prior art and has the normal means and capacity for routine work and experimentation (G-VII,3). He is oriented towards practicalities (**T5/81**), but the development of the art normally expected by him does not include solving technical problems by performing scientific research in areas not yet explored (**T500/91** r.2.2). He is constantly occupied with the elimination of deficiencies, with the overcoming of drawbacks and with the improvement of known devices and/or products (**T15/81** r.3; **T195/84** r.8.1). The skilled person is a captive of established prejudices in his field (**T455/91** r.5.1.3.3).

The skilled person has no ability for creative thinking (**T455/91** r.5.1.3.8) and has no inventive imagination (**T223/92** r.5.5). Since the decisions do not define what creative thinking and inventive imagination is, these characteristics are of limited value in the assessment of inventive step. **T39/93** r.7.8.4 states that all definitions of the skilled person have in common that he has no inventive capability. Application of this characteristic in the assessment under **Art.56** is neither useful, as it will probably result in a circle reasoning.

The terms and objects of the EPC require that essentially the same professional competence must be attributed to the skilled person and an EPO examiner. Since an examiner is technically qualified according to **Art.18** and is neither professionally competent to evaluate non-technological art nor to assess ideas in a non-technological field, the person skilled in the art must be competent in a technical field but not competent in non-technological fields, such as business, actuary or accountancy. Hence, the skilled person assessing a management system for order placement was regarded to be a software project team, not including any business expert, but having knowledge of business-related features of the order management method in the form of a requirements specification. (**T172/03** r.6, 16)

See Case Law of the BoA, I.D.8.1.3 for a definition of a skilled person in the field of biotechnology.

Nationality makes no difference. For instance there is no difference between a European and an American skilled person; knowledge is accessible everywhere (**T124/85**).

For the purpose of **Art.56** and **83** the same level of skill is required from the person skilled in the art. However, for the assessment of inventive step he has knowledge of the prior art only; for evaluating sufficiency he has knowledge of the prior art and of the invention as disclosed (**T694/92** r.7). Hence, the knowledge of the skilled person is different for the purpose of **Art.56** and **83**. Where the prior art and the disclosed invention cover different technical fields, evaluation of sufficiency requires a team of skilled persons from these different technical fields (G-VII,3).

The characteristics of the skilled person in terms of knowledge, abilities and impediments will be set out in the following three sections.

3 Knowledge of skilled person

3.1 PRIOR ART

The skilled person has access to the state of the art in full. The state of the art is mentioned in **Art.56**, stating that an invention involves an inventive step if it is not obvious 'having regard to the state of the art'. The state of the art is also called 'prior art'. Although **Art.56** does not refer to **Art.54** for a definition of the state of the art, self-evidently novelty and inventive step must be assessed in view of the same state of the art (Empel §96; **T107/82** r.11). Thus the state of the art for the purpose of **Art.56** is as set out in **Art.54(2)** and notes thereto.

However there is an important difference from novelty. The second sentence of **Art.56** excludes documents within the meaning of **Art.54(3)** from the prior art to be considered in relation to inventive step. Such documents, also called European prior rights, are European patent applications filed before the date of filing of the application in issue and published on or after that date. Prior rights are only used in the assessment of novelty, in relation to which the entire subject-matter of a European prior right is fictitiously regarded as prior art. The exclusion of prior rights from the assessment of inventive step mitigates the otherwise harsh effect of the whole contents approach (see **Art.54(3):1**). National prior rights (i.e. earlier filed and later published national patent applications) are not prior art and therefore not used in the assessment of inventive step.

Since the term 'state of the art' should be understood as 'state of technology', only information relevant to some field of technology is included. Not included is information on e.g. commerce and business methods. (**T172/03** hn1; G-VII,2)

The prior art must be evaluated for the purpose of inventive step at the end of the day before the date of filing or, where appropriate, the date of priority of the invention (G-VII,4; **T24/81** hn2). This is not stated in **Art.56**, apparently because the legislator considered it self-evident (Empel §97). It follows that a prior art document should be construed in the light of knowledge that has become available to the skilled person since publication and up to the relevant date (G-VII,4). Note that this is different from the position in relation to novelty, where the prior art must be evaluated on the date the document became available to the public precisely to avoid such further development of its subject-matter in the mind of the skilled person (G-VI,3).

The technical disclosure in a prior art document should be considered in its entirety. It is not justified to isolate arbitrarily parts of such a document from their context in order to derive therefrom technical information which would be distinct from, or even in contradiction with, the integral teaching of the document (**T56/87** hn). Knowledge known to the applicant only is not prior art (**T181/95**).

3.2 TECHNICAL FIELD

The person skilled in the art is knowledgeable about the technical field of the invention. The reference to 'art' in **Art.56** should not be construed as to refer to technology in general but to the specific field of technology with which the invention is concerned. The skilled person will not consult prior art in remote technical fields (**T11/81**; see below).

The specific technical field of the skilled person is defined by the technical problem to be solved (**T422/93** hn.1). If the problem prompts the skilled person to seek the solution in another technical field, that field is the specific technical field of the skilled person (**T26/98**). For example, if the problem is wear of a metal scraper on a conveyor belt, the skilled person for the invention is the man skilled in materials, not in conveyor belts (**T32/81** Conveyor belt; r.4.2).

Where the technical fields of the problem and solution are different, the skilled person is the expert in the field of the problem, not the solution (**T422/93** hn.2, established case law). The problem should be formulated not to contain pointers to the solution to avoid an ex post facto view of inventive step (**T422/93** r.3.6.1; **T164/98** r.2.4.2).

In some cases a team of skilled persons from different specific technical fields is required, in particular where different parts of the problem relate to different technical fields (**T141/87** r.3.7; **T986/96** r.3.1.1). For example, a person skilled in electronics may consult a computer programmer if confronted with a program listing (**T164/92** hn.II).

When his own knowledge is insufficient to solve the problem, the skilled person may search the patent literature in his own, neighbouring and broader general technical fields (**T176/84**; **T195/84**).

3.3 NEIGHBOURING TECHNICAL FIELD

The skilled person will take into account the prior art in a neighbouring field where the same or similar problems occur, of which the skilled person can be expected to be aware (**T176/84** hn), i.e. the skilled person has an incentive to search in that field, e.g. because similar problems play a role. Neighbouring fields in this sense must have sufficient technical affinity so that methods and products from one field will be regarded as being of obvious application in the other. If the connection from one field to another can only be made via a broader general field, the two fields are not neighbouring fields (**T176/84** r.5.3.2).

Examples of neighbouring fields:

- gas chromatography and absorption spectral analysis (**T454/87**),

- moulding technology in dentistry and prosthodontics (**T358/90**),
- fuse links for programmable ROMs and ultra-miniaturised integrated switches (**T1037/92**),
- pharmaceutics and cosmetics (**T838/95**).

3.4 BROADER GENERAL TECHNICAL FIELD

Likewise the skilled person will look in a non-specific, broader general technical field if the same or similar problems occur in that field and he can be expected to be aware of them (**T195/84** hn). The IPC class in which a document is classified is less relevant to the status of broader general technical field than the presence of the same or similar problems (**T195/94** r.8.4). For example, a skilled person in the field of ophthalmic lenses who is confronted with the technical problems of adhesion and abrasion resistance of a coating on the surface of the lens, will also refer to the state of the art in the more general field of coated plastic sheets, in which the same problems of adhesion and abrasion resistance of the coating arise and of which he is aware (**T891/91** r.4.1.4). Similarly, the skilled person faced with a problem of wrapping hay bales would consult the broader general field of packaging methods of large diameter objects (**T189/92** r.6.1.4).

3.5 REMOTE TECHNICAL FIELD

The skilled person will not search remote fields because he would not expect to find a solution in such fields due to the different products and methods used (**T11/81** r.3).

Examples of remote fields:

- wigs and carpets (**T767/89**),
- closure for means of transporting money and bulk goods packaging, because of the different security risk (**T675/92**),
- door for computer cabinet and door of aeroplane hangar (**T9/82**),
- pencil sharpener with automatically closing container and saving box having comparable automatic closing (**T176/84** r.5.3).

If an application in suit refers to a remote technical field, the reference does not make that field a neighbouring field the skilled person would search; hence, that field should not be considered during examination of the application (**T28/87** r.5.4).

Nevertheless, a skilled person will look for a solution in a remote technical field if prompted to do so, for example by a statement in a prior art patent application about a relationship between materials used in the field of the application and in a remote field (**T560/89** hn, r.5.2; G-VII,3).

It could be argued that the skilled person is aware of the field of 'everyday items' and therefore might use knowledge in this field as prior art, even if this field is a remote field and not a neighbouring or broader general field. For example, the skilled person trying to motorise a soap dispenser drawer in a washing machine would refer to the familiar motorised disc tray of a CD player (**T234/96**, not followed in later decisions). The relevance of such knowledge for inventive step depends very much on the circumstances of the individual case (**T1043/98**, not followed). Most boards are reticent to use everyday items as prior art (see e.g. **T397/87**, **T349/96**).

3.6 COMMON GENERAL KNOWLEDGE

The class of prior art called 'common general knowledge' has a special position in the assessment of substantive issues, which warrants separate discussion. Common general knowledge is knowledge which the skilled person has at his immediate disposal (**T206/83** r.5), either because he knows it or is aware of the place where to find it.

Common general knowledge is important for the following substantive issues. In the assessment of novelty under **Art.54(1)**, common general knowledge may be used for curing insufficiency of a prior art disclosure, e.g. to obtain starting materials for a process to make a specific chemical compound (see **Art.54(2):4.3** on sufficiency of disclosure). When assessing inventive step, the skilled person regards it as obvious to combine the teachings of a prior art document with the common general knowledge (see below). An invention is sufficiently disclosed in the sense of **Art.83**, if the disclosure of the application allows the skilled person, using his common general knowledge, to carry out the invention. Common general knowledge also determines whether or not an error in an application can be corrected under **R.139**.

Common general knowledge is the knowledge the skilled person has in his specific technical field (**T939/92** r.2.3). It is defined as the knowledge an experienced man in his field is expected to have, or at least to be aware of, to the extent that he knows he can look it up if he needs it (**T766/91** r.8.2). The skilled person does not necessarily have knowledge of the whole technology (**T206/83** r.5). Since the common general knowledge available to the skilled person is part of the prior art, its extent must be evaluated for the purpose of inventive step on the day before the date of filing or, where appropriate, the date of priority of the invention.

Common general knowledge need not be in writing and may be part of the unwritten mental furniture of the skilled person, which may require oral evidence for proof (**T939/92** r.2.3). Proof of an allegation that something is part of the common general knowledge is only required if this is challenged by another party or the EPO (see e.g. **T1877/07** r.5). This manner of proceeding is necessary as otherwise examination and opposition procedures would drown in a flood of textbook and encyclopaedia extracts concerning facts which turn out not to be in dispute, and is justified because the parties can be presumed not to be taken by surprise by anything that is common general knowledge in the particular art concerned (**T766/91** r.8.1).

Information in writing is only common general knowledge when it complies with each of the following three requirements, which are common to all cases: the skilled person must be able to 1. select the right reference book, 2. identify the appropriate section of the book without undue effort and 3. derive the correct information from that section without further investigation (**T890/02** r.3, giving a summary of the case law):

i) Common general knowledge is normally represented by the contents of reference books (**T890/02** r.3). These include basic handbooks and textbooks on the subject (**T20/81** r.5; **T206/83** r.5; **T171/84** r.5; F-II,4.1). Subject-matter appears in such books because it is already general common knowledge; it does not become so because of the publication in a handbook or textbook (**T766/91** r.8.2). A hand- or textbook relating to a broader general field may also represent common general knowledge, even if it provides specific applications in certain technical fields only (**T426/88** hn.I). The language of the book is irrelevant for its status as general reference book (**T426/88**).

   The contents of patent documents normally do not belong to the common general knowledge (**T171/84** r.5). The same applies to scientific papers (**T893/98** r.2.5). On the other hand, when a field of research is so new that the technical knowledge is not yet available in textbooks, a skilled person may derive his knowledge from sources such as patents and scientific papers. In these special circumstances patents (**T51/87** r.9) and scientific papers (**T772/89** r.3.3) may be regarded as representing common general knowledge. A scientific study is, exceptionally, also regarded as common general knowledge when the most recent and best information required for the skilled person to carry out his work is not immediately available from textbooks (**T676/94** r.10(iii)).

ii) A skilled person must be able to identify the appropriate section(s) of the reference book without this requiring any significant effort. A search of the literature covering nearly the whole state of the art is regarded as an undue effort (**T171/84** r.12). Therefore, searching a database such as Chemical Abstracts or Biological Abstracts, covering virtually the complete state of the art and in total representing much more than the skilled person's common general knowledge, is an unacceptable burden (**T206/83** r.6; **T890/02** r.12). In contrast, some nucleotide sequence databases, set up as a handbook or encyclopaedia, are regarded as common general knowledge because they do not require sophisticated search strategies as with the Abstracts, but allow the extraction of unambiguous and straightforward information about an enzyme without undue effort simply by providing its name (**T890/02** r.8, 9).

iii) The relevant section(s) of the reference book must provide the correct information or unambiguous data that can be used without further research work (**T890/02** r.3(c)). It may also refer the skilled person to articles describing specifically what to do or at least giving a generally applicable and unambiguous method for the relevant purpose (**T206/83** r.5).

3.7 ERRORS IN PRIOR ART DOCUMENTS

Prior art documents may contain errors which the skilled person may be able to interpret or ignore. When assessing the relevance to patentability of a document with a potential error, if the skilled person:

a) can immediately see that the document contains an error and immediately identify what the only possible correction should be, then the document is considered to contain the correction (**T591/90**);

b) can immediately see that the document contains an error but is able to identify more than one possible correction, then the part of the document containing the error is not taken into account (**T422/07** r.5.2.2);

c) cannot immediately recognise that an error has occurred in the document, then the literal disclosure is taken into account as is. (G-IV,9; not in GL2017)

4 Abilities of the skilled person

The skilled person has the ability to search the prior art and, using the results of the search and the common general knowledge, develop the prior art. This ability of the skilled person is used to assess whether an invention involves an inventive step as required for patentability and governed by **Art.56**. The invention as defined by the set of features in a claim of a patent or patent application is a solution of a technical problem of the prior art (see **Art.52(1):1**).

The starting point of the assessment is a prior art embodiment, e.g. a known device, product or method. The technical problem facing the skilled person is to provide a certain technical effect over the prior art embodiment (G-VII,5.2, third paragraph). The technical effect is achieved by combining the teachings of several prior art items and possibly routine experiments, which together disclose the features of the invention, i.e. the features of the claim. The combined teachings and any routine experiments is called the solution of the problem. The solution of the problem is a result of the prior art search.

It must now be assessed whether a development of the prior art embodiment according to the solution is obvious for a skilled person who tries to solve the problem: would he use said teachings and any routine experiments to solve the problem? If the solution is obvious for him, the invention does not include an inventive step, if the solution is not obvious, the invention does include an inventive step.

The skilled person is limited in this development by his knowledge, abilities and impediments.

The technical effects to be provided over the prior art embodiment are often new properties. Examples of such properties are an improved control of an electric motor, a reduced weight of a gear box, reduced side effects of a medical compound. The technical effect may relate to adding new functionality to a prior art item, such as finding a new medical compound for a specific disease. The technical effect may also be an alternative to a known solution of a problem (**T92/92**).

The prior art items may include the common general knowledge of his specific technical field. The skilled person will only use teachings from that part of the prior art that belongs to his technical field as set out in the above section on technical field. If a solution requires combining teachings from different technical fields, the solution will probably be not obvious for the skilled person.

The determination of the actual prior art embodiment forming the starting point of the development, often called 'the closest prior art', and the formulation of the technical problem to be solved is set out below in the section on the problem-solution approach.

A combination of a first and second prior art item will be obvious if the skilled person has a pointer that guides him from the first prior art item to the second. Such a pointer is usually linked to the problem to be solved. For example, a prior art device has as a problem that it consumes too much energy. When a second prior art document discloses features that are described as reducing energy consumption, then the reduction of energy consumption is a pointer that guides the skilled person from the first prior art document to the second. The solution in the form of the combination of the teachings of the two prior art documents is therefore obvious. Inclusion of the features in the prior art device is thus also obvious.

4.1 INDICATIONS FOR AND AGAINST COMBINATION OF PRIOR ART ITEMS

The solution may use several measures, which may involve applying the teaching of a prior art document or a teaching from common general knowledge or carrying out routine experiments. The combination of the prior art embodiment with such measures is referred to below as the combination of prior art items.

A skilled person will apply a specific measure from the prior art if he has a reasonable expectation of some improvement or advantage (**T2/83**). The 'reasonable expectation' is based on a scientific appraisal of available facts; it cannot be replaced by 'hope to succeed', which is merely the expression of a wish (**T296/93**; **T207/94**). The reasonable expectation may be based on a known pointer to combine prior art items.

Note that **T91/98** r.8 deviates from the requirement of 'reasonable expectation' in view of difficulties experienced in realising inventions in the field of genetic engineering. It decided that it is sufficient to apply a 'try and see' approach when testing the activity of a certain compound against a retrovirus.

The following two sections give examples of circumstances in which first the skilled person regards the combination as obvious and where he will combine the teachings, and secondly the skilled person regards the combination as non-obvious and where he will not combine the teachings. The examples apply equally to prior art documents and prior art made available to the public in another way, e.g. by use.

4.1.1 Examples of circumstances where the skilled person would have combined two prior art items

- The prior art item disclosing the prior art embodiment may be combined with another prior art item if this other prior art item includes a pointer in the form of a reference to the technical problem and is in the same, neighbouring or broader general technical field. The combination must have been obvious for a skilled person without knowledge of the claimed solution to that problem (**T745/92** r.1.3).

  The reference in the other prior art item to the technical problem need not be explicit but may be implicit. An example of an implicit indication is that preferred features contribute to avoid conditions known to be a cause of the problem. (**T716/07** r.4.3; G-VII,5.3)
- The combination of two prior art items is obvious if one of them contains a clear and unmistakable reference to the other (G-VII,6(iii)).
- It is obvious to combine the teachings of one or more prior art items with the common general knowledge, even without pointer (G-VII,6(iii)).
- The combination of two parts of the same prior art item, e.g. disclosing different embodiments, is obvious if there is a reasonable basis on which to associate these parts with one another (**T95/90**; G-VII,6(iii)).
- The combination of a prior art item disclosing the prior art embodiment and normal design procedures, workshop modifications and routine experiments is obvious. See the section below on Routine work and experimentation.

4.1.2 Examples of circumstances against combining prior art items

- Prior art items cannot readily be combined if there is an inherent incompatibility in disclosed features essential to the invention (G-VII,6(i)).
- A combination of prior art items is not obvious if one of them is from a remote technical field.
- The mere fact that two prior art items are from the same technical field is not a sufficient reason for combining their teachings.

4.2 ROUTINE WORK AND EXPERIMENTATION

The skilled person has at his disposal the means and the capacity for routine work and experimentation (G-VII,3). This means and capacity is similar to the common general knowledge. The extent of the means and capacity must be evaluated for the purpose of inventive step at the end of the day before the date of filing or, where appropriate, the date of priority of the invention.

The skilled person will only carry out routine work or experimentation if he has a reasonable expectation of some improvement or advantage (**T2/83**).

Routine work includes workshop modifications, such as simple extrapolation of a property to a new range, repeating a known measure to improve the result (i.e. more of the same), choosing parameter values from a limited range of possibilities by routine experimentation or by normal design procedures. An example of a routine experiment is where the yield of a chemical process can be increased with a modification which is known to increase yield, and the positive effect can easily be shown in a routine experiment

(**T199/84, T132/86**). See G-VII, Annex 3.1(ii) and (iii) for examples of obvious design procedure and extrapolation.

The recognition of a problem during routine experiments does not contribute to inventive step (**T532/88** r.3.2, established case law).

Starting from an amorphous form of a pharmaceutically active compound as prior art, it is obvious to try a crystalline form of the same compound if there are no prejudices or unexpected properties, because the skilled person in the field of pharmaceutical drug development will screen for polymorphs (**T777/08** hn).

4.2.1 *Ranges*

The skilled person will only carry out experiments over a range of parameter values if he has a reasonable expectation of some improvement or advantage. For example, a chemical manufacturing process is known to have an increasing yield for temperatures in a range from 20 °C to 120 °C. The skilled person facing the problem of selecting a temperature providing a high yield will select a temperature near 120 °C. He will not carry out experiments to determine the yield over the temperature range, because he does not have a reasonable expectation of a higher yield other than at the highest temperature. Hence, the skilled person will not find any sub-range having a unexpectedly high yield. However, the skilled person would have made experiments if there was a pointer toward such a sub-range.

4.2.2 *Optimisation of parameters*

A routine optimisation of the value of a parameter is treated as a normal activity of a skilled person. The result of such optimisation is obvious for a skilled person (G-VII, Annex 3.1(iii)), unless an unexpected effect is produced (G-VII, Annex 3.2(i)). Hence, it was obvious to optimise the value of a physical parameter to achieve a compromise acceptable for the intended use, where two effects had contrary dependence on the value (**T410/87** r.3.4). Similarly, the simultaneous optimisation of a number of lens properties leading to a quality formula was obvious (**T263/86**). The concurrent optimisation of two parameters by the simultaneous solution of two known equations expressing the parameters was obvious for the skilled person where the prior art suggested that this calculation might give favourable results (**T36/82**).

4.3 OBVIOUS SOLUTIONS

The skilled person will usually be able to solve a technical problem if the solution involves merely the application of known measures using their known properties. In such a case the prior art item discloses that the properties can be achieved by applying certain measures. He will regard the application of these measures to the prior art embodiment as an obvious measure to solve the problem; hence, the solution is obvious. Therefore, an invention involving the application of known measures using their known properties will in general not involve an inventive step.

The following examples of obvious solutions have been taken from the Guidelines G-VII Annex 1.1.

- The invention fills a gap in the prior art. Example: the new use of aluminium for a known building structure made from lightweight material. When referring to the prior art for a lightweight building material, the skilled person will know from common general knowledge that aluminium is a lightweight material that can be used in the field of building.

- The invention uses a well-known equivalent. Example: the new use of a hydraulic motor for a pump, where the use of an electric motor for this purpose was known. The problem is the provision of an alternative for the electric motor. Since well-known equivalents are part of the common general knowledge, the skilled person will apply a hydraulic motor replacing the electric motor. Hence, the solution of the problem is obvious.
- The invention merely uses a well-known material employing its known properties in a new use. Example: the problem is to improve the cleaning power of a known washing composition. The skilled person knows that the property of lowering the surface tension of water is essential for detergents. If an item of prior art discloses that a known compound has the property of lowering the surface tension of water, it is obvious to add this compound to the washing composition in order to improve its cleaning power. The improvement of the washing powder is within the ability of the skilled person and is therefore obvious to him.

  In deciding whether a new use of a measure in a specific field is obvious, where another use of the measure is known in the same field, the problems to be solved by use of this measure, both in the case to be decided and in the known case, must be taken into account (**T39/82** hn). If there is no fundamental difference between the two problems, there is no inventive step (**T142/84** r.8.2).
- The invention substitutes in a known device a recently developed material obviously suitable for that use (analogous substitution). Example: the new use of a newly developed adhesive known to be suitable for polymer-metal bonding in an electric cable comprising a polyethylene sheath bonded to a metallic shield by an adhesive.
- The invention consists merely of the use of a known technique in a closely analogous situation (analogous use). Example: the new use of a pulse control technique to control the electric motor for driving the auxiliary mechanisms of a fork-lift truck, the use of this technique to control the electric propulsion motor of the truck already being known.
- If a known device is modified by adding a feature which has no technical function, this modification cannot contribute to inventive step (**T72/95** r.5.4). If the invention is a modification of the prior art which the skilled person could clearly predict to be disadvantageous, there is no inventive step in the absence of an unexpected technical advantage (**T119/82,T155/85**).

4.4 NON-OBVIOUS SOLUTIONS

The skilled person cannot solve a problem that involves unknown measures or new properties of known measures. If no prior art item discloses the properties and the measures to achieve them, the skilled person has no reason to apply the measures. Hence, a combination of the prior art embodiment with the measures to achieve the new properties is beyond the abilities of the skilled person and therefore non-obvious for him; the invention thus includes an inventive step.

Examples of non-obvious solutions:

- The invention uses a known method or means for a different purpose involving a new, surprising effect. Example: the new use of high-frequency power for conductive butt welding, where the use for inductive butt welding was known; the new use surprisingly made scale removal not necessary. Since a prior art search for the needlessness of scale removal during conductive butt-welding will not provide any results, the skilled person will not use conductive butt welding. (G-VI, Annex 1.2(i))

- The invention applies a known device or material in a new use, thereby overcoming technical difficulties not resolvable by routine techniques. Example: the new use of a known device for supporting and controlling the rise and fall of gas holders, where a similar device was known from floating docks but practical difficulties not encountered in the known applications needed to be overcome. Note that this example assumes that the technical fields of gas holders and floating docks are neighbouring. (G-VII, Annex 1.2(ii))
- A combination of two known measures achieve a new technical effect. Example: a mixture of a painkiller and a tranquilliser has an unexpected strong painkilling effect through effect of the tranquilliser on the painkiller. The effect was unknown and could not have been predicted from the known properties of both substances. (G-VII, Annex 2.2)

  However, if the strong painkilling effect does not occur, the mixture will not produce a new synergistic effect or working inter-relationship. Such a mixture will just show a juxtaposition of the known properties of the substances. A skilled person looking for a combination of said properties will arrive at said mixture, which is therefore obvious. (G-VII, Annex 2.1)

4.5 SOLUTIONS INVOLVING SELECTION

Whether or not a skilled person will regard it obvious to make a certain selection from a set or a range depends on the presence of an unexpected technical effect in the selection. In the absence of such an effect the selection is obvious to a skilled person.

For example, the problem is to provide an alternative for an electric heat supply for a chemical process, where a number of equally likely alternative ways of so supplying the heat is known. The solution of the problem of finding an alternative heat supply is to select the heat supply according to the invention (G-VII, Annex 3.1(i)). Note, that there is no pointer to this particular heat supply. The choice of the skilled person appears to be based on hindsight: he could have chosen any alternative; however, this is the only way to make a choice without improvement or advantages obvious in the sense of **Art.56**.

The same reasoning applies to selecting a sub-set of compounds from a set of compounds, the selected compounds having known properties (G-VII, Annex 3.1(iv)). Such a selection from a set of known suitable compounds amounts to an arbitrary choice and does not involve an inventive step (**T939/92** r.2.5.3; **T967/97** hn). However, the selection is not obvious if the selected compound has unexpected advantages; a skilled person has no pointer guiding him to this compound (see G-VII, Annex 3.2(ii) for an example).

A selection of a sub-range of parameter values from a known range of values in a process or device is within the abilities of the skilled person if the properties over the sub-range are known from the prior art (see G-VII, Annex 3.1(ii) for an example). However, if the properties over the sub-range are not known and show unexpected effects, the skilled person will not be guided to this sub-range. In that case the selection of the sub-range is not obvious (see G-VII, Annex 3.2(i) for an example).

A sub-set or sub-range displaying a technical effect different from that of the known broader set or range is novel (see **Art.54(1):6**). The sub-set or sub-range is not obvious if no hints lead the skilled person to the selection. The criterion of 'seriously contemplating' in relation to the novelty test of overlapping ranges, should not be confused with the assessment of inventive step. This former criterion is based on technical feasibility, whereas the latter depends on whether the skilled person would have made the selection of the sub-range claimed in the expectation of solving a technical problem or in the expectation of some improvement or advantage. (G-VII,12)

5 Impediments of the skilled person

5.1 PURPOSE

The skilled person is purpose driven; his goal is to solve a technical problem. He will not act out of idle curiosity but rather with a specific technical purpose in mind (**T939/92**). The skilled person will not carry out frivolous or random research; such research is a known source of solutions involving an inventive step. The skilled person has no desire to know how things work; research driven by this desire often produces creative solutions.

5.2 COULD-WOULD

The development of the prior art is not determined by what the skilled person could have done but by what he would have done in the expectation of solving the underlying technical problem, i.e. in the expectation of some improvement or advantage (**T2/83; T7/86**). When a problem is not known in the prior art, the skilled person could have applied measures to solve the problem, but he would not have done so, because the prior art does not prompt him (**T2/83**; G-VII,5.3).

The incentive or prompting to apply certain measures need not be explicit but may be implicit, for example as a statement that preferred features avoid conditions known to be a cause of the problem solved by the patent (**T257/98; T35/04**; G-VII,5.3).

Hence, an invention is not obvious if the skilled person *could* have arrived at the solution claimed by modifying the closest prior art. On the other hand if, but only if, in expectation of solving the problem, he *would* have made such a modification, the invention is obvious (**T2/83** r.7; **T414/98** r.6.1). This so-called 'could-would approach' reduces the risk of an ex post facto analysis wrongly suggesting that an invention was obvious.

5.3 CROSS-FERTILISATION

A skilled person will only make combinations of prior art in his specific technical field, neighbouring and broader general technical fields. He will not consider remote prior art (**T11/81** r.3).

Research workers often change technical field, thereby facilitating cross-fertilisation between fields. Solutions known in one field often lead to creative solutions in other fields. Therefore, great care should be taken when comparing the knowledge of the skilled person with that of actual research workers or scientists (see e.g. Case Law of the BoA, I.D.8.1.1 and 8.1.3).

5.4 PREJUDICES

The skilled person is a captive of prejudices. A prejudice that might have diverted the skilled man away from the alleged invention is an indication of the presence of an inventive step in relation to an invention that rejects the prejudice. Prejudice of the skilled person is often used by applicants to argue the presence of inventive step. However, the EPO seldom accepts the existence of a prejudice (see Case Law of the BoA, I.D.10.2).

A prejudice must reflect the common thinking in the relevant technical field. A single opinion should not be taken in isolation; the whole relevant prior art should be taken into consideration to gauge the common thinking. A prior patent stating that a claimed invention is not realizable does not create a prejudice (**T206/83**). Such a statement expressed in a patent is regarded as not being the expression of general opinion and is no proof of an existing prejudice because the specification of the prior art patent may be based on special premises or on the view of the drafter (**T19/81**). A prejudice may be based on a significant scientific publication (**T148/83**) or on a specialized manual (**T18/81** r.8). A standard textbook is also accepted as representing the opinion of the skilled person (**T19/81, T104/83**). See G-VII, Annex 4 for an example of a prejudice.

A party who wishes to rely on a prejudice has the onus of demonstrating its existence (**T119/82** r.14; **T48/86** r.4.2.3).

6 Problem-solution approach

The EPO assesses the presence of an inventive step using the problem-solution approach. The method is based on the requirement in **R.42(1)(c)** that the invention must be disclosed in terms of a technical problem and its solution. Although this means of analysing inventive step is not mandatory, it is very unusual for the EPO to take any other approach. If, exceptionally, some other method is adopted, the reasons for not using the problem-solution approach should be stated (Case Law of the BoA, I.D.2).

In decision **T465/92** the Board of Appeal used an alternative approach. **T188/09** permitted the use of the alternative approach, provided that one of the situations of **T465/92** applies: either there is no close prior art because the invention breaks new ground or there are several equally close relevant citations. Moreover, the alternative approach must provide the same result as the problem-solution approach. (**T188/09** r.1-9)

Note, that the objectivity of the assessment of inventive step under **Art.56** is in part based on the use of a single method for the assessment (G-VII,5). Different methods are unlikely to give the same result in all situations. The objectivity is also reflected in that the problem is called the 'objective technical problem'; different methods could result in a 'subjective technical problem'.

The problem-solution approach is intended to give objectivity to the assessment of inventive step and to avoid ex post facto analysis of the prior art, i.e. hindsight.

The problem-solution approach consists of three stages (G-VII,5):

1. Identifying the closest prior art from a prior art search (G-VII,5.1).
2. Establishing the objective technical problem in view of the closest prior art. The problem is based on technical effects of the invention not present in the closest prior art (G-VII,5.2).
3. Starting from the closest prior art and the objective technical problem, considering whether the solution of the problem would have been obvious to the skilled person at the relevant date. The obviousness of the solution is commonly determined by assessing whether it was obvious to combine the closest prior art with other prior art to arrive at the invention.

6.1 CLOSEST PRIOR ART

An invention involves an inventive step only if the solution of the problem is not obvious in view of all items of prior art. Therefore, the problem-solution approach should be applied to each item of prior art. This task is simplified by selecting the closest prior art and assessing whether the invention is obvious in view of that item as the starting point. If the closest prior art does not result in an obvious solution, it is unlikely that a more remote prior art will lead to an obvious solution. This does not rule out alternative arguments in relation to alternative items proposed as the closest prior art.

The closest prior art is that which in one single reference discloses the combination of features which constitutes the most promising starting point for a development leading to the invention (**T432/92**; G-VII,5.1). The primary consideration in the selection of the closest prior art is that it should be directed to a similar purpose or effect as the invention (**T696/89**) or at least belong to the same or a closely related technical field as the claimed invention (**T989/93**).

In practice, the closest prior art is generally that which corresponds to a similar use and has the most relevant technical features in common, i.e. requiring the minimum of structural and functional modifications to arrive at the claimed invention (**T606/89**). A second consideration for the selection of the closest prior art is the similarity of the problem to be solved (**T495/91**).

If there is a group of prior art documents and the choice of the closest prior art is not unambiguous, the problem-solution approach should be repeated for each of these prior art documents. If the invention is obvious for at least one of these documents, the invention lacks inventive step and the choice of starting point needs no specific justification. (**T1742/12** r.6.5, 6.6)

However, in opposition proceedings, applying the problem-solution approach from different starting points is only permitted if it has been convincingly shown that these documents are equally valid springboards (G-VII,5.1; not in GL2017). Accordingly, various attacks starting from different prior art documents cannot be freely developed by the opponent (**T320/15** r.1.1.2). The EPO appears to have brought this into the Guidelines to expedite oppositions in view of Early Certainty targets.

6.2 PROBLEM

In the second stage the invention is compared with the closest prior art, from which the distinguishing features of the invention over the closest prior art are identified. The distinguishing features have certain technical effects as disclosed in the application or known from common general knowledge. The 'objective technical problem' is the aim and task of the skilled person to modify the closest prior art to provide the technical effects that the distinguishing features furnish over the closest prior art (G-VII,5.2; **T1019/99**). This 'aim and task' is better conveyed by the word 'Aufgabe' (i.e. 'task') in the German version of **R.42(1)(c)** than by 'problem' and 'problème' in the other two languages.

The problem must be a technical problem which the skilled person in the particular technical field might have been asked to solve at the relevant date. The problem should not refer to matter of which the skilled person would only have become aware by knowledge of the solution claimed (G-VII,5.4.1).

The 'objective technical problem' need not be the same as the problem stated in the application as filed (the 'subjective technical problem'). However, the problem stated in the application as filed may be a good starting point. If the invention does not solve this problem or if closer prior art is found, a reformulation of the problem may be necessary, possibly to meet a less ambitious goal (**T246/91**). Any effect provided by the invention and derivable from the application as filed may be used as a basis for the reformulation (**T386/89**), provided all information necessary to achieve the effect is at the disposal of the skilled person (**T1639/07** r.2.5). Thus, new effects submitted by the applicant during the proceedings may also be used, provided that the skilled person would recognise these effects as implied by or related to the technical problem initially suggested in the application as filed (**T184/82**). (G-VII,5.2)

Alleged advantages to which the application merely refers, without proper evidence, cannot be used as a basis for a problem; in such a case a reformulation of the problem is necessary (**T20/81**). The advantage must be plausible. In **T210/02** the advantage was a specific effect of a drug on a complex system such as the immune system of an animal. A mere allegation of an effect without any concrete evidence was not sufficient. Since the inventive step hinged on this effect for a second-medical use claim, the lack of plausibility resulted in lack of inventive step.

The problem must be formulated sufficiently broadly that it does not contain pointers to the solution, since inclusion of elements of the invention in the problem necessarily results in hindsight (**T229/85**). On the other hand, a problem should not be formulated so generally as to circumvent indications in a prior art document towards the claimed solution (**T1019/99** r.3.3).

The examiner should not abstract the problem such that it leads away from the way of reasoning of the skilled person and in this way leads to a problem already solved in the state of the art (**T5/81**), (**T176/84** Pencil sharpener; looks like a saving box). Instead, he must determine the problem, examine how the inventor solved it, and decide on the obviousness of the claimed solution (**T24/81**, **T1/80**).

If no objective technical problem can be established, e.g. the objective problem relates to non-technical issues only, the invention does not have an inventive step because there is no technical contribution to the art. On the other hand, where the claim refers to an aim to be achieved in a non-technical field, this aim may appear in the formulation of the problem as part of the technical framework of the problem to be solved, in particular where it was a constraint that had to be met (G-VII,5.2).

Where the technical problem is both known and solved in the closest prior art, in a way different from the invention, a redefinition of the problem is not necessary. The objective technical problem may be to provide an alternative solution to a known problem. (**T92/92**).

6.3 SOLUTION

6.3.1 Question to be asked

In the third stage of the problem-solution approach an assessment is made whether or not the solution of the problem is obvious for the skilled person. The assessment depends on the precise question that is being asked. There are two possible questions.

The first question that could be asked is: would a development by the skilled person starting from the closest prior art and guided by the problem to be solved result in the claimed invention? If yes, the invention is obvious. The skilled person must develop the closest prior art, which involves a prior art search for a solution of the problem. There are three issues with the first question. The first one is that there are usually many ways in which a problem can be solved. It is therefore a matter of chance that the search of the skilled person will result in the invention. The second issue is that the Guidelines and case law do not mention a search in the third stage. The third issue is whether or not the skilled person will find a certain prior art item in his search. The third issue would give rise to arguments for and against finding the relevant prior art. However, such arguments are not addressed in the Guidelines. Rather, the Guidelines merely discuss whether or not a combination of certain prior art is obvious.

The second question is: is the solution, i.e. the combination of prior art that together disclose the features of the invention and found during the search under **Art.92**, obvious for a skilled person in view of the problem of the closest prior art to be solved? The solution found during the search is presented to the skilled person and the question is whether the combination of prior art in the solution is obvious for him in view of the problem. If yes, the invention is obvious. An issue with this question is that it involves more hindsight than the first question. In the second question the complete solution is presented to the skilled person. In the first question only the closest prior art and the problem are given to the skilled person. Another important difference with the first question is, that no search is carried out in the third stage of the problem-solution approach.

The Guidelines and case law do not explicitly state which question should be asked. However, section I.D.5 of the Case Law of the BoA appears to imply that the second question is the correct one. The second question is also consistent with the procedure followed by EPO examiners during the assessment of inventive step. In the following sections the second question is used.

6.3.2 Obviousness of the solution

In the third stage it is determined whether or not the claimed invention, starting from the closest prior art and the objective technical problem, would have been obvious to the skilled person. In practice this amounts to determining whether the skilled person would have modified the teaching of the closest prior art in the way indicated by the solution in the expectation of solving the problem. The invention is obvious if a pointer in the teaching obtained from the prior art would have prompted the skilled person to make such a modification.

Often the solution is based on the combination of the closest prior art with one further prior art item. It is also permissible to combine the closest prior art with more than one prior art item, but if more than one is needed in order to arrive at the invention, that may be a sign that there is an inventive step (G-VII,6; **T113/82** r.7.2).

Proof of non-obviousness in view of the closest prior art according to the problem-solution approach cannot be replaced merely by showing the technical progress of the claimed invention in comparison with marketed products (**T164/83**, **T181/82**).

If the solution of a problem does not require any technical skills, but e.g. merely administrative or financial skills, the invention does not meet the requirement of inventive step (**T641/00**, r.13, Mobile telephone system). The solution need not be a technical improvement over the prior art (**T588/93**).

6.3.3 Examples

The following situations may arise in the third stage:

- The closest prior art and further prior art disclose all features of the claimed invention and the combination is obvious. Hence, the invention lacks inventive step.
- The closest prior art and common general knowledge disclose all features. Such a combination is always obvious and so is the invention.
- The closest prior art and further prior art disclose all features of the invention, but the combination is not obvious. In such a case the invention includes an inventive step.

- The closest prior art and any further prior art do not disclose all features of the invention. It must be assessed whether routine work and experiments can fill the gap between the combined teaching and the invention. If they can and the steps of combining the prior art and carrying out the routine work and/or experiments are obvious, the invention is obvious.

6.4 SEARCH

The search under **Art.92**, carried out before the assessment of inventive step under **Art.56**, is based on the problem-solution approach. For that reason, the problem-solution approach should be a four instead of a three-stage method with the search as the first stage.

Prior to the search, the examiner identifies in the application the problem underlying the invention, the inventive concept leading to its solution, the features essential to the solution as claimed and the results and effects obtained (B-III,3.2; B-IV,1.1). The search will cover the essential features and the results and effects. The search for the results and effect may show documents that disclose pointers that can be used in the third stage of the problem-solution approach.

The search is carried out in the technical fields relevant for the invention (B-III,2.3). The document having the most features in common with the invention will be regarded as the closest prior art. Since the document is from a technical field relevant for the invention, the document will usually be directed to a similar purpose or effect as the invention, as required for the closest prior art.

The retrieved closest prior art may necessitate a change of the problem stated in the application (B-III,3.2.2). A redefined problem requires a new search.

The search report should not only cite the parts of documents describing the features, but also the parts relating to the problem solved by the features (B-I,9.4). The documents describing the claimed features are the basis of the solution of the problem. The obviousness of this solution is assessed in the third stage of the problem-solution approach.

The search provides all key elements for the problem-solution approach: closest prior art, problem and solution, and allows the preparation of consistent obviousness arguments.

7 Secondary indicia

The EPO has identified secondary indicia or indications which point to the presence of an inventive step. They can be used to strengthen or weaken arguments in the problem-solution approach. As their name indicates, their importance is secondary. Any argument to show the presence of an inventive step should start with an assessment of the prior art by a person skilled in the art, not with secondary indicia. Secondary indicia alone do not suffice to show inventive step, but they do indicate the possible presence of an inventive step (**T24/81** r.15; **T181/82**; **T330/87** r.8.3). A mix of indicia can be found in **T181/85** (decaffeination of coffee). An overview of secondary indicia is given in Case Law of the BoA, I.D.10.

The secondary indicium 'prejudice' has been dealt with in the above section on impediments of the skilled person, since prejudice is a characteristic of the skilled person.

7.1 LONG-FELT NEED

The age of the closest prior art and a long inactivity in the state of the art may be an indication of inventive step, provided that during this time an urgent need for solving the problem demonstrably existed (**T79/82** r.4; **T109/82** r.5.5).

For example, if a long standing method is modified to become more expensive but less environmentally damaging, then the long existence of the method is no indication of inventive step where the new method was not used previously because of cost and became attractive only recently because of stricter environmental regulations (**T24/81** Steel production with CO2 instead of O2 blowing; gives steps for assessing inventive step). An example of a long-felt need is the need for a reduction in the risk of explosion in the mass manufacture of ethylene oxide (**T41/84**).

A fingertip sized piece of waffle on a waffle with outer glazing solved a long-felt need to avoid smudgy fingers; the solution was simple and not known (**T330/87**).

The removal of a known disadvantage of a product that had been commercially successful for 20 years, in spite of its disadvantages, is an indication of inventive step (**T271/84** r.5,6,9, **T165/85** r.8,7). A real inventive step, e.g. a combination with a new effect must, of course, always be present.

Seven years is regarded as a long period for a strongly felt need relating to health problems (**T106/84** r.8.6). Six years is regarded as a long time for a strongly felt need in a quickly developing technological field (**T145/84**). Examples where a period of 11 to 80 years between publication of the prior art document and the filing of the application was regarded as a secondary indicium in support of inventive step are given in Case Law of the BoA, I.D.10.3.

7.2 COMMERCIAL SUCCESS

Commercial success alone is not by itself an indicator of inventive step, but may become so when coupled with a long-felt need and evidence that the commercial success derives from technical features and not from other influences such as selling techniques or advertising (**T1212/01** (Viagra)) (G-VII,10.3). A positive result from the examination of an application can be strengthened by the economic success of the invention (**T335/86**).

The economic effect of an invention is often no indicium, though occasionally a minor indicium (**T91/83, T69/82, T270/84**). A small increase in the yield (0.5%) of a large-scale process indicated the economic value of the invention, which was not overlooked in the assessment (**T38/84**). Examples of cases where commercial success was taken into account as a secondary indicium are **T677/91** and **T626/96.**

In **T754/89** (Epilady) the technical facts were by themselves amply convincing of the involvement of an inventive step, such that the commercial success of the invention as secondary indicium was of no relevance.

7.3 SIMPLE SOLUTION

A simple solution without sacrificing quality, which has escaped those concerned despite considerable activity in the field, may be a secondary indicium of the presence of inventive step (**T106/84** hn2; **T229/85** r.7).

An example of a major improvement by a simple solution concerned a paper fastener in the form of an elongate hollow profile strip having a slit along its underside; a sheet of paper inserted into the slit was captured by glass spheres inside the hollow strip; the invention was the surface roughening of the glass spheres to improve the suspension of sheets of heavy paper (**T349/95**).

7.4 SURPRISING EFFECT - BONUS EFFECT

A surprising effect can be regarded as an indication of an inventive step (**T181/82** hn.I). Such an effect must be proved by comparative tests, in particular in the field of chemistry, and it must be shown convincingly to have its origin in the characterising features of the invention (**T181/82** r.3; **T197/86**; G-VII,10.2). A chemical compound can exhibit an inventive step if it has properties not suggested by the prior art (**T20/83** hn3).

An additional, surprising effect does not point towards an invention if the skilled person would already have arrived at the invention because another advantageous effect could be achieved by combining prior art documents (**T21/81**; **T69/83**). The additional effect is merely a bonus effect. For example, the state of the art already recommended a specific measure to improve the resistance to wear of an electric relay; an additional advantageous effect (possibly unforeseen), namely that the measure caused the relay to produce a chatter before the end of its life did not make the measure inventive (**T21/81**).

Similarly, an additional, surprising effect occurring in a 'one-way street' situation is not an indication of an inventive step (**T192/82** hn2; G-VII,10.2). In a 'one-way street' situation the skilled person has only one available approach for modifying the closest prior art to choose from.

8 Special inventions

8.1 PARTIAL PROBLEMS

An invention is based on partial problems if it contains two sets of features relating to solutions to separate parts of a problem, without any interaction between these two sets of features that brings about a technical effect in excess of the sum of their individual effects, the said sets of features being merely juxtaposed (**T389/86** r.4.2).

For example, an invention related to a door comprising a profile surrounded on all sides with PVC skin foam; the first partial problem was to reinforce the edges of the foam, the second partial problem was to improve the aesthetic appearance; the two sets of features in the claim solving these two partial problems (applying a strong cover layer on the edges and imprinting a wood-like profile on the foam) appeared not to have functional reciprocity (**T130/89**). The two sets were only an aggregate or juxtaposition of features. Another example is presented in **T552/89**, in which the objective problem comprised two partial problems, the first partial problem being solved by combining the closest prior art with a second document and the second partial problem by combining the closest prior art with a workshop modification of the teaching of a third document; the invention was therefore obvious.

In these cases the assessment of inventive step involves carrying out the problem-solution approach twice, once for each partial problem using its own closest prior art. The invention is not obvious if at least one of the two approaches shows the presence of an inventive step (**T130/89**).

8.2 NON-CONTRIBUTING FEATURE

A claim may have a mix of technical and non-technical features, as is often the case with computer-implemented inventions (see **Art.52(2):6**). However, the problem-solution approach must be applied such that inventive step is not acknowledged on the basis of features that do not contribute to the technical character of the invention (**T641/00** (Comvik) hn1). To this end, the Guidelines give the following steps for the problem-solution approach (G-VII,5.4).

i) The features of the claim that contribute to the technical character of the invention are determined on the basis of the technical effects achieved by the invention. All claimed features must be assessed on their contribution (**T172/03** r.11). Since the assessment is usually complex, the determination in step (i) is usually on a prima facie basis; it is done more thoroughly in step (iii).

ii) The selection of the closest prior art is based on the features contributing to the technical character as identified in step (i).

iii) The features that distinguish the claim from the closest prior art are determined and whether or not these features have a technical effect in the context of the claim as a whole (**T756/06** r.5). The technical effects must be derivable from the application as filed when considered in the light of the closest prior art (G-VII,5.4.1).

    Care should be taken to avoid missing any feature that might contribute to the technical character of the claim, for example by a wording of the claim loosely paraphrased by the examiner (**T756/06** r.6). A non-technical feature may interact with other features so as to produce a technical effect (**T154/04** r.13). The more thorough assessment of the technical contribution of features in step (iii) may reveal that a feature considered prima facie in step (i) as not contributing to the technical character of the invention, does make such a contribution or vice versa. In such cases the selection of the closest prior art in step (ii) may have to be revised.

    a) If there are no distinguishing features, not even a non-technical feature, a novelty objection is raised.

        Note, that the Guidelines suggest that a non-technical feature can make a claim novel. However, some case law holds that novelty can only be established on the basis of the technical features of an invention (**T154/04** r.14, 15).

    b) If the distinguishing features do not make any technical contribution, an objection of lack of inventive step is raised with the reasoning that there cannot be an inventive step if the subject-matter does not provide a technical contribution to the prior art.

    c) If the distinguishing features make a technical contribution, the objective technical problem is formulated based on the technical effects of these features. Any distinguishing feature that does not give a technical contribution or any non-technical effect achieved by the claimed features may be used in the formulation of the problem, as part of what is 'given' to the skilled person (**T641/00** hn2; **T1461/12**, following T641/00; G-VII,5.4.1).

        The inclusion of non-technical features and effects in the problem to be solved by the skilled person, thereby 'giving' them to the skilled person, is not hindsight, because not including features of the solution in the problem applies only to features that do make a technical contribution.

G-VII,5.4.2 gives four examples illustrating the above assessment.

T756/06 r.5 compares the above assessment of a claim including a mix of technical and non-technical features with the related assessment of **T931/95** (Pension benefit systems). Two examples of the consequences of non-technical features are given below.

A claim relating to a conventional computer system for controlling an improved pension benefits plan had, as the sole novel feature, an improvement of the plan. Assessment of inventive step first considered the technical character of the claim as a whole. The computer system gave the claim a technical character, making the claim in principle patentable. The claim was novel in view of the closest prior art, i.e. existing pension plans. The improvement of the pension plans could not contribute to inventive step because the improvement lay in the non-technical field of economy. The only technical contribution was the programming of the computer system. The inventive step was assessed from the point of view of a programmer as the skilled person, having knowledge of the improved pension benefits plan and the underlying schemes of information processing. Note that in the assessment of inventive step the novel non-technical features were treated as not new. The claim did not involve an inventive step since the technical features of the apparatus claimed were functionally defined by known steps of information processing and the use of computer systems was known in the economic sector. (**T931/95** r.8)

T1227/05 r.3 held that procedural steps of a computer-implemented method for simulating the performance of an electronic circuit subject to 1/f noise do not constitute a mathematical method as such nor a computer program as such, but contribute to the technical character of the method because they serve a technical purpose. The simulation of a circuit subject to 1/f noise having inputs and outputs whose performance is described by differential equations is an adequately defined technical purpose. The simulation provides a realistic prediction of the performance of a designed circuit, which allows a wide range of designs to be virtually tested before the expensive fabrication process starts. The simulation is therefore to be regarded as an essential part of the fabrication process. In that light, such a simulation method cannot be denied a technical effect merely on the ground that it does not yet incorporate the physical end product, i.e. the circuit. Hence, the procedural steps must be considered in the assessment of inventive step because of their technical character.

It should be noted that a simulation method is not necessarily to be equated with a circuit design method (**T1227/05** r.3.4.2). **T453/91** hn. regarded a method for the design of a physical VLSI-chip to lack technical character, the resulting design being a mere abstract notion, which did not and possibly never would exist in the real world. The method could be given technical character by adding a step for actually manufacturing the designed chip (see also G-II,3.3).

8.3 PROBLEM INVENTION

A problem invention is based on the discovery of an unrecognised problem. The discovery may give rise to an inventive step even if the claimed solution is, once the problem has been identified, trivial and obvious (**T2/83** hn.I). A minimum requirement of a problem invention is that the problem must be clearly and unambiguously disclosed in the application as filed (**T971/92** r.3.7.1). However, the posing of a problem does not represent a contribution to the inventive merits of the solution if the problem could have been posed by the skilled person (**T109/82** hn.I). The skilled person is assumed to be constantly occupied with the elimination of deficiencies and achievement of improvements; such aims are inherently obvious (**T15/81** r.3). Since problem inventions are generally not recognised by the boards (see Case Law of the BoA I.D.9.10), the Guidelines do not refer to them anymore.

The unrecognised problem cannot be used as the objective technical problem, because the unrecognised problem contains pointers to the solution, which is incompatible with the problem-solution approach (see **Art.56:6.2**). Instead, a broader problem should be formulated and the unrecognised problem should be cited after recitation of the first claim in the introductory part of the patent application as support for the presence of an inventive step. For example, the objective technical problem can be to improve the functioning of a device, where the unrecognised problem is that the malfunctioning is caused by a specific component of the device.

8.4 CHEMICAL INVENTIONS

The properties of chemical compounds depend strongly on the chemical structure of the compounds. Hence, a denial of inventive step based on structural similarity to known compounds is only justified if the skilled person knows that similar structural differences between the known compounds are sufficiently small to have no essential bearing on the claimed properties (**T852/91** r.8.2).

If the technical effect of a group of compounds is the sole reason for the alleged inventiveness of these compounds, the technical effect of the solution should be achieved by all compounds claimed; there is no inventive step if not all compounds covered possess the desired effect. (**T939/92** hn.II)

New intermediates that are essential in an advantageous complete process involve an inventive step (**T22/82** hn.I). The mere novelty of the intermediate is not sufficient to impart inventive step; there must be other factors, such as inventive further processing (**T163/84** hn and **T18/88**; denied in **T648/88**). **T65/82** requires that the intermediates in a non-inventive analogy process (see below) must provide a structural contribution to the end product.

An analogy process is a method which is analogous to a known method and used for making a chemical substance. The process derives its patentability solely from the patentability of the end product. Hence, an analogy process for making a compound is patentable in so far as the compound is new and inventive (**T119/82**). This formerly provided a way of indirectly obtaining product protection in contracting states which excluded direct claiming of a chemical substance protection under **Art.167(2)(a)** EPC 1973. **Art.167** EPC 1973 was deleted by EPC 2000.

Art. 57 Industrial application

An invention shall be considered as susceptible of industrial application if it can be made or used in any kind of industry, including agriculture.

1 Industry

'Industry' should be understood in a broad sense as including any physical activity of technical character (G-III,1). The concept of 'industry' implies that an activity is carried out continuously, independently and for financial gain (**T144/83** r.5). Industrial application does not include applications for private use (see e.g. **T74/93**; however see **T1165/97** hn) and commercial and financial applications (**T953/94**). It should be noted that a product for use in a non-industrial application, such as a paint brush for use in creating art, may be industrially manufactured.

Formerly under EPC 1973, medical treatments were considered to lack industrial applicability under **Art.52(4)** EPC 1973. Under EPC 2000 this legal fiction no longer applies, and these activities are considered industrially applicable but excluded from patentability on social-ethical grounds under **Art.53(c)**.

Agriculture is specifically mentioned in **Art.57** to clarify the position of the EPC in view of the diverging national laws at the time of drafting the Convention (Empel §116).

2 **Manufacturability and industrial application**

Industrial applicability requires that the invention can be manufactured, which entails a.o. that the invention is sufficiently disclosed (**Art.83**) and does not violate physical laws. A claim stating perpetual motion as intended function or purpose is not industrially applicable as violating physical laws and will be objected to under **Art.57** and **Art.83**. However, a perpetuum mobile claimed merely as a device having a particular construction is insufficiently disclosed and is objectionable only under **Art.83** (**T85/82**). (F-III,3; G-III,1)

A perpetuum mobile is an example of an invention based on an erroneous physical theory. Patentability requires that where an invention is based on a specific theory, the theory must be valid or, where validity has not yet been proven, it must have a reasonable prospect of being proven to be valid. Acknowledgment of the theory by the scientific community at large may be regarded as such proof.

The industrial application of an invention must be stated in the application if this is not obvious (**R.42(1)(f)**). The industrial application of sequences of genes is regarded not self-evident and must be disclosed in the application (**R.29(3)**; F-II,4.9; G-III,4). A sequence without indication of a function is not a patentable invention (G-III,4). The indication of the function must be substantial, specific and credible; a speculative use does not suffice (Dec. Opp. Div, OJ 2002, 293 r.11(ii)). See also **R.29(3):1**.

Although industrial applicability and technical character of an invention are intimately related (**T854/90** r.2.1; G-III,1), they are not synonymous and constitute two distinct, non-equivalent requirements under the EPC (**T953/94** r.3.11; **T619/02** r.2.6.2).

3 **Medical and cosmetic methods**

A method of contraception applied in the private and personal sphere of a human being is not susceptible of industrial application; **Art.57** may be regarded as an expression of the general idea that any natural person has the right to have his or her privacy respected (**T74/93** r.2.2.6).

Whereas treatment by therapy and surgery is excluded from patentability (**Art.53(c)**), cosmetic treatment is not (**T36/83**, **T144/83** r.5 appetite reducer, **T780/89**). If a substance has both a cosmetic and a therapeutic effect, the cosmetic treatment is not rendered unpatentable (**T144/83**). However, an extensive discussion in a patent application on the simultaneous cosmetic and therapeutic effects of a substance might make a claimed cosmetic treatment unpatentable, because it is no longer considered a purely cosmetic treatment (**T290/86**). See also **Art.53:3**.

Chapter II *Persons entitled to apply for and obtain a European patent – Mention of the inventor*

Art. 58 Entitlement to file a European patent application

A European patent application may be filed by any natural or legal person, or any body equivalent to a legal person by virtue of the law governing it.

1 **Open filing system**

The EPC is an open filing system. Any person may file a European patent application, irrespective of whether he is a national of or has his residence or place of business in a contracting state of the EPC. In contrast, the PCT is a closed system. For example, an Argentine person living in Argentina may file a European patent application, whereas he may not file an international patent application, because Argentina is not a contracting state of the PCT.

The European patent application may be filed by any natural or legal person. National law decides who are natural and legal persons. Even a person incapable to act can file an application; the following steps must then be taken by a representative or a curator. The entitlement of the person to the patent is governed by **Art.60(3)** and the requirement that the person is duly represented by **Art.133**.

Art. 59 Multiple applicants

A European patent application may also be filed either by joint applicants or by two or more applicants designating different Contracting States.

1 **Joint applicants and two or more applicants**

A European application may be filed by one or more applicants according to **Art.58** and **59**, respectively. The filing by multiple applicants is in line with **Art.71**, which allows splitting up the application by the transfer of the application for one or more designated contracting states to several applicants.

Art.59 distinguishes joint applicants and applicants designating different contracting states. This implies that joint applicants are applicants designating the same contracting states.

Art.59 requires that applicants designating the same contracting states act as joint applicants. Similarly, **Art.118** states that applicants designating different contracting states are regarded as joint applicants. Hence, all applicants of an application are regarded as joint applicants.

Joint applicants have the procedural status of a single applicant and can only act in common to maintain the unitary character of the application and procedure before the EPO (see **Art.118:1**). They cannot acquire a procedural status different from that of a single applicant, because otherwise each of them could perform different and contradictory procedural acts (**J2/01**, r.2.5.1). There will be one, uniform text of the application for the designated states resulting in a uniform patent protection (see **Art.118:2** for exceptions).

The joint applicants may appoint one applicant or a representative as common representative in the Request for Grant form (**R.41(3)**) and be represented by him. Otherwise, the EPO, wanting a single contact that speaks for and commits the applicants, applies **R.151** to appoint a common representative.

When different applicants are entered in the Register for different designated states, **R.72** provides that the patent is granted for each designated state to the applicant(s) registered in respect of that state. See EP 0 166 725 for an example.

Art. 60 Right to a European patent

1 **General**
The right to a patent belongs to the person who made the invention or to his successor in title (**Art.60(1)**). When two or more persons independently made and filed the same invention, the right to the patent belongs to the person who first filed the application (**Art.60(2)**). In proceedings before the EPO the applicant, and not the person of **Art.60(1)**, is regarded as entitled to the patent.

Art. 60(1) The right to a European patent shall belong to the inventor or his successor in title. If the inventor is an employee, the right to a European patent shall be determined in accordance with the law of the State in which the employee is mainly employed; if the State in which the employee is mainly employed cannot be determined, the law to be applied shall be that of the State in which the employer has the place of business to which the employee is attached.

1 **Inventor**
Art.60(1) lays down as substantive law that the inventor or his successor in title is entitled to the right to a European patent. If there is more than one inventor, each of them has the same rights. Although this is not dealt with explicitly in the EPC, it can be derived from the fact that in all contracting states co-inventors have the same rights as a sole inventor. The necessary contribution to the application to become (co-)inventor is assessed differently in different states.

The EPC does not define the term 'inventor' and has left its interpretation as a matter of national law (Empel §152). When the inventor is an employee, **Art.60(1)** states that his right to the patent must be determined by the law of the state in which the inventor is mainly employed or, if this state cannot be determined, by the law of the state where the employer has his place of business. The differences in national labour laws decide whether an employer or employee has the right to a patent. See also Prot. Rec. Art.4. Similarly, the provision does not define the successor in title of the inventor, which must also be determined according to national law. The successor in title is often an employer, a transferee or an heir.

The moral right of the inventor to be acknowledged is safeguarded by **Art.62** and realized in **Art.81**, first sentence and **R.19** and **R.20**. If the applicant is not the inventor or is not the sole inventor, he must state the origin of his right to the patent (**Art.81**, second sentence).

2 **Assessment of substantive rights**
The EPC deems the applicant, i.e. the person filing the application (**Art.58**), to be entitled to exercise the right to the patent (**Art.60(3)**). This procedural right is not attributed to the inventor or his successor in title; hence, they have no procedural status before the EPO. Whether the applicant entered in the EPO Register is the rightful inventor or his successor in title is a matter of national law. The EPO is not concerned with entitlement questions (see e.g. **R.19(2)**) and has no power to determine such questions (**G3/92**, r.3). Any entitlement issue should be dealt with by a national court, as is clear from

Art.61 and the Protocol on Recognition. The provisions on continuation after a national entitlement procedure in **Art.61** and on transfer in **Art.72** and **R.22** define the conditions under which the EPO may exceptionally take into account questions of substantive law and procedural acts by a person other than the registered applicant (**J2/01** r.3). Issues of substantive law also arise in the assessment of the transfer of opponent status (see **Art.99(1):1.4**).

Art. 60(2) If two or more persons have made an invention independently of each other, the right to a European patent therefor shall belong to the person whose European patent application has the earliest date of filing, provided that this first application has been published.

Art.93 Publication of a European patent application

1 **Transitional provision EPC 2000**

The above revised **Art.60** is applicable to EP applications filed on or after the date of EPC 2000 entry into force. (Spec. Ed. 4, OJ 2007)

The person whose application has the earlier date of filing will have the right to the patent, because his application will become prior art for a subsequent application. The revision of **Art.54** has changed the prior art by deleting paragraph 4 on the territorial extent of the prior rights. The EPC 1973 restricted the prior right effect to the contracting states commonly designated in the application as published and the application under examination, whereas the EPC 2000 extends the prior right effect to all contracting states of the EPC. During the transitional period, the territorial extent of the prior right effect of the earlier filed application will depend on the filing date, not the priority date, of the application under examination. If the application under examination is filed before the date of EPC 2000 entry into force (13.12.2007), the prior right effect of the earlier filed application will exist only for the commonly designated states; if filed on or after that date, the prior right effect of the earlier filed application will exist for all contracting states.

2 **First-to-file principle**

The person who first files an application has the right to the patent. Although this first-to-file principle puts an administrative burden on the inventor in having to file the application as soon as possible, the resulting patent system is less complex, gives more legal certainty and results in fewer cases of double patenting than a patent system based on the first-to-invent principle.

The person will obtain this right only if the application is validly published under **Art.93**. If the application has been withdrawn shortly before publication and is still published invalidly, a later applicant may have the right to the patent (see **J5/81**). The right to the patent exists only in validly designated contracting states.

The date of filing for the purpose of **Art.60(2)** is the priority date for applications claiming priority (**Art.89**).

Two applications relating to the same subject-matter, with different applicants and filed on the same date can result in double patenting (G-IV,5.4).

The case of two applications claiming the same or overlapping subject-matter and the same applicant is not dealt with explicitly in the EPC. However, it is an accepted principle in most patent systems to avoid this type of double patenting. In such a case, e.g. the one relating to a divisional application and a parent application (C-IX,1.6), the examining division must request the applicant either to amend the applications in such a manner that they no longer claim the same invention or to choose which one of the applications he wishes to proceed to grant (G-IV,5.4). See also **Art.139(3):3**.

3 **Realisation of right to patent**
The first-to-file principle is embodied in the definition of the prior art in **Art.54**. The first filed application forms part of the prior art for a later filed application, thereby taking away the novelty of claims in the later filed application the subject-matter of which is disclosed in the first filed application.

Art. 60(3) In proceedings before the European Patent Office, the applicant shall be deemed to be entitled to exercise the right to a European patent.

1 **Entitlement to the patent**
According to **Art.60(3)** the EPO assumes by way of legal fiction that the person identified in the Request for Grant form as applicant (**R.41(2)(c)**; **Art.81**, second sentence) is entitled to exercise the right to the patent. The legal fiction also applies to joint applicants who are entitled to exercise the right to the patent in common (**J2/01** r.2.5.1; see also **Art.59:1**). The EPC attributes the entitlement to exercise the right to the patent to the applicant and not to the person having the substantive right to the patent; note that the applicant is not mentioned in **Art.60(1)** on substantive right. Even though, as a consequence of the legal fiction contained in **Art.60(3)**, a European patent application may as a matter of fact be filed by a person other than the inventor or his successor in title, contrary to the legal right of the latter, as a matter of law only the inventor or his successor in title is entitled to apply for the grant of a European patent (**G3/92** r.2). The relation between the applicant and the person having the substantive right is governed by national law.

According to **J2/01**, r.2.6, the right to the patent in **Art.60(3)** is a formal, procedural right, which derives from the status of being the registered applicant, in contrast with the right to the patent in **Art.60(1)**, which is a substantive right. The distinction between the procedural right and the substantive right is deliberate and allows the EPO not to be concerned with questions of entitlement in terms of substantive law. In fact, the EPO has no power to determine disputes regarding substantive entitlement (**G3/92**, r.3). **Art.60(3)** allows the EPO to decide issues on entitlement to procedural rights, such as the right to file a divisional application, by reference to the Register.

The fiction of correct entitlement relieves the EPO from the need to investigate the validity of any substantive entitlement. When a person referred to in **Art.60(1)**, other than the applicant, disputes the entitlement to grant before a national court, the entitlement may be changed under the conditions provided in **Art.61**. A change in entitlement is also allowable under **R.139**, first sentence, as a correction of a mistake, provided there is sufficient evidence to support the request for correction. (**J18/93** r.1)

The EPO may have to investigate the validity of entitlement if the legal entity of a party in appeal is not the same as in the preceding proceedings and if the applicant contests a request for transfer of the application filed by a third party (in derogation from **G3/92** r.3).

Art. 61 European patent applications filed by non-entitled persons

1 **General**

Art.61 deals with the remedies available where a person other than the applicant is held by a national court to be the person entitled to the grant of a European patent. **R.14** and **R.16** specify a number of conditions which must be met for such remedies to be available. **R.16** also makes a connection with the Protocol on Recognition, which lays down in Art.1(1) that the courts of the contracting states have jurisdiction to decide entitlement claims. It also governs in Art.9(1) the recognition of the final decision of a court given in a contracting state in other contracting states.

Art. 61(1) If by a final decision it is adjudged that a person other than the applicant is entitled to the grant of the European patent, that person may, in accordance with the Implementing Regulations:
(a) prosecute the European patent application as his own application in place of the applicant;
(b) file a new European patent application in respect of the same invention; or
(c) request that the European patent application be refused.

Implementation:
R.14 Stay of proceedings
R.15 Limitation on withdrawals
R.16 Procedure under Art.61(1)
R.17 Filing a new application
R.18 Partial transfer of right
R.51(6) Renewal fee for a new application

1 **Entitlement procedure**

If a person is of the opinion that he is entitled to the grant of a European patent instead of the person whom the EPO has registered as applicant, he can obtain his rights only through a national court. The choice of the court and the recognition of its decision by other contracting states designated in the application is set out in the Protocol on Recognition. The EPO will stay its proceedings according to **R.14(1)** after the entitled person has provided proof to the EPO that he has opened proceedings before the national court. The proceedings will only be stayed after the publication of the application. The stay prevents the application from being amended to the detriment of the entitled person. **R.15** prohibits withdrawal of the application or any designation. **R.14** and **R.15** secure the rights of the entitled person during the time the national court takes to reach a final decision. After the final decision of the court has been issued, the entitled person may exercise the rights of **Art.61(1)** on the application. The entitled person has three options to exercise the rights: continue the prosecution of the pending application, file a new application, request refusal of the application. The three options will be discussed in the following sections.

Art.99(4) provides the procedure for an entitled person to obtain his rights where a patent has already been granted and is implicated in opposition proceedings.

2 **Prosecute application (Art.61(1)(a))**

The new applicant must inform the EPO in writing of his intention to prosecute the application; he then takes the place of the original applicant and continues the grant procedure (A-IV,2.4).

Options (a) and (b) each have their advantages: (a) does not require payment of several fees, whereas (b) allows a new start of the examination including subject-matter which may have been abandoned by the original applicant during prosecution.

Option (a) is in general only open for a third party who has become entitled to the entire subject-matter of the application for either all or some of the designated states. If he is entitled to only a part of the subject-matter, he must file a new application under **Art.61(1)(b)** (see also **R.18(1)**). (C-IX,2.3)

If it is adjudged that the third party and the original applicant have the right to the grant for different designated states, option (a) may be used to allow the third party to replace the original applicant for the states adjudged to the third party and prosecute the application for these states. Consequently, the application will have different applicants for different states and may have different claims, description and drawings for these different states (**R.18(2)**).

Option (a) may also be used if the third party is entitled to part of the right to grant and, exceptionally, the application cannot be divided for the application of **R.18**. The third party can then use option (a) to become an additional applicant. (Singer, Art. 61, rdn.28)

3 **File new application (Art.61(1)(b))**

The rules for filing a new application are given in **R.17**. The new application is regarded as a divisional application in many respects (**Art.61(2)** and notes thereto). The original application is deemed to be withdrawn at the filing date of the new application (**R.17(1)**).

If the third party is entitled to the patent in only some of the designated states and he does not replace the original applicant for these states under paragraph (1)(a) but files a new application for these states, then the original application continues for the remaining states.

Subject-matter disclosed in the original application may be disclaimed in the new application (**G2/10** r.4.6).

In **G3/92** hn the Enlarged Board of Appeal decided, based on the EPC 1973, that the not yet granted original usurping application need not still be pending before the EPO at the time the new application is filed. In such a case, the entitled applicant can only file a new application (**G3/92** r.5.8; A-IV,2.1). The right of the lawful applicant outweighs the legal uncertainty of third parties. A third party having commenced infringing commercial activities after the lapse of the usurping application and before the filing of the new application must seek his rights in an infringement procedure before a national court in an application of **Art.122(5)** mutatis mutandis. (**G3/92** r.6)

A minority of the members of the Enlarged Board in the above case held the opinion that the words 'not yet' in **Art.61(1)** EPC 1973 suppose that the usurping application is still in the granting stage, and that the article is not applicable to lapsed applications, thereby giving more legal security to third parties than the above decision (likewise **T146/82**). It is the intention of the EPO that the solution of **G3/92** also applies to the revised EPC 2000.

4 **Refusal of application (Art.61(1)(c))**

The EPO must accede to the request to refuse the original application; the decision to refuse is open to appeal (**Art.106(1)**; A-IV,2.6). The refusal may only relate to those designated states and that subject-matter of the application to which the third party has become entitled.

Art. 61(2) Article 76, paragraph 1, shall apply mutatis mutandis to a new European patent application filed under paragraph 1(b).

Art.76(1) European divisional applications

1 **Similarity between new application and divisional application**

A new application filed under **Art.61(1)(b)** is regarded in most respects as a divisional application because of the reference in **Art.61(2)** to **Art.76(1)**. Hence, the provisions of **Art.76(1)** for a divisional application apply also to a new application. In particular, since **Art.76(1)** refers to the Implementing Regulations for filing a divisional application, these rules should also be applied to a new application in so far as the Implementing Regulations have no specific ruling for filing a new application. **Art.61(1)** refers to such specific rules. A new application and a divisional application are similar in respect of the following issues:

- The new application must be filed with a filing office of the EPO (**Art.76(1)**, **R.36(2)**; A-IV,2.5).
- The language of the new application must be the language of the proceedings of the original application or the language of the original application as filed if that was not an official EPO language (**R.36(2)**; A-VII,1.3).
- The new application has the same filing and priority date as the earlier application, provided the content of the new application does not extend beyond the subject-matter of the earlier application (**Art.76(1)**, **G3/92** r.5.4, see also **Art.100(c)**).
- The new application should be filed when the original earlier application is pending (**R.36(1)**). However, this is in conflict with **G3/92** and A-IV,2.1, as explained below.

Under EPC 1973 **Art.61(2)** did not refer to **Art.76(3)**, which stated that the procedure for filing the divisional application was laid down in the Implementing Regulations. A new application was bound by its own provisions (**R.15** and **16** EPC 1973). Hence, a new application was not bound by **R.25** EPC 1973 (**R.36** EPC 2000), which ruled that a divisional application may only be filed during pendency of the parent application; hence, a new application could be filed even if the earlier application was no longer pending (**G3/92** r.5.5, 5.6).

In EPC 2000 the reference to the procedure for filing the divisional has been transferred from **Art.76(3)** to **Art.76(1)**. Hence, the reference in **Art.61(2)** to **Art.76(1)** now includes a reference to the procedure for filing a divisional application. This procedure includes **R.36(1)**, for which there is no equivalent for a new application. Hence, a new application should be filed only relating to a pending earlier application. The change in the EPC has caused a conflict with one of the bearing motives of **G3/92**, causing uncertainty about whether or not a new application may still be filed where the earlier application is no longer pending. The EPO may amend the Implementing Regulations to make the law and the decision consistent.

It was the intention of the legislator to maintain the applicability of **G3/92** in view of the references to this decision in the footnote to **Art.61** in the 13th edition of the EPC (the blue book) and in A-IV,2.1 and C-IX,2.2). Hence, the Guidelines permit filing where the earlier application is no longer pending.

2 **Differences between new application and divisional application**
Art.61(1) refers to the Implementing Regulations for the filing of a new application. These rules should be applied instead of equivalent rules for filing a divisional application as referred to via **Art.61(2)** and **Art.76(1)**, since the former rules form leges speciali. Several rules specific for a new application lay down the same procedure as the rules for a divisional application.

- The application number of the earlier application must be given in the Request for Grant form (**R.41(2)(f)**).
- **Art.61(2)** does not refer to **Art.76(2)**, because the national entitlement decision may limit the designations to only some of the contracting states designated in the earlier application (see **R.17(1)**).
- The designation of inventor is governed by **R.60(2)**.
- The filing fee, search fee and designation fee must be paid in accordance with **R.17(2)** and (3).
- The renewal fees for a new application are only due in respect of the years following the year of its filing (**R.51(6)**). In contrast, for a divisional application they are due from the filing date of the parent application (**R.51(3)**).

Art. 62 Right of the inventor to be mentioned

The inventor shall have the right, vis-à-vis the applicant for or proprietor of a European patent, to be mentioned as such before the European Patent Office.

See for the implementation:
R.19 Designation of the inventor
R.20 Publication of the mention of the inventor
R.21 Rectification of the designation of an inventor

1 **Moral right of inventor**
The moral right of the inventor to be mentioned as expressed in **Art.62** is realized in **Art.81**, which requires that the inventor is designated in the European patent application.

Chapter III *Effects of the European patent and the European patent application*

1 **General**
Art.2(2) provides that a European patent shall have the same effect as a national patent, unless otherwise provided. This chapter gives provisions implementing some of these rights, relating to patent applications and patents which are binding on the contracting states and allowing national law to influence the effect of and conditions for European patent applications and patents. See NatLaw tables III, IV, V and IX for the specific provisions of the contracting states affecting European patent applications and patents.

The provisional protection conferred by a published application is governed by **Art.67**. This provisional protection is deemed not to have existed if the application does not lead to a patent (**Art.67(4)**). If it does lead to a patent, the provisional protection is replaced by the normal protection conferred by the patent under **Art.64** on the date of the grant. A revocation of the patent in subsequent opposition proceedings or limitation or revocation under **Art.105a** has as a result that the provisional and normal protection are deemed never to have existed (**Art.68**). A lapse or surrender of the patent ends the protection, but it does not change the rights up to the surrender or lapse. The extent of the provisional and normal protection is a matter of national law.

Art. 63 Term of the European patent

Art. 63(1) The term of the European patent shall be 20 years from the date of filing of the application.

1 **Term of patent**
A European patent has a uniform term of 20 years for all contracting states. The 20 year term is based on the legislator's opinion that by the expiry of the term the cost to society of the patent monopoly begins to exceed the benefits.

The relevant date for calculation of the 20-year term of the patent is the date of filing and not the priority date, which finds its basis in the Paris Convention **Art.4bis(5)**.

The EPC does not define the calculation of the expiry of the 20-year term; **R.131** defines the calculation of ‘periods’ and not ‘terms’. It neither defines whether or not the day of filing is included in the patent term. This lapse of the legislator in defining accurately one of the standard rules of a European patent has caused a divergence between contracting states. A difference of a day in the date of lapse may be important for the revenue of a party; it is also important for requesting a Supplementary Protection Certificate under **Art.63(2)**, which has to be made before lapse of the patent.

Some contracting states include the day of filing in the patent term, in this case ‘from the date of filing’ in **Art.63(1)** is interpreted as in **R.14(4)** and **R.142(4)**. Other contracting states regard the following day as the first day of the term. The 20 years may be calculated as ‘full years’. Hence, if the day of filing is 26.11.1979, the last day of validity of the patent will be 25.11.1999 for the validity starting on the day of filing and 26.11.1999 for it starting on the next day. Alternatively, the 20 years may be calculated according to **R.131(3)** with the day of filing as the day of the relevant event or the first day of validity as the day of relevant event in the sense of **R.131(2)**. In that case the last day of validity is 26.11.1999 or 27.11.1999.

The EPO intends to use the calculation of **R.131(3)** with the date of filing as the day of the relevant event for the patent term of the unitary patent (P:4.2), for which they will enter the date of lapse in the Register. The last day of validity using this calculation agrees with the method used by the EPO to calculate the patent years for the purpose of renewal fee payments (OJ 1984, 272; see also **Art.86(1):1**).

Note, that the term is not extended under **R.134** on account of non-working days of the EPO.

After expiry of the term, each designated state informs the EPO of the date of lapse of the patent for its territory, which information is entered in the Register (**R.143(1)(p)**) during the opposition period and any opposition proceedings and in a special section of the Register thereafter. The date of lapse is not defined in the EPC. Some contracting states define it as the date of expiry of the term, i.e. the last day of validity of the patent; other states define it as the first day of invalidity.

The lack of proper definitions for the patent term and the date of lapse is visible in the Register. For example, the following data is given for the European patent EP 11 844: priority dates: 02.12.1978 and 10.08.1979, date of filing: 26.11.1979, date of lapse: 25.11.1999 (CH), 25.11.1999 (GB), 26.11.1999 (NL), 27.11.1999 (SE). For more legal certainty about the lapse of a specific patent, the national register should be inspected and the national patent office consulted about the meaning of the data in the national register. However, the information provided by national patent offices is not always consistent.

Harmonisation of the patent term is difficult, because the differences in interpretation have been enshrined in national practice and law. A forced harmonisation could be achieved through **Art.173**.

Art. 63(2) Nothing in the preceding paragraph shall limit the right of a Contracting State to extend the term of a European patent, or to grant corresponding protection which follows immediately on expiry of the term of the patent, under the same conditions as those applying to national patents:

- **(a) in order to take account of a state of war or similar emergency conditions affecting that State;**
- **(b) if the subject-matter of the European patent is a product or a process for manufacturing a product or a use of a product which has to undergo an administrative authorisation procedure required by law before it can be put on the market in that State.**

1 **Extended term of patent**

Any state using or intending to make use of **Art.63(2)(b)** must inform the EPO of the conditions and duration of any extension of the term of patents or of a corresponding protection, in order to permit exchange of views within the Administrative Council (Act revising Art.63, Resolution on mutual information, OJ 1992, 1).

Art.63(2)(b) gives a proprietor of a patent a compensation in the form of an extended patent term for a delayed market introduction due to a lengthy administrative authorisation procedure, as is common for pharmaceuticals. Whereas the time from conception to market is usually between 5 and 8 years for an electronic device, it is in general more than 12 years for a medicament. All EU states must provide such Supplementary Protection Certificates for medicinal products under EU Regulation 1768/92. Switzerland also has corresponding national provisions.

According to EU regulation 1610/96 which entered into force on 08.02.1997, EU states may also grant supplementary protection certificates for plant protection products. The certificate provides for the extension of patent protection by up to five years and corresponds fully to the certificate for medicinal products. (OJ 1997, 77)

Art. 63(3) Paragraph 2 shall apply mutatis mutandis to European patents granted jointly for a group of Contracting States in accordance with Article 142.

Art.142 Unitary patent for group of states

Art. 63(4) A Contracting State which makes provision for extension of the term or corresponding protection under paragraph 2(b) may, in accordance with an agreement concluded with the Organisation, entrust to the European Patent Office tasks associated with implementation of the relevant provisions.

Art. 64 Rights conferred by a European patent

The provision is an elaboration of **Art.2(2)**, laying down the rights of a European patent in comparison with a national patent.

Art. 64(1) A European patent shall, subject to the provisions of paragraph 2, confer on its proprietor from the date on which the mention of its grant is published in the European Patent Bulletin, in each Contracting State in respect of which it is granted, the same rights as would be conferred by a national patent granted in that State.

1 **Rights conferred by patent**
The main right granted in most states is to prevent others from using the invention. Other rights may provide what acts of third persons constitute infringement and what remedies are available in respect of any infringement.

Many EPC states have made the conferment of rights dependent on the filing of a translation of the specification (see **Art.65**). The rights are effective immediately after the publication of the mention of the grant, but become void ex tunc if the national requirements have not been met (NatLaw table IV, note 2). See also the comments on the London Agreement under **Art.65(1)**.

Art. 64(2) If the subject-matter of the European patent is a process, the protection conferred by the patent shall extend to the products directly obtained by such process.

1 **Protection of product directly obtained by a process**
Art.64(2) extends the protection conferred by a process patent to the products obtained directly by the process, even if the products are not patentable per se. Hence, the protection may extend to a known product (not patentable under **Art.52(1)**) or a plant variety (not patentable under **Art.53(b)**). The non-patentability of the product does not affect the examination of the process claim, because **Art.64** does not belong to the requirements of the EPC on patentability to be examined (**Art.52-57**) but to the provisions concerning the effects of patents and patent applications to be applied by national courts deciding on infringement. (**G1/98** r.4)

Similarly, the examination of the patentability of product or product-by-process claims is not affected by the extent of the protection conferred by the claims (**G2/12** r.VIII,2(6)(b); F-IV,4.12).

Art.64(2) was particularly important historically for contracting states having made reservations under **Art.167(2)** EPC 1973, not giving protection for certain products: Greece for pharmaceutical products, Spain for chemical and pharmaceutical products. The reservations terminated on 07.10.1992.

Art.64(2) does not confer the novelty of the process to the product (**T248/85** hn1). If the product itself is not inventive, it may not be claimed in the form of a product claim, not even in the form of a product-by-process claim (**T150/82** r.10).

The protection of a product by a process claim under **Art.64(2)** applies to all processes, i.e. to processes producing products completely different from the starting materials as well as to processes producing only superficial changes as polishing and painting (F-IV,4.12).

Most national laws assume that a new product, the production process of which has been patented and which is manufactured by a third party, is made according to the patented process, unless the third party provides proof to the contrary. The UPC uses the same reversal of the burden of proof for product-by-process infringement for a new product (Art. 55(1) UPC). The EPC has not taken over this provision, because infringement of a European patent must be sued nationally or under the UPC.

The UPC Agreement and harmonised national law of the contracting states extend the protection of the direct product to import of the product and further use of it (Art. 25(c) UPCA). Proof of infringement of an imported product may be difficult when the importer has discharged the burden of proof and the process has been carried out in a country where the process is not protected and no access to the production facilities is possible. Evidence that novel features of the product, such as impurity concentrations, point toward the patented process may be helpful.

2 Product-by-process claim

The automatic product-by-process protection of **Art.64(2)** should be distinguished from the protection provided by a product-by-process claim. The special protection of **Art.64(2)** extends even to products which are not patentable per se, and covers known products, but it is limited to products which are directly obtained by the patented process (**Art.64(2)**).

A product-by-process claim is a product claim that defines the product in terms of a manufacturing process (F-IV,4.12). It covers the product made by any process and gives the broadest possible protection. However, the product itself must be patentable, and, therefore, the claim may not cover known products. (**G1/98** r.4; **T150/82**)

Product-by-process claims should be restricted to those cases where another definition of the product is not possible. Product-by-process claims are only allowed in so far the products themselves are patentable, i.e. comply with the provisions of **Art.52** to **57**, and there is no other information available in the application which could enable the applicant to define the product satisfactorily by reference to its structure, composition or any testable parameter. (**T150/82, T248/85, T664/90; T1242/06** r.45)

As an example, the limit of a range in a product claim can only be satisfactorily given in terms of a process feature, because the alternative, a feature in the form of a desired property, is not allowed in some contracting states (**T129/88** r.2.2.3/4). An improved product quality alone is not generally considered a structural feature allowing a product-by-process claim (**T394/03**).

Art. 64(3) Any infringement of a European patent shall be dealt with by national law.

1 **Infringement**

Although the unitary patent does not yet exist, the infringement procedure in one state may have already effects in other states due to the Brussels I Regulation on jurisdiction of courts and the recognition and enforcement of judgements in civil and commercial matters in EU countries (cross-border injunctions).

The EPC lays down only two rules for the substantive law during a national infringement procedure: the scope of protection (**Art.69**) and the product-by-process protection (**Art.64(2)**). In an infringement procedure the EPO is only competent to give a technical opinion on request (**Art.25**). All other questions must be solved by national law.

The authentic text of the patent specification in the national infringement proceedings is determined by **Art.70**.

A third party can start a procedure for obtaining a ruling on infringement after the mention of the grant of the patent, because the proprietor obtains his rights at that moment (**Art.64(1)**). If during an opposition procedure before the EPO an infringement procedure is started, the alleged infringer can intervene in the opposition procedure (**Art.105**). National law determines whether or not the national court will postpone taking a decision on the infringement till after the decision in the opposition procedure.

Art. 65 Translation of the European patent

1 **Validation of the European patent**

The steps to be carried out to obtain a valid patent in a designated contracting state after grant of a European patent are called validation. This validation of a patent should be distinguished from the validation of a non-contracting state for a European patent application as set out in **Art.79(2):2.2**, which is a kind of designation.

The requirements for validation are different for different contracting states and are set out in the brochure NatLaw table IV, where the html version on the EPO web site is more up to date than the pdf version. The steps may include:

- Filing a translation of the claims or the entire specification in an official language of a state if the patent is not granted in an official language of that state (**Art.65(1)**); mark the special requirements for some states. Several states have limited their translation requirements by becoming party to the London Agreement (see **Art.65(1):2**).
- Appointment of a professional representative authorised to act before the national office.
- Payment of a fee for publishing the translation (**Art.65(2)**).
- Payment of a national renewal fee.
- Use of a prescribed form.

CH and LI must be validated together (**Art.142(1)**).

For most contracting states the validation must be carried out within three months from the publication of the grant. A few states have a longer period. However, a proprietor may already have to act within two months from publication. If a national renewal fee falls due within two months of publication, it must be paid before expiry of the two months (**Art.141(2)**); payment should not be postponed to expiry of the three month period. It is unfortunate that the legislator has chosen different periods for filing the translations and paying the national renewal fee. Note, that the invitation to pay the national renewal fee will be sent to the proprietor and not to his representative if no different address for service has been recorded with the national office. A proprietor may regard such an invitation as a hoax letter (see OJ 2014 A42).

Several states that have acceded to the London Agreement have no requirements for filing a translation and paying a fee for publishing. When a European patent is granted, it becomes automatically and immediately a valid patent in these countries. Such a patent will lapse if the national renewal fee is not paid. The automatic validation may have consequences for co-pending national patents under **Art.139(3)**. If e.g. the proprietor has prosecuted a national GB application to grant and a co-pending European application claiming priority from the GB application is also granted with the same scope of protection, the GB patent will be revoked at expiry of the unavailed opposition period or closure of the opposition proceedings where the European patent has been maintained. The proprietor can avoid the loss of the GB patent by having different scopes of protection, withdrawing the GB designation before grant of the European patent or surrendering the EP(GB) patent before the GB patent will be revoked.

States that do have requirements regarding translation and fee for publishing will regard the European patent to be void ab initio in that state if the requirements have not been complied with (**Art.65(3)**). Hence, the above problem for a co-pending national patent does not occur.

2 **Translation of the patent**

The EPO publishes a European patent in the language of the proceedings with claims in all three official EPO languages (**Art.14(6)** and **R.71(3)**). Since a patent may have a considerable effect on commercial activities, a state may request under **Art.65(1)** a translation in one of its official languages in order to improve the understanding of the patent. A contracting state may request such a translation after grant when the patent is validated for that state and after amendment or limitation in opposition or limitation proceedings. The London Agreement limits the options to request a translation for contracting states acceded to it, thereby relaxing the translation requirements for the patent proprietor.

A country demanding a translation may publish the translation and request the proprietor to pay at least part of the cost of publication (**Art.65(2)**). When the proprietor does not file the translation or pay any fee for publishing for a contracting state, the patent may be deemed void ab initio in that state (**Art.65(3)**).

Art. 65(1) Any Contracting State may, if the European patent as granted, amended or limited by the European Patent Office is not drawn up in one of its official languages, prescribe that the proprietor of the patent shall supply to its central industrial property office a translation of the patent as granted, amended or limited in one of its official languages at his option or, where that State has prescribed the use of one specific official language, in that language. The period for supplying the translation shall end three months after the date on which the mention of the grant, maintenance in amended form or limitation of the European patent is published in the European Patent Bulletin, unless the State concerned prescribes a longer period.

Relevant provisions:
Art.97(3) Publication of the mention of the grant
Art.98 Content of specification (no abstract)
Art.103 Publication of a patent maintained in amended form

R.71(3) Invitation to approve text to be granted

1 **Translation of patent in language of contracting state**

Art.65(1) allows a contracting state to request a translation of the European patent when it is not drawn up in one of its official languages. A group of states has reduced the translation requirements by acceding to the London Agreement (see next section).

The translation requirements for each contracting state and extension state can be found in the regularly updated html version of NatLaw, Table IV on the EPO website (search for 'national law html'). The paper and pdf versions of NatLaw are often outdated. NatLaw also provides details relating to the appointment of a national representative, the period for filing the translation and any extension, the way to file and payment of fees (relatively high for some states) for validation.

The translation must be provided of the patent as granted, amended in opposition (**R.82(2)**) or limited in limitation (**R.95(3)**) proceedings. All contracting states allow correction of the translation under the conditions of **Art.70(3)** and (4). Whereas a contracting state may require translation of the complete patent under **Art.65(1)**, it may only require a translation of the claims of a patent application for obtaining provisional protection under **Art.67**.

According to **Art.65(1)** the translations of the patent in an official language of a designated state must be provided within a period of at least 3 months from the publication date of mention of the grant. All contracting states have a period of 3 months, except Iceland, allowing 4 months, and San Marino, allowing 6 months. Note that the translation of the claims of the patent in two official EPO languages must be filed earlier, i.e. within the time limit for response to the **R.71(3)** communication, requesting the applicant to approve of the text intended for grant.

2 **London Agreement**

The optional 'Agreement on the application of Article 65 EPC' or 'London Agreement' has the objective to reduce the cost of European patents by at least partly waiving the translation requirements of **Art.65(1)** (OJ2001, 550). It has a legal basis in **Art.149a** and entered into force on 01.05.2008 (OJ 2008, 123). Information on the contracting states bound by the Agreement and their translation requirements is available in the html version of NatLaw on the epo website. A list of contracting states to the Agreement is provided in **Art.169:1.1**.

A state party to the Agreement having an official EPO language, English, German or French, as an official language will not require a translation of any European patent under **Art.65(1)**.

A state not having English, German or French as official language will neither require a translation in its official language if the patent is granted in the official EPO language prescribed by that state or translated into that language. However, such a state may request that the claims be translated in one of its official languages. Note, that requesting a translation of the claims only is probably outside the scope of **Art.65(1)**, which merely provides for requesting 'a translation of the patent'.

A state may prescribe that in the case of a dispute the proprietor must supply at the request of an infringer or a court a translation of the patent in an official language of the state concerned.

Art. 65(2) Any Contracting State which has adopted provisions pursuant to paragraph 1 may prescribe that the proprietor of the patent must pay all or part of the costs of publication of such translation within a period laid down by that State.

1 **Fee for publishing**
A state that prescribes that a translation of a European patent must be supplied, may also demand payment of a fee for publishing the translation. NatLaw table IV indicates for each state whether a translation and payment of the fee are required.

The fee for publishing does not have a well-defined name. The following names are also used: fee for publication, special fee, publication fee, national validation fee. The fee of **Art.65(2)** should not be confused with the validation fee for extending the effect of a European patent application and patent to a non-contracting state (see **Art.79(2):2.2**).

Art. 65(3) Any Contracting State may prescribe that in the event of failure to observe the provisions adopted in accordance with paragraphs 1 and 2, the European patent shall be deemed to be void ab initio in that State.

1 **Failure to provide translation**
All states that require a translation have made use of this provision (NatLaw introduction to table IV, note 2). Re-establishment in the case of a late filing cannot be made under **Art.122**, because the non-observed time limit is not vis-à-vis the EPO (**Art.122(6)**); a possible re-establishment must be made under national law.

The Court of Justice of the European Communities has ruled in its decision C-44/98 of 21.09.1999 that the right of a contracting state to prescribe the filing of a translation on penalty of loss of the patent does not contravene the EC Treaty; the division of the EU market in a protected and an unprotected area, caused by the limitation of protection to fewer than the desired number of states due to the costs of translations, is not regarded as an obstacle to the free movement of goods as enshrined in the EC Treaty.

Art. 66 Equivalence of European filing with national filing

A European patent application which has been accorded a date of filing shall, in the designated Contracting States, be equivalent to a regular national filing, where appropriate with the priority claimed for the European patent application.

1 **European filing equivalent to national filing**
The provision brings the European application in line with the Paris Convention: the filing must be recognized by all states of the Paris Convention for the right of priority (**Art.4A(1),(2)** Paris Convention).

The extension of the equivalence to priority rights gives the European patent application a much stronger right in a state than only the right to a filing date. The right of priority also applies to utility models and utility certificates (**Art.87(1)**).

The priority rights in the designated states allow a conversion of the European application into a national application while maintaining its priority claim (**Art.135**).

According to **Art.140** a European patent application is also equivalent to a national utility model and a utility certificate.

The equivalence is the basis for the provisional protection under **Art.67**.
The date of filing is given when the Receiving Section has come to the conclusion according to **Art.90(1)** that the application fulfils the requirements of **Art.80**. The claimed priorities are also included in this provision.

Art. 67 Rights conferred by a European patent application after publication

Art. 67(1) A European patent application shall, from the date of its publication, provisionally confer upon the applicant the protection provided for by Article 64, in the Contracting States designated in the application.

Art.64 Rights conferred by a European patent

1 **Provisional rights conferred by application**
This provision states the basic principle that the application after publication gives the same rights in a designated contracting state as the granted patent (**Art.2(2)**), albeit provisionally. The extent of protection is defined in **Art.69(2)**. **Art.67(2)** gives a possibility for states to escape this far-reaching provision by providing a reduced protection. The countries giving the same protection as the granted patent are given in NatLaw table III.A, column 2.

Since the publication of an application designates all contracting states, the application enjoys provisional protection in all contracting states. However, this effect is deemed never to have occurred if the relevant designation is withdrawn or deemed to be withdrawn (**Art.79(3)**.

The provisional protection starts on the day of publication of the application. It is immaterial whether or not the search report or the mention of the publication in the Patent Bulletin is published at the same date (**Art.127**, **R.143(1)**, **Art.129(a)**). A third party can start an opposition or revocation procedure only after the grant of the patent. The applicant is informed of the intended publication date by a communication of the EPO issued about 4 weeks prior to the **Art.93(1)** publication (see **R.67(2):1**).

A not-regularly published application does not give rise to provisional protection (**Art.67(4)**). An application is not regularly published if it is withdrawn before the date of publication but too late to prevent publication.

The provisional protection is also applicable to the designated extension states according to the Extension Ordinance, Art.4 (OJ 1994, 80). See PCT §5.5 for the provisional protection conferred by an international application.

Art. 67(2) Any Contracting State may prescribe that a European patent application shall not confer such protection as is conferred by Article 64. However, the protection attached to the publication of the European patent application may not be less than that which the laws of the State concerned attach to the compulsory publication of unexamined national patent applications. In any event, each State shall ensure at least that, from the date of publication of a European patent application, the applicant can claim compensation reasonable in the circumstances from any person who has used the invention in that State in circumstances where that person would be liable under national law for infringement of a national patent.

1 **Minimum rights conferred by application**
All contracting states regard a European application as a national application in regard of the provisional protection. See NatLaw table III.A for the different provisions for each state: all states have provided for either compensation reasonable in the circumstances or damages.

Art. 67(3) Any Contracting State which does not have as an official language the language of the proceedings may prescribe that provisional protection in accordance with paragraphs 1 and 2 above shall not be effective until such time as a translation of the claims in one of its official languages at the option of the applicant or, where that State has prescribed the use of one specific official language, in that language:
(a) has been made available to the public in the manner prescribed by national law, or
(b) has been communicated to the person using the invention in the said State.

1 **Translation for provisional protection**
A state that does not have the language of the proceedings as an official language may make the provisional protection dependent on the filing of a translation of the claims in one of its official languages. NatLaw table III.B indicates which states have made use of this provision. The table gives for each state any requirements for appointing a national representative, any fee payable and the permitted languages.

All states, except Malta and Switzerland, require a translation of the claims under **Art.67(3)** if the language of proceedings is not an official language of that state (NatLaw table III.A, column 3). The translation is made available to the public by inspection, by mention in a bulletin, by a printed publication, or by entry in the national patent register.

The translations required for obtaining provisional rights are not governed by the London Agreement, which relates only to translations after grant (**Art.65(1):2**). For example, when the language of proceedings is English, France requires a French translation of the claims for provisional protection but does not require a translation of the granted patent specification. Note, that the granted claims will be available in the three EPO languages, one in the language of proceedings and two in translation under **Art.14(6)**.

There is no time limit for filing the translation. However, the protection is only effective after publication of the translation (**Art.67(3)(a)**) or after communication to the person using the invention (**Art.67(3)(b)**). See NatLaw table III.A, column 4 for the start of protection for each state. Most states use provision (a) and about a fifth of them in addition provision (b). As an exception, the protection in the Netherlands begins 30 days after the user has been notified of the applicant's rights by a so-called writ accompanied by a translation of the claims in Dutch or an indication that the translation has been entered in the patent register.

The EPO provides information on the requirements of **Art.67(3)** in a communication sent about four weeks prior to the publication of the patent application, in which it also informs the applicant of the intended publication date (OJ 1991, 224; see **R.67(1):1**).

The provisional protection also applies to Euro-PCT applications after their publication (**Art.153(2), Art.93, Art.67**). If the international application is not published in an official language of the EPO, the provisional protection under **Art.67** starts only after publication of the translation by the EPO (**Art.153(4)**). For example, where the international application is published in Japanese and an English translation is published by the EPO under

Art.153(4), the protection for Great Britain starts on the date of publication of the English translation (**Art.67(1)**) but the protection for Germany starts only after a translation of the claims in German has been published or sent to the user (**Art.67(3)**).

Art. 67(4) The European patent application shall be deemed never to have had the effects set out in paragraphs 1 and 2 when it has been withdrawn, deemed to be withdrawn or finally refused. The same shall apply in respect of the effects of the European patent application in a Contracting State the designation of which is withdrawn or deemed to be withdrawn.

1 **Retroactive effect of withdrawal and refusal of application**
The application is finally refused at the end of the period for filing an appeal following a decision to refuse, or, if appealed, at the end of the appeal procedure (see **Art.106(1):2**).

The provisional protection of an allowable application ends the day before the day of publication of the grant of the patent. It is then replaced by the normal protection of the patent.

Art. 68 Effect of revocation or limitation of the European patent

The European patent application and the resulting European patent shall be deemed not to have had, from the outset, the effects specified in Articles 64 and 67, to the extent that the patent has been revoked or limited in opposition, limitation or revocation proceedings.

Art.64 Rights conferred by a European patent
Art.67 Rights conferred by a European patent application after publication

1 **Retroactive effect of limitation and revocation of patent**
Art.68 uniformly establishes the retroactive effect of limitation and revocation. A European patent application and patent are deemed not to have conferred any rights ex tunc in the designated contracting states to the extent that the patent is revoked or limited in opposition proceedings according to **Art.101(2)** and (3), in limitation or revocation proceedings under **Art.105a** or in national revocation proceedings. The same provision for withdrawal and refusal is given in **Art.67(4)**. The inclusion of national revocation proceedings in **Art.68** formalises the achieved harmonisation in all contracting states of the ex tunc effect of the revocation of European patents. (Spec. Ed. 4 of OJ 2007)

Since a European patent has the effect of a national patent (**Art.64(1)** and **Art.2(2)**), the annulment of the rights according to the EPC is binding on all designated contracting states, also on those states having different national provisions.

The revoked patent remains valid prior art. Renewal fees cannot be refunded. A refund of already paid licence fees depends on the particular conditions of the licence contract and national law. An infringer may be liable to pay compensation if the proprietor has taken action against him before the date of revocation, depending on national law.

Art. 69 Extent of protection

1 **General**

The extent of protection of a patent determines the outcome of infringement proceedings and thereby the actual value of the patent. Since a European patent shall confer the same rights as a national patent (**Art.64(1)**) and infringement of European patent is dealt with by national law (**Art.2(2)** and **64(3)**), it is accepted that a European patent will confer different protection in different contracting states. **Art.69(1)** tries to limit this divergence by giving guidance to national courts for the harmonization of the historically diverging interpretations of patents. A unified interpretation of the European patent and a determination of the extent of protection in accordance with **Art.69** will give the proprietor more legal certainty. To strengthen the provision, a Protocol on the Interpretation of **Art.69** has been appended. The provision prevents a wide interpretation by the national courts, including the protection of the general inventive concept, as in Germany; it also prevents a narrow interpretation adhering to the exact wording of the claims, as in the United Kingdom. The overview of national case law in Singer Art.69, rdn. 7 shows the present degree of harmonization of patent interpretation.

Note that the extent of protection of a European patent need not be the same for all designated contracting states in consequence of European or national prior rights (**R.138**), reservations under former **Art.167(2)** EPC 1973, or a partial transfer of right (**R.18**).

Art. 69(1) The extent of the protection conferred by a European patent or a European patent application shall be determined by the claims. Nevertheless, the description and drawings shall be used to interpret the claims.

See for the implementation: Protocol on the interpretation of Art.69 of the Convention

1 **Extent of protection determined by claims**

Pursuant to **Art.69(1)**, the extent of protection conferred by a patent or a patent application is determined by the claims, the description and drawings being used to interpret those claims (see also **Art.84**, **R.43 - 45**).

Note that under EPC 1973 the English version of **Art.69(1)** referred to the 'terms of the claims', pointing to the literal meaning, whereas the German and French versions referred to 'Inhalt' and 'teneur', suggesting a broader interpretation. **Art.69(1)** EPC 2000 refers only to the claims as such, not their terms.

In combination with the Protocol on the Interpretation of **Art.69**, it is made clear that the interpretation of the claims serves not only to resolve any ambiguities in the claims but also to clarify the technical terms used therein, as well as to clarify the significance and scope of the invention. The interpretation must be made by the skilled person, not by a philologist. Terms in the claims and description must therefore be construed as they would be by the skilled person in view of the overall content of the specification, according to the idea behind the invention, having regard to the problem and solution as derived from the patent (see **R.42(1)(c)**). (German Federal Court of Justice, OJ 2001,259)

Where the description states that a feature is necessary for the invention, the claims can be interpreted to contain this feature, even if they do not explicitly state so (**T416/87**). The drawings have a comparable function (**T169/83**).

If an applicant has declared during grant proceedings that he does not seek protection for a particular embodiment, he may not broaden the extent of protection of his patent to cover this embodiment. The principle of good faith requires him to adhere to his declaration. (German Federal Court of Justice, OJ 1998,141)

Art. 69(2) For the period up to grant of the European patent, the extent of the protection conferred by the European patent application shall be determined by the claims contained in the application as published. However, the European patent as granted or as amended in opposition, limitation or revocation proceedings shall determine retroactively the protection conferred by the application, in so far as such protection is not thereby extended.

1 **Extent of protection before and after grant**

The extent of the protection of a patent application before grant is determined by the latest filed claims contained in the publication of the application (**Art.69(2)**). This is either the European patent application published under **Art.93** or the Euro-PCT application published pursuant to **Art.153(3)** (WO publication) or (4) (translation published by EPO). Since **Art.69(2)**, second sentence, refers to the limitation proceedings and national revocation proceedings, a limitation of the patent in any of these proceedings retroactively limits the extent of protection conferred by the application. (Spec. Ed. 4 of OJ 2007)

The applicant may amend the claims after receipt of the search report (**Art.123** and **R.137(1)**). If he makes use of this opportunity before the end of the technical preparations for publication (**R.67(1)**, five weeks before publication), the application will be published including the claims as filed and the amended claims (**R.68(4)**); the amended claims determine the extent of the provisional protection. Voluntary amendment is only allowed together with the first substantive response (**R.137(2)**).

The extent of the protection of a patent after grant is determined by the claims as granted or amended in opposition or limitation proceedings (**Art.69(1)**). Any amendment of the claims during opposition or limitation proceedings may not extend the protection (**Art.123(3)**). The claims as granted or amended in opposition or limitation proceedings also determine retroactively the provisional protection of the application provided this protection is not extended compared with the protection of the claims of the published application (**Art.69(2)**, second sentence).

In other words: even if the claims of the patent as granted are broader than those of the application as published, which may be the case provided there is a basis for that in the application as filed, third parties' rights are not affected by such broadening for the period up to grant of the patent; if on the other hand, the claims of the patent as granted are narrower than those of the application as published, third parties are benefiting from this as from the outset. (**G1/93** r.10)

When a patent is maintained in opposition or limitation proceedings with amended claims and scope making a started infringement procedure without grounds, an already paid compensation or damages must be reimbursed. If the patent is not granted or is revoked in opposition or revocation proceedings, the effects are regarded as non-existent ex tunc (**Art.67(4)**, **Art.68**); this retroactively takes away all rights to a compensation.

Art. 70 Authentic text of a European patent application or European patent

1 **General**
This provision determines the authentic text of the application and patent. It indicates the importance of the language of the proceedings in procedures before the EPO and before authorities in each contracting state.

Art. 70(1) The text of a European patent application or a European patent in the language of the proceedings shall be the authentic text in any proceedings before the European Patent Office and in any Contracting State.

1 **Authentic text of application and patent in proceedings**
The language of the proceedings is the language in which the application or its translation has been filed (**Art.14(3)**). The wording of the claims of a European patent in other official EPO languages as filed under **R.71(3)** carries no legal weight (A-VII,8).

Mistakes in the specification of a patent (**Art.98**) arising in the course of its production have no effect on the content of the patent granted. The published specification is for information purposes only and has no legally binding character. Only the text on which the decision to grant the patent (**Art.97(1)** and **R.71a(1)**) is based is decisive. (C-V,10)

Art. 70(2) If, however, the European patent application has been filed in a language which is not an official language of the European Patent Office, that text shall be the application as filed within the meaning of this Convention.

See for the implementation:
R.7 Legal authenticity of the translation of the European patent application

1 **Authentic text of the application as filed**
Art.70(2) establishes that if a European patent application is filed in a language which is not an official language of the EPO, that text is the 'application as filed' for:
- **Art.14(2)**: bringing translation into conformance with application as filed;
- **Art.54(3)**: establishing content of a prior right (A-VII,7; G-IV,5.1);
- **Art.61(1)(b)** and **(2)**: determining extension of subject-matter for a new application filed after an entitlement suit;
- **Art.76(1)**: extension of subject-matter of a divisional application;
- **Art.100(c)**: extension of subject-matter of a patent in opposition proceedings;
- **Art.123(2)**: extension of subject-matter when amending a patent application; and
- **Art.138(1)(c)**: extension of subject-matter in national revocation proceedings. (Spec. Ed. 4 of OJ 2007)

The EPO need not investigate the correctness of the translation of its own motion; it may assume the translation is correct (**R.7**, which is a lex specialis of **Art.114**, D-V,6.1), unless someone provides proof to the contrary. Although the EPO is not obliged to check the correctness, it may do so if it suspects errors.

If the translation in an official EPO language or an amendment during prosecution has extended the subject-matter of the application, **Art.70(2)** prescribes the use of the original text in the non-EPO language for determining the extension. An extension of the subject-matter is a ground for opposition (**Art.100(c)**) and revocation (**Art.138(1)(c)**).

Whether the original filing in a non-EPO language is also 'the application as filed' for a Euro-PCT application filed with the EPO as receiving Office depends on whether or not the filing referred to in **Art.70(2)** must have been with the EPO. If the filing is restricted to the EPO, **Art.70(2)** will not be applicable, because a Euro-PCT application can only be filed with the EPO in an official EPO language (**R.157(2)**). The issue has not been settled. See also **R.159(1):2.1**.

Note, that a correction of a translation during opposition proceedings will not be allowed if it extends the protection conferred, thereby offending against **Art.123(3)** (A-VII,7).

Art. 70(3) Any Contracting State may provide that a translation into one of its official languages, as prescribed by it according to this Convention, shall in that State be regarded as authentic, except for revocation proceedings, in the event of the European patent application or European patent in the language of the translation conferring protection which is narrower than that conferred by it in the language of the proceedings.

1 **Authentic text in the case of narrow translation**

States may request a translation of the claims of the application (**Art.67(3)**) and of the patent (**Art.65(1)**). Such a translation can become the authentic text under **Art.70(3)** in the case that the translation provides a narrower scope of protection than the text in the language of the proceedings. In revocation proceedings the text in the language of the proceedings is authentic.

Belgium and Germany have not made use of **Art.70(3)** and the authentic text is always that in the language of the proceedings (see NatLaw table V).

Art. 70(4) Any Contracting State which adopts a provision under paragraph 3:

(a) **shall allow the applicant for or proprietor of the patent to file a corrected translation of the European patent application or European patent. Such corrected translation shall not have any legal effect until any conditions established by the Contracting State under Article 65, paragraph 2, or Article 67, paragraph 3, have been complied with;**

(b) **may prescribe that any person who, in that State, in good faith has used or has made effective and serious preparations for using an invention the use of which would not constitute infringement of the application or patent in the original translation, may, after the corrected translation takes effect, continue such use in the course of his business or for the needs thereof without payment.**

Art.65(2) Payment for publication of the translation of the patent in an official language of a state

Art.67(3) Publication of the translation of the claims of the application in an official language of a contracting state

1 **Correction of narrow translation**

All countries that regard the translation with a narrower scope of protection as the authentic text have provisions pursuant to paragraph (b). See NatLaw table V, column 2. See OJ2011, 398 for an example of the legal effect of a translation error in a patent.

See **Art.122(5)** for a right of continued use after re-establishment of rights equivalent to the right of paragraph (b).

Chapter IV *The European patent application as an object of property*

1 **Transfer and licencing**

A patent application can have a considerable economic and financial value. It must therefore be able to take part in legal actions, such as transfer and licensing, in each state. The legal matters related to property aspects of national applications and patents have been provided in national law. As the European patent application extends its effect over several states, some emerging property questions must be settled in the EPC. Therefore, the EPC has provided a uniform provision for transfer and licensing of applications and their registration in the European Patent Register.

Changes in the name of an applicant or proprietor, not involving a transfer of a right, will be entered in the Register on production of supporting evidence (E-XIV,5).

The transfer of an application before the EPO has effect in all designated states, and takes place through an act in law (**Art.72**), e.g. because of a sale, a gift, a last will, or because of a law, e.g. an inheritance. The rights in connection with an application may be the grant of a licence, rent, loan, usufruct, pawning, seizure. The requirements for the act of transfer of the application are laid down in **Art.72**. The EPC has no special provisions for the establishment of rights, apart from licensing (**Art.73**). Such rights must be established in conformance with national law (**Art.74**). The transfer becomes valid before the EPO only after payment of the appropriate fee and entry of the transfer in the European Patents Register (**R.22(1), (2)**).

2 **Competence**

The EPC provisions relating to the transfer of patent applications and patents primarily aim at ensuring that the EPO knows the correct applicant or proprietor during proceedings before it. The EPC does not have explicit provisions for the competence of the EPO and the national offices relating to the transfer and for national legal effects of a transfer registered with the EPO. The following reasoning gives a caesura for competence and legal effects at the date of mention of the grant. The reasoning is in line with the decisions of national courts published in OJ 1984, 276 and 1987, 438.

The EPC is a system of law, common to the contracting states, for the grant of patents (**Art.1**). Hence, only the EPO is competent in all matters provided for in the EPC relating to a European patent application, such as according a filing date, designation of inventor and registering of transfers. Therefore, **Art.71-73** and **R.22-24** pertaining to transfers and licensing are binding on the contracting states. In consonance, most contracting states have no provisions in their national law for registering a transfer of a European patent application other than copying the register information transmitted by the EPO. Thus, the registration of the transfer of an application before the EPO must have legal effect for the designated contracting states. As a consequence, national offices should not be competent to register the transfer of a European patent application. Legal matters relating to the property of European patent applications not provided for in the EPC follow national law (**Art.74**). Entitlement disputes for an application, for example, can only be decided by national courts (see **Art.61(1)** and Prot. on Rec.)

Art.2(2) and **Art.97(3)** delimit the periods during which the EPO and the national offices respectively are competent to decide on requests for the registration of transfers and licences. The European patent is subject to national law in matters of transfer according to **Art.2(2)**, because the EPC does not provide otherwise. Hence, after publication of the mention of the grant (**Art.97(3)**) the European Patents Register is for registration purposes only, and registration of a transfer as required by **R.85** has no national legal effects. **R.85** merely enables the EPO to keep up the Register till the end of the opposition period or opposition proceedings and it should not take precedence over national provisions for transfer of patents. The national offices alone are competent for effectively registering the transfer of a European patent with national legal effect. This applies also during the opposition period and opposition proceedings. Several states recognize under special conditions a transfer registered by the EPO under **R.85** (NatLaw table IX, column 6). The national requirements for registering a transfer of a European patent in the national patent registers are given in NatLaw table IX.

If, for example, a person to whom a European patent has been transferred wants to sue an infringer, he must have the transfer registered with the national office of the contracting state where the infringer is domiciled; a registration of the transfer of the patent with the EPO does not suffice.

A future Unitary Patent Regulation may centralize the registration of rights in respect of unitary patents. In that case, a transfer of or a licence in respect of a unitary patent will have effect vis-à-vis third parties in all contracting states after entry in the Register.

Art. 71 Transfer and constitution of rights

A European patent application may be transferred or give rise to rights for one or more of the designated Contracting States.

See for the implementation:
R.22 Registering a transfer of the patent application
R.85 Transfer of the European patent

1 **Transfers and licences**

The European patent application is treated as a unity according to uniform rules in the proceedings before the EPO (**Art.118**). This principle applies only partly to the application as an object of property due to the needs of the trade, which vary between states. Hence, a transfer of an application need not be made for all designated states as a whole but may be made for one or more states (**Art.71**). This is in concord with **Art.59**, allowing different applicants for different states. The transfer of the application and the associated rights applies to the whole territory of a contracting state (**Art.71**), whereas the transfer of licenses can be for part of the territory of a contracting state (**Art.73**).

The procedure and requirements for registering a transfer of a patent application before the EPO are provided in **R.22**. The transfer becomes effective for the EPO when the required documents have been filed and the fee paid (**R.22(3)**).

Although **Art.71** is applicable to transfers of applications only, according to **R.85** a transfer of a patent during the opposition period or the opposition proceedings and a possible appeal (**R.100(1)**) must also be entered in the Register in the same way as the transfer of an application, as prescribed in **R.22**, to become valid before the EPO. The registration is necessary for the EPO to know the correct parties in opposition proceedings.

Art. 72 Assignment

An assignment of a European patent application shall be made in writing and shall require the signature of the parties to the contract.

1 **Requirements for assignment**
An assignment is a legal transfer (Dutch: rechtsgeldige overdracht, German: rechtsgeschäftliche Übertragung). The formal document of the transfer of a patent application may not be made orally but must be in writing. The document must be signed by the parties to the contract according to **Art.72** (E-XIV,3). The practice of the EPO to accept a declaration of transfer signed by the assignor only has been abolished (E-XIV,3). A representative may sign an assignment only if he is authorised to do so. If one of two applicants wants to transfer his right to the application to another party, he can do so without the consent of the other applicant, provided national law or a contract do not rule differently.

National laws may prescribe different requirements for the transfer of a national application, such as authorisation by a notary, entry in a patent register, publication of the assignment, etc (see e.g. **J16/05** r.2.1). In contrast, an assignment of a European patent application complying with **Art.72** and **R.22** will be effective vis-à-vis the EPO and have legal effect in all contracting states (see **Art.74:1**).

In general, the EPO does not require the filing of the instrument of transfer but only of a document providing evidence that the transfer has taken place (**R.22(1)**). In case of doubt, the EPO may request filing of a certified copy of the instrument of transfer.

Art. 73 Contractual licensing

A European patent application may be licensed in whole or in part for the whole or part of the territories of the designated Contracting States.

See for the implementation:
R.22 Registering a transfer of the licence
R.23 Registering of licences and other rights
R.24 Special entries for licence registrations

1 **Registering of licences**
Licences are entered in the Register of European Patents according to **R.23** in the same way as transfers; see **R.143(1)(w)**. Before entry, a fee must be paid and evidence of the existence of the licence must be provided (**R.23(1)**, referring to **R.22(1)**, **(2)**).

Beware, **Art.73** applies to applications only, not to patents (see **R.85**). So, licences in respect of a patent cannot be registered with the EPO, not even during the opposition period, as the EPC has no provisions for it (see **R.23:1**). Licence registration for patents must satisfy national requirements, independently of the opposition procedure.

Art. 74 Law applicable

Unless this Convention provides otherwise, the European patent application as an object of property shall, in each designated Contracting State and with effect for such State, be subject to the law applicable in that State to national patent applications.

1 **Application of national law**

Art.74 is one of the provisions of the EPC, together with **Art.66** (equivalence of European filing with national filing) and **Art.67** (rights conferred by a European patent application after publication), that makes a choice between a harmonized system and a system with different laws for each state. The envisaged uniform provision for the application as object of property turned out not to be possible. The present compromise can cause difficulties in certain cases; see e.g. **J4/10.**

Art.71-73 and **R.22-24, 85** are examples of the 'otherwise specified'; hence, these EPC provisions overrule national law.

Art.148 allows a group of contracting states to specify property rules uniform for the group and not depending on national law. The rules may deviate from **Art.71-73.** It allows the group to move towards a unified patent application that can be transferred, mortgaged or executed only collectively for all states of the group.

The EPO makes an entry of a transfer (**Art.71, 72, 73**) only if its validity is clear. Because the transfers are often complex international civil law affairs, the assessment of the validity by the EPO is kept within sensible bounds according to **R.22(1).**

The competence of an applicant to perform legal acts related to the property rights of his application or patent must be decided by national law, because such an issue is of a property nature not laid down in the EPC, and hence falling under **Art.74** (**J900/85** r.9, sometimes referred to as JXX/XX).

PART III THE EUROPEAN PATENT APPLICATION

Chapter I *Filing and requirements of the European patent application*

Art. 75 Filing of a European patent application

1 **Transitional provision EPC 2000**
The revised **Art.75** is applicable to European patent applications filed on or after the time of the EPC 2000 entry into force. (Spec. Ed. 4, OJ 2007)

2 **General**
A European patent application must be filed with the EPO according to **Art.75** and **R.35(1)** using a method of filing permitted by **R.2**. The date of filing accorded to the application will be the date of receipt by an office permitted by **R.35(1)** in a form allowed by **R.2**, provided the requirements of **Art.80** are met. An application filed with an office other than the ones mentioned in **R.35(1)** may be forwarded by that office to the EPO as a courtesy service and will be accorded as date of receipt, the date on which the application arrives at the EPO.

An applicant has, in general, the choice of filing his European patent application with the EPO or with a national authority of a contracting state (**Art.75(1)**). However, national law may restrict the choice by prescribing that the applicant must file the European patent application with a national authority (**Art.75(2)**). A European divisional application and a new application under **Art.61** must always be filed directly with the EPO (**Art.61(2)** and **Art.76(1)**).

Art. 75(1) A European patent application may be filed:
(a) with the European Patent Office, or
(b) if the law of a Contracting State so permits, and subject to Article 76, paragraph 1, with the central industrial property office or other competent authority of that State. Any application filed in this way shall have the same effect as if it had been filed on the same date with the European Patent Office.

Art.76(1) European divisional applications
See for the implementation:
R.35 Filing of the patent application

1 **EPO filing offices** (**Art.75(1)(a)**)

Any applicant may, subject to national security provisions under **Art.75(2)**, file his European patent application with the EPO. The filing offices of the EPO are specified in **R.35(1)**. The reference to **Art.76(1)** in subparagraph (b) is a reminder that a divisional application must be filed directly with the EPO.

Promptly after receipt of the application the EPO issues a receipt to the applicant stating the application number and the date of receipt of the documents making up the application (**R.35(2)**). Subsequently, the Receiving Section carries out the examination on filing according to **Art.90**, determining amongst others, whether the requirements for accordance of a date of filing are satisfied.

2 **National filing offices** (**Art.75(1)(b)**)

All contracting states except the Netherlands allow applicants to file European patent applications with their national authorities (NatLaw table II, column 1). NatLaw Table II, column 3 gives the languages in which a European application must or may be filed with a national office. See **Art.14(2):1**.

A few states that do not have an EPO language as official language, e.g. Cyprus and Spain, require that a European patent application filed with its national patent office and which is not in an official language of that state must be accompanied or followed by a translation in an official language of the state (NatLaw Table II, column 5).

Most contracting states limit the choice of filing office pursuant to **Art.75(2)** on grounds of national security (NatLaw Table II, column 2). They require that their residents and/or citizens must file a first application with its national authority under **Art.75(2)** (see NatLaw table II, column 2). For example, a Greek must file in Greece if he does not claim the priority of an earlier Greek application.

Promptly after receipt of the application, the national authority issues a receipt to the applicant stating the application number and the date of receipt (**R.35(2)**) and informs the EPO of the same data (**R.35(3)**). Most national authorities examine whether the subject of the application is liable to secrecy. The national authority forwards those applications evidently not liable to secrecy within six weeks of filing, or, where further examination as to liability to secrecy is required, 4 months of filing or, if priority has been claimed, 14 months of the date of priority (**R.37(1)**), to the EPO according to the provisions of **Art.77** and **R.37**. The EPO notifies the applicant under **R.35(4)** of the receipt of the application forwarded by the national authority and starts the examination on filing according to **Art.90**.

Before receipt of the communication under **R.35(4)** from the EPO, the applicant may send further documents relating to the application to the national authority. The national authorities accept (automatic) debit orders for deposit accounts according to **ADA.5.6.1-5.6.3**, notes to **AAD.5** and A-II,1.6. Hence, payment of the filing, search and claims fees other than by debit order should not be made to national offices. After the applicant has received the communication under **R.35(4)**, further documents must be sent directly to the EPO (A-II,3.2). Documents nevertheless sent to a national authority may be forwarded by the authority to the EPO as a courtesy service; the EPO will accord the documents as date of receipt, the date on which the documents arrive at the EPO (see a.o. OJ 2005, 445).

3 **Form of documents**

The form of the application documents is prescribed by **R.49** for the written pages and **R.46** for the drawings.

Art. 75(2) Paragraph 1 shall not preclude the application of legislative or regulatory provisions which, in any Contracting State:

(a) govern inventions which, owing to the nature of their subject-matter, may not be communicated abroad without the prior authorisation of the competent authorities of that State, or

(b) prescribe that any application is to be filed initially with a national authority, or make direct filing with another authority subject to prior authorisation.

1 **National security**

The EPC has no provisions for handling applications that should be kept secret in the interest of national security. **Art.75(2)** allows the contracting states to apply national provisions regarding secrecy to European applications, using one of the following two options. A contracting state may require that a European application that includes subject-matter to be kept secret may not be communicated abroad without authorisation (**Art.75(2)(a)**) and must be filed with a national authority. European applications not containing such subject-matter may be filed abroad without prior authorisation. Alternatively, a contracting state may require that each European application must be filed initially with a national authority, allowing a check on subject-matter that must be kept secret; filing directly with another authority is only allowed after prior authorisation **Art.75(2)(b)**). Authorisation for foreign filing may sometimes be obtained from a national office within a few hours.

If the national authority decides that the subject-matter of the application should be kept secret, it will not forward the application to the EPO (**Art.77(2)**) and it will subject the application to the national procedure for secret applications. Otherwise, the application will be forwarded to the EPO (**Art.77(1)**).

The provisions of each contracting state under both paragraph (a) and (b) can be found in NatLaw Table II, column 2. Limited information on other states can be found in Section B1 of the PCT Applicant's Guide. Some contracting states do not require national filing of any European application. Other contracting states require applicants having a residence or place of business in that state or being a national of that state to file any European application with an authority of that state (paragraph (b)). This requirement is waived in most cases if the European application claims priority of an earlier national application. Several contracting states require that only European applications important to the defence of the state must be filed with the national authority (paragraph (a)); they leave the initial assessment of the significance of the application's subject-matter to national security to the applicant.

Where two or more states require the same application to be filed first with their patent offices, the applicant should apply for a foreign filing licence from the most lenient states and make the first filing with the least lenient state. In case the first filing must be made with the USPTO, the applicant will need a licence from the USPTO to apply for a foreign filing licence in another state.

Art. 76 European divisional applications

1 **Transitional provision EPC 2000**

The revised **Art.76** is applicable to divisional applications received at the EPO on or after the date of the EPC 2000 entry into force (13.12.2007), regardless of whether the parent application was filed under the EPC 1973 or the EPC 2000. (Spec. Ed. 4, OJ 2007; Trans. Pract. §5, 10.1)

See the transitional provisions of **Art.54(3)** for extent of the prior art for the divisional application.

2 **General**

An applicant may divide an application by filing one or more divisional applications ('divisionals') (A-IV,1.1). A divisional may be divided in turn (**G1/06** r.10.2; see also **R.36(1):2** and Spec. Ed. 4, OJ 2007, Art.76).

A divisional may be filed of the applicant's own volition (voluntary division) or at the request of the EPO to meet an objection under **Art.82** that the application lacks unity (mandatory division). The limitation of the parent application ('parent') must be clear and unconditional. The EPO may refuse an application if an applicant does not limit the application to a single invention within the period set in a communication requiring him to limit the application due to lack of unity. (C-IX,1.2)

A divisional is regarded as a new European patent application and its procedure is in principle independent from the procedure of the parent (**G4/98** r.5). Hence, the provisions in the EPC for a European patent application should be applied mutatis mutandis, unless otherwise provided (see e.g. **Art.76** and **R.36**). The 'otherwise provided' relates to the date of filing, designations, periods for payment of fees and extension of subject matter beyond the content of the parent application. Another consequence of the independence is that the fate of the parent after filing of the divisional cannot affect the divisional (**G1/06** r.12.2, case consolidated with **G1/05b**).

Art. 76(1) A European divisional application shall be filed directly with the European Patent Office in accordance with the Implementing Regulations. It may be filed only in respect of subject-matter which does not extend beyond the content of the earlier application as filed; in so far as this requirement is complied with, the divisional application shall be deemed to have been filed on the date of filing of the earlier application and shall enjoy any right of priority.

See for the implementation:
R.36 Provisions for filing divisional application

1 **Filing of divisional application**

A divisional is based on an earlier application and takes over the effective date of that application (**Art.76(1)**). The earlier application may be any European patent application. The earlier application may be a divisional, since a divisional is treated as an ordinary application and a divisional is included in 'any pending application' of **R.36(1)** (**G1/06** r.10.2).

A divisional must be filed directly with the EPO (**Art.76(1)**, first sentence). **R.36(2)** specifies the offices in Munich, The Hague and Berlin as filing offices. National offices are not competent to receive divisionals, since this would cause too much delay for a prompt publication of the divisional. They may, as a service, forward the divisional to the EPO. However, the documents are regarded as received only when the EPO has received them. (A-IV,1.3.1)

A divisional must be filed using a method of filing permitted by **R.2(1)**.

A divisional may be filed by reference to the parent following **R.40(1)(c).** (A-IV,1.3.1; see also **R.36(2):2**)

The claims may be filed after the date of filing of the divisional as a consequence of **R.40(1)**, even if the parent is no longer pending at the date of filing the claims (A-IV,1.2.1).

The Request for Grant Form should be used (**R.41(1)**) and the box for a divisional (**R.41(2)(e)**) ticked.

At the time of filing the divisional and up to compliance with the requirements of **R.40(1)**, the parent must still be pending, i.e. not granted, withdrawn, deemed to be withdrawn or finally refused (**R.36(1)**). See **R.36(3)** and (4) for the filing, search, and designation fee to be paid at filing, **R.38(3)** and (4) for any page fee and divisional fee, and **R.45(1)** for the claims fees and **R.51(3)** for the renewal fees.

When a divisional meets the requirements of **Art.80** and **R.40(1)**, it will be accorded the same date of filing as the parent (A-IV,1.2.1). The date it meets the requirements of **R.40(1)** will be regarded as the date of receipt for the purpose of **R.36(1)**; although this has not been stated explicitly in the Guidelines, it is tacitly assumed. The requirement of **Art.76(1)** regarding confinement to subject matter contained in the parent is assessed during the substantive examination (A-IV,1.2.1). See **Art.76(1):6** for the procedure after filing.

A divisional that does not meet the requirements of **Art.80** and **R.40(1)**, even after correction, will not be dealt with as a divisional application (**Art.90(2)**).

Note, that the Guidelines regard **R.40** applicable to divisionals (A-IV,1.2.1 and 1.3.1), whereas the Travaux Préparatoires of the EPC 2000 state: 'As no individual filing date is accorded to a divisional, **R.40** is not applicable to divisionals' (Spec. Ed. 1 of OJ 2003, p.159).

The reason for the impedimental wording of **Art.76(1)** is given in **G1/06** point VIII and reason 2.

2 Applicant

The issue of who is entitled to file a divisional is not raised in **Art.76**, because it was regarded self-evident that Art.4G Paris Convention applies, which states that 'the applicant may divide the application'. Hence, the applicant of the parent is entitled to file a divisional, confirmed by **R.36(1)**. (**J2/01** r.2.4)

The right to file a divisional is a procedural right that derives from the applicant's status as applicant for the earlier application (**J2/01**, r.5.1). As a consequence of **Art.60(3)**, dealing with the procedural status of the applicant, the applicant named in the Register is regarded as entitled to file a divisional.

Multiple applicants are joint applicants, each of which can only exercise his party rights in common with the other applicant(s) (see **Art.59:1**). Hence, a divisional of a parent filed by multiple applicants must be filed by the same multiple applicants. If not complied with, the application will not acquire divisional status (**J2/01** r.12 and point III of Summary of facts and submissions); the application can neither be dealt with as an independent application with the date of receipt as filing date (**G1/06** r.11.1). Any substantive rights of applicants to part of the subject-matter of the parent under **Art.60(1)** are not relevant for the procedural status of the applicant, because **Art.60(1)** does not refer to 'the applicant'. (**J2/01** r.6)

A representative may act on the basis of an individual authorisation in respect of the parent only if it expressly empowers him to file divisionals (A-IV,1.6). See **R.152(6)** for the consequences of not filing an authorisation if requested to do so.

The designation of the inventor for a divisional is preferably contained in the request for grant form (**R.19(1)**). If not made in the request for grant form, the EPO will invite the applicant to make the designation within a period to be specified (**R.60(2)**) of at least two months. Since a divisional normally relates to part of the subject-matter of the parent, only those inventors designated in the parent who contributed to that part of the subject-matter need be designated in the divisional.

3 Transfer of application

R.36(1) lays down that only the applicant of the parent or his successor in title entered in the Register (**R.143(1)(f)**) may file a divisional. In the case of a transfer the new applicant may file a divisional only on or after the date that the transfer of the parent was duly registered with the EPO under **R.22** (A-IV,1.1.3). If a representative of the applicant must file an authorisation, he may only act on the basis of the authorisation filed in respect of the parent if it expressly empowers him to file divisionals (A-IV,1.6).

Where the parent is filed by joint applicants, the divisional should also be filed by the same joint applicants. There are two possibilities to reduce the number of applicants of a divisional. Suppose the parent disclosing a first and a second invention is filed by a first and second applicant. The divisional relates only to the second invention, in which the first applicant is not interested and in which the second applicant has a substantive right. The second applicant can file the divisional as sole applicant only if the first applicant has notified the EPO under **R.22** before the filing of the divisional. The **R.22** notification can take the form of a transfer of the right to the second invention from the first applicant to the second applicant, or an agreement of the first applicant that the divisional is being prosecuted further in the sole name of the second applicant (**J2/01**, r.8). Alternatively, both applicants can file the divisional and the first applicant subsequently notifies the EPO under **R.22** as above and withdraws as applicant.

4 Language

A divisional must, according to **R.36(2)**, be filed in the language of the proceedings of the parent or the language in which the parent was filed if that language was not an official EPO language (A-IV,1.3.3).

5 Priority

If the parent claims priority from one or more earlier applications, then the divisional retains this priority according to **Art.76(1)**, last sentence, even though the date the divisional was filed is well outside the priority year. A declaration of priority need not be filed a second time, as the right of priority is granted automatically for a divisional, provided the priority claim of the parent is valid on the date the divisional is filed. A lapse of the priority right may occur through abandonment of priority or an unjustified claim to priority. Priority documents also need not be filed again; the EPO places them in the file of the divisional. If the priority documents have not yet been filed for the parent, they must be filed for both the parent and divisional to the extent the applicant wants to enjoy the right of priority for these applications. (A-IV,1.2.2; see also **R.53(1):1** and **(2):1**)

If the priority claim of the parent has been withdrawn before filing of a divisional, the divisional cannot claim that priority anymore; a withdrawal of the priority claim of the parent after filing of the divisional does not affect the priority of the divisional. A withdrawal of a priority claim of a divisional does not affect the priority claim of the parent. (A-IV,1.2.2)

An example: The priority application P1 has a filing date D1: 02.01.2008 and contains subject-matter A and B. A subsequent application P2 is filed at date D2: 20.12.2008 with subject-matter A, B, C and D, claiming priority of P1 for A and B. Non-unity is noticed between A-C and B-D. On 01.06.2010 P2 is divided and a divisional P3 with subject-matter A and C is filed, automatically obtaining the priority of P1. The effective date for subject-matter A in P3 is D1 and for C D2.

6 Examination on filing, search and publication

The divisional will in principle be dealt with as a new, independent application (**G4/98** r.5). It will be treated in the same manner as ordinary applications and subject to the same requirements, unless specific provisions of the EPC, in particular those of **Art.76** or **R.36**, require something different (**G1/06** r.3.1, 9.1).

After filing, the divisional is searched, published and examined in the same way as other European patent applications (A-IV,1.8). During the examination compliance with the requirement of **Art.76(1)**, second sentence, will also be assessed, i.e. whether the subject matter of the divisional does not extend beyond the content of the parent (C-IX,1.4). If complied with, the divisional is accorded the date of filing of the parent. Any amendment of the divisional after filing is assessed on extension of subject matter beyond the content of the divisional as filed (**Art.123(2)**).

The filing and search fee (**R.36(3)**) and any page fee or divisional fee (**R.38(3), (4)**) must be paid within one month of filing. Any claims fees must be paid within one month of filing the first set of claims (**R.45(2)**). The designation fee must be paid within six months of the mention of the publication of the search report for the divisional (**R.36(4)**). Examination must be requested within the same six month period (**R.70(1)**).

The EPO has not provided guidance on the time of publication of the divisional. In practice, the divisional will be published two to four months after its filing. If the claims are filed later than the application and are not available by this time, the publication will be postponed until they are available (see **Art.93(1):1**). The publication will include a search report if available at the completion of the technical preparations for publication. If not available, the search report will be published later.

7 Scope of claims

The applicant is free to determine the scope of protection he desires by including or excluding specific subject-matter disclosed in the description (**G2/10** r.4.5.5). A divisional may disclaim subject-matter disclosed positively in the parent (**G2/10** r.4.6).

The claims of a divisional as filed need not be limited to the subject-matter already claimed in claims of the parent. However, their subject-matter may not extend beyond the content of the parent as filed (**Art.76(1)**). (C-IX,1.4; see the following section for the extent of the subject-matter)

The claims of the divisional may be amended after its filing to aspects of the parent disclosed in the divisional as filed but not encompassed by the claims of the divisional as filed (**G1/06** r.9.2). The amendment may not extend the subject-matter of the divisional (not the parent!) as filed because of **Art.123(2)**). (**T441/92** r.4.2)

The parent and divisional may not claim the same subject-matter in order to avoid double patenting. However, one application may claim its own subject-matter in combination with that of the other application; e.g. if the parent and divisional claim separate and distinct elements A and B respectively which may operate in combination, one of the two applications may also include a claim on A plus B. (C-IX,1.6 in view of G-IV,5.4; see **Art.139(3):5**)

An independent claim in the parent may include all the features of an independent claim in the divisional combined with an additional feature (**T587/98** hn).

An independent claim of a divisional may be restricted to only a part of the subject-matter claimed in the parent, if this part is directly and unambiguously derivable from the parent as being a separate part or entity, i.e. one which can even be used outside the context of the invention of the parent (**T545/92**; C-IX,1.4).

As an exception to the prohibition of identical claims, the claims of a divisional may have the same scope as that of the parent, provided that, by the time the claims of the divisional are submitted, the parent has ceased to exist. In that case the question of double patenting does not arise. (**T441/92** r.2.2; see also **G1/06** r.13.4, 13.5)

A decision in appeal for a parent case is binding for the same subject matter in a divisional case, and claims refused on appeal for the parent case cannot be pursued on appeal in the divisional case (**T51/08**).

The practice of filing a sequence of substantially identical divisionals and pending for up to twenty years for strategic reasons was regarded unsatisfactory by the Enlarged Board of Appeal (**G1/06** r.13.5). See **R.36(1):1** for the consequential amendments of **R.36(1)** to reduce abuse of the divisional system.

8 Subject-matter of divisional application

The subject-matter of a divisional may not extend beyond the content of the earlier application or parent, according to **Art.76(1)**. The content of the parent is the total technical information content of the disclosure, including the description, claims and drawings (**G1/06** r.9.2; **T1409/05** r.3.1.2). The content does not include the abstract (**Art.85** and **T246/86** applied analogously).

The same test as for extension of subject-matter under **Art.123(2)**, i.e. the disclosure test, must be used for assessment of the extension (**G1/06** r.5.1 and **G2/10** r.4.3, 4.6). The subject-matter of a divisional must be objectively and unambiguously derivable from the parent (**T423/03**). The divisional will be accorded the filing date of the parent including any priority claim only if its subject-matter does not extend beyond the content of the parent (**Art.76(1)**, second sentence).

The subject matter of the divisional must be disclosed in the parent as filed and not be unequivocally and definitively abandoned by the time of filing the divisional (**G1/06** r.11.2). Subject-matter deleted from an application, e.g. on grounds of non-unity, may be used for a divisional. When deleting subject-matter, the applicant should avoid any statements which could be interpreted as abandonment (C-IX,1.3). Explicitly abandoned subject-matter cannot be used for a divisional because such subject-matter is regarded as given to the public (**J15/85**, r.4, 5; **J2/01** r.6). As an exception, an expressly declared abandonment of claims may be revoked later in order to reinstate claims in a divisional, provided this was the real intention of the party when deleting the claims (**T910/92**).

Material in the pending parent only relevant for the invention of the divisional should be removed from the parent, as being irrelevant matter in the sense of **R.48(1)(c)** (F-V,11.1). Likewise, material in the divisional unrelated to or inconsistent with the invention of the divisional should be removed, but only where it is absolutely necessary (C-IX,1.5).

Amendment of the divisional after its filing is subject to the restrictions of **Art.123(2)** (**G1/06** r.9.2) with respect to the divisional as filed, not with respect to the parent as filed (**T441/92** r.4.2). After the filing of the divisional, no interchange of subject-matter between the parent and divisionals is possible.

9 Test for extension of subject-matter

The test for extension of subject-matter corresponds to that under **Art.123(2)** (**T514/88** r.2.1; **T441/92** r.4.3; **T276/97** r.2.4; **G1/06** r.5.1). The generally accepted test is the disclosure test: the overall change in the content of the divisional in view of the parent, whether by way of addition, alteration or excision, may not result in the skilled person being presented with information which is not directly and unambiguously derivable from that presented in the parent, even when account is taken of matter which is implicit to a person skilled in the art (**T194/84** mutatis mutandis). The following discussion focusses on the claims of the divisional and assumes that the description and drawings of the divisional do not contain subject-matter that extends beyond the content of the parent as filed.

The set of features in an independent claim of a divisional must be disclosed in the parent as filed for compliance with **Art.76(1)**. Several cases can be distinguished.

If the parent discloses an embodiment, either in its description, drawings or claims, that contains exactly the same features as the independent claim of the divisional, not more and not fewer, there will be no extension of subject-matter. However, if the claim and the embodiment use different terminology for the same features, the correspondence between the features must be shown. The use of different terminology in parent and divisional should be strongly discouraged. If there is no one-to-one correspondence, one of the following cases applies.

If the claim contains one or more features not shown in an embodiment of the parent, the disclosure test is not met and the subject-matter extends beyond the content of the parent.

If the claim contains a subset of features of an embodiment of the parent, the claim may cover devices or methods not disclosed in the parent and, hence, extend the subject-matter of the parent. A claim may not contain an arbitrary subset of the features that make up an embodiment of the parent. The objection may be overcome if it can be proven that the extra features of the embodiment not included in the claim are not essential for the invention. There are three common cases of non-essential features.

1. An extra feature of the embodiment is regarded as non-essential if the parent states that the claimed subset has a special technical advantage.
2. An extra feature is not essential if the parent clearly states that it is optional.
3. An extra feature which is not stated as being optional can still be regarded as not essential for the invention if it complies with the so-called three-point test (**T331/87**), namely that a skilled person will directly and unambiguously recognize that:
   a) the feature is not explained as essential in the disclosure,
   b) it is not, as such, indispensable for the function of the invention in the light of the technical problem it serves to solve, and

c) the replacement or removal of the feature from the embodiment requires no real modification of other features to compensate for the change.

The 'invention' used in item b) is the solution of the technical problem of the application provided by the features in the claim.

10 **Correction of extension of subject-matter**

If the subject-matter of the divisional as filed extends beyond that of the parent, the examining division will ask the applicant to remove the added matter or have the divisional refused under **Art.97(2)** (C-IX,1.4). An interpretation of the second sentence of **Art.76(1)** that a divisional not complying with the substantive requirement of extension of subject-matter on the date of filing of the divisional is invalid is not correct (**G1/05b** r.2.9, consolidated with **G1/06**). Since a divisional must be treated in the same manner as ordinary applications and subject to the same requirements, the applicant has a right to amend the deficiency after filing in proceedings before the EPO according to **Art.123(1)** (**G1/06** r.3.1 & 3.4), even during opposition proceedings (**G1/06** r.3.6). The proceedings of **G3/06** relating to correction of extension of subject-matter during opposition proceedings were terminated, because all appeals in the referring case were withdrawn (OJ 2007, 312). Pendency of the parent at the time of the amendment is not relevant (**G1/06** r.8.2). If the added matter is not removed, the divisional will be refused under **Art.97(2)** as not meeting the requirements of **Art.76(1)** (**G1/06** r.2.4).

Decision **G1/06** overturned **T1158/01**, **T720/02**, **T797/02**, **T39/03** and **T90/03**.

It is not possible to convert a divisional into an application with its own filing date, because the EPC does not provide for it (**T555/00** hn.3, r.1.6; **G1/06** r.11.1, overturning **T904/97** r.4.1.2). It is neither allowed to file a divisional on subject-matter added to the earlier application and claiming as filing date the date on which that subject-matter was added (**G1/06** r.11.1). Content omitted on filing from a divisional cannot be re-introduced into that application or into any divisional filed on that application (**G1/06** r.11.2).

A divisional divided from a divisional is examined applying **Art.76(1)** mutatis mutandis, i.e. by regarding the first-generation divisional as the earlier application out of which the second-generation divisional has been divided. If the first-generation divisional does not comply with the requirements of **Art.76(1)**, the second-generation divisional is likewise invalid (**T1158/01** hn).

Once the divisional has been filed and the conditions of **Art.76(1)** have been met, the divisional is treated quite separately from the parent and must itself comply independently with all requirements of the EPC. Hence, in view of **Art.123(2)**, amendments after filing of the divisional may not extend the subject-matter beyond the contents of the divisional as filed. Note that the requirement of **Art.76(1)** is separate from that of **Art.123(2)** and that a divisional must meet both requirements; i.e. the divisional must neither extend its subject matter beyond the content of the parent nor be amended after its filing in such a way that it extends its subject matter beyond the content of the divisional as filed. (**T441/92** r.4.1-4.2)

The following is an example of the application of both requirements. The parent discloses only subject matter A+B. The divisional on filing discloses only A. The EPO regards the broadening as extension of subject matter beyond the content of the parent and requests the applicant to amend the divisional to A+B to comply with **Art.76(1)**. However, the introduction of B in the divisional would violate **Art.123(2)** by extending the subject matter of the divisional beyond its content on filing. Hence, the two requirements may form an inescapable trap.

It is therefore recommended to include all subject matter of the parent in a divisional; if the divisional includes amended claims, the claims of the parent should be included in the description of the divisional, e.g. as clauses. The divisional is preferably filed in the language of filing of the parent if the parent was not filed in an official EPO language, thereby making it possible to correct translation errors in the divisional (see **R.36(2):1**).

Extension of the subject-matter beyond the content of the parent and beyond the content of the divisional as filed is a ground for opposition (**Art.100(c)**). Since the EPO will keep the file of the parent for at least the same time as the file of the divisional (**R.147(5)**), it will be available for inspection to assess the extension, even if the parent has been withdrawn before publication (**Art.128(3)**) or abandoned later on.

Art. 76(2) All the Contracting States designated in the earlier application at the time of filing of a European divisional application shall be deemed to be designated in the divisional application.

1 **Designation of contracting states**
All contracting states designated in the parent, i.e. not withdrawn or deemed withdrawn, at the time of filing a divisional are deemed designated in the divisional (**Art.76(2)**; A-IV,1.3.4; see also **G4/98** r.5). The designation fee for the divisional must be paid in accordance with **R.36(4)**. If the designation fee is not paid in due time, the application will be deemed withdrawn (**R.39(2)**.

Similarly, all extension states and validation states designated in the parent at the time of filing a divisional are deemed designated in the divisional (A-IV,1.3.5).

Art. 77 Forwarding of European patent applications

Art. 77(1) The central industrial property office of a Contracting State shall forward to the European Patent Office any European patent application filed with it or any other competent authority in that State, in accordance with the Implementing Regulations.

See for the implementation:
R.37 Forwarding of patent applications by national authorities

Art. 77(2) A European patent application the subject of which has been made secret shall not be forwarded to the European Patent Office.

Art. 77(3) A European patent application not forwarded to the European Patent Office in due time shall be deemed to be withdrawn.

1 **Failure to forward application to EPO**
If the application does not reach the EPO before the end of the fourteenth month after filing or, where priority has been claimed, after priority, the applicant will be notified that the application is deemed withdrawn and all fees are refunded (A-II,3.2). Hence, apart from the filing, page, search and designation fee, the claims fees and examination fee are also refunded (**R.37(2)**, last sentence).

Re-establishment of rights under **Art.122(1)** is not possible, because the non-observance of the time limit is not the fault of the applicant (J3/80). However, a request for conversion into a national patent application under **Art.135(1)(a)** may be filed (A-II,1.7). See **Art.135(2)** for special provisions relating to this conversion. The European filing date (**Art.66**) will no longer be recognized, if the request for conversion is not transmitted within 20 months after filing, or, where priority has been claimed, after the date of priority (**Art.135(4)** and **R.155(3)**). The only remedy is to re-file the application with loss of the earlier filing date.

If the time limit expires on a day on which there is an interruption or subsequent dislocation in the delivery of mail within the meaning of **R.134(2)**, the time limit will extend to the first day following the end of the period of interruption or dislocation. (A-II,1.7)

Art. 78 Requirements of a European patent application

1 **Meaning of 'application'**

The EPC uses the word 'application' in three different meanings. The first one is the set of documents, making up the European patent application; the second one is the European patent application itself, i.e. description, claims, abstract and drawings and the third one is use, e.g. in industrial application in **Art.57**. Beware which meaning the word has in the different articles. **Art.78**, for instance, uses the first, broad meaning, whereas **Art.83** uses the second, narrow meaning of 'application'.

Art. 78(1) A European patent application shall contain:
(a) a request for the grant of a European patent;
(b) a description of the invention;
(c) one or more claims;
(d) any drawings referred to in the description or the claims;
(e) an abstract,
and satisfy the requirements laid down in the Implementing Regulations.

See for the implementation:
(a) **R.41** Request for grant
(b) **Art.83** Disclosure of the invention
R.42 Contents of the description
R.30 Requirements relating to nucleotide and amino-acid sequences
R.31 Deposit of biological material
R.32 Expert solution
R.33 Availability of biological material
R.34 New deposit of biological material
(c) **Art.82** Unity of invention
Art.84 Claims
R.43 Form and content of claims
R.44 Unity of invention
(d) **R.46** Form of the drawings
(e) **Art.85** Abstract
R.47 Form and content of the abstract
R.48 Prohibited matter
R.49 Presentation of application documents
R.50 Documents filed subsequently

Items a) and b) are checked during the examination of **Art.90(1)** for accordance of a date of filing (**Art.80**). Items a) to e), i.e. all documents making up the application, are checked during the subsequent formalities examination (**Art.90(3)**) and have to be complied with at the conclusion of the formalities examination.

The method of filing the application must be in accordance with **R.2(1)**. Common methods of filing are by mail, by fax or electronically.

1 **Request for grant form**

The use of the EPO Request for Grant Form 1001 is not necessary for obtaining a date of filing. However, use of the Form is a formal requirement for an application (**R.41(1)**). When not provided on filing, the EPO will invite the applicant to remedy the deficiency, without which the application will be refused (**Art.90(5)**).

2 **Description**

If an application discloses an nucleotide or amino acid sequence, a sequence listing must be provided in an annex to the description. The sequence listing must be filed in a specific format according to **R.30**.

An application relating to biological material that is not publicly available and that cannot be described in an enabling manner requires deposition of the biological material with a depositary institution under **R.31** for sufficient disclosure as prescribed in **Art.83**. The availability of a sample of the material is governed by **R.32** and **33**.

3 **Drawings**

Art.78(1) does not state that drawings are necessary; the necessity is to be determined by the applicant, heeding **Art.83** (sufficiency of disclosure). Formulas are not drawings, and need not comply with the requirements for drawings. Beware, the USA requires drawings for all drawable features of the claims.

If drawings referred to in the description are missing, the Receiving Section will apply **Art.90(4)** and **R.56** for correction, which may result in redating of the application. Deficiencies in the drawings must be corrected under **Art.90(4)** and **R.58**. The formal requirements of the drawings are provided in **R.46**.

Art. 78(2) A European patent application shall be subject to the payment of the filing fee and the search fee. If the filing fee or the search fee is not paid in due time, the application shall be deemed to be withdrawn.

See for the implementation:
R.38 Period for payment of filing fee, search fee and page fee
R.45 Claims fees, period for payment and sanction on non-payment
Rfees2(1)1 Amount of filing fee
Rfees2(1)1a Amount of page fee
Rfees2(1)1b Amount of divisional fee
Rfees2(1)2 Amount of search fee
Rfees2(1)15 Amount of claims fee

1 **Filing fee and search fee**

The filing and search fee must be paid within one month of filing the application, according to **R.38(1)**.

Payment of the filing fee and search fee for divisional applications is dealt with in **Art.76(1)** & **R.36(3)**, for new applications in **Art.61(1)** & **R.17(2)**, and for Euro-PCT applications in **Art.153(1)** & **R.159(1)**.

See **Rfees9** and notes thereto for any refund of the filing and search fee.

2 **Other fees payable at filing**

The claims fees for an application due under **R.45(1)** must be paid within one month of filing the first set of claims (**R.45(2)**, **Rfees2(1)15**). When the claims are filed together with the application, any claims fees must be paid within the same one month period as the filing and search fee. See **R.45** for the sanction on not paying the claims fees.

The page fee due under **R.38(2)** must be paid within the later of one month of filing the application, the first set of claims or the certified copy of the previously filed application. See **R.38(3):1** for the sanction on not paying the fee in due time and **Rfees2(1)1a** for the amount of the fee.

The divisional fee due under **R.38(4)** must be paid within one month of filing a divisional application; the amount is given in **Rfees2(1)1b**.

3 **Missing filing fee or search fee**

Payment of the filing fee and search fee is checked under **Art.90(3)** and **R.57(e)**. If payment of any of these fees according to **Art.78(2)** has not been made, the application is deemed withdrawn (**Art.78(2)**, second sentence. The loss of rights ensues on expiry of the one-month period, not at expiry of the period for requesting further processing (A-III,16.2). The applicant will be notified of any loss of rights (**R.112(1)**). Further processing under **Art.121** and **R.135** is possible and must be requested within two months from the notification of the loss of rights. Re-establishment in the one month period is excluded under **R.136(3)**, but re-establishment is available for the two month period for further processing. A possible remedy, if applicable, is to prove within two months after notification of the loss of rights that the payment was actually made in due time (**R.112(2)**).

Another remedy is to re-file the application and claim priority from the failed application and any earlier application if still possible. Such refiling does not require the payment of the further processing fee at the cost of a later date of filing.

The communication of the loss of rights noted under **R.112(1)** presupposes a validly filed application (J18/96 r.3.2). Hence, an applicant can derive from the receipt of a **R.112(1)** communication that his application has been accorded a date of filing, and the application may still be used as priority document if he does not pay the fees due.

After deemed withdrawal it is sometimes allowed to convert to a national application under **Art.135**. See NatLaw table VII. Another remedy is to file a new European application and, if possible, claim the priority of an earlier application or of the withdrawn application, which must have received a date of filing for that purpose.

Art. 79 Designation of Contracting States

1 **Designation system**

Art.3 allows the grant of a European patent for one or more of the contracting states. **Art.79** provides the system by which an applicant can indicate those contracting states in which he desires protection for his invention.

Since 2009 all contracting states are deemed designated on filing and remain so until grant, unless designations are withdrawn before grant (see **Art.79(3)**). After grant the proprietor can decide in which contracting states he desires protection by complying with the national requirements of those states, such as filing any translation and paying fees (see **Art.65:1**). A single, flat-fee is payable for designating all contracting states (**R.39**).

The designation system in force till 2009 required payment of a designation fee for a valid designation of a contracting state in which protection was desired. A designation for which the designation fee was not paid in due time was regarded withdrawn. The effects of the old system may still be noticeable for prior rights (**Art.79(2):3**, **Art.54(3):3** and 4) and in the fee schedule (**RFees2(2)3**). A description of the old system can be found in Guidelines 2007 A-III,11, available on the EPO website.

Art. 79(1) All the Contracting States party to this Convention at the time of filing of the European patent application shall be deemed to be designated in the request for grant of a European patent.

1 **Designation of contracting states**

All contracting states party to the EPC at the filing date of the application are deemed designated according to **Art.79(1)**. Any other state indicated in the form will be disregarded (A-III,11.1). See **Art.169(1):1,2** for the effect of the designation of a state for which the EPC enters into force shortly after filing of the application.

A designation is effective as from the date of filing. To maintain the effect a designation fee must be paid according to **Art.79(2)** and **R.39**. If the designation fee is not paid, the application will be deemed withdrawn (**R.39(2)** as valid from 01.04.2009). Non-payment of a designation fee under the previous system results in the corresponding designation being deemed withdrawn (**R.39(2)** as valid before 01.04.2009).

Where an application is filed by two or more applicants, the applicants may designate different contracting states according to **Art.59**.

In addition to the designated EPC contracting states, the application can be extended to non-EPC contracting states which have concluded an Extension Agreement with the EPO. The box in the Request for Grant form for extending the application to all extension states is pre-crossed; hence, the form is deemed to be a request to extend the application to all non-contracting states with which such an Extension Agreement exists on the filing date. See **Art.169:5** for the list of extension states and provisions of the Extension Agreement. The extension to a state takes effect only if the extension fee for that state is paid within the period for payment of the designation fee.

The applicant can also validate his European patent applications and patents for a state not being an EPC contracting state. The patent will confer essentially the same protection in that state as a patent granted by the EPO for the EPC contracting states. Whereas an extension state should in due time become a contracting state of the EPC, a validation state does not have this prospect. See **Art.169:6** for the list of validation states and the Validation Agreement.

Art. 79(2) The designation of a Contracting State may be subject to the payment of a designation fee.

See for the implementation:
R.17(3) Designation fee for a new application
R.36(4) Designation fee for a divisional application
R.39 Designation fee, period for payment and sanction

R.159(1)(d) Designation fee for a Euro-PCT application
Rfees2(1)3 Amount of designation fee

1 Designation fee

1.1 AMOUNT OF DESIGNATION FEE AND PERIOD FOR PAYMENT

Art.79(2) enables the EPO to request payment of a designation fee to maintain the validity of a designation made at filing of the application. **R.39(1)** provides the requirement to pay a designation fee.

All contracting states of the EPC at the time of filing of the application are deemed designated (**Art.79(1)**). A joint designation fee must be paid for the designations of an application (**Rfees2(1)3**). The designation fee does not cover extension fees (OJ 2009, 124 footnote 6).

The designation fee is due upon mention of the publication of the search report under **Art.92** (A-X,5.2.2) and, according to **R.39(1)**, must be paid within six months of the date of that mention. The period for payment expires on the same date as the period for filing the request for examination (**R.70(1)**). The designation fee has the character of a non-refundable surcharge on the examination fee.

The applicant is reminded of the expiry of the six-month period in the communication of **R.69(1)**, informing him of the publication date of the search report. The period may be extended under **R.134** due to non-working days. The search report allows the applicant to make an adequate assessment of the prospects of his application, following which he can decide whether to continue the prosecution or to terminate it by not paying the designation fee. The period of six months from the publication of the search report for paying the designation fee also applies to a new application (**R.17(3)**), divisional application (**R.36(4)**) and a Euro-PCT application (**R.159(1)(d)**).

Irrespective of payment of the designation fee, the designations of all contracting states remain valid until expiry of the period for payment of the designation fee (**R.39(1)**).

1.2 EFFECT OF NON-PAYMENT OF DESIGNATION FEE AND REMEDIES

The EPO checks payment of the designation fee under **Art.90(3)** (C-II,4). Where the designation fee is not paid in due time, the application will be deemed withdrawn (**R.39(2)**). Similarly, if the applicant withdraws all designations, the application is deemed withdrawn (**R.39(2)**). The EPO notifies the loss of rights under **R.112(1)**.

If applicable, the applicant may prove within two months from the notification of the loss of rights under **R.112(1)** that the payment of the designation fee was in time (**R.112(2)**).

The applicant may use further processing according to **Art.121** and **R.135** to pay as yet the designation fee and the further processing fee within two months of notification of the communication. Re-establishment is excluded.

The loss of the application ensues on expiry of the normal period of **R.39(1)** and not at expiry of the two-month period for requesting further processing (A-III,11.2.3, applying **G4/98** r.7.2 mutatis mutandis).

2 Extension and validation of states not party to the EPC

2.1 DESIGNATION OF EXTENSION STATE

On filing the applicant may mark in the Request for Grant form the extension states for which, at the time of filing, he intends to pay the extension fees. An extension fee is payable for each extension state where protection is desired. See **Art.169:2** for the Extension Ordinance. The system of extension fees has not changed with the introduction of the flat fee for designation of EPC contracting states on 01.04.2009.

The amount of the extension fee for each extension state is laid down in Art.3 of the Extension Ordinance (euro 102, OJ 1994, 82; see also Schedule of fees). There is no maximum number of extension fees. The extension fees must be paid within the same period as the designation fee as laid down in **R.39(1)** and **R.159(1)(d)** (OJ 1997, 215, point 12). Under the automatic debiting system only extension fees will be debited for extension states for which the Request for Grant form indicates an intention to pay the extension fee (**AAD.3.2(r)** and notes thereto).

2.2 VALIDATION OF NON-CONTRACTING STATE

On filing the applicant may mark in the Request for Grant form the non-contracting states for which, at the time of filing, he intends to have his application and patent validated and to pay the validation fees. See **Art.169:6** for validation of states.

The validation fee for validating a non-contracting state must be paid to the EPO within six months from the publication of the search report. The amount of the fee depends on the validation state. The grace period for payment and the remedy are the same as for payment of the extension fee (see the following section).

If the validation fee is not paid in due time, the request for validation is deemed withdrawn. (Dec. Pres. OJ 2018 A15)

2.3 NON-PAYMENT OF EXTENSION AND VALIDATION FEES AND REMEDIES

If the extension or validation fee is not paid in due time, the corresponding extension is deemed withdrawn. The following two remedies are available if the basic period of **R.39(1)** or **R.159(1)(d)** has not been observed.

An extension or validation fee not paid in the basic period may still be paid with a 50% surcharge in a grace period of two months from expiry of the basic period (OJ 2009, 603; see also extension agreement OJ 1994, 75, Art.2; A-III,12.2). The grace period is an aggregate period (**R.131(2):3**).

The EPO will not issue a loss of rights communication for unpaid extension or validation fees. In the special case that a designation fee is not validly paid, the EPO will issue a loss of rights communication for the designation fee, allowing the applicant to pay the designation fee and also any extension or validation fee using further processing. See A-III,12.2 for the conditions.

EPC remedies and appeals not explicitly referred to in the extension agreement do not apply to actions taken by the EPO under the extension or validation procedure (**J22/10** r.3.3.3; A-III,12.1). Hence, re-establishment of rights under **Art.122** and **R.136** is excluded for the extension and validation fees. (A-III,12.2)

3 Publication of designations

The application as published indicates the designated contracting states (**R.68(3)**).

The designations valid at publication of the application are important for European prior rights under the EPC 1973. Under **Art.54(4)** EPC 1973 a prior right was only effective for contracting states validly designated on publication of the application. Whether the published application indicates valid designations depends on whether the application was filed before or after the 1997 fee reform. Under **Art.54(3)** EPC 2000 the validity of the designations in the publication is no longer relevant. See **Art.54(3):4** for details of the effect the published designations have on the prior right effect.

Applications not claiming priority and filed before 01.07.1996 and applications claiming a priority before 31.05.1996 indicate only valid designations in the publication.

Applications filed on or after 01.07.1997 indicate all contracting states in the publication. The Register must be consulted for the valid designations.

Applications filed within the interval from 31.05.1996 and 01.07.1997 either publish the valid designations or all designations, depending on the transitional provisions as set out in OJ 1997, 479.

The Register and Bulletin will, likewise, mention the extension states for which the extension fees have been paid (OJ 1997, 479, point 7).

Art. 79(3) The designation of a Contracting State may be withdrawn at any time up to the grant of the European patent.

1 **Withdrawal of all designations**

The applicant may withdraw a designation at any time up to the grant of the patent (**Art.79(3)**), for example to avoid collision in a contracting state between a European patent application or patent and a national application or patent of the same family (**Art.139(3)**). The designation fee will not be refunded in most cases (see **R.39(3):1**).

Withdrawal of a designation is not possible from the date a third party proves before the EPO to have initiated proceedings concerning entitlement up to the date of resumption of the grant proceedings (**R.15**).

Art. 80 Date of filing

The date of filing of a European patent application shall be the date on which the requirements laid down in the Implementing Regulations are fulfilled.

See for the implementation:
R.40 Requirements for date of filing
R.55 Redating after remedy of deficiencies
R.56 Redating after late filing of missing parts or drawings

1 **General**

The requirements for the accordance of a date of filing laid down in **R.40** reflect the worldwide standard laid down in Art.5 of the Patent Law Treaty 2000 (PLT). The EPO intends to become a Contracting Party to the PLT and would then be bound by this standard.

In view of the many details contained in Art.5 PLT, it was regarded appropriate to consolidate the EPO provisions on the accordance of a filing date in the Implementing Regulations. (Spec. Ed. 4 of OJ 2007)

R.55 provides a date of filing for an application of which deficiencies are remedied after the examination revealed that it did not meet the requirements of **R.40. R.56** allows an applicant to make up missing parts of the description or missing drawings after accordance of the date of filing with a possible re-dating of the application.

2 **Transitional provision EPC 2000**

The revised **Art.80** is applicable to European patent applications filed on or after the time of EPC 2000 entry into force. (Spec. Ed. 4 of OJ 2007)

This also applies to **R.55** and **R.56**, which implement **Art.80**. (for **R.56** see **J10/07** r.1.3)

3 **Legal effects of date of filing**

The date of filing of an application is the date of receipt of the application documents complying with the requirements of **Art.80**, by one of the offices referred to in **Art.75(1)** using a method permitted by **R.2(1)**. A valid date of filing has, amongst others, different legal effects, discussed below (see **T1409/05** r.3.2.6).

The following effects will ensue immediately when the filing date has been accorded:

- a European patent application is pending as of that date (**Art.80** in conjunction with **Art.90(1), (2)**);
- the applicant formally claims to have deposited his invention with the EPO on the filing date as notional date, from which his right to the patent arises under **Art.60(2)**;
- a European patent application gives rise to a right of priority for subsequent European, national or international patent applications as from the date of filing (**Art.87(2)**).
- the state of the art and hence the extent of search and examination is defined by the filing date (**Art.54(2)** and **(3)**);

Upon publication the following legal effect of the date of filing will unfold:

- the application will count as prior right under **Art.54(3)** for other applications as from its date of filing;

The date of filing an application will be replaced by the date of filing of an earlier application to the extent that the priority claim is valid (**Art.89**).

4 **Requirements and examination**

The requirements for according a date of filing are set out in **R.40**. The procedure on filing, the examination of the requirements for according a date of filing, and the correction of deficiencies are given in **Art.90(1), (2), (4)** and **R.55** and **56**.

Art. 81 Designation of the inventor

The European patent application shall designate the inventor. If the applicant is not the inventor or is not the sole inventor, the designation shall contain a statement indicating the origin of the right to the European patent.

See for the implementation:
R.19 Filing the designation of inventor
R.20 Publication of the mention of the inventor
R.21 Rectification of the designation of an inventor
R.60 Subsequent designation of the inventor

1 **Designation of the inventor**
Art.81 realizes the right of the inventor according to **Art.62** to be mentioned before the EPO. The inventor is also mentioned in the published application and specification; he may waive this right according to **R.20(1)**.

Co-inventors should be mentioned in the application in the order indicated by the applicant. The order may be based on the contribution of the inventors to the subject-matter of the application; being mentioned first can be regarded in such a case as a moral right of the main inventor.

R.19 gives the requirements for designating an inventor and, where required, the origin of the applicant's right to the patent, and the duty of the EPO to send information to the inventor where the applicant is not the inventor or is not the sole inventor. **R.21** governs the rectification of the designation of the inventor. See also A-III,5.

2 **Missing or deficient designation**
If the designation of the inventor is not filed at the date of filing or is deficient, e.g. the name, address or signature is missing, the applicant will be invited to remedy the deficiency as set out in **R.57(f)** and A-III,5.5 and 5.6. Not complying with **Art.81** results in refusal of the application (**R.60(1)**). The procedure for correction is set out in **R.57:7**.

Corrections of the designation made on the instigation of the inventor or applicant can be made at any time (A-III,5.6).

Art. 82 Unity of invention

The European patent application shall relate to one invention only or to a group of inventions so linked as to form a single general inventive concept.

See for the implementation:
R.44 Unity of invention
R.64 European search report where the invention lacks unity
R.137(5) Amendment of claims to unsearched subject-matter lacking unity
R.164 Unity of invention and further searches of a Euro-PCT application

1 **General**
Art.82 has a regulatory function in the interest of a rational procedure in that it prohibits unjustified saving of fees by lumping together non-related inventions and ensures a minimum degree of ready comprehensibility of the invention. (**T110/82** r.5)

2 **Unity of invention**
Art.82 defines unity of invention as relating to one invention only or to a group of inventions so linked as to form a single general inventive concept. **R.44** defines a single general inventive concept as a technical relationship among inventions involving one or more of the same or corresponding special technical features. The special technical features are features that define a contribution which each of the inventions considered as a whole makes over the prior art.

A group of inventions may be formed by a plurality of independent claims in the same or in different categories or a plurality of alternative embodiments defined in a single independent claim (F-V,2; see **R.43(2):1**).

Lack of unity should not be raised or persisted on a narrow, literal or academic approach. The benefit of doubt is for the applicant. (F-V,4)

There is no lack of unity if a dependent claim states features comprising an independent invention, as the claim comprises all the features of the claim it depends on (F-V,2.1). Intermediate products of a process may form unity with the final products (see F-V,2.2.2.4). A claim including alternatives ('OR'-claim or a Markush grouping) may be unitary (F-V,2.2.2.2).

3 **Examination of unity**

The unity of invention is examined by both the search division and the examining division. Lack of unity may be noticed a priori, i.e. before prior art is taken into account, or a posteriori, i.e. after prior art is taken into account, which may cause e.g. the the first claim to fall, leaving non-unity between the remaining dependent claims (F-V,4).

The procedure of the search division where the application lacks unity is given in **R.64(1)**. If the search division considers that the invention lacks unity, it will search one invention and search the one or more other inventions only after payment of one or more further search fees. Since a patent can be granted for one invention only, other inventions should be prosecuted in a divisional application (F-V,6.2; **R.48(1)(c)**; **R.36(1)**; **R.63(3)**; **G2/92**).

The requirement of unity of invention is also applied in the following situations. After a Euro-PCT application has entered the European phase, R.164 gives the procedure for searching, where the requirement of unity of invention determines whether further search fees have to be paid to have all claims searched. During proceedings before the EPO unity of invention is also used to determine whether an amendment of claims switches the subject-matter to another invention, which is prohibited by **R.137(5)**.

Lack of unity is no ground for opposition (**Art.100**; **T162/85** r.9) or revocation in national proceedings (**Art.138(1)**). In opposition proceedings it is irrelevant that the patent as granted or amended does not meet the requirement of unity (**G1/91** hn). Thus, after an opposition procedure a patent maintained in amended form need not meet the requirement of unity (**G1/91** hn).

Art. 83 Disclosure of the invention

The European patent application shall disclose the invention in a manner sufficiently clear and complete for it to be carried out by a person skilled in the art.

See for the implementation:
R.30 Requirements relating to nucleotide and amino acid sequences
R.31 Requirements relating to biological material
R.34 New deposit of biological material
R.42 Contents of the description

1 **Principle of disclosure**

Art.83 is one of the basic provisions of the patent law. The general principle of the law is that the applicant may obtain a monopoly protecting his invention only if he provides a complete disclosure of his invention, thereby enriching the technology. **Art.83** governs the adequacy of the teaching in the disclosure. An insufficient disclosure may result in refusal of the application under **Art.97(2)**; it is also a ground for opposition (**Art.100(b)**) and revocation (**Art.138(1)(b)**). See **Art.84**, note 2.2 for the relation between **Art.83** and **Art.84**.

The disclosure of the priority application and the disclosure of the priority claiming application have to be interpreted in the same way to avoid inconsistencies between claiming priority and amending the application (**G1/03** r.4; **Art.88(4):2; Art123(2):1.2**).

2 Sufficiency of disclosure

The disclosure of the patent application must be sufficient for the skilled person to enable the invention, availing himself of contemporaneously available common general knowledge and the literature referred to in the description. The last two elements widen the scope of the disclosure.

When assessing sufficiency of disclosure, a feature of an embodiment must be given an interpretation that is meaningful for the function the feature is expected to perform; the skilled person will exclude other interpretations as being irrelevant for working the invention. (T521/12 r.9)

The EPO seldom raises an objection of insufficient disclosure. When raised, it is often based on insufficient disclosure for a broad claim, an essential feature of the invention not being disclosed or inconsistencies. Insufficiency is more often raised in opposition and national proceedings.

2.1 CONTENT OF THE DISCLOSURE

Sufficiency of disclosure must be judged on the basis of the application as a whole, including the description and the claims (**T14/83** r.3). Any sequence listing filed under **R.30** and biological material deposited under **R.31** or **R.34** must be included in the content for assessing sufficiency.

2.1.1 Common general knowledge

The skilled person may use the common general knowledge to cure insufficiencies or errors of the disclosure to enable him to carry out the invention (**T206/83** hn, r.5). The required research or experiments should not involve an undue effort of the skilled person (**T171/84** r.12). Documents not belonging to the common general knowledge and not referred to in the application as filed cannot be used to contribute to the clarity and sufficiency of the disclosure (**T580/88** r.2.3). The scope of the common general knowledge has been set out in **Art.56:3.6**.

An error in the description is immaterial to the sufficiency of the disclosure if the skilled person could recognise and rectify it without undue effort using his common general knowledge (**T171/84** hn, r.12).

Applicants are well advised not to be unduly influenced by their excessive experience in the field to which the invention relates, so as to neglect providing all the detailed instructions in the specification which are necessary for carrying out the invention without difficulties and to rely immoderately on the possibility of using common general knowledge to fill gaps and to rectify any deficiency in the disclosure (**T171/84** r.13).

2.1.2 Referenced document

The disclosure of a patent application may be supplemented by the disclosure of a document it refers to. The requirement that the application must enable the skilled person to work the invention without undue effort is complied with if the teaching is completed by reference to a document cited in the application as filed (**T611/89** r.3.1; **T267/91** r.2). The language of the document referred to is irrelevant (**T920/92** r.2).

The reference document must be available to the public. It will only be considered if it was publicly available on the date of filing of the application or, if this was not the case, it was available on or before the filing date to the EPO or to the receiving Office of a Euro-PCT application that was not filed with the EPO, and also available to the public on or before the date of publication of the application (e.g. by being present in the file of the application) (**T737/90**; H-IV,2.2.1).

A feature from a referenced document relating to an essential feature of the invention is not only important for sufficiency of disclosure but also for the definition of the invention. Since a patent application must itself identify all the features of the invention for which protection is sought, such a feature may not merely be referred to but must be included in the claim by amendment (**T689/90** r.1.4; F-III,8). The rules for inclusion by amendment are stricter than the above rules for incorporation, because in such a case the feature must be regarded as being part of the content of the application as filed according to **Art.123(2)**. By way of exception such features can be introduced in a claim by amendment without violating **Art.123(2)** if the description of the application as filed leaves no doubt to the skilled reader that (**T689/90** r.2.2; case law summarized in H-IV,2.3.1):

1 protection is or may be sought for such features;
2 such features contribute to solving the problem of the invention;
3 such features at least implicitly belong to the description of the invention as filed;
4 such features are precisely defined and identifiable in the reference document.

All essential features in the reference document which belong together must be incorporated into the claim; it is not permissible to single out a particular one of their number (**T6/84** hn). See **T1819/07** r.3.4 for an insufficiently defined feature; a claimed particle size range was regarded as unclear because no method for measuring the size was specified; a reference in the description to a document disclosing both a method of making and of measuring the particles was of no avail, because the reference was only to the method of making the particles and not to that of measuring.

2.2 SUFFICIENCY

Sufficiency of disclosure requires that the teaching of the application enables the skilled person to carry out the whole subject-matter which is defined in the claims, often using functional formulations, without undue burden. A broad claim requires in general the disclosure of a number of alternatives over the range of the claim; one embodiment may suffice where the skilled person can perform the invention over the whole claimed range (F-III,1; F-IV,6.3; **T435/91** r.2.2.3). If the only embodiment disclosed does not have the technical advantages of the invention as stated in the application, it cannot be the basis for generalisation over the range of the claim; therefore, the disclosure is insufficient (**T1173/00** r.3.1).

A disclosure of a composition defined by its function must comprise the technical teaching to make the composition (**T435/91**). An insufficient disclosure is a ground for opposition (**Art.100(b)**). The requirements for disclosure in the USA and JP are stricter than those of the EPC.

Although the skilled person for the purpose of **Art.56** and **Art.83** has the same level of skill, the knowledge for both purposes is different (**T60/89**). The skilled person when assessing inventive step is aware of the common general knowledge in the art at the relevant date and has all prior art in the relevant technical field at his disposal (G-VII,3). The skilled person when assessing sufficiency of disclosure of a patent has knowledge of the invention as disclosed, i.e. knowledge of both the prior art, the problem and its solution, and is aware of documents cited in the patent and the common general knowledge in the art (**T6/84**, **T171/84**).

3 Insufficient disclosure

An insufficient disclosure cannot be remedied later because of **Art.123(2)**. If no embodiment is sufficiently disclosed in order to avoid easy copying of the invention and the missing information is not available from the general knowledge of a skilled person, the application will be refused (**T219/85** Marking of gem stones). This is rather unlikely to happen. If some embodiments are insufficiently disclosed, the claims must be restricted to the sufficiently disclosed embodiments, the other embodiments being deleted. (F-III,2)

There can be a fundamental insufficiency in the invention, as shown in the following examples, which is irreparable (F-III,3).

A first example is where the successful performance depends on chance, i.e. results are unrepeatable or success in achieving these results is unreliable, e.g. in a micro-biological process involving mutations. The description or the knowledge of the skilled person must then suffice to identify the desired or erroneous product and/or show how to correct the process. In the absence of such information, reliance on chance events amounts to undue burden. (**T14/83**, **T226/85**, **T727/95** r.11)

A second example of a fundamental insufficiency is an invention violating established physical laws, e.g. a device having a specified construction and alleged to operate as a perpetuum mobile. A claim on a perpetuum mobile relating merely to its structure does not comply with **Art.83**. Since the structure does not solve the problem, i.e. achieve a perpetuum mobile, there is also an inventive step problem under **Art.56**. If a claim on a perpetuum mobile is directed to its function and not merely to its structure, it will be objected to under **Art.83** and also **Art.57** as not being industrially applicable (e.g. **T541/96**, Cold nuclear fusion). Where the technical effect in the form of a function is part of the claim, the effect cannot be used to define the problem in the problem-solution approach. (see also F-III,12)

A third example is an invention defined in terms of a functional feature where the actual implementation of the feature is an undue burden for the skilled person (**T1063/06** hn.II; see **Art.84:1.6**).

Time-consuming and ethically questionable tests, e.g. to establish whether a particular product has a claimed pharmaceutical effect, are unreasonable if the claim could have been defined by features making the tests superfluous; such a claim does not comply with **Art.83** (**T1635/09** r.7.3).

If there is an error in the description (e.g. a wrong number), this is immaterial for the sufficiency of the disclosure, if the skilled person can recognize and correct it using the common general knowledge (**T171/84**). An erroneous disclosure that cannot be corrected using common general knowledge should not be considered part of the state of the art under **Art.54(2)** (**T77/87** hn1).

3.1 INSUFFICIENCY AND INVENTIVE STEP

Lack of reproducibility of a claimed invention may become relevant for sufficiency of disclosure or inventive step, depending on the way the invention is claimed. If a technical effect expressed in the claim is not achieved, the claim will be regarded insufficiently disclosed. Since the technical effect is presented as part of the solution, it cannot be part of the problem to be solved. If a technical effect is not expressed in the claim but is part of the problem, not achieving the technical effect is an inventive step issue. (**G1/03** r.2.5.2; **T5/06** r.7; **T380/05** r.7.2; F-III,12)

Art. 84 Claims

The claims shall define the matter for which protection is sought. They shall be clear and concise and be supported by the description.

See for the implementation:
R.43 Form and content of claims
R.62a Plurality of independent claims during search
R.63 Incomplete search due to not clear subject-matter

1 Clarity and interpretation of claims

Art.84 in combination with **R.43(1)** stipulates the requirements that the claims shall be clear and define the matter for which protection is sought in terms of technical features of the invention. Those requirements serve two purposes: - ensuring that the public is not left in any doubt as to which subject-matter is covered by a particular claim and which is not; - delimiting the subject-matter from the prior art in order not to give rise to uncertainty regarding the technical contribution to the art it provides. (**T728/98** r.3.1)

The clarity of the claims is of utmost importance, as the claims define the scope of the matter for which protection is sought. The clarity requirement applies to independent and dependent claims alike and to the claims as a whole (F-IV,4.1; **G3/14** r.49). The words should have their ordinary meaning; if a specific meaning has been given, this must be clear from the wording; this is important, as only the claims of the European patent will be translated in the other official languages.

A patent may be its own dictionary and may define technical terms and determine how a skilled person has to interpret a specific word when used in the description or in the claims. This will not be necessary if the patent does not depart from the meaning a word normally has in the respective technical field and which a skilled person would attribute to it. If, however, it is intended to use a word which is known in the art to define a specific subject-matter to define a different matter, the description may give this word a special, overriding meaning by explicit definition. (**T500/01** r.6)

Complexity of a claim is not tantamount to lack of clarity. The simplicity of a claim is not a criterion for the granting of a patent. (**T1020/98** hn.I)

Art.84 requires that the claims must be clear in themselves, without including any knowledge derived from the description of the patent application. The description is mentioned in **Art.84** only for the requirement of support. (**T988/02** r.3.3.1)

Art.69(1) should not be invoked to interpret the claims in terms of the description for the purpose of **Art.84**, because **Art.69** concerns only the extent of protection and **Art.84** the definition of the matter to be protected by a claim (**T1129/97**; established case law, confirmed in **T56/04**).

1.1 INCONSISTENCIES

Inconsistencies between the claims and the description may cast doubt on the extent of protection. A first example is a simple verbal inconsistency. E.g. the description does not emphasize a feature, while the claims are limited to the inclusion of the feature, or vice versa. The description should be limited or the claims broadened. A second example is an inconsistency regarding apparently essential features. E.g. an independent claim does not mention a feature which is essential to the invention according to general knowledge or to the description. The claim is then unclear, as **Art.84** and **R.43(1)** require not only that the claim must be technically comprehensible, but must also clearly define the object of the invention, i.e. indicate all the essential features thereof (**T32/82** r.15). The claim need not be amended if the applicant shows that the feature is not essential. Apparently unessential features do not incite a reaction from the EPO. A third example of an inconsistency is when part of the subject-matter of the description and/or drawings is not covered by the claims. E.g. the claims specify a circuit with semiconductors, but the embodiments in the description also show a circuit with electronic tubes. The amendment consists in broadening the claims or limiting the description. This inconsistency is absent for examples presented in the description to improve the understanding, but which are not embodiments of the invention. (F-IV,4.3)

General statements in the description which imply an expanded extent of the protection in vague terms, e.g. to everything covered by the spirit of the invention or, if the invention relates to a combination of features, to the separate features, are objected to.

1.2 ESSENTIAL FEATURES

An independent claim must specify all essential features needed to define the invention (**T133/85** r.2) except in so far as such features are implied by the generic terms used, e.g. a bicycle implies the presence of wheels. The essential features should in particular comprise those features which distinguish the invention from the closest prior art (**T1055/92** hn.III). This implies that it is not always necessary for a claim to identify technical features or steps in detail (r.4). It is sufficient if a claim modifying a known product clearly identifies the product and states the modifications. There is an inconsistency and lack of clarity if a claimed process does not lead to the desired product. Such an objection could be raised based on common general knowledge or the description.

There is a large amount of case-specific case law on essential features, where the discussion concentrates on a specific technical question. If the EPO raises an objection of lack of an essential feature in an independent claim, the applicant must argue why the features present in said claim achieve the claimed effect and solve the technical problem.

If a non-technical feature is regarded as constitutive for defining an invention, it must be included as an essential feature in the independent claim. An example is a method step of making a deductive decision about a pathology in a diagnostic method: if its essentialness is unambiguously inferable from the patent or patent application, it is to be included in the independent claim. (**G1/04** r.6.2.4).

1.3 RELATIVE TERMS

A claim is not clear in the sense of **Art.84** if it comprises an unclear technical feature for which no unequivocal, generally accepted meaning exists in the relevant art (**T728/98** hn.I). Examples of these features are relative terms as 'thin', 'wide' or 'strong'. Such a feature should be replaced by a more precise wording from the description. If there is no such basis and the term is not essential to the invention, it should be retained to avoid an extension of subject-matter. In opposition proceedings, a replacement may enlarge the scope of the claim, which is not allowed according to **Art.123(3)**. If the relative term is essential for the definition of the invention, it is not allowed in the claim. Such a term may not be used to distinguish from the prior art. The words 'about', 'approximately' and 'substantially' may be applied mainly to numerical values and only if they do not prevent an unambiguous distinction from the prior art and the skilled person knows within which tolerance a certain effect can be obtained. (F-IV,4.6 and 4.7; see also **G2/88** r.2.5)

A vague term can be made slightly more acceptable by adding 'in practical circumstances'; the skilled person will then understand the meaning.

The provision of **Art.69(1)** according to which the description and the drawings shall be used to interpret the claims, applies also to the clarity requirement of **Art.84**, provided that the claims are not self-contradictory. Where a claim specifies an undefined, relative quality, e.g. a product should be 'water-soluble', it is not normally necessary to identify any method for its determination. The claim is clear in the sense of **Art.84**, if to the skilled person the quality has a sufficiently precise meaning taking into account the common general knowledge and having regard to its context in the light of the description. (**T860/93**, criticising the broad statements in **T454/89**)

Where a claim is self-contradictory in that it has mutually incompatible features, it is not permissible to rely on the description to resolve the contradiction. (**T860/93** r.5.7; **T454/89**)

1.4 UNCLEAR EXPRESSIONS

Expressions like 'preferably', 'for example', 'such as', 'more particularly' in a claim may introduce ambiguity and give rise to a clarity objection. The feature following the expression is entirely optional and can be ignored when assessing the scope of the claim (F-IV,4.9). See also **R.137(5):5**.

In an expression such as 'about 200 C' or 'approximately 200 C' the value is interpreted as being as accurate as the method used to measure it or as having an error margin specified in the application or, if no error margin is specified, as having a margin determined by rounding off to the last decimal place. The Guidelines do not indicate when to use which interpretation. (F-IV,4.7, not in GL 2017)

Terms such as 'substantially' and 'approximately' applied to a structural unit, e.g. a tray plate with a substantially circular circumference, is interpreted as a feature of the unit being produced within the tolerance of the method used to manufacture it. (F-IV,4.7.1, not in GL 2017)

Unclear expressions will be objected to if the application suggest that they extend the interval beyond the above-mentioned error margins or manufacturing tolerance. (F-IV,4.7.2, not in GL 2017)

Use of the word 'in' to define a relation between entities and/or activities in a claim may cause ambiguity in the scope of the claim. Examples are: cylinder head in an engine; in a telephone apparatus including a dial-tone detector, the dial-tone detector including ...; in a device for ..., the improvement consisting of ... It is essential to define the scope clearly; therefore, the use of the word 'in' for defining relations should normally be avoided. (F-IV,4.15)

Use of brackets in a claim defining a feature may lack clarity. For example, it is unclear whether or not a '(concrete) moulded brick' is limited to concrete. Use of brackets with a generally accepted meaning is allowable, such as in '(meth)acrylate', meaning 'acrylate' and 'methacrylate', and in formulae. (F-IV,4.19)

Trade marks and the like are only allowed if they are unavoidable and have a precise meaning (see e.g. **T480/98** (unclear) and **T623/91** (clear)).

Claims defining the invention by the result to be achieved should not be allowed, unless the invention can only be defined in such terms and the result can be verified by described tests involving nothing more than trial and error.

1.5 PARAMETER FEATURES

A parameter in a claim which depends on a mode of operation of a device such as the adjustable pulse time of a laser, i.e. on a human factor irrelevant to the device per se, makes the extent of protection ambiguous and indefinite. Such a claim lacks clarity under **Art.84**. (**T227/91** r.3)

A claim for a product characterized by parameters related to its physical structure is allowed, provided the parameters can be clearly and reliably determined objectively by a method for measuring (**T94/82**). The method must either belong to common general knowledge, so that no explicit description is needed, or the method needs to be identified (**T860/93**). The claim need not describe the manufacture of such a product, but the description must enable a skilled person to make the product (**T94/82**). An opponent alleging that the measurement of a parameter is unclear must provide proof that a skilled person was unable to determine the value of the parameter (**T525/99**, r.3.1.2: a party making an allegation must prove the correctness of the allegation).

1.6 DEFINITION IN TERMS OF EFFECT

A claim must be defined in terms of technical features according to **R.43(1)**. A technical feature is a feature that can be read by a skilled person as an instruction as to the technical procedure to be followed to achieve a given result. Such an instruction may be explicit or functional, i.e. defined in terms of an effect. (**T68/85** r.8.4.1)

A definition in terms of effect is often chosen to provide a broad scope. The Guidelines distinguish between two types of definition in terms of effect: functional feature and result to be achieved. The requirements for allowing the two types of definition are different (F-IV,4.10)

1.6.1 Functional features

A functional feature in a claim is a feature defined in terms of function rather than structure. A functional feature is a feature known to the skilled person. It often defines its function without reference to other features ('means for mixing powder') or with reference to another feature ('means for transmitting the signal to an input port').

A functional feature has a scope extending to all means providing the same effect, where structurally disclosed means within that scope only represent examples. Note, that the EPO sometimes makes a prior art document relevant in the assessment of patentability by giving a 'means for' feature in the document the function it has in the patent application although the feature in the document has a different function but can, unintentionally, perform the function of the patent application.

A functional definition is acceptable if the broad scope cannot be obtained easily with a definition in structural terms, the skilled person can provide some means of performing this function without undue burden (F-IV,2.1) and he would appreciate that means other than those disclosed in the description could be used for the same function (F-IV,6.5).

A functional feature is sufficiently disclosed if the examples given in the description allow a skilled person to implement other embodiments. For example, the feature 'terminal position detecting means' supported only by a limit switch can obviously also be realised by a photoelectric cell or a strain gauge. The EPO may require limitation of the scope of a functional feature if the description shows only one particular way of implementing the feature and alternatives are not obvious. (F-IV,6.5)

A medicament claim may define the illness to be treated in a functional way, e.g. an illness that requires as treatment the selective occupation of a specific receptor, provided the skilled person has instructions either from the application or from common general knowledge to recognise which medical conditions fall within this definition (**T241/95** r.3.1.1; F-IV,4.22)

Functional features are less common in chemistry than in other technical fields. **Art.83** requires that a claim defining a chemical compound using a functional feature is allowable provided the feature can be reduced to practice without undue burden (r.5). This requirement is met if the number of alternative compounds covered is finite (r.5.5). However, if the number of alternatives is infinite and includes compounds not yet structurally defined on the priority date, the burden is undue (r.3.2). This is the case for a claim defining a compound having a specific medical effect, the compound to be selected by testing every conceivable compound with a newly discovered screening method. Such a compound claim is not patentable, although a claim relating to the screening method as such could be patentable. The compound claim is an example of a 'reach-through' claim, having a scope broader than the applicant's actual contribution to the art and claiming unexplored fields of research. (**T1063/06**)

1.6.2 *Result to be achieved*

The second type of definition in terms of effect consists of a feature defining the invention by a result to be achieved (F-IV,4.10). For example, a claim relating to an agent for selective weed control contains as feature a specified compound 'in an amount producing a synergistic herbicidal effect' (**T68/85** r.2), or to a device having flanges 'so dimensioned as to enable the device to be moved by facial muscles and to hold it firmly in the speaking position' (**T204/90**).

The result to be achieved is often related to the technical problem solved by the invention and is normally not part of the state of the art, in contrast with the above functional feature. It is therefore important that the description or common general knowledge provides tests and criteria to allow the skilled person to assess whether the desired result is achieved (**T241/95** hn.II). As a general rule, claims which attempt to define the invention by a result to be achieved should not be allowed, in particular if they only amount to claiming the underlying technical problem (F-IV,4.10). A claim that defines a result to be achieved that essentially corresponds to the problem to be solved must include all features necessary to achieve the result (**T809/12** r.2.8).

A definition in terms of a result to be achieved is allowed if all of the following requirements are met:

1 the feature cannot otherwise be defined more precisely without restricting the scope;
2 the feature provides instructions sufficiently clear to be reduced to practice without undue burden, if necessary with reasonable experiments; the result can be verified directly and positively; and
3 the state of the art does not stand in the way of using such functional and therefore general and broad terminology. (**T204/90** r.3.2, following **T68/85** hn, r.8.4.1-3; F-IV,4.10)

1.7 DISCLAIMERS

Generally, the subject-matter of a claim is defined in terms of positive features (F-IV,4.20). However, in special circumstances the extent of a claim may be limited by a negative feature, i.e. a disclaimer, without contravening the clarity requirement of **Art.84**. A disclaimer is allowed if the subject-matter remaining in the claim cannot be defined more clearly and concisely in terms of positive features (**T4/80** hn). A disclaimer is also accepted if the subject-matter cannot be defined in terms of positive features without unduly restricting the scope of the claim (**T1050/93** r.3.6).

There are three common cases where subject-matter can be excluded using a negative feature (**G2/03**). In the first case a claim is limited in view of a prior right to restore novelty. In the second case the exclusion restores novelty over an accidental anticipation. An accidental anticipation is so unrelated to and remote from the claimed invention that the skilled person would never have taken it into consideration. In the third case subject-matter must be excluded because it is not patentable under **Art.52-57** for non-technical reasons, e.g. a possible therapeutic use of a method must be excluded to avoid a conflict with **Art.53(c)**.

A disclaimer can restore the novelty of a claim; however, it cannot impart inventive step to a teaching which is obvious (**T170/87** r.8.4.4). A range is not rendered novel by the fact that the values from an example of a prior art document are excepted by a disclaimer, at least not if these values cannot be regarded as individual (**T188/83**).

A disclaimer may be introduced in a claim by way of amendment under **Art.123(2)**. The conditions for allowance of such an amendment are given in **Art.123(2):2.4**.

1.8 PRODUCT-BY-PROCESS CLAIMS

Claims for products defined in terms of a process are allowed only if the product is patentable (new and inventive) and the product cannot be defined in a better way. A product is not novel because of a novel process (**T150/82**). According to **T20/94** hn.2 it is immaterial whether the claim uses the words 'product X obtainable by process Y', 'obtained by' or 'directly obtained by' (F-IV,4.12). Since courts and patent offices other than the EPO may interpret words differently, it is recommended to use the broadest term 'obtainable' when drafting a patent application.

1.9 USE FEATURES

A use feature in a claim, e.g. 'product X for use in application Y', 'device for mixing powders' or 'component A connectable to component B', is interpreted as 'suitable for the use' and limits the scope of the claim only to the extent of suitability for the specified use (see T304/08).

In contrast, the 'use' in a claim to a known substance for use in a medical method or features of the form 'means for ...' in the data-processing / computer program field are interpreted as means adapted co carry out the relevant steps or functions rather than merely means suitable for carrying them out. (F-IV,4.13, not in GL 2017)

Lack of clarity can result if a claim for a first entity specifies the relationship of the first entity to a second entity related to it through use but not included in the scope of the claim. For example, clarity is lacking in a claim relating to a plug for fitting in a wall, the length of the plug being related to the thickness of the wall. There is no lack of clarity, if the features of the second entity are standardized ('a box for storing audio cassettes which project out of the box for easy removal') or are usual in the art ('a cover sheet for a hay bale, the size of the sheet being related to the dimensions of the bale' **T455/92**). Initially, such a claim is interpreted as not including the second entity or its features and the first entity is limited to being suitable for use with the second entity. If the claim is without any doubt directed to a combination of the first and second entities or where the use causes unclarity, the claim must be reworded to define the combination, e.g. by changing 'connectable' to 'connected'. (F-IV,4.14)

Use features are common in distributed inventions, where the invention relates to an improvement in two separate but inter-related products which may be sold separately, but each carry out the same inventive idea, such as an electric plug and socket or transmitter and receiver (F-IV,3.2). The use feature in such an invention relates the two independent claims in respect of each of the products and causes a co-operative functionality between them. This effect of the use feature must be taken into account when assessing the clarity of the claims (**T1194/97** r.2.4). For example, the independent claims relate to a reading device and a record medium for use in the device, on which digital data is recorded in a specified data structure. The reference to the reading device explains the data structure and thus clarifies the subject-matter for which protection is sought. The claim is limited in so far as the 'for use' excludes interpretations which would be incompatible with this use (**T1194/97** r.2.2).

'Use of the substance X as insecticide' is not a claim directed to the substance X, but is equivalent to the process claim 'the process of killing insects using substance X'. 'Use of a transistor in an amplifying circuit' is a process claim for the process of amplification using a circuit with a transistor, and not a claim for an amplifying circuit comprising a transistor, and neither a claim for the process of using the transistor in building such a circuit. (F-IV,4.16)

See **Art.54(1):7** on the extent of conformance for the effect of a use feature on the assessment of prior art.

1.10 COMPRISING VS. CONSISTING

The terms 'comprising' and 'consisting' have a specific meaning in patents that deviates from everyday language. 'Comprising' is not limiting; 'consisting' is limiting. Hence, a claim directed to a compound comprising components A and B does not exclude the presence of other components. However, a claim directed to a compound consisting of components A and B does not include other components. The expression 'consisting essentially of' or 'consisting substantially of' may be used to indicate the presence of other components that do not materially affect the essential characteristics of the compound. (F-IV,4.21, not in GL 2017)

2 Conciseness

Single claims as well as the totality of the claims must be concise (F-IV,5). A large number of claims does not meet the requirement of clarity and conciseness of **Art.84** and **R.43(5)** (**T246/91** r.7). The number of independent claims in the same category is also limited by **R.43(2)**.

A Markush formula is the concisest means of defining a class of chemical compounds (**T1020/98** hn.II).

The EPO tries to force applicants to comply with **Art.84** before it carries out the search. It levies claims fees, increasing with the number of claims, on filing (**R.45**; see in particular **R.45(1):2** for reduction of claims fees). The EPO will ask an applicant to indicate the independent claims to be searched if a plurality of independent claims in the application does not comply with the requirements of **R.43(2)** (**R.62a**). If the application is not sufficiently clear to carry out a search, the applicant will be requested to indicate the subject-matter to be searched (**R.63**). Any unsearched subject-matter may not be used for amendment of claims during prosecution of the application (**R.137(5)**).

3 **Support in the description**

The claims must be supported by the description according to **Art.84**. This means that there must be a basis in the description for the subject-matter of every claim and that the scope of the claims must not be broader than is justified by the extent of the description and drawings and also the contribution of the invention to the art (**T409/91** r.3.3; F-IV,6.1).

Support by the description is generally assumed, unless exceptionally there are reasons to believe that the skilled person would be unable to extend the invention to the scope of the claims on the basis of the description by exercising routine methods. The support must be of a technical character. The examiner should only raise an objection of non-support if he has well-founded reasons, preferably supported by a published document. (F-IV,6.3)

An embodiment presented in the application as filed as not being part of the invention but e.g. as belonging to the state of the art or as a comparative example cannot be claimed (**G2/10** r.4.5).

Subject-matter clearly disclosed only in a claim may later be added to the description. Where the claim is dependent, it may suffice if the description mentions that the claim gives a particular embodiment of the invention. (F-IV,6.6)

3.1 BROAD CLAIMS

Most claims are generalisations of one or more examples. A claim should not be so broad that it goes beyond the description nor yet so narrow as to deprive the applicant of a just reward for disclosing his invention. An invention in a new field permits wider claims than an advance in a known field. The applicant should be allowed to cover all obvious modifications, equivalents to and uses of the invention. Later additions should not contravene **Art.123(2)**.

A claim may broadly define a feature in terms of its function, even when it is supported by only one example, provided that example suffices the skilled person to see alternatives. If the description suggests that the function should be carried out in a particular way and other ways appear inappropriate, the claim must be restricted to this particular way. (see F-IV,4.23)

A broad claim concerning a group of chemical compounds per se does not lack support for the sole reason that the description does not make it sufficiently credible that an alleged technical effect (which is not, however, part of the claim) is obtained by all compounds. 'Supported by the description' means that the technical features stated in the description as being essential features of the described invention must be the same as those in the claims (**T409/91** r.3.2), for otherwise the claims would not be true definitions but mere descriptions. The question of achievement of the technical effect by all compounds arises under **Art.56**, if this effect is the sole reason for the alleged inventiveness of the compounds. (**T939/92** hn.I, II, r.2.2.2)

3.2 BROAD CLAIM IN OPPOSITION

Art.84 is no ground for opposition. If a very broad claim has been granted, it cannot be opposed based on **Art.84**. However, lack of support can also be considered as insufficient disclosure (**Art.83**), which can be used as ground for opposition. Although **Art.83** and **Art.84** relate to different parts of the application, they give effect to the same legal principle that the patent monopoly should be justified by the technical contribution to the art. The claims should not extend to subject-matter which, after reading the description, would still not be at the disposal of the skilled person. Claiming not only the technical contribution to the art actually described but also to monopolise overtly covetously a technical area extending well beyond it would be contrary to the requirement of support in **Art.84**. Hence, an essential feature must be included in the main claim. The disclosure of the invention is only sufficient if it enables the skilled person to obtain substantially all embodiments falling within the ambit of the claims (**T226/85**). The disclosure of only a single way of performing the invention is only sufficient if it allows the skilled person to perform the invention in the whole range that is claimed. (**T409/91** hn, r.3; see also **T595/90** hn.II)

3.3 AMENDMENT OF CLAIMS

The scope of the claims may be extended during the examination of the application, provided there is support for the extension in the description. After grant, e.g. during opposition proceedings, extension is not allowed any more (**Art.123(3)**). It is not permitted by **Art.123(2)** to delete a feature from an independent claim if the application as filed presents the feature as essential (**T260/85**).

4 Relation between Art.83 and 84

T94/82 gave the following relation between the requirements of **Art.83** and **84**, where a claim defined a product in terms of parameters relating to its physical structure. The requirement of **Art.83** is fulfilled if the description enables the skilled person to obtain the product; the requirement of **Art.84** is met if the parameters in the claim can be clearly and reliably determined by objective procedures.

However there are situations where the requirements overlap. This is relevant for examination: the requirements of both **Art.83** and **Art.84** will be examined during grant proceedings; during opposition proceedings compliance with **Art.83** will be examined without restriction, but compliance with **Art.84** will be examined only in relation to an amendment of the patent (**T127/85** r.2.1; **T301/87** hn.I; see **Art.100:2** and **Art.101(3):1**). The overlap of requirements broadens the issues to be examined and objections that can be raised during opposition, allowing issues of support and clarity to be objected to under **Art.83**.

4.1 LACK OF SUPPORT

Sufficiency and support give effect to the same legal principle that the patent monopoly should be justified by the technical contribution to the art (**T409/91** hn). The protection conferred by a patent should correspond to the technical contribution to the art made by the disclosure, which excludes the patent monopoly from being extended to subject-matter which, after reading the patent specification, would still not be at the disposal of the skilled person (**T435/91** r.2.2.1; F-IV,6.1).

An objection under **Art.83** of non-availability of some embodiments and the requirement of enablement to carry out the invention may lead to an objection under **Art.84** that the claims are not properly supported. It has to be decided on a case by case basis whether broad functional terminology in the claims is the only possible way to define the invention to provide fair protection. (**T292/85** r.3)

Only if the whole scope of a claim is affected by an ambiguity such that it is impossible to carry out at all the invention, an objection under **Art.83** will be raised. Otherwise an objection under **Art.84** is appropriate (**T608/07**; F-III,11).

4.2 LACK OF CLARITY

The EPO has no uniform way of handling clarity objections relating to parameters. A claim using parameters that are not defined and lack details of the measuring method in the application may be objected to under **Art.83** or **84**, depending on the particular board of appeal, although there is a tendency to use **Art.83** in opposition proceedings (see Case Law of the BoA, II.C.7.2).

An ill-defined parameter in a claim may give rise to objections under both **Art.83** and **84** (T593/09; F-III,11)

Art. 85 Abstract

The abstract shall serve the purpose of technical information only; it may not be taken into account for any other purpose, in particular for interpreting the scope of the protection sought or applying Article 54, paragraph 3.

Art.54(3) Prior rights
See for the implementation:
R.47 Form and content of the abstract
R.66 Definitive content of the abstract

1 **Informative character of abstract**

An application must contain an abstract (**Art.78(1)(e)**). The purpose of the abstract is to inform the public of the invention of the application. It is therefore included in the publication of the application (**R.68**). The abstract should also assist the EPO in searching in the particular technical field of the invention (**R.47(5)**).

The informative character of the abstract means that it cannot be regarded as content of the application as filed in the sense of **Art.123(2)** (**T246/86**) and of **Art.54(3)** (**Art.85**). After publication under **Art.93(2)** the abstract is available to the public in the sense of **Art.54(2)** and may be used as state of the art for assessing both novelty and inventive step (**T160/92** hn.I). However, if an abstract and its cross-referenced original document contain conflicting teachings, the disclosure of the abstract should be interpreted by reference to the original document; if the disclosure of the abstract is erroneous, it should not be considered as part of the state of the art (**T77/87** hn2).

2 **Missing abstract**

If the abstract is lacking in the application documents, the Receiving Section will notify the applicant (**Art.90(3)**, **R.57(d)**), and invite him to file the abstract within a period of two months (**R.58**). If not filed in time, the application will be refused (**Art.90(5)**). Remedy is possible with re-establishment. The final contents of the abstract are determined by the search division (**R.66**).

Art. 86 Renewal fees for the European patent application

1 Character of renewal fees

Art.86 governs the payment of renewal fees for patent applications which are still pending after 2 years from the date of filing of the application. Renewal fees differ from most of the other fees in that they do not entitle the payer to a service of the EPO. It is a generally accepted fund-raising provision for patent offices which allows to keep the initial costs of patenting in the form of filing, search and examination fees below the break-even level and reduce the financial hurdle at the start of the patenting process. The annually recurring renewal fees are a stimulus for an applicant or proprietor to leave the invention to the public domain as soon as protection is no longer needed (**T1402/13** r.4.4.3).

The renewal fees to be paid to the EPO under **Art.86(1)** relate only to patent applications. After grant, renewal fees must be paid to the national offices of contracting states where the patent is validated (**Art.86(2)**). Part of the renewal fees received by the national offices for European patents is paid to the EPO under **Art.39(1)**.

Art.86 and **R.51** provide a self-contained set of rules relating to the payment of renewal fees, aimed at a simple administration for the EPO (**J4/91** r.2.4.2). The periods for payment of renewal fees are different from other periods in the EPC. A renewal fee must be paid on a specific date, the due date, not within a period of specified duration. The due date is the last day of the month containing the anniversary of the date of filing (**R.51(1)**).

Most fees can only be paid validly within a normal period running from the due date (see **Rfees4** for the meaning of 'due date'). A payment before the due date is invalid; often a payment with surcharge may be made in a grace period following the normal period. In contrast, a renewal fee may be paid up to three or six months before the due date (**R.51(1)**). A renewal fee may be paid in an additional period of six months from the due date, provided an additional fee is paid (**R.51(2)**).

Special provisions govern the payment of renewal fees for a divisional application, with two concurrent periods (**R.51(3)**), for cases of re-establishment of rights under **Art.122** (**R.51(4)**) and for the case of a petition of review under **Art.112a** (**R.51(5)**).

The terminology of renewal fees differs from the terminology of other fees. The surcharge for late payment of a renewal fee is called an 'additional fee'. The 6-month period for payment of this fee **R.51(2)** is called an 'additional period'.

Art. 86(1) Renewal fees for the European patent application shall be paid to the European Patent Office in accordance with the Implementing Regulations. These fees shall be due in respect of the third year and each subsequent year, calculated from the date of filing of the application. If a renewal fee is not paid in due time, the application shall be deemed to be withdrawn.

See for the implementation:
R.51 Date for payment of renewal fees
Rfees2(1)4 Amount of renewal fee
Rfees2(1)5 Additional fee

1 **Patent years**

No renewal fee is due for an application in respect of the first two patent years. The first renewal fee to be paid to the EPO is due in respect of the third patent year (**Art.86(1)**). The last renewal fee to be paid to the EPO is due in respect of the patent year in which the mention of the grant is published (**Art.86(2)**). The renewal fees for the European patent in respect of the subsequent years must be paid to the national offices (**Art.141(1)**). If the mention is published in the first or second patent year, no renewal fees for the EPO are due.

A patent year runs from the day after the anniversary of the application until the next anniversary (based on **R.131(2)**, first sentence). Patent years are counted from the date of filing, not from the priority date, because **Art.89** does not refer to **Art.86(1)**. A renewal fee in respect of the coming year is due on the last day of the month containing the anniversary of the date of filing (**R.51(1)**). (A-X,5.2.4)

An example: an application is filed on 04.06.2018, the anniversary is 04.06, the first patent year runs from 04.06.2018 to 04.06.2019 (based on **R.131(3)**), the second patent year from 05.06.2019 to 04.06.2020 and the third patent year from 05.06.2020 to 04.06.2021. The first renewal fee payable, i.e. the renewal fee in respect of the third patent year, is due on 30.06.2020. There is no renewal fee due if the mention of the grant is published on or before 04.06.2020. The renewal fee in respect of the third year is due if the mention is published on or after 05.06.2020. See A-X,5.2.4 for more examples.

2 **Payment of renewal fee**

The amount of the fee is determined by **Rfees2(1)4** as valid at the date the payment is considered to have been made to the EPO pursuant to **Rfees7** (A-X,5.1.2 and for example OJ 1997, 12, Art.2). An increase in fee can be avoided by an early payment up to three or six months before the due date (**R.51(1)**; OJ 1987, 4).

The renewal fee must be paid at the latest on the due date and may be paid up to three or six months before this date (**R.51(1)**). If the renewal fee has not been paid on the due date, the renewal fee plus an additional fee (**Rfees2(1)5**) can be paid within an additional period of six months of the due date (**R.51(2)**).

3 **Notification of non-payment of renewal fee**

If the renewal fee has not been paid on or before the due date, the EPO informs, as a courtesy service, the applicant as soon as possible of the possibility of payment with additional fee in the already running six-month period of the due date (A-X,5.2.4). The EPO is not compelled to send this notice. Hence, the applicant cannot derive rights from the omission of such a reminder (**J1/89** hn.I.2). Re-establishment under **Art.122** cannot be based on the absence of such a notice (**J12/84** hn2). Where the EPO does send the notice, the applicant can rely on its accuracy; a late payment due to a misleading notice will be regarded as in due time (**J1/89**).

If the renewal fee and additional fee are not even paid within the six-month period, the EPO will send a communication under **R.112(1)**, notifying the applicant of the loss of rights. In contrast with the courtesy service, the EPO is obliged to send the communication under **R.112(1)**.

4 **Effect of non-payment**

Non-payment of the renewal fee on or before the due date does not result in a loss of the application. If the renewal fee and the additional fee have not been paid within the six-month period, the application will be deemed withdrawn upon expiry of the six-month period (**Art.86(1)**, second sentence, and **R.51(2)**, second sentence). Hence, a divisional application can be validly filed in the six-month period, even if the renewal fee for the parent application is not paid before expiry of the six-month period.

Note, that the onset of the sanction on non-payment of the renewal fee is inconsistent with the principle that deemed withdrawal takes effect at expiry of the normal period and not at expiry of a grace period (**J4/86**, endorsed by **G4/98** r.7). The European patent with unitary effect does follow said principle in that the patent will lapse on the date the renewal fee was due if the renewal fee and any additional fee are not paid in due time (OJ 2016 A39 R.14(2)).

5 **Remedy**

Failure to pay the renewal fee before or on the due date may be redressed by paying the renewal fee with additional fee within the six-month additional period of **R.51(2)**. Further processing and re-establishment are probably excluded, because the due date is not a proper time limit in the sense of **Art.121(1)** and **Art.122(1)**. Moreover, the remedy of **R.51(2)** is more reliable.

Failure to pay the renewal fee and additional fee within the six-month additional period cannot be redressed using further processing, because the period is excluded in **R.135(2)**. Because of this exclusion re-establishment under **Art.122** and **R.136** is possible (**R.136(3)**). The fatal period of one year within which the request for re-establishment must be filed starts running at the expiry of the six-month additional period (**R.136(1)**). Re-establishment must be requested within two months from removal of the cause of non-compliance, the fee for re-establishment, the renewal fee and the additional fee must be paid and all due care must be proven.

6 **Refund of renewal fee**

Renewal fees paid for an application not anymore pending on the due date are refunded (A-X,10.1.1). If no request for examination has been filed, also not in the further processing period of **R.135(1)**, the paid renewal fee that became due after the expiry of the normal 6-month period of **R.70(1)** is refunded, because the application ceased to exist at the expiry of the normal period (**J4/86**).

If the anniversary is e.g. on 15.07.2018, then a renewal fee is due on 31.07.2018. A payment made on 10.07.2018, i.e. before the due date, is a pre-payment, which will be refunded as having no basis if the application is (deemed) withdrawn on or before the due date, i.e. on or before 31.07.2018.

Art. 86(2) The obligation to pay renewal fees shall terminate with the payment of the renewal fee due in respect of the year in which the mention of the grant of the European patent is published in the European Patent Bulletin.

1 **Last renewal fee for EPO**

The last renewal fee payable to the EPO is in respect of the patent year in which the mention of the grant is published. The payment of this last renewal fee is checked before the grant of the patent as provided for in **Art.97(1)** and **R.71a(4)**. Renewal fees for the following years are to be paid to the national offices. This is stated implicitly in **Art.141(1)** and **Art.39(1)** and explicitly in NatLaw table VI. The transition of the obligation to pay from the EPO to the national offices is laid down in **Art.86(2)** and **Art.141**.

See **Art.86(1):1** for an example of the payment of the last renewal fee to the EPO.

Chapter II *Priority*

1 **General**
The right of priority has the effect that the date of filing of an application will be replaced by the date of filing of an earlier application (**Art.89**).

The EPC has its own complete, self-contained code of rules on priority. It has not taken over the exact wording of the Paris Convention (see note 3 to the Preamble). The EPC allows an internal priority and thereby extends beyond the minimum standards of the Paris Convention, which only regulates external priorities (Art.4A(1) PC). The Paris Convention is ambiguous on whether a patent application can claim the priority of an industrial design or a trademark, which has been clarified in the EPC as being not allowed. (J15/80; A-III,6.1)

The priority rules of the EPC apply not only to direct European applications but also to Euro-PCT applications that have entered the European phase (see **Art.150(2):2**).

Art. 87 Priority right

Art. 87(1) Any person who has duly filed, in or for
(a) any State party to the Paris Convention for the Protection of Industrial Property or
(b) any Member of the World Trade Organization,
an application for a patent, a utility model or a utility certificate, or his successor in title, shall enjoy, for the purpose of filing a European patent application in respect of the same invention, a right of priority during a period of twelve months from the date of filing of the first application.

1 **General**
Art.87 deals with the recognition of priority rights. **Art.87(1)** is aligned with Article 2 of the TRIPs Agreement, which requires that priority rights also be extended to first filings made in any WTO member state. Note however that **Art.87(2)** and (4) still refer only to a State, not to a Member. The lacking 'member of the WTO' in these paragraphs is an omission that should be rectified in the next Diplomatic Conference.

2 **'Duly filed in or for any state'**
According to **Art.87(1)**, the first application used as basis for a priority claim must be 'duly filed'. The 'duly' refers to the requirement that the first application must be filed in such a way that a date of filing is accorded, giving the application the status of a regular national filing according to **Art.87(3)**, which the EPC in **Art.87(2)** recognizes as giving rise to a right of priority.

The first application must be filed in or for any state party to the Paris Convention, or a member of the WTO. Therefore, an application filed in a state not party to either agreement cannot serve as a basis for claiming the right of priority (subject to **Art.87(5)**). Such an application is not a first application in the sense of **Art.87(1)** and a subsequent filing in a state party to the Paris Convention or a WTO member will still be considered as a first application in the sense of **Art.87(1)**. See also **Art.87(5)** for states not party to either agreement.

The first application may be a national application filed with the national authorities of a state ('filed *in* a state') or an international or regional application in which the state is designated ('filed *for* a state'). Hence, the priority may be claimed of an earlier national, European or PCT application (F-VI,1.3).

The state in or for which a first application is filed, may be designated in the subsequent priority claiming European application (internal priority), because **Art.87(1)** has no restrictions on the Paris Convention state in or for which the first application is filed ('any') and **Art.3** allows the designation of any contracting state. The Paris Convention provides for external priority only (Art.4A(1) PC).

3 **'An application'**

The application must be

for a patent or

for the registration of a utility model or

for a utility certificate.

The list is exhaustive. Hence, a priority claim based on the deposit of an industrial design is not recognized (**J15/80**). Inventor's certificates are no longer referred to in EPC 2000, as such provisions are obsolete.

4 **'A person or his successor in title'**

Any person who has duly filed a patent application or his successor in title enjoys a right of priority (**Art.87(1)**).

If the applicant of the first application also files the subsequent application, he is entitled to priority. The same applies if several applicants file the first application and the same applicants file the subsequent application. The following subsection deals with the situation in which several applicants file one application and not all of them file the other application.

The successor in title of the applicant of the first application also enjoys a right of priority. The issue of which right he must be successor in title to, the law applicable to the transfer of the title and the possibility of a retro-active transfer are discussed in the following subsections.

It should be borne in mind, that if the transfer is not valid, there is no provision in the EPC to remedy the resulting loss of priority right, although national law may provide a remedy (R. Wieczorek *Die Unionspriorität im Patentrecht* (Köln, 1975)). If the transfer cannot be effected in due time for practical reasons, a valid priority claim may still be established, if the subsequent application is filed in the name of the applicant of the first application; the applicant can transfer the priority right and the right to the subsequent application to his successor in title after the filing of the subsequent application.

4.1 MULTIPLE APPLICANTS

Two different cases with different number of applicants for the first and subsequent application must be distinguished.

In the first case the first application is filed by applicant X and the subsequent application by applicants X and Y. Both X and Y may be one or more applicants. The right of priority of X extends to X and Y, provided that the one or more applicants of the first application are among the applicants of the subsequent application (A-III,6.1). There is no need for a transfer of the priority right to the other applicants (A-III,6.1). **T1933/12** is one of the very few decisions on this issue and supports the above point of few of the Guidelines. Its sole reasoning is 'as the board understands', **Art.87(1)** does not exclude the sharing of a priority right (r.2.4), which is poor.

In the second case the first application is filed by applicants X and Y and the subsequent application by applicant X. The priority right belongs simultaneously and jointly to the applicants X and Y of the first application, which thus constitute a legal unity. **Art.87(1)** and **88(1)** imply identity for applicants of the first and later application. If there is no transfer of the priority right from Y to X, the priority application is not a first application within the meaning of **Art.87(1)** and there is no valid priority (**T788/05** r.2). The same reasoning is used for identity of applicants for a parent and a divisional application (**J2/01**).

If the reasoning of **T788/05** where applied to the first case, the priority would not be valid, since the legal unity X changes to the different legal unity X & Y without a transfer. The established practice of the EPO in both cases could be regarded as inconsistent. Another consequence of the practice in the first case is, that if X withdraws as applicant after filing of the subsequent application, Y has obtained the right of priority whereas he is neither the applicant nor the successor in title in the sense of **Art.87(1)** because there has been no transfer of the right. If Y would join as applicant only after filing of the subsequent application, it is not clear whether he would enjoy the right of priority without a transfer.

4.2 RIGHTS SUBSISTING IN AN APPLICATION

The filing of a first application in or for a state creates two distinguishable rights for the applicant. The first one is the right to the grant of a patent having effect in that state. The second one is the right to claim priority from this application in a subsequent application filed in or for a state recognizing the first filing as giving rise to a right of priority. When, for instance, the first filing was made in a state party to the Paris Convention, other states party to the Paris Convention must recognize a priority claim from this first application.

Since ownership of the application and ownership of the right to priority can usually be separated, the applicant may transfer the right of priority to a successor in title independently of the right to the grant of the patent. If the applicant of a first application transfers his rights to a successor in title, he must transfer at least the right of priority for his successor in title to be able to claim priority of the first application (**T577/11** hn.3).

4.3 LAW APPLICABLE TO TRANSFER

The right to the first application is determined by the law of the state of filing the first application. For a European application **Art.60** and **61** apply. **Art.87(1)** vests the right of priority in the applicant of the first application or his successor in title. The inventorship of the first and subsequent applications is irrelevant for priority; it is the identity of the applicant which is decisive for the priority entitlement (**T5/05**). The transfer of the right of priority to a successor in title is the exclusive concern of national law (**T205/14** r.3.6.3). **T205/14** gives a three-step test for determining which national law is applicable to the transfer.

Since the right to priority is not the same as the right to the grant of a patent, the requirements of **Art.71, 72** and **R.22**, relating to the transfer of the right to grant, do therefore not apply to the transfer of a right to priority (**T205/14** r.3.6.1).

T1201/14 adds to the transfer the requirement that it must have been completed before filing of the subsequent application. That requirement could be regarded as interference with national law.

4.4 RETRO-ACTIVE TRANSFER

Where the applicant of the first application has omitted to transfer the right of priority to the applicant of the subsequent application within the priority year, he may try to include a retro-active clause in the transfer causing the transfer to occur before the date of filing the subsequent application. Several national laws permit such retro-active clauses.

However, **T1201/14** rejects a transfer with retro-active effect. **Art.87(1)** implies that a transfer must have been effected before the filing of the subsequent application (r.3.1.1.1). It held that such a retro-active effect would cause legal uncertainty for third parties about the status of the priority. However, a similar uncertainty about the status of the priority is created by the EPC in **R.52**, which allows filing a declaration of priority after the filing of the subsequent application. Case law has imposed the requirement on such a late declaration that the priority must be settled by the time the application is published.

The applicant should make every effort to conclude the transfer before the subsequent application is filed. If he does not succeed, he should convince the EPO that a retro-active transfer does not violate the EPC, using the above arguments and those in two legal opinions submitted on 29.06.2015 and 17.03.2016 in case EP1540227. The EPO should leave the transfer to national law and only require that the applicant provides certainty about the priority before publication of the application.

5 **'A European patent application in respect of the same invention'**

The EPC does not explicitly define the meaning of 'the same invention'. Opinion **G2/98** has ruled that a narrow or strict interpretation of 'the same invention' is appropriate, equating it with 'the same subject-matter' referred to in **Art.87(4)**. Consequently, the requirement for the right of priority is that the subject-matter of a claim defining the invention, i.e. the specific combination of features present in the claim, must be specifically disclosed in the first application as a whole, either explicitly or implicitly (**G2/98** r.2). Whether or not a feature is related to the function and effect of the invention is irrelevant (**G2/98** r.8.3). This interpretation is consistent with Art.4 of the Paris Convention and the EPC, in particular **Art.87(4)** and **Art.88(2)-(4)** (**G2/98** r.5, 6.8). A broad interpretation of the same invention would recognise the priority of a claim including a feature not disclosed in the priority document and not related to the function and effect of the invention (see e.g. **T73/88**, Snackfood). The broad interpretation is inappropriate, because it is at variance with the principle that the right to the patent should be associated with the application which discloses the subject-matter first (r.8.1), it gives an inconsistency between the same invention of **Art.87(1)** and the same subject-matter of **Art.87(4)** (r.8.2), and results in legal uncertainty because the relation of the feature to the effect and function of the invention depends on the prior art that happens to be found (r.8.3).

The characteristics of specific disclosure are dealt with in **Art.88(4):2**. Section F-VI,2.2 of the Guidelines reflects the ruling of **G2/98** on specific disclosure and determining priority dates. **Art.88(2)** and **(3)** discuss the effect of multiple priorities and alternative embodiments in a claim.

The wording of **Art.87(1)** is open to different interpretations regarding exhaustion of the priority right in the sense of whether or not the same priority right may be validly claimed in more than one European patent application. Case law has endorsed the practice of the EPO to allow claiming of the same priority right in more than one European patent application; hence, there is no exhaustion of priority rights (**T15/01** hn.1, r.33, 34; **T5/05**). The earlier decision **T998/99** should not be followed, as being an 'exception' (**T15/01** r.40).

6 **'A right of priority'**
A valid right of priority has the effect that the date of filing of the first application, i.e. the priority date, will count as the date of filing of the subsequent application for the purpose of establishing the prior art relevant for the application and for the right to the patent (**Art.89**).

The EPO examiner does normally not investigate the validity of the right to priority. He does so, however, if there is prior art (**Art.54(2)**) published on or after the priority date and before the date of filing, e.g. in the form of an intermediate document, or if the content of the application is totally or partly identical with the content of another European application within the meaning of **Art.54(3)**, such other application claiming a priority date within that period and designating one or more of the same states.

See **Art.88:3, 4** and A-III,6.9-10 for non-entitlement to and loss of the priority right.

7 **'During a period of twelve months'**
The European patent application must be filed within a period of twelve months from the date of filing of the first application (**Art.87(1)**). There are only limited remedies for failing to meet the 12-month period for claiming priority. Further processing cannot be used, because the period is excluded under **Art.121(4)**. The application of re-establishment is permitted according to **Art.122**, but the request must be filed within two months of the expiry of the 12 month priority period (**R.136(1)**).

The periods are extended when they expire on a non-working day (**R.134(1)**) and when the postal delivery is interrupted (**R.134(2)**) as published by the President or the EPO is on strike (implicit in **R.134(4)**, explicit in Art.4C(3) Paris Convention). Note that the priority period of **Art.87(1)** is also extended for non-working days of national offices when the European application is filed there (see **R.134(3)** and notes thereto).

The application may be regarded as received within the priority period even if actually received after its expiry, provided the conditions for despatch of **R.133** or the conditions of **R.134(5)** are met.

If the Receiving Section notices that the date of the earlier filing precedes the date of filing of the application by more than one year, it notifies the applicant that there will be no priority right, unless either a corrected date is indicated in accordance with **R.52(3)** within four months of the filing date of the application, or sixteen months from the priority date (A-III,6.6); or re-establishment is requested within two months from expiry of the priority period (**Art.122, R.136(1)**). The date of filing accorded, from which the 12-month term runs, can be later than the date of receipt of the document, e.g. if drawings have been added later (**R.56**).

8 **'The first application'**
The application of which priority is claimed must be 'a duly filed first application' in the sense that it must be the application in which the applicant describes for the first time the subject-matter of the European application claiming the priority. This principle is expressed in the EPC by the use of the ordinal number 'first' in **Art.87(1)** interpreted in view of its use in **Art.87(4)**. It should be noted that the 'first' in **Art.87(1)** appears prima facie to make a reference to the 'duly filed application' in the same provision, merely distinguishing between the 'duly filed application' and the 'subsequent, priority claiming application'.

If the subject-matter has been disclosed in a still earlier application originating from the same applicant or his predecessor in title, the priority claim does not comply with the requirements of **Art.87(1)** and the priority right for the earlier described subject-matter will be lost, even if the still earlier application had been withdrawn, to make cascading of applications impossible (see **R.57(g)**). See case **T788/05** (discussed in 'a person or his successors in title') for comments on the identity between applicants for first and second applications.

By way of exception, a subsequent application will be considered as a first application in spite of a previous first application relating to the same subject-matter, if the requirements of **Art.87(4)** have been fulfilled.

The EPC applies the priority right at the level of the claims of the patent application claiming priority, as implied by **Art.88(2)-(4)**. Hence, the priority right of a claim in an application can only be based on a first application, i.e. an earlier application specifically disclosing for the first time all subject-matter of that claim. If the earlier application is not the first application describing the subject-matter, but the subject-matter has been described in a still earlier application originating from the same applicant or his predecessor in title, the priority right for that claim is invalid. The effective date of the claim is the date of filing of the application. This claim is not novel if the still earlier application was published prior to the effective date of the application (**Art.54(2)**), or the still earlier application is a European application published on or after the effective date of the application (**Art.54(3)**). The priority right is valid for a claim relating to subject-matter not described in the still earlier application but described for the first time in the earlier application. See **Art.88(2):1** for the effect of multiple priorities on the effective date of a claim.

Art. 87(2) Every filing that is equivalent to a regular national filing under the national law of the State where it was made or under bilateral or multilateral agreements, including this Convention, shall be recognised as giving rise to a right of priority.

1 **Claiming priority from a regular national filing**

A European patent application may claim the priority of a regular national filing in or for a state. The latter filing can be under EPC or PCT. Conversely, a European filing having a filing date according to the EPC (**Art.80**) is equivalent to a regular national filing in a designated contracting state (**Art.66**).

Art. 87(3) A regular national filing shall mean any filing that is sufficient to establish the date on which the application was filed, whatever the outcome of the application may be.

1 **Regular national filing**

The requirements to establish a filing date at a national office are governed by national law. For example, in the United Kingdom an application without claims, a so-called provisional application, will be accorded a filing date, as the British patent law does not require claims for according a filing date.

Art.87(3) has the effect that a withdrawal, abandonment or refusal of the earlier application after its filing does not affect the right to priority. For example, if the designation fee of a European first application is not paid, the application will be deemed withdrawn upon expiry of the period of **R.39(1)** without having effect on the validity of the filing date accorded (**G4/98** r.5)

It is possible to file in the US a so-called 'provisional application for patent', requiring only a description and any drawings necessary for understanding the invention for according a filing date and giving rise to priority for a subsequent, non-provisional national application. The provisional application as such cannot lead to grant; however, the subsequent fate of a first filing is immaterial for the EPC. Hence, the EPO regards the provisional application as a duly filed national application in the sense of **Art.87(3)** which gives rise to a right of priority within the meaning of **Art.87(1)**. (OJ 1996,81)

Art. 87(4) A subsequent application in respect of the same subject-matter as a previous first application and filed in or for the same State shall be considered as the first application for the purposes of determining priority, provided that, at the date of filing the subsequent application, the previous application has been withdrawn, abandoned or refused, without being open to public inspection and without leaving any rights outstanding, and has not served as a basis for claiming a right of priority. The previous application may not thereafter serve as a basis for claiming a right of priority.

1 **Priority claim from a first application**

The purpose of the provision is to give the applicant the possibility to replace a previous application by a subsequent application as a basis for priority. The previous application may have been filed in too early a stage of research and does not describe the invention properly, as revealed by subsequent investigations. **Art.87(4)** allows the applicant to file a subsequent, improved application which will be regarded as a first application. Within twelve months from the filing of this subsequent first application he can file an application claiming priority of the subsequent first application.

The text of the provision implies that the right of priority may only be based on a first application, i.e. the application in which the applicant has disclosed the subject-matter for the first time. This requirement is consistent with the interpretation of the term 'first application' in **Art.87(1):8**.

See **Art.87(1):5** for the interpretation of the phrase 'the same subject-matter' in **Art.87(4)**.

2 **Requirements for regarding a subsequent application a first application**

Each of the following conditions contained in **Art.87(4)** must be met, if a subsequent application for the same subject-matter as the previous application will be regarded as a first application for priority purposes (F-VI,1.4.1).

1 The previous and subsequent application must have been filed in or for the same State. Note that 'State' appears to refer only to States party to the Paris Convention (**Art.87(1)**); there is no mention of being able to replace a first filing made in a WTO member. However, this must be interpreted in accordance with MR/12/00, which notes that priority rights -presumably including all aspects of priority- are to be extended to any WTO member.

The purpose of this requirement may be not to allow an applicant to circumvent difficulties in the prosecution of a first application in one country by filing a subsequent application in another country (Verlust des Prioritätsrechts, P. Wiegand, GRUR 1936, 351).

The fact that a previous application that has not left any rights outstanding, was not filed in or for the same state as the subsequent application will only be revealed during a file inspection in the applicant's office, as might be carried out in a discovery procedure under national law.

2 At the filing date of the subsequent application, the previous application must have been withdrawn, abandoned or refused. The previous application may not have been open for public inspection on or before the filing date of the subsequent application (see also the German text of **Art.87(4)**). Hence, a publication after the filing date of the subsequent application is not an obstacle to the subsequent application being regarded as a first application. The previous application may not leave any rights outstanding.

3 The previous application may not have served as a basis for claiming a right of priority before the filing date of the subsequent application. After the filing date of the subsequent application, the previous application may not serve either as a basis for claiming a right of priority. The last sentence of **Art.87(4)** is an implementation of the requirement in the same provision that the previous application does not leave any rights outstanding. After the replacement of a previous application by a subsequent application, priority on the basis of the previous application may no longer be recognized (Paris Convention, G.H.C. Bodenhausen (BIRPI 1968), commentary on the identical sentence in **Art.4C(4)** PC).

4 The applications must have been filed by the same applicant or his successor in title. Although this condition is not explicitly stated in **Art.87(4)**, it is a consequence of **Art.87(1)**, which states that only the applicant or his successor in title enjoys the right of priority of a first application. Hence, an application can solely claim priority from first applications that have been filed by the same applicant or his successor in title. Only such first applications are relevant for the application of **Art.87(4)**. Applications having different applicants face each other as prior art under **Art.54(2)** or (3). (**T5/05** r.4)

If any of these requirements is not fulfilled, the subsequent application will not be regarded as a first application, and a priority claim based on the subsequent application will be invalid in so far as it relates to subject-matter in the subsequent application already described in the previous application. The EPO will consider this issue only if there is evidence of the existence of a previous application and the priority is relevant in view of prior art. It will request the applicant to provide evidence, usually from a patent office, that the requirements of **Art.87(4)** are complied with (F-VI,1.4.1). A priority claim based on a US continuation-in-part is evidence for the existence of an earlier application; however, priority may be validly claimed for any subject matter first disclosed in the continuation in part. A priority claim based on a US continuation or a divisional application is always invalid because of the existence of an earlier application pending at the date of filing and the absence of added subject-matter.

3 Example

The effect of **Art.87(4)** is shown in decision **T1056/01**. Application A was filed with the UK patent office on 08.04.1991 and withdrawn in favour of application B, filed on 07.04.1992. Application A surfaced because the UK patent office published as part of their normal procedure its title, the name of the applicant and the withdrawal before publication of the application. European application C was filed on 07.04.1993 claiming priority from B. The applicant could not prove to the satisfaction of the EPO that A had been withdrawn on the filing date of B, as required for the application of **Art.87(4)**. As the UK patent office had destroyed the file of A five years after the withdrawal, it could not provide evidence of the actual date of withdrawal. Since applications A and B disclosed the same invention, B was not the first application in the sense of **Art.87(1)** and the priority claim was invalid. A publication on 16.02.1993 was therefore prior art and destroyed the novelty of the main claim of C.

Art. 87(5) If the first filing has been made with an industrial property authority which is not subject to the Paris Convention for the Protection of Industrial Property or the Agreement Establishing the World Trade Organization, paragraphs 1 to 4 shall apply if that authority, according to a communication issued by the President of the European Patent Office, recognises that a first filing made with the European Patent Office gives rise to a right of priority under conditions and with effects equivalent to those laid down in the Paris Convention.

1 **Recognition of priority from a state not party to Paris Convention and not WTO member**

Art.87(5) enables the President to issue a communication that the patent office of a state not party to the Paris Convention and not WTO member recognises that a first filing with the EPO gives rise to a priority effect according to the Paris Convention. This communication indicates that a first filing with that patent office will be dealt with as a first filing according to **Art.87(1)** to (4); hence, the EPO will recognize the priority right of the first filing. At present, 15.11.2017, the President has not issued a communication under **Art.87(5)** (A-III,6.2).

Since the recognition must be given by the industrial property authorities rather than the state, no agreements have to be concluded between that state and the EPO and the EPO contracting states. (Spec. Ed. 4 of OJ 2007)

The decisions **G2/02** hn = **G3/02** hn, relating to claiming priority from an application filed in a country being WTO member but not Paris Convention party, does no longer apply under the revised **Art.87(1)**. A still relevant reason of the decisions holds that the EPO itself is not bound directly by TRIPS (**G2/02** r.8.2, 8.3).

Art. 88 Claiming priority

1 **General**

Art.88 contains a first paragraph relating to procedural aspects of claiming priority and three paragraphs relating to substantive requirements for claiming priority.

2 **Effect of priority claim and its abandonment on time limits**

The priority date determines the expiry of certain time limits, such as the designation of the inventor (16 months, **R.60(1)**) and the publication of the application (18 months, **Art.93(1)**). Furthermore, the priority date is important for determining the state of the art and for determining which of two applications from independent persons for the same invention is to proceed to grant (**Art.54(2)**, **Art.60(2)**, **Art.89**).

An applicant can abandon the right of priority in order to meet a certain period running from the date of priority. The abandonment has no effect on periods which have already expired (A-III,6.11).

For example, an applicant can abandon the right of priority to avoid publication of the application 18 months after the priority date. However, when the technical preparations for publication have been completed (**R.67(2)**), then the application will still be published 18 months after the priority date; it will be a normal publication under **Art.54(2)**, with effect under **Art.54(3)** from the filing date and not from the priority date. (G-IV,5.1.1)

The right of priority can be abandoned for a European application even after publication of the application. This also applies to a PCT application (was forbidden after publication of the application by old R.32bis PCT, now deleted). In the regional phase, the possibility of withdrawal is governed by national law.

3 **Invalid priority claim**

An application has no right of priority if:
- The applicant of the application is not the same as the applicant or his successor in title of the earlier application (**Art.87(1)**).
- the application is not filed in the 12-month period of **Art.87(1)**, possibly extended according to **R.133** or **R.134(1) - (4)**, or the applicant failed to indicate a corrected date of priority after invitation in accordance with **R.52(3)**;
- the earlier application did not seek an industrial property right giving rise to a priority right, e.g. an industrial design (**Art.87(1)**);
- the earlier application does not give rise to a priority right in respect of the state or WTO member in or for which the later application was filed (**Art.87(1)**).
- the earlier application is not a first application in the sense of **Art.87(1)**.
- the application includes features which are not implicitly or explicitly disclosed in the earlier application (**Art.88(4):2** and **Art.87(1):5**); the application includes features for which the earlier application does not provide an enabling disclosure (see **Art.88(4):2**; the priority right for claims including such features is invalid, the priority right of other claims in the application may still be valid;
- The earlier application does not contain an enabling disclosure of the invention (**T206/83**, **T193/95**).

4 **Loss of priority right**

The right of priority is lost where:
- the declaration of priority is not filed in due time (**Art.88(1)**, **R.52(2)**, **R.41(2)(g)**);
- the certified copy of the earlier application or of any requested translation of the earlier application is not filed in due time (**R.53(1), (3)**).

The applicant is notified (**R.112(1)**) of any non-entitlement to or loss of priority right (**Art.90(5)**). The computation of not yet expired time limits that run from the priority date will take this new situation into account. This also applies where entitlement to priority is surrendered. (A-III,6.11)

Art. 88(1) An applicant desiring to take advantage of the priority of a previous application shall file a declaration of priority and any other document required, in accordance with the Implementing Regulations.

See for the implementation:
R.52 Declaration of priority
R.53 Priority documents
R.54 Issuing priority documents

1 **Formalities for claiming priority**

Art.88(1) governs the formal requirements for claiming priority by requiring the filing of a declaration of priority and any other document as set out in the Implementing Regulations.

The application will only have the benefit of the priority of a previous application if the applicant fulfils the following three requirements:

1 File a declaration of priority stating the date of the previous application, the state or WTO member in or for which it was made and the file number (**R.52(1)**). See **R.52(2)**, (3) for the time limit and correction of errors.

2 File a copy of the previous application. See **R.53(1)** for the time limit, and **R.53(2)** for cases where a copy need not be filed.

3 File a translation of the previous application or a declaration that the application and the previous application are identical, if the previous application is not in an official EPO language and the validity of the priority claim is relevant to patentability. See **R.53(3)** for the time limit and correction of errors.

The priority data is published in the patent application and in the patent specification (**R.52(5)**). A priority claim may be added or corrected under the circumstances and time limit as set out in **R.52(3)**; later correction may, exceptionally, be allowed under **R.139** (A-III,6.5.2).

Art. 88(2) Multiple priorities may be claimed in respect of a European patent application, notwithstanding the fact that they originated in different countries. Where appropriate, multiple priorities may be claimed for any one claim. Where multiple priorities are claimed, time limits which run from the date of priority shall run from the earliest date of priority.

1 **Multiple priorities**

The first sentence of **Art.88(2)** allows the claiming of multiple priorities and corresponds in substance to the first part of the first sentence of Art.4F Paris Convention. The second sentence of **Art.88(2)** allows multiple priorities to be claimed for a single claim. The legislative intent of this sentence can only be derived from the preparatory documents of the Convention, as set out in **G2/98** r.6.1-6.7. These documents distinguish 'AND' and 'OR' claims.

Where a first priority application discloses a feature A and a second priority application discloses a feature B for use together with A, then an 'AND' claim directed to A+B cannot enjoy a partial priority from the first priority date, because the invention A+B was disclosed only at the date of the second priority application. Hence, multiple priorities cannot be claimed for an 'AND' claim. (**G2/98** r.6.6)

Where a first priority application discloses a feature A and a second priority application discloses a feature B as an alternative to feature A, then an 'OR' claim directed to A or B can enjoy the first priority for part A of the claim and the second priority for part B of the claim ('partial priorities'). It is also acceptable to claim the two priorities for a claim directed to C, if the feature C, either in the form of a generic term or formula, or otherwise (a generic 'OR' claim), encompasses feature A as well as feature B. (**G2/98** r.6.7)

2 **Partial priority**

A partial priority is a situation in which only a part of the subject matter of a claim is entitled to the priority date of an earlier application. The entitlement to partial priority is relevant for patent families where the subject-matter of a patent application has been extended beyond that of its priority application, for example by introducing a generalisation of a more specific disclosure in the priority application.

Boards of appeal have applied the proviso of **G2/98** for determining entitlement to partial priority of a generic 'OR' claim. Decision **G2/98** r.6.7 held that a generic 'OR' claim for which multiple priorities are claimed is acceptable, provided it gives rise to the claiming of a limited number of clearly defined alternative subject-matters (the 'proviso'). Boards of Appeal have given different interpretations of the proviso for generic 'OR' claims, resulting in the referral to **G1/15**.

G1/15 assessed the relevance of the proviso for the entitlement to partial priority of a generic 'OR' claim. It concluded, that the only substantive requirement under **Art.87** and 88 for partial priority is the 'same invention', in line with **G2/98**. The proviso is not a requirement for recognising a partial priority claim. (**G1/15** r.5.3)

G1/15 did not cancel the proviso. The EBoA held that the proviso applies to multiple priorities and not to a partial priority (**G1/15** r.6.3). However, it did not explain how the proviso affects multiple priorities. A suggestion, compatible with both **G2/98** and **G1/15**, is to regard the proviso as a requirement under **Art.84** to impose clarity on cases claiming multiple priorities. The proviso does not apply to the claim itself, as was held by the decisions leading to the referral, but to the priority claims. The different priority claims should not cause an unclear legal situation, for example by overlapping ranges. This interpretation of the proviso has not yet been confirmed by case law.

G1/15 r6.4 gave a two-step test for assessing whether a generic 'OR' claim may enjoy partial priority. In the first step the relevant invention of the priority application is determined, using the disclosure test. The burden of proof of the disclosure lies with the applicant. In the second step it is determined whether the same invention is encompassed by the generic 'OR' claim of the subsequent application. If so, the claim is conceptually divided in a part corresponding to the invention disclosed in the priority application and enjoying priority, and in a remaining part not enjoying this priority. The priority document must disclose the invention for the first time, directly or at least implicitly, unambiguously and in an enabling manner (**G1/15** hn).

For example, when a priority document discloses an embodiment using iron and the claim of the subsequent application defines embodiments using metal, the embodiment using iron is entitled to priority and the embodiments using other metals do not enjoy the priority. See also **T260/14** r.2 for an example.

T1519/15 broadened the generic 'OR' claim to absence of a feature in the claim of the subsequent application. It applied **G1/15** to a case where the priority application discloses a circuit having four sensing capacitors and seven transistors and the claim of the subsequent application having at least two sensing capacitors but not specifying any transistors. Since the claim does not specify transistors, it encompasses the specific embodiment including seven transistors. The four sensing capacitors are also encompassed by the at least two sensing capacitors in the claim. Hence, the claim enjoys a partial priority for the embodiment of the priority application, but not for the remaining embodiments covered by the claim, for example embodiments including a number of sensing capacitors other than four, since these embodiments are not disclosed in the priority application.

G1/15 made clear that poisonous priorities (e.g. **T571/10**) and toxic divisionals (e.g. **T557/13**), both caused by an incorrect application of the proviso to partial priority, do not occur under the EPC.

3 **Examples of effective dates of claims**
An independent 'AND'-claim defines a single embodiment of an invention and can only have a single effective date. If the application containing the claim does not claim priority, the effective date of the claim is the filing date of the application. If the application claims the priority of one earlier application, the effective date of the claim is the filing date of the earlier application, i.e. the priority date (**Art.89**), provided the earlier application discloses all features of the claim (**Art.88(3)**). If the previous application does not disclose all features, the effective date of the claim is the filing date of the application itself. If multiple priorities are claimed, the effective date of the claim is the filing date of the earliest application that by itself discloses all features of the claim. Note that a combination of features from priority documents is only itself entitled to priority where an explicit direction to make the combination is given in the priority application (F-VI,1.5).

Multiple priorities for an independent claim can only result in multiple effective dates if the claim defines multiple embodiments. Such an 'OR'-claim may contain for example the feature 'made of copper *or* tin', thereby defining two different embodiments. The conjunction 'and/or' between features defines three embodiments. For a priority assessment, such claims should be divided into separate claims, each defining a single embodiment, without alternatives, and each having a single effective date.

A claim dependent on an independent claim defines an embodiment of the invention containing the features of both the independent claim and the dependent claim. A claim dependent on an 'OR'-claim defines two embodiments. The effective date of the dependent claim is the filing date of the priority application that discloses the features of both the independent claim and the dependent claim or, if the disclosure of the priority applications is insufficient, the filing date of the application itself.

An example of multiple priorities is given in **Art.88(3):2**.

Art. 88(3) If one or more priorities are claimed in respect of a European patent application, the right of priority shall cover only those elements of the European patent application which are included in the application or applications whose priority is claimed.

1 **Element**
The term 'element' in **Art.88(3)** constitutes subject-matter as defined in a claim of the application (**G2/98** r.6.2). Note, that in older case law the term is sometimes interpreted as a 'feature' (e.g. **T73/88** r.2.4).

An application claiming priority of an earlier application can itself serve as a basis for priority for a later application in as far as the application contains elements or subject-matter not included in the earlier application (**Art.87(4)**).

2 **Effective date of a claim**
A claim without alternative embodiments, also called an 'AND'-claim, can be accorded only one effective date, i.e. the filing date of the earliest application disclosing all features of the claim. See **Art.88(2):1** and the examples in F-VI,2.4.

The following example relates to a device which may comprise one or more of the different features A, B and C. A first application having filing date D1 describes three embodiments: the device, the device comprising feature A and the device comprising feature B. A second, subsequent application having filing date D2 describes the device comprising feature C and the device comprising both features B and C. A third, subsequent, application having filing date D3 claims the priority of both earlier applications, where

D3 is filed within one year from D1. Claim 1 of the third application defines the device itself. Claim 2 depends on Claim 1 and has as features 'A or C'. Claim 3 depends on Claim 1 or 2 and has as a feature 'B'. The effective date of Claim 1 is D1. Claim 2 defines two embodiments of the invention. The embodiment including A has effective date D1, the embodiment including C has effective date D2. Claim 3 defines three embodiments. The first embodiment, in dependence on Claim 1, includes only B and has effective date D1. The second embodiment, in dependence on Claim 2, includes the combination of A and B and has effective date D3, provided neither the first nor second application describes the combination of features. The third embodiment, also in dependence on Claim 2, includes the combination of B and C and has effective date D2. All time limits of the third application running from the priority date run from the filing date of the earliest date of priority, i.e. from D1 (**Art.88(2)**, last sentence). (See also F-VI,1.5)

Art. 88(4) If certain elements of the invention for which priority is claimed do not appear among the claims formulated in the previous application, priority may nonetheless be granted, provided that the documents of the previous application as a whole specifically disclose such elements.

1 **Disclosure in application as a whole**

The term 'element' in **Art.88(4)** constitutes subject-matter as defined in a claim of the application (**G2/98** r.6.2). The requirement for the right of priority of a claim is that its subject-matter must be specifically disclosed in the priority application as a whole, either explicitly or implicitly (**G2/98** r.2). According to **Art.88(4)**, it is irrelevant whether the subject-matter appears in the claims or in any other part of the priority application. Since drawings are an integral part of an application, a feature may also be disclosed only in a drawing (**T169/83**).

According to the Guidelines, in the determination of the priority date no account should be taken of subject-matter solely found in that part of the description referring to prior art or in an explicit disclaimer (F-VI,2.2). Note, however, that for the assessment of novelty the disclosure of a prior art document does include prior art explicitly described and any matter explicitly disclaimed (G-IV,5.1). See **Art.123(2):2.4.4** for the effect of an added undisclosed disclaimer on priority.

2 **Specific disclosure**

The specific disclosure in **Art.88(4)** requires that the subject-matter of a claim, i.e. all its features, must be derivable directly and unambiguously from the disclosure of the invention in the priority document. This disclosure test should be the same as the test for compliance of an amendment to an application with the requirement of **Art.123(2)** (**G2/98** r.1 and 2; F-VI,2.2; **Art.123(2):1.2**). The disclosure test differs from the novelty test as used for **Art.54(1)** (**G2/98**, point II(v)).

Specific disclosure includes features which a skilled person regards as implicit in what is expressly mentioned in the document. For example, a claim to an apparatus including 'releasable fastening means' would be entitled to the priority date of a disclosure of that apparatus in which the relevant fastening means were a nut and bolt, a spring catch or a toggle-operated latch, provided the general concept of 'releasable' is implicit in the disclosure of such means (F-VI,2.2; e.g. **T809/95**).

Conversely, specific disclosure means that it is not sufficient if the disclosure refers merely in broad and general terms to a detailed feature of the claim (F-VI,2.2; e.g. **T409/90**). Exact correspondence of features is not required. It suffices if, on a reasonable assessment, there is in substance a disclosure of all the features of the claim (F-VI,2.2). For example, a claim to an apparatus including a nut and bolt would not be entitled to the priority date of a disclosure of that apparatus including releasable fastening means but not disclosing the nut and bolt as an embodiment of the fastening means. In other words, a species may give rise to priority of a genus, a genus generally does not give rise to priority of a species.

A later application may disclaim subject-matter disclosed as a positive feature in the priority application without jeopardizing the right to priority (**G2/10** r.4.6).

Since a disclosure is only effective if a skilled person can carry out its teaching (**T206/83**), the priority document must give an enabling disclosure of the subject-matter for which priority is claimed. It could become a misuse of the priority system if some parties in a competitive situation were allowed to jump ahead of others on the basis of mere expectations, omitting the critical feature of the invention altogether (**T81/87** r.12). For example, a priority document disclosing a new chemical compound without a reproducible method for its preparation, the method not being part of the common general knowledge, does not give rise to a right of priority for the compound.

The skilled person and the common general knowledge appearing in r.9 of **G2/98** should only serve to interpret the meaning of a technical disclosure and place it in context; they cannot be used to complete an otherwise incomplete technical disclosure (**T744/99**). The common general knowledge may be used to interpret implicit features in the disclosure but not to introduce equivalents, which are not relevant for priority but only for the assessment of inventive step.

According to **G2/98** r.8.4, a selection invention has no right of priority if it is 'novel' in view of the priority document. It is not clear why the EBoA has chosen here the novelty criterion, whereas the same opinion holds that the criterion for the right to priority is 'disclosure' and not 'novelty' (cf. **G2/98**, point II(v) and r.9 last sentence). The difference in effect is clear from the following example. A priority document discloses a broad numerical range and the subsequent application claims a sub-range without a different technical effect. The sub-range is not novel in view of the broad range (no purposive selection, see e.g. **T279/89**). According to the novelty criterion in **G2/98** r.8.4, the claim is not excluded from priority, whereas according to the stricter disclosure test of **G2/98** r.2 the sub-range is not disclosed in the priority document and, hence, the priority of the claim should not be acknowledged.

Opinion **G2/98** overrules all case law using the broad interpretation of 'the same invention', which interpretation recognises the priority of a claim including a feature not specifically disclosed in the priority document. In **T81/87** only the essential features of the claim, i.e. those feature that define the invention over the prior art, must be disclosed in the priority document. In **T73/88** (Snackfood) a claim was regarded as entitled to priority in spite of an added non-essential feature, i.e. not related to the function and effect of the invention, and not disclosed in the priority document. **T136/95** recognized priority of a claim where the skilled person could infer features not disclosed in the priority document by performing simple operations to carry out the invention. An example is a feature that constitutes nothing more than a routine choice of parameter values (**T581/89**). In **T255/91** a claim relating to a broad range and the same claim but relating to a sub-range were regarded as relating to the same invention because both ranges had the same technical effect; this statement is no longer relevant (Case Law of the BoA, II.D.2.1.1).

When drafting a subsequent application, it is recommended to take the literal text of the priority document as a starting point for the subsequent application and add any subject-matter as needed to avoid unnecessary divergence between the texts of the first and subsequent application. Any differences can easily be interpreted as being an extension of the first document. The burden of proof of the equivalence of the subject-matter is on the applicant.

3 **Effect of intermediate document on claims not entitled to priority**

A document published during the priority interval, the technical contents of which corresponds to that of the priority document, constitutes prior art against an application claiming that priority, to the extent such priority is not validly claimed, e.g. because of added subject-matter. **Art.93(1):2** gives reasons for requesting an early publication of the priority document.

Suppose on 01.01.1990 an applicant files an application P1 comprising features A+B. On 01.02.1990 a document D is published comprising features A+B. On 01.03.1990 the same applicant files an application P2 comprising features A+B+C. On 01.06.1990 the same applicant files a European patent application with claim 1 containing the features A+B and a claim 2 containing the features A+B+C; priority is claimed from P1 and P2. Claim 1 contains the same invention as disclosed in P1; claim 2 contains the same invention as the one disclosed in P2; the invention disclosed in P1 is not the same as the one disclosed in P2, although there is unity of invention within the meaning of **Art.82**. Since claim 2 cannot derive priority from application P1 (**Art.87(1)**), document D is valid prior art for claim 2. (**G3/93**, overturning T301/87 hn4 Biogen)

Art. 89 Effect of priority right

The right of priority shall have the effect that the date of priority shall count as the date of filing of the European patent application for the purposes of Article 54, paragraphs 2 and 3, and Article 60, paragraph 2.

Art.54(2) State of the art
Art.54(3) European prior rights
Art.60(2) Right to a European patent

1 **General**

Art.89 provides that the date of priority counts as the date of filing for three provisions of the EPC relating to prior art and right to a patent. The same effect is also incorporated in the text of several procedural provisions.

The articles referred to in **Art.89** make it clear that the provision applies only to substantive patent law. Procedural provisions in the EPC use the actual filing date unless stated otherwise.

2 **Priority date counts as the date of filing for:**

Art.54(2) Definition of the state of the art
Art.54(3) Prior rights
Art.60(2) Right to a patent
Art.93(1) Publication of the European patent application
R.31(2)(a) Statement of depositary institution and file number of culture

R.37(1)(b), (2) Forwarding of applications to the EPO by national offices
R.52(2) Indication of the file number of a previous filing
R.53(1) Filing of a copy of previous application
R.60(1) Designation of the inventor
R.155(3) Transmission of a request for conversion to a national application
R.157(3) Forwarding of Euro-PCT application to EPO as receiving Office
R.159(1) Entry of Euro-PCT application in regional phase

3 **Filing date is NOT replaced by the priority date for:**
Art.55 Non-prejudicial disclosures
Art.63(1) Term of the patent
Art.83 Disclosure of the invention
Art.86(1) Payment of renewal fees
Art.123(2) Extension of subject-matter beyond application as filed
R.31(1)(a) Deposition of culture
R.38 Payment of filing and search fee
R.56(2) Correction of parts or drawings missing from application

4 **Effect of priority right on state of the art**
A justified priority claim has the effect that a document published on or after the priority date but before the filing date of the application claiming the priority does not belong to the state of the art under **Art.54(2)**. Likewise, a European application filed before the priority date and published on or after that date is a prior right under **Art.54(3)**; an application filed after the priority date but published before the filing date is not a prior right (**J21/82** r.3).

The priority date is also decisive for determining the right to a patent when several applicants independently file an application (**Art.60(2)**).

See **Art.55(1):1** for the interpretation of the missing reference in **Art.89** to **Art.55**.

PART IV PROCEDURE UP TO GRANT

1 Examination of the patent application

The examination of a European patent application can be divided into three stages: examination on filing, examination as to formal requirements and substantive examination.

1 The first examination after receipt of the application documents is the examination on filing according to **Art.90(1)**. The Receiving Section examines whether the application meets the requirements of **Art.80** for accordance of a date of filing. Non-compliance results in that the application will not be dealt with as a European patent application (**Art.90(2)**). The Receiving Section also examines whether the filing and search fee have been paid in time and the translation under **Art.14(2)** has been filed. Non-compliance results in the application being deemed withdrawn.

2 The second stage is the examination as to formal requirements according to **Art.90(3)** by the Receiving Section and by the examining division once the application has been transferred to the latter (A-I,2). The procedure and the objects of the second stage are clearly separated from the first stage to avoid that the results of the examination in the second stage influence the conclusion of the examination on filing (**J22/03** r.3.2).

The second stage starts only after the application has been accorded a date of filing (**Art.90(3)**). The Receiving Section checks amongst others the representation of the applicant, the correctness of the Request for Grant form and, where appropriate, the priority claim, the presence of the abstract, designation of inventor and drawings, and the layout of the application documents. Non-compliance with the requirements most often results in the application being refused. An application which passes the examination as to formal requirements is ready for publication under **Art.93**.

The search is carried out in parallel with the formalities examination (B-IV,1.2). The search division will draw up the search report (**Art.92(1)**) accompanied by the search opinion on patentability (**R.62(1)**).

3 In the substantive examination under **Art.94** an examining division assesses whether the application is patentable in the sense of **Art.52(1)**, i.e. whether the invention to which the application relates is new, has an inventive step and is susceptible of industrial application. If the applicant does not reply in time to an invitation of the examining division to file observations, the application will be deemed to be withdrawn. The EPO may take decisions on specific issues prior to the decision terminating the grant procedure. The findings in **T713/02** r.2 that no such prior decisions in the applicant's favour may be taken is not followed by the departments of first instance (Not. EPO OJ 2006, 293). If the application does not meet the requirements of the EPC, it will be refused, otherwise the patent will be granted.

2 **Possible negative outcomes of the examination**
If deficiencies in the application are noted and not corrected during the examination proceedings, the application is not dealt with as a European patent application, is refused or is deemed to be withdrawn. A refusal is an appealable decision of the EPO based on the documents filed so far. A withdrawal is a decision of the applicant, actively withdrawing the application. A 'deemed to be withdrawn' is an observation of the EPO after failure of an applicant to respond in due time. The legal consequences can normally be remedied using further processing or re-establishment. The observation becomes an appealable decision only after a request for a decision by the applicant (**R.112(2)**).

Art. 90 Examination on filing and examination as to formal requirements

1 **Patent Law Treaty**
The Patent Law Treaty (PLT) entered into force on 28.04.2005 and aims to harmonize and streamline formal procedures. The implementation of the PLT in the EPC 2000 has modified the procedures before the EPO. Firstly, it has harmonized the various remedies in the procedures. Secondly, it has made the requirements for according a date of filing more lenient and has broadened considerably the possibilities for correcting deficiencies in the application after filing. The applicant has more options available at filing at the expense of a more complex remedial system and increased legal uncertainty. The addition and correction options at filing may prolong the procedures considerably and give rise to many unclear cases.

The EPO has implemented all options of the PLT because it intends to become party to the PLT. If a more restricted version had been adopted in the EPC 2000, a widening later on would be difficult. The EPO can tailor the requirements to their need when it has gained experience with the procedures. The PCT, in contrast, could only implement a subset of the PLT provisions, because the articles of the PCT could not be amended.

2 **Options at filing**
Most options at filing introduced by the implementation of the PLT are remedial in character; see in particular **R.40** on filing an application without claims, **R.40(1)(c)** on filing by reference, **R.52** on late filing of the declaration of priority, and **R.56** on adding missing parts to the application after its filing. Because of this remedial character, the options are not intended for common use and for amending the application but only for correcting deficiencies and filing in special circumstances. The EPO strongly recommends to use the filing practice under the EPC 1973 as a safe procedure, i.e. file the patent application including one or more claims with the Request for Grant form, not using filing by reference. Other options for filing do not provide the same legal certainty as this preferred method.

The option of filing by reference (**R.40(1)(c)**) may be useful if there is not sufficient time to prepare a complete application or for filing a divisional application, having the same description and drawings as the parent application.

Late filing of missing parts of the description or drawings under **R.56** should be used for remedying an incorrect transmission of the application documents or of incomplete documents submitted.

Filing without claims as allowed by **R.40(1)** should be used only in case of emergency, e.g. when rights must be safeguarded quickly by filing a priority document. A major drawback of filing without claims is that the later filed claims may not extend the subject matter of the application as filed.

Art. 90(1) The European Patent Office shall examine, in accordance with the Implementing Regulations, whether the application satisfies the requirements for the accordance of a date of filing.

See for the implementation:
R.55 Correction of deficiencies on filing

1 **Procedure on filing**
After filing of the application documents with the EPO, the EPO (or the national authority when filed according to **Art.75(1)(b)**) marks the documents with the date of receipt, checks the nature and number of the received documents and issues a receipt to the applicant stating the date of receipt of the documents making up the application (**R.35(2)**).

If the documents have been filed with a national authority, this authority immediately issues a receipt to the applicant (**R.35(2)**) and informs the EPO of the receipt of the documents (**R.35(3)**, see also A-II,3.2). Applications not liable to secrecy must be forwarded to the EPO within six weeks after filing (**R.37(1)(a)**), extendable to four months after filing or, where priority has been claimed, to fourteen months after the date of priority where further examination as to liability to secrecy is necessary (**R.37(1)(b)**). Applications received by the EPO after expiry of fourteen months after filing or, where priority has been claimed, after the date of priority are regarded as withdrawn (**R.37(2)**). When the EPO has received the application, it informs the applicant accordingly (**R.35(4)**).

The Receiving Section is competent to examine the application documents and determine whether they satisfy the requirements for the accordance of a date of filing as set out in **Art.80** and **R.40** according to **Art.90(1)** (**Art.16**; see also A-II,4.1). A national authority with which an application is filed is not competent to carry out this examination. Hence, a possible re-dating of a deficient application under **R.55** will be substantially later when the application has been filed with a national authority than when filed directly with the EPO.

2 **Examination on filing, correction and sanction**
The examination on filing distinguishes five different types of requirements: those mentioned in **R.55**, information about the applicant (**R.40(1)(b)**), certified copy of previous application (**R.40(3)**, first sentence), translation of previous application (**R.40(3)**, second sentence), and missing parts (**R.56**), each having its own correction procedure and sanction on non-compliance, as set out in the notes to **R.40**.

The invitation under **Art.90(4)** and **R.55** to correct the application documents should always precede a communication under **R.112(1)** that the application is deemed withdrawn because of non-payment of the filing and search fees (**J18/96** r.3.2-3). If the application is redated under **R.55**, all periods running from the date of filing also shift. The application will not be dealt with as a European patent application if the deficiencies are not duly remedied (**R.55**).

An error in the application documents, for instance an erroneous identity of the applicant, may be corrected under **R.139** (**J7/90** hn.I). Such a correction has a retroactive effect and, hence, does not result in redating of the application (**J4/85**).

3 **According of date of filing**
The date of receipt of the application documents will be accorded as date of filing if the application documents meet the requirements of **R.40** or the date on which the deficiencies were rectified (A-II,4.1.5). As an exception, where the application is filed by reference to a previously filed application and the applicant files the certified copy only within two months of invitation under **R.55**, the application maintains its original date of filing (A-II,4.1.5). The application may be re-dated if the applicant inserts parts of the description or drawings after the date of filing (see **R.56**).

If the application documents meet the requirements of **R.40** on the date of receipt of the application documents and the date of filing accorded is the date of receipt, the EPO does *not* inform the applicant of the date of filing. However, if the application is redated after correction of deficiencies or addition of missing parts not contained in the earlier application, the applicant is informed of the new date of filing (**R.55**, last sentence; **R.56(2)**, last sentence).

The EPO does not take a decision when a date of filing is accorded. The question of compliance with the requirements of **R.40** may be raised during the entire grant proceedings. Correspondingly, the EPC does not set a period for issuing the **R.55** communication informing the applicant of a new date of filing after correction of the application documents. The communication may be issued even after the formalities examination of **Art.90(3)**, in spite of the time order of the two stages of examination set in **Art.90(3)**. The EPO is not negligent when the communication is issued half a year after the filing of the application. Hence, an applicant may not rely on having received a date of filing when this communication has not been received. (J22/03 r.2, 3)

See **Art.169:1.2** for the date of filing of an application filed just prior to the coming into force of the EPC in a designated state.

Art. 90(2) If a date of filing cannot be accorded following the examination under paragraph 1, the application shall not be dealt with as a European patent application.

1 **Date of filing not accorded**
If the deficiencies are not corrected, the EPO will send the applicant a **R.112(1)** communication, informing him that the documents filed will not be dealt with as a European patent application (**Art.90(2)**). Any fees paid will be refunded as lacking a legal basis (A-II,4.1.4).

If the applicant is of the opinion that the communication is inaccurate, he can file his arguments with the EPO and ask for an appealable decision under **R.112(2)**. Alternatively, the applicant can re-file the application without the deficiencies, to avoid the time delay and uncertainty involved in correcting the application.

Art. 90(3) If the European patent application has been accorded a date of filing, the European Patent Office shall examine, in accordance with the Implementing Regulations, whether the requirements in Articles 14, 78 and 81, and, where applicable, Article 88, paragraph 1, and Article 133, paragraph 2, as well as any other requirement laid down in the Implementing Regulations, have been satisfied.

Art.14 Languages
Art.78 Requirements of an application
Art.81 Designation of the inventor
Art.88(1) Declaration of priority

Art.133(2) Compulsory representation
See for the implementation:
R.57 Examination as to formal requirements

1 **Examination as to formal requirements**
The purpose of the examination of **Art.90(3)** is to make the application ready for publication under **Art.93**. The examination is carried out by the Receiving Section (**Art.16**) after the application has been accorded a date of filing (**Art.90(3)**).

The issues to be examined, the action taken if deficiencies are noted, sanctions and remedies are set out in the notes to **R.57**.

Art. 90(4) Where the European Patent Office in carrying out the examination under paragraphs 1 or 3 notes that there are deficiencies which may be corrected, it shall give the applicant an opportunity to correct them.

See for the implementation:
R.55 Correction of deficiencies on filing
R.56 Missing parts of description or missing drawings
R.58 Correction of deficiencies in the application documents
R.59 Deficiencies in claiming priority
R.60 Subsequent designation of the inventor

1 **Correction of deficiencies on filing and formal deficiencies**
The provision gives an applicant an opportunity to correct any deficiencies in the application. There are two different procedures for correcting deficiencies: a first procedure for deficiencies noted during the examination on filing under **Art.90(1)** and a second procedure for deficiencies noted during the formalities examination under **Art.90(3)**.

Details of the examination on filing are dealt with in **Art.90(1):1** and **R.40**. The procedure for correction of deficiencies under **Art.90(4)** is set out in **Art.90(1):1, R.55** and **R.56**. The sanction on not correcting the deficiencies in due time is provided in **Art.90(2)**.

The examination as to formalities is provided in **Art.90(3)** and **R.57**. Deficiencies noted during this examination can be corrected according to the procedure of **Art.90(4)** in conjunction with **R.58** to **60**. The examination, invitation and sanction for each formal requirement is set out in the notes to **R.57**. **Art.90(5)** is the general provision for the sanction on not correcting formal deficiencies.

Art. 90(5) If any deficiency noted in the examination under paragraph 3 is not corrected, the European patent application shall be refused unless a different legal consequence is provided for by this Convention. Where the deficiency concerns the right of priority, this right shall be lost for the application.

1 **Effect of non-corrected deficiencies**
The legal effect of any deficiencies established by the EPO and not corrected by the applicant is provided by **Art.90(5)**. All deficiencies concern obligations that must, in principle, be fulfilled on filing. (Spec. Ed. 4 of OJ 2007)

The default sanction of **Art.90(5)** on not correcting formal deficiencies noted in the examination as to formalities under **Art.90(3)** is refusal of the application. The EPC may provide different legal consequences, such as the application being deemed withdrawn when the requirements of **R.57(a)** or (e) are not complied with. The notes to **R.57** for the different formal requirements indicate the appropriate sanctions.

Receipt of the communication of loss of rights under **R.112(1)** presupposes a validly filed application (**J18/96** r.3.2). Hence, an applicant can derive from the receipt of a such a communication that his application has been accorded a filing date, and the application may still be used as priority document if he chooses not to correct the deficiency.

After a deemed withdrawal it is sometimes permitted to convert the European application to a national application under **Art.135**. See NatLaw table VII. Another remedy is to file a new European application and, if possible, claim the priority of an earlier application or of the deemed withdrawn or refused application, which must have received a date of filing to give rise to a right of priority.

2 **Date on which sanction takes effect**

As a rule, a sanction for not complying with a requirement takes effect upon expiry of the normal period set for complying with the requirement, and not upon expiry of any subsequent remedial period, such as the two month period of **R.135(1)** for requesting further processing. Any act performed after the sanction of loss of the application has taken effect is without legal consequence. Hence, a divisional application should be filed before the sanction takes effect.

- Where the designation fee is not paid, the application is deemed withdrawn at expiry of the normal six-month period under **R.39(1)** (A-III,11.2.3)
- Failure to pay the filing or search fee results in the application being deemed withdrawn on expiry of the one-month period of **R.38**. (A-III,16.2)

Non-observance of the two-month period of **R.58** for correction of deficiencies in the application may lead to the application being refused under **Art.90(5)** or being deemed withdrawn. The deemed withdrawal takes effect at expiry of the two-month period (**G4/98** r.7); the refusal becomes final two months after notification of the decision to refuse (**G1/09** r.4.2).

Art. 91 (deleted)

Art. 92 Drawing up of the European search report

The European Patent Office shall, in accordance with the Implementing Regulations, draw up and publish a European search report in respect of the European patent application on the basis of the claims, with due regard to the description and any drawings.

See for the implementation:
R.61 Content of the European search report
R.62 Extended European search report
R.62a Plurality of independent claims
R.63 Incomplete search
R.64 Search report where the invention lacks unity
R.65 Transmittal of the search report to the applicant

R.66 Definitive content of the abstract
R.68 Form of the publication of the search report
R.69 Information about publication of the search report

1 **General**

The provision obliges the EPO to draw up a search report in respect of a European patent application. The search is an important element of the grant procedure, determining the state of the art for the application. The assessment of the patentability of the invention by the EPO is based on the documents mentioned in the search report (see **R.61(1)**).

The reference in **Art.92** to 'the European patent application' implies that a search is only performed on an application which has a filing date (otherwise it is not a European patent application, see **Art.90(2)**) and is pending when the search is performed (Spec. Ed. 4 of OJ 2007).

2 **Start of the search**

The search is carried out in parallel with the formalities examination under **Art.90(3)** (B-IV,1.2). Since the EPO usually renders a service only after payment of the corresponding fee, the search will start only after payment of the filing fee and search fee. Where the application is not filed in an official EPO language, the search will not start before receipt of a translation into one of those languages (see **R.6(1)**). The date of start of the search is recorded in the file (B-IV,1). The date is relevant for refund of the search fee if the application is (deemed) withdrawn or refused before that date (**Rfees9(1)**).

The search can only start if the application documents on filing are complete enough for the search to be performed. Since the search must be based on the claims according to **Art.92**, the search can only start after the claims and any translation have been filed (see **R.57:2** and **4**). It should be noted that in certain cases the filing of the translation may be made up to about one month before publication of the application, making it difficult to publish the search report together with the application.

If the Search Division has despatched a communication under **R.62a** (multiple independent claims), **63** (unsearchable subject-matter) or **64** (non-unity) the search can only proceed after receipt of the applicant's response or expiry of the period for response. (OJ 2015 A93 §10, 11)

3 **Drawing up of the European search report and the opinion**

The search report for a European patent application will be drawn up by a search division (**Art.17**). A search division consists normally of one search examiner; for inventions covering several fields a division may consist of two or three search examiners (B-I,2).

At the same time the search division draws up the search report, it also determines the definitive content of the abstract according to **R.66** and F-II,2.2.

Telephone conversations and informal interviews are normally only possible during substantive examination (B-II,1.1, also giving exceptions for the search).

Under BEST the search examiner will also be the primary examiner in the substantive examination of the patent application (see **Art.15:1**). For increased efficiency the examiner prepares, already at the search stage, an opinion on whether the application and the invention to which it relates seem to meet the requirements of the EPC, also called the opinion on patentability. The search report and the opinion are issued together to the applicant in the form of an extended European search report. The content of the search report is specified in **R.61**. Details of the opinion are given in **R.62**.

4 Basis and extent of search

The search will be based on the claims with due regard to the description and any drawings (**Art.92**). Hence, the search is not restricted by the literal wording of the claims (B-III,3.2). The search division has the discretionary power to make a complete search of the invention, even if essential features are not defined in the claims but only in the description or drawings (**T708/00** r.4). The searcher must also anticipate amendments and should cover subject-matter to which claims might reasonably be amended during prosecution (B-III,3.5, **R.137(5)**). However, a single broad claim in the application as filed without dependent claims does not give entitlement to a search to all features of a large number of disclosed embodiments covered by the claim (**T1679/10** r.4.2; B-III,3.5).

If the application contains a plurality of independent claims not complying with **R.43(2)**, the search division will ask the applicant to indicate the independent claims to be searched (**R.62a**).

If the search division considers that a complete search is not possible because the application does not comply with the EPC or relates to subject-matter excluded from patentability, it will ask the applicant to indicate the subject-matter to be searched; in such a case the search division may make a partial search or no search at all (see **R.63**).

If the search division considers that the application lacks unity, it invites the applicant to pay further search fees to search the further inventions and informs him that only the part of the application that relates to the inventions for which search fees have been paid will be searched (see **R.64**). Any unsearched subject-matter may not be used for amendment of claims during prosecution of the application (**R.137(5)**).

Claims above the number of fifteen for which no claims fees have been paid will not be searched (**R.45(3)** and B-III,3.4).

The extent of the search in terms of publication dates is given in **R.61(3):1**. In general, the examiner accepts the validity of any priority claim of the application being searched. However, if the examiner finds prior art under **Art.54(2)** published on or after the priority date and before the date of filing or prior art under **Art.54(3)** filed on or after the priority date and before the filing date, he will allocate effective dates to the claims of the application being searched, depending on the presumed validity of the priority claim. If the prior art application also claims priority, effective dates will also be allocated to the parts of the prior art application. (F-VI,2.1)

Since the applicant is not allowed under **R.137(1)** to amend the claims before receiving the search report, the search is on the claims as filed on the date of filing or filed later of the applicant's own volition or as correction under **R.57(c)** and **R.58** (B-III,3.3). See **R.63(1)** for an exception. Claims abandoned because of non-payment of claims fee (**R.45(3)**) are not searched (B-III,3.4).

5 Transmittal and publication of the search report

The search report is important for the applicant, giving him a basis for the decision whether to continue prosecution of the application. Hence, the law provides for the possibility to request examination only after the search report has become available (**R.70(1)**). When the search report has been drawn up, it will be transmitted to the applicant under **R.65**. Voluntary amendment is only allowed together with the first substantive response (**R.137(2)**).

The search report is also important for third parties, in particular for competitors, giving an impression of the scope of protection of a possibly granted patent. The law has provided for publication of the search report in **Art.92**, because the accessibility of the published document provided legal certainty for third parties before online inspection became available, informing them about the search results and the start of the period for requesting examination.

The EPO informs the applicant of the date on which the Bulletin will mention the publication of the search report (**R.69(1)**). This communication is despatched immediately after the publication of the search report.

The EPO will publish the search report together with the application if the former is available before termination of the technical preparations for publication (A-VI,1.3). If not available, the search report will be published separately (**R.68(1)**; A-VI,1.5). The form of the publication is governed by **R.68**. The search opinion (**R.62(2)**) and the search strategy (OJ 2017 A106 §4(d)) will not be published but are available via file inspection under **Art.128** (A-VI,1.3).

6 Top-up search

When the examiner carries out the main search, the search files will usually not be complete. Prior art under **Art.54(3)**, so-called European prior rights, are available to the examiner and can be searched. However, they may only be cited after they have been published because of **Art.128(1)**. The publication is also a requirement for the application to become prior art under **Art.54(3)**. It will only become known whether it is published 18 months after the priority or filing date of the application. Only when the examiner has ascertained that the application is published, will he cite the prior right. The latest citable European prior right is an application filed the day before the filing date of the application being examined and published 18 months later. (C-IV,7.1)

A PCT application may also constitute prior art under **Art.54(3)** (**Art.153(5)** and **R.165**). If the EPO does not handle the PCT application in the international phase, the application will become available to the examiner only after publication (the EPO has not made use of Art.13(1) PCT). Hence, the examiner can examine such prior rights only after 18 months from the filing or priority date. If he regards the application under examination novel in view of these prior rights, he can continue the examination and even issue a **R.71(3)** communication, without waiting for any translation or an effective entry of the prior international application into the European phase. (**T1849/12** r.3.3)

Hence, the examiner usually carries out a top-up search at the earliest 18 months after the priority or filing date of the application being examined. The top-up search is usually the first step of the substantive examination (**Art.94(3):3**). If the priority claim of the application being examined is valid for the whole content of the application, the top-up search may be carried out at the earliest 18 months from the priority date. (C-IV,7.1 and **T1849/12** r.3.2)

The top-up search also takes into consideration potentially relevant prior art cited by other patent offices on applications of the same family and therefore needs to be performed for any file at the start and end of examination (C-IV,7.1).

The results of the top-up search may be included in the search report or in the first **Art.94(3)** communication. If not yet available by that time, the examiner must ensure that the top-up search is completed before the application is reported to be in order for grant. In the rare case the prosecution is accelerated and the top-up search is not yet completed before the application is considered ready for grant, the grant should be postponed till the top-up search is completed. (C-IV,7.1)

7 **Completion of the search**

The EPO always performs an accelerated search for direct European patent applications; no PACE request is needed. The EPO strives to issue the search report within six months from the date of filing the application (OJ 2015 A93 §6, 8). As a transitional provision, the search of a direct European application filed before 01.07.2014 and claiming priority will only be accelerated after a PACE request (OJ 2015 A93 §1-6, 9).

The search division will only be able to complete the search in due time if the workload of the search division is not too high and the start of the search is not delayed (see above section **2**; OJ 2015 A93 §6, 10).

If the search report of an application filed on or after 01.06.2014 has not been issued within six months from the date of filing and the applicant files an enquiry about the status of the file using Form 1012 (see **Art.94(1):6**), the EPO will issue the search report within one month from receipt of the enquiry. As a transitional provision, the EPO will issue the search report within six months from receipt of the enquiry if the search report of an application filed before 01.06.2014 and claiming priority has not been issued and the applicant files an enquiry using Form 1012. (OJ 2016 A66 §6; E-VIII,7)

8 **Legal effect of publication of the search report**

The mention of the publication of the search report has the following legal implications:

- **R.39(1)**: The mention triggers the six-month period for payment of the designation fee.
- **R.70(1)**: The mention triggers the six-month period for filing the request for examination and, where appropriate, filing comments on the search opinion attached to the search report under **R.70a**. If the request was filed before the EPO transmitted the search report to the applicant, the applicant is invited to confirm the request for examination (**R.70(2)**). After the filing of the request or receipt of the confirmation, the examining division starts the examination of the application (**Art.18(1)** and **R.10**).

Note, that the publication under the PCT of the international search report of a Euro-PCT application takes the place of the publication of the search report under the EPC (**Art.153(6)**).

Art. 93 Publication of the European patent application

1 **General**

In return for patent protection, the patent application is made public with the intention to foster innovation. The information in the published application may be used without infringing for further research by third parties to improve the invention or to develop a non-infringing alternative.

Art.93 is the basis for the publication of the application. The publication of the search report is governed by **Art.92**. Preferably the application and the search report are published together. If the search division cannot complete the search report in time for publication together with the application, the application will be published timely in the interest of the public and the search report will be published later (**R.68(1)**).

Art. 93(1) The European Patent Office shall publish the European patent application as soon as possible
(a) after the expiry of a period of eighteen months from the date of filing or, if priority has been claimed, from the date of priority, or
(b) at the request of the applicant, before the expiry of that period.

See for the implementation:
R.67 Technical preparations for publication
R.68 Form of the publication of the patent application

1 **Form and date of publication**
The publication of a patent application contains a front page, the description, claims and any drawings as filed, the abstract, and the search report if available (**R.68(1)**). The form of the publication is determined by **R.68(1)**. The application is published in the language of the proceedings (**Art.14(5)**). The front page mentions bibliographic data, the designated states (**R.68(3)**) and the abstract.

Timely filed new or amended claims will be included in the publication (**R.68(4)**). Even if claims are deemed abandoned because of non-payment of the claims fees under **R.45(3)**, the complete first set of claims as filed by the applicant will be included in the publication. The publication will indicate if the claims were filed after the date of filing (**R.68(4)**). Since the publication must include the claims (**R.68(1)**), the publication will be postponed if the first set of claims is filed after the date of filing and is not yet available (see also **Art.69(2)**, first sentence).

Any timely requested and allowed correction under **R.139** is incorporated in the publication. If a decision is pending on such a correction, a warning is printed on the first page if the correction influences rights of third parties, e.g. a correction of a priority claim. (A-VI,1.3)

The EPO informs the applicant of the completion of the technical preparations for publication under **R.67(1)**) and of the publication number and the date on which it intends to publish the patent application (A-VI,1.1). This communication is despatched about four weeks before the intended date of publication, i.e. after the completion.

The publication date is a Wednesday (OJ 1997, 542), usually the first Wednesday after expiry of the 18-month period of **Art.93(1)(a)**, irrespective of whether this day is a public holiday or not. At the publication date an entry is made in the Register of European Patents (**R.143(1)(a)-(i)** and **(2)**) in the three EPO languages (**Art.14(8)**). At the same date the European Patent Bulletin mentions the date of publication of the search report and, if published earlier, also the date of publication of the application together with bibliographic data (**Art.129(a)**). See **Art.79(2):3** for the publication of the designated contracting states.

2 **Early publication on request**

The application can be published before expiry of the 18 months on request of the applicant provided that the filing fee and search fee have been paid (A-VI,1.1). Reasons for such an early publication can be to obtain rights under **Art.67** with respect to third parties, or to prevent a third party to come too close to the subject matter of the application with his later filed application: the third-party application only needs to be novel over a not-yet-published application, but needs to have an inventive step over a published application.

3 **Deferred publication**

If the applicant abandons his priority claim, the publication is deferred until 18 months after the date of filing, provided the notification of abandonment reaches the EPO before termination of the technical preparations for publication (**R.67(2)**). If received later, the publication will not be deferred and the abandonment will be published in the Bulletin. The same procedure applies if the priority right is lost under **Art.90(5)**. (A-VI,1.1)

4 **Invalid publication**

The application will not be published if it has been finally refused or withdrawn or deemed withdrawn before the termination of the technical preparations for publication (**R.67(2)**). The application is, however, published if, upon said termination, a request for a decision under **R.112(2)** has been received but no decision has yet been taken or if there is a pending request for re-establishment (A-VI,1.2). If after said termination the application is withdrawn to avoid publication, non-publication cannot be guaranteed and the application may still be published (see **R.67(2):1**). Such a publication of the application is not according to **Art.93** and is sometimes referred to as an invalid publication. If the applicant wants to have the option of continuing the prosecution if the application is still published after a late withdrawal of the application, he should make the withdrawal conditional on prevention of the publication (see **R.67(2):3**).

An invalid publication has the following legal implications:

- **Art.54(2)**: The content of the publication may be used as prior art
- **Art.54(3)**: Since the publication is not valid, the application does not have the effect of a European prior right.
- **Art.67(4)**: The application is deemed never to have conferred provisional protection under **Art.67(1)**.
- **Art.128(4)**: The publication does not give rise to the possibility of inspecting the files (OJ 1993, 56).
- **Art.139(1)**: The publication does not give rise to a national prior right effect (**J5/81** r.3).

5 **Legal effect of publication of the patent application**

The publication of the application triggers certain periods and provides the opportunity to undertake certain actions:

- **Art.54(2)**: After publication the contents of the application forms part of the state of the art.
- **Art.54(3)**: The prior right effect comes into force.
- **Art.67**: The applicant can exercise his rights of the provisional protection, where the extent of protection is determined by the latest filed claims included in the publication (**Art.69(2)**).
- **Art.115**: After publication of the application third parties may file observations to be considered during examination.
- **Art.127**: Data of the application is entered in the Register of European Patents.

- **Art.128(4)**: After publication of the application the file at the EPO is open for public inspection.

See **Art.92:8** for the legal effect of the publication of the search report.

Art. 93(2) The European patent application shall be published at the same time as the specification of the European patent when the decision to grant the patent becomes effective before the expiry of the period referred to in paragraph 1(a).

1 **Early publication after early grant**

The application will be published before expiry of the 18 months in the exceptional case that the patent is granted before the expiry. The application and the patent will then be published simultaneously (**Art.93(2)**; A-VI,1.1). If in this case the application were to be published after expiry of the 18 months, i.e. after the patent, there would arise problems with the prior right effect according to **Art.54(3)**. Therefore, in practice, the EPO does not grant patents before a top-up search has been done.

The examiner usually carries out a top-up search for European prior rights after 18 months (see **Art.92:6**). PCT applications should also be searched for potential prior rights; only if they enter the European phase, usually 31 months after the filing or priority date, will they become a European prior right. If the EPO does not act as international office for a PCT application, it is not available to the EPO until its publication. Only in the unlikely event that the examiner considers the claims of the application patentable in view of the prior art before expiry of the 18 months period, can a patent be granted before said expiry. (**T1849/12** r.3 and 4)

Art. 94 Examination of the European patent application

1 **General**

Art.94 deals with the initiation of the examination (paragraphs (1) and (2)) as well as the conduct of the examination procedure (paragraphs (3) and (4)).

Art. 94(1) The European Patent Office shall, in accordance with the Implementing Regulations, examine on request whether the European patent application and the invention to which it relates meet the requirements of this Convention. The request shall not be deemed to be filed until the examination fee has been paid.

See for the implementation:
R.6(3) Reduction of examination fee on account of language
R.70 Request for examination
R.70a Response to extended search report
R.142(4) Interruption of time limit because of interruption of proceedings
R.159(1) Time limit for requesting examination for Euro-PCT application
Rfees2(1)6 Amount of the examination fee
Rfees14(1) Amount of reduction of examination fee

1 Examination on request

The substantive examination of the application is the second stage of the grant procedure, which follows the formalities examination of **Art.90(3)**. The substantive examination will only be carried out if the applicant has filed a request for examination in accordance with **R.70**. The requirement of a request allows the applicant to stop the grant procedure after the first stage, possibly because of prejudicial prior art found in the search, thereby relieving him from payment of the examination fee.

The Implementing Regulations may provide for filing the request by means other than in writing (Spec. Ed. 4 of OJ 2007, Art.94). They may permit a deferred examination, e.g. to cope with an excessive workload of the examiners; since **Art.94(1)** does not state who may file the request, the deferred examination may be combined with allowing third party requests (Spec. Ed. 4 of OJ 2007, Art.95).

The examining division which will carry out the examination takes over the competence from the Receiving Section at receipt of the request for examination when the request is filed after transmission of the search report (**R.10(2)**), or at receipt of the confirmation of the request for examination upon invitation under **R.70(2)** when the request has been filed before transmission of the search report (**R.10(3)**). When the request has been filed before transmission of the search report and the applicant has waived the invitation under **R.70(2)**, the examining division becomes competent on the day the search report is transmitted to the applicant (**R.10(4)**).

2 Filing the request for examination

The request for examination consists of two acts according to **Art.94(1)**. The first act is the filing of the written request for examination ('request' in **Art.94(1)**), the second act is the payment of the examination fee (**Art.94(1)**, last sentence). The request is valid only if both the filing and payment have been made in due time (**Art.94(1)**, last sentence).

A written request for examination is preprinted on the Request for Grant form with the appertaining box already ticked. The use of the Request for Grant form is mandatory when filing a patent application (**R.41(1)**), but an omission can be corrected under **R.58**. The written request for examination is thus always filed together with the Request for Grant form. Hence, no separate filing of the written request is necessary. An applicant who must be represented under **Art.133(2)** may file the Request for Grant himself (**Art.133(2)**) and, hence, also the written request for examination.

The examination fee is due when the request for examination is filed (see **Rfees4(1):1**). Since the request is preprinted in the Request for Grant form, the examination fee can be paid as from the date of filing the Request for Grant form.

The examination fee must be paid within the period of **R.70(1)**, i.e. within six months from publication of the search report. Since the written request has been filed together with the application, the payment of the examination fee is the only act still to be performed within the period of **R.70(1)**. The applicant can base his decision to pay the examination fee on the results of the search and the accompanying opinion. If the results do not justify continuing the prosecution, the applicant can terminate the procedure by not paying the examination fee (**Art.94(2)**).

Anybody may pay the examination fee (see **Rfees6(1):1**). See the notes to **R.70** for details of filing the request for examination, consequence of failure to file it in due time and remedies.

Where the search opinion states deficiencies in the application, which is usually the case, the applicant must not only pay the examination fee but also file a response to the objections before expiry of the period of **R.70(1)** (R.70a).

3 Examination fee, reduction and refund

The amount of the examination fee is laid down in **Rfees2(1)6.**

The examination fee will be reduced by 30% if an entitled applicant files the request for examination in an admissible non-EPO language (see **R.6(3):2** for entitlement) (**G6/91** r.21). Only the request for examination must be filed in an admissible non-EPO language for entitlement to the reduction of the examination fee. Whether or not the description and the claims of the application or responses to communications from the EPO are in an admissible non-EPO language is irrelevant for the entitlement. See **R.6(3):3.3** for the filing of the request. See **Rfees14(2)** for reduction of the examination fee for a Euro-PCT application.

The examination fee will be refunded in part or in total if the EPO does not carry out a substantive examination. The amount of the refund depends on the moment where the procedure terminates, either due to refusal by the EPO, being deemed withdrawn or withdrawal by the applicant. See **Rfees11** for details of the refund conditions.

4 Acceleration of examination

The examination of a direct European application can be accelerated in several ways, such as omitting procedural steps and reducing the response time of the EPO. See Not. EPO OJ 2015 A94 for a summary.

The applicant can request the EPO to use the Patent Prosecution Highway, which expedites the grant procedure by allowing the EPO to make use of work results of another patent office (see **Art.94(3):7**).

If the examination fee is paid on filing of the application and the invitation under **R.70(2)** is waived, examination is requested unconditionally, irrespective of the results of the search (see **R.70(2):3**). The first examining communication under **Art.94(3)** instead of the search opinion under **R.62(1)** will be despatched together with the search report.

The examination can be further accelerated by filing a PACE request as set out in the section below. After receipt of the request, the examining division will strive to issue a communication within three months from receipt of a response of the applicant. The applicant must respond to the communication within the period set, and he should deal with all the points raised in the communication and co-operate with the EPO. In about 2/3 of the cases the EPO manages to respond within three months (situation 2014).

The grant can also be accelerated as set out in **Art.97(1):2.**

See **R.159:4** for accelerating the processing of a Euro-PCT application.

5 PACE request

The programme for accelerated prosecution of European patent applications (PACE) enables a faster processing of applications during examination (Not. EPO, OJ 2015 A93).

An applicant can apply for accelerated examination by filing a PACE request. The EPO may restrict the number of allowed requests depending on technical field and applicant. The PACE request for acceleration must be filed online on a special EPO form. The EPO will acknowledge receipt promptly. A request not filed online or not on the special EPO form will not be processed. The request must be filed for one application at a time. It will not be published and will be excluded from file inspection. (OJ 2015 A93 §1-3, 6)

It should be noted that the request is a 'document' in the sense of **R.2** the filing of which is governed by the Decisions of the President taken under **R.2**. A Notice of the EPO limiting the ways of filing a PACE request to online only appears to violate **R.2**.

See **R.114(2):1** for triggering of PACE by receipt of third party observations.

The search is always accelerated; there is no need for a PACE request (**Art.92:7**).

Accelerated examination can only be requested after the examining division has become responsible for the application according to **R.10** (see **R.70(1):1; (2):1** and C-II,1). Hence, a PACE request filed during search will not accelerate examination. The EPO enters the date on which responsibility for an application passes to the examining division in the Register. (OJ 2015 A93 §12)

When accelerated examination has been requested, the examining division strives to issue a communication within three months from receipt of the request or the applicant's response to a previous communication, whichever is latest (OJ 2015 A93 §14, 15). The applicant can enquire with the EPO customer services as to the status of an application for which a PACE request has been filed (OJ 2015 A93 §7).

The examination will no longer be accelerated if the applicant withdraws the PACE request or requests an extension of a period, or if the application has been refused, withdrawn or deemed withdrawn. Since a PACE request may be filed only once during each stage of the procedure, a removal from the PACE programme cannot be undone by refiling the PACE request. Hence, an allowed request for further processing will continue the proceedings but not the accelerated examination. (OJ 2015 A93 §2, 4)

Accelerated examination will be suspended in the event of failure to pay the renewal fee by the due date (OJ 2015 A92 §5). After payment, accelerated prosecution will be resumed.

6 Status enquiry

A party to proceedings may contact the EPO to enquire about the progress of his file. The enquiry must be filed online using Form 1012 (OJ 2016 A66; C-VII,2.1; E-VIII,7). The EPO will acknowledge receipt of the form. Enquiries and responses will be entered in the file and are open to public inspection.

The response of the EPO indicates the period within which it intends to issue the next communication. Although Form 1012 is not a PACE request, it will speed up processing in the following cases. If a communication was not issued within the committed period, and additionally the application is processed under PACE or a previous enquiry has been filed, the next communication will be issued within one month from receipt of the enquiry. (OJ 2016 A66; E-VIII,7)

7 Deferral of examination

The EPC has a fixed time limit for requesting examination laid down in **R.70(1)**. A deferred examination, of interest for applicants having a long time to market, is currently not available. At the moment, an applicant can extend the duration of the prosecution by using the remedy of further processing (**Art.121**) to extend each period for response by approximately three months. Alternatively or in addition he can ask the examiner to delay the processing of the application, starting with the issue of the first communication under **Art.94(3)**.

When an applicant requests the EPO the status of an application, the application will be moved forward in the processing queue. Hence, no status requests should be made for applications for which the prosecution must be slowed down.

Art. 94(2) If no request for examination has been made in due time, the application shall be deemed to be withdrawn.

See for the implementation:
R.70(1) Six month period for requesting examination

1 **Effect of non-payment of the examination fee**
The request for examination must be filed 'in due time', i.e. within the period laid down in **R.70(1)**. If the request for examination is not made within a six-month period of mention of publication of the search report of **R.70(1)**, the application is deemed withdrawn under **Art.94(2)** (A-VI,2.3). See **R.70(1):2** for further processing according to **Art.121** and **R.135** as remedy.

The two-month period for requesting further processing according to **Art.121** and **R.135** is not an extension of the six-month period, but a remedy with retrospective effect (**J4/86** r.4 applied mutatis mutandis, equating the remedial character of the grace period of **R.85b** EPC 1973 with that of the two-month period of **R.135(1)** EPC 2000). Hence, when the request is neither filed in the normal period nor in the two-month period, the application is deemed to be withdrawn at the end of the six-month period, not at the end of the grace period (**G4/98** mutatis mutandis; see also A-III,11.2.3). The Guidelines do not contain a statement relating to this issue.

As a consequence, a renewal fee which becomes due after expiry of the normal six-month period must be refunded if the request for examination is not filed (**J4/86** hn, mutatis mutandis). Likewise, a divisional application filed after expiry of the six-month period will only be regarded as a divisional application if further processing has been granted and the examination fee for the parent application has been paid within the two-month period (see **R.36(1):3.1.3**). The fiction of **Art.94(2)** has the effect that the application is deemed never to have had the effect of conferring rights provided for in **Art.67** (**Art.67(4)**).

Art. 94(3) If the examination reveals that the application or the invention to which it relates does not meet the requirements of this Convention, the Examining Division shall invite the applicant, as often as necessary, to file his observations and, subject to Article 123, paragraph 1, to amend the application.

Art.123(1) Amendments
See for the implementation:
R.71(1) Invitation to correct deficiencies
R.71(2) Content of communication

1 **General**
Details of the procedure can be found in
R.71: Examination procedure
R.112: Noting of loss of rights
R.113: Signature, name and seal on notices and communications
C-I,4: Examination procedure in general

The main principle of the examination procedure is speed. Hence, the applicant does not have the benefit of the doubt: if he does not show sufficient progress, the examiner might refuse the application (T84/82). See **Art.94(1):4** for acceleration of the examination.

The communications during the examination may be in an admissible non-EPO language (with a subsequent translation) for documents bound to a time limit (**Art.14(4)**), and only in an official EPO language if not bound to a time limit (**R.3(1)**).

2 **Substantive examination**

The EPO will invite the applicant to file his observations on all deficiencies found in the application and to amend the application. The first substantive examination is carried out together with the search, i.e. before the request for examination must be filed, and the first report is issued as an opinion annexed to the search report (**R.62(1)**). The applicant must respond to any objections raised in the opinion within the period for filing the request for examination (**R.70a**). Subsequent reports with deficiencies are issued as communications under **Art.94(3)**. Although the search opinion has the character of a communication under **Art.94(3)**, it is not called so because of legal reasons.

The applicant is the master of the examination according to **Art.113(2)**: the EPO is bound to the text filed or approved by the applicant. However, the examining division may propose amendments.

If the examiner does not find an inventive step, the burden of proof of the presence of an inventive step is on the applicant; the examiner need not prove the lack of inventive step (T2/81). The burden to propose amendments to enable progress in the examination procedure is on the applicant (T300/89 r.9.1).

When the examiner challenges the unity of the claims, the applicant need not file both amended claims and description in reply to the communication. First the main question of unity must be settled, only after that should the examiner request the applicant to amend the description. (T544/88)

An amendment of the application will be objected to by the examiner if it is objectionable under the EPC, e.g. introducing obscurity or extending the subject-matter of the application beyond the content of the application as filed. See H-IV,2.2 and **Art.123(2)** for extension of subject-matter.

Addition of subject-matter to the application is exceptionally allowed if it introduces further information regarding relevant prior art (H-IV,2.3.7), if it is a clarification of an obscurity or the resolution of an inconsistency (H-IV,2.3.8). For example, an additional description of a relevant document in the state of the art is allowed and often necessary because of **R.42(1)(b),(c)**. However, later filed statements of advantages, additional examples or explanations extending the subject-matter may be taken into account for assessing inventive step. This material will be added to the file, and is open to inspection, thus becoming part of the state of the art. The presence of such material will be mentioned on the cover page of the patent specification (H-V,2.3).

3 **Start of examination**

Once the request for examination has been filed and the examining division has assumed responsibility under **R.10**, the substantive examination of the application will start.

One of the first steps is a top-up search for additional prior art as set out in **Art.92:6**. The date of launch of the top-up search is recorded in the file (C-IV,7.1). The date is relevant for refund of the examination fee if the application is (deemed) withdrawn or refused before that date (**Rfees11**).

The examiner will use the results of the top-up search and any arguments and amendments filed by the applicant under **R.70a** for a direct European application or under **R.159(1)(b)** or **161(1)** for a Euro-PCT application for drafting the first communication.

4 **First communication**

The first communication of the EPO in the examination phase should cover, where appropriate, all objections to the application (**R.71(2)**), including not only substantive matters, but also formal matters, e.g. matter regarding the requirements in **R.41-43, 46, 48, 49** and **50**. The communication must contain a reasoned statement covering, where appropriate, all grounds against the grant (**R.71(2)**). The communication must state clearly and unequivocally on what issues the applicant must reply, e.g. an opinion on inventive step, a deletion or limitation of the scope of a claim, division because of lack of unity (**J13/84**). Apart from objections, a first communication may also include positive statements on patentability and suggestions how to overcome objections (C-III,4.1.2). The communication must state the time limit for reply, in general between 2 and 4 months from notification of the communication (**R.132**). A communication containing erroneous information which misleads a party into taking action causing his application to be refused is void in its entirety, because the principle of good faith applies to all procedural matter between the applicant and the EPO (**J2/87**).

The first communication may be minutes of a telephone conversation with the applicant. The examiner may inform the representative of the intention to issue summons to oral proceedings. (C-VII,2,7)

The first communication may also be a summons for oral proceedings. This happens only in exceptional cases where despite the applicant's reply to the search opinion no possibility of a grant can be envisaged. The summons will justify why they are issued as first action. (C-III,5)

If the applicant makes a genuine effort to overcome the objections stated in the summons, the oral proceedings may be cancelled or postponed (C-III,5). It is recommended to file auxiliary requests and arrange a telephone interview with the examiner.

5 **Response, further communication and immediate refusal**

The communication under **Art.94(3)** will state the period within which the applicant must file a response (**R.71(1)**). The consequences of failure to observe the period are dealt with in **Art.94(4)**.

In his reply to the first communication the applicant may put forward any arguments (both legal and technical) against the objections raised by the examining division, in support of the text of the application as filed or already amended.

He need not co-operate with the examiner in the sense of accepting the latter's objections. An applicant may try to obtain a patent with a certain extent of protection, whereas the examining division has the duty only to grant a patent which complies with the requirements of the EPC; in this situation there is no possibility of collaboration in the above sense. Lack of such collaboration or weak legal or factual reasons are no grounds for refusing the application immediately after only one previous communication (**T640/91** r.10).

It is established case law that the examining division may send an immediate refusal after a first communication, provided the decision to refuse complies with **Art.113(1)**; a prior warning is not required (**T1002/03** r.5). Such an immediate refusal is in principle allowable when the decision to refuse is based solely on grounds on which the applicant has had an opportunity to comment (**T201/98**; C-IV,3). In case **T1002/03** the first communication raised objections on clarity of claim 1 and inventive step of claims 1 and 5; in his response the applicant filed an amended claim 1 to meet the clarity objection and provided three pages of arguments on inventive step; since the examining division did not regard the arguments as convincing, they refused the application. The applicant can only continue prosecution after a refusal by filing an appeal.

The examiner must consider discussing remaining objections, e.g. by telephone, to draw the attention of the applicant to deficiencies not yet dealt with or to resolve unclear issues (C-IV,3).

The decision to invite further observations under **Art.94(3)** depends on whether or not there is a reasonable prospect that such an invitation could lead to the grant of the application (**T84/82, T162/82, T640/91**). There might be no reasonable prospect when there is no reasonable co-operation in procedural matters or lack of good faith from a party. Lack of good faith arises only in exceptional circumstances, e.g. if an applicant deliberately tries to mislead the EPO in relation to relevant facts. Since lack of good faith is a very serious matter, the EPO has a legal obligation under **Art.113(1)** to invite further observations from an applicant before issuing an adverse decision, such as an immediate refusal of an application, on the ground that the party has shown lack of good faith. (**T640/91** r.8)

The risk of an immediate refusal can be avoided by requesting oral proceedings in the response to the first communication under **Art.94(3)** (**T300/89** r.9.2) or to the search opinion (see **R.70a(1):1**). Since such a request may not be ignored (**Art.116(1)**) and the arrangements for oral proceedings involve a substantial amount of work for the EPO, the examiner will usually send a second communication.

If, in response to a unfavourable communication, the applicant decides to withdraw a European application, it is recommended not to answer the communication and let the case be deemed withdrawn. A response to the communication may result in a refusal, which decision may have a negative bearing on the prosecution of the case before other patent offices or courts.

6 Auxiliary requests

Where an applicant is uncertain about the patentability of a set of claims, filing one set of claims as a main request and one or more alternative sets of claims as auxiliary requests may clarify the procedural position and expedite the procedure without requiring the applicant to abandon his position. It allows the applicant to defend a request without abandoning a higher-ranking request which is regarded as not-allowable. An applicant may have a refused request re-examined by a board of appeal. The following requirements for and the examination of such requests are set out in H-III,3.3.

Auxiliary requests will be admitted, provided they are in a clear order, relate to one invention and do not re-introduce unallowable subject-matter already removed by the applicant (H-III,3.3.1.1). If the requests are filed late, the requests must additionally represent a convergent development, in that the most broadly worded set of claims is filed as main request and sequentially limiting sets of claims as auxiliary requests (H-III,3.3.1.2; **T1685/07** r.6.5-6.6).

Identical claims in auxiliary requests may be replaced by references. The number of requests should not be excessive (**T907/91**). The examining division examines the requests in the order presented by the applicant. If it considers an alternative set patentable, it will propose this set in a communication under **Art.94(3)** or a communication under **R.71(3)** or, where appropriate, during oral proceedings and state why the higher ranking requests, including the main request, are not acceptable. Requests ranking lower than the allowable request will not be examined.

The procedure for grant in the case of auxiliary requests has been set out in **R.71(3):5.1** and **R.71(6):6**.

7 Patent Prosecution Highway pilot programme

Several patent offices have concluded an agreement with the EPO providing a pilot Patent Prosecution Highway (PPH) programme for linking their fast-track patent examination procedures to grant patents faster and more efficiently and permitting each office to use the work previously done by other offices. The EPO will publish a notice if the pilot programme is terminated before 05.01.2020. An overview of the PPH for the IP5 offices (EP, JP, KR, CN, US) is given in OJ 2016 A106.

A list of the bilateral PPH agreements of the EPO with other patent offices, including their duration, can be found on the WIPO website (search **'PCT-PPH'** on the internet). For each of these countries, the bilateral agreement covers both PCT and national work. In addition to the countries listed therein, the EPO has an agreement with BR. The requirements for a specific country can be found by searching on the internet for 'EPO Journal PPH [name country]', which will give the OJ reference for that country as one of the first results.

An applicant can request PPH for a European application if he wants to use before the EPO the results of the examination of a corresponding application carried out by another one of the nine offices. The European application and the corresponding application must have the same earliest date, whether this be the priority or filing date. The corresponding application may be a national application or a PCT application. Hence, the results of the examination may be the results of an examination by a national office or a written opinion of the ISA or an international preliminary examination of one of the IP5 offices as IPEA.

For example, an application filed in the US has been examined by the USPTO and the applicant may use the results of the examination for a European application claiming priority from the US application by requesting PPH for the European application. An exhaustive list of possible combinations of national and PCT applications and first filings and priority-claiming applications that can be used for PPH is given in OJ 2016 A106 Annex 1 and 2.

The results of the examination by the other office must indicate that at least one claim is patentable or allowable. The claims in the EP application must sufficiently correspond to the patentable or allowable claim(s), i.e. are of the same or a similar scope or narrower and are of the same category. Substantive examination of the EP application may not yet have begun. The examination starting date is visible for an unpublished EP application by file inspection using the MyFiles service and for a published EP application in the register.

For participation in the PPH pilot programme of an office, the applicant must file a request using the recommended form 1009 as set out in OJ 2016 A44 and file a series of documents as listed in the overview for that office, also published in the OJ. Once the request is granted, the application will be processed in an accelerated manner using the results of the earlier examination. The conditions of the PACE programme (**Art.94(1):5**) apply by analogy.

It is strongly recommended to check any restrictions offices may apply during PPH prosecution, such as prohibiting amendment of claims by inclusion of features from the description.

Art. 94(4) If the applicant fails to reply in due time to any communication from the Examining Division, the application shall be deemed to be withdrawn.

1 **Period for responding**

The period for response to the communication under paragraph 3 is in general between two and four months from notification of the communication and can be extended to a total time limit of six months by a request according to **R.132**, filed before the expiry of the period (E-VIII,1.6). See **R.132(2):2** for details of the extension. Note, that the examiner has no time limit for issuing a new communication following a response; delays of over a year are common (situation 2017). He does have a time limit if the prosecution is accelerated (see **Art.94(1):4**).

A response within the meaning of **Art.94(4)** is a substantive response to the communication in which the applicant exercises his rights in accordance with **Art.113(1)** to present comments. The reply need not be (substantively) complete or convincing to qualify as a reply within the meaning of **Art.94(4)** (**T160/92**). A reply of an applicant who wants to close the debate by not responding in substance but requesting a decision on the file as it stands is in effect a waiver of the applicant's right in accordance with **Art.113(1)** to comment (**T685/98** r.3.2; see also C-V,15). The EPO may regard both replies as the applicant's definitive reply, even if the time limit for reply has not expired, and continue the proceedings by inviting the applicant to indicate his approval of the text to be granted, by sending a further communication under **R.71(1)**, or refuse the application pursuant to **Art.97(2)**. (**T685/98**)

A reply devoid of any substantive implications and which cannot be understood as a waiver, express or implied, of the rest of the time limit set for reply is not a reply within the meaning of **Art.94(4)** and allows the applicant to file a substantive reply or any request (e.g. according to **R.132** or **Art.121**) during the not-elapsed part of the time limit. The former reply does not trigger the procedure leading to the application being deemed withdrawn for failure to reply under **Art.94(4)**. A refusal pursuant to **Art.97(2)** without a reply within the meaning of **Art.94(4)** is a substantial procedural violation, because **Art.97(2)** expressly precludes refusal where 'this Convention provides for a different legal consequence', the sanction being the 'deemed to be withdrawn' of **Art.94(4)** (**T685/98** hn2). In unclear cases there can be no presumption that an applicant has waived his right to be heard under **Art.113(1)**. (**T685/98**)

2 **Sanction on late filing and remedies**

If the reply to the invitation of **Art.94(3)** is not filed within the period specified in the invitation, including a possible extension, the application is deemed withdrawn under **Art.94(4)** and the EPO notifies the applicant of the loss of rights according to **R.112(1)**. In practice, the **R.112(1)** communication is despatched about one month after expiry of the period. Within two months from the notification under **R.112(1)** the applicant can request further processing (**Art.121** and **R.135**) by paying the fee for further processing and filing his reply. A request for further processing thus extends the period for reply, including a possible extension according to **R.134**, by three to four months at the expense of the moderate further processing fee (**Rfees2(1)12**).

Instead of or in addition to a request for further processing the applicant can, within two months from the **R.112(1)** notification, apply for an appealable decision according to **R.112(2)** if he is of the opinion that the EPO did receive the reply in due time. (see **R.112(2):1**)

Failure to meet the two-month period of **R.135(1)** or **R.112(2)** can only be remedied by requesting re-establishment in the two-month period according to **Art.122** and **R.136**: file the request, prove all due care, pay the fee and file the reply, all within two months from removal of the cause of non-compliance but not later than one year from expiry of the period in which re-establishment is requested.

Art. 95 (deleted)

Art. 96 (deleted)

Art. 97 Grant or refusal

Art. 97(1) If the Examining Division is of the opinion that the European patent application and the invention to which it relates meet the requirements of this Convention, it shall decide to grant a European patent, provided that the conditions laid down in the Implementing Regulations are fulfilled.

See for the implementation:
R.71 Examination procedure
(3) Communication of text to be granted
(4) Additional claims fees
(5) Approval of text to be granted
(6) Filing of amendments or corrections
(7) Sanction
R.71a Conclusion of the grant procedure
(1) Decision to grant
(2) Resumption of examination
(5) Crediting of already paid fees
(6) Refund of fee for grant and publishing
R.72 Grant of the European patent to different applicants
R.140 Correction of errors in decisions

1 **Intention to grant the patent**
If the examining division considers that the text of the patent application meets the requirements of the EPC, it must establish that several requirements are met before it can take the decision to grant.

The period for payment of the designation fee in **R.39(1)** may expire after the notification of the **R.71(3)** communication. In such a case the EPO informs the applicant that the mention of the grant will not be published until the designation fee has been paid (**R.71a(3)**). Applications filed before 01.04.2009 require payment of a designation fee for each contracting state.

Similarly, if a renewal fee falls due in the period between the communication and the next possible day for publication of the mention of the grant, the EPO informs the applicant that the grant will be deferred till after payment of the renewal fee (**R.71a(4)**).

The requirements to be met for grant are given in:

- **R.71(3)**, approval of the text of the application to be granted by filing translations of the claims in the official EPO languages other than the language of the proceedings and paying the fee for grant and publishing;
- **R.71(4)**, payment of any additional claims fees;
- **R.71a(3)**, payment of still unpaid designation fee;
- **R.71a(4)**, payment of any renewal fee due.

The examining division will issue a **R.71(3)** communication informing the applicant of the text it proposes to grant and inviting him to meet the requirements. The requirements stated in **R.71(3)** must be met within a period of four months from notification of the **R.71(3)** communication. Non-observance results in the application being deemed withdrawn under **R.71(7)**. **R.71(6)** gives the applicant the possibility to disapprove the text proposed to be granted and to request grant based on a different text. The examining division may resume the substantive examination or proceed towards grant of the different text.

2 **Acceleration of the grant**

The **R.71(3)** communication will be issued within tight deadlines if accelerated examination has been requested (see **Art.94(1):5**). The following steps in the grant procedure cannot be quickened by filing a request for acceleration but only by promptly responding to the EPO communications.

An applicant can accelerate the grant of the patent by complying with all requirements immediately after receipt of the **R.71(3)** communication: file the translations of the claims and pay all necessary fees (fee for grant and publishing (**R.71(3)**); any claims fees (**R.71(4)**); any designation fee (**R.71a(3)**); and any renewal fee (**R.71a(4)**). It is recommended to pay the next renewal fee if the response is made less than three months before its due date; the fee will be reimbursed if the mention of the grant is published in the current patent year.

Note, that applicants using the automatic debiting procedure may have to pay the above fees separately to ensure rapid grant (see notes to **AAD.3.2(d)**, **(e)** and **(g)**). The applicant is informed of this situation in the **R.71(3)** communication.

If the applicant files amendments in response to a **R.71(3)** communication, he can waive a further **R.71(3)** communication. Provided the amendments are allowable, the examining division will not send a further **R.71(3)** communication, but will issue the decision to grant forthwith. (see **R.71(6):4**)

3 **Disapproval of the text to be granted**

Art.97(1) does not provide for the case when an applicant disapproves of the text proposed by the examining division for grant. In such a case the examining division can no longer decide upon the proposed text, because the applicant has not approved the text as required under **Art.113(2)**. The procedures developed for the case where disapproval is expressed have been set out in **R.71(6)** and notes thereto.

Explicit disapproval of the text to be granted occurs mainly in cases where a main request and one or more auxiliary requests are pending (see **R.71(6):6**).

In the common case where only one set of claims is pending, an explicit disapproval of the text proposed for grant is usually accompanied by an approval of a text including an amended set of claims. The examining division will not decide upon the text it proposed, but will allow, further examine or refuse the amended text (**R.71(6):3, 5**).

4 Decision to grant

When the requirements have been complied with in due time, the examining division will decide to grant the patent and start the preparations for publication of the patent specification under **Art.98**. The written decision under **Art.97(1)** states which text forms the basis for the grant (**R.71a(1)**, last sentence) by referring to the **R.71(3)** communication. It also states the designated contracting states, the requirement for translation of the specification in an official language of a contracting state under **Art.65(1)** and the date of publication of the mention of the grant (C-V,10). The decision is notified by registered letter to the applicant under **R.126** when the technical preparations for publication of the patent specification (**R.73** juncto **R.67(1)**) have been completed (C-V,10; OJ 2006, 409).

The decision takes effect on the date of publication of the mention of the grant in the Bulletin (**Art.97(3)**), i.e. it does not take effect on the date the decision is taken. In practice the mention of the grant is published four weeks after issue of the decision (OJ 2006,409). As soon as possible after the publication of the mention, the EPO publishes the specification in a form determined by **R.73(2)** and enters the date of publication of the mention in the Register (**R.143(1)(o)**). From the date of publication of the mention the rights of the patent are conferred on its proprietor (**Art.64(1)**). The EPO publishes the patent specification as soon as possible after the mention of the grant (**Art.98**). Promptly after the publication of the specification the EPO sends a certificate for a patent to the proprietor (**R.74**).The specification is sent only if it has been duly requested (Dec. Pres., Spec. Ed. 3 of OJ 2007 D.2). See **R.73(2):2** for withdrawal before publication of the specification.

After the decision has been taken, both the EPO and the applicant are bound by the decision as far as the text of the patent to be granted is concerned (**R.140:3.1**). See **R.140:3.2** for correcting the published specification of the patent where it does not conform to the text as granted.

5 Appealability of decision to grant

The decision to grant is, in principle, appealable. However, since the applicant has given his approval under **R.71(3)** for the text to be granted, situations where the applicant is adversely affected by the decision are rare. An example of such a situation is where the decision is not based on the text approved. This may happen if the examining division grants the patent in spite of a request of the applicant to disregard his earlier approval and amend the application (see e.g. **T1093/05** hn). An appeal filed with the object of amending the patent as granted will be inadmissible, because the applicant is not adversely affected by the decision to grant (**J12/83** r.3). A published specification of the patent not in conformance with the text as approved is no ground for appeal and should be corrected under **R.140**.

The relation between approval and adverse affection is different in grant proceedings and opposition proceedings. Since in grant proceedings there is no opposing party and no translation costs are incurred prior to the issue of an appealable decision refusing the application, there is no reason to issue an interlocutory decision as in opposition proceedings; rather, the final decision refusing the application is issued immediately. As set out in the above section, there is no adverse affection where a decision to grant is based on a text approved by the applicant. In contrast, a proprietor may be adversely affected by a decision maintaining the patent in amended form, even though he has approved the amended text before the decision was taken (and provided he has not withdrawn any higher-ranking requests). The adversity resides in the fact that the scope of the patent as maintained is smaller than that of the patent as granted. Hence, the proprietor can appeal the decision to maintain the patent in amended form.

Another difference between grant and opposition proceedings arises when auxiliary requests have been filed. If in grant proceedings the examiner indicates the allowable request in the **R.71(3)** communication, he will ask the applicant to approve this request and abandon the higher-ranking requests. A decision to grant based on the remaining, approved request is not appealable because the applicant is not adversely affected. If the applicant wants to maintain a higher-ranking request, he should not approve the request proposed by the examiner but refuse to withdraw the higher-ranking request; as a consequence, the application will be refused by an appealable decision. Subsequently, the applicant can defend the higher-ranking request in appeal. In opposition proceedings the proprietor is deemed to have approved all requests by the act of filing them. He is not requested to withdraw requests before a decision is taken, but the decision is taken on all requests. The decision states which requests have been rejected and which request is allowed. The proprietor can appeal this decision if the patent according to the allowed request has a scope that is smaller than that of the patent as granted. See **R.71(6):6** and **R.81(3):1** for details of handling auxiliary requests.

Art. 97(2) If the Examining Division is of the opinion that the European patent application or the invention to which it relates does not meet the requirements of this Convention, it shall refuse the application unless this Convention provides for a different legal consequence.

1 **Refusal of the application**

An application will be refused if it does not meet the formal and/or substantive requirements of the EPC (**Art.97(2)**).

The application is refused in total, without considering possible patentable matter in it (**T5/81**). For example, when the examiner considers one of the claims not allowable, and the applicant does not amend this claim, the entire application is refused; there will be no interlocutory decision on the non-allowable claim, which could be appealed separately from the allowed claims. The appeal should relate to a main request including the allowable and non-allowable claims and a subsidiary request for only the allowable claims. If the refusal of the entire application is appealed, the board of appeal will examine again the allowable claims, with the risk of a refusal (**G10/93** hn allows an appellant to be put in a worse position). A better way of securing the rights in the allowable claims is to remove the non-allowable claim and have the patent granted; the prosecution of the non-allowable claim should be continued by filing a divisional application for that claim before a decision is taken (**Art.76, R.36(1)**).

The decision to refuse the application must be reasoned (**R.111(2)**) and be based on facts known to the applicant and on which he has had an opportunity to comment **Art.113(1)**). The omission of the reason for the decision is a substantial procedural violation, which entitles the applicant to reimbursement of the appeal fee (**R.103**). The applicant can appeal the decision to refuse the application. If an appeal has been lodged, the examining division can revise its decision in the light of the statement of grounds under **Art.109(1)**. If the examining division does not revise its decision, the case will be remitted to the board of appeal. After the board has taken a decision, it can remit the case to the examining division for further prosecution, back to the same examiner (**Art.111(2)**).

An example of 'a different legal consequence' as mentioned in **Art.97(2)** is the fiction of withdrawal of the application after non-payment of renewal fees (**Art.86(1)**), a not-timely filed response (**Art.94(4)**), non-payment of the fee for grant and publishing, non-payment of the claims fee or not filing the translation of the claims under **R.71(7)**.

Art. 97(3) The decision to grant a European patent shall take effect on the date on which the mention of the grant is published in the European Patent Bulletin.

See for the implementation:
R.71a Conclusion of the grant procedure
(3) Designation fee
(4) Renewal fee

1 **Publication of decision to grant**

The communication notifying the decision to grant informs the applicant of the date of the publication of the mention of the grant. The communication is sent to the applicant when the technical preparations for publishing the patent specification have been completed (C-V,10). The scheduled date of publication is four weeks after issue of the decision to grant (OJ 2006, 409).

The mention of the grant will not be published until any designation fee or renewal fee under **R.71a(3)** and (4) have been paid.

If the decision to grant is notified to the applicant, but the mention of the grant has not yet been published, the applicant can still withdraw designations of states, because the decision to grant is not effective at that time (**Art.97(3)**, **J7/96** r.6.3).

The patent specification is published as soon as possible after the publication of the mention of the grant (**Art.98**). The effect of the grant is that it confers the rights of **Art.64(1)** on the proprietor. A deficiency in the mention of the grant does not necessarily render the decision to grant ineffective (J14/87). See also **Art.98:1**.

The European patent has, in each designated state, the effect of a national patent from the date of publication of the mention of the grant (**Art.2(2)**, **Art.64(1)**). Many contracting states require translation of the granted patent or part of it under **Art.65(1)**, which gives the applicant at least three months after the publication of the mention of the grant for filing the translations of the granted claims or the specification in the languages of those designated contracting states requiring such a translation. The EPO does not inform the applicant about the states that require translation; the information is available on the EPO website.

A granted patent is subject to national law, unless otherwise provided (**Art.2(2)**). The opposition is an example of the 'otherwise provided', where the patent is still bound by the EPC.

2 **Legal effect of the mention of the grant**

Art.2(2) The European patent has the effect of a national patent
Art.64(1) The European patent confers the same right as a national patent
Art.65(1) Requirement to file translation of European patent
Art.99(1) The 9-month opposition period starts
Art.105a Centralised limitation and revocation possible
Art.138 Grounds in national revocation proceedings are restricted

Art.141 Renewal fees must be paid to the national patent offices

Art. 98 Publication of the specification of the European patent

The European Patent Office shall publish the specification of the European patent as soon as possible after the mention of the grant of the European patent has been published in the European Patent Bulletin.

See for the implementation:
R.73 Content and form of the specification
R.74 Certificate for a European patent

1 **Publication of the specification**
The specification of the granted patent will be published as soon as possible after publication of the mention of the grant (**Art.98**), which in practice is on the first Wednesday following the publication of the mention of the grant. The purpose of the publication is to inform the public of the grant of the patent and its content; the published specification has no binding character (**R.140:3.2**).

The applicant has been informed of the date of publication by the decision to grant, sent to him after the completion of the technical preparations for publishing (C-V,10).

The mention of the grant of the patent is published in the European Patent Bulletin (**Art.97(3)**). As soon as possible thereafter, the EPO publishes the patent specification, the form and contents of which are governed by **R.73**.

After the publication of the specification, the EPO sends the proprietor a certificate of entitlement to the patent (**R.74**). If no notice of opposition is recorded within nine months of publication, the proprietor is informed and an appropriate entry is published in the Bulletin (C-V,13).

Possibilities to correct errors in the published specification are dealt with in **R.140:3.2**.

PART V OPPOSITION AND LIMITATION PROCEDURE

1 **General**

The EPC provides for an opposition procedure after the grant procedure in order to improve the quality of the patents by allowing other parties to bring forward prejudicial facts which are difficult of access to examiners, such as oral disclosure and public prior use. The opposition procedure has the character of a centralised revocation procedure affecting all national rights originating from a European patent. The EPC has chosen for a post-grant instead of a pre-grant opposition because some contracting states did not want to recognize the rights of an unexamined application, it would take too long for the rights to become effective if the application could only become a patent after opposition, and to exclude the possibility for a third party to delay the grant by an unjustified opposition.

Revocation of the patent in opposition has an effect ex tunc in that the patent is deemed never to have conferred the rights of **Art.64** (**Art.68**). The opposition and its effects are an exception to the rule that after grant the European patent is subject to national law (see **Art.2(2)**).

An overview of the opposition procedure is published in OJ 2016 A42. The opposition proceedings may be accelerated in the case of a pending infringement action (see **Art.101(1):4**). About 4.0% of all patents granted by the EPO are opposed (situation 2016). The average duration of an opposition from filing till final decision is 25 months (situation 2016).

Art. 99 Opposition

Art. 99(1) Within nine months of the publication of the mention of the grant of the European patent in the European Patent Bulletin, any person may give notice to the European Patent Office of opposition to that patent, in accordance with the Implementing Regulations. Notice of opposition shall not be deemed to have been filed until the opposition fee has been paid.

See for the implementation:
R.75 Opposition to lapsed or surrendered patent
R.76 Content of the notice of opposition

1 Person entitled to oppose

1.1 ADMITTED PERSONS

Any person has the right to file an opposition according to **Art.99(1)**. Since an opposition is not only in the interest of the opponent, but also in the interest of the public, making a bar to admissibility of a person is undesirable. 'Any person' must be construed in line with **Art.58** as meaning: (a) any natural person, (b) any legal person or (c) any body equivalent to a legal person by virtue of the law governing it (**G3/99** r.9). A fictional person, i.e. a person having no legal existence, cannot validly file an opposition (**T1165/03**). If an opposition is filed by a body that may lack legal personality under national law (such as a UK partnership) and if no evidence in support of the status as a legal person can be produced, the EPO will treat the opposition as being filed by several persons acting in common (**T482/02** hn).

A (single) notice of opposition may also be filed by several persons acting in common (**R.51(1)**, last sentence). Such persons are filing only one opposition, need to pay only one opposition fee, and are joint opponents (or common opponents) throughout the proceedings. The joint opponents must act through a common representative (see **R.151(1):2**). The common representative is either appointed by the persons filing the opposition or by the EPO according to **R.151** (**G3/99** r.14). Each of the persons must be of the type (a), (b) or (c) mentioned above. (**G3/99** r.3, 9, 10)

A party filing two notices of opposition to the same patent acquires party status as opponent only once (**T9/00**).

Multiple oppositions against the same patent are dealt with in a single procedure. Prior art filed in an inadmissible opposition may be taken into account by the opposition division under **Art.114(1)** if also an admissible opposition has been filed and the material is considered relevant (**T966/02** r.2.4).

The identity of the opponent must be clear before the end of the opposition period (**T25/85**). See **R.76(2):2.2** for correction of the identity.

The fact that according to **Art.99(1)** the opposition is open to 'any person' is incompatible with a requirement that the opponent must have a commercial or other interest in the opposition (**G1/84** r.3, **G3/97** r.3.2). The opponent can for example desire to assess the inventive step out of mere curiosity or to supplement his professional training (**T798/93** hn.I).

An opposition is not inadmissible because the opponent is a licensee of the patent, even if the licence agreement includes a no-challenge provision (**G3/97** r.3.3.2).

1.2 OPPOSITION BY STRAW MAN

A straw man in opposition is a person who filed the opposition in his own name but is acting on behalf of a usually unnamed principal. Opponents may resort to the use of a straw man to hide their identity from the patentee, e.g. to avoid showing an interest in the technology or to attack a patent during negotiations with the patentee. Some companies offer the service of acting as a strawman in opposition; the professional representative will represent before the EPO such a company instead of the principal; see e.g. **T616/08**.

The EPO accepts a straw man as opponent since decision **G3/97**, provided that the use of a straw man does not circumvent the law.

The status of the opponent is a procedural status. Hence, the opponent is the person who fulfils the requirements of the EPC for filing an opposition; in particular, the person must be identifiable (see **R.76(2)(a)**). The status of the opponent is similar to that of an applicant, who is 'deemed' to be entitled to the patent (**Art.60(3)**). It is irrelevant for the opposition proceedings whether the opponent is a nominal opponent, also called a straw man, acting on behalf of a, possibly unnamed, principal. Hence, an opposition is not inadmissible only because it is filed by a straw man. (**G3/97** r.2.1; case consolidated with **G4/97**; overturning **T10/82**, **T219/86** hn1, **T635/88**, **T798/93** hn2)

However, an opposition is inadmissible if the action of a straw man is to be regarded as a circumvention of the law by abuse of process. This is the case if a straw man represents the proprietor's interests, because the proprietor is not entitled to oppose his own patent (see below). A straw man should also not be used to circumvent the provisions on representation. This is the case, if a person not entitled to act as a professional representative files an opposition in his own name on behalf of a client, in the context of activities which, taken as a whole, are typically associated with professional representatives. (**G3/97** r.4)

The challenge to the admissibility of the opposition based on the opponent's identity may be raised before the department of first and second instance by the patent proprietor or the EPO of its own motion (**G3/97** r.5). The burden of proof on the basis of clear and convincing evidence is to be borne by the person raising the issue. As a rule, the EPO has no indication that a straw man has filed an opposition on the proprietor's behalf, and the inadmissibility of the opposition will not be detected. Indications of an opponent acting as a straw man for the proprietor are where the opponent is bound by the proprietor's instructions as a subsidiary company within a large group or as an employee of the proprietor (**G3/97** r.5.1.1). An indication that a straw man is used to circumvent the provisions on representation is where a person, not being a professional representative, regularly acts as an opponent in his own name, creating the impression that these activities are part of his normal professional activities (**G3/97** r.5.1.2). However, the law is not circumvented purely because a professional representative files an opposition in his own name on behalf of a client, or because an opponent having either a residence or place of business in one of the contracting states, acts on behalf of a principal who does not meet these requirements (**G3/97** r.4.2).

1.3 SELF-OPPOSITION

Under EPC 1973 patent proprietors could oppose their own patents ("self-opposition") to amend the granted patent in a central procedure before the EPO. Decision **G1/84** had allowed such self-opposition. However, **G9/93** overruled the earlier decision and forbade self-opposition. Hence, despite the term 'any person' in **Art.99(1)**, the proprietor may not oppose his own patent. Opposition can be filed by an inventor who is not also proprietor (**T3/06** r.2).

In order to provide a central procedure for amending a patent after grant, the EPC 2000 has introduced the limitation procedure of **Art.105a - c.**

1.4 TRANSFER OF THE OPPOSITION

According to general principles of procedural law, a party to proceedings does not have the discretion to transfer its party status to another person. The EPC contains exceptions for the transfer of the status of applicant and proprietor in **Art.71** and **R.85**. The only exception for opponents in the EPC is implicitly provided in **R.84(2)**, which accepts a transfer of opponent status to the opponent's heirs. The legislator did not want to provide for cases of transfer of opponent status other from universal succession. Hence, the status as an opponent cannot be freely transferred. The public interest in a speedy conduction of opposition proceedings does not allow the time-consuming examination of contested questions arising in transfers resulting from a liberal admission of transfers or the lengthening of the procedure caused by the introduction of new lines of attack by a new party. (**G2/04**, r.2.1.2, r.2.2.2, hn.Ia; see also **G3/97**, r.2.2)

The EPO has the duty to consider the opponent status at all stages. The validity of a transfer of opponent status may therefore be raised at all stages during the proceedings, even for the first time in appeal. If the alleged opponent files an appeal, his status as opponent is not protected by the prohibition on reformatio in peius. If the board denies the validity of the transfer, the opposition procedure has to be redone from the time of the transfer, this time with an entitled opponent. (**T1178/04**)

Examples of universal succession are succession from a deceased person and incorporation and merging of legal persons (**T355/86**; **T349/86**; **T475/88**). **G4/88** also allowed the transfer of opponent status to a third party in a case where a company filed an opposition in the interest of a part of the company without legal personality and subsequently transferred the assets of that part to the third party. The opposition, which is an inseparable part of the assets, must be regarded as transferable when the assets are transferable in accordance with the principle that an accessory object follows the principal object. Hence, an opposition may be transferred as part of the opponent's assets together with the assets in the interest of which the opposition was filed. Case law has not extended the rationale of **G4/88** to other situations. See also **T670/95** and **T711/99**. In **T74/00**, it was held that, unlike a legal transfer of an opposition, a transfer arising from the death of the opponent need not be accompanied by any specific assets of the deceased. The new opponent gains its status purely from being the heir of the previous opponent.

G2/04 refused the transfer of opponent status to a third party where a company filed an opposition in the interest of one of its subsidiaries having legal personality and subsequently transferred the assets of the subsidiary to the third party. Since the company in **G4/88** was the sole legal entity and could not file an opposition in the name of the part of the company, whereas the company in **G2/04** could file an opposition in the name of its subsidiary, the Board concluded that the two cases are essentially different. The Board decided to interpret **G4/88** restrictively and not to extend its rationale to other situations because there was no overriding interest of the parties or the public. (**G2/04** r.2.2; see also **T711/99**, reaching the same conclusion based on **G3/97**)

The status of party may be transferred within the above bounds at any stage of the opposition and opposition appeal; the right to lodge an appeal may also be transferred (**T563/89** r.1.1). The transfer must be substantiated (**T670/95**). The previous party retains its rights until the required proof has been provided (**R.22(3)**; **T870/92a**). If a purported notice of appeal does not indicate how a transfer of status has taken place, it is not the duty of the Board of Appeal to investigate further (for example, by examination of appropriate trade registers) to substantiate the transfer (**T428/08**). A transfer may be to only one successor party to avoid other persons becoming party to the proceedings after expiry of the time limits and without payment of fees (**T298/97** r.7.6).

The following precautions can be taken to avoid problems in a transfer.

- File the opposition or opposition appeal in the name of both the company and the subsidiary if the latter has legal personality; the company can withdraw from the opposition after the transfer (**G2/04** r.2.1.2). See **T960/08** r.3.1 for necessary conditions and **T9/00** for a failed variant of this precaution.
- File the opposition or opposition appeal in the name of the company as a main request and in the name of the subsidiary as an auxiliary request (**G2/04** r.3.2; see e.g. **T1877/08** r.1).

- Ask the EPO for advice before filing the opposition or appeal, noting date and persons contacted for later proof. In case the EPO refuses the transfer, the principle of good faith may be invoked to correct the name of the opponent (see **Art.125:2**).
- File the opposition and opposition appeal through a straw man as legally accepted by **G3/97**, because any transfer of the straw man's principal need not be entered in the Register of the EPO.

1.5 WITHDRAWAL OF THE OPPOSITION

Withdrawal of an opposition does not directly end the opposition procedure, as the opposition division may continue the proceedings of its own motion in the public interest (**Art.114(1)** and **R.84(2)**). Moreover, the Division must take a decision to be entered in the Register (**R.143(1)(r)**). (**T197/88**)

The opposition proceedings are also continued if one or more common opponents withdraw from the opposition, since otherwise a single one of the common opponents, not being the common representative, could of its own motion end the opposition (**G3/99** r.13). The common representative should notify the EPO of any withdrawal. A withdrawal of the common representative should also be communicated to the EPO; the new common representative must be appointed either by the remaining common opponents or by application of **R.151**. See also **R.151(1):2**.

See also **R.84** for surrender of the patent, death of the opponent and withdrawal of the opposition during first instance proceedings and **Art.108:1** for withdrawal in opposition appeal.

2 Filing

2.1 PERIOD FOR FILING

Opposition can only be raised against a granted patent within nine months from the publication of the mention of the grant under **Art.97(3)** (**Art.99(1)**), not from the publication of the patent specification under **Art.98**. An opposition filed before the mention of the publication of grant of the patent is not regarded as an opposition. In that case the opposition documents become part of the public file and the opposition fee is refunded (D-IV,1.1).

Since the nine-month period and the payment of the opposition fee are regarded as essential requirements, they are provided in the Convention and not in the Implementing Regulations.

2.2 FORMAL REQUIREMENTS

The notice of opposition must be in writing (**R.76(1)**) and signed (**R.76(3)**, **R.50(3)**, D-III,3.4). It must be filed with an EPO filing office using a method permitted under **R.2(1)**. The notice may be filed e.g. by fax (**R.2(1):6**) or electronically (**R.2(1):7**), but not using Web-Form Filing (D-III,3.2).

The notice must be in one of the three languages of the EPO, not necessarily the language of the proceedings (**R.3(1)**). Since the notice is a document to be filed within a time limit, it may also be filed in an official language of a contracting state according to **Art.14** if the opponent (not his representative, **T149/85**) has his residence or place of business in that state or is a national of that state. In that case a translation in one of the three EPO languages must be filed within the longer of one month from filing the notice and the end of the opposition period (**R.6(2)**). Failing the time limit for filing the translation cannot be corrected according to **Art.121** or **122**, because the opponent is not an applicant or proprietor (**T702/89**).

2.3 OPPOSITION FEE AND LATE FILING

The opposition will be deemed not to have been filed until the opposition fee has been paid (**Art.99(1)**, second sentence). The amount of the opposition fee is fixed in **Rfees2(1)10**. A single opposition filed by two or more persons acting in common is admissible on payment of only one opposition fee (**G3/99** r.10). A late filing of the notice of opposition or a late payment of the opposition fee cannot be remedied with **Art.121**, **Art.122** or **R.139**, because an opponent is not an applicant or proprietor as required by **Art.121** and **122** and the acts of late filing and payment are not errors or mistakes in documents as required by **R.139**. (**T702/89** r.3, **T323/87** r.5, **T128/87** r.2)

3 **Notice of opposition deemed (not) to have been filed**

On receipt of the notice of opposition the EPO assesses whether the opposition is regarded as filed on the basis of the received documents (D-IV,1.2.1). Only after the notice is regarded as filed will the EPO assess the admissibility of the opposition under **Art.101**. All cases where a notice of opposition is regarded as not filed can be derived directly from the EPC. See **T765/08**, r. 9-11 for the legal status of a document deemed not to have been received.

An opposition will be regarded as not filed if:

- The opposition fee is not paid in due time (**Art.99(1)**), causing the opposition being deemed not to have been filed.
- The notice has no signature (**R.76(3)** in conjunction with **R.50(3)**), or the signature has not been provided in time, causing the notice being deemed not to have been filed (D-IV,1.2.1(ii)). Further processing and re-establishment are not available for the opponent. If, after invitation by the formalities officer, it is provided in due time, the notice retains its date of filing (**R.50(3)**). The reproduction of the signature on a notice of opposition by fax will be accepted as signature (D-III,3.4).
- The notice has been sent by fax and no confirmation copy has been filed in due time after invitation, causing the notice being deemed not to have been received (**R.2(1)**; OJ 2007 se3 p.7 Art.7(2)).
- When the opponent is represented and the authorisation has not been filed on invitation by the EPO within the time set (**R.152(2)**). The act of filing is deemed not to have been carried out (**R.152(6)**).
- The notice of opposition is not in an official language of the EPO according to **R.3(1)** nor in an admissible non-EPO language according to **Art.14(4)**, e.g. in Japanese. The opposition will be regarded as not filed, unless the opposition is filed in an admissible language before the end of the opposition period (**Art.14(4)**). Beware, **R.6(2)** does not apply to an opposition filed in Japanese, because the filed opposition is not a translation relating to a document filed in an admissible non-EPO language according to **Art.14(4)**.
- The notice of opposition is filed in an official language of a contracting state but the opponent is not entitled to use the language according to **Art.14(4)**. Hence, a notice of opposition in Dutch of a German opponent is deemed not to have been filed, even if the opponent is represented by a Dutch representative (**Art.14(4)**; **T149/85**).
- The notice is filed in an admissible non-EPO language but the translation of the notice required under **Art.14(4)** is not filed within the longer of one month after filing the notice or the end of the opposition period (**R.6(2)**). Hence, the notice is regarded as not received (this applies to all further documents entering the EPO) (**Art.14(4)**). (**T193/87**; D-IV,1.2.1(v))

4 **Procedure after filing**
An opposition division is the competent department of the EPO to assess the notice of opposition (**Art.19(1)**). It first assesses whether the notice of opposition is deemed to have been filed or not, next it examines the admissibility of the opposition (**Art.101(1)** and **R.77**) and finally it examines the allowability of the opposition, i.e. whether the invoked grounds for opposition prejudice the maintenance of the patent (**Art.101(1)**).

The following four cases may arise from filing an opposition:

- No opposition has been started, because the notice of opposition is deemed not to have been filed, e.g. due to late filing of the notice of opposition or late payment of the opposition fee. An already paid opposition fee will be refunded. See **Art.101(1):1** and D-IV,1.4.1.
- An opposition has been started but not yet the procedure due to major errors in the notice of opposition. The errors must be remedied according to **R.77(1)** within the opposition time limit, otherwise the opposition is inadmissible. The fee paid for an inadmissible opposition is not refunded. See **R.77(1):1** and D-IV,1.2.2.1.
- An opposition has been started and a procedure has been started conditionally, because of small errors in the notice of opposition. The errors must be corrected according to **R.77(2)** within a period to be set by the EPO (normally 2 months) (D-IV,1.3.2, 1.4.2), otherwise the notice is inadmissible. See **R.77(2)** and D-IV,1.2.2.2.
- An opposition and procedure have been started according to **Art.101**.

Art. 99(2) The opposition shall apply to the European patent in all the Contracting States in which that patent has effect.

1 **Territorial extent of opposition**
The opposition is in respect of all designated states. An opposition filed in respect of only some of the designated states is treated as if it were filed in respect of all designated states (D-I,3). The outcome of the opposition proceedings also applies to the extension states and validation states, based on their national law (see **Art.169:4** and e.g. OJ 2016 A5 §17 for Morocco)

The patent in opposition may have different claims, description and drawings for different designated states because of national prior rights (**R.138**), European prior rights under EPC 1973 (see **Art.54(3):3**), or a transfer of the patent to an entitled third party for some but not all designated states (**R.18(2)**; **R.78(2)**).

Art. 99(3) Opponents shall be parties to the opposition proceedings as well as the proprietor of the patent.

1 **Parties to opposition proceedings**
In the formal examination by the formalities officer of the notice of opposition to assess whether the notice is deemed filed and admissible, the proprietor is not involved. This part of the examination is in fact ex parte (D-IV,3; Empel no. 472). The subsequent substantive examination is inter partes.

If an opposition is withdrawn or finally rejected as inadmissible, the opponent is no longer a party in the proceedings (D-I,6). An assumed infringer who intervenes according to **Art.105** becomes party to the opposition proceedings. A third person who has filed an observation according to **Art.115** is not a party to the proceedings.

Art. 99(4) Where a person provides evidence that in a Contracting State, following a final decision, he has been entered in the patent register of such State instead of the previous proprietor, such person shall, at his request, replace the previous proprietor in respect of such State. Notwithstanding Article 118, the previous proprietor and the person making the request shall not be regarded as joint proprietors unless both so request.

Art.118 Unity of patent
See for the implementation:
R.78 Procedure where the proprietor is not entitled

1 **Opposition and entitlement procedure**
If during the opposition period or the opposition procedure a third person provides proof to the EPO that he has started court proceedings seeking a judgement that he is entitled to the patent, the opposition procedure will be stayed, unless the third person consents to continuation of the opposition procedure (**R.78(1)**).

The Protocol on Recognition, according to which entitlement decisions of national courts must be recognized in all EPC Contracting States, applies only to patent applications and not to patents. Therefore, a national decision on entitlement to a patent is not recognized by the other states designated in the patent on the basis of the Protocol. However, such a decision can be recognised in the EU based on EU Regulation 1215/2012 and in most EFTA countries based on the Lugano Convention.

When the entitled person has replaced the first proprietor for some but not all designated states and the entitled person and first proprietor do not request to become joint proprietors, there will be two opposition procedures running at the same time before the same opposition division. This allows the new proprietor to defend independently the part of the patent right transferred to him against the opposition. In such a case, the outcome of the opposition can be different for the respective states (see **R.78(2)**).

Art. 100 Grounds for opposition

Opposition may only be filed on the grounds that:
(a) the subject-matter of the European patent is not patentable under Articles 52 to 57;
(b) the European patent does not disclose the invention in a manner sufficiently clear and complete for it to be carried out by a person skilled in the art;
(c) the subject-matter of the European patent extends beyond the content of the application as filed, or, if the patent was granted on a divisional application or on a new application filed under Article 61, beyond the content of the earlier application as filed.

Art.52 Patentable inventions
Art.53 Exceptions to patentability
Art.54 Novelty
Art.55 Non-prejudicial disclosures
Art.56 Inventive step
Art.57 Industrial application
Art.61 Application filed by non-entitled person

1 Grounds for opposition

The list of grounds for opposition in **Art.100** is exhaustive in view of the word 'only' in **Art.100.**

The grounds for opposition must, in principle, be set out in the notice of opposition. The EPO has restricted the possibilities for introducing new grounds during the opposition procedure, i.e. after expiry of the 9-month opposition period (see **R.76(2)(c):3**). See **R.76(2):4.3.3** for a discussion what grounds are regarded as separate grounds.

1.1 PATENTABILITY (ART.100(A))

The ground of **Art.100(a)** applies if the subject-matter of the claims of the patent as granted is considered not to be an invention under **Art.52**, if it falls under one of the exceptions to patentability (**Art.53**), if it is not new (**Art.54**), if it does not involve an inventive step (**Art.56**) or if it is not susceptible to industrial application (**Art.57**). The opposition procedure is especially suitable for revealing unpatentability in view of oral disclosure or prior use.

A notice of opposition indicating only national prior rights is inadmissible, because these rights are not European prior rights within the meaning of **Art.54(3)** and are accordingly not comprised in the state of the art; they can, therefore, not support the ground of **Art.100(a)** (D-III,5; **T550/88** hn1 and hn2). Nevertheless, during the opposition proceedings the patent may be amended in view of national prior rights (**R.138**, H-II,3.3, see also **R.80**).

1.2 DISCLOSURE (ART.100(B))

Art.100(b) relates to not compliance with the requirement of sufficiency of disclosure of **Art.83**.

If an embodiment of the invention is not sufficiently disclosed, that embodiment should be deleted from the patent. If the proprietor does not remove it, the embodiment itself cannot be revoked, because the EPO can only decide on the patent in the text submitted or approved by the proprietor (**Art.113(2)**); in this case the entire patent has to be revoked.

1.3 EXTENSION (ART.100(C))

Art.100(c) corresponds to **Art.123(2)** and provides a sanction in case the claims of the patent lack basis in the application as filed, and for a patent granted on a divisional application also in case the claims as granted lack basis in the earlier application as filed (**Art.76(1)**).

If the application as filed is in a non-EPO language, the claims as granted must have a basis in the application as filed in the non-EPO language (**Art.70(2)**). The opposition division may assume that the translation of the application filed during the grant procedure is correct (**R.7**), unless evidence to the contrary is provided, for example by the opponent (D-V,6.1).

2 Invalid grounds for opposition

Other grounds than those of **Art.100** cannot be used in the notice of opposition. Examples of invalid grounds:

- The claims do not comply with the unity requirement of **Art.82** (**T162/85** r.9; see **Art.82:3**).
- The claims are not clear and concise in the sense of **Art.84** (see **Art.84:4** and **T409/91** for the relation between **Art.83** and **Art.84**). **Art.84** was not included as ground of opposition, because the other grounds for opposition were regarded adequate to deal with these issues and clarity objections would delay the opposition proceedings too much (Travaux Préparatoires EPC 1973, see **G3/14** r.69).

The check of **Art.84** is only made if the claims are amended in the opposition procedure; claims unclear from the outset can be maintained (**T23/86**). Clearness and conciseness are only relevant in as far as they can influence the decisions on issues under **Art.100** or arise in amendments in consequence of these issues (**T127/85**; **T23/86**). See also **Art.101(3):1**.
- A claim is not divided in preamble and characterizing part as required by **R.43(1)**. This is merely a matter of the grant procedure (**T99/85**).
- Inadequate acknowledgment of the state of the art in the patent (**T220/85** r.3).
- A re-establishment of rights during the grant procedure is unfounded (**Art.122**).
- A mere allegation that a priority claim is invalid. However, this may introduce relevant state of the art supporting one of the grounds of **Art.100(a)**.

Art. 101 Examination of the opposition – Revocation or maintenance of the European patent

1 **Opposition division**
The examination of the opposition is carried out by an opposition division, which consists of three technically qualified examiners and, if necessary, one legally qualified examiner. Only one of the technically qualified examiners has taken part in the grant procedure, and he is not the chairman of the opposition division (**Art.19(2)**, D-II,2). This examiner normally makes the preparations for taking a decision. Part of the preparatory work is done by a formalities officer. All decisions are taken by and oral proceedings conducted before all three or four examiners. An outline of the opposition procedure is given in OJ 2016 A42.

Art. 101(1) If the opposition is admissible, the Opposition Division shall examine, in accordance with the Implementing Regulations, whether at least one ground for opposition under Article 100 prejudices the maintenance of the European patent. During this examination, the Opposition Division shall invite the parties, as often as necessary, to file observations on communications from another party or issued by itself.

See for the implementation:
R.77 Rejection of the opposition as inadmissible
R.79 Preparation for the examination of the opposition
R.80 Amendment of the patent
R.81 Examination of the opposition
R.83 Request for documents
R.84 Continuation of the proceedings by the EPO of its own motion
R.85 Transfer of the patent
R.86 Documents in opposition proceedings
R.142 Interruption of proceedings

1 **Procedure prior to assessment of admissibility**
As soon as the EPO receives an opposition, it enters the filing date in the Register, publishes the filing date in the Bulletin (D-I,8) and sends a copy of the opposition to the proprietor for information (D-IV,1.1).

If the formalities officer notes deficiencies which may cause the notice of opposition being deemed not to have been filed (see **Art.99(1):3**) and which can still be remedied, he may at his own discretion, as a courtesy service, invite the opponent to remedy them within the time limits within which it is still possible to remedy the deficiencies (D-IV,1.3.3). Notification of a missing signature is not to the formalities officer's discretion; this notification must be carried out according to **R.50(3)**.

If the deficiencies are not remedied in time, the formalities officer will notify the opponent that the opposition is deemed not to have been filed (**Art.119**, **R.112(1)**); the opponent can request the opposition division to take an appealable decision on this matter under **R.112(2)**. If not requested within 2 months after notification, and if there is no other valid opposition pending, the proceedings are closed and the parties informed accordingly. The documents submitted with the notice will become part of the file, and regarded as observations under **Art.115**. The opposition fee is refunded in this case, as there is no legal basis for the payment (D-IV,1.4.1, **T193/87** hn). Since the opposition is not in existence, the assessment of admissibility under **R.77** will not be carried out.

2 **Assessment of admissibility**

When the opposition is regarded as filed, the admissibility of the opposition will subsequently be assessed according to **R.77** on the basis of the contents of the notice of opposition as filed and any correction filed within the opposition period (**T522/94** hn.II). Serious deficiencies must be corrected before expiry of the opposition period (**R.77(1)**), whereas minor deficiencies must be corrected within a period set by the EPO, which may expire after the end of the opposition period (**R.77(2)**). The formalities officer may, as a courtesy service, notify the opponent of deficiencies under **R.77(1)** which can still be remedied; in contrast, he must notify deficiencies as required by **R.77(2)** (D-IV,1.3.3). These notifications may be made together with the courtesy notification in the preceding section. See **R.77** and notes thereto for deficiencies and the procedure for remedy. If the deficiencies are corrected in due time, the opposition will be regarded as admissible.

If the opposition is regarded as inadmissible and the opponent does not refute the opinion, the formalities officer will take a decision to reject the notice of opposition as inadmissible, which decision is also communicated to the proprietor under **R.77(3)** (D-IV,1.4.2). Where the inadmissibility relates to facts, evidence or arguments, the file is submitted to the opposition division to take the decision (D-IV,1.4.2; D-IV,3). There is no refund of opposition fee if the notice is inadmissible, because the opposition has in fact started (but early terminated) and a substantial amount of work has already been done. The opposition division will not consider the substance of an inadmissible notice of opposition (**T925/91**), although provided one admissible opposition has been filed, the division may consider of its own motion any relevant art cited in an inadmissible opposition (**T966/02** r.2.4).

The question of admissibility may be raised all through the opposition procedure, even in opposition appeal (**T289/91**). The EPO must check the admissibility ex officio in every phase of the opposition and ensuing appeal (**T522/94** r.3). The EPO or the proprietor may challenge the admissibility, e.g. on lack of facts, evidence or arguments (**T222/85**; D-IV,5.1). The decision on admissibility is normally taken together with the final decision.

3 **Preparation of the examination**

If the opposition is regarded as admissible, the formalities officer will start the preparation of the examination and will invite the parties to file observations regarding the opposition. The formalities officer will first invite the proprietor to file his observations and any amendments to the patent (**R.79(1)**). The amendments must comply with **R.80**. The EPO forwards the response of the proprietor to the opponent and invites him to reply, if considered expedient (**R.79(3)**). The dossier is subsequently forwarded to the opposition division. During the examination the EPO may invite parties to reply on specific issues (**R.81(2), (3)**).

The usual period for responding to communications under **R.79** and **81** is four months for matters of substance and two months for other matters. This periods may be extended exceptionally on a reasoned request (see **R.132(2):2**; E-VIII,1.6).

4 **Acceleration of the procedure**

The total time needed for a decision in straightforward cases is 15 months from expiry of the opposition period (OJ 2016 A43).

The processing will be accelerated if an infringement action is pending before a national court of a contracting state and a party to the opposition proceedings files a reasoned request with the EPO or the national court informs the EPO. The EPO will make every effort to issue the next procedural step within three months from the request. The parties should cooperate in making their submission promptly and in full. Extension of periods above the normal four months will be granted only in exceptional, duly substantiated cases. (E-VIII,5)

Further reasons for acceleration are given in D-VII,1.2, e.g. where the opposition proceedings are of a considerably longer duration than usual. The PACE program is not applicable in opposition (OJ 2015 A94 §9).

5 **Extent of substantive examination**

The extent of the substantive examination is restricted by the extent of the opposition stated in the notice of opposition according to **R.76(2)(c)**. The grounds given in the notice of opposition define the legal framework of the examination. Addition of grounds during the procedure is restricted as set out in **R.76(2):4**. Facts and evidence should be provided in the notice of opposition (**R.76(2)(c)**). If filed later, they may be disregarded (**Art.114(2)**; **R.76(2):4.3**). Amendments of the patent made during the opposition procedure are open to all possible objections according to **Art.101(3)**.

The opposition division is not obliged to consider all the grounds for opposition referred to in **Art.100**. The examination of grounds for opposition is guided by the following principles developed by the Enlarged Board. The opposition division is obliged to examine only those grounds for opposition listed in the opponent's statement under **R.76(2)(c)**. In addition to this, the opposition division may in accordance with **Art.114(1)** examine of its own motion any ground for opposition under **Art.100** not invoked by the opponent where said ground is relevant and prejudices the maintenance of the European patent. (**G10/91** hn.2)

The practice of the office is to consider mainly the grounds set out in the notice of opposition, following **G10/91** and laid down in **Art.101(1)** and **R.81(1)**. However, the EPO will not be very strict in restricting the grounds to those of the notice of opposition; it will make an effort to consider as many grounds as possible as compliant with a fast procedure.

6 Substantive examination of the opposition

The substantive examination of the opposition must be carried out in accordance with **R.81.** Chapter D-V of the Guidelines gives details of the examination of the grounds of **Art.100.**

The patent may be amended only when the amendments are occasioned by grounds of **Art.100** (**R.80**). The amendment may not extend the subject-matter of the patent beyond the original disclosure (**Art.100(c)**) nor extend the protection conferred (**Art.123(3)**). It is permissible to replace a granted single independent claim by two or more independent claims, if this is the most appropriate response to the grounds of opposition (**T263/05**). Subject matter in the description of the application which was deleted during prosecution as no longer relevant to the claimed invention will not generally be allowed to be reinstated during opposition (**T684/02**).

If parties in an opposition procedure take different views, the burden of proof is on the opponent (**T219/83**). If the opponent proves that the teaching of the patent does not lead to the claimed result and the opposition division shares this view, the proprietor must prove to the contrary (F-III,4).

According to **Art.101(1)** and **R.79(1)**, the proprietor has a right to file observations on a notice of opposition. Any further observations of parties are only admissible if the opposition division deems them necessary and expedient. This is in the interest of the efficient conduct of the opposition proceedings. The parties must follow the guidance of the opposition division, and not proceed of their own motion. (**T295/87**)

The opposition division may invite parties to file further observations to clarify issues. All communications and replies thereto are communicated to all parties (**R.81(2)**). The proprietor will be invited, where appropriate, to file amendments to the patent (**R.81(3)**). To comply with the requirement of **Art.113(1)**, any communication to the proprietor will contain a reasoned statement, covering all grounds against maintenance of the patent, where necessary (**R.81(3)**). Oral evidence may be taken (**Art.117**, **R.117**, D-VI,1; E-IV,1.2 and 1.4) or an additional search may be carried out, where necessary (D-VI,5).

The format of the documents sent to the EPO must comply with **R.35-50** according to **R.86**; for example the documents must be signed (**R.50(3)**).

The period for filing the observations is normally fixed at four months (D-VI,3.1 & E-VIII,1.2(ii)), which may be extended on request to six months (E-VIII,1.6). No direct loss of rights occurs when failing the time limit fixed for filing observations in opposition proceedings (**G1/90** r.8). The EPO regards submissions and requests from parties as received in time when they have been filed before closure of the proceedings (see **G12/91** hn); however, facts and evidence may be disregarded under **Art.114(2)** when not filed in due time (E-VIII,1.8, similar to **R.83**, second sentence). To speed up the procedure, the EPO may send the proprietor a courtesy reminder if he has not filed observations in due time; if the proprietor does not respond to the reminder, the proceedings will be continued without his observations.

Oral proceedings are being held if requested by a party or considered expedient by the opposition division (**Art.116(1)**). The parties will be summoned in accordance with **R.115(1)** and their attention will be drawn to the points to be discussed (**R.116**). The conduct of oral proceedings has been set out in **Art.116:3**.

Art. 101(2) If the Opposition Division is of the opinion that at least one ground for opposition prejudices the maintenance of the European patent, it shall revoke the patent. Otherwise, it shall reject the opposition.

1 Decision to revoke the patent by the EPO

After the observations of the proprietor have been received, the opposition division is in a position to decide the case. The proprietor can avoid the risk of an unexpected decision revoking the patent by asking for oral proceedings, thereby deferring the decision.

The revocation can be on any of the grounds mentioned in **Art.100**, not necessarily those put forward by the opponent. The opposition division may of its own motion add grounds to those relied on by the opponent which are prima facie prejudicial to the maintenance of the patent (**R.81(1)**, second sentence; **G10/91** hn1). If the opposition division adds new grounds of its own motion, the parties can expect to be given an opportunity to comment on those grounds (**T515/05**). See **R.76(2):4.3** for adding grounds during the procedure.

For the European patent to be revoked, it is sufficient for one of the grounds for opposition to prejudice its maintenance. The patent is maintained where none of the grounds for opposition prejudices its maintenance. (OJ 2007 se4 (EN) p.110)

2 Revocation of the patent at the proprietor's request

A proprietor has several options to have the patent revoked by the EPO without substantive reasoning on patentability in the decision revoking the patent. Such reasoning could otherwise affect proceedings of other patents in the same patent family before patent offices or courts.

If the proprietor requests that the patent be revoked during opposition proceedings, the EPO will revoke the patent. The EPO also revokes the patent if the proprietor states that he no longer approves the text in which the patent was granted and does not submit an amended text, in view of **Art.113(2)** (D-VI,2.2; D-VIII,1.2.5; **T73/84**). If the proprietor unambiguously declares to the EPO the surrender, abandonment or renunciation of the patent, this is interpreted as equivalent to a request that the patent be revoked (D-VIII,1.2.5). Generally, a statement by the proprietor making it unambiguously clear that he no longer wishes his patent to be maintained is considered to be a request for its revocation, irrespective of the wording used (**T237/86**, hn; D-VII,5.1).

The proprietor can also effect the revocation of the patent by refraining from paying the fee for publishing the new patent or filing translations of the amended claims, leading to revocation under **R.82(3)**.

Note, that a proprietor cannot request the EPO to terminate the opposition procedure without decision. Even if the patent has been surrendered before the national offices of all states, **R.84(1)** gives the opponent the right to continue the opposition proceedings.

A request to revoke the patent during opposition proceedings should be distinguished from a request for revocation under **Art.105a(1)**. The former request will be dealt with in the inter-partes opposition procedure, whereas the latter request normally starts an ex-parte revocation procedure based on **Art.105a**. However, a request for revocation under **Art.105a(1)** filed during pending opposition proceedings is not admissible (**Art.105a(2)**). Conversely, if an opposition is filed while revocation proceedings are pending, the revocation will take precedence (**R.93(2):1**).

Art. 101(3) If the Opposition Division is of the opinion that, taking into consideration the amendments made by the proprietor of the European patent during the opposition proceedings, the patent and the invention to which it relates

(a) meet the requirements of this Convention, it shall decide to maintain the patent as amended, provided that the conditions laid down in the Implementing Regulations are fulfilled;

(b) do not meet the requirements of this Convention, it shall revoke the patent.

See for the implementation:
R.82 Maintenance of the European patent in amended form

1 **Maintenance of patent in amended form**

Art.101(2) limits the jurisdiction of the EPO during opposition to the grounds for opposition mentioned in **Art.100** when it relates to an unamended patent. In contrast, when it relates to an amended patent, **Art.101(3)** confers jurisdiction to decide upon the patent in the light of the requirements of the EPC as a whole. Objections based upon articles other than **Art.100** are not allowed if the objections do not arise out of the amendments made (**T301/87** hn1).

The claims of an amended patent may be examined for compliance with the requirements of **Art.84**, such as clarity, only when, and then only to the extent that an amendment introduces non-compliance with **Art.84**. Hence, an amendment of the patent does not open the door for a thorough assessment of the patent for compliance with all requirements of the EPC. A dormant lack of clarity in the patent as granted that becomes critical because of an amendment is no reason for a clarity examination. Similarly, a combination of an independent claim and a dependent claim does not introduce a new claim and should therefore not be assessed on clarity. However, a claim must be examined for compliance with **Art.84** if a feature from a dependent claim as granted is introduced into an independent claim as granted and the introduction disconnects this feature from other features of that dependent claim and causes an alleged lack of compliance with **Art.84**. (**G3/14**; see D-V,5 for more clarity examples)

Unity is no ground for opposition, because **Art.100** does not refer to **Art.82**. The patent to be maintained under **Art.101(3)** need not comply with the requirements of unity of **Art.82** because of **G1/91**. **T263/05** extends **G1/91** such that other requirements of the EPC only apply where it is reasonable that they do so to the documents of the amended patent. In particular, once an amendment is established to be necessary and appropriate, purely administrative provisions of the EPC may not be requirements.

See **R.82** for the procedure for maintenance in amended form. If the proprietor does not approve the text and neither submits a new text, the patent is to be revoked (**T73/84**).

The subject-matter of the patent must not extend beyond the application as filed, and the scope of the claims may not have been enlarged (**Art.123(2)**, (3)). The opposition division does not assess independent claims which are not opposed; however, where a process claim is opposed, a product-by-process claim referring to the process is considered to be implicitly covered by the extent of opposition (**G9/91**; D-V,2.1).

2 **Revocation of the patent**

The patent will still be revoked in spite of the Division's favourable opinion if:

1 The fee for publishing the new patent specification has not been paid in 3 months (**R.82(2)**), nor has the fee for publishing with surcharge been paid within 2 months of notification of the failure to pay (**R.82(3)**).

2 The translations of the amended claims in the other two languages of the EPO have not been filed in 3 months (**R.82(2)**), nor have they been filed with surcharge 2 months after notification (**R.82(3)**).

3 No new representative has been appointed within 2 months after an interruption of the proceedings because of death or legal incapacity of the representative (**R.142(1)(c)**), while representation is necessary according to **Art.133(2)**. (**R.142(3)(a)**)

The proprietor can remedy failure to meet the above time limits with re-establishment (**Art.122**). Further processing is not available because the periods do not relate to a patent application but to a patent.

Art. 102 (deleted)

Art. 103 Publication of a new specification of the European patent

If the European patent is maintained as amended under Article 101, paragraph 3(a), the European Patent Office shall publish a new specification of the European patent as soon as possible after the mention of the opposition decision has been published in the European Patent Bulletin.

Art.101(3)(a) Maintenance of the patent in amended form
See for the implementation
R.87 Content and form of the new specification

1 **Publication**

The words 'as soon as possible' in the provision indicate that it is not always technically possible to publish the new specification on the same day as the mention of the opposition decision is published in the Bulletin (OJ 2007 se4 (EN) p.112). The new specification is published in electronic form (**R.87** referring to **R.73(2)**).

Art. 104 Costs

1 **General**

Each party to proceedings pays its own costs unless the opposition division orders a different apportionment of costs (**Art.104(1)**), where one party has to pay some or all of the costs incurred by another party. For example, the division may order an opponent to pay to the proprietor the costs incurred by the proprietor for attending oral proceedings. A cost apportionment is given where reasons of equity demand so, i.e. for reasons of fairness. Since the different apportionment is the only exception in the EPC to the principle that each party pays its own costs, there is no room for a practice that the losing party reimburses the costs of the winning party.

Art. 104(1) Each party to the opposition proceedings shall bear the costs it has incurred, unless the Opposition Division, for reasons of equity, orders, in accordance with the Implementing Regulations, a different apportionment of costs.

1 **Reasons for apportionment**

A decision to apportion costs differently requires special circumstances such as improper behaviour which make it equitable to award costs against one of the parties (T170/83). A cost apportionment can be given in case of conduct of a party which is not in keeping with the care required to assure the effective exercise of the rights involved or which stems from culpable actions of an irresponsible or even malicious nature (T765/89). Since apportionment of costs is a matter of equity, no absolute rules can be given for when a cost apportionment is justified or not. Costs may even be apportioned against the winning party ; e.g. in case a prior art document is filed late by the opponent without justification and the revocation of the patent is based on that document, a cost apportionment may be given against the opponent.

Art.16(1) RPBA gives a few examples where a different apportionment of costs may be given in appeal: amendment of a party's case, extension of a period, acts or omissions prejudicing the timely and efficient conduct of oral proceedings, failure to comply with a direction of the board, abuse of procedure. Additionally, the requirement of equity of **Art.104** must of course be complied with.

Examples from the Guidelines and case law:

- The proprietor requests revocation of the patent (see **Art.99(3):1**) just before the proceedings and it was already clear that the proprietor had no case when the summons were issued. The unnecessary costs for preparing oral proceedings incurred by the opponent may be charged to the proprietor. (see D-IX,1.4)
- Relevant facts and evidence, including prior art, are submitted at a late stage without a good reason (T117/86); the same applies for requests.
- Notification just prior to the oral proceedings that a party will not appear and the non-attendance renders the oral proceedings unnecessary (T937/04 r.5.2). A different apportionment may not be appropriate in cases as sudden serious illness. A party summoned to oral proceedings has the equitable obligation to inform the EPO as soon as he knows that he will not be attending (T212/07).
- Culpably making inaccurate or false statements, thereby requiring the other party to incur cost for gathering further evidence (T952/00).

Apportionment of costs cannot be based on withdrawal of an appeal, because such withdrawal is an absolute right. Based on the principle of free party disposition, this right may not be restricted, not even implicitly by the threat of cost apportionment (T490/05). The Board can decide on apportionment of costs even after withdrawal of the (sole) appeal (T765/89).

Art. 104(2) The procedure for fixing costs shall be laid down in the Implementing Regulations.

See for the implementation

R.88 Procedure for fixing cost

1 **Procedure**

The procedure for fixing costs has been set out below for the opposition division. Boards of appeal can also apportion costs according to **Art.104(1)** and also fix the costs under **Art.104(2)** directly in appeal (see e.g. **T930/92** r.4.1 and **T934/91** hn1). They derive such power from **Art.111(1)**, second sentence. A decision of a board fixing the costs cannot be appealed (**T934/91** hn2).

The procedure for apportioning and fixing costs involves the following three steps.

1 The first step in a cost apportionment is a decision taken by the opposition division under **Art.104(1)** which orders an apportionment of costs different from the one where each party pays its own costs (**R.88(1)**). The EPO may take such a decision of its own motion or on request of a party (D-IX,1.2). The decision states which costs are differently apportioned. See **R.88(1)** for the kind of costs that can be taken into consideration. The costs ordered to be paid may be all or part of the costs incurred by the party, e.g. 75% of the opponent's costs for attending oral proceedings. The actual amounts are determined in the second step.

A Board may express the costs ordered directly as a specific amount (Art.16(2) RPBA). The decision apportioning costs cannot be the sole subject of an appeal (**R.97(1)**).

2 In the second step at least one party requests the opposition division to fix the actual amount of the costs to be paid under the above decision apportioning them (**R.88(2)**). The request may only be filed after the decision apportioning the costs has become final (**R.88(2)**), i.e. after any appeal, or unavailed appeal period, and directly if the decision cannot be appealed under **R.97(1)**. The request must be accompanied by a bill of costs and supporting evidence (**R.88(2)**). A formalities officer with specialist knowledge examines the credibility of the costs (**R.88(2)**), fixes the costs and notifies the parties (D-IX,2.1).

3 The third step provides the possibility for a review by the opposition division of the costs fixed by the formalities officer. The party desiring such a review must file a reasoned request for a decision by the opposition division and pay the prescribed fee within one month of the communication on the fixing of costs (**R.88(3)**). The opposition division takes its decision without oral proceedings (**R.88(4)**). The decision is appealable, but only if the amount of the costs exceeds the amount of the appeal fee (**R.97(2)**). It is not clear whether the amount of the costs relates to the total amount to be paid by a party or the amount which is in dispute.

Art. 104(3) Any final decision of the European Patent Office fixing the amount of costs shall be dealt with, for the purpose of enforcement in the Contracting States, in the same way as a final decision given by a civil court of the State in which enforcement is to take place. Verification of such decision shall be limited to its authenticity.

1 **Enforcing payment**

Art.104(3) provides means to enforce payment of the apportioned costs. Since the EPO cannot enforce payment from an unwilling party, the final decision by the EPO is given the same status as a national decision, allowing enforcement under national law. The decision referred to also covers the final fixing of the costs by the opposition division, according to D-IX,3. A party that wishes to enforce payment under national law should request a review of the fixing of the costs, because only such a review results in a decision that will have national effect.

Art. 105 Intervention of the assumed infringer

1 **General**

The purpose of **Art.105** is to safeguard an assumed infringer as far as possible against costly and time-consuming revocation proceedings before various national courts by relying on the centralised procedure before the EPO as long as it is within the competence of the EPO to deal with the question of validity of the patent concerned. Because the 9-month opposition period of **Art.99(1)** has often lapsed before infringement court proceedings are started, **Art.105** gives the assumed infringer a period to intervene in a pending opposition procedure or pending opposition appeal procedure concerning the patent (**G1/94**); after a valid intervention the intervener is treated as an opponent. The intervention may be based on any ground for opposition under **Art.100**, even a new ground (**G1/94**). A new ground raised by an intervention during appeal proceedings may cause the case to be remitted to the first instance (**G1/94** r.13). The intervenor cannot challenge any board of appeal decision taken in the opposition and which has become final at the time of the intervention (**T694/01** hn).

Art. 105(1) Any third party may, in accordance with the Implementing Regulations, intervene in opposition proceedings after the opposition period has expired, if the third party proves that
- **(a) proceedings for infringement of the same patent have been instituted against him, or**
- **(b) following a request of the proprietor of the patent to cease alleged infringement, the third party has instituted proceedings for a ruling that he is not infringing the patent.**

See for the implementation:
R.89 Filing of notice of intervention

1 **Person and time limit for intervention**

An alleged infringer must file the notice of intervention within three months (**R.89(1)**) from the institution of the first action between him and the proprietor, and pay the opposition fee in the same period (**R.89(2)**).The first action is either proceedings for infringement instituted by the proprietor or proceedings for a ruling on non-infringement instituted by the alleged infringer (**Art.105(1)(a)** and **(b)**; **T296/93** hn). In the former case the serving of a writ under national law, making the alleged infringer aware of the proceedings, is regarded as the institution of the proceedings from which the three-month period runs (**T694/01**, r.2.3). Likewise, for an interim injunction granted in ex parte proceedings, i.e. without the alleged infringer being involved, the date the order is served on the intervener is regarded as the trigger for the period, on the basis that the intervener is not aware of the ex parte proceedings until service of the order (**T452/05** r.1.2).

Under **Art.105(1)(b)**, the intervener must show both that he has received a 'request' of the proprietor and that this demands the intervener to 'cease' infringement. A criminal complaint against the alleged infringer may also be accepted as a trigger (**T1713/11** r.2). Mere warnings of infringement and threats of legal action are however insufficient (**T887/04** r.2.1). National law determines whether the proceedings for a non-infringement ruling are to be instituted before a court or before another body (OJ 2007 se4 (EN) p.114).

1.1 INTERVENTION DURING OPPOSITION PROCEEDINGS

According to **Art.105(1)** a third party may intervene 'in opposition proceedings'; hence, opposition proceedings must be in existence at the time of filing the intervention (**G4/91** hn1). The intervenor must pay the opposition fee (**R.89(2)**).

An intervention filed before expiry of the 9-month opposition period will be regarded as a normal opposition according to **Art.99**.

After the intervenor has complied with all requirements of **Art.105**, his status corresponds to that of an opponent under **Art.99**. In particular, he is entitled to file an appeal under **Art.107**, first sentence, or participate in an appeal as party as of right under **Art.107**, second sentence. A valid filing of the appeal requires that the intervenor pays the appeal fee as required under **Art.108**. (**G3/04** r.4, 10, 11)

The above intervenor has an independent right to continue the proceedings in case all other oppositions are withdrawn. The intervenor who has filed an appeal also has the right to continue the appeal proceedings on his own when the other appellants have withdrawn their appeals. (**G3/04** r.10)

1.2 INTERVENTION DURING TWO-MONTH APPEAL PERIOD

If the intervention is made after the decision terminating the opposition proceedings has been issued by the opposition division but before the expiry of the two-month appeal period, and the decision is not appealed, then the intervention is inadmissible because there are no pending proceedings as required by **Art.105(1)** (**G4/91** hn.IV). The decision is regarded as issued in written proceedings on the day the decision is handed over to the EPO postal service (**T631/94**, **G12/91**, notes ante **R.111**). An intervention filed after the announcement of the decision of the Opposition Division in oral proceedings, but before the notification of the written decision, was held in **T791/06** to be filed in the appeal proceedings, not in the opposition proceedings. If the decision is appealed, opposition proceedings are still pending and the intervention is admissible (**G4/91** r.6; D-VII,6).

1.3 INTERVENTION DURING APPEAL PROCEEDINGS

An intervention filed during pending appeal proceedings is admissible, as the term 'opposition proceedings' in **Art.105(1)** also includes subsequent appeal proceedings (**G1/94**, following **T338/89**, overruling **T390/90**).

According to **Art.107**, the entitlement to appeal is restricted to parties to the first instance proceedings that led to the decision under appeal. A party that intervened during the appeal proceedings has not been party to the first instance proceedings, and, hence, has no right to appeal; he becomes party as of right. If the sole, or each, appeal are withdrawn, he may not continue the proceedings and the appeal proceedings are terminated for all parties as regard the substantive issues, including any new grounds raised by the intervenor. (**G3/04** r.6, 10)

The question of the independent right to continue was also referred in **G4/03**, but the proceedings have been terminated because of the withdrawal of the remaining intervention in the referring decision (OJ 2004 p.542).

If the precise time of filing on the same day of the sole appellant's notice of withdrawal of appeal and a notice of intervention can be established, their chronological order must be taken into account (**T517/97**). Withdrawal of an appeal is a procedural act which has immediate effect; its effect is not postponed to midnight of the date of filing (**T517/97** r.4).

Art. 105(2) An admissible intervention shall be treated as an opposition.

1 **Formal requirements for notice of intervention**

A valid intervention requires the filing of a notice of intervention including the proof of institution of the proceedings (**Art.105(1)**), an admissible, i.e. written and reasoned notice of opposition and payment of the opposition fee (**R.89(2)**), all before the end of the 3 month period (**R.89(1)**). Re-establishment after failing this period is not possible, because re-establishment is in principle only available for an applicant and proprietor, not for an intervenor.

When the intervention is filed during pending appeal proceedings, no appeal fee need be paid, because the EPC has no provisions requiring this (**G3/04** r.11; overruling **T1011/92** and **T517/97** r.2). Note, that **R.89(2)** does require payment of the opposition fee in such a case (**G3/04** r.5). The intervenor becomes party as of right in the appeal proceedings (**G3/04** r.6).

Although the intervention is treated as an opposition, as an exception the opposition division may dispense with forwarding some communications and invitations to the intervenor (**R.79(4)**, D-IV,5.6). The intervenor can obtain copies of these documents by file inspection.

Art. 105a Request for limitation or revocation

1 **General**

Art.105a-c provide for a central limitation and revocation of European patents by an administrative procedure before the EPO. An important reason to introduce the limitation procedure in the EPC 2000 was the impossibility of a central review of the patent by the proprietor after self-opposition was prohibited by **G9/93**. The examining division is competent to take decisions in the limitation and revocation procedures (**R.91**).

Art.105a–c are applicable to European patents already granted at the time of EPC 2000 entry into force and to European patents granted in respect of European patent applications pending at, or filed on or after that time. (OJ 2007 se4 (EN) p.118)

The limitation procedure is designed to avoid costly national disputes over the validity of a European patent and to enhance legal certainty. The procedure may be useful where relevant prior art is discovered after grant of the patent, or the patent is granted with too broad a scope. A request for limitation must include amended claims that constitute a limitation vis-à-vis the claims as granted or amended in opposition or limitation proceedings (**R.95(2)**). The limitation may relate to a dependent claim only (D-X,4.3).

The amended claims may be tailored to products that have come on the market. It is not permissible to introduce non-limiting amendments in the description or in the claims that are not a consequence of the limitation of the claims, e.g. tidying up unclear claims, making amendments to improve the patent or cosmetic changes. Adding dependent claims is neither permissible if not directly caused by the limitation introduced in the claims. (D-X,4.3)

The provisions also create a centralised revocation procedure. The revocation has ex tunc effect. The revocation proceedings allow the proprietor to react immediately in the case of controversial patents in technologies that attract a good deal of public interest, thereby limiting damage to his reputation. Another reason for central revocation is to minimise the costs for proprietors without sufficient funds to defend their patents in numerous national proceedings.

Art. 105a(1) At the request of the proprietor, the European patent may be revoked or be limited by an amendment of the claims. The request shall be filed with the European Patent Office in accordance with the Implementing Regulations. It shall not be deemed to have been filed until the limitation or revocation fee has been paid.

See for the implementation:
R.90 Subject of proceedings
R.91 Competence of the examining division
R.92 Requirements of the request
Rfees2(1)10a Limitation and revocation fee

1 **Requirements of the request**
Under **Art.105a(1)** a European patent may be revoked or limited (by an amendment of the claims) at the request of the proprietor, subject to payment of a fee. **R.92** sets out the criteria for admissibility. In particular a request must be filed in writing (**R.92(1)**). Electronic filing is possible (see R.2(1):7).

The request must include details of the patent proprietor (**R.92(2)(a)**). Where a patent is held by different proprietors in different states, details of these proprietors and evidence that the requester is entitled to act on their behalf must also be included (**R.92(2)(c)**).

The patent number must be identified, and a list of contracting states in which the patent has effect given (**R.92(2)(b)**).

The amended claims, and where appropriate description and drawings must be given (**R.92(2)(d)**).

R.90 makes clear that only the patent as granted or amended by the EPO may be the subject of limitation or revocation proceedings. Amendments made before national courts or patent offices will not be taken into account, although the proprietor may of course request limitation before the EPO in order to bring the European patent into line with amendments made nationally.

The request is deemed not filed until the limitation or revocation fee has been paid (**Art.105a(1)**). The amount of the limitation and revocation fees is fixed in **Rfees2(1)10a**.

A request for revocation or limitation may be withdrawn at any time (D-X,9).

Art. 105a(2) The request may not be filed while opposition proceedings in respect of the European patent are pending.

See for the implementation:
R.93 Precedence of opposition proceedings

1 **Precedence of opposition proceedings**
Art.105a(2) governs the relation between the limitation procedure and opposition proceedings. The priority it gives to opposition proceedings prevents limitation procedures occurring where opposition has already been lodged. In this case, the request is deemed not to be filed (**R.93(1)**). Where an opposition is filed while limitation proceedings are pending, the limitation proceedings terminate and the limitation fee is refunded (**R.93(2)**). If revocation proceedings are pending, the revocation continues.

The European limitation procedure does not however take precedence over national proceedings (revocation proceedings in particular). Where parallel cases do occur, the national proceedings can be stayed or continued in accordance with the provisions of the relevant national law. Where national proceedings resulting in limitation have already been concluded, the limitation can be extended to further contracting states via European limitation proceedings. It is also emphasised that limitation of a European patent in proceedings before the EPO does not preclude further limitation in national proceedings. (OJ 2007 se4 (EN) p.116)

Art. 105b Limitation or revocation of the European patent

Art. 105b(1) The European Patent Office shall examine whether the requirements laid down in the Implementing Regulations for limiting or revoking the European patent have been met.

See for the implementation:
R.94 Rejection of the request as inadmissible

1 **Examination of the request**
Under **R.94** the requirements of **R.92** are examined, and any deficiencies noted. The requester will be notified to correct any such deficiencies within a period to be fixed by the EPO. If they are not corrected, the request will be rejected as inadmissible. If admissible, the proceedings progress to the next stage.

The limitation procedure requires the EPO to examine whether the requirements laid down in **R.95** for a requested limitation or revocation have been met. With limitation, this means in particular establishing whether the requested amendment of the claims actually limits the patent or is designed to protect something else, and whether the requirements of **Art.84** are met. Here too, moreover, the EPO has to apply the Convention's relevant general rules of procedure, in particular **Art.123(2)** and (3) EPC. The EPO is not required to examine whether the aim of the limitation - e.g. delimitation with respect to a particular prior art - is achieved, or whether the subject matter of the limited patent is patentable under **Art.52-57** EPC.

In the event that the requirements of **R.95** are not met, the examining division will offer one opportunity to correct deficiencies and to offer further amendments to the claims (and description and drawings, if appropriate). The time limit is to be specified by the division (**R.95(2)**).

Art. 105b(2) If the European Patent Office considers that the request for limitation or revocation of the European patent meets these requirements, it shall decide to limit or revoke the European patent in accordance with the Implementing Regulations. Otherwise, it shall reject the request.

See for the implementation:
R.95 Decision on the request

1 **Allowance or rejection of request**
After examination of the request under **Art.105b(1)** is concluded, the examining division is required to limit or revoke the European patent, provided the requirements of **Art.105b(1)** are met. Otherwise the request must be rejected. Limitation should be based on the revised version of the claims submitted by the proprietor. The communication notifying the patent proprietor that the request for limitation can be allowed will invite him to file a translation of the amended claims and to pay the fee for publishing (**R.95(3)**). He thus has the opportunity to check the version of the patent before the decision to limit is taken. Any obvious mistakes or typing errors may be rectified on request. On the other hand, he may no longer make any substantive amendments to the claims, as the request for limitation has already been examined and allowed. If no response to this communication is submitted, the request will be rejected (**R.95(4)**). Decisions of the examining division in limitation proceedings are subject to appeal in accordance with **Art.106**. (OJ 2007 se4 (EN) p.118)

Art. 105b(3) The decision to limit or revoke the European patent shall apply to the European patent in all the Contracting States in respect of which it has been granted. It shall take effect on the date on which the mention of the decision is published in the European Patent Bulletin.

1 **Effect of decision**
When the decision to revoke or limit the European patent in accordance with **Art.105b(3)** is published, the effects of the European patent are cancelled ab initio (see **Art.68**) in full or in part in respect of all the contracting states in which it is or was valid. (OJ 2007 se4 (EN) p.118)

The decision may include different sets of claims for different contracting states. Such a situation can arise where the limitation takes into account one or more national prior rights. The requester must inform the EPO of the existence of such national prior rights under **R.138**, without which a request for limitation including different sets of claims will be refused. Different sets of claims may only be based on European prior rights under **Art.54(3)** where the patent is granted in respect of an application filed before the date of the EPC 2000 entry into force (13.12.2007) (see **Art.54(3):4** for the transitional provisions). **R.87** EPC 1973 remains applicable to such patents. (D-X,10.1)

The limitation may also be different for different contracting states because the claims forming the basis of the limitation procedure were different in different contracting states. This situation can occur where the patent has different claims for different contracting states because of national prior rights or European prior rights under **Art.54(3)** (taking into account the above transitional provisions), or where a partial transfer of rights has taken place (**Art.61** and **R.18(2)**). (D-X,10.2)

Where for example a European patent has been limited in Germany in national proceedings and the proprietor requests limitation under **Art.105a** for all contracting states, the examiner will compare both limitations. If the patent is more limited in Germany than in the request, there will be different sets of claims; if the patent is more limited in the request than in Germany, the requested limitation will apply in all contracting states.

Once the decision has been taken, the limitation will become effective in the designated contracting states. If any translation requirements under **Art.65** have not been met or any fees not paid to the national offices, a contracting state may prescribe that the patent is void ab initio (**Art.65(3)**).

Art. 105c Publication of the amended specification of the European patent

If the European patent is limited under Article 105b, paragraph 2, the European Patent Office shall publish the amended specification of the European patent as soon as possible after the mention of the limitation has been published in the European Patent Bulletin.

See for the implementation:
R.96 Content and form of the amended specification

1 **Publication of amended specification**
Under **Art.105c**, when the EPO publishes the decision to limit the European patent, it will publish an amended European patent specification containing, in accordance with **R.96**, the new version of the claims, a translation thereof into the two other official languages of the EPO and, where appropriate, the description and drawings as amended. The patent in the amended form has retroactive effect (**Art.68**).

Contracting states may require the filing of a translation of the amended specification under **Art.65** in the same way as for a granted European patent (OJ 2007 se4 (EN) p.118; see NatLaw table IV, column 2 for the requirements of each state).

PART VI APPEALS PROCEDURE

1 **Second instance**
The appeal procedure before a board of appeal is the last instance of the grant and opposition procedure of the EPO. The possibility to continue nationally with an application rejected by the EPO is provided for in exceptional cases by **Art.135(1)**; a few states have made use of this possibility by allowing conversion to a utility model in special cases. To ensure a uniform application of the law, a board of appeal or the President may refer important points of law to an Enlarged Board of Appeal.

The decisions of the Boards of Appeal form the basis of the Guidelines for the examination. The Guidelines contain general instructions as to the practice and procedure within the EPO. The examining staff acts as a general rule in accordance with the Guidelines and may depart from these instructions only in exceptional cases. The Guidelines do not constitute legal provisions. Hence, the Boards of Appeal are not bound by the Guidelines (**Art.23(3)**). The Guidelines are amended annually to comply with recent case law.

Art. 106 Decisions subject to appeal

Art. 106(1) An appeal shall lie from decisions of the Receiving Section, Examining Divisions, Opposition Divisions and the Legal Division. It shall have suspensive effect.

See for the implementation:
R.98 Appeal against surrendered or lapsed patent

1 **Appealable decisions**
The Boards of Appeal are responsible for the examination of appeals (**Art.21(1)**). The competence and composition of the Technical and Legal Boards of Appeal are governed by **Art.21(2)-(4)**.

The list of appealable decisions in **Art.106(1)** is exhaustive: decisions of other organs of the EPO, such as directors, are not appealable to the Boards. The search divisions are not incuded in **Art.106(1)** because search divisions do not issue decisions; instead, they issue opinions, which are not appealable. Hence, the search division's opinion on lack of unity (**R.64(1)**) is not appealable and is made final with the decision of the examining division (see **R.64(1):3**). Since a decision on a request for limitation or revocation is taken by an examining division (**R.91**), such a decision is also appealable (see also OJ 2007 se4 (EN) p.118).

A notification of loss of rights under **R.112(1)**, is not a decision and is not appealable (**J13/83** r.4). If the applicant does not agree with the findings in the notification, he must ask for a decision of the EPO under **R.112(2)**. The decision is appealable. If he does not ask for a decision within 2 months from the notification, the loss of rights ceases to be contestable.

If the board of appeal decides on failure to meet the time limit of **R.112(2)**, e.g. after failure to reply to an invitation of the board of appeal (**R.100(3)**), then the decision cannot be appealed from, because the decision has not been taken by a department mentioned in **Art.106(1)**. Likewise, a decision of the President, e.g. on classification of patents (**R.11(1)**) or on exemption from requirements for professional representatives (**Art.134(7)**), cannot be appealed from, because the President is not mentioned in **Art.106(1)**. A separate appeal is not possible against a decision taken by a director of a department on an objection to a member of an opposition division on the ground of suspected partiality under **Art.24**; the decision may be challenged in appeal against a final decision of the division or against an interlocutory decision allowing separate appeal (**G5/91** hn.II).

Only decisions are appealable, not statements reflecting a preliminary opinion. Whether or not a communication is a decision can be recognized in last resort by its contents (**J8/81**). Not repeating the words of **Art.106-108** does not make a decision invalid (**R.111(2)**, **T42/84**). In exceptional circumstances a notice from the EPO that unlawfully takes away rights of a party, such as a **R.71(3)** communication not allowing the applicant to disapprove the text proposed, may be regarded as an appealable decision (**T1181/04** r.2.4).

2 **Suspensive effect**

An appeal has suspensive effect, according to **Art.106(1)**, second sentence. Suspensive effect means that the consequences of a decision are suspended; it prevents the impugned decision to have any legal consequences until the decision in appeal is taken (**T1/92** r.3.1). The following actions are not taken: entry in the Register, mention in the Bulletin, and, where appropriate, publication of a new specification of the patent (E-XII,1). Renewal fees should always be paid up to the final decision in appeal to avoid a subsequent loss of rights due to non-payment of renewal fees.

The suspensive effect does not cancel the appealed decision. Only the final decision in appeal can either set aside the impugned decision with the effect to put back a procedure to the status where it was before the first instance took its decision or it can confirm the impugned decision and so terminate its pending status. (**J28/03** r.12, 13)

The suspensive effect during an appeal against the grant of a patent follows the above rule. The admissibility of every further action, not only the filing of a divisional application, depends on the outcome of the appeal proceedings. The final decision of the board is decisive for the further consequences. Hence, a divisional filed during the appeal proceedings is invalid if the appeal is not allowed. (**J28/03** r.11)

By way of exception, an appeal against the refusal of a patent application allows a valid filing of a divisional application during the appeal procedure, independently of the outcome of the appeal, even if the refusal is confirmed. (**J28/03** r.10, 11; Not. EPO OJ 2002 p.112; see also **R.36(1):3.1.2**).

Recently, during an appeal against a correct refusal of the application, the applicant was allowed to correct the deficiency that caused the refusal (**J18/08**); the application was refused under **R.163(5), (6)** for failing to appoint a representative as required by **Art.133(2)**; the deficiency was corrected in appeal by appointing a representative. However, according to **J1/05** r.4e, the suspensive effect during an appeal against a **R.112(2)** decision does not provide an opportunity to correct a deficiency on which the decision was based.

The suspensive effect occurs only if an admissible appeal has been filed. A decision to reject the appeal as inadmissible puts the party back to the legal situation existing at the time the impugned decision was taken as if no appeal had been lodged. It is irrelevant whether the appeal is obviously inadmissible from the very beginning or if it was rejected as inadmissible at a later stage (**J28/03** r.17, 18). The effects of a purported suspension cannot be invoked to support the admissibility or otherwise of an appeal; the admissibility must be determined first (**T591/05** r.2.5). **G1/09** decided that the possibility to file a divisional application in the two-month appeal period following a first-instance refusal did not depend on the suspensive effect of a possible appeal (r.3 and 4); the board did not answer whether a divisional application can be filed after the two-month appeal period if the appeal is (obviously) inadmissible (r.4.3.3; see also **R.36(1):3**).

A less strict position was taken in Münchner Gemeinschaftskommentar, Art.108, §38, according to which the suspensive effect occurs only if an effective appeal has been filed, i.e. the notice of appeal has been filed and the fee for appeal has been paid in accordance with **Art.108** and the appeal is not obviously inadmissible (Münchner Gemeinschaftskommentar, Art.108, §38, 39; this position is also expressed by the President of the EPO in **G1/09**, submission VII.5). The suspensive effect should not be used for an unjustified procrastination of a decision to take effect. Note, that there is no basis in the EPC for denying suspensive effect to an obviously inadmissible appeal.

If re-establishment is granted to a late-filed notice of appeal, the suspensive effect should become effective with the allowance of the re-establishment (Singer Art.106, rdn.28).

The following is an example of the effect of confirmation of a first instance decision in appeal. A loss of rights arising by operation of law, without a decision, and notified under **R.112(1)**, for example the deemed withdrawal of an application after failure to reply to a communication under **Art.94(3)**, takes effect on expiry of the unobserved period. If the decision under **R.112(2)** is confirmed in appeal, the deemed withdrawal has still taken effect on expiry of the unobserved period. Any divisional application should have been filed before the expiry.

Art. 106(2) A decision which does not terminate proceedings as regards one of the parties can only be appealed together with the final decision, unless the decision allows a separate appeal.

1 Interlocutory decision

An interlocutory decision is a decision that does not terminate the proceedings for any party. For example, in a first instance opposition procedure, at the end of oral proceedings the decision that a patent in amended form meets the requirements of the EPC is taken as interlocutory decision according to EPO practice (**R.82(1):2**). Such a decision is interlocutory because the opposition division issues the final decision to maintain the patent in amended form only later when, after any appeal proceedings, the proprietor has filed the translated claims and paid the prescribed fee (**R.82(1):1**). Interlocutory decisions are exceptional during other first instance proceedings and are normally given only if the duration or cost of the proceedings as a whole is thereby reduced (E-X,3). A department taking an interlocutory decision on an issue has no power thereafter to continue examination of that issue; any further submissions of parties relating to that issue are inadmissible (**T390/86**).

Examples of interlocutory decisions: interlocutory decision refusing a refund of paid further search fees (**T2526/17**), decision on the admissibility of an opposition taken by an opposition division (see e.g. **T376/90**), or a board of appeal (see e.g. **T482/02**), exclusion of and objection to members of any department (**G5/91** hn.II; **G1/05a**), and referral to the Enlarged Board of Appeal under **Art.112(1)(a)**.

2 **Appealability of interlocutory decision**

The EPC does not specify when an interlocutory decision is to be made separately appealable. An interlocutory decision of an opposition division that a patent in amended form meets the requirements of the EPC is always made appealable according to EPO practice (**R.82(1):1**). Otherwise, an interlocutory decision will be made separately appealable for instance if the continuation of the proceedings depends on a ruling in appal on a fundamental point of law (E-X,3). If an interlocutory decision allows a separate appeal, as permitted by **Art.106(2)**, the requirements for an admissible appeal must still be complied with, e.g. that the decision is taken by a department mentioned in **Art.106(1)**. Hence, (interlocutory) decisions by a body not mentioned in **Art.106(1)** are never appealable, e.g. a decision of a director objecting to a member of an opposition division (**G5/91** hn.II), or an intorlocutory decision of a board of apeal (see e.g. **T482/02**). The first instance proceedings are suspended until the decision in appeal has become final (E-X,3).

An interlocutory decision that allows separate appeal will state so and will be issued in writing and be reasoned; if no separate appeal is allowed, the reasons may be given later in the final decision (E-X,3).

If no appeal is filed against an appealable interlocutory decision, the decision will become *res judicata* and can no longer be impugned in an appeal against the final decision (T55/90, r.2.3). Any decision of the Board remitting an opposition to the opposition division with the order to maintain the patent in amended form (after filing of the translated claims and payment of the fee) cannot be challenged thereafter, neither before the opposition division nor in a later appeal against the final decision (T55/90, r.2.4). In such a case, any appeal against the final decision to maintain a patent in amended form can only concern the formalities of **R.82(2)** (T55/90, r.2.6).

Art. 106(3) The right to file an appeal against decisions relating to the apportionment or fixing of costs in opposition proceedings may be restricted in the Implementing Regulations.

See for the implementation:
R.97 Appeal against apportionment and fixing of cost

1 **Decision apportioning costs**

A decision apportioning costs cannot be the sole subject of an appeal (**R.97(1)**). A decision fixing the amount of the cost cannot be appealed unless the amount exceeds that of the fee for appeal (**R.97(2)**).

If part of the cost is apportioned to the victorious party, that party cannot appeal the apportionment, because he must at the same time appeal a decision relating to the patent. However, he cannot do so, because as victorious party he is not adversely affected by the decision (**Art.107**). Where a valid appeal has been filed by the losing party, the victor cannot separately appeal against the apportionment of costs (**T1237/05**).

When a party has lost an opposition on good grounds and is ordered to pay part of the costs of another party in accordance with **Art.104(1)**, the party can appeal the apportionment by simultaneously appealing the decision of the opposition division. He may base the appeal of the latter decision on less than solid grounds. The board of appeal has to consider the appeal relating to the rejection of the opposition, but may reject it because of invalid grounds. The apportionment must then also be dealt with. In this way, a party can circumvent **Art.106(3)**. However, if the second subject of appeal is rejected as inadmissible, e.g. because of lack of grounds, then the remaining subject of appeal, i.e. the apportionment, becomes the sole subject, which according to **R.97(1)** must fail (**T154/90** r.1.3).

Art. 107 Persons entitled to appeal and to be parties to appeal proceedings

Any party to proceedings adversely affected by a decision may appeal. Any other parties to the proceedings shall be parties to the appeal proceedings as of right.

1 **Persons entitled to appeal**

Appeal is open to any party adversely affected by a decision (**Art.107**, first sentence). The party must have been party to the first instance proceedings which led to the decision under appeal. The German and French versions of **Art.107** make this clearer than the English version and state that 'any party to the proceedings that led to a decision may appeal the decision in so far as the party is adversely affected by the decision' (**T656/98** r.1). A 'party' is confined to the parties entered in the Register in the first instance proceedings. A successor in title based on an assignment becomes party only after having been duly recorded in the Register (see **R.22**). When a transfer of a patent takes place during the appeal period, and an appeal is filed in the name of the new proprietor, evidence of this transfer must be given to the EPO before the expiry of the appeal period for the appeal to be considered admissible (**T956/03** r.7). To overcome this, an appeal may be filed naming the original proprietor in a main request, and the new proprietor in an auxiliary request (**G2/04**).

If a party consists of a plurality of persons, an appeal against a decision which adversely affects this party has to be filed on behalf of all these persons (**T755/09** r.1). An appeal filed in common by several persons must be filed by the common representative, which applies both to joint opponents (**G3/99** r.18), joint proprietors (**T1154/06** r.1), and joint applicants.

Where the validity of an opponent's status after an alleged transfer of opposition is disputed in appeal, the appeal of the opponent is admissible - a 'party' is someone who took part in the first instance proceedings; however, his procedural status up to the decision in appeal is limited to the issue of his entitlement; should opponent status be revoked on appeal, he is no longer entitled to take part in the proceedings, but it is not the case that he never assumed party status (**T1178/04**).

When a party ceases to exist, his universal successor in law immediately acquires party status (**T15/01** r.11, 12). The existence of a legal entity such as a party is determined by national law (**G1/13** r.5.1). National law is not followed when it confers procedural rights contrary to the EPC, such as transfer of an opposition before the EPO (**G1/13** r.8). When a party ceases to exist during proceedings before the EPO, for example because the company is dissolved, and is restored with retroactive effect under national law, the EPO will recognise the retroactive effect (**G1/13** hn). See **R.101(2):1** for correction of a deficient name or address of an appellant.

A person who was not a party to opposition proceedings can, as an exception, become party to the opposition appeal by intervening under **Art.105**.

Appeal is open only to the parties to proceedings which led to the appealed decision (**Art.107**). The party in grant proceedings is the applicant. Parties in opposition proceedings are the proprietor and the one or more opponents, as well as any intervenor (**Art.105**). Both the requester and the applicant or proprietor are party for decisions on a request for correction of the mention of the inventor (**R.21**), for stay (or resumption) of the proceedings (**R.14**), for registering of a transfer or licence (**R.22, 23**), or for inspection of files (**Art.128, J27/87**). The proprietor is party in limitation or revocation proceedings under **Art.105a**. A person who has filed observations under **Art.115** is a "third party" and is not a party to the proceedings. The EPO or its employees are never party to appeal proceedings under **Art.106**.

The Board checks the requirements of **Art.107**. If not complied with, the appeal is rejected as inadmissible (**R.101(1)**).

2 Adverse affect

A party may file an appeal only if he is adversely affected (**Art.107**, first sentence, see also **G1/99** r.6.3). An applicant is only adversely affected if a decision does not agree with his explicit request (**J12/85**). If the applicant has not agreed to the text of the application as granted, contrary to **Art.113(2)**, he can appeal the decision to grant.

An appeal may be filed by the patentee on the basis of a decision recorded in the minutes that the then sole request does not meet the requirements of the EPC (**T537/05**), even though a subsequently-amended main request has been submitted and upheld. Once the sole request has been refused, the first instance procedure ends; any subsequent acts are ultra vires.

A sufficient ground for appeal is a not-allowed request of the proprietor to revoke the patent, filed after filing the notice of appeal. A request for revocation by the proprietor must be granted, as it is not in the interest of the public to maintain a patent against the will of the proprietor (**T459/88**). A request for revocation by the proprietor in the appeal stage of opposition proceedings is equivalent to withdrawal of his agreement to the text of the patent as granted (**Art.113(2)**); on this basis the patent must be revoked without examination of the substantive grounds for opposition (**T237/86**).

A party in opposition proceedings is adversely affected where only an auxiliary request, and not the main request, is granted. When an opposition results in the patent being maintained on the basis of an auxiliary request, both parties clearly have a right to appeal. The proprietor is adversely affected because he is still entitled to his main request, as he has not abandoned it by his approval of the text of the amended patent (**T123/85, T155/88, T506/91**). **T386/04** hn. held that an appeal to reinstate the scope of the patent as granted was generally admissible, even if the main request of the proprietor during opposition proceedings was more limited; the narrowing of a patent in opposition is considered to affect the proprietor adversely.

A request of an opponent for revocation of the entire patent during appeal is not admissible, if only partial revocation was requested during first instance proceedings. During appeal his entitlement is determined by the scope of the opposition. There is no adverse effect within the meaning of **Art.107** that justifies an appeal which exceeds that scope. (**T299/89** r.3)

The discovery of relevant prior art by the proprietor after the decision to grant does not mean the proprietor was adversely affected by that decision, if it reflected his main request at the time (**T591/05** r.2.3). Under EPC 2000, this situation could now be remedied by limitation under **Art.105a**.

An appeal is inadmissible if the grounds have been taken away before the start of the proceedings, e.g. where inspection of the file of a not-yet published application was refused by the Receiving Section and the application was published before the appeal proceeding, thereby removing the adverse affection (**J27/87**).

If an opponent is invited to give his observations under **R.82** on the text of the amended patent that is to be maintained and he fails to do so, he can still appeal if he does not agree with the text (**G1/88**).

3 Party as of right

3.1 GENERAL

Parties to the proceedings that have led to the appealed decision and which have not appealed are party to the appeal proceedings as of right (**Art.107**, second sentence). For example, a proprietor or one or more opponents that have not filed an appeal are parties as of right in opposition appeal proceedings.

A party whose appeal is found to be inadmissible or deemed not to have been filed also becomes a party as of right in appeal proceedings based on an admissible appeal filed by another party. The same applies to a party who withdraws his appeal. An opponent who withdraws his opposition during appeal, ceases to be a party as far as the substantive issues are concerned.

In appeal proceedings, an appealing party is referred to as appellant and a party as of right opposing the appellant is referred to as respondent.

The rights of a party as of right are restricted compared with those of an appellant. In particular, a party as of right has no right to continue the proceedings if the sole appellant withdraws his appeal. If there are several appellants and one of them withdraws his appeal, the further appellants have the right to continue the appeal and are therefore not party as of right, and the appeal fees paid by them are not reimbursed, unless **R.103** applies. (**G2/91**, see also **Art.110:9**)

3.2 REFORMATIO IN PEIUS

The Boards of Appeal have introduced the principle of the 'prohibition of reformatio in peius', i.e. the prohibition to put (a person) in a worse position, in appeal proceedings. The principle prevents the Boards from going beyond a request of an appealing party and put it in a worse position than it was in before it appealed (**T60/91** r.7). The prohibition does not apply to an appeal of a decision refusing to grant a patent, because the appeal cannot put the appellant in a worse position (**G10/93** r.2, 3). The board of appeal has the power to examine in such an appeal whether the application meets all requirements of the EPC, even if some requirements have not been considered by the examining division or were regarded as having been met (**G10/93** hn; see **Art.114(1)** and notes thereto).

The prohibition affects the different parties in an opposition appeal in different ways. The prohibition of reformatio in peius is applied in inter partes proceedings where either the proprietor or the opponent is not appellant. This is the case if one of the parties has withdrawn from the proceedings or one of the parties is party as of right. A party as of right is supposed not to be adversely affected by the decision of the first instance, and, therefore, a request by it which goes beyond the appellant's original appeal request is not admissible. A party as of right may only make submissions in the appeal proceedings to defend the results obtained before the first instance (**G9/92** r.11; case consolidated with **G4/93**). If this is combined with the finding that a board of appeal cannot amend a contested decision to the appellant's disadvantage (**G9/92** r.12), the following points in opposition appeals emerge.

3.2.1 Opponent as party as of right

First: if the patent proprietor is the sole appellant against an interlocutory decision maintaining the patent in amended form, neither the board of appeal nor the non-appealing opponent may challenge the maintenance of the patent as amended in accordance with the interlocutory decision (**G9/92** hn.I).

3.2.2 Proprietor as party as of right

Secondly: if the opponent is the sole appellant against an interlocutory decision maintaining a patent in amended form, the patent proprietor is primarily restricted during the appeal proceedings to defending the form in which the patent was maintained by the opposition division in its interlocutory decision. Amendments proposed by the proprietor as a party as of right may be rejected as inadmissible if they are neither appropriate nor necessary (**G9/92** hn.II). Thus the rights of the appellant outweigh the principle of ex officio examination under **Art.114(1)** (**G9/92** r.2-6). **G9/92** follows **T369/91** and overrules **T576/89** and **T123/85**. Although the scope of amendment available to the proprietor is restricted, this does not give the appellant/opponent the right to dictate the form of such amendments; this is still a matter for the patentee (**T23/04** r.2.5.3).

In the second case, a claim may in principle not be amended to widen the scope of the claims as maintained in first instance, which would put the opponent and sole appellant in a worse position than if it had not appealed. As an exception, based on equity, such an amendment may be allowed if the patent would otherwise have to be revoked as a direct consequence of an inadmissible or unallowable amendment that was regarded allowable in the impugned decision of the opposition division, e.g. if an added feature violates **Art.123(2)** (**G1/99** hn, r.13.1, 13.2) or if an added feature is unclear. The exception applies not only in case of an error of judgment of the opposition division but also in case the factual and/or legal basis on which the patentee had added the feature changes, provided that the patentee would otherwise be prevented from adequately defending its patent against new facts and objections introduced into the proceedings at the appeal stage (**T1843/09**).

The nature and order of the requests to be filed by the proprietor in order to benefit from the exception (see **G1/99** hn) can be summarized as follows: (1) introduce a further limiting feature (i.e. add a feature), (2) only if this is not possible, introduce a feature which extends the scope of the claims held allowable by the opposition division but does not extend the scope of the patent as granted (i.e. replace the feature at issue with another feature), (3) finally, if such amendments are not possible, delete the feature; provided that each request complies with **Art.123(2)** and (3). Hence deleting the feature objected to is only allowable if the amendments under (1) and (2) cannot be made, e.g. because the application as filed discloses neither more specific nor more general embodiments of the feature objected to.

The prohibition applies in principle until the final settlement of the opposition, including continued opposition proceedings (and any further appeal proceedings) following remittal (**T1843/09** hn).

3.2.3 Extent of prohibition

The prohibition of reformatio in peius does not apply to requests not allowed by the opposition division or to any request made for the first time in appeal (**T226/98** r.9.2). For example, if a request in appeal includes a claim not comprised in a set of claims allowed by the opposition division or a claim amended in view of such a set, the prohibition does not apply and the board of appeal has the power and duty pursuant to **Art.111(1)** and **R.82** to assess the patentability of this claim. If the Board regards the claim not allowable, it will dismiss the entire request, in spite of the presence of claims allowed by the opposition division (see e.g. **T226/98** r.12.11). This is a consequence of the fact that a request can only be decided on as a whole (**T303/94** r.2; **T401/95** r.2). An appellant desiring to make use of the prohibition of reformatio in peius must file at least one request before the board of appeal which contains only claims as allowed by the opposition division.

The prohibition of reformatio in peius is not applicable to separate points decided by the opposition division; it applies only to an allowed request as a whole (**T372/92** r.1.2; **T401/95** r.2; **T266/98** r.9). For example, if an appeal is lodged against an adverse decision of the first instance about the main request, then the whole request is before the board of appeal and within its jurisdiction. E.g., even if the opposition division had decided that a claim of this main request was novel but lacked inventive step, the Board is empowered to reopen and to decide upon the issue of novelty (**T303/94** r.2; **T583/95** r.2; **T1341/04** r.1.4).

The prohibition of reformatio in peius does neither apply to the question of opponent status; the EPO have a duty to examine this at any stage of the proceedings (**T1178/04**).

3.3 CHOICE BETWEEN PARTY AND PARTY AS OF RIGHT

A party as of right is rather restricted in appeal proceedings: he cannot continue the appeal after the sole appellant has withdrawn his appeal, he is restricted to defend the results of the decision in first instance, he can only come off worse (see also **T239/96** r.2-6). Hence, it is in general disadvantageous to be merely party as of right. It is possible for a party to become appellant when there is an appeal and at the same time not lose the appeal fee if another party does not lodge an appeal. He should file a notice of appeal and pay the appeal fee within the two-month period for appeal. If, after enquiry with the EPO, it turns out that no other party has filed an appeal, he can withdraw his appeal before expiry of the 4-month period and have the appeal fee reimbursed under **R.103(1)(b)**. If another party has filed an appeal, he can file his statement of grounds and become appellant in the appeal proceedings.

Art. 108 Time limit and form

Notice of appeal shall be filed, in accordance with the Implementing Regulations, at the European Patent Office within two months of notification of the decision. Notice of appeal shall not be deemed to have been filed until the fee for appeal has been paid. Within four months of notification of the decision, a statement setting out the grounds of appeal shall be filed in accordance with the Implementing Regulations.

See for the implementation:
R.99 Content of the notice of appeal and the statement of grounds

1 **Filing an appeal**

The filing of an appeal against a decision of a department of first instance involves two steps. The first step includes filing a notice of appeal and pay the fee for appeal, both within two months from the date of notification of the impugned decision. The second step is filing a statement setting out the grounds of appeal within four months from the date of notification.

If there are several parties, only one of which, the appellant, has paid the appeal fee the others being party as of right (**Art.107**, second sentence), and the sole appellant withdraws his appeal, the appeal proceedings will be terminated. Only parties who have paid the appeal fee have an independent right to continue the proceedings. If several parties have paid the appeal fee, no appeal fees will be refunded for that reason. (**G2/91**)

An appeal can be withdrawn by the appellant, because it is not expressly forbidden as it is for the request for examination (**R.70(1)**, last sentence; a contrario reasoning). A partial withdrawal is also allowed, if that part relates to a special issue dealt with separately in the appeal (**J19/82**). If an appeal has been withdrawn, the board of appeal may decide to continue with issues related to the appeal, such as a request for reimbursement of the appeal fee (**T41/82**) or for apportionment of the costs according to **Art.104** (**T117/86**).

2 **Form of the notice of appeal**

The notice of appeal must comply with **R.50** (form of subsequently filed documents). The appeal must be filed at the EPO in Munich, The Hague or Berlin, using a means of communication allowed under **R.2(1)**; documents in respect of appeal proceedings may not be filed using Web-Form Filing. (see **R.2(1):7.4**).

The content of the notice of appeal is governed by **R.99**: name and address of the appellant and the impugned decision and a request defining the subject of the appeal. An appeal filed as a subsidiary request, i.e. conditional on the main request not being allowed, is inadmissible (**J16/94** hn); nor is any other form of conditionally filed appeal (**T254/03** r.1.3). Note that the appellant may be named conditionally, i.e. a first appellant as main request and a second appellant as auxiliary request, if the entitlement to appeal is not clear (**G2/04** hn.II; see e.g. **Art.99(1):4** on transfer).

3 **Time limit and remedies**

The legislator regarded two months for filing both the notice and grounds as too short a period for the appellant to prepare his grounds, whereas three months for filing the notice and grounds leaves the proprietor and third parties in uncertainty for too long a time. The two periods in this article are a compromise between a short period of uncertainty for the proprietor and sufficient preparation time for the appellant.

The decision appealed from, notified according to **Art.119, R.126(1)**, is deemed to be delivered 10 days after the date stamp on the letter (**R.126(2)**). The 2-month period for filing the notice of appeal runs from the tenth day, even if this day is a Saturday or Sunday (**T743/05**). The 4-month period for filing the statement of grounds also runs from the tenth day. The 2-month period for appealing a decision given in oral proceedings is not triggered by the pronouncement of the decision during the oral proceedings but by the subsequent notification of the written decision (see **R.111(1):1**). An appeal can be validly lodged immediately after the pronouncement of the decision during oral proceedings, well before the notification of the decision (**T389/86**).

Failure to meet the 2 or 4 month period by the applicant or proprietor can be remedied with re-establishment (**Art.122**). Re-establishment is generally not available for opponents (**Art.122, T210/89** hn1). As an exception, the opponent as appellant can apply for re-establishment in the 4-month period for filing the statement of grounds. (**G1/86; T210/89** hn2; E-VIII,3.1.2)

4 **Payment**

A valid appeal requires payment of the appeal fee within two months after the date of notification of the decision appealed from (**Art.108**, first and second sentence; **J21/80**). The amount of the appeal fee is fixed in **Rfees2(1)11**.

If no appeal fee has been paid, there is not an inadmissible appeal but the appeal is deemed not to have been filed (**Art.108**, second sentence); a notice of appeal without payment has no legal effect. An appeal fee which has been paid late is refunded as lacking a legal basis, even of the EPO's own motion, without request, because the appeal is deemed not filed. Refunding the appeal fee is established EPO practice since **J2/78, J21/80**, and **J24/87**. In referrals leading to **G1/14** and **G2/14**, it was suggested that the appeal should be held inadmissible instead of deemed not filed and the appeal fee should not be refunded. However, the Enlarged Board did not decide on the issue in both cases (see also OJ 2015 A13). Subsequently, **R4/15** held that the sanction on late payment of the fee for a petition for review is that the petition is deemed not filed; **T1553/13** of 23.11.2016 applied the same sanction to a late paid appeal fee and deemed the appeal not filed (also **T2406/16**). However, **T1897/17** maintained that the sanction is that the appeal is inadmissible. Accordingly, the President referred the question to the EBoA whether an appeal is inadmissible or is deemed not to have been filed if a notice of appeal is filed late and/or the appeal fee is paid late. The case is pending as **G1/18** (OJ 2018 A71).

If the amount paid falls short by a small amount, the fee is regarded as paid in time, if the circumstances justify overlooking the amount lacking (**T130/82**). See **Rfees8** for what amount is defined as small. The small amount must be paid as yet afterwards.

See **Art.125:2** on good faith for the question whether the BoA must notify an appellant of a missing appeal fee when the notice of appeal is filed sufficiently early to allow correction.

The appellant is notified of a late payment of the appeal fee according to **R.112(1)**. If he does not agree with the finding of the EPO, he can request, within two months of the **R.112(1)** notification, a decision of the EPO according to **R.112(2)** and provide proof that the fee was timely paid. If he fails the two-month time limit of **R.112(2)**, he may request re-establishment according to **Art.122**. Since the decision of **R.112(2)** and the decision on re-establishment are both taken by the board of appeal, they cannot be appealed (**Art.106(1)**). See the previous section for remedies of failure to meet the two month time limit of **Art.108**.

5 Notice of appeal deemed (not) to have been filed

Before the admissibility of the appeal is assessed, the EPO assesses whether the notice of appeal is regarded as filed on the basis of the received documents. In case the appeal is regarded as not filed and the deficiencies are not remedied in the procedure set out in **Art.110:1**, there will be no appeal. All cases where a notice of appeal is regarded as not filed can be derived directly from the EPC. An appeal will be regarded as not filed in the following cases:

1 The appeal fee is not paid in time, causing the appeal being deemed not to have been filed (**Art.108**, second sentence, **J16/82** hn.II, **T324/90** r.9).

2 The notice of appeal is not filed within the 2-month time limit of **Art.108** (**T41/82** r.1). A payment of the appeal fee cannot take the place of an omitted written notice of appeal that contains an identification of the appellant and an explicit declaration of the wish to contest a particular decision by means of an appeal as required by **R.99** (**J19/90**;**T778/00** r.2; **T377/11**). If the notice of appeal is not duly filed, the appeal fee must be reimbursed as having no legal basis (**T41/82** r.1).

3 The notice of appeal bears no signature (**R.99(3)** in conjunction with **R.50(3)**), or the signature has not been provided in time after invitation by the formalities officer, causing the notice being deemed not to have been filed ; if provided in due time, the notice retains its date of filing. The signature on the notice of appeal should be assessed analogously to the signature on a notice of opposition. If a notice of appeal is signed by a person not being the appellant, a representative or an employee, the notice is regarded as not signed, and the appellant is requested to correctly sign the notice according to **R.50(3)** (analogous to **T665/89** r.1.4 relating to a notice of opposition).

4 The notice of appeal has been sent by fax and no confirmation copy has been filed in due time after a request to that effect, causing the notice being deemed not to have been received (**R.2(1)**, OJ 2007 se A3 Art.7(2)).

5 The translation of the notice of appeal required under **Art.14(4)** is not filed within the longer of one month after filing the notice or the end of the 2-month appeal period (**R.6(2)**); the document is deemed not to have been filed (this applies to all documents entering the EPO) (**Art.14(4)**). (**T323/87**)

6 The notice of appeal is not in an admissible official language of a contracting state, e.g. Japanese. The notice is deemed not to have been filed (**R.3(1)** & **Art.14(4)**).

7 The notice of appeal is in an admissible official language of a contracting state, but the appellant is not entitled to use the language, e.g. a German living in Munich and writing in Italian. The notice is deemed not to have been filed (**R.3(1)** & **Art.14(4)**).

6 Statement of grounds of appeal

The statement of grounds must be filed in writing within four months of notification of the decision appealed from (**Art.108**, last sentence; **R.1**). If not filed within this period, the appeal will be inadmissible (**R.99(2)** and **R.101(1)**).

The statement of grounds of appeal and the reply of the respondent must contain a party's complete case. They must set out clearly and concisely the reasons why it is requested that the decision under appeal be reversed, amended or upheld, and should specify expressly all facts, arguments and evidence relied on (Art.12(2) RPBA). Any later submission of such reason, fact, argument or evidence is treated as an amendment to a party's case and may be admitted or not at the Board's discretion (Art. 13(1) RPBA). The same applies for claim requests with claim amendments.

The statement must state the legal and factual reasons why the decision should be set aside. It does not suffice that the statement asserts that the impugned decision is incorrect: **Art.108** requires that the legal and factual grounds are given why the decision should be set aside. A mere presentation of facts is neither sufficient; the inferences from the facts must be made adequately clear (**T220/83**). If a decision declares an opposition inadmissible because of insufficient substantiation, and the grounds for appeal discuss merely patentability, not the admissibility of the opposition, then the appeal is inadmissible because of lack of adequate substantiation (**T213/85**). An appeal may be based on a new fact that is crucial to the maintenance of the decision (**J902/87**).

The statement of grounds must enable the board to understand the facts and why the appealed decision is alleged to be incorrect; the board should not be expected to have to make further investigation (**T809/06**).

The request in the notice of appeal must indicate whether the decision under appeal is contested as a whole or only partially. The appellant is not obliged to maintain the same extent in his statement of grounds. The EPO recognises that requiring an appellant to argue for claims he no longer wants simply in order to validate the notice of appeal is unnecessary. The grounds of appeal may therefore be more limited in extent than the initial indication in the notice (**R.99(1):3** and **T642/05**).

Art. 109 Interlocutory revision

1 General

Interlocutory revision is a procedure where an appeal against a decision will be handled and decided by the department of first instance that took the contested decision instead of by a board of appeal. The procedure is substantially faster than appeal. The filed appeal will be considered by the department that took the decision. If it regards the appeal admissible and well founded, it will examine the allowability. The department will grant interlocutory revision when it considers the appeal allowable within three months from receipt of the statement of grounds. If the appeal is not regarded allowable, no interlocutory revision will be made and the appeal will be remitted to a board of appeal without comments as to its merit. The appellant will know that interlocutory revision will not be allowed if he receives a communication informing him of the commencement of proceedings before the board of appeal and of the number of the appeal.

The appeal is well founded if the submissions of the party in its main request clearly meet the objections on which the refusal of the application was based (**T139/87**). If for example an application is refused on the ground of novelty and the amended claims filed with the appeal are clearly novel, interlocutory revision must be granted and the examining division will continue the prosecution by examining inventive step. If the independent claims clearly do not meet the requirements of **Art.123(2)** or do not overcome other objections raised by the examining division, no interlocutory revision will be granted (E-XII,7.4.2). However, **T1060/13** r.4, criticises the examples in E-XII,7.4.2.

The department of first instance will rectify its decision if the applicant amends the wording to a proposal of the examiner he has previously rejected or if the department made an error, e.g. not taking into account available material or disregarding a request for oral proceedings. If a substantial procedural violation has occurred, interlocutory revision must be made, even if new objections arise (E-XII,7.4.2(a); E-XII,7.4.1). The new objections should be dealt with in continued examination. Interlocutory revision will also be applied where new information overcomes the objections of the decision under appeal (E-XII,7.1).

The appellant may file amended claims. Interlocutory revision will be granted if the amendments are substantial (**T47/90**) and clearly overcome the grounds for the refusal even if further new objections arise; the appellant is entitled to have the new objections examined in two instances (**T219/93**). Possible other grounds against the grant of the patent shall not be taken into account for the interlocutory revision; they can be dealt with in the continued procedure before the first instance (**T139/87**). For example, a refusal is based on novelty only and inventive step has not been discussed in the procedure; interlocutory revision must be allowed if the new claims are clearly novel but do not include an inventive step (E-XII,7.4.2(b)).

Interlocutory revision is never possible on the basis of an auxiliary request, since the applicant has the right to have his main request examined by a board of appeal (**T919/95**; E-XII,7.4.3)

If re-establishment in the time limit of **Art.108** has been requested, the first instance will allow interlocutory revision only if it can take the decision on re-establishment within the three-month time limit of **Art.109(2)** for remittance and the conditions for granting interlocutory revision are fulfilled. In all other cases the appeal and the application for re-establishment will be submitted to a board of appeal. (E-VIII,3.3)

Interlocutory revision does not automatically result in reimbursement of the appeal fee. Even if the examining division allows an interlocutory revision, there is no obligation to reimburse the appeal fee. The proper interpretation of **R.103** is that also in the case of interlocutory revision a substantial procedural violation must have taken place in the proceedings up to the contested decision in order to allow a reimbursement. (**T79/91** r.4.2)

A department of first instance is not competent to refuse a request for reimbursement of the appeal fee in an interlocutory revision, because a decision in interlocutory revision may not adversely affect the appellant (**G3/03** hn.I, r.2). If the requirements for interlocutory revision are fulfilled but the request for reimbursement of the appeal fee is considered not allowable, the department of first instance must grant the interlocutory revision and remit the request to a board of appeal, which will give a decision solely on the reimbursement. The board of appeal competent to deal with the substantive issues if no interlocutory revision had been granted is competent to decide on the request (**G3/03** hn.II). If the appeal is no longer pending at the time of a request for reimbursement (for example, because the department of first instance has dealt with the appeal by interlocutory revision), then there is no basis for refunding the appeal fee (**T21/02** hn).

An interlocutory revision can be regarded as an extension of the grant procedure, albeit rather costly because of the expense of filing an appeal. Parties often use interlocutory revision to redress the consequences of a refusal which has taken them unaware. In many cases this expensive procedure can be avoided by asking for a personal or telephone interview near the end of the grant procedure to clarify the position of the examining division. In 2012 about 6% of all appeals filed in ex parte proceedings resulted in interlocutory revision.

Art. 109(1) If the department whose decision is contested considers the appeal to be admissible and well founded, it shall rectify its decision. This shall not apply where the appellant is opposed by another party to the proceedings.

1 **Rectification of decision**
In grant proceedings an interlocutory revision of a refusal decision in grant proceedings is possible even if there are several applicants because these are as a rule joint applicants (**Art.118**). In opposition, interlocutory revision is only possible in special cases, e.g. if all oppositions are withdrawn and the proprietor appeals. An interlocutory revision is not possible for decisions regarding mention of the inventor (**R.21**), stay of the proceedings (**R.14**) or registering a transfer (**R.22**), because there are opposing parties. If interlocutory revision is not possible under **Art.109(1)**, last sentence, the first instance department sends the notice of appeal immediately to the board of appeal.

See **Art.110:2** on the assessment of admissibility of the appeal. An appeal is considered well founded if the grounds of the appeal contain an amendment to the application which meets the objections on which the contested decision of the examining division was based. In that case the department that issued the decision must rectify that decision in an interlocutory revision. (T139/87)

An interlocutory revision is a decision; the decision is not appealable because an allowed interlocutory revision has granted the party's request and does not adversely affect him.

Art. 109(2) If the appeal is not allowed within three months of receipt of the statement of grounds, it shall be remitted to the Board of Appeal without delay, and without comment as to its merit.

1 **Remittal to Board of Appeal**
On expiry of the three month period, the board of appeal becomes responsible for the case. The department of first instance loses jurisdiction and interlocutory revision is no longer possible. (T778/06)

The first instance department remits the appeal to the board of appeal without comment as to the merit of the appeal, according to **Art.109(2)**. Even when the board of appeal considers that interlocutory revision would have been justified, it is not open to the board to criticise the refusal of interlocutory revision in view of the requirement for silence. (T704/05 r.5.3)

Art. 110 Examination of appeals

If the appeal is admissible, the Board of Appeal shall examine whether the appeal is allowable. The examination of the appeal shall be conducted in accordance with the Implementing Regulations.

See for the implementation:
R.100 Examination procedure
R.101 Rejection of the appeal as inadmissible

1 **Assessment on filing of the notice of appeal**
The assessment of the notice of appeal on filing is similar to that of the notice of opposition, which is apparent from the equivalence of **Art.101(1)**, **R.77** and **R.79** on the one hand and **Art.110**, **R.100** and **R.101** on the other hand. The provisions for the appeal procedure have not been worked out in detail in the Guidelines, because the boards of appeal are not bound by the Guidelines but only by the EPC (**Art.23(3)**).

If the formalities officer notes deficiencies which may cause the notice of appeal being deemed not to have been filed (see **Art.108:5**) and which can still be remedied, he may, as a courtesy service, invite the appellant to remedy them within the 2 month period of **Art.108** (similar to D-IV,1.3.3). Notification of a missing signature is not at the formalities officer's discretion; this notification must always be made according to **R.50(3)**.

If not remedied in time, the formalities officer will notify the appellant that the appeal is deemed not to have been filed (**Art.119, R.112(1)**); the appellant can apply for a decision on this matter according to **R.112(2)**. The documents submitted with the notice will become part of the file, and regarded as observations under **Art.115**. Since the appeal is not in existence, examination for its admissibility under **R.101** does not come into question and an already paid appeal fee is refunded.

2 **Assessment of admissibility**

If the notice of appeal is regarded as filed, the admissibility of the appeal will subsequently be assessed. An appeal is admissible if it does not contain any of the deficiencies listed in **R.101**. In simple cases the department of first instance that took the impugned decision will decide on the question of admissibility (**T473/91**). Major deficiencies in the notice and grounds must be corrected before expiry of the relevant period of **Art.108** (**R.101(1)**), minor deficiencies may be corrected later but, after invitation, at the latest in a period set by the EPO (**R.101(2)**).

The appellant will be informed about the admissibility of his appeal. This notice is not a decision; the question of admissibility may be raised all through the appeal procedure. The admissibility of an appeal must be checked ex officio in every phase of the appeal proceedings (**T15/01 r.1**). The decision about the admissibility is normally taken together with the final decision. There is no refund of appeal fee if the notice is inadmissible, because the appeal has in fact started (but early terminated), and a substantial amount of work has already been done (**T89/84**).

3 **Examination of allowability**

The 'examination of allowability' under **Art.110** should be construed as an examination whether the grounds on which the appeal is based warrant a rectification of the impugned decision, as can be inferred from the French text of the provision. See also **Art.109(2)** German text compared with the English text. The examination of allowability has been implemented by **R.100**. The examination is carried out by the first instance under **Art.109** where the case can be allowed immediately on the basis of the appeal submissions themselves; the second instance has exclusive jurisdiction over more complicated cases (**T473/91**).

4 **Rules of procedure**

R.100(1) states that in general the same procedural rules apply in appeal as in proceedings before the first instance, especially the general procedural rules in **Art.113-126**: fair hearing, examination of its own motion, oral proceedings, taking of evidence, and **R.26-36**: filing of documents. Rules specific for the boards are provided in **Art.106-112** and **R.97-103** and in the Rules of procedure of the Boards of Appeal (OJ 2007 p.536, see **R.12c(2)**). In particular, Art.12(2) RPBA prescribes that the statement of grounds shall contain the appellant's complete case, including all facts, arguments and evidence relied on. The same applies for the reply of the respondent. Any amendments to a party's case as set out in the statement of grounds or the reply thereto are admitted at the discretion of the board (Art.13(1) RPBoA); this applies to late filed facts, evidence, requests (including amended claims), and in principle also to late filed arguments. See also the Guidance for parties in OJ 2003 p.419 §2.

The appeal procedure is in principle in writing, but can include oral proceedings on request of a party or of the board of appeal (**Art.116**). The board can reject a request for a further oral proceedings (**Art.116(1)**). In the invitation for the oral proceedings, the board may indicate issues which are important for the decision or questions that have to be settled (**R.116(1)**). In general, oral proceedings are concluded by a final decision and form the end of the appeal procedure.

5 Extent of examination

In a grant appeal proceedings the board of appeal has the power to examine whether the application meets the requirements of the EPC, including any requirements the examining division did not consider or regarded as having been met (**G10/93** hn, following **J4/80** hn.I and **T105/87** r.1).

In opposition appeal the board of appeal may not examine subject-matter not covered by the extent of opposition as stated in the notice of opposition (**G9/91** r.11). The board of appeal may consider only the grounds for opposition on which the contested decision was based, unless the patentee agrees to the additional fresh ground (**G10/91** hn3). A ground for opposition put forward in the notice of opposition, but subsequently not maintained at oral proceedings, is considered a fresh ground if reintroduced on appeal (**T376/04** r.1.1). This applies also to further appeal proceedings after an initial remittal to the opposition division. Any ground raised in the first opposition proceedings, but not relied on in the second, will be considered a fresh ground of opposition if reintroduced to the proceedings in the further appeal (**T986/04**). The grounds that are regarded as separate grounds for opposition have been given in **Art.100:1**. See **R.76(2):4** for details of the grounds and extent.

The purpose of an opposition appeal is mainly to give the losing party a possibility to challenge the decision of the opposition division on its merits (**G9/91**). Accordingly, under Art.12(4) RPBA the board has the discretionary power to hold inadmissible facts, evidence and requests which could have been presented in the first instance proceedings or which were rejected as inadmissible by the first instance department in both grant and opposition appeals .

6 Filing new set of claims

A new set of claims filed with the notice of appeal following a refusal by the examining division must be assessed according to **R.137(3)** (**T1/80**; **T63/86**). If major amendments are proposed, the case is remitted to the first instance, while the applicant remains entitled to file an appeal against a decision regarding the assessment as well as the patentability of the amended claims. The same rules apply for filing new claims as for amending claims.

The admissibility into the appeal proceedings of all late-filed matter, including main and auxiliary requests consisting of amended or new claims, is at the board's discretion. Late filed requests may be excluded from the proceedings if the reasons for their lateness are not acceptable. If the reasons are accepted, late-filed requests may still be excluded if they are not clearly allowable. Conversely, a clearly allowable request may be excluded if the late filing is not justified. (**T583/93** r.2.1)

An alternative set of claims should normally be filed together with the statement of grounds of appeal or as soon as possible thereafter during the stage of examination of the appeal, to avoid disruption of the proceedings and to allow time for consideration. A board of appeal may refuse to consider alternative claims filed at a later stage, such as during oral proceedings, if such claims are not clearly allowable. A board of appeal may exceptionally decide to consider late-filed claims, provided both the board and all parties have sufficient opportunity to consider the allowability of such claims. (**T153/85** r.2.1(e))

Filing of a new set of claims based on a combination of the original claims at a late stage in the proceedings will not necessarily be allowed (**T1060/04**). Although an opposition to an independent claim implicitly covers all dependent claims, this does not mean that the Board or patentee must be prepared to argue in respect of the dependent claims at any time in the proceedings. See **T470/04** for a case in which late-filed claims were admitted, on the basis that they did not change the subject of proceedings, and **T70/04** and **T1273/04** for cases in which they were not, as they were considered to raise new issues and shift the scope of the invention, respectively.

The filing of an appeal not only to reverse a decision on a request considered by the opposition division, but also on the basis of a new request raising issues not considered by the opposition division is not in accordance with the purpose of the appeal proceedings. The board should confine itself to a judicial review of the requests considered by the opposition division. A late filed request is only admitted if it is the last chance for the patentee to obtain a patent. (**T840/93** r.3.1, 3.2, 3.2.2). Filing a request on appeal which was abandoned during opposition proceedings is not necessarily considered abuse where the appellant had unsuccessfully tried to persuade the Opposition Division to consider the request (**T1276/05** r.1.3).

7 **Closure of debate in oral proceedings**

During oral proceedings a party may make submissions until the chairman closes the debate, after which the board deliberates and then issues its decision based on the submissions (**G12/91** r.3). The announcement of a negative decision often takes parties by surprise; had they expected a negative decision, they would have filed a further request. The inability to file a further request is a commonly used ground in petitions for review, the inability being regarded as a fundamental violation of **Art.113**. These petitions are usually rejected as unallowable.

The uncertainty in oral proceedings frequently prompts applicants to file a divisional application prior to oral proceedings, pay the fees only after a negative decision, and continue prosecution with the divisional application. If the facts and objection in the case of the divisional are the same and the previous board has already dealt with the objection, the new board has no power to examine the objection again (**T51/08** r.3, 4).

The last moment in time a party can file a further request in oral proceedings is the moment the chairman declares the debate closed for deliberation. The party must then request that the debate be re-opened and file his request. (**R10/08** r.8)

However, at closure of the debate the outcome of the deliberation will not be clear. Hence, it is recommended that a party files an auxiliary request, when setting out his case at the start of the oral proceedings, to be given the opportunity to file a further request if all pending requests will be rejected.

8 **Accelerated processing**

A party with a legitimate interest may file a reasoned request for an accelerated processing of the appeal. A court of an EPC contracting state may also use this possibility. Valid reasons are: pending or envisaged infringement proceedings, the validity of the patent affects pending licence negotiations, the appeal is from a decision taken in accelerated opposition proceedings (see **Art.101(1):4**). Exceptionally, the board may accelerate the procedure ex officio, e.g. because of disadvantages due to the suspensive effect of the appeal. Allowance of the request to accelerate the proceedings is at the board's discretion. (Not. of Vice-Pres., OJ 2008 p.220)

9 **Termination of proceedings**

When the sole appellant withdraws the appeal, appeal proceedings are terminated in ex parte and inter partes proceedings alike, in so far as the substantive issues settled by the contested decision at first instance are concerned (**G8/91** hn). Withdrawal of the opposition by the sole appellant and opponent is regarded as withdrawal of the appeal (**G8/93**). The board of appeal is not allowed to continue an opposition appeal proceedings of its own motion, as would follow from the exception for opposition proceedings in **R.84(2)** in conjunction with **R.100(1)**, because opposition proceedings and opposition appeal proceedings are of a different nature (**G7/91** r.7). In contrast to the purely administrative character of the opposition procedure, the appeal procedure is to be considered as a judicial procedure, which is by its nature less investigative than an administrative procedure. (**G7/91, G8/91, T357/89, T695/89**)

As a consequence, appeal proceedings are terminated after the sole appellant and opponent has withdrawn his opposition, irrespective of whether the proprietor agrees to termination and even if in the board of appeal's view the requirements under the EPC for maintaining the patent are not satisfied. (**G8/93** hn; see also **G7/91** r.10, 11)

When a party as of right, e.g. an opponent and respondent to an appeal, withdraws his opposition, the procedure continues but he ceases to be party as far as the substantive issues are concerned (**T340/05**). Evidence submitted prior to withdrawal can still be used in the appeal. However, he remains party for the issue of apportionment of costs under **Art.104**. (**T789/89**)

Art. 111 Decision in respect of appeals

1 **General**

The board of appeal reviews the impugned decision and decides on the appeal. If the board sets aside the impugned decision, it may exercise any power within the competence of the department of first instance that took the decision or remit the case to that department for further prosecution (**Art.111(1)**). After remittal the department of first instance is bound by the decision of the board (**Art.111(2)**). The content of the decision, such as the reasons and signature, are governed by **R.102**. The form of the decision must comply with **R.111(2)**.

All decisions of the boards are published on the EPO website unless they are excluded from file inspection under **Art.128(1)**. Some decisions are published in the three languages in the OJ. The date of a decision in appeal finally refusing a patent application is published in the European Patent Bulletin and Register according to **Art.127, 129, R.143(1)(n)**.

Art. 111(1) Following the examination as to the allowability of the appeal, the Board of Appeal shall decide on the appeal. The Board of Appeal may either exercise any power within the competence of the department which was responsible for the decision appealed or remit the case to that department for further prosecution.

See for the implementation:
R.102 Form of decision of the Board of Appeal
R.103 Reimbursement of appeal fees

1 **Decision in appeal proceedings**
A decision in appeal may be interlocutory, not terminating proceedings, or final, terminating proceedings (see e.g. **Art.106(2)**). The word 'final' is also used in the expression 'a decision has become final', where it has the different meaning of 'a decision has become res judicata', i.e. the decision is no longer open to appeal (see the section below).

The investigative powers of the Boards of Appeal given by **Art.114(1)** are limited in inter partes proceedings to the extent of the initial requests of the parties (**G9/91** r.1, see also **G10/91**, **G9/92** and **Art.108:6** and **R.76(2):4.2**).

If the appellant has filed a set of auxiliary claims with the notice of appeal, the board of appeal will first decide on the main set of claims, and, if not acceptable, on the auxiliary set of claims (**T156/87**). When the board of appeal decides to grant a patent, the case will be remitted to the department of first instance with instructions on the exact scope of the patent to be granted, so the first instance can then take care of the administrative procedure necessary for grant as set out in **R.71** and **71a**.

A decision of the board of appeal must comply with the requirements of **R.102**. A decision will be based on a request of a party. Hence, a request in oral proceedings is not a mere basis for a discussion, but a procedural declaration to the Board for a decision to be made on that basis. A request for the grant of a patent includes the applicant's approval of the text in the sense of **Art.113(2)**. (**J8/98**)

2 **Remittal to first instance**
According to **Art.111(1)** a board of appeal may remit a case to the department which was responsible for the decision appealed. It will remit a case to the department of first instance if fundamental deficiencies are apparent in the first instance proceedings (**Art.11** RPBA). However, this is not always the case; for example, if the appellant was not disadvantaged by the deficiency and was permitted to present their arguments before the board of appeal (**T515/05**). A ground for remittal is a substantial procedural error by the first instance, e.g. no fair hearing, oral proceedings not allowed as not fit for the purpose, essential points not been decided. **T1505/06** concerns a case where the board were unable to determine whether the right to be heard had been violated, so had no choice but to remit the case to the first instance to ensure that the party was not disadvantaged. Another ground can be new facts and evidence, e.g. a new, essential prior art document, introduced for the first time in the appeal stage of opposition proceedings. They will be taken into consideration when the principle of examination by the EPO of its own motion so requires. If such prior art appears to be crucial, the case must be remitted to first instance to give the applicant again two levels of jurisdiction (**T273/84, T253/85, T133/87**). If a decision revoking a patent because of lack of novelty is revoked in appeal on the same ground, the case must be remitted to assess the inventive step. An essential amendment of the claims during appeal often leads to remittal of the case; after remittal, the first instance assesses the allowability of the amendment under **R.137(3)** (**T63/86**). Cases

where a new ground of objection is raised late in the appeal should only be remitted where the admittance of the new ground would result in the revocation of the patent (**T97/90**). Late filed matter which substantially changes a case should lead to an apportionment of costs against the party responsible for the late filing (**T97/90**).

3 Res judicata effect of board of appeal decision

A decision of the board of appeal becomes formally res judicata as soon as it is issued, i.e. it is not open to appeal (**G1/97**, r.2a). The principle of res judicata is based on public policy that there should be an end to litigation (**T167/93**, r.2.7). This applies both to interlocutory and final decisions. An appeal decision can only be set aside by a petition for review that is successful for one of the grounds stated in **Art.112a(2)**. **T167/93** r.2.5 lists six criteria a decision must comply with for res judicata to apply.

The substance of a board of appeal decision is binding both on the board and on the parties to the proceedings (substantive res judicata). If the same parties in new proceedings before the EPO dispute the same issue, the EPO is bound by the substance of the earlier decision. If proceedings are resumed before the same board following an interlocutory decision that has become final, the board must take the substance of its decision as the basis for its subsequent decision. (**T694/01**, r.2.10)

See **Art.111(2)** for the substantive res judicata effect or binding effect of a board of appeal decision.

Art. 111(2) If the Board of Appeal remits the case for further prosecution to the department whose decision was appealed, that department shall be bound by the ratio decidendi of the Board of Appeal, in so far as the facts are the same. If the decision under appeal was taken by the Receiving Section, the Examining Division shall also be bound by the ratio decidendi of the Board of Appeal.

1 Binding effect of board of appeal decision

The binding effect of a decision applies only to the extent determined by the nature of the proceedings and the provision of the law.

According to **Art.111(2)**, first sentence, a department to which a case is remitted is bound by the ratio decidendi of the decision of the board of appeal, in so far as the facts are the same. For example, if a board of appeal has rejected certain claims and has remitted the case for further prosecution of the remaining claims, the examination of the rejected claims cannot thereafter be reopened, either by the examining division or by the board of appeal in any subsequent appeal proceedings (**T79/89**). The competence of the latter board of appeal is restricted in the same way as that of the examining division.

An appeal decision for a parent case is binding for the same subject matter in a divisional case, and claims refused on appeal for the parent case cannot be pursued on appeal in the divisional case (**T51/08**).

1.1 BINDING EFFECT IN SAME CASE

The binding effect of **Art.111(2)** does not extend to any subsequent department. For example, a decision of a board of appeal from an examining division has no binding effect in subsequent opposition proceedings or on appeal therefrom, not only because different parties are involved but also because the EPC does not give such a decision binding effect for opposition proceedings (**T167/93**, hn, r.2.10; E-X,4). By way of exception, according to **Art.111(2)**, second sentence, the examining division is bound by the assessment of the Legal Board of Appeal of a decision taken by the Receiving Section. In this way procedural questions settled for the first instance by the Legal Board of Appeal are not being questioned again by the examining division. There is no need for such an exception for the opposition division, as most procedural questions relate to the grant procedure, and the opposition division need only assess the grounds of opposition of **Art.100**, which are not procedural but substantive in nature.

1.2 BINDING EFFECT ON OTHER CASES

A decision of a board of appeal has a binding effect only in the individual case which the board has remitted to the department of first instance. It has no binding effect on other cases but may serve as guiding principle. In general the departments of first instance follow the decisions of the boards of appeal in order to maintain a consistent practice and to avoid unnecessary appeals. There is, however, no principle in the EPC preventing the first instance from having a question, already decided by a board, reconsidered in another case by the same or another board. This may in appropriate cases contribute to developing the law. (**J27/94** r.4)

A party may legitimately expect that the first instance departments will not deviate from the established case law if this case law has become part of the consistent practice of the department of first instance, in particular if this practice has been published in the Guidelines or Notice from the EPO. (**J27/94** r.5)

If there is no solid body of consistent case law on the interpretation of a substantive provision governing patentability but only a very limited number of individual decisions, there can be no legitimate expectation that the EBoA will not overrule the interpretation (**G2/07** r.2.5).

Art.20 RPBA stipulates, that, where a board departs from an earlier decision on a point of law, the board must explain the departure in the reasons for the decision and inform the President. The President may decide to refer the point of law to the Enlarged Board of Appeal (**Art.112(1)(b)**). Should a board consider it necessary to deviate from an interpretation or explanation of the EPC in an earlier opinion or decision of the Enlarged Board of Appeal, the question must be referred to the Enlarged Board of Appeal (**Art.21** RPBA).

Art.111(2) refers only to the ratio decidendi, i.e. the bearing motives (**T843/91**), and not to the obiter dicta, i.e. findings that do not support the order of the decision. Therefore, the binding effect of a board of appeal decision does not apply to obiter dicta.

Decisions of the EPO in proceedings for grant, grant appeal, opposition and opposition appeal have no substantive res judicata effect for national courts in revocation proceedings pursuant to **Art.138**, even if the same parties are involved (**T694/01**, r.2.12). Hence, the assessment of prior art by the EPO has no binding effect on the revocation proceedings. In Germany the decisions of the EPO are regarded as expert opinions which must be acknowledged but which are without further legal effect (OJ 1999 p.322; OJ 2010 p.622).

Art. 112 Decision or opinion of the Enlarged Board of Appeal

1 **Competence and composition of Enlarged Board of Appeal**
The purpose of the Enlarged Board of Appeal (EBoA) is to ensure a uniform application of the law and to resolve important points of the law (**Art.112(1)**). Therefore it has the competence according to **Art.22(1)** to give decisions on points of law referred to it by the boards of appeal (BoAs) and to give opinions on points of law referred to it by the President. The EBoA also has competence under **Art.22(1)(c)** to undertake a judicial review role, in deciding on petitions for review of Board of Appeal decisions. See **Art.112a** and notes.

In early drafts of the EPC a European Patent Court was to have jurisdiction on further appeals from decisions of the BoAs in grant proceedings. However, during the negotiations leading to the EPC 1973, no agreement could be reached about such a court. Hence, it was decided that a decision of a BoA is final and cannot be appealed further under EPC 1973 (Empel §521). **Art.112a** EPC 2000 later added a limited possibility of review of decisions of a BoA for procedural errors.

The instrument set up to attain a certain degree of uniformity is the EBoA. When a BoA refers a point of law to the EBoA, the EBoA will settle this point only and does not rule on any other issue in the appeal case. The final decision in a case is then always taken by the BoA, using the decision of the EBoA.

The wording of **Art.112(1)** is modelled on now abolished German law around 1970; hence, the legislator has given the EBoA a limited power to achieve the desired uniformity. The power of the President to refer questions to the EBoA is very limited; since he is in an executive position, he should not have too much legislative powers.

According to **Art.112(1)**, the EBoA has jurisdiction only over referrals by BoAs and the President. The EBoA may not investigate legal issues of its own motion. Moreover, the legislator decided to restrict the number of referrals further by including several conditions in **Art.112(1)**, to be discussed below. As a consequence, some lack of uniformity in the application of the law has arisen over the past 30 years, causing legal uncertainty for users of the EPC.

The EBoA comprises about thirty members, who are appointed by the Administrative Council under **Art.11(3)**. They are drawn from the members of the BoAs, who for their part, according to **Art.23(2)**, may not be members of the departments of first instance. Under **Art.11(5)** the Administrative Council may appoint legally qualified members of the national courts of the EPC states as members of the EBoA. The aim is to further the harmonisation of patent law.

For each referral, the EBoA consists of seven members from the above list, five legally and two technically qualified, as governed by **Art.22(2)**. At least four members may not have taken part in the proceedings before the BoA referring the point of law (Art.2(4) RPEBoA) to avoid members of the referring board having a majority in the EBoA. Partiality of the EBoA's members is dealt with in **Art.24(3)**. The Rules of Procedure of the EBoA are adopted by the Boards of Appeal Committee of the Administrative Council under **R.12c** and are subject to the approval of the Administrative Council (**Art.23(4)**).

Art. 112(1) In order to ensure uniform application of the law, or if a point of law of fundamental importance arises:

(a) the Board of Appeal shall, during proceedings on a case and either of its own motion or following a request from a party to the appeal, refer any question to the Enlarged Board of Appeal if it considers that a decision is required for the above purposes. If the Board of Appeal rejects the request, it shall give the reasons in its final decision;

(b) the President of the European Patent Office may refer a point of law to the Enlarged Board of Appeal where two Boards of Appeal have given different decisions on that question.

1 **Conditions for referral by a board of appeal** (**Art.112(1)(a)**)

A BoA may only refer a question to the EBoA under **Art.112(1)(a)** if the following two conditions are met:

- the question must relate to ensuring uniform application of the law or to a point of law of fundamental importance and
- the board must consider that a decision is required.

A BoA will refuse a request for referral if both conditions are not met. Under EPC 1973, the provision was for referral if an 'important point of law' arises; it remains to be seen whether the change to refer only to points of law 'of fundamental importance' has any impact. The conditions limit considerably the number of cases referred by the boards of appeal, as shown in the following examples. Moreover, a board of appeal may not want to hand over the power to decide to another department of the EPO.

A referral presupposes an admissible appeal; this does not apply when the referral concerns the admissibility (**G2/04**, r.1.2).

The EBoA itself, when acting on a petition for review under **Art.112a**, is not a board of appeal in the meaning of **Art.112(1)(a)**, and cannot refer questions to the EBoA for a decision (**R7/08**).

The question must be of a legal, not of a factual nature (**T118/89**). Hence, a technical question, such as the extent of the abilities of a skilled person (**T181/82** r.14) or a question relating to appreciation of evidence in a concrete case (**T845/90** r.4.1) will not be referred to the EBoA.

A referral to ensure uniform application of the law is not necessary if there is no contradictory case law and earlier decisions can be followed (see e.g. **J47/92** r.5). Two decisions are not contradictory if they are based on different circumstances (**T143/91** r.5.9.5; **T248/88** r.3.3). There is no contradictory case law if an isolated decision deviates from established case law (**T248/88** r.3.3), nor if EPO case law diverges from national jurisprudence (**T154/04**). See also **Art.111(2):1.2.**

There is no important point of law if there is no general interest in clarifying a specific issue, e.g. if the question is geared essentially to the specific facts of the case on hand (**T601/92** r.5; **T939/92** r.4.1). An important point of law is normally derived from the bearing motives of a decision; however, obiter dicta may also concern important points of law that can give rise to legal uncertainty and can justify a referral (**G3/93** r.2; **G3/08b** hn.5).

Most requests for a referral by a party are refused on the ground of the second condition, i.e. the necessity for a decision. The necessity is generally determined in view of the functioning of the EPO, not in view of legal certainty for the public. If a BoA can answer an important point of law beyond doubt by reference to the EPC, the question need not be referred to the EBoA (**J5/81** hn.2). A decision is not required either if the appeal would have to be dismissed for reasons not related to the question to be referred (**J16/90** r.1.2). A referral is ruled out if the question does not arise in the case under appeal (**J14/91** r.5.2; **T26/88**). When a BoA intends to take a favourable decision on an issue for which a party has requested a referral, there is no need anymore for a referral and the BoA will refuse any request for referral (**T461/88** r.10; **T301/87** r.4.9).

The attitude of the BoAs towards the necessity of referral in the case of contradictory decisions does not appear to be consistent, for which Van Empel warned as early as 1975 (Empel, §523). The following examples will make this clear. The board of **T998/99** took a decision relating to the exhaustion of priority right which contradicted the uniform practice of the EPO; the decision was published in the OJ. It deemed that a referral was not required, because 'it is first and foremost for the boards of appeal to decide on this question', without reference to the conditions of **Art.112(1)** (r.6). On the other hand, in an earlier case an isolated decision **J22/95** interpreted the notion of effective designation of a contracting state in a way that conflicted with standing practice of the EPO. In order not to increase legal uncertainty, publication of this decision in the OJ was delayed until the President's referral of the case to the EBoA was published (OJ 1998 p.569). The decision **T15/01** contradicted the earlier decision **T998/99** based on similar facts. The BoA deemed that a referral for ensuring uniform application of the law was not required, because the first and second instance practice of the EPO was uniform, with the exception of this earlier decision (**T15/01** r.40). Such a practice of refusing requests for referral creates legal uncertainty until a sufficient number of contradictory cases have been decided to warrant a referral. Reference is made to notes on **Art.53(c)** on the patentability of diagnostic methods, where a considerable body of contradictory case law accumulated over more than fifteen years before the President made a referral to the EBoA (**G1/04**). The decision **J15/98**, published in the OJ, on the language requirement for according a date of filing was contrary to the practice of the office; the issue of referral was not mentioned. In a later, similar case in which neither the appellant nor the BoA referred to **J15/98**, the practice of the office was implicitly endorsed (**J9/01**, not published in the OJ). Due to the fact that the Guidelines referred only to the unpublished decision **J9/01**, the public was supposed to know that the EPO did not follow **J15/98**. Similarly, the EPO publication Case Law of the BoA informs the public in its 6th edition that decision **T465/92** on use of the problem-solution approach in the assessment of inventive step is a one-off decision; however, the 7th and 8th edition do not anymore mention the 'one-off' character. Decisions of the EBoA could create more legal certainty in these cases.

2 Procedure in the case of referral by a Board of appeal

During proceedings, a BoA may refer a question to the EBoA either of its own motion or following a request from a party to the appeal (**Art.112(1)(a)**). The board has the discretion to grant or refuse such a request from a party. If the BoA rejects the request, it must give the reasons in its final decision (**Art.112(1)(a)** last sentence). The referral is in the form of an interlocutory decision.

When a BoA refers a question, the proceedings which gave rise to the question will be stayed and will be continued after the EBoA has given its decision, which is binding on the board of appeal (**Art.112(3)**). The parties to the appeal proceedings remain parties to the proceedings before the EBoA (**Art.112(2)**). Any third party may send its views on the referred question of law in a written statement (amicus curiae brief) to the EBoA, which may then take it into account (Art.10 RPEBoA). The EBoA may publish an invitation in the OJ under Art.11b(2) RPEBoA to submit such statements (see e.g. OJ 2004 p.157).

If oral proceedings take place before the EBoA, the decision of the EBoA is usually not pronounced at the end of the oral proceedings, but will be handed down in writing afterwards.

If two or more points of law have been referred with the same or similar subject-matter, the EBoA may consider them in consolidated proceedings (Art.8 RPEBoA, see e.g. **G2/99** and **G3/99**). Where the proceedings of the BoA referring a question to the EBoA are terminated during pending proceedings of the EBoA, e.g. if the sole opponent/appellant withdraws his appeal, the proceedings of the EBoA are also terminated as lacking legal basis (see e.g. **G4/03** in OJ 2004 p.542).

Art.20(1) RPBA requires that a board gives the grounds for deviating from an earlier decision of a BoA, unless the grounds are in accordance with an earlier decision or opinion of the EBoA, and that the BoA informs the President of its decision. If the decision gives a different interpretation of the EPC to that given in the Guidelines, the BoA may give the grounds for its action (Art.20(2) RPBA). Where a BoA considers it necessary to deviate from an interpretation or explanation of the EPC in an earlier opinion or decision of the EBoA, the question must be referred to the EBoA (Art.21 RPBA, see e.g. **T301/95**).

3 Conditions for referral by the President (Art.112(1)(b))

The President of the EPO may refer a question to the EBoA under **Art.112(1)(b)**, provided the following two conditions are met:

- the question must relate to ensuring uniform application of the law or to an important point of law and
- two boards of appeal must have given different decisions on that question.

These conditions limit the freedom of the President to refer questions to the EBoA. The first condition is discussed in the above notes.

The 'different decisions' in **Art.112(1)(b)** must be interpreted in view of the purpose of the provision to establish uniformity of law and is to be understood restrictively in the sense of 'conflicting decisions' (**G3/08b** hn.3). In both **G3/95** and **G3/08b** the EBoA decided that the referral was inadmissible, because it found that the decisions referred by the President were not in conflict.

A difference between two decisions caused by a legal development cannot on its own form the basis for a referral (**G3/08b** hn.4). The EBoA regarded a period of seven years between the two decisions as compatible with the notion of development of the case law (**G3/08b** r.10.9). The EBoA did not address the resulting legal uncertainty for the users of the system.

A legal development may be caused by changing moral concepts, such as an increasing sensitivity to partiality. Such changing concepts require a dynamic interpretation of the law and, hence, changes in case law over time. (**R19/12** r.23; **G3/98** r.2.5)

A restrictive interpretation of the condition that the decisions must stem from two boards of appeal would unduly restrict the power of the President, since it would not allow referral of two conflicting decisions of the Legal BoA, being one organisational unit only. In accordance with the purpose of **Art.112**, to ensure a uniform application of the law, the condition of two different boards is deemed met if the two decisions were given by the same board in different compositions. (**G4/98** r.1.2; **G3/08b** hn.2)

A reason for not referring contradicting decisions to the EBoA can be that the practice of the EPO is uniform, in spite of a one-off decision (e.g. **T465/92, J15/98**), or the question is not regarded as an important point of law. The views on what constitutes an important point may differ between the EPO and the users of the EPC, i.e. applicants, proprietors and patent attorneys. Whereas the EPO regarded the competence of a department to reimburse the appeal fee (**G3/03**) an important point of law, the users regarded the exhaustion of the priority right (**T15/01**) as being of vital importance. The users can inform the President of the importance they attach to a point of law and request referral, as happened in cases **G4/98** and **G1/04**.

4 **Procedure in the case of referral by the President**
A BoA must inform the President if it takes a decision deviating from earlier decisions. When the President has decided to refer a case to the EBoA, he delegates the drafting of the questions and reasons to DG5, the legal directorate of the EPO. The procedure before the EBoA when giving an opinion is similar to the procedure when giving a decision, as described above. There are no parties to the proceedings. However, any third party may submit his views on the question in a written statement, which may be taken into account (Art.10(1) RPEBoA).

When the President refers a question to the EBoA, the EBoA issues an opinion, not a decision (**Art.22(1)(b)**). The opinion has no bearing on the decisions that have given rise to the referral, because the proceedings which led to the contradictory decisions have already been closed.

Art. 112(2) In the cases referred to in paragraph 1(a) the parties to the appeal proceedings shall be parties to the proceedings before the Enlarged Board of Appeal.

Art. 112(3) The decision of the Enlarged Board of Appeal referred to in paragraph 1(a) shall be binding on the Board of Appeal in respect of the appeal in question.

1 **Binding effect of decision of Enlarged Board of Appeal**
A decision of the EBoA is binding on the board of appeal which referred the question (**Art.112(3)**). The binding effect applies to the order of a decision and the conclusion of an opinion and to the supporting reasons of the EBoA; it does not apply to any obiter dicta of the EBoA (**T389/95** r.2.6-2.9; see also **Art.111(2)** for the similar binding effect of a decision of a BoA).

A decision or opinion of the EBoA has no effect on decisions which have already become final. The decision or opinion may affect the opinion of the BoA in pending cases.

A decision or opinion of the EBoA does not bind the BoA in future cases. However, if a BoA considers it necessary to deviate from a decision or opinion of the EBoA, it must refer the question to the EBoA according to Art.21 RPBA (see e.g. **T788/90**). The EBoA is not bound by its own decisions either (compare **G9/93**, overruling **G1/84**).

When a decision or opinion of the EBoA changes the interpretation of the EPC, parties are entitled to expect that the EPO applies its previous interpretation up to the date on which the decision or opinion was made available to the public (**G5/93** r.2.3). A decision can be considered to be made public when published on the EPO website. The EBoA may also prescribe up to when the previous interpretation is applicable (see e.g. **G2/08b** r.7 and Not. EPO OJ 2010 p.514)

The EPC does not provide that a department of first instance is bound by a decision or opinion of the EBoA. If a decision of such a department deviates from a decision or opinion of the EBoA and is appealed, the BoA will usually set the decision aside but it may in exceptional cases refer the matter again to the EBoA. Hence, departments of first instance tend to follow established case law.

2 **Effect of referral on pending cases**

A board usually stays appeal proceedings if their outcome depends on the answers the EBoA will give to questions of law referred to it (**T1145/09** r.3).

First instance proceedings will be stayed by the department of first instance or on request of a party if a referral to the EBoA is pending and the outcome of the examination and opposition proceedings depends entirely on the decision of the EBoA (E-VII,3). For specific cases the President may decide to stay ex officio all first instance substantive proceedings the outcome of which depend entirely on the outcome of the EBoA decision (see e.g. Not. EPO OJ 2016 A105).

3 **Pending referrals to the Enlarged Board of Appeal**

A list of decisions and opinions of the EBoA is given in the case law index of this book. The following case is pending (situation 15.11.2018):

G1/18 Appeal inadmissible or deemed not filed. See OJ 2018 A71 and **Art.108:4**.

4 **Overruled decisions of the Enlarged Board of Appeal**

The following decisions of the EBoA or part thereof are overruled by a subsequent decision of the EBoA or a change in law:

G1/83, G5/83, G6/83 Swiss-type claim, overruled by G2/08b r.7
G1/84 Self-opposition, overruled by G9/93
G2/12, G2/13 overruled by amendment of R.27 and R.28 (OJ 2017 A56)

The following decisions of the EBoA or part thereof are overruled by the EPC 2000:

G3/91 Re-establishment on entry into European phase
G5/92, G6/92 Re-establishment in period for requesting examination
G1/97 hn.I No revision of final decision of BoA

Art. 112a Petition for review by the Enlarged Board of Appeal

1 **General**

Decision **G1/97** noted that the EPC1973 has no possibility of reviewing a final decision of a board of appeal, whereas this was different in the contracting states. In response, the EPC 2000 provides a limited judicial review of decisions of the boards of appeal in **Art.112a**, which gives the Enlarged Board of Appeal the competence to decide on petitions for review of board of appeal decisions (OJ 2007 se4 (EN) p.126). **Art.112a** makes the EBoA a further instance, but with a limited scope.

Art. 112a(1) Any party to appeal proceedings adversely affected by the decision of the Board of Appeal may file a petition for review of the decision by the Enlarged Board of Appeal.

1 **Entitlement to file petition**
Under **Art.112a(1)** EPC a party adversely affected by the decision in appeal may file a petition for review. Both interlocutory and final decisions may be the subject of a petition (**R5/08**, see **Art.111(1)**). For a discussion of adverse effect, see **Art.107:2**.

Art. 112a(2) The petition may only be filed on the grounds that:
(a) a member of the Board of Appeal took part in the decision in breach of Article 24, paragraph 1, or despite being excluded pursuant to a decision under Article 24, paragraph 4;
(b) the Board of Appeal included a person not appointed as a member of the Boards of Appeal;
(c) a fundamental violation of Article 113 occurred;
(d) any other fundamental procedural defect defined in the Implementing Regulations occurred in the appeal proceedings; or
(e) a criminal act established under the conditions laid down in the Implementing Regulations may have had an impact on the decision.

Art.24(1) Exclusion and objection
Art.24(4) Decision on exclusion and objection
Art.113 Right to be heard and basis of decisions
See for the implementation:
R.104 Further fundamental procedural defects
R.105 Criminal acts
R.106 Obligation to raise objections

1 **Grounds for filing petition**
Under **Art.112a(2)** a petition for review may only be based on the grounds defined in the EPC. These are, on the one hand, fundamental procedural defects which occurred in appeal proceedings, and, on the other hand, the existence of a criminal act which may have had an impact on the decision.

Fundamental procedural defects are, in the first place, the deficiencies defined in **Art.112a(2)(a)** to **(c)**, i.e. a breach of **Art.24** governing the exclusion of and objection to members of a Board of Appeal, the participation of persons not appointed as a member of the Boards of Appeal, and fundamental violation of **Art.113**. **Art.112a(2)(d)** refers to further fundamental procedural defects defined in **R.104**. These defects include, for example, a fundamental procedural defect arising from failure to take into account a request made by a party.

The examples in **Art.112a(2)(a)** to (c) and particularly the wording of **Art.112a(2)(d)** make it clear that only fundamental (but not minor) procedural defects can be the basis for a petition for review. Under no circumstances may the petition for review be a means to review the application of substantive law. This restriction is justified because the function of the petition for review is to remedy intolerable deficiencies occurring in individual appeal proceedings, not to further the development of EPO procedural practice or to ensure the uniform application of the law.

To succeed on the basis of a fundamental violation of **Art.113**, the petitioner must show both that the decision under review was based on grounds or evidence of which the petitioner was not aware, and on which he had no opportunity to comment; and that there is a causal link between the defect and the decision. In the absence of such a link, the violation cannot be considered fundamental (**R1/08**).

The petition in **R7/09** was successful on the basis that the patentee's right to be heard under **Art.113** was fundamentally violated when the EPO did not forward an appeal by the opponent to the patentee, and a decision on the appeal was taken without further correspondence. The EBoA also confirmed that a patentee or professional representative is under no obligation to monitor the online file of a case to ensure that they are aware of all correspondence.

The EBoA has competence to consider violations of the Rules of Procedure of the Boards of Appeal with a view to determining whether such violations led to a fundamental violation of **Art.113** (**R2/08**).

It is not yet clear if not applying the rules for referral to the EBoA is a fundamental procedural defect that can be used as ground for a petition for review.

R.106 provides that a petition for review shall only be admissible if the defect was objected to during appeal proceedings and the objection rejected by the Board of Appeal, unless the objection could not have been raised during appeal proceedings. Case **R1/08** admitted a petition on the basis that, although the petitioner did not object during the appeal proceedings, the Board of Appeal revoked the patent at oral proceedings directly after deliberation, and the written decision was based on grounds and arguments of which the petitioner was not aware. Hence objection could not have been raised during the appeal proceedings.

One of the most serious defects from which a decision might suffer is that criminal behaviour might have had an impact on the decision. Also in these cases the possibility of review by the Enlarged Board of Appeal should exist. However, the EPO has no power to establish whether a certain behaviour was an offence within the meaning of criminal law. Thus **R.105** states that a petition may be based on a decision by a competent court or authority that a criminal act has occurred; a conviction is not necessary.

If criminal proceedings against the person concerned are not possible, in particular in the event of the death of this person, no petition for review is possible: even an implicit examination of the issue whether there is a criminal act fails because the boards which are only subject to the EPC have no international penal code at hand suitable as yardstick in order to decide on criminally relevant behaviour.

In view of national differences relating to the definition of behaviour which is 'criminal' within the meaning of penal law or subject to other sanctions, the definition of what constitutes a 'criminal act' within the meaning of **Art.112a(2)(e)** is left to the case law of the Enlarged Board of Appeal. (OJ 2007 se4)

The list of **Art.112a** and **R.104** is exhaustive. Only a revision of the EPC or the Administrative Council may add violations to the list.

2 Procedural violation

The occurrence of a procedural violation may be proven by statements from witnesses that attended oral proceedings or by the minutes of the oral proceedings drafted under **R.124**. Since the content of minutes of oral proceedings before a board of appeal are often brief, the minutes are normally not useful as evidence. It is not yet clear how the boards can be forced to draft more elaborate minutes. See also **R.105:1, 106** and **124**. The EBoA noted in petitions **R7/08** and **R10/08** that the petitioner may reasonably be expected to object to minutes which do not indicate evidence of a procedural violation, if such a violation did indeed occur.

Art. 112a(3) The petition for review shall not have suspensive effect.

1 **Lack of suspensive effect**
Art.112a(3) makes clear that the petition for review is an extraordinary legal remedy, the filing of which does not affect the force of res judicata of the decision under attack. Implicitly it follows that a decision of the board of appeal has legal effect until a successful petition for review results in a decision of the EBoA which sets the decision of the board of appeal aside, i.e. overturns its res judicata effect, and re-opens appeal proceedings. This is further clarified in **Art.112a(5)**. (OJ 2007 se4)

Note the difference with the filing of an appeal, which does have suspensive effect (**Art.106(1)**).

Art. 112a(4) The petition for review shall be filed in a reasoned statement, in accordance with the Implementing Regulations. If based on paragraph 2(a) to (d), the petition shall be filed within two months of notification of the decision of the Board of Appeal. If based on paragraph 2(e), the petition shall be filed within two months of the date on which the criminal act has been established and in any event no later than five years from notification of the decision of the Board of Appeal. The petition shall not be deemed to have been filed until after the prescribed fee has been paid.

See for the implementation:
R.107 Contents of the petition for review

1 **Filing of petition for review**
Art.112a(4) provides for the form, the time limits and the fee for the petition for review. The contents of the statement setting out the grounds for the petition for review are further defined in **R.107**. This provides that the petition for review shall contain:

1 the name and address of the petitioner as provided in **R.41(2)(c)**;
2 a statement identifying the decision to be reviewed;
3 a statement setting out the grounds on which the petition is based as well as an indication of the facts, evidence and arguments presented in support of these grounds.

The possibility of filing a petition for review must not cause long-lasting legal uncertainty for third parties. The outcome of the new appeal proceedings following successful review proceedings might be that a failed patent or patent application is revived so that protection already lost will be re-established. Thus, it is important that the deadline for filing such petitions is short.

As with opposition and appeal proceedings, the statement of grounds must indicate the reasons for the petition, and must be sufficient for the EBoA (and third parties) to understand immediately why the decision concerned suffers from a fundamental procedural violation (**R5/08**).

The short time limit under **Art.112a(4)**, second sentence, i.e. two months after the notification of the decision of the Board of Appeal, would make it nearly impossible to base a petition for review on criminal behaviour. In these exceptional and particularly serious cases, the period therefore starts when the conviction by the criminal court becomes final. The protection of a party adversely affected by criminal behaviour prevails over legal certainty for third parties. However, there is an absolute time limit after the expiry of which no petition for review will be admissible; a period of five years is appropriate. This period should be sufficient to obtain a national decision on a criminal act.

The periods under **Art.112a(4)** are excluded from further processing under **Art.121(4)**. Re-establishment according to **Art.122** and **R.136** is available to applicants and proprietors.

A high fee for a petition for review is payable (**Rfees2(1)11a**). However, **R.110** provides that the fee for the petition for review shall be reimbursed if the Enlarged Board re-opens the proceedings before the Board of Appeal, unless reimbursement is not considered equitable.

The filing of a petition for review will be entered in the European patent register. (OJ 2007 se4)

Art. 112a(5) The Enlarged Board of Appeal shall examine the petition for review in accordance with the Implementing Regulations. If the petition is allowable, the Enlarged Board of Appeal shall set aside the decision and shall re-open proceedings before the Boards of Appeal in accordance with the Implementing Regulations.

See for the implementation:
R.108 Examination of the petition
R.109 Procedure in dealing with petitions for review
R.110 Reimbursement of the fee for petitions for review

1 **Examination of petition for review**
Examination of the petition is governed by the provisions of **R.108** to **R.110**. These note that:

1 The petition for review shall be rejected as inadmissible if
   a) it is not filed by a party adversely affected by the decision under attack;
   b) it has not been filed in due time;
   c) the reasoned statement setting out the grounds for the petition does not sufficiently substantiate the reasons why the decision under attack should be set aside;
   d) the alleged procedural defect was not objected to as prescribed in **R.106**(see notes **Art.112a(2):1**); or
   e) the alleged criminal act is not established as provided for in **R.105** (see notes **Art.112a(2):1**).

2 If the petition for review is admissible, the Enlarged Board of Appeal shall examine whether the alleged procedural defect occurred in appeal proceedings or whether the established criminal act might have had an impact on the decision.

3 If the petition for review is allowable, the Enlarged Board of Appeal shall set aside the decision of the Board of Appeal and shall re-open appeal proceedings before the Board of Appeal which rendered the decision. If appropriate the Enlarged Board of Appeal may order that the Board of Appeal be composed differently. In exceptional cases, the Enlarged Board of Appeal may re-open appeal proceedings before another Board of Appeal.

R.109(1) provides that in deciding on a petition for review, the provisions relating to proceedings before the Boards of Appeal shall apply, unless otherwise provided.

Each alleged procedural deficiency in the decision is to be considered separately by the EBoA for admissibility and allowability (**R3/08**).

The EBoA examines a petition for review in a two-stage procedure as set out in R.109(3):1. See also the RPEBoA (OJ 2015 A35), especially Art. 11, Art. 12, and Art. 17.

If the petition for review is allowed, the consequence shall be that the decision of the board of appeal is set aside and appeal proceedings reopened before the boards of appeal. This decision overturns the res judicata effect of the previous decision. The result of the second appeal proceedings may be the same as in the first appeal proceedings, or different. (OJ 2007 se4)

Art. 112a(6) Any person who, in a designated Contracting State, has in good faith used or made effective and serious preparations for using an invention which is the subject of a published European patent application or a European patent in the period between the decision of the Board of Appeal and publication in the European Patent Bulletin of the mention of the decision of the Enlarged Board of Appeal on the petition, may without payment continue such use in the course of his business or for the needs thereof.

1 **Third party right to continue use**

The revival of lost patent protection may prejudice third-party interests. Thus, provision must be made for intervening rights such as intermediate use. **Art.112a(6)** governs this issue in terms similar to those of **Art.122(5)** concerning the protection of third-party interests in case of re-establishment of rights after missing a time limit despite observance of all due care. The requirement of good faith guarantees that no rights can be acquired in an abusive way. (OJ 2007 se4)

2 **Renewal fees**

The EPC 2000 Diplomatic Conference decided that payment of renewal fees in the Contracting States for a European patent during review proceedings is a matter of national law. The lack of a uniform procedure has caused uncertainty about the fate of a patent after a review procedure. In particular, the EPC does not stipulate that retroactive payment of renewal fees after grant must be possible in the Contracting States if a patent is revoked by a first decision in appeal, this first appeal decision is set aside by a decision on a petition for review, and the patent is then maintained in a second decision in appeal.

PART VII COMMON PROVISIONS

Chapter I *Common provisions governing procedure*

1 **Applicability of provisions**
All provisions in this Part are applicable to any procedure before the EPO, unless stated otherwise.

Art. 113 Right to be heard and basis of decisions

See for the implementation:
R.111 Form of decisions
R.112 Noting of loss of rights
R.113 Signature, name, seal

Art. 113(1) The decisions of the European Patent Office may only be based on grounds or evidence on which the parties concerned have had an opportunity to present their comments.

1 **Opportunity to comment**
The provision lays down the principle that the EPO may base its decisions only on grounds or evidence on which a party has had an opportunity to comment. Parties cannot be surprised by negative decisions. The opportunities to comment have been worked out in the provisions for written or oral comment, time limits, remedy of a failure, and taking of evidence. The EPO must discuss the arguments of the parties. All evidence used for the decision must be or become public. Minutes of oral proceedings may be important as evidence of respect for the right to be heard (C-III,10.3).

There is a substantial procedural violation if arguments of the parties are not discussed or if not enough time has been provided for reply. For example, when a party announces the filing of further evidence, and the EPO does not give him a reasonable period for filing, there is a substantial procedural violation (J4/82). See **R.115(2):1** for the right to be heard in oral proceedings where a party is absent.

The opposition division must give an express opportunity to parties to present observations after remittal to it of a case by a board of appeal for further prosecution on the basis of new evidence, even if submissions with respect to this new evidence have already been made during the preceding appeal proceedings. An immediate termination of the opposition proceedings after remittal constitutes a substantial procedural violation in the sense of **R.103**. (T892/92)

Art. 113(2) The European Patent Office shall examine, and decide upon, the European patent application or the European patent only in the text submitted to it, or agreed, by the applicant or the proprietor of the patent.

1 **Consent of party to text**
The party controls the text of the application or patent which the EPO considers during grant and opposition proceedings, both in first and second instance. He decides the text under discussion and its amendments under **Art.123**. The EPO can only propose amendments. An implementation of **Art.113(2)** is the approval of the text to be granted under **R.71(5)**. The board of appeal and the first instance are not competent to grant a patent in a version different from that submitted or agreed by the applicant (**T32/82**).

If an applicant agrees with only part of the text in an opposition or appeal procedure, and does not provide an amended text, the department can only revoke the entire patent. However, in a national revocation procedure it may be possible to revoke the patent in part (**Art.138(2)**).

Art. 114 Examination by the European Patent Office of its own motion

Art. 114(1) In proceedings before it, the European Patent Office shall examine the facts of its own motion; it shall not be restricted in this examination to the facts, evidence and arguments provided by the parties and the relief sought.

1 **Examination of own motion**
The basic principle of examination of its own motion, also called ex-officio examination, applies in principle to all procedures before the EPO, from the Receiving Section to the Enlarged Board of Appeal. However, the application of ex-officio examination in opposition procedures in first and second instance is restricted. The post-grant opposition procedure under the EPC resembles a national revocation procedure, and, consequently, the opposition proceedings under the EPC must likewise be considered as contentious proceedings between two parties normally representing opposite interests, who should be given equally fair treatment (**G9/91** r.2). **Art.114(1)** must be applied in an even more restrictive manner in the appeal procedure in opposition, which is to be considered as a judicial procedure (**G1/99** r.6.6).

An ex-officio examination in opposition proceedings might be interpreted as favouring one party. The EPO will therefore mainly examine the request as formulated in the notice of opposition. This view of the opposition procedure has led to more emphasis on procedural matters than on compliance of the patent maintained in opposition with the requirements of the EPC. Note, that in this case the applicability of an Article is restricted by applying considerations not derived from the EPC (see also the minority opinion on own motion in **G9/92** r.17).

Examples of restrictions on the ex-officio examination can be found below and in **R.76(2):4**.

The EPC 2000 has not changed **Art.114(1)** to solve the apparent conflict with case law, because the EPO wants to keep the option open of going back to a broader use of own motion, but at the same time being able to restrict own motion to accelerate the procedure. At the time of drafting the EPC 2000 the EPO had no intention to change the procedure.

2 **Examination of facts and evidence**

The ex-officio examination has its major impact in the exact determination of the state of the art used in the examination.

The EPO may carry out a top-up search providing facts to complement the state of the art given in the application and the search report (B-XI,3.9).

The applicant cannot leave the fact-finding to the EPO, he must cooperate. He must e.g. formulate proposals for claims, and look for patentable matter outside the claims. The EPO stops the examination of its own motion if the necessary cooperation of a party is lacking, e.g. if a party claiming prior public use withdraws from the proceedings and the facts are difficult to establish without his cooperation (**T129/88**). When two parties in an opposition procedure assert opposite facts without proper evidence, and the EPO cannot provide the evidence of its own motion, then this disadvantage is put on the opponent (**T219/83**).

The opposition division or the board of appeal may introduce documents from the search report in the proceedings if they regard them to be relevant (**Art.114(1)**), although it is not their duty to redo the examination for grant (**T387/89**). Documents cited in the opposed patent are not automatically part of the opposition proceedings; however, the most relevant state of the art on which the patent is based, is part of the proceedings (**T536/88**).

Art.114(1) does not mean that a board of appeal must conduct a rehearsing of the first instance proceedings without regard to how late submissions were made. If in first instance a late-filed submission is not taken into account, the second instance need neither take it into account. (**T97/90**)

The board of appeal decides on reimbursement of appeal fees of its own motion (**J7/82**).

3 **Examination of grounds**

In an appeal from a grant refusal the board of appeal has the power to examine whether the application meets the requirements of the EPC, including requirements the examining division did not consider or regarded as having been met (**G10/93** hn; see e.g. **T1158/01**, r.2).

The extent of opposition as indicated according to **Art.101** and **R.76(2)(c)** may not be widened by using **Art.114(1)**, because **Art.114(1)** is subject to **Art.101** with **R.76(2)(c)** as far as the extent is concerned (**G9/91**, confirming **T9/87**). Note, that this limitation of the applicability of an Article by a Rule has a strained relation with **Art.164(2)**.

During opposition proceedings new grounds for opposition may be added to those indicated in the notice of opposition under **R.76(2)(c)** but only when deemed prima facie relevant; new grounds are not allowed in appeal proceedings, unless the proprietor agrees to it (**G10/91**, overruling **T122/84**, **T9/87**, **T227/88**, **T493/88** and **T182/89**).

In so far as the substantive issues settled by the contested decision at first instance are concerned, appeal proceedings are terminated, in ex parte and inter partes proceedings alike, when the sole appellant withdraws the appeal. (**G8/91** hn)

Art. 114(2) The European Patent Office may disregard facts or evidence which are not submitted in due time by the parties concerned.

1 Late-filed submissions

The EPO may disregard late-filed facts or evidence according to **Art.114(2)**. It allows a normal course of the proceedings and makes tactical abuse of late submission of facts impossible (**T273/84**). The admissibility of late submitted facts and evidence is determined by their importance for the case, the state of the proceedings and the reasons for the late submission (E-VI,2). Because 'arguments' are not mentioned in paragraph 2, a late submission of new arguments is allowed, being indispensable for oral proceedings. However, if a new argument changes a case substantially, the argument may be disregarded or a case in appeal may be referred to first instance with an apportionment of costs (**T124/87** hn3, **T97/90** hn2). The late filing of amendments is also not covered by **Art.114(2)**. The admissibility of a late-filed amendment in grant proceedings is a matter of discretion of the examining division according to **R.137(3)** (see also **R.71(6):2**). Late-filed amendments in opposition proceedings may be refused if the examination of the opposition or appeal is substantially complete (**T406/86** hn2).

2 Grounds for considering late-filed submissions

Summary of the grounds for deciding to act of its own motion, specially with respect to late submissions of facts and evidence:

1 Basis for the examination of its own motion is that the EPO is obliged to the public not to grant patents of which it is certain that they have no legal basis.
2 The EPO must check the relevance of late submissions and communicate the result.
3 In contrast to timely submitted facts and evidence, late submission may be rejected without extensive reasoning.
4 Something will only be considered as being late submitted if a careful preparation of the case would have given rise to an earlier submission.
(**T156/84**)

The check as to relevance is not required if the late submission could have been filed earlier and forms an abuse of procedure; a department may refuse such a document without assessing its relevance (**T951/91** r.5.9, **T534/89** hn2).

The grounds for admitting late-filed grounds, facts and evidence are given in **R.76(2):4**.

3 Examples

Where late-filed evidence or arguments in appeal raise a case substantially different from that decided in first instance, the case will be remitted to the first instance with an award of costs against the tardy filer. A late-filed new ground of objection in an opposition appeal should only be referred to the first instance where it might result in the revocation of the patent. Where the maintenance of the patent is not at risk, the Board can either refuse to admit the new ground or admit it in the proceedings and decide it against the opponent (**T97/90**).

A relevant document for the first time submitted in an opposition appeal often incites the board of appeal to remit the case to the opposition division (**Art.111(1)**).

Evidence of common general knowledge may introduce new facts and thereby change the framework of the appeal. If filed only with the notice of appeal, the Board is empowered to disregard such evidence, even though a document indicating common general knowledge merely serves to confirm what is already commonly known in the field. (**T85/93** hn r.1)

If an alleged prior public use is not adequately substantiated, it is immaterial and, if not submitted in due time, may be disregarded under **Art.114(2)** (**T93/89**).

An alleged prior public use deliberately filed late in order to abuse the procedure may be disregarded irrespective of its potential relevance (**T534/89**). Even an assertion of prior public use based on the opponent's own activities which is filed after the expiry of the opposition period without good reasons is an abuse of the proceedings and a breach of the principle of good faith; such an assertion should be disregarded irrespective of its potential relevance (**T17/91**).

Supporting evidence for a restatement of the problem of a patent application is regarded as submitted in due time if submitted together with the grounds of appeal (**T1/80** hn.II). An allegation of insufficient disclosure made for the first time during oral proceedings in opposition appeal is in general rejected because of its late submission (**T294/85** r.4). The delay in the proceedings must be weighed against the requirement of examination of its own motion. An alleged prior use submitted for the first time in the notice of appeal was regarded as inadmissible although close to the subject-matter of the impugned patent, because it was submitted too late in view of the uncertainty in the result and duration of the taking of the evidence (there was no proof that the object claimed was indeed identical with the object asserted to have been sold) (**T262/85**).

If the parties to opposition proceedings make contrary assertions which they cannot substantiate and the EPO is unable to establish the facts of its own motion, the patent proprietor is given the benefit of the doubt (**T219/83**).

Art. 115 Observations by third parties

In proceedings before the European Patent Office, following the publication of the European patent application, any third party may, in accordance with the Implementing Regulations, present observations concerning the patentability of the invention to which the application or patent relates. That person shall not be a party to the proceedings.

See for the implementation:
R.114 Filing and communication of observations

1 General

Art.115 gives a third party the possibility to file his observations on a case pending before the EPO and have them examined. Although observations usually contain arguments against patentability, they may also give arguments in favour of patentability. Such observations help to avoid the grant of invalid patents. It is an easily accessible route, because there are no fees to be paid (OJ 2017 A86 §1), in contrast with the opposition procedure.

Observations can be filed during pending proceedings but only after publication of the application. Filing is possible both in grant and opposition proceedings because **Art.115** refers to 'application' and 'patent'. They will be taken into account during first and second instance proceedings.

Details of the filing and subsequent procedure are provided in **R.114**. The EPO prefers online filing of third party observations using a structured online form to facilitate and promote their use because of the proven usefulness of the observations in examination (OJ2011, 418 and 420).

2 Third person

The title of the article is confusing in that 'parties' are not 'parties to the proceedings'. The French and German texts of the article are clearer.

Since only a 'third party' may file observations, the applicant or any other party to proceedings may not file observations under **Art.115** (E-VI,3). It is not clear whether a third party not living or working in or being a national of a contracting state must be represented in view of **Art.133(2)** for filing his observations.

The language requirements and procedure are laid down in **R.114**.

Observations may be filed anonymously with departments of first instance (OJ 2017 A86 §3.2). See e.g. the observations dated 12.05.1998 and 07.12.1999 in the case EP 0451216 filed by the cartoon character Buzz Lightyear.

The boards of appeal have not reached a unanimous view on considering anonymous observations. They may be considered in ex parte appeal (**T1336/09** r.2.2). Whereas in opposition appeal **T735/04** r.2 did consider an anonymous observation, **T1439/09** r.1.7 regarded an anonymous observation as not filed if not signed after a **R.50(3)** invitation. The latter board held that an anonymous observation could be used by a party for late submissions in opposition proceedings to avoid apportionment of cost. However, this is not a sound reason, because even if the board can identify a third party that sent an observation, it will not know whether the third party was instructed by a party to the proceedings. The Enlarged Board of Appeal does not consider anonymous statements (**G1/03**, Summary of facts and submissions VI(3)).

3 Issues to be raised

Only patentability questions can be raised according to **Art.115**. Since 'Patentability' is the title of the chapter of the EPC containing **Art.52-57**, the questions could be interpreted to relate only to these provisions. The EPO notice OJ 2017 A86 §3.4 restricts observations to 'substantive requirements of the EPC, e.g. Articles 52-57'. However, the Guidelines use a broader interpretation (E-VI,3). The case law on which the interpretation is based, uses the broad interpretation usually without giving any grounds.

The EPO considers also clarity objections under **Art.84** (see e.g. **T598/97** r.3) and insufficient disclosure under **Art.83** (see e.g. **T918/94** r.9). Hence, lack of unity (**Art.82**) could also be considered. The EPO also accepts observations relating to non-technical subject-matter under **Art.52(2)** and **(3)**, exclusions under **Art.53**, industrially not applicable according to **Art.57** and unallowable amendments under **Art.76(1)** and **123(2)** (E-VI,3). Formal issues, such as the validity of an authorisation or the allowability of a request for re-establishment, will not be considered. Non-entitlement of the proprietor to the patent can only be raised in a national procedure (**Art.138(1)(e)**). During opposition, non-unity issues will not be considered (**Art.100:2**) and clarity issues only if relating to amendments (**Art.101(3):1**).

4 Time limit for filing

There is no provision in the EPC defining circumstances during pending proceedings wherein the information filed under **Art.115** should not be taken into account. Since the person of **Art.115** is not a party referred to in **Art.114(2)**, **Art.114(2)** may not be applied for the information filed under **Art.115**, and, hence, late filed information should always be taken into account (**T156/84** r.3.7 and E-VI,3). The information is in time if it reaches the EPO before the final decision is pronounced in oral proceedings or issued in written proceedings (**Ante R.111:1**). See E-VI,3 for the fate of observations received late. A submission under **Art.115** putting forward prior public use should give all required evidence as to what, who and where, because the EPO will not invite him to provide this information (**T908/95** r.4.1; E-VI,3).

Decision **T951/91** held that **Art.115** does not extend the rights of third parties beyond the rights of parties to proceedings; observations under **Art.115** should therefore be subject to **Art.114(2)** and may be disregarded if filed late, depending on their relevance and possible abuse of procedure. In **T667/92** a new ground raised in an **Art.115** submission during opposition appeal was not admitted because of the restricted applicability of **Art.114(1)** to opposition appeal. The Guidelines have not been amended in view of these decisions (E-VI,3).

Art. 116 Oral proceedings

See for the implementation:
R.4 Language in oral proceedings,
R.111(1) Form of the decision in oral proceedings,
R.115 Summons to oral proceedings,
R.116 Preparation of oral proceedings,
R.124 Minutes of oral proceedings
E-II Oral proceedings

1 **Oral proceedings and consultations**

Although the procedure before the EPO is in principle in writing, the parties are by way of exception entitled to oral proceedings, as they may speed up the procedure. In some situations, a consultation in the form of a face to face interview or a telephone call may be useful.

An examining division will send at least one **Art.94(3)** communication before considering to issue summons to oral proceedings. It should be noted that a search opinion, a supplementary search or an opinion or report from the PCT procedure is not an **Art.94(3)** communication. (E-III,5.1)

Oral proceedings will be held in the place where the relevant department of the EPO is located (**T1012/03** r.37). Since the question of venue of oral proceedings is a matter of organisational nature belonging to the management of the EPO pursuant to Art.10(2), an examining division is not competent to decide on a request to change the venue and such a request is therefore not allowable (**T1012/03; T1142/12** hn; E-III,2). A calendar of public oral proceedings is available on the EPO website.

Interviews and oral proceedings before an examining division may be held in the form of a video conference (OJ 2012, 354; E-III,11). Note, that the EPO uses a hardware video conferencing system and not a software-based system. During such a video conference, the applicant may file documents by e-mail (OJ2012, 348; **R.2(1):8.1**). A party has no right to have oral proceedings by video conference; high travel cost to Munich to attend oral proceedings before a BoA is no reason for allowing video conferencing (**T2068/14** r.1.3.18).

See **Art.134(1):2** for submissions by accompanying persons during oral proceedings.

2 **Telephone consultation and interview**

A consultation is a formless discussion between an applicant and an examiner or formalities officer and not a kind of oral proceedings; it may speed up a procedure but it is not part of the formal procedure. Moreover, statements of the examiner during a consultation are not binding for the division (C-VII,2.5; **T160/92** r.3.3). The grant of a request for a consultation is a discretionary matter for the examiner (C-VII,2); its refusal is not a procedural violation (**T951/92** r.3(ix)). Consultations during the search stage are usually not permitted (B-II,1.1). Consultations in inter-partes proceedings are usually refused, because of the contentious character of such proceedings (E-III,1). Whereas oral proceedings are always before the complete examining division, a consultation is usually attended only by the primary examiner.

A consultation may be in the form of a face to face interview or a telephone consultation. In the case of a telephone consultation it is advisable to agree on a date of discussion, so both the party and the EPO employee have an opportunity to prepare the case. When in grant proceedings an examiner states what he regards as allowable, it is possible to negotiate towards allowable claims acceptable to the applicant. In this way a satisfactory decision is often reached more quickly than in written proceedings. The EPO draws up minutes of the interview or telephone consultation, places them in the file and sends a copy to the party. (C-VII,2)

3 Conduct of oral proceedings

The EPO summons the parties for oral proceedings at the request of a party or where the EPO considers it expedient (**Art.116(1)**). The invitation may contain an opinion and an indication of points of view of the parties and items to be discussed (E-III,5). Parties attending oral proceedings must take into account the time required for the security inspection of persons entering the premises of the EPO and items they carry (OJ 2017 A6).

The oral proceedings start with a formal part, including identification of the parties (E-III,8.3.1). The substantive part of the proceedings begins with submissions of the parties; in opposition cases first the opponent(s) and then the proprietor (E-III,8.5). Late filed submissions may cause adjournment of the proceedings if it is of crucial importance and the parties cannot reasonably be expected to familiarise themselves in the time available with the new facts or evidence or the proposed amendments (E-III,8.6). Submissions during oral proceedings may be typed or handwritten (E-III,8.5; 8.7; **R.82(2):4**).

The following discussion is intended to clarify facts for the EPO. If the department intends to depart from a previous legal assessment of the situation or from a prevailing legal opinion, or if facts are seen in a different light, causing the case to take a significant turn, the parties should be so informed (E-III,8.9).

After a deliberation, the department closes the oral proceedings by pronouncing the decision or by announcing that the procedure will be continued in writing (E-III,8.11). The reasoning of the decision need not be made at this time; the subsequently notified written decision must contain the reasoning (**R.111**; E-III,9). The decision is usually notified two to six months after the date of the oral proceedings, however, the notification may be more than 20 months after the oral proceedings (see e.g. **T307/03**).

A party desiring to contest a decision taken by a department of first instance in oral proceedings must file the notice of appeal within two months after the date of notification of the decision (**Art.108**), not after the date the decision is delivered in oral proceedings. The form of the decision is determined by **R.111**, while signatures are required by **R.113** and by **R.102** for decisions of the board of appeal. Any fact submitted to the department of first instance after a decision in oral proceedings has been pronounced is not taken into account anymore. Such facts must be put forward in an appeal. If the department considers timely filed facts relevant, it might revise its decision under **Art.109**.

Art. 116(1) Oral proceedings shall take place either at the instance of the European Patent Office if it considers this to be expedient or at the request of any party to the proceedings. However, the European Patent Office may reject a request for further oral proceedings before the same department where the parties and the subject of the proceedings are the same.

1 **Right to oral proceedings**
A request for oral proceedings of a party is not assessed on expediency; exceptions are a further request (**Art.116(1)**) and a request to the Receiving Section (**Art.116(2)**). A first request for oral proceedings may not be refused by the EPO (**T19/87**) subject to **Art.116(2)**. The request must be granted even if filed after the issue of the **R.71(3)** communication but before the termination of the proceedings, which occurs three days prior to the date stamped on the decision (**T556/95** hn r.6). Not granting oral proceedings requested by a party having a right to it is a substantial procedural violation (**T93/88**) that may give rise to reimbursement of the appeal fee under **R.103**; a decision taken after an unjustified refusal to grant oral proceedings must be set aside as null and void (**T556/95** r.7). To avoid unnecessary oral proceedings, a request for it should be filed on condition that the case put forward is not allowed. If the department considers oral proceedings requested by a party as inexpedient, it will consult the requester (E-III,2).

The EPO will in general offer new oral proceedings after a change in composition of an Opposition Division after oral proceedings (**T862/98** hn, r.2.3; **T315/03** r.15.2).

Art. 116(2) Nevertheless, oral proceedings shall take place before the Receiving Section at the request of the applicant only where the Receiving Section considers this to be expedient or where it intends to refuse the European patent application.

1 **Oral proceedings before Receiving Section**
The right to oral proceedings before the Receiving Section is restricted in the interest of procedure economy. Oral proceedings will take place at the request of the applicant if the Receiving Section intends to refuse the application, e.g. if the application is not rectified after invitation to do so (**Art.90(5)**, **R.58**). Oral proceedings will also take place at the request of the applicant if the Receiving Section considers it expedient. Oral proceedings are expedient if they can clarify questions which speed up the procedure; they are not expedient when they only delay without providing clarification, e.g. if a deficiency cannot be corrected. Oral proceedings may be expedient if a loss of rights will occur because of a deficiency of the application, e.g. when during the examination on filing or the examination as to formal requirements the application may be refused under **Art.90(5)**, first sentence, deemed withdrawn under **R.37(2)** or **R.39(2)**; or when the right of priority may be lost (**Art.90(5)**, second sentence), or the missing parts are not regarded as completely contained in the sense of **R.56(3)**.

Art. 116(3) Oral proceedings before the Receiving Section, the Examining Divisions and the Legal Division shall not be public.

Art. 116(4) Oral proceedings, including delivery of the decision, shall be public, as regards the Boards of Appeal and the Enlarged Board of Appeal, after publication of the European patent application, and also before the Opposition Divisions, in so far as the department before which the proceedings are taking place does not decide otherwise in cases where admission of the public could have serious and unjustified disadvantages, in particular for a party to the proceedings.

1 **Publicly accessible proceedings**
Oral proceedings are in principle publicly accessible to allow the public to verify that justice is done. This applies in particular to boards of appeal, which operate like courts. As an exception, oral proceedings as regards the boards of appeal before publication of the application are not public, analogous to **Art.128**.

Oral proceedings before departments of first instance may be public only in proceedings after grant.

2 **Not-publicly accessible proceedings**
According to **Art.116(3)** oral proceedings before the Receiving Section, examining divisions and the Legal Division are not public.

Oral proceedings before the Disciplinary Board of Appeal are in general not public (see e.g. **D20/99**). Oral proceedings relating to partiality are in general not public in view of **R.144(a)** (see e.g. **T190/03**, Summary of facts and submissions VII).

Oral proceedings in opposition proceedings in cases relating to genetically modified products are often not publicly accessible in view of the antipathy the subject-matter arouses in the public.

Art. 117 Means and taking of evidence

See for the implementation:
R.117 Decision on taking of evidence

1 **General**
Many articles and rules of the EPC state that the EPO gives opinions, which a party may prove to be not true. In principle, no absolutely certain proof is required, which is most often not possible either, but a declaration of probability to make the fact credible. If a declaration by the EPO is equivocal, the advantage is for the applicant or the proprietor. The reliability of an item of evidence determines its weight; e.g. an unsigned statement by an unknown and unnamed person has minimal weight (**T750/94** hn.II r.8).

Thus, decisions on evidence brought forward in opposition proceedings must be arrived at on the basis of the overall balance of probability, as distinct from ‘beyond all reasonable doubt’, ‘up to the hilt’ or ‘absolute conviction’. Each of the parties must therefore seek to prove facts alleged by it to that degree of proof. (**T270/90**). However, it is the established practice of the boards of appeal to apply the criterion of ‘absolute conviction’ rather than the ‘balance of probabilities’ in cases of prior public use for which the evidence lies entirely within the sphere of the opponent (**T738/04** r.3.4).

The more serious the issue, e.g. refusal or revocation, the more convincing must be the evidence, for example in a case of alleged prior publication or public prior use (**T750/94** hn.I, **T472/92** hn.I).

Art.117 and **R.117** to **124** set out the procedure for formal taking of evidence. The procedure involves as a first step and as a precondition for its use a decision to take evidence in the sense of **Art.117** (**R.117**); such a decision must set out all matters prescribed in **R.117**. (G4/95 r.8(a))

Art. 117(1) In proceedings before the European Patent Office the means of giving or obtaining evidence shall include the following:
(a) hearing the parties;
(b) requests for information;
(c) production of documents;
(d) hearing witnesses;
(e) opinions by experts;
(f) inspection;
(g) sworn statements in writing.

1 **Departments**
In proceedings before the EPO, the following EPO departments have the power to take evidence: the Receiving Section (see **J20/85**), the examining divisions, the opposition divisions, the legal division, the boards of appeal and the Enlarged Board of Appeal (see also **Art.112a**). (Spec. Ed. 4 of OJ 2007)

Evidence before the Receiving Section may relate to proof of timely payment of fees, proof that **Rfees7(3)** applies for a late payment, use of due care (**Art.122(1)**), requirements for corrections under **R.139** (**J20/85**).

2 **Means of giving evidence**
The list of means of taking evidence is not exhaustive, but shows merely examples. The EPO is not able to force persons to provide information. Hence, if the EPO cannot obtain the information, it may request a national court according to **R.120** to obtain the information under legal force.

The hearing of **Art.117(1)(a)** is to give assertions conclusive force, while the hearing in an oral proceedings is to clarify facts and opinions. The EPO cannot force somebody to be heard.

An example of a request for information under **Art.117(1)(b)** is asking the publisher the date of publication of a book. See e.g. **T750/94**.

Any document is allowed under the production of documents of **Art.117(1)(c)**. The probative value of any such documents depends on the particular circumstances (**T482/89**).

A witness being heard under **Art.117(1)(d)** cannot be party to the proceedings. See **T84/83** for hearing of witnesses about an asserted public prior use. Whether the hearing before a national court is under oath or not depends on the national law.

If a party persists in contesting assertions of a witness made in an unsworn declaration, e.g. on public prior use, a request of the party to hear the witness must, as a rule, be granted before a decision based on these assertions is taken against him. The hearing permits to scrutinize the reliability of the witness testimony. (**T474/04** hn, r.8)

In case the facts to be proven by a witness are no longer relevant, the witness will not be heard (E-IV,1.6.8).

Under **Art.117(1)(e)** the opinion of an expert may be used as evidence. An expert is a person, who based on his expertise, can pronounce empiric theses (Erfahrungssätze), which are normally used to draw conclusions from facts. A person pronouncing facts for the observation of which a special expertise is required, is not an expert, but an expert witness. The opinion of an expert goes in two stages: written advice followed by hearing of the expert. An opinion of an expert without a decision thereto by the EPO is not regarded as an opinion according to **Art.117(1)(e)**, but as an assertion supporting the claim of a party. An opinion is asked if the EPO deems it expedient (**R.117**, first sentence). If a party requests an opinion, the procedure follows **R.117**, second sentence. Other parties can object to the expert (**R.121(4)**). Expert evidence may be useful for determining the common general knowledge; it should not be used for the assessment of inventive step, which requires an act of evaluative judgment outside the competence of an expert (see OJ 2005, 145).

A sworn statement under **Art.117(1)(g)** is known in English as affidavit. It is a written declaration under oath, made before a competent person who takes the oath and indicates the consequences of a false declaration (e.g. up to three year imprisonment in Germany). As the EPC does not contain any indication of the probative value of such a document the principle of free evaluation of evidence applies (**T482/89**). It is not proper to request the filing of statements under oath having a content suggested by a department of the EPO, which involves the risk of leading witnesses and could seriously undermine the probative value of such statements (**T804/92**).

3 **Language of evidence**

The languages of evidence that can be used in written and oral proceedings are given in **R.3(3)**, **R.4(3),(5),(6)**.

When producing documents (**Art.117(1)(c)**) any language can be used, provided a translation in an official language of the EPO is filed on invitation within a period to be specified (**R.3(3)**). The EPO may disregard such a document if no translation has been filed in due time (**R.3(3)**), which an applicant can remedy using further processing (**Art.121** and **R.135**) or a proprietor using re-establishment (**Art.122** and **R.136**).

When hearing parties, witnesses or experts, any language may be used, provided the party requesting the taking of evidence makes provisions for interpretation into an EPO language as permitted under **R.4(3)**.

Statements made during oral proceedings in an official language of the EPO are entered in the minutes of the hearing in that language. Statements made in another language are entered in the official EPO language into which they have been translated (**R.4(6)**).

Art. 117(2) The procedure for taking such evidence shall be laid down in the Implementing Regulations.

See for the implementation:
R.118 Summons to give evidence before the EPO
R.119 Examination of evidence before the EPO
R.120 Hearing by a competent national court
R.121 Commissioning of experts
R.122 Costs of taking of evidence
R.123 Conservation of evidence
R.124 Minutes of oral proceedings and of taking of evidence
E-III Taking and conservation of evidence

Art. 118 Unity of the European patent application or European patent

Where the applicants for or proprietors of a European patent are not the same in respect of different designated Contracting States, they shall be regarded as joint applicants or proprietors for the purposes of proceedings before the European Patent Office. The unity of the application or patent in these proceedings shall not be affected; in particular the text of the application or patent shall be uniform for all designated Contracting States, unless this Convention provides otherwise.

See for the implementation:
R.138 Different claims for different states

1 **Unity of application and patent**

The unity of application, procedure and patent is a basic principle of the EPC: a unitary procedure for the grant of a unitary patent. The principle is not explicitly provided for in the Convention; however, **Art.118** is formulated as a confirmation of the unitary character of the application and patent in a specific case ('the unity ... shall not be affected'), **R.138** allows an exception from unity of application in special cases and the Preamble mentions 'a single procedure'. The principle of uniform patent protection is mentioned in **G1/98** r.3.5.

According to the principle of unity of application, the application will be dealt with in a single procedure and in a single text. **Art.59** allows that an application is filed by joint applicants or two or more applicants designating different states. For the latter case **Art.118** provides that the applicants will be regarded as joint applicants; their Request for Grant is regarded as a single request and not as separate requests by the applicants for the different designated states. Hence, the applicants are forced to act in common. The EPC also provides that there is a single address for correspondence during the grant proceedings by the appointment of a common representative (**R.130** with **R.41(3)** and **R.151**). The requirement of unity also applies to European patents in opposition proceedings, although the opponents need not act in common (**T272/95** r.4.7).

2 **Exceptions from unity**

The 'unless otherwise provided' in **Art.118** allows a deviation from the unity of application or patent, both for a single as well as for multiple applicants. The EPC provides the following exceptions:

1 Applications filed before 13.12.2007, i.e. the date of the EPC 2000 entry into force, follow the EPC 1973 in respect of European prior rights, which are effective only for validly designated contracting states (see **Art.54(3)**:3.1). Hence, such applications may have different claims for different states and, if necessary, also a different description and drawings in the case of European prior rights (**R.87** EPC 1973). The different claims may only be submitted after the EPO has noted the existence of the prior rights.

Under the EPC 2000 European prior rights are effective in all contracting states. Hence, it is not allowed to file different claims for different states for applications filed on or after 13.12.2007 in the case of European prior rights.

2 In the case of national prior rights, different claims may be filed for different states, and, if necessary, also a different description and drawings (**R.138**). The different claims may only be submitted after the EPO has noted the existence of the prior rights.
3 A third party adjudged to be partly entitled to the application may prosecute the application as his own (**Art.61(1)(a)**) and amend the description, drawings and claims or file a new application under **Art.61(1)(b)** for the states for which he is entitled (**R.18(2)**). The same applies in the case of an opposition procedure before the EPO (**Art.99(4)**, **R.78(2)**).
4 An application filed on or before 07.10.1992 in which a state (e.g. Greece or Spain) is designated which has made a reservation under **Art.167(2)(a)** EPC 1973 may have different claims, even at filing. (H-III,4.4)

The claims fee (**R.45**) for an application with multiple sets of claims is calculated only for the set with the highest number of claims (A-III,9). All sets of claims must be translated in the two official EPO languages other than the language of the proceedings under **R.71(3)**.

Art. 119 Notification

Decisions, summonses, notices and communications shall be notified by the European Patent Office of its own motion in accordance with the Implementing Regulations. Notification may, where exceptional circumstances so require, be effected through the intermediary of the central industrial property offices of the Contracting States.

See for the implementation:
R.125 General provisions on notification
R.126 Notification by post
R.127 Notification by technical means of communication
R.128 Notification by delivery by hand
R.129 Public notification
R.130 Notification to representatives

1 **Notification**
Notification is the act by which the addressee is given the opportunity to take notice of a communication sent by the EPO in the way prescribed by the EPC. The notification is of special importance for the calculation of periods under **Art.120**.

R.125 prescribes the permitted means of communication of the EPO with a party. The means that may be used in the reverse communication from the party to the EPO is governed by **R.2**.

2 **Receipt theory**
The EPO uses the receipt theory for its communication with parties. When a party has to file a document, the date of receipt by the EPO is the relevant event for determining whether a time limit has been met (**T702/89** r.2.2; Not. EPO OJ 2005, 44 §5). Similarly, when the EPO despatches a communication from which a time limit is reckoned, the receipt by the party on the date of notification triggers the time limit. In contrast, in the despatch theory the date of despatch is the relevant event.

The EPC does not explicitly state that the receipt theory is used. The use of the receipt theory for despatch from the EPO to a party is clear from **R.131(2)**, last sentence, stating that the event considered for calculating a period is the receipt of the document notified. The use of the receipt theory for mailing from a party to the EPO can only be inferred indirectly from the EPC: provisions for interruption in the mail delivery (**R.133** and **R.134(2)**) do not make sense in a despatch theory; payments also follow in general the receipt theory (**Rfees7(1)**). The five-day fail-safe rule of **R.133** for documents and the ten-day fail-safe rule of **Rfees7(3)** for payments are exceptions where the EPC uses the despatch theory.

3 **Documents to be notified**

The following documents must be notified:

1 Decisions, also if the decision has already been pronounced in oral proceedings (**R.111(1)**); the notification triggers the period for appeal (**Art.108**).
2 Summons, e.g. for oral proceedings (**R.115(1)**) and for taking evidence (**R.118(1)**).
3 Notices and communications triggering a period, e.g.
   a) a communication of the Receiving Section under **R.55** (pointing out failure to comply with the requirements to be accorded a date of filing for an application); **R.56** (correcting missing parts); **R.58** (inviting to rectify deficiencies in the application documents); **R.60** (subsequent identification of the inventor).
   b) The notification of the search report by the search division under **R.65**.
   c) The notices and communications by the examining division under **Art.94** and **R.71**.
   d) The notices and communications by the opposition division under **Art.101** ff and **R.81** ff.
   e) The notices and communications by the board of appeal under **Art.110** and**R.100** ff.
   f) The notification of loss of rights under **R.112(1)** by departments of all instances.
4 Notices and communications required by other provisions of the EPC.
5 Notices and communications required by the President; up to now the President has not prescribed such notifications.

The notification can be made through a national patent authority if in an important case delivery by post is unsuccessful and public notification is not expected to be successful. See **R.125(3)**.

Art. 120 Time limits

The Implementing Regulations shall specify:

(a) the time limits which are to be observed in proceedings before the European Patent Office and are not fixed by this Convention;

(b) the manner of computation of time limits and the conditions under which time limits may be extended;

(c) the minima and maxima for time limits to be determined by the European Patent Office.

See for the implementation:
R.131 Calculation of periods
R.132 Periods specified by the EPO

R.133 Late receipt of documents
R.134 Automatic extension of periods when:
(1) the EPO is closed
(2) general dislocation in the postal delivery or transmission
(3) a national office is closed for receipt of a patent application
(4) publication of period of dislocation
(5) local dislocation in the postal delivery or transmission
R.142 Interruption of proceedings

1 **General**

R.132(1) of the Implementing Regulations specifies the duration of periods not fixed in the Articles or Rules (**Art.120(a)**), **R.131** and **134** the computation and extension of periods (**Art.120(b)**), and **R.132(2)** the minimum and maximum duration of periods to be determined by the EPO (**Art.120(c)**).

2 **Terminology**

A period having a well defined start and end is called a 'period', 'Frist' and 'délai' in the English, German and French version of the EPC, respectively. However, the English version also uses the term 'time limit' for the same notion. This is undesirable from a legal point of view, where terminology should be unequivocal. Moreover, **R.131** defines the calculation of periods, whereas the EPC does not define the calculation of time limits.

Decision **J18/04** r.21, 26 recognized this confusing terminology and decided that the term 'time limit' is an equivalent of 'period' in the EPC 1973. (E-VIII,1.1)

The EPC 2000 has addressed this issue and uses 'time limit' in the more English meaning of 'a fixed point in time beyond which something ceases to be possible or allowable' (Oxford English Dictionary). In the terminology of the EPC 2000 'a time limit is the expiry of a period'. Hence, the legislator has for the sake of consistency replaced the term 'time limit' in the Rules of the EPC 2000 by 'period' wherever possible (Spec. Ed. 1 of OJ 2003, p.159, Introduction). The replacement has no legal consequences (**J19/10** r.7.1). The 'time limit' in **R.50(3)** still used in the meaning of 'period' is probably an oversight.

It should be noted that this correction has not been made in the earlier drafted Articles of the Convention of the EPC 2000. Therefore, the Articles frequently refer to 'time limit' where the corresponding Rules refer to 'period'. In recent amendments of the Rules the legislator appears to have lapsed back into the pre-EPC 2000 terminology, which is still the common terminology within the EPO (see e.g. **R.125(1)**).

3 **Periods**

The periods used in the provisions of the EPC can be divided in two classes.

The first class contains the periods of a legally indicated length fixed for carrying out a particular procedural act (**J24/03** hn.I). In the EPC 1973 such periods were called 'time limits'. Examples are the one-month period for payment of the filing fee and search fee (**R.38**), the two-month period of **R.58** for correcting formal deficiencies in the application, the period to be specified for correcting substantive errors under **R.71(1)**, the 12-month period for claiming priority (**Art.87(1)**), the period for responding to a communication from an examiner (**Art.94(3)**) and the opposition period (**Art.99(1)**). The period is not necessarily equal to the period during which the procedural act may be validly performed. In many cases the EPC allows applicants to perform acts even before the period starts to run (**J18/04** r.30).

The second class contains periods within which a party need not perform an act before the EPO and internal periods of the EPO. Examples are the term of a patent (**Art.63(1)**), the patent years for the payment of renewal fees in **Art.86** (OJ 1984, 272), the eighteen-month period of **Art.93(1)(a)** (see e.g. J32/89 r.3), internal periods as in **Art.109(2)**, the ten-day period of **R.126(2)** and the 'negative' periods of six months in **Art.55(1)** and two and five weeks in **R.67** (see e.g. J32/89 r.3)

Art.120 deals with time limits, i.e. the expiry of periods of the first class. Their triggering and computation are governed by **R.131**. Some periods may be extended upon request under **R.132** and periods will be extended automatically under **R.134(1)-(3)**. **R.133** and **R.134(5)** provide a legal fiction that a late received document may be deemed received in due time. In special cases a period may be interrupted (**R.14(4)**, **R.142(4)**).

Periods calculated from the priority date must be calculated anew from the filing date if the priority claim has been withdrawn before the expiry of the period as calculated from the priority date (A-III,6.11). Failure to observe a period of the first class can be remedied using either further processing or re-establishment. Time limits or periods of the second class are not open for the legal remedies of further processing and re-establishment.

A condition that must be complied with for carrying out an act cannot be equated with a period; for the former the duration is determined by the occurrence of the condition, whereas for the latter the duration is predetermined from the outset. E.g. the filing of a divisional requires compliance with the condition of pendency of the parent application (**R.36(1)**); the last day on which the divisional can be filed, i.e. the last day of pendency of the parent application, is not predetermined from the outset but determined by occurrence of the condition of pendency. Therefore, **R.36(1)** does not impose any time limit for filing a divisional application but rather sets a condition. (J24/03 hn.II, III)

The computation of periods of the second class is not explicitly provided for in the EPC. However, it is generally accepted to apply mutatis mutandis the computation of the periods of the first class as set out in **R.131**; however the extensions under **R.132** and **134** are not applicable.

4 Convention period and office period

The EPC distinguishes two types of periods: convention periods and office periods.

A convention period is a period of which the duration is fixed in the Articles or Rules of the EPC, such as the periods for the payment of filing and search fee (**R.38**), for the filing of the request for examination (**R.70(1)**) and for filing the notice of appeal (**Art.108**). A convention period cannot be extended on request under **R.132**.

An office period is a period the duration of which is not fixed by the EPC but by the EPO in each specific case as set out in **R.132**. Examples are the period for responding to a communication of an examiner under **Art.94(3)** and the period of **R.70(2)** inviting the applicant to indicate whether he desires to proceed further. An office period may be extended on request under **R.132**.

5 Non-observance of period

Possible consequences of not observing a time limit or period:

- The application will not be dealt with as a European patent application (**Art.90(2)**).
- The application is refused or the right of priority is lost (**Art.90(5)**).
- The application is deemed withdrawn (**Art.94(2)**, **94(4)**).
- The patent is revoked (**R.82(3)**).

If non-observance leads to a direct loss of rights, the affected party is notified according to **R.112(1)**.

Art. 121 Further processing of the European patent application

1 **Remedy**
Further processing is the main remedy for non-observance of a time limit vis-à-vis the EPO in the grant procedure and related ex parte appeal proceedings. It allows further processing of the application merely by paying a fee; no written request is necessary. If further processing is possible, re-establishment according to **Art.122** is not possible (**R.136(3)**). Further processing is a reliable remedy. In contrast, re-establishment is not reliable (see **Art.122:1**; Spec. Ed. 4 of OJ 2007, Art.121), because it requires the applicant to prove exercise of all due care. A summary of the requirements for further processing are given in **Art.121(2):1**.

Art. 121(1) If an applicant fails to observe a time limit vis-à-vis the European Patent Office, he may request further processing of the European patent application.

1 **Applicability**
The reference in **Art.121(1)** to 'applicant' restricts the application of further processing to patent applications; patents are excluded. Hence, further processing can be used in grant proceedings and subsequent ex-parte appeal proceedings but not in opposition proceedings.

Since **Art.121(1)** allows only the applicant to request further processing, an applicant to whom the application has been transferred may only request further processing after the transfer has been registered at the EPO (**R.22(3)**).

Further processing is available both for Convention periods, i.e. periods fixed by the EPC, such as the one month period of **R.38** for paying the filing and search fee, and for office periods, i.e. periods fixed by the EPO, such as the period of **R.50(3)** for redressing an unsigned document. Further processing is excluded for the periods mentioned in **Art.121(4)** and **R.135(2)**.

The applicability of further processing does not depend on the sanction on failing a time limit. It is irrelevant whether the sanction is a total loss of rights such as refusal of the application or a partial loss of rights such as loss of a priority claim.

A refusal of an application under **Art.97(2)** cannot be remedied using further processing, because the refusal does not follow a failure to observe a time limit, as required by **Art.121(1)**. A refusal is a consequence of the fact that the application itself does not meet the requirements of the EPC. The only remedy is to appeal the refusal.

2 **PCT**
Further processing can be applied to Euro-PCT applications, in particular to the period for entering the regional phase before the EPO (see **R.160**). When the receiving Office declares in the international phase the application as withdrawn, further processing may be possible before the EPO in connection with the review and excuse procedure (PCT §7.6).

Art. 121(2) The European Patent Office shall grant the request, provided that the requirements laid down in the Implementing Regulations are met. Otherwise, it shall reject the request.

See for the implementation:
R.135(1) Requirements for request
R.135(3) Department competent to decide

1 **Requirements for further processing**
The requirements for an allowable request for further processing as provided in **Art.121** and **R.135** are:

1. The request must be filed by an applicant (**Art.121(1)**). A request filed by any other party, such as a proprietor or an opponent, is not allowable.
2. The request must relate to a failed time limit (**Art.121(1)**). A loss of rights due to any other cause cannot be remedied using further processing.
3. The time limit must be vis-à-vis the EPO (**Art.121(1)**). **Art.121** is not applicable to a time limit vis-à-vis a national office, e.g. for filing a translation of a European patent under **Art.65(1)**.
4. The period is not excluded from further processing under **Art.121(4)** and **R.135(2)**.
5. The fee for further processing must be paid (**R.135(1)**, **Rfees2(1)12**).
6. The omitted act must be completed (**R.135(1)**). The omitted act may relate to a payment, the filing of a document, or both.
7. The payment of the fee and the completion of the omitted act must be carried out within two months from notification of the communication concerning the failed time limit (**R.135(1)**).

More details of the requirements are set out in the cited provisions. The requirements do not include a written request. A failed fee payment can therefore be remedied by merely paying the omitted fee and the fee for further processing.

If the requirements are met, the EPO will grant the request for further processing (**Art.121(2)**). The requirements to be met are merely formal in nature; hence, compliance is simple, making further processing a reliable remedy. The request will be decided on by the department competent to decide on the omitted act (**R.135(3)**).

2 **Rejection of request for further processing**
If the requirements for requesting further processing have not been met, the EPO will reject the request (**Art.121(2)**, second sentence). After rejection of the request or not requesting further processing, the legal consequence of not observing the time limit takes effect at expiry of the unobserved, normal period, not at the end of the two-month period for requesting further processing (the Guidelines apply **G4/98** r.7 mutatis mutandis, see A-III,11.2.3).

Art. 121(3) If the request is granted, the legal consequences of the failure to observe the time limit shall be deemed not to have ensued.

1 **Grant of request for further processing**
If a request for further processing is granted, the European patent application must be treated as if the non-observance of the time limit had not happened and has been pending throughout. If the request is refused, the loss of rights will have occurred on expiry of the relevant period and the application ceased to be pending then (**J4/11** r.22; A-IV,1.1.1).

Art. 121(4) Further processing shall be ruled out in respect of the time limits in Article 87, paragraph 1, Article 108 and Article 112a, paragraph 4, as well as the time limits for requesting further processing or re-establishment of rights. The Implementing Regulations may rule out further processing for other time limits.

Art.87(1) Priority period
Art.108 Periods for filing appeal
Art.112a(4) Periods for filing petition for review
See for the implementation:
R.135(2) Exclusion of other periods from further processing

1 **Periods excluded from further processing**
The EPC excludes several periods from further processing. The more important periods, the non-observance of which affects third parties most, are laid down in **Art.121(4)**. Other periods, mainly relating to periods that have a remedial character, are contained in the easier amendable Rules.

Art.121(4) excludes eight periods from further processing: the priority period under **Art.87(1)**, the two periods for appeal in **Art.108**, the three periods for petition for review in **Art.112a(4)** and the periods for requesting further processing and re-establishment of rights. The first seven periods allow re-establishment (see **Art.122(4):1** and **R.136(3):1** for reasons to allow only re-establishment). A remedy of failing these important periods should be based on specific grounds, as required by re-establishment, and should not be possible by the easy further processing.

The exclusion of the periods for requesting further processing and re-establishment prevents chaining of remedies. Note that further processing is not possible for the period for requesting re-establishment, whereas re-establishment is possible for the period for requesting further processing (see **R.136(3):1**).

Further exceptions to the applicability of further processing have been provided for in **R.135(2)**. This affords the flexibility needed to adapt the scope of application of **Art.121** to changing practical requirements and new periods. It is not the purpose of the second sentence of **Art.121(4)** to enable the scope of application of further processing to be generally restricted. Only if an adequate legal remedy is already provided by the law will it be possible to rule out application of **Art.121.** (MR/24/00)

Art. 122 Re-establishment of rights

1 **Remedy**
The remedy of re-establishment can restore an applicant or proprietor in his rights lost after non-observance of a time limit. The remedy causes true party intention to prevail over procedural certainty about loss of rights; therefore, precise limited circumstances and conditions are defined to avoid legal uncertainty for third parties (**T824/00** r.6). Re-establishment requires that the requester has exercised all due care, which must be proven convincingly. The required proof makes re-establishment an unreliable remedy. This is supported by the fact that the prevention of hardship ensuing from the application of **Art.122** was the whole point of introducing **R.133** and **134** (**J13/05** r.3.2).

The requirements for re-establishment conform to Art.12(1) PLT. This article offers a choice between 'all due care' and 'unintentional delay', the latter requirement being used by the USPTO, because no agreement could be reached on a single requirement. The EPO decided not to use the more party-friendly 'unintentional delay', because they were more familiar with the 'all due care' criterion.

Other provisions to avert the consequences of non-observance of time limits are given in **Art.121** (further processing), **R.51(2)** (additional period for renewal fee), **R.132(2)** (extension of time limit upon request), **R.133** (excuse of late receipt), **R.134** (automatic extension of periods), **R.142** (interruption of proceedings), **Rfees7(3)** (late payment) and **Rfees8** (small amount missing). It is strongly recommended to use, where possible, these remedies instead of re-establishment, because they are reliable for not requiring proof of all due care and do not give rise to third parties rights as in **Art.122(5)**.

Art. 122(1) An applicant for or proprietor of a European patent who, in spite of all due care required by the circumstances having been taken, was unable to observe a time limit vis-à-vis the European Patent Office shall have his rights re-established upon request if the non-observance of this time limit has the direct consequence of causing the refusal of the European patent application or of a request, or the deeming of the application to have been withdrawn, or the revocation of the European patent, or the loss of any other right or means of redress.

1 **Entitled person**

According to the wording of the provision both an applicant and a proprietor may apply for re-establishment. Third parties have been excluded from re-establishment, because they have national remedies available, which are not available to the applicant and proprietor.

Exceptionally, an appellant already known as opponent, who has validly filed a notice of appeal, may request re-establishment of rights for filing the grounds of appeal within the 4 month time limit (**G1/86**). The extension of the applicability is based on the principle of equal treatment of parties to judicial proceedings. The decision **G1/86** must be interpreted narrowly: an appellant known as opponent cannot apply re-establishment to the 2 month time limit for filing an appeal (**T210/89**). If the application has been transferred, the new owner may request re-establishment only after the EPO has received the transfer documents referred to in **R.22(1)**.

Re-establishment can be requested by the applicant of a Euro-PCT application in the transitional phase and the regional phase because of the fiction of **Art.153(2)**. The procedure in the transitional phase is described in PCT §7.6 on the review and excuse procedure. Re-establishment can be used for time limits not excluded under **Art.122(4)** and **R.136(3)**.

2 **Failed time limit**

Re-establishment is only applicable to a loss of rights due to non-observance of a time limit according to **Art.122(1)**. The period defining the time limit must have a starting date and a duration; time restrictions imposed by the EPO but not having these elements are not regarded as time limits for the purposes of **Art.122** (**J18/04** hn.II).

The time limit is defined as the expiry of a period of a legally indicated length fixed for carrying out a particular procedural act. In procedural law, an act to be carried out within a time limit is different from a conditional act, which can only be validly carried out during the circumstances forming the condition; the circumstances are not created to carry out the act, whereas the period of specified duration is created to carry out the act. Hence, as an example, the condition of pendency of the earlier application in **R.36(1)** for filing a divisional application is not a time limit in this sense and therefore not open to re-establishment. Note that these decisions do not use the EPC 2000 definition of 'time limit' as the expiry of a period. (**J24/03**, hn.I, r.4; **J18/04** r.7-11)

Similarly, re-establishment of rights is not possible for failure to be present on the date appointed for oral proceedings (E-VIII, 3.1.1).

No re-establishment is possible in a non-observed time limit that does not give rise to one of the consequences of **Art.122(1)**. An example is the period for the submission of the observations by the proprietor on a statement of another party to the opposition proceedings or on communications from the opposition division (**R.79(1)**). Also excluded are periods to be observed by third parties before the EPO, e.g. by the opponent or intervenor (**Art.99, 105**). As an exception, the 4-month time limit for filing grounds by an opponent in the appeal procedure is not excluded (**G1/86**). The national authorities that must forward the application within 14 months (**Art.77**) are also third parties for whose failures re-establishment does not apply.

Art.122(4) and **R.136(3)** exclude from re-establishment the period for requesting re-establishment and the periods for which further processing is available. Hence, re-establishment is not applicable for most periods in the grant procedure, where further processing is the main remedy.

Re-establishment in the priority period of **Art.87(1)**, implementation of which is required by Art.13 PLT, and the period for filing a petition for review under **Art.112a(4)** is explicitly allowed in **R.136(1)**.

The principle of proportionality, which makes a sanction proportional to the number of days a time limit was missed, cannot be relied on. Although older case law does use the principle, more recent case law holds that only the conduct before expiry of the period is decisive, not the length of the ensuing delay (see **T439/06** r.15).

3 Loss of rights

The loss of rights to be remedied can be any total loss of an application or a patent as expressly stated in the provision. The loss may relate to 'any other right', i.e. a partial loss of rights, such as the right of priority and the right of designating states. The loss may also concern 'any means of redress', such as the right to request further processing.

Art.122(1) requires that the loss of rights must be the 'direct consequence' of the non-observance of a time limit. The 'direct consequence' means that the non-observed time limit must have been a time limit which was explicitly and specifically provided by the EPC for the performance of the procedural act in question (**J18/04** r.12).

Non-observance of the priority period of **Art.87(1)** has the direct consequence of causing the loss of priority, a partial loss of rights, by virtue of **Art.90(5)**. Non-observance of the period for requesting further processing during the grant procedure has the direct consequence of the loss of the right to file such a request under **Art.121(1)**. In opposition non-observance of the time limit for paying the fee for publishing or filing a translation of amended claims has as the direct consequence the revocation of the patent (**R.82(3)**).

Re-establishment is not available for a loss of rights that is not the direct consequence of the non-observance of a time limit. An example of an indirect loss of rights is where the applicant fails the 12-month priority period, resulting in lack of novelty because of intermediate prior art. The refusal of the application cannot be remedied using re-establishment, because it is not a direct consequence of the failure to meet the 12-month priority period. See **J18/04** r.13 for another example.

4 **All due care**

Re-establishment of rights will only be allowed if the party can prove that all due care required by the circumstances has been taken, in other words, that the party has been diligent and careful and the delay was caused by unforeseeable factors; errors of law, however, do not constitute grounds for re-establishment (**D6/82**). All due care usually requires proof that the non-observance was caused by a one-time error in an otherwise properly working system, involving an exhaustive description of the time limit monitoring system employed.

All due care requires the presence of a system for monitoring time limits and, for larger offices, at least one effective cross-check (**T428/98** r.3.5). An isolated procedural mistake of an otherwise properly functioning administration is an admissible ground for re-establishment (**J2/86**).

If a professional representative runs a one-person office, appropriate provisions should be made so that, in the case of an absence through illness, the observance of time limits can be ensured with the help of other persons (**J41/92** r.4.4).

The requirement of all due care by the applicant or proprietor extends to his representative and to the personnel of the representative (**J5/80**). The extent of the due care depends on the person concerned. The representative is responsible for the instruction and supervision of the personnel and the heaviness of the delegated tasks. The personnel must have been selected, trained and supervised properly, and be up to the delegated tasks (**J5/80**); the same applies to temporary personnel.

A culpable error of an assistant is not to be imputed to the representative, if the latter has exercised all due care. The extent of the due care depends on the specific circumstances according to **Art.122(1)**. It always includes the above mentioned instruction and supervision. However, the kind of time limit that needs to be observed and the legal consequences of missing it has also to be taken into consideration. Hence, time limits without further ordinary remedy require more care than other time limits. A representative must therefore verify the calculation of time limits such as those for filing an appeal once the file has been handed over to him. (**T439/06**)

All due care may be proven in the case of natural events and inevitable circumstances (force majeure) (**J18/82** r.11). Workload and long-lasting illness are not sufficient grounds, but a sudden illness is (**T525/91** hn). A human error occurring for the first time, due to pressure and not to negligence, may be regarded as an isolated mistake (**T111/92** r.4). Unexpectedly long delivery times are valid grounds (**T81/83** r.3, see also **T777/98** hn). An incorrect interpretation of the EPC by the party is not a valid ground (**D6/82** hn4). Shortness of money is a valid ground for re-establishment, provided the shortness was due to circumstances beyond the control of the applicant and he has exercised all due care in seeking financial assistance (**J22/88**). Reliance on a courtesy service such as the EPO's reminder for payment of a renewal fee (A-X,5.2.4) is no exercise of due care (**J12/84** hn2).

5 **Examples**

A few examples of cases where re-establishment is possible:

- payment of a renewal fee plus additional fee (**R.51(2)**);
- filing of a priority claiming patent application within the priority period (**Art.87(1)**);
- filing a notice of appeal (**Art.108**);
- filing a translation of an application (**R.6(1)**);
- filing a request for further processing (**Art.121**).

Art. 122(2) The European Patent Office shall grant the request, provided that the conditions of paragraph 1 and any other requirements laid down in the Implementing Regulations are met. Otherwise, it shall reject the request.

See for the implementation:
R.136(1) Requirements for filing request
R.136(2) Grounds and facts, completion of omitted act
R.136(4) Competent department

1 **Requirements for re-establishment**
The requirements for an allowable request for re-establishment as provided in **Art.122** and **R.136** are:
1 The request must be filed by an applicant or proprietor (**Art.122(1)**). A request filed by any other party, such as an opponent, is in principle not allowable. See **Art.122(1):1** for an exception.
2 The request must relate to a failed time limit (**Art.122(1)**). A loss of rights due to any other cause cannot be remedied using re-establishment.
3 The time limit must be vis-à-vis the EPO (**Art.122(1)**). **Art.122** is not applicable to a time limit vis-à-vis a national office, e.g. for filing a translation of a European patent under **Art.65(1)**.
4 The time limit is not excluded from re-establishment under **Art.122(4)** and **R.136(3)**.
5 The written request must be filed and the fee for re-establishment must be paid (**R.136(1), Rfees2(1)13**).
6 The omitted act must be completed (**R.136(2)**). The omitted act may relate to a payment, the filing of a document, or both.
7 The filing of the request, payment of the fee and the completion of the omitted act must be carried out within 2 months from removal of the cause of non-compliance and within one year from expiry of the unobserved period (**R.136(1)**, note the two exceptions therein).

More details of the requirements are set out in the cited provisions. If the requirements are met, the EPO will grant the request for re-establishment (**Art.122(2)**) and the legal consequences of the failure to observe the time limit shall be deemed not to have ensued (**Art.122(3)**).

2 **Rejection of request for re-establishment**
If the requirements for requesting re-establishment have not been met, the EPO will reject the request (**Art.122(2)**, second sentence). The decision will state the grounds for the rejection (**R.111(2)**, E-VIII,3.3).

After rejection of the request or not requesting re-establishment, the legal consequence of not observing the time limit takes effect at expiry of the unobserved, normal period, not at the end of the 2 month period for requesting re-establishment (similar application of the principle set out in A-III,11.2.3 for further processing, applying **G4/98** r.7 mutatis mutandis).

Art. 122(3) If the request is granted, the legal consequences of the failure to observe the time limit shall be deemed not to have ensued.

1 **Grant of request**
Art.122(3) states the principle underlying the re-establishment of rights, i.e. that the consequences of failure to observe a time limit will be deemed not to have ensued where a request for re-establishment of rights is granted.

The grounds of the decision need only be stated in case the request is not granted. However, in opposition proceedings the grounds must always be given, as the opponents are party to the re-establishment proceedings. (E-VIII, 3.3)

Art. 122(4) Re-establishment of rights shall be ruled out in respect of the time limit for requesting re-establishment of rights. The Implementing Regulations may rule out re-establishment for other time limits.

See for the implementation:
R.136(3) Other periods excluded from re-establishment of rights

1 **Periods excluded from re-establishment of rights**
Art.122(4) rules out re-establishment in the period for requesting re-establishment to avoid chaining of remedies.

Other periods are ruled out by **R.136(3)**. Periods excluded from re-establishment for other reasons are given in **Art.122(1):2**.

Art. 122(5) Any person who, in a designated Contracting State, has in good faith used or made effective and serious preparations for using an invention which is the subject of a published European patent application or a European patent in the period between the loss of rights referred to in paragraph 1 and publication in the European Patent Bulletin of the mention of re-establishment of those rights, may without payment continue such use in the course of his business or for the needs thereof.

1 **Right to continue use**
Since the request for re-establishment of rights does not have a suspensive effect on the proceedings, the legal consequences of the failure to meet a time limit will remain in force until re-establishment is allowed. Therefore, any person may use the invention to the extent rights to its subject-matter have been lost.

The right of continued use of an invention after allowance of re-establishment is equivalent to the right of continued use in the case of an incorrect translation according to **Art.70(4)(b)**. The meaning of 'use' is determined by national law. The use must have been made in good faith. Use includes preparations for use. There is no equivalent rule for further processing.

A loss of rights and subsequent re-establishment before the publication of the application, i.e. before provisional protection has commenced, does not give a third party rights to continue use of the invention, because such a right can only arise after the publication of the application and a granted request for re-establishment. (J5/79)

Art. 122(6) Nothing in this Article shall limit the right of a Contracting State to grant re-establishment of rights in respect of time limits provided for in this Convention and to be observed vis-à-vis the authorities of such State.

1 **Re-establishment before national offices**
The EPC contains a few time limits which a party has to observe before a national office, e.g. filing of a translation of the patent (**Art.65**), filing of a request for conversion (**Art.135(2)**), payment of renewal fees for European patents (**Art.141**). **Art.122(1)** restricts the application of re-establishment by the EPO to non-observed time limits vis-à-vis the EPO. **Art.122(6)** allows national authorities to apply re-establishment in the case of non-observance of EPC time limits vis-à-vis national authorities.

Art. 123 Amendments

1 **General**
The right to amend an application as provided in **Art.123** is important for meeting objections of the EPO in grant and opposition proceedings or for implementing a shift in the desired scope of protection. During the grant procedure and a possible opposition procedure a more complete view of the state of the art is obtained, which often necessitates amendment of the text of the application or patent. Amendments usually relate to the claims of an application to meet objections about patentability and clarity and sometimes to the description for removing inconsistencies. An amendment may be an amendment of addition, replacement or deletion.

The first paragraph of **Art.123** restricts amendments in time, the second paragraph limits the extent of amendments of a patent application or a patent and the third adds a further restriction to the extent of amendments of a granted patent.

Art. 123(1) The European patent application or European patent may be amended in proceedings before the European Patent Office, in accordance with the Implementing Regulations. In any event, the applicant shall be given at least one opportunity to amend the application of his own volition.

See for the implementation:
R.137 Opportunities for amendment
R.138 Different claims, description and drawings for different states
R.139 Correction of errors in documents filed with the EPO
R.140 Correction of errors in decisions

1 **Opportunity to amend**
Art.123(1) provides the basic right to amend the application and, where applicable, the patent. The provision makes clear that the conditions under which amendments may be made (**R.137-140**) but also other matters such as the form of the amendments (**R.50(1)**, first sentence) are laid down in the Implementing Regulations. It leaves open the possibility for the Implementing Regulations to limit, under certain circumstances, the right to make amendments to the description. (Spec. Ed. 1 of OJ 2003, p.159)

The right of the applicant to amend at least once of his own volition in the second sentence of the provision and the implementation in **R.137** restricting the right to amend strike a balance between the interest of the applicant and the efficiency of the procedure before the EPO. The applicant will be given a single opportunity at the start of the substantive examination to file voluntary amendments; any further voluntary amendment requires consent of the EPO. This restricts the 'at least one' in **Art.123(1)** to 'only one' except where the EPO admits further voluntary amendments (**R.137(2)** combined with **R.137(3)**).

The exceptional case of an amendment in view of a prior right leading to different claims, descriptions and drawings for different states is governed by **R.138**. Whereas **Art.123** deals with amendments of the application and patent, **R.139** and **140** deal with correction of mistakes in documents filed with the EPO and decisions of the EPO, bringing them back in the form as intended at the time of filing or issue. See **R.139:1** for a discussion of the relation between amendment and correction.

Art. 123(2) The European patent application or European patent may not be amended in such a way that it contains subject-matter which extends beyond the content of the application as filed.

1 **Extension of subject-matter**

The underlying idea of **Art.123(2)** is that an applicant shall not be allowed to improve his position by adding subject-matter not disclosed in the application as filed, which would give him an unwarranted advantage and could be damaging to the legal security of third parties relying on the content of the original application (**G1/93** r.9).

The applicant does not have the benefit of the doubt in matters of **Art.123(2)**. Where the content of the application relating to a requested amendment is essentially speculative, the amendment is not allowable. (**T400/94**)

A reformulation of a phrase in an application is in principle allowable but is not recommended because of the inherent danger of extension of subject-matter. Reformulation should only be used to remove inconsistencies from the application.

Note, that the terms 'disclosed in' and 'having a basis in' are used for **Art.123(2)** and **R.137(4)** and the terms 'having support in' and 'supported by' for **Art.84** (see also **G2/10** r.3.7).

1.1 CONTENT OF THE APPLICATION AS FILED

Whether an amendment extends the subject-matter must be assessed with respect to the content only of the application as filed. This content does not include the abstract (consequence of **Art.85**; **T246/86**) and the content of priority documents, even when filed together with the application (**T260/85**). Thus, it is not permissible to amend an application by adding matter which is only present in a priority document.

Since the title of the application is not mentioned in **Art.78(1)**, it is not part of the content of the application (H-V,8).

As an exception, missing drawings and missing parts of the description may be taken from a priority document and inserted in the application as filed without re-dating of the application, provided the conditions of **R.56(3)** are complied with. This possibility is only available at the filing stage of the application and cannot be applied at later stages. (H-IV,2.2.2)

Amendment of the divisional application after its filing is subject to the restrictions of **Art.123(2)** with respect to the divisional application as filed (not with respect to the parent application as filed) (**T441/92** r.4.2).

If the application is filed in a non-EPO language, the original text in that language constitutes the basis for determining the extension and not the translation filed under **Art.14(2)** (**Art.70(2)**). The EPO assumes that the translation conforms to the original text, except if proven to the contrary, e.g. by an opponent (**R.7**). (A-VII,7)

For a Euro-PCT application the application 'as originally filed' is the PCT application as originally filed (B-VIII,6).

Features only described in a cross-referenced document are prima facie not part of the content of the application. The conditions under which they may be introduced into the application are given in **Art.83:2.1.2.**

1.2 DISCLOSURE TEST FOR EXTENSION OF SUBJECT MATTER

The EPO uses the so-called disclosure test for determining whether an amendment extends the subject-matter beyond the content of the application as filed: an amendment is not allowable if the overall change in content of the application results in the skilled person being presented with information which is not directly and unambiguously derivable, seen objectively and relative to the date of filing, from the whole content of the application as filed, even when account is taken of matter which is implicit to a person skilled in the art using common general knowledge (**G3/89** r.2; **G2/10** r.4.3; H-IV,2.2).

A disclosure may be explicit or implicit. An implicit disclosure is a clear and unambiguous consequence of what is explicitly disclosed. Hence, a literal basis for an amendment is not required by the wording of **Art.123(2)** (**T667/08** r.4.1.4). An implicit disclosure is technical matter of the application that is not explicitly mentioned in the application but is clearly and unambiguously derivable by the skilled person from matter explicitly mentioned in the application. Common general knowledge is taken into account in deciding what is clearly and unambiguously implied by the explicit disclosure of the application. An implicit disclosure is *not* technical matter that the disclosure of the application renders obvious for the skilled person in view of the common general knowledge; such technical matter does not belong to the disclosure of the application and is relevant for the assessment of inventive step. (**T823/96** r.4.5)

The Guidelines emphasise that a patent application is directed to a technical audience and its disclosure is what it teaches a skilled person, without a disproportionate focus on the structure of the claims. (H-IV,2.3; **T2619/11** & **T1363/12** hn)

The disclosure test is the generally accepted test for any amendment (**G2/10** r.4.3). The test is also used for extension of subject-matter in the ground of opposition **Art.100(c)** (**G1/93** hn.I, **G2/10** r.4.3), for identity of invention when claiming priority (**G2/98** r.9), for extension of subject-matter of a divisional application (**G1/06** r.5.1 and **G2/10** r.4.3) and for correction under **R.139**, second sentence (**G3/89** hn.I). The uniform application of the disclosure test preserves the structural relationship established in the EPC, based on the first-to-file system, between the provisions defining the prior art and their impact on patentability, the substantive requirements for validly claiming priority or for filing divisional applications and for the right to amend the application (**G2/10** r.4.6).

The Enlarged Board of Appeal has allowed a departure from the disclosure test only for two specific amendments of a claim, where addition of an undisclosed feature is necessary to exclude subject-matter for legal reasons and where the feature does not provide a technical contribution to the claimed invention (**G2/10** r.4.3). Firstly, an amendment of a claim for escaping from the **Art.123(2)-(3)** trap may be based not only on a disclosed feature complying with the disclosure test but also on an undisclosed feature that does not provide a technical contribution to the invention (**G1/93** hn.II, r.16). Secondly, an undisclosed disclaimer may be added to a claim under specific conditions (**G1/03** r.2).

The above specific amendments depart from the disclosure test. Since the added undisclosed feature and undisclosed disclaimer are technical features, and the validity of a priority claim is assessed strictly using the disclosure test, both specific amendments will probably affect the right to priority of a claim (see **Art.123(2):2.4.4**).

The novelty test, according to which an amendment complies with **Art.123(2)** if it does not generate novel subject-matter, is no longer used (Case Law of the BoA, II.E.1.7.3).

An amendment introducing a new range based on the lower limit of a broad range and the lower limit of an enclosed narrow, preferred range meets the disclosure test (**T1170/02** r.4.5; however, see **G2/10** r.4.5.3). The feature on which the amendment is based, for example in a drawing, must not be accidental but be disclosed as a deliberate measure directed to the solution of the technical problem (**T398/00** r.3.4; H-V,6). If the description discloses a genus, a species is part of the content of the application as filed if the skilled reader would seriously contemplate such species as a possible practical embodiment of the invention, having regard to its context in the remainder of the application as filed, and subject to any understanding of the skilled reader to the contrary (**T187/91**).

2 Amendment of the claims

2.1 DELETION OF A FEATURE

The deletion of a feature in a claim is allowable and required, if it clarifies the claim and removes an inconsistency (**T172/82**). A specific feature may not be replaced by an encompassing, general expression, when such an expression introduces special features for the first time (**T416/86**). It is not allowed to delete features from an independent claim that are presented as essential in the description (**T260/85**). A feature described in the application as optional and which later-on has become essential to delimit the invention from prior art found after the filing date, may be introduced into a claim, provided that the resulting combination of features still corresponds to the teaching of the application (**T583/93** r.4.5). In general, introduction into a claim of a feature described as non-essential is not ruled out by **Art.123(2)** (**T583/93** hn.II).

Extending the scope of a claim by deleting a technical feature is allowed, if the description contains at least one embodiment without this feature, whether or not the feature is relevant for the invention; it suffices if the embodiment is only shown in the drawings in a manner clear and unequivocal for the skilled person (**T66/85**). **T331/87** developed a three-point essentiality test for the allowability of the replacement or deletion of a feature from a claim: a skilled person would directly and unambiguously recognize that

1 the feature was not explained as essential in the originally filed disclosure,
2 the skilled person would directly and unambiguously recognise that it is not, as such, indispensable for the function of the invention in the light of the technical problem it serves to solve, and
3 the skilled person would directly and unambiguously recognise that the replacement or removal requires no modification of one or more of the features to compensate for the change, i.e. it does not in itself alter the invention (followed in H-V,3.1; see also **Art.76(1):9**).

In some situations the application of the three-point test may not be appropriate (**T1118/10**; **T2311/10**) and **T1852/13** even recommends to replace the three-point test by the disclosure test. The two tests will give different results in many situations. In contrast, the Guidelines require that the amendment complies with both tests (H-V,3.1).

The removal from a claim of a feature which 'does not provide a technical contribution to the subject-matter of the claimed invention' within the meaning of **G1/93** and the removal of which broadens the protection of the claim, does not contravene **Art.123(2)** (**T802/92**, ohmic contacts on a photovoltaic cell, all embodiments showing the contacts). The latter decision reduces the proper regard to the wording of the claims in favour of an increased emphasis on the general inventive concept and might not be tenable in view of **G2/98** (see also Protocol on **Art.69**).

Whether deletion or limitation of a claim is regarded as substantive abandonment of the relevant subject-matter without possibility of reinstatement or for use in a divisional application depends on the circumstances and wording of the request for amendment (**J15/85**; **G1/05b**; **G1/06**). An express and unambiguous abandonment of a claim and the relevant parts of the description is a substantive abandonment (**T61/85**). A declaration of abandonment must be interpreted taking into account all the circumstances: if the party's real intention is to meet an objection and not a substantive abandonment, reinstatement of a claim is permitted without violating legal security of third parties (**T910/92**).

2.2 REPLACEMENT OF A FEATURE

The above (Art.123(2):2.1) three-point test also applies to replacement of a feature in a claim.

A generalisation in the form of an amendment which replaces a disclosed specific feature either by its undisclosed function or by a more general undisclosed term and thus incorporates undisclosed equivalents into the content of the application as filed is not allowable under **Art.123(2)** (**T416/86**; **T284/94** r.2.1.6; established case law). In general, a species may not be replaced by a genus as such an amendment contravenes the disclosure test. However, a specific expression in a claim which does not suitably describe a feature present in the cited state of the art and in the invention may be replaced by a more general expression which gives a better description, without extending the subject-matter (**T52/82**).

Claims originally directed to a general notion or a wide range may be amended to reduce the scope. The new claim should not be novel in regard of the application as filed. A genus may not be replaced by a species if this species is not disclosed in the application as filed. See **Art.54(1):6** on selection inventions and the notes below on disclaimers.

Amendment of an incorrect chemical formula of a substance to a correct one is not allowed, even if the substance is the inevitable unambiguous result of a method completely disclosed in the application (**T552/91**).

An error in a claim or description caused by a wrong calculation, which correction is not obvious, may be corrected according to **Art.123(2)** if the amendment follows unequivocally for a skilled reader from the application as filed. If there are more correction possibilities, that one must be chosen which is closest to the application in its entirety. (**T13/83**)

See **Art.123(3):2** for amendments changing the category of a claim.

2.3 ADDITION OF A FEATURE

A technical feature from an embodiment of the description or drawings may be added to a claim. However, adding a feature derived from a measurement in a drawing is not allowed in general. See **Art.83:2.1.2** for adding a feature from a cross-referenced document.

When a feature taken in isolation from an embodiment in the description is added to a claim as filed, the amended claim forms an intermediate generalisation, i.e. a generalisation of the embodiment intermediate the claim as filed and the embodiment. Such an intermediate generalisation does not extend beyond the subject-matter of the application as filed if the feature is not related or inextricably linked to the other features of the embodiment and the overall disclosure justifies the generalising isolation of the feature and its introduction into the claim. The amended claim should not be a particular combination created artificially from individual features pertaining to separate embodiments; the application is not a reservoir from which any features can be combined. (H-V,3.2.1)

An intermediate generalisation reducing the scope of a claim does not contravene **Art.123(2)** if the new combination of features solves a problem unambiguously derivable from the application in isolation from any other element of the embodiment not included in the claim (**T17/86**; followed by **T284/94** hnI; **T470/05** r.2.4; established case law).

Examples of intermediate generalisation are given in H-V,3.2.1.

It should be noted, that rejection of a claim under **Art.123(2)** because of inadmissible intermediate generalisation has no strong legal basis in the EPC. It makes the clear concept of extension of subject-matter dependent on the definition of the problem, which may change in time (see also **G2/98** r.8.3). **Art.123(2)** is not related to the problem-solution approach of **Art.56** but relates to extension of disclosed subject-matter. When the set of features in a claim including features added in isolation from an embodiment in the description is disclosed in said embodiment, the selection should, according to **Art.123(2)**, be regarded as not extending beyond the application as filed, whether or not the set of features solves a specific problem. Hence, if a claim contains an arbitrary selection of features from a specific disclosed context caused by adding an isolated feature from that context to the claim, which selection does not serve any meaningful technical purpose, the requirements of **Art.123(2)** should be regarded as being complied with, and in the subsequent assessment of inventive step the lack of technical purpose should result in rejection of the claim under **Art.56**.

2.4 ADDITION OF A DISCLAIMER

A claim may be amended by inserting a disclaimer into a claim. A disclaimer is a negative technical feature that excludes specific subject-matter from the scope of the claim. The excluded subject-matter may be one or more specific embodiments, a subgroup or an area. Since a disclaimer can be present in a claim of an application as filed and be added as an amendment during prosecution, a disclaimer should not be defined as a specific type of amendment as in **G2/10** r.2.2, which definition is not consistent with r.2.1 of the decision either.

The amended claim including the disclaimer must meet the requirements of the EPC. The insertion of a disclaimer in a claim must comply with the clarity requirement of **Art.84**; it may be allowed if the subject-matter cannot be defined more clearly and concisely in terms of positive features (see F-IV,4.20 and **Art.84:1.7**). The excluded subject-matter cannot be taken into account for the assessment of clarity, conciseness and support (**Art.84**), sufficiency of disclosure (**Art.83**) and inventive step (**Art.56**). In respect of inventive step the question becomes relevant whether the problem has been solved over the whole breadth of the claim or whether an advantageous effect obtained by the remaining subject-matter can be deduced from the application as filed. (**G1/03** hn.II.4; **G2/10** r.4.5.5)

The allowability of an amendment inserting a disclaimer depends on whether or not the disclaimer or the subject-matter excluded by it has a basis in the application as filed. The following three cases can be distinguished:

- A 'disclosed disclaimer', in which the negative feature is disclosed in the application as filed. For example, the disclaimer is 'not A', and 'not A' is disclosed.
- A 'disclaimer excluding disclosed subject-matter', where the subject-matter of the disclaimer is disclosed as a positive feature but the disclaimer as such is not disclosed. For example, the disclaimer is 'not A', and 'A' is disclosed but 'not A' is not disclosed.
- An 'undisclosed disclaimer', where neither the disclaimer nor the excluded subject matter is disclosed. For example, the disclaimer is 'not A', and neither 'A' nor 'not A' are disclosed.

2.4.1 Disclosed disclaimer

A disclaimer based on a negative feature disclosed in the application as filed may be inserted in a claim by way of amendment. The negative feature may be disclosed in an explicit way (**T245/91** r.3.2; **T255/91** r.2.1.7) or in an implicit way (**T278/88** r.3; **T170/87** r.8.3). An originally disclosed feature defined in negative terms may also be used as a disclaimer (see e.g. **T154/06**).

2.4.2 Disclaimer excluding disclosed subject-matter

Subject-matter originally disclosed in the application as a positive feature of the invention may be excluded from the scope of a claim by inserting a disclaimer in the claim. The applicant is free to determine the scope of protection by including or excluding specific subject-matter in the claims. The EPC does not oblige him to seek the broadest possible protection offered by the disclosure, nor to include a preferred embodiment in the scope of the claims. Note, that an embodiment presented as belonging to the prior art or as a comparative example may not be claimed at all.

A legitimate reason to choose a narrow scope is an interest in a quick grant of a preferred embodiment and a prolonged prosecution of the general teaching in a divisional application, possibly with a disclaimer for the preferred embodiment. Licensing could be another reason for splitting an application. (**G2/10** r.4.5.5, overturning **T1102/00**)

The insertion of a disclaimer excluding disclosed subject-matter may not violate **Art.123(2)** by adding subject-matter and, like any amendment of an application or patent, must pass the disclosure test. Since the disclaimer does not as such define a feature of the claimed invention, the test must be applied to the subject-matter remaining in the claim after amendment. Hence, the inclusion of the disclaimer infringes **Art.123(2)** if the remaining subject-matter presents the skilled person with technical information which is not directly and unambiguously derivable from the application as filed, the information being explicitly or implicitly disclosed for a skilled person using common general knowledge. (**G2/10** hn.1a, r.4.5.2; confirming **T4/80** and **T1107/06**)

The test requires an assessment of the relationship of the excluded subject-matter and the remaining subject-matter. The remaining subject-matter will normally not be modified by a disclaimer excluding one specific embodiment from an invention disclosed in general terms including different embodiments. However, insertion of a disclaimer that confines the remaining subject-matter to a subgroup or intermediate generalisation that is not disclosed in the application as filed, or singles out any hitherto not disclosed individual compound or group of compounds, or leads to a particular not disclosed meaning of the remaining subject-matter contravenes **Art.123(2)**. (**G2/10** hn.1b, r.4.5.4, following **T615/95** hn.1)

Note, that the so-called rules of logic: if the application discloses an embodiment or smaller region B within a broad region A, the logical complement or remaining subject-matter A-B is logically and inevitably disclosed, do not apply for determining disclosure of the remaining subject-matter. As a consequence, a claim to A disclaiming B does not inevitably comply with **Art.123(2)**. On the other hand, a reasoning solely suggesting that the introduction of the disclaimer modifies the subject-matter would be insufficient to motivate an objection under **Art.123(2)**. (**G2/10** r.4.5.3)

The requirements set out in **G1/03** are only applicable to an undisclosed disclaimer and not to a disclaimer excluding disclosed subject-matter (**G2/10** r.3; overturning **T1050/99**, **T1102/00**, **T868/04**, **T795/05** and **T1559/05**). If the remaining subject-matter after insertion of a disclaimer excluding disclosed subject matter extends the subject-matter of the application as filed, the insertion is not allowable; the strict requirements of **G1/03** should not be applied for determining the allowability of the insertion (**G2/10** r.4.7).

2.4.3 *Undisclosed disclaimer, allowability*

In specific cases an undisclosed disclaimer, where neither the disclaimer per se nor the excluded subject matter is disclosed in the application as filed, may be inserted in a claim by way of amendment under **Art.123(2)**. The allowability of such undisclosed disclaimers has been analysed in **G1/03** using the test for extension of subject matter developed in **G1/93** (see also H-V,4). The EBoA concluded that an amendment to a claim by the insertion of a disclaimer may not be refused under **Art.123(2)** for the sole reason that neither the disclaimer nor the subject-matter excluded by it from the scope of the claim have a basis in the application as filed (**G1/03** hn.I, case consolidated with **G2/03**).

The decision **G1/03** analyses the use of a disclaimer in the following cases, confirmed by **G1/16**.

1 A claim is not novel over prior art under **Art.54(3)**. An undisclosed disclaimer may be used for establishing novelty over a prior right. The purpose of **Art.54(3)** is to avoid double patenting. A delimitation of a claim from an earlier application by means of a disclaimer achieves this purpose by splitting the subject-matter of an invention in two parts: a part identical with the first application, the right to which is preserved for the first applicant, and the rest, disclosed for the first time in the second application, for the applicant of the second application. Such a disclaimer excludes subject-matter for legal reasons and has no bearing on the technical information in the application. Its insertion is therefore not in contradiction to **Art.123(2)**. (**G1/03** hn.II.1 and r.2.1, **G1/16** r.37 and r.45)

2 A claim is not novel over an accidental anticipation under **Art.54(2)**. An undisclosed disclaimer may be inserted into the claim to restore novelty over such an anticipation.

An anticipation is accidental if it is so unrelated to and remote from the claimed invention that the person skilled in the art would never have taken it into consideration when working on the invention. Accidental anticipation often occurs in the fields of chemistry and biotechnology. For example, a claim relates to a large group of chemical compounds with certain properties which are advantageous for a specific use. Prior art disclosing a single compound falling within the group but for a completely different use and, therefore, only properties irrelevant to the new use constitutes an accidental anticipation. It would be unfair if such a disclosure represented a bar to patenting the entire group in the absence of a basis for a disclaimer of the known compound in the application as filed. Since an accidental anticipation has nothing to do with the teaching of the claimed invention, a disclaimer excluding the subject-matter of the anticipation does not change the technical information relating to the invention and therefore does not contravene **Art.123(2)**. (**G1/03** hn.II.1 and r.2.2, **G1/16** r.37 and r.45)

3 A claim is not novel in view of an anticipation under **Art.54(2)** that is not accidental. The Enlarged Board of Appeal ruled that an undisclosed disclaimer may not be used to make the claim novel in such a case. The prohibition avoids the unrestricted use of disclaimers. An applicant could otherwise wait for the state of the art revealed by the EPO and tailor the patent around it using disclaimers, thereby reducing the importance of a detailed description, e.g. by claiming a broad class of compounds with yet unknown properties, disclaiming those which turn out to be known and test the rest for advantageous properties to be used in the inventive step arguments. (**G1/03** r.2.3)

4 A claim includes subject-matter excluded from patentability, e.g. inventions the exploitation of which is contrary to 'ordre public' or morality under **Art.53(a)** or methods for medical treatment under **Art.53(c)**. An undisclosed disclaimer may be used to exclude this subject-matter. Since the disclaimer is not related to the technical teaching of the invention and merely excludes subject-matter its insertion is allowable. An example of such a disclaimer is the exclusion of human beings in a claim related to a method for avoiding economically undesirable offspring. (**G1/03** hn.II.1, r.2.4; **G1/16** r.37 and r.45)

5 A claim covers non-working embodiments. A disclaimer may not be used to excise non-disclosed non-working embodiments. If there is a large number of conceivable alternatives and the disclosure provides criteria to find appropriate alternatives with reasonable effort, the inclusion of non-working embodiments in a claim is of no harm (see **T238/88**, **T292/85** and **T301/87**). Therefore, a disclaimer is neither necessary nor appropriate. If this is not the case and the claimed invention lacks reproducibility, there are two possibilities. First, if the claim expresses an effect, there is lack of sufficient disclosure. A lack of disclosure cannot be remedied during proceedings before the EPO (**T170/87** and **T313/86** not to be followed). Secondly, if the claim does not express the effect, but the effect is part of the problem to be solved, there is lack of inventive step (see **T939/92**). A disclaimer cannot help in supporting inventive step. (**G1/03** r.2.5; see also **G2/10** r.3.5-9; F-III,5.1)

If a limitation of a claim by an undisclosed disclaimer later turns out to be of technical relevance (**T323/97** r.3), it does contribute technical teaching and adds technical subject-matter within the meaning of **Art.123(2)**; hence, the disclaimer must be considered inadmissible ex post (**G1/03** hn.II.3, r.2.6). Addition of an undisclosed disclaimer having effects which go beyond the purpose set out in the above points 1, 2 or 4 is not allowable (**G1/03** r.2.6.5). The evaluation of inventive step has to be carried out disregarding the undisclosed disclaimer. In this way, any unallowable modification of the original technical teaching in the assessment of inventive step is avoided (**G1/16** r.46.4).

Even though G2/10 r.4.5.1 states that all amendments must comply with the disclosure test (the 'golden standard'), G1/16 decided that the disclosure test should not be applied to an amendment that introduces an undisclosed disclaimer, even though such an amendment does introduce technical subject-matter. Instead, an undisclosed disclaimer must comply with the above criteria of G1/03. Additionally, an undisclosed disclaimer may not change the identity of the invention as originally filed, and it may not become relevant for the assessment of inventive step or for the question of sufficiency of disclosure. (G1/16 hn, r.42, 44, 47)

2.4.4 *Undisclosed disclaimer, formal issues*

An undisclosed disclaimer must comply with the following two requirements. Firstly, the disclaimer should not remove more than is necessary either to restore novelty or to disclaim subject-matter excluded from patentability for non-technical reasons (G1/03 hn.II.2). The insertion of a necessary disclaimer is not on opportunity for the applicant to reshape his claims arbitrarily. To keep the patent transparent, the specification should mention the presence of an undisclosed disclaimer and the reason for its insertion. (G1/03 r.3)

Secondly, the subject-matter remaining in the claim must be disclosed in the application as filed to comply with **Art.123(2)**. This requirement has been added by **G2/10** r.4.7 as interpreted by **T1870/08** hn and **T2464/10** hn (see also H-V,4.1). See the above section **2.4.2** for a discussion of the requirement.

The first requirement may be difficult to comply with where the prior art discloses the subject-matter to be disclaimed in several, possibly speculative or insufficiently disclosed variants; if the disclaimer is too narrow, the claim is not novel; if the disclaimer is too broad, the added matter violates **Art.123(2)**. The first and second requirement together may make it impossible to define an undisclosed disclaimer. According to **T2130/11** hn it is allowed to remove more than strictly necessary to restore novelty, without arbitrary reshaping the claim, in order to satisfy the clarity requirement of **Art.84**. A safer solution may be not to use an undisclosed disclaimer but to define the claim in terms of sub-ranges or groups disclosed in the application, which may result in a smaller scope but does not suffer from the problems of the undisclosed disclaimer.

The requirements on the undisclosed disclaimer tend to make the claim complex. However, the claim must remain clear under **Art.84**. These requirements are often incompatible, making it impossible to include an undisclosed disclaimer. The solution is again to define the claim in sub-ranges or groups disclosed in the application. See **T2130/11** as an example.

Inserting a disclaimer not disclosed in the application as filed nor in a novelty-destroying prior art document contravenes **Art.123(2)** (**T596/96** r.2; **T597/92** r.3).

G1/03 r.4, referring to **G2/98**, holds that the insertion of an undisclosed disclaimer not providing a technical contribution to the invention, which is allowable during the prosecution, does not change the identity of the invention within the meaning of **Art.87(1)**, and, therefore, does not affect the right to priority from a first application not containing the disclaimer.

Note, that this conclusion could be regarded as dubious. **G2/98** r.9 requires that even technical features which are not related to the function and effect of the invention must be taken into account for assessing the validity of a priority claim. Hence, an undisclosed disclaimer should be taken into account. Moreover, a disclaimer is a technical feature that inevitably provides a technical contribution to the invention, the invention being the subject-matter of the claim as defined in **G2/98** hn.

G1/03 r.2 also holds, that a feature without a technical meaning would not restrict the scope of a claim. Since an undisclosed disclaimer does restrict the scope and thereby the technical content of a claim, the undisclosed disclaimer is not a feature without technical meaning. In a later decision, **G2/10** r.4.3, the EBoA states that the disclosure test (see **Art.123(2):1.2**) must be applied to any amendment without exception and irrespective of the context of the amendment made. **G2/10** appears not to leave room for the exceptions of **G1/03**, and, as a consequence, the introduction of technical content in a claim in the form of an undisclosed disclaimer should comply with the disclosure test (**T437/14** r.8.1.3). Application of the disclosure test would make most undisclosed disclaimers not allowable, because a disclaimer excluding undisclosed subject-matter almost by definition contravenes **Art.123(2)** (**T437/14** r.8.1). Different decisions of BsoA since **G2/10** have applied different standards for **Art.123(2)** relating to undisclosed disclaimers. **T437/14** has referred the question of applicability of the disclosure test to undisclosed disclaimers to the EBoA, pending under **G1/16**.

3 Amendment of the description

Important amendments of the description are the reformulation of the problem (**T184/82**) and the compulsory completion of the state of the art (**T11/82**).

A closer prior art may be incorporated in the description; such an amendment may only consist of features that follow directly and unequivocally from the prior art (**T11/82** r.20-22). However, if the incorporation of the reference to the prior art expressly or implicitly extends the subject-matter for which protection is sought, then **Art.123(2)** will be contravened (**T11/82** r.23; F-II,4.3; H-IV,2.1). A reformulation of the problem and solution, also part of the content of the application, is allowed if the man skilled in the art can derive it from the state of the art (**T13/84**). The reformulation necessary in view of a closer state of the art is also allowed during appeal proceedings; the board of appeal may apply the same provisions as the examining division (**R.100(1)**, **T1/80**).

A claim which does not include a feature which is described in the description as essential, is not supported by the description according to **Art.84**. An amendment of the description making the feature unessential is not allowed, because it extends the subject-matter of the application. (**T133/85**)

Common general knowledge or what is implied by the description may indicate that a described feature not mentioned in an independent claim is essential for the invention. The EPO will request insertion of the feature into the claim. However, the applicant or proprietor may retain the unamended claim if he convinces the EPO that the feature is in fact not essential. (F-IV,4.3(ii))

An additional explanation of the functioning of a sufficiently disclosed technical feature is allowed if the functioning could be derived from the original application by a skilled person (**T37/82**).

A clarification of a technical effect of a feature may be added without contravening **Art.123(2)**, provided the effect can be deduced without difficulty by a person skilled in the art from the application as filed (H-V,2.1).

Later filed embodiments to show the validity of a broad claim are carefully assessed by the examining division for extension of the subject-matter, because the embodiments could provide indications for the skilled person which were not evident from the original application, even when taking into account subject-matter not expressly mentioned but read into it by the skilled person (H-V,2.2).

The same applies to the inclusion of additional advantages in support of inventive step, e.g. an advantage of a fluid for cleaning wool products stated in the description cannot be supplemented by the not-mentioned advantage of moth-proofing. Such later filed examples or new effects, even if not allowed into the application, may under circumstances be taken into account by the examiner as evidence in support of the patentability of the claimed invention (H-V,2.2).

Such supplementary technical information is put in the file, and becomes public together with the other contents of the file. This additional information submitted after the application was filed and not included in the specification is pointed out to the public by a notice on the front page of the patent specification (H-V,2.3).

Art. 123(3) The European patent may not be amended in such a way as to extend the protection it confers.

1 Prohibition to extend protection during opposition

According to **Art.123(3)**, the European patent as a whole (i.e. the claims, description and drawings, if any) may not be amended in such a way as to extend the protection it confers (see **T1149/97**). This principle is applicable in all proceedings before the EPO, including limitation proceedings, as well as in national proceedings. (Spec. Ed. 4 of OJ 2007)

The provision gives legal security to the public: the protection of the patent as granted shall not be extended in opposition proceedings. An amendment extending the protection will be declared inadmissible, because the amendment does not comply with **Art.123(3)**. Extension of the protection is a ground for revocation in national revocation procedure (**Art.138(1)(d)**).

The provision applies both to amendments of granted claims as well as to adding new claims. The scope is also determined by the content of the description (Protocol on the interpretation of **Art.69**). Hence, changes in the description must also be checked when assessing compliance with **Art.123(3)** (**T1149/97** hn.II; **T142/05** hn). Reinstatement in the patent of subject-matter deleted from the application or indicated as no longer relating to the invention before the grant, is as a rule not admissible under **Art.123(3)**; the grant has a cut-off effect, in that it reduces the original disclosure to the subject-matter relating to the invention and retained in the patent specification (**T1149/97** hn.III).

It is allowed to amend a granted claim so as to replace an inaccurate technical statement, which is evidently inconsistent with the total of the disclosure of the patent, by an accurate statement of the technical features involved. (**T108/91**)

A limitation of a claim by restricting the number of components of a composition may have the undesired effect of extending the protection it confers. For example, the claim as granted defines 'a composition having 1-10% halogens by weight'. When the claim is limited in opposition proceedings to '1-10% halogens by weight, the halogens being chlorine', the amount of fluorine is no longer defined and may be more than 10%, which is an unallowable extension of the protection. (H-IV,3.4; GL2017 H-IV,3.5; **T2017/07** hn)

2 Change of claim category

A change of category of a claim by way of amendment after a patent has been granted will be allowed in exceptional cases only (**T378/86** hn.I) and on condition that the amendment is necessitated by a ground of opposition (**R.80**). Such a change in claim category is not open to objection under **Art.123(3)**, if it does not result in extension of the protection conferred by the claim (**G2/88** hn.I). Examples of change of category:

1 A product claim may be amended to a claim to a particular use of the product. The use must define the use of a physical entity to achieve an effect and may not define such a use to produce a product. Since a product claim confers protection upon the product for all uses, the use claim confers less protection. Hence, the amendment does not violate **Art.123(3)**. (**G2/88** hn.II; H-V,7.1)

2 A product claim may be amended to a claim directed to a method for producing the product, provided that the method only results in the product previously claimed. As it is a fundamental principle of the EPC that the protection conferred by a product claim covers all methods for production of the product, the limitation to one of these methods cannot extend the protection conferred originally. Note, that a process claim confers protection to all products directly obtained by the process according to **Art.64(2)**. (**T5/90**; **T54/90**; H-V,7.2)

3 A claim relating to a method of operating a device may be replaced by a claim relating to the device itself, if the method claim is merely a definition of the device in terms of the function of its components (**T426/89**; **T378/86** r.3.1). However, such an amendment is not allowed if the method claim protects a device when in use and the device claim includes only technical features protecting the device whether or not it is in use (**T82/93** r.2.5, cardiac pacer). The summary of these cases in H-V,7.3 is unclear.

Note, that a change of category from a method in which an apparatus is used to the apparatus itself is not allowable (**T86/90**). (H-V,7.3)

4 An amendment of a claim from a method in which a certain product is used to the use of the product in performing that same method is allowable (**T332/94**). However, a claim to a process for the preparation of a product may not be amended to the use of the product for a purpose other than previously claimed (**T98/85**; **T194/85**). (H-V,7.4)

3 **Art.123(2)-(3) trap**

An amendment made during the grant procedure, introducing a limiting feature in a claim that extends the subject-matter and is approved by the examiner, should be removed in an opposition procedure because of **Art.123(2)**. However, such a removal violates **Art.123(3)**. Hence, with or without amendment, the applicant loses his application. This seemingly inescapable trap is partly caused by the examining division allowing the amendment. The Enlarged Board of Appeal (**G1/93**) has indicated in what cases an escape from this trap is possible. To that end the board gave a new, broader interpretation of **Art.123(2)** based on the purpose of both **Art.123(2)** and (3). The board distinguished the following four cases.

1 The added feature can be replaced by another feature disclosed in the application without violating **Art.123(3)**, and the patent can be maintained in amended form (**G1/93** hn.I r.11, 13). For example, an added feature 'alcohol' can be replaced by its disclosed species 'ethanol'.

2 The added subject-matter does not limit the scope of the claim, which allows the added matter to be removed without violating **Art.123(3)**, and the patent to be maintained in amended form (**G1/93** r.11). For example, the term 'flat' added to define a not specified torsion spring was regarded as lacking an unambiguous and useful technical meaning, and did therefore not limit the scope of a claim comprising a flat torsion spring (**T231/89** hn.II, r.3.3).

3 The added matter limits the scope of protection and provides a technical contribution to the subject-matter of the claimed invention; the addition would give an unwarranted advantage to the patentee, contrary to the purpose of **Art.123(2)**. Hence, the patent must be revoked. An example is the case where the limiting feature creates an inventive selection not disclosed in the application as filed. Such an added feature may not be removed, thereby making the claim unpatentable. (**G1/93** hn.I r.16, overturning **T231/89** hn.I)

An added feature is regarded as providing a technical contribution to the invention as claimed, if it interacts with the remaining features of the claim such that it influences the solution of the technical problem (**T384/91** hn.II, added feature of freedom of striae in optical membrane influences process parameters for making the membrane).

4 The added feature limits the scope of protection by merely excluding protection for part of the subject-matter of the application as filed and does not provide a technical contribution to the subject-matter of the claimed invention. Such a feature need not be removed as violating **Art.123(2)**, because it is not subject-matter extending the content of the application as filed. An example of an added feature not violating **Art.123(2)** is a disclaimer in a parameter range (**G1/93** r.7; see also **Art.123(2):2.4**). (**G1/93** hn II r.16)

Decision **G1/93** departs from the strict interpretation of **Art.123(2)** as laid down in the disclosure test by allowing the addition of an undisclosed feature that merely excludes protection for part of the subject-matter of a claimed invention without providing a technical contribution to the subject-matter, for legal reasons, i.e. to avoid the trap. The decision distinguishes between added features providing a technical contribution to the subject-matter of the claimed invention and features that do not provide such a contribution. The latter feature is unrelated to the teaching of the claimed invention and its addition does not contravene **Art.123(2)**, because it does not give an unwarranted advantage to the patentee nor does it adversely affect the interests of third parties (**G1/93** r.16).

The mere exclusion of protection by an added feature in **G1/93** is a different legal situation from 'identity of invention' for a priority claim in **G2/98** (**G1/03** r.2.1.2). Since the added feature does not change the identity of the invention within the meaning of **Art.87(1)**, it does not affect the right to priority from a first application without this feature (**T175/03**). However, see the note at the end of section **Art.123(2):2.4.4**.

National courts may take a view on adding an undisclosed feature different from **G1/93** and revoke a patent with an added feature on the ground of **Art.138(1)(c)**. German courts interpret **Art.123** differently from the EPO and do not consider the deletion of an undisclosed feature from a granted claim as an extension of protection (OJ 1998, 617). They neither require a patent to be revoked if a claim contains an undisclosed feature, provided the feature narrows the protection and does not lead to another teaching (OJ 2015 A78).

Art. 124 Information on prior art

1 General

The provision allows the EPO to request the applicant to provide information on prior art relevant for a patent application. The EPO uses this provision to improve the quality of the examination and to make the grant procedure faster and more efficient.

The EPO may invite the applicant to provide information about prior art cited during proceedings of parallel patent applications and patents and punish failure with deemed withdrawal. The EPC does not oblige an applicant to disclose all relevant prior art known to it, in contrast with for example US patent law which may penalize non-disclosure of relevant prior art with unpatentability.

A limited use of **Art.124** would have been expected in view of the fact that the EPO does already have relevant material for the examination from the European search, the work sharing between patent offices, and the worldwide public data retrieval systems which have made it easy to obtain information about national and regional patent applications. Moreover, the EPO can request information on prior art from other patent offices under **Art.130(1)**.

Art. 124(1) The European Patent Office may, in accordance with the Implementing Regulations, invite the applicant to provide information on prior art taken into consideration in national or regional patent proceedings and concerning an invention to which the European patent application relates.

See for the implementation:
R.70b Invitation to file search results
R.141 Procedure for requesting information on prior art

1 **Information on corresponding applications**
Each applicant claiming priority must provide the results of any search carried out by the office of first filing on the priority application (**R.141(1)**). If not provided voluntarily on filing or regional entry, the EPO will request them under **R.70b**.

The EPO may also invite an applicant to provide information on prior art taken into account in corresponding national and regional patent proceedings (**R.141(3)**). He must also provide the information for corresponding utility models and utility certificates filed in EPC contracting states, i.e. not for those filed in non-contracting states (**Art.140** referring to **Art.124**). Espacenet shows the cited documents for family members.

The EPO may not request information other than prior art. Hence, the applicant need not forward communications and decisions from national authorities to the EPO. Similarly, **Art.42** PCT forbids elected Offices to require the applicant to furnish copies of such documents relating to the same international application in any other elected Office.

Art. 124(2) If the applicant fails to reply in due time to an invitation under paragraph 1, the European patent application shall be deemed to be withdrawn.

1 **Failure to provide information**
If the applicant does not respond to an invitation under **Art.124(1)** within the specified period, the application will be deemed withdrawn and the EPO will notify the applicant under **R.112(1)**. The applicant can request an appealable decision according to **R.112(2)**. The non-observance of the period can be remedied with further processing (**Art.121**).

Note that there is no sanction on not providing information on all relevant prior art.

Art. 125 Reference to general principles

In the absence of procedural provisions in this Convention, the European Patent Office shall take into account the principles of procedural law generally recognised in the Contracting States.

1 **Procedural law of the EPC**

Since the EPC is an independent system based on the legal systems of the contracting states, any holes in the procedural law of the EPC must be closed by taking account of the generally accepted legal principles of the contracting states. These principles are often based on maxims of Roman Law, as these have proved themselves in practice over many centuries (**T167/93**, r.2.3). Not much use has been made of this provision. In most cases holes were open questions which could be answered by a further development of the EPC in line with the generally accepted legal principles. The provisions of the EPC are by necessity formulated in a generalizing and abstract way. Hence, an apparent hole on application of a provision to a specific case can often be filled by interpretation of the provision (**J6/86** hn.II). The reference to impartiality as a general principle of law in **G5/91** r.3 can be regarded as an application of **Art.125**.

The provision applies only to procedural law, not to material patent law (**J15/86** hn.IV). Holes in the material law must always be closed by changes in the EPC or by further development of the EPC.

1.1 EXAMPLES OF CLOSED HOLES:

- An accompanying person may plead at oral proceedings only with permission of the EPO and under supervision of the responsible representative. See **Art.134(1)**:2.
- Errors in documents include missing indications (**J8/80**).
- The right of the applicant has been confirmed that he can withdraw his application at all times; but due to the rule of publication after 18 months and the technical preparations for it, the applicant has no right up to this time limit to demand non-disclosure. Although the application cannot be guaranteed not to be published if it is withdrawn after completion of the technical preparations, the EPO must make an effort to prevent its publication. (**J5/81**)
- If an appeal has lost its grounds, the procedure will not be continued, as is common practice in legal procedures (**J20/85**).
- Referring to national law, the correction of the mention of the inventor has been allowed, showing, however, that this matter is solved differently in the various contracting states (**J8/82**).

1.2 LEGAL PRINCIPLES

Some general legal principles are not contained in the EPC; they can be drawn in, as these principles form a recognized legal source. One such principle is the procedural equality of all parties to proceedings. This is the basis of the decision (**G1/86**) that an appellant, being an opponent, has the right to re-establishment when not having observed the time limit for filing the grounds of appeal. The applicant of a Euro-PCT application has the same rights as the applicant of a direct European application (**J8/83** r.8). Other general legal principles are the narrow interpretation of provisions that exclude subject-matter from patentability (**G5/83** r.22) and the principle of good faith, as set out below.

In most cases such legal principles could be developed from the relation between individual procedural provisions in connection with the goal of the EPC. The Legal Board did not need to analyse national law in such cases, but interpreted the EPC out of itself.

1.3 EXAMPLES OF EPO'S OWN PROCEDURAL PRINCIPLES:

- A withdrawal will only be recognized if it is unconditional and unequivocal (**J11/80**).

- A published withdrawal cannot be revoked, because of public interests (**J15/86**).
- A notice of withdrawal of an application need not be phrased in specific terms (**J7/87**), but must be clear, and the circumstances must make clear that it expresses the true intention of the applicant (**J11/87**).
- A decision of a board of appeal in grant proceedings has no binding effect in subsequent first instance opposition proceedings or on appeal therefrom. The explicit provisions of the EPC regarding the assessment of the grant of a patent both at a first examination and at an opposition stage precludes that a decision of the board of appeal in grant proceedings is regarded as an estoppel per rem judicatam in subsequent opposition proceedings. (**T167/93**)

2 Good faith

According to **Art.31(1)** of the Vienna Convention treaties shall be interpreted in good faith. Since the rules of the Vienna Convention are also applicable to the EPC (see Preamble **2.2**), the EPC must be interpreted in good faith, even though the EPC does not explicitly refer to the principle. The relation between the EPO and a party is based on the EPC and, therefore, is likewise governed by the principle of good faith. The principle of good faith, also referred to as the principle of protection of legitimate expectations, is generally recognised among the contracting states and is well established in European Community law. (**G5/88** r.3.2)

The principle of good faith may provide a remedy for a loss of rights in cases which might otherwise be irremediable. However, the principle also causes uncertainty for parties in that its applicability is not well defined. The application of the principle by the EPO, as derived from case law, allows the distinction of two cases, a first case where the EPO deviates from a course expected by a party and a second case where a party deviates from a course expected by the EPO.

2.1 DEVIATION BY EPO

The most common deviations by the EPO are unexpected changes in procedure and erroneous or ambiguous notifications. The application of the principle of good faith to procedures before the EPO requires that measures taken by the EPO should not violate the reasonable expectations of parties (**G5/88** r.3.2).

A party may legitimately expect that the first instance will not deviate from the established case law if this case law has become part of the consistent practice of the department of first instance, in particular if this practice has been published in the Guidelines or a Notice from the EPO. In such a situation, an applicant may legitimately expect that a practice allowing or even recommending a certain procedural conduct will not be changed without appropriate advance information. (**J27/94** r.5; **J2/08** r.6)

If there is doubt whether an established practice exists, a party must seek clarification by means of an enquiry to the EPO (**J25/95**). See also **R.103(1):3** when a deviation from a procedure set out in the Guidelines is regarded as a substantial procedural violation.

A party relying on a lenient practice of the EPO must obtain the legitimately expected result. However, he should not stretch the practice to his advantage. If the practice is unclear, he should seek clarification from the EPO and not jump to conclusions. (**T905/90** r.6, 7)

A party who embarked in good faith on proceedings, e.g. a self-opposition, which cannot adversely affect the rights of any third party, can continue such proceedings if the interpretation of the EPC changes after initiation of the proceedings, e.g. by forbidding self-opposition (**G9/93** r.6.1).

The applicant can, on the basis of the principle of good faith, rely on information from the EPO on procedural matters (**J10/84**). If an applicant performs a wrong act because of an erroneous message from the EPO or a request the true nature of which is uncertain and loses his application, then the acts of the applicant and the EPO are totally null and void. If good faith requires so, consequences due to the EPC shall not enter into force: an erroneous or ambiguous message from the EPO shall not be detrimental to the applicant (**J2/87**; **J3/87**; **J15/92**). The ambiguous message may be a courtesy service, a message in writing or an oral communication (**J27/92**). Note, that no claim may be based on an omitted courtesy service (**J12/84**). **J19/10** r.8 held that the legal accuracy of the wording of an examination report may not be simply relied on because of the inexperience of examiners in handling procedural issues.

In contrast with the above examples of procedural errors by the EPO, an amendment of an application or patent following an erroneous proposal by the EPO cannot be corrected by relying on good faith, even if it results in a final refusal of the application or revocation of the patent (see e.g. **Art.123(3):3**). The ultimate responsibility for any amendment of an application or patent always remains that of the applicant or the patentee (**G1/93** r.13). Hence, in such matters a party cannot rely on advice from the EPO: the principle of good faith does *not* apply.

2.2 DEVIATION BY PARTY

The most common deviation from the expected course by a party is the filing of a deficient request. The request may be a request for further processing, a notice of opposition or appeal. The deficiency may be an incomplete written request or an omitted payment. The application of the principle of good faith to such cases should not be interpreted to expect the EPO always to warn the party in time. This would take the principle of good faith too far. It is incumbent on both the EPO and a party to act in good faith (**J12/94**). A party cannot shift its own responsibility for complying with the provisions of the EPC to the EPO (**J41/92**). The following balance between the responsibility of the EPO and that of a party has been confirmed by the Enlarged Board of Appeal (**G2/97**).

A party can expect a warning from the EPO in good faith, if the deficiency in the request is readily identifiable for the EPO and can be remedied within the period for filing the request (**T14/89**; **J13/90**; **J12/94**). In the case of a request whose true nature is uncertain, the EPO should clarify the matter by asking the requester (**J15/92**). The EPO will draw the appellant's attention to missing grounds and facts in an application for re-establishment (**T14/89**).

Since payments are often made in a way which is not apparent from the letter containing the request (cf. **Rfees5(1)**), a request without accompanying payment is not a readily identifiable deficiency. The EPO can often only establish whether a specific fee has been paid after the expiry of the time limit, when it disposes of the complete data on all payments made during the relevant period. Hence, in general a warning in respect of a missing payment should not be expected. (**J41/92**; **G2/97** hn, r.3.3, 3.4)

However, the EPO will warn a party in respect of a payment if the request contains erroneous information on the payment and the party would, without warning, inadvertently miss the time limit (**G2/97**). This is the case where a letter refers to an enclosed payment which is in fact missing (**T128/87**), or it is clear from a letter that a party is in error with regard to the need to make payment of a fee within a certain period (**J13/90**). The EPO is also obliged to give prompt reliable information on a specific question (**J27/92**).

In **J15/90** hn. it was held that a period of 18 days is sufficient to remedy a deficient payment; in **J13/90** r.8 nine days were sufficient to warn a party of an omitted act under **R.136(2)**. In **T923/95** a period of one week was regarded as too long for the EPO to remain inactive after it had received an underpayment for the appeal fee; in contrast, **T161/96** r.8 held that the labour-intensive processing of payments in the EPO excluded the issue of a warning within seven days from receipt of an underpayment of an opposition fee.

2.3 COMPLAINTS

Anyone may make a complaint when dissatisfied with a service of the EPO. The complaint should preferably be filed online (www.epo.org/contact; OJ 2013, 608). The department DQMS, handling the complaints, aims to reply within 30 days. See for more information chapter 8 of the 'Handbook of Quality procedures before the EPO', available on the EPO website.

When the complaint relates to the behaviour of a specific examiner, such as applying an improper procedure or responding unsatisfactorily, a party may, before launching an official complaint, contact the director of the examiner. No complaint should be raised about lack of progress in examination; instead, a request for acceleration should be filed.

Correspondence relating to complaints is normally not available in the public file. However, if it has a substantive and/or procedural bearing on an opposition, the EPO will usually put it in the public file. (**T1691/15** r.3; E-VI,4)

428 complaints were registered in 2015, 39% of which related to the work of examiners.

Art. 126 (deleted)

Chapter II *Information to the public or to official authorities*

1 **General**

The EPO provides information to the public and official authorities about European patent applications and patents and about issues of the EPO of a general character that are relevant for parties and authorities. The provisions in this chapter deal with the keeping and inspection of the Register of European patents and files (**Art.127, 128**), public availability of information (**Art.128, 129**) and the exchange of information between the EPO and other authorities (**Art.130-132**).

2 **Information relating to patents and patent applications**

The EPO publishes patent applications as prescribed in **Art.93** to enrich the technical knowledge with the content of the applications. The publication also informs the public of the property right of applicants. The publication of granted patents under **Art.98** and patents amended in opposition under **Art.103** inform the public similarly of the right obtained by the patent proprietor.

The legislator regarded the possibility of access to the application merely by file inspection as insufficient (Empel §421). The publications used to be on paper but are now available via the internet on a publication server at 'https://data.epo.org/publication-server', which is the sole legally authoritative publication medium for European A and B patent documents (OJ 2005, 126). The search report is also published under **Art.92** on the publication server. The publication server provides a link to the Register entries of each patent document. The website has a translation service for patent documents.

The EPO records data about the procedures in the European Patent Register (**Art.127**) to inform third parties and users of the EPC. Part of the data is published in the Bulletin under **Art.129(a)**, formerly on paper, now only online at the EPO website. The Register can be inspected online at 'https://register.epo.org'; each page of the Register has a link to the file of the application or patent.

Documents in the EPO files of published European applications and patents are available for on-line inspection under **Art.128**. Complete patent documents of several patent offices can be found on 'http://worldwide.espacenet.com'. European patent documents retrieved from this site contain a link to the Register, which in turn has a link to the file.

3 **Other information**

The main entry to the EPO websites is through www.epo.org and provides links to a.o. the publication server, Register and search engines, and discloses decisions and information of a general nature. The mentioned EPO websites are publicly accessible and free of charge. The EPO does not guarantee completeness and accuracy of the data and information available on the websites; this does not apply to documents on the publication server, the files, the content of the Register and issues of the Bulletin (see Terms of Use §4 on the website). Updates of the websites are published on 'http://www.epo.org/service-support/updates.html' (OJ 1999, 133).

Information of a general character issued by the EPO, such as selected decisions of the Boards of Appeal, is published in the Official Journal on the EPO website (see **Art.129(b)**). The publication of the paper version of the Official Journal was discontinued on 01.01.2014 (Not. EPO OJ 2013, 93).

Users of the European patent system can find information for contacting the EPO on the customer services page 'www.epo.org/contact'. The EPO will provide free of charge assistance by telephone; international freephone numbers are available for the EPC contracting states. (OJ 2013, 91)

The EPO publishes each fortnight an e-mail newsletter providing announcements and recent news (www.epo.org/service-support/contact-us/newsletter.html).

The list of professional representatives is kept up to date by the Legal Division (**Art.20**, **Art.134(1)**). The list is open for public inspection on the EPO website under the same rules as the files, i.e. **R.145** and **R.146** (OJ 1985 p.42). The EPC has no provisions for the keeping and inspection of the list of professional representatives.

An overview of forms and publications available from the EPO and a price list is published in OJ 2015 A10 and on the EPO website.

Art. 127 European Patent Register

The European Patent Office shall keep a European Patent Register, in which the particulars specified in the Implementing Regulations shall be recorded. No entry shall be made in the European Patent Register before the publication of the European patent application. The European Patent Register shall be open to public inspection.

See for the implementation:
R.143 Entries in the European Patent Register

1 **Entries in the Register of European Patents**
Entries in the Register are made in the three official EPO languages (**Art.14(8)**). The Legal Division is responsible for the entries (**Art.20(1)**). A request to the Legal Division for changing an entry aimed at revision of a final decision of a board of appeal must be refused (**G1/97** hn.IV).

On filing of a European application, particulars of the application are entered in a non-public shadow register. At publication of the application, the content of the shadow register is transferred to the public Register. Entries in the Register are made up to the expiry of the opposition period or the termination of the opposition proceedings. Entries relating to transfers (**R.143(1)(w)** & **R.22**) are entered in the Register up to the mentioned time because of **R.85**, referring to **R.22**. On the other hand, entries relating to licences (**R.143(1)(w)** & **R.23**) are entered only up to the grant of the patent, because **R.85** does not refer to **R.23**. The entries in the Register will be published in the European Patent Bulletin after the entry has been made (**Art.129(a)**).

See **R.143(1):2** for the means of inspection of the Register.

Art. 128 Inspection of files

Art. 128(1) Files relating to European patent applications which have not yet been published shall not be made available for inspection without the consent of the applicant.

1 **Files not available for inspection**
Art.128(1) is the counterpart of Art.127, second sentence, and lays down that the files of an unpublished application are not publicly accessible. The unpublished state of the application takes care that the application does not become part of the state of the art, allowing the applicant to withdraw the application and, where appropriate, re-file it in amended form.

A file may be inspected before publication with consent of the applicant (Art.128(1)). If the consent of the applicant is not provided together with a request for inspection, the EPO will ask the applicant for consent. (A-XI,2.5)

When an application is not-regularly published under Art.93, e.g. it was withdrawn after the termination of the technical preparations of R.67 but before the publication, its file will not be available for public inspection.

The prohibition in Art.128(1) is not absolute and the phrase 'unless otherwise provided' should have been added. The following provisions enable certain persons or authorities to inspect files of unpublished applications without consent of the applicant:

Art.128(2) Person against whom rights under the application have been invoked

Art.128(3) Anybody, after a divisional application or a new application has been published

Art.130 National industrial property offices

Art.131 Courts or authorities of the contracting states

The applicant can access the file of his own application before its publication date as set out in **R.145(2):1**.

Art. 128(2) Any person who can prove that the applicant has invoked the rights under the European patent application against him may obtain inspection of the files before the publication of that application and without the consent of the applicant.

1 **Inspection after invocation of rights under application**
A person may inspect the file of an unpublished application without the consent of the applicant, if the latter has invoked the rights under the application against him. Such an invocation can be an early warning of a user of the invention of the rights the applicant may assert against him under **Art.67** after publication of the application or under **Art.64** after grant. The rights within the meaning of **Art.128(2)** are also invoked when the invocation of rights has been made in respect of a first filing in a contracting state, provided the subsequent European application is mentioned at the same time (J14/91 hn.I). The procedure for inspection is set out in A-XI,2.5.

Art. 128(3) Where a European divisional application or a new European patent application filed under Article 61, paragraph 1, is published, any person may obtain inspection of the files of the earlier application before the publication of that application and without the consent of the applicant.

Art.61(1) European patent applications filed by non-entitled persons

1 **Inspection of file of parent application**
Art.128(3) allows a third person to check the origin of the divisional or new application and a possible extension of subject-matter immediately on publication of the divisional or new application. It may be used in cases where, after the filing of the divisional application, the parent application is withdrawn before publication. Without **Art.128(3)** the file of this parent application would remain closed. The same applies to checking the content of a new application filed under **Art.61(1)(b)** in view of the claimed application.

Art. 128(4) After the publication of the European patent application, the files relating to the application and the resulting European patent may be inspected on request, subject to the restrictions laid down in the Implementing Regulations.

See for the implementation
R.144 Parts of the file excluded from inspection
R.145 Procedure for the inspection of files
R.146 Communication of information contained in the files
R.147 Maintenance of files

1 **Inspection of file of published application**
The content of the file of an application becomes public upon publication of the application. It allows a third person to check the validity of the created exclusive right based on the filed application. A file can be inspected without request; the 'request' in the provision relates only to the old way of inspection by requesting paper copies of documents.

The restrictions to the inspection mentioned in **Art.128(4)** relate to parts of the file not available for inspection under **R.144** and to the availability of the file in view of the time the files are kept according to **R.147**. The procedure for inspecting the files is set out in **R.145**, **R.146** and A-XI,2.

Art. 128(5) Even before the publication of the European patent application, the European Patent Office may communicate to third parties or publish the particulars specified in the Implementing Regulations.

Art.128(5)(a)-(e) deleted in EPC 2000

1 **Communication by EPO of data prior to publication**
The particulars that may be communicated to third parties before publication of the application are specified in **R.19(3)**.

The EPO sends information to the inventors, being third parties, under **R.19(3)**. A publication of biographic data under **Art.128(5)** is the entry in the patent register of the application number of the parent application on publication of a divisional application in the rare case where the parent is withdrawn before its publication (e.g. EP application 89100942.5).

The EPO publishes on its publication server the publication numbers of applications for which the publication of the application and/or search report were announced in the Bulletin, but were not actually published. Possible reasons for not publishing include that the application was withdrawn by the applicant and that the publication was erroneous because formal requirements had not yet been fulfilled. (A-XI,2.6)

Art. 129 Periodical publications

The European Patent Office shall periodically publish:
(a) a European Patent Bulletin containing the particulars the publication of which is prescribed by this Convention, the Implementing Regulations or the President of the European Patent Office;
(b) an Official Journal containing notices and information of a general character issued by the President of the European Patent Office, as well as any other information relevant to this Convention or its implementation.

1 **European Patent Bulletin (Art.129(a))**
The bulletin contains particulars and information of a general character, in particular bibliographic and procedural data of published applications and patents, as prescribed by the EPC or the President, e.g. in **Art.97(3), 105b(3), 112a(6), 122(5), 153(3), (6); R.21(2).** The Bulletin contains only part of the information contained in the Register. The provisions for the Register are laid down in **Art.127** and **R.143.**

In the pre-internet era the paper-publications of the Bulletin were the primary source of data about applications and patents. The Bulletin is now published weekly on Wednesday in digital form in the three official languages of the EPO (**Art.14(7)(a)**) and is available on the EPO website free of charge.

2 **Official Journal (Art.129(b))**
The Official Journal of the European Patent Office (OJ) publishes decisions of the Enlarged Board of Appeal and selected decisions of the Boards of Appeal, changes to the Guidelines and other information relevant to the EPC and its implementation. The OJ is published only on the EPO website 'www.epo.org'; the paper version was discontinued per 01.01.2014 (OJ 2013, 444, 606).

The translations of the official text of decisions of boards of appeal as published in the OJ are legally irrelevant to the interpretation of the official text in the language of the proceedings (**T952/92** hn.V, r.2.2). Occasionally, the decision is arrived at in another EPO language if the rapporteur of the board is less competent in the language of the proceedings (R.5(6) RPBoA; **J18/90** r.1.1; **G4/08** r.4.8). Hence, a German 'translation' of a decision may be more intelligible than the text in the language of proceedings.

Art. 130 Exchanges of information

Art. 130(1) Unless this Convention or national laws provide otherwise, the European Patent Office and the central industrial property office of any Contracting State shall, on request, communicate to each other any useful information regarding European or national patent applications and patents and any proceedings concerning them.

1 **Exchange of information with patent offices of contracting states**
The EPO and the central industrial property office of any Contracting State communicate on request to each other any useful information not only regarding European or national patent applications, but also regarding European or national patents. Such an exchange of information takes place unless the EPC or the national law provides otherwise. (Spec. Ed. 4 of OJ 2007)

Art. 130(2) Paragraph 1 shall apply to the communication of information by virtue of working agreements between the European Patent Office and
(a) the central industrial property offices of other States;
(b) any intergovernmental organisation entrusted with the task of granting patents;
(c) any other organisation.

1 **Exchange of information with other patent offices**
Examples of offices with which EPO exchanges information:
a) patent offices of US, JP, extension states;
b) OAPI patent office; not the International Bureau under PCT of the WIPO, as it does not grant patents;
c) International Bureau of the WIPO.

Art. 130(3) Communications under paragraphs 1 and 2(a) and (b) shall not be subject to the restrictions laid down in Article 128. The Administrative Council may decide that communications under paragraph 2(c) shall not be subject to such restrictions, provided that the organisation concerned treats the information communicated as confidential until the European patent application has been published.

Art.128 Inspection of files

1 **Restrictions to information exchange**
The restrictions of Art.128 are specifically the non-disclosure before publication of the application, in view of the last sentence of Art.130(3). The parts of the file excluded from inspection under R.144 are not included in the exchange of information, because they relate to matter which is not useful ('sachdienlich') (Art.130(1)).

Art. 131 Administrative and legal co-operation

Art. 131(1) Unless this Convention or national laws provide otherwise, the European Patent Office and the courts or authorities of Contracting States shall on request give assistance to each other by communicating information or opening files for inspection. Where the European Patent Office makes files available for inspection by courts, Public Prosecutors' Offices or central industrial property offices, the inspection shall not be subject to the restrictions laid down in Article 128.

Art.128 Inspection of files
See for the implementation:
R.148 Communication between EPO and national authorities
R.149 Inspection of files by courts or national authorities

1 **Exchange of information between EPO and other authorities**
If an authority listed in Art.131(1), second sentence, such as a court, requests information from an EPO file, the restrictions of non-disclosure of the file prior to publication of the application and of exclusion of parts of the file from inspection (R.144) do not apply (Art.131(1), second sentence). A request of any authority not listed in the second sentence, e.g. fiscal authorities, is subject to the restrictions of Art.128. Since Art.131(1) relates to authorities,

private individuals and firms cannot use the provision for gaining access to information (OJ1993, 588).

Under **Art.131(1)** the EPO may request information from a personnel file of a national patent office (**J5/99** r.3.2) or request information about national law (**J18/99** r.3.1).

Art. 131(2) At the request of the European Patent Office, the courts or other competent authorities of Contracting States shall undertake, on behalf of the Office and within the limits of their jurisdiction, any necessary enquiries or other legal measures.

See for the implementation:
R.150 Procedure for letters rogatory
The most important application is the taking of evidence (see the more explicit German version of provision) according to **R.120**.

Art. 132 Exchange of publications

Art. 132(1) The European Patent Office and the central industrial property offices of the Contracting States shall despatch to each other on request and for their own use one or more copies of their respective publications free of charge.

1 **Publications exchanged**
The publications include the Official Journal, the Patent Bulletin, the published applications and the granted patents. This exchange has resulted in an outstanding search collection in The Hague.

Art. 132(2) The European Patent Office may conclude agreements relating to the exchange or supply of publications.

1 **Competence to conclude agreements**
The President is competent to make such agreements according to **Art.33(4)**.

Chapter III *Representation*

Art. 133 General principles of representation

1 **General**

Art.133 contains the general principles governing representation with respect to proceedings under the Convention.

In general, a person (e.g. applicant, proprietor, opponent) need not be represented in proceedings before the EPO (**Art.133(1)**). As an exception, a person not having a residence or place of business in a contracting state must be represented (**Art.133(2)**). Although not required by law, representation is recommended for a person having a residence or place of business in a contracting state. Professional handling of the case is in the interest of both the person and the EPO, ensuring that the person achieves the desired goal and the procedure before the EPO is conducted efficiently. The representation may only be undertaken by a person on the list of professional representatives before the EPO (**Art.134(1)**) and, exceptionally, by an employee (**Art.133(3)**) or a legal practitioner (**Art.134(7)**). A party choosing to act in oral proceedings through a person not entitled to represent is equivalent to not at all appearing at the oral proceedings (**T927/05** r.2).

2 **Appointment and authorisation of representative**

Due representation before the EPO comprises the two separate procedural acts of appointment and authorisation (A-VIII,1.1; **J17/98** r.4.2, 4.3).

2.1 APPOINTMENT OF A REPRESENTATIVE

The appointment informs the EPO of the representative that will act before the EPO on behalf of the applicant, proprietor or opponent.

For each case where a party wishes or is obliged to be represented, an appointment must be filed in which the EPO is informed of the fact and of the name of the representative who will handle the case. A representative is normally appointed by entering his name in the Request for Grant form (**R.41(2)(d)**) or in the notice of opposition (**R.76(2)(d)**). The proprietor in opposition and the parties in appeal are known to the EPO and are supposed to act through the already appointed representative unless indicated otherwise.

Either the party or the representative must sign the Request for Grant form. In the latter case, the representative identifies himself to the EPO as the appointed representative. Similarly, in the case of several applicants, each one of them or their representative(s) must sign.

A party may appoint several representatives (**R.152(10)**). The name of the representative to whom the EPO will notify all communications must be entered in the form followed by the words 'et al' (see also **R.130(2)**); the names of the further representatives must be given on an additional sheet. In the case of a general authorisation, only one representative and the registration number of the authorisation must be entered in the form; the names of the further representatives need not be given. (OJ 2013, 535 section II)

A group of representatives can be registered with the EPO as an association, allowing appointment of all of them by merely entering the name of the association and the registration number in the same box of the form (see **R.152(11):1**).

Several parties acting jointly may each appoint a representative, but they must act through a common representative (**R.41(3)**, **R.151**). See **R.41(3):1** for the appointment of the common representative.

2.2 AUTHORISATION OF A REPRESENTATIVE

The second procedural act for representation is the filing of an authorisation, which serves the purpose of establishing whether a representative acting before the EPO on behalf of a party has indeed been enabled by the party to do so. An authorisation or letter of engagement may be filed in respect of a single case or in respect of all transactions of a party with the EPO (general authorisation, **R.152(5)(b)**).

R.152(1) establishes the exceptional cases where the EPO requires the filing of an authorisation. In such cases the first act of a party before the EPO should refer to a (general) authorisation filed together with the first act or to a previously filed general authorisation of a single representative or an association of representatives (**R.152(11)**). Note, that the filing of a general authorisation without a link between a case and the authorisation does not imply the appointment of a representative for that case (**J17/98** hn.I). Since, as a rule, a representative is not obliged to file an authorisation, he is deemed to be entitled to act in the name of the respective party, unless he fails to file an authorisation in due time if invited to do so (**G2/04** r.1.1.2).

A party may authorise one or more representatives by means of an individual authorisation in respect of one or more individually mentioned cases of the party, preferably using Form 1003.

A party may instead use a general authorisation in respect of all cases of the party. A general authorisation, preferably using Form 1004, must be filed with the Legal Division, who will register it and issue a registration number. The registration number can be used when appointing a representative for a case. (OJ 2013, 535 section II)

3 Authorisation under PCT

Representation before an international authority according to the PCT (receiving Office, ISA, IPEA) is governed by the law of the receiving Office where the international application is filed (**Art.49, R.83** PCT, see PCT §8.3). If the EPO is receiving Office, **Art.133** & **134** EPC apply (**Art.27(7)** PCT). However, a non-resident applicant (**Art.133(2)** EPC) may himself initiate processing of the application by the EPO as designated or elected Office (Euro-PCT Guide §466). The processing starts the day following that on which the procedural steps of **Art.22(1)** or **39(1)(a)** PCT in conjunction with **Art.153(5)** and **R.159(1)** EPC were taken. The representative of a non-resident applicant in the international phase, who is not entitled to act before the EPO, is not allowed to act on the applicant's behalf before the EPO as designated or elected Office; the representative may not even initiate the regional European phase. Under **Art.49** PCT he is not entitled to practise before the EPO as designated or elected Office. Any procedural steps he nonetheless takes (apart from payments) have no effect (**R.152(6)**).

If a national office is receiving Office, the national law determines the requirements for the representation in the entire international phase. If an international application is filed in the USA, the USA representative may act before the EPO as ISA and IPEA. However, when entering the national phase, he must give way to a representative complying with **Art.134** EPC, because representation before the designated or elected Office follows the national law of that office. This makes sense, as the international application is regarded in the national phase as a European application when the EPO is designated or elected Office (Euro-PCT application).

Art. 133(1) Subject to paragraph 2, no person shall be compelled to be represented by a professional representative in proceedings established by this Convention.

1 **Non-compulsory representation**
A person need not be represented in proceedings before the EPO. However, a person without residence or place of business in a contracting state must, according to paragraph 2, be represented. A not represented person must be legally competent.

Art. 133(2) Natural or legal persons not having their residence or principal place of business in a Contracting State shall be represented by a professional representative and act through him in all proceedings established by this Convention, other than in filing a European patent application; the Implementing Regulations may permit other exceptions.

1 **Compulsory representation**
The compulsory representation of persons without residence or place of business in a contracting state stems from the desire to run the procedure before the EPO efficiently, requiring familiarity of a party with the legal system and avoiding postal delays. Improvements in the postal services have made the latter point less relevant than at the time of drafting of the Convention. Whereas for use of an admissible non-EPO language in further documents the residence and nationality of the party are important (**Art.14(4)**), for representation solely the residence is important: the EPO needs a letter box within a contracting state. Note that an extension state is not a contracting state.

From a comparison of the French, German and English texts of **Art.133(2)** it appears that the adjective 'principal' in the English text is incorrect. It is generally accepted that 'a place of business' in the sense of having legal presence in a contracting state, suffices; a company need not have its headquarters in a contracting state.

The Administrative Council has hitherto not created any exceptions to the compulsory representation as allowed by **Art.133(2)**.

2 **Allowed acts**
Art.133(2) excludes only the filing of a European patent application from the compulsory representation. Hence, a person not having his residence or place of business within a contracting state may file a European patent application without being represented. The filing includes all acts leading to the accordance of a date of filing (A-VIII,1.1 and **R.55**). Only after a date of filing has been accorded, i.e. during the formalities check of **Art.90(3)** and **R.57(h)**, will the EPO check the requirement of representation.

In the case of compulsory representation the EPO requires a representative for all acts following the accordance of a date of filing, such as the appointment of a representative under **R.57(h)** and **R.58**. Note, that payments may be made by any person, also those obliged to be represented (**Rfees6(1):1**).

3 **Assessment and sanction**
Compliance with the requirement of compulsory representation is assessed when a party enters proceedings before the EPO. Any sanction on non-compliance is adapted to the particular proceedings and included in the part of the EPC dealing with the proceedings.

In grant proceedings the assessment is carried out during the formal examination under **R.57(h)**. The procedure for correcting any deficiencies is given in **R.57:9**. If the representation is not duly rectified, the application will be refused according to **Art.90(5)**.

On entry in the European phase, the EPO checks compliance with the requirements of **Art.133(2)** for an international application. If not corrected after invitation under **R.163(5)**, the application is refused under **R.163(6)**.

At the start of opposition proceedings the EPO assesses the representation of the opponent. The sanction is created in the Guidelines in D-IV,1.2.2.2(iv) by making non-compliance a deficiency under the 'cover-all' provision **R.77(2)**, causing the opposition to be inadmissible if the deficiency is not duly corrected.

There are no provisions for assessment of representation and sanction in the appeal stage, because normally no new parties enter the proceedings. The EPC has neither an expressly stated sanction on non-representation of a party who enters opposition proceedings through intervention under **Art.105**.

Art. 133(3) Natural or legal persons having their residence or principal place of business in a Contracting State may be represented in proceedings established by this Convention by an employee, who need not be a professional representative but who shall be authorised in accordance with the Implementing Regulations. The Implementing Regulations may provide whether and under what conditions an employee of a legal person may also represent other legal persons which have their principal place of business in a Contracting State and which have economic connections with the first legal person.

1 **Representation by employee**

The representation of an enterprise by an employee is restricted to enterprises having a place of business in a contracting state according to **Art.133(3)**, first sentence. The employee need not be a professional representative. The employee is strictly not regarded as a true representative but as a person through whom the party acts, as is clear from the distinction made between 'vertreten' versus 'handeln durch' in the German version and 'représenter' versus 'agir par' in the French version of **Art.133(2)**, (3) and **134**; the distinction is lost in the English version.

The director of a company represents the company, as he expresses the will of the company. He need not be authorised. An employee, on the other hand, must be authorised (**R.152**). There is no provision in the Rules allowing an employee to act on behalf of another legal person, even when economically connected. Hence, an employee is not allowed to act for economically connected companies (see e.g. **T298/97** hn.II).

Art. 133(4) The Implementing Regulations may lay down special provisions concerning the common representation of parties acting in common.

See for the implementation:
R.151 Appointment of a common representative

Art. 134 Representation before the European Patent Office

1 **General**

Art.134 deals with issues of professional representation, determining who may represent persons in proceedings established under the Convention and in particular, the conditions under which a person may be entered on the list of professional representatives. Furthermore, it deals with the entitlement of national representatives of a state acceding to the EPC to be entered on that list.

Representation in proceedings before the EPO may only be undertaken by persons whose names appear on the list of professional representatives of **Art.134(1)** or by certain legal practitioners under **Art.134(8)**. The purpose of this arrangement is to create a corpus of professional representatives with a monopoly status who possess the necessary qualification for their work. This is designed to protect the parties that have to rely on the services of a professional representative and to ensure the efficient conduct of proceedings before the EPO. (**G3/97** r.4.2.1)

Art. 134(1) Representation of natural or legal persons in proceedings established by this Convention may only be undertaken by professional representatives whose names appear on a list maintained for this purpose by the European Patent Office.

See for the implementation:
R.152 Authorisations
R.154 Amendment of the list of professional representatives

1 **List of representatives**

All representation before the EPO must be undertaken exclusively by professional representatives entered on the list, employees according to **Art.133(3)** or by legal practitioners according to **Art.134(8)**.

The entries in the list of representatives are in alphabetical order of the first part of the surname. On request, a second entry will be made at a location in the list easier to find for surnames having a prefix such as 'de' and 'von'. The Legal Division is responsible for entries in and deletions from the list (**Art.20(1)**). A person fulfilling the requirements of **Art.134(2)** will be entered on the list on request. A person will be deleted from the list on request or on account of **R.154**.

Entries of the list can be inspected on the EPO website. Requests for (re) entry on, changes or deletion from the list must be sent in writing to the Legal Division of the EPO (OJ 2015 A55).

2 **Submissions by accompanying person during oral proceedings**

A person not entitled to represent parties before the EPO and accompanying a professional representative during oral proceedings has a limited procedural status. He is not entitled to make formal requests, such as requests relating to patentability (see e.g. **T1178/04** r.33). He may make submissions during oral proceedings on specific legal or technical issues (**G2/94** hn.I; **G4/95** hn.I). The submissions may relate to facts, evidence or arguments (**G4/95** r.8). Note, that the admissibility of facts and evidence filed at a late stage in proceedings is always a matter of discretion for the EPO (**Art.114(2)**; E-III,8.6).

The submissions must be made under the continuing responsibility and control of the professional representative and only in addition to his complete presentation of the case (**G4/95** hn.I, II(b) (iv)). Submissions may be made during oral proceedings in ex-parte and inter-partes proceedings, both in first and second instance (**G2/94** hn.I, emphasis on grant appeal proceedings; **G4/95** hn.I, emphasis on opposition proceedings).

Submissions by a non-entitled person cannot be made as a matter of right, but only with the permission of and under the discretion of the EPO (**G2/94** hn.II(a), **G4/95** hn.II(a)). The professional representative must request permission for the submissions to be made, stating the name and qualifications of the accompanying person, specifying the subject-matter of the proposed submissions, and stating that the submissions will be made under the continuing responsibility and control of the professional representative (**G4/95** hn.II; E-III,8.5). The request must be filed on or before the date fixed for written submissions in the summons for the oral proceedings according to **R.116(1)**; a late filed request will only be allowed in exceptional circumstances or if all other parties agree to the making of the submissions (**G4/95** hn.II(b)(ii); E-III,8.5).

Decisions **G2/94** and **G4/95** do not state the meaning of the 'subject-matter' of the proposed submission to be specified in the request. In the context of the decisions it is reasonable to assume that the subject-matter comprises facts and evidence but does not include arguments.

Parties are not accompanying persons in the sense of **G4/95** (**T621/98** r.2). They have the right to make submissions in oral proceedings by virtue of their status as party to the proceedings. (E-III,8.5)

A non-entitled person cannot use the taking of evidence under **Art.117** as a basis for entitlement to make oral submissions involving the presentation of facts and evidence (**G4/95** r.8(a)).

Additional provisions specific for ex-parte and inter-partes proceedings are given below.

2.1 EX PARTE PROCEEDINGS

An accompanying person may be allowed to make oral submissions on legal and technical issues during oral proceedings in ex parte appeal proceedings. The request must be made in advance of the day of the oral proceedings. The Board must be informed of all relevant matters before deciding on the request. (**G2/94** hn.I, II(a), r.2)

2.2 INTER PARTES PROCEEDINGS

An accompanying person may be allowed to make oral submissions on legal and technical issues, other than under **Art.117**, during oral proceedings in opposition or opposition appeal. The request must be made sufficiently early so that all parties are able to prepare themselves properly in relation to the proposed submissions. A request made shortly before or at the oral proceedings will normally be refused, unless all parties agree to the making of the oral submissions. (**G4/95** hn.I, II)

2.3 FORMER MEMBER OF BOA

The EPO will normally refuse permission for a former member of the boards to make oral submissions during oral appeal proceedings either ex parte or inter partes, unless at least three years have elapsed following termination of his appointment to the boards. After three years have elapsed, the EPO will grant permission, except in very exceptional circumstances, so that the boards could not reasonably be suspected of partiality. (**G2/94** hn.II(b))

Art. 134(2) Any natural person who
(a) is a national of a Contracting State,
(b) has his place of business or employment in a Contracting State and
(c) has passed the European qualifying examination
may be entered on the list of professional representatives.

1 **Conditions for entry on the list**
During a transitional period a person not having passed the qualifying examination may be entered on the list (**Art.134(3)**). On 31.12.2007 60% of the persons on the list were registered on the basis of **R.134(2)** and 40% on the basis of the grandfather clause **Art.134(3)**.
See **Art.134a(1)(b)** for the European qualifying examination.

Art. 134(3) During a period of one year from the date on which the accession of a State to this Convention takes effect, entry on that list may also be requested by any natural person who
(a) is a national of a Contracting State,
(b) has his place of business or employment in the State having acceded to the Convention and
(c) is entitled to represent natural or legal persons in patent matters before the central industrial property office of that State. Where such entitlement is not conditional upon the requirement of special professional qualifications, the person shall have regularly so acted in that State for at least five years.

1 **Grandfather clause**
The provision allows a representative under national law of a contracting state acceded to the EPC to be entered on the list of European professional representatives without the requirement to pass the European qualifying examination within one year from the date of accession.

Art. 134(4) Entry shall be effected upon request, accompanied by certificates indicating that the conditions laid down in paragraph 2 or 3 are fulfilled.

Art. 134(5) Persons whose names appear on the list of professional representatives shall be entitled to act in all proceedings established by this Convention.

Art. 134(6) For the purpose of acting as a professional representative, any person whose name appears on the list of professional representatives shall be entitled to establish a place of business in any Contracting State in which proceedings established by this Convention may be conducted, having regard to the Protocol on Centralisation annexed to this Convention. The authorities of such State may remove that entitlement in individual cases only in application of legal provisions adopted for the purpose of protecting public security and law and order. Before such action is taken, the President of the European Patent Office shall be consulted.

1 **Place of business in Germany or the Netherlands**
Proceedings established by the EPC are conducted in Germany and the Netherlands. Hence, this provision allows a non-German representative to set up his business in Germany and a non-Dutch representative to set up his business in the Netherlands.

See the website of the EPO for the text of the Protocol on Centralisation.

Art. 134(7) The President of the European Patent Office may grant exemption from:
(a) the requirement of paragraphs 2(a) or 3(a) in special circumstances;
(b) the requirement of paragraph 3(c), second sentence, if the applicant furnishes proof that he has acquired the requisite qualification in another way.

1 **Exemption from nationality requirement**
The President has delegated his powers to grant exemptions to the Vice-President of DG5 (Dec. Pres. OJ 2012, 13). An exemption under paragraph (a) is usually granted if the person has lived for at least four years in an EPC contracting state, is employed at a patent law firm or patent department of a company, and has shown a real intention to stay there on a permanent basis and practice as a European patent attorney. Proof of the intention must be provided.

Art. 134(8) Representation in proceedings established by this Convention may also be undertaken, in the same way as by a professional representative, by any legal practitioner qualified in a Contracting State and having his place of business in that State, to the extent that he is entitled in that State to act as a professional representative in patent matters. Paragraph 6 shall apply mutatis mutandis.

1 **Representation by legal practitioner**
Art.134(8) is a special rule limited in scope to the profession of legal practitioners in a contracting state that act as an organ of the judicial machinery and as a representative in all legal matters. 'Legal practitioner' covers the profession Rechtsanwalt in Germany and solicitor and barrister in Great-Britain. A patent attorney under national law cannot be regarded as such a 'legal practitioner' (**J19/89**). **Art.134(8)** allows the legal practitioner to act before the EPO as professional representatives to the extent that he is entitled to act as such in his contracting state in patent matters.

The EPC draws a distinction between professional representatives and legal practitioners because of the professional representative's closer connection with the EPO:

- professional representatives are subject to the disciplinary authority of the epi or the EPO (**Art.134a(1)(c)**), whereas legal practitioners are subject to disciplinary authority under national law;
- the professional representative's entitlement to act can be ascertained by consulting the list of **Art.134**, whereas a legal practitioner's entitlement is much harder to establish, as it is based on his qualification in a contracting state, his place of business and the right to act as a professional representative in patent matters in that state;
- a professional representative is always technically qualified, whereas a legal practitioner may not be.

The requirement for legal practitioners to submit always an authorisation (see **R.152(1):1**) creates transparency for clients whether they are being represented by a professional representative or a legal practitioner (**J8/10** r.2.3, 8, 9).

Art. 134a Institute of Professional Representatives before the European Patent Office

1 **General**
Art.134a anchors the existence of the epi in the Convention and sets forth the powers of the Administrative Council to adopt provisions governing the standards for admission as a professional representative, the conducting of qualifying examinations and the disciplinary powers to be exercised by that institute or the EPO.

Art.134a(1)(d) confers on the Administrative Council the competence to create an evidentiary exception modelled on the US attorney-client privilege, applying solely to proceedings before the EPO (see **R.153**).

Art.134a(2) anchors in the Convention the principle clearly formulated in Article 5(1) of the Regulation on the Establishment of the Institute, to the effect that any person entered on the list of professional representatives shall be a member of the epi. (Spec. Ed. 4 of OJ 2007)

Art. 134a(1) The Administrative Council shall be competent to adopt and amend provisions governing:
(a) the Institute of Professional Representatives before the European Patent Office, hereinafter referred to as the Institute;
(b) the qualifications and training required of a person for admission to the European qualifying examination and the conduct of such examination;
(c) the disciplinary power exercised by the Institute or the European Patent Office in respect of professional representatives;
(d) the obligation of confidentiality on the professional representative and the privilege from disclosure in proceedings before the European Patent Office in respect of communications between a professional representative and his client or any other person.

See for the implementation:
R.153 Attorney evidentiary privilege

1 **Epi (Art.134a(1)(a))**
The institute of professional representatives has been established and is called 'The Institute of Professional Representatives before the EPO' (*epi*). See Suppl. to OJ 1/2011, 105 for the Regulation on establishment of the institute. Membership is compulsory for professional representatives (Regulation on the establishment of an institute of professional representatives before the European Patent Office, **Art.5(1)**, Suppl. to OJ 1/2012, 106).

Membership requires payment of an annual fee (Regulation, **Art.6(1)**), which may be paid through standard banking procedure or by direct debiting mandate (see **ADA.8**). If the fee is not paid in due time, the entry of the professional representative will be deleted from the EPO list of professional representatives (**R.154(1)**).

2 **European qualifying examination (Art.134a(1)(b))**
The consolidated Regulation on the European qualifying examination (REE) mentioned in **Art.134a(1)(b)** are available on the EPO eqe website; the examination fee is fixed in OJ 2014 A35 §9. Since 2012 a pre-examination determines the admission to the main examination (Art.1(7), R.10(1)). The announcement of the European qualifying examination 2019 is published in OJ 2018 A30. See for preparation the articles on the examination published in the *epi* Information journal. Instructions to candidates are published in OJ 2014, sp2 p.38. A useful collection of still relevant notices from the EPO

and decisions of the President is the Ancillary Regulations to the EPC, published at irregular intervals (OJ 2016 A51).

Compendia containing the papers of the Examination of previous years can be ordered from the EPO (OJ 2004, 621) and are available on the EPO website. The examination tests the candidate's knowledge of the law and its interpretation as valid at 31 October of the year prior to the examination in question (OJ 2017 A88 Art.1). Details of the marking of papers can be found in the decision of the disciplinary board of appeal **D7/05** r.4, 5. The examination is an open-book examination (OJ 2014, sp2, p.43).

For admission to the qualifying examination a candidate must possess a level of scientific or technical knowledge equivalent to a university level qualification, and at least two years of training in the patent field for the pre-examination and a total of at least three years for the main examination. As from 2013 admission to the main examination will require a pass grade in the pre-examination. (Regulation Art.11(2) and (7))

The training must be under the supervision of a person entered on the list of professional representative or under an employee in the sense of **Art.133(3)** (**Art.10(2)(a)** REE, **D25/96**). A reduction of the three-year period is possible in the circumstances listed in OJ 2016 A108 II. §5.2. Training under supervision of a legal practitioner entitled under **Art.134(8)** to act before the EPO does not count, because legal practitioners 'do not normally possess the scientific or technical knowledge required with a view to activities pertaining to European patent applications and patents' (**D14/93** hn, r.2.2).

Candidates intending to enrol for the eqe for the first time must register at the start of their training. The period of training after registration counts for the three-year period; previous periods of professional activity can also be registered. (OJ 2017 A24, A78)

Information about the CEIPI training courses is available on the website www.ceipi.edu and in the OJ (OJ 2018 A39-41). For epi tutorials see the website www.patentepi.com and OJ 2006, 305. The European Patent Academy (see **Art.4(2):2**) also provides training in the form of seminars and in-house training (OJ 2017 A99).

3 **Discipline (Art.134a(1)(c))**

The purpose of disciplinary proceedings is to serve the public interest in the orderly and proper exercise of professional representation before the EPO, not for individuals to pursue their interests vis-à-vis others. Claims of individuals arising from a representative's infringement of the rules of professional conduct are a matter for national courts under civil, criminal or administrative law. (**D25/05** r.3, published in epi 3/2007)

The disciplinary power extends to all activities related to the EPC. The activities include the acts of filing translations and payment of renewal fees for European patents before national authorities. (**D25/05** r.4, published in epi 3/2007)

The disciplinary power is exercised by the Disciplinary Committee of the *epi*, the Disciplinary Board of the EPO and the Disciplinary Board of Appeal of the EPO. See OJ 2003, 523 for the *epi* Code of Conduct of Professional Representatives, Suppl. to OJ 1/2013, 119 and OJ 2018 A57 for the Regulation on Discipline for professional representatives (RDR); Suppl. to OJ 1/2013, 131, 141 and 50 for the Additional Rules of Procedure of the Disciplinary Committee, the Disciplinary Board and the Disciplinary Board of Appeal. Point 2 of the Code sets rules for advertising by professional representatives (see e.g. **D12/88**).

The Disciplinary Committee, consisting of professional representatives, considers breaches of the Code of Conduct and can dismiss a case, warn a representative or refer the case to the Disciplinary Board (**Art.6(2)** RDR). The Disciplinary Board and the Disciplinary Board of Appeal, both consisting of legally qualified members of the EPO and professional representatives (**R.12b(6)** EPC and Art.9 and 11 RDR), may impose a fine or delete the name of a professional representative from the list of professional representatives. The deletion may be for an indefinite period (see e.g. **DB2/92**, OJ 1994, 750; **D11/91** Summ.I).

4 **Confidentiality and attorney client privilege** (**Art.134a(1)(d)**)
The Administrative Council may adopt provisions governing the obligation of confidentiality on the professional representative. It may also adopt provisions on the privilege from disclosure in proceedings before the European Patent Office in respect of communications between a professional representative and his client or any other person. The provision on privilege from disclosure as laid down in **R.153** is in response to the US practice of requiring disclosure of documents to all parties in discovery proceedings.

Art. 134a(2) Any person entered on the list of professional representatives referred to in Article 134, paragraph 1, shall be a member of the Institute.

Art.134(1) Representation before the European Patent Office

PART VIII IMPACT ON NATIONAL LAW

Chapter I *Conversion into a national patent application*

1 **General**

A European patent application not leading to a European patent can in some cases be converted into a national application for states designated in the application. The EPC provides conversion only in two cases. The first case is where a European application has not been filed with the EPO but with a national authority, and has not been forwarded to the EPO in time. The second case is where a designated state has explicit provisions for the conversion of a European application which has become ineffective or for the conversion of a patent which has been revoked. All states must allow the conversion in the first case. The states are free to formulate the conditions for conversion in the second case.

The basis for the conversion is **Art.66**, stating that a validly filed European patent application is regarded as a national application with the same filing or priority date. This means that the converted national application will be accorded the same filing date as the European application. Other European or national applications filed on or after the filing date will not be prejudicial for the converted national application. The applicant will only enjoy this effect of **Art.66** when he complies with the requirements for conversion as laid down in **Art.135** and 137.

The request for conversion must be filed with the EPO, except where the application has not been forwarded to the EPO in due time on grounds of national security or error (**Art.77(3)**), in which case the request must be filed with the filing office.

A conversion can also be applied to utility models and utility certificates (**Art.140**, referring to **Art.135** and 137).

Art. 135 Request for conversion

Art. 135(1) The central industrial property office of a designated Contracting State shall, at the request of the applicant for or proprietor of a European patent, apply the procedure for the grant of a national patent in the following circumstances:

(a) where the European patent application is deemed to be withdrawn under Article 77, paragraph 3;

(b) in such other cases as are provided for by the national law, in which the European patent application is refused or withdrawn or deemed to be withdrawn, or the European patent is revoked under this Convention.

Art.77(3) Forwarding of European patent applications
See for the implementation:

R.155 Filing and transmission of the request for conversion
R.156 Information to the public in the event of conversion

1 **Conversion when application deemed withdrawn (Art.135(1)(a))**
When an application duly filed with a national patent office has not been forwarded to the EPO within 14 months (**R.37(2)**), it is regarded as withdrawn (**Art.77(3)**). This might happen in the case of national security or error of the national patent office.

2 **Conversion in other cases (Art.135(1)(b))**
Excessive use of this provision could seriously reduce the importance of the uniform grant procedure of the EPC. Hence, there has been strong opposition against inclusion of the provision; it has been pushed through by Germany. The contracting states have made very limited use of **Art.135(1)(b)**. The following possibilities have been created under national law (see Nat-Law table VII, column 1 and 5):

2.1 MISSING TRANSLATION
Several states allow conversion if an application filed in a non-EPO language is deemed to be withdrawn, because the translation in an EPO language (**Art.14(2)**) was not filed in due time (**R.6(1)**).

2.2 WITHDRAWAL, REFUSAL OR REVOCATION
A few states allow conversion where a European patent application is withdrawn, deemed withdrawn or refused and a European patent is revoked in opposition.

2.3 UTILITY MODEL
In general, states having a utility model with less stringent requirements for inventive step than a patent allow conversion of a failed European patent application into a national utility model. Hence, several states allow conversion into a national utility model for European patent applications deemed withdrawn pursuant to **Art.77(3)**. Other states allow conversion into a national utility model for European patent applications deemed withdrawn because a translation in the language of the proceedings was not filed in time (**Art.14(2)**). Some states allow conversion into a national utility model of a European patent application withdrawn, regarded as withdrawn or refused by the EPO. Conversion into a utility model is also allowed in Italy for European patents revoked for Italy. See OJ 1987, 175 for the derivation of a German utility model from a European application.

Art. 135(2) In the case referred to in paragraph 1(a), the request for conversion shall be filed with the central industrial property office with which the European patent application has been filed. That office shall, subject to the provisions governing national security, transmit the request directly to the central industrial property offices of the Contracting States specified therein.

1 **Submission of request with national office**
An application filed with a national office which has not reached the EPO within 14 months after the date of filing or priority is deemed to be withdrawn (**R.37(2)**). When a request for conversion has been filed with the national office and national secrecy does not prohibit it, the national office will forward the documents to the national offices of the states specified in the request. If the national office does not transmit the application within the twenty months from the filing or priority date (**R.155(3)**), the effect of **Art.66**

lapses (**Art.135(4)**). A late forwarding cannot be remedied with re-establishment, because the failure is not due to the applicant.

Art. 135(3) In the cases referred to in paragraph 1(b), the request for conversion shall be submitted to the European Patent Office in accordance with the Implementing Regulations. It shall not be deemed to be filed until the conversion fee has been paid. The European Patent Office shall transmit the request to the central industrial property offices of the Contracting States specified therein.

1 **Submission of request with EPO**
In the case of **Art.135(1)(b)**, the applicant must submit his request for conversion to the EPO and pay the conversion fee (**Rfees2(1)14**). The request must be filed within three months of withdrawal or of the communication that the application is deemed to be withdrawn, or of the decision refusing the application or revoking the patent. The effect of the application under **Art.66** lapses if the request is not filed within the three month period (**R.155(1)**). The EPO forwards a duly submitted request and the file of the application or patent to the national offices of the states specified in the request.

Art. 135(4) The effect of the European patent application referred to in Article 66 shall lapse if the request for conversion is not submitted in due time.

Art.66 A European application with a filing date is equivalent to a regular national filing
See for the implementation:
R.155(1), (3) Period for filing the request for conversion

1 **Period for filing request**
The effect referred to in **Art.66** is that the converted application retains the priority and filing date of the spawning European application (see national decision in OJ 1982, 66).

The due time for filing the request as laid down in **R.155(1)** is within three months of withdrawal, or notification of the communication that the application is deemed withdrawn, or notification of the decision refusing the application or revoking the patent. Where the application is deemed withdrawn under **Art.77(3)** because a national office has not forwarded a European application to the EPO in due time, the request must be filed within twenty months from the date of filing or, if priority has been claimed, the date of priority (**R.155(3)**).

Art. 136 (deleted)

Art. 137 Formal requirements for conversion

1 **General**
This provision allows national authorities to levy a filing fee and request a translation of the application. The file of the application to be converted is opened for public inspection according to **R.156**, allowing the public to know the origin of the application.

Art. 137(1) A European patent application transmitted in accordance with Article 135, paragraph 2 or 3, shall not be subjected to formal requirements of national law which are different from or additional to those provided for in this Convention.

Art.135(2) Request for conversion where application is deemed withdrawn under Art.77(3)
Art.135(3) Request for conversion in other cases

Art. 137(2) Any central industrial property office to which the European patent application is transmitted may require that the applicant shall, within a period of not less than two months:

(a) pay the national application fee; and
(b) file a translation of the original text of the European patent application in an official language of the State in question and, where appropriate, of the text as amended during proceedings before the European Patent Office which the applicant wishes to use as the basis for the national procedure.

1 **Period for paying fee and filing translation**
The period of at least two months runs from receipt of the request by the national office.

Chapter II *Revocation and prior rights*

1 **Revocation and prior rights in national proceedings**

Art.138 and **139** of this chapter contain provisions for the further existence of the uniform and centrally granted European patent in the contracting states and the mutual effects of European and national patents and patent applications.

A European patent can be revoked in central opposition proceedings (**Art.99** ff.), started within 9 months after publication of the grant, which may lead to a revocation with effect for all designated states. The patent can also be revoked centrally by the revocation procedure of **Art.105a**. The other possibility to revoke a patent is in a revocation procedure before a court of a contracting state, leading to a revocation with effect only in that state.

The question of revocation often arises in national infringement procedures. Some states (e.g. DE, AT) start from the principle of the validity of the patent; a revocation must be requested in a special revocation procedure. In other states (e.g. NL) a revocation can be requested as a counterclaim in an infringement procedure. When requested in an infringement procedure, the decision of courts in some states (CH, IT) is only effective between the parties (inter partes), without automatic effect for everybody (erga omnes). A mixed form is also possible (FR), where apart from the nullity inter partes a court can also pronounce the nullity for the entire state.

The purpose of **Art.138** is to harmonize the national revocation and limitation procedures by imposing minimum rights for the proprietor. A proprietor has the right to limit his patent in view of grounds for revocation during national revocation proceedings; he also has the right of self-limitation. The essential parts of the revocation are thus bound by the EPC, which is an exception to the fact that the European patent is subject to the conditions applicable to national patents (**Art.2(2)**). These measures increase the legal certainty of the proprietors and leads to a further harmonization of the legal effect of a European patent.

Whether or not a revocation procedure started within the opposition period is allowed, depends on national law. For instance, Germany does not allow it, Austria allows it if the party is not opposing the patent.

Art. 138 Revocation of European patents

Art. 138(1) Subject to Article 139, a European patent may be revoked with effect for a Contracting State only on the grounds that:

(a) the subject-matter of the European patent is not patentable under Articles 52 to 57;

(b) the European patent does not disclose the invention in a manner sufficiently clear and complete for it to be carried out by a person skilled in the art;

(c) the subject-matter of the European patent extends beyond the content of the application as filed or, if the patent was granted on a divisional application or on a new application filed under Article 61, beyond the content of the earlier application as filed;

(d) the protection conferred by the European patent has been extended; or

(e) the proprietor of the European patent is not entitled under Article 60, paragraph 1.

Art.52 Patentable inventions
Art.53 Exceptions to patentability

Art.54 Novelty
Art.55 Non-prejudicial disclosures
Art.56 Inventive step
Art.57 Industrial applications
Art.60(1) Right to a European patent
Art.61 European patent application filed by non-entitled person
Art.139 Prior rights and rights arising on the same date

1 **Grounds for national revocation**

Art.138(1) provides an exhaustive list of grounds for revocation of a European patent in national proceedings. Since the provision does not refer to national law, it is clear that **Art.138** does not make national revocation of European patents conditional on the adoption of special national provisions (Spec. Ed. 4 of OJ 2007).

Art.138 limits the number of possible grounds on which a national court may revoke a European patent. This gives legal certainty to the proprietor: a patent granted by the EPO may only be revoked in a national procedure on the grounds of **Art.138**. The only allowed additional ground is the revocation of a patent claiming subject-matter falling under a reservation according to **Art.167(2)** EPC 1973; the revocation is the only sanction for not complying with **Art.167(2)**. The EPC does not compel the contracting states to use all five grounds for revocation.

Grounds (a) - (c) are equivalent to the opposition grounds of **Art.100(a)-(c)**. The additional ground (d) relates to the case where the patent has been maintained in opposition proceedings (**Art.101(3)(a)**) or amended in a limitation procedure (**Art.105b**), but the scope of protection has been extended, contrary to **Art.123(3)**.

Ground (e) covers the case where the proprietor is not entitled to the patent. If proof is provided that the proprietor is not entitled, the court of a state may revoke the patent for that state.

2 **National prior rights**

In a revocation procedure, the court has to take into account the compulsory provision of **Art.139(1)** and (2) on the equivalence of European and national rights in a national revocation or infringement procedure. Hence, national prior rights are also taken into account in a revocation procedure. The EPC (**Art.139(3)**) leaves it to national law to allow grant of a patent through a national and European route, and, hence, to include or exclude this from the grounds for revocation.

Art. 138(2) If the grounds for revocation affect the European patent only in part, the patent shall be limited by a corresponding amendment of the claims and revoked in part.

1 **Revocation in part**

The wording of **Art.138(2)** makes it clear that limitation and partial revocation of a European patent are always to take the form of a corresponding amendment to the patent claims. This does away with the opportunity provided for under **Art.138(2)**, second sentence, EPC 1973 to pronounce partial revocation simply by amending the description or drawings.

The provision does not refer to national law, thereby making it directly applicable without provisions in national law.

Art. 138(3) In proceedings before the competent court or authority relating to the validity of the European patent, the proprietor of the patent shall have the right to limit the patent by amending the claims. The patent as thus limited shall form the basis for the proceedings.

1 **Right to limitation of patent**

Art.138(3) establishes the right to self-limitation of the patent by the proprietor and is binding in national proceedings relating to the validity of European patents, thereby extending the degree of harmonisation.

It is designed to give the patent proprietor the right in such proceedings to submit an amended, i.e. limited, version of his claims which in his view meets the objections to the validity of his patent. This limited version of the patent must then form the basis for subsequent proceedings. If the court or authority dealing with the case considers that the proprietor's own limitation is insufficient, it may further limit the patent or revoke it in full.

As in European opposition proceedings and in accordance with the limitation procedure (see **Art.105a** ff), the effect of limiting or revoking a European patent in national revocation proceedings is retroactive. Therefore, **Art.68** refers to national revocation proceedings. (Spec. Ed. 4 of OJ 2007)

Art. 139 Prior rights and rights arising on the same date

1 **Double patenting**

This article deals with avoiding double patenting by European and national applications or patents. The provision is split up in three parts: first the case where the European right is the older right, secondly where the national right is the older right, and thirdly where the same invention is patented via a national and the European route. According to paragraphs 1 and 2, the European right has the same effects as a national right. This equivalence causes the European right to be maintained or revoked dependent on whether it is the older or younger one of the two rights. If the European right is the younger one, **Art.139(2)** gives a ground for revocation under **Art.138(1)(a)**.

The prior right effect in extension states is governed by **Art.7** and **8** of the Extension Agreement (OJ 1994, 75). An earlier European application extending to an extension state has the same prior art effect for a subsequent application filed in that state as a national application. Likewise, an earlier national application is prejudicial to a later European application extending to the extension state. This prior art effect is only obtained if the extension fee has been paid.**Art.101(2):1** Where an extended European application and a national application have the same effective date, the former takes precedence, to the extent that it protects the same invention.

See **Art.140:1** for the effect of national prior utility models and utility certificates.

Art. 139(1) In any designated Contracting State a European patent application and a European patent shall have with regard to a national patent application and a national patent the same prior right effect as a national patent application and a national patent.

1 **Prior right effect of European application and patent**

The provision mentions the prior right effect of a European patent in order to cover the prior right effect of a European application granted before its publication (see **Art.93(2)**).

A not-regularly published European application does not have a national prior right effect, just as it does not have a European prior right effect (**J5/81** r.3).

Note that until 2008 Switzerland and Liechtenstein, in contrast with the EPC, used the prior claim approach in the assessment of prior rights instead of the whole contents approach. See **Art.54(3):1**.

Art. 139(2) A national patent application and a national patent in a Contracting State shall have with regard to a European patent designating that Contracting State the same prior right effect as if the European patent were a national patent.

1 **Prior right effect of national application and patent**

The EPC deals differently with European and national prior rights during the European grant and opposition procedure. A European prior right is comprised in the state of the art according to **Art.54(3)** for all contracting states under the EPC 2000 and for the overlapping contracting states under **Art.54(4)** EPC 1973 and may form a bar to the grant of a European patent. In contrast, national prior rights are never comprised in the state of the art considered under the EPC. Consequently, the existence of a national prior right is neither an obstacle to patentability under **Art.52-Art.57** nor a ground for opposition under **Art.100**. During the search of the European application, national prior rights are not specifically looked for, but if found, the applicant is informed accordingly (B-VI,4.2). During substantive examination the applicant may limit the claims and amend the description and drawings for the appropriate states in view of the national prior rights after the EPO has evaluated the prior right (**R.138**; G-IV,6; H-III,4.5). After grant national prior rights can be taken into account in limitation proceedings (D-X,10.1) and asserted in national revocation proceedings according to **Art.138(1)(a)** with **Art.139(2)**.

Art. 139(3) Any Contracting State may prescribe whether and on what terms an invention disclosed in both a European patent application or patent and a national application or patent having the same date of filing or, where priority is claimed, the same date of priority, may be protected simultaneously by both applications or patents.

1 **Protection through single route and double protection**

The purpose of **Art.139(3)** is to avoid that for a single invention both a European and a national patent is granted. The provision was intended as a first step in the abolition of national patents (Travaux Préparatoires 1962, 3076/IV/62-D, p. 114a). After the decision was taken to restrict the EPC to a system for only granting patents, it was left to the contracting states whether or not to allow an invention to be granted through both the national route and the European route.

The provision is not intended as a general prohibition on double patenting. Although the Munich Diplomatic Conference of 1973 regarded the prohibition of double patenting as a generally recognised principle of procedural law in the Contracting States (M/PR/I, point 665, page 62), it did not include a prohibition on double patenting in the EPC and left it to the contracting states to permit or prohibit double patenting.

Many national laws do not have a broad prohibition against double patenting. National laws sometimes use the faculty given by **Art.139(3)** and include a provision prohibiting double patenting where a European application and a national application having the same applicant and same date of filing both proceed to grant.

2 **Simultaneous protection by European and national patent**

The provision assumes that the European patent application or patent and the national application or patent have the same applicant or proprietor. Obviously, two European applications and patents having the same priority date but two different applicants may protect the same invention simultaneously (G-IV,5.4, last sentence; see also **Art.60(2):2**).

The provision does not cover, probably unintentionally, the common case where a European application claims priority of a national application and designates the state in which the national application was filed. The phrase 'having the same date of filing ... of priority' should read 'having the same effective date'.

Some contracting states do not exclude the protection of an invention by both a European patent and a national patent having the same effective date (see NatLaw table X, column 1). Other contracting states give priority to the European patent: to the extent that it protects the same invention, the national patent ceases to have effect. The date on which the national patent ceases to have effect is different for most states: see NatLaw table X, column 1. Germany does not allow simultaneous protection for national patent applications or patents, but it does allow simultaneous protection for utility models (NatLaw table X). See also **Art.65:1** for the consequence of automatic validation.

Double protection by applications or by applications and patents is not excluded. The EPO should not check collision during the grant procedure. After the grant it has to be sorted out according to national law.

3 **Double patenting**

The issue of double patenting can arise not only where the same invention is protected through the European and a national route, but also between parent and divisional application and between two applications filed on the same day by the same applicant. The EPC has no provision explicitly prohibiting double patenting. Nevertheless, the EPO applies the prohibition increasingly.

The EPO has developed guidelines to be applied during the grant procedure to avoid double patenting (G-IV,5.4 and C-IX,1.6) and examining divisions refuse applications when they violate these guidelines. A few decisions of the board of appeal have endorsed this practice, other decisions have rejected it. **T587/98** r.3 held that there is no basis in the EPC to refuse a divisional application relating to the same invention as the parent on the ground of double patenting.

In its decision **G1/06** r.13.4, the Enlarged Board of Appeal accepted in an obiter dictum that 'the principle of prohibition of double patenting exists on the basis that an applicant has no legitimate interest in proceedings leading to the grant of a second patent for the same subject-matter if he already possesses one granted patent therefor'; it did not give an explicit legal basis for the prohibition. The later decision **T307/03** discovered a basis for the right of an inventor to the grant of only one patent for a particular invention in the first sentence of **Art.60(1)** by interpreting the indefinite article 'a' in the provision as 'one', which interpretation is rather unusual in the field of patents. The decision has not been cited in later decisions. Other decisions reject the use of **Art.60** as basis; see e.g. **T1423/07** hn.3. The prohibition has, however, been upheld in several later decisions of the boards of appeal. The examining and opposition divisions do not allow double patenting (G-IV,5.4). **T936/04** r.2.3 allowed raising an objection on the ground of double patenting in opposition proceedings even though it is not a ground of opposition.

Note, that the Enlarged Board of Appeal emphasised the procedural character of double patenting, permitting introduction of the prohibition into the EPC via **Art.125** as a general procedural principle. **T307/03** has not followed this line and, instead, tried to find a basis for the prohibition in substantive law (see r.2.7).

T51/08 used a different tool to avoid duplicating judgements. It regarded an appeal in the case of a divisional inadmissible because the claims submitted were identical to claims of the parent on which already a decision in appeal had been taken. Therefore, the principle of res judicata prevented the board from examining the same claims again (r.3, 4). The board did not investigate whether the use of this principle complied with **Art.125**.

4 Definition of double patenting

Application of the prohibition requires a definition of 'double patenting', which has not yet been provided by the EPO. The definition should give guidance on at least the following three issues, as discussed in an article by Harrison and Bremi in the journal *epi Information* 2/2009.

When are the applicants of two applications the same? The EPO may follow the same strict line as in **T788/05**, where applicants were regarded as not being the same because the sole applicant of one application was one of several joint applicants of another application.

Another issue is which claims must be compared and at what moment in time. **T307/03** r.3.1 compared the latest filed claims of the divisional with the claims of the granted parent. By making the comparison during proceedings before the EPO, the board used the prohibition to avoid multiple grant procedures defending the same invention in parent and divisional; even abandonment of the parent application would not remove the objection (r.3.2). From the perspective of an alleged infringer, the issue of double patenting is only relevant when assessing infringement before a national court, at which time any amendment of claims in opposition or limitation proceedings can be taken into account; in this case abandonment of one of patents would solve the double patenting issue. From this perspective, the assessment of double patenting should be deferred to national infringement or revocation proceedings.

The third issue for which guidance is necessary is the degree of similarity required for 'the same invention' and is dealt with in the following section.

5 Same invention

The above cited decision of the Enlarged Board of Appeal held that the double patenting issue involves granting two patents 'for the same subject-matter' (**G1/06** r.13.4). When the wording of **Art.139(3)** 'an invention ... protected simultaneously by both applications or patents' is combined with the two statements of **G2/98** equating 'the same invention' with 'the same subject-matter' (r.5) and defining the invention by the subject-matter of a claim (r.2), the following statement can be derived: double patenting requires protection of the same invention by two patents including claims having the same subject-matter (see also **T2461/10**).

The interpretation of 'the same invention' as 'the same subject-matter' is used consistently by the EPO in fields as diverse as double patenting (**T118/91** r.2.4.1; **T587/98** r.3.3), claiming priority (**G2/98** hn), and prior rights under **Art.54(3)** where double patenting is avoided by requiring novelty. Hence, a difference of a single feature between two claims makes the claims relate to different inventions. The Guidelines follow this interpretation for double patenting as from the June 2012 edition (G-IV,5.4).

The above sections of the Guidelines appear to be consistent with the statement in that double protection only occurs where two applications claim the same invention, i.e. the same subject-matter. Decisions **T587/98** and **T1391/07** r.2.4 are in agreement with the statement. The Guidelines and the decision **T587/98** give examples of embracing claims of different scope (i.e. totally overlapping), **T877/06** of partially overlapping claims that do not violate the prohibition. The Guidelines allow an applicant to obtain a first quicker protection for a preferred embodiment and pursue the general teaching in a divisional (G-IV,5.4; see **G2/10** r.4.5.5; overturning **T307/03** r.5.3).

Chapter III *Miscellaneous effects*

Art. 140 National utility models and utility certificates

Articles 66, 124, 135, 137 and 139 shall apply to utility models and utility certificates and to applications for utility models and utility certificates registered or deposited in the Contracting States whose laws make provision for such models or certificates.

Art.66 Equivalence of European filing with national filing
Art.124 Information concerning national patent applications
Art.135 Request for the application of national procedure
Art.137 Formal requirements for conversion
Art.139 Rights of earlier date or the same date

1 **General**

The national law of several contracting states provides protection for utility models, the national law of France for utility certificates (see NatLaw table VII, column 5).

According to **Art.66**, a European filing is regarded as a valid national filing for a utility model or certificate in the designated states giving protection for them.

The applicability of **Art.124** entails that the applicant on request by the EPO must mention the contracting states in which he has filed utility models or certificates. Beware, **Art.124** requires an applicant to mention all states, i.e. not only contracting states, in which he has filed corresponding patent applications.

Art.135 and **137** allow a European patent application to be converted into a national utility model or certificate. See **Art.135(1):2** and NatLaw table VII for the states that make use of this possibility.

The applicability of **Art.139(1)** means that a European patent application or patent has the same prior right effect in regard of utility models and certificates as national patent applications and patents. All contracting states use the 'whole contents' approach. The prior rights are only taken into account for assessing novelty, not for inventive step of the utility model and certificate.

The applicability of **Art.139(2)** means that national filings of utility models and certificates are effective as prior rights for European patents in the same way as they are effective as prior rights for national patents. Hence, prior utility models and certificates filed in a contracting state may be prejudicial to later-filed European patent applications designating such a state. A utility model in Germany is not prejudicial for a later-filed European patent designating Germany, but the rights of the patent may not be exercised until the lapse of the utility model.

The applicability of **Art.139(3)** means that it is up to national law to arrange for double protection. In Germany, for instance, simultaneous protection by a patent and utility model is allowed (NatLaw table X).

Art. 141 Renewal fees for European patents

1 **Transition of payment**

While the renewal fees for a European patent application are to be paid to the EPO, the renewal fees for the granted patent are to be paid to the national patent offices. **Art.141** lays down the transition of the obligation to pay. See NatLaw table VI. The renewal fees for a patent are payable to the national office in order to allow national offices to levy the fees according to their own scales of fees.

The national patent offices pay their expenses mainly from the renewal fees of granted European patents. The national offices must transfer 50% of the renewal fees paid for European patents to the EPO as decided by the Administrative Council (OJ 1984, 296 and **Art.39(1)**).

Art. 141(1) Renewal fees for a European patent may only be imposed for the years which follow that referred to in Article 86, paragraph 2.

Art.86(2) Termination of the obligation to pay renewal fees to the EPO

1 **Example of renewal fee payment**

The patent application is filed on 02.06.1978; the patent year then ends on 02.06, the next patent year begins on 03.06. A possible priority right has no influence on these dates. When the mention of the grant is published on 02.06.1980, no renewal fees need be paid to the EPO anymore, but instead from the third year onwards renewal fees must be paid to the national offices of the contracting states where the patent is to be kept in force. When the mention is published on 03.06.1980, the renewal fee in respect of the third year must still be paid to the EPO and is due 30.06.1980, while the renewal fees in respect of the fourth and following years must be paid to the national offices according to their national rules.

NatLaw table VI indicates the national requirements for the payment of renewal fees, such as the amount of the renewal fees, due date, grace period and the requirement to appoint a representative. Particulars about the bank accounts of the national offices are given in NatLaw table VIII. The moment the patent lapses if a due renewal fee is not paid to the national office is governed by national law and is not stated in NatLaw.

Art. 141(2) Any renewal fees falling due within two months of the publication in the European Patent Bulletin of the mention of the grant of the European patent shall be deemed to have been validly paid if they are paid within that period. Any additional fee provided for under national law shall not be charged.

1 **Two-month period before national office**

The two months is a safety period to allow for different rules in different states. If the renewal fees are paid within this period, they must be regarded as paid in time, irrespective of national law. See **Art.65:1** for the concurrence of the two-month period and the period of **Art.65(1)** for filing a translation of the patent.

PART IX SPECIAL AGREEMENTS

1 **Unitary patent for several states**
This part is included in the EPC to make it possible that a patent granted according to the EPC becomes a unitary patent for the EU. See **P:4.2** for progress of the negotiations. The articles in this part have already made it possible that a European patent for Switzerland and Liechtenstein is treated as a unitary right.

The agreement between Switzerland and Liechtenstein and the EU Regulation setting up a unitary patent (see **P:4.2**) are special agreements in the meaning of **Art.142** and regional patent agreements in the meaning of **Art.45** PCT.

Art. 142 Unitary patents

Art. 142(1) Any group of Contracting States, which has provided by a special agreement that a European patent granted for those States has a unitary character throughout their territories, may provide that a European patent may only be granted jointly in respect of all those States.

Switzerland and Liechtenstein form such a group (OJ 1980 p.407). See **P:4.2** for the agreements setting up unitary patent protection in the EU.

Art. 142(2) Where any group of Contracting States has availed itself of the authorisation given in paragraph 1, the provisions of this Part shall apply.

The provisions of this Part IX are **Art.142-149a**.

Art. 143 Special departments of the European Patent Office

Art. 143(1) The group of Contracting States may give additional tasks to the European Patent Office.

1 **Additional tasks**
Additional tasks to be given to the EPO under the unitary patent scheme are: the administration of the requests for the new patent, administration of renewal fees and the register for the unitary patent.

Art. 143(2) Special departments common to the Contracting States in the group may be set up within the European Patent Office in order to carry out the additional tasks. The President of the European Patent Office shall direct such special departments; Article 10, paragraphs 2 and 3, shall apply mutatis mutandis.

Art.10(2) Functions and powers of the President
Art.10(3) Replacement of President by Vice-President

Art. 144 Representation before special departments

The group of Contracting States may lay down special provisions to govern representation of parties before the departments referred to in Article 143, paragraph 2.

Art.143(2) Special departments of the European Patent Office

1 **General**
Professional representatives allowed to act before the EPO are also allowed to act before the special departments of the EPO.

Art. 145 Select committee of the Administrative Council

Art. 145(1) The group of Contracting States may set up a select committee of the Administrative Council for the purpose of supervising the activities of the special departments set up under Article 143, paragraph 2; the European Patent Office shall place at its disposal such staff, premises and equipment as may be necessary for the performance of its duties. The President of the European Patent Office shall be responsible for the activities of the special departments to the select committee of the Administrative Council.

Art.143(2) Special departments of the European Patent Office

Art. 145(2) The composition, powers and functions of the select committee shall be determined by the group of Contracting States.

1 **Powers of select committee**
The select committee for the unitary patent is governed by Art.9(2) EU Regulation 1257/2012.

The powers of the select committee are: governance and supervision of the additional tasks of Art.143(1), setting the amount of the renewal fees, and the distribution of the renewal fees over the participating member states and the EPO. See OJ 2016 A39-41 for three published decisions relating to Unitary Patent Protection adopted by the select committee.

The Rules relating to Unitary Patent Protection lay down the competences and duties of the select committee, establish a Unitary Patent Protection Division within the EPO, and provide the rules governing the procedures before the EPO. (OJ 2016 A39)

Art. 146 Cover for expenditure for carrying out special tasks

Where additional tasks have been given to the European Patent Office under Article 143, the group of Contracting States shall bear the expenses incurred by the Organisation in carrying out these tasks. Where special departments have been set up in the European Patent Office to carry out these additional tasks, the group shall bear the expenditure on staff, premises and equipment chargeable in respect of these departments. Article 39, paragraphs 3 and 4, Article 41 and Article 47 shall apply mutatis mutandis.

Art.39(3), (4) Payments by the Contracting States in respect of renewal fees for European patents
Art.41 Advances
Art.47 Provisional budget
Art.143 Special departments of the European Patent Office

Art. 147 Payments in respect of renewal fees for unitary patents

If the group of Contracting States has fixed a common scale of renewal fees in respect of European patents, the proportion referred to in Article 39, paragraph 1, shall be calculated on the basis of the common scale; the minimum amount referred to in Article 39, paragraph 1, shall apply to the unitary patent. Article 39, paragraphs 3 and 4, shall apply mutatis mutandis.

Art.39(1) The part of the renewal fees to be paid to the EPO
Art.39(3), (4) Payments by the Contracting States in respect of renewal fees for European patents
The provision is applied in the treaty between Switzerland and Liechtenstein.

1 **Renewal fees for Switzerland and Liechtenstein**
Switzerland and Liechtenstein have made use of **Art.147** and a single renewal fee is due for a European patent designating the two states.

2 **Renewal fees for the European patent with unitary effect**
Renewal fees for European patents with unitary effect must be paid to the EPO. The amounts are laid down in the Rules relating to Fees for Unitary Patent Protection (OJ 2016 A40).

The EPO deducts a 50% share of the renewal fees and any fees for late payment for its own benefit (**Art.39(1)**). Before paying the other 50% share to the member states participating in the unitary patent protection, the EPO deducts from this share the expenditure for the special tasks under **Art.146** (see Budgetary and Financial Rules, OJ 2016 A41 Art.3).

Art. 148 The European patent application as an object of property

Art. 148(1) Article 74 shall apply unless the group of Contracting States has specified otherwise.

Art.74 Application of national law to a European patent application as an object of property

Art. 148(2) The group of Contracting States may provide that a European patent application for which these Contracting States are designated may only be transferred, mortgaged or subjected to any legal means of execution in respect of all the Contracting States of the group and in accordance with the provisions of the special agreement.

Art. 149 Joint designation

Art. 149(1) The group of Contracting States may provide that these States may only be designated jointly, and that the designation of one or some only of such States shall be deemed to constitute the designation of all the States of the group.

1 **Joint designation of states**
Switzerland and Liechtenstein have made use of this possibility, so that both states can only be designated together. See OJ 1980 p.407 for the treaty.

Art. 149(2) Where the European Patent Office acts as a designated Office under Article 153, paragraph 1, paragraph 1 shall apply if the applicant has indicated in the international application that he wishes to obtain a European patent for one or more of the designated States of the group. The same shall apply if the applicant designates in the international application one of the Contracting States in the group, whose national law provides that the designation of that State shall have the effect of the application being for a European patent.

Art.153(1) PCT applications

1 **Liechtenstein-Switzerland designation**
If a Euro-PCT application indicates that the applicant wants to obtain a regional patent for Liechtenstein or Switzerland, this is interpreted as a wish to obtain a European patent for both these states. If a Euro-PCT applicant does not indicate that he wishes to obtain a regional patent, it is assumed that the applicant wishes to obtain a national patent for these two states, granted by the Swiss Patent Office.

Art. 149a Other agreements between the Contracting States

1 **General**
Art.149a creates a legal basis for any future agreements between the EPC contracting states concerning such matters as translation requirements or litigation concerning European patents.

The Paris Intergovernmental Conference of 1999 has mandated two working parties to submit to the governments of the EPC contracting states and to the EPC Revision Conference proposals aiming at reducing the cost of European patents and improving litigation concerning European patents (OJ 1999 p.545).

Art. 149a(1) Nothing in this Convention shall be construed as limiting the right of some or all of the Contracting States to conclude special agreements on any matters concerning European patent applications or European patents which under this Convention are subject to and governed by national law, such as, in particular

(a) an agreement establishing a European patent court common to the Contracting States party to it;

(b) an agreement establishing an entity common to the Contracting States party to it to deliver, at the request of national courts or quasi-judicial authorities, opinions on issues of European or harmonised national patent law;

(c) an agreement under which the Contracting States party to it dispense fully or in part with translations of European patents under Article 65;

(d) an agreement under which the Contracting States party to it provide that translations of European patents as required under Article 65 may be filed with, and published by, the European Patent Office.

Art.65 Translation of the European patent

1 **Special agreements on patent court and translation regime**

Art.149a(1) expressly underlines that the Convention does not prevent any contracting state from concluding with other contracting states agreements on any matters which under the EPC are governed by national law, in particular Art.2, 64(2) and 65 (OJ 2007 se4). Sub-paragraph (a) covers the Unified Patent Court Agreement. Sub-paragraph (c) covers the 'London Agreement' on translations, which has in the meantime entered into force (see Art.65(1):2).

Art. 149a(2) The Administrative Council shall be competent to decide that:

(a) the members of the Boards of Appeal or the Enlarged Board of Appeal may serve on a European patent court or a common entity and take part in proceedings before that court or entity in accordance with any such agreement;

(b) the European Patent Office shall provide a common entity with such support staff, premises and equipment as may be necessary for the performance of its duties, and the expenses incurred by that entity shall be borne fully or in part by the Organisation.

1 **Support of the EPO staff**

Art.149a(2) addresses the involvement of the European Patent Organisation once an agreement under paragraph (1)(a) or (b) has been concluded and entered into force (OJ 2007 se4). It is not envisaged to make use of Art.149a(2)(a) for the Unified Patent Court Agreement.

PART X INTERNATIONAL APPLICATIONS UNDER THE PATENT COOPERATION TREATY - EURO-PCT APPLICATIONS

1 **General**
Art.150 is the basic provision for Euro-PCT applications. It is followed by two articles defining the EPO's functions as a receiving Office and an international authority in the international phase of the PCT and a final article combining the provisions relating to the European phase.

A synopsis of the PCT procedures can be found in the Chapter *Notes to the Patent Cooperation Treaty* of this book. The synopsis indicates the relationship between the EPC and the PCT by reference to **Art.150-153** and **R.157-165**. The notes below refer to the relevant sections of the Chapter of this book relating to the PCT in the form: PCT §3.2.1.

Art. 150 Application of the Patent Cooperation Treaty

1 **Relationship between PCT and EPC**
This article lays down the principles governing the interaction between the EPC and PCT, i.e. the prevalence rule for the provisions of the PCT over those of the EPC.

Art. 150(1) The Patent Cooperation Treaty of 19 June 1970, hereinafter referred to as the PCT, shall be applied in accordance with the provisions of this Part.

'This Part' refers to Part X of the EPC and appertaining implementing regulations, i.e. **Art.150 - 153** and **R.157 - 165**.

Art. 150(2) International applications filed under the PCT may be the subject of proceedings before the European Patent Office. In such proceedings, the provisions of the PCT and its Regulations shall be applied, supplemented by the provisions of this Convention. In case of conflict, the provisions of the PCT or its Regulations shall prevail.

1 **General**
This provision expressly refers to the PCT Regulations, as the PCT itself lacks a provision corresponding to **Art.164(1)** EPC declaring the PCT Regulations to be an integral part of the Treaty. (OJ 2007 se4 (EN) p.178)

2 **Prevalence of the PCT**

An international application may be subject to proceedings before the EPO, both in the international phase with the EPO acting as receiving Office (rO, **Art.151**), International Searching Authority or International Preliminary Examining Authority (ISA or IPEA, **Art.152**), and in the regional phase with the EPO acting as designated Office or elected Office (**Art.153**). Details of the procedures are given in the chapter 'Notes to the PCT' in this book.

In both phases the EPO must apply the provisions of the PCT, supplemented by those of the EPC acting as international office for filling in details and making choices where options are available (**Art.150(2)**, second sentence). Some PCT provisions refer to specific national procedures, such as Art.48(2) and R.82*bis*.2 PCT referring to national remedies.

In the international phase the EPO applies the PCT for both procedural and substantive issues, supplemented by a few procedural provisions of the EPC, e.g. **Art.75, 151, R.157-158** and Rfees for payments to the EPO. The EPO uses the provisions of the PCT for substantive issues, such as for priority (Art.8 PCT), search (Art.15 PCT) and examination (Art.33 PCT). The EPO boards of appeal held that they have no jurisdiction in the international phase unless the PCT or EPC explicitly states so (**J20/89; J14/98** r.2.1).

The entry of a Euro-PCT application into the European phase is governed by Art.22 and 39 PCT, supplemented by **R.159-165** EPC. Art.23 PCT prohibits the EPO to process the application under its regional procedure before entry. On the other hand, the regional procedure requires a.o. payment of certain fees before entry. The conflict is solved by giving prevalence to the provisions of the PCT, as required by **Art.150(2)**, last sentence: **R.159(1)** extends the periods for payment till the date of entry. The EPC requirements for form and content may not be used to supplement those of the PCT (Art.27(1) PCT). Hence, an international application complying with the PCT requirements regarding form and content may not be objected to because of different requirements of the EPC after entry.

The processing of the Euro-PCT application by the EPO as designated and elected office after it has entered the regional phase is governed by the procedural provisions of the EPC, because the PCT has no procedural provisions for the period after entry into the regional phase.

Art.27(5) PCT allows a PCT contracting state to apply national law in respect of patentability of an invention claimed in an international application. The EPO as designated and elected office makes use of this provision and applies its own substantive requirements. Since the validity of a claimed priority has a direct effect on the patentability, the EPO applies the provisions of the EPC for determining the validity of a priority claim of a Euro-PCT application. However, the filing of the declaration of priority for the international application follows the provisions of the PCT, because the filing is a purely formal requirement to be fulfilled before the receiving Office. (**T577/11** r.6.2 and 6.5.8; see also **Ante Art.87:1**)

A Euro-PCT applicant has the same rights as an applicant of a direct European application with regard to refund of the examination fee. See **Rfees11** and OJ 2009 p.544.

Art. 151 The European Patent Office as a receiving Office

The European Patent Office shall act as a receiving Office within the meaning of the PCT, in accordance with the Implementing Regulations. Article 75, paragraph 2, shall apply.

Art.75(2) Compulsory national filing because of national law relating to secrecy and national security
See for the implementation:
R.157 The EPO as receiving Office

1 **EPO acting as receiving Office**
Art.151 deals with the role of the EPO as a PCT receiving Office (rO) and the regulations for the filing and transmittal of international applications.

PCT §2.3.2 describes the provisions applied by the EPO when it acts as rO.

2 **Filing and transmittal of the international application**
The EPO acts as a receiving Office in accordance with the provisions of **R.157**. These provisions permit residents and nationals of EPC contracting states to file international applications with the EPO as receiving Office. The reference to **Art.75(2)** in **Art.151** allows national law to prescribe filing of international applications with its national office, e.g. for reasons of national security, which national office will transmit the applications to the EPO as receiving Office.

Certain EPC contracting states prescribe that residents must always file the 'first' application with their national office, for example residents of France may file directly with the EPO or the IB only if claiming priority from an earlier application filed in France at the INPI. (AG-General Information, Annex B1; **Art.75(2)** EPC)

The Guidelines do not provide information about the EPO acting as receiving Office and refer to the Euro-PCT Guide (E-IX,1). See **R.157** for the implementation. The general requirements for filing an international application and the procedure for transmittal are set out in PCT §2.3. The specific requirements for the EPO as rO are given in PCT §2.3.2.

Art. 152 The European Patent Office as an International Searching Authority or International Preliminary Examining Authority

The European Patent Office shall act as an International Searching Authority and International Preliminary Examining Authority within the meaning of the PCT, in accordance with an agreement between the Organisation and the International Bureau of the World Intellectual Property Organization, for applicants who are residents or nationals of a State party to this Convention. This agreement may provide that the European Patent Office shall also act for other applicants.

See for the implementation:
R.158 Non-unity before EPO as ISA or IPEA

1 **EPO acting as ISA**
Art.152 governs the operation of the EPO as international searching authority (ISA) and as international preliminary examining authority (IPEA) under the PCT.

The procedure for an ISA in general is given in PCT §4.1.

See OJ 2017 A115 for the agreement between the European Patent Organisation and WIPO. See PCT §4.8 for the EPO acting as ISA.

The EPO acts as ISA for several rOs according to **Art.16(3)(b)** and **R.35** PCT. In principle, the EPO acts as ISA for all EPC contracting states according to the Protocol on Centralisation, Section II. By way of exception, under Section III(1) a patent office of an EPC contracting state in which the official language is not an EPO language may act as ISA and IPEA for international applications filed by nationals or residents of that state and of adjacent states. At present (November 2018) this applies to the national offices of Austria, Finland, Spain, Sweden and Turkey, the Nordic Patent Institute and the Visegrad Patent Institute (Euro-PCT Guide §203).

The PCT defines residency and nationality in **R.18.1**: residency and nationality are determined by national law, possession of a real and effective industrial or commercial establishment is considered residency, and a legal entity constituted according to national law is considered a national.

If the EPO acts as ISA, the applicant must pay the EPO a search fee. The Rules of the EPC do not expressly provide for this (although there is provision for a transmittal fee in **R.157(4)** EPC). However, basis for the search fee may be found in **Rfees2(1)2**, which directly refers to **R.16.1** PCT. In **Rfees2(1)2**, the search fee is referred to as 'a search fee in respect of an international search', whereas **R.158(1)** EPC refers to 'an additional international search fee' (see **R.158** EPC for related provisions). See OJ 2017 A95 for details about a refund of the international search fee when the EPO as ISA can make use of an earlier search (see also PCT §2.8.6.1). Details about the use of the international search report in the procedure before the EPO are given in **Art.153(6)-(7)** EPC (see also **R.164(2)** EPC).

See **R.158(1)** and **R.158(3)** EPC and section 4 below for the procedure following a non-unity finding by the EPO acting as ISA.

2 EPO acting as SISA

The EPO can also act as an International Searching Authority competent to carry out supplementary international searches (SISA) according to **R.45bis** PCT. See OJ 2017 A115 (Art.3(4) of the agreement between the European Patent Organisation and WIPO.

The fee for a supplementary international search carried out by the EPO is set at the same level as the fee for an international search. This fee, along with the supplementary international search handling fee, should be paid to the IB (not the EPO). The scope of a supplementary international search by the EPO is the same as the scope of an international search by the EPO. Although no separate Written Opinion is established, the EPO will provide explanations under **R.45bis.7(e)** PCT that are of equal value to a Written Opinion established by the EPO as ISA. (OJ 2017 A115, Art. 3(4); PCT §4.9.1).

3 EPO acting as IPEA

The procedure for an IPEA in general is given in PCT §6.

See OJ 2017 A115 for the agreement between the European Patent Organisation and WIPO. PCT §6.6 indicates the special provisions for the EPO as IPEA.

The purpose of international preliminary examination is to provide in the international phase a notice for the offices elected by the applicant, containing a non-binding advice on the patentability of the claimed invention (**Art.33(1)** PCT). The advice relieves the burden on the grant procedure in the respective states. Details of the examination are contained in **Art.34** and **R.66** PCT. The Guidelines do not provide information about the EPO as IPEA and refer instead to the Euro-PCT Guide (E-IX,1). There is no direct provision in the EPC for paying the preliminary examination fee if the EPO acts as IPEA, but there is a direct link to R.58 PCT in **Rfees2(1)19**.

See **R.158(2)-(3)** EPC and section 4 below for the procedure following a non-unity finding by the EPO acting as IPEA.

The EPO may act as an IPEA according to **Art.32** PCT for all states for which it can act as ISA. However, the possibilities are reduced considerably by the limitation that the international search report must have been established by the EPO or by an ISA located in and operating for an EPC contracting state (see OJ 2017 A115, Annex A).

4 **Non-unity**

The provision for payment of an additional fee in the case of a non-unity finding by the ISA is given in **Art.17(3)(a)** and **R.40** PCT. **R.16.1** PCT allows an ISA to request a fee for carrying out the international search and other tasks such as additional searches in the case of non-unity.

The EPO levies a search fee for additional international searches according to **R.158(1)** EPC and **Rfees2(1)2.** See PCT §4.3 and §4.8 for the procedure followed by the EPO acting as ISA.

In the case of a non-unity finding by the EPO acting as IPEA, the applicant will be requested to restrict the claims or to pay an additional fee for a further examination (**Art.34(3)(a)**, **R.68** PCT). The EPO levies a fee for each additional invention examined according to **R.158(2)** EPC, **Rfees2(1)19.**

When the EPO acts as ISA or IPEA, the additional fees may be paid under protest, (R.40.2(c-e), R.68.3(c-e) PCT, **R.158(3)** EPC). The EPO is obliged to examine the protest, see PCT §4.3.2, §4.8. §6.3.3 and §6.6.4. (OJ 2010p. 322)

Non-unity can also occur if the EPO acts as SISA; a protest procedure is available (**R.45bis.6** PCT; OJ 2010 p.316, 320). At the supplementary search stage there is no opportunity for the applicant to have further inventions searched upon payment of additional search fees (OJ 2010 p.316, §9).

Art. 153 The European Patent Office as designated Office or elected Office

See for the implementation:

R.159 The EPO as a designated or elected Office - Requirements for entry into the European phase
R.160 Consequences of non-fulfilment of certain requirements
R.161 Amendment of the application
R.162 Claims incurring fees
R.163 Examination of certain formal requirements by the EPO
R.164 Unity of invention and further searches of a Euro-PCT application
R.165 The Euro-PCT application as conflicting application under Art.54(3)

1 **General**

PCT §7 outlines the general procedure for entry into the national or regional phase before a designated Office and PCT §7.4 gives the specific provisions for the EPO as designated Office. The EPO publication 'Euro-PCT Guide' gives a overview of important procedural steps the applicant has to carry out before the EPO as a designated or elected Office.

Art. 153(1) The European Patent Office shall be

(a) a designated Office for any State party to this Convention in respect of which the PCT is in force, which is designated in the international application and for which the applicant wishes to obtain a European patent, and

(b) an elected Office, if the applicant has elected a State designated pursuant to letter (a).

1 **Designation**
An international application designates all contracting states of the PCT which are contracting states on the international filing date (**R.4.9(a)(i)** PCT) both national and regional, because of the all-inclusive designation system of **R.4.9** PCT. The EPO is designated Office only for designated states which are contracting states to the EPC at the date of filing of the international application. The effect of the designation of EPC contracting states in an international application is set out in PCT §2.9.1.2 and the entry into the regional phase before the EPO in PCT §7.4.

Art. 153(2) An international application for which the European Patent Office is a designated or elected Office, and which has been accorded an international date of filing, shall be equivalent to a regular European application (Euro-PCT application).

1 **Euro-PCT applications**
This provision governs, in addition to **Art.11(3)** PCT, the conditions under which an international application has the effect of a European application and defines the term 'Euro-PCT application'.

When an international application has been accorded an international filing date (**Art.11(3)** PCT), it is regarded as a regular national application, and, according to **Art.45** PCT, also as a regular application for a European patent (note the similarity with **Art.66** EPC for equivalence of a European filing with a national filing). It should be noted that the EPO is designated in each international application because of its all-inclusive designation. From then on, the application is called a Euro-PCT application. In 2015 about 78% of all applications filed with the EPO were PCT applications and 22% were direct European applications. See PCT §1.6 and §7.4.

The international application may enter the regional phase before the EPO within 31 months from the date of filing or, where priority has been claimed, from the date of priority (**R.159(1)** EPC), and is deemed to be a regular European patent application.

Art. 153(3) The international publication of a Euro-PCT application in an official language of the European Patent Office shall take the place of the publication of the European patent application and shall be mentioned in the European Patent Bulletin.

1 **International publication**
Art.153(3) and **Art.153(4)** EPC are closely related and deal with two different situations.

Art.153(3) EPC deals with an international application which was published in the international phase (**Art.21** PCT) in English, French or German. In this situation the effects of the international publication, such as provisional protection (**Art.29** PCT) take effect immediately at the time of the international publication.

Art.153(4) EPC deals with the situation that the international publication was published in a language other than English, French or German. Upon entry into the European regional phase, the applicant has to furnish to the EPO a translation into English, French or German which is subsequently published by the EPO. In line with **Art.29(2)** PCT and subject to **Art.67(3)** EPC, the provisional protection only starts when the EPO publishes the translation and other national requirements are fulfilled. (see also PCT §5.5.1)

Note, that **Art.153(3)** does not define the start of the provisional protection when the international application is published in an official EPO language and **Art.153(4)** does not define which publication will take the place of the publication of the European patent application when the international publication is not in an official EPO language.

2 **Effect of international publication**
Art.153(3) lays down that the publication of an international application under **Art.21** PCT in an official EPO language takes the place of the publication of the European patent application. This is of special importance for the equalisation of an international application and a European prior right and for the start of provisional protection. Since the provisional protection laid down in **Art.67** starts at the date of publication of the European patent application, it starts at the date of the publication under **Art.21** PCT for an international application published in an official EPO language.

The publication of the international application is set out in PCT §5 and the effect of the international publication (**Art.29** PCT) in PCT §5.5.

The accuracy of any translation made in the international phase is not checked by the EPO; it forms the basis of the grant procedure before the EPO. Correction of errors in the translation is allowed under **Art.26** and **28** PCT.

See **Art.153(5):2** for the prior right effect of an international application.

Art. 153(4) If the Euro-PCT application is published in another language, a translation into one of the official languages shall be filed with the European Patent Office, which shall publish it. Subject to Article 67, paragraph 3, the provisional protection under Article 67, paragraphs 1 and 2, shall be effective from the date of that publication.

Art.67(1) Rights conferred by a European patent application after publication
Art.67(2) Minimum rights conferred by application
Art.67(3) National requirements for publication and communication

1 **Publication of translation and provisional protection**
An international application published in a non-EPO language will be re-published by the EPO in an official EPO language.

Although not explicitly specified in **Art.153(4)**, payment of the 'national fee' (**Art.22(1)** PCT) equal to the 'filing fee' (**Rfees2(1)1**) is one of the requirements for entry into the regional phase before the EPO (see also **R.159(1)(c)**; **R.165** EPC; Euro-PCT Guide §541). The EPO may only act and proceed to publish the translated application after entry into the European regional phase (**Art.23(1)** PCT). The provisional protection will be effective from the date of that publication (**Art.153(4)**, second sentence), provided any national requirements have been met. The required publication by the EPO may cause a later start of the provisional protection for a state than for an international application with a national designation of that state.

The EPO has not published guidance on the time of publication of the translation. In practice, the translation of the international application including the international search report will be published approximately 6 weeks after entry into the European phase; however, occasionally the publication may be up to 12 weeks after regional entry.

All EPC contracting states must give provisional protection for un-examined European applications (**Art.67** EPC). An international application will not be published if the USA is the only designated country and the applicant has explicitly requested non-publication (**Art.64(3)(a), (b)** PCT).

If the language of the publication is not an official language of a contracting state, national law may provide that the provisional protection for that state is effective from the date of publication or communication to the alleged infringer of a translation of the claims in an official language of that state (**Art.67(3)** EPC).

Art. 153(5) The Euro-PCT application shall be treated as a European patent application and shall be considered as comprised in the state of the art under Article 54, paragraph 3, if the conditions laid down in paragraph 3 or 4 and in the Implementing Regulations are fulfilled.

Art.54(3) European prior right
See for the implementation:
R.159(1) Requirements for entry into European regional phase
R.165 Euro-PCT as conflicting application

1 **Treatment as European application**

This provision combines the conditions for two cases: (1) the conditions to be complied with for the Euro-PCT application to be treated as a European patent application and (2) for the Euro-PCT application to be treated as a prior right under **Art.54(3)**.

Since the Travaux Préparatoires EPC 2000 state that this provision gives the conditions for entry into the European phase and those for considering a Euro-PCT application as a European prior right, it must be concluded that the word 'treated' refers to 'processed' and 'examined' in the sense of **Art.23** PCT. Since this processing and examining is independent of the publication of the Euro-PCT dealt with by **Art.153(3)** and (4), the reference to these two paragraphs in **Art.153(5)** should pertain to the conditions for the European prior right only. The conditions for entry into the European phase are provided in **R.159(1)**.

2 **Treatment as European prior right**

The PCT allows in **Art.27(5)** that a PCT contracting state may define the extent of the state of the art that is taken into account when determining the patentability of a PCT application; hence, the EPC may define under what conditions other PCT applications will have a prior right effect. This is done in **Art.153(5)**.

Art.153(5) stipulates that a Euro-PCT will be considered as comprised in the state of the art under **Art.54(3)**, i.e. as a European prior right, only if the conditions in **Art.153(3)** and (4) and the Implementing Regulations are fulfilled. According to **Art.54(3)** EPC, the state of the art includes the contents of earlier European patent applications filed before and published on or after the effective date of the application being examined. The purpose of **Art.153(5)** is to avoid that all Euro-PCT applications, even those that do not enter the European phase, become European prior rights. **Art.153(5)** can be regarded as lex specialis of **Art.54(3)**.

The reference to **Art.153(3)** and (4) stipulates that a Euro-PCT application must be published in an EPO language, similar to **Art.54(3)**. If the international publication is in another language, a translation in an EPO language must be filed with the EPO, which will publish it. The publication will be mentioned in the Bulletin (**Art.153(3)**).

The reference to the Implementing Regulations must be read as a reference to **R.165**, according to the EPO, further requiring payment of the filing fee under **R.159(1)(c)** and **Rfees2(1)1**.

When these two conditions have been complied with, a Euro-PCT application will be regarded as a European prior right.

Under the EPC 2000, the EPO is continuing its practice under the EPC 1973 by requiring only submission of a translation and payment of the filing fee. The EPO may in the future publish the translation even after abandonment of the application after payment of the fee and filing of the translation and before the intended date of publication.

Art. 153(6) The international search report drawn up in respect of a Euro-PCT application or the declaration replacing it, and their international publication, shall take the place of the European search report and the mention of its publication in the European Patent Bulletin.

1 **General**

The provisions relating to the international search authority (ISA) and the international search report are given in PCT §4, those relating to the international publication in PCT §5. **Art.152** includes the provision for the EPO acting as ISA. The Guidelines do not provide information about the EPO as ISA and refer to the Euro-PCT Guide. Details for the supplementary European search are given in paragraph (7) of this article, **R.164**, B-II, 4.3 and B-VII, 2.3.

2 **International search report takes place of European search report**

In principle, the 6-month period for filing a request for examination (**R.70(1)**) starts to run from publication of the international search report. The end of the period for requesting examination also depends on the prevailing PCT rules (**Art.150(2)**; **R.159(1)(f)**): if publication of the international search report is delayed until after 25 months from the filing/priority date, then the 6-month period of **R.70(1)** for filing the request will not end before the start of the regional phase before the EPO, i.e. before 31 months from the priority date (**R.159(1)**). The PCT processing prohibition in **Art.23(1)** PCT prevents national offices from processing an international application before expiry of 30 months from priority, unless expressly requested to do so by the applicant (**Art.23(2)** PCT). The EPC has used **Art.22(3)** [**Art.39(1)(b)**] PCT to fix a later time limit for national phase entry at 31 months from priority (implemented in **R.159(1)** EPC).

The 6-month period for payment of the designation fee has a form similar to that for requesting examination (**R.39(1)**; **R.159(1)(d)**).

The drawing up of a supplementary European search report pursuant to **Art.153(7)** or the republication of the application pursuant to **Art.153(4)** does not affect the 6-month period for payment of the designation and examination fees. A supplementary European search report entitles an applicant to the invitation of **R.70(2)** (E-IX,2.5.3). See also **R.164(4):2**.

If the ISA finds that no meaningful search can be made (**Art.17(2)(a)** PCT), it publishes a declaration stating so instead of publishing a search report (**Art.21(3)** PCT); this publication also takes the place of the mention of the publication of the European search report (see **Art.153(6)** EPC).

Art. 153(7) A supplementary European search report shall be drawn up in respect of any Euro-PCT application under paragraph 5. The Administrative Council may decide that the supplementary search report is to be dispensed with or that the search fee is to be reduced.

1 **Supplementary European search report**

The legal basis in the PCT which allows for a supplementary search in the national phase is **Art.27(7)** PCT.

Art.153(7) governs when a supplementary European search report will be drawn up and authorises the Administrative Council to make exceptions. Provisions for timely and late payment of the supplementary search fee are given in **R.159-160; R.164** provides an opportunity to have further claimed inventions searched.

The EPO will in principle draw up a supplementary European search report under **Art.92** and a search opinion pursuant to **R.62** for any Euro-PCT application. The Administrative Council may decide for which Euro-PCT applications no supplementary European search report is required; see section 3 below. No time limit has been set for the completion of the supplementary search report; in exceptional cases it may take more than six years after regional entry, e.g. as in EP1120644. Under current practice, the EPO always accelerates the supplementary search (OJ 2015 A93).

The supplementary European search report is not published as such, although its establishment is mentioned in the Bulletin. However, the supplementary search report is available from file inspection and is marked as 'A4'. (B-X,4)

European supplementary search reports are accompanied by a search opinion in which the search division gives an opinion on whether the application and the invention to which it relates seem to satisfy the requirements of the EPC (**R.62(1)**; B-X, 1).

2 **Search fee for the supplementary European search**

The search fee for the supplementary European search report is in principle equal to the usual European search fee (**Rfees2(1)2**), but may be reduced or dispensed with by a decision of the Administrative Council in accordance with **Art.153(7)**.

When the EPO is a designated or elected Office (see PCT §7.4), this search fee must be paid within 31 months from the priority date (**R.159(1)** and **R.159(1)(e)**). If not paid in due time, the application is considered withdrawn (**R.160(1)**). Further processing is available for payment of supplementary search fees (**Art.121** and **R.135**).

See **Rfees9** for a refund of the search fee in respect of the supplementary European search.

3 **No supplementary European search report required**

No supplementary European search report will be drawn up for an international application entering the European phase for which an international search report has been drawn up by the EPO as ISA or for which the EPO as SISA has drawn up explanations under **R.45bis.7(e)** PCT. Hence, no search fee pursuant to **Art.153(7)** is payable. (OJ 2018 A26 §3(a))

4 **Reduction of search fee for the supplementary European search**

The amount of the search fee for the supplementary European search report is set out in **Rfees2(1)2**.

If a (S)ISA of a contracting state of the EPC (the Austrian, Spanish, Finnish, Swedish or Turkish Patent Office, or the Nordic or Visegrad Patent Institute) has carried out the (supplementary) international search, the amount of the search fee for the supplementary European search will be reduced (see OJ 2016 A2; A3, Art.2 ; 2017 A57).

The reduction of the search fee where a non-European ISA (AU, CN, JP, KR, RU, US) carried out the international search is no longer available for search fees paid on or after 01.04.2018 (OJ 2018, A3).The reduction of the EPO search fee is abolished because the non-European ISAs do not give similar reductions (CA/102/17 §12.2-18).

Art. 154 (deleted)

Art. 155 (deleted)

Art. 156 (deleted)

Art. 157 (deleted)

Art. 158 (deleted)

PART XI TRANSITIONAL PROVISIONS (DELETED)

PART XII FINAL PROVISIONS

Art. 164 Implementing regulations and protocols

Art. 164(1) The Implementing Regulations, the Protocol on Recognition, the Protocol on Privileges and Immunities, the Protocol on Centralisation, the Protocol on the Interpretation of Article 69 and the Protocol on Staff Complement shall be integral parts of this Convention.

1 **Parts of the Convention**
The Implementing Regulations and the Protocols have the same legal effect as the EPC; the rules for their validity, revision, languages, etc. are the ones given in the EPC (see **Art.164(2)** and notes).

The Rules relating to Fees do not form part of the Convention and have been added after the Munich Diplomatic Conference. **Art.51(4)** contains a reference to the Rules relating to Fees.

The text of the Protocols on Recognition and on the Interpretation of **Art.69** are included in this book. The texts of the Protocols on Privileges and Immunities, on Centralisation and on Staff Complement are available on the website of the EPO.

Art. 164(2) In case of conflict between the provisions of this Convention and those of the Implementing Regulations, the provisions of this Convention shall prevail.

1 **Priority rules**
Rules of priority for provisions:

1 the PCT has priority over the EPC (**Art.150(2)** EPC, second sentence);
2 the Protocol on Recognition has priority over the EPC (Article 11 Prot. Recogn.);
3 the Protocol on Centralisation has priority over the EPC (Section VII Prot. Centr.);
4 the Articles of the EPC have priority over the Rules of the EPC (**Art.164(2)** EPC).

2 **Conflict and ambiguity**
Up to now, the board of appeal has not indicated a conflict between the Articles and Rules of the EPC, in spite of allegations by appellants.

R.67(1) allows the President to determine the time at which the technical preparations for publication are ready. The board decided that the theoretical possibility of abuse of the rule does not make it invalid or in conflict with other provisions (J5/81).

If rules are ambiguous, the provisions and principles of the EPC must be consulted. The phrase 'deemed to have been completed' in **R.67(1)** is interpreted with the requirement of **Art.93** that all applications must be published promptly after 18 months (**J5/81**).

A rule will not be applied if the goal of the rule has already been reached. For example, a request for correction will not be issued if the applicant has already made the correction. (**G1/88** r.5.2.3)

The provisions of most protocols prevail over any contradictory provisions of the Convention and of agreements (see e.g. Prot. Centr. Section VII, Prot. Recogn. Article 11).

See **Art.23(4):1** for conflicts between the EPC and the Rules of Procedure of the BoA and **Art.177(2)** for conflicts between texts of the Convention in a language other than English, French or German and the texts in English, French and German.

Agreements drafted together with the EPC form part of the EPC. The EPC prevails in the case of conflicting provisions.

Art. 165 Signature - Ratification

Art. 165(1) This Convention shall be open for signature until 5 April 1974 by the States which took part in the Inter- Governmental Conference for the setting up of a European System for the Grant of Patents or were informed of the holding of that conference and offered the option of taking part therein.

1 **Signatory, participating and invited states**

The following states signed the Convention until 5 April 1974: Belgium, Denmark, France, Federal Republic of Germany, Greece, Ireland, Italy, Liechtenstein, Luxembourg, Netherlands, Norway, Sweden, Switzerland and the United Kingdom.

The following states only took part in the negotiations: Austria, Finland, Monaco, Portugal, Spain, Turkey and Yugoslavia.

The following states were invited but did not take part in the negotiations: Cyprus and Iceland.

Art. 165(2) This Convention shall be subject to ratification; instruments of ratification shall be deposited with the Government of the Federal Republic of Germany.

Art. 166 Accession

Art. 166(1) This Convention shall be open to accession by:
- **(a) the States referred to in Article 165, paragraph 1;**
- **(b) any other European State at the invitation of the Administrative Council.**

Art.165(1) States which took part in the Inter-Governmental Conference for setting up the EPC or were offered to take part

Art. 166(2) Any State which has been a party to the Convention and has ceased to be so as a result of the application of Article 172, paragraph 4, may again become a party to the Convention by acceding to it.

Art.172(4) A state ceased to be a party after not ratifying a revised text of the EPC

Art. 166(3) Instruments of accession shall be deposited with the Government of the Federal Republic of Germany.

Art. 167 (deleted)

1 **Reservations for pending patent applications**
Art.167 offered contracting states the possibility of making certain reservations regarding the implementation of the EPC, for a limited period of time. Only three contracting states made reservations and all of them have now expired. Since newly acceding contracting states cannot make further reservations, **Art.167** is now otiose and has been deleted in the EPC 2000. However, **Art.167(5)** remains applicable to European patents granted on European patent applications filed during the period in which the reservation was effective. (Spec. Ed. 4 of OJ 2007)

The reservation for Spain that European patents are ineffective in Spain in so far as they confer protection on chemical or pharmaceutical products as such is still effective for applications filed before 08.10.1992 and divisional applications having an effective date of filing before said date and still pending before the EPO (OJ 1992, 301).

Since 01.01.1996 Spain is bound by the TRIPS agreement, which permits patents for any inventions, whether products or processes, without discrimination as to the field of technology. In spite of the fact that Spain has not yet withdrawn the reservation, the EPO recommends not to maintain a separate set of restricted claims for Spain. If an applicant maintains the separate set of claims, he will not enjoy protection for chemical or pharmaceutical products as such in Spain. (Not. EPO, OJ 2007, 258 and 439)

The reservation for Greece is still applicable. (Not. EPO, OJ 2007, 258)

Art. 168 Territorial field of application

Art. 168(1) Any Contracting State may declare in its instrument of ratification or accession, or may inform the Government of the Federal Republic of Germany by written notification at any time thereafter, that this Convention shall be applicable to one or more of the territories for the external relations of which it is responsible. European patents granted for that Contracting State shall also have effect in the territories for which such a declaration has taken effect.

1 **Territorial extent**
NatLaw table X, column 2 states the territorial field of application of the EPC. A few special cases are listed below.

The EPC is applicable to New Caledonia (FR), French Polynesia (FR), the Southern and Antarctic territories (FR), Wallis (FR), Département St-Pierre-et-Miquelon (FR), Mayotte (FR) and the Isle of Man (UK). The territory of the Federal Republic of Germany includes the territory of the former DDR for applications filed since 3.10.1990. A European patent granted for the Netherlands will also be valid for Bonaire, Sint Eustatius and Saba as part of the Netherlands and for Curaçao and Sint Maarten.

The EPC is *not* applicable to Greenland (DK), the Faroe Islands (DK) and Aruba (NL). A European patent granted in respect of the UK may be registered in overseas states and territories as indicated in OJ 2004, 179. The procedure to extend a European patent designating GB to Hong Kong is set out in OJ 2009, 546.

Art. 168(2) If the declaration referred to in paragraph 1 is contained in the instrument of ratification or accession, it shall take effect on the same date as the ratification or accession; if the declaration is notified after the deposit of the instrument of ratification or accession, such notification shall take effect six months after the date of its receipt by the Government of the Federal Republic of Germany.

Art. 168(3) Any Contracting State may at any time declare that the Convention shall cease to apply to some or to all of the territories in respect of which it has given notification pursuant to paragraph 1. Such declaration shall take effect one year after the date on which the Government of the Federal Republic of Germany received notification thereof.

Art. 169 Entry into force

1 Contracting states EPC

1.1 LIST

Contracting states of the EPC, the date of entry into force of the EPC for each state, membership of the European Union (EU), the European Monetary Union (EMU, states using the Euro currency; see **Rfees5**) and the London Agreement (LA, see **Art.65(1):2**) (published annually in the fourth issue of the OJ, situation November 2018).

Albania	AL	01.05.2010			LA
Austria	AT	01.05.1979	EU	EMU	
Belgium	BE	07.10.1977	EU	EMU	
Bulgaria	BG	01.07.2002	EU		
Croatia	HR	01.01.2008	EU		LA
Cyprus	CY	01.04.1998	EU	EMU	
Czech Republic	CZ	01.07.2002	EU		
Denmark	DK	01.01.1990	EU		LA
Estonia	EE	01.07.2002	EU	EMU	
Finland	FI	01.03.1996	EU	EMU	LA
France	FR	07.10.1977	EU	EMU	LA
Germany	DE	07.10.1977	EU	EMU	LA
Greece	GR	01.10.1986	EU	EMU	
Hungary	HU	01.01.2003	EU		LA
Iceland	IS	01.11.2004			LA
Ireland	IE	01.08.1992	EU	EMU	LA
Italy	IT	01.12.1978	EU	EMU	
Latvia	LV	01.07.2005	EU	EMU	LA
Liechtenstein	LI	01.04.1980			LA
Lithuania	LT	01.12.2004	EU	EMU	LA
Luxembourg	LU	07.10.1977	EU	EMU	LA
Macedonia	MK	01.01.2009			LA
Malta	MT	01.03.2007	EU	EMU	
Monaco	MC	01.12.1991		EMU	LA
Netherlands, the	NL	07.10.1977	EU	EMU	LA

Norway	NO	01.01.2008			LA
Poland	PL	01.03.2004	EU		
Portugal	PT	01.01.1992	EU	EMU	
Romania	RO	01.03.2003	EU		
San Marino	SM	01.07.2009		EMU	
Serbia	RS	01.10.2010			
Slovakia	SK	01.07.2002	EU	EMU	
Slovenia	SI	01.12.2002	EU	EMU	LA
Spain	ES	01.10.1986	EU	EMU	
Sweden	SE	01.05.1978	EU		LA
Switzerland	CH	07.10.1977			LA
Turkey	TR	01.11.2000			
United Kingdom	GB	07.10.1977	EU		LA

1.2 TRANSITIONAL PROVISION

A state for which the EPC enters into force after the filing date of a European application cannot be designated in that application (**J14/90**). Similarly, the EPO can only act under the PCT as designated Office for states designated in an international application in respect of which the EPC was in force on the date on which the international application was filed (**J30/90**).

A state for which the EPC entered into force, for example for Albania on 01.05.2010, can be designated in a European application filed on or after 01.05.2010. From that date such a state is included in the designation of the EPC contracting states in the Request for Grant form. To allow such a new contracting state to be designated, however, the EPO will accord a European patent application filed in April 2010 the filing date of 01.05.2010 if the applicant expressly requests that filing date when filing the application. (OJ 2010, 96)

Nationals, residents and persons having their place of business in such a state may file international applications with the EPO as receiving Office as from 01.05.2010. The state may only be designated for a European patent in international applications filed on or after 01.05.2010. (OJ 2010, 96)

See OJ 2010, 394 for the accession of Serbia.

2 Extension ordinance

Since 1994 several states, not being contracting states, have concluded an Extension Agreement with the European Patent Organisation. The president of the EPO is authorised by the Administrative council to conclude such agreements under **Art.33(4)**. The agreements provide European patent applicants a cost-effective way of obtaining protection in those states. The rules under national law governing the extension of European patents to an extension state are set out in an Extension Ordinance for that state. See OJ 1994, 75 for the complete text of an Extension Ordinance. The extension states have not (yet) become contracting states, and have therefore no right to vote in the Administrative Council (**Art.34(1)**). The expected number of patent applications from these states does not justify at the moment a full membership with the accompanying influence in the European Patent Organisation.

The designation of such states, called an extension, extends the protection of a patent to those states. The extension is not based on direct application of the EPC but on national law modelled on the EPC. The extension procedure and the legal effects of the extension are governed solely by national law. Only those provisions of the Convention, Implementing Regulations and the Rules relating to Fees will apply which are referred to in the Extension Ordinance. The provisions referred to relate only to time limits and arrangements for paying the extension fee. Thus the EPC provisions concerning applicant's legal remedies and appeals do not apply in respect of actions taken by the EPO under the extension procedure. The principle of good faith is applicable when the EPO is acting within the framework of the EPC; hence, the principle does not apply to acts carried out under an extension agreement (**J14/00** r.1.4). The EPO merely assist the extension state by undertaking the administrative task of collecting the fees and passing the greater part of the fee to the extension state (**J14/00** r.1.2.2).

3 **Extension system**

An extension for a state can be requested for any European patent application filed on or after the Extension Agreement has entered into force for that state. The request for extension is automatically deemed to be made for any application filed on or after the entry into force of the Extension Agreement. The request may be indicated on the Request for Grant form, which indication is merely for information purposes.

Only by paying the extension fee for each extension state where protection is desired (see **Rfees3(1)**), comparable to the designation fee, the applicant decides to extend the protection of his application. The extension fee must be paid to the EPO within the period of **R.39(1)** or **R.159(1)(d)**; see **Art.79(2):2.1**; Ext. Agr. and **J14/00** for remedies. The Rules relating to Fees apply mutatis mutandis. When extension fees are paid, the states for which they are intended must be specified. The extension fee is euro 102 and is included in the schedule of EPO fees regularly published in the OJ. (OJ 1994, 75)

Any adverse decision of the Receiving Section in relation to the designation of an extension state or payment of the extension fee is not open to appeal under **Art.106**, but a remedy should be sought under the national jurisdiction of the extension state (**J14/00** r.1.3.4).

The request for extension is deemed withdrawn if the extension fee is not paid in due time, or the application is refused, withdrawn or deemed withdrawn. The extension fees are not refunded. A divisional application may be extended to the same states as to which the earlier application is extended.

A Euro-PCT application can also be extended to a PCT contracting state which has concluded an Extension Agreement, provided that both the EPO and that state are designated. An application can be extended to a state irrespective of whether the national phase before the patent office of that state has already been opened or not. The extension fee must be paid to the EPO in the same way as the designation fee in **R.159(1)(d)**.

Renewal fees are payable to the national offices for the years following that in which the mention of the grant is published.

A flow chart of the Euro-direct and Euro-PCT extension procedure is published in OJ 1994, p.86 and 87.

4 **Effects of extension**

A European patent application for which extension has been requested is equivalent to a duly filed national application, and after publication confers a provisional protection corresponding to that of **Art.67**. The granted European patent has the same effect as a national patent, provided that, if the state prescribes so, a translation of the specification or claims is filed and a publication fee is paid equivalent to **Art.65**. National law may provide for rules covering cases of collision between and double protection of European and national patents or applications, similar to **Art.139(1)** and **(2)**. The specific requirements for each extension state are provided in **NatLaw**.

The provisional protection is lost ab initio if the request for extension subsequently lapses. Similarly, to the extent that the patent granted for the application is revoked in EPO opposition proceedings, the provisional protection and other effects of the patent are again lost ab initio.

The extension states publish in their national register data of European applications and patents extending to their territory (A-III,12.5). The Register of European Patents, the European Patent Bulletin and the patent documents published by the EPO, on the other hand, will not contain any information about the extension of European patents.

Detailed information about the extension system is published in OJ 1994, 75; A-III,12 gives a summary. NatLaw Introduction and Tables contain details of the extension system for each extension state.

5 Extension states

States having concluded an Extension Agreement with the EPO and the date of entry into force of the Agreement for each state:

Bosnia and Herzegovina	BA	01.12.2004
Montenegro	ME	01.03.2010

The Extension Agreements of Albania, Croatia, Macedonia and Serbia terminated with the entry into force of the EPC in these countries. As from the date of entry into force European patent applications and patents can no longer be extended to this country. The extension system will continue to apply to all European and international applications filed prior to that date as well as to all European patents granted in respect of such applications. (OJ 2007, 638 §4; OJ 2008, 507 §4; OJ 2010, 96 §4; 394 §4).

On 01.11.2004 an extension agreement entered into force for the union of Serbia and Montenegro (OJ 2004, 563). After the declaration of independence of Montenegro on 03.06.2006 the Extension Agreement did not apply anymore to the country (Not. EPO, OJ 2007, 406). On 01.03.2010 a new Extension Agreement entered into force for Montenegro (OJ 2010, 10).

6 Validation Agreement

The EPO can conclude a bilateral international agreement with a state not being an EPC contracting state that European patent applications and patents can be validated for that state and will confer essentially the same protection as patents granted by the EPO for the EPC contracting states. Whereas an extension state should in due time become a contracting state of the EPC, a validation state does not have this prospect.

Validation for such a state is deemed requested for any European patent application filed on or after entry into force of the agreement and for any Euro-PCT application designating both the EPO and the validation state and having an international filing date on or after the entry into force. Validation is not available for applications filed prior to that date or for any European patents resulting from such applications. The request is deemed withdrawn if the validation fee is not paid in due time. (**Art.79(2):3.2**; A-III,12)

The following table gives the states that can be validated and the date of entry into force:

Cambodia	KH	01.03.2018
Moldova	MD	01.11.2015
Morocco	MA	01.03.2015
Tunisia	TN	01.12.2017

The agreement to validate European patents in Cambodia is published in OJ 2018 A16 and the validation fee and the period for payment for Cambodia in OJ 2018 A15. See the EPO website for the validation agreements and validation fees for the other countries; search for '**EPO validation system**'. Specific requirements for each validation state are provided in **NatLaw**.

The procedure for extension and validation is the same. The distinction between them is mainly geographical. Validation Agreements are not limited to Europe and can be concluded with non-European states, even though they have no prospect of acceding to the European Patent Organisation. The advantage of a Validation Agreement for users is that the state commits itself to bringing its IP laws into line with the EPC.

The unfortunate choice of the word 'validation' for this type of extension may cause confusion with the validation of a European patent after grant to obtain a valid patent in a contracting state (see **Art.65:1**).

Art. 169(1) This Convention shall enter into force three months after the deposit of the last instrument of ratification or accession by six States on whose territory the total number of patent applications filed in 1970 amounted to at least 180 000 for all the said States.

1 **Entry into force of EPC**
The condition of this paragraph was fulfilled on 07.10.1977. The EPC went into force on this date for Belgium, France, Federal Republic of Germany, Luxembourg, Netherlands, Switzerland, and the United Kingdom. The EPO opened on 01.06.1978.

Art. 169(2) Any ratification or accession after the entry into force of this Convention shall take effect on the first day of the third month after the deposit of the instrument of ratification or accession.

Art. 170 Initial contribution

Art. 170(1) Any State which ratifies or accedes to this Convention after its entry into force shall pay to the Organisation an initial contribution, which shall not be refunded.

Art. 170(2) The initial contribution shall be 5% of an amount calculated by applying the percentage obtained for the State in question, on the date on which ratification or accession takes effect, in accordance with the scale provided for in Article 40, paragraphs 3 and 4, to the sum of the special financial contributions due from the other Contracting States in respect of the accounting periods preceding the date referred to above.

Art.40(3), (4) Level of fees and payments-Special financial contributions

Art. 170(3) In the event that special financial contributions were not required in respect of the accounting period immediately preceding the date referred to in paragraph 2, the scale of contributions referred to in that paragraph shall be the scale that would have been applicable to the State concerned in respect of the last year for which financial contributions were required.

Art. 171 Duration of the Convention

The present Convention shall be of unlimited duration.

Art. 172 Revision

Art. 172(1) This Convention may be revised by a Conference of the Contracting States.

1 **Revision of Art.63**
A Diplomatic Conference of the contracting states on 17.12.1991 in its competence according to **Art.172(1)** drew up an act revising **Art.63** relating to extension of the term of a European patent. This first revision of the EPC entered into force on 04.07.1997.

2 **Overall revision of the EPC (EPC 2000)**
A first Diplomatic Conference for the overall revision of the EPC convened in November 2000 and adopted on 29.11.2000 a revised text of the EPC, referred to as the EPC 2000. The Act revising the Convention has been printed in Special edition No. 4 of OJ 2001, pages 1-53 and is also available on the EPO website (OJ 1999, 54; 2000, 173). The aim of the revision was to take into account developments in international law, in particular the TRIPs Agreement and the Patent Law Treaty 2000, introduction of a limitation procedure (Art.105a-c) and a review possibility of board of appeal decisions (Art.112a), both at the request of the user community, deregulation and transfer of procedural detail to the Implementing Regulations to enhance flexibility.

A Conference Resolution expresses the need for another diplomatic conference to deal with subjects not dealt with in the first Diplomatic Conference, such as provisions on software and biotechnological inventions and the Community patent (Special Edition No. 4 of OJ 2001, page 52).

The travaux préparatoires to the Diplomatic Conference are available on the web site www.epo.org/patents/law/legal-texts/archive/epc2000.html.

The Diplomatic Conference has authorized the Administrative Council (Art.3 of the Act revising the Convention) to draw up a new text of the revised EPC, including the amendments adopted by the Diplomatic Conference and align its wording in the three languages, and transitional provisions. The Administrative Council made minor amendments to the text adopted by the Diplomatic Conference and adopted the new text and the transitional provisions by its decision of 28.06.2001 (Special Edition No.4 of OJ 2001, page 54-140). The complete text of the Articles of the EPC 2000 as adopted by the decision of the Administrative Council on 28.06.2001, the Implementing Regulations as adopted by decision of the Administrative Council of 12.12.2002 and explanatory remarks about the amendment of the Rules and the transitional provisions have been reproduced in Special edition No. 1 of OJ 2003, pages 1-208. A trilingual version of the Articles and the Implementing Regulations is published in Special Edition no.1 of OJ 2007. Special Edition no.4 of OJ 2007 synoptically presents the EPC 1973 and EPC 2000, showing the changes with explanatory remarks and detailed transitional provisions. Gaps in the transitional provisions are being closed by case law; see e.g. **J10/07** r.1 and **T616/08** r.5-17.

The Diplomatic Conference was convened before the anticipated accession of several new contracting states. The new member states that joined the EPC since 2002 had to ratify the EPC 2000. Since 11 new states had joined since 2002, the minimum of 15 states to start the procedure for entry into force was already achieved on 13.12.2005.

The EPC 2000 entered into force on 13.12.2007. All contracting state had ratified the EPC 2000 at that date.

Art. 172(2) The Conference shall be prepared and convened by the Administrative Council. The Conference shall not be validly constituted unless at least three-quarters of the Contracting States are represented at it. Adoption of the revised text shall require a majority of three-quarters of the Contracting States represented and voting at the Conference. Abstentions shall not be considered as votes.

Art. 172(3) The revised text shall enter into force when it has been ratified or acceded to by the number of Contracting States specified by the Conference, and at the time specified by that Conference.

Art. 172(4) Such States as have not ratified or acceded to the revised text of the Convention at the time of its entry into force shall cease to be parties to this Convention as from that time.

1 **No ratification or accession**
The severe punishment for not ratifying or acceding a revision aims at keeping the text of the Convention identical for all contracting states. A state which has ceased to be party may accede again to the Convention according to **Art.166(2)**. See **Art.175** and **176** for the consequences of the cessation to be party to the EPC.

Art. 173 Disputes between Contracting States

Art. 173(1) Any dispute between Contracting States concerning the interpretation or application of the present Convention which is not settled by negotiation shall be submitted, at the request of one of the States concerned, to the Administrative Council, which shall endeavour to bring about agreement between the States concerned.

1 **Dispute resolution**
If the contracting states cannot reach agreement on interpretation of the EPC, a contracting state may submit the issue to the Administrative Council, which will endeavour to bring about agreement.

An example of an issue where the contracting states have not been able to reach agreement on is the definition of the patent term (see **Art.63(1):1**). Since the contracting states could not reach agreement on the definition during preparatory discussions in epi committees, it is unlikely that the same contracting states will reach agreement in the Administrative Council.

If after six months the Administrative Council has not reached agreement, a contracting state may submit the dispute to the International Court of Justice under **Art.173(2)** for a binding decision.

Art.173 thus provides a method for forced resolution of disputes on the interpretation of the EPC. Such a resolution requires that at least one contracting state is willing to submit the dispute to the Administrative Council and to the International Court of Justice.

Art. 173(2) If such agreement is not reached within six months from the date when the dispute was referred to the Administrative Council, any one of the States concerned may submit the dispute to the International Court of Justice for a binding decision.

Art. 174 Denunciation

Any Contracting State may at any time denounce this Convention. Denunciation shall be notified to the Government of the Federal Republic of Germany. It shall take effect one year after the date of receipt of such notification.

Art. 175 Preservation of acquired rights

Art. 175(1) In the event of a State ceasing to be party to this Convention in accordance with Article 172, paragraph 4, or Article 174, rights already acquired pursuant to this Convention shall not be impaired.

Art.172(4) Revision
Art.174 Denunciation

Art. 175(2) A European patent application which is pending when a designated State ceases to be party to the Convention shall be processed by the European Patent Office, as far as that State is concerned, as if the Convention in force thereafter were applicable to that State.

Art. 175(3) Paragraph 2 shall apply to European patents in respect of which, on the date mentioned in that paragraph, an opposition is pending or the opposition period has not expired.

Art. 175(4) Nothing in this Article shall affect the right of any State that has ceased to be a party to this Convention to treat any European patent in accordance with the text to which it was a party.

Art. 176 Financial rights and obligations of former Contracting States

Art. 176(1) Any State which has ceased to be a party to this Convention in accordance with Article 172, paragraph 4, or Article 174 shall have the special financial contributions which it has paid pursuant to Article 40, paragraph 2, refunded to it by the Organisation only at the time when and under the conditions whereby the Organisation refunds special financial contributions paid by other States during the same accounting period.

Art.40(2) Level of fees and payments-Special financial contributions
Art.172(4) Revision
Art.174 Denunciation

Art. 176(2) The State referred to in paragraph 1 shall, even after ceasing to be a party to this Convention, continue to pay the proportion pursuant to Article 39 of renewal fees in respect of European patents remaining in force in that State, at the rate current on the date on which it ceased to be a party.

Art.39 Payments by the Contracting States in respect of renewal fees for European patents

Art. 177 Languages of the Convention

The provision determines the languages in which the Convention is drawn up and the mutual relation of the three language versions of the Convention.

Art. 177(1) This Convention, drawn up in a single original, in the English, French and German languages, shall be deposited in the archives of the Government of the Federal Republic of Germany, the three texts being equally authentic.

1 **Three languages of the EPC**
The authentic text of the EPC is the text as set out in the hard-copy edition of the EPC as published by the EPO (see e.g. OJ 2008, 1).

All three texts are equally authentic. None of the three texts is a translation. The three texts can help to find the clear, well-defined will of the legislator. According to **Art.33(3)** of the Vienna Convention, all terms in each of the three texts should have the same meaning. If there is a discrepancy between the texts, the term should be interpreted in line with the goal of the EPC. Therefore, the Boards of Appeal often refer to the other texts to find the correct interpretation. A few examples:

A combination preparation comprising two sequentially administered medications can be seen as a product, especially a compound according to **Art.53(c)** and **Art.54(4)**, and, hence, can be protected as chemical substance as a first medical indication. The German term 'Stoffgemische' does not cover such a kit of parts, but the wider English and French term 'composition' does. (**T9/81**)

A substantial procedural violation is required for reimbursement of the appeal fee (**R.103**). The German text of the provision is clearer than the English and French texts: 'wesentlicher Verfahrensmangel' indicates an objective deficiency affecting the entire proceedings. (**J7/83**)

The proprietor can file an opposition against his own patent, as decided on the ground of text comparison (**G1/84**). If there were a difference between 'any person' and 'any third person' the text would have made that clear. Note that self-opposition is not allowed anymore after **G9/93**.

Art. 177(2) The texts of this Convention drawn up in official languages of Contracting States other than those specified in paragraph 1 shall, if they have been approved by the Administrative Council, be considered as official texts. In the event of disagreement on the interpretation of the various texts, the texts referred to in paragraph 1 shall be authentic.

There are no official texts yet in other languages.

Art. 178 Transmission and notifications

Art. 178(1) The Government of the Federal Republic of Germany shall draw up certified true copies of this Convention and shall transmit them to the Governments of all signatory or acceding States.

Art. 178(2) The Government of the Federal Republic of Germany shall notify to the Governments of the States referred to in paragraph 1:
- **(a) the deposit of any instrument of ratification or accession;**
- **(b) any declaration or notification received pursuant to Article 168;**
- **(c) any denunciation received pursuant to Article 174 and the date on which such denunciation comes into force.**

Art.168 Territorial field of application
Art.174 Denunciation of Convention by contracting state

Art. 178(3) The Government of the Federal Republic of Germany shall register this Convention with the Secretariat of the United Nations.

Implementing Regulations to the Convention on the Grant of European Patents

of 5 October 1973

as last amended by decision of the Administrative Council

of the European Patent Organisation

of 28 June 2018

Part I
IMPLEMENTING REGULATIONS TO PART I OF THE CONVENTION

Part II
IMPLEMENTING REGULATIONS TO PART II OF THE CONVENTION

Part III
IMPLEMENTING REGULATIONS TO PART III OF THE CONVENTION

PART I IMPLEMENTING REGULATIONS TO PART I OF THE CONVENTION

Chapter I *General provisions*

R. 1 Written proceedings

In written proceedings before the European Patent Office, the requirement to use the written form shall be satisfied if the content of the documents can be reproduced in a legible form on paper.

EPC 1973: no corresponding provision

1 **General**
R.1 provides the possibility of electronic filing and all-electronic two-way communication. It specifies what documents fulfil the requirement to use the written form. (Spec. Ed. 1, OJ 2003, p. 159)

2 **Form of written documents**
In written proceedings a document is regarded as being a written document if it can be reproduced in a legible form on paper (**R.1**). Hence, an electronic file that can be processed by a computer program to produce a legible print on paper is considered to be a written document.

Further requirements relating to physical properties and layout of the documents making up the patent application are governed by **R.49** and those for further documents, filed after the application, are given in **R.50**.

The permitted means for filing written documents are governed by **R.2**.

R. 2 Filing of and formal requirements for documents

EPC 1973: **R.24, R.36(3), (5)**

R. 2(1) In proceedings before the European Patent Office, documents may be filed by delivery by hand, by postal services or by means of electronic communication. The President of the European Patent Office shall lay down the details and conditions and, where appropriate, any special formal or technical requirements for the filing of documents. In particular, he may specify that confirmation must be supplied. If such confirmation is not supplied in due time, the European patent application shall be refused; documents filed subsequently shall be deemed not to have been received.

Amended by decision of the Administrative Council of 15.10.2014, which entered into force on 01.04.2015. (OJ 2015 A17, A36 §1, 5)

1 **Filing of documents**

The President of the EPO is responsible for deciding through what route and in what form, and in particular by what technical means, documents may be filed with the EPO which fulfil the requirement to use the written form (**R.2(1)**). The provision applies to both filing of patent applications and further documents, i.e. documents filed subsequently to the filing of the patent application.

The Decisions of the President give an exhaustive list of the methods by which European patent applications and further documents may be filed. An application filed in another way, such as by telegram, telex or similar means, will be regarded as not received (Dec. Pres., Spec. Ed. 3 of OJ 2007 A.3 Art.1(3); see also **R.40(1):1.1**). The same applies to further documents (A-VIII,2.5). E-mail cannot be used to perform a procedural act; however, see section **8.1** below (OJ 2000, 458; A-VIII,2.5).

The President may specify that confirmation of filed documents must be supplied (**R.2(1)**). He has done so only for filing by fax and by e-mail (see below).

Whereas **R.2** relates to methods by which a party may communicate with the EPO, **R.125** governs the methods by which the EPO communicates with a party.

2 **Acknowledgment of receipt**

The EPO or national authority will always acknowledge receipt of a patent application (see **R.35(2)** and A-II,3.1 for direct European applications and **R.157(1):3** for Euro-PCT applications). See below for special provisions for confirmation of receipt of applications filed by fax or in electronic form.

The EPO acknowledges receipt of further documents from a (third) party only on request. The acknowledgment is on EPO form 1037 for further documents that have been signed and form 1038 for further documents that have not been signed. The filled-in form must be sent to the EPO together with the further documents. The EPO will return the form marked with the date of receipt to the sender. The form will normally be returned by mail; it will be returned by fax on request and payment of a fee. (Dec. Pres., Spec. Ed. 3 of OJ 2007 A.3 Art.8)

The general rules for acknowledgment of receipt of documents sent to the EPO under the EPC 1973 were provided in Not. of the EPO of 06.12.2004 (OJ 2005, 44 §6). These rules have been copied for the EPC 2000 to Dec. of Pres. of 12.07.2007 concerning 'the filing of patent applications and other documents by facsimile' (Dec. Pres., Spec. Ed. 3 of OJ 2007 A.3 Art.8). Notwithstanding the title of the Decision, its rules for acknowledgment should be applicable to acknowledgment of receipt of documents sent to the EPO by any method, not only by facsimile, except where specific rules for acknowledgement are provided (see e.g. Dec. Pres., OJ 2018 A45, Art. 11 for electronic filing of documents with the EPO and Dec. Pres., Spec. Ed. 3 of OJ 2007 A.6, Art.5 for electronic filing of European patent applications with the German Patent and Trade Mark Office)

See **R.126(1):1** for acknowledgement of receipt of communications from the EPO to a party.

3 **Filing by delivery by hand**

R.2(1) allows European patent applications and further documents to be filed by delivery by hand with the EPO or a national authority under **Art.75**. The application documents may be handed over personally in one of the EPO filing offices during office hours. The date of filing accorded will be the date of handing over. See Not. EPO, OJ 2018 A18 for the EPO office hours and the first issue of the OJ of each year for a list of holidays observed by the EPO and the national authorities.

Use may be made at any time of the automated mailboxes of the EPO offices in Munich (at the Pschorrhöfe building) and Berlin. The Isar building in Munich (as from 01.04.2017) and the office in the Hague have no automated mailbox; outside office hours documents may be handed to the porter at all the filing offices. (Dec. Pres., OJ 2017 A11 Art.1(3))

4 **Filing by delivery service**

The postal services in **R.2(1)** cover both postal authorities of a state, commonly called 'the post', and private delivery services, such as courier services (CA/47/14 §11, 16).

Delivery services or courier services require a visiting address, i.e. street plus house number, and not a post office box for delivery. They do not in general deliver outside office hours, as they require a signature when delivering goods (see OJ 2017 A12 for office hours).

5 **Filing by post**

R.2(1) allows European patent applications and further documents to be filed in writing with the EPO or a national authority under **Art.75** by post. However, debit orders may only be filed electronically (ADA5.1.2); see ADA5.6.1 for an exception if an application is filed with a national authority under **Art.75 (A-II,1.6; not in GL 2017)**.

The mail addresses of the EPO filing offices are given in the Not. EPO, Spec. Ed. 3 of OJ 2007 A.2, those of the national authorities in NatLaw Table II, first column. Registered mail will only be delivered during office hours. Business mail, such as mail for patent offices, is not delivered during weekends and national holidays. The date of filing accorded to an application filed with the EPO by post is the date of receipt at an EPO filing office (Not. of the EPO, OJ 2005, 44 §5.5). The date of filing accorded to an application filed with a national authority under **Art.75** is the date of receipt by the national authority (**Art.75(1)(b)**, last sentence).

6 **Filing by fax and confirmation**

Documents can be sent to the EPO using fax. Fax can be used in any procedure and for any type of document, except authorisations and priority documents (Dec. Pres., Spec. Ed. 3 of OJ 2007). Debit orders may not be filed by fax (ADA5.1.3).

Fax numbers of the EPO filing offices are given in OJ 2017 A12. European patent applications may also be filed by fax with national authorities of those contracting states which so permit (see A-II,1.2).

The EPO will request a written confirmation of a document sent by fax only if the fax is of inferior quality but still legible (A-II,1.2; A-VIII,8.5). The EPO issues a confirmation of receipt of the document by fax on request (A-II,3.1).

Fax can be used close to oral proceedings and during interviews and oral proceedings held as a video conference as a fast means of communication (C-VII,2.8.4; E-III,11.3.1).

The use of fax for transmitting documents to the EPO has been decreasing rapidly and the EPO would like to abolish it as permitted means under **R.2(1)** (see epi Information 02/2018 p.10). However, parties prefer to keep the fax with its dependable telephone line as fallback in case of outages of electronic communication. The number of outages of fax attributable to the EPO is less than one a year, and of electronic filing is about three per month (based on publications on the EPO website; see also **R.134(1):1**).

An alternative to filing by fax is web-form filing (**R.2(1):7.3**).

7 **Electronic filing**

Documents, including European patent applications, may be filed electronically with the EPO as set out in Dec. Pres. OJ 2018 A45 and Not. EPO OJ 2018 A46. Detailed information on the different electronic filing methods is given on www.epoline.org. The EPO encourages online filing of applications by a reduced filing fee (see **Rfees2(1)1**).

European patent applications may be filed electronically also with national authorities of those contracting states which so permit (OJ 2018 A45 Art.2(2)). See e.g. Not. EPO, Spec. Ed. 3 of OJ 2007, 19 for electronic filing of European patent applications with the German patent office.

The EPO has provided four different methods for electronic filing, each having different requirements for software and a different scope of the documents that can be filed. The methods are Online Filing using internet (OLF), Online Filing using a data carrier (OLF), Case Management System (CMS) and Web-Form Filing. All methods use the internet for transmission of the documents to the EPO except Online Filing using a data carrier.

Where required, documents can be signed using a facsimile signature, i.e. an image of a handwritten signature, a text string between two forward slashes, or an enhanced electronic signature, e.g. a smart card signature. (OJ 2018 A45 Art.10)

Sequence listings must be filed electronically in a text-only format, for example txt. If they are not available in the correct format on filing, they can first be submitted in pdf format and subsequently in the correct format along with payment of the late furnishing fee (see **R.30(3)**). See OJ 2011, 372; OJ 2013, 542 and user guides of the electronic filing methods for details.

Electronic filing, except Web-Form Filing, allows the filing of a pre-conversion archive in addition to the filed documents. The pre-conversion archive may contain original documents, i.e. before conversion into pdf or xml, in the format in which they were created, e.g. docx format. The original documents may be helpful in the event of quality issues and submission of colour documents. They will not become publicly available. (OJ 2018 A45 Art.9; Spec. Ed. 3 of OJ 2007 A5 Art.3 and user guides)

The date of receipt of documents filed electronically is the date the patent application documents were received at the EPO or national authority; or the date of completion of the transmission of the documents or the date of receipt of the data carrier (OJ 2018 A46, 2nd par. & OJ 2015 A91 Art.9).

Electronic filing does not require confirmation by paper document (OJ 2018 A46, 2nd par. & OJ 2015 A91 Art.12).

An electronic document that is illegible or incomplete, is infected, or has been filed using a method not allowing the filing of such a document (e.g. notice of opposition via Web-Form Filing) will be deemed not to have been received and the EPO will notify the sender without delay (OJ 2018 A45 Art.12, Art.3).

The provisions for electronic filing apply not only to the filing of European patent applications and further documents but also to the filing of international applications and further documents filed with the EPO in the international phase (OJ 2018 A45 Art.2(1)).

Third parties can use a special method of electronic filing for observations set out in **Art.115:1.**

An applicant may use the MyFiles service (see **R.127:1**) to notify the EPO of changes in representation (Dec. Pres. OJ 2012, 352).

7.1 ONLINE FILING USING INTERNET (OLF)

Documents to be filed online with OLF are prepared, signed where required, packaged on a local computer and submitted by the sender in encrypted form to a secure server of the EPO (OJ 2018 A45 Art.8(1)). The software to be used on the local computer can be downloaded free of charge from the EPO website (OJ 2017 A59).

Submitting through OLF requires an activated smart card and certificates issued or accepted by the EPO. A smart card can be ordered **online** from the EPO website. The authorities issuing certificates are listed in Spec. Ed. 3 of OJ 2007 A5.

OLF can be used for filing any type of document in all proceedings under the EPC, including opposition proceedings, limitation and revocation proceedings, appeal proceedings and proceedings for review under **Art.112a** (OJ 2018 A45 Art.2(1)). However, it can be used for filing priority documents only if they have been digitally signed by the issuing authority and the EPO accepts the signature (OJ 2018 A45 Art. 4). At present (situation November 2018) the EPO accepts the electronic filing of US priority documents only. A filed priority document that is not duly signed is deemed not to have been received and the EPO will inform the sender without delay (OJ 2018 A45 Art.4).

The format of the technical documents to be filed must be xml or pdf or, for sequence listings, a text-only format (OJ 2018 A45 Art.9(1), Art.5 and user guide OLF). The EPO provides software to generate documents in xml format and to convert documents to pdf format with embedded fonts. The EPO will provide an acknowledgement of receipt within the submission session (OJ 2018 A45 Art.11(1)(a)).

7.2 ONLINE FILING USING A DATA CARRIER (OLF)

Documents can be filed electronically with the EPO using a data carrier (OJ 2018 A45 Art1(2)). The data carrier can be used for filing documents in all proceedings under the EPC. The permitted types and formats of documents are the same as for the Online Filing using internet in the above section **7.1.** Before online filing was possible a data carrier was the only means filing a long sequence listing.

The documents are prepared, signed where required, and packaged by the sender on a local computer using the same software as described in the above section for Online RFiling using internet (OLF). The packaged file must be stored on a data carrier of the CD-R or a DVD±R type (Spec. Ed. 3 OJ 2007 A5 Art. 2).

The data carrier must be accompanied by a paper document stating the applicant and/or his representative, an address for correspondence and a listing of the files stored. (OJ 2018 A45 Art.8(2))

The data carrier and the document must be filed with the EPO by hand, delivery service or post (OJ 2018 A45 Art.11)).

The EPO will send an acknowledgement of receipt as set out in the above section **2.** Note, that the rules set out in OJ 2018 A45 Art.11(1) apply only to methods of filing using the internet.

The inadvertent name OLF of this method of filing, which actually is not online, may stem from the use of the OLF software for preparing the documents.

7.3 CASE MANAGEMENT SYSTEM (CMS)

The Case Management System (CMS) is a secure web-based application for preparing forms and documents online and submitting them online with the EPO. In contrast with OLF in the above sections 7.1 and 7.2, no software need be installed on the local computer and no updating carried out, except for installing the smart card software. The service uses a case management system, which allows managing applications online. EPO documents often refer to CMS using its former name 'New online filing (CMS)'.

Use of CMS requires a smart card registered for CMS and certificates issued by the EPO (OJ 2018 A45 Art.6(2), 7(2)).

The format of the documents to be filed must be xml or pdf , except sequence listings, which must be filed in a text-only format.

CMS can be used for filing any type of document in all proceedings under the EPC, except priority documents and authorisations (OJ 2018 A45 Art.4(2)). The EPO will provide an acknowledgement of receipt in the CMS (OJ 2018 A45 Art.11(1)(b)).

7.4 WEB-FORM FILING

Web-Form Filing is a secure web-based service on the EPO website for filing solely pdf documents with the EPO through the internet. The service is an alternative to filing by fax and can also be used as a fallback for OLF and CMS.

Web-Form Filing can be used for filing European and PCT applications and further documents relating to such applications. It cannot be used for filing authorisations, priority documents and documents relating to opposition, limitation and revocation proceedings, appeal proceedings, and proceedings for review under **Art.112a.** (OJ 2018 A45 Art.3(1))

A sequence listing can be filed in Web-Form Filing only in pdf format. It must be filed later in a text-only format using another method of filing.

Access to the Web-Form Filing requires prior registration on the EPO website. It does not require a smart card or certificates; internet access and an email address are sufficient. It also allows filing on a smartphone. Further information is provided on www.epoline.org under Web-Form Filing.

The EPO will provide an acknowledgement of receipt on the website once the files have been transferred. An email acknowledgement will be sent on request. (OJ 2018 A45 Art.11(1)(c))

8 E-mail

E-mail has no legal force in proceedings under the EPC and PCT and thus can in general not be used to perform validly any procedural act and in particular to comply with time limits (OJ 2000, 458).

8.1 E-MAIL DURING VIDEO-CONFERENCES

As an exception, e-mail may be used for document exchange during video-conferences held for conducting interviews and oral proceedings. The EPO will provide an e-mail address to which the further documents referred to in **R.50** can be sent. Amended application documents must be attached in pdf format, other attachments may be sent in any format that can be opened by the examiner or examining division and reproduced in a legible form. Authorisations may not be filed by e-mail. (Dec. Pres., OJ 2012, 348)

No confirmation on paper is necessary, unless the EPO requests so during the video-conference. Where a signature is required, this may be included in the attachment or in the e-mail. Documents are deemed not filed if they do not comply with the above requirements, if they are illegible or incomplete, or if a requested confirmation is not received within two months. The e-mail submission will be added to the file, except for documents excluded from file inspection under **R.144**. A routine confidentiality note in e-mails will not be regarded as a request to exclude the submission from file inspection. (Dec. Pres., OJ 2012, 348)

8.2 OTHER USE OF E-MAIL

The Guidelines allow e-mail for arranging a date for an interview, communicating amendments during a telephone consultation, and providing the examining division with amended claims shortly before oral proceedings in addition to an official submission, e.g. by fax. (C-VII,2.8.1)

Any exchange of information by e-mail has to be agreed previously between the examiner and the applicant, e.g. by telephone. An e-mail relating to procedural or substantive matters received by the examiner without prior agreement to use of e-mail, must also be put in the file (see **T599/06** r.4.2); the applicant should be invited to resend the submission using permitted means. (C-VII,2.8.2)

R. 2(2) Where the Convention provides that a document must be signed, the authenticity of the document may be confirmed by handwritten signature or other appropriate means the use of which has been permitted by the President of the European Patent Office. A document authenticated by such other means shall be deemed to meet the legal requirements of signature in the same way as a document bearing a handwritten signature which has been filed in paper form.

1 **Signature on document**

The EPC provides that the Request for Grant form (**R.41(2)(h)**) and further documents (**R.50(3)**) must be signed. The EPC states explicitly that the following documents must also be signed: assignment of an application (**Art.72**), designation of inventor (**R.19(1)**), and authorisation (**R.152(1)**). The documents may be included as an annex in a further document; the designation and authorisation may also form part of the application documents.

R.2(2) defines the permitted forms of signature. Paper documents that must be signed require a handwritten signature (**R.2(2)**). The signature reproduced on a fax is an appropriate form of signing (Spec. Ed. 3 of OJ 2007 A.3 Art.4). Documents filed in electronic form may have a text string signature or an enhanced electronic signature (when using OLF) or their authenticity may be confirmed by a facsimile signature (OJ 2018 A45; OJ 2016 A21; Spec. Ed. 3 of OJ 2007, 17 Art.1).

2 **Incorrect or missing signature**

R.2(2) and the decisions of the President do not state the legal consequences of non-compliance with the form requirement for the signature. The following consequences can be derived from the EPC.

The EPO will request under **R.57(b)** and **R.58** correction of a Request for Grant form not signed in accordance with **R.41(2)(h)**. Accordance with **R.41(2)(h)** should include compliance with **R.2(2)**, signature by an authorised person and one signature for each applicant. The sanction on failure to correct after invitation in accordance with **R.58** is refusal of the application under **Art.90(5)**.

If a further document, filed after filing the application, has not been signed, the EPO will invite the party to provide a signed document; if not provided, the document will be deemed not filed (**R.50(3)**). The same applies to the designation of inventor according to **R.19(1)**. A signature not complying with **R.2(2)** should probably be regarded as a missing signature for the purpose of **R.50(3)**.

R. 3 Language in written proceedings

Implementation of: **Art.14(3)**
EPC 1973: **R.1**

R. 3(1) In written proceedings before the European Patent Office, any party may use any official language of the European Patent Office. The translation referred to in Article 14, paragraph 4, may be filed in any official language of the European Patent Office.

Art.14(4) Translation of further document filed in admitted non-EPO language

1 **Derogation from language of proceedings by party**
Written submissions of parties are usually in the language of the proceedings (**Art.14(3)**). However, **R.3(1)** allows parties to file their documents, except those mentioned in **R.3(2)**, in an official EPO language (**Art.14(1)**) other than the language of proceedings, without a requirement to file a translation into the language of the proceedings. This situation occurs most often in opposition proceedings, where an opponent might prefer an official EPO language other than the language of the proceedings. Since **R.3(1)** refers to **Art.14(4)**, an entitled party may file a document to be filed within a time limit in an admissible non-EPO language. He must file a translation in an official EPO language under **R.3(1)**, not necessarily being the language of proceedings. The translation must normally be filed within one month of the filing of the document (**R.6(2)**).

2 **Derogation from language of proceedings by EPO**
In written proceedings the EPO will only use the language of the proceedings as determined by **Art.14(3)** (**G4/08** r.3.11; A-VII,2; overruling **J18/90**).

R. 3(2) Amendments to a European patent application or European patent shall be filed in the language of the proceedings.

1 **Language of amendments**
Any amendment of the application or patent must be filed in the language of the proceedings according to **R.3(2)**.

However, since **Art.14(4)** takes precedence over **R.3(2)**, an amendment in response to a communication of the EPO which has to be filed within a specified period, may be filed by an entitled party in an admissible non-EPO language within that time limit. Such an amendment must be translated in the language of the proceedings (**Art.14(4)** and **R.3(2)**) and be filed within one month of the filing of the amendment (**R.6(2)**). During proceedings the amendment must be discussed with reference to the text in the language of the proceedings. (**J18/90** r.1.2, 1.3)

Art.14(4) does not apply to an amendment not to be filed within a specified period. Hence, such an amendment must be filed in the language of proceedings.

R. 3(3) Documentary evidence and, in particular, publications may be filed in any language. The European Patent Office may, however, require that a translation in one of its official languages be filed, within a period to be specified. If a required translation is not filed in due time, the European Patent Office may disregard the document in question.

1 **Documents used as evidence**
A document used as evidence may be filed in any language (**R.3(3)**). The EPO often requests a translation into an official EPO language, for which it may set a period between 2 and 6 months depending on the language and the length of the document. The EPO may disregard the document if the translation is not filed in due time. (A-VII,5)

R. 4 Language in oral proceedings

Implementation of: **Art.14(3)**
EPC 1973: **R.2**

R. 4(1) Any party to oral proceedings before the European Patent Office may use an official language of the European Patent Office other than the language of the proceedings, if such party gives notice to the European Patent Office at least one month before the date of such oral proceedings or provides for interpretation into the language of the proceedings. Any party may use an official language of a Contracting State, if he provides for interpretation into the language of the proceedings. The European Patent Office may permit derogations from these provisions.

1 **Language in oral proceedings**
In oral proceedings the EPO will use the language of proceedings as determined by **Art.14(3)**. A derogation is provided in **R.4(2)**.

R.4(1) allows a party to use an official EPO language other than the language of the proceedings. In such a case the EPO will make provisions for interpreting in the language of proceedings when the party gives the EPO at least one month notice (**R.4(5)**); otherwise the party itself must make provisions for interpreting. If all parties have indicated that they will use another official language, an opposition division may depart from the language of proceedings to manage with fewer or no interpreters (E-V,1; not in GL 2017). The EPO will send a notice to parties when arranging a date for oral proceedings in an opposition procedure, requesting them to refrain from interpretation in view of the costs (OJ 1994, 583).

A party in oral proceedings may use any official language of any contracting state, because in **R.4(1)** the use of such languages is not limited by the residence and nationality of the party as it is in **Art.14(4)**. The party has to provide always for interpretation in the language of the proceedings. See E-V,3 for possible postponement of oral proceedings if a party is unable to arrange for the translation.

If a party uses an official EPO language not being the language of the proceedings in oral proceedings before a department of first instance, he is only allowed to use this language again in subsequent oral proceedings before a department of second instance after filing a new request for use of this language, because the proceedings of the second instance are not a continuation of, but wholly separate and independent from the first instance proceedings (Comm. Vice-Pres., Spec. Ed. 3 of OJ 2007, 118; **T34/90**).

R. 4(2) In the course of oral proceedings, employees of the European Patent Office may use an official language of the European Patent Office other than the language of the proceedings.

1 **Change to other official EPO language**
The employees of the EPO will normally use the language of proceedings during oral proceedings. By way of exception, **R.4(2)** allows the use of another EPO language in oral proceedings. However, the EPO should not depart from the use of the language of the proceedings without good reason. The parties need not agree to such a departure. The EPO informs them prior to oral proceedings, unless they have equally requested to use the other EPO language. If parties are not competent in that language, the EPO will provide for interpretation in the language of proceedings under **R.4(5)** at its own expense. (E-V,5)

R. 4(3) Where evidence is taken, any party, witness or expert to be heard who is unable to express himself adequately in an official language of the European Patent Office or of a Contracting State may use another language. Where evidence is taken upon request of a party, parties, witnesses or experts expressing themselves in a language other than an official language of the European Patent Office shall be heard only if that party provides for interpretation into the language of the proceedings. The European Patent Office may, however, permit interpretation into one of its other official languages.

R. 4(4) If the parties and the European Patent Office agree, any language may be used.

There will be no interpretation or prior notice (E-V,2).

R. 4(5) The European Patent Office shall, if necessary, provide at its own expense interpretation into the language of the proceedings, or, where appropriate, into its other official languages, unless such interpretation is the responsibility of one of the parties.

R. 4(6) Statements by employees of the European Patent Office, parties, witnesses or experts, made in an official language of the European Patent Office, shall be entered in the minutes in that language. Statements made in any other language shall be entered in the official language into which they are translated. Amendments to a European patent application or European patent shall be entered in the minutes in the language of the proceedings.

See **R.124** for drawing up of the minutes and E-V,6 for language used.

R. 5 Certification of translations

Where the translation of a document is required, the European Patent Office may require that a certificate that the translation corresponds to the original text be filed within a period to be specified. If the certificate is not filed in due time, such document shall be deemed not to have been filed, unless otherwise provided.

Implementation of: **Art.14**
EPC 1973: **R.5**

1 **General**
The EPO will only require a certificate of translation if it has serious doubts as to the accuracy of the translation of a document. If the certificate is not filed in the period specified, the document will be deemed not to have been received (**R.5**, second sentence). This partial loss of rights can be remedied with further processing (**Art.121**). (A-VII,7)

R. 6 Filing of translations and reduction of fees

Rule 6(3) amended and Rule 6(4)-(7) inserted by decision of the Administrative Council of 13.12.2013, which entered into force on 01.04.2014. The previous R.6(3) was mainly used by applicants who filed the written request for examination in an admissible non-EPO language, e.g. Dutch, to benefit from the reduction in examination fee, and filed all subsequent documents in an EPO language. This is not in line with the original intention of the provision, i.e. to provide a financial compensation for the translation requirements of the EPC. Moreover, R.6(3) was hardly ever used for fees other than the filing and examination fee.

The amendment limits the scope of the application of the fee reduction to two fees and to limited categories of applicants and increases the rate of reduction. The new system of language-related fee reductions supports small enterprises, natural persons and non-profit organisations.

The amended provision applies to European patent applications filed on or after 01.04.2014 and to international applications entering the European phase on or after that date. Oppositions, appeals, petitions for review or requests for limitation or revocation filed on or after 01.04.2014 will not anymore benefit from the fee reduction. (OJ 2014 A4, A23)
Implementation of: **Art.14**
EPC 1973: **R.6**

R. 6(1) A translation under Article 14, paragraph 2, shall be filed within two months of filing the European patent application.

Art.14(2) Translation of an application

1 **Period for filing translation of application**
The filing of the translation is checked under **Art.90(3)** and **R.57(a)**. If the two-month period of **R.6(1)** is not observed, the EPO will issue an invitation under **R.58** to correct the omission within two months. The final time limit for filing the translation may be about five months from filing.

The periods of **R.6(1)** and **R.58** are excluded from further processing under **R.135(2)** but re-establishment under **Art.122** is available, provided all due care can be proven. See also **Art.14(2):3**.

R. 6(2) A translation under Article 14, paragraph 4, shall be filed within one month of filing the document. This shall also apply to requests under Article 105a. Where the document is a notice of opposition or appeal, or a statement of grounds of appeal, or a petition for review, the translation may be filed within the period for filing such a notice or statement or petition, if that period expires later.

Art.14(4) Further documents in admitted non-EPO language
Art.105a Request for limitation or revocation

1 **Period for filing translation of further document**
A translation of a further document filed in an admissible non-EPO language under Art.14(4) into an official EPO language must be filed within one month of filing the document (**R.6(2)**, first sentence). If the document is sent by fax, the one month period is triggered by the day the fax is received (A-VII,2.5), not by the date the confirmation of the fax is received. Where the document is a notice of opposition or appeal, a statement of grounds of appeal or a petition for review, the translation may be filed within the period for filing such document if that expires later than the one-month period (**R.6(2)**, third sentence).

The reference to the request for limitation and revocation under **Art.105a** in **R.6(2)** is a lex specialis allowing the request to be filed in another language, provided a translation is filed (CA/PL/29/06 Add.1), even though the request need not be filed in a time limit as required by **Art.14(4)**. It should be noted that the Guidelines limit the languages of the request to those of **Art.14(4)**, i.e. admissible non-EPO languages (D-X,2.1(iv)), but it is not stated that the person filing the request must comply with the requirements of **Art.14(4)**. Hence, it appears to allow a Uruguayan party to file such a request in Spanish, although this is probably not intended.

If the time limit is not observed in grant proceedings, further processing (**Art.121** and **R.135**) may be requested. Re-establishment is excluded under **R.136(3)**. In opposition further processing is not available (**Art.121(1)**). An opponent has no remedy for late filing a translation, because both further processing and re-establishment are not available for him (see **Art.122(1):1**).

R. 6(3) Where a person referred to in Article 14, paragraph 4, files a European patent application or a request for examination in a language admitted in that provision, the filing fee or examination fee shall be reduced in accordance with the Rules relating to Fees.

Art.14(4) Person entitled to use admissible non-EPO language
Implementation of **Art.94(1)**
EPC 1973: **R.6(3)**

1 **Reduction of fees in the event of translations**
The provision gives a financial compensation for the cost of translations to be made by a party using an admissible non-EPO language, i.e. an official language of an EPC contracting state other than English, French or German. The amount of the reduction is fixed in **Rfees14(1)**.

The following three requirements must be complied with for entitlement to the reduction:

- The applicant must expressly declare that he is an entity or natural person covered by **R.6(4)** (**R.6(6)**). The declaration may be made by ticking the box in section 14.1 of the Request for Grant form or by filing a separate declaration, for which a pre-printed form may be used. The declaration must be filed at the latest by the time of payment of the (reduced) filing or examination fee. (OJ 2014 A23 p.4-6)
- At least the essential elements of a first act in the proceedings, i.e. the documents to be filed in a time limit, must be in an admissible non-EPO language. Essential elements are set out below for each of the fees to be reduced.

- The reduction is allowed if the translation in one of the official EPO languages is filed no earlier than simultaneously with the application or document (**G6/91** hn.1; A-X,9.2.1). However, if the application or document subject to a time limit is first filed in the language of the proceedings and subsequently in an admissible non-EPO language, the reduction is not allowed; nevertheless, see decision **J21/98** below.

The reduction is not applicable to the opposition fee, appeal fee, fee for the petition for review, and the limitation and revocation fee, because **R.6**(3) does not mention them.

2 Persons entitled to fee reduction

The persons entitled to a reduction of the filing and examination fee must comply with each of the following two requirements.

According to **R.6**(3), the fee reduction is available for a person referred to in **Art.14**(4), i.e. a person having his residence or place of business within a contracting state or who is a national of that state and resident abroad, using an official language of that contracting state other than English, French or German. The compensation is not available for a party having a residence or place of business outside a contracting state and who is not a national of a contracting state, e.g. a Uruguayan person living in India, nor is it available for use of a language other than an admissible non-EPO language, e.g. Japanese. (see also A-X,9.2.1)

Secondly, the applicant must be a small or medium-sized enterprise, a natural person, or a non-profit organisation, university or public research organisation (**R.6**(4)). The detailed definition of small and medium-sized enterprises **R.6**(5) refers to is given in A-X,9.2.1.

If there are multiple applicants, each one must comply with the language-residence requirement of **Art.14**(4) and with the small applicant requirement of **R.6**(4) (FAQ on EPO website and **R.6**(7)). For example, the examination fee will not be reduced when a request for examination is filed in Dutch by two applicants, an SME with place of business in the Netherlands and an SME with place of business in Germany, because the German co-applicant may not file a document in Dutch under **Art.14**(4).

No evidence of entitlement need be provided when filing the application or request for examination. In case of reasonable doubt, the EPO may request evidence (**R.6**(6)). If the applicant doubts about his entitlement to the reduction, he should pay the full fee as a precaution and request a refund of the reduction (30%) (see **Rfees14:1**).

If the evidence is not filed or is not convincing, the fee is underpaid and the EPO will regard the fee as not paid. As a consequence, the application will be deemed withdrawn (**Art.78**(2) or **94**(2)) and the EPO will issue a loss of rights communication under **R.112**(1). As a remedy further processing (**Art.121**) can be applied within two months of the communication by paying the deficit and the further processing fee, i.e. 50 % of the full fee. If the applicant regards the opinion of the EPO incorrect, he can also ask for a decision under **R.112**(2). (A-X,9.2.1 and FAQ on EPO website)

3 Fees to be reduced

3.1 FILING FEE

The essential element of the first act in filing a patent application is the description (not the claims) (**J4/88** together with **G6/91** r.18-22, adapted to the EPC 2000 in A-X,9.2.2). The filing fee (not the search fee) is reduced if at least the description (**J4/88**) is filed in an admissible non-EPO language and a translation in an official EPO language is filed at the earliest at the same time as the application.

The reduction also applies where an application is filed by reference under **R.40(1)(c)** to a previously filed application in an admissible non-EPO language and the applicant is entitled to a reduction (A-X,9.2.2). The reduction applies likewise in cases where the description is filed by reference to a previously filed application in an admissible non-EPO language, even when the claims are filed in an official EPO language after the date of filing, because the essential element, the description, has been filed in an admissible non-EPO language (A-II,4.1.3.1).

3.2 PAGE FEE AND DIVISIONAL FEE
Since the page fee is part of the filing fee according to **R.38(2)**, the page fee will also be reduced when the application is filed in a language as stated in **Art.14(4)**. (Not. EPO, OJ 2009, 118 §3.2; A-III,13.2; A-X,9.2.2)

The divisional fee is also part of the filing fee according to **R.38(4)**; hence, the divisional fee is reduced (A-X,9.2.2).

3.3 EXAMINATION FEE
The essential element of the first act in requesting examination is the written request for examination. The examination fee is reduced if the request for examination is in an admissible non-EPO language. A translation of the request need not be filed, because the Request for Grant form already contains a preprinted box for the written request for examination in the official EPO languages; the written request for examination in the admissible non-EPO language can be entered in the box for the request for examination. The Request for Grant form has a link to examples of the wording of the request in these languages on the EPO website.

Alternatively, the applicant may file the request for examination in an admissible non-EPO language at a later time before expiry of the 6-month period of **R.70(1)**, provided a translation of the request in an official EPO language is filed no earlier than simultaneously with the request (**J21/98** r.14). The Notes to the Request for Grant form recommend to enter the translation in the form on filing.

In order to benefit from the reduction it is not necessary to file subsequent documents during the examination procedure in an admissible non-EPO language, only the language of the first document is relevant. (A-X,9.2.3; see **G6/91**)

R. 6(4) The reduction referred to in paragraph 3 shall be available for:
(a) small and medium-sized enterprises;
(b) natural persons; or
(c) non-profit organisations, universities or public research organisations.

1 **Entitled applicants**
The definition of a small applicant entitled to fee reduction is given in OJ 2014 A23, p.7-11. Changes in the status of an applicant which occur after filing the declaration will not have a retroactive effect on the fee reductions that were justified when granted (OJ 2014 A23, p.10). If reasonable doubt arises as to the veracity of the declaration of the applicant, the EPO may request appropriate evidence (**R.6(7)**; OJ 2014 A23, p.11).

See **R.6(3):2** for the consequence of not filing a declaration or filing an incorrect declaration.

R. 6(5) For the purposes of paragraph 4(a), Commission recommendation 2003/361/EC of 6 May 2003 concerning the definition of micro, small and medium-sized enterprises as published in the Official Journal of the European Union L 124, p. 36 of 20 May 2003 shall apply.

R. 6(6) An applicant wishing to benefit from the fee reduction referred to in paragraph 3 shall declare himself to be an entity or a natural person within the meaning of paragraph 4. In case of reasonable doubt as to the veracity of such declaration, the Office may require evidence.

R. 6(7) In case of multiple applicants, each applicant shall be an entity or a natural person within the meaning of paragraph4.

R. 7 Legal authenticity of the translation of the European patent application

Unless evidence is provided to the contrary, the European Patent Office shall assume, for the purpose of determining whether the subject-matter of the European patent application or European patent extends beyond the content of the application as filed, that the translation filed under Article 14, paragraph 2, or Rule 40, paragraph 3, is in conformity with the original text of the application.

Art.14(2) Language and translation of application
R.40(3) Filing of translation of previously filed application
Implementation of: **Art.14(2), 70(2)**
EPC 1973: **R.7**

1 **Incorrect translation**
The EPO assumes that a translation of a patent application or patent is in conformity with the original text of the application, unless proof to the contrary is given (**R.7**). The proof may be provided by an opponent during opposition proceedings or by a third party after file inspection according to **Art.128**. A correction of a translation during an opposition procedure is permitted under **Art.14(2)**, provided the correction does not extend the scope of the claims of the translation (**Art.123(3)**).

R. 8 Patent classification

The European Patent Office shall use the classification referred to in Article 1 of the Strasbourg Agreement concerning the International Patent Classification of 24 March 1971, hereinafter referred to as the international classification.

EPC 1973: **R.8**

1 **Strasbourg agreement on classification**
See B-V on the classification of the application. Other references to classification: **R.11(1)**: assignment of duties to departments of first instance; **R.61(6)**: mention of the classification in the search report; and **R.143(1)(d)**: entry in the Register.

The complete International Patent Classification (IPC) is available on www.wipo.int/classifications/ipc/en/.

Since 01.01.2013 the EPO uses the Cooperative Patent Classification (CPC) system, developed jointly with the USPTO and compliant with the IPC (see www.cooperativepatentclassification.org). The USPTO uses the CPC since 01.01.2013 and the SIPO since 01.01.2014.

R. 9 Administrative structure of the European Patent Office

R.9(1) amended by decision of the Administrative Council of 30.06.2016, which entered into force on 01.07.2016 (OJ 2016 A100). The decision changes the BsoA and the EBoA in Art.15(f) and (g) from a directorate-general under R.9(1) into a separate organisational unit under R.12a.

Implementation of: **Art.15**

EPC 1973: **R.12**

R. 9(1) The European Patent Office shall be divided administratively into Directorates-General, to which the departments specified in Article 15(a) to (e), and the services set up to deal with legal matters and the internal administration of the Office, shall be assigned.

R. 9(2) Each Directorate-General shall be directed by a Vice-President. The assignment of a Vice-President to a Directorate-General shall be decided by the Administrative Council, after the President of the European Patent Office has been consulted.

R. 10 Responsibility of the Receiving Section and the Examining Division

Implementation of: **Art.16**

EPC 1973: **Art.16, Art.18(1)**

1 **General**

R.10 delimits the period of the Receiving Section's responsibility for examination on filing and as to formal requirements and lays down the rules on the transition of responsibility to the examining divisions.

To avoid parallel responsibility, paragraph 1 provides that the Receiving Section ceases to be responsible when the examining division's responsibility begins.

Under **Art.94(1)**, the EPO examines, on request and in accordance with the Implementing Regulations, whether the application and the invention to which it relates meet the requirements of the EPC. The request is deemed not to have been filed until the examination fee has been paid. Therefore, under paragraph 2 of the new rule, the examining division becomes responsible, subject to paragraphs 3 and 4, once a request for examination has been filed.

In the event that the request for examination is filed before the European search report has been transmitted to the applicant, paragraph 3 provides that the examining division is not responsible until the indication under **R.70(2)** has been received. The EPO interprets the phrase 'the European search report has been transmitted to the applicant' as 'the European search report has been handed over to the EPO postal service for notification'; this moment is three days prior to the date stamped on the communication (see **G12/91** r.9.1)

Paragraph 4 is a separate provision governing cases in which the applicant has waived the right under R.70(2). The responsibility provisions are entirely consistent with the practice under the EPC 1973. (CA/PL17/06)

R.10 allows an examining division after having assumed responsibility to take care of formal requirements, such as checking payment of fees.

R. 10(1) The Receiving Section shall be responsible for the examination on filing and the examination as to formal requirements of a European patent application up to the time when the Examining Division becomes responsible for the examination of the European patent application under Article 94, paragraph 1.

Art.94(1) Examination of the European patent application

R. 10(2) Subject to paragraphs 3 and 4, the Examining Division shall be responsible for the examination of a European patent application under Article 94, paragraph 1, from the time when a request for examination is filed.

Art.94(1) Examination of the European patent application

R. 10(3) If a request for examination is filed before the European search report has been transmitted to the applicant, the Examining Division shall, subject to paragraph 4, be responsible from the time when the European Patent Office receives the indication under Rule 70, paragraph 2.

R.70(2) Invitation to proceed after early request for examination

R. 10(4) If a request for examination is filed before the European search report has been transmitted to the applicant, and if the applicant has waived the right under Rule 70, paragraph 2, the Examining Division shall be responsible from the time when the search report is transmitted to the applicant.

R.70(2) Invitation to proceed after early request for examination

R. 11 Allocation of duties to the departments of first instance

Implementation of: Art.15
EPC 1973: R.9

1 **General**

R.11 reflects the administrative grouping into directorates of the departments involved in the grant procedure – i.e. the search divisions, examining divisions and opposition divisions, made up of technically qualified examiners.

R. 11(1) Technically qualified examiners acting as members of Search, Examining or Opposition Divisions shall be assigned to Directorates. The President of the European Patent Office shall allocate duties to these Directorates by reference to the international classification.

R. 11(2) The President of the European Patent Office may allocate further duties to the Receiving Section, the Search, Examining and Opposition Divisions, and the Legal Division, in addition to the responsibilities vested in them under the Convention.

See **Art.20** for the allocation of duties to the Legal Division.

R. 11(3) The President of the European Patent Office may entrust to employees who are not technically or legally qualified examiners the execution of duties falling to the Search, Examining or Opposition Divisions and involving no technical or legal difficulties.

1 **Formalities officers**
Certain duties normally the responsibility of the examining or opposition division have been entrusted to non-examining staff for operational efficiency (Dec. Pres. OJ 2014 A6; Not. EPO OJ 2014 A32; Dec. Pres. 2015 A104).

The employees of the non-examining staff are called formalities officers, allocated to the Receiving Section, examining and opposition divisions and Boards of Appeal. Formalities officers may take decisions concerning matters not involving legal or technical difficulties, such as concerning the inadmissibility of an opposition (**G1/02** hn). It is a substantial procedural violation in the sense of **R.103** if a formalities officer takes a decision not within his competence; such a decision will be set aside (see e.g. **T178/01**).

The competence of the Boards of Appeal to hear appeals is not affected by the entrustment of duties to formalities officers (**G2/90** hn.II). Hence, an appeal of a decision taken by a formalities officer of an examining or opposition division must be heard by a board of appeal competent under **Art.21** to hear the appeal had the decision been taken by the division itself. See **Art.20(1):1** for an exception regarding delegated duties normally the responsibility of the Legal Division.

R. 12a Organisation and management of the Boards of Appeal Unit and President of the Boards of Appeal

By decision of 30.06.2016 the Administrative Council inserted R.12a. The provisions entered into force on 01.07.2016 (OJ 2016 A100).
Implementation of: **Art.21**

1 **Reform of the boards of appeal and their independence**
The boards of appeal were reformed in 2016 following decision **R19/12**, which objected to the chairman of the EBoA for suspected partiality because of his connection as vice-president of Directorate-General 3 with the management of the EPO. The reform intends to increase the managerial autonomy, perception of independence and the efficiency of the boards by

- changing the boards from a directorate-general headed by a vice-president (**R.9**) to a BoA unit headed by a president of the BoA, who is also the chairman of the EBoA (**R.12a(1)**), thereby separating the administrative head of the BoA from the President of the EPO. The president of the BoA is hierarchically independent of the President of the EPO and responsible to the Administrative Council;
- delegation of powers of the President of the EPO relating to the management of the BoA Unit to the president of the BoA (**R.12a(2)**);
- creation of a BoA Committee as a subsidiary body of the Administrative Council (AC) for advising the Council (**R.12c**); and
- relocating the BoA to a separate building (see **Art.6:3**)

2 **Independence of BoA members**

The reform does not guarantee the envisaged independence of members of the boards under **Art.23** for several reasons.

Firstly, since the reform, re-appointment of a member after a five-year term requires under **R.12d(3)** a positive opinion of the president of the BoA on his performance, which is a subjective criterion. The President of the BoA may only propose a member for re-appointment (**R.12d(2)**); the decision is taken by the AC (**Art.11(3)**). Hence, re-appointment depends on the AC, an organ that is not part of the Boards of Appeal Unit and whose abidance with the rule of law is not guaranteed (see notes to **Art.23(1)** for incidents).

Secondly, in disciplinary proceedings against a board of appeal member the AC can suspend a member indefinitely without the proposal from the EBoA for removal as required by **Art.23(1)** (see **Art.23(1):3**).

Thirdly, the AC and the President of the EPO can still exert influence on the boards through denying re-appointment of the President of the BoA (**R.12a(1):1**); adopting the rules of procedure of the boards through a subsidiary body (**R.12c(2)**); influencing the above performance criteria (**R.12d(3)**); and the possibility that the President of the EPO revokes the delegation of powers to the President of the BoA (**R.12a(2):1**).

Users of the EPC cannot ascertain the independence of the BoA members, because the AC does usually not publish their (re-)appointments and accompanying grounds. The lack of transparency makes it impossible to check whether the AC has applied the rule of law when denying a member re-appointment.

It appears that the independence of the board members can only be guaranteed by deletion of the five-year term in **Art.23(1)**, requiring a diplomatic conference under **Art.172**, which is unlikely to be convened in the short term.

R. 12a(1) The Boards of Appeal and the enlarged Board of appeal, including their registries and support services, shall be organised as a separate unit (the "Boards of Appeal Unit") and be directed by the President of the Boards of Appeal. The Chairman of the Enlarged Board of Appeal shall act as President of the Boards of Appeal. the President of the Boards of Appeal shall be appointed by the Administrative Council on a joint proposal made by the Committee established under Rule 12c, paragraphs 1, and the President of the European Patent Office. If the President of the Boards of Appeal is absent or indisposed, one of the members of the Enlarged Board of Appeal shall take his place in accordance with the procedure laid down by the Administrative Council.

1 **President of the Boards of Appeal**

R.12a(1) lays down that the President of the BoA is appointed by the AC on a joint proposal by the President of the EPO and the Boards of Appeal Committee, established by the AC under **R.12c(1)**. Note, that **R.12a(1)** governs only the appointment of the President of the BoA, not his re-appointment.

The term of the President of the BoA is five years (**Art.23(1)**). Each five years the AC may re-appoint the president of the BoA under **Art.11(3)** after consultation of the President of the EPO (see Annex 1of CA/43/16 Rev. 1e, in particular Annex 3, §5 and Art.3(c) of the Act of Delegation). The five-yearly re-appointment makes the president of the BoA dependent on the President of the EPO and the AC, in contradiction to his independence under **Art.23**.

The president of the BoA also acts as chairman of the EBoA in a long and successful tradition; the involvement of the administrative head also in judicial activities reinforces his expertise and standing (CA/43/16 Rev. 1, Annex 1, §5 and Annex 3 §5; see also **R.12d(1)**). In 2016 the AC appointed the first President of the BoA (OJ 2017 A1) and the President of the BoA appointed his deputy (OJ 2017 A70).

A deputy shall take the place of the president of the BoA if he is absent or indisposed (**R.12a(1)**, fourth sentence). The president of the BoA has the power to designate the deputy (see OJ 2018 A85).

R. 12a(2) The President of the Boards of Appeal shall manage the Boards of Appeal Unit and, to this end, have the functions and powers delegated to him by the President of the European Patent Office. In exercising the delegated functions and powers, the President of the Boards of Appeal shall be responsible solely to the Administrative Council and shall be subject to its hierarchical and disciplinary authority.

1 **Delegation of powers**

The President of the EPO will delegate some of his functions and powers to the President of the BoA to allow him to manage the BoA Unit. The President of the EPO may revoke the delegation on his own initiative.

According to OJ 2017 A19 the President of the EPO signed the act of delegation on 14.02.2017, which entered into force on 01.03.2017. The text of the signed act has not been published but the proposal for the text is available in CA/43/16 Rev. 1e, Annex 3, Part II.

On 01.07.2018 the next President of the EPO also signed an act of delegation, which also entered into force on 01.03.2017. It is not clear why the delegation was made twice.

R. 12a(3) Without prejudice to Article 10, paragraph 2(d), and Article 46, the President of the Boards of Appeal shall prepare a substantiated budget request for the Boards of Appeal Unit. This request shall be examined and discussed with the relevant departments of the European Patent Office, and be presented by the President of the Boards of Appeal to the Committee established under Rule 12c, paragraph 1, for opinion, before being forwarded to the President of the European Patent Office for consideration for the yearly draft budget. The President of the European Patent Office shall provide the President of the Boards of Appeal with the necessary resources, as set out in the adopted budget.

Art.10(2)(d) Power of President EPO to prepare and implement the budget
Art.46 Preparation and adoption of the budget

R. 12a(4) The President of the European Patent Office shall make the services mentioned in Rule 9, paragraph 1, available to the President of the Boards of Appeal as far as necessary and within the limits of the adopted budget.

R.9(1) Services dealing with legal matters and internal administration

R. 12b Presidium of the Boards of Appeal and business distribution scheme for the Boards of Appeal

By decision of 30.06.2016 the Administrative Council amended R.12 and changed its number to R.12b. The provisions entered into force on 01.07.2016 (OJ 2016 A100).
Implementation of: **Art.21**
EPC 1973: **R.10**

1 **General**
The members of the Boards of Appeal are appointed by the Administrative Council (**Art.11(3)**). They elect from their ranks the Presidium of the Boards of Appeal, consisting of a chairman and twelve members (**R.12b(1)**). The chairman is the President of the BoA. The Presidium is in charge of the day-to-day functioning of the BoA.

The Presidium advises the President of the BoA on the Rules of Procedure of the Boards of Appeal and the Enlarged Board of Appeal (**R.12b(3)(c)**), which are to be approved by the BoA Committee (**R.12c**). The Presidium designates the members of the Boards of Appeal and allocates their duties (**R.12(4)**). The composition of the Presidium and the Boards of Appeal is published annually in the OJ (see Supplementary publication to OJ of January).

R. 12b(1) The autonomous authority within the Boards of Appeal Unit (the "Presidium of the Boards of Appeal") shall consist of the President of the Boards of Appeal, who shall act as chairman, and twelve members of the Boards of Appeal, six being Chairmen and six being other members.

R. 12b(2) All members of the Presidium shall be elected by the Chairmen and members of the Boards of Appeal for two working years. If the full composition of the Presidium cannot be reached, the vacancies shall be filled by designating the most senior Chairmen and members.

R. 12b(3) The Presidium shall
- **(a) adopt the Rules of Procedure for the election and designation of its members;**
- **(b) adopt, without prejudice to regulations adopted in accordance with Article 10, paragraph 2(c), and Article 33, paragraph 2(b), a Code of Conduct for the members and Chairmen of the Boards of Appeal and of the Enlarged Board of Appeal, which shall be subject to the approval of the Administrative Council;**
- **(c) advise the President of the Boards of Appeal on proposals for amendments to the Rules of Procedure of the Boards of Appeal and of the Enlarged Board of Appeal;**
- **(d) advise the President of the Boards of Appeal on matters concerning the functioning of the Boards of Appeal Unit in general.**

Art.10(2)(c) Power of President EPO to propose regulations
Art.33(2)(b) Competence of Administrative Council to adopt Service Regulations

R. 12b(4) Before the beginning of each working year, the Presidium, extended to include all Chairmen, shall allocate duties to the Boards of Appeal. In the same composition, it shall decide on conflicts regarding the allocation of duties between two or more Boards of Appeal. The extended Presidium shall designate the regular and alternate members of the various Boards of Appeal. Any member of a Board of Appeal may be designated as a member of more than one Board of Appeal. These measures may, where necessary, be amended during the course of the working year in question.

R. 12b(5) The Presidium may only take a decision if at least five of its members are present; these must include the President of the Boards of Appeal or his deputy, and the Chairmen of two Boards of Appeal. Where the tasks mentioned in paragraph 4 are concerned, nine members must be present, including the President of the Boards of Appeal or his deputy, and the Chairmen of three Boards of Appeal. Decisions shall be taken by a majority vote; in the event of parity of votes, the Chairman or his deputy shall have the casting vote. Abstentions shall not be considered as votes.

R. 12b(6) The Administrative Council may allocate duties under Article 134a, paragraph 1(c), to the Boards of Appeal.

Art.134a(1)(c) Disciplinary power over professional representatives

R. 12c Boards of Appeal Committee and procedure for adoption of the Rules of Procedure of the Boards of Appeal and of the Enlarged Board of Appeal

By decision of 30.06.2016 the Administrative Council inserted R.12c. The provisions entered into force on 01.07.2016 (OJ 2016 A100).
Implementation of: Art.21

R. 12c(1) The Administrative Council shall set up a committee (the "Boards of Appeal Committee") to advise it and the President of the Boards of Appeal on the Boards of Appeal Unit in general and to adopt the Rules of Procedure of the Boards of Appeal and of the Enlarged Board of Appeal. the committee shall be composed of six members appointed by the Administrative Council, three from among the delegations of the Contracting States within the meaning of Article 26, and three from among serving or former judges of international or European courts or of national courts of the Contracting States. The President of the European Patent Office and the President of the Boards of Appeal shall have the right to attend the Committee's meetings. Further details, in particular as to the Committee's composition, alternate members, working arrangements and functions in advising the Boards of Appeal Unit, shall be determined by the Administrative Council in the decision setting up the Committee.

1 **Boards of Appeal Committee**
The Boards of Appeal Committee is a subsidiary body of the Administrative Council and advises and assists the Administrative Council and the President of the Boards of Appeal on the Boards of Appeal Unit in general and adopts the Rules of Procedure of both the Boards of Appeal and the Enlarged Board of Appeal. The Committee among others monitors the independence of the Boards of Appeal Unit, a corner stone of the rule of law, and provides guidance on criteria for performance evaluation. (Dec. Adm. Council, OJ 2016 A101)

The Committee has six members, not being members of the Boards of Appeal, appointed by the Administrative Council. The President of the BoA and the President of the EPO may participate in all meetings of the Committee. The advisory and supervisory functions of the Committee are limited to a general level; the day-to-day functioning of the BoA is in charge of the Presidium of **R.12b(1)**.

It should be noted, that the Administrative Council and the President of the EPO have a decisive role in a committee that monitors the independence of the boards, whereas both have shown on several occasions to have other priorities than the rule of law (see e.g. **Art.23(1):2** and **3**).

R. 12c(2) On a proposal from the President of the Boards of Appeal and after the President of the European Patent Office has been given the opportunity to comment, the Committee set up under paragraph 1 shall adopt the Rules of Procedure of the Boards of Appeal and of the Enlarged Board of Appeal.

1 **Rules of procedure of Boards of Appeal**
The Boards of Appeal Committee adopts the Rules of Procedure for both the Boards of Appeal and the Enlarged Board of Appeal (**R.12c(1)**), while the Presidium may advise on proposals for amendment (**R.12b(3)(b)**). Whereas before 01.07.2016 the rules were adopted by only members of the boards of appeal, after that date there are no members anymore in the committee that adopts the rules.

The latest consolidated version of the Rules of Procedure of the Boards of Appeal is published in OJ2015 sp1, III.2. The latest consolidated version of the Rules of Procedure of the Enlarged Board of Appeal is published in OJ 2015 A35.

R. 12d Appointment and re-appointment of the members, including the Chairmen, of the Boards of Appeal and of the Enlarged Board of Appeal

By decision of 30.06.2016 the Administrative Council inserted R.12d. The provisions entered into force on 01.07.2016 (OJ 2016 A100).
Implementation of: **Art.21**

1 **General**
R.12d deals with the appointment and re-appointment of the members of the EBoA and the chairman and members of the boards of appeal. The appointment of the chairman of the EBoA, who is also the President of the Boards of Appeal, is not governed by **R.12d** but by **R.12a(1)**; his re-appointment by **Art.11(3)** (see **R.12a(1):1**).

R. 12d(1) The Chairman of the Enlarged Board of Appeal shall, on his appointment, also be appointed as a legally qualified member of the Boards of Appeal.

R. 12d(2) Upon delegation from the President of the European Patent Office, the President of the Boards of Appeal shall exercise the right to propose the members, including the Chairmen, of the Boards of Appeal and the members of the Enlarged Board of Appeal for appointment by the Administrative Council, and the right to be consulted on their re-appointment of external legally qualified members (Article 11, paragraph 5).

1 **Proposal for chairmen and members of boards**
The President of the Boards of Appeal may propose the chairmen and members of the boards of appeal and the members of the Enlarged Board of Appeal for appointment to the Administrative Council and he is consulted on their re-appointment (**R.12d(2)**). The President of the EPO may propose the chairman of the Enlarged Board of Appeal and is consulted on his re-appointment (CA43/16 Rev.1 en, Annex 3, §5).

R. 12d(3) The President of the Boards of Appeal shall exercise the right under paragraph 2 to be consulted on re-appointments by submitting a reasoned opinion, including an evaluation of the member's or Chairman's performance, to the Administrative Council. The criteria for evaluating performance shall be set by the President of the Boards of Appeal in consultation with the Committee established under Rule 12c, paragraph 1. Subject to a positive opinion and performance evaluation and the number of posts under Article 11, paragrap 3, available in the adopted budget for the Boards of Appeal Unit, the members, including the Chairmen, of the Boards of Appeal and the members of the Enlarged Board of Appeal shall be re-appointed at the end of their five-year term under Article 23, paragraph 1.

Art.11(3) Appointment of board of appeal members by the Administrative Council
Art.23(1) Term of board of appeal members

R. 13 Business distribution scheme for the Enlarged Board of Appeal and adoption of its Rules of Procedure

Before the beginning of each working year, the members of the Enlarged Board of Appeal appointed under Article 11, paragraph 3, shall designate the regular and alternate members of the Enlarged Board of Appeal in proceedings under Article 22, paragraph 1(a) and (b), and the regular and alternate members in proceedings under Article 22, paragraph 1(c). Decisions may only be taken if at least five members are present, including the Chairman of the Enlarged Board of Appeal or his deputy; in the event of parity of votes, the Chairman or his deputy shall have the casting vote. Abstentions shall not be considered as votes.

By decision of 30.06.2016 the Administrative Council amended R.13 by deleting paragraph 2 and combining paragraphs 1 and 3. The provision entered into force on 01.07.2016 (OJ 2016 A100).
Art.11(3) Appointment by the Administrative Council

Art.22(1)(a) Referral by board of appeal
Art.22(1)(b) Referral by the President of the EPO
Art.22(1)(c) Petition for review of a decision of a board of appeal
Implementation of: **Art.22**
EPC 1973: **R.11**

1 **Members of the Enlarged Board of Appeal**

The members of the Enlarged Board of Appeal are appointed by the Administrative Council (**Art.11(3)**) on a proposal from the President of the Boards of Appeal (**R.12d(2)**).

R.13 allows to designate specifically members for the proceedings under **Art.112**, i.e. referrals to the Enlarged Board of Appeal, and for the proceedings under **Art.112a**, i.e. petitions for review, to enable more members to work regularly on petitions for review. (Spec. Ed. 5 of OJ 2007)

The composition of the Enlarged Board of Appeal is published annually in the OJ (see Suppl. to OJ of January).

PART II IMPLEMENTING REGULATIONS TO PART II OF THE CONVENTION

Chapter I *Procedure where the applicant is not entitled*

R. 14 Stay of proceedings

Implementation of: **Art.61**
EPC 1973: **R.13(1), (2), (3) + (5)**

1 **General**
The stay of the EPO proceedings during entitlement proceedings secures the rights of a third party and allows him time to prove his entitlement to the patent before a national court of a contracting state (**J6/03** r.2). After the court's decision has become final, the third party has three months to take one of the actions mentioned in **Art.61(1)**. The Legal Division is competent in procedures where the applicant or proprietor is not entitled to the grant of the European patent (**Art.61(1), 99(5), R.14, 15, 18**) (OJ 2013, 600).

Whereas **R.14 - 18** concern an applicant who is not entitled, **R.78** applies to a patent proprietor who is not entitled.

R. 14(1) If a third party provides evidence that he has instituted proceedings against the applicant seeking a decision within the meaning of Article 61, paragraph 1, the proceedings for grant shall be stayed unless the third party communicates to the European Patent Office in writing his consent to the continuation of such proceedings. Such consent shall be irrevocable. However, proceedings for grant shall not be stayed before the publication of the European patent application.

Art. 61(1) European patent application filed by non-entitled person

1 **Procedure for requesting stay of grant proceedings**
If a third party provides satisfactory evidence to the EPO that he has instituted entitlement proceedings at a national court and the conditions of **R.14(1)** are met, the EPO will stay the proceedings ex officio to safeguard the rights of the third party (A-IV,2.2.3). The stay takes effect on the date an allowable request is filed (**J9/12** r.11). If, exceptionally, the third party consents in writing to the continuation of the proceedings, the proceedings will not be stayed (**R.14(1)**). The meaning of 'institution of proceedings' is determined by national law (**J7/00** r.3).

The EPO does not have to give the applicant an opportunity to comment or take a formal decision. The applicant will be informed of the stay. He can request to lift the stay by providing arguments and evidence, upon which the EPO will take a decision. The decision can be appealed by the adversely affected party. (**J28/94** r.2.2.1; **J18/06** r.2; A-IV,2.2.3)

The EPO will reject a request for staying the proceedings if e.g. the grant proceedings are terminated or the conditions of **R.14(1)** are not met. The rejection is in the form of a formal decision. The third party can appeal the decision, the applicant becoming party as of right. (**J28/94** r.2.2)

The immediate stay of the proceedings makes it impossible for the applicant to withdraw the application (**R.15**), securing the rights of the third party (**J15/06** r.7). During the stay, a transfer of the application may not be recorded in the register (**J17/12** hn) and no divisional may be filed on the application (**J9/12** r.5).

However, if the proceedings continue on express request of the third party, the applicant cannot be prevented from withdrawing the application (**R.15**), giving rise to an insecure situation for the third party. Withdrawal of the request for staying is interpreted as consent to continue the proceedings (**J1/06** r.3).

Grant proceedings can be interrupted by a request for staying if filed before the date on which the Bulletin mentions the grant according to **Art.97(3)**, even if the request is filed after the decision to grant has been taken (**J7/96** hn, r.9).

Proceedings cannot be stayed before publication of a direct EP application (**R.14(1)**, last sentence) and before entry into the EP phase of a Euro-PCT application (A-IV,2.2).

R. 14(2) Where evidence is provided that a final decision within the meaning of Article 61, paragraph 1, has been taken, the European Patent Office shall inform the applicant and any other party that the proceedings for grant shall be resumed as from the date stated in the communication, unless a new European patent application under Article 61, paragraph 1(b), has been filed for all the designated Contracting States. If the decision is in favour of the third party, the proceedings may not be resumed earlier than three months after the decision has become final, unless the third party requests the resumption.

Art. 61(1)(b) New European patent application filed by entitled person

R. 14(3) Upon staying the proceedings for grant, or thereafter, the European Patent Office may set a date on which it intends to resume the proceedings for grant, regardless of the stage reached in the national proceedings instituted under paragraph 1. It shall communicate this date to the third party, the applicant and any other party. If no evidence has been provided by that date that a final decision has been taken, the European Patent Office may resume proceedings.

1 **Date of resumption of the proceedings**

The EPO communicates the date of resumption of the proceedings to the third party and the applicant (A-IV,2.2.5). The date is chosen with regard to the interests of the parties (see A-IV,2.2.5). If at the date set the judgement is expected soon, there will be a further stay. The proceedings will be resumed if delaying tactics by the third party are suspected. The decision to resume is appealable (see e.g. **J33/03** r.1).

The parties may request a change of date or an end of the stay (**T146/82**).

R. 14(4) All periods other than those for the payment of renewal fees, running at the date of the stay of proceedings, shall be interrupted by such stay. The time which has not yet elapsed shall begin to run from the date on which proceedings are resumed. However, the time still to run after such resumption shall not be less than two months.

1 **Interruption of periods**

All periods running at the date of stay of proceedings are interrupted, except the period for payment of renewal fees. Therefore, the third party must make sure that the applicant continues to pay the renewal fees which fall due during the stay, otherwise the third party has to pay them. Note, that any automatic debit order ceases to be effective if the proceedings are stayed; after resumption a new order must be given if automatic debiting is to be used again (**AAD.13.1(e)**).

The phrase 'from the date' in **R.14(4)** is interpreted such that the date of resumption of proceedings is included in the time still to run; for example, a date of resumption of 5 January and a non-elapsed period of 2 months result in a time limit of 4 March.

The stay of proceedings under **R.14(4)** has a different effect on running periods than an interruption of the proceedings under **R.142**: after the stay the period continues with the not yet elapsed time, after the interruption the period starts again.

2 **Example interruption of periods**

The 6-month period of **R.70(1)** was triggered by the mention of the publication of the search report on 28.06.2017; thus the computation of the period (**R.131(2)**) starts on 29.06.2017 and would normally have ended 28.12.2017. Proceedings are stayed on 22.09.2017 and resumed on 03.08.2018. The last day of the elapsed period is 21.09.2017. The non-elapsed period thus runs from 22 September to 28 December. The length of this period is 7 days (from 22 September, which is the first day of the period, to 28 September), plus 3 months (from 28 September to 28 December), making 3 months and 7 days in total. This non-elapsed period begins on 03.08.2018, which is already the first day of the period (**R.14(4)**: 'from the date'), and thus ends on 9.11.2018. (A-IV,2.2.4; see D-VII,4.3 for another example)

Note, that the extension under **R.134(1)** of the non-elapsed period should be included in the length of the non-elapsed period, although neither the EPC nor the Guidelines state so. In the above-case it would mean that the expiry of the extended, non-interrupted period on 02.01.2018, would have resulted in a non-elapsed period of 3 months and 11 instead of 7 days in total, and thus expiry of the non-elapsed period on 13.11.2018.

Moreover, neither the EPC nor the Guidelines state how the duration of the non-elapsed period should be calculated: first days and then weeks, first days and then months, first months and then days or any other combination. Since the length of the period depends on the way of calculation, the date of resumption is indeterminate. In practice, the EPO resumes the proceedings at a date promptly after the longest non-elapsed period that can be calculated.

R. 15 Limitation on withdrawals

From the date on which a third party provides evidence that he has instituted national proceedings under Rule 14, paragraph 1, and up to the date on which the proceedings for grant are resumed, neither the European patent application nor the designation of any Contracting State may be withdrawn.

R.14(1) Entitlement suit
Implementation of: **Art.61**
EPC 1973: **R.14**

1 **Prohibition to withdraw**
R.15 is an implementing regulation of **Art.61**, securing the right of the third party. Beware, **R.15** applies only if the third party has provided proof to the EPO of the initiation of entitlement proceedings and has not consented to continuation of the grant proceedings; if there is no stay of proceedings, the original applicant may still withdraw the application or designations of contracting states. The prohibition of withdrawal sets in on the day the EPO receives the evidence required under **R.14(1)** (**R.15**); there is no retro-active effect (A-IV,2.3).

R. 16 Procedure under Article 61, paragraph 1

Implementation of: **Art.61**
EPC 1973: **Art.61(1)**

R. 16(1) A person entitled to the grant of a European patent may only avail himself of the remedies under Article 61, paragraph 1, if:
(a) he does so no later than three months after the decision recognising his entitlement has become final, and
(b) the European patent has not yet been granted.

1 **Period for requesting remedy under Art.61(1)**
R.135(2) excludes the three-month period under **R.16(1)(a)** from further processing. Re-establishment is available, because the exclusion in **R.135(2)** implicitly recognises that, in principle, the entitled person under **Art.61(1)** has access to the remedies provided by the EPC to deal with failure to observe time limits. (Special Edition no. 1, OJ 1/2003, p. 159)

The 'European patent has not yet been granted' in **R.16(1)(b)** probably means before publication of the mention of the grant (see **Art.97(3)**).

R. 16(2) Such remedies shall only apply in respect of Contracting States designated in the European patent application in which the decision has been taken or recognised or must be recognised on the basis of the Protocol on Recognition.

1 **Protocol on Recognition**
The Protocol on Recognition lays down in Art.1(1) that the courts of the contracting states have jurisdiction to decide entitlement claims. It also governs in Art.9(1) the recognition of the final decision of a court given in a contracting state in other contracting states.

The Protocol of Recognition is an integral part of the EPC according to **Art.164(1)**. Adherence to the Protocol is not an absolute requirement for the EPO to recognize the court's decision; this would be too narrow an interpretation, which is not justifiable in respect of the rights of applicants from outside the contracting states (**J34/86**). Before 07.10.1987 it was possible for states acceding to the EPC to exclude under **Art.167(2)(d)** EPC 1973 being bound by the Protocol of Recognition. The background of this provision was to avoid delaying the accession of the state to the EPC due to matter not related to patent law, such as recognition of decisions of foreign courts.

R. 17 Filing of a new European patent application by the entitled person

Implementation of: **Art.61**
EPC 1973: **R.15(1) + (2)**

1 **General**
The new application according to **Art.61(1)(b)** has many characteristics of a divisional application (see **Art.61(2)**; A-IV,2.5).

R. 17(1) Where the person adjudged by a final decision to be entitled to the grant of the European patent files a new European patent application under Article 61, paragraph 1(b), the original application shall be deemed to be withdrawn on the date of filing the new application for the Contracting States designated therein in which the decision has been taken or recognised or must be recognised on the basis of the Protocol on Recognition.

Art.61(1)(b) Filing of a new application by the entitled person

1 **Designation of states**
All contracting states have to recognize a national entitlement decision, because the reservations on recognition according to **Art.167** EPC 1973 have expired.

If it is adjudged that a third party is entitled to the grant for only some of the contracting states and the third party files a new application for these states, for the remaining states the earlier application continues to be in the name of the earlier applicant (A-IV,2.7).

R. 17(2) The filing fee and search fee shall be paid within one month of filing the new application. If the filing fee or search fee is not paid in due time, the application shall be deemed to be withdrawn.

1 **Filing fee and search fee for new application**
The amount of the filing fee and search fee is fixed in **Rfees2(1)1** and **Rfees2(1)2**, respectively.

If the filing fee and search fee are not paid within one month from filing the new application, the application shall be deemed withdrawn (**R.17(2)**). The EPO will send the applicant a communication informing him of the loss of rights according to **R.112(1)**. The applicant may request further processing under **Art.121** and **R.135** within two months from notification of the communication.

The search fee for the new application must always be paid, even if a search fee has already been paid for the earlier application in respect of the same invention (A-IV,2.5(iii) and A-IV,1.4.1). The search fee for the new application will be refunded fully or in part if the search report can be based on the search report of the earlier application (**Rfees9(2)**).

On filing, a page fee and claims fee may be payable. See **R.38** and **45**.

R. 17(3) The designation fee shall be paid within six months of the date on which the European Patent Bulletin mentions the publication of the European search report drawn up in respect of the new application. Rule 39, paragraphs 2 and 3, shall apply.

Amended by decision of the Administrative Council of 21.10.2008, which entered into force on 01.04.2009. (OJ 2008, 513; OJ 2009, 118 footnote 1)
R.39(2) Non-payment of the designation fee
R.39(3) Non-refundability of the designation fee

1 **Designation fee for new application**
For new applications filed on or after 01.04.2009 a flat designation fee must be paid within six months of the date on which the Bulletin mentions the publication of the search report for the new application (**R.17(3)**). The procedure on non-payment is the same as for a normal application because of the references to **R.39** in the provision.

If the designation fee is not paid in due time, the new application will be deemed withdrawn under **R.39(2)**. The loss of rights will be communicated under **R.112(1)** to the applicant, who can request further processing under **Art.121** and **R.135** within two months from notification of the communication. The loss of rights takes effect upon expiry of the six month period, not upon expiry of the period for further processing (**G4/98** hn.II, r.7.2 mutatis mutandis; A-III,11.2.3)). See **Art.92** for the publication of the search report.

2 **Other fees for new application**
If there are more than 15 claims, claims fees must be paid within one month of filing (**R.45(1)**). Renewal fees are only due for the years following the year of filing the new application (**R.51(6)**).

R. 18 Partial transfer of the right to the European patent

Implementation of: **Art.61**
EPC 1973: **R.16(1) + (2)**

1 **General**
The partial transfer of right may relate to the transfer of only part of the subject-matter of an application to another party (**R.18(1)**), to the transfer of the application for only some of the designated states (**R.18(2)**), or to the transfer of the patent for only some of the designated states (**R.78(2)**).

R. 18(1) If a final decision determines that a third party is entitled to the grant of a European patent in respect of only part of the subject-matter disclosed in the original European patent application, Article 61 and Rules 16 and 17 shall apply to such part.

Art.61 Application filed by non-entitled person
R.16 Procedure for entitled person
R.17 Filing of new application by entitled person

1 **Options for partially entitled person**
R.18(1) applies **Art.61** and **R.17**, which normally deal with the entire application, to part of the subject-matter of an application. It follows that a new application can be filed for part of an original application.

A third party entitled to only part of the subject-matter does not have the option of **Art.61(1)(a)**. He may only file a new application under **Art.61(1)(b)**, confined to that part of the original subject-matter to which it has become entitled. Similarly, the original application must be confined to the subject-matter to which the original applicant remains entitled. The relation between the new application, the amended original application and the original application is similar to the relation between a first divisional application, a second divisional application and a parent application. Hence, the requirements for divisional applications concerning extension of subject-matter beyond the subject-matter of the original application as filed, amendment of the description and claiming identical subject-matter as set out in C-IX,1.4-6, are applicable to this situation. (C-IX,2.3)

R. 18(2) Where appropriate, the original European patent application shall contain, for the designated Contracting States in which the decision was taken or recognised or must be recognised on the basis of the Protocol on Recognition, claims, a description and drawings which are different from those for the other designated Contracting States.

1 **Different applications for different states**
If by a final decision a third party is entitled to the grant of a patent in only some of the designated states, the third party and the original applicant may each prosecute under **Art.61(1)(a)** the application for the designated states adjudged to them; the original application may subsequently contain different claims, description and drawings for the different states according to **R.18(2)**. This is an example of the 'unless otherwise provided for' of **Art.118**, second sentence, allowing a deviation from the requirement of unity of the application.

Where the final decision divides the right to the grant so that the third party and the original applicant may apply for the entire subject-matter of the application for different designated states, the EPO will examine each application without regard to the other (C-IX,2.4). The subject-matter of each application may not extend beyond that of the original application as filed (C-IX,2.1).

Chapter II *Mention of the inventor*

R. 19 Designation of the inventor

Implementation of: **Art.81**
EPC 1973: **R.17**

R. 19(1) The request for grant of a European patent shall contain the designation of the inventor. However, if the applicant is not the inventor or is not the sole inventor, the designation shall be filed in a separate document. The designation shall state the family name, given names and full address of the inventor, contain the statement referred to in Article 81 and bear the signature of the applicant or his representative.

Art.81 Statement indicating the origin of the right to the patent

1 **Designation**
The designation of the inventor must be signed by the applicant or the appointed representative, or, in the case of several applicants, by each applicant or the respective representative, or, if a common representative has been appointed, the signature of said common representative suffices (see also A-VIII,1.3). The signature is also required if the designation is filed as a separate document annexed to the Request for Grant (exception to the 'exception of annexed documents' in **R.50(3)**).

The 'statement referred to in Article 81', i.e. the statement of the right to the patent by the applicant, can be short. In the case of a transfer, it need only state: 'by agreement of...'. In the case of employment it suffices to state that the inventor is an employee of the applicant. In the case of inheritance, the applicant can state his capacity of legatee of the inventor.

See **R.21** and **R.57(f)** for rectification of a missing or deficient designation of inventor.

R. 19(2) The European Patent Office shall not verify the accuracy of the designation of the inventor.

1 **Correction of designation**
An error in a designation can be corrected under **R.21**, e.g. by deleting, changing or adding a name. The EPO informs the applicant of a missing designation under **R.60**.

R. 19(3) If the applicant is not the inventor or is not the sole inventor, the European Patent Office shall communicate to the designated inventor the information in the document designating him and the following data:

(a) the number of the European patent application;
(b) the date of filing of the European patent application and, if priority has been claimed, the date, State and file number of the previous application;
(c) the name of the applicant;
(d) the title of the invention;
(e) the Contracting States designated.

1 **Information concerning designation of inventor**

This provision protects the rights of the inventor. The notification by the EPO of information about the application to the inventor might trigger him to initiate a corrective action according to **Art.61** or **81.**

If the address is incorrect, the EPO will try once more at another address supplied by the applicant. If that also fails, no further attempt is made.

The inventor can waive the right to be sent the communication of **R.19(3)** by filing together with the designation of the inventor a written waiver of the right of notification, containing all necessary data of the application (filing date; priority date, state and number; name of applicant, etc.), i.e. all information otherwise contained in the communication under **R.19(3)**. In this way the safeguards for the inventor provided in the EPC are ensured while the amount of work involved by the inventors and their representatives and the EPO is reduced. (A-III,5.4)

R. 19(4) The applicant and the inventor may invoke neither the omission of the communication under paragraph 3 nor any errors contained therein.

R. 20 Publication of the mention of the inventor

Implementation of: **Art.81**
EPC 1973: **R.18**

R. 20(1) The designated inventor shall be mentioned in the published European patent application and the European patent specification, unless he informs the European Patent Office in writing that he has waived his right to be thus mentioned.

1 **Mention of inventor in application and patent**

The inventor's waiver of his right to be mentioned in the published application and patent under **R.20(1)** is separate from his waiver of the communication containing data relating to the designation of inventor under **R.19(3)**. Both waivers do not affect his inventor status in the application and patent.

After a renunciation to be mentioned, the entry in the patent register under **R.143(1)(g)** will not be made, and the designation of the inventor in the file of the application will be excluded from file inspection (**R.144(c)**).

R. 20(2) Paragraph 1 shall apply where a third party files with the European Patent Office a final decision determining that the applicant for or proprietor of a European patent is required to designate him as an inventor.

1 **Inventor dispute**

The EPO assumes that the correct inventor has been designated and does not verify the accuracy of the designation (**R.19(2)**). The EPC has no provisions to resolve a dispute about the status of a person as inventor. Any dispute should be decided under national law. A court decision is not an absolute requirement. The EPO will apply **R.20(1)** where it receives a decision that a third party must be designated as inventor (**R.20(2)**) and will mention him in the patent application and specification, unless he has waived this right.

R. 21 Rectification of the designation of an inventor

Implementation of: **Art.81**
EPC 1973: **R.19**

R. 21(1) An incorrect designation of an inventor shall be rectified upon request and only with the consent of the wrongly designated person and, where such a request is filed by a third party, the consent of the applicant for or proprietor of the patent. Rule 19 shall apply mutatis mutandis.

R.19 Designation of the inventor

1 **Rectification of the designation of inventor**
The impervious wording of the provision has been interpreted by case law and Guidelines as set out below.

A designation of inventor is incorrect if a wrong inventor is named, an inventor is not named or data of an inventor is incorrect. See **R.60** for the subsequent designation of an inventor.

The designation may be rectified voluntarily under **R.21** or mandatorily upon invitation under **R.60** if the EPO has noticed a deficiency under **R.57(f)** during the examination as to formalities. A voluntary rectification may be made at any time, even after termination of the proceedings (A-III,5.6). Mandatory rectification must be made within the period of **R.60(1)**.

A wrongly designated inventor will be cancelled from the designation of inventor upon request, provided the request contains the consent of the wrongly designated inventor and, where the request is filed by a third party, the consent of the applicant or proprietor (**R.21(1)**, first sentence; A-III,5.6).

An inventor can be added to the designation upon request. The addition does not require the consent of any already named inventor, because an already named inventor is not 'wrongly designated' (**J8/82** hnI). The request must contain the data of the added inventor and must be duly signed as required by **R.19(1)**; the added inventor will be notified of his designation according to **R.19(3)** (see reference to **R.19** in the provision). (A-III,5.6)

A request to correct data of an inventor can be filed at any time under **R.21(1)**.

R. 21(2) Where an incorrect designation of the inventor has been recorded in the European Patent Register or published in the European Patent Bulletin, its rectification or cancellation shall also be recorded or published therein.

Chapter III *Registration of transfers, licences and other rights*

1 **Competence to register a transfer**
The Legal Division is competent for decisions in respect of entries in the Register of European Patents (**Art.20**). However, routine requests for entry and correction of entries, i.e. when a request is not disputed, are handled by the Receiving Section or the examining division depending on the stage of the grant procedure. The same applies to decisions applying **R.21** (rectification of the designation of the inventor). (**J18/84**)

R. 22 Registration of transfers

Implementation of: **Art.71** and **73**
EPC 1973: **R.20**

1 **General**
The provision ensures that the EPO knows the parties to the proceedings. Hence, the EPO registers transfers of applications and patents up to the expiry of the opposition period or opposition procedure (**R.85**) or a possible subsequent appeal (**R.100(1)**) (**J17/91**). The EPO will regard a person as a party to proceedings only if he is duly recorded as such. A successor of a party will be recognized by the EPO as party only if the necessary formalities have been completed. In the case of an applicant or proprietor the formalities are laid down by **R.22**. The simple registration under **R.22** is mandatory in first and second instance proceedings. The registration allows a precise and simple determination of the parties, thereby avoiding that the EPO is tangled up in complicated investigations as to the relations between the original parties and later would-be parties (**T656/98** r.1.1). The EPO has no jurisdiction to decide disputes as to entitlement, for which reason **Art.60(3)** confines the applicant to the person on record.

The requirements for a valid transfer of an application before the EPO are: the filing of a written request for registering a transfer, providing written proof of the transfer and paying a fee. The transfer can be entered in the Register only after publication of the application (**Art.127**, second sentence). See also E-XIII. The corresponding PCT provisions can be found in **R.92bis** PCT.

A mere change of name, not involving a modification of the legal identity of the applicant, will be registered upon request and production of relevant documentary evidence and is free of charge (E-XIV,5).

2 **Time of transfer**
A transfer effected before publication of the application will be entered in a shadow Register and recorded in the public Register only after publication (consequence of **Art.127**).

The EPO records transfers for applications and patents that are or can become subject to proceedings before the EPO. When they can no longer be the subject of proceedings, there is no legal justification for recording transfers. Hence, the EPO will still record transfers for applications that are (deemed) withdrawn or refused as long as procedural rights are pending. Also, the EPO will record transfers for granted patents during the nine-month opposition period and while opposition proceedings are pending.

An example of such procedural rights is the right to priority during 12 months from filing. A transfer of a deemed withdrawn priority application during the priority year will therefore be recorded, which is necessary for complying with the 'successor in title' requirement of **Art.87(1)**.

Another example is the right to a remedy such as further processing during two months from the notice of the loss of rights or re-establishment during the two-month and one-year periods of **R.136(1)**. However, the EPO will only record a transfer of an application to be revived if the successor in title has taken remedial steps, such as requesting further processing and/or re-establishment. The steps should be taken at the latest when filing the request for recording the transfer for reasons of legal certainty of the public. (J10/93 hn and r.4)

R. 22(1) The transfer of a European patent application shall be recorded in the European Patent Register at the request of an interested party, upon production of documents providing evidence of such transfer.

1 **Request for transfer**

The request must be in one of the official EPO languages (**R.3(1)**). The document can be filed in any language, as such a document is not part of the request but a document used for the purpose of evidence (**R.3(3)**). The EPO can ask for a translation of the document.

It is not necessary to file formal transfer documents as defined in **Art.72**; any written evidence of the transfer is admissible, provided that the documents bear the name and signature of the parties appearing on the documents. If the evidence is unsatisfactory, the EPO will invite the parties to remedy the deficiency. (E-XIV,3)

The request may be filed by any interested party (**R.22(1)**).

R. 22(2) The request shall not be deemed to have been filed until an administrative fee has been paid. It may be rejected only if paragraph 1 has not been complied with.

1 **Fee for transfer**

Payment of the fee for transfer is a requirement for recording a transfer in the Register. The fee is fixed by the President under **Rfees3(1)**.

R. 22(3) A transfer shall have effect vis-à-vis the European Patent Office only at the date when and to the extent that the documents referred to in paragraph 1 have been produced.

1 **Effective date of the transfer**

A transfer becomes effective before the EPO only when all formalities of registering the transfer have been carried out, i.e. filing the request for transfer and payment of an administrative fee. The express wording 'only when' of **R.22(3)** makes any earlier date mentioned in the text of an assignment and effective between the parties to the assignment irrelevant for the EPO. Hence, a new owner is entitled to file an appeal only if the transfer has been recorded with the EPO before the filing. (**T656/98** r.3.5, 4.1; **G1/12** r.45.1)

R.22(3) does not apply to universal succession in law when a party ceases to exist, e.g. due to death or a merger. When a party ceases to exist, he loses party status. Since in general the authorisation of his representative does not terminate (**R.152(9)**), the proceedings will not be interrupted (**R.142(1)(a)**), the representative immediately represents the successor in law and can act in proceedings (**T15/01** r.11). The successor in law automatically becomes party before the EPO. In appeal the change in name of the party may be corrected under **R.101(2)** (**T15/01** r.14).

R. 23 Registration of licences and other rights

Implementation of **Art.73**
EPC 1973: **R.21**

1 **General**
The requirements for a valid registration of a licence in the European Patents Register (**R.143(1)(w)**) are: the request must be in writing and signed (**R.23(1)**, **R.22**, and **R.50(3)**), proof of establishment or transfer of the right must be given (**R.23(1)** and **R.22(1)**), the fee must be paid (**R.23(1)** and **R.22(2)**). The amount of the fee is fixed by the President under **Rfees3(1)**.

A request for registration of a licence can be filed by any interested party (**R.22(1)** with **R.23(1)**). However, registration of an exclusive licence must be requested by the applicant and the licensee (**R.24(a)**).

Licences and other rights cannot be registered after the decision to grant has become effective (**Art.97(3)**), because **R.85** (transfer of the patent) does not refer to **R.23** and **24**, and there are no other provisions in the EPC. See also **J17/91**, refusing registration by the EPO of a licence on a patent after all proceedings before the EPO and the opposition period had terminated.

Such other rights that can be registered are for example a security interest (a pledge). This requires a formal written request (i.e. a letter) for which no specific form should be used as well as evidence i.e. a copy of an official document or extract thereof or a declaration signed by both parties.

R. 23(1) Rule 22, paragraphs 1 and 2, shall apply mutatis mutandis to the registration of the grant or transfer of a licence, the establishment or transfer of a right in rem in respect of a European patent application and any legal means of execution affecting such an application.

R.22 Registering a transfer

R. 23(2) A registration under paragraph 1 shall be cancelled upon request, supported by documents providing evidence that the right has lapsed, or by the written consent of the proprietor of the right to the cancellation of the registration. Rule 22, paragraph 2, shall apply mutatis mutandis.

R.22(2) Payment of fee

1 **Cancellation of registration**
The fee for cancelling a registration is fixed by the President under **Rfees3(1)**.

R. 24 Special entries for licence registrations

A licence in respect of a European patent application shall be recorded

(a) as an exclusive licence if the applicant and the licensee so request;

(b) as a sub-licence where it is granted by a licensee whose licence is recorded in the European Patent Register.

Implementation of **Art.73**
EPC 1973: **R.22**

1 **Types of licences**

An exclusive licence confers a right in respect of an application or a patent on the licensee to the exclusion of all other persons, including the licensor, i.e. the applicant or proprietor. Plural exclusive licences may be granted under a single application or patent for separate rights, such as the right of manufacture, distribution, use or relating to different territories (see **Art.73**). A non-exclusive licence places no restriction on the licensor to grant further licences for the same right.

A sole licence confers a right on the licensee to the exclusion of persons other than the licensor; the licensor may continue to use the licensed rights himself.

A licence may authorise the licensee to grant sub-licences to a third party without reference to the licensor. Such a sub-licence can be recorded in the Register, provided the licence is also recorded.

Chapter IV *Certificate of exhibition*

R. 25 Certificate of exhibition

Within four months of filing the European patent application, the applicant shall file the certificate referred to in Article 55, paragraph 2, which:

(a) is issued at the exhibition by the authority responsible for the protection of industrial property at that exhibition;
(b) states that the invention was in fact displayed there;
(c) states the opening date of the exhibition and, where the invention was disclosed later than on that date, the date on which the invention was first disclosed; and
(d) is accompanied by an identification of the invention, duly authenticated by the above-mentioned authority.

Art.55(2) Non-prejudicial disclosures
Implementation of: **Art.55(2)**
EPC 1973: **R.23**

1 **Certificate and identification**
If the applicant files a statement under **Art.55(2)** that his invention has been displayed at an international exhibition, he has to provide a supporting certificate and identification of the invention within four months of filing the application (**R.25**). See **Art.55(2):1** for the procedure.

R.159(1)(h) governs the filing of the certificate for a Euro-PCT application.

Chapter V *Biotechnological inventions*

1 **EU Biotechnology Directive**
Chapter V, containing **R.26** to **29**, was inserted (as Chapter VI, R.23b to 23e EPC 1973) by decision of the Administrative Council of 16.06.1999 which entered into force on 01.09.1999 (OJ 1999, 437). The Chapter implements the EU Directive on the legal protection of biotechnological inventions (see OJ 1999, 101 for the text of the Directive and OJ 1999, 573 for a notice of the EPO concerning its implementation).

The EU Directive intends to harmonize the protection of biotechnological inventions within the EU. Even though the relevant national provisions predating the Directive are most often taken from the EPC, the differing interpretations to which these provisions are open are liable to give rise to divergencies of practice prejudicial to the proper operation of the internal market. The EU has chosen to effect the harmonization by a Directive rather than by the more indirect and unpredictable approach of seeking to amend the wording of the EPC. (OJ 2002, 231 r.2, 16, 22)

Although **R.26** to **29** are intended to implement the Directive, the EBoA held in **G2/06** r.2-11 that there was no mechanism in the EPC whereby questions relating to the interpretation of the Rules, and hence the Directive, could be referred to the European Court of Justice.

The provisions **R.26** to **R.29** are not only applicable to cases filed on or after the date the rules took effect but also to cases pending on that date (**T315/03** hn.I; **G2/06**).

R. 26 General and definitions

Implementation of: **Art.53(b)**
EPC 1973: **R.23b**

R. 26(1) For European patent applications and patents concerning biotechnological inventions, the relevant provisions of the Convention shall be applied and interpreted in accordance with the provisions of this Chapter. Directive 98/44/EC of 6 July 1998 on the legal protection of biotechnological inventions shall be used as a supplementary means of interpretation.

1 **Reference to EU Biotechnology Directive**
R.26(1) expresses a common purpose of the set of provisions in **R.26** to **29**. Its only function is to supply provisions for the application and interpretation of the provisions already contained in the EPC. The provisions did not change the bars to patentability of animals. (**T315/03** r.5.1).

The reference to the Directive aims to ensure that the recitals preceding the provisions of the Directive are also taken into account and to promote a uniform Europe-wide interpretation of the provisions. The text of the Directive is reproduced in OJ 1999, 101. (OJ 1999, 573)

R. 26(2) "Biotechnological inventions" are inventions which concern a product consisting of or containing biological material or a process by means of which biological material is produced, processed or used.

R. 26(3) "Biological material" means any material containing genetic information and capable of reproducing itself or being reproduced in a biological system.

1 **Biological material**
An animal, consisting of a material containing genetic information and capable of reproduction, is a product consisting of biological material in accordance with **R.26(3)** (**T315/03** r.5.2).

R. 26(4) "Plant variety" means any plant grouping within a single botanical taxon of the lowest known rank, which grouping, irrespective of whether the conditions for the grant of a plant variety right are fully met, can be:
(a) defined by the expression of the characteristics that results from a given genotype or combination of genotypes,
(b) distinguished from any other plant grouping by the expression of at least one of the said characteristics, and
(c) considered as a unit with regard to its suitability for being propagated unchanged.

R. 26(5) A process for the production of plants or animals is essentially biological if it consists entirely of natural phenomena such as crossing or selection.

1 **Essentially biological processes**
R.26(5) provides a definition of the term 'essentially biological' in **Art.53(b)**. However, the provision is self-contradictory in stating that crossing and selection are examples of natural phenomena, whereas crossing and selection in the context of processes for the production of plants (**Art.53(b)**) are not natural phenomena but method steps generally involving human intervention. The wording of the provision and the legislative history of the Biotech Directive do not provide sufficient guidance for interpreting the term. (**G2/07** r.4, 5)
See **Art.53:2.2** for the definition of the term.

R. 26(6) "Microbiological process" means any process involving or performed upon or resulting in microbiological material.

R. 27 Patentable biotechnological inventions

Biotechnological inventions shall also be patentable if they concern:
(a) biological material which is isolated from its natural environment or produced by means of a technical process even if it previously occurred in nature;
(b) without prejudice to Rule 28, paragraph 2, plants or animals if the technical feasibility of the invention is not confined to a particular plant or animal variety;
(c) a microbiological or other technical process, or a product obtained by means of such a process other than a plant or animal variety.

Amended by decision of the Administrative Council of 29.06.2017, which entered into force on 01.07.2017 (OJ 2017 A56).
R.28(2) exception for products obtained by essentially biological process
Implementation of: **Art.53(b)**
EPC 1973: **R.23c**

1 **Patentable inventions**

The list of items in **R.27** that are explicitly considered patentable is non-exclusive (G-II,5.2).

The reference to **R.28(2)** in sub-paragraph (b) of the provision excludes the patentability of plants and animals exclusively obtained by means of an essentially biological process. If a technical feature of a claimed plant or animal could be the result of either a technical intervention or of an essentially biological process, a disclaimer is necessary to delimit the claimed subject matter to the technically produced product (G-II,5.4). Examples are given in GII,5.4.2.1.

Item (c) excludes product claims for plant or animal varieties from patentability even if the variety is produced by means of a microbiological process. However, a variety will enjoy protection under **Art.64(2)** as a direct product of a patented process. (OJ 1999, 573)

R. 28 Exceptions to patentability

Amended by decision of the Administrative Council of 29.06.2017, which entered into force on 01.07.2017 (OJ 2017 A56). The decision changed the previous R.28 to paragraph (1) and inserted a new paragraph (2).
Implementation of: **Art.53(a)**
EPC 1973: **R.23d**

R. 28(1) Under Article 53(a), European patents shall not be granted in respect of biotechnological inventions which, in particular, concern the following:

(a) processes for cloning human beings;
(b) processes for modifying the germ line genetic identity of human beings;
(c) uses of human embryos for industrial or commercial purposes;
(d) processes for modifying the genetic identity of animals which are likely to cause them suffering without any substantial medical benefit to man or animal, and also animals resulting from such processes.

Art.53(a) Inventions contrary to morality

1 **Exclusion from patentability**

The provision contains four categories of inventions in the field of biotechnology that must be excluded from patentability under **Art.53(a)**. The words 'in particular' in **R.28(1)** indicate that the rule is not intended to provide an exhaustive list of inventions excluded from patentability but that, on the contrary, it is limited to four categories - its effect is simply that a case falling within one of the four categories (a) - (d) must ipso facto be denied a patent under **Art.53(a)** and there is no need to consider that article further; but, on the contrary, a case not falling within one of those categories must be considered further under **Art.53(a)** (**T315/03** hn.II.1). See **Art.53:1.2** and **R.28(1):3** below for details of tests for exclusion.

2 **Use of human embryos (R.28(1)(c))**

R.28(1)(c) forbids the patenting of a claim directed to a human embryonic stem cell culture which - as described in the application - at the filing date could be prepared exclusively by a method which necessarily involved the destruction of the human embryos from which the cultures are derived, even if the method is not part of the claim. A later development making the destruction of human embryos not necessary to carry out the invention is of no significance; the applicability of **R.28(1)(c)** must be assessed at the time of filing the application. To do otherwise would reduce legal certainty, and might be to the detriment of any third party who later provided an innocuous way to carry out the invention. (**G2/06** hn.2; r.33; see also later decision C-34/10 of the CJEU)

The exact wording of the claims is not relevant; rather the exploitation of the invention is the critical issue. To restrict the application of **R.28(1)(c)** to what an applicant chooses explicitly to claim would have the undesirable consequence that merely skilful drafting of such a claim could avoid the patenting prohibition. (**G2/06** r.22)

As a consequence of **G2/06**, a method claim including destruction of human embryos is not patentable. The point in time at which such destruction takes place is irrelevant (**T2221/10** r.37; G-II,5.2(ii)). However, human embryos may be excluded by way of a disclaimer, even if the disclaimer has no basis in the application as filed. (**T329/06** r.2-8)

3 **Modification of genetic identity (R.28(1)(d))**

The exclusion test for category (d) requires the consideration of the likelihood of only three issues: animal suffering, medical benefit and the necessary relation between the two in terms of the animals in question (**T315/03** hn.V). The three issues require support by evidence (**T315/03** r.9.5). The level of proof of suffering and of substantial benefit required for **R.28(1)(d)** is not more than 'likelihood' (**T315/03** r.6.2, r.9.3). The criteria must be assessed on the effective date of the subject-matter, as with all criteria for the assessment of patentability (**T315/03** r.8.2).

The criterion 'substantial medical benefit to man or animal' in the provision constitutes a sub-range of benefits completely within the broader range 'usefulness to mankind' in the test of **T19/90** (see **Art.53:1.2**). Hence, if the former criterion is established, the latter is necessarily established (**T315/03** r.7.1).

The provision requires that the benefit is obtained for all animals likely to suffer and within the scope of a claim. Hence, a claim must be excluded from patentability if one animal covered by the claim is likely to suffer without evidence of medical benefit. (**T315/03** r.12.2.2-3). See also **T606/03**; here claims were allowed to animals which would not be expected to suffer, regardless of the potential medical benefit.

R. 28(2)Under Article 53(b), European patents shall not be granted in respect of plants or animals exclusively obtained by means of an essentially biological process.

Art.53(b) varieties and essentially biological processes

1 **Products of essentially biological processes**

The provision excludes from patentability plants and animals exclusively obtained by means of an essentially biological process. See **Art.53:2.2** for the definition of an essentially biological process. (G-II,5.4)

In 2015 decisions **G2/12** and **G2/13** held that, whereas a claim directed to an essentially biological process is excluded from patentability under **Art.53(b)**, a claim directed to the product of an essentially biological process is not excluded, because **Art.53(b)** must be interpreted narrowly and does not apply to a different category of claims such as product claims.

However, a notice of the European Commission on the Biotech Directive (2016/C 411/03) dated 08.11.2016 states that the EU legislator's intention was to exclude from patentability products that are obtained by means of essentially biological processes. The Administrative Council held in 2017, that the EU Biotechnology Directive, from which **R.26-29** were taken, is a supplementary means of interpretation of the EPC provisions and the notice has the function of harmonising the application and implementation of EU law. Hence, the Administrative Council decided to align its law by amending **R.27** and **28** (CA56/17; OJ 2017 A56, A62). The amendment of the law overrules **G2/12** and **G2/13**.

R. 29 The human body and its elements

Implementation of: **Art.53(a), (b)**
EPC 1973: **R.23e**

R. 29(1) The human body, at the various stages of its formation and development, and the simple discovery of one of its elements, including the sequence or partial sequence of a gene, cannot constitute patentable inventions.

R. 29(2) An element isolated from the human body or otherwise produced by means of a technical process, including the sequence or partial sequence of a gene, may constitute a patentable invention, even if the structure of that element is identical to that of a natural element.

R. 29(3) The industrial application of a sequence or a partial sequence of a gene must be disclosed in the patent application.

1 **Industrial application of sequence or gene**

Whereas the industrial applicability, required by **Art.57**, is self-evident for most inventions and needs no clarification in the description (see **R.42(1)(f)**), the industrial applicability of sequences is not obvious and, according to **R.29(3)**, must be stated explicitly in the application.

In particular, the disclosure must indicate what function is performed by the sequence and the protein built from it (OJ 1999, 573 §27). A protein may have several equally valid ways of describing its function - molecular, cellular, biological - and none is more fundamental than the others for the purposes of **R.29(3)** (**T898/05** hn.3). Further, the industrial application of a gene is not related to any foreseeable economic benefit.

T1329/04 noted that, while post-published evidence may be used to support a suggested industrial application of a gene or protein, it could not provide the sole basis for this. The application itself must at least make it plausible that the technical problem addressed by the invention and its industrial application is solved.

R. 30 Requirements of European patent applications relating to nucleotide and amino acid sequences

Implementation of: **Art.78(1)(b)**
EPC 1973: **R.27a(1)+(4)**

1 **Filing of sequence listings**
An application disclosing nucleotide or amino acid sequences must contain a sequence listing in an annex to the description, complying with the requirements of **R.30**. The EPO has adopted the same requirements for representation of sequence listings in a standardized layout in European applications as apply to international applications under R.5.2 PCT and provided for in the PCT Administrative Instructions.

Sequence listings must be filed electronically in txt format according to the provisions in Dec. Pres. OJ 2011, 372 and Not. EPO OJ 2013, 542.

When filing a divisional application, the sequence listing must be filed again for this application (OJ 2013, 542 §I.1.7). This does not apply when filing by reference. See A-IV,5.1-3 for sequence listings inserted as missing part under **R.56**, sequence listings filed by reference to a previous application under **R.40(1)(c)** and sequence listings of a divisional.

A sequence listing may be corrected under **R.139** or amended under **Art.123(2)**. In this case a complete new sequence listing must be filed. (H-IV,2.3.4)

R. 30(1) If nucleotide or amino acid sequences are disclosed in the European patent application, the description shall contain a sequence listing conforming to the rules laid down by the President of the European Patent Office for the standardised representation of nucleotide and amino acid sequences.

1 **Obligation to include sequence listing**
The rule covers disclosures of nucleic acid and amino acid sequences, regardless of whether such sequences are claimed in the application. Sequences which belong to the prior art and are publicly available in a database need not be listed in the application if they have been identified as set out in OJ 2013, 542 §I.1.5.

The rules for the standard representation of sequence listings and details of the procedure for filing them are laid down in the decision of the President OJ 2011, 372. The sequence listing must comply with the WIPO standard ST.25 (see WIPO website) and be filed in electronic form in txt format. The sequence listing should not be filed on paper or, when filing electronically, in pdf format. (OJ 2013, 542 §I.1.4)

R. 30(2) A sequence listing filed after the date of filing shall not form part of the description.

1 **Late-filed sequence listing**
A sequence listing may be filed after the date of filing of the application for use in the search. Such a late-filed sequence listing will not be part of the description and the disclosure of the application and will not be published with the application (OJ 2013, 542 §I.2.5).

R. 30(3) Where the applicant has not filed a sequence listing complying with the requirements under paragraph 1 at the date of filing, the European Patent Office shall invite the applicant to furnish such a sequence listing and pay the late furnishing fee. If the applicant does not furnish the required sequence listing and pay the required late furnishing fee within a period of two months after such an invitation, the application shall be refused.

1 **Late filing of sequence listing**

The amount of the fee for late furnishing is fixed in **Rfees2(1)14a**.

In the event no sequence listing or a sequence listing not complying with this rule has been filed on the date of filing, the Receiving Section invites the applicant to file the sequence listing together with payment of the late furnishing fee within a two-month period of notification of the invitation (**R.30(3)**). See **J7/11** for an example of a correction of a sequence listing. The late-filed sequence listing must be accompanied by a statement that the sequence listingdoes not extend the subject-matter of the application as filed (**OJ 2011, 372 Art. 2(2)**).

Where a sequence listing filed with the EPO is incorrect, the search will be postponed until a correction has been filed. The late furnishing fee is intended to cover the additional administrative costs entailed and to encourage applicants to supply a listing conforming to the relevant standard as quickly as possible.

Pages with sequence listings are exempted from the page fee of **Rfees2(1)1a** because examiners do not read but only search them. However, the EPO will charge the page fee for sequence listing not filed in the standardised representation required by **R.30(1)** (see **Rfees2(1):4.2.1**).

A late filed sequence listing will be used for the search. However, a late filed sequence listing will not be published together with the application or specification, because it does not form part of the description (**R.30(2), 68(1), 73**). Where a sequence listing can be included under **R.56** from a previous application, it will be considered as integral part of the description on the date of filing (which may or may not have changed because of the inclusion) (A-IV,5.2).

The sanction for failure to meet the two month period is refusal of the application under **R.30(3)**. Further processing under **Art.121** may be used if this time limit is not met; note that further processing may apply to the two separate acts of filing the sequence listing and payment of the late furnishing fee. Accordingly two fees for further processing may be needed (see **Rfees2(1)12**). These provisions also apply to Euro-PCT applications.

R. 31 Deposit of biological material

Implementation of: **Art.78(1)(b)**
EPC 1973: **R.28(1)+(2)**

1 **Requirement for deposition of biological material**

Deposition of a sample of biological material under **R.31** for compliance with the disclosure requirement of **Art.83** is only required if the biological material to which the application relates is not available to the public and cannot be described in the application in an enabling manner. The requirements of **R.31** are satisfied for an application filed by reference if the referred to application already satisfied these requirements.

A consolidated notice on disclosure and deposition of biological material is published as Not. EPO OJ 2010, 498. The requirements for deposition of biological material in R.31-33 apply to direct European applications. See §5-13 of said notice for Euro-PCT applications.

2 **Availability of deposited material**

The material must be available as from the date of filing of the application (Not. EPO OJ 2010, 498 §3.6). Access of the public is controlled by R.33(1).

The disclosure of the invention is considered to be insufficient if repeated requests to the depositary institution are necessary, and techniques considerably more sophisticated than those recommended by the depositary institution must be applied (T418/89).

R. 31(1) If an invention involves the use of or concerns biological material which is not available to the public and which cannot be described in the European patent application in such a manner as to enable the invention to be carried out by a person skilled in the art, the invention shall only be regarded as being disclosed as prescribed in Article 83 if:

(a) a sample of the biological material has been deposited with a recognised depositary institution on the same terms as those laid down in the Budapest Treaty on the International Recognition of the Deposit of Microorganisms for the Purposes of Patent Procedure of 28 April 1977 not later than the date of filing of the application;

(b) the application as filed gives such relevant information as is available to the applicant on the characteristics of the biological material;

(c) the depositary institution and the accession number of the deposited biological material are stated in the application, and

(d) where the biological material has been deposited by a person other than the applicant, the name and address of the depositor are stated in the application and a document is submitted to the European Patent Office providing evidence that the depositor has authorised the applicant to refer to the deposited biological material in the application and has given his unreserved and irrevocable consent to the deposited material being made available to the public in accordance with Rule 33.

Art.83 Disclosure of the invention
R.33 Availability of biological material

1 **Deposition of biological material**

1.1 PRIORITY (R.31(1)(A))

The depositary institution must be an international authority under the Budapest Treaty or a depositary institution recognised by the EPO by virtue of a bilateral agreement. The recognised institutions are published annually under R.33(6) in the 4th issue of the OJ.

A priority claim of an application relating to deposited biological material is valid only if the priority application has a sufficient disclosure of the invention by referring to a deposition of the material made no later than the priority date. (Not. EPO OJ 2010, 498 §1.4)

1.2 RELEVANT INFORMATION (R.31(1)(B)-(D))

The application as filed must disclose relevant information on the characteristics of the biological material (**R.31(1)(b)**), such as classification of the material, morphological or physiological characteristics relevant for recognition, and propagation of the material if it cannot replicate itself (F-III,6.3(i)). An accession number alone without a written description of a micro-organism does not provide a sufficient disclosure in the sense of **Art.83** (T418/89).

If biological material is deposited as part of the disclosure of an application, the application must state the depositary institution and the accession number of the deposit (**R.31(1)(c)**). If this information is provided after the date of filing as allowed by **R.31(2)**, the application must supply at the date of filing a reference that enables the deposit to be related to the later filed accession number. It is recommended to file the deposit receipt issued by the depositary institution, if available, already at the date of filing. (F-III,6.3(ii); OJ 2010, 498 §3.3, 3.11)

Communication of the information on the depositary institution, the accession number and, where applicable, details of a depositor other than the applicant to the EPO is considered as consent of the applicant to the biological material being made publicly available under **R.33** (**R.31(2)**, last sentence).

See Not. EPO OJ 2010, 498 §3.7-3.9 for a deposit made by a person other than the applicant.

1.3 INFORMATION OF DEPOSIT

The Receiving Section checks, during the examination of formal requirements under **Art.90(3)**, whether the requirements of **R.31(1)(c)** are fulfilled. It notifies the applicant of any deficiencies and points out that the requirements must be fulfilled by the end of the period specified in **R.31(2)** (see **R.57:16**).

R. 31(2) The information referred to in paragraph 1(c) and (d) may be submitted

(a) within sixteen months after the date of filing of the application or, if priority has been claimed, after the priority date, this period being deemed to have been observed if the information is communicated before completion of the technical preparations for publication of the European patent application;

(b) up to the date of submission of a request under Article 93, paragraph 1(b);

(c) within one month after the European Patent Office has communicated to the applicant that the right to inspect the files under Article 128, paragraph 2, exists.

The ruling period shall be the one which is the first to expire. The communication of this information shall be considered as constituting the unreserved and irrevocable consent of the applicant to the deposited biological material being made available to the public in accordance with Rule 33.

Art.93(1)(b) Early publication of the application at applicant's request
Art.128(2) Inspection of files after invocation of rights
R.33 Availability of biological material

1 **Period for submission of information on deposition**
The information concerning the accession number of the deposited material according to **R.31(1)(c)** and, if applicable, the name, address and authorisation of the depositor according to **R.31(1)(d)** may not be submitted after expiry of the time limit set out in **R.31(2)(a)**, because of their relevance for the disclosure of the application (**G2/93**). For euro-PCT cases, the relevant time limit is that of publication of the PCT application (**T328/04**).

2 **Consequence of failure to provide information on deposition**
Where the requirements of **R.31(1)(c)** or **(d)** and **31(2)** are not fulfilled, the biological material is not regarded as disclosed under **Art.83** by reference to the deposit. (F-III,6.3)

The period of **R.31(2)** is excluded from further processing by **R.135(2)**. Re-establishment is available according to **T227/97** hn. However, the EPO Notice OJ 2010, 498 §3.10 holds that re-establishment is not possible (A-IV,4.1), based on an interpretation of **G2/93** that was disapproved of by **T227/97**, published before the notice; moreover the interpretation also appears to violate the EPC (**Art.122(4)** and **R.136(3)**).

It is recommended to complete duly sections 34-37 of the Request for Grant form to allow the EPO to draw the applicant's attention to any deficiencies before expiry of the period of **R.31(2)**. (Not. EPO OJ 2010, 498 §3.11)

R. 32 Expert solution

Amended by decision of the Administrative Council of 28.06.2017, which entered into force on 01.10.2017 (OJ 2017 A55). The amendment abolishes the list of experts as not being sufficiently flexible in view of the pace of technological evolution (CA/29/17; OJ 2017 A61).

Implementation of: **Art.78(1)(b)**

EPC 1973: **R.28(4)+(5)**

1 **Expert solution**
A third party can easily work a biological invention by requesting a sample from the biological material deposited under **R.31** and simply growing the sample according to the instructions given in the application. An applicant wishing to avoid a competitor catching up using the deposited material can restrict its availability by opting for the so-called 'expert solution'. In that case a sample of the material will be made available only to an expert nominated by the requester and not to the requester himself. A third party must request the EPO under **R.33** to make a sample available to an expert recognised by the EPO under **R.32(2)**; the requester can ask the expert to perform specific experiments on the sample and report the results.

The expert solution makes part of the disclosure of an application not available to the public, as an exception to **Art.83**.

Details of the expert solution are set out in Not. EPO OJ 2010, 498 §4 and A-IV,4.3.

R. 32(1) Until completion of the technical preparations for publication of the European patent application, the applicant may inform the European Patent Office that,

(a) until the publication of the mention of the grant of the European patent or, where applicable,

(b) for twenty years from the date of filing, if the application is refused or withdrawn or deemed to be withdrawn,

the availability referred to in Rule 33 shall be effected only by the issue of a sample to an independent expert nominated by the requester.

R.33 Availability of biological material

1 **Indicating expert solution and period of applicability**
The applicant must, according to **R.32(1)**, notify the EPO of his choice for the expert solution before completion of the technical preparations for publication (see **R.67**). The applicant can indicate his choice in the Request for Grant form. The fact that said solution has been chosen will be mentioned on the front page of the published application. If the EPO is not notified in time, the material will be available as provided for in **R.33** without an expert acting as intermediary (OJ 2010, 498, §4.4).

The expert solution applies until publication of the mention of the grant or, where applicable, twenty years from the date of filing if the application is refused, withdrawn or deemed to be withdrawn (**R.32(1)**).

R. 32(2)Any natural person may be nominated as an expert, provided that he complies with the requirements and obligations laid down by the President of the European Patent Office. The nomination shall be accompanied by a declaration from the expert that he undertakes to comply with the aforementioned requirements and obligations and that he knows of no circumstances which might give rise to justified doubts as to his independence or which might conflict in any other way with his function as expert. The nomination shall also be accompanied by a declaration from the expert vis-à-vis the applicant in which he enters into the undertaking given under Rule 33 until either the date on which the patent expires in all the designated States or, where the application is refused, withdrawn or deemed to be withdrawn, the date referred to in paragraph 1(b), the requester being regarded as a third party.

R.33 Availability of biological material

1 **Recognition of experts**
A third party may nominate any natural person as expert to whom deposited biological material may be made available under **R.33**. The request for nomination must be sent to the EPO accompanied by two declarations. The natural person must declare to the EPO that he will comply with the requirements and obligations laid down in Dec. Pres. OJ 2017 A60 and declare to the applicant that he enters into the undertaking given under **R.33** (**R.32(2)**, second and third sentence). The requirements relate among others to knowledge, availability of facilities and to independence and impartiality. Only in cases of reasonable doubts as to the independence would the EPO turn to the requester before certifying the request (OJ 2017 A61 §7). The third party can use forms on the EPO website for the request and the declarations (OJ 2017 A61 §8).

The third party does not need the consent of the applicant for the nominated expert. If an applicant were to withhold his consent, deposited material would not be available, contrary to **Art.83** on sufficiency of disclosure.

R. 33 Availability of biological material

Implementation of: **Art.78(1)(b)** and **Art.83**

EPC 1973: **R.28(3), (6), (7), (8)+(9)**

1 **General**

The depositary institution will store deposited material for a period of at least five years after the most recent request for the issue of a sample was received by the institution and, in any case, for a period of at least 30 years after the date of the deposit; the depositor may not withdraw the material before expiry of this period. (Budapest Treaty)

The availability of the material is not affected by refusal or withdrawal of the application nor by lapse of the patent or expiry of the patent term (OJ 2010, 498, §16). The issue of a sample may be restricted to an expert if the declaration under **R.32(1)** has been made, which restriction is mentioned on the front page of the published application.

Prescribed forms for requesting samples are available on the EPO website. The request must be submitted to the EPO (**R.33(4)**), who forwards it to the depositary institution (**R.33(5)**). The EPO does not charge a fee for the request, but the depositary institution may request a fee. The requester must also file a declaration agreeing to restrict the use of the biological material during pendency of the application and patent as set out in **R.33(2)**. See OJ 2010, 498 §26 for the handling of the request within the EPO. The sample will be issued to the requester or, if the applicant has chosen the expert option of **R.32**, to the expert.

Details of the availability of deposited biological material and requests for the issue of samples are given in Not. EPO OJ 2010, 498 §14-27.

R. 33(1) Biological material deposited in accordance with Rule 31 shall be available upon request to any person from the date of publication of the European patent application and to any person having the right to inspect the files under Article 128, paragraph 2, prior to that date. Subject to Rule 32, such availability shall be effected by the issue of a sample of the biological material to the person making the request (hereinafter referred to as "the requester").

R.31 Deposit of biological material
R.32 Expert solution
Art.128(2) Inspection of files before publication

R. 33(2) Said issue shall be made only if the requester has undertaken vis-à-vis the applicant for or proprietor of the patent not to make the biological material or any biological material derived therefrom available to any third party and to use that material for experimental purposes only, until such time as the patent application is refused or withdrawn or deemed to be withdrawn, or before the European patent has expired in all the designated States, unless the applicant for or proprietor of the patent expressly waives such an undertaking. The undertaking to use the biological material for experimental purposes only shall not apply in so far as the requester is using that material under a compulsory licence. The term "compulsory licence" shall be construed as including ex officio licences and the right to use patented inventions in the public interest.

R. 33(3) For the purposes of paragraph 2, derived biological material shall mean any material which still exhibits those characteristics of the deposited material which are essential to carrying out the invention. The undertaking under paragraph 2 shall not impede any deposit of derived biological material necessary for the purpose of patent procedure.

R. 33(4) The request referred to in paragraph 1 shall be submitted to the European Patent Office on a form recognised by that Office. The European Patent Office shall certify on the form that a European patent application referring to the deposit of the biological material has been filed, and that the requester or the expert nominated by him under Rule 32 is entitled to the issue of a sample of that material. After grant of the European patent, the request shall also be submitted to the European Patent Office.

R.32 Expert solution

R. 33(5) The European Patent Office shall transmit a copy of the request, with the certification provided for in paragraph 4, to the depositary institution and to the applicant for or the proprietor of the patent.

R. 33(6) The European Patent Office shall publish in its Official Journal the list of depositary institutions recognised for the purpose of Rules 31, 33 and 34

Amended by decision of the Administrative Council of 28.06.2017, which entered into force on 01.10.2017 (OJ 2017 A55).
R.31 Deposit of biological material
R.33 Availability of biological material
R.34 New deposit of biological material.
See OJ issue 4 of each year under *International Treaties.*

R. 34 New deposit of biological material

If biological material deposited in accordance with Rule 31 ceases to be available from the recognised depositary institution, an interruption in availability shall be deemed not to have occurred if a new deposit of that material is made with a recognised depositary institution on the same terms as those laid down in the Budapest Treaty on the International Recognition of the Deposit of Microorganisms for the Purposes of Patent Procedure of 28 April 1977, and if a copy of the receipt of the new deposit issued by the depositary institution is forwarded to the European Patent Office within four months of the date of the new deposit, stating the number of the European patent application or of the European patent.

R.31 Deposit of biological material
Implementation of: **Art.78(1)(b)**
EPC 1973: **R.28a**

1 **Biological material not longer available**
Deposited biological material ceases to be available if the material has degraded or the depositary institution no longer qualifies for that kind of material. In this case the applicant must make a new deposition under **R.34** as set out in A-IV,4.1.1.

PART III IMPLEMENTING REGULATIONS TO PART III OF THE CONVENTION

Chapter I *Filing of the European patent application*

R. 35 General provisions

Implementation of: **Art.75(1)**
EPC 1973: **R.24**

R. 35(1) European patent applications may be filed in writing with the European Patent Office in Munich, The Hague or Berlin, or the authorities referred to in Article 75, paragraph 1(b).

Art.75(1)(b) Filing of a European patent application

1 **Filing offices**
The application may be filed with a filing office of the EPO or a national authority as allowed under **Art.75** (see NatLaw table II, col. 1; **Art.75(1)(b)**). The filing offices of the EPO are in Munich, The Hague and Berlin (**R.35(1)**). Details of the EPO filing offices are given in OJ 2017 A11; OJ 2018 A18; A75and **R.2(1)**:3.

The EPO sub-office in Vienna is not a filing office for the purpose of **Art.75(1)(a)** and applications filed there will be forwarded to one of the filing offices and will only be accorded a filing date on receipt by the latter (OJ 2017 A11 Art.1(2)).

The EPO filing offices can also receive international applications, other documents and fees payable to the EPO.

The means for communication with the EPO filing offices is governed by **R.2**. If a national authority allows means of communication not allowed by the EPO and an applicant uses such means to file a European application at that office, the EPO will accord the application a date of filing under **Art.75(1)(b)**, second sentence (J20/84).

R. 35(2) The authority with which the European patent application is filed shall mark the documents making up the application with the date of their receipt, and issue without delay a receipt to the applicant including at least the application number and the nature, number and date of receipt of the documents.

1 **Confirmation of receipt**
The authority with which the application is filed may be a filing office of the EPO or a national authority under **Art.75(1)(b)** or **Art.75(2)**. The same authority that receives the application must issue a receipt to the applicant (**R.35(2)**).

The applicant may fill in the receipt form and send it together with the other application documents to the competent filing office. The filing office checks the nature and number of documents received and returns a copy of the form marked with the date of receipt as a confirmation of the receipt of the documents.

The receipt for applications filed on line will be acknowledged electronically during the submission session. On request, the EPO as filing office provides a confirmation of the receipt by fax for a fee (A-II,3.1; see also **R.2(1):2**).

On receipt the EPO does not check the number of sheets, does not confirm the presence of drawings when the applicant has not indicated their presence on the receipt form, and does not check the matching of titles in the Request for Grant form and the beginning of the description. This is examined later under **Art.90(3)**. The returned receipt form only serves to communicate the application number, the nature and number of the documents and the date of receipt. Therefore, no conclusions regarding the content of the documents on the filing date can be drawn from a lack of a notification by the filing office in response to deficiencies. (**J21/94** r.1 and note in Section 47 of the Request for Grant form, page 'Receipt for documents')

Confirmation of receipt does not imply the accordance of a filing date.

R. 35(3) If the European patent application is filed with an authority referred to in Article 75, paragraph 1(b), such authority shall without delay inform the European Patent Office of the receipt of the application, and, in particular, of the nature and date of receipt of the documents, the application number and any priority date claimed.

Art.75(1)(b) Filing of a European patent application

R. 35(4) Upon receipt of a European patent application forwarded by the central industrial property office of a Contracting State, the European Patent Office shall inform the applicant accordingly, indicating the date of its receipt.

1 **Confirmation of receipt of nationally filed application**
When the EPO has received an application which has been forwarded by a competent national authority under **Art.77**, the EPO issues a **R.35(4)** communication to the applicant confirming receipt of the application.

After receipt of the communication the applicant must file all further documents directly with the EPO and not with the national authority (A-II,3.2). Documents erroneously filed with the national authority may be forwarded to the EPO, but the date of receipt will be the date of receipt by the EPO.

R. 36 European divisional applications

Implementation of: **Art.76(1)**
EPC 1973: **R.4** + **R.25**

R. 36(1) The applicant may file a divisional application relating to any pending earlier European patent application.

Amended by decision of the Administrative Council of 16.10.2013, which entered into force on 01.04.2014. Amended R.36(1) applies to divisional applications filed on or after 01.04.2014. (OJ 2013, 501; OJ 2014 A22).
Art.82 Unity of invention
Art.94(3) Invitation to correct deficiencies
R.71(1) Invitation to correct deficiencies
R.71(2) Content of communication
R.71(3) Invitation to approve text to be granted

1 **Amendmends of R.36(1)**

R.36(1) as valid until 01.04.2014 restricted the filing of divisionals by two 24 months periods with the intention to reduce the number of divisionals (OJ 2009, 481) and to avoid the protracted public uncertainty caused by a sequence of divisionals abusively kept pending up to twenty years (see also **G1/06** r.13.5). However, the number of divisionals filed increased, mainly because the restrictive periods prompted applicants to file precautionary divisionals. **R.36(1)** has therefore been amended again and reverted to the form it had before 01.04.2010, allowing to file divisionals on any pending application. The filing of sequences of divisionals is discouraged by levying an additional fee for divisionals filed on divisionals (**R.38(4)** and **Rfees2(1)1b**).

2 **Divisional application**

An applicant may divide a Euro-direct application, a Euro-PCT application or a divisional European application by filing a divisional application ('divisional'). **G1/06** r.10.2 has accepted sequences of divisional applications. The word 'any' in **R.36(1)** clarifies that it is irrelevant what kind of application the earlier application is (A-IV,1.1; OJ 2002, 112).

The term 'earlier application' in the provision refers to the immediate parent application on which the divisional application is based. The 'earliest application' is the first-filed application in a sequence of predecessor applications where a certain event occurred. In the case of a first-generation divisional application, i.e. where the immediate parent is not itself a divisional, both terms refer to the same application. (A-IV,1.1)

The divisional application may be a voluntary or a mandatory divisional. A voluntary divisional is a divisional filed on the applicant's own initiative, even if no lack-of-unity objection has been raised. It may be filed because of procedural reasons, e.g. as a fallback position in case of an unexpected refusal during oral proceedings in appeal, or economic reasons, e.g. to focus an independent claim on a marketed product. A mandatory divisional is a divisional filed in response to a non-unity objection.

3 **Opportunity for filing**

An applicant may file a divisional application relating to a European application as from the date of filing of this application and during its subsequent pendency. Two further provisions may limit the possibility to file a divisional (**G1/09** r.4.2.3). **R.14** prevents the filing of a divisional if the proceedings for the earlier application are stayed (**J9/12** r.3-5). Although an international application designating the EPO is regarded as equivalent to a European application (**Art.153(2)**), no divisional application relating to this application may be filed before the international application has entered into the European phase, because the processing prohibition of Art.23(1) PCT takes precedence over **R.36(1)** (**Art.150(2)**; see also OJ 2002, 112 and **R.159:3**).

The following sub-sections set out until when the earlier application is pending. See **R.36(1):4** for possible remedies if the divisional is filed too late.

3.1 PENDING EARLIER APPLICATION

According to **R.36(1)** the divisional application may only be filed when the earlier application is pending. In the case the earlier application is itself a divisional application, it is sufficient that this divisional is still pending at the filing date of the second divisional (A-IV,1.1.1). Pendency of still earlier applications is not required. During opposition proceedings and a related appeal, there is only a pending patent and no pending application anymore; as a consequence, filing of a divisional application is not possible.

G1/09 r.3 distinguishes between a pending application and pending proceedings, which need not coincide in time. For example opposition proceedings can only be made pending after grant of the patent, i.e. when the patent application is no longer pending. According to **R.36(1)** the pendency of the application rather than the proceedings is relevant for the right to file a divisional application. An (earlier) application is pending as long as substantive rights deriving therefrom are still in existence. Examples of substantive rights which the applicant is entitled to exercise are provisional protection and the right of filing a divisional application. The EPC lays down in **Art.67(4)** when the provisional protection exists, and, hence, when the application is pending. The Enlarged Board decided that the right of filing a divisional application exists as long as provisional protection exists. Using this rule, the decision sets out the pendency of the application in the case of grant and refusal.

A Euro-PCT application is pending in the sense of **R.36(1)** only if the requirements of **Art.22** PCT for entering the European phase have been fulfilled (**J18/09** hn).

3.1.1 *Filing divisional and grant of earlier application*

The provisional protection of a patent application is in existence until the date of publication of the mention of the grant under **Art.97(3)** (consequence of **Art.64(1)**). Since a substantive right for the application is in existence until the mention of the grant, the application is pending up to but not including the day the mention of the grant is published. The substantive right of filing a divisional application therefore exists up to but not including the day of publication of the mention of the grant of the earlier application. (**G1/09** r.4.3; A-IV,1.1.1)

The actual date the decision to grant is taken is not relevant, only the date the mention of the grant is published (cf. **J7/96** hn). The EPO informs the applicant of the intended date of publication of the mention (see **Art.97(1):4**). A divisional application can be filed at the latest on the day before the date the mention of the grant is published (**J24/03** r.4).

When filing an appeal against the decision to grant, the suspensive effect of the appeal means that the consequences of the appealed decision will not immediately occur. If the appeal is dismissed, the appealed decision is confirmed, thereby putting the applicant back at the legal situation at the time of the grant as if no appeal had been lodged. Hence, a divisional filed during the appeal period after grant will not be dealt with as a divisional. (**J28/03**)

Since **R.36(1)** does not lay down a period of predetermined duration within which a certain act must be carried out but rather a condition that must be complied with when filing a divisional, provisions of the EPC relating to periods are not applicable to the determination of the last day of validly filing a divisional, such as **R.133** for late receipt of documents and **R.134** for extension of periods (**J24/03** hn.III; **J19/10** r.5-7). Hence, the divisional must be filed at the latest on the last day before the publication of the mention of the grant on which the EPO is open for receipt of documents filed by the particular method of **R.2(1)** chosen by the applicant. (A-IV,1.1.1)

For example, if the mention of the grant is published on Wednesday, 04.10.2017, a divisional can be filed by fax or electronically at the latest on 03.10.2017; by post or delivery service to EPO Munich or Berlin at the latest on 02.10.2017 (03.10.2017 being a national holiday in DE) and to EPO The Hague at the latest on 03.10.2017. Filing by deposition in the automated mailbox in Munich or delivery by hand to the porter of EPO The Hague, Munich or Berlin can be made at the latest on 03.10.2017. (see **R.2(1):3, 4** and **5** for acceptance of deliveries)

3.1.2 Filing divisional and refusal of earlier application

The substantive right of provisional protection conferred by an application may continue to exist until the application is finally refused according to **Art.67(4)**. The application is finally refused in first instance upon expiry of the period for filing an appeal. Hence, an application which has been refused in first instance is still pending until the expiry of the period for filing an appeal and, on the day after, is no longer pending if no appeal is filed. This applies both where the decision to refuse is given in written proceedings and where it is pronounced in oral proceedings. (**G1/09** r.4.2, overruling OJ 2002, 112)

Hence, the last day for filing a divisional application is the expiry of the 2-month period of **Art.108** for filing an appeal, triggered by the notification of the written decision of the examining division refusing the earlier application. It is not necessary to appeal a refusal to be able to file a divisional after the decision (**G1/09** r.4.3.3).

The period for filing a divisional application can be extended by appealing the refusal; see e.g. **J23/13** r.8. If the notice of appeal is deemed not to have been filed (see **Art.110:1**), the period is not extended. If the notice of appeal is validly filed but the grounds of appeal are not filed, the pendency of the application ends on expiry of the period for filing the grounds (**J23/13** r.8.3). An application will be pending till the end of proceedings of an admissible appeal, even if the board would subsequently confirm the refusal of the parent application (A-IV,1.1.1).

An appeal against a decision to grant is in general inadmissible and, according to **J28/03** r.11, 15, does not have the benefit of the possibility to file a divisional application during the appeal procedure. Although the issue was raised, **G1/09** did not answer the question whether an (obviously) inadmissible appeal extends the period (see r.4.3.3).

A decision in appeal enters into force on pronouncement in oral proceedings or on notification in written proceedings (**G12/91** r.2, 3). Therefore, following **G1/09** r.4.2.1, in an appeal following refusal of an application, the application is pending until pronouncement or notification of the decision of the board of appeal.

In written appeal proceedings a divisional might be filed until notification of the decision. Since a communication from the EPO is usually received a few days prior to deemed notification on the tenth day (**R.126(2)**), the applicant would still have a few days to file a divisional. This direct consequence of **G12/91** has not yet been confirmed by a board of appeal, nor by internal guidelines of the EPO.

An applicant fearing a refusal at oral proceedings in appeal should file a divisional before the decision in oral proceedings and pay the fees for the divisional after the oral proceedings (but within the period of **R.36(3)**) only if the decision is not satisfactory. An unsatisfactory decision in first instance can be followed by an appeal or by prosecuting a divisional.

3.1.3 *Filing divisional and deemed withdrawal*
Where the application is deemed withdrawn due to non-observance of a period (e.g. **Art.94(4)**), the deemed withdrawal takes effect at expiry of the non-observed period (**G4/98** r.7; A-IV,1.1.1), i.e. the application is pending until midnight at the end of the last day of the non-observed period. Where the application is deemed withdrawn because of non-payment of a renewal fee, the application is pending until expiry of the six-month period of **R.51(2)** (A-IV,1.1.1).

When the applicant receives the communication of the loss of rights under **R.112(1)**, the application is already no longer pending. A mere filing of a request for further processing or re-establishment does not make the application pending again. The application will only become pending, retroactively from the expiry of the non-observed period, if the request is granted, possibly only in appeal. Hence, a divisional filed after an application has been deemed withdrawn will only be validly filed if a remedy is applied successfully. (**J4/11** hn, relating to re-establishment; extended in A-IV,1.1.1 to cover also further processing).

3.1.4 *Filing divisional and withdrawal of parent*
A withdrawal of an application takes effect the moment the EPO receives the notice of withdrawal. A divisional application can be filed only till the moment the withdrawal is received (**T517/97** r.4 mutatis mutandis). A late filing of the divisional may be remedied by reviving the withdrawn parent application by retracting the withdrawal, which may exceptionally be allowed as set out in **R.139:3.2**.

4 **Remedy for late filing**
If the EPO considers that the divisional application is filed too late, the divisional will not be accorded the date of filing (and priority) of the earlier application (**Art.76(1)**). If applicable, a remedy is to ask for an appealable decision under **R.112(2)** within two months after the notification of late filing and provide proof that filing of the divisional did in fact occur in due time.

If a divisional is filed when the earlier application is no longer pending, **R.133** and **R.134** cannot be invoked, because these provisions apply only to periods and not to conditions such as the pendency of **R.36(1)**. Further processing cannot be used, because the loss of rights does not relate to failure to observe a time limit. Re-establishment can neither be used because the pendency in **R.36(1)** does not lay down a time limit within the meaning of **Art.122(1)** (**J24/03** hn.III; **J10/01** r.15). Other remedies relating to pendency of the earlier application are indicated in the above sub-sections.

R. 36(2) A divisional application shall be filed in the language of the proceedings for the earlier application. If the latter was not in an official language of the European Patent Office, the divisional application may be filed in the language of the earlier application; a translation into the language of the proceedings for the earlier application shall then be filed within two months of the filing of the divisional application. The divisional application shall be filed with the European Patent Office in Munich, The Hague or Berlin.

Amended by decision of the Administrative Council of 25.03.2009, which entered into force on 01.04.2010. Amended R.36(2) applies to divisional applications filed on or after that date. (OJ 2009, 296)

1 **Language of divisional application**

A divisional application may be filed in the language of the proceedings of the earlier application (**R.36(2)**, first sentence). It may also be filed in the language of the earlier application if this application was not filed in an official EPO language and translated into the language of proceedings of the earlier application (**R.36(2)**, second sentence).

When filing the divisional in a non-EPO language, the applicant has the possibility of **Art.14(2)**, second sentence, to bring the translation into conformity with the divisional in the non-EPO language at any stage of the procedure. The fee reduction under **R.6(3)** also applies. If the divisional is filed in the language of proceedings of the parent, the applicant has only the limited possibility to correct a translation error under **R.139**, second sentence, which requires a basis for the correction in the divisional itself.

When filing a divisional application by reference to a previous application following **R.40(1)(c)**, the previous application must be the parent application. The parent may be in a non-EPO language. If the previous application was a direct European application or an international application filed with the EPO as receiving Office, no copy of the previous application need be filed under **R.40(3)**. If the previous application was an international application not filed with the EPO as receiving Office, a certified copy must be filed. (A-II,4.1.3.1 and A-IV,1.3.1)

The EPC nor the Guidelines provide the sanction on filing a divisional in a language that is neither an official EPO language nor the language of the earlier application. The application will probably not be dealt with as a European patent application under **Art.90(2)**. If the applicant considers the language admissible, he should request a decision under **R.112(2)**. A remedy is to re-file the divisional in an admissible language, heeding the time constraint of **R.36(1)**.

2 **Translation of divisional application**

R.36(2), second sentence, requires that a translation of the divisional application into the language of the proceedings must be filed within two months of the filing if the divisional was filed in the non-EPO language of the earlier application.

The filing of the translation is checked under **R.57(a)** and if not yet filed, an invitation will be sent under **R.58** to file the translation within two months. If not filed, the application will be deemed withdrawn according to **Art.14(2)**. Further processing is excluded for the period in **R.58** (**R.135(2)**); only re-establishment is available. (A-III,14)

Where the divisional is filed by reference to the parent under **R.40(1)(c)** **and a translation of the parent is available,** no translation need be filed and the EPO will include a copy of the translation of the parent into the file of the divisional (OJ 2009, 486 §4; A-II,4.1.3.1). As admitted by the EPO, its publications on the requirement to file a translation in this situation are ambiguous (compare the previous two references with OJ 2009, 481 §II and A-IV,1.3.3).

3 **Filing offices for divisional application**

A divisional application must be filed with the EPO office in Munich, The Hague or Berlin (**R.36(2)**, last sentence); filing with a national office is not permitted. Details of the EPO filing offices are given in Spec. Ed. 3 of OJ 2007, Dec. Pres. A.1 and Not. EPO A.2.

R. 36(3) The filing fee and search fee shall be paid within one month of filing the divisional application. If the filing fee or search fee is not paid in due time, the application shall be deemed to be withdrawn.

1 **Payment of filing fee and search fee**

The amount of the filing fee and search fee is fixed in **Rfees2(1)1** and **Rfees2(1)2**, respectively.

The requirements, including the fees, for filing a divisional application are similar to those for filing a first application.

The filing and search fee must be paid within one month after filing (**R.36(3)**). The search fee must always be paid, even when a search fee has already been paid for the same invention in the parent application. The search fee will be refunded fully or in part if the search report is based entirely or partly on the earlier search report of the parent application (**Rfees9(2)**).

If the filing fee or search fee is not paid, the divisional will be deemed withdrawn (**R.36(3)**, second sentence) with effect upon expiry of the one month period, not upon expiry of the two-month period for requesting further processing (G4/98 r.7.2; A-III,16.2). The EPO informs the applicant of the loss of rights using the communication of **R.112(1)**. The applicant may request further processing under **Art.121** and **R.135** within two months of the notification of the communication.

If there are more than 15 claims, claims fees must be paid also within one month after filing (**R.45(1)** and **Rfees2(1)15**), even if for the same claims in the parent application the claims fees have already been paid (A-IV,1.4.2).

If the application comprises more than 35 pages, the filing fee will include a page fee (see **R.38(2)** and **Rfees2(1)1a**). If the earlier application is a divisional application, i.e. the divisional is of the second or subsequent generation, the filing fee will include a divisional fee (see **R.38(4)** and **Rfees2(1)1b**). The above sanction and remedy for not paying the filing fee are also applicable to not paying any page fee and divisional fee. See **R.6(3)** for a reduction of the filing, page and divisional fee. (A-IV,1.4.1.1)

See **R.51(3)** and **Rfees2(1)4** for renewal fees payable for a divisional application.

Any fees paid for the divisional will be refunded if the application is not accepted as a divisional, i.e. if it does not have the benefit of the date of filing and priority, if any, of the earlier application (J11/91 hn4).

R. 36(4) The designation fee shall be paid within six months of the date on which the European Patent Bulletin mentions the publication of the European search report drawn up in respect of the divisional application. Rule 39, paragraphs 2 and 3, shall apply.

Amended by decision of the Administrative Council of 21.10.2008, which entered into force on 01.04.2009 and applies to divisional applications received on or after that date. The term 'designation fees' has been replaced by 'designation fee', implementing the switch from payment per designated state to a flat designation fee. (OJ 2008, 513; OJ 2009, 118 footnote 1)
R.39(2) Non-payment of the designation fee
R.39(3) Non-refundability of the designation fee

1 **Payment of designation fee**

A designation fee, covering all contracting states, must be paid for a divisional application, the amount of which is fixed in **Rfees2(1)3**.

The designation fee must be paid within six months of the publication date of the search report drawn up in respect of the divisional application according to **R.36(4)**. If the designation fee is not paid in due time, the application will be deemed withdrawn (**R.39(2)**).

The EPO will inform the applicant of the loss of rights using the communication of **R.112(1)**. Further processing under **Art.121** and **R.135** is available. The withdrawal takes effect upon expiry of the six month period, not upon expiry of the two-month period for requesting further processing (**G4/98** hn.II). See **R.39(3):1** for a possible refund of the designation fee.

Within the same six-month period the request for examination (**R.70**) and a response to the search opinion (**R.70a**) must be filed.

R. 37 Forwarding of European patent applications

Implementation of: **Art.77**
EPC 1973: **Art.77**

1 **General**
R.37 contains details regarding the forwarding of a European patent application from the central industrial property office of the Contracting State with which the application was filed to the EPO.

R. 37(1) The central industrial property office of a Contracting State shall forward European patent applications to the European Patent Office in the shortest time compatible with its national law relating to the secrecy of inventions in the interests of the State, and shall take all appropriate steps to ensure such forwarding within:
(a) six weeks of filing, where the subject of the application is evidently not liable to secrecy under the national law; or
(b) four months of filing or, if priority has been claimed, fourteen months of the date of priority, where the application requires further examination as to its liability to secrecy.

1 **Forwarding of applications under national security**
There are no sanctions if the 6-week or 4-month periods in paragraph 1 are not met (A-II,1.7). Hence, these periods will often be extended to the 14-month period of paragraph 2.

R. 37(2) A European patent application not received by the European Patent Office within fourteen months of filing or, if priority has been claimed, of the date of priority, shall be deemed to be withdrawn. Any fees paid in respect of this application shall be refunded.

1 **Failed forwarding**
If the EPO does not receive the application within 14 months from filing or priority, the application will be deemed withdrawn and all fees will be refunded (**R.37(2)**). The term 'fees' includes any additional fees or surcharges which may have been paid (Spec. Ed. 5 of OJ 2007).

R. 38 Filing fee and search fee

Amended by decision of the Administrative Council of 21.10.2008, which entered into force on 01.04.2009 and applies to European applications filed on or after that date and international applications that entered the regional phase on or after that date. The amendment introduced the page fee to be paid on filing the application. (OJ 2008, 513)
Implementation of: **Art.78(2)**
EPC 1973: **Art.78(2)**

1 **Transitional provision**

For European applications filed before 01.04.2009 and international applications that entered the European phase before that date, **R.38** as in force before 01.04.2009 continues to apply:

R.38 The filing fee and search fee shall be paid within one month of filing the European patent application.

Under **R.38** as valid before 01.04.2009, only the filing and search fee were payable. The fee for any excess pages is levied as fee for grant and printing at grant and is due on notification of the **R.71(3)** communication. The amount payable for more than 35 pages is fixed in **Rfees2(2)7.2** as valid before 01.04.2009. **R.38** as valid before 01.04.2009 will continue to apply till grant of the last application filed before 01.04.2009, which is probably till at least 2014.

The amendment of **R.38** moves the payment for excess pages from grant to filing, thereby covering also the 50% of the filed applications that do not reach grant. The fees at grant do not anymore depend on the number of pages of the specification.

R. 38(1) The filing fee and search fee shall be paid within one month of filing the European patent application.

1 **Period for payment of filing and search fee**

The filing and search fee must be paid within one month of the filing the application (**R.38(1)**). The EPO does not send an invitation to pay within the one month period.

The 'filing of the application' in **R.38(1)** is interpreted as the date of filing (A-III,13.1). Where the application as received does not satisfy the requirements for accordance of a date of filing, the one month period starts on the date of filing as accorded after rectification. The date of filing is the first date on which the application meets the requirements of **Art.80**. See also **G3/98** r.2.2.

The amount of the filing fee is fixed in **Rfees2(1)1.** The amount of the filing fee is reduced if the application documents are filed online (**Rfees2(1):3**). The amount of the search fee is fixed in **Rfees2(1)2.**

See also **Art.78(2):1.**

R. 38(2) The Rules relating to Fees may provide for an additional fee as part of the filing fee if the application comprises more than 35 pages.

1 **Page fee**

The additional fee is provided for in **Rfees2(1)1a.** Its purpose is to reduce the number of pages in filed patent applications.

The amount of the additional fee is fixed in **Rfees2(1)1a** and must be paid for applications comprising more than 35 pages. The way of counting pages is set out in **Rfees2(1):4.** The period for payment is set by **R.38(3).**

Note that the term 'additional fee' is also used in the EPC for the surcharge for belated payment of a renewal fee (**Rfees2(1)5** and for the surcharge for filing a divisional on a divisional (**R.38(4)**). Therefore, the additional fee of **R.38(2)** is referred to in this book as 'page fee'; see also Euro-PCT Guide §543.

R. 38(3) The additional fee referred to in paragraph 2 shall be paid within one month of filing the European patent application or one month of filing the first set of claims or one month of filing the certified copy referred to in Rule 40, paragraph 3, whichever period expires last.

R.40(3) filing copy of previously filed application

1 **Payment of page fee**
The page fee is not included in the filing fee, because it would then be payable within one month of filing and at that time the number of pages of the application will not be known if the claims are filed later or the application is filed by reference to a not yet available previously filed application under **R.40(1)(c)**. Hence, the page fee is separate from the filing fee and must be paid within the later of one month of filing the application, the first set of claims, or the certified copy of the previously filed application (**R.38(3)**).

The page fee for a Euro-PCT application must be paid on entry into the European phase (**R.159(1):4.1**).

Since the page fee is part of the filing fee according to **R.38(2)**, non-payment of the page fee will result in the application being deemed withdrawn (**Art.78(2)**, **R.160(1)**). Failure to meet the one-month period can be remedied using further processing under **Art.121** and **R.135**. (A-III,13.2)

R. 38(4) The Rules relating to Fees may provide for an additional fee as part of the filing fee in the case of a divisional application filed in respect of any earlier application which is itself a divisional application.

Added by decision of the Administrative Council of 16.10.2013, which entered into force on 01.04.2014. The provision applies to divisional applications filed on or after 01.04.2014. (OJ 2013, 501; OJ 2014 A22)

1 **Divisional fee**
The additional fee is a surcharge on the filing fee levied for divisionals that are filed in respect of an earlier divisional application. The additional fee tries to discourage filing of sequences of divisionals. The amount of the additional fee is fixed in **Rfees2(1)1b** and must be paid as part of the filing fee within one month of filing the divisional application (**R.36(3)**). If not paid in due time, the EPO will notify the applicant under **R.112(1)** that the application is deemed withdrawn (**R.36(3)**); further processing is available as a remedy.

Since the term 'additional fee' is used for several other fees, the additional fee of **R.38(4)** is referred to in this book as 'divisional fee'.

R. 39 Designation fees

Amended by decision of the Administrative Council of 21.10.2008, which entered into force on 01.04.2009 and applying to European applications filed on or after that date and international applications that entered the European phase on or after that date. The term 'designation fees' has been replaced by 'designation fee', implementing the switch from payment per designated state to a flat designation fee (see **Art.79**). (OJ 2008, 513)

The Administrative Council has unfortunately not yet amended the title of the provision to reflect the singular character of the fee.

Implementation of: **Art.79(2), (3)**
EPC 1973: **Art.79(2), Art.91(4)** and **Art.79(3)**

1 **General**
Explanatory notes to **R.39** are given under **Art.79(2)**.

R. 39(1) The designation fee shall be paid within six months of the date on which the European Patent Bulletin mentions the publication of the European search report.

1 **Designation fee**
The amount of the designation fee is fixed in **Rfees2(1)3**.

R. 39(2) Where the designation fee is not paid in due time or the designations of all the Contracting States are withdrawn, the European patent application shall be deemed to be withdrawn.

R. 39(3) Without prejudice to Rule 37, paragraph 2, second sentence, the designation fee shall not be refunded.

R.37(2) Non-forwarded application deemed withdrawn

1 **Non-refund of designation fee**
The initial half-sentence of **R.39(3)** makes it clear that the principle whereby the designation fee is not refunded does not apply in the special case referred to in **R.37(2)**, where a national authority with which a European application had been filed has not forwarded the application to the EPO in due time.

R.39(3) is in conflict with two situations where the designation fee must be refunded. The first one is where the designation fee is paid on filing and the application is not dealt with as a European patent application because the requirements of **R.40** have not been complied with or a divisional application will not be dealt with as such (**J11/91** r.4.2).

The second situation is where the designation fee is paid and the application is subsequently (deemed) withdrawn or refused before publication of the search report. Since the designation fee is only due on the date of publication of the search report (**Rfees4(1):1**), a payment before that date has no legal basis. Based on the general principle that payments that lack a legal basis must be refunded (see **Rfees9:1**), the designation fee should be refunded in this situation. (see also the EPO brochure 'How to get a European patent' §122a, last par.)

The EPO accepts payment of the designation fee before the due date (A-X,5.2.2), thereby not adhering to the principle that a fee paid before the due date lacks legal basis and must be refunded (A-X,10.1.1). In the second situation the EPO will refund the payment only if before the due date both the payment was made and the application was lost.

R. 40 Date of filing

Implementation of: **Art.80**
EPC 1973: **Art.80**

1 **General**
R.40 specifies the requirements for a date of filing. The wording of **R.40(1)** follows the model of Art.5(1) and (7) PLT 2000.

Under Art.5(7) and R.2(5)(a) PLT, contracting parties are obliged to accept a reference to a single, previously filed application instead of a description and any drawings, provided that the previously filed application is properly identified. These requirements are inserted in **R.40(2)**.

In such a case, **R.40(3)** requires the filing of a copy of the previously filed application (R.2(5)(b) PLT) – unless such a copy is already available to the contracting party (R.4(3) PLT) – and, where appropriate, of a translation of that application. (OJ 2003 se1 p.159)

See **Art.90:2** about the usefulness of the different options for filing an application allowed under **R.40**. The application of **R.40** to filing divisionals has been set out in **Art.76(1):1**.

R. 40(1) The date of filing of a European patent application shall be the date on which the documents filed by the applicant contain:
(a) an indication that a European patent is sought;
(b) information identifying the applicant or allowing the applicant to be contacted; and
(c) a description or reference to a previously filed application.

1 **Requirements for according date of filing**

Documents filed by the applicant will be accorded a date of filing if they contain the items listed under **R.40**. The word 'filed' in **R.40** must be interpreted as duly filed in the sense of **Art.75** with an office allowed by **Art.75** and **R.35(1)**, using a method of filing permitted by **R.2(1)**. Hence, the minimum requirements for according a European patent application a date of filing are given explicitly in **R.40** and implicitly in **Art.75, R.35(1)** and **R.2(1)**.

The examination for according a date of filing is carried out under **Art.90(1)**, the sanction on non-compliance is provided in **Art.90(2)** and the procedure for correcting deficiencies in **Art.90(4)**. The consequences of non-compliance with the requirements of **R.40** and any re-dating of the application are dealt with **Art.90(2)** and **R.55**.

1.1 PLACE AND MEANS OF FILING (ART.75, R.35 AND R.2)

The place where the application is filed and the means used for communicating the application are important for according a date of filing and must therefore be regarded as requirements for according a date of filing, even though they are not mentioned in **R.40**.

A determining factor for according the date of filing of a patent application is the date of receipt of the application documents at a filing office of the EPO according to **Art.75(1)(a)** and **R.35(1)** or at a competent national authority according to **Art.75(1)(b)** and **(2)**. Application documents filed with another office, e.g. the EPO sub-office in Vienna or the Dutch national authority, will be forwarded to a competent filing office as a courtesy service and the date of receipt at the competent filing office determines the date of filing.

The application must be filed using a means of communication permitted under **R.2(1)**, where appropriate with written confirmation. Application documents transmitted by other means, such as telex or telegram, will be deemed not to have been received (OJ 2007 se3, 7 Art.1(3)) and cannot be accorded a date of filing. Where a national filing office allows means of communication not allowed by the EPO and an applicant uses such means to file a European patent application at that office under **Art.75(1)(b)**, the EPO will accord the application a date of filing (**J20/84**).

1.2 INDICATION THAT A EUROPEAN PATENT IS SOUGHT (R.40(1)(A))

The indication that a patent is sought need be in no particular form to obtain a date of filing (A-III,4.1). The EPO Request for Grant form (**R.41(1)**) contains a statement that a European patent is sought. Use of the form is not required to obtain a date of filing. However, the Request for Grant form must be provided at a later stage or the application will be refused according to **Art.90(3)**, **R.57(b)**, **R.41(1)** and **Art.90(5)**.

If no indication is provided, the EPO will send a **R.55** communication, requesting the applicant to correct the deficiency within two months. If corrected, the application will be redated to the date of receipt of the correction. If not corrected, the application will not be dealt with as a European patent application (**Art.90(2)**, **R.55**). (A-II,4.1.4 and 4.1.5)

If the EPO cannot read the language of the application documents, it will probably keep the documents and defer the examination on filing until a translation has been provided.

1.3 INFORMATION IDENTIFYING THE APPLICANT (R.40(1)(B))

R.40(1)(b) requires that information is provided to identify the applicant or allow him to be contacted. If there are multiple applicants, the information has to be provided for only one of them (A-II,4.1.2). The EPO will take into account all data contained in the documents filed to determine whether this requirement is met (**J25/86** r.3). Any kind of information which allows the applicant to be contacted will be considered to fulfil the requirement of **R.40(1)(b)**, in particular the name and address of the applicant's representative, a fax number,r a PO box number or a phone number (A-II,4.1.2).

The information need not be sufficient to determine whether the applicant must be represented under **Art.133(2)** (A-II,4.1.2).

A signature of the applicant or his representative is not required for according a date of filing. If the signature is not provided in due time, the application will be refused according to **Art.90(3)**, **R.57(b)**, **R.41(2)(h)** and **Art.90(5)**.

Since there is no language requirement for the information, the EPO may receive applications of which it cannot read the address. In such cases the EPO will probably keep the documents and wait for the applicant to approach the EPO. There is no legal basis not to treat the filing as a European patent application. Note that the procedure for correcting deficient information set out in A-II,4.1.4 is not applicable in this case, since there is no deficiency. In this case the invitation under **R.58** to file a translation cannot be notified publicly under **R.129**, even though this may be in conflict with **Art.128**.

The passage in A-II,4.1.4 stating that there is a deficiency under **R.40(1)(b)** if the address 'does not enable the EPO to contact the applicant' appears to be intended for the case where the address is deficient such that it does not enable the EPO to contact the applicant, and not to the case where the EPO is merely unable to read the address.

Since **R.55** does not refer to **R.40(1)(b)**, no invitation for correction will be sent under **R.55** if the information to contact the applicant is missing or insufficient. However, if the applicant corrects the deficiency of his own motion within two months from the date of receipt of the original documents, then the date of filing is the date on which the requirements of **R.40** are regarded as met. If not corrected by the end of the two month period, the application will not be dealt with as a European patent application (**Art.90(2)**). (A-II,4.1.4)

Note that the EPC does not provide a legal basis for the two-month period, although the period is similar to the one mentioned in **R.40(3)**.

1.4 DESCRIPTION (R.40(1)(C))

The documents must contain a description or reference to a previously filed application.

The description does not require close scrutiny at this stage of examination. It is sufficient to identify a document which appears to include a description (A-II,4.1.3).

If no description is provided, the EPO will send a **R.55** communication, requesting the applicant to correct the deficiency within two months. If corrected, the application will be redated to the date of receipt of the application. If not corrected, the application will not be dealt with as a European patent application (**Art.90(2)**, **R.55**). (A-II,4.1.4 and 4.1.5)

1.5 REFERENCE TO A PREVIOUSLY FILED APPLICATION (R.40(1)(C))

Instead of a description, the filing documents may contain a reference to a previously filed application. The previously filed application may be a priority application (A-II,4.1.3.1) or a parent application (A-IV,1.3.1).

The reference must comply with the requirements of **R.40(2)** and a certified copy of the previously filed application must be supplied under **R.40(3)**. More detail is provided in the notes to these provisions.

Although **R.40(1)(c)** states 'reference to *a* previously filed application', it is the intention that the reference is to a *single* previous application, which follows from the Explanatory Remarks on new Rule 25d in OJ 2003 se1, p.168; and from Section 26.1 of the Request for Grant form, which allows entry of details for only one previous application.

When filing by reference using the Request for Grant form, the reference replaces the description and any drawings. Optionally, the reference may also replace the claims. If no reference is made to the claims of the previous application, the claims may be filed as part of the application documents or filed later. It is not permitted to refer to a previous application and also include a description in the application documents; similarly, no additional set of claims may be filed before receipt of the search report if reference is made to the claims of the previous application. (see A-II,4.1.3.1)

The PLT has not defined the words 'previous' and 'application'. The EPO may use the definition of Art. 2 PCT for an application, corresponding to that used in **Art.87(1)**. It is recommended to use one of the applications mentioned in **Art.87(1)** as previous application, for which the certified copy required under **R.40(3)** can also be obtained. The application need not necessarily claim the priority of the previous application it refers to.

If the Request for Grant form is not used, it is recommended to indicate clearly what is referred to. E.g. a reference to the description only does not include the drawings and claims. Each referenced item must be specifically stated.

2 Issues irrelevant for according date of filing

2.1 LANGUAGE OF THE APPLICATION

R.40 does not contain any requirement as to the language of the application, which implies that the language of the application is not relevant for according a date of filing, as required by the PLT (A-VII,1.1). **Art.14(2)**, relating to the examination as to formalities, implies that an application may be filed in any language. The indication that a European patent is sought and the information identifying the applicant or allowing the applicant to be contacted may also be filed in any language. The PLT did not want to define 'language'. A minimum condition should be the ability to make a reliable translation, requiring the availability of a dictionary. For online filing there must be an ISO code for the characters of the language, because the EPO uses the ISO codes.

It is not possible to file the application documents in the wrong language. The EPO does not require that these documents are all in the same language (A-VII,1.1; EPO practice changed in 2014; see A-VII,4.1, edition November 2014).

The requirements as to language provided in Art.14(2) are examined in the formalities examination under **Art.90(3)** and **R.57(a)**, i.e. after the examination for according a date of filing. If the application is not filed in one of the official languages of the EPO, i.e. English, German or French (**Art.14(1)**), a translation into one of these languages must be provided under **Art.14(2)**.

2.2 CLAIMS

The presence of one or more claims is not a requirement for according a date of filing. If no claims are present on filing, the EPO will invite the applicant to file claims under **R.58**. The applicant may file the claims of his own volition before being so invited (A-III,15). As a formal requirement, the at least one claim of **Art.78(1)(c)** must be on file at the time of the formalities examination under **Art.90(3)** and **R.57(c)**. Note, that the application is not re-dated on receipt of late-filed claims. The EPO will publish the application always with claims.

Claims filed after the date of filing are regarded as amendments under **Art.123(2)** and may not extend the subject matter of the application as filed (A-III,15). Since claims usually form the broadest definition of the invention in an application, it is difficult to achieve a broad scope in late filed claims without violating **Art.123(2)**. Late filing of claims should therefore be used only in cases of emergency, for example where it is necessary to safeguard the rights of an inventor quickly and claims will be added only to a subsequent application claiming the priority of the first application without claims.

The EPO may request the applicant under **R.137(4)** to indicate the basis of the late-filed claims in the application as filed, since late-filed claims are regarded as an amendment (H-III,2.1.1(i)).

The applicant may indicate at filing that the claims of the previous application take the place of claims in the application as filed. The indication can be made in Section 26 of the Request for Grant form. If the indication is made, the claims of the previous application will form the basis of the search and examination (A-II,4.1.3.1).

Claims filed after the date of filing of the application are regarded as an amendment to the application and must comply with **R.3(2)**, i.e. they must be filed in the language of proceedings. When the claims are filed before the translation of the application under **R.6(1)** has been filed, the language of the claims must be the language in which the application will be translated, as the application must be in one language.

2.3 FORM OF THE APPLICATION

R.40 does not give requirements for the form of the application. Hence, an identifiable description suffices for the purpose of according a filing date, even if it deviates from the EPC requirements. The documents making up the application must be sufficiently legible to enable the information to be discerned (A-II,4.1). Note that the documents as filed also determine the content of the application beyond which extension is not allowed during subsequent proceedings (**Art.123(2)**).

2.4 DESIGNATION OF CONTRACTING STATES

On filing no indication of designation of contracting states need be provided. All contracting states are automatically designated under **Art.79(1)**. See **Art.79(3):1** for withdrawing designations during the grant procedure.

2.5 FEES

Payment of fees is not necessary for according a date of filing, which makes a European patent application an economical way of securing a filing date for a priority document. If the filing fee and search fee are not paid within one month after filing, the application will be deemed to be withdrawn (**Art.78(2)**). The withdrawal does not affect the right to claim priority of this application (**Art.87(2)** and (3)).

2.6 MISSING PARTS OF DESCRIPTION AND MISSING DRAWINGS

The EPO will check during the examination on filing whether any parts of the description or any drawings appear to be missing. Where such items are missing but the requirements of **R.40(1)** have been fulfilled, the application documents will initially be accorded a date of filing corresponding to the date they were received; any correction of the missing parts may change this date.

The applicant may file missing parts of his own motion or on invitation by the EPO. The application will be re-dated to the date of receipt of the missing parts. However, the application will retain the original date of filing if the missing part of the description or the missing drawings are contained in a priority application.

See **R.56** and notes thereto for details.

R. 40(2) A reference to a previously filed application under paragraph 1(c) shall state the filing date and number of that application and the Office with which it was filed. Such reference shall indicate that it replaces the description and any drawings.

1 **Reference to previous application**

When a reference to a previously filed application is filed instead of a description, the following information must be provided according to **R.40(2)** for accordance of a date of filing (A-II,4.1.3.1):

i) the filing date of the previous application
ii) its file number, i.e. the application number
iii) the office where it was filed and
iv) an indication that this reference replaces the description and any drawings.

It is possible to indicate in the Request for Grant form, Section 26, that the reference also replaces the claims (see **R.57(c)**).

The previous application is normally a patent application, but alternatively it may be an application for a utility model (A-II,4.1.3.1).

The reference to 'office' in **R.40(2)** should read 'state', similar as for priority. This will be corrected in the near future.

2 **Late filing of data of previous application**

The information of the previous application must be provided when filing the application. Its presence is a requirement for according a date of filing to an application filed by reference.

If any of the items is not included in the application documents, the EPO will invite the applicant to provide it as yet within two months of invitation (**R.55**, first sentence). If not provided, the application will not be dealt with as a European patent application (**R.55**, first sentence). If provided in due time, the EPO will redate the application to the date of receipt of the information and inform the applicant of the date of filing (**R.55**, second sentence). (A-II,4.1.4)

If the filing date of the previous application is not known when filing an application by reference, any date can be given and, when the filing date is known, correction requested under **R.139**, first sentence.

Where the filing number is incorrect, a request for correction under **R.139**, second sentence, is unlikely to be granted because of the difficulty to prove that the correction is obvious. Moreover, a correction would amount to replacement of the complete document forming the patent application, which is prohibited by **G2/95**. If a later date of filing is acceptable, the applicant should re-file the application.

R. 40(3) Where the application contains a reference under paragraph 2, a certified copy of the previously filed application shall be filed within two months of filing the application. Where the previously filed application is not in an official language of the European Patent Office, a translation thereof in one of these languages shall be filed within the same period. Rule 53, paragraph 2, shall apply mutatis mutandis.

R.53(2) Copy previous document in EPO file

1 **Copy of previous application**

Where the application refers to a previously filed application under **R.40(1)(c)**, the applicant must file a certified copy of this previous application (**R.40(3)**, first sentence). A certified copy rather than a normal copy is required, since the previously filed application is not necessarily published or the previous application is an application from which priority is claimed which requires the filing of a certified copy under **R.53(1)**.

According to **R.40(3)**, last sentence, the requirement to file a copy is dispensed with if the previous application is already available to the EPO. The previous application is only available where it is a European patent application or an international application filed with the EPO as receiving Office. Hence, a divisional application referring e.g. to a Euro-PCT application that was not filed with the EPO as receiving Office, requires filing of a certified copy of the international application as originally filed with the receiving Office. (A-II,4.1.3.1 and A-IV,1.3.1)

Note that the availability under **R.40(3)** is different from that under **R.53(2)** for previous applications from which priority is claimed.

Since it is difficult to obtain a certified copy of an application from a patent office within the relatively short period of **R.40(3)**, it is recommended to use filing by reference only where the certified copy is available on filing or where the EPO will include the copy in the file.

2 **Period for filing copy of previous application**

A copy of the previously filed application must be filed within two months of filing the application (**R.40(3)**). If the copy is available at the expiry of the two-month period, the application will retain its original date of filing. Note, that the provision of a copy is a requirement for according a date of filing that need not be complied with at the date of filing, as usual for such requirements, but only two months later.

If the copy is not filed within two months of filing the application, the applicant will receive a communication setting a time limit of a further two months under **R.55**. If the copy is supplied within that period, the original filing date will be retained (A-II,4.1.5). If no copy is available by expiry of the period, no filing date will be accorded and the application will not be dealt with as a European patent application (**R.55**, first sentence). (A-II,4.1.4)

The EPO has an interest in receiving the copy of the previous application and, where applicable, the translation as early as possible for the purpose of publishing the application, in particular if the European application is filed towards the end of the priority period. Therefore, the two-month periods in **R.40(3)** and **R.55** for filing the copy are excluded from further processing under **R.135(2)**. However, re-establishment is available for both periods.

3 Translation of previous application

If the previous application is not in an official EPO language, a translation in English, French or German must be filed in addition to the certified copy of the application (**R.40(3)**, second sentence). The translation must be presented in the same form as the application documents (**R.49(1)**). If the translation is already available to the EPO, it need not be filed again (**R.40(3)**, last sentence) and the EPO will include a copy in its file (A-II,4.1.3.1).

The provision of a translation is not a requirement for according a date of filing (A-II,4.1.4, last sentence). The mention of furnishing of a translation in a provision on requirements for according a date of filing is therefore unsuitable. The legislator has allegedly included the requirement in this provision to reduce the amount of law text.

When the previous application is in an admissible non-EPO language according to **Art.14(4)**, the applicant may be entitled to a reduction of the filing fee (see **R.6(3)**).

The translation may subsequently be brought into conformity with the previously filed application (A-VII,7; **Art.14(2)**, second sentence). It should be noted that, in contrast to **R.6(1)**, **R.40(3)** does not refer to **Art.14(2)**; however, **Art.14(2)** is regarded as applicable to all rules relating to translations of the application.

4 Period for filing translation of previous application

A translation of the previously filed application must be filed within two months of filing the application (**R.40(3)**, second sentence). This period is the same as the period for filing a translation under **R.6(1)**.

If the translation is not filed in time, the EPO will, as part of the formalities examination under **R.57**, invite the applicant under **R.58** to supply the translation within two months. If neither filed in this period, the application will be deemed withdrawn under **Art.14(2)**, last sentence (A-III,16.2). However, the application retains its date of filing. The procedure is accelerated if the translation is filed as early as possibly, preferably within the period of **R.40(3)**.

The two-month periods of **R.40(3)** and **R.58** are excluded from further processing (**R.135(2)**) but are open to re-establishment under **Art.122**.

Chapter II *Provisions governing the application*

R. 41 Request for grant

Implementation of: Art.78(1)(a)
EPC 1973: R.26

R. 41(1) The request for grant of a European patent shall be filed on a form drawn up by the European Patent Office.

1 **Request for Grant form**
Use of the Request for Grant form (Form 1001) is a compulsory formal requirement for filing a European patent application (**R.57(b)**). If the Form is not used on filing and not supplied after invitation, the application will be refused (**Art.90(5)**). However, use of the Form is not a requirement for according a date of filing (**R.40(1)(a)**). The form is made available free of charge by the EPO. Use of the EPO Request for Grant form is not applicable to Euro-PCT applications (**R.49.4** PCT).

Apart from preprinted versions available from the EPO information desks, the EPO also accepts a print of the Request for Grant form downloaded from the EPO website and filled in by computer (OJ 1997, 344) and an electronic filing of the form when the application is filed electronically (**R.2(1):7**).

R. 41(2) The request shall contain:
(a) a petition for the grant of a European patent;
(b) the title of the invention, which shall clearly and concisely state the technical designation of the invention and shall exclude all fancy names;
(c) the name, address and nationality of the applicant and the State in which his residence or principal place of business is located. Names of natural persons shall be indicated by the person's family name, followed by his given names. Names of legal persons, as well as of bodies equivalent to legal persons under the law governing them, shall be indicated by their official designations. Addresses shall be indicated in accordance with applicable customary requirements for prompt postal delivery and shall comprise all the relevant administrative units, including the house number, if any. It is recommended that the fax and telephone numbers be indicated;
(d) if the applicant has appointed a representative, his name and the address of his place of business as prescribed in sub-paragraph (c);
(e) where appropriate, an indication that the application constitutes a divisional application and the number of the earlier European patent application;
(f) in cases covered by Article 61, paragraph 1(b), the number of the original European patent application;
(g) where applicable, a declaration claiming the priority of an earlier application and indicating the date on which and the country in or for which the earlier application was filed;
(h) the signature of the applicant or his representative;
(i) a list of the documents accompanying the request. This list shall also indicate the number of sheets of the description, claims, drawings and abstract filed with the request;

(j) the designation of the inventor, where the applicant is the inventor.

Art.61(1)(b) Filing new application by entitled person

1 **Examination of the Request for Grant**
See **R.57(b)** for the examination of compliance with the requirements of R.41(2) during the examination of formal requirements of the application under **Art.90(3)**.

2 **Information on the applicant (R.41(2)(c))**
An applicant who may act without a representative may indicate an address for correspondence in a contracting state other than his address of residence or principal business (A-III,4.2.1).

Where an application is filed by multiple applicants, the information of R.41(2)(c) must be provided for each applicant (A-III,4.2.1).

R. 41(3) If there is more than one applicant, the request shall preferably contain the appointment of one applicant or representative as common representative.

1 **Appointment of common representative**
A common representative can be appointed by entering details of the representative in section 15 of the Request for Grant form, including the indication 'common representative' (see Point 14 and 15 of the Notes to the Request for Grant form).

In all other cases, e.g. where an applicant instead of a representative is common representative or where more than one representative is appointed, the common representative should be appointed on a signed additional sheet.

If the form mentions several applicants but not a common representative, a common representative is appointed by the EPO applying **R.151**.

If the authorisation of the representative entitles him to act for all applicants, he can sign the form. If all applicants sign the form, the form itself is a basis for his entitlement to act. An authorisation need be filed only on request by the EPO (**R.152(1)**). See also **Art.133:2** for appointment and authorisation.

R. 42 Content of the description

Implementation of: **Art.78(1)(b)** and **Art.83**
EPC 1973: **R.27**

1 **General**
The purpose of this rule is to ensure that the technical information in the application suffices the skilled person to put the invention into practice as required by **Art.83**, and to enable a reader to understand the contribution to the art. Thereto the description must disclose:

- the technical field (paragraph (1)(a))
- the prior art (paragraph (1)(b))
- a disclosure of the invention facilitating the identification of the problem and the solution to said problem (paragraph (1)(c))
- a brief description of the drawings (paragraph (1)(d))
- an embodiment (paragraph (1)(e))
- a way of exploitation in industry if necessary (paragraph (1)(f)).

R. 42(1) The description shall:

(a) specify the technical field to which the invention relates;

(b) indicate the background art which, as far as is known to the applicant, can be regarded as useful to understand the invention, draw up the European search report and examine the European patent application, and, preferably, cite the documents reflecting such art;

(c) disclose the invention, as claimed, in such terms that the technical problem, even if not expressly stated as such, and its solution can be understood, and state any advantageous effects of the invention with reference to the background art;

(d) briefly describe the figures in the drawings, if any;

(e) describe in detail at least one way of carrying out the invention claimed, using examples where appropriate and referring to the drawings, if any;

(f) indicate explicitly, when it is not obvious from the description or nature of the invention, the way in which the invention is industrially applicable.

1 **Prior art (R.42(1)(b))**

The term 'background art' in **R.42(1)(b)** and **(c)** has the same meaning as 'prior art' (T11/82 hn.II).

Only the most appropriate prior art need be mentioned (F-II,4.4).

A prior right document must be clearly identified as such, and it should be indicated that said document is not relevant for the assessment of inventive step. Adding references to prior art documents after filing of the application does not extend the subject-matter in the sense of **Art.123(2)**. The later-added prior art references must be purely factual. The subject-matter of the application is understood to consist of those features which relate to the invention, starting off from the prior art. (F-II,4.3)

A reference to a priority document is not allowed.

A reference to a document giving information necessary to understand the invention must be given in the application as filed. A later inclusion of such a reference introduces new matter. If such a document is not available to the public at the date of filing, a copy must be furnished to the EPO on or before the date of filing, and the document must be published before or on the date of publication of the application. (F-III,8 and H-V,2.5)

If the application refers to knowledge in the state of the art which cannot be classified as being in a relevant field, that knowledge cannot be used to the applicant's disadvantage as being in a neighbouring field merely on account of that reference. The link to said field is the inventor's internal state of the art. (**T28/87**)

The relevant content of a document referred to in the application as filed is regarded as forming part of the application for the purpose of prior right (**Art.54(3)**) against later applications. (F-III,8)

If necessary to put the contribution to the art made by the invention into proper perspective, the EPO may request that references to documents from the search report are cited (**T11/82**). Although the indication of prior art in the description is not worded in **R.42(1)(b)** as a requirement, it becomes mandatory if the EPO has indicated the prior art to be acknowledged (**T11/82** r.17, 25). If the applicant or proprietor does not follow the invitation to amend the references to the prior art, the application will be refused (**Art.97(2)** & **R.42(1)**) or the patent revoked (**Art.101(2)** & **R.42(1)**).

2 **Disclosure of the invention (R.42(1)(c))**

The description must disclose the invention as claimed making the technical problem and its solution understandable; it may state any advantages in view of the state of the art (**R.42(1)(c)**). If the subject-matter of a dependent claim is self-explanatory, no additional explanation is necessary. If the invention resides in the recognition of a problem, i.e. the invention is a so-called problem invention, this should be indicated. Advantageous effects must not be presented in a way disparaging the prior art (**R.48(1)(b)**. If an independent claim defines a patentable invention, the underlying problem must be derivable from the application; only then is the requirement of **R.42(1)(c)** fulfilled (**T26/81**; F-II,4.6).

R.42(1)(c) is not a separate formal criterion independent of **Art.52**. The EPC does not require that an invention must have an advantageous effect to be patentable; it may provide a mere alternative to the prior art (G-VII,5.2).

3 **Description of an embodiment (R.42(1)(e))**

Details of well-known features need not be given, as the reader is assumed to be skilled in the art. The required number of embodiments depends on how broad the claimed field is. Normally a single embodiment renders it obvious how to put the invention into practice, but where the claims cover a broad field, a series of embodiments or variants extending over the field is necessary to satisfy **Art.83**. (F-III,1)

The requirements of sufficient disclosure of the invention (**Art.83**) and support of the claims by the description (**Art.84**) are based on the same legal principle that the patent monopoly should be justified by the technical contribution to the art. Therefore, the extent to which an invention is sufficiently disclosed is also highly relevant for the answer to the question of support. (**T409/91**)

The PCT requires that the best mode for carrying out the invention be described (**R.5.1(a)(v) PCT**). This is especially important if the USA is designated, where this is also a requirement.

In order to clarify the invention, it should be described not only in structural terms, but also in functional terms, unless the function of the elements is immediately clear. In some fields, e.g. computers, a functional description is often clearer than a structural one. (F-III,1)

4 **Industrial application (R.42(1)(f))**

In most cases the way in which an invention can be exploited in industry is self-evident, and needs no further clarification in the description. Since the industrial application of certain biotechnological inventions, i.e. sequences and partial sequences of genes, is not self-evident, the industrial application of such sequences must be disclosed in the application according to **R.29(3)**. (F-II,4.9 and G-III,4)

R. 42(2) **The description shall be presented in the manner and order specified in paragraph 1, unless, owing to the nature of the invention, a different presentation would afford a better understanding or be more concise.**

1 **Departure from R.42(1)**

The clarity of the description is the responsibility of the applicant. Hence, an examiner should not be too strict when the applicant requests amendments departing from **R.42(1)**. (F-II,4.10)

R. 43 Form and content of claims

Implementation of **Art.78(1)(c)** and **Art.84**
EPC 1973: **R.29**

R. 43(1) The claims shall define the matter for which protection is sought in terms of the technical features of the invention. Wherever appropriate, claims shall contain:

(a) a statement indicating the designation of the subject-matter of the invention and those technical features which are necessary for the definition of the claimed subject-matter but which, in combination, form part of the prior art;

(b) a characterising portion, beginning with the expression "characterised in that" or "characterised by" and specifying the technical features for which, in combination with the features stated under subparagraph (a), protection is sought.

1 **Form and content of claims**

Specifying a result to be achieved, i.e. a statement of purpose, is allowed if it helps in defining the invention. Functional features are allowed as long as a skilled person does not have to exercise inventive skills to provide means for performing the function in question. Claims to the use of an invention, in the sense of the technical application thereof, are allowed. (F-IV,2.1)

R.43(1)(a) applies only to independent claims and not to dependent claims. Only relevant features of the prior art have to be mentioned. If one or more features in the characterizing part of a claim are known in combination with the features of the preamble of the claim (i.e. the first part reciting the prior art) and, in that combination, have the same effect as in the full combination of the invention, those features must be transferred to the preamble. (F-IV,2.2)

The two-part form need not be used, if this gives a misleading picture of the contribution made to the art. Examples are where the invention lies solely in the combination of known elements of equal status; modification of a known process by omitting a substance or substituting a substance for another one; a complex system of interrelated parts, the invention residing in changes in several of these parts or in their inter-relationships. A two-part claim should be avoided if the prior art is a prior right (F-IV,2.3). If a one-part claim is used, the description should clearly identify the prior art (T170/84).

Although not prescribed by the EPC, claims are normally drafted as a single sentence. Claims comprising more than one sentence are exceptional (see as an example EP 0 293 769 B1, Claim 1).

R. 43(2) Without prejudice to Article 82, a European patent application may contain more than one independent claim in the same category (product, process, apparatus or use) only if the subject-matter of the application involves one of the following:

(a) a plurality of interrelated products,

(b) different uses of a product or apparatus,

(c) alternative solutions to a particular problem, where it is inappropriate to cover these alternatives by a single claim.

Art.82 Unity of invention

1 **One independent claim per category**

The intention of **R.43(2)** is to limit the number of independent claims in an application. It legally defines the principle of 'one independent claim per category'. The only admissible exceptions to this principle are explicitly stated. The rule allows an examiner to object to large numbers of independent claims without lengthy substantive argumentation. An applicant wishing more than one independent claim in the same category to obtain the desired scope of protection for the invention must, if the EPO objects, convincingly demonstrate that all the additional independent claims come under one of the exceptions explicitly given in the rule. So the onus is on the applicant. (OJ 2002, 112)

The EPO can raise an objection to multiple independent claims in the same category already at the search stage under **R.62a** and during substantive examination (F-IV,3.3).

T263/05 r.5.19 regards **R.43(2)** as an administrative provision designed to help refuse without difficulties applications contravening **Art.82** and **84**; therefore, the rule is not applicable in opposition proceedings.

When after an objection under **R.43(2)** an applicant maintains a plurality of independent claims without convincing arguments that one of the three situations in the provision applies, the application may be refused under **Art.97(2)** (F-IV,3.3).

The provision aims at reducing the amount of work spent on the substantial number of applications drafted in the so-called US style, containing an excessive number of independent claims, which do not comply with the requirement of conciseness (**Art.84**). A proliferation of dependent claims is counteracted by **R.43(5)** (see also F-IV,5).

R.43(2) allows in principle one independent claim in each of the following four categories: product, process, apparatus and use. Basically, there are only two different claim types: physical entities (product, apparatus) and activities (process and use) (F-IV,3.1; **G6/88** r.2.2)). Different categories of claims may help to obtain full protection for the invention (F-IV,3.1). Note that a claim for a method and a claim for an apparatus using the method are independent claims (see also **R.43(4):1**).

The independent claims, whether in the same or different categories, must comply with the requirement of unity according to **Art.82** ('without prejudice' in **R.43(2)**). See **R.44(1):1** for examples of claims in different categories having the same inventive concept.

2 **Several independent claims per category**

In three specific cases **R.43(2)** allows an application to have two or more independent claims in the same category (see F-IV,3.2 for the examples):

1 A plurality of inter-related products having the same inventive concept, e.g. plug and socket, transmitter and receiver, intermediate and final product, gene - gene construct - host - protein - medicament.

The 'interrelated products' must relate to different objects that complement each other or work together; it does not cover different embodiments of essentially the same object (**T56/01** r.4.1).

Note, that **R.43(2)(a)** should cover interrelated methods, although they are not mentioned; for example a method for coding data and a method for decoding data.

2 Different uses of a product or apparatus, e.g. a substance disclosed for a number of distinct cosmetic or medical uses (second and further medical indication).

3 Alternative solutions to a particular problem based on the same inventive concept, where it is not appropriate to cover these alternatives by a single claim, e.g. where the invention resides in a group of new chemical compounds or in a number of processes for the manufacture of such compounds.

When two independent claims have a considerable overlap, they may be regarded as not relating to alternative solutions and it is appropriate to cover them by a single claim (**T56/01** r.4.3). Combining two independent claims relating to alternative solutions in one more general claim is not appropriate if it might cause extension of subject-matter or loss of priority (**T525/03** r.4.5).

When an objection under **R.43(2)** arises, the burden of proof that multiple independent claims can be maintained is on the applicant (**T56/01** r.5).

Examples of sets of claims for a computer-implemented invention complying with **R.43(2)** are given in F-IV,3.9.

R. 43(3) Any claim stating the essential features of an invention may be followed by one or more claims concerning particular embodiments of that invention.

R. 43(4) Any claim which includes all the features of any other claim (dependent claim) shall contain, if possible at the beginning, a reference to the other claim and then state the additional features. A dependent claim directly referring to another dependent claim shall also be admissible. All dependent claims referring back to a single previous claim, and all dependent claims referring back to several previous claims, shall be grouped together to the extent and in the most appropriate way possible.

1 **Independent and dependent claims**

According to **R.43(4)** a claim is dependent if it includes all the features of any other claim. Some special cases are given below.

A claim without a reference to another claim is only independent if it does not include all features of another claim. In the case where Claim 1 relates to a device and Claim 2 to the device including feature A without a reference to Claim 1, Claim 2 is a dependent claim, because it includes all features of Claim 1. The EPO will raise a clarity objection against Claim 2 and request compliance with the requirement of **R.43(4)** that the claim contain a reference to Claim 1.

A claim referring only to another claim of a different category is independent. First example: Claim 1 for a process and Claim 2 for an apparatus for carrying out the process of claim 1. Second example: Claim 1 for a product and Claim 2 for a process for the manufacture of the product of claim 1. Third example: Claim 1 for a product and Claim 2 for a use of the product of claim 1. See also F-IV,3.8.

A claim referring to another claim but not including all features of the other claim is independent. First example: Claim 1 for a machine having part X and Claim 2 for the machine according to claim 1 modified in that X is replaced by Y. Here the reference between the claims is used for claiming alternative features (see F-IV,3.7). Second example: Claim 1 for a device including element A and Claim 2 for element B adapted for cooperation with element A of claim 1. It has to be carefully considered which elements of the claim referred to are necessarily comprised in the subject-matter of the referring claim and which are not.

If a product claim is patentable, an independent process claim for obtaining the product is also patentable, provided all features of the product result from the process (**T169/88**). Similarly, the patentability of a product claim implies the patentability of a claim for the use of the product, the use relating to the claimed features of the product (**T642/94**). In all other circumstances, the patentability of the independent claim referred to does not necessarily imply the patentability of the independent claim containing the reference. (F-IV,3.8)

2 **Form of dependent claims**
The phrases 'characterised in that' or 'characterised by' are not necessary in dependent claims, but are permissible (F-IV,3.4). Where the two-part form is used for the independent claim(s), dependent claims may relate to further details of features not only of the characterizing portion but also of the preamble (F-IV,3.6). A dependent claim may refer back to one or more independent claims, dependent claims or to a combination thereof (F-IV,3.4). A claim can include a number of alternatives which can fairly be substituted one for another, as long as the number and presentation of alternatives in a single claim does not make the claim obscure or difficult to construe (F-IV,3.7).

3 **Use of dependent claims**
Dependent claims are useful during the grant and opposition procedure, because they define embodiments that can be used as fallback positions when the scope of an independent claim must be limited, e.g. in view of prior art discovered after filing of the application. In the absence of such dependent claims, a fallback position must be obtained by adding one or more features from embodiments in the disclosure to the independent claim. The EPO may object to inclusion of isolated features from an embodiment on the ground of inadmissible intermediate generalisation (see **Art.123(2):2.3**).

The extent of protection conferred by a patent is defined mainly by the independent claims. However, dependent claims in a patent may be used to define specific embodiments covered by the independent claim, thereby avoiding any ambiguity in the meaning of features in an independent claim.

Dependent claims may also be useful in a patent as fallback position during national limitation proceedings, where national law does not allow post-grant limitation by including features from the description (see **Art.138(3)**).

It should be noted that the EPO makes an effort to reduce the number of dependent claims to decrease their workload, in spite of the usefulness of dependent claims to the applicant and proprietor. An important step was the introduction of the two-tier system for claims fees in 2009 (see **Rfees2(1)15**). See also the response of applicants in **R.45(1):2**.

R. 43(5) The number of claims shall be reasonable with regard to the nature of the invention claimed. The claims shall be numbered consecutively in Arabic numerals.

1 **Number of dependent claims**
A multiplicity of trivial claims will be objected to (F-IV,5). A large number of claims gives rise to high claims fees (**R.45(1)**).

R. 43(6) Except where absolutely necessary, claims shall not rely on references to the description or drawings in specifying the technical features of the invention. In particular, they shall not contain such expressions as "as described in part ... of the description", or "as illustrated in figure ... of the drawings".

1 **Reference to description and drawing in claim**
An omnibus claim, i.e. a claim relying on references to the description or drawings for all its technical features, is not allowed (F-IV,4.17).

The applicant must show that a reference in a claim to the description or drawings is absolutely necessary (**T150/82**). Such an exceptional case can be a reference to a peculiar shape, illustrated in a drawing, an item hard to define in words or formulae, or a chemical product defined with reference to a graph or diagram.

A method of measuring a claimed parameter need not be included in the claim if i) its length or complexity makes the claim unclear; in that case a reference to the description should be included in the claim; ii) there is one commonly known method or the skilled person knows what method to use; or iii) all methods yield the same result within measurement accuracy. (F-IV,4.18)

Examples of accepted references in claims:
- reference to a US patent for a measuring technique (EP 0 187 491 B1, Claim 7);
- reference to a diagram in a Figure of the specification for a chemical composition (EP 0 503 901 B1, Claim 3);
- reference to an international standard for a measurement procedure (EP 0 432 501 B1, Claim 1).

R. 43(7) Where the European patent application contains drawings including reference signs, the technical features specified in the claims shall preferably be followed by such reference signs relating to these features, placed in parentheses, if the intelligibility of the claim can thereby be increased. These reference signs shall not be construed as limiting the claim.

1 **Reference signs**
Reference signs are an aid to understanding the claim and may not be construed as limiting the scope of the claim; a comment to that effect in the description is acceptable (**T237/84**). A claim requiring reference signs for intelligibility may be refused, if reference signs are not inserted after a request to this effect by the EPO (**T237/84** r.6). However, the requirement to insert reference signs may be lifted if the applicant convincingly argues that if the claims without reference signs are clear in the sense of **Art.84** they must also be intelligible and emphasises that the insertion of reference signs is not obligatory but only preferable according to **R.43(7)**.

If there is a large number of embodiments, only the reference signs of the most important embodiment need be incorporated in the independent claim(s) (F-IV,4.19). Reference signs should be inserted both in the preamble and the characterising part of a two-part claim (F-IV,4.19).

R. 44 Unity of invention

Implementation of: **Art.82**
EPC 1973: **R.30**

R. 44(1) Where a group of inventions is claimed in a European patent application, the requirement of unity of invention under Article 82 shall be fulfilled only when there is a technical relationship among those inventions involving one or more of the same or corresponding special technical features. The expression "special technical features" shall mean those features which define a contribution which each of the claimed inventions considered as a whole makes over the prior art.

1 **Unity of invention**

A group of inventions is unitary according to **Art.82** if they are linked so as to form a single general inventive concept. A single general inventive concept linking a group of inventions is a technical relationship among those inventions involving one or more of the same or corresponding special technical features (consequence of **R.44(1)**, first sentence, implementing **Art.82**).

A special technical feature defines a contribution over the prior art (**R.44(1)**, second sentence); hence, it is a novel technical feature. According to case law, a special technical feature must also contribute to the inventive step (W6/90 r.3.3), briefly called 'an inventive feature'. Since an invention is defined by an independent claim, there is a single general inventive concept and, hence, unity of invention only if a group of independent claims have a technical relationship involving one or more of the same or corresponding novel and inventive technical features. Since **R.44(1)** uses the word 'only', a unity argument must refer to special technical features; a unity argument for example based on single general inventive step not mentioning special technical features therefore lacks legal basis.

There is a technical relationship between claims if:

- one or more special technical features of the claims are the same. 'Same' means identical wording (W2/95 r.6.3).
- one or more special technical features of the claims have the same technical effect (W11/99 r.2.7). Features have the same effect if, for example, they solve the same problem in a different way (W17/03 r.2.4) or if they are alternatives of a similar nature, such as in a Markush claim (W3/92 r.10).
- one or more special technical features of the claims have a causal relation. For example, a particular step in a manufacturing process causes a structural feature in the product (W6/90 r.3.2), or different uses of a product have their basis in a particular structural feature of the product.
- one or more special technical features of the claims are interrelated to achieve a certain technical effect. The interrelation may that the features complement each other or that they co-operate. For example, a specially formed prong of a plug co-operates with a slot of a socket to form an electrically conductive connection, or a special algorithm in a coding method complements an inverse algorithm in a corresponding de-coding method.

The first example in the above list relates to the 'same special technical features' in **R.44(1)**, the following examples to the 'corresponding special technical features' in **R.44(1)**. The technical relationship among the claims with corresponding special technical features may be for example a same technical effect, a causal relation or an interrelation causing a technical effect.

The assessment of unity involves determining the closest prior art for each independent claim, establishing the novel and inventive technical features of each claim and comparing whether these features define a technical relationship because they are the same or corresponding. If there is such a technical relationship among the claims, they are unitary.

2 **Independent claims in different categories**

The claims in each of the following groups are unitary according to the Guidelines (F-V,2.2.1):

- a claim for a product, a claim for a process specially adapted for the manufacture of said product, and a claim for use of said product;
- a claim for a process, a claim for an apparatus specifically designed for carrying out the process;
- a claim for a product, a claim for a process specially adapted for the manufacture of said product, and a claim for an apparatus specifically designed for carrying out the process. (F-V,2.2.1)

The expressions 'specifically adapted' and 'specifically designed' mean new and suited for carrying out the process and having a technical relation as set out in **R.44(1)**. It is not sufficient for unity of invention if the apparatus is merely able to carry out the process. The expressions do not imply that the product could not also be manufactured by a different process or that a similar process could not also be used for the manufacture of other products. (F-V,2; **W11/99** r.2.1)

The unitary character of the above groups is based on R.30 EPC 1973 in the version before its amendment in 1991. The amendment introduced the special technical features as a requirement for unity. Since the unitary character of the above groups is not based on the presence of special technical features but on a pre-1991 interpretation of single general inventive concept, its legal basis is questionable.

The Guidelines give several examples of unitary claims without indicating the special technical features of these claims, for example Markush claims (F-V,2.2.2.2) and intermediate and final product claims (F-V,2.2.2.4). Since the unity reasoning for these examples is not based on R.44(1), it lacks proper legal basis. The same applies to case law on unity not discussing the special technical features; such case law should be regarded as overruled.

R. 44(2) The determination whether a group of inventions is so linked as to form a single general inventive concept shall be made without regard to whether the inventions are claimed in separate claims or as alternatives within a single claim.

R. 45 Claims incurring fees

Implementation of: **Art.78(2)**
EPC 1973: **R.31**

1 **General**

The purpose of requiring payment of claims fees (**R.45(1)**) is not primarily fiscal but to keep the number of claims within reasonable limits (cf. **R.43(5)**), particularly for the purposes of the European search (**J9/84**; **J6/12** r.10).

R. 45(1) Any European patent application comprising more than fifteen claims shall, in respect of the sixteenth and each subsequent claim, incur payment of claims fees as laid down in the Rules relating to Fees.

Amended by decision of the Administrative Council of 06.03.2008 and entered into force on 01.04.2008 (OJ 2008, 124).

1 **Amount due**

The amount of the claims fee is fixed in **Rfees2(1)15**.

Claims fees are due for 'any' European patent application, i.e. for Euro-direct applications, divisional applications, new applications (**Art.61**) and Euro-PCT applications. The claims fee must be paid for each claim numbered 16 and up. The fees are also due for claims of a divisional application, even if they have already been paid for the corresponding claims of the parent application (A-IV,1.4.2). When there are several sets of claims, the fees are payable only for the set with the highest number of claims (A-III,9).

If an application contains what can clearly be seen to be claims, especially in a section identified as such, then these claims contain the matter for which the applicant wants protection. All other matter, even in the form of a list of numbered clauses, is not regarded as claims for the purpose of determining the amount of claims fees under **R.45** (**J15/88**). However, if the applicant indicates an intention to regard the clauses as claims, they will be regarded as claims for the purpose of **R.45** (**J5/87**).

2 **Reduction of claims fees**

The increases in claims fees in 2008 and 2009 has resulted in a reduction of the number of claims in applications filed with the EPO. However, dependent claims form necessary fallback positions both during and after the grant procedure (see **R.43(4):3**).

Due to the high claims fees, applicants tend to obtain simultaneously a reduction in claims fees and maintenance of fallback positions by including alternatives in a single claim, by adding features for dependent claims as preferred options in a main claim (using expressions as 'preferably', 'for example'; see **Art.84:1.4**), and by adding claim-like passages to the description of the figures from which claims may be derived if required. These passages must be deleted prior to grant (F-IV,4.4, not in GL2017) or rewritten to remove the claim-like character. It is also possible to file multiple applications each with a smaller number of claims; however, the total cost of these applications over their term should be balanced with the reduction in claims fees. Alternatively, the EPO may be bypassed by filing national applications.

Note that when the number of claims in a Euro-PCT application is reduced in response to the **R.161** invitation, i.e. after entry into the European regional phase, excess claims fees paid on national entry will be refunded (**R.162(3)**).

R. 45(2) The claims fees shall be paid within one month of filing the first set of claims. If the claims fees have not been paid in due time, they may still be paid within one month of a communication concerning the failure to observe the time limit.

1 **Period**

The fees must be paid within one month of filing the first set of claims (**R.45(2)**). When the claims are filed together with the application documents, the claims fees have to be paid within the same period as the filing and search fee under **Art.78(2)**. This applies also to divisional applications and new applications. See **R.162** for Euro-PCT applications.

2 **Insufficient payment**

In the event that the amount of claims fees paid is insufficient to cover all claims numbered 16 and up and no indication has been given for which of these claims the amount must be used, then the applicant will be invited to indicate this (**Rfees6(2)**). Since only the claims numbered 1 to 15 as filed are exempt from claims fee, it is not possible to transfer the fee exemption to a claim numbered 16 or higher (**J9/84** r.2). If an application (particularly from the USA) contains a series of 'clauses' resembling claims, but not referred to as such, then no claims fees need be paid for them, and the subject-matter in them is not regarded as abandoned if no claims fees are paid for the clauses (**T490/90, J15/88**). If the claims fees for an application comprising several sets of claims are not paid, the claims numbered 16 and higher of each set are deemed to be abandoned under **R.45(3)**.

3 **Sanction on non-payment and remedy**

If the claims fees have not been paid within one month of filing the first set of claims, the EPO will send the applicant a communication pointing out the failure and invite him to pay the claims fees without surcharge within a grace period of one month from notification of the communication (**R.45(2)**). If not paid within the one month grace period, the claims concerned are being deemed abandoned (**R.45(3)**).

The applicant is notified of this loss of rights (**R.112(1)**). There are two remedies: if applicable, prove that the claims fees were paid in time (**R.112(2)**), or, within two months from notification of the loss of rights request further processing under **Art.121** and **R.135**, pay the further processing fee (equal to 50% of the missing claims fees) and pay the missing claims fees. (A-III,16.2)

R. 45(3) If a claims fee is not paid in due time, the claim concerned shall be deemed to be abandoned.

1 **Loss of rights**

Deemed abandonment of claims need not result in a loss of rights if their subject-matter can be found in the description and drawings. The abandoned claims can then be re-introduced in an amendment under **Art.123(1)**, as they do not extend the subject-matter of the application as filed (A-III,9). However, beware of intermediate generalisation (see **Art.123(2):2.3**).

Abandoned claims will not be searched (B-III,3.4) and amendments may not relate to unsearched subject-matter (**R.137(5)**). Any claims fees for the re-introduced claims will be levied under **R.71(4)** just before the grant of the patent.

Forced abandonment of subject-matter, in reliance on only one Implementing Regulation (**R.45(3)**) appears to be rather in conflict with principles of higher law. The right expressed in **Art.123(2)** to derive subject-matter for claims from any part of the description prevails over the forced abandonment. (**J15/88** r.7)

Abandonment of claims can only cause a substantive loss of subject-matter if the subject-matter of the claims was contained only in the claims and not also in the description or drawings (**J15/88** r.6; A-III,9).

See **Art.93(1):1** for the effect of abandonment on publication of the application.

R. 46 Form of the drawings

Implementation of: **Art.78(1)(d)**
EPC 1973: **R.32**

1 **Examination of drawings**

The Receiving Section checks the presence of drawings under **Art.90(1)** and **R.55** and will invite the applicant to provide missing drawings under **R.56**. The drawings will be examined under **Art.90(3)** on compliance with the formal requirements of **R.46** and the applicant will be invited to correct deficiencies in accordance with **Art.90(4)** and **R.58**.

2 **Photographs**

The EPC makes no express provision for photographs in applications; they are nevertheless allowed where it is impossible to present in a drawing what is to be shown and provided that they are in black and white, directly reproducible and fulfil the applicable requirements for drawings (e.g. paper size, margins, etc.). Colour photographs are acceptable but will be available in the file in black and white only. Information coded in colour only may be lost. (A-IX,1.2; F-II,5.3)

T1544/08 hn.3 allowed a proprietor to base an amendment on colour information in a drawing of the application as filed, even though the published application did not show the information, because **Art.123(2)** refers to the application as filed and not as published. The opponent could not know the colour information, as all documents in the public files of the EPO are black and white. The use of colour information in **T1544/08** is detrimental to public certainty if applications are not published in colour: a published patent application may contain information only accessible to the applicant and the EPO. The only solution appears to be that the EPO scan all filed documents in full colour and delete the words 'without colourings' in **R.46(2)(a)**. The EPO and WIPO are discussing how to introduce the filing of colour drawings (situation 2018).

R. 46(1) On sheets containing drawings, the usable surface area shall not exceed 26.2 cm x 17 cm. The usable or used surface shall not be surrounded by frames. The minimum margins shall be as follows:

top 2.5 cm
left side 2.5 cm
left side 2.5 cm
left side 2.5 cm

R. 46(2) Drawings shall be executed as follows:

(a) **Drawings shall be executed without colourings in durable, black, sufficiently dense and dark, uniformly thick and well-defined lines and strokes.**
(b) **Cross-sections shall be indicated by hatching which should not impede the clear reading of the reference signs and leading lines.**
(c) **The scale of the drawings and their graphical execution shall be such that electronic or photographic reproduction with a linear reduction in size to two-thirds will allow all details to be distinguished without difficulty. If, exceptionally, the scale is given on a drawing, it shall be represented graphically.**
(d) **All numbers, letters, and reference signs appearing on the drawings shall be simple and clear. Brackets, circles or inverted commas shall not be used in association with numbers and letters.**
(e) **Generally, all lines in the drawings shall be drawn with the aid of drafting instruments.**
(f) **Elements of the same figure shall be proportional to one another, unless a difference in proportion is indispensable for the clarity of the figure.**
(g) **The height of the numbers and letters shall not be less than 0.32 cm. For the lettering of drawings, the Latin and, where customary, the Greek alphabets shall be used.**

(h) **The same sheet of drawings may contain several figures. Where figures drawn on two or more sheets are intended to form a single figure, the figures on the several sheets shall be so arranged that the whole figure can be assembled without concealing any part of the partial figures. The different figures shall be arranged without wasting space, preferably in an upright position, clearly separated from one another. Where the figures are not arranged in an upright position, they shall be presented sideways with the top of the figures at the left side of the sheet. The different figures shall be numbered consecutively in Arabic numerals, independently of the numbering of the sheets.**

(i) **Reference signs not mentioned in the description and claims shall not appear in the drawings, and vice versa. Reference signs to features shall be consistent throughout the application.**

(j) **The drawings shall not contain text matter. Where indispensable to understand the drawings, a few short keywords, such as "water", "steam", "open", "closed" or "section on AB", may be included. Any such keywords shall be placed in such a way that, if required, they can be replaced by their translations without interfering with any lines of the drawings.**

1 **Form of drawings**

No indications like 'actual size' are permitted, as this does not allow reduction of the drawing (A-IX,7.4).

An apostrophe (') after a number is allowed under **R.46(2)(d)** (A-IX,7.5).

If an application is amended by taking out references to features in the drawings, the corresponding reference signs must be removed from the drawings. If the removal is tedious, the examiner should not be too strict in requiring this removal. The reverse situation, where reference signs in the description do not appear in the drawings, should never occur. A key to the reference signs is recommended for complex subject-matter incorporating a large number of drawings (A-IX,7.5.4).

If an invention has many variants with features with basically the same function, such a feature may be numbered with a reference sign common to the features, preceded by the number of the figure or the variant, e.g. 115, 215, 315, etc. (A-X,7.5.5).

Symbols and keywords in flow sheets and functional diagrams are often regarded as indispensable for understanding the drawing and are therefore allowed under **R.46(2)(j)** (A-IX,8; F-II,5.1). The PCT does not make use of this possibility because translations of text in the drawings have to be made. One can still use symbols like those for a diode or a low-pass filter to indicate the function of a block.

R. 46(3) Flow sheets and diagrams shall be deemed to be drawings.

R. 47 Form and content of the abstract

Implementation of: **Art.78(1)(e)** and **85**
EPC 1973: **R.33**

1 **Examination of the abstract**

The Receiving Section checks for obvious errors in the abstract under **Art.90(3)** and **R.57(d)** (A-III,10.2). The search division checks compliance of the abstract with the requirements of **R.47** under **Art.92** and **R.66** (F-II,2.2).

R. 47(1) The abstract shall indicate the title of the invention.

R. 47(2) The abstract shall contain a concise summary of the disclosure as contained in the description, the claims and any drawings. The summary shall indicate the technical field to which the invention pertains, and shall be drafted in a manner allowing the clear understanding of the technical problem, the gist of the solution of that problem through the invention, and the principal use or uses of the invention. The abstract shall, where applicable, contain the chemical formula which, among those contained in the application, best characterises the invention. It shall not contain statements on the alleged merits or value of the invention or on speculative applications thereof.

R. 47(3) The abstract shall preferably not contain more than one hundred and fifty words.

R. 47(4) If the European patent application contains drawings, the applicant shall indicate the figure or, exceptionally, the figures of the drawings which should be published with the abstract. The European Patent Office may decide to publish one or more other figures if it considers that they better characterise the invention. Each essential feature mentioned in the abstract and illustrated by a drawing shall be followed by a reference sign placed in parentheses.

1 **Figure to accompany the abstract**
The figure must be chosen from the drawings accompanying the application; a special figure for the abstract, not contained in the drawings, is not allowed. If the application contains figures, and no figure for the abstract is indicated, the search division will decide on the figure to be used. (A-III,10.3, F-II,2.4)

R. 47(5) The abstract shall be drafted in such a manner as to constitute an efficient instrument for the purpose of searching in the particular technical field. In particular, it shall make it possible to assess whether consultation of the European patent application itself is necessary.

R. 48 Prohibited matter

Implementation of: Art.78(1)
EPC 1973: R.34

R. 48(1) The European patent application shall not contain:
- **(a) statements or other matter contrary to "ordre public" or morality;**
- **(b) statements disparaging the products or processes of any third party or the merits or validity of the applications or patents of any such party. Mere comparisons with the prior art shall not be considered disparaging per se;**
- **(c) any statement or other matter obviously irrelevant or unnecessary under the circumstances.**

1 **Prohibited matter**
A mere comparison with prior art, as required by **R.42(1)(b)**, (c), is not regarded as disparaging. Advertising with trade marks or industrial designs or models falls under paragraph (c). Excision of non-unitary subject-matter from an application may also be requested under **R.48(1)(c)**. See A-III,8 and F-II,7 for more examples of prohibited matter.

R. 48(2) If the application contains matter prohibited under paragraph 1(a), the European Patent Office may omit such matter from the application as published, indicating the place and number of words or drawings omitted.

R. 48(3) If the application contains statements referred to in paragraph 1(b), the European Patent Office may omit them from the application as published, indicating the place and number of words omitted. Upon request, the European Patent Office shall furnish a copy of the passages omitted.

R. 49 General provisions governing the presentation of the application documents

Implementation of: **Art.78(1)**
EPC 1973: **R.35**

1 **OCR readable documents**
The applicant can ease the EPO's task of converting the text of the application into digital format by making the text OCR readable (optical character recognition). The application documents should then comply with slightly stricter requirements than those of **R.49**. The main additional requirements are: unbend A4 format paper; one typeface per page; a pitch of 10 or 12 cpi (characters per inch); a minimum character height of 10 points, while upper-case characters must be at least 2.1 mm high; a line spacing of 1½; preferably no handwritten amendments (however, see **R.50(1):2**); preferably no word-breaks at the end of a line; tables and chemical or mathematical formulae must be integrated into the text and not on separate sheets at the end of the description. (OJ 1993, 59; A-VIII,2.1)

The Receiving Section examines, according to **Art.90(3)**, those requirements of **R.49** as specified in **R.57(i)**, and invites the applicant to remove any deficiencies (**Art.90(4)** and **R.58**).

R. 49(1) Any translation filed under Article 14, paragraph 2, or Rule 40, paragraph 3, shall be deemed to be a document making up the European patent application.

Art.14(2) Application filed in non-EPO language
R.40(3) Previously filed application in a non-EPO language

R. 49(2) The documents making up the application shall be presented so as to allow electronic and direct reproduction, in particular by scanning, photography, electrostatic processes, photo offset and microfilming, in an unlimited number of copies. All sheets shall be free from cracks, creases and folds. Only one side of the sheet shall be used.

1 **Number of copies to be filed**
The number of copies to be filed is specified in the Guidelines. Documents relating to more than one application or patent, e.g. a general authorisation, or having to be communicated to more than one party, only need to be filed in one copy. However, letters accompanying documents must be filed in one copy for each file to which the document they accompany relates. (A-VIII,2.4)

For example, where two different applications share a common priority claim, the applicant only needs to file one copy of the priority document, but this must be accompanied by two different, signed letters, one for each application. (A-VIII,2.4)

R. 49(3) The documents making up the application shall be on A4 paper (29.7 cm x 21 cm) which shall be pliable, strong, white, smooth, matt and durable. Subject to paragraph 9 and Rule 46, paragraph 2(h), each sheet shall be used with its short sides at the top and bottom (upright position).

Amended by decision of the Administrative Council of 21.10.2008, which entered into force on 01.04.2009. The amendment replaced the erroneous reference '10' by '9'. (OJ 2008, 513)
R.46(2)(h) Drawing with figure presented in landscape

1 **Paper quality**
Pliability means, in practice, that the paper weight should be 80 - 120 g/m^2, admitting automatic feed through a copying machine. This is particularly relevant for drawings, which were often filed on stiff cards. (OJ 1994,74; A-IX,3)

The EPO recommends to use the paper quality prescribed in **R.49(3)** for application documents also for notices of opposition (D-III,3.1)

R. 49(4) Each of the documents making up the application (request, description, claims, drawings and abstract) shall commence on a new sheet. The sheets shall be connected in such a way that they can easily be turned over, separated and joined together again.

R. 49(5) Subject to Rule 46, paragraph 1, the minimum margins shall be as follows:
top: 2 cm
left side: 2.5 cm
right side: 2 cm
bottom: 2 cm
The recommended maximum for the margins quoted above is as follows:
top: 4 cm
left side: 4 cm
right side: 3 cm
bottom: 3 cm

R.46(1) Margins for sheets containing drawings

1 **Margins of sheets**
The provision specifies the minimum margins on sheets of the application documents. However, sheets of the application documents containing drawings must have minimum margins as set in **R.46(1)**.

Margins need not be completely blank, as required in the deleted **R.35(7)** EPC 1973; in practice text in margins, e.g. reference numbers or imprints by the fax machine, is not objected to.

R. 49(6) All the sheets contained in the application shall be numbered in consecutive Arabic numerals. These shall be centred at the top of the sheet, but not placed in the top margin.

1 **Numbering of pages**
There shall, preferably, be three series of page numbers: one for the request, one for the description with the claims and the abstract, and one for the drawings. The last two series may be combined into one. (A-IX,4.2)

R. 49(7) The lines of each sheet of the description and of the claims shall preferably be numbered in sets of five, the numbers appearing on the left side, to the right of the margin.

1 **Numbering of text elements**
In February 1999 the EPO introduced paragraph numbering in the text of the description in published applications and specifications, instead of page and line numbering. The change applies to the description only, as the patent claims are already numbered. (OJ 1998, 598)

R. 49(8) The request for grant of a European patent, the description, the claims and the abstract shall be typed or printed. Only graphic symbols and characters and chemical or mathematical formulae may, if necessary, be drawn or written by hand. The typing shall be 1½ spaced. All text matter shall be in characters, the capital letters of which are not less than 0.21 cm high, and shall be in a dark, indelible colour.

1 **Font size**
The minimum height of capital letters must be 0.21 cm according to **R.49(8)**. This corresponds to 8.5 point Times New Roman and 9.0 point Arial, two common fonts available in Windows computer operating systems. Note that conversion from text processor format to pdf may involve scaling of the text.

The text content of a page approximately doubles when going from 12.0 point Times New Roman, often used for filing patent applications, to 8.5 point font size. This should be born in mind when filing an application exceeding 35 pages in view of the page fee (see **Rfees2(1):4.2.1**)

See **R.50(1)** for the consequences of **R.49(8)** for handwritten amendments.

R. 49(9) The request for grant of a European patent, the description, the claims and the abstract shall not contain drawings. The description, claims and abstract may contain chemical or mathematical formulae. The description and abstract may contain tables. The claims may contain tables only if their subject-matter makes the use of tables desirable. Tables and chemical or mathematical formulae may be placed sideways on the sheet if they cannot be presented satisfactorily in an upright position. Tables or chemical or mathematical formulae presented sideways shall be placed so that the tops of the tables or formulae are at the left-hand side of the sheet.

1 **Formulas, tables and listings**
Formulae and tables may be grouped on a separate sheet (A-IX,1.1), each provided with a reference sign (A-IX,11.1). However, they are preferably integrated into the text (A-IX,11.1).

Computer program listings cannot be used as the sole disclosure. A description, preferably accompanied by flow diagrams, is required. (F-II,4.12)

R. 49(10) Values shall be expressed in units conforming to international standards, wherever appropriate in terms of the metric system using SI units. Any data not meeting this requirement shall also be expressed in units conforming to international standards. Only the technical terms, formulae, signs and symbols generally accepted in the field in question shall be used.

Amended by decision of the Administrative Council of 21.10.2008, which entered into force on 01.04.2009. The amendment deleted the superfluous 'conventions'. (OJ 2008, 513)

1 **Values and technical terms**
Since **R.57(i)** does not refer to **R.49(10)** and (11), compliance with these requirements is not examined by the Receiving Section but by the examining division (A-III,3.2).

An overview of the SI units can be found in F-II Annex 2.

R. 49(11) The terminology and the signs shall be consistent throughout the European patent application.

R. 49(12) Each sheet shall be reasonably free from erasures and shall be free from alterations. Non-compliance with this rule may be authorised if the authenticity of the content is not impugned and the requirements for good reproduction are not thereby jeopardised.

R. 50 Documents filed subsequently

EPC 1973: **R.36**

1 **General**
Documents filed subsequent to the filing of the patent application, also called 'further documents', may be filed in a form and by a method permitted by **R.2(1)**, relying on decisions of the President for details.

An applicant can file further documents in a single copy, even when the EPO must communicate such documents to several persons, because the EPO keeps the files electronically (Spec. Ed. 5 of OJ 2007).

2 **Filing office**
All further documents should normally be filed with a filing office of the EPO as mentioned in **R.35(1)**. There is no legal basis for this rule, with exception for two specific cases. Further documents transmitted by fax must be filed with the filing offices of the EPO (Spec. Ed. 3 of OJ 2007, 7 Art.3). The second case is where the application has been filed with a national authority under **Art.75(1)(b)**; further documents may be forwarded to that authority until the applicant receives the EPO communication of **R.35(4)**, after which all further documents must be forwarded to an EPO filing office (A-II,3.2). Documents nevertheless sent to a national authority may be forwarded by

the authority as a courtesy service to the EPO; the EPO will give them a date equal to the date it has received the documents.

To expedite the procedure documents relating to appeal proceedings should preferably be sent directly to Munich (OJ 2005, 44 §2).

3 **Form of documents**

The only physical requirements for documents filed directly or by post are that they must be typewritten or printed and have 2.5 cm left margin (**R.50(2)**). However, replacement pages of the patent application or patent must comply with the requirements for application documents (**R.50(1)**, **R.86**). The documents may in general be filed in a single copy (see **R.49(2):1** for an exception). The documents must be signed in accordance with **R.50(3)** and the language of the documents must comply with the provisions of **R.3**.

The EPC has no sanction for non-compliance with the layout requirements of **R.50(2)**. See **R.50(3)** for the sanction on failure to sign documents. A document filed in a language not admissible by the EPO or duly translated will be deemed not to have been filed (**Art.14(4)**).

4 **Acknowledgment of receipt**

See **R.2(1):2** for acknowledgment of receipt of further documents.

R. 50(1) Rules 42, 43 and 46 to 49 shall apply to documents replacing documents making up the European patent application. Rule 49, paragraphs 2 to 12, shall also apply to the translation of the claims referred to in Rule 71.

R.42 Contents of the description
R.43 Form and content of claims
R.46 Form of the drawings
R.47 Form and content of the abstract
R.48 Prohibited matter
R.49 General provisions governing the presentation of the application documents
R.71 Examination procedure

1 **Replacements for application documents**

According to **R.50(1)**, documents filed after filing of the patent application and replacing documents of the patent application or patent or part of it are bound by the same formal requirements for content and form as the patent application itself. Hence, further documents replacing documents making up the application and relating to the description, claims and abstract must present the content as in the application documents (**R.42, 43, 47**). The replacement documents may not contain prohibited matter (**R.48**) and must have the same form as the application documents (**R.46, 47, 49**).

Replacement document filed during opposition and appeal must comply with the same requirements (**R.86** and **R.100(1)**).

2 **Handwritten amendments**

Since **R.49(8)** requires the description, claims and abstract to be typed or printed, any replacement document must also be typed or printed according to **R.50(1)**. As permitted under **R.49(8)**, graphic symbols and characters and chemical and mathematical formulae may in exceptional cases be drawn or written by hand; however, it is recommended to type or print them (A-IX,11.1). The EPO enforces this rule strictly as of 01.01.2014. Hence, any amendment of the description or claims must be typed or printed, handwritten amendments are deficiencies that must be corrected (A-III,3.2). (Not. EPO OJ 2013, 603)

Amendments of an application should be filed with the EPO both as clean, typed replacement pages and as replacement pages with the amendments clearly marked. The amendments are preferably marked with a text editor but they may be in handwritten form (H-III,2.2). Filing the amendments online in character-coded format will give entitlement to a reduced fee for grant once the EPO applies amended **Rfees2(1)7** (OJ 2018 A28).

Handwritten amendments will normally be accepted during oral proceedings as a basis for discussion. A final decision granting a patent may be taken only on the basis of a typed or printed document. The EPO provides computers, pdf printers, copiers and internet access for preparing typed documents during oral proceedings. If a typed or printed document is not available during oral proceedings, the EPO will continue in writing and request to file a compliant document within two months. Where handwritten amendments are filed in examination proceedings, the EPO will request to submit a typed or printed version if there is agreed patentable subject-matter. (E-III,8.7.2)

The opposition divisions and boards of appeal do not apply **R.49(8)** to documents filed during oral proceedings. After the oral proceedings the EPO will, where necessary, request the applicant or proprietor to submit documents complying with **R.49(8)** for preparing the 'Druckexemplar'. (**R.82(2)**:4; **T1635/10** r.5; **T37/12** r.3.4-3.7; OJ 2016 A22).

3 **Form of translations**

The translation of the claims in the two official EPO languages other than the language of the proceedings to be filed in response to the **R.71(3)** communication must be presented as set out in **R.49**. Filing the translation online in character-coded format will give entitlement to a reduced fee for grant once the EPO applies amended **Rfees2(1)7** (OJ 2018 A28).

The translation under **Art.14(2)** or **R.40(3)** of a patent application is considered to be included in the 'documents making up the European patent application' (**R.49(1)**). Hence, the translation must also meet the requirements of **R.42, 43** and **46** to **49**.

R. 50(2) All documents other than those making up the application shall generally be typewritten or printed. There shall be a margin of about 2.5 cm on the left-hand side of each page.

R. 50(3) Documents filed after filing the application shall be signed, with the exception of annexed documents. If a document has not been signed, the European Patent Office shall invite the party concerned to do so within a time limit to be specified. If signed in due time, the document shall retain its original date of receipt; otherwise it shall be deemed not to have been filed.

1 **Signature on further documents**

Further documents filed with the EPO must be signed by a person authorised to act before the EPO, such as the applicant or proprietor who is not obliged to be represented under **Art.133(2)** or his representative (A-VIII,3.1). The name and position of that person must be clear from the signature. The EPO does not check entitlement of a person to sign on behalf of a legal person, except where it has reason to doubt the authorisation of the person (A-VIII,3.3). The reason to require a signature is to show clearly that the content of a document is authorised by the person who has filed it.

In general, an applicant obliged to be represented may only sign the application documents when filing a patent application (**Art.133(2)**) but not further documents.

If there are several applicants, further documents need only be signed by the applicant or a representative who has been appointed as common representative in the Request for Grant form (**R.41(3)**), in a notice of opposition or in a separate notice of appointment, or who has been deemed to be a common representative by force of **R.151(1)**. (A-VIII,3.4)

All further documents except annexes must be signed (**R.50(3)**). As lex specialis, the following annexes must be signed: assignment of an application (**Art.72**), designation of inventor (**R.19(1)**) and authorisation (**R.152(1)**).

Documents such as priority documents or translations should bear a note addressed to the EPO or be accompanied by a separate letter; the note or letter must be signed by a person authorized to act before the EPO. This also applies to a designation of inventor signed by an applicant obliged to be represented (A-VIII,3.1).

Since the second sentence of **R.50(3)** refers to 'the party', the provision relates to documents submitted by parties; hence, an observation filed by a third party under **Art.115** need not be signed (**T1336/09**, r.2.2; however, see **T146/07**, r.3).

The signature must comply with the requirements of **R.2(2)**.

2 **Missing signature**

R.50(3) provides a remedy only for a missing signature. The signature of an unauthorised person, such as the secretary of an authorised representative, is regarded as a missing signature; this applies both to a handwritten signature (**T665/89** r.1.4; A-VIII,3.1) and to an electronic signature (**T1427/09** r.8). Similarly, any signature not complying with **R.2(2)** should probably be regarded as a missing signature, which can be corrected under **R.50(3)**.

The EPO informs a party of a missing signature on a further document and invites him to supply a duly signed document within a period set by the EPO (**R.50(3)**). The period is fixed at two months as a rule, i.e. the same period as for correcting minor deficiencies (D-IV,1.2.1(ii) and E-VIII,1.2(i)). If signed in due time, the document retains its original date of receipt; otherwise it will be deemed not to have been filed (**R.50(3)**).

An applicant may remedy failure to meet the two-month period with further processing according to **Art.121** and **R.135**.

A missing signature on a patent application is not dealt with under **R.50(3)** but under **Art.90(3)**, **R.57(b)**, **R.41(2)(h)** and **Art.90(5)** (see **R.57(b):3**).

Chapter III *Renewal fees*

R. 51 Payment of renewal fees

Implementation of: **Art.86**
EPC 1973: **R.37**

1 **General**
Renewal fees are fees that must be paid annually for a pending application or patent. In contrast with most other fees, the EPO does not provide a service for renewal fees.

Renewal fees have a dual purpose. The first one is budgetary, making up for fees that do not cover the cost of the EPO, such as the search and examination fee and the opposition and appeal fee. The second purpose is to provide an incentive for the applicant or proprietor to withdraw an application or patent in which he is no longer interested. Unnecessary restrictions to free trade should be removed.

R. 51(1) A renewal fee for the European patent application in respect of the coming year shall be due on the last day of the month containing the anniversary of the date of filing of the European patent application. The renewal fee in respect of the third year may not be validly paid more than six months before it falls due. All other renewal fees may not be validly paid more than three months before they fall due.

Amended by decision of the Administrative Council of 13.12.2017, which entered into force on 01.04.2018 (OJ 2018 A2).

1 **Payment of renewal fee**
A renewal fee of a European patent application must be paid on a due date (**R.51(1)**). Normally, a fee becomes due on the due date and may be paid within a fixed period following the due date. In contrast, the due date of a renewal fee is both the day on which a renewal fee becomes due and the last day on which it can be paid without an additional fee; it can be regarded as a period of zero days or no period at all. The EPC has provided flexibility for applicants by allowing valid payment of a renewal fee in a period before the due date.

The law distinguishes between a pre-payment period for the renewal fee in respect of the third year, i.e. the first renewal fee to be paid for a patent application, and for renewal fees in respect of all subsequent years. The EPO prefers a short pre-payment period of three months to reduce the opportunity for applicants to pay the old fee amount in the case of a fee increase (see OJ 1987, 4). The law provides, exceptionally, a longer pre-payment period for the first renewal fee to simplify payment for a Euro-PCT application when entering into the European phase, by allowing payment of all fees necessary, including the first renewal fee, in one step on entry. A three-month pre-payment period would make it necessary to pay the first renewal fee in a second step if this period has not yet started when entering the European phase. That occurs if the Euro-PCT application claims priority and the last day of the calendar month containing the filing date lies more than nine months after the priority date. The beneficial longer pre-payment period is not only available for Euro-PCT applications but also for Euro-direct applications because of the principle of equal treatment (**Art.153(2)**).

Hence, the renewal fee in respect of the third year may be paid validly up to six months before the due date (**R.51(1)**, second sentence) and the renewal fee in respect of the fourth and following years may be paid validly up to three months before the due date (**R.51(1)**, third sentence). The Guidelines calculate the first day of the negative pre-payment period 'de ultimo ad ultimo' in the sense of **J4/91**, i.e. from the last day of the month to the last day of the month. For example for the three-month pre-payment period, the first date for valid payment is 31 August if the due date is 30 November; the first date for valid payment is 28 February 2011 where the due date is 31 May 2011. (A-X,5.2.4)

A renewal fee paid up to one month before the start of the pre-payment period will, for practical reasons, be retained by the EPO, but the payment will not take effect until the first day of the pre-payment period (A-X,5.2.4; OJ 2009, 118 §3.5).

The amount of the renewal fee is fixed in **Rfees2(1)4**.

2 **Due date for renewal fees**

A renewal fee of a European patent application in respect of the coming year is due on the last day of the month containing the anniversary of the date of filing at the beginning of that year (**R.51(1)**). Hence, the first renewal fee payable for an application is due on the last day of the month in which the second anniversary of the date of filing falls.

When the due date falls on a date the EPO cannot receive mail in the sense of **R.134(1)**, (2) or (4), the due date is not changed, because the due date is not a period which can be extended. Instead, the last day for valid payment is deferred to the first working day. (**J4/91** r.3.2)

The calculation of the due date may be summarised mathematically as follows. When an application is filed in month m of the year y, then the renewal fee in respect of the kth year ($k \geqslant 3$) is due on the last day of month m of the year (y+k-1), possibly with deferred payment on account of **R.134**. Note in this respect that the last day of December and the next day are holidays.

3 **Deviant due date**

Two cases can be distinguished, where the due date for the renewal fee is not the last day of a month defined in **R.51(1)**; in these cases the due date has a deviating legal basis.

The first case is where the due date moves forward to a date where a specific event takes place. A first example of such an event is the filing of a divisional application, where the renewal fees for the divisional application accrued before the date on which it is filed fall due on that date (**R.51(3)**). A second example is the date of notification of a decision granting a request for re-establishment, where a renewal fee that would have fallen due between the loss of rights and said date falls due on that date (**R.51(4)**). A third example is the date of notification of the decision granting a petition for review and re-opening proceedings, where a renewal fee that would have fallen due between the decision of the board of appeal subject to the petition and said date falls due on that date (**R.51(5)(a)**). A fourth example is the resumption of proceedings after an interruption under **R.142**, e.g. due to death of the applicant, where a renewal fee that would have fallen due during the interruption falls due on the date of resumption (**R.142(4)**).

In the first case the due date does not shift to the first working day if it falls on a non-working day, because the due date is not the expiry of a period (**J4/91** r.3.2).

The second case is where the due date is deferred to the expiry of a period. This happens when the renewal fee for a Euro-PCT application would have fallen due under **R.51(1)** earlier than the expiry of the 31-month period of **R.159(1)**, in which case the due date is deferred to the expiry of the 31-month period (**R.159(1)(g)**).

In the second case the due date shifts to the first working day if it falls on a non-working day, together with the expiry of the 31-month period.

Note, that there is no deviant due date for a new application filed under **Art.61(1)(b)**, because the new application is in effect a continuation of the usurped original application and takes over the obligation to pay renewal fees (see **R.51(6)**).

R. 51(2) If a renewal fee is not paid on the due date under paragraph 1, the fee may still be paid within six months of the said date, provided that an additional fee is also paid within that period. The legal consequence laid down in Article 86, paragraph 1, shall ensue upon expiry of the six-month period.

Amended by decision of the Administrative Council of 14.12.2016, which entered into force on 01.01.2017 (OJ 2016 A102, A103). The amendment defines the date the sanction on non-payment takes effect, without changing the practice of the office. It removes the discrepancy noted in **T1402/13** between the previous text of the law and the practice of the office.
Art.86(1) Legal consequence of not paying renewal fee

1 **Six-month additional period**

R.51(2), first sentence, provides for a six-month remedial period for payment of a renewal fee with additional fee if the renewal fee has not been paid on or before the due date.

The six-month period starts on the due date, i.e. the last day of the month referred to in **R.51(1)**, even if the EPO cannot receive mail on that date because of holidays or other disruptions as set out in **R.134(1)**, (2), and (4). These circumstances do not postpone the due date for payment of renewal fees. Hence, the six-month period is not an aggregate period. (**J4/91** hn.II)

The six-month period expires on the last day of the sixth month after the due date (following **R.51(1)**), and not on the day of that month corresponding in number to the due date (according to **R.131(4)**). **R.51(1)** and **R.51(2)** are regarded as a lex specialis of **R.131(4)**. Thus, the calculation must be made from the last day of the month to the last day of the month (de ultimo ad ultimo). If the due date is 28 February, then the end of the 6-month period is 31 August, and not 28 August. (**J4/91** hn.I, de ultimo ad ultimo)

R.134 may be applied to the expiry of the six-month period, extending the period of six months to the first date on which the EPO can again receive mail (**J4/91** r.3.2, last paragraph).

Notification of non-payment of a renewal fee, sanction and remedies are set out in **Art.86(1):3 - 5**.

First example:

15 December	filing date
31 December	due date for renewal fee
2 January	last day for payment without additional fee (**R.134(1)**);
30 June	expiry of 6-month period for payment with additional fee; if this is a Sunday, then under **R.134(1)**
1 July	last day for payment with additional fee.

Second example:

15 February	filing date
28/29 February	due date for renewal fee
31 August	expiry of 6-month period for payment with additional fee; if this is a Saturday, then under **R.134(1)**
2 September	last day for payment with additional fee.

2 **Six-month period for deviant due date**

Where the due date has moved to a date on which a specific event has taken place, i.e. the first case in **R.51(1):3**, the start of the six-month period is the due date (see e.g. **R.51(4)(b)**). The due date does not shift to the first working day if it falls on a non-working day (**J4/91** r.3.2). The expiry of the six-month period is not calculated 'de ultimo ad ultimo', but as a normal period using **R.131(4)** for the calculation of duration of a period expressed in months. The six-month period may be extended on account of **R.134**. For the first three examples of the first case there is a four-month period running parallel to the six-month period in which the renewal fee can be paid without surcharge. See **R.51(3):3** and **R.159(1):8** for examples.

Note that the due dates of renewal fees falling due after the date on which the divisional was filed are not deviant due dates and the 'de ultimo ad ultimo' calculation is used for the six-month period.

Where the due date has moved to the expiry of a period, i.e. the second case in **R.51(1):3**, the six-month period is calculated from the expiry of the period, possibly extended under **R.134**. The expiry of the six-month period is not calculated 'de ultimo ad ultimo', but as a normal period using **R.131(4)**. The six-month period may be extended on account of **R.134**, making the six-month period an aggregate period (**R.131(2):3**). See **R.159(1):8.3** for an example.

3 **Start of the six-month period**

After the amendment of **R.51(2)** on 01.01.2017, the provision explicitly defines the period for payment with additional fee as six months of the due date stated in **R.51(1)**, i.e. six months of the last day of the month containing the anniversary of the date of filing of the European patent application. The purpose of this amendment was to clarify that a renewal fee can still be paid with additional fee if the renewal fee has not been paid on the due date under **R.51(1)** (CA/99/16 §32).

Whereas the amendment is appropriate for the normal due dates defined in **R.51(1)**, it does not take into account the deviant due dates in **R.51(1):3**. Under the previous provision the additional period for a deviant due date was six months from the deviant due date and not from the normal due date as stipulated by the amended **R.51(2)**.

The Guidelines apply the previous practice and determine the six-month period for deviant due dates from the deviant due date. Hence, the determination of these six-month periods does not take the amended **R.51(2)** into account and, as a consequence, does not have a legal basis anymore. The six-month periods for deviant due dates in this book are based on the Guidelines.

R. 51(3) Renewal fees already due in respect of an earlier application at the date on which a divisional application is filed shall also be paid for the divisional application and shall be due on its filing. These fees and any renewal fee due within four months of filing the divisional application may be paid within that period without an additional fee. Paragraph 2 shall apply.

1 **Renewal fees for divisional application**

A divisional application is deemed filed on the filing date of the parent application (**Art.76(1)**). Therefore, the renewal fees for the divisional application are due in respect of the third year and subsequent years calculated from the filing date of the parent application (A-IV,1.4.3). The renewal fees accrued before the filing of the divisional application are due on the filing of the divisional application (**R.51(3)**, first sentence). They may be paid without an additional fee within four months from the filing of the divisional application (**R.51(3)**, second sentence). If the accrued renewal fees are not paid within the 4-month period, they may be validly paid within a 6-month period from the filing, provided the additional fee is paid (**R.51(3)**, last sentence).

Since the due date of the renewal fee of the divisional application is the date on which the divisional application is filed, it usually does not fall on the last day of the month, as it does under **R.51(1)**. Because this due date is not the expiry of a period which can be extended under **R.134** (**J4/91** r.3.2), the due date does not shift to the first working day if it falls on a non-working day. The 4- and 6-month periods of **R.51(3)** run from the due date, irrespective of whether or not the due date is a non-working day. If the last day of the period is a non-working day, the extension under **R.134** may be applied. (**J4/91** r.3.2, last paragraph)

Re-establishment in the 4- and 6-month period of **R.51(3)** is possible and must be requested within two months from removal of the cause of non-compliance (**R.136(1)**). The request must be filed at the latest within one year from the expiry of the 4- or 6-month period, depending on whether re-establishment is requested in the 4- or 6-month period (**R.136(1)**; the view on the start of the one-year period in A-IV,1.4.3 is probably incorrect).

2 **Period for paying renewal fee for divisional application**

R.135(2) excludes the periods under **R.51(3)** from further processing. If the four-months period provided for in **R.51(3)** for the payment of renewal fees without a surcharge expires and the renewal fees have not been paid, the remedy is already provided for in **R.51(3)**, last sentence, namely the payment with surcharge within six months as of filing the divisional application. The reference in **R.135(2)** to the whole paragraph 3 of **R.51** clarifies that also the six-months period of **R.51(3)** is excluded from further processing like the period under **R.51(2)** EPC. Similarly, also the periods under **R.51(4)** and **(5)** are excluded. (CA/PL17/06)

Failure to meet the 4- and 6-month periods can be remedied using re-establishment under **Art.122** and **R.136**.

3 **Example of renewal fee payment for divisional application**

Example of the due dates for renewal fees for a parent and divisional application:

Parent application:

03.02.2013	filing date of parent application
28.02.2015	due date renewal fee in respect of the 3rd year
02.03.2015	last day of valid payment (28.02.2015 Saturday)

31.08.2015	last day of 6-month period with additional fee for the 3rd year
29.02.2016	due date renewal fee in respect of the 4th year
31.08.2016	last day of 6-month period with additional fee for the 4th year.

Divisional application:

13.02.2016	filing date of divisional application = due date for renewal fee in respect of 3rd year
29.02.2016	due date renewal fee in respect of the 4th year
13.06.2016	last day of 4-month period without additional fee for the 3rd and 4th year
16.08.2016	last day of 6-month period with additional fee for the 3rd year (13.08.2016 Saturday, 15.08.2016 holiday)
31.08.2016	last day of 6-month period with additional fee for the 4th year
13.06.2017	expiry of the one-year period under R.136(1) for re-establishment in the 4-month period for the renewal fee in respect of the 3rd and 4th year
16.08.2017	expiry of the one-year period for re-establishment in the 6-month period for the renewal fee in respect of the 3rd year
31.08.2017	expiry of the one-year period for re-establishment in the 6-month period for the renewal fee in respect of the 4th year.

R. 51(4) If a European patent application has been refused or deemed to be withdrawn as a result of non-observance of a time limit, and if the applicant's rights are re-established under Article 122, a renewal fee

(a) which would have fallen due under paragraph 1 in the period starting on the date on which the loss of rights occurred, up to and including the date of the notification of the decision re-establishing the rights shall be due on that latter date. This fee and any renewal fee due within four months from that latter date may still be paid within four months of that latter date without an additional fee. Paragraph 2 shall apply.

(b) which, on the date on which the loss of rights has occurred, was already due but the period provided for in paragraph 2 has not yet expired, may still be paid within six months from the date of the notification of the decision re-establishing the rights, provided that the additional fee pursuant to paragraph 2 is also paid within that period.

Art.122 Re-establishment of rights

1 **Renewal fees and re-establishment of rights**

R.51(4) concerns the case where an application has been refused or deemed withdrawn as a result of failing a time limit and renewal fees have fallen due in the period starting on the date on which the loss of rights has occurred up to and including the date of notification of the decision granting the re-establishment of rights of the applicant under **Art.122**. Because of the retrospective effect of the re-establishment decision, these renewal fees will become due only on the date of notification (**R.51(4)(a)**, first sentence) and can still be paid without additional fee within a period of four months after that date (**R.51(4)(a)**, second sentence). If not paid within this period, **R.51(2)** applies, i.e. the fees can still be paid with an additional fee within a period of six months after that date (**R.51(4)(a)**, last sentence). (CA/PL17/06)

Where the loss of rights occurs during a pending six-month period, the renewal fee may still be paid within 6-months from the date of the notification of the decision. In other words, the six-month period will begin again as from the day of notification. The renewal fee can be validly paid in this deferred six-month period, provided the additional fee is paid. (**R.51(4)(b)**)

This provision is applicable only if the whole application has been refused or deemed to be withdrawn because the time limit was not observed, as expressly stated in its introductory passage. It would not be appropriate in the case of so-called partial losses of rights, since a European patent application, for which renewal fees have to be paid at regular intervals, continues in force even if, for example, a priority right or the designation of a state is lost. (CA/PL29/06 Add.1)

R. 51(5) If the Enlarged Board of Appeal reopens proceedings before the Board of Appeal under Article 112a, paragraph 5, second sentence, a renewal fee

(a) **which would have fallen due under paragraph 1 in the period starting on the date when the decision of the Board of Appeal subject to the petition for review was taken, up to and including the date of the notification of the decision of the Enlarged Board of Appeal re-opening proceedings before the Board of Appeal, shall be due on that latter date. This fee and any renewal fee due within four months from that latter date may still be paid within four months of that latter date without an additional fee. Paragraph 2 shall apply.**

(b) **which, on the day on which the decision of the Board of Appeal was taken, was already due but the period provided for in paragraph 2 has not yet expired, may still be paid within six months from the date of the notification of the decision of the Enlarged Board of Appeal re-opening proceedings before the Board of Appeal, provided that the additional fee pursuant to paragraph 2 is also paid within that period.**

Art.112a(5) Petition for review by the Enlarged Board of Appeal

1 **Renewal fee and petition for review**

A situation analogous to **R.51(4)** above exists where a petition for review under **Art.112a** is successful. Therefore **R.51(5)** likewise provides that the renewal fees, which would be due retrospectively by the effect of the decision of the Enlarged Board of Appeal, becomes due only on the date of the notification of the decision of the Enlarged Board ordering re-opening of proceedings. (CA/PL17/06)

Note that the delayed payment of a renewal fee applies only to patent applications and not to granted patents. In the latter case the proprietor is advised to continue to pay any renewal fees due to the national offices if there are no provisions for delayed payment under national law.

R. 51(6) A renewal fee shall not be payable for a new European patent application filed under Article 61, paragraph 1(b), in respect of the year in which it was filed and any preceding year.

Art.61(1)(b) New application filed by entitled applicant

1 **Renewal fees for new application**
Renewal fees for a new application under **Art.61(1)(b)** need not be paid for the year in which it was filed and any preceding year. These previous renewal fees have already been paid for by the original applicant for the earlier application, deemed withdrawn according to **R.17(1)**.

Chapter IV *Priority*

1 **General**
R.52, 53 and **54** set out the requirements to be met when claiming priority under **Art.88(1)**. **R.52** deals with the declaration of priority and its correction; **R.53** and **54** concerns the priority documents.

2 **Examination of priority claim**
The declaration of priority is checked during the examination of the application as to formal requirements under **R.57(g)**. The provisions for notification of errors and rectification are given in **R.59** and **R.52(3)**.

The validity of the priority claim and the contents of the priority documents are normally not checked, only obvious errors are communicated to the applicant (A-III,6.4, 6.6). It is checked only when prejudicial documents published within the priority term (**Art.54(2)**) or European applications filed in the priority term (**Art.54(3)**) are found during the search or examination (C-IV,7.1-7.4).

3 **Correction of priority claim**
Priority claims may be added after filing of the application and data of existing priority claims may be corrected within a restricted period as set out in **R.52(2)** and **(3)**. After this period addition and correction is possible only to a limited extent under **R.139**. To avoid adversely affecting the public interest, the correction must in general be requested before publication of the patent application. In exceptional circumstances a later filed request may be allowed.

R. 52 Declaration of priority

Implementation of: **Art.88(1)**
EPC 1973: **R.38(1), (2) + (6)**

1 **General**
R.52 governs the filing of the declaration of priority as required by **Art.88(1)** for applications that should benefit from an earlier date of filing. The contents of the declaration are set out in **R.52(1)**.

R.52(2) recommends to file the declaration on filing the patent application, but permits a later filing of a priority claim or a later addition of a further priority claim. A declaration of priority may be corrected as set out in **R.52(3)**. A correction in the sense of **R.52(3)** is a correction of particulars of an already filed priority claim; the late filing of a first priority claim or the addition of a further priority claim is not a correction under **R.52(3)** but a filing under **R.52(2)** (see Spec. Ed. 5 of OJ 2007, p.96). The possibility of addition and correction is a requirement of the PLT (Art.13(1), R.14(1) and (3)), the periods have been taken from R.26*bis*.1(a) PCT. Whereas addition and correction under PCT are dealt with in a single rule, the EPC splits them in two separate paragraphs.

R.52(4) prohibits adding and correcting priority claims after requesting early publication of the application and **R.52(5)** requires inclusion of the declaration of priority in the published patent application and patent.

R. 52(1) The declaration of priority referred to in Article 88, paragraph 1, shall indicate the date of the previous filing, the State party to the Paris Convention or Member of the World Trade Organization in or for which it was made and the file number. In the case referred to in Article 87, paragraph 5, the first sentence shall apply mutatis mutandis.

Art.87(5) First filing in recognised state not subject to Paris and WTO
Art.88(1) Declaration of priority

1 **Formal requirements for declaration of priority**
The date and state or member in or for which the priority application was made and the file number should preferably be provided on filing and indicated in the Request for Grant form (**R.41(2)(g)**). This is not however a formal requirement.

R. 52(2) The declaration of priority shall preferably be made on filing the European patent application. It may still be made within sixteen months from the earliest priority date claimed.

1 **Period for making declaration of priority**
The declaration of priority is preferably made on filing the application. However, late filing of a declaration of priority as a first priority claim or as a further priority claim is allowed within 16 months from the earliest priority date (**R.52(2)**). For the time being, the EPO does not intend to make use of Art.13(4) PLT and prescribe that a fee be paid if priority is claimed late or a correction of the priority declaration is made.

An example of calculation of the period:

Filing date: 06.02.2018; priority claimed on filing: none; added priority date: 06.02.2017; deadline for adding priority claim: 06.06.2018.

A late filing of the declaration will delay the start of the search and may make it impossible to publish the search report together with the application. The applicant can tick a box on the Request for Grant form to indicate that he will not file a later priority declaration, thereby allowing the search division to start the search promptly (see **Art.92:6**).

Non-observance of the 16 month period may be remedied using re-establishment according to **Art.122** and **R.136**. In view of the publication of the application, the period for late declaration of priority under **R.52(2)** does not permit further processing and is excluded in **R.135(2)** (Spec. Ed. 1 of OJ 2003, p.159).

In exceptional cases an omitted priority claim may be corrected under **R.139**, first sentence (**R.139:3.1.1**).

2 **Information to applicant about priority errors**
During the examination as to formal requirements, the EPO does not inform the applicant of an omitted date and/or state in a priority claim (**R.58**), but an omitted file number will be notified (**R.59**). Only if the date of the first filing precedes the date of the application by more than one year, will the EPO invite the applicant to correct the deficiency within the period set by **R.52(3)**, or to request re-establishment in respect of meeting the 12 month priority period.

3 **Indication of date, state, and file number and provision of copy priority document**

When claiming priority, the date, state, and file number of the previous filing must be indicated within 16 months of the claimed priority date, according to **R.52(2)**. The indications must be in an official EPO language (A-III,6.5). Any errors in these data may be corrected under **R.52(3)**. See also **R.57:8.**

A copy of the priority document has to be provided within the same 16-month period (**R.53(1)**). See also **R.53(2):1.**

4 **Euro-PCT applications**

To safeguard a priority claim based on a PCT application, it suffices to indicate only one of the states designated or elected in an earlier application (**R.4.10** PCT). A correction of particulars in the priority declaration of Euro-PCT applications is possible under the same conditions as for European applications (J2/92, see **R.139:3.1**).

R. 52(3) The applicant may correct the declaration of priority within sixteen months from the earliest priority date claimed, or, where the correction would cause a change in the earliest priority date claimed, within sixteen months from the corrected earliest priority date, whichever sixteen-month period expires first, provided that such a correction may be submitted until the expiry of four months from the date of filing accorded to the European patent application.

1 **Period for correcting declaration of priority**

A declaration of priority may be corrected within sixteen months from the earliest priority date, taking into account priority dates before and after correction; the correction may always be made up to four months from the date of filing of the application (**R.52(3)**). There are no further restrictions on the ability to correct the declaration within the sixteen month / four month period, other than that this may not be done after a request for early publication of the application has been filed (**R.52(4)**). The reason for the time limit is to ensure that any correction is made before publication of the application promptly after eighteen months from the claimed earliest priority date.

Correction of errors under **R.139** may also be invoked outside this period. For corrections of the date and state of filing, this may be done before publication (see **R.139:3.1.2**); again, this ensures that any correction is made before publication of the application, and so can be communicated to the public. A wrong file number may be corrected under **R.139**, first sentence, even after publication of the application. The public interest is not adversely affected if the relevant priority document is in the file, open for public inspection. (J3/91 r.5)

The wording of **R.52(3)** is somewhat unclear; the effect of the provision is to ensure that an applicant may always request correction of a priority claim in the four months after filing the application, while in many circumstances a request for correction may be submitted after this date (A-III,6.5.2). The request for correction may be submitted by the later of:

1 four months from the date of filing the application; and
2 the earlier of
   a) 16 months from the originally-claimed earliest priority date; and
   b) 16 months from the corrected earliest priority date.

The four / sixteen month period for correcting a priority claim is excluded from further processing under **R.135(2)** for the same reason as the period under **R.52(2)**. Re-establishment according to **Art.122** and **R.136** is available.

2 **Examples**

- Filing date: 04.02.2018; priority claimed on filing: 13.03.2017; corrected priority date: 13.02.2017; deadline for requesting correction: 13.06.2018.
  16 months from the corrected priority date is 13.06.2018; this is the earlier of the two dates calculated from the priority claims. This is also later than 4 months from the filing date, and so it is the relevant deadline.
- Filing date: 13.02.2018; priority claimed on filing: 16.02.2017; corrected priority date: 16.03.2017; deadline for requesting correction: 18.06.2018.
  16 months from original priority date is 16.06.2018, which is a Saturday, so extended to 18.06.2018. This is earlier than 16 months from the corrected priority date, and later than 4 months from filing date, so it is the relevant deadline.
- Filing date: 06.02.2018; priority claimed on filing: 14.11.2017; corrected priority date: 14.12.2017; deadline for requesting correction: 14.03.2019.
  16 months from original priority date is 14.03.2019, which is the earlier of the two dates calculated from the priority claims. This is also later than 4 months from the filing date, so it is the relevant deadline.

3 **Transitional provision EPC 2000**
R.52(3) applies to applications pending at the time of entry into force of EPC 2000, i.e. on 13.12.2007. Where an application was filed before the entry into force of EPC 2000, but the time limit under **R.52(3)** has not yet expired, the applicant may request correction of the priority claim until the expiry of said time limit. (Trans. Pract. §2.5)

R. 52(4) However, a declaration of priority may not be made or corrected after a request under Article 93, paragraph 1(b), has been filed.

Art.93(1)(b) Request for early publication of application

1 **Addition or correction only before request for early publication**
This provision takes care that the priority data as published in the application is accurate.

R. 52(5) The particulars of the declaration of priority shall appear in the published European patent application and the European patent specification.

1 **Publication of priority data**
The priority data will be published with the application under **R.68(1)** and with the granted patent under **R.73(1)**.

R. 53 Priority documents

Implementation of: **Art.88(1)**
EPC 1973: **R.38(3), (4) + (5)**

R. 53(1) An applicant claiming priority shall file a copy of the previous application within sixteen months of the earliest priority date claimed. This copy and the date of filing of the previous application shall be certified as correct by the authority with which that application was filed.

1 **Period for filing copy of priority document**

The 16-month term is relatively long because it is often difficult to obtain certified copies of priority documents from national patent offices. The copy should be filed well before the publication of the application to allow the EPO to publish the priority claim. **R.54** governs the issue by the EPO of certified copies of applications for claiming priority before other patent offices.

If the priority document is not provided within 16 months after priority, the EPO will invite the applicant according to **R.59** to provide it within two months (J1/80; A-III,6.7). If the priority document is not filed in due time, priority will be lost pursuant to **Art.90(5)**. See **Art.54(3):2** for the effect of the loss of priority right on the prior right effect of the application. The only possible remedy is re-establishment (**Art.122**). Further processing is excluded under **R.135(2)**.

Note the difference between failure to file the priority document and failure to observe the 16-month time limit for the designation of the inventor (**Art.90(5)**): the legal consequence in the latter case (the application is refused) directly follows at the expiry of the 16-month time limit. The omission of the designation of the inventor is a deficiency on the date of filing or priority, and to be remedied within 16 months. In contrast, the omission of the priority document only becomes a deficiency 16 months after the date of priority, and is to be remedied in a subsequent period to be specified by the EPO. (J1/80 r.3, 4)

2 **Form of copy of priority document**

According to **R.53(1)** the copy of the priority document to be filed must be certified as an exact copy of the previous application. This is usually a paper copy issued by the authority which received the previous application (A-III,6.7). The copy must be original, i.e. it must contain the original certificate issued by the receiving authority and state the date of filing. See **R.49(2):1** for the number of copies to be filed.

A copy of the previous application may also be filed on physical media other than paper, e.g. CD-R, provided the three conditions set out in A-III,6.7 are met.

R. 53(2) The copy of the previous application shall be deemed to be duly filed if a copy of that application available to the European Patent Office is to be included in the file of the European patent application under the conditions determined by the President of the European Patent Office.

1 **Exemption from filing copy of priority document**

No copy of a priority document has to be filed by the applicant where the previous application is available to the EPO. The EPO will add a copy of the priority document to the file without request and free of charge, if that application was a European patent application, an international application filed with the EPO as receiving Office, a CN, JP or KR patent or utility model application, or a US provisional or non-provisional patent application (Dec. Pres. OJ 2012, 492 Art.1; OJ 2012, 494).

Note that the availability under **R.53(2)** is different from that under **R.40(3)** for a previously filed application in filing by reference.

The Notices of the EPO in OJ 2007, 472 and 473 give practical aspects of the automatic exchange of priority documents. When filing a US priority application, the USPTO will by default permit a participating foreign IP office to access the priority document (opt-out system).

The EPO participates as of 01.11.2018 in the WIPO digital access system (DAS) for exchanging certified priority documents. The EPO will include free of charge a priority application retrievable via DAS in the fileof EP-applications and international applications entering the EP phase (Dec. Pres. OJ 2018 A78 Art.1). To this end the applicant must indicate in the request for grant form the DAS access code of the priority application, which code was generated on filing of the priority application (Not. of EPO OJ 2018 A79 with details of the retrieval procedure). The EPO informs the applicant if retrieval of the priority document via DAS was not possible (Dec. Pres. OJ 2018 A78 Art.2). The EPO intends to extend the use of the DAS-system to PCT-applications in the international phase in 2019.

The application claiming priority may be a Euro-direct application or a Euro-PCT application entering the regional phase before the EPO as a designated or elected Office (**R.163(2)**).

The EPO will inform the applicant that it has included a copy of the priority document in the file, unless the previous application is a European patent application or an international application filed with the EPO as receiving Office. If a copy cannot be included, it shall be deemed not duly filed and the EPO will invite the applicant to file the copy under **R.53(1)**. (Dec. Pres. OJ 2012, 492 Art.2).

The EPO will in general also add a copy of the priority document and any translation of a previous application to the file of a divisional application and a new application under **Art.61(1)(b)** free of charge (Special Edition No 3 OJ 2007, B.2). If at filing of the divisional application no priority documents have been filed in respect of the parent application, they must be filed in respect of the divisional application and, if the priority of the parent application's remaining subject-matter is to be retained, in respect of the parent application also. (A-IV,1.2.2)

R. 53(3) Where the previous application is not in an official language of the European Patent Office and the validity of the priority claim is relevant to the determination of the patentability of the invention concerned, the European Patent Office shall invite the applicant for or proprietor of the European patent to file a translation of that application into one of the official languages within a period to be specified. Alternatively, a declaration may be submitted that the European patent application is a complete translation of the previous application. Paragraph 2 shall apply mutatis mutandis. If a requested translation of a previous application is not filed in due time, the right of priority for the European patent application or for the European patent with respect to that application shall be lost. The applicant for or proprietor of the European patent shall be informed accordingly.

Amended by decision of the Administrative Council of 27.06.2012, which entered into force on 01.04.2013. Amended **R.53(3)** applies to all applications and patents for which a **R.53(3)** invitation is issued on or after 01.04.2013. (OJ 2012, 442)

1 **Translation of priority document or declaration**

If the language of the priority document as filed is not one of the official languages of the EPO, the EPO will invite the applicant or, as the case may be, the patentee to file a translation into one of these official EPO languages if the validity of the priority claim is relevant to the determination of the patentability of the invention (**R.53(3)**, first sentence). In other cases the EPO will not request a translation of the priority document. This is in line with the requirements of Art.4(4) PLT. The advantage for the applicant not having to file a translation was regarded to outweigh the increased legal uncertainty of the public that has to make its own translation for verifying the validity of a priority claim.

Even if the EPO does not request so, an applicant may voluntarily file a translation (or a declaration) at any time (A-III,6.8.5). If a translation is required, the applicant will be invited to file it within a time limit to be set by the Office (**R.53(3)**). This requirement may arise during search, examination, opposition or appeal proceedings (A-III,6.8; F-VI,3.4; D-VII,2; see also Not. EPO OJ 2013, 150 §1-3).

The translation or declaration of the priority documents of a divisional application need not be filed if they are in the file of the parent application at the time of filing of the divisional application. Otherwise, they need be filed only for those priorities claimed in the parent application to which the subject-matter of the divisional application relates. If the divisional application is filed before the relevant document is filed for the parent application, the applicant can, within the period for filing the documents for the divisional application, also inform the EPO that he has in the meantime submitted these documents in respect of the parent application. (A-IV,1.2.2)

2 **Complete translation**

It is not necessary to file the translation if the applicant declares that the application claiming priority is a complete translation of the priority document (**R.53(3)**, second sentence). The declaration can be made by crossing a box in the Request for Grant form or in the form for entry into the European phase. An application is a 'complete' translation in the sense of **R.53(3)**, if the text of the description, the claims and, where applicable, text matter in the drawings of the application is a full translation of the corresponding texts/words of the priority document. The translation may not add or omit anything vis-à-vis the text of the priority document. Allowed changes are transposing the claims from the beginning to the end, and changing the letter type of the reference numerals. Examples of not-allowed changes are changing the order of the claims, adding reference signs, and changing sections such as listing of components, headings and words in drawings. If the application did not contain claims on the date of filing, the description of the application must be an exact translation of the description of the priority document. (A-III,6.8.6)

Where a declaration cannot be accepted for any of the above reasons, a complete translation must be filed (A-III,6.8.6). Since the period of **R.53(3)** will normally have expired when the EPO notifies the party, the translation must be filed together with a remedy (see below).

3 **Period for filing the translation or declaration**

The period for filing the translation is specified by the EPO in A-III,6.8.1. Only a single invitation to provide the translation or declaration is issued by the Office (A-III,6.8).

Where the search division opines that a translation of a priority document is required, the invitation will be issued at about the same time as the **R.70a(1)** communication inviting the applicant to comment on the search opinion or the **R.70(2)** communication inviting the applicant to comment on the search opinion and to indicate whether he wants to proceed further with the application. In both cases the translation for a direct European application must be provided within six months from the publication of the search report. The translation for a Euro-PCT application where a supplementary search report is drafted must be filed within six months from notification of the **R.70(2)** communication. Where the period between notification of the invitation and expiry of the six-month period is less than two months, the period will be extended till two months after the notification. (A-III,6.8.1)

When the examining division or the opposition division requests a translation, an invitation with a four month period will be sent separately or together with an **Art.94(3)** or **Art.101(1)** communication. For a Euro-PCT application where the EPO acted as (S)ISA, the invitation may only be sent after expiry of the six-months period of **R.161(1)**. No summons to oral proceedings will be issued until the earlier of receipt of the translation and expiry of the period for further processing in respect of the **R.53(3)** period. (A-III,6.8.2; C-IV,3.1)

4 **Effect of missing translation or declaration**

If the Office does not receive the requested translation or declaration in due time, the right to priority is lost and the applicant is informed accordingly (**R.53(3)**, third and fourth sentence; **R.112(1)**). The intermediate documents which led to the validity of the priority claim being considered relevant to patentability will become prior art under **Art.54(2)** or (3) as applicable (A-III,6.8.3). See **Art.54(3):2** for the effect of the loss of priority right on the prior right effect of the application.

5 **Remedies**

The loss of rights caused by not responding to the **R.53(3)** invitation can be remedied during grant proceedings using further processing (**Art.121** and **R.135**). During opposition proceedings it can be remedied using re-establishment (**Art.122** and **R.136**). Additionally, a decision under **R.112(2)** may be requested if the invitation is unjustified because the translation had already been filed. (A-III,6.8.3)

When the applicant or proprietor opines that the validity of the priority claim is not or no longer relevant for patentability, e.g. because of amendment of the claims, and that the request for a translation is inappropriate, he still has to file a translation of the priority application. If he submits arguments instead of the translation in response to the **R.53(3)** invitation, the right of priority will be lost because arguments cannot replace the translation. If he requests subsequently a decision under **R.112(2)**, he should auxiliary apply a remedy and file the translation in case the decision is negative and the priority would be lost. In these circumstances it could be considered to file merely a machine translation of the priority document or supplement the filed application with a machine translation of the difference between the filed application and the priority document. It is doubtful whether the **R.53(3)** procedure safeguards the right to be heard under **Art.113(1)**.

R. 54 Issuing priority documents

On request, the European Patent Office shall issue to the applicant a certified copy of the European patent application (priority document), under the conditions determined by the President of the European Patent Office, including the form of the priority document and the circumstances under which an administrative fee shall be paid.

Implementation of: **Art.88(1)**
EPC 1973: **R.38a**

1 **Issuing certified copies**

The EPO makes certified copies of a priority document available on request of the applicant in the form of paper copies (Dec. Pres., Spec. Ed. 3 of OJ 2007, 123 Art.2(3)). The fee for this service has been set under **Rfees3(1)**.

After publication of the application, the EPO will provide to anyone certified copies of any document on file on request and against payment of a fee (A-XI,5.1).

If the deficiencies are not remedied within two months of notification of the invitation, no filing date will be accorded and the application will not be dealt with as a European patent application (**Art.90(2)**, **R.55**). The Receiving Section informs the applicant by means of a **R.112(1)** communication; if the applicant regards the communication as inaccurate, he may ask for an appealable decision. Further information on the filing date requirements and correction can be found in the notes to **R.40**.

The two-month period of **R.55** is not extendable under **R.132**, because it is not an office time limit. **R.135(2)** excludes the two-month period from further processing. Re-establishment (**Art.122** and **R.136**) is possible. The established practice of the Receiving Section is to accord a date of filing corresponding to the last day of the two-month period of **R.55** where re-establishment is granted.

Instead of applying for re-establishment, the applicant may file a corrected application, provided the date of filing is not critical. This remedy is cheaper than re-establishment and does not have the uncertainty of re-establishment. Any fees paid in respect of the earlier application will be refunded as lacking legal basis (A-II,4.1.4).

R. 56 Missing parts of the description or missing drawings

Implementation of: **Art.90(4)**
EPC 1973: **R.41** + **R.43**

1 **Correction of missing parts by later filing**
The purpose of **R.56** is to correct parts of the description or drawings that are missing in the filed applications, caused by e.g. faulty fax transmission or received only after midnight. It implements Art.5(6) PLT. The provision should be used for correcting true errors and not for amending the application after filing by incorporating specific parts from an earlier application, the priority of which may even have been added after the date of filing (H-IV,2.2; **J27/10** hn.1).

If during the examination on filing the EPO finds that any parts of the description or drawings appear to be missing, it will invite the applicant under **R.56(1)** to file these parts within two months from invitation. The applicant may also file missing parts of his own motion within two months of the date of filing (**R.56(2)**). The application will be re-dated to the date of receipt of the missing parts (**R.56(2)**). The applicant may withdraw subsequently filed parts of the description or drawings in order to retain his original filing date (**R.56(6)**).

If the application claims priority and the missing part of the description or drawings was completely contained in the priority application, that missing part may be included in the application without loss of the original date of filing, provided the requirements of **R.56(3)** are met. (Spec. Ed. 1 of OJ 2003, p. 159)

R.56 refers only to missing parts of the description and missing drawings. Hence, inclusion of claims from a previous application using **R.56** is not permitted. See A-IV,5.1 for a missing sequence listing. **R.56** cannot be used to amend or replace originally filed documents; it can only be used to supplement missing parts of the description and missing drawings (**J15/12** r.4). However, in a case where the drawings filed with the application were obviously incorrect, the applicant was allowed to file a new set of drawings, because there was no doubt that the drawings referred to in the description were missing; the drawings filed with the application remained part of the application, thereby avoiding the prohibited replacement of the drawings

PART IV IMPLEMENTING REGULATIONS TO PART IV OF THE CONVENTION

Chapter I *Examination by the Receiving Section*

R. 55 Examination on filing

If the examination under Article 90, paragraph 1, reveals that the application fails to meet the requirements laid down in Rule 40, paragraph 1(a) or (c), paragraph 2 or paragraph 3, first sentence, the European Patent Office shall inform the applicant of any deficiencies and advise him that the application will not be dealt with as a European patent application unless such deficiencies are remedied within two months. If the applicant does this, he shall be informed of the date of filing accorded by the Office.

Art.90(1) Examination on filing
R.40(1)(a) Indication that European patent is sought
R.40(1)(c) Description or reference to previously filed application
R.40(2) Filing date and number of previously filed application
R.40(3) Certified copy of previously filed application
Implementation of: **Art.90(4)**
EPC 1973: **R.39**

1 **Accordance of date of filing and re-dating**
R.55 deals with the examination under **Art.90(1)** as to whether the requirements for the accordance of a date of filing are fulfilled. If the examination reveals deficiencies relating to **R.40(1)(a)** or **(c)**, **R.40(2)** or **(3)**, the EPO will invite the applicant under **Art.90(4)** and **R.55** to correct the deficiencies within two months. If the deficiency relates to parts of the description or drawings that are missing, the EPO will follow the procedure of **R.56** instead of **R.55**.

A correction filed in response to the **R.55** invitation may cause a redating of the application, depending on the deficiency corrected. The actual rules for redating, and hence for according a date of filing, after correction are not laid down in the EPC but only in the Guidelines.

If a deficiency relating to **R.40(1)(a)**, **(c)**, or **R.40(2)** is corrected in due time, the date of receipt of the correction will become the date of filing of the application. The applicant will be informed of this date under **R.55**, last sentence. (A-II,4.1.4)

If a deficiency relating to **R.40(3)**, first sentence, is corrected in due time, the original date of filing is retained (A-II,4.1.5).

See the notes to **R.40** for the effect of specific corrections on the date of filing.

(J2/12 r.10, 11). **R.56** cannot be used to add drawings of proper quality, because the original low-quality drawings were not missing (J12/14 r.7).

The 'content of the application as filed' for the purpose of determining extension of subject-matter under **Art.123(2)** includes missing parts of the description and missing drawings allowed under **R.56(3)** (H-IV,2.2.2).

Where the applicant has filed missing parts, the publication under **Art.93** contains the description, the claims and any drawings as filed (**R.68(1)**) and any late-filed missing parts of the description or drawings, provided that these were not subsequently withdrawn (A-VI,1.3).

2 **Correction of missing drawings under R.139**

Since **R.56** does not exclude application of **R.139** (J4/85), an applicant may try to insert a missing drawing or replace one or more erroneously filed drawings by way of a correction under **R.139**, second sentence, without re-dating the application. The applicant must prove that the skilled person would have derived the correction from the application at the date of filing ('obvious' in the sense of **R.139**) and that the application contained the matter of the correction already at the date of filing (no extension of subject-matter as required by **Art.123(2)**, **G3/89**). The disclosure of the drawings in a priority document may not be used as evidence, making the proof difficult (**G3/89** r.7, **G11/91** r.7; H-IV,2.3.5). The description of the application may be useful as evidence, if it discloses a good portrait of the drawings. Since the correction may not add new subject-matter to the application, the usefulness of adding a drawing under **R.139** is doubtful.

A request to add a drawing by way of correction under **R.139** should be accompanied by an auxiliary request either to add the drawing and re-date the application or to delete the references to the missing drawings under **R.56**. In cases where the decision on the request for correction requires a technical examination, the Receiving Section must leave the decision to the examining division (J4/85). The publication of the application will not be delayed by this procedure (J4/85).

R. 56(1) If the examination under Article 90, paragraph 1, reveals that parts of the description, or drawings referred to in the description or in the claims, appear to be missing, the European Patent Office shall invite the applicant to file the missing parts within two months. The applicant may not invoke the omission of such a communication.

Art.90(1) Examination on filing

1 **Nomenclature**

R.56 refers to 'missing parts of the description' and 'missing drawings'.

A drawing means a single numbered figure. If part of a drawing is missing, the drawing will be regarded as completely missing for the purpose of **R.56** and the EPO will invite the applicant to resubmit a complete drawing (A-II,5.3; CA/PL17/06). The EPO does not want to assemble a complete drawing by cutting and pasting.

A drawing of low visual quality is not considered a missing part and cannot be remedied under **R.56** (J12/14).

The missing parts of the description and the missing drawings are referred to together as 'missing parts' or, once filed with the EPO, as 'late-filed parts' (A-II,5).

2 **Missing parts and missing drawings noted by EPO**
During the examination on filing under **Art.90(1)** the EPO checks whether parts of the description or drawings referred to in the description or claims appear to be missing. If noted, the applicant will be invited to file the missing parts within two months of notification of the invitation. No check will be made of missing claims, because the presence of claims is not a requirement for a date of filing (see **R.40(1):2.2**).

If the missing parts are filed in due time, the application will either be re-dated under **R.56(2)** or, where the missing parts are contained in a priority document and the criteria of **R.56(3)** are met, retain the original date of filing.

Failure to file the missing parts within the two month period leads to deletion of any references to the missing parts in the description and claims and no re-dating of the application (**R.56(4)(a)**).

3 **Period for filing**
The missing parts must be filed within two months of notification of the invitation. The two-month period is excluded from further processing by **R.135(2)**. Re-establishment under **Art.122** and **R.136** may be used as a remedy.

It is also possible to re-file the application with the correct description and drawings, which has the same effect as re-dating, although fees paid for the first application may not be refunded (see **Rfees9(1)**).

R. 56(2) If missing parts of the description or missing drawings are filed later than the date of filing, but within two months of the date of filing or, if a communication is issued under paragraph 1, within two months of that communication, the application shall be re-dated to the date on which the missing parts of the description or missing drawings were filed. The European Patent Office shall inform the applicant accordingly.

1 **Missing parts and missing drawings noted by applicant**
The applicant may of his own volition file missing parts of the description and missing drawings (not missing claims) within two months of the date of filing (**R.56(2)**). However, if the EPO invites the applicant to file missing parts, the period under **R.56(1)** takes precedence (A-II,5.2) and the applicant can file any missing parts within two months from the invitation.

The two-month period from the date of filing is excluded from further processing by **R.135(2)**. Re-establishment under **Art.122** and **R.136** is available. Alternatively, the applicant may re-file the application in corrected form.

It is advisable to file the missing parts as soon as possible, because in the case of re-dating, the application will be accorded the date of receipt of the missing parts as the date of filing. Moreover, if the EPO does not notice any missing parts are missing and does not send the invitation under **R.56(1)**, the possibility to file the missing parts ends two months after the original date of filing (A-II,5.2).

2 **Re-dating of the application**
Where missing parts are filed, the EPO will re-date the application to the date on which the missing parts were filed (**R.56(2)**, first sentence) and inform the applicant of the new date of filing (**R.56(2)**, last sentence).

However, there will be no re-dating when the special criteria of **R.56(3)** apply.

Re-dating of an application need not result in a loss of rights, if the new date of filing is still within the priority year of an earlier application from which it claims priority, and the earlier application discloses the missing parts. If re-dating causes a later effective date of the application, the applicant must balance on the one hand the risk of pertinent prior art between the original date of filing and a later effective date when the application is re-dated and on the other hand insufficiency of disclosure of the application (**Art.83**) if the later filed parts are withdrawn to retain the original date of filing (i.e. the priority date or the original filing date).

R. 56(3) If the missing parts of the description or missing drawings are filed within the period under paragraph 2, and the application claims priority of an earlier application, the date of filing shall, provided that the missing parts of the description or the missing drawings are completely contained in the earlier application, remain the date on which the requirements laid down in Rule 40, paragraph 1, were fulfilled, where the applicant so requests and files, within the period under paragraph 2:

(a) a copy of the earlier application, unless such copy is available to the European Patent Office under Rule 53, paragraph 2;

(b) where the earlier application is not in an official language of the European Patent Office, a translation thereof in one of these languages, unless such copy is available to the European Patent Office under Rule 53, paragraph 3; and

(c) an indication as to where the missing parts of the description or the missing drawings are completely contained in the earlier application and, where applicable, in the translation thereof.

R.40(1) Requirements for according date of filing
R.53(3) Application or translation available in EPO file

1 **Missing parts based on priority**

The application will not be re-dated but retains the original date of filing if the missing parts are contained in an earlier application from which priority is claimed and the following criteria are satisfied within the period of **R.56(2)** (A-II,5.4):

i) the missing parts of the description or the missing drawings have been filed;
ii) the application claims priority of an earlier application;
iii) a request has been filed that the missing parts or missing drawings be based on the earlier application to avoid redating;
iv) the missing parts or missing drawings are 'completely contained' in the earlier application;
v) a copy of the earlier application has been filed, unless such copy is already available to the EPO under **R.53(2)**;
vi) a translation of the earlier application in one of the official EPO languages has been filed if the earlier application is not in one of these languages, unless such translation is already available to the EPO under **R.53(3)**;
vii) an indication as to where the missing parts or missing drawings are 'completely contained' in the earlier application and, where applicable, in the translation thereof.

1.1 PRIORITY CLAIM (ITEM II)

The priority claim in question must have been in existence no later than the filing of the request in iii) above. Hence, the missing parts may also be based on a priority added after the original date of filing. The priority may not be added after the filing of the request in iii) above. An added priority claim must be filed within the period of **R.52(2)**, i.e. sixteen months from the earliest priority date. (see also A-II,5.4.1)

R.56(3) uses the term 'earlier application' intentionally to ensure that the paragraph covers only the case of missing parts contained in priority applications and not in any previously filed application (CA/PL17/06).

1.2 COMPLETELY CONTAINED IN EARLIER APPLICATION (ITEM IV)

The requirement of **R.56(3)** that the missing part be 'completely contained in the earlier application' is met only if the parts of the earlier application identified according to **R.56(3)(c)** contain the same drawings, with the same annotations or, for missing parts of the description, contain the same text. The missing part must be inserted in the description in a manner that does not add technical content. (A-II,5.4.2)

If a translation of the earlier application is required under **R.56(3)(b)**, the missing parts must be completely contained in the translation. (A-II,5.4.2)

The assessment of 'completely contained' is a formal matter that can be carried out by an examiner who is not technically qualified. The EPO may require photographic identity.

Lawyers in the EPO hold that an addition to the description of an application must be taken from the description of the priority application, not from the claims of the priority application.

1.3 COPY AND TRANSLATION OF EARLIER APPLICATION (ITEM III, VI)

If no copy of the priority application is available to the EPO under **R.53(2)**, the applicant must furnish a copy (**R.56(3)(a)**), which need not be certified (A-II,5.4.2).

Where the priority application is not in English, French or German, the applicant must file a translation into one of these languages, unless such a translation is already available under **R.53(3)** (**R.56(3)(b)**). Instead of a translation, the applicant may file a declaration that the late-filed missing parts of the description, or drawings, are an exact translation of the identified parts of the priority application (A-II,5.4.4). See A-II,5.4.4 where the priority application and the application under examination are in two different EPO languages.

At this stage the language of the proceedings may not yet be known; hence, the EPO cannot require filing of the translation into the language of the proceedings and therefore requires a translation into one of the official languages. In the unlikely case that the applicant translates the priority application into another official language than the priority claiming application, the EPO will probably request a translation into the language of proceedings of only those parts of the priority document that correspond to the missing parts or a declaration that the late-filed missing parts are an exact translation of the corresponding parts of the priority document (A-II,5.4.4 last paragraph mutatis mutandis).

1.4 INDICATION OF MISSING PARTS (ITEM VII)

The indication facilitates the processing of the missing parts of the description and the missing drawings by the EPO (CA/PL17/06).

2 **Effect of non-compliance**
Where criterion i) is not complied with, i.e. the missing parts have been filed after expiry of either of the two-month periods of **R.56(2)**, the missing parts are deemed not to have been filed and any references to these missing parts will be deemed deleted according to **R.56(4)(a)**. The application will not be re-dated and the missing parts will not be introduced into the application.

Non-compliance with one or more of the criteria ii)-iv) leads to redating of the application to the date on which the missing parts were filed under **R.56(2)**.

Non-compliance with one or more of the criteria (v)-(vii) results also in redating to the date on which the missing parts were filed, but in this case under **R.56(5)**.

The EPO will inform the applicant of the non-compliance and the consequences under **R.56(4)(a)**, (2) or (5), whichever applies.

3 **Decision on late-filed missing parts**
The Receiving Section will inform the applicant of its decision on late-filed parts, in particular the requirement that the missing parts are 'completely contained' in the priority document. The decision will be reviewed by the search division (B-XI,2.1) and the examining division (C-III,1), who may also check any translation of a priority application, which may result in a change of the date of filing. An opposition division is probably not allowed to change the date of filing, since this is not covered by **Art.100**, to which it is bound.

R. 56(4) If the applicant:
(a) fails to file the missing parts of the description or the missing drawings within the period under paragraph 1 or 2, or
(b) withdraws under paragraph 6 any missing part of the description or missing drawing filed under paragraph 2,
any references referred to in paragraph 1 shall be deemed to be deleted, and any filing of the missing parts of the description or missing drawings shall be deemed not to have been made. The European Patent Office shall inform the applicant accordingly.

1 **Late filing or withdrawal of missing parts**
The missing parts are deemed not to have been filed if the applicant files the missing parts after expiry of two months from invitation under **R.56(1)** or from the date of filing under **R.56(2)**, or if he withdraws any missing part under **R.56(6)**. In that case any references in the description or claims to these parts will be deemed to be deleted.

When a reference to a missing figure is deemed to be deleted, then reference signs referring to that figure are also deemed to be deleted. Technical information still meaningful without the reference will be retained. (A-II,5.5)

R. 56(5) If the applicant fails to comply with the requirements referred to in paragraph 3(a) to (c) within the period under paragraph 2, the application shall be re-dated to the date on which the missing parts of the description or missing drawings were filed. The European Patent Office shall inform the applicant accordingly.

1 **Non-compliance with requirements of R.56(3)**
R.56(5) provides for the sanctions applicable where the requirements referred to in paragraph (3)(a) to (c) are not complied with in due time. In such a case, the application will be re-dated to the date on which the missing parts of the description or missing drawings were filed. Alternatively, the applicant can withdraw the missing parts of the description or missing drawings under **R.56(6)** so as to avoid any modification of the filing date. (CA/PL17/06)

R. 56(6) Within one month of the notification referred to in paragraph 2 or 5, last sentence, the applicant may withdraw the missing parts of the description or the missing drawings filed, in which case the re-dating shall be deemed not to have been made. The European Patent Office shall inform the applicant accordingly.

1 **Withdrawal of missing parts or missing drawings**
Where an applicant files missing parts of the description or missing drawings under **R.56(2)** that are not based on a priority document, the EPO sends a communication informing him of the new date of filing. The applicant may reconsider the filing of the missing parts or missing drawings and withdraw the late-filed parts within one month of the notification of the communication. As a result, the re-dating is deemed not to have been made and all references to the missing parts of the description and missing drawings are deemed deleted under **R.56(6)**. (A-II,5.5)

Where the late filed parts are based on a priority application and one or more of the criteria ii) to (vii) in the notes of **R.56(3)** are not met, the application will be re-dated. If the applicant prefers the original date of filing, he may withdraw the late-filed parts within one month of the communication informing the applicant of the re-dating. In such a case the re-dating will be deemed not to have been made (**R.56(6)**) and all references to the missing parts of the description and missing drawings will be deemed to be deleted under **R.56(4)(b)**.

The examining division may review the finding of the Receiving Section concerning the added missing parts or drawings. If the examining division finds that the "completely contained"-criterion is not satisfied, it will inform the applicant accordingly and invite him to comment. The applicant can reply by withdrawing the added missing parts or drawings, or by arguing on why they are indeed "completely contained" in the priority application. If in the latter case the examining division is not convinced, it will inform the applicant of re-dating of the application. Thereafter, the applicant can still withdraw the added missing parts or drawings within two months from the communication. (C-III 1.1.1)

The publication under **Art.93** will not contain any late-filed missing parts of the description or drawings if these were subsequently withdrawn under **R.56(6)** (A-VI,1.3). See **R.56(3):3** for the taking of a decision on late-filed missing parts.

R. 57 Examination as to formal requirements

If the European patent application has been accorded a date of filing, the European Patent Office shall examine, in accordance with Article 90, paragraph 3, whether:

(a) a translation of the application required under Article 14, paragraph 2, under Rule 36, paragraph 2, second sentence, or under Rule 40, paragraph 3, second sentence, has been filed in due time;

(b) the request for grant of a European patent satisfies the requirements of Rule 41;

(c) the application contains one or more claims in accordance with Article 78, paragraph 1(c), or a reference to a previously filed application in accordance with Rule 40, paragraphs 1(c), 2 and 3, indicating that it replaces also the claims;

(d) the application contains an abstract in accordance with Article 78, paragraph 1(e);

(e) the filing fee and the search fee have been paid in accordance with Rule 17, paragraph 2, Rule 36, paragraph 3, or Rule 38;

(f) the designation of the inventor has been made in accordance with Rule 19, paragraph 1;

(g) where appropriate, the requirements laid down in Rules 52 and 53 concerning the claim to priority have been satisfied;

(h) where appropriate, the requirements of Article 133, paragraph 2, have been satisfied;

(i) the application meets the requirements laid down in Rule 46 and Rule 49, paragraphs 1 to 9 and 12;

(j) the application meets the requirements laid down in Rule 30.

Amended by decision of the Administrative Council of 21.10.2008, which entered into force on 01.04.2009. (OJ 2008, 513)

Amended by decision of the Administrative Council of 25.03.2009, which entered into force on 01.04.2010 (OJ 2009, 296)

Art.14(2) Application filed in non-EPO language

Art.78(1) Requirements for application

Art.90(3) Examination as to formal requirements

Art.133(2) Compulsory representation

R.17(2) Period for paying filing and search fee for new application

R.19(1) Content of designation of the inventor

R.30 Requirements of application relating to nucleotide and amino acid sequences

R.36(2) Language of divisional application

R.36(3) Period for paying filing and search fee for divisional application

R.38 Period for paying filing and search fee for application

R.40(1)(c) Replacement of application by previous application

R.40(2) Bibliographic data of previous application

R.40(3) Translation of previous application

R.41 Content of Request for Grant

R.46 Form of the drawings

R.49 General provisions governing the presentation of the application documents

R.52 Declaration of priority

R.53 Priority documents

Implementation of: **Art.90(3)**

EPC 1973: **Art.91(1)** + **R.40**

1 **Formalities examination**

Examination as to formal requirements under **R.57** concerns the formalities examination to be conducted under **Art.90(3)** after a date of filing has been accorded.

In addition to the ten requirements listed in **R.57**, the Receiving Section also checks (A-III,1.2; A-III,8):

i) clarity and conciseness of the title (**R.41(2)(b)**), preliminary check;
ii) payment of claims fees under **R.45(1)** where appropriate;
iii) the certificate of exhibition under **R.25** where the invention has been displayed under **Art.55(1)(b)**;
iv) whether the information pursuant to **R.31(1)(c)** and **(d)** is complete where the application relates to biological material;
v) check where required a sequence listing has been filed (**R.30**);
vi) matter prohibited by **R.48**, preliminary check.

The check of payment of the designation fee and extension fees is part of the formalities examination. This examination can only be made after expiry of the period for payment of these fees, i.e. six months after publication of the search report.

The examination set out below applies to direct European patent applications, including divisional and new applications. Euro-PCT applications are examined on entry into the European phase according to **R.159**, rather than to **R.57**.

Where the EPO notices non-compliance with one of the requirements of **R.57**(a) to **(d)**, **(h)** and **(i)**, it will send an invitation under **R.58** to correct the deficiency, the sanction on non-compliance being refusal of the application unless another sanction is provided (**Art.90(5)**). There are special provisions for an invitation to correct and a sanction for non-compliance with each one of the requirements of **R.57(e)** to **(g)**, **(j)** and the above further requirements i to v, as set out in the sections below.

See **Art.90(5):2** for the time a sanction takes effect.

2 **Translation of application (R.57(a))**

Where a filed application is not in one of the official EPO languages, a translation into such a language must be filed according to **Art.14(2)** within two months of filing the application (**R.6(1)**). Where a divisional application is filed in the language of the earlier application and this language is not an official EPO language, a translation must be provided within two months of filing the application (**R.36(2)**). Where the application is filed by reference to a previously filed application as allowed by **R.40(1)(c)** and the previous application is not in an official EPO language, a translation into one of these languages must be filed within two months of filing the application according to **R.40(3)**.

The EPO will check under **R.57(a)** whether the translation has been filed at expiry of the two months; if not, it will invite the applicant to rectify the deficiency under **R.58** within a further period of two months (A-III,14).

Non-compliance results in the application being deemed withdrawn under **Art.14(2)**, last sentence. The EPO will notify the applicant of the loss of rights according to **R.112(1)**. Where applicable, the applicant can prove within two months of the notification that he did file the translation in due time (**R.112(2)**) or request re-establishment under **Art.122**.

It should be noted that the Travaux Préparatoires of the EPC 2000 state that non-compliance with filing the translation of **R.40(3)** will result in the application being refused under **Art.90(5)** (Spec. ed. 5, OJ 2007, p.106). The EPO has admitted that this statement is not correct.

The periods of **R.6(1)**, **R.40(3)** and **R.58** are excluded from further processing by **R.135(2)**. Re-establishment in the periods is possible under **Art.122** and **R.136**. It is also possible to convert the European application to a national application under **Art.135(1)(b)**.

See also A-III,16 and **Art.14(2):3**.

3 **Request for grant (R.57(b))**

The Receiving Section examines whether the Request for Grant form complies with the requirements of **R.41**, several of which are dealt with below (A-III,4.2).

Use of the appropriate Request for Grant form is mandatory (**R.41(1)**). The form already contains a preprinted petition for the grant of a European patent, which is required under **R.41(2)(a)**.

The Request must contain the title of the invention (**R.41(2)(b)**). See the separate section below on examination of the title.

The Request must properly identify the name, address and nationality of the applicant (**R.41(2)(c)**), and, if a representative has been appointed, his name and address (**R.41(2)(d)**, see also **R.57(h)**). When there are several applicants, the name, address and nationality of each of them must be given (A-III,4.2.1).

Where applicable, the Request must indicate that it relates to a divisional application and state the number of the earlier application (**R.41(2)(e)**). The same applies to a new application under **Art.61(1)(b)** (**R.41(2)(f)**).

The Request must be signed (**R.41(2)(h)**). The description, claims and drawings are not stated as requiring a signature; hence, they need not be signed separately. Other application documents requiring a signature are the separately filed designation of inventor (**R.19(1)**) and the authorisation (**R.152**). The documents, with the exception of the authorisation of a representative, may be signed by an appointed representative instead of the applicant. (A-VIII,3.2)

If there is more than one applicant, each applicant or his representative must sign the request for grant and, where applicable, the appointment of a common representative. This also applies if one of the applicants is considered common representative under **R.151(1)**, first sentence. The common representative may sign the designation of inventor and all further documents. An authorisation on behalf of more than one applicant must be signed by all applicants. (A-VIII,3.4)

The Request must identify the documents annexed to the application (**R.41(2)(i)**).

The Request must contain the designation of the inventor where the applicant is the inventor (**R.41(2)(j)**). Otherwise, the designation must be filed in a separate document according to **R.19(1)**. The inventor may renounce his title as inventor, in which case his name does not appear on the front page of the published application, and is not entered into the Register (**R.20(1)**, **R.143(1)(g)**). The examination of the designation is provided in **R.57(f)**.

If the Receiving Section notes that the Request for Grant form has not been filed or any error in the Request for Grant form (with the exception of designation of inventor (see **R.57(f)**), priority claim (see **R.57(g)**) and title (see section below)), it will invite the applicant under **R.58** to remedy the deficiencies within two months of invitation. Further processing is excluded by **R.135(2)**; however, re-establishment according to **Art.122** and **R.136** is available. Non-compliance will result in the application being refused under **Art.90(5)**. An applicant may request correction of his own volition under **R.139**, first sentence.

4 **Claims (R.57(c))**
Since the presence of one or more claims in the application is not a prerequisite for accordance of a date of filing under the EPC 2000, the presence of claims is not examined on filing but in the subsequent formal examination (see A-III,15).

An applicant has three opportunities to file claims. On filing the application documents he may also file claims, either by supplying a set of claims or referring to claims in a previous document. If no claims are available on filing of the application, an applicant may file claims of his own volition up to the time the EPO invites him to do so under **R.58**. If he has not provided claims on the date of filing or later of his own volition, an invitation under **R.58** will be issued for mandatory filing of claims. (A-III,15)

The applicant can use only one of the three opportunities for filing claims. A second filing of claims before receipt of the search report is not permitted under **R.137(1)**. Claims can only be filed by reference to a previous document on the date of filing, later filing of claims by reference is not allowed (A-II,4.1.3.1).

Claims filed after the date of filing must have a basis in the application as filed in order not to extend subject-matter in the sense of **Art.123(2)** (A-III,15).

Late-filed claims are regarded as an amendment and must be filed in the language of the proceedings according to **R.3(2)**.

During the formalities examination it is checked if at least one claim is present in the application, as required by **Art.78(1)(c)**. If not, the EPO will invite the applicant under **R.58** to remedy the deficiency within two months from invitation. Failure to do so will result in refusal of the application according to **Art.90(5)**.

The EPO will notify the applicant of the decision under **R.111**. The two-month period of **R.58** is excluded from further processing according to **R.135(2)**. Re-establishment under **Art.122** and **R.136** is available.

5 **Abstract (R.57(d))**
Where the abstract, required under **Art.78(1)(e)**, is missing or obviously inappropriate, the Receiving Section will invite the applicant to correct the deficiency under **R.58** (A-III,10.2). If the application contains drawings, and the applicant has not indicated the drawing to accompany the abstract (**R.47(4)**), the search division will decide which figure to publish (A-III,10.3).

Non-compliance will result in refusal of the application under **Art.90(5)** (A-III,16.2). No further processing is possible for the two-month period of **R.58** (**R.135(2)**); however, re-establishment under **Art.122** and **R.136** is available.

The definitive content of the abstract is the responsibility of the search division (**R.66**) which checks compliance with all requirements of **R.47**.

6 **Filing fee, page fee, divisional fee and search fee (R.57(e))**
The Receiving Section checks whether payment of the filing and search fees as required by **Art.78(2)** has been made by expiry of one month of filing (**R.38(1)**). The filing fee may be reduced if an admissible non-EPO language is used (**R.6(3)**) (A-XI,9.2.2). See **Rfees9** for refund of search fees.

For a divisional application under **Art.76(1)** or a new application under **Art.61(1)(b)** the filing and search fees must be paid within one month of filing the application (**R.36(3)** and **R.17(2)**, respectively). For a divisional of second or higher generation the divisional fee must also be paid (**R.38(4)**).

A page fee as part of the filing fee must be paid within the later of one month of filing the application, the first set of claims or the certified copy of **R.40(3)** (**R.38(3)**).

The EPO does not issue an invitation to pay the filing, page, divisional and search fees. Note, that **R.58** does not refer to **R.57(e)**.

If any of these fees is not paid in due time, the application is deemed withdrawn according to **Art.78(2)**. The EPO will notify the applicant of the loss of rights under **R.112(1)**. Further processing according to **Art.121** and **R.135** may be requested for the one-month time limit within two months of the notification of the loss of rights. The further processing fee is equal to 50% of the missing fee (**Rfees2(1)12**).

7 **Designation of inventor (R.57(f))**

An application must designate the inventor according to **Art.81**. The EPO does not verify the accuracy of the designation (**R.19(2)**); it only checks whether the designation conforms to **R.19(1)**. The EPO sends the filed designation for information to any inventor who is not an applicant (**R.19(3)**). According to **Art.81** the designation must contain the entitlement to the application if the applicant is not the inventor. The entitlement is not verified (**Art.60(3)** & **R.19(2)**). However, when the inventor receives his designation under **R.19(3)**, he can assess the entitlement and may request correction if necessary. The applicant can request correction of the designation under **R.139** of his own volition during the proceedings before the EPO. A designation of an incorrect inventor may be corrected according to **R.21(1)**. A rectification of an incorrect designation already entered in the Register will be published in the Bulletin (**R.21(2)**). See also A-III,5.

A deficient designation is no ground for opposition (**Art.100**) or revocation (**Art.138**).

If the designation on filing is missing or does not comply with **R.19** (e.g. inventor's name or address or the signature of the applicant is missing), the EPO will follow the procedure under **R.60**.

8 **Priority claim (R.57(g))**

When claiming the priority of an earlier application, the Request for Grant must indicate so and state the date and state of filing of the earlier application (**R.41(2)(g)**). See **Art.87, Art.88, R.52, R.53** and **R.139** for requirements for claiming priority, addition and correction of a priority claim of the applicants own volition.

The Receiving Section need not examine the content of the priority document. However, where the document obviously relates to subject-matter different from the application, the applicant should be informed that the priority document appears not to be the relevant document. (A-III,6.4)

Where a priority right is lost because deficiencies have not been corrected in due time, the applicant is notified. Periods depending on the priority will take the new situation into account. The loss of priority right has no effect on a period which has already expired. (A-III,6.11)

8.1 DECLARATION OF PRIORITY

The declaration of priority is preferably made on filing the application (**R.52(2)**). The Receiving Section examines in the Request for Grant form under **R.57(b)** whether the declaration of priority of **Art.88(1)** contains the date and state of filing and the file number, as required by **R.52(1)**. If the information is missing or obviously incorrect, the EPO will invite the applicant under **R.58** to file a corrected Request for Grant form (implied by A-III,6.5). It will not send such an invitation for deficiencies in priority claims added or corrected after the Request for Grant form has been filed (A-III,6.5). The applicant will be given more time to correct the file number than to correct the date and state.

The date and state may be corrected voluntarily within the sixteen/four month time limit of **R.52(3)**. If an incorrect priority claim has not been corrected by expiry of this period, the priority right is lost according to **Art.90(5)**. The period of **R.52(3)** is excluded from further processing (**R.135(2)**), but re-establishment under **Art.122** and **R.136** is available. (A-III,6.5.3)

If a missing file number is not provided within the sixteen/four month time limit of **R.52(3)**, the EPO will invite the applicant again to file it within a period to be specified (**R.59**). The period is between two and four months (**R.132(2)**). Non-observance of the period of **R.59** results in the loss of the priority right under **Art.90(5)**, last sentence. The period of **R.59** is excluded from further processing according to **R.135(2)**. Re-establishment under **Art.122** and **R.136** is available for this period. See also **R.59:1**; A-III, 6.5.3 and 16.2.

An incorrect file number may be corrected at any time under **R.139** (A-III,6.5.3).

8.2 PRIORITY PERIOD

Where the date of filing of the application falls after expiry of the priority period, the EPO invites the applicant to correct the priority date within the sixteen/four month period of **R.52(3)** or the applicant may request re-establishment in the priority period within two months of the expiry of the priority period according to **Art.122** and **R.136(1)**. The omitted act is the establishment of a date of filing by filing the application documents within the same two-month period, claiming the appropriate priority. The priority period may be extended on account of **R.133** or **R.134**. (A-III,6.6 and 6.9(i)(a), (b))

When the deficiency is not corrected in due time, the priority right is lost according to **Art.90(5)**.

8.3 COPY OF PRIORITY DOCUMENT

Before expiry of sixteen months of the earliest priority date a copy of the priority document must be filed (**R.53(1)**), either on paper or on physical media other than paper, e.g. CD-R (A-III,6.7). The certificate of correctness of the document must be included. No copy need be filed if it is already available to the EPO, which will include a copy in the file free of charge (**R.53(2)**); see Dec. Pres. OJ 2012, 492 for conditions). The EPO participates as of 01.11.2018 in the WIPO's digital access system (DAS) for exchanging certified priority documents; for the time being DAS is available for EP applications and international applications entering the EP phase (Dec. Pres. OJ 2018 A78 Art.1; see **R.53(2):1** for more details).

If no copy is filed within the sixteen-month period, the EPO will invite the applicant to file it within a two month period (**R.59**; A-III,6.7). Non-observance of the period results in loss of the priority right under **Art.90(5)**, last sentence. The period of **R.59** is excluded from further processing according to **R.135(2)**, but can be extended under **R.132(2)**. Re-establishment under **Art.122** and **R.136** is available for this period. See also **R.59:1**; A-III,6.7 and 16.2.

8.4 TRANSLATION OF PRIORITY DOCUMENT

The EPO will request a translation into an official EPO language of a priority document in an non-EPO language only where the validity of the priority claimed is relevant to the assessment of the patentability of the invention concerned (**R.53(3)**). This invitation may be sent during the examination or the opposition procedure. The applicant or proprietor may also send the translation of his own motion (A-III,6.8). Instead of a translation, the applicant or proprietor may file a declaration that the application is a complete translation of the priority document (R.53(3)). The EPO will include a copy of the translation in the file where the translation is already available to the EPO (R.53(3), R.53(2)).

The translation must be filed within a period specified in the invitation (R.53(3); A-III,6.8). If no translation is provided before expiry of the period, the priority right is lost according to **R.53(3)**, 4th sentence). During grant proceedings further processing under **Art.121** and **R.135** is available; during opposition proceedings only re-establishment under **Art.122** and **R.136** can be used as remedy.

9 Compulsory representation (R.57(h))

An applicant who does not have a residence or place of business in a contracting state must be represented according to **Art.133(2)**. He may only file the application himself; subsequent acts must be carried out by a duly appointed representative (**Art.133(2)**). If there are several applicants, each one of them has to comply with **Art.133(2)**. In such a case one applicant or representative must be appointed as common representative, either by the applicants in the Request for Grant form (**R.41(3)**) or by the EPO using **R.151(1)**.

During the examination of formal requirements under **Art.90(3)** the Receiving Section checks whether the applicant has complied with the requirements of representation as set out in **Art.133(2)**. If he is incorrectly not represented, the EPO will invite him according to **Art.90(4)** and **R.58** to appoint a representative within two months of invitation (**R.58**). The first communication of the Receiving Section to the applicant should cover this deficiency, besides other obvious deficiencies (A-III,16.1).

In special cases the Receiving Section will also request the applicant to file a signed authorisation according to **R.152(1)** within the same period as for appointing a representative (**R.152(3)**). If the authorisation is not filed in time, all acts of the representative are void (**R.152(6)**). (A-VIII,1.7)

If the representative is not appointed within the two months of **R.58**, the application is refused (**Art.90(5)**). Further processing is excluded by **R.135(2)**. Re-establishment under **Art.122** and **R.136** is available.

10 Physical requirements to be satisfied (R.57(i))

The Receiving Section checks under **R.57(i)** whether the application documents comply with the physical requirements of **R.57(i)**, such as paper, layout, tables, formulae (**R.49**) and for drawings margins, scale, numbering, reference signs, text matter (**R.46**).

R.57(i) clarifies that the examination as to formal requirements does not encompass the question whether values are expressed in units conforming to international standards and, where appropriate in terms of the metric system using SI units (**R.49(10)**); also the consistence of the terminology and the signs used in the application (**R.49(11)**) is not examined in this stage of proceedings (CA/PL17/06). These matters are considered by the examining division, including the more physical requirements as listed in A-III,3.2.

Where the application is filed by reference to a previously filed application according to **R.40(1)(c)**, the certified copy of the previous application must satisfy the physical requirements. However, if the previous application has to be translated under **R.40(3)**, the translation must comply with the physical requirements instead. (A-III,3.2.2)

Late-filed application documents, such as late-filed claims (**R.57(c)**), inserted missing parts (**R.56**), replacement documents (**R.50(1)**) or translations (**R.49(1)**), must also comply with the physical requirements (A-III,3.2; A-VIII,2.2).

10.1 EXAMINATION OF PHYSICAL REQUIREMENTS

If the application documents do not comply with the physical requirements examined under **R.57(i)**, the Receiving Section will invite the applicant under **R.58** to remedy the deficiencies within two months of invitation (A-III,16.1). Any correction may not extend the subject-matter of the application (H-IV,2.1). If the period is not observed, the application is refused under **Art.90(5)**. Further processing is excluded for the two-month period under **R.135(2)**; however, re-establishment according to **Art.122** and **R.136** is available. (A-III,3.2)

See A-III,3.2.2 for the examination of late-filed application documents, in particular inserted missing parts under **R.56**.

10.2 INFORMAL DRAWINGS

The EPO allows filing of informal drawings which depart substantially from the physical requirements laid down in **R.46**. Informal drawings are often filed when an applicant does not have sufficient time to prepare formal drawings before filing the application (A-IX,10). The Receiving Section permits filing of amended or replacement drawings complying with the requirements, provided that no subject-matter is added in violation of **Art.123(2)**. (A-IX,10)

The inclusion of the amended or replacement drawings in the published application merely signifies that the drawings have been accepted for publication, not that they comply with **Art.123(2)**. The final examination of the drawings is carried out by the substantive examiner. (OJ 1987, 123)

11 Sequence listing (R.57(j))

Where a sequence listing is required, it must comply with the requirements of **R.30**.

If the Receiving Section notes that a required sequence listing has not been filed or that the filed sequence listing contains deficiencies, it will invite the applicant to file a correct sequence listing and pay the late furnishing fee (**Rfees2(1)14a**) within two months of invitation according to **R.30(3)**. If not complied with in due time, the application is refused under **R.30(3)**, last sentence. Further processing under **Art.121** and **R.135** is available: file the sequence listing, pay the late furnishing fee and pay the further processing fee, being the fixed fee for late submitting the sequence listing plus 50% of the late furnishing fee for late payment (**Rfees2(1)12**). See also Dec. Pres. OJ 2011, 372; Not. EPO OJ 2013, 542; A-III,3.2 and A-IV,5.

See A-IV,5 for sequence listings filed by reference to a previous application under **R.40(1)(c)** and sequence listings inserted as missing part under **R.56**.

12 Title

The Receiving Section makes a preliminary check that the title of the invention which will appear in the published application is in general accord with the requirements of **R.41(2)(b)**, i.e. it must clearly and concisely state the technical designation of the invention and exclude fancy names (A-III,7.1). The EPO will change an obviously non-complying title of its own motion, informing the applicant upon transmission of the search report (A-III,7.2). The communication announcing the forthcoming publication will inform the applicant of the wording of the title in the three official EPO languages. The ultimate responsibility for ensuring that the title conforms with the Rules rests with the examining division (A-III,7.2).

A missing title, which is not available from the application documents as a whole, will result in a request for correction under **R.58**.

13 **Claims fees**

An application comprising more than fifteen claims incurs payment of a claims fee in respect of each claim over and above that number (**R.45(1)**). The EPO checks the number of claims at the time they are filed, either (A-III,9):

i) on the date of filing accorded under **Art.90(1)**;
ii) on receipt of a response to a **R.58** invitation indicating their absence; or
iii) when filed by the applicant of his own motion after the date of filing but before the **R.58** invitation.

The claims fees must be paid within one month of whichever of the above dates of filing the claims applies (**R.45(2)**, first sentence). If not paid within the one-month period, the EPO will invite the applicant to pay them as yet within one month from invitation (**R.45(2)**, second sentence) without surcharge.

Where the application was filed by reference to a previous application under **R.40(1)(c)** and it is indicated that the claims of the previous application take the place of claims in the application as filed, the claims fee are due within one month of the date of filing. However, the EPO will send the invitation under **R.45(2)**, second sentence, only after receipt of the copy of the previous application, when it can check how many claims fees are due. (A-III,9)

If a claims fee is not paid within the period of grace, the claim concerned is deemed abandoned (**R.45(3)**) and the applicant is notified to that effect (A-III,9). Further processing under **Art.121** and **R.135** can be used as a remedy.

14 **Prohibited matter**

The application may not contain matter prohibited in the sense of **R.48(1)**.

The Receiving Section will carry out a cursory examination to ensure that the application does not contain such matter (A-III,8). The search division may also inform the Receiving Section of the existence of prohibited matter in the application (A-III,8.1 and 8.2). The examining division also examines prohibited matter (F-II,7.5).

The Receiving Section may take action to prevent publication of such matter under **R.48(3)**, notifying the applicant of the omitted matter (A-III,8).

15 **Certificate of exhibition**

The certificate of exhibition, accompanied by an identification of the invention, must comply with the requirements of **R.25**. The certificate and identification must be filed within four months of filing the application (**R.25**).

The Receiving Section acknowledges receipt of the certificate and identification of the invention (A-IV,3.2). The Receiving Section draws the applicant's attention to any manifest defects in the certificate or the identification in case it is possible to rectify the deficiencies within the four-month period allowed (A-III,1.2(iii); A-IV,3.2). If not rectified in due time, **Art.55(1)(b)** will not apply to the display at the exhibition (**Art.55(2)**) and the display will be regarded as belonging to the state of the art.

The applicant is notified according to **R.112(1)** if the certificate or identification is not furnished within the time allowed. The applicant may request further processing in respect of this loss of rights according to **Art.121** and **R.135**. (A-IV,3.2)

16 **Deposit of biological material**

Where an application relates to biological material and the material has been deposited, the information pursuant to **R.31(1)(c)** (the depositary institution and the accession number of the deposit) and, where applicable, **R.31(1)(d)** (details of depositor other than the applicant) must be provided within the time limit of **R.31(2)**. Where information pursuant to **R.31(1)(c)** is missing on the date of filing, the accession number must be traceable without ambiguity from the application as filed (see A-IV,4.2).

Where the application refers to a previous application under **R.40(1)(c)** and the previous application does not provide the information of **R.31(1)(c)**, the deficiency must still be rectified in the time limit of **R.31(2)**, even though the EPO can invite the applicant only after receipt of the copy of the previous application or its translation (A-IV,4.1.2).

The examining division assesses whether the available information sufficiently discloses the biological material to make it available to the public (F-III,6.2). If the information is insufficient, the biological material will not be considered disclosed pursuant to **Art.83** (F-III,6.2).

17 **Designation fee**

The designation fee must be paid within six months of the mention of the publication of the search report (**R.39(1)**), i.e. within the same time limit in which the request for examination must be filed (**R.70(1)**).

See **Art.79**, **R.39** and A-III,11 for particulars about the payment of the designation fee and the change on 01.04.2009 from a designation fee for each contracting states to a flat rate designation fee for all contracting states.

18 **Extension fees**

The extension fee must be paid within the same period as the designation fee. If not paid in due time, the request for extension is deemed withdrawn. A communication of loss of rights to extensions will only be issued if a communication for loss of rights to designations is issued. Only in this case further processing according to **Art.121** and **R.135** will be available for payment of the extension fees. A grace period of two months from expiry of the basic period is available in which an extension fee can be paid with 50% surcharge (OJ2009, 603). Re-establishment is not possible. (see **Art.79(2):2.3**; A-III,12.2)

R. 58 Correction of deficiencies in the application documents

If the European patent application does not comply with the requirements of Rule 57(a) to (d), (h) and (i), the European Patent Office shall inform the applicant accordingly and invite him to correct the deficiencies noted within two months. The description, claims and drawings may be amended only to an extent sufficient to remedy such deficiencies.

R.57 Examination as to formal requirements
Implementation of: **Art.90(4)**
EPC 1973: **R.41(1)**

1 **Invitation to correct deficiencies in the application**
Where the formalities examination under **Art.90(3)** reveals that the application does not comply with the requirement of **R.57(a)** to **(d)**, **(h)** and **(i)**, the EPO will invite the applicant to correct them within two months of notification of the invitation (**R.58**). See the notes to **R.57** for the invitation in the cases where the requirements of **R.57(e)** to **(g)** and **(j)** are not complied with. **R.135(2)** excludes the non-extendable two-month period of **R.58** from further processing. Hence, re-establishment according to **Art.122** and **R.136** is available.

The sanction on failure to meet the period of **R.58** is refusal of the application unless another sanction is provided (**Art.90(5)**). The notes to **R.57** mention the specific sanctions provided for not meeting the requirements and any remedies.

If the sanction is refusal, an appeal may be filed as remedy, correcting the deficiency on filing the appeal. **J18/08** allowed correction of not appointing a representative in this manner. In contrast, if the sanction is deemed withdrawn and a decision under **R.112(2)** is requested, an appeal against a negative decision will merely be a re-examination of the loss of rights communication. The communication will only be regarded inaccurate if the act was performed in due time. Hence, in such a case an appeal cannot be used to correct a deficiency (**J18/08** r.5).

2 **Amendment of the application documents**
Prior to the receipt of the search report the applicant may amend his application only if the Receiving Section has invited him under **R.58** to remedy particular deficiencies (see **R.137(1)**).

After receipt of the search report and before the receipt of the first communication from the examining division the applicant may amend the application of his own volition (**Art.123(1)**, last sentence and **R.137(2)** as valid before 01.04.2010), taking care not to extend the subject-matter (**Art.123(2)**) (A-V,2.1). When the search report is drawn up on or after 01.04.2010, a voluntary amendment is only allowed when filed together with the first substantive response (**R.137(2)** as valid from 01.04.2010).

An applicant may correct any errors in the application of his own volition by filing a request according to **R.139** (A-V,3).

R. 59 Deficiencies in claiming priority

If the file number of the previous application under Rule 52, paragraph 1, or the copy of that application under Rule 53, paragraph 1, have not been filed in due time, the European Patent Office shall inform the applicant accordingly and invite him to file them within a period to be specified.

R.52(1) Content of declaration of priority
R.53(1) Priority document
Implementation of: **Art.90(4)**
EPC 1973: **R.41(2), (3)**

1 **Correction of file number or filing copy of priority document**
Under **R.59** the applicant will be invited to indicate the file number of the previous application or to file a copy thereof if this has not already been done within the 16-month period under **R.52(2)** and **R.53(1)**. In accordance with **Art.90(5)**, the right of priority will be lost if the deficiencies noted in the invitation are not corrected within the period specified. (Spec. Ed. 1 of OJ 2003, p.159)

The EPO specifies a period of two months for responding to the invitation (A-III,6.5.3 for the file number; A-III,6.7 for the copy).

Since the period of response is specified by the office, it can be extended by filing a request under **R.132(2)** before expiry of the period. **R.135(2)** excludes the two-month period of **R.59** from further processing. Re-establishment of rights according to **Art.122** and **R.136** will be available as a legal remedy.

See **R.57(g):8** for more detail.

R. 60 Subsequent designation of the inventor

Implementation of: **Art.90(4)**
EPC 1973: **R.42**

1 **Omission of the designation of inventor**
If it is difficult to obtain the data of a sole inventor within 16 months from the date of filing or priority, another person may be designated temporarily as inventor to avoid the more expensive remedies stated below. After the data of the inventor have been obtained, the designation can be rectified under **R.21**, whereby the signature of the other person is required because he was wrongly designated. The other person may be an employee of the applicant. If the other person is the representative, the EPO might not accept the designation and request correction under **R.60**, which provides less time for correction than **R.21**. Note, that a change in designation of inventor may require an oath of inventorship for a corresponding patent application filed in the US.

R. 60(1) If the designation of the inventor has not been made in accordance with Rule 19, the European Patent Office shall inform the applicant that the European patent application will be refused unless the designation is made within sixteen months of the date of filing of the application or, if priority is claimed, of the date of priority, this period being deemed to have been observed if the information is communicated before completion of the technical preparations for the publication of the European patent application.

1 **Invitation to correct designation of the inventor**
The application must designate the inventor according to **Art.81**. Compliance of the designation with the requirements of **R.19(1)** or **R.41(2)(j)** is checked during the formalities examination under **Art.90(3)** and **R.57(f)**. The applicant will be informed of a missing or incorrect designation in accordance with **R.60(1)**. See **R.57:7** for the content of the designation.

2 **Period for filing designation of inventor**
The designation of inventor must be submitted on the date of filing. There is a deficiency if it is not filed together with the application documents or the designation is not correct. In that case the EPO will invite the applicant to file the designation or correction within sixteen months of the date of filing or, if priority is claimed, of the date of priority (**R.60(1)**). The period is deemed to have been observed according to **R.60(1)** if the deficiency is remedied before the completion of the technical preparations for publication of the application (see **R.67(1):1**). The timing of the remedy allows the EPO to mention the designation in the published application as required by **R.20(1)**.

If the designation is not filed before completion of the technical preparations, the application will be published without the designation; since the EPO can check the requirement of **R.60(1)** only after said completion, the publication cannot be stopped anymore. After the publication the EPO will inform the applicant according to **R.60(1)** about its reasons for refusal, allow him to comment, and subsequently issue the decision to refuse under **R.60(1)**. The refusal can be remedied using further processing under **Art.121** and **R.135**, in spite of the fact that the 16-month period has a remedial character (see **R.135(2):1**).

In the case of an early publication of the application, at the request of the applicant or because of an early decision to grant (**Art.93(1)**, (2)), the 16-month period is not shortened and the applicant may file the designation after the publication of the application if this is still within the period. The application will not be re-published with designation; the designation will be published in the Bulletin and will be available in the register (reason 3.2; not republishing appears to be in conflict with **R.20(1)**). (**J1/10** r.1-3; A-III,5.5)

The quasi-extension of the 16-month period, modelled on the PCT, was included in the provision to give the applicant more time; however it obfuscates the expiry of the period and complicates the procedure.

R. 60(2) Where, in a divisional application or a new application under Article 61, paragraph 1(b), the designation of the inventor has not been made in accordance with Rule 19, the European Patent Office shall invite the applicant to make the designation within a period to be specified.

Art.61(1)(b) Application filed by non-entitled person
R.19 Content of designation of the inventor

1 **Designation of inventor for divisional and new application**
The designation of inventor for a divisional application and a new application under **Art.61(1)(b)** is also due on filing. If the designation is not made on filing the application, the EPO will invite the applicant to file it within a period to be specified, which is at least two months (**R.132(2)**). (Spec. Ed. 1 of OJ 2003, p.159)

Chapter II *European search report*

R. 61 Content of the European search report

Implementation of: **Art.92**
EPC 1973: **R.44**

1 **Contents**
The search report transmitted to the applicant contains the search report proper, mentioning the prior art documents retrieved in the search (**R.61**), the search strategy used for retrieving the documents (**R.61(1):2**), and the search opinion, giving an opinion on the patentability of the invention in view of the prior art (**R.62**). The search report will be published under **Art.92** and **R.68**. The publication includes the search report proper. Neither the search strategy (OJ 2017 A106 §4(d)) nor the search opinion (**R.62(2)**) will be published; they are available via file inspection.

R. 61(1) The European search report shall mention those documents, available to the European Patent Office at the time of drawing up the report, which may be taken into consideration in deciding whether the invention to which the European patent application relates is new and involves an inventive step.

1 **Cited documents**
The search report cites only those prior art documents which are present in the search files or to which the search division has access in another way (B-VI,6.1). Although the report usually cites written documents, it may also cite video and audio media fragments available on the internet (B-X,11.6). Instead of a document published before the filing date in an inconvenient language, the search examiner may cite from a translation published after the filing date, such as another member of the same patent family (B-VI,6.2).

Apart from the documents mentioned in paragraph 1, the search report could also mention (B-X,8):

- Claims not searched because the claims fee is not paid (**R.45(3)**);
- Lack of unity: identification of groups of claims searched (**R.64(1)**);
- Claims for which no meaningful search could be made (**R.63**), together with reason, e.g. not patentable (**Art.52(2)**, **Art.53**), insufficiently clear claims (**Art.84**).

2 **Search strategy**
The search examiner uses a search strategy as set out in B-IV,2 for retrieving relevant prior art documents. Details of the strategy useful for applicants and third parties, such as the databases consulted and keywords used, are included in an information sheet that will be attached to each search report drawn up by the EPO. The information sheet will be sent to the applicant together with the search report (B-X,3.4). The information sheet is not published but will be available via file inspection. (OJ 2017 A106)

R. 61(2) Each citation shall be referred to the claims to which it relates. Where appropriate, relevant parts of the documents cited shall be identified.

R. 61(3) The European search report shall distinguish between cited documents published before the date of priority claimed, between such date of priority and the date of filing, and on or after the date of filing.

1 **Documents published before and after priority and filing date**

The date of filing is the date when all documents required for an application have been received and comply with the requirements of **Art.80**; this date can be later than the date of receipt of the first documents if these are insufficient to accord a date of filing.

Only European applications can be regarded as prior rights under **Art.54(3)**. Under PCT, international, European and national prior rights will be mentioned in the international search report and the international preliminary examination report (**R.33.1**(c) and **R.64.3** PCT), but will not be considered prior art for the international preliminary examination (**R.64.3** PCT). The PCT has no equivalent of **Art.55** EPC, i.e. it has no provisions for non-prejudicial disclosure.

If the claimed priority dates cannot be verified, uncertainty will exist as regards their validity and the search will be extended to all published patent applications with an earliest priority date up to the filing date (not the claimed priority date) of the application under consideration (B-VI,3). The search takes into account not only documents published before the earliest priority date, but also intermediate documents, published between the earliest priority date and the filing date of the application under consideration (B-VI,5.2). Since it is the examining division's responsibility to assess the validity of the priority claim, the search division does not check it. However, documents pointing to an unjustified priority claim are indicated, e.g. an earlier filing for the same invention by the same applicant of which no priority has been claimed, or a USA continuation in part (CIP) of which the priority is claimed but where the priority of the parent of the CIP has not been claimed (B-VI,5.3).

2 **Categories of documents in search report**

The search report uses the following categories to distinguish between the cited documents (B-X,9.2):

X: particularly relevant document when taken alone;
Y: particularly relevant document when taken in combination with another document classified as Y;
A: document defining the general state of the art and not particularly relevant ('A' of German allgemein = general);
O: non-written disclosure ('O' of oral);
P: intermediate document published in the priority interval or on the date of priority ('P' of priority);
T: document published after the filing or priority date and cited for the principle or theory underlying the invention ('T' of theory);
E: potentially conflicting patent document (prior right) published after the filing date of the application searched but having a filing or priority date earlier than that date; also a patent document having the same priority date ('E' of the German älteres Recht = prior right).
D: document cited in the application searched ('D' of description);
L: document throwing doubt on a priority claim, establishing the publication date of another citation or relevant for double patenting.

The Register also uses the category 'I' to indicate a document which, taken alone, casts doubt on inventive step.

R. 61(4) Any document which refers to an oral disclosure, a use or any other means of disclosure which took place before the date of filing of the European patent application shall be mentioned in the European search report, together with an indication of the date of publication, if any, of the document and the date of the non-written disclosure.

1 **Oral disclosure**
The search mentions a non-written disclosure only if there is a written confirmation or if the searcher is convinced that the facts can be proved. **Art.54** does consider a public oral description as prior art (B-VI,2). The PCT recognizes this only as prior art if it is substantiated by a written disclosure.

R. 61(5) The European search report shall be drawn up in the language of the proceedings.

R. 61(6) The European search report shall contain the classification of the subject-matter of the European patent application in accordance with the international classification.

1 **Classification of documents in search report**
The code is the IPC (International Patent Classification) code (**R.8**).
A classification is given for each invention when the application lacks unity (B-V,3.3).

R. 62 Extended European search report

Implementation of: **Art.92**
EPC 1973: **R.44a**

1 **Opinion on patentability**
To increase its efficiency the EPO issues the search report and the first opinion on patentability together. The measure helps to streamline the granting procedure, reduce the time applications are pending, and encourage early withdrawals. Since the BEST project (see **Art.15:1**) the search examiner is also the primary substantive examiner, it increases efficiency if the examiner prepares an opinion on patentability already at the search stage. As the opinion will cause more amendments to be filed upon entering substantive examination, it also helps to reduce the average time for granting a patent to the desired 36 months.

Since the Convention does not provide for integration of the search and substantive examination, the EPO has introduced the Extended European Search Report (EESR) as an interim solution. The EESR contains the European search report and a non-binding opinion on whether the application and the invention to which it relates seem to meet the requirements of the Convention. Although the opinion is prepared in the context of the search, it is not part of the search report drawn up under **Art.92** and it is independent of the subsequent substantive examination under **Art.94**. The opinion may be used by the applicant to assess the patentability of his application and decide whether to continue the prosecution or not.

Search and examination have been further integrated by making a response to an opinion that notes deficiencies compulsory. The response is to be filed before expiry of the period for requesting examination (**R.70a**). The contents of the opinion and the compulsory response make the search opinion effectively a first Art.94(3) communication. However, since it is drawn up during search and not during substantive examination, it is, in a legal sense, not an Art.94(3) communication and it is therefore called an opinion. Moreover, the opinion does not bind the EPO, as emphasised by the word 'seem' in R.62(1). (OJ 2005, 435 §I.1)

R. 62(1) The European search report shall be accompanied by an opinion on whether the application and the invention to which it relates seem to meet the requirements of this Convention, unless a communication under Rule 71, paragraph 1 or 3, can be issued.

R.71(1) Communication of the Examining Division
R.71(3) Invitation to approve text for grant

1 **Extended European Search Report**
The EPO will draft an opinion on patentability, also called 'search opinion', to accompany the search report for European applications and Euro-PCT applications for which a supplementary search report must be drawn up under **Art.153(7)**. The opinion may include objections, suggestions to overcome the objections and positive statements about patentability (B-XI,3).

The 'unless' in the provision refers to the case where the examination fee has been paid before the search report is transmitted to the applicant and the right to the communication under **R.70(2)** has been waived (**R.10(4)**). In this special case the examination can start immediately after completion of the search report and no opinion will be sent. Instead, a first communication of the examining division under **R.71(1)** or **R.71(3)** will be sent. The **R.71(1)** communication will be issued as soon as possible after completion of the search report if the application does not meet the requirements of the EPC (C-VI,3). This communication is legally binding, in contrast with the search opinion. A **R.71(3)** communication will be issued if the application is ready for grant and a final search does not reveal additional prior rights (C-VI,3). In all other cases the search report is accompanied by the opinion on patentability.

If the EESR contains a positive opinion, the applicant can pay the examination fee in the usual way. He will then receive the **R.71(3)** communication, provided the top-up search carried out about 18 months after the filing date (**Art.92:6**) does not reveal additional prior art under **Art.54(3)** and the examining division assigned concurs with the opinion. (B-XI,3.9)

If the EESR contains objections to patentability, the applicant must respond within six months from publication of the search report to meet the objections (**R.70a**). He may file voluntary amendments in the same period (**R.137(2)**). The substantive examination starts after completion of the requirements set out in **R.70**.

R. 62(2) The opinion under paragraph 1 shall not be published together with the search report.

1 **Transmittal and non-publication of opinion**
When the EPO transmits the search report to the applicant under **R.65**, it includes the opinion on patentability (B-X,12).

The opinion is not published together with the search report under **Art.92**, because it is not part of the search report. However, it is accessible to the public. Once the EESR is despatched to the applicant, it is part of the file and will become available for inspection under **Art.128(4)** after publication of the application. (A-VI,1.3)

R. 62a Applications containing a plurality of independent claims

Inserted by decision of the Administrative Council of 25.03.2009, which entered into force on 01.04.2010. (OJ2009, 299)
Implementation of **Art.92**

1 **General**
The purpose of **R.62a** is to reduce the number of independent claims in the same category to within the scope of **R.43(2)** and define the invention more clearly at the start of the search stage, thereby reducing the problems of multiple independent claims in the same category during search and examination and providing legal certainty for the public about the scope of the application at an early stage. **R.62a** makes **R.43(2)** enforceable already at the search stage.

R. 62a(1) If the European Patent Office considers that the claims as filed do not comply with Rule 43, paragraph 2, it shall invite the applicant to indicate, within a period of two months, the claims complying with Rule 43, paragraph 2, on the basis of which the search is to be carried out. If the applicant fails to provide such an indication in due time, the search shall be carried out on the basis of the first claim in each category.

R.43(2) Several independent claims in one category

1 **Multiple independent claims during search**
If the search examiner opines that the application contains multiple independent claims in the same category that do not comply with **R.43(2)**, he will invite the applicant to indicate the claims complying with **R.43(2)** on which he will base his search. The invitation need not be reasoned. The applicant may respond by indicating the claims complying with **R.43(2)** that he wants to have searched. These claims must be pending and may not be deemed abandoned because of non-payment of claims fees (B-VIII,4.4). Claims dependent on an unsearched independent claim will likewise not be searched (B-VIII,4.6).

Alternatively he may contest the opinion of the search examiner, arguing that the independent claims do comply with the law or that apparently independent claims are in fact dependent. See **R.43(4):1** for the definition of an independent claim. If he convinces the search examiner that the objection was not justified, the examiner will search all claims. If his arguments are not convincing, the search will be based on the first independent claim (B-VIII,4.2.2). At this stage of the prosecution amendments of the application will not yet be admitted (**R.137(1)**).

The period for response to the invitation is two months according to **R.62a(1)**, first sentence. If no response is filed in time, the search will be based on the first independent claim in each category (**R.62a(1)**, second sentence). Further processing for the two-month period is ruled out by **R.135(2)** to have the search report ready before publication of the application; re-establishment is available.

2 **Multiple independent claims and non-unity**
The EPC does not provide for payment of a further search fee for searching subject-matter of claims not complying with **R.43(2)**. Such further search fees are only provided for non-unitary inventions (**R.64**).

When an application to be searched has two non-unitary independent claims in the same category, the search examiner can choose between (1) objecting against multiple independent claims and sending the applicant an invitation under **R.62a(1)** to indicate the claims to be searched and (2) issuing a non-unity objection and inviting the applicant under **R.64** to pay further search fees. The first option does not provide an opportunity to have both claims searched. The choice of the examiner depends on the specific application being searched (B-VIII,4.5).

R. 62a(2) The Examining Division shall invite the applicant to restrict the claims to the subject-matter searched unless it finds that the objection under paragraph 1 was not justified.

1 **Restriction of claims during examination**
R.62a(2) and **R.137(5)** ensure that no patent is granted with claims relating to unsearched subject-matter. During the substantive examination the applicant will be invited under **R.62a(2)** to restrict the claims to the searched subject-matter. During examination amendments introducing unsearched subject-matter in the claims will not be allowed under **R.137(5)**.

The applicant may respond to the invitation under **R.62a(2)** by arguing that the objection under **R.62a(1)** was not justified. If the examiner agrees, the invitation will be withdrawn ('unless' in **R.62a(2)**) and a new search made.

If the applicant does not convince the examiner and he does not restrict the claims as requested, the application may be refused under **Art.97(2)** as not meeting all the EPC requirements (F-IV,3.3).

Subject-matter covered by claims not searched on account of **R.62a(1)** may not be used for amending claims (**R.137(5)**). Protection for such subject-matter can only be obtained by filing a divisional application.

R. 63 Incomplete search

Amended by decision of the Administrative Council of 25.03.2009, which entered into force on 01.04.2010. Amended **R.63** applies to applications for which the search report or the supplementary search report is drawn up on or after 01.04.2010. (OJ2009, 299)

The provision for applications where the search report is drawn up before 01.04.2010 has been set out in the notes below.
Implementation of **Art.84** and **Art.92**
EPC 1973: **R.45**

1 **Unsearchable subject-matter**
R.63 provides an exception to the EPO's obligation to carry out a search for each application. The EPO will not search claims that are not properly drafted or relate to unpatentable subject-matter. In such cases it will invite the applicant to indicate the subject-matter to be searched. The indication, to be submitted before the search, should improve the quality of the search. If the applicant does not respond or the indicated subject-matter does not overcome the deficiency, the EPO will issue a partial search report or a declaration that no search could be carried out. Unsearched subject-matter cannot be used anymore for amending the claims.

R.63 should induce applicants to comply with the clarity requirement of **Art.84** already at the search stage and avoid additional searches during the substantive examination.

R. 63(1) If the European Patent Office considers that the European patent application fails to such an extent to comply with this Convention that it is impossible to carry out a meaningful search regarding the state of the art on the basis of all or some of the subject-matter claimed, it shall invite the applicant to file, within a period of two months, a statement indicating the subject-matter to be searched.

1 **Reasons for incomplete search**
According to **R.63** the search division will not search applications or parts thereof that do not comply with the requirements of the EPC to such an extent that no meaningful search can be made. Important requirements are that the subject-matter must have technical character (**Art.52(2)**), not be excluded from patentability (**Art.53**) and be sufficiently clear and complete (**Art.83**), and that the claims are clear, concise and supported by the description (**Art.84**), and are susceptible of industrial application (**Art.57**). As an example, a claim having eight independent numerical parameters was regarded unclear and therefore unsearchable (EP1540227).

R.63 may also be applied where the claims extend the subject-matter of the application as filed (**Art.123(2)**) or of the parent application (**Art.76(1)**, B-VIII,3(iv)). Non-compliance may also occur for only some of the claims or for part of a claim (B-VIII,1). The above considerations are similar to those set out in R.39.1 PCT, which are regarded as applicable to searches under the EPC (B-VIII,1).

The Search Division determines what is or is not 'meaningful' as a question of fact. **R.63** should not be invoked because a search is difficult. **T1242/04** held that **R.63** relates only to the practicability of a search and not to the potential relevance of its results in subsequent substantive examination (see hn.I, r.8.5). B-VIII,3 gives examples where **R.63** may be applied.

R.63 constitutes an exception to the EPO's obligation to carry out a search as an essential element of the grant procedure and as such must be interpreted narrowly (**T1242/04** r.8.2). Hence, a declaration under **R.63** may be issued only in exceptional cases in which the claimed subject-matter, i.e. the entire set of claims including all independent and dependent claims, clearly has no technical character (**T1242/04** hn.II).

1.1 SUBJECT-MATTER LACKING TECHNICAL CHARACTER UNDER ART.52(2) AND (3)
The search division will not search subject-matter excluded from patentability because of lacking technical character (**Art.52(2), (3)**).

A feature that is non-technical when taken in isolation may nonetheless contribute to the technical character if in the context of the invention it contributes to produce a technical effect. Claimed features must therefore be analysed in the light of the description and drawings to determine if they produce a technical effect and form part of a technical solution of a technical problem. The search opinion must indicate which claimed features do not contribute to the technical character of the invention. (B-VIII,2.2)

Hence, a claim merely relating to no more than a method of doing business will not be searched. A declaration under **R.63** to this effect will take the place of the search report. Where the claimed subject matter involves technical means, a search report or partial search report will be issued. When the technical means are notorious knowledge, i.e. so conventional that they were widely available to everyone at the date of filing and no documentary evidence is considered required because of their notoriety, such as a standard computer, the search report will state so and will not cite a document (Not. EPO, OJ 2007, 592; **T1411/08** r.4.1, 4.2). A search report not citing any document can only be issued for computer-implemented business methods (B-VIII,2.2.1).

The existence of notorious knowledge cannot be reasonably disputed. This should be distinguished from common general knowledge, which can in general be reasonably questioned (B-VIII,2.2.1; **Art.56:3.6**). The examining division must provide documentary evidence if the notoriety of the knowledge is challenged (**T2467/09** r.7-10).

1.2 SUBJECT-MATTER EXCLUDED FROM PATENTABILITY UNDER ART.53

The EPO will not search subject-matter excluded from patentability because its commercial exploitation contravenes morality (**Art.53(a)**), it relates to a plant or animal variety or a biological method for the production of plants or animals (**Art.53(b)**), or it relates to a method for medical treatment or diagnosis (**Art.53(c)**).

A claim relating to a medical method should be searched in the case that the determining technical feature is the effect of a substance, which can be searched (B-VIII,2.1).

1.3 SUBJECT-MATTER NOT COMPLYING WITH ART.83 AND 84

Important requirements are those for sufficiency of disclosure (**Art.83**), clarity and conciseness of the claims and support by the description (**Art.84**) (see also OJ 2000, 228). Non-compliance with **Art.83** and **84** often occurs as a direct result of the applicant's drafting style. The following four examples clarify the problems posed by this non-compliance.

A broad claim supported by a limited disclosure covering a small part of the scope of the claim may lack support and sufficient disclosure. Such a claim may be searched only on the basis of the narrower, disclosed invention or even disclosed examples (B-III,3.6; B-VIII,3(i)). The searcher may base his search on what he considers to be the extent to which the claims are defensible in a subsequent substantive examination.

A large number of claims or possibilities within a claim is not concise. The large number may make it burdensome to determine the subject-matter for which protection is sought and make a complete search de facto impossible or useless in view of the indefensibility of the claims or claim (B-VIII,3(ii); see example **T1873/06**). See also **R.62a** for a restriction on the number of independent claims.

A claim defined in terms of desiderata may violate **Art.83** and/or **Art.84**, leading to an incomplete search (OJ 2000, 228).

The definition of a claim in terms of a particular parameter may make a meaningful search impossible, e.g. because the prior art does not use the parameter; in such a case a partial search may be made for the disclosed examples or the way in which the parameter is obtained (B-VIII,3(iii)).

2 **Statement indicating subject-matter to be searched**
If the search division is of the opinion that a normal search cannot be carried out, it will invite the applicant to file a statement more clearly defining the subject-matter to be searched (**R.63(1)**). The invitation is reasoned (B-VIII,3.1). The statement may (Not. EPO OJ 2009,533 §3.2; B-VIII,3.2):
- indicate that part of the description, e.g. a specific embodiment, which can be used for interpreting the claims, or
- consist of an explanation in the form of an improved claims wording; the amended claims will only become a formal amendment if requested so in the response to the extended European search report.

Note, that a search based on the statement may conflict with the EPC, because amendment of claims at this stage is prohibited by **R.137(1)**, **R.63** not qualifying as an exception (see also OJ 2009, 533 §7.1 and the excuse in B-VIII,3.2.2), and the search must be based on the claims and not on a part of the description according to **Art.92**.

The applicant may, instead of indicating subject-matter to be searched, argue that the claimed subject-matter is searchable (B-VIII,3.2).

Any improvement of the claims during the substantive examination to improve compliance with **Art.53, 83** and **84** will very likely introduce unsearched subject-matter and will not be admissible under **R.137(5)**. Hence, the statement filed before the search will probably limit the scope of the claims, without a possibility to enlarge the scope later-on during the substantive examination.

Any further interaction with the search examiner after filing the amendment is not provided for in the EPC and Guidelines.

R. 63(2) If the statement under paragraph 1 is not filed in due time, or if it is not sufficient to overcome the deficiency noted under paragraph 1, the European Patent Office shall either issue a reasoned declaration stating that the European patent application fails to such an extent to comply with this Convention that it is impossible to carry out a meaningful search regarding the state of the art on the basis of all or some of the subject-matter claimed or, as far as is practicable, draw up a partial search report. The reasoned declaration or the partial search report shall be considered, for the purposes of subsequent proceedings, as the European search report.

1 **Procedure before search division**
The applicant must file the statement indicating the subject-matter to be searched within two months from invitation (**R.63(1)**). Further processing is not possible according to **R.135(2)** to allow publication of the search report together with the application; however, re-establishment is available.

If the statement is not filed within two months from invitation, if it is not sufficient to overcome the deficiencies, or if the arguments that the claimed subject-matter is searchable are not regarded convincing, the EPO will issue either a declaration that no meaningful search could be carried out or a partial search report covering only some of the subject-matter claimed. A statement may be insufficient if it refers to subject-matter without basis in the application as filed.

The declaration that no search could be carried out must be reasoned according to **R.63(2)**, first sentence, i.e. the search division must state why it regards the claims as not searchable. The partial search report must also give the reasons for restricting the search (B-X,8(iii)). The applicant cannot contest the opinion of the search division at the search stage; however, he may argue the reasoning of the search division during the substantive examination (see **R.63(3)**).

If a document cited in the application appears to be essential for the search and the document is not available at the EPO, the search division will ask the applicant to file a copy of it. If the applicant fails to comply, a partial search may result or a declaration that no meaningful search could be made. (B-IV,1.3)

2 **Additional searches**

The search division can make an additional search report on request of the examining division because of amendments of claims (but see **R.137(5)**), clarification of obscurities (**R.63**), reversal of the provisional opinion of the search division on unity (**R.64**) or exclusion from patentability, or imperfections in the initial search. (B-II, 4.2; C-IV,7.2; H-II,5 and 6)

In the exceptional case where a **R.63** declaration has been issued, it is not always necessary to carry out an additional search. An objection of lack of inventive step may be raised without documented prior art, e.g. if the claimed subject-matter is obvious from the common general knowledge. However, if the claim features do not form part of the common general knowledge and the applicant does not acknowledge them to be known, an additional search must be carried out. (**T1242/04** r.9.2)

R. 63(3) When a partial search report has been drawn up, the Examining Division shall invite the applicant to restrict the claims to the subject-matter searched unless it finds that the objection under paragraph 1 was not justified.

1 **Procedure before examining division**

If the search division has issued a partial search report, the examining division will invite the applicant to restrict the claims to the subject-matter searched (**R.63(3)**), because according to **G2/92** r.2 the EPO will only examine searched subject-matter. The applicant may in response contest the restricted search. If the argument convinces the examiner, no restriction of the claims is necessary (**R.63(3)**) and an additional search may be carried out (B-VIII,3.2; C-IV,7.2).

If the applicant does not convince the examiner and he does not restrict the claims as requested, the application will not meet the requirements of the EPC and may be refused under **Art.97(2)**.

Since **R.137(5)** does not allow amended claims to relate to subject-matter not searched in accordance with **R.63**, protection for such subject-matter can only by pursued in a divisional application.

If a declaration has been issued and the applicant cannot convince the examiner, his application will not contain any searched subject-matter. Although **R.63(3)** implies that he cannot maintain any claims and that the application should be refused, the applicant may amend his claims again before the examining division (C-IV,7,2(i)).

R. 64 European search report where the invention lacks unity

Implementation of **Art.82** and **Art.92**
EPC 1973: **R.46**

R. 64(1) If the European Patent Office considers that the European patent application does not comply with the requirement of unity of invention, it shall draw up a partial search report on those parts of the application which relate to the invention, or the group of inventions within the meaning of Article 82, first mentioned in the claims. It shall inform the applicant that, for the European search report to cover the other inventions, a further search fee must be paid, in respect of each invention involved, within a period of two months. The European search report shall be drawn up for the parts of the application relating to inventions in respect of which search fees have been paid.

Amended by decision of the Administrative Council of 25.03.2009, which entered into force on 01.04.2010 (OJ2009, 299).
Art.82 Unity of invention

1 **Non-unity opinion**
The search division assesses whether the application complies with the unity requirement of **Art.82**, i.e. whether the application relates to one invention or a linked group of inventions. The search division considers lack of unity both a priori and a posteriori. See **R.44** for the definition of unity of invention. Lack of unity a priori arises before considering prior art, where independent claims do not have a common inventive concept. The inventions may also be hidden in a Markush claim, i.e. a claim in which features are connected by 'or'. Lack of unity a posteriori arises after considering prior art, e.g. where an independent claim is shown to be not novel and leaving two or more claims, which, when made independent, are without a common inventive concept. (F-V,7)

The opinion of the EPO on unity may change during prosecution of the application in the light of new facts and evidence (B-VII,1.4). Hence, a non-unity objection may be raised for the first time by the examining division.

2 **Procedure before search division**
If the search division considers that the application does not comply with the unity requirement, it will draw up a partial search report for the invention first mentioned in the claims (**R.64(1)**, first sentence). It will send the applicant a communication including the partial search report and a provisional opinion of the patentability of the invention first mentioned in the claims, a specification of the separate inventions and the reasons for non-unity (OJ 2017 A20; B-VII,1.1, 1.2; B-XI,5; F-V, 6.1, not in GL2017). The opinion and the reasons allow the applicant to form a reasoned opinion about his chances. No reply is required and, if filed, will not be considered by the search division.

The communication also invites the applicant to pay a further search fee equal to the search fee (**Rfees2(1)2**) for each further invention to be searched; the fees must be paid within two months of invitation (**R.64(1)**, second sentence; B-VII,1.2). If the automatic debiting procedure is used, the applicant must inform the EPO within this period if he does not want all or any of the further inventions to be searched. Otherwise all the further search fees will be debited automatically on the last day of the period (**AAD.6.1**; B-VII,1.2)

When an applicant pays fewer further search fees than the number of further inventions, he must indicate to which further inventions the fees pertain. Without such an indication the purpose of the payment is not clear and the examiner will issue a communication under **Rfees6(2)** to establish the purpose.

If the applicant does not pay any further search fee(s), no further inventions will be searched.

After completion of the search, the search division issues a search report and opinion covering the first invention and any further invention for which the search fee has been paid (**R.64(1)**, third sentence; B-XI,5). The report also contains the non-unity objection and the reason for it. If the search can be extended over all inventions of a non-unitary application without much effort, e.g. in case of unity a posteriori and/or conceptually very close inventions, the search division will not ask further search fees and issues a search report and search opinion stating the non-unity opinion (B-VII,2.2). The non-unity opinion cannot be contested in the search stage; this can be done during the substantive examination.

The search opinion will also invite the applicant to limit his claims to subject-matter that has been searched (B-VIII,3.3).

Subject-matter relating to unsearched inventions may not be used for amending the claims during the substantive examination (**R.137(5)**).

3 **Review of opinion by examining division**

The examining division is obliged to review the non-unity opinion of the search division (C-III,3.1; F-V,11.1; **T631/97** r.3.9.2). Decision **T631/97** interpreted an unclear paragraph in **G2/92** (r.3) relating to this obligation in the above sense. The examining division will also consider the question of unity if the search division did not raise it (C-III,3.1).

Under BEST the search examiner and the substantive examiner are the same person (see **Art.15:1**). Hence, an ex-officio review of the non-unity opinion during the substantive examination appears not very likely. Instead, an applicant who does not agree with the opinion should send his arguments in favour of unity in his response to the search opinion and request a review of the non-unity opinion.

If the examiner considers the opinion justified, the examination will proceed on the basis of the searched invention or, where several inventions have been searched, the searched invention selected by the applicant (C-III,3.1.2). Non-payment of further search fees deprives the applicant of the right to choose with which invention to continue the application; he is bound to the searched invention (**G2/92** hn). The non-unity issue will not be the subject of an interlocutory decision. An applicant desiring a review by a board of appeal of the unity objection, should have the application refused in first instance on the ground of non-unity and appeal the refusal. Lack of substantiation of a non-unity decision may be regarded as a substantial procedural violation, justifying reimbursement of an appeal fee under **R.103** (**T708/00** r.20).

Subject-matter not relating to the invention to be examined must be excised from the application and may be used for one or more divisional applications (**G2/92** hn). Any further search fee paid for a non-unitary invention gives entitlement to a refund under **Rfees9(2)** of the search fee for a divisional application filed for this invention.

If the examiner considers the non-unity opinion not justified, the examination will proceed on the basis of the unitary inventions, possibly supplemented by an additional search ordered by the examiner (B-II,4.2(iii)). Further search fees paid by the applicant will be refunded only if a refund has been requested under **R.64(2)**.

4 **Basis of substantive examination**

The EPO will only carry out a substantive examination of an invention if the invention has been searched (**G2/92** r.2). Hence, when no further search fee has been paid, the applicant is deemed to have elected the searched invention (C-III,3.1.1) and the opinion on patentability, included in the EESR (see **R.62**), will relate to the searched invention and include an invitation to excise the non-unitary claims and related subject-matter (C-III,3.1.1). When a search fee has been paid for more than one invention, the applicant must inform the EPO on which searched invention the substantive examination is to be based (C-III,3.1.2). There are several opportunities for the applicant to inform the EPO of the invention to be examined.

If at the beginning of the substantive examination the examiner maintains the objection of lack of unity and the applicant has not yet stated on which one of several searched inventions the examination is to be based, the examiner will invite him to do so and to limit the application by excising the parts belonging to the other inventions. The applicant may file divisional applications for the other inventions. (C-III,3.1.1; 3.2; F-V,11.1)

During the examination the applicant may request a refund of further search fees under **R.64(2)**, if the Examining Division finds that the non-unity opinion of the Search Division was not justified.

The above procedure applies to a non-unitary direct European application. The procedure for a non-unitary Euro-PCT application is governed by **R.164**.

5 **Period for paying further search fees**

The period for paying further search fees is two months from invitation (**R.64(1)**, second sentence). **R.135(2)** excludes the period from further processing. Re-establishment under **Art.122** and **R.136** is available.

R. 64(2) Any fee paid under paragraph 1 shall be refunded if, during the examination of the European patent application, the applicant requests a refund and the Examining Division finds that the communication under paragraph 1 was not justified.

1 **Refund of further search fee**

If an applicant has paid further search fees under **R.64(1)** and considers that the application does comply with the requirement of unity, he should request a refund of one or more of the paid further search fees under **R.64(2)**. The request will be dealt with by the examining division, not by the search division (**R.64(2)**).

Since **R.64(2)** refers to the communication in **R.64(1)** expressing the non-unity opinion, the decision of the examining division need not deal with other objections such as an objection that the search report was not drawn up in accordance with the Guidelines. In such a case the examining division may arrange for an additional search if it considers a search report incomplete. (**J24/96** r.4)

If the examiner opines that the request should be refused, he will communicate his opinion in an **Art.94(3)** communication and give the applicant a period for response before issuing the decision. (C-III,3.3)

A decision on the request for refund of further search fees is usually given in the form of an interlocutory decision. The applicant may also request an appealable interlocutory decision on the matter. If the examiner has come to a conclusion on the request early in the grant procedure, an interlocutory decision should be issued promptly and not be left until the final decision on the application. If the conclusion is reached near the end of the procedure, an interlocutory decision on the request should be issued with the **R.71(3)** communication or the decision on the request should be included in the decision refusing the application. (C-III,3.3)

The interlocutory decision on a request for refund is separately appealable (C-III,3.3). The appeal of such an interlocutory decision runs in parallel with the grant proceedings (**J21/09** r.11) and is usually decided well after grant of the patent. Hence, its outcome cannot affect the grant proceedings. If the board of appeal decides that the non-unity decision of the examining division is to be reversed and the further search fees refunded, the scope of the already granted claims complying with the non-unity decision of the examining division cannot be broadened anymore (see e.g. **J24/96**, where the decision of the board of appeal was issued three years after the decision to grant). If an applicant is not interested in broadening the scope of the claims but only in a refund of further search fees, he should request an appealable interlocutory decision when requesting a refund of the further search fees.

If an applicant does want to have the option of broadening the scope of the claims following a reversal of the non-unity decision in appeal, he should request the examining division to issue a non-appealable interlocutory decision or to include the decision on refund in the decision to grant or refuse the application (**J21/09** r.8). In that case it is possible to contest the non-unity decision and, if successful, amend the scope of the claims accordingly

R. 65 Transmittal of the European search report

Immediately after it has been drawn up, the European search report shall be transmitted to the applicant together with copies of any cited documents.

Implementation of **Art.92**
EPC 1973: **Art.92(2)**

1 **Transmission of the search report**
Together with the search report and the copies of the cited documents, the EPO also forwards to the applicant:

- an annex to the search report listing the families of the patent documents cited in the search report (B-X,9; OJ 1999, 90),

- information relating to restriction of the subject of the search because of not-paid claims fees, non-unity or impossibility to make a meaningful or complete search (B-VIII.3.3; B-X,8),
- the translation of the title into the two other EPO languages (B-X,7),
- the definitive content of the abstract (B-X,7),
- the opinion on patentability (**R.62(1)**).

The annex listing the patent families, included in the publication, may be relevant to third parties (OJ 1984, 381).

Additional copies of the cited documents may be ordered from the EPO at a charge fixed under **Rfees3**.

If after completion of the search report but before the preparations for the publication of the search report are completed a further relevant document is found, it is added to the search report. If found before the filing of a request for examination, the late discovered document is sent to the applicant and the information is published. Thereafter, it is brought to the attention of the examining division. (B-IV,3.2)

R. 66 Definitive content of the abstract

Upon drawing up the European search report, the European Patent Office shall determine the definitive content of the abstract and transmit it to the applicant together with the search report.

Implementation of **Art.85** and **Art.92**
EPC 1973: **R.47**

1 **Purpose and content of abstract**

The sole purpose of the abstract is to provide information to the public (**Art.85**). The dissemination of information is the responsibility of the EPO. Hence, the EPO assesses the contents of the abstract. The search division examines the abstract, checking that it constitutes an efficient instrument for searching (F-II,2.2). After the search division has approved or modified the abstract, the EPO will transmit the definitive abstract to the applicant together with the search report (F-II,2.6).

Chapter III *Publication of the European patent application*

R. 67 Technical preparations for publication

Implementation of **Art.93(1)**
EPC 1973: **R.48**

R. 67(1) The President of the European Patent Office shall determine when the technical preparations for publication of the European patent application are deemed to have been completed.

1 **Completion of technical preparation**
The preparations are deemed to have been completed at the end of the day that comes five weeks before expiry of the eighteenth month from the day of filing or, if priority is claimed, from the earliest date of priority (Dec. of Pres. Spec. Ed. 3 of OJ 2007, D.1).

Example: priority date: Tuesday 18.04.2017, expiry of the 18 months for publication under **Art.93(1)**: Thursday 18.10.2018, 5 weeks before that date: Thursday 13.09.2018. The preparations are deemed to have been completed at the end of Thursday 13.09.2018 (adapted from **J11/80**, Summary of facts and submissions I and II).

Beware, **R.134** for extension of periods due to holidays does not apply to the 18-month period and the 5-week period.

After completion of the technical preparations, the application will be published. The publication is always on a Wednesday (OJ 1997, 542).

Note, that the technical preparations for PCT applications are completed by the 15th day prior to the date of publication (AG-IP §9.013) and the publication date is a Thursday.

R. 67(2) The application shall not be published if it has been finally refused or withdrawn or is deemed to be withdrawn before the termination of the technical preparations for publication.

1 **Non-publication of application**
The application will not be published if it has been finally refused, withdrawn or deemed withdrawn before the completion of the technical preparations as set out in paragraph 1. In the case illustrated above, it would be necessary to withdraw the application before the end of Sunday 13.09.2009 to guarantee non-publication.

The EPO is not obliged to prevent publication of an application which is withdrawn after the completion of the technical preparations as set out in **R.67(1)**. The EPO endeavours to prevent publication in such cases as well, provided the actual circumstances still so permit. This is checked on a case-by-case basis. The EPO cannot guarantee non-publication (**J5/81**). In practice, publication can often be prevented if the declaration of withdrawal is received by the Receiving Section at the latest two weeks before the scheduled date of publication (Not. EPO OJ 2006, 406 §3). If the scheduled date of publication in the above case is Wednesday 28.10.2009, then the withdrawal must have been received at the latest on Wednesday 14.10.2009.

The courtesy communication 'Notification of European publication number and information on the application of Article 67(3) EPC' informing the applicant when the technical preparations are completed, the publication number and the intended publication date of the application (A-VI,1.1), issued about four weeks before the scheduled date of publication, can be regarded as a final notification or warning of the date of publication (OJ 2006, 406 §3).

To ensure immediate recognition of a declaration of withdrawal intended to prevent publication as such, the applicant should send the declaration to the EPO separately, not combined with other declarations, clearly indicating the intention of preventing the forthcoming publication. The declaration may be sent by fax, for which no confirmation is necessary. (Not. EPO OJ 2006, 406)

See **Art.93(1):3** for deferred publication after abandonment of a priority claim.

2 **Invalid publication**

An invalid publication, i.e. a publication of an application withdrawn before publication, is not a publication under **Art.93** and does not give rise to a prior right effect under **Art.54(3)**, but only under **Art.54(2)** (G-IV,5.1.1). Moreover, it gives no provisional protection under **Art.67(1)**. See also **Art.93(1):4**.

If the publication of the application according to **Art.93(1)** can still be prevented, it might be possible that the publication of the mention thereof in the Bulletin according to **Art.129(a)** can no longer be prevented. In that case, the erroneous mention will be revoked by a subsequently published announcement in the Bulletin, thereby avoiding the file being opened for inspection (**Art.128(4)**).

3 **Conditional and unconditional withdrawal**

The application can only be withdrawn by a clear, signed declaration; if the request of the withdrawal is ambiguous, the search division must invite the applicant to clarify his request (J11/80). The applicant is bound by the request to withdraw. The only exception is withdrawal by mistake, for instance due to a wrong file number provided, in which case **R.139** may be applicable (J4/97).

A withdrawal can be made on condition of non-publication. This takes into account the procedural peculiarity that the applicant who makes his declaration of withdrawal later than five weeks before expiry of the 18-month period cannot know whether publication can still be prevented. (A-VI,1.2)

When requesting the EPO to withdraw an application to avoid publication, any pending priority application should also be withdrawn, because otherwise the subject-matter might still be published.

R. 68 Form of the publication of European patent applications and European search reports

Implementation of **Art.93(1)** and **Art.92**
EPC 1973: **Art.93(2)** + **R.49**

R. 68(1) The publication of the European patent application shall contain the description, the claims and any drawings as filed, and the abstract, or, if these documents making up the application were not filed in an official language of the European Patent Office, a translation in the language of the proceedings, and, in an annex, the European search report, where it is available before the termination of the technical preparations for publication. If the search report or the abstract is not published at the same time as the application, it shall be published separately.

1 **Contents of publication**

The description, claims and drawings of an application are published as filed, according to **R.68(1)**. The abstract, possibly amended by the EPO under **R.66**, is included in the publication. Any sequence listing filed at the date of filing of the application will also be published with the application (OJ 2013, 542 §IV.1)

If the application was not filed in an official EPO language, the text in the language of filing is the 'application as filed' (**Art.70(2)**). However, **Art.14(5)** stipulates that the application must be published in an official EPO language. Therefore, the lex specialis in the second half of the first sentence of **R.68(1)** makes it clear that in such a case the translation into the language of the proceedings will be published. The provisions of **Art.14(2)**, second sentence and **Art.70(2)** are unaffected. (CA/PL29/06 Add.1)

If the search report is available in time, it will be included in the publication; else it will be published separately (**R.68(1)**).

R. 68(2) The President of the European Patent Office shall determine the form of the publication of the application and the data to be included. The same shall apply where the European search report and the abstract are published separately.

1 **Form of publication**

All publications of European patent applications, European search reports and European patent specifications will be published only in electronic form by means of a publication server from which they can be downloaded (Dec. Pres., Spec. Ed. 3 of OJ 2007, D.3 Art.1(1)). See **R.145(1):1** for the publication server. Publication on paper has been discontinued (OJ 2005, 126).

A list of patent and non-patent literature cited in the description will be included at the end of applications and specifications published as from 13.09.2006. The list is made by the EPO and is for information only and does not form part of the application or specification. (Dec. Pres. Spec. Ed. 3 of OJ 2007, D.4)

2 **Identification of the publication**

The published application is given a serial number and an identification of the types of publication document (A-VI,1.3; OJ 2001, 117). As from 01.01.2002, the serial number of an application reflects the filing year in its first two positions (OJ 2001, 465). The publication numbers are consecutive numbers given according to the order of publication of the applications; the patent number is the same as the publication number. In all proceedings before the EPO the application and the possible patent are identified by the serial number. The EPO uses the following publication document codes:

A1 Patent application, front page with abstract (as approved or determined by search division) and search report

A2 Patent application and front page with abstract (as approved or determined by search division) without search report

A3 Search report and front page with abstract (as approved or determined by search division)
A4 Supplementary search report
A8 Corrected title page of an A document
A9 Complete reprint of a corrected A document
B1 Patent specification
B2 Patent specification as amended in opposition
B3 Patent specification as amended after limitation
B8 Corrected title page of a B document
B9 Complete reprint of a corrected B document

R. 68(3) The designated Contracting States shall be indicated in the published application.

1 **Designations in published application**
The publication of the application indicates all contracting states party to the EPC on the date of filing of the application (A-VI,1.3). The publication also indicates all extension states. See **Art.79:1** for changes in the designation system.

R. 68(4) If the claims were not filed on the date of filing of the application, this shall be indicated when the application is published. If, before the termination of the technical preparations for publication of the application, the claims have been amended under Rule 137, paragraph 2, the new or amended claims shall be included in the publication in addition to the claims as filed.

Amended by decision of the Administrative Council of 21.10.2008, which entered into force on 01.04.2009. The amendment deleted the superfluous word 'patent'. (OJ 2008, 513)
R.137(2) Voluntary amendment of application

1 **Publication of late-filed claims**
The first sentence in **R.68(4)** concerns cases where a European patent application is accorded a date of filing in accordance with **R.40(1)**, but the claims are only filed later. Since this later filing of claims may result in extension of subject-matter within the meaning of **Art.123(2)**, the fact that the claims were only filed after the date of filing is pointed out when the application is published. (CA/PL29/06, A-VI,1.3)

R. 69 Information about publication

Amended by decision of the Administrative Council of 25.03.2009, which entered into force on 01.04.2010. (OJ2009, 299)
Implementation of **Art.92**
EPC 1973: **R.50**

R. 69(1) The European Patent Office shall inform the applicant of the date on which the European Patent Bulletin mentions the publication of the European search report and shall draw his attention to Rule 70, paragraph 1, Article 94, paragraph2, and Rule 70a, paragraph 1.

Art.94(2) Sanction on not filing request for examination
R.70(1) Request for examination

R.70a(1) Compulsory response to opinion attached to search report

1 **Information about publication of search report**
The communication under **R.69(1)** informs the applicant about the date the search report was published and, to avoid a loss of rights, draws his attention to the period of six months from that date for filing the request for examination (**R.70(1)**) and to the sanction on not filing the request in due time (**Art.94(2)**). It reminds the applicant of the requirement of **R.70a(1)** to respond to a negative opinion attached to the search report within the same six month period. The communication also draws the applicant's attention to the period of **R.39(1)** for the payment of designation and extension fees (A-VI,2.1).

The communication is normally despatched a few days, typically one week, after the actual date of publication of the search report, both for A1 and A3 publications.

There is no such communication for PCT applications (the communication was prescribed in **R.32bis.1(c)** PCT, which has been deleted).

R. 69(2) If a date of publication is specified in the communication under paragraph 1 which is later than the actual date of publication, that later date shall be the decisive date as regards the periods referred to in Rule 70, paragraph 1, and Rule 70a, paragraph 1, unless the error is obvious.

R.70(1) Request for examination
R.70a(1) Compulsory response to opinion attached to search report

1 **Erroneous date in communication**
The 6-month period for filing the request for examination normally runs from the actual date of publication of the search report (**R.70(1)**). If the communication under **R.69(1)** mentions erroneously a later date of publication, this date will be the trigger for the 6-month period for filing the request for examination and the response to the search opinion, unless the error in the date of publication is obvious (**R.69(2)**, second sentence). Although not stated explicitly, the later date should also be the trigger for the 6-month period for payment of the designation and extension fees.

R. 70 Request for examination

Implementation of **Art.94(1)**
EPC 1973: **Art.94(2)** + (3) + **Art.96(1)** + **R.51(1)**

R. 70(1) The applicant may request examination of the European patent application up to six months after the date on which the European Patent Bulletin mentions the publication of the European search report. The request may not be withdrawn.

1 **Period for filing request for examination**
According to **Art.94(1)**, requesting examination includes filing a request for examination and payment of the examination fee (**Rfees2(6)**). Usually the request for examination is made on filing, because it is preprinted on the Request for Grant form. The completion of the request is then determined by the payment of the examination fee.

The examination fee may be paid at any time between the filing of the application and six months of publication of the search report (**R.70(1)**). The communication of **R.69(1)**, informing the applicant of the date of publication of the search report, draws the attention of the applicant to the time limit for payment of the examination fee (**R.70(1)**). Although the time limit for filing the request for examination and filing the mandatory response under **R.70a(1)** is the same, both acts need not be carried out simultaneously.

The applicant has to observe the 6-month period without any further reminder from the EPO. An early payment of the examination fee, e.g. together with the filing and search fee, has the advantage that the six-month time limit need not be monitored and any fee increases may be avoided. **R.70(2)** provides for the refund of the examination fee where payment has been made before transmission of the search report and the application has been withdrawn after the transmission, e.g. because of prejudicial prior art mentioned in the search report. Payment near the end of the six-month period has the advantage that no interest on the amount of the fee is lost and the payment can be made contingent on the contents of the search report.

If the applicant has filed an automatic debit order, the examination fee will be debited on the last day of the six-month period (**AAD.3.2(f)**, **6.1(a)**). According to **AAD.6.1(b)** on early payment of the examination fee under the automatic debiting procedure, the examination fee will be deemed to have been paid on the day of receipt of the waiver for the invitation under **R.70(2)**, which may be ticked in the Request for Grant form, and on the day of receipt of the request for accelerated examination under the PACE programme (see Spec. ed. no. 3, OJ 2007, F1).

The six-month period expires about 24 months from the date of filing, or, if priority has been claimed, from the date of priority, because the search report is normally published immediately after 18 months from priority or filing (**Art.93(1)**). A delay in the publication of the search report results in a later expiry of the period for filing the examination. Where the applicant requests an early publication under **Art.93(1)(b)**, i.e. before 18 months from priority or filing, the search report might also be published early, resulting in an earlier expiry of the period for filing the request for examination and also an earlier start of the examination.

The six-month period for requesting examination for a divisional application is triggered by the mention of the publication of the search report for the divisional application (A-IV,1.8; see **Art.76(1):6**).

The period may be extended on account of non-working days (**R.134(1)**) or mail interruption (**R.134(2)**, **(5)**). The period may be interrupted when the proceedings are stayed because a third party has opened entitlement proceedings (**R.14(1)**) or when the proceedings are interrupted on account of death or legal incapacity of the applicant or his representative (**R.142(3)**).

If the applicant does not desire to proceed further with the application after receipt of the search report, he need not take any action and the application will be deemed withdrawn under **Art.94(2)**. Only if he has paid the examination fee early and waived the invitation under **R.70(2)** should he withdraw the application as soon as possible to receive a full refund of the examination fee under **Rfees11(a)**.

2 **Effect of non-payment and remedies**

If the examination fee is not paid within the six-month period, the application will be deemed withdrawn under **Art.94(2)**. The EPO will notify the loss of rights according to **R.112(1)** (A-VI,2.3). The applicant can request further processing under **Art.121** and **R.135** by paying the examination fee and the further processing fee within two months of notification of the loss of rights. The further processing fee is 50% of the examination fee (**Rfees2(1)12**).

Re-establishment is not available for the six-month period but it is available for the two-month period for requesting further processing (**R.136(3)**).

See **Art.94(2):1** for the moment in time the loss of rights ensues.

3 **Prohibition to withdraw request for examination**

The prohibition in the last sentence of **R.70(1)** to withdraw the request for examination provides legal certainty, as it avoids problems about the conditions of withdrawal and the possibility of subsequently filing a new request. Nevertheless, the applicant can still terminate the grant procedure after having filed the request for examination by withdrawing the application (**Art.67(4)**), not answering a communication (**Art.94(4)**) or not paying a renewal fee (**Art.86(1)**).

R. 70(2) If the request for examination has been filed before the European search report has been transmitted to the applicant, the European Patent Office shall invite the applicant to indicate, within a period to be specified, whether he wishes to proceed further with the application, and shall give him the opportunity to comment on the search report and to amend, where appropriate, the description, claims and drawings.

1 **Confirmation of request for examination**

R.70(2) relates to the case where the applicant has filed the request for examination, i.e. filed the written request and paid the examination fee, before he has received the search report. It obliges the EPO to invite the applicant after transmission of the search report to indicate whether he desires to continue with the application, because the content of the search report may have changed the applicant's opinion about continuing the prosecution.

The **R.70(2)** communication also invites the applicant to comment on the search report and, where appropriate, amend the application in view of the prior art cited in the search report, as allowed under **Art.123(1)** and **R.137(2)** (**R.70(2)**). If the opinion attached to the search report is negative, the applicant is obliged to respond by filing comments and / or amendments together with the indication to proceed further (**R.70a(2)**). Note, that the invitation in the **R.70(2)** communication appears to duplicate the invitation of **R.70a(2)**.

The relevant date for determining whether the request for examination (written request and payment) is filed early or late is, according to **R.70(2)**, 'the transmission of the search report' to the applicant under **R.65**. The EPO has not provided guidance on whether the transmission is the date of despatch or the date of notification of the search report, i.e. the tenth day after the date stamp on the search report according to **R.126(2)**.

R.70(2) is applied to all Euro-PCT applications for which a supplementary search report is drawn up. For such applications the request for examination must be filed on entry into the European phase, which is before receipt of the supplementary search report. (E-IX,2.5.3)

2 **Procedure, withdrawal and refund**

The EPO specifies the period in which the applicant must file the indication whether to proceed (**R.70(2)**). It sets the period to six months from the publication of the search report (E-VIII,1.2), giving the same expiry date as the 6-month period of **R.70(1)**. Hence, the examination can start at the latest at the same date for both routes. The ten-day rule of **R.126(2)** does not apply to the six-month period, because the period is not triggered by a notification.

For Euro-PCT applications where a supplementary search report is drawn up, the period for filing the indication whether to proceed is six months from the notification of the invitation under **R.70(2)** (E-IX,2.5.3). Since the supplementary search report is not published, the publication date cannot be used to trigger the period for response. The invitation is usually sent a few weeks after notification of the supplementary search report. The ten-day rule of **R.126(2)** applies to the six-month period.

On receipt of the applicant's indication that he desires to proceed further, the Receiving Section transfers its responsibility to an examining division for the substantive examination of the application (**R.10(3)**). If the applicant withdraws the application, the examination fee will be refunded at a rate depending on the date of withdrawal (see **Rfees11**). The withdrawal may be made conditional on the refund (E-VIII,7.3).

The applicant's response to the search opinion is interpreted as the confirmation required by **R.70(2)**, even where not explicitly expressed as such (C-II,1.1).

If the applicant desires not to continue, e.g. in view of prejudicial prior art mentioned in the search report, he can actively withdraw the application. Alternatively, the applicant can omit to respond to the invitation according to **R.70(2)**; after expiry of the 6-month period the EPO will deem the application to be withdrawn under **R.70(3)** and notify the applicant according to **R.112(1)** of the loss of rights. Since the substantive examination has not yet begun, the examination fee is refunded in full (**Rfees11(a)**).

Failure to file the indication within the period of **R.70(2)** may be remedied by further processing according to **Art.121** and **R.135**). If no response has been filed to the **R.70a(2)** communication either, two further processing fees are due when filing the indication and the response. If the response cannot be prepared in time, the indication should still be filed within the six-month period to avoid having to pay two further processing fees.

3 **Waiver of invitation**

An early payment of the examination fee may be made unconditional by waiving the right to the invitation for the confirmation of the request for examination pursuant to **R.70(2)**. A waiver has been preprinted on the Request for Grant form and can be put into effect by placing a cross in the relevant place. The waiver relieves the applicant from watching the 6-month period of **R.70(2)** and accelerates the procedure, because the examining division need not wait for the applicant's reply to the **R.70(2)** invitation but can assume responsibility the day the search report is transmitted to the applicant (**R.10(4)**).

If the applicant desires to proceed further with the application after having taken cognizance of the search report, he need not take action. If, instead, he wants to withdraw the application, he should notify the EPO as soon as possible. The examination fee will be fully, partially or not refunded depending on the date of withdrawal (see **Rfees11**).

R. 70(3) **If the applicant fails to reply in due time to the invitation under paragraph 2, the application shall be deemed to be withdrawn.**

R. 70a Response to the extended European search report

Inserted by decision of the Administrative Council of 25.03.2009, which entered into force on 01.04.2010. **R.70a** applies to applications for which the search report or the supplementary search report is drawn up on or after 01.04.2010. (OJ2009, 299)

Implementation of **Art.94**
EPC 1973: no provision

1 **Compulsory response to opinion**
R.70a obliges the applicant to respond to a negative opinion of the search division within six months from publication of the search report, i.e. within the period for requesting examination under **R.70(1)**. Note, that both acts need not be carried out simultaneously. The mandatory response should speed up the examination procedure, because the EPO does not have to issue a first communication under **Art.94(3)** identical to the opinion in the case the applicant has not responded to the opinion, as was common under previous practice. The requirement to respond makes the opinion for the applicant effectively a communication under **Art.94(3)**, although legally it is not. Hence, the EPO cannot refuse the application directly following the response.

The EPO may refuse an application if the response to a first communication from the examining division under **Art.94(3)** does not bring the application closer to grant. This can be avoided by including a conditional request for oral proceedings in the response (see **Art.94(3):5**; C-III,4).

See Art.94(3):4 in case the first communication is a summons for oral proceedings.

It should be noted that new **R.70a** appears to violate **Art.94**. **Art.94(3)** obliges the EPO to invite the applicant to file observations and to amend the application if the substantive examination reveals deficiencies. This examination can only be started after the request for examination has been filed according to **Art.94(1)**. New **R.70a** compels the applicant to correct deficiencies at the same time he files his request for examination. Hence, the EPO carries out a substantive examination of the application before the applicant has filed the request for examination and the applicant must file the first response before the EPO can start the examination and invite him.

This legal problem has arisen because the diplomatic revision conference in 2000 did not have sufficient time to amend **Art.15, 92** and **94** and merge the search and examination. Note, that in 1999 one of the triggers for the revision was to give a sound legal basis to the BEST system (bringing examination and search together; see **Art.15:1**) (OJ1999, 545 §5).

R. 70a(1) In the opinion accompanying the European search report the European Patent Office shall give the applicant the opportunity to comment on the extended European search report and, where appropriate, invite him to correct any deficiencies noted in the opinion accompanying the European search report and to amend the description, claims and drawings within the period referred to in Rule 70, paragraph 1.

R.70(1) Request for examination

1 **Invitation to comment on opinion**
The opinion accompanying the search report under **R.62** gives the applicant the opportunity to comment on the search report and the opinion. The comment may include corrections under **R.139** and voluntary amendments of the application as permitted by **R.137(2)**.

The opinion, 'where appropriate', also invites the applicant to correct any deficiencies noted in the opinion and amend the application.

A response to the search opinion is not required and it is appropriate not to issue the invitation if either the opinion is positive because there are no deficiencies and the examining division can issue the **R.71(3)** communication or the opinion is negative but there are only minor deficiencies which the examining division will correct in the **R.71(3)** communication. A response to the search opinion is required and it is appropriate to issue the invitation if the opinion is negative and there are deficiencies which the applicant must correct.

The mandatory response to the invitation and any voluntary response to the opportunity to amend must both be filed within the period of **R.70(1)**, i.e. within six months from publication of the search report. Hence, the request for examination and the response to the opinion must be filed within the same period. The **R.69(1)** communication informs the applicant of the duration of the period. The sanction on not responding to the invitation is given in **R.70a(3)**. Admission of any voluntary amendment filed after expiry of this period is at the discretion of the examiner (**R.137(3)**).

A few days after publication of the search report, the EPO sends the applicant a communication under **R.69(1)**, drawing his attention to the obligation under **R.70a(1)**.

R. 70a(2) In the case referred to in Rule 70, paragraph 2, or if a supplementary European search report is drawn up on a Euro-PCT-application, the European Patent Office shall give the applicant the opportunity to comment on the extended European search report and, where appropriate, invite him to correct any deficiencies noted in the opinion accompanying the European search report and to amend the description, claims and drawings within the period specified for indicating whether he wishes to proceed further with the application.

R.70(2) Confirmation of early filed request for examination

1 **Invitation where request for examination was filed early**
If the request for examination has been filed before transmission of the search report by early payment of the examination fee (**R.70(2)**), the period to respond to the opinion and to file any voluntary amendment will be equal to the period specified in the **R.70(2)** communication for indicating whether the applicant wishes to proceed further with the application. The Guidelines specify this period as six months from publication of the search report (E-VIII,1.2). This period is extendible only exceptionally (E-VIII,1.6).

When the EPO has drawn up a supplementary search report and opinion for a Euro-PCT application, it will also invite the applicant to respond to deficiencies noted in the opinion and file any voluntary amendment (**R.70a(2)**; E-IX,2.5.3). The response must be filed in the period for confirming to continue the prosecution of the application (**R.70a(2)**), i.e. within six months from notification of the invitation pursuant to **R.70(2)** and **R.70a(2)** (E-IX,2.5.3; Not. EPO OJ 2009, 533 §5.1.5). See also **R.159(1):6**.

If the applicant filed the request for examination early and waived the right to the **R.70(2)** communication, no search opinion and no **R.70a** communication will be issued. Instead an **Art.94(3)** communication will be issued.

R. 70a(3) If the applicant neither complies with nor comments on an invitation in accordance with paragraph 1 or 2, the application shall be deemed to be withdrawn.

1 **Sanction on not responding to invitation**

If the applicant does not file comments or amendments in response to an invitation within the period of **R.70a(1)** or (2), the application will be deemed withdrawn. Further processing under **Art.121** and **R.135** is available.

Since a positive opinion does not include an invitation, the sanction will not apply and a response to the opinion is voluntary.

Chapter IV *Examination by the Examining Division*

R. 70b Request for a copy of search results

Inserted by decision of the Administrative Council of 28.10.2009, which entered into force on 01.01.2011. **R.70b** applies to all European applications and international applications filed on or after 01.01.2011. (OJ 2009, 585)
Implementation of **Art.124(1)**
EPC 1973: no provision

1 **Prior art information of priority application**
R.70b implements part of the procedure under **Art.124(1)** and **R.141(1), (2)** in which the applicant must provide a copy of the search results of a priority application. The complete procedure is set out in **R.141(1):2.**

R. 70b(1) Where the European Patent Office notes, at the time the Examining Division assumes responsibility, that a copy referred to in Rule 141, paragraph 1, has not been filed by the applicant and is not deemed to be duly filed under Rule 141, paragraph 2, it shall invite the applicant to file, within a period of two months, the copy or a statement that the results of the search referred to in Rule 141,paragraph 1, are not available to him.

R.141(1) Request for search results of priority application

1 **Invitation to provide search results**
An applicant must file with the EPO a copy of search results of any priority application (**R.141(1)**). He should do so on filing of the direct European application or on entry into the EP phase of a Euro-PCT application. No copy need be filed if the copy is available to the EPO (see **R.141(2)**).

The EPO checks availability of the copy when the examining division assumes responsibility under **R.10**. If neither the applicant has filed a copy nor the EPO has included a copy in the file, the EPO will invite the applicant to file a copy or a statement that no search results are available to him (**R.70b(1)**).

The applicant must respond to the invitation within two months (**R.70b(1)**). If he does not respond, the application will be deemed withdrawn (**R.70b(2)**). Further processing under **Art.121** is available as remedy.

A response to the **R.70b** invitation for a divisional is not required if the search results have already been filed for the parent (OJ2010, 410 §3.2).

R. 70b(2) If the applicant fails to reply in due time to the invitation under paragraph 1, the European patent application shall be deemed to be withdrawn.

R. 71 Examination procedure

Paragraphs (1) and (2) are an implementation of **Art.94(3)**; paragraphs (3) to (7) of **Art.97(1)**.
EPC 1973: **R.51(2)-(8)**.

R. 71(1) In any communication under Article 94, paragraph 3, the Examining Division shall, where appropriate, invite the applicant to correct any deficiencies noted and to amend the description, claims and drawings within a period to be specified.

Art.94(3) Examination of the European patent application
Implementation of **Art.94(3)**
EPC 1973: **R.51(2)**

1 **Invitation to correct deficiencies**
Where the examiner notes any deficiencies in the application, he invites the applicant to correct them. These corrections have a compulsory character: the applicant either amends the application or convinces the examiner that the proposed corrections are inappropriate. If he does not amend or convince, the application will be refused.

The invitation will only be sent 'where appropriate', i.e. where the examiner expects a positive reaction. If no positive reaction is expected, no invitation will be sent and the application will be refused (C-IV,3).

The applicant must respond within a period to be specified. The duration of the period, consequences of non-observance and remedies are dealt with in the notes to **Art.94(4)**.

The applicant must file a first substantive response to the search opinion if the opinion notes deficiencies (**R.70a**; **R.161(1)**). The response preferably includes any voluntary amendment the applicant wishes to make (**R.137(2)**).

R. 71(2) Any communication under Article 94, paragraph 3, shall contain a reasoned statement covering, where appropriate, all the grounds against the grant of the European patent.

Implementation of **Art.94(3)**
EPC 1973: **R.51(3)**

1 **Reasoned statement in communication**
The 'where appropriate' in the rule makes the extent to which the grounds are covered in a communication a matter of procedural expediency, at the examiner's discretion (**J32/95** r.3.2). If, for example, the claims are not clear, the first communication should cover the ground of clarity and, after the meaning of all features in the claims has been made clear, the second communication should cover the grounds of novelty and inventive step.

However, the grounds on which a decision is based must have been stated in earlier communications, because a decision based on a finding in a communication without the essential legal and factual reasoning contravenes **Art.113(1)** (**T951/92** hn.II).

R. 71(3) Before the Examining Division decides to grant the European patent, it shall inform the applicant of the text in which it intends to grant it and of the related bibliographic data. In this communication the Examining Division shall invite the applicant to pay the fee for grant and publishing and to file a translation of the claims in the two official languages of the European Patent Office other than the language of the proceedings within four months.

Amended by decision of the Administrative Council of 26.10.2010, which entered into force on 01.04.2012 and applies to applications for which a **R.71(3)** communication is despatched on or after 01.04.2012 (OJ 2010, 637).
Implementation of **Art.97(1)**
EPC 1973: **R.51(4)**

1 **Amendment of grant procedure**

The decision of the Administrative Council of 26.10.2010 has amended **R.71** and inserted **R.71a**. The amendment defines the procedure involving amendments and/or corrections following a **R.71(3)** communication and postpones the formal requirements of payment of fees and filing translations till after agreement has been reached on the text of the patent to be granted. It should simplify the procedure and reduce delays.

2 **General**

R.71(3) to (7) are an implementation of **Art.97(1)** and provide details of the procedure from the moment the examining division intends to grant the patent to the approval of the text to be granted. An overview of the procedure is given in Not. EPO OJ 2012, 52.

When the EPO considers that a patent can be granted on an application, it sends the applicant a **R.71(3)** communication in which it informs the applicant of the text it intends to grant and the bibliographic data and invites him to pay the fee for grant and publishing and to file translations of the claims. The communication will also inform the applicant if any claims fees are due (**R.71(4)**). The applicant can approve of the text by paying the fees and filing the translations (**R.71(5)**), after which the decision to grant will be taken (**Art.97(1)** and **R.71a**) and the patent will be published (**Art.98**).

If the applicant does not agree with the proposed text, he can request a grant based on a different text in response to the **R.71(3)** communication (**R.71(6)**); in that case neither fees need be paid nor translations filed. The EPO may send a new **R.71(3)** communication if it approves the different text. If it disapproves, the examination will be resumed (**R.71(6)**), which may involve an immediate refusal.

The sanction on non-payment of the fees or not filing the translation is set out in **R.71(7)**.

3 **R.71(3) communication**

When the examining division is of the opinion that the application is ready for grant, it must obtain the applicant's approval of the text to comply with **Art.113(2)** before it can take a decision. The approval is obtained by the procedure set out in **R.71(3)-(7)**.

3.1 TEXT INTENDED FOR GRANT

In the **R.71(3)** communication the examining division informs the applicant of the text in which it intends to grant the patent (the 'Druckexemplar'). The transmission of the complete text allows the applicant to check the text without the need to assemble the text from previous communications, as is customary with some national patent offices. It also informs him of the related bibliographic data.

The text intended for grant may include amendments and corrections made by the examining division on its own initiative. It can make the amendments without consulting the applicant if the applicant can reasonably be expected to accept them. Examples are corrections of minor errors, but also amendments which, although changing the scope of an independent claim, would very clearly have to be made. The examiner should contact the applicant, e.g. by telephone, if he wants to make more substantial amendments, such as an amendment that can be made in different ways and that significantly changes the scope of a claim, or deleting or combining claims. (C-V,1.1)

Until 2014 amendments of the examining division were made in handwriting on the latest, scanned version of the text submitted by the applicant. As of 2014 the EPO prepares the Druckexemplar electronically by converting the text submitted by the applicant by OCR from a scanned filed paper or fax version or directly from a filed pdf version to XML format. The examining division will make any amendments of the text electronically (C-V,1.1 and C-V, Annex).

The applicant must make his amendments to the Druckexemplar also electronically; handwritten amendments are no longer allowed, unless they relate to graphic symbols and characters and formulae (C-V,1.1). He can make the amendments in an XML or pdf version of the text, available on the publication server and in the EPO file.

The approved text of the Druckexemplar will be the text of the granted patent. Corrections of the text after grant are not possible anymore (**R.140:3.1**). Hence, the check of the Druckexemplar is the last opportunity of the applicant for correcting any errors. Until 2014 a check of the text was relatively easy as amendments were usually handwritten on the applicant's own version of the text. Since 2014 the check has become more burdensome, because the text of the Druckexemplar is a converted text and correction of any errors made by the EPO in the conversion is the sole responsibility of the applicant. A full text comparison of the Druckexemplar with the application as filed is recommendable. When the EPO has introduced full electronic processing, the conversion will be made on filing of the application, giving the applicant more opportunities during the procedure for correcting errors.

3.2 ACTS TO BE COMPLETED

The **R.71(3)** communication invites the applicant to perform the following acts:

1 Payment of the fee for grant and publishing within the period of R.71(3). The amount of the fee is set in **Rfees2(1)7**, or in **Rfees2(2)7** for applications filed before 01.04.2009.. (C-V,1.2)

2 Filing of a translation of the claims in the two official EPO languages other than the language of the proceedings, as required by **Art.14(6)**. Where the application contains different sets of claims for different contracting states, a translation of all sets must be filed (C-V,1.3). The translations must be filed within the period of **R.71(3)**.

3 Payment of any claims fees (**R.71(4)**, **Rfees2(1)15**) within the period of **R.71(3)** (C-V,1.4).

4 Payment of the designation fee (**Rfees2(1)3**) under **R.71a(3)** within the period of **R.39(1)** if the period expires after the **R.71(3)** communication (C-V,2).

5 Payment of any renewal fee under **R.71a(4)** before the due date of **R.51(1)** if the due date falls after the **R.71(3)** communication (C-V,2).

6 Correction of any errors in documents other than the application documents, such as bibliographic data and designation of inventor (see **R.71(3):5.2**).

7 Instead of the first six acts, request grant based on a different text (**R.71(6)**).

3.3 FURTHER INFORMATION IN THE R.71(3) COMMUNICATION

The **R.71(3)** communication must inform the applicant of the different options to approve the text, to amend the text and, where an auxiliary request is regarded allowable, to disapprove the text of this request and maintain the higher-ranking request(s) (**T1255/04** r.3.1). Note, that although **R.71** does not explicitly mention disapproval as a response, the applicant may not be deprived of this option (**T1255/04** r.3.1).

The **R.71(3)** communication informs the applicant also of the requirement of contracting states and extension states to file a translation of (part of) the specification under **Art.65**.

The payment of fees and filing of translations under **R.71(3)** as a requirement for the decision to grant has as a consequence that oral proceedings in the grant procedure cannot be closed with a decision to grant the patent, but only with the prospect of a grant. In the subsequent written continuation of the procedure the fees can be paid and the translations filed, after which the decision to grant will be taken.

Any sanctions on non-performance of these acts have been set out in the following notes and in the provisions referred to.

4 **Period for response and sanction on non-response**

The response to the **R.71(3)** communication must be filed within a period of four months of notification of the communication. The period will be extended under **R.134** if it expires on a non-working day or in case of dislocation of mail; the period cannot be extended on request under **R.132(2)** (C-V,1.1).

If the applicant does not respond within four months to the communication by either 1) paying the fees and filing the translations or 2) requesting grant based on a different text, the application will be deemed withdrawn (**R.71(7)** and C-V,3). Further processing is available under **Art.121**, where the omitted act is 1) payment of the fee for grant and publishing or any claims fees or filing of the translations or 2) requesting grant based on a different text. The fee for further processing is set by **Rfees2(1)12**.

5 **Response to R.71(3) communication**

The applicant can respond to the **R.71(3)** communication in one of the following four ways.

5.1 APPROVAL

If the applicant agrees to the text to be granted and the bibliographic data, he must pay the fee for grant and publishing and any claims fees and file a translation of the claims in the two EPO languages other than the language of the proceedings within four months of the **R.71(3)** communication (**R.71(3)**). Compliance with these requirements is regarded as an implicit approval of the text, including any amendments and corrections made by the examiner, and verification of the bibliographic data (**R.71(5)**). The approval of the text is not binding on the EPO or the applicant; see **R.71a(2)**.

The payment of any designation fee or renewal fee after the four-month period will not affect the approval of the text to be granted but will delay issue of the decision to grant and publication of the grant until payment of the fees (see **R.71a(3)** and (4)). If the designation fee or renewal fee is not paid in due time (**R.39(1)**; **R.51**), the application will be deemed withdrawn (**R.39(2)**; **Art.86(1)**).

If the text intended for grant is based on an auxiliary request, the **R.71(3)** communication will include the reasons why the higher-ranking requests are not allowable. Payment of the fees and filing of the translations is regarded as approval of the text of the auxiliary request and abandonment of all higher-ranking requests (C-V,2).

When the acts required in the **R.71(3)** communication have been carried out, the procedure for grant continues as set out in the notes to **Art.97(1)**.

See **Art.97(1):2** for acceleration of the grant procedure.

5.2 DIFFERENT TEXT

If the applicant desires a grant based on a text different from the one included in the **R.71(3)** communication, he must request so within the four-month period of **R.71(3)**. This occurs in about 15% of all responses to the **R.71(3)** communication. The procedure is set out in **R.71(6)**.

The filing of the request removes the obligation to pay the fee for grant and publishing and any claims fees and to file the translations within the four months of **R.71(3)**. It interrupts the grant procedure and the procedure is continued as set out in **R.71(6)**. Note, that **R.71** does not explicitly state that compliance with **R.71(3)** requires either payment of the fees and filing of translations *or* filing of amendments and corrections to the text; it is only clearly stated in C-V,4.1.

In the event amendments and corrections relate to the text to be granted, no fees need be paid and no translations filed within the four-month period of **R.71(3)** (C-V,4). If the filed amendments or corrections relate solely to other documents, such as the bibliographic data or the designation of inventor, the fees must be paid and the translations filed, otherwise the application will be deemed withdrawn under **R.71(7)**.

When requesting grant based on a different text, it is allowed, although not required, to pay the fees in response to the **R.71(3)** communication. The voluntary paid fees will be credited towards the amount due in response to the second **R.71(3)** communication (**R.71a(5)**) or may be refunded (**R.71a(6)**). See also **R.71(6):3**.

5.3 DELAY

If an applicant needs more time for preparing the response to the **R.71(3)** communication, he can delay the procedure by not responding to the communication, i.e. not paying the fees and not filing any translations, amendments or corrections. Consequently, the application will be deemed withdrawn under **R.71(7)**. Using further processing under **Art.121**, the applicant may gain about three months time.

Note, that the four-month period of **R.71(3)** cannot be extended on request under **R.132(2)** because it is not a period specified by the EPO.

5.4 NO GRANT

If, exceptionally, the applicant does not want the application to grant, he can end the procedure in two ways. The first one is not to respond to the **R.71(3)** communication and let the application be deemed withdrawn under **R.71(7)**.

The second way is to inform the EPO of the disapproval and not to pay any fees or file translations. The application will be refused under **Art.97(2)** for failure to comply with **Art.113(2)**, because there is no text agreed to by the applicant, provided that (i) the examining division did not propose any amendments or corrections under **R.71(3)**, (ii) the text was based on a main request, and (iii) the applicant did not file amendments or corrections together with his disapproval of the text. If amendments were proposed by the examining division, the disapproval is interpreted as a rejection of the proposal, and the procedure of **R.71(6)** will be followed. The same applies if the **R.71(3)** communication was based on an auxiliary request, in which case the disapproval is interpreted as a request for a higher ranking request to be the basis for grant. (C-V,4.9)

The refusal of the application is appealable. The sanction of deemed withdrawn would deprive the applicant of the possibility to appeal the rejection of the application. (**T1181/04** r.3.3)

Note, that the sanction of refusal in the present case appears to be contrary to **Art.97(2)**, since **R.71(7)** provides in this case for the different sanction of deemed withdrawn.

R. 71(4) If the European patent application in the text intended for grant comprises more than fifteen claims, the Examining Division shall invite the applicant to pay claims fees in respect of the sixteenth and each subsequent claim within the period under paragraph 3 unless the said fees have already been paid under Rule 45 or Rule 162.

Amended by decision of the Administrative Council of 26.10.2010, which entered into force on 01.04.2012. (OJ 2010, 637)
R.45 Claims fees on filing of direct European application
R.162 Claims fees on entry into the European phase
Implementation of **Art.97(1)**
EPC 1973: **R.51(7)**

1 **Claims fees**

If the number of claims in the allowable text is larger than fifteen, **R.71(4)** obliges the applicant to pay claims fees (**Rfees2(1)15**) for claims numbered 16 and higher, unless the claims fees for these claims have already been paid on filing of the application (**R.45**) or on entry into the European phase (**R.162**). If the text to be granted contains fewer claims than on filing or entry, no claims fees will be refunded. (C-V,1.4)

Where the allowed text is based on an auxiliary request, the claims fees are due only for the claims of the allowed text (C-V,1.4).

If the response to the **R.71(3)** communication does not amend the text to be granted, the claims fees must be paid within the four-month period of **R.71(3)**. Non-payment of the claims fees leads to the entire application being deemed withdrawn according to **R.71(7)**. The remedy has been set out in **R.71(7):1.**

If in response to the **R.71(3)** communication the applicant requests a grant based on a different text, the claims fees need not be paid within this period; instead, payment can be deferred to the 4-month period of the second **R.71(3)** communication (C-V,4.1). However, if the applicant pays the claims fee voluntarily in response to the first **R.71(3)** communication, the amount paid will be credited to the payment of claims fees for a second **R.71(3)** communication (**R.71a(5)**, C-V,4.2, 4.8.1). The onerous rules for the crediting are given in A-X,11.2 and C-V,4.2.

Note, that non-payment of the claims fees on filing or entry in the European phase results in abandonment of the claims for which no fees are paid (**R.45(3)**). The aggravation of the sanction on non-payment in the grant phase is necessary to avoid the legal complication of an abandonment of claims in an already approved application.

R. 71(5) If the applicant, within the period laid down in paragraph 3, pays the fees under paragraph 3 and, where applicable, paragraph 4 and files the translations under paragraph 3, he shall be deemed to have approved the text communicated to him under paragraph 3 and verified the bibliographic data.

Amended by decision of the Administrative Council of 26.10.2010, which entered into force on 01.04.2012. (OJ 2010, 637)
Implementation of **Art.97(1)**
EPC 1973: **R.51(4)**

1 **Implicit approval**
If the applicant pays the fees and files the translations in due time in response to the **R.71(3)** communication, he is deemed to have approved the text intended for grant and verified the bibliographic data (**R.71(5)**). Hence, the approval of the text intended for grant is given implicitly. The approval is not binding (see **R.71a(2):1**).

However, if the response to the **R.71(3)** communication additionally includes amendments or corrections, no approval is given (implied by C-V,4.2) and the procedure under **R.71(6)** is followed. The voluntarily paid fees may be credited to a second **R.71(3)** communication (**R.71a(5)**).

R. 71(6) If the applicant, within the period under paragraph 3, requests reasoned amendments or corrections to the communicated text or keeps to the latest text submitted by him, the Examining Division shall issue a new communication under paragraph 3 if it gives its consent; otherwise it shall resume the examination proceedings.

Amended by decision of the Administrative Council of 26.10.2010, which entered into force on 01.04.2012. (OJ 2010, 637)
Implementation of **Art.97(1)**
EPC 1973: **R.51(5)** and **(6)**

1 **Different text for grant**
If the applicant desires a grant based on a text different from the one proposed by the examining division in the **R.71(3)** communication, he must request so within the four-month period of **R.71(3)**. The following three cases can be distinguished.

- The applicant no longer approves the latest text submitted by him and allowed by the examining division and wants to change the text. He must submit amendments and/or corrections in response to the **R.71(3)** communication. The amendments or corrections must be reasoned (**R.71(6)**), i.e. the response must indicate why the amended documents comply with the EPC or why the corrections are evident in accordance with **R.139** (C-V,4.3). The basis of amendments in the application as filed must be indicated (H-II,2.5.5). If the amendments or corrections concern the claims, it is recommended to provide at the same time any corresponding amendments to the description to avoid delay in the procedure (C-V,4.5).

  The amendments to the application must be typed or printed. Handwritten amendments are not accepted, unless they relate to graphic symbols and characters and formulae (C-V,1.1; see also **R.71(3):3.1** and **R.50(1):2**).

- The allowed text is an auxiliary request and the applicant desires grant of a higher ranking request. He must inform the EPO of his disapproval of the communicated text and request grant of a higher ranking request. The request must be reasoned (**R.71(6)**).

  This request is not explicitly mentioned in **R.71(6)**, but can be regarded as a special case of amendment (see **T1255/04** r.4.1).
- The applicant does not approve the amendments and/or corrections proposed by the examining division in the text intended for grant. He must inform the EPO that he rejects the communicated text and keeps to the latest text submitted by him. Although **R.71(6)** does not require so, it is recommended to provide reasons for keeping to the latest text (C-V,4.6.1).

  This case is explicitly mentioned in **R.71(6)** to provide a legal basis for the practice of the examining division to make amendments and/or corrections on its own initiative.

In these three cases, no fees need be paid nor translations filed within the four-month period of **R.71(3)** (see **R.71(3):5.2**).

The request for amendment or correction or rejection of the examiner's amendments must be filed within four months from notification of the **R.71(3)** communication. If no response has been filed in the four-month period, the application will be deemed withdrawn under **R.71(7)** because of not paying the fees and filing the translations. This can be remedied using further processing by paying the further processing fee and completing the omitted act by submitting the request.

If the examining division gives its consent, it issues a new **R.71(3)** communication. If the examining division does not consent, it resumes the examination proceedings.

2 Admissibility of amendments and corrections

R.71(6) allows the applicant to submit a different text for grant in response to the invitation under **R.71(3)**. However, the admissibility of the submission depends on the circumstances of the case.

The examining division will exercise its discretion in accordance with **R.137(3)** in admitting amendments filed in response to the **R.71(3)** communication, taking into account the late stage of the proceedings at which the substantive examination has already been completed and the applicant has already had at least one opportunity to amend the application. At this stage the outcome of the earlier procedure should not be called into question; allowance of a request for amendment will be an exception rather than the rule. Only amendments which do not appreciably delay the preparations for grant will be admitted. However, the filing of separate sets of claims for states for which national prior rights exist or for which **Art.167(2)** EPC 1973 applies is always admissible. (**G7/93**, also applicable to the amended **R.71** according to **T1064/04** and H-II,2.5.1).

Where the **R.71(3)** communication includes amendments to the claims carried out by the examining division on which the applicant has not yet had an opportunity to comment, any comment of the applicant relating to such amendments must be admitted under **Art.113(1)**. (C-V,4.6.1 and 4.7.1)

In the exceptional case that receipt of the **R.71(3)** communication triggers the opportunity to file voluntary amendments under **R.137(3)** as valid till 01.04.2010, amendments filed in response to the communication are always admissible under **R.137(2)** (C-V,4.4; H-II,2.5.4).

R.71(6) mentions corrections of errors under **R.139** separately from amendments under **R.137(3)**. As a consequence, the admissibility of corrections is not at the discretion of the EPO. Corrections are possible up to the decision to grant (H-VI,2.1; **J42/92**).

3 **Second R.71(3) communication**

If the request for grant based on a different text filed in response to the **R.71(3)** communication is admissible and allowable, the examining division will issue a second **R.71(3)** communication including the text based thereon (**R.71(6)**, C-V,4.6). The examining division may propose amendments of its own volition in this second **R.71(3)** communication (C-V,4.6.3).

The applicant can indicate his approval of the text by paying the fee for grant and publishing and any claims fees and filing the translations of the claims (see **R.71(3):3**). Instead, the applicant can again submit a different text in response to the second **R.71(3)** communication (C-V,4.10).

4 **Waiving a further R.71(3) communication**

An applicant wishing to accelerate the grant procedure may file his amendments and waive a further **R.71(3)** communication (Not. EPO OJ 2015 A52; C-V,4.11). Such a waiver is regarded as an approval of the amended or corrected text to be granted and of the bibliographic data. It deprives the applicant of the opportunity to check the text of the patent before approval after a further **R.71(3)** communication. Errors remaining in the text cannot be corrected under **R.140** (see **R.140:3.1**).

The applicant has to fulfil the following conditions within the four-month period of **R.71(3)**:

- Expressly indicate the wish to waive the right to a further **R.71(3)** communication.
- Comply with acts 1, 2, 3 of **R.71(3):3.2**. Fee payments should be made separately, because they are not debited automatically under the automatic debiting procedure in the case of a waiver.
- Identify the amendments or corrections and, where applicable, indicate their basis in the application as filed and file the relevant pages of the Druckexemplar that contain the amendments or corrections.

If all formal requirements have been fulfilled and the examining division has no objection to the requested amendments or corrections (e.g. because they relate to minor corrections), it will consent to the waiver and no further **R.71(3)** communication will be sent. Instead, it publishes Form 2004W, informing the applicant and the public of the text to be granted. Next, the decision to grant is issued, provided any designation or renewal fees have been paid.

If the examining division does not consent to the waiver because of lacking formal requirements or considers additional changes necessary, it will send a further **R.71(3)** communication. In the case of not allowable amendments or corrections, it will resume the examination procedure and send an **Art.94(3)** communication. The examining division will never consent to a waiver if the **R.71(3)** communication was based on an auxiliary request and the applicant replies by requesting grant of a higher request; in such a case the examination will be resumed.

5 **Resumption of examination proceedings**

If the request for grant based on a different text is not admissible or allowable, e.g. because the argumentation or evidence provided by the applicant in his response to the **R.71(3)** communication are not convincing, the examining division will resume the examination proceedings (**R.71(6)**; C-V,4.7).

Where the grounds and/or evidence for the non-admissibility or non-allowability have not yet been dealt with in examination proceedings, the examining division will issue an **Art.94(3)** communication setting out its findings. Oral proceedings may have to be appointed before taking a decision (see C-V,4.7.1). If agreement is reached on the text, a second **R.71(3)** communication will be sent, based on the agreed text (C-V,4.7.2). If no agreement can be reached, the application will be refused (C-V,4.7.3).

The application may be refused directly after receipt of the response to the **R.71(3)** communication if 1) the grounds and evidence for the non-admittance or non-allowance have already been dealt with in examination proceedings (**Art.113(1)**), 2) at least one **Art.94(3)** communication has been issued, and 3) the applicant's right to oral proceedings has been respected (**Art.116(1)**) (C-V,4.7.1).

6 Auxiliary requests

During grant proceedings the applicant may file one set of claims as a main request and one or more alternative sets of claims as auxiliary requests as set out in **Art.94(3):6**. When the examining division regards an auxiliary request allowable, it issues the **R.71(3)** communication in regard of that set of claims, stating the reasons why the higher-ranking requests are not considered allowable (**T1255/04** r.3.2; C-V,1.1). The applicant can proceed in one of the following ways:

- He agrees to the opinion expressed in the communication and expresses his approval of the text to be granted by paying the fees and filing the translations under **R.71(3)**, thereby making the allowable set his sole request and abandoning the higher-ranking requests (C-V,2). This option deprives the applicant of the possibility to appeal the rejection of higher-ranking requests. Hence, an applicant wanting to maintain the option of appeal should not yield to a request of the examining division to make the allowable request his sole request.
- The applicant refuses to approve the text regarded allowable and maintains a higher-ranking request in his response under **R.71(6)**. The application will usually be refused under **Art.97(2)** (see **Art.97(2):1**) in the resumed examination proceedings. The application may be directly refused, provided the applicant's right to be heard has been respected and the **R.71(3)** communication has provided sufficient information about the objections, to allow the applicant to comment on them (C-V,4.7.1.1; not in GL2017).The decision refusing the application should state the reasons why the higher-ranking requests were considered not allowable. However, if arguments of the applicant in his response to the **R.71(3)** communication convince the examining division that the higher-ranking request meets the requirements of the EPC, a new **R.71(3)** communication will be issued. (C-V,4.6.2)
- The applicant files amendments to the claims of the request regarded allowable as permitted under **R.71(6)**, without paying the fee for grant and publishing and without filing the translations of the claims. If the examining division agrees, it will issue a new **R.71(3)** communication. If the examining division does not agree, it will resume the examination proceedings under **R.71(6)**.

An applicant may, on request, obtain an immediate decision on the non-patentability of the higher-ranking requests before the **R.71(3)** communication is issued. In that case the examining division issues the appealable final decision refusing the application immediately. (C-V,15)

If the applicant appeals the decision refusing the application and requests grant on the basis of the set of claims considered to be allowable, the examining division will rectify its decision by interlocutory revision under **Art.109**. Otherwise, the case will be remitted to the board of appeal without comments as to its merits; the board is not bound by the examining division's positive assessment of an auxiliary request.

R. 71(7) If the fee for grant and publishing or the claims fees are not paid in due time, or if the translations are not filed in due time, the European patent application shall be deemed to be withdrawn.

Amended by decision of the Administrative Council of 26.10.2010, which entered into force on 01.04.2012. (OJ 2010, 637)
Implementation of Art.97(1)
EPC 1973: **R.51(8)**

1 **Sanction on non-compliance and remedies**
The application will be deemed withdrawn under **R.71(7)** if the fee for grant and publishing or any claims fees are not paid or the translations of the claims not filed within four months from notification of the **R.71(3)** communication. If a different text is proposed under **R.71(6)** in response to the **R.71(3)** communication, no fees need be paid or translations submitted and the sanction does not apply (C-V,3). See **R.71(3):5.4** for a refusal following non-compliance with the requirements of **R.71(3)**.

The loss of rights is notified according to **R.112(1)** and can be remedied using further processing under **Art.121**. The omitted act must be completed and a further processing fee paid within two months from the notification of the loss of rights. The nature of the omitted act is determined by the desired course of action of the applicant. Firstly, if the applicant wants the application to grant, the omitted act is payment of fees and filing translations of the claims. The further processing fee is a fixed fee for the fee for grant and publishing and the translations; the further processing fee for the claims fees is 50% of the unpaid amount (**Rfees2(1)12**). Secondly, if the applicant wants a different text for grant, the omitted act is filing amendments and / or corrections, filing a rejection of the amendments proposed by the examining division, or filing a request for grant of a higher request than the allowed auxiliary request (C-V,8). The further processing fee in this case is the fee 'other cases' in **Rfees2(1)12**.

If the applicant did perform the required acts in time, he should request a decision under **R.112(2)** as main request and further processing as auxiliary request. Re-establishment is not available for the four-month period of **R.71(3)** but it is available for the two-month period of **R.112(2)** and **R.135(1)**.

Note that non-payment of a fee or not filing a translation results in a loss of the application without an appealable decision being taken. In that case a fee for grant and publishing paid in response to the **R.71(3)** communication will be refunded under **R.71a(6)**. Any paid claims fees may be refunded (**R.71a(6):1**).

See **R.71a(3):1** and **(4):1** for the consequence of non-payment of the designation fee and renewal fee.

R. 71a Conclusion of the grant procedure

Inserted by decision of the Administrative Council of 26.10.2010 and entering into force on 01.04.2012. **R.71a** applies to applications for which a **R.71(3)** communication is despatched on or after 01.04.2012. (OJ2010, 637)

See **R.71(3):2** for a summary of the revised grant procedure.
Implementation of **Art.97(1)** and **(3)**.
EPC 1973: **R.51(6)**, **(8a)** and **(9)**.

R. 71a(1) The decision to grant the European patent shall be issued if all fees have been paid, a translation of the claims in the two official languages of the European Patent Office other than the language of the proceedings has been filed and there is agreement as to the text to be granted. It shall state which text of the European patent application forms the basis for the decision.

Implementation of **Art.97(1)**
EPC 1973: **R.51(11)**

1 **Decision to grant**
Once the applicant has approved the text intended for grant by paying the fees and filing the translations of the claims in response to the **R.71(3)** communication, the EPO will issue the decision to grant the patent (**R.71a(1)**). The decision to grant is usually taken between two and three weeks after the EPO has received the approval of the text according to **R.71(5)**, provided no further requests are filed together with or after the approval.

Issue of the decision will be delayed if designation or renewal fees have to be paid after notification of the **R.71(3)** communication (**R.71a(3)** and **(4)**).

The decision does not include the text of the application forming the basis of the decision but refers to the text included in the **R.71(3)** communication that has been approved by the applicant. The decision is not reasoned because it does not adversely affect the party (**R.111(2):1**).

See **R.140:2** for correction of errors in the decision and **R.140:3** for errors in the publication of the patent specification.

R. 71a(2) Until the decision to grant the European patent, the Examining Division may resume the examination proceedings at any time.

Implementation of **Art.97(1)**

1 **Resumption of examination**
After approval of the text according to **R.71(3)**, the examining division may resume the examination procedure at any time up to the moment the decision to grant is handed over to the EPO's internal postal service for transmittal to the applicant (**G12/91** hn; C-V,6.1).

An approval of the text notified under **R.71(3)** does not bind an applicant (**G7/93** hn.I). The approval is considered withdrawn if the applicant files an amendment to the text of the application after his approval and before the issue of the decision to grant (**G10/92** r.5, 7). The examining division has a discretion under **R.137(3)** whether or not to allow such an amendment and resume the examination proceedings.

In view of the late stage in the granting procedure, resumption of the proceedings will be an exception (**G7/93** hn.I, II) but may be justified if the applicant or a third party informs the EPO of very relevant prior art or the applicant requests amendments or corrections (C-V,6.1). Although the two G-decisions relate to an earlier version of **R.71(3)** and **(6)**, they appear also applicable to the present version of the provisions.

Resumption of the proceedings cancels the previous approval of the text and a new **R.71(3)** communication will be issued if a new text is regarded allowable (C-V,6.2).

R. 71a(3) If the designation fee becomes due after the communication under Rule 71, paragraph 3, the mention of the grant of the European patent shall not be published until the designation fee has been paid. The applicant shall be informed accordingly.

Implementation of **Art.97(3)**
EPC 1973: **R.51(8a)**

1 **Designation fee**
The period for payment of the designation fee as provided in **R.39(1)** is 6 months of publication of the search report. In the rare case that the expiry of the 6-month period falls after notification of the **R.71(3)** communication, the decision to grant and the publication of the mention of the grant will be postponed until the designation fee has been paid (**R.71a(3)**). **R.71a(3)** ensures that in the case the patent is ready for grant before the expiry of this period, the mention of the grant will only be published after payment of the designation fee. The applicant is informed accordingly (C-V,2).

If the designation fee is not paid within the six-month period, the application will be deemed withdrawn (**R.39(2)**) and the mention of the grant will not be published. Further processing according to **Art.121** and **R.135** can be used as remedy.

Note, that the word 'due' in the provision refers to the expiry of the period for payment of the fee. This meaning conflicts with the definition of the word in **Rfees4(1)**.

R. 71a(4) If a renewal fee becomes due after the communication under Rule 71, paragraph 3, and before the next possible date for publication of the mention of the grant of the European patent, the mention shall not be published until the renewal fee has been paid. Theapplicant shall be informed accordingly.

Implementation of **Art.97(3)**
EPC 1973: **R.51(9)**

1 **Renewal fee**
Art.86(2) provides that the renewal fee in respect of the patent year in which the mention of the grant is published must be paid to the EPO. Since the sanction in **Art.86(1)**, last sentence, that the application is deemed withdrawn on failure to pay the renewal fees is not applicable anymore after the grant of the patent, the EPC has to secure payment of the renewal fees due before grant by deferring the grant until they have been paid.

R.71a(4) relates to the case where the due date of a renewal fee falls between notification of the **R.71(3)** communication and the next possible date for publication of the mention of the grant. The decision to grant and the publication of the mention of the grant will be postponed until the renewal fee has been paid. The applicant is informed accordingly (C-V,2). The renewal fee must be paid before or on the due date or, with additional fee, within six months from the due date (**R.51(2)**). If the renewal fee is not paid in due time, the application will be deemed withdrawn under **Art.86(1)**, last sentence, and the mention of the grant will never be published. Further processing is excluded by **R.135(2)**, but re-establishment according to **Art.122** and **R.136** is available.

The case where the due date for payment of the renewal fee falls before the **R.71(3)** communication and the expiry of the six-month period of **R.51(2)** after that communication is not dealt with in the EPC 2000, whereas it was covered by **Art.97(2)(c)** EPC 1973. There is no legal basis to delay the publication of the mention of the grant until after payment of such a renewal fee. It is to be expected, however, that the EPO will delay the **R.71(3)** communication or the issue of the decision to grant to ensure payment of the renewal fee.

R.71a(4) does not apply to the case where the anniversary of the date of filing and a subsequent publication of the grant fall within the same month, because in that case the renewal fee for the coming year must be paid to the EPO according to **Art.86(2)** but the due date of the renewal fee, i.e. the last day of that month (**R.51(1)**), is in general after the publication of the grant. To avoid this reversal of due date and publication date, the EPO avoids publication of the mention of the grant in the month containing the anniversary.

R. 71a(5) If, in response to an invitation under Rule 71, paragraph 3, the applicant has already paid the fee for grant and publishing or the claims fees, the paid amount shall be credited if a further such invitation is issued.

Implementation of **Art.97(1)**

1 **Crediting of fees paid**

The EPO expects many applicants to pay the fees in response to the **R.71(3)** communication when amendments are filed. If the EPO were to refund the fees as having no legal basis, the refund and the obligation to pay the fees in response to a quickly issued second **R.71(3)** communication could cross, causing a confusing situation for the applicant. **R.71a(5)** avoids this situation by regarding the fees paid in response to the first **R.71(3)** communication as voluntarily paid and by not refunding the fees but crediting them to the fees to be paid in response to a further **R.71(3)** communication.

The EPO distinguishes two cases for crediting fees.

i) If an applicant responds to the **R.71(3)** communication by requesting a grant based on a different text, no approval of the text for grant is given and the fee for grant and publishing and the claims fees need not be paid within the four month period of **R.71(3)** (C-V,4.1). If the fees are paid voluntarily, they will be credited to the fees to be paid for the second **R.71(3)** communication (**R.71a(5)**, C-V,4.2).

   The EPO will accept such voluntarily paid fees, in spite of the principle that fees lacking a legal basis are to be refunded (**Rfees9:1**; A-X,10.1.1(ii)).

ii) Similarly, if an applicant approves the text to be granted by paying the fee for grant and publishing and the claims fees and subsequently the examination is resumed (see **R.71a(2)**), the approval is withdrawn, but the fees were validly paid. The mandatory paid fee for grant and publishing and the claims fees are also credited to the fees to be paid for the second **R.71(3)** communication (**R.71a(5)**, C-V,6.3).

If in cases i. and ii. the fee for grant and publishing for the second **R.71(3)** communication is different, e.g. because of amendment of the fee rates, a shortfall has to be paid and an excess will be refunded (A-X,11.1, 11.2; C-V,4.2).

If in cases i. and ii. the claims fees for the second **R.71(3)** communication are higher, e.g. because of an increased number of claims, the shortfall must be paid (A-X,11.2).

If in case i. the claims fees for the second **R.71(3)** communication are lower, an excess will be refunded (C-V,4.2). However, if in case ii. the claims fees for the second **R.71(3)** communication are lower, an excess will *not* be refunded (A-X,11.2).

See **R.71a(6)** for refund of fees in the event that the application ceases to exist.

R. 71a(6) If the European patent application is refused, withdrawn prior to notification of the decision on the grant of a European patent or, at that time, deemed to be withdrawn, the fee for grant and publishing shall be refunded.

Implementation of **Art.97(1)**

1 **Refund of fees**

The fee for grant and publishing will be refunded under **R.71a(6)** if the application is refused, withdrawn or deemed to be withdrawn prior to notification of the decision to grant (C-V,4.2).

In such a situation, the claims fees will be refunded if they have been paid voluntarily (**R.71a(5):1** case i.). However, if the claims fees have been paid mandatory (**R.71a(5):1** case ii.), they will *not* be refunded (A-X,10.2.5; GL2017 A-X,10.2.7).

R. 72 Grant of the European patent to different applicants

Where different persons are recorded in the European Patent Register as applicants in respect of different Contracting States, the European Patent Office shall grant the European patent for each Contracting State accordingly.

Implementation of **Art.97(1)**
EPC 1973: **R.52**

Chapter V *The European patent specification*

R. 73 Content and form of the specification

Implementation of Art.98
EPC 1973: R.53

R. 73(1) The specification of the European patent shall include the description, the claims and any drawings. It shall also indicate the period for opposing the European patent.

1 **Content of the specification**
The contents of the specification are governed by **R.73(1)**. The specification is published in the language of the proceedings (**Art.14(6)**), and contains the description, claims (in the three EPO languages (**Art.14(7)**) and any drawings (**R.73(1)**, first sentence). The text in the language of the proceedings is the authentic text in any subsequent proceedings (**Art.70(1)**). The specification may contain different descriptions, drawings and sets of claims for different designated contracting states due to the existence of different national prior rights (**R.138**).

R. 73(2) The President of the European Patent Office shall determine the form of the publication of the specification and the data to be included.

1 **Publication of the specification**
Under **R.73(2)** the President has prescribed that the specifications of European patents are published in electronic form only and are available by means of downloading from a publication server (Dec. Pres., Spec. Ed. 3 of OJ 2007 D.3). See **R.145(1):1** for the publication server.

The publication of the specification is as soon as possible after the publication of the mention of the grant (**Art.98**).

See **R.140:3.2** for errors in the published specification.

2 **Withdrawal before publication**
Withdrawal of the application before publication of the specification follows the same principles as withdrawal of the application before publication under **R.67(2)**, in particular the avoidance of publication by withdrawing the application before the termination of the technical preparations for publication (C-V,11). In practice, publication can often be prevented if withdrawal is received at least two weeks before the scheduled date of publication. See **R.67(2):3** for the binding nature of the declaration of withdrawal and the limited possibility to retract it under **R.139**.

The technical preparations for publication are completed five weeks before the scheduled date of publication of the specification (OJ 2006, 409). The completion is about one week before the internal decision to grant is taken (OJ 2006, 409). The written decision, notified to the applicant when the technical preparations have been completed, states the date of publication of the mention of the grant in the Bulletin (C-V,10); this date is four weeks after the decision to grant was taken (OJ 2006, 409). The patent specification is published as soon as possible after the publication of the mention of the grant (**Art.98**) (C-V,10).

3 **Data in specification**

The front page of the published specification shows the title and the designated contracting states (see **R.73(3)**). Information on the surrender or lapse of the patent in the contracting states can be obtained from the Register (see **R.143:2**) and the national patent offices. The front page mentions the same serial number as the front page of the published application and an identification of the kind of publication document (see **R.68(2):2**).

The front page of the specification will mention the presence of supplementary technical information in the file that has been introduced after the application has been filed. Such information may have been used by the examiner in support of the patentability of the invention but could not be included in the application by way of amendment because of **Art.123(2)**. The information is contained in the part of the file that is open to public inspection (**Art.128(4)**), unless access is excluded under **R.144(d)**. (H-V,2.3)

A list of patent and non-patent literature cited in the description will be included at the end of applications and specifications published as from 13.09.2006. The list is made by the EPO and is for information only and does not form part of the application or specification. (Dec. Pres. Spec. Ed. 3 of OJ 2007, D.4).

R. 73(3) The designated Contracting States shall be indicated in the specification.

1 **Designations published**

The publication of an application under **Art.93** mentions all EPC contracting states (**R.68(3)**); likewise the specification of the corresponding patent. States for which the designation has been withdrawn under **Art.79(3)** before completion of the technical preparations for publication of the application or patent will not be mentioned.

R. 74 Certificate for a European patent

As soon as the specification of the European patent has been published, the European Patent Office shall issue to the proprietor of the patent a certificate for a European patent. The President of the European Patent Office shall prescribe the content, form and means of communication of the certificate and determine the circumstances in which an administrative fee is payable.

Implementation of **Art.98**
EPC 1973: **R.54**

1 **Form of certificate**

The certificate for a patent as granted or amended will be supplied in paper form to the proprietor or to each proprietor if there are several proprietors. The certificate states the patent number and certifies that the patent has been granted to the person(s) named in the certificate, for the invention described and the states designated, or has been maintained in amended form. (Dec. Pres. OJ 2013, 416)

A certified copy of the certificate with the patent specification annexed will be issued to the proprietor only upon request and payment of an administrative fee as fixed under **Rfees3(1)**. (Dec. Pres. OJ 2013, 416 and Not. EPO OJ 2013, 418)

Specifications of granted patents are available electronically on the internet publication server (Dec. Pres., Spec. Ed. 3 of OJ 2007 D.3; see **R.145(1):1**).

PART V IMPLEMENTING REGULATIONS TO PART V OF THE CONVENTION

Chapter I *Opposition procedure*

R. 75 Surrender or lapse of the patent

An opposition may be filed even if the European patent has been surrendered in all the designated Contracting States or has lapsed in all those States.

Implementation of **Art.99(1)**
EPC 1973: **Art.99(3)**

1 **Opposition to surrendered or lapsed patent**
An opposition against a surrendered or lapsed patent may be useful, because revocation of the patent by the EPO has an effect ex tunc (**Art.68**), thereby changing rights previously established under **Art.64** and **Art.67**. In contrast, a lapse of the patent in a designated has, depending on national law, usually an effect ex nunc (not changing previously established rights). The effect of surrender of patent in a designated state is also a matter of national law and may be ex tunc or ex nunc.

A proprietor may inform a national office of a state that he surrenders his European patent for that state. Lapse of a European patent for a state occurs most often by non-payment of a renewal fee to a national patent office. See **R.84(1)** for continuation of opposition proceedings after lapse or surrender of the patent.

R. 76 Form and content of the opposition

Implementation of **Art.99(1)**
EPC 1973: **R.55**

R. 76(1) Notice of opposition shall be filed in a written reasoned statement.

1 **Written reasoned statement**
The term 'written' in this provision excludes the filing of oppositions orally, but does not exclude electronic filing (OJ 2007 se5 (EN) p.128). See the notes to **R.2(1)** for permitted methods of filing.

The phrase 'reasoned statement' in **R.76(1)** implies the requirement of providing arguments in the notice of opposition (D-III,6). The arguments must present the reasoning why the grounds for opposition have been raised against the patent in suit and show how the facts and evidence submitted under **R.76(2)(c)** support these grounds.

R. 76(2) The notice of opposition shall contain:
(a) particulars of the opponent as provided in Rule 41, paragraph 2(c);
(b) the number of the European patent against which opposition is filed, the name of the proprietor of the patent and the title of the invention;
(c) a statement of the extent to which the European patent is opposed and of the grounds on which the opposition is based, as well as an indication of the facts and evidence presented in support of these grounds;
(d) if the opponent has appointed a representative, particulars as provided in Rule 41, paragraph 2(d).

R.41(2)(c) Particulars of applicant
R.41(2)(d) Particulars of representative

1 **General**

R.76 gives requirements for entry of a second party in a procedure before the EPO; it resembles **R.41** for filing an application. EPO Form 2300 can be used as check list for the information to be provided for an opposition.

If the requirements are not complied with, **Art.101(1)** & **R.77** will be applied for the correction and sanction. Any deficiency of **R.76** to which **R.77(1)** refers must be corrected before expiry of the opposition period. Deficiencies in other items can be corrected after the opposition period on invitation by the EPO (**R.77(2)**). Failure to correct in due time results in inadmissibility of the notice of opposition (**R.77(1), (2)**).

2 **Identity of the opponent (R.76(2)(a))**

2.1 REQUIREMENT

At the start of the opposition proceedings the identity of the opponent must be known and verifiable to both the EPO and the proprietor, because the opposition proceedings started with **Art.99(1)** are new proceedings with new parties, the identity of which must be known from the start. Hence, at the end of the opposition period the identity of the opponent must be known, as he becomes party to the proceedings; then it must be known which language he is allowed to use (**R.3(1)**), whether a representative is required (**Art.133(2), (3)**), and whether the general requirements as to the person's legal capacity have been met. (**T25/85** r.6)

2.2 ERROR IN IDENTITY

An error in details of the designation of the opponent can be corrected according to **R.76(2)(a)** in conjunction with **R.77(2)**, even after the end of the opposition period. This interpretation of **R.76(2)(a)** with **R.77(2)** is equal to the interpretation of **R.40(1)(b)** with **Art.90(4)**: an applicant must be identified on filing, whereas details about the applicant as required under **R.41(2)(c)** may be provided subsequently under **Art.90(4)**. The same applies to the appeal proceedings: mark the similar wording of **R.99(1)(a)** and **R.101(2)** for appeal on the one hand and **R.76(2)(a)** and **R.77(2)** for opposition on the other hand.

A correction of the identity of the opponent under **R.139** after the end of the opposition period is only allowed if the error was due to a genuine mistake; the mistake must be proven. The correction has retrograde effect, making the opponent deemed known at the end of the opposition period. The same possibility for correction applies to the applicant in the case of **R.40(1)(b)** or an appellant in the case of **Art.106(1), 107** and **108. R.76(2)(a)** and **R.77(2)** do not form a lex specialis in respect of **R.139** for the opponent (reversal of **T25/85**). **R.139** is of general applicability and other rules relating to remedying deficiencies are simply complementary to **R.139.** An invitation to remedy under **R.77(2)** has merely to be responded to, whereas a voluntary correction of a mistake under **R.139** may involve proving that an error was made, what the error was and what the correction should be. (**T219/86**, see also **T590/93**)

See **Art.99(1):1.2** for the entitlement of a straw man to oppose and **Art.99(1):1.4** for transfer of opposition.

A genuine error in the identity of the opponent can be corrected under **R.139**, even if evidence of the original intention is filed after expiry of the opposition period (**T615/14** hn).

3 **Patent opposed (R.76(2)(b))**

The sole purpose of **R.76(2)(b)** is to make a correct identification of the opposed patent possible (**T317/86**). The identification of the patent may be corrected under **R.77(2)**, even after expiry of the opposition period, because **R.77(1)** does not refer to **R.76(2)(b)** (**T344/88**).

4 **Extent of opposition, grounds, facts and evidence (R.76(2)(c))**

4.1 GENERAL

R.76(2)(c) has the double function of governing (together with other provisions) the admissibility of the opposition and of establishing at the same time the legal and factual framework within which the substantive examination of the opposition in principle shall be conducted. The latter function is of particular importance in that it gives the patentee a fair chance to consider his position at an early stage of the proceedings. (**G9/91** r.6)

The facts and evidence must be supplemented by arguments showing how they support the grounds for opposition (see **R.76(1):1**; D-IV,1.2.2.1(v)).

4.2 STATEMENT OF THE EXTENT OF THE OPPOSITION

The extent of opposition defines the formal competence of the opposition division to investigate the validity of the patent. In the unusual case where an opposition is limited to a part of the patent, the investigation must also be limited to the opposed part (**G9/91** r.9).

Subject-matter not covered by the extent of opposition may not be subject to opposition, both in the opposition proceedings and in a possible appeal. Such subject-matter is not subject to any opposition in the sense of **Art.101**, nor are there any proceedings in the sense of **Art.114** and **115.** (**G9/91** r.10, confirming **T9/87**)

However, if the opposition is explicitly directed only to an independent claim, then the dependent claims are considered as being implicitly covered by the extent and may be examined, provided their validity is prima facie in doubt on the basis of already available information (**G9/91** r.11, confirming **T293/88**).

The extent of the opposition can be reduced during the proceedings by a partial withdrawal of the opposition. For example, a sole opponent requests revocation of the entire patent in the notice of opposition and, during the proceedings, states that he will withdraw his opposition if the claims are amended in a specified way. The BoA will regard the offer as a partial withdrawal of the opposition, which is now no longer directed against the amended claims. After the amendment has been made, the BoA will assess the allowability of the amendment (no abuse of procedure and no violation of **Art.123**). Since there is no opposition against the amended claims, the patent in amended form must be maintained without further substantive examination. (**T6/92**)

4.3 STATEMENT OF THE GROUNDS

The statement of grounds gives the legal framework for the attack on the patent, where the part of the patent which is being attacked has been defined by the extent of the opposition. The possible grounds are given in **Art.100**. Opposition is most times based on lack of novelty (**Art.54**) or lack of inventive step (**Art.56**).

4.3.1 Added grounds in first instance

In principle, the opposition division should examine only those grounds which have been properly submitted by the opponent (**G10/91** hn.2). Since it is the aim of the first instance opposition procedure to avoid invalid patents, the opposition division must examine any ground raised (**G10/91** r.16). Therefore, the opposition division may of its own motion raise a ground for opposition not covered by the indication of the grounds (**Art.114(1)** is applicable to opposition proceedings (see also D-V,2.2)) or consider such a ground raised by the opponent or a third party (**Art.115**) during the opposition proceedings. This deviation from the indicated grounds should only take place where, prima facie, the grounds are believed to be relevant (**G10/91** hn.2).

The opposition division may not disregard a new ground without examination of its relevance (**T736/95**). A late-submitted ground disregarded by the opposition division may be considered by the board of appeal if the board considers that the division was wrong in this respect (**T986/93** hn). Grounds should not be excluded merely for being late; the division should at least consider whether the grounds prima facie prejudice the maintenance of the patent (**T798/05**). A new ground against foreseeable amendments to the claims is regarded as late filed (E-VI,2.1). A limitation to a dependent claim is a foreseeable amendment; a limitation by including a feature from the description is not (E-VI,2.1).

A ground will only be admitted if the ground is substantiated (**T222/85**). A ground is substantiated if the requirement of **R.76(2)(c)** is met, i.e. an indication of the facts, evidence and arguments presented in support of these grounds is given (see the following sections). A ground indicated as being relied upon in the notice of opposition, or on EPO form 2300, but not substantiated, is not considered part of the proceedings (**R2/08**). An opposition division need not consider a ground substantiated in the notice of opposition but subsequently not maintained during the opposition, unless the ground is likely to prejudice the maintenance of the patent (**T274/95** hn.I). Such a ground is not regarded as a fresh ground of opposition and may be re-introduced during appeal proceedings without agreement of the proprietor, in the exercise of the discretion of the board of appeal (**T274/95** hn.II). However, a ground withdrawn at oral proceedings is considered a fresh ground if reintroduced on appeal (**T376/04**).

An opponent may substantiate a ground of opposition against a single claim of each request on file. If he succeeds in establishing that a claim of each request is not allowable, the patent will be revoked. Thus an opponent is under no obligation to 'overkill' requests put forward by the proprietor by substantiating grounds for opposition against more than one claim of such request. (**T926/93** hn)

4.3.2 *Added grounds in second instance*

The aim of the opposition appeal is to give the losing party the opportunity to contest the opposition division's decision. Issues outside the subject-matter of the decision under appeal are not part of the appeal (**G1/99** r.6.1). Hence, during opposition appeal, in principle only the grounds considered in the first instance proceedings are considered. A fresh ground filed during appeal is allowed very exceptionally if it is prima facie highly likely to prejudice the maintenance of the patent and if the patentee agrees to it (**G10/91** hn.3). If such a fresh grounds is admitted, the case should be remitted to the first instance (see **G9/91** r.16, 18). Following these decisions, **T1007/95** held an appeal to be inadmissible because the appeal was based on the new ground of lack of novelty in view of a new document, whereas the appealed decision of the opposition division was based only on lack of inventive step, the appeal therefore amounting to a new opposition; in this case the proprietor did not consent to consideration of novelty in appeal.

Decision **G10/91** overrules on the one hand **T122/84**, **T9/87** and **T182/89**, which restricted the grounds to those put forward in the notice of opposition because of speed of procedure and legal certainty, and on the other hand **T227/88** and **T493/88**, which allowed fresh grounds in order to deliver a sound patent in the interest of the public.

4.3.3 *Separate grounds*

The grounds of **Art.100(b)** and **(c)** each are single, separate grounds for opposition (**G1/95** r.4.2). The ground of unpatentable subject-matter according to **Art.52(2)** is another ground than novelty and inventive step (**G1/95** hn). Likewise, novelty and inventive step are also separate grounds for opposition (**G7/95** hn). However, novelty as a new ground may be considered in view of the same document used for deciding upon the ground of lack of inventive step (**G7/95** hn). In a case where a patent has been opposed on the ground of novelty and inventive step and only the ground of novelty has been substantiated in view of a prior art document, lack of inventive step in view of the same prior art document is not a fresh ground in appeal and can consequently be examined without the agreement of the patentee (**T131/01** hn). Since the assessment of inventive step requires that an invention is novel, a simultaneous substantiation of lack of novelty and lack of inventive step in view of the same document is contradictory (**T131/01** hn, r.3.1).

4.4 INDICATION OF FACTS

The notice must give an indication of the facts presented in support of the grounds for opposition (**R.76(2)(c)**). The opponent has to make clear with the help of the facts why he uses the mentioned grounds. He must indicate how the facts, in particular when not taken from published documents, have been made available (**T328/87**).

The facts provided in the notice must be sufficient to make it objectively clear to a skilled person how the opposition is based on the grounds presented. A poor quality formulation can lead to inadmissibility. An opponent cannot ask the opposition division to find the facts itself (**T222/85** r.4, 5, 6: 16 patents filed by opponent as facts without indicating specific passages).

If the facts are not logical, the opposition may still be admissible (**T234/86**).

Facts and evidence filed late during the opposition procedure are only exceptionally admitted if they appear prima facie to prejudice the maintenance of the patent (**T1002/92** hn.I). A late submitted document may be taken into account in view of an amendment of the contested patent (**T501/94** r.2.7). No final decision on the opposition can be taken until such an examination has been performed. The EPO communicates the result to the parties, although it need not give a detailed reason for not taking into account late-filed facts. (**T156/84,T273/84,T271/84,T142/84,T258/84 ,T122/84**). Late filed facts submitted without good reason and causing extra cost to other parties for oral proceedings or taking of evidence, may be taken into account in an apportionment of costs under **Art.104**.

During appeal new facts, evidence and related arguments in support of the grounds on which the opposition is based are only very exceptionally admitted if they are prima facie highly relevant in the sense that they highly likely prejudice the maintenance of the patent; other relevant factors are possible objections of the patentee to the admission and added procedural complications. (**T1002/92** hn.II).

Evidence of common general knowledge should also be filed at an early stage before the opposition division, similar to other documents; it may be rejected as inadmissible if filed late in appeal proceedings, because a possible change in the factual framework of appeal proceedings outweighs the fact that the evidence merely serves to confirm what was already commonly known in the field (**T85/93**).

The strict rules of **T1002/92** have been relaxed in recent case law; fixed time limits for the submission or the criterion of the relevance of the facts are no longer regarded as appropriate. According to **T633/97** the admission must be governed by a general interest in the appeal proceedings being conducted in an effective manner, i.e. in dealing with as many of the issues raised by the parties as possible, while still being brought to a close within a reasonable time. In oral proceedings new evidence will be disregarded if its complexity prevents the board and parties to deal with it without adjournment of the oral proceedings. The assessment does not require consideration of the relevance of the evidence (**T633/97** hn2).

See Chapter IV.C.1 of Case Law of the BoA on the transition from the strict to the less rigorous approach to admission of late-filed submissions.

4.5 INDICATION OF EVIDENCE

The notice of opposition must contain at least an indication of evidence. The evidence itself ('Beweismittel' in the German version of the law) should preferably be filed with the notice of opposition to expedite the opposition proceedings. Otherwise, if the opposition is admissible, the EPO will invite the opponent under **R.83** to file it as a rule within two months. (D-IV,1.2.2.1(v))

The opposition division will assess the evidence only after it has formed an opinion on the admissibility of the opposition. It checks whether a priority claim is justified, whether the cited documents have been published before the priority date, and whether the documents disclose the arguments of the opponent (**T234/86**).

It does not suffice to provide only facts and evidence in a notice of opposition; a logical connection must be made between them. The 'reasoned statement' in **R.76(1)** implies the arguments that provide the required 'logical connection'. (D-IV,1.2.2.1(v); **T222/85** r.6, based on **R.55(c)** EPC1973, which mentioned 'arguments')

For written evidence the opponent must indicate the date of publication of the document and the relevant technical subject-matter.

If a document provided as evidence is not in an official EPO language, the EPO may request a translation in an official EPO language (**R.3(3)**; D-III,3.4); in practice the opponent will always be requested to file a translation. The document may be disregarded if the requested translation is not filed (**R.3(3)**).

The prior art taken into account by the examining division is not automatically subject-matter in the opposition procedure, because the opposition procedure is a special procedure, and not a continuation of the grant procedure (**T198/88** hn.1). However, the document quoted in the patent as the closest prior art does form part of the opposition (**T536/88** hn.II; D-V,2.2). For oral evidence the witnesses must be identified with their testimony, date of publication and the group of people attending the disclosure. The same applies to public prior use.

See **Art.54(2):3.6** on public prior use and **T328/87** for an extensive discussion of **R.76(2)(c)** when the state of the art is a prior use: the facts must indicate 'when, where, what, how'.

An expert opinion according to **Art.117(1)(e)** is not often used in opposition proceedings. The search report, possible additional searches and the technical knowledge of the members of the Division are often sufficient. However, use is often made of sworn statements under **Art.117(1)(g)**.

5 **Identity of the representative (R.76(2)(d))**

If a third party is represented, this party is opponent, not his representative. The authorisation of the representative must be filed on request only (**R.101(1)**).

If a representative acts as a straw man, as permitted by **G3/97**, r.2.1, he should be entered as opponent in the notice of opposition.

R. 76(3) Part III of the Implementing Regulations shall apply mutatis mutandis to the notice of opposition.

1 **Applicability of Part III of the Rules**

R.76(3) clarifies that also in opposition proceedings the general provisions on proceedings before the EPO and the provisions of Part III of the Implementing Regulations (**R.35-54**) shall apply mutatis mutandis. (CA/PL17/06)

Close analysis shows that numerous provisions in Part III of the Implementing Regulations can play an important role in these proceedings. In cases where Part III is generally to be applied mutatis mutandis, it will be necessary to establish whether and how a rule is actually applicable to a particular set of circumstances. Consequently, it will not matter if the reference is irrelevant in the case of one or the other provision. (CA/PL29/06)

R. 77 Rejection of the opposition as inadmissible

Implementation of **Art.101(1)**
EPC 1973: **R.56**

1 **Assessment of admissibility**

After the examination upon receipt of the notice of opposition whether the opposition is regarded as filed (see **Art.101(1):1** and **Art.99(1):3**), the formalities officer assesses the opposition for admissibility. Major deficiencies must be remedied before expiry of the opposition period on penalty of inadmissibility, minor deficiencies must be remedied usually within 2 months from invitation, also on penalty of inadmissibility.

Note that a failure to pay the opposition fee is not a deficiency under **R.77** but a deficiency under **Art.99(1)**, causing the notice of opposition deemed not to have been filed.

2 **Procedure for corrigible deficiencies**
When a notice of opposition which is deemed to have been filed reveals serious deficiencies under **R.77(1)**, the EPO will notify the opponent of the deficiencies if it is still possible to correct the deficiencies before the expiry of the opposition period. Since the EPO is not obliged to issue the notification, the opponent can seek no remedy against failure to issue it. (D-IV,1.3.3)

Minor deficiencies under **R.77(2)** must be remedied within a time limit after invitation set by the EPO, which may expire later than the expiry of the opposition period. The EPO is obliged to issue an invitation to correct the deficiencies (**R.77(2)**). If the invitation is inadvertently omitted, the opponent may remedy deficiencies at his own initiative, even after expiry of the opposition period without suffering adverse legal consequences. (D-IV,1.3.3)

Failure to meet the period of **R.77(2)** for correction cannot be remedied: it is not a time limit failed by the applicant (**Art.121(1)**) or loss experienced by the applicant or proprietor (**Art.122**). The period may be extended on request under **R.132**.

3 **Procedure for incorrigible deficiencies**
If there are deficiencies which can no longer be remedied and which have not been communicated to the opponent because the opposition period or a later time limit for correction has expired, the formalities officer notifies the deficiencies to the opponent, as required under **Art.113(1)**, allowing him in general two months to submit comments, and points out that the notice of opposition is likely to be rejected as inadmissible. On expiry of the period for comments or of the period of the invitation to remedy, the decision is taken to reject the opposition as inadmissible and is communicated to the parties (**R.77(3)**). (D-IV,1.4)

4 **Inadmissibility**
The decision that the opposition is admissible is generally taken together with the final decision of the procedure. This procedure is followed, because the opposition can become inadmissible during the proceedings. This is not ruled out by a communication indicating the admissibility according to **R.79(1)** (**T222/85**). (D-IV,5.5)

When the opposition is inadmissible, the opposition fee is not refunded.

R. 77(1) If the Opposition Division notes that the notice of opposition does not comply with Article 99, paragraph 1, or Rule 76, paragraph 2(c), or does not sufficiently identify the patent against which opposition has been filed, it shall reject the opposition as inadmissible, unless these deficiencies have been remedied before expiry of the opposition period.

Amended by decision of the Administrative Council of 21.10.2008, which entered into force on 01.04.2009. (OJ 2008 p.513)
Art.99(1) Opposition
R.76(2)(c) Statement of extent of opposition

1 Deficiencies to be corrected before expiry of the opposition period

1.1 ART.99(1) NON-COMPLIANCE

The identity of the opponent is not known at the end of the opposition period (D-IV,1.2.2.1(vi), **T590/94** r.1.2.2; **Art.99(1):1.1** and **R.76(2)(a):2**). See **R.76(2):2.2** for correction possibilities.

The notice is not filed with an EPO office in Munich, The Hague or Berlin, and the national office has not transmitted it to the EPO within the nine-month period. (D-IV,1.2.2.1(i))

The notice is not in writing. **R.86** requires that all documents must comply with Part III of the Rules (35-54), in which **R.50(2)**, applying also to opposition documents, states that it shall generally be typewritten or printed. Hence, the notice may be handwritten.

The notice does not contain a statement of grounds. (D-IV,1.2.2.1(iv))

Late payment of the opposition fee is not a ground for inadmissibility of the opposition but for deemed not filed of the opposition (**Art.99(1):2.3**).

1.2 R.76(2)(C) NON-COMPLIANCE

The notice does not state the extent of the opposition. If no indication of the extent of the opposition has been given, it suffices when the extent is clear from the notice in its entirety. See **R.76(2)(c):4.2**. (D-IV,1.2.2.1(iii))

The notice does not give the grounds of opposition. If non-patentability is given as ground, the statement must at least implicitly indicate which conditions for patentability (**Art.52 - 57**) are considered not fulfilled.

The notice does not contain the facts and evidence to support the grounds of opposition (D-IV,1.2.2.1(v)). On invitation under **R.83**, the evidence can be filed within a term of usually 2 months. If the facts and evidence to support the grounds are based on national prior rights only, the grounds are not valid, and the opposition will be inadmissible (**T550/88**). Abstracts of European prior rights cannot be used as facts (**Art.85**). The evidence for prior use in an opposition need not be filed together with the facts and arguments, provided that the information on the prior use given in the facts and arguments is comprehensible enough for its merits to be examined (**T538/89**). If the indication of facts, evidence and arguments is not beyond any shadow of doubt, the public interest may lie in the examination of the opposition on its merits; thus the benefit of the doubt as regards admissibility of the opposition should be given to the opponent (**T925/91** r.2.2 and **G1/84** r.3).

1.3 INSUFFICIENT IDENTIFICATION OF THE OPPOSED PATENT

This requirement is less strict than the requirement under **R.76(2)(b)**. It is complied with if the particulars available to the EPO are together sufficient to identify the patent easily and without doubt, i.e. either the publication number or application number normally suffices (**T317/86**). The indication of only the name of a large company does not suffice. However, a mere number suffices, provided no conflicting information is given, e.g. an inconsistent name of the proprietor (D-IV,1.2.2.1(ii)).

R. 77(2) If the Opposition Division notes that the notice of opposition does not comply with provisions other than those referred to in paragraph 1, it shall communicate this to the opponent and shall invite him to remedy the deficiencies noted within a period to be specified. If the deficiencies are not remedied in due time, the Opposition Division shall reject the opposition as inadmissible.

Amended by decision of the Administrative Council of 20.10.1977 which entered into force on 01.02.1978 (OJ 1978 p.12).

1 **Deficiencies to be corrected in an office time limit**
Examples of deficiencies under **R.77(2)** are (D-IV,1.2.2.2):
- Incomplete name or address and state of residence or business of opponent (**R.76(2)(a)** & **R.41(2)(c)**; **T25/85**).
- Incorrect identity of opponent. The identity may be corrected under **R.77(2)** if the correction does not involve a change of mind and the identity was clear at the expiry of the opposition period (**G1/12** r.11, 30 and **T615/14** r.1.6). A correction under **R.139**, first sentence is also possible, even where the identity was not clear at expiry of the opposition period (**G1/12** r.37; **T615/14** r.1.4, 1.5; see also **R.139:3**). The true intention may be proven using evidence filed after the opposition period (**T615/14** r.1.7).
- Incomplete number, name of proprietor or title of opposed patent (**R.76(2)(b)**). If the particulars available to the EPO are together sufficient to identify the patent easily and without doubt, no deficiency exists within the meaning of **R.77(2)** with regard to the title (**T317/86**).
- Incomplete name or address of representative (**R.76(2)(d)** & **R.41(2)(d)**).
- The opponent must be represented according to **Art.133(2)**, but has not appointed a representative. The opponent will be invited to appoint a representative and arrange for the signature or approval of the notice of opposition by the representative. (D-IV,1.2.2.2(iv))

Another deficiency is the omission of the signature of the opponent or his representative. When the omission is not rectified on invitation, the opposition is regarded as not filed (**R.50(3)** is lex specialis); the opposition is not regarded as inadmissible. Hence, the signature is checked before the application of **R.77** (D-IV,1.2.1(ii); see **Art.99(1):3**).

Failure to correct the deficiencies in the notice of opposition in time cannot be redressed by further processing, because the failure does not relate to an application, neither by re-establishment because that remedy is in principle not open for opponents. (D-IV,1.4.2)

R. 77(3) The decision to reject an opposition as inadmissible shall be communicated to the proprietor of the patent, together with a copy of the notice of opposition.

1 **Communication of inadmissibility**
The decision to reject a notice of opposition can be taken without the participation of the proprietor. The proprietor is not asked for comments, and, if no other notices of opposition have been filed, amendments filed by him are not taken into consideration by the EPO, because there is no opposition procedure (D-IV,1.4.1; see e.g. **T550/88**). Without **R.77(3)**, the EPO would not have been obliged to inform the proprietor.

R. 78 Procedure where the proprietor of the patent is not entitled

Implementation of **Art.99(4)**
EPC 1973: **R.13(4)** + **R.16(3)**

1 **General**
R.78 deals with the procedure to be followed where the registered proprietor of a patent was not entitled to the grant of the patent (D-VII,4). The procedure for handling a third party claim to the patent, including a possible stay of the proceedings, during the opposition procedure parallels the procedure for a non-entitled applicant during the grant procedure in **R.14** to **18**. Note, that the entitlement procedure does not apply to limitation and revocation proceedings.

R. 78(1) If a third party provides evidence, during opposition proceedings or during the opposition period, that he has instituted proceedings against the proprietor of the European patent, seeking a decision within the meaning of Article 61, paragraph 1, opposition proceedings shall be stayed unless the third party communicates to the European Patent Office in writing his consent to the continuation of such proceedings. Such consent shall be irrevocable. However, proceedings shall not be stayed until the Opposition Division has deemed the opposition admissible. Rule 14, paragraphs 2 to 4, shall apply mutatis mutandis.

Art.61(1) European patent application filed by non-entitled person
R.14(2)-(4) Resumption of proceedings

1 **Procedure for requesting stay of opposition proceedings**
Whereas **R.14(1)** applies only to stay of grant proceedings, **R.78(1)** provides for staying opposition proceedings. During the stay the third party can await the final decision(s) on entitlement to the patent taken by a national court(s), without the risk of steps being taken by the proprietor detrimental to the third party.

Proceedings are resumed when evidence is provided that a final decision within the meaning of **Art.61(1)** has been taken. If the decision is in favour of the third party, the proceedings may not be resumed earlier than three months after the decision has become final, unless the third party requests resumption (D-VII,4.2.1). The Legal Division is responsible for stay and resumption of the opposition procedure (OJ 2013 p.600; D-VII,4.4).

R. 78(2) Where a third party has, in accordance with Article 99, paragraph 4, replaced the previous proprietor for one or some of the designated Contracting States, the patent as maintained in opposition proceedings may, for these States, contain claims, a description and drawings different from those for the other designated States.

Art.99(4) Replacement of non-entitled proprietor

1 **Different patents for different states**
After a decision of a national court becomes final and the third party is entered in the national patent register of a state instead of the previous proprietor, the third party can replace the previous proprietor for that state (**Art.99(4)**, first sentence). Since the Protocol on Recognition does not apply to patents, it is possible that the third party becomes the new proprietor for some but not all of the designated states. The previous proprietor then remains the proprietor for the other designated states. By derogation from **Art.118**, the previous proprietor and the new proprietor will not be joint proprietors unless both so request (**Art.99(4)**, second sentence). Hence, they can act independently in the opposition procedure and the patent may be

maintained in different forms for the different states as allowed by **R.78(2)** (D-VII,3.2).

R. 79 Preparation of the examination of the opposition

Implementation of **Art.101(1)**
EPC 1973: **R.57**

1 **Communication of documents**
R.79 provides for the distribution of documents between parties and for inviting them to submit observations and any amendments.

The opposition division will transmit a notice of opposition it has received to the proprietor of the patent in suit (**R.79(1)**). If several notices of opposition have been filed, the opposition division will also send a copy to the other opponents (**R.79(2)**). Any observations and amendments filed by the proprietor will be sent to the opponents (**R.79(3)**).

To reduce the amount of paper transmitted between the EPO and the parties, the opposition division does not transmit copies of patent documents to parties; paper copies are available only upon request. All documents will be available online via the Register (see **R.143(1):2**). Parties are advised to inspect the Register before oral proceedings to ensure they have all relevant documents. (Not. EPO OJ 2009 p.434)

R. 79(1) The Opposition Division shall communicate the notice of opposition to the proprietor of the patent and shall give him the opportunity to file his observations and to amend, where appropriate, the description, claims and drawings within a period to be specified.

1 **Communication of opposition to proprietor**
After the opposition period, any period for remedying deficiencies under **R.77(2)**, or a period for presenting evidence, the formalities officer invites the proprietor to file his observations and any amendments of the patent within a four-month period (**R.79(1)**; D-IV,5.2), unless the opposition is already finally rejected as inadmissible under **R.77(3)**. The proprietor should submit a full response to the opposition. An extension of the period will be granted in exceptional cases only and only on a duly substantiated request (OJ 2016 A42).

There is no sanction on late filing of submissions and requests. If they are received before a decision is issued, they are regarded as received in due time (**G12/91**); any late filed facts and evidence are, however, to be treated as not filed in due time (**Art.114(2)**) (E-VIII,1.8). Such facts and evidence will be disregarded, unless they are prima facie relevant, i.e. they would affect the outcome of the decision to be taken (OJ 2016 A42 §5).

If there are several opponents, the formalities officer will send the notices of opposition also to the other opponents (**R.79(2)**).

R. 79(2) If several notices of opposition have been filed, the Opposition Division shall communicate them to the other opponents at the same time as the communication under paragraph 1.

R. 79(3) The Opposition Division shall communicate any observations and amendments filed by the proprietor of the patent to the other parties, and shall invite them, if it considers this expedient, to reply within a period to be specified.

1 **Communication with opponent**
The formalities officer will communicate observations of any of the parties immediately to the other parties for information. The opposition division can issue a separate invitation with a period of normally four months for filing a reply, if it considers that further submissions are necessary for the procedure (D-IV,5.4). In most cases, however, the opposition division will issue summons to oral proceedings directly after receiving the proprietors reply under **R.79(1)** (OJ 2016 A42 §3).

An opponent has no obligation to respond, and non-response has no legal consequences. However, an opponent who does not respond, runs the danger that later filed facts and evidence may be disregarded under **Art.114(2)** (E-VIII,1.8).

In the case of oral proceedings, the first substantive communication of the opposition division is annexed to the summons (D-VI,3.2).

R. 79(4) In the case of an intervention under Article 105, the Opposition Division may dispense with the application of paragraphs 1 to 3.

1 **Limited communication with intervenor**
The application of the provisions in paragraphs 1 to 3 to a late-filed intervention (**Art.105**) might slow down the procedure too much. Therefore, the intervenor is normally notified of all communications so far in the proceedings, and from then on he participates as an opponent in the proceedings. (**G1/94** r.8)

R. 80 Amendment of the European patent

Without prejudice to Rule 138, the description, claims and drawings may be amended, provided that the amendments are occasioned by a ground for opposition under Article 100, even if that ground has not been invoked by the opponent.

Art.100 Grounds for opposition
R.138 Different claims, description and drawings for different states
Implementation of **Art.101(1)**
EPC 1973: **R.57a**

1 **Amendment of patent in opposition**
R.80 addresses substantive requirements for admissibility of amendments made in opposition. The amendments must be occasioned by a ground for opposition, which ground need not have been invoked by the opponent (H-II,3.1). For example, in opposition proceedings admissibly opened on grounds of non-patentability, the proprietor could also make amendments to remove added subject-matter. (Not. EPO OJ 1995 p.416)

Hence, the right to amend in opposition proceedings cannot be used merely to tidy up and improve the disclosure of the patent (**T127/85**). The mere addition of new claims to the claims as granted is inadmissible because such an amendment is neither appropriate nor necessary to meet a ground for opposition (**T674/96** r.3.10). However, replacing one independent claim as granted with multiple independent claims, each directed to a respective specific embodiment of the independent claim as granted, is admissible if the replacement is occasioned by a ground for opposition (**T223/97**, H-II,3.1). Furthermore, if an independent claim is amended, further consequential amendments of other claims and the description comply with **R.80** (H-II,3.2).

The amended claims must comply with the requirements of **Art.123(2)** and (3). The amendments themselves must also comply with the requirement of clarity under **Art.84** (see **G3/14**). Amended claims in opposition need not comply with the requirement of unity of invention under **Art.82** (see **Art.82:3**) and, according to **T263/05** hn.II, neither with the limitation of the number of independent claims of **R.43(2)**. Hence, an amendment changing a single independent claim to a plurality of independent claims is allowed if the amendment is a necessary and appropriate response to a ground of opposition; the number of independent claims is restricted by the requirement that 'the amendment is a necessary and appropriate response to a ground of opposition' (**T263/05** hnI; r.5.19).

According to the provision, **R.80** does not limit the application of **R.138**. Hence, apart from the above, amendments occasioned by national prior rights are admissible during opposition proceedings (H-II,3.3).

Where a patent has been granted with different sets of claims for different contracting states (**R.138**), the proprietor may apply a limitation of one set to another set or file a single set for all contracting states (H-III,4.5).

R.80 is a lex specialis and prevails over **R.79(1)**. It gives the proprietor the right to amend of his own volition. Amendments not related to the grounds of opposition, e.g. corrections or clarifications, will be taken into consideration up to the pronouncement of the decision in oral proceedings or until the date the decision taken in written proceedings is handed over to the EPO's internal postal service|(H-II,3.2; **G12/91**).

2 **Correction of patent in opposition**

Errors and mistakes in the patent as granted may be corrected during opposition proceedings by an amendment under **R.80** based on a ground for opposition, or, where the errors or mistakes concern texts or drawings of the patent that remain unamended, by a correction under **R.139**. A correction under **R.140** is not possible (**G1/10**). (**T657/11** hn; r.3)

3 **Non-binding character of limitation of claim in opposition**

If the proprietor has reduced the scope of protection during opposition proceedings, he can enlarge the scope again later-on during the proceedings (**T123/85**). A limitation to meet objections does not irrevocably abandon subject-matter not anymore covered by the limited claim (**T123/85** r.3.1.5). See **G1/99** for a redress in appeal of an inadmissible amendment held allowable by the opposition division.

4 **Extension of protection and shift to unsearched subject-matter**

The opposition division and board of appeal have a discretion to allow amendments in opposition (appeal), and may refuse them if filed at a late stage, or if neither appropriate nor necessary (**T406/86**; D-VI,4.2). An amendment of the claims may not extend the protection conferred (see **Art.123(3)** and notes). An amendment during appeal proceedings enlarging the scope of protection as maintained in first instance proceedings is only allowed if the proprietor is appellant and not merely party as of right (see **Art.107:3**).

If the amended claims have shifted to subject-matter of a dependent claim of subordinate importance, or to elements previously not set out in the claims, an additional search may be required. In exceptional cases an additional search by the search division can be set in train (D-VI,5)

R. 81 Examination of opposition

Implementation of **Art.101(1)**
EPC 1973: **R.58(1)**, (2) + (3)

1 **General**
R.81 gives the details of the examination during the opposition procedure. **R.81(1)** governs which grounds of opposition the opposition division must examine. The communication with the parties is controlled by **R.81(2)**. According to **R.81(3)** the proprietor must, where necessary, be given an opportunity to amend the patent; a communication may contain a reasoned statement covering the grounds against maintenance of the patent.

Any party can request oral proceedings during the opposition procedure (**Art.116(1)**). The summons for oral proceedings are accompanied by a review of the items to be discussed and, usually, a non-binding opinion of the opposition division on the positions of the parties (D-VI,3.2).

R. 81(1) The Opposition Division shall examine those grounds for opposition which are invoked in the opponent's statement under Rule 76, paragraph 2(c). Grounds for opposition not invoked by the opponent may be examined by the Opposition Division of its own motion if they would prejudice the maintenance of the European patent.

R.76(2)(c) Extent of opposition

1 **Examination of grounds for opposition**
Paragraph 1 incorporates the principles established by the Enlarged Board of Appeal regarding the examination of grounds for opposition by the opposition division (see **G10/91**; OJ 1993 p.420; D-V,2.2). (OJ 2003 se1, p.159)

The extent of examination by the opposition division of its own motion is restricted by case law, as set out in **Art.114(1):1**.

R. 81(2) Communications under Article 101, paragraph 1, second sentence, and all replies thereto shall be sent to all parties. If the opposition division considers this expedient, it shall invite the parties to reply within a period to be specified.

Art.101(1) Examination of the opposition

1 **Information to all parties**
In view of **R.81(2)**, the EPO does not allow informal personal interviews and telephone conversations in opposition proceedings in which more than one party is involved. An exception is for example proceedings concerning the inadmissibility of a notice of opposition (see **R.77(3):1**). (E-III,1)

R. 81(3) In any communication under Article 101, paragraph 1, second sentence, the proprietor of the European patent shall, where necessary, be given the opportunity to amend, where appropriate, the description, claims and drawings. Where necessary, the communication shall contain a reasoned statement covering the grounds against the maintenance of the European patent.

Art.101(1) Examination of the opposition-Revocation or maintenance of the European patent

1 **Auxiliary requests**

The proprietor can file a main request in the form of the set of claims as granted or a new set of claims, and one or more auxiliary requests each in the form of an alternative set of claims. The auxiliary requests must be presented in order of preference. If the opposition division decides to maintain the patent in amended form based on an auxiliary request, the decision includes a rejection of the main request and of any higher ranking auxiliary requests, thereby providing the possibility to file an appeal against the decision to reject the higher ranking requests.

The number of requests should not be excessive (**T907/91**). The most broadly worded claims should be filed as main request and more limited claims as auxiliary request.

The opposition division examines the main and auxiliary requests as submitted by the proprietor and in the order indicated by the proprietor up to and including the highest-ranking allowable request, if any. If the opposition division considers a request allowable, and all parties have had an opportunity to comment as required by **Art.113(1)**, the opposition division immediately issues an interlocutory decision stating that the patent in amended form according to that request meets the requirements of the EPC and giving the reasons why the request is allowable and the higher ranking requests are not allowable. The decision is separately appealable under **Art.106(2)**. Any requests lower ranking than the allowable request will not be examined.

Decision **T926/93** holds, that an opponent need only substantiate a ground of opposition against a single claim of each request. If he succeeds in establishing that a claim of each request is not allowable, the patent will be revoked. The decision reduces the overkill of attacks usually launched on all claims of a request.

Before issuing a decision revoking a patent solely on the basis of a proprietor's main request, the opposition division must ensure that the proprietor has expressly withdrawn all auxiliary requests (**T5/89**).

Both proprietor and opponent may appeal against an (interlocutory) decision to maintain the patent in amended form, since both are adversely affected: the proprietor in that the opposition is not rejected, the opponent in that the patent is not revoked.

R. 82 Maintenance of the European patent in amended form

Implementation of **Art.101(3)**
EPC 1973: **R.58(4), (5), (6), (7) + (8)**

1 **General**

R.82 concerns the maintenance of the European patent in amended form. The legal consequences of failure to pay the fee or file the translation in due time are set out in paragraph 3; the amount of the fee and surcharge is laid down in the Rfees. (OJ 2003 se1 p.159)

R. 82(1) Before the Opposition Division decides to maintain the European patent as amended, it shall inform the parties of the text in which it intends to maintain the patent, and shall invite them to file their observations within two months if they disapprove of that text.

1 **EPO practice of interlocutory decision**

Provisions **R.82(1)** and **R.82(2)**, first sentence, are rarely used. Instead, the opposition division normally uses an interlocutory decision, as approved by **G1/88**, r.7, to avoid that the proprietor has to provide a translation in first instance and again in second instance if the patent is further amended in appeal. The normal practice of the EPO in opposition proceedings is set out in the following paragraphs.

If the opposition division considers that the patent can be maintained in amended form, it issues an interlocutory decision (see **Art.106(2)**) stating that, taking into consideration the amendments, the patent and the invention to which it relates meet the requirements of the EPC. This is not yet the final decision of the opposition division according to **Art.101(3)(a)** to maintain the patent in amended form. The interlocutory decision is appealable. (D-VI,7.2.2.)

If no appeal is filed, the opposition division issues the invitation of **R.82(2)**, second sentence, to pay the fee for publishing the new specification and to file the translations of the amended claims in the two other official languages of EPO, and in case of handwritten amendments, to file a typed text under **R.82(2)**, third sentence (D-VI,7.2.3). Only after these formal requirements have been met, the final decision to maintain the patent in amended form of **Art.101(3)(a)** (and **R.82(4)**) is taken. The new patent specification is then published, thereby starting the period for filing translations of the amended patent with national patent offices under **Art.65(1)** (D-VII,1.4.1).

If the interlocutory decision is appealed, a BoA will review the interlocutory decision. The Board may decide to maintain the patent in amended form based on the interlocutory decision or based on another specified text, reject the opposition as inadmissible, reject the opposition and maintain the patent unamended, or revoke the patent. If the Board maintains the patent in amended form, it will remit the case to the opposition division, which will issue the invitation of **R.82(2)**, second sentence, and proceed as in the previous paragraph.

The interlocutory decision closes the debate before the opposition division on the issues decided in it and the opposition division has thereafter no power to consider those issues anymore (**T390/86** hn.2). Since the interlocutory decision is appealable, any matters decided in it can no longer be challenged later in an appeal against the final decision under **R.82(4)**. The final decision is only appealable in as far as it relates to issues occurring before the opposition division after the appealable interlocutory decision (see e.g. **T91/08** r.1).

2 **Remaining use of R.82(1)**

If an opposition division has made amendments of its own motion in written proceedings, it can issue an invitation under **R.82(1)** to the proprietor to comment (D-VI,7.2.1). An opponent that has not replied to the **R.82(1)** invitation can still appeal the decision to maintain the patent in amended form (**G1/88**). The invitation of **R.82(1)** is not often used, even in written opposition proceedings. The reason is that the prerequisites for an interlocutory decision to maintain the patent in amended form are 1) that the patent proprietor has submitted the new text (as main or auxiliary request), or has approved the new text in case of amendments by the opposition division (**Art.113(2)**) and 2) that the opponent has had sufficient opportunity to comment on the proposed new text, in view of **Art.113(1)**. In written proceedings, a communication under **Art.101(1)** can be used for meeting both prerequisites by giving the opponent the opportunity to comment and inviting the proprietor to approve the text in case of amendments by the opposition division. Once these requirements have been met, a separate communication under **R.82(1)** is neither necessary nor appropriate (**G1/88**).

R. 82(2) If a party disapproves of the text communicated by the Opposition Division, examination of the opposition may be continued. Otherwise, the Opposition Division shall, on expiry of the period under paragraph 1, invite the proprietor of the patent to pay the prescribed fee and to file a translation of any amended claims in the official languages of the European Patent Office other than the language of the proceedings, within a period of three months. Where, in oral proceedings, decisions under Article 106, paragraph 2, or Article 111, paragraph 2, have been based on documents not complying with Rule 49, paragraph 8, the proprietor of the patent shall be invited to file the amended text in a form compliant with Rule 49, paragraph 8, within the three-month period.

Amended by decision of the Administrative Council of 14.10.2015, which enters into force on 01.05.2016, and applies to all patents for which a decision under Art.106(2) or Art.111(2) is taken on or after that date (OJ 2015 A82).
Art.65(1) Translation of patent required by contracting state
Art.106(2) Interlocutory decision in first instance
Art.111(2) Remittal of case to first instance
R.49(8) Requirement of typed version of text

1 **Procedure around interlocutory decision**

The first sentence of **R.82(2)** is hardly used; see R.82(1):1. If an opposition division considers that a patent can be maintained in amended form according to a certain text and **Art.113** is complied with, an appealable interlocutory decision is issued to that effect. Once the interlocutory decision can no longer be impugned and becomes '*res judicata*', i.e. after expiry of the appeal period or after the appeal procedure, the opposition division issues the invitation of **R.82(2)**, second sentence (**G1/88** r.7). Hence, the word 'otherwise' in **R.82(2)**, second sentence, does not mean that the invitation of **R.82(1)** must be issued first, but that the examination of the opposition is closed.

2 **Fee for publishing**

The fee for publishing of a new specification is fixed in **Rfees2(1)8.** No claims fees are due, even if the number of claims has increased.

3 **Translations**

The **R.82(2)** communication also includes an invitation to file translations of the amended claims in the two EPO languages other than the language of the proceedings.

Contracting States may prescribe that a translation of the amended patent specification is filed with the national patent office within three months from the publication of the patent in amended form (**Art.65(1)**).

4 **Typed version of amended text**

During oral proceedings in opposition and opposition appeal the proprietor may file handwritten amendments in documents replacing parts of the patent (see **R.50(1):2**). These documents can serve as the basis of the interlocutory decision or the appeal decision. In such cases the **R.82(2)** invitation includes a request to file amended text passages compliant with **R.49(8)**, i.e. typed, for preparing the 'Druckexemplar' for publication (**R.82(2)**, third sentence). The formally deficient document with handwritten amendments remains the authentic text of the patent maintained in amended form. (OJ 2016 A22; D-VI,7.2.3; E-III,8.7.3).

R. 82(3) If the acts required under paragraph 2 are not performed in due time, they may still be performed within two months of a communication concerning the failure to observe the time limit, provided that a surcharge is paid within this period. Otherwise, the patent shall be revoked.

1 **Grace period for payment of fee and filing of translations and typed text**

If payment of the fee for publishing, filing of the translations of amended claims or, where necessary, filing a typed version of the amended text has not been carried out within the three month period of **R.82(2)**, the opposition division will invite the proprietor under **R.82(3)** to complete the omitted act(s) and pay the fixed surcharge of **Rfees2(1)9** within two months. A divergence between a document with handwritten amendments and a typed version of the document submitted under **R.82(2)** will also trigger the communication under **R.82(3)** (OJ 2016 A22 §12).

In case the **R.82(3)** communication was not justified, the proprietor may provide proof that the acts required under **R.82(2)** had been carried out in time, and, if required, on an auxiliary basis carry out the acts and pay the surcharge.

Re-establishment in the three-month period of **R.82(2)** does not make sense, because the amount of the surcharge of **R.82(3)** is lower than the amount of fee for re-establishment. Further processing is excluded, because the failure does not relate to a patent application but to a patent.

If the requested acts have not been carried out and the surcharge paid on expiry of the two-month period, the patent will be revoked (**R.82(3)**, last sentence; **G1/90** hn). The proprietor may appeal the decision, if he considers that the decision was incorrect, e.g. he disputes the facts or the interpretation of the law (**G1/90** r.13). If the proprietor has failed the two-month period, he may apply for re-establishment, even if the decision to revoke has not yet been delivered (**G1/90** r.14): within 2 months from removal of the cause of non-compliance but within 1 year following the expiry of the two-month period by completing the omitted acts, which always includes payment of the surcharge of **Rfees2(1)9**, requesting re-establishment, paying the fee for re-establishment and proving compliance with the all-due-care criterion.

R. 82(4) The decision to maintain the European patent as amended shall state which text of the patent forms the basis for the decision.

R. 83 Request for documents

Documents referred to by a party to opposition proceedings shall be filed together with the notice of opposition or the written submissions. If such documents are neither enclosed nor filed in due time upon invitation by the European Patent Office, it may decide not to take into account any arguments based on them.

Implementation of **Art.101(1)**
EPC 1973: **R.59**

1 **Documents filed in opposition**
In opposition proceedings, documents should be filed in a single copy. (Spec. Ed. 5 of OJ 2007; D-III,6(iii); D-IV,1.2.2.1(v))If the documents are not submitted within the opposition period, the EPO will request the party to file them as a rule within two months (D-IV,1.2.2.1).

R. 84 Continuation of the opposition proceedings by the European Patent Office of its own motion

Implementation of **Art.101(1)**
EPC 1973: **R.60**

R. 84(1) If the European patent has been surrendered in all the designated Contracting States or has lapsed in all those States, the opposition proceedings may be continued at the request of the opponent filed within two months of a communication from the European Patent Office informing him of the surrender or lapse.

1 **Continuation of proceedings after surrender or lapse of patent**
The EPO requests the opponent to notify within 2 months after the mention of the surrender or lapse whether he wants to continue the opposition. The patent may lapse by non-payment of the renewal fees for the designated states. The lapse or surrender must be proven to the EPO by means of excerpts from the national patent registers. If the proprietor renounces his rights ex tunc or no request for continuation is filed by the opponent, the opposition proceedings will be terminated and the parties informed accordingly. **R.84(1)** also applies in appeal proceedings through **R.100(1)** (see e.g. **T870/92b**).

R. 84(2) In the event of the death or legal incapacity of an opponent, the opposition proceedings may be continued by the European Patent Office of its own motion, even without the participation of the heirs or legal representatives. The same shall apply where the opposition is withdrawn.

1 **Continuation of proceedings after death of opponent**
The opposition division has a discretion to continue the opposition proceedings after withdrawal of the opposition or in the event of the death or legal incapacity of the opponent. A continuation without heirs of the deceased opponent provides the possibility to continue the opposition speedily and give the proprietor his rights, even if the heirs take a long time to settle their affairs.

The opposition division will continue the proceedings if these are likely to result in limitation or revocation of the patent and it can do so without assistance of the opponent and without too much effort. Otherwise, the proceedings are closed by issuing a decision. (D-VII,5)

If a notice according to **R.82(1)** has been issued, the opposition division should always continue the opposition in the public interest. (**T197/88**)

The decision to terminate the proceedings is appealable (**T197/88**, Sum. F&S IV).

In spite of the general reference in **R.100(1)** to **R.84(2)**, relating to first instance proceedings, **R.84(2)** is not applicable to appeal proceedings in opposition because of the different legal nature of the two proceedings (**G7/91** r.7). Hence, withdrawal of the appeal by the opponent as sole appellant terminates the appeal proceedings in so far as the substantive issues settled by the contested decision at first instance are concerned (**G7/91** hn). The termination of the appeal is irrespective of whether the proprietor agrees to the termination or whether the patent satisfies the requirements of the EPC (**G8/93** hn).

R. 85 Transfer of the European patent

Rule 22 shall apply to any transfer of the European patent made during the opposition period or during opposition proceedings.

R.22 Registration of transfers
Implementation of: **Art.71**and**Art.101(1)**
EPC 1973: **R.61**

1 **Registering a transfer of the patent**
R.22 provides a rule for transferring patent applications. **R.85** makes this rule also applicable to the transfer of patents during the opposition period and during the opposition proceedings. The registration of the proprietor of a patent is mandatory, because the EPO must know the parties in the opposition proceedings. The transfer becomes effective if the EPO has received the related documents verifying the transfer. The new proprietor takes the place of the previous proprietor both in the opposition and the appeal proceedings. His entitlement may not be questioned in these proceedings, as for the proceedings the legal fiction of **Art.60(3)** applies. An opposition division is not competent to decide on the entitlement, only the Legal Division is competent as it is responsible for entry of transfers in the Register (**Art.20(1)**). (**T553/90**)

If and under what conditions a registration of a transfer of a patent with the EPO is recognised by a contracting state is determined by national law (see NatLaw table IX, col.6). If a transfer does not automatically take effect in a designated state, the transfer must also be registered in that state to sue and infringer in such a state.

R.85 does not cover the transfer of licences (**R.23**) during opposition period or procedure. Hence, the EPO no longer registers licences once a patent is granted (**J17/91**).

R. 86 Documents in opposition proceedings

Part III of the Implementing Regulations shall apply mutatis mutandis to documents filed in opposition proceedings.

Implementation of: **Art.101(1)**
EPC 1973: **R.61a**

1 **Applicability of Part III of Rules**
According to **R.86**, the provisions of Part III of the Implementing Regulations (**R.35-54**) are to be applied mutatis mutandis in opposition proceedings.

Close analysis shows that numerous provisions in the third part of the Implementing Regulations can play an important role in these proceedings. In cases where Part III is generally to be applied mutatis mutandis, it will be necessary to establish whether and how a rule is actually applicable to a particular set of circumstances. Consequently, it will not matter if the reference is irrelevant in the case of one or the other provision. (CA/PL29/06)

The mutatis mutandis in **R.86** is interpreted to mean that the provision can only be taken to refer to those requirements which it would still be reasonable to demand of the new documents relating to the amended patent (G1/91 r.3.2). See also **T263/05** r.5.6-5.20, which decided that **R.43(2)** is not applicable in opposition.

R. 87 Content and form of the new specification of the European patent

The new specification of the European patent shall include the description, claims and drawings as amended. Rule 73, paragraphs 2 and 3, and Rule 74 shall apply.

R.73(2) Form of the specification
R.73(3) Indication of designated contracting states
R.74 Certificate for a European patent
Implementation of **Art.103**
EPC 1973: **R.62** + **R.62a**

R. 88 Costs

Implementation of **Art.104(2)**
EPC 1973: **R.63**

R. 88(1) The apportionment of costs shall be dealt with in the decision on the opposition. Such apportionment shall only take into consideration the expenses necessary to assure proper protection of the rights involved. The costs shall include the remuneration of the representatives of the parties.

1 **Apportionable costs**
A cost apportionment takes into consideration only the expenses that were necessary to assure proper protection of the rights involved (**R.88(1)**). The costs shall be limited to expenses that are necessarily and reasonably incurred (see **Art.16(2)** RPBA).

Generally, the costs to be paid are the expenses incurred by the receiving parties and caused by the culpable conduct of the party against whom the cost apportionment is ordered. Unlike Art.104 EPC 1973, the costs are not limited to expenses incurred during the taking of evidence or in oral proceedings. Examples of such expenses are given in D-IX,1.3 and **T930/92** hn.III.

R. 88(2) The Opposition Division shall, on request, fix the amount of costs to be paid under a final decision apportioning them. A bill of costs, with supporting evidence, shall be attached to the request. Costs may be fixed once their credibility is established.

1 **Fixing the amount of costs**
The costs may only be fixed on the basis of a final decision apportioning them (**R.88(2)**, first sentence), i.e. after a decision in appeal (however, see **R.97(1)**) or an unavailed appeal period. See **Art.104(2):1** for the procedure of fixing the costs.

R. 88(3) A request for a decision by the Opposition Division may be filed within one month of the communication on the fixing of costs under paragraph 2. The request shall be filed in writing and state the grounds on which it is based. It shall not be deemed to be filed until the prescribed fee has been paid.

Rfees2(1)16 Fee for the awarding of costs

R. 88(4) The Opposition Division shall decide on the request under paragraph 3 without oral proceedings.

R. 89 Intervention of the assumed infringer

Implementation of **Art.105(1)**
EPC 1973: **Art.105**

R. 89(1) Notice of intervention shall be filed within three months of the date on which proceedings referred to in Article 105 are instituted.

Art.105 Intervention of the assumed infringer

R. 89(2) Notice of intervention shall be filed in a written reasoned statement; Rules 76 and 77 shall apply mutatis mutandis. The notice of intervention shall not be deemed to have been filed until the opposition fee has been paid.

R.76 Form and content of the opposition
R.77 Rejection of the opposition as inadmissible

1 **Notice of intervention**
The reference in paragraph 2 to **R.76** makes it clear that on filing a notice of intervention, particulars must be given corresponding to a complete notice of opposition. The provisions of the Implementing Regulations governing opposition, in particular **R.76** and **R.77**, shall equally apply to the admissibility of the intervention. (CA/PL17/06; CA/PL29/06)

The requirements for the notice of intervention have been set out in **Art.105(2):1**.

Chapter II *Procedure for limitation or revocation*

1 **General**
R.90–96 contain the provisions governing the details of the limitation procedure (**Art.105a, 105b, 105c** EPC 2000). As indicated in the notes to these Articles, the limitation procedure is designed as an ex parte procedure which does not provide for the participation of third parties. However, third parties may present observations under **Art.115.** (OJ 2003 se1 p.159)

R. 90 Subject of proceedings

The subject of limitation or revocation proceedings under Article 105a shall be the European patent as granted or as amended in opposition or limitation proceedings before the European Patent Office.

Implementation of **Art.105a(1)**
EPC 1973: No corresponding provision

1 **Subject of proceedings**
R.90 defines the subject of the centralised limitation or revocation procedure before the EPO. The provision makes it explicit that only the European patent as granted or amended by the EPO is to be the subject of such proceedings (OJ 2003 se1 p.159). Where previous limitations have been made before the EPO, the patent as limited will be the subject of future proceedings.

A country may have legal provisions for limiting a European patent before national authorities, which has effect for that country only. Amendments made before such national authorities are not taken into account in proceedings before the EPO. However, the proprietor may submit in limitation proceedings before the EPO the same amendments as made earlier in national proceedings.

R. 91 Responsibility for proceedings

Decisions on requests for limitation or revocation of the European patent under Article 105a shall be taken by the Examining Division. Article 18, paragraph 2, shall apply mutatis mutandis.

Art.18(2) Composition of examining division
Implementation of **Art.105a(1)**
EPC 1973: No corresponding provision

1 **Competence of the examining division**
According to **R.91** the examining division is responsible for deciding on requests for limitation or revocation (already implied in **Art.21(3)(a)**; OJ 2003 se1 p.159). Entrusting the examining division with the limitation and revocation proceedings is expedient because the amended claims are examined under **R.95(2)** not only for formal requirements but also for e.g. clarity (**Art.84**).

The formalities examination is entrusted to a formalities officer (Dec. Pres. OJ 2014 A6, Art1 items 25 and 26). The substantive examination up to the decision is as a rule entrusted to one examiner (**Art.18(2)** mutatis mutandis).

R. 92 Requirements of the request

Implementation of **Art.105a(1)**
EPC 1973: No corresponding provision

1 **General**
R.92 sets out the details of the requirements to be met by a request for limitation or revocation of a European patent.

R. 92(1) The request for limitation or revocation of a European patent shall be filed in writing in one of the official languages of the European Patent Office. It may also be filed in an official language of a Contracting State, provided that a translation is filed in one of the official languages of the European Patent Office within the period specified in Rule 6,paragraph 2. Part III of the Implementing Regulations shall apply mutatis mutandis to documents filed in limitation or revocation proceedings.

Amended by decision of the Administrative Council of 21.10.2008, which entered into force on 01.04.2009. (OJ 2008 p.513)

1 **Procedure for filing request**
R.92(1) requires that the request be filed in writing in one of the official languages of the EPO or in an official language of a contracting state. Although not stated in the provision, the latter language must comply with **Art.14(4)**, i.e. it must be an official language of the contracting state of which the patentee is resident or national (D-X,2.1(iv)). A translation of the request in an official EPO language must be filed within one month of filing the request (**R.6(2)**). In accordance with **R.3(2)**, the text of the amended claims and, as the case may be, the amended description must be filed in the language of the proceedings in which the patent was granted.

R.92(1) refers to Part III of the Implementing Regulations (**R.35-R.54**). This means that the provisions of Part III are to be applied mutatis mutandis in limitation and revocation proceedings. Since the reference is to Part III in general, it will be necessary to establish whether and how a provision of Part III is actually applicable to a particular set of circumstances. Consequently, it will not matter if the reference is irrelevant in the case of one or the other provision. (CA/PL29/06 Add.1)

The request must indicate whether limitation or revocation is sought. Under **Art.105a(1)**, the request is only deemed to be filed when the limitation or revocation fee has been paid. The amount of the appropriate fee is laid down in **Rfees2(1)10a**. The request does not have to be accompanied by a statement of reasons, but this can be expedient where, for example, the requester's entitlement or the limiting effect of the requested amendment of the claims are not unambiguously apparent from the request documents. (OJ 2003 se1 p.159)

The reasons underlying the request need not be given, and are not relevant to the allowability of the request (D-X,4.2).

R. 92(2) The request shall contain:

(a) particulars of the proprietor of the European patent making the request (the requester) as provided in Rule 41, paragraph 2(c), and an indication of the Contracting States for which the requester is the proprietor of the patent;

(b) the number of the patent whose limitation or revocation is requested, and a list of the Contracting States in which the patent has taken effect;

(c) where appropriate, the names and addresses of the proprietors of the patent for those Contracting States in which the requester is not the proprietor of the patent, and evidence that the requester is entitled to act on their behalf in the proceedings;

(d) where limitation of the patent is requested, the complete version of the amended claims and, as the case may be, of the amended description and drawings;

(e) where the requester has appointed a representative, particulars as provided in Rule 41, paragraph 2(d).

R.41(2)(c) Particulars of applicant
R.41(2)(d) Particulars of representative

1 **Contents of request**

R.92(2) specifies the information and the documents which the request must contain. Sub-paragraphs (a), (b) and (e) deal with the identification of the requester and, where appropriate, the representative, as well as the patent to which the request relates (see the corresponding provisions in R.76(2)).

Paragraph 2(c) refers to the cases in which the requester is not the patent proprietor for all the contracting states in which the European patent has become valid (i.e. granted, validated and not revoked). In these cases, he must indicate the further patent proprietors concerned and show that he is entitled to act on their behalf in the limitation or revocation proceedings. The request must also provide evidence that a proprietor is acting for a certain state. In view of the ex tunc effect of limitation and revocation under **Art.68**, this requirement also applies to patent proprietors in states where the European patent has already expired. The EPO must rely on the information provided by the proprietor, because changes in proprietor are not recorded in the Register of the EPO.

Limitation of the European patent under **Art.105a(1)** is only possible by an amendment of the claims. Paragraph 2(d) prescribes accordingly that the request must contain the complete text of the amended claims. A limitation of a dependent claim without limiting an independent claim is acceptable (D-X,4.3). A separate set of claims for a particular Contracting State may also be presented under **R.138** (see **Art.105b(3):1**).

The filing of a description modified in accordance with the amended text of the claims is not prescribed, since the text granted will normally support the claims as amended. If the requester nevertheless wishes to amend the description, he may do so, appending the amended version to his request. The same applies in respect of the drawings.

In accordance with **R.3(2)**, the text of the amended claims and, where appropriate, of the description must be filed in the language of the proceedings in which the patent was granted. Since the amended claims form the basis for limitation and for the publication of the amended specification of the European patent, they must comply with the general provisions concerning the form of documents filed with the EPO (**R.50**). (OJ 2003 se1 p.159)

R. 93 Precedence of opposition proceedings

Implementation of **Art.105a(2)**
EPC 1973: No corresponding provision

1 **General**
An overview of the relation between limitation and revocation proceedings, opposition proceedings and national procedures is given in Art.105a(2):1. **R.93** governs the precedence of opposition proceedings over limitation and revocation proceedings.

R. 93(1) The request for limitation or revocation shall be deemed not to have been filed if opposition proceedings in respect of the patent are pending at the time of filing the request.

1 **Request for limitation or revocation while opposition is pending**
R.93(1) governs the situation where, at the time of filing the request for limitation or revocation, opposition proceedings relating to the patent are pending. **Art.105a(2)** stipulates that the request may not be filed while opposition proceedings are pending. **R.93(1)** clarifies that in such a case the request will be deemed not to have been filed. Accordingly, the fee for limitation or revocation is reimbursed. (OJ 2003 se1 p.179)

The EPC does not define when opposition proceedings are pending. It appears reasonable that they are regarded as pending after valid filing of the notice of opposition and payment of the opposition fee; the effect of manifest inadmissibility of an opposition on the pendency is not clear. The opposition proceedings are no longer pending once the opposition division has taken a decision terminating the procedure, unless the decision is appealed (G4/91 r.7). A limitation or revocation request filed in an unavailed appeal period is hence validly filed (see also **Art.105(1):1.2**).

R. 93(2) If, at the time of filing an opposition to a European patent, limitation proceedings in respect of that patent are pending, the Examining Division shall terminate the limitation proceedings and order the reimbursement of the limitation fee. The reimbursement shall also be ordered in respect of the fee referred to in Rule 95, paragraph 3, first sentence, if the requester has already paid this fee.

R.95(3) Fee for publishing limited specification

1 **Filing opposition while limitation proceedings are pending**
R.93(2) provides that, if an opposition is filed against the European patent while limitation proceedings are already pending for that patent, the limitation proceedings are terminated by the EPO of its own motion. The limitation fee is reimbursed. This complies with the principle of the precedence of opposition proceedings as laid down in **Art.105a(2)**, allowing the patentee to defend his patent against the opponent in the opposition procedure. (OJ 2003 se1 p.179)

R.93(2) does not apply where an opposition is filed during a pending revocation procedure. In this case, the revocation proceedings will continue, leading to revocation of the patent, which makes the opposition pointless. Opposition proceedings will only start if the request for revocation is withdrawn or rejected.

R. 94 Rejection of the request as inadmissible

If the Examining Division finds that the request for limitation or revocation fails to comply with the requirements of Rule 92, it shall invite the requester to correct the deficiencies noted, within a period to be specified. If the deficiencies are not corrected in due time, the Examining Division shall reject the request as inadmissible.

R.92 Requirements of the request
Implementation of **Art.105b(1)**
EPC 1973: No corresponding provision

1 **Inadmissible request**

R.94 concerns the examination as to admissibility of requests under **Art.105a**. Prior to the examination of admissibility, the request may already be rejected as deemed not filed because of formal deficiencies (**R.92**), precedence of opposition proceedings (**R.93**), or an unpaid fee (**Art.105a(1)**). **R.94** is analogous to **R.77(2)** for opposition proceedings.

Non-observance of the period set for correcting the deficiencies cannot be remedied using further processing, because further processing is only available during grant proceedings. Re-establishment of rights under **Art.122** is available. The decision rejecting the request as inadmissible is open to appeal (D-X,2.2).

R. 95 Decision on the request

Implementation of **Art.105b(2)**
EPC 1973: No corresponding provision

R. 95(1) If a request for revocation is admissible, the Examining Division shall revoke the patent and communicate this to the requester.

1 **Revocation of patent**

R.95(1) deals with the request for revocation. If the request for revocation is admissible, the examining division revokes the patent and communicates this to the requester (D-X,3). The decision takes effect on the date the mention of the decision is published in the Bulletin (**Art.105b(3)**); the revocation of the patent is effective ab initio.

R. 95(2) If a request for limitation is admissible, the Examining Division shall examine whether the amended claims constitute a limitation vis-à-vis the claims as granted or amended in opposition or limitation proceedings and comply with Article 84 and Article 123, paragraphs 2 and 3. If the request does not comply with these requirements, the Examining Division shall give the requester one opportunity to correct any deficiencies noted, and to amend the claims and, where appropriate, the description and drawings, within a period to be specified.

Art.84 Requirements for claims
Art.123(2), (3) Amendments

1 **Limitation**

R.95(2) requires that the amendment constitutes a limitation vis-à-vis the claims before limitation, i.e. a reduction in extent of protection conferred. An amendment leading to an *aliud* or for clarification only is not a limitation in the sense of **R.95(2)** (D-X,4.3).

A limitation must reduce the extent of protection conferred by the independent claims. Limitation of a dependent claim only, without any independent claim being limited, is acceptable. However, it is not permissible to introduce non-limiting amendments in the description or claims that are not a consequence of the limitation of the claims (e.g. for tidying up unclarities or improving the text). Adding dependent claims is not permissible if not directly caused by the limitation of the claims. (D-X,4.3)

The claims before limitation are the most recent claims. Hence, if claims are restricted in a first limitation procedure, the claims cannot be broadened in a second limitation procedure.

2 **Examination of request for limitation**

Paragraph 2 concerns the examination for compliance with the substantive requirements for limitation of the European patent. It must be established whether the requested amendment of the claims actually constitutes a limitation and whether the requirements of **Art.84** and **Art.123(2)** and **(3)** have been met, and, where appropriate, whether the amendments to the description or the drawings comply with these requirements. This examination is carried out on the basis of the amended claims and the amended description as submitted by the requester in accordance with **R.92(2)(d)**.

In principle, there should be no examination as to whether the subject-matter of the limited patent is patentable under **Art.52** to **57** or whether the supposed aim of the limitation – e.g. delimitation with respect to particular prior art – is actually achieved by the requested amendment of the claims. (OJ 2003 se1 p.181)

An amendment of the claims need not be accompanied by a corresponding amendment of the description; only the requirements of **Art.84** and **Art.123** must be met.

3 **Opportunity to correct deficiencies**

If the request does not comply with the requirements set out above, the examining division will give the requester only one opportunity to amend the claims and the description within a period of normally two months which is extendable, but only under exceptional circumstances (D-X,4.4). If the response gives rise to new objections, a further communication is issued giving the requester an opportunity to comment; normally no further amendments may be made in reply to that communication (D-X,4.4). Errors of transcription or obvious mistakes can be rectified on request or by the EPO of its own motion (D-X,4.4). Since the request for limitation can be filed again at any time, restricting the requester to one round of amendments during a limitation procedure does not seem unreasonably harsh.

A request for oral proceedings according to **Art.116** must be granted if the request for limitation is not allowable. No further amendments may be submitted during oral proceedings if the opportunity to make amendments has already been taken. (D-X,4.4).

4 **Observations by third persons during limitation proceedings**
Third persons may file observations under **Art.115** during limitation and revocation proceedings. Such observations must relate to patentability, which is interpreted to include **Art.84** and **Art.123(2)**. The EPO forwards the observations to the proprietor, who may take them into account and introduce further limitations in response to the invitation under **R.95(2)**, or, if there is no such invitation, by filing another request for limitation. (D-X,4.5)

R. 95(3) If a request for limitation is allowable under paragraph 2, the Examining Division shall communicate this to the requester and invite him to pay the prescribed fee and to file a translation of the amended claims in the official languages of the European Patent Office other than the language of the proceedings, within a period of three months; Rule 82, paragraph 3, first sentence, shall apply mutatis mutandis. If the requester performs these acts in due time, the Examining Division shall limit the patent.

Amended by decision of the Administrative Council of 26.10.2010, which entered into force on 01.04.2012 (OJ 2010 p.637).
Art.65(1) Translation of patent required by contracting state
R.82(3) Two-month grace period with surcharge

1 **Allowance of request for limitation**
According to paragraph 3, if a request for limitation of the European patent is to be allowed, the requester has to file with the EPO a translation of the amended claims in the two other official languages and pay the fee for publishing the amended patent specification (**Rfees2(1)8**). Only thereafter, the decision to limit the patent is taken. (OJ 2003 se1 p.182)

A contracting state may require that a translation of the patent as limited into the national language of that state be filed under **Art.65**. If not complied with, the patent can be deemed to be void ab initio (**Art.65(3)**). See NatLaw Table IV.

If the payment of the fee and the filing of the translation have not been completed within the period of three months, the EPO will send a communication concerning the failure to observe the period to the proprietor and invite him to perform the acts within two months of the communication, and pay the surcharge of **Rfees2(1)9** within this period (**R.95(3)**, reference to **R.82(3)**).

Non-observance of the three-month period for filing the translation and payment of the fee cannot be remedied using further processing, since further processing is restricted to grant proceedings (**Art.121(1)**); the same applies for the two-month period for performing the acts with surcharge. Re-establishment according to **Art.122** and **R.136** is available.

R. 95(4) If the requester does not respond in due time to the communication issued under paragraph 2, or if the request for limitation is not allowable, or if the requester fails to perform the acts required under paragraph 3 in due time, the Examining Division shall reject the request.

1 **Rejection of request for limitation**
Under paragraph 4, the request for limitation of the European patent is rejected if the request is not allowable, or if the requester does not respond to a communication under paragraph 2 or fails to perform the acts required under paragraph 3 in due time. (OJ 2003 se1 p.182)

The decision to reject the request is appealable. However, since the appeal fee is higher than the limitation fee, it is recommended to file a new request for limitation. If an appeal is filed, the competence of the board of appeal is limited to that of the examining division in limitation proceedings (see **R.95(2)**).

R. 96 Content and form of the amended European patent specification

The amended European patent specification shall include the description, claims and drawings as amended. Rule 73, paragraphs 2 and 3, and Rule 74 shall apply.

R.73(2) Form of the specification
R.73(3) Indication of designated contracting states
R.74 Certificate for a patent
Implementation of **Art.105c**
EPC 1973: No corresponding provision

1 **Content of specification after limitation**
The content of the specification after limitation as set out in **R.96** is the same as the content after opposition, which is governed by **R.87**. A certificate is issued after publication of the amended specification (**R.74**).

PART VI IMPLEMENTING REGULATIONS TO PART VI OF THE CONVENTION

Chapter I *Appeals procedure*

R. 97 Appeal against apportionment and fixing of costs

Implementation of **Art.106(3)**
EPC 1973: **Art.106(4)** and **(5)**

R. 97(1) The apportionment of costs of opposition proceedings cannot be the sole subject of an appeal.

R. 97(2) A decision fixing the amount of costs of opposition proceedings cannot be appealed unless the amount exceeds that of the fee for appeal.

1 **Decision fixing costs**
The decision fixing the amount of costs is a review of the fixing of the costs by the opposition division (**R.88(4)**). According to **R.97(2)**, the amount of costs must be in excess of the appeal fee.

R. 98 Surrender or lapse of the patent

The decision of an Opposition Division may be appealed even if the European patent has been surrendered in all the designated Contracting States or has lapsed in all those States.

Implementation of **Art.106(1)**
EPC 1973: **Art.106(2)**

1 **Decision relating to lapsed or surrendered patent**
This is the equivalent of **R.75** for opposition and is important because revocation and surrender or lapse have different legal consequences: revocation has effect ex tunc (**Art.68**), while surrender and lapse have only effect ex nunc. See **Art.67(2), (4)**.

R. 99 Content of the notice of appeal and the statement of grounds

Implementation of **Art.108**
EPC 1973: **R.64**

R. 99(1) The notice of appeal shall contain:
(a) the name and the address of the appellant as provided in Rule 41, paragraph 2(c);
(b) an indication of the decision impugned; and
(c) a request defining the subject of the appeal.

R.41(2)(c) Particulars of applicant

1 **Name and address (R.99(1)(a))**
The identification of the name and address of the appellant is similar to that required for the first instance in **R.41(2)(c)**. The identification may be corrected under **R.101(2)**. Since a transfer of opposition may cause uncertainty as to entitlement to appeal (see **Art.99(1):1.4**), it is allowed to file the appeal in the name of a first person and, as an auxiliary request, in the name of a second person (**G2/04** hn.II).

The requirement of **R.99(1)(a)** is satisfied if the appellant can be identified. Hence, an address is not required. (**T662/09** r.1.2)

2 **Impugned decision (R.99(1)(b))**
The notice must identify the impugned decision. The Board may infer the contested decision from the file (**T925/91** r.1.1). However, the notice must contain an explicit and unequivocal statement of a definite intention to contest an appealable decision (**T460/95** hn). Hence, a notice accompanying the payment of the appeal fee that merely states 'payment of the appeal fee relating to the aforementioned application' leaves the aim of the appeal unclear, and does not comply with **R.99(1)(b)** (**T460/95** r.5). Likewise, an appeal filed as an auxiliary request, i.e. a conditional appeal, does neither comply with **R.99(1)(b)** (**J16/94** hn).

The extent of the appeal need no longer be stated expressly or be implied in the notice, contrary to the position under EPC 1973 (**T7/81** hn, **T32/81** r.1), and has been moved to the statement of grounds (see **R.99(2)**).

3 **Request (R.99(1)(c))**
The appellant's initial request, according to **G9/92** r.1 (=**G4/93**) and **G1/99** r.6.2, defines the subject of the appeal and thereby the framework of the appeal proceedings. As a rule, the notice of appeal should already clarify whether the decision under appeal is contested as a whole or only partially (**T358/08** hn, r.4.11).

R. 99(2) In the statement of grounds of appeal the appellant shall indicate the reasons for setting aside the decision impugned, or the extent to which it is to be amended, and the facts and evidence on which the appeal is based.

1 **Statement of grounds**
The statement of grounds must indicate the extent to which the decision is appealed. Under **R.64** EPC 1973, this was required in the notice of appeal. This rarely presented a problem in appeals filed by an opponent; as a rule, an opponent will request that the decision impugned be set aside and the patent be revoked (partially or in its entirety). However, where the appellant is the patent proprietor, the amended patent claims are nearly always filed with the statement of grounds for appeal, and it is only then that the precise nature of the requested amendment of the decision impugned becomes apparent. Consequently, this requirement is moved to the statement of grounds, defining the content of the statement of grounds of appeal, which up to now has only been concretized by board of appeal case law under

Art.108, third sentence. As an exception, the extent is sufficiently identified if an application has been refused by the decision impugned and it is stated that an appeal is being lodged against that decision in its entirety; in such a case it can initially be assumed that the appellant adheres to his submission on which the impugned decision was based (**T7/81**).

The part of the decision not attacked in the appeal becomes legally valid at the end of the appeal period (**J27/86** r.2).

R. 99(3) Part III of the Implementing Regulations shall apply mutatis mutandis to the notice of appeal, the statement of grounds and the documents filed in appeal proceedings.

1 **Procedural provisions**
R.99(3) refers to Part III of the Implementing Regulations (**R.35-R.54**). This means that the provisions of Part III are to be applied mutatis mutandis in appeal proceedings. Close analysis shows that numerous provisions in the third part of the Implementing Regulations can play an important role in these proceedings. In cases where Part III is generally to be applied mutatis mutandis, it will be necessary to establish whether and how a rule is actually applicable to a particular set of circumstances. Consequently, it will not matter if the reference is irrelevant in the case of one or the other provision. (CA/PL29/06)

R. 100 Examination of appeals

Implementation of **Art.110**
EPC 1973: **Art.110(2)** + (3) + **R.66(1)**

R. 100(1) Unless otherwise provided, the provisions relating to proceedings before the department which has taken the decision impugned shall apply to appeal proceedings.

1 **Applicability of first-instance provisions**
Examples of the applicability of provisions of departments of first instance in appeal proceedings are given in the notes to **Art.110**.

Examples of the 'otherwise provided' in **R.100(1)** are provisions in the EPC specifically relating to the appeal procedure (**Art.106-112, R.97-103**) and the Rules of Procedure of the Boards of Appeal (see **R.12c(2)**). The Rules of Procedure of the Boards of Appeal may deviate from the EPC provisions for the first instance, but not from those for the second instance; **R.116(1)** is an example of the former (**G6/95**).

R. 100(2) In the examination of the appeal, the Board of Appeal shall invite the parties, as often as necessary, to file observations, within a period to be specified, on communications issued by itself or observations submitted by another party.

R. 100(3) If the applicant fails to reply in due time to an invitation under paragraph 2, the European patent application shall be deemed to be withdrawn, unless the decision impugned was taken by the Legal Division.

1 **No response from applicant**
The provision serves the purpose of avoiding inappropriate delays in the prosecution of an application during appeal proceedings in a way similar to **Art.94(4)** during first instance grant proceedings. The provision does not apply to proprietors and opponents, because it mentions only the 'applicant'. Hence, it is applicable in grant proceedings only. The provision itself states, that it is also not applicable to appeals against a decision taken by the Legal Division, which decisions relate in general to transfers of right and not to the grant of an application. (**J29/94** r.1.2)

The applicant is notified of loss of rights in the appeal procedure (**R.112(1)**); he can apply for a formal decision under **R.112(2)**, but he has no right to appeal that decision. The legal consequence of **R.100(3)** can be removed by requesting further processing under **Art.121**. The sanction of deemed withdrawal of the entire application also applies where the appealed decision did not refuse the application but related only to a request to add a designation of a contracting state (**J29/94** hn).

The only sanction for a party not being an applicant is that late filed observations may not be taken into account (see Art.12(4) RPBA). He cannot use further processing, because that is only available for an applicant. When a respondent in an admissible opposition appeal does not file a request or reply, the board of appeal may not allow the appeal without examination, but it must examine and decide whether the appeal is allowable (**T501/92** hn.IV). Where the BoA allows an appeal and the respondent (proprietor) has not had the opportunity to comment, this is a fundamental violation of the right to be heard (**R7/09**).

R. 101 Rejection of the appeal as inadmissible

Implementation of **Art.110**
EPC 1973: **R.65**

R. 101(1) If the appeal does not comply with Articles 106 to 108, Rule 97 or Rule 99, paragraph 1(b) or (c) or paragraph 2, the Board of Appeal shall reject it as inadmissible, unless any deficiency has been remedied before the relevant period under Article 108 has expired.

Art.106 Decisions subject to appeal
Art.107 Persons entitled to appeal and to be parties to appeal proceedings
Art.108 Time limit and form of notice of appeal
R.97 Appeal against apportionment and fixing of costs
R.99 Content of the notice of appeal and the statement of grounds

1 **Grounds for inadmissibility**
If the formalities officer has decided that the appeal is deemed to have been filed, he will assess the admissibility of the appeal under **Art.110(1)**.

The following cases of inadmissibility of an appeal may arise under **R.101(1)**.

1.1 ART.106: APPEALABLE DECISION
An appeal lying from a non-appealable impugned decision is inadmissible. Examples of non-appealable decisions:

- The decision was not taken by a department mentioned in **Art.106(1)**, e.g. by the President.
- An intermediate decision which does not allow separate appeal (**Art.106(2)**).

- The decision relates only to an apportionment of costs in an opposition (**Art.106(3), R.97(1)**).
- A decision fixing the costs where the costs do not exceed the required amount (**R.97(2)**).

1.2 ART.107: ENTITLEMENT OF PARTY

An appeal by a party not entitled to appeal will be inadmissible. Examples of non-entitled parties:

- The party is not adversely affected. E.g. the proprietor appeals a decision of an opposition division to maintain the patent based on a main request and in a form as amended by the proprietor himself.
- The party is a third party, e.g. a person who filed observations under **Art.115** against the maintenance of the patent by the opposition division (**T89/84**).
- The appellant has not been identified by the end of the appeal period (**T25/85** r.10). Deficiencies in the name and address may be corrected under **R.101(2)** and **R.139**, first sentence (**G1/12**).

1.3 ART.108: FILING FORMALITIES

Non-compliance with filing formalities in general results in an inadmissible appeal. Examples of filing deficiencies:

- The notice of appeal is not in writing (**R.99(3)** and **R.50(2)**).
- The grounds are filed after the 4 month period (**T13/82**). A notice of appeal not giving any legal or factual reasons why the impugned decision should be set aside, but merely stating that the importance of a warning from the EPO was not recognized and an omitted act would be completed, is not regarded as a valid statement of grounds (**T22/88**).
- The grounds are inadequate. A mere reference in general terms to passages in the literature showing the state of the art and to the Guidelines without making their inference sufficiently clear will not suffice as grounds. Lack of such inferences will cause the appeal to be inadmissible according to **R.101(1)**. (**T220/83**)
- If the notice of appeal or the appeal fee is not received in time, **Art.108** gives as consequence that the appeal is deemed not to have been filed. In this case the appeal is not inadmissible (see **Art.108:5**).

1.4 R.99: IDENTIFICATION OF DECISION, REQUEST, REASONS AND FACTS

An appeal is inadmissible if the notice of appeal does not indicate the decision impugned (**R.99(1)(b)**) or if the notice does not include a request defining the subject of the appeal (**R.99(1)(c)**).

An appeal is also inadmissible if the statement of grounds does not indicate the reasons for setting aside the decision impugned or the extent to which it is to be amended, and does not indicate the facts and evidence on which the appeal is based (**R.99(2)**).

1.5 R.3(1): LANGUAGE

The notice of appeal and statement of grounds may be filed in any official EPO language or an admissible non-EPO language, in the latter case with a translation (**R.3(1), R.6(2), Art.14(4)**). When these language requirements are not adhered to the notice of appeal or statement is deemed not to have been received (**Art.14(4)**), resulting in the notice of appeal being regarded as not filed (see **Art.108:5**).

1.6 R.50(3): SIGNATURE
Note that the omission of the signature of the appellant or his representative will result in the appeal to be deemed not filed; the appeal will not be regarded as inadmissible. Hence, the signature is checked prior to the assessment of admissibility under **R.101** (see **Art.108:5**). The EPO will invite the appellant to correct the omission according to **R.50(3)**.

2 **Correction of deficiencies**
The deficiencies must be rectified before the end of the 2 month or, where appropriate, the 4-month period of **Art.108** (**R.101(1)**). If there is time to correct the deficiencies, the registry of the board of appeal will invite the appellant to correct the deficiencies. If there is not sufficient time for correction, the registry will inform the appellant and invite him to file his observations. Before taking the decision to dismiss an appeal as inadmissible, the appellant is invited to file his observations on the findings of the EPO (**Art.113(1)**). The appeal fee is not refunded if the appeal is inadmissible (**T89/84**).

Failure to meet the 2 or 4 month time limit can be remedied with re-establishment under **Art.122**, if the appellant is the applicant or the proprietor, or, as an exception for the 4-month time limit only, the opponent if he did not file the grounds in time (**G1/86**).

R. 101(2) If the Board of Appeal notes that the appeal does not comply with Rule 99, paragraph 1(a), it shall communicate this to the appellant and shall invite him to remedy the deficiencies noted within a period to be specified. If the deficiencies are not remedied in due time, the Board of Appeal shall reject the appeal as inadmissible.

R.99(1)(a) Indication of name and address appellant

1 **Correction of name and address of appellant**
Deficiencies in the name or address of the appellant may be corrected using **R.101(2)** on invitation of the Board of Appeal or using **R.139** on a party's own initiative. The deficiency may be a wrong designation of the appellant (**T97/98** correction under **R.101(2)**; **T814/98** correction under **R.139**).

The nature of the deficiency is not relevant, because **R.99(1)(a)** and **R.101(2)** do not make a distinction in this respect. A correction under **R.101(2)** must comply with two requirements. In the first place the deficiency must be a genuine error. The correction may not reflect a later change of mind as to whom the appellant should be, but on the contrary, only express what was intended when filing the appeal (confirmed by **G2/04** r.3.1). The true intention must be shown when making the correction, for which the data in the file relating to the first instance proceedings may be useful. In the second place, the indication must be such that the appellant is identifiable at expiry of the period for filing the appeal (requirement of **R.101(1)**), even though it is allowed to make the correction after that point in time. It must then be possible to determine whether or not the appeal was filed by a person entitled to appeal in accordance with **Art.107**. It is sufficient therefor that it is possible to derive from the information in the appeal, if necessary with the help of other information on file, with a sufficient degree of probability by whom the appeal should be considered to have been filed. (**T97/98** r.1.4, endorsed by **G1/12** r.29; **T124/10**). Free evaluation of evidence must be used (**G1/12** r.31).

The identity of the appellant may also be corrected using the general procedure for correcting errors under **R.139**, first sentence (**G1/12** r.32-40; **T445/08**). See also **R.139:3**.

The EBoA has decided that 'true intention' can be used, and not only objective criteria, to establish deficiency of an identification in the sense of **R.101(2)** (**G1/12**).

A request for a change of the name of the appellant is not allowable if the name first provided was in conformity with the true intentions of the author of the declaration; in such a situation there is no deficiency which may be remedied in accordance with **R.99(1)(a)** in conjunction with **R.101(2)** (**G2/04** r.3.1).

Examples of allowed corrections: supplying a missing address (**T613/91**), correction of the name (**T1/97**), substitution of named appellant for another natural or legal person if evidence is provided this was the true intention (**T97/98** hn), substitution of named appellant for universal successor in law (**T15/01** r.14). Example of not-allowed correction: substitution of named appellant for another natural or legal person without evidence of transfer of the related business assets (**T298/97** hn.III).

The use of a previous and therefore incorrect name does not have the consequence that the party status is to be denied or that procedural acts have to be regarded as invalid, as long as the identity of a legal person is not at issue (**T15/01** r.3).

R. 102 Form of decision of the Board of Appeal

The decision shall be authenticated by the Chairman of the Board of Appeal and by the competent employee of the registry of the Board of Appeal, either by their signature or by any other appropriate means. The decision shall contain:

(a) a statement that it was delivered by the Board of Appeal;
(b) the date when the decision was taken;
(c) the names of the Chairman and of the other members of the Board of Appeal taking part;
(d) the names of the parties and their representatives;
(e) the requests of the parties;
(f) a summary of the facts;
(g) the reasons;
(h) the order of the Board of Appeal, including, where appropriate, a decision on costs.

Implementation of **Art.111(1)**
EPC 1973: **R.66(2)**

1 **Authentication of decision**
Decisions of boards of appeal are usually authenticated under **R.102(a)** by electronic means, indicated on the decision (OJ 2018 sp1 V.1).

R. 103 Reimbursement of appeal fees

Amended by decision of the Administrative Council of 13.12.2013 and entered into force on 01.04.2014 (OJ 2014 A3). The amendment extends the reimbursement possibilities of the appeal fee by the insertion of paragraph 2; the intention is to increase the number of appeals that will be withdrawn and thereby reduce the workload of the boards. The amended rule applies to appeals pending on 01.04.2014 and appeals filed thereafter.
Implementation of **Art.111(1)**
EPC 1973: **R.67**

R. 103(1) The appeal fee shall be reimbursed in full

(a) in the event of interlocutory revision or where the Board of Appeal deems an appeal to be allowable, if such reimbursement is equitable by reason of a substantial procedural violation, or

(b) if the appeal is withdrawn before the filing of the statement of grounds of appeal and before the period for filing that statement has expired.

1 **Conditions for full reimbursement on procedural violation**

The reimbursement of the appeal fee in full by reason of a substantial procedural violation can only take place if all three conditions below are met (OJ 1996 p.342 §1.1.5):

- the appeal must be allowable, i.e. the board of appeal or, in the case of interlocutory revision, the department of first instance, in substance at least, follows the relief sought by the appellant, and allows his requests,
- there must be a substantial procedural violation, and
- the reimbursement because of this error must be equitable.

The board of appeal remains competent to decide on reimbursement of the appeal fee, even after the appeal has been withdrawn (**T41/82**).

2 **Substantial procedural violation**

A substantial procedural violation is an objective deficiency affecting the entire proceedings (**J7/83**). A procedural violation is in principle that the rules of procedure have not been applied as prescribed by the Convention, but also includes giving incorrect information which may have the same consequences as the incorrect application of those rules (**J6/79** r.8).

In decisions **J21/98** r.16, fifth paragraph, **J22/98**, **J6/99**, **J14/99** and **J15/99** it was decided that a procedural violation which had not played any part in the decision could not be considered substantial. In decision **T682/91** r.4.2 it was emphasised that a procedural violation which did not adversely affect anyone could not be considered substantial; the seriousness of a procedural violation derived from its adverse effects.

T347/04 distinguishes the four J-decisions and decided that where the rules of procedure have not been applied in the manner prescribed in the EPC, a procedural violation has occurred. Even when it has not played any part in the decision, it is considered by the Board as a substantial procedural violation due to its consequences and, particularly, its possible worst case consequences for the applicant.

A reimbursement is not equitable if a party can at least in part be blamed for the procedural violation, e.g. where oral proceedings were not being held because the proprietor requested them very late in the proceedings due to tardiness (**T1544/06** r.5.2).

A few examples of substantial procedural violations: no reasoning of decision in first instance; unjustly disregarding a relevant document; no opportunity of party to comment on reasoning of first instance; giving parties insufficient time to study new amended claims before oral proceedings (**T783/89**); a letter lost in the EPO, so its content is not taken into account (**T205/89**); not providing the opportunity to comment under **R.71(6)** (**T1255/04** r.2.2); contradictory statements in a decision (**T616/08** r.4). A delay of three years between oral proceedings and issue of the written decision is a substantial procedural violation (**T900/02** r.3). A delay of ten years in opposition proceedings is a procedural violation (**T315/03** r.15.6). An extensive list of substantial procedural errors is given in Singer Art.111, rdn. 40-58.

3 **Examples of rejected requests for reimbursement**
An erroneous assessment of patentability cannot lead to reimbursement (**T153/84**).

A wrong interpretation of prior art or of a letter of the applicant is neither a procedural error. A misleading notification of the EPO can lead to a substantial procedural error (**J3/87**).

Non-observance of a procedure set out in the Guidelines, which is not a rule of law, is not a substantial procedural error if not at the same time the EPC is violated (**T42/84**). Where the EPC or established case law does not lay down unambiguously the procedure to be followed in a given situation, use of an incorrect procedure does not constitute a substantial procedural violation (**T234/86** hn.3). Hence, taking a different line from an as yet isolated appeal decision - as opposed to established case law - cannot be regarded as a substantial procedural violation (**T208/88** r.6).

Equity and efficiency of the examining division cannot be matter for an appeal (**T398/86**). An example where the reimbursement is not equitable is an appeal allowed because of a substantial procedural error, but in which the appellant gave rise to the flawed procedure by filing wrong documents (**J18/96** r.5).

An interlocutory revision is in itself no reason for reimbursement of the appeal fee; a substantial procedural violation is necessary, without which there will be no reimbursement of appeal fees. (E-XII,7.3)

Since **R.103(1)** requires allowability of the appeal as a condition for reimbursement, the appeal fee will not be reimbursed if the appeal is rejected as inadmissible or as unallowable (**T13/82**).

4 **Reimbursement on withdrawal of appeal**
Paragraph 1(b) goes some way towards compensating for the lack of a cross-appeal facility. Appeals filed as a precaution – in case the other party appeals – can be withdrawn, if the other party does not file an appeal, at an early stage of the proceedings, during the period between the expiry of the respective periods for filing the notice of appeal and filing the statement of grounds of appeal, i.e. before any great expense of effort by the parties or the EPO. (OJ 2003 se1 p.159, notes to R.67)

R.103(1)(b) does not state the consequence of the withdrawal. If the consequence is that the appeal has existed but now withdrawn, it opens the possibility of filing a divisional application after refusal in first instance proceedings by filing an appeal, filing a divisional application and subsequently withdrawing the appeal and having the appeal fee reimbursed. On the other hand, if the consequence of the withdrawal is that the appeal is regarded as not filed, there will not be the possibility of filing a divisional application. The EPO has not yet made a statement on this issue.

R. 103(2) The appeal fee shall be reimbursed at 50% if the appeal is withdrawn after expiry of the period under paragraph 1(b), provided withdrawal occurs:
- **(a) if a date for oral proceedings has been set, at least four weeks before that date;**
- **(b) if no date for oral proceedings has been set, and the Board of Appeal has issued a communication inviting the appellant to file observations, before expiry of the period set by the Board for filing observations;**
- **(c) in all other cases, before the decision is issued.**

1 **Partial reimbursement**
If the period for filing the statement of grounds has already expired, the appeal fee can still be reimbursed at 50% if the appeal is withdrawn. The withdrawal must be made at least four weeks before the date for oral proceedings, if such date has been set. If no date for oral proceedings has been set and the board has issued a communication inviting the appellant to file observations, the withdrawal must be made before expiry of the period set for filing the observations; any second and further communication also opens the possibility for reimbursement (**T265/14**). In all other cases, the withdrawal must occur before the decision is issued; the date of the decision will only become known to the appellant after the decision has been notified.

R. 103(3) The department whose decision is impugned shall order the reimbursement if it revises its decision and considers reimbursement equitable by reason of a substantial procedural violation. In all other cases, matters of reimbursement shall be decided by the Board of Appeal.

1 **Department competent to reimburse**
Paragraph 3 codifies the case law of the Legal Board of Appeal (**J32/95**). (OJ 2003 se1 p.159)

In case interlocutory revision under **Art.109** is granted by the department of first instance, the department of first instance shall order the reimbursement of the appeal fee if it considers the reimbursement equitable by reason of a substantial procedural violation. However, this department may not refuse a request for reimbursement in interlocutory revision; in such a case only the board of appeal is competent to decide on the request (**G3/03** hn). Hence, if interlocutory revision is granted by the department of first instance but not a request for reimbursement, the appeal is forwarded to the board to decide on the reimbursement only.

Chapter II *Petitions for review by the Enlarged Board of Appeal*

R. 104 Further fundamental procedural defects

A fundamental procedural defect under Article 112a, paragraph 2(d), may have occurred where the Board of Appeal,

(a) contrary to Article 116, failed to arrange for the holding of oral proceedings requested by the petitioner, or

(b) decided on the appeal without deciding on a request relevant to that decision.

Art.112a(2)(d) Review because of any other fundamental procedural defect
Art.116 Obligation to arrange oral proceedings
Implementation of **Art.112a(2)(d)**
EPC 1973: No corresponding provision

1 **Further fundamental procedural defects**

The right to oral proceedings, addressed in **R.104(a)**, is an important aspect of the 'right to be heard'. Ignoring a request for oral proceedings may therefore constitute a fundamental procedural defect, which in proceedings under **Art.112a** merits the same treatment as the cases covered by **Art.112a(2)** (a) to (c). It is up to the Enlarged Board of Appeal to assess the seriousness of the procedural defect. Only non-appointment of oral proceedings which contravenes **Art.116** is to be a reason for re-opening appeal proceedings.

The seriousness of the fundamental procedural defect addressed in **R.104(b)** is also to be assessed by the Enlarged Board of Appeal, which must interpret the terms 'fundamental' and 'relevant' to this end. The assumption is that only requests submitted in writing or requests which the party had recorded in the minutes of the oral proceedings will fall within the ambit of that provision. Furthermore, the wording of **R.104(b)** implies that the fundamental procedural defect must have occurred with respect to the appeal. Therefore, requests relating to the apportionment of costs, the reimbursement of the appeal fee or other requests concerning collateral issues are not addressed by the present provision. A partial re-opening of appeal proceedings with respect to collateral issues only is not desirable. (OJ 2003 se1 p.159)

R. 105 Criminal acts

A petition for review may be based on Article 112a, paragraph 2(e), if a competent court or authority has finally established that the criminal act occurred; a conviction is not necessary.

Art.112a(2)(e) Review because of criminal act
Implementation of **Art.112a(2)(e)**
EPC 1973: No corresponding provision

1 **Criminal acts**

R.105 provides that only a criminal act finally established by a competent court or authority can serve as the basis for proceedings under **Art.112a(2)(e)**. The act may be 'finally established' in any of the following ways:

- by a final judgment under (criminal) law;
- by another final decision of a competent court,

- by a final decision of a competent authority (e.g. under administrative criminal law, to the extent that such a breach of law can be liable to influence the decision of the Board of Appeal).

The operative criterion is not whether the (criminal) court or authority has passed sentence, as this would leave out cases where, for example, the perpetrator dies before sentence can be pronounced, or where a finding of diminished capacity makes sentencing impossible. Instead, the crucial issue is whether an act constituting a criminal offence has actually occurred, and whether the fact of its having occurred has been definitely established by a competent court or authority. (OJ 2003 se1 p.159)

Examples of acts that may be regarded as criminal acts are: forging or manipulating prior art documents, bribery, intimidating or threatening a board member and perjury by a witness. Under most national laws there is always perjury if the witness gives wrong evidence under oath and sometimes perjury if he gives wrong evidence without oath. The EPO cannot hear witnesses under oath, but it can ask for witnesses to give testimony under oath before a national court (**R.120**).

R. 106 Obligation to raise objections

A petition under Article 112a, paragraph 2(a) to (d), is only admissible where an objection in respect of the procedural defect was raised during the appeal proceedings and dismissed by the Board of Appeal, except where such objection could not be raised during the appeal proceedings.

Art.112a(2) Grounds for review
Implementation of **Art.112a(2)**
EPC 1973: No corresponding provision

1 **Raising of objections**

R.106 establishes the obligation to raise any procedural objections already during the appeal proceedings, in so far as the party adversely affected by the defect is – or should be – aware of it. It will be up to the Enlarged Board of Appeal to interpret the term 'could not be raised' and to develop an appropriate standard for assessing whether or not such objection 'could not be raised' during appeal proceedings. (OJ 2003 se1 p. 159; see also comments on **R1/08** in **Art.112a(2):1**)

Where a decision is based on grounds of which the petitioner was not aware, it is apparent that any objections could not be raised during the appeal proceedings (**R1/08, R2/08**).

If no objection is raised during appeal proceedings, although it could have been so raised (for example, where the petitioner responded to the alleged defect by proceeding with the appeal), then the petition is not admissible (**R3/08**).

Where an objection is raised during the appeal, it is necessary that it be dismissed by the board of appeal for there to be a defect (**R3/08, R4/08**).

It is recommended to raise objections arising during oral proceedings in writing and to request the objection be included in the minutes.

Where a suspicion of partiality only arises after the decision in appeal, the petition will probably be admissible.

R. 107 Contents of the petition for review

Implementation of **Art.112a(4)**
EPC 1973: No corresponding provision

1 **Petition for review**
R.107 implements **Art.112a(4)**, first sentence, particularly in respect of the petitioner's duty to substantiate his allegations. The 'reasoned statement' prescribed in **Art.112a(4)**, first sentence has to be filed within the time limits laid down in **Art.112a(4)**, second and third sentences. Its contents must meet the requirements laid down in **R.107**. **R.107(3)** clarifies that the general provisions on proceedings before the EPO and the provisions of Part III of the Implementing Regulations shall apply mutatis mutandis. (OJ 2003 se1 p.159)

The petition must present the complete case. The indication of the decision to be reviewed, the reasons, facts and evidence must all be filed within the same period of **Art.112a(4)**, i.e. two months for grounds other than criminal acts. There is some flexibility in that the EBoA may consider further submissions under Art.12(1) of the Rules of Procedure of the EBoA.

R. 107(1) The petition shall contain:
(a) the name and the address of the petitioner as provided in Rule 41, paragraph 2(c);
(b) an indication of the decision to be reviewed.

R.41(2)(c) Particulars of applicant

R. 107(2) The petition shall indicate the reasons for setting aside the decision of the Board of Appeal, and the facts and evidence on which the petition is based.

1 **Content of the petition**
Note that the petition does not require formal requests, but need only make clear the decision of the board of appeal that is to be set aside (**R5/08**). It must however be clear from the petition why the decision in question suffers from a fundamental procedural defect.

R. 107(3) Part III of the Implementing Regulations shall apply mutatis mutandis to the petition for review and the documents filed in the proceedings.

R. 108 Examination of the petition

Implementation of **Art.112a(5)**
EPC 1973: No corresponding provision

R. 108(1) If the petition does not comply with Article 112a, paragraphs 1, 2 or 4, Rule 106 or Rule 107, paragraph 1(b) or 2, the Enlarged Board of Appeal shall reject it as inadmissible, unless any defect has been remedied before the relevant period under Article 112a, paragraph 4, expires.

Art.112a(1) Person entitled to file petition for review
Art.112a(2) Grounds for review
Art.112a(4) Form of review, period for filing, fee

R.106 Obligation to raise objections
R.107 Contents of the petition for review

1 **Examination of admissibility of petition**
R.108(1) lists the major admissibility requirements to be met by a petition for review. Any defect of the petition relating to these requirements must be remedied within the two-month or five-year period specified in **Art.112a(4)**. If not remedied in due time, the petition will be rejected as inadmissible (**R.108(1)**).

R. 108(2) If the Enlarged Board of Appeal notes that the petition does not comply with Rule 107, paragraph 1(a), it shall communicate this to the petitioner and shall invite him to remedy the deficiencies noted within a period to be specified. If the deficiencies are not remedied in due time, the Enlarged Board of Appeal shall reject the petition as inadmissible.

R.107(1)(a) Name and address of petitioner

1 **Remedy of deficiencies in petition**
R.108(2) is drafted on the model of **R.101(2)**, which applies to appeal proceedings and provides that the Board shall invite the appellant to remedy minor defects, i.e. deficiencies in the particulars required under **R.99(1)(a)**, within a specified period if it notes that the appeal does not comply with the said rule. Petitioners for review should not be barred from a similar possibility to remedy deficiencies. Even if the required particulars are limited to 'the name and the address' as suggested above with respect to **R.107(1)(a)**, it would still be an unnecessary hardship if any missing element in name and address would lead automatically to the inadmissibility of a petition. (OJ 2007 se5 (EN) p.166)

R. 108(3) If the petition is allowable, the Enlarged Board of Appeal shall set aside the decision of the Board of Appeal and order the re-opening of the proceedings before the Board of Appeal responsible under Rule 12b, paragraph 4. The Enlarged Board of Appeal may order that members of the Board of Appeal who participated in taking the decision set aside shall be replaced.

R.12(4) Allocation of duties to boards of appeal by Presidium
By decision of 30.06.2016 the Administrative Council changed the reference R.12 to R.12b. The amendment entered into force on 01.07.2016 (OJ 2016 A100).

1 **Allowable petition**
Paragraph 3 concerns the decision of the Enlarged Board of Appeal if the petition is allowable. In accordance with the legal character of the petition as a special remedy, the Enlarged Board will set aside the decision of the Board of Appeal (by 'cassatory' decision or iudicium rescindens) and order that the proceedings be re-opened. There is no discretionary element to this part of the remedy, therefore requests as such are unnecessary. The consequence of an allowable petition is as defined. The proceedings are re-opened before the Board of Appeal responsible under the business distribution scheme enacted under **R.12b(4)**; however, the Enlarged Board of Appeal may order that members of the board be replaced.

R. 109 Procedure in dealing with petitions for review

Implementation of **Art.112a(5)**
EPC 1973: No corresponding provision

R. 109(1) In proceedings under Article 112a, the provisions relating to proceedings before the Boards of Appeal shall apply, unless otherwise provided. Rule 115, paragraph 1, second sentence, Rule 118, paragraph 2, first sentence, and Rule 132, paragraph 2, shall not apply. The Enlarged Board of Appeal may specify a period deviating from Rule 4, paragraph 1, first sentence.

Art.112a Petition for review by the Enlarged Board of Appeal
R.4(1) One month notice to use other language in oral proceedings
R.115(1) Two months' notice of summons oral proceedings
R.118(2) Two months' notice of summons to give evidence
R.132(2) Duration of office periods

1 **Procedure in dealing with petition**
Paragraph 1 is the parallel provision to **R.100(1)**. The provisions relating to appeal proceedings apply in particular to proceedings before the Enlarged Board of Appeal in the five-member composition under paragraph 2(b). The special rules for proceedings before the Enlarged Board in the three-member composition no longer apply if the Enlarged Board of Appeal has to decide in the composition provided in **R.109(2)(b)**. (OJ 2003 se1, p.159)

In the interest of procedural efficiency, the EBoA may shorten the following periods under **R.109(1)**, second sentence:
- the minimum period of two months for the summons to oral proceedings (**R.115(1)**, second sentence)
- the minimum of two months for periods specified by the EPO (**R.132(2)**)
- the period for a notice of summons to give evidence issued to a party, witness or expert (**R.118(2)**, first sentence)
- the period for requesting interpretation in the language of proceedings (**R.4(1)**, first sentence). (OJ 2007 se5 (EN) p.166)

The EPO will probably decide that confidential documents will be excluded from file inspection.

R. 109(2) The Enlarged Board of Appeal
(a) consisting of two legally qualified members and one technically qualified member shall examine all petitions for review and shall reject those which are clearly inadmissible or unallowable; such decision shall require unanimity;
(b) consisting of four legally qualified members and one technically qualified member shall decide on any petition not rejected under sub-paragraph (a).

1 **Composition of Enlarged Board of Appeal**
According to Art.3(2) of the Rules of Procedure of the EBoA the board under **R.109(2)(b)** will consist of the three members of the board under **R.109(2)(a)** and two additional members.

To cope with the expected large number of petitions, the initial examination of the petitions will be carried out in a fast procedure before a three-member panel of the EBoA. If the petition is not rejected as clearly inadmissible or clearly unallowable by a unanimous decision of the three-member panel, the EBoA in five-member composition will examine the petition in full. The unanimity requirement applies only to the EBoA in the three-member composition. (OJ 2007 se5 (EN) p. 168)

R. 109(3) The Enlarged Board of Appeal composed according to paragraph 2(a) shall decide without the involvement of other parties and on the basis of the petition.

1 **Rejection of petition as clearly inadmissible or unallowable**
The petition for review is assessed in a two-stage procedure before the EBoA. The first stage (**R.109(2)(a)**) filters out cases which are clearly inadmissible or clearly unallowable. In the second stage (**R.109(2)(b)**) the petition for review can be allowed or rejected. The two stages reflect the fear of the EPO that many petitions for review will be filed that are clearly inadmissible or clearly unallowable.

In the first stage proceedings are conducted in accordance with paragraph 3; in the interests of legal certainty, review proceedings which clearly have no chance of succeeding must be ended swiftly. Proceedings under paragraph 3 are therefore conducted without involving the other parties (**R5/08**). The involvement of other parties is not necessary at this stage, because the three-member panel cannot allow a petition. If the petition is rejected as clearly inadmissible or clearly unallowable, the other parties are not adversely affected, as proceedings on the petition for review are terminated and the legal situation remains as stated by the Board of Appeal.

If the three-member panel intends to reject the petition, the petitioner will be invited to attend oral proceedings if he has so requested, or if the Enlarged Board of Appeal considers this expedient, in which case it will issue an invitation of its own motion. If necessary, the period to be observed for issuing the invitation may be shortened. At the end of the oral proceedings, the three-member panel will either reject the petition for review as clearly inadmissible or clearly unallowable, or forward the petition to the five-member panel. If the petition is forwarded, the petition is examined by the EBoA in the five-member composition under **R.109(2)(b)** with the involvement of the other parties. The three-member panel decides 'on the basis of the petition', i.e. on the basis of the reasons submitted, within the period laid down in **Art.112a(4)** and supported by facts and evidence, for setting aside the decision.

The decisions of the EBoA must be reasoned, in accordance with general principles.

From **Art.106** and **112a** it follows that there is no right of further appeal against a decision of the Enlarged Board of Appeal concerning a petition for review. (OJ 2003 se1 p.159)

R. 110 Reimbursement of the fee for petitions for review

The Enlarged Board of Appeal shall order the reimbursement of the fee for a petition for review if the proceedings before the Boards of Appeal are reopened.

Implementation of **Art.112a(5)**
EPC 1973: No corresponding provision

PART VII IMPLEMENTING REGULATIONS TO PART VII OF THE CONVENTION

Chapter I *Decisions and communications of the European Patent Office*

1 Date of decisions

1.1 EFFECT OF FINAL DECISION

A final decision closes proceedings. The decision enters into force the moment in time a party can take cognizance of it. A party cannot file submissions up to this moment, because the decision-making department must be able to take the submissions into account. The last moment in time for filing depends on the type of proceedings, as indicated below. The last moment will only become known to a party after the decision has been taken. All documents filed subsequently serve no purpose in those proceedings any more. The date of notification of the decision in writing to a party does not end the proceedings; it might trigger a period, e.g. for filing an appeal.

See **R.36(1):3.1** for the relation between the date of the decision and the pendency of an application.

1.2 DECISION IN ORAL PROCEEDINGS

In oral proceedings a party can make submissions up to the closing of the debate and after reopening of the debate, which reopening is at the Board's discretion (**T595/90**). A decision pronounced at the end of the oral proceedings enters into force the moment it is pronounced (**G12/91** r.2, 3). It is subsequently notified in writing to a party (**R.111(1)**).

1.3 DECISION IN WRITTEN PROCEEDINGS OF SECOND INSTANCE

In written proceedings of the second instance a party can make submissions up to the date of the decision. This date is communicated in the written decision according to **R.102(b)**. The decision enters into force the date it is notified (**G12/91** r.2).

1.4 DECISION IN WRITTEN PROCEEDINGS OF FIRST INSTANCE

In contrast, the EPC has no provision to communicate to parties the date of a decision in first instance. The legislator did therefore not intend to bind the division to its signed decision from the date the decision was taken and prevent it from taking account of important developments occurring after this date but before the decision left its hands. (**G12/91** r.7.4)

After the decision in first instance has been taken, the formalities section postdates the decision by three days and hands the decision over to the EPO postal service. The decision is thereby taken from the file and thus removed from the power of the department that issued it, completing the proceedings. The EPO postal service despatches the decision for notification exactly on the date stamped on the decision. The practice of stating the date of despatch on the decision allows parties to calculate the date of notification under **R.126(2)** as the tenth day following despatch. (**G12/91** r.6.2, 9)

Therefore, in written proceedings of the first instance the department can take submissions into account and amend the already taken decision up to three days prior to the date stamped on the decision, which therefore corresponds to the closing of the debate in oral proceedings. The date is easy to ascertain by a party, albeit only once the decision has been notified, which provides legal certainty. (**G12/91** r.9; overruling **T598/88** and **T584/88**).

As an example, the first instance decision was stamped 06.03.1996 (Wednesday) and, hence, was handed over to the EPO postal service three *working* days prior to that date, i.e. on 01.03.1996 (Friday); therefore, a party could expect account to be taken of a submission filed before 01.03.1996 (**T394/96** r.4)

The decision taken in written proceedings enters into force when notified, i.e. on the tenth day following the date stamped under **R.126(2)** (**G12/91** r.2).

R. 111 Form of decisions

Implementation of **Art.113**
EPC 1973: **R.68**

R. 111(1) Where oral proceedings are held before the European Patent Office, the decision may be given orally. The decision shall subsequently be put in writing and notified to the parties.

1 **Decision during oral proceedings**
The decision given during oral proceedings is, in general, not reasoned and merely states whether a request is allowed or not. After conclusion of the oral proceedings the decision is completed to the form prescribed in **R.111(2)** by the addition of reasons and notified in written form to the party or parties. The written decision is usually notified a few months after the oral proceedings.

The two-month period of **Art.108** for filing an appeal is triggered by the notification of the written decision in first instance proceedings and not by the pronouncement of the decision during the oral proceedings, because the 'notification' in **Art.108** refers to the notification of the written decision in **R.111(1)** (**T390/86** r.2). See also **Art.116** on the procedure for oral proceedings.

R. 111(2) Decisions of the European Patent Office which are open to appeal shall be reasoned and shall be accompanied by a communication pointing out the possibility of appeal and drawing the attention of the parties to Articles 106 to 108, the text of which shall be attached. The parties may not invoke the omission of the communication.

Art.106 Decisions subject to appeal
Art.107 Persons entitled to appeal and to be parties to appeal proceedings
Art.108 Time limit and of notice of appeal

1 **Form of written decision**
The EPC does not prescribe a particular form for a decision; **R.111(2)** requires only the presence of reasons and a written communication drawing attention to the possibility of appeal and referring to **Art.106-108**.

A decision open to appeal must give reasons why any not withdrawn request is inadmissible, allowable or rejected (**R.111(2)**; E-X,2.6). In the case of several subordinate requests (main request and auxiliary requests) reasons must be provided why each request of higher ranking than the allowed request is not allowed (**T406/86**). Since **R.111(2)** refers to 'decisions open to appeal', a decision not open to appeal, e.g. a decision that does not adversely affect a party, such as granting a request for re-establishment, need not comply with **R.111(2)** and, hence, need not be reasoned. **R.111(2)** does not apply to a decision of a board of appeal because of lex specialis **R.102(g)**, which requires that such a decision must be reasoned, in spite of the fact that it is not open to appeal on account of **Art.106(1)**.

The reasons must contain the logical chain of facts and reasons on which the decision is based and at least some motivation on crucial points of dispute in this line of argumentation, in so far as this is not immediately apparent from the reasons given, in order to give the party concerned a fair idea of why his submissions were not considered convincing (see a.o. **T740/93**, r.5.4). Other case law holds that **R.111(2)** has sufficiently been complied with when some reasons, even if incomplete and inadequate, were given (see a.o. **T856/91**, r.6.2). A decision not reasoned in conformity with **R.111(2)**, e.g. because the reasoning is not intelligible, amounts to a substantial procedural violation and may result in reimbursement of the appeal fee under **R.103** (see e.g. **T755/96** r.5.5, **T278/00** hn.3; **T2467/09** r.6, 13).

A party may not invoke the omission of the written communication stating the possibility of appeal and referring to **Art.106-108** according to the last line of **R.111(2)**. It may neither invoke failure of the EPO to attach the text of the articles to the communication (**T42/84** hn.II).

2 Decision versus communication

The EPC makes a clear distinction between a decision and a communication, as is apparent from **R.111** and **R.113(1)**; this distinction is not always apparent from the form in which the EPO sends them to parties. The EPC and case law do not prescribe a specific form for a decision. A decision may appear as a communication and vice versa without affecting its legal status. Case law has legalized the freedom of form of decisions and communications.

An appealable decision must contain a reasoning but it need not state the possibility of appeal nor provide the text of **Art.106-108** (see previous section). A document providing the contents of a decision is not merely a communication when the requirements of **R.111(2)** are not fully complied with (**J8/81** r.2). A decision may be sent as a mere letter (**T713/02** r.2.1.4), contravening the prescribed form of notification in **R.126(1)**.

Whether a document issued by the EPO constitutes a decision or a communication depends on the substance of its contents, not upon its form (**J8/81**, hn.I).

The contents of a communication never constitute a decision. A communication may express a preliminary view or opinion of the EPO, in particular the communication that gives the party an opportunity to comment on a view of the EPO as required by **Art.113(1)** before the EPO takes a decision. Such a view or opinion is not binding. In contrast, a decision always closes the discussion on an issue and binds the department that issues it and can only be challenged by way of appeal (**T222/85**, r.3). Even the use of the word 'decision' does not make a document a decision in the sense of the EPC (**T713/02** r.2.1.4).

See **R.112(1):2** and **3** for the difference between a decision incurring a loss of rights and a communication under **R.112(1)** informing a party of a loss of rights arisen without a decision.

R. 112 Noting of loss of rights

Implementation of: **Art.113**
EPC 1973: **R.69**

R. 112(1) If the European Patent Office notes that a loss of rights has occurred, without any decision concerning the refusal of the European patent application or the grant, revocation or maintenance of the European patent, or the taking of evidence, it shall communicate this to the party concerned.

1 **Loss of rights**
Under the EPC a loss of rights can arise with or without a decision, depending on the phrasing of the law. The following sections indicate the cases where a decision is taken and where not and the differences in procedure between the two cases.

2 **Loss of rights with a decision**
A loss of rights will be based on a decision if the law states that the EPO will 'decide' or take a 'decision'. Examples of decisions that (may) incur a loss of rights are maintenance of a patent as amended (**Art.101(3)(a)**), apportionment of costs in opposition proceedings (**Art.104(1)**), a decision on an appeal (**Art.111(1)**), a decision on a request for further processing (**R.135(3)**) or on a request for re-establishment (**R.136(4)**; **G1/90**, r.14), a decision to take evidence (**R.117**). The grant of a patent according to **Art.97(1)** will be a loss of rights if the scope of the patent is less broad than desired. Note that a refusal, rejection or revocation implies a decision, which is also clear from the wording of **R.112(1)** (see also **G1/90**, r.5, 7). Examples are a refusal of an application (**Art.90(5)** and **Art.97(2)**), a rejection of a notice of opposition or appeal as inadmissible (**R.77(1)**, **R.101(1)**), a revocation of a patent (**Art.101(2)**, first sentence), a rejection of an opposition (**Art.101(2)**, second sentence).

In general, a decision is taken in cases where the EPO has to carry out an examination, often substantive in nature. After the examination the EPO informs the party of its view and gives him an opportunity to comment under **Art.113(1)**. Subsequently the EPO takes a decision, which is notified to those concerned under **Art.119** and **R.126**.

A party adversely affected by a decision taken in first instance may appeal (**Art.107**). The appeal can be used as a re-examination of the grounds of the first instance decision, but also as a procedure to correct the deficiency that caused the loss of rights. In **J18/08** the application was refused under **R.163(5)**, **(6)** for failing to appoint a representative as required by **Art.133(2)**; the deficiency was corrected in appeal by appointing a representative. Such a correction in appeal is not possible if the decision appealed was taken under **R.112(2)** (see below).

If the notice of appeal is not filed within the period of **Art.108**, the decision cannot be contested anymore and becomes final. As soon as a decision is final, it is entered in the Register and published in the Bulletin, provided the patent application concerned has been published (**Art.127**, **128**). The public can rely on the loss of rights as published. In the event of a change in legal position caused by re-establishment, a third party is protected by the right of continued use under **Art.122(5)**.

3 **Loss of rights without a decision**

The legislator has introduced the concept of 'loss of rights without a decision' to settle clear-cut cases and relieve the EPO from the task of writing a reasoned decision as required by **R.111(2)**. In such cases the loss of rights occurs automatically by operation of law (**G1/90**, r.6). The loss of rights is in general noted by a formalities officer simply by establishing the facts of the case and applying the law (E-VIII,1.9.2). A loss of rights without a decision arises in all cases where no decision is taken. Such cases are in general expressed in the EPC by the standard phrase 'deemed to be ... ' (**G1/90**, r.4). See the above section for the cases where a decision is taken. The list of decisions in **R.112(1)** should be regarded as examples of decisions, not as an exhaustive list.

The loss of rights must result from the Convention. A loss of rights caused by failing the time limit of **Art.65(1)** for filing a translation of a European patent in a contracting state is not a loss under **R.112(1)**, because the time limit and the loss are determined by national law (see **Art.65(3)**; **J43/92**, r.6). The loss of rights may be total, e.g. the application is deemed withdrawn, or partial, e.g. the right of priority is lost.

The most common cause of a clear-cut loss of rights is failure to meet a time limit resulting in a 'deemed to be withdrawn'. Most instances of **R.112(1)** relate to the grant procedure. Examples are the deemed withdrawn of the patent application (**Art.86(1)**, **Art.94(4)**, **R.37(2)**, **R.70(3)**, **R.71(7)**, **R.100(3)**, **R.160(1)**), loss of the right of priority (**Art.90(5)**; A-III,6.10), the deemed not filed of the notice of opposition (**Art.99(1)**), of the notice of appeal (**Art.108**, e.g. **G2/97**, Summ.II) and of a document (**Art.14(4)**, **R.5**, **R.2(1)**, **R.50(3)**), the application not being dealt with as a European patent application (**Art.90(2)**), procedural steps deemed not to have been taken (**R.152(6)**).

4 **Communication of the loss of rights**

The EPO notifies its finding about the loss of rights to the person concerned as a communication under **Art.119**. The communication is despatched under **R.126** by registered letter without advice of delivery. In contrast with decisions, the communication of the loss of rights is not preceded by an invitation to comment on the view of the EPO.

The EPC does not prescribe the form of the communication distinguishing it from a decision, other communication or notice from the EPO. Normally the communication indicates that it refers to a noting of loss of rights pursuant to **R.112(1)**. If this indication is not provided, the content of the communication will be decisive; the content has at least to indicate which of the person's rights is concerned by a loss (**J43/92**, r.4).

Since the communication is not a decision but merely an opinion of the EPO about the effect of the operation of the law, it is not open to appeal (see also **J13/83**, r.4).

The procedure under **R.112(1)** is an efficient way to conclude proceedings of an application in which the applicant has lost interest: the applicant simply refrains from responding to a communication from the EPO and the EPO need not formulate a decision but merely sends a communication under **R.112(1)**. In case the communication under **R.112(1)** is inaccurate or the loss of rights is not desired, a party can ask for a review under **R.112(2)** or apply a legal remedy to retract the legal consequences of the loss of rights, respectively.

5 **Remedies**

A loss of right resulting from the EPC and communicated under **R.112(1)** can be remedied in several ways, depending on the type of loss.

- If the finding of the EPO causing the loss of rights is inaccurate, a review of the finding should be requested by applying for a decision under **R.112(2)**. Such a request is preferably accompanied by requesting one or more remedies in auxiliary requests in case the EPO upholds its finding. Examples of multiple requests are given in **R.112(2):3**.
- The loss may be remedied using further processing under **Art.121** and **R.135**, provided the conditions for further processing have been complied with.
- If further processing is not available, re-establishment under **Art.122** and **R.136** may be used, provided the conditions for re-establishment have been met.
- No remedy is necessary if the loss of rights is intentional. For example, when a PCT application designates the EPO and the applicant decides not to enter into the European phase, the EPO will send a **R.112(1)** communication (see **R.159(1):1.3**).

R. 112(2) **If the party concerned considers that the finding of the European Patent Office is inaccurate, it may, within two months of the communication under paragraph 1, apply for a decision on the matter. The European Patent Office shall take such decision only if it does not share the opinion of the party requesting it; otherwise, it shall inform that party.**

1 **Application for a decision**

If the person affected by the loss of rights considers that the finding of the EPO is inaccurate, he may apply for a decision under **R.112(2)** (E-VIII,1.9.3). A good overview of the procedure is given in Legal Advice **L16/85**, OJ 1985, 141 (cancelled by Dec. Pres. OJ 2012, 446). Possible inaccuracies of the EPO may be an incorrect calculation of a period or not applying provisions for late receipt such as **R.133, Rfees7(3), ADA.4.1** and **5.5**. The person must state the facts and arguments contesting the finding of the EPO in his request and provide evidence where necessary.

The application for a decision under **R.112(2)** must be filed within two months from notification of the loss of rights under **R.112(1)**, taking into account the ten-day rule of **R.126(2)**. Failure to meet the two-month period makes the finding of loss of rights incontestable, unless the person concerned successfully applies for re-establishment according to **Art.122** and **R.136** (E-VIII,1.9.3). **R.135(2)** excludes the two-month period of **R.112(2)** from further processing.

The decision is in general taken by the same formalities officer that noted the loss of rights (see e.g. **G1/02**, Summary of proc. I). According to **R.112(2)**, second sentence, the EPO will give a decision only if it does not share the opinion of the person requesting it; in cases where the EPO accepts the arguments of the requester, it will not issue a decision but inform the requester that the communication under **R.112(1)** will be set aside and the proceedings will continue. The possibility to 'apply for a decision on the matter' in **R.112(2)** is in fact to 'request a review of the communication under **R.112(1)**'.

An adverse decision, reasoned in accordance with **R.112(2)**, is open to appeal, provided the decision was taken by a department of first instance. The two- and four-months periods of **Art.108** for filing the appeal are triggered by the notification of the decision. The board of appeal will only re-examine the finding in the loss of rights communication under **R.112(1)**; the deficiency that caused the loss of rights cannot be corrected during the appeal procedure (**J18/08** r.5; **J1/05** r.4e).

2 **Remedies and R.112(2)**

If the person concerned regards the communication under **R.112(1)** accurate but the resulting loss of rights undesirable, an application for a decision under **R.112(2)** is not useful. The decision will merely confirm the accuracy of the communication but it will not retract the legal consequences of the loss of rights. Instead, such a person must apply a legal remedy appropriate for the loss. Possible remedies are: further processing (**Art.121**), re-establishment (**Art.122**), invoking the principle of good faith in exceptional cases (e.g. **J14/94**; see **Art.125:2**). The period for requesting further processing is triggered by the notification of the **R.112(1)** communication (**R.135(1)**). The period for requesting re-establishment is triggered by the event that makes the party aware of the loss of rights (**R.136(1)**). This event may be the actual receipt of the **R.112(1)** communication.

When the person regards the **R.112(1)** communication inaccurate and applies for a decision under **R.112(2)**, he will be informed of the result only several months after filing the request for a decision. If the result is a justified adverse decision, an appeal will not retract the loss of rights. Since the periods for requesting remedies of the loss of rights run parallel to the two months of **R.112(2)**, these will normally have expired by the time the party receives the decision under **R.112(2)**. Therefore, the party should apply for any remedy together with the application for a decision in the form of a main and auxiliary requests. The requests should be in order of increasing cost.

3 **Example of requests under R.112(2)**

The form of the requests will be clarified in the following example, where an applicant pays the examination fee for his European patent application by giving an order to his bank in Montreal eleven days before expiry of the period of **R.70(1)**. Subsequently the EPO sends a **R.112(1)** communication to the applicant's representative, pointing out that the fee was actually entered in the bank account held by the EPO after expiry of the period and that the application is deemed withdrawn under **Art.94(2)**. The representative files the following series of requests:

- main request: application for a decision under **R.112(2)** arguing that the time limit was considered to have been observed because of the ten-day fail-safe provision of **Rfees7(3)**;
- first auxiliary request: request re-establishment under **Art.122** and **R.136**, pay the fee for re-establishment, arguing that the delay in transfer of the payment was exceptionally long;
- second auxiliary request: request further processing under **Art.121** and **R.135** and payment of the further processing fee equal to 50% of the examination fee.

The EPO takes one decision, dealing with all requests in the order presented by the representative. The EPO will respond as follows:

- the main request is not allowed, because **Rfees7(3)** does not apply to payments from outside the contracting states;
- the first auxiliary request is not allowed, because **R.136(3)** and **R.135** excludes the period of **R.70(1)** from re-establishment;

- the second auxiliary request is allowed.

The fee for re-establishment and the fee for further processing are kept by the EPO. The representative can appeal the decision within two months from notification of the decision.

If the order of the first and second auxiliary request had been reversed, the fee for re-establishment would have been refunded as having no legal basis: the second auxiliary request would not have been dealt with because the higher ranking request for further processing was allowable. Had the EPO allowed the main request, the fees for re-establishment and further processing would both have been refunded.

R. 113 Signature, name, seal

Implementation of **Art.113**
EPC 1973: **R.70**

R. 113(1) Any decisions, summonses, notices and communications from the European Patent Office shall be signed by, and state the name of, the employee responsible.

R. 113(2) Where a document referred to in paragraph 1 is produced by the employee responsible using a computer, a seal may replace the signature. Where the document is produced automatically by a computer, the employee's name may also be dispensed with. The same shall apply to pre-printed notices and communications.

See OJ 2003, 612 for the form of the seals of the various departments.

Chapter II *Observations by third parties*

R. 114 Observations by third parties

Implementation of **Art.115**
EPC 1973: **Art.115**

R. 114(1) Any observations by a third party shall be filed in writing in an official language of the European Patent Office and state the grounds on which they are based. Rule 3, paragraph 3, shall apply.

1 **Method of filing and language of observation**
Observations by a third party in accordance with **Art.115 may be filed by any means permitted under R.2(1), but preferably by electronic means (E-VI,3).**

R.114 stipulates that observations must be filed in an official language of the EPO. If filed in another language, the EPO will request a translation from a non-anonymous third party. The reference to **R.3(3)** makes clear that the third party can file documentary evidence and, in particular, publications in any language. The Office may request a non-anonymous third party to supply a translation of the document and may disregard it if the translation is not filed in due time. (Not. EPO OJ 2017 A86 §3; A-VII,3.5)

R. 114(2) Any such observations shall be communicated to the applicant for or proprietor of the patent, who may comment on them.

1 **Procedure for observations**
The EPO places a received third-party observation in the public part of the file and forwards it to the applicant or proprietor for comment (**R.114(2)**).

The EPO does not send communications in the procedure to the third party other than an acknowledgment of receipt and any request for translation under **R.114(1)**, as he is not a party to the proceedings. The EPO must give its opinion on the observations either in the next substantive communication or as a substantive comment in the Register. Both are available through file inspection (**Art.128(4)**), where an email alert service may be used.

The examining or opposition division must consider the observation and comment on its relevance in the next substantive communication to the parties. If an observation received close to or after issue of the **R.71(3)** communication is regarded not relevant, the EPO will not issue a substantive communication but put a substantive comment in the Register. If an observation received close to or after issue of the **R.71(3)** communication is regarded relevant, the EPO will continue the examination and issue a substantive communication. (OJ 2017 A86 §4)

The EPO will make every effort to issue the next communication within three months of the receipt of the observation, provided the observation is substantiated and not filed anonymously. A non-anonymous filing allows the EPO to check that the person filing the observation is not the applicant or proprietor; if they want to accelerate the proceedings, they must file a PACE request. The filing of a third-party observation does not have the effect of a PACE request, which accelerates not only the next substantive communication but all subsequent actions of the EPO (see **Art.94(1):5**). (OJ 2017 A86 §5)

A third-party observation filed in the international phase of a Euro-PCT application will be taken into account after entry into the EP phase. The EPO will make every effort to issue the next substantive communication within three months after expiry of the **R.161** period if the third party filed the observation non-anonymously and expressly requested expedited issue of the next communication. The express request is not necessary if the observation is (re-)filed after entry. (OJ 2017 A86 §5)

If the applicant or proprietor does not respond to the substantive communication by filing his comments under **Art.94(3)**, **Art.101(1)** or **R.100(2)**, the application is regarded as withdrawn (**Art.94(4)**, **R.100(3)**) or the patent may be revoked if the observations are prejudicial to the maintenance of the patent (**Art.101(2)**).

Chapter III *Oral proceedings and taking of evidence*

R. 115 Summons to oral proceedings

Implementation of **Art.116**
EPC 1973: **R.71**

1 **General**
It is one of the goals of the oral proceedings to make the case ripe for decision at the end of the oral proceedings (see a.o. Art.15(6) RPBoA). The summons inviting the party allow the parties to prepare for the proceedings by setting out the points to be discussed.

R. 115(1) The parties shall be summoned to oral proceedings under Article 116, drawing their attention to paragraph 2 of this Rule. At least two months' notice of the summons shall be given, unless the parties agree to a shorter period.

1 **Summons to oral proceedings**
The EPO invites a party to oral proceedings by means of a summons. The summons states the date, time and location of the oral proceedings. The summons gives parties at least four months notice in examination and six months in opposition, unless the parties agree to a shorter period; a two to four months' notice can be given without preliminary agreement in specific circumstances (E-III,6). The summons indicates the consequences of not appearing (**R.115(2)**) and the points to be discussed (**R.116(1)**). It may contain the provisional and non-binding opinion of the Division. It normally sets a term for filing written submissions (**R.116(1)**). In this way attention during the oral proceedings may be concentrated on the essential issues. (E-III,6)

In opposition proceedings summons are despatched as a rule at least six months before the date set for oral proceedings. The summons contain the opposition division's provisional and non-binding opinion and fixes a date, normally two months before the oral proceedings, for filing observations and amendments. (OJ 2016 A42 §8)

The summons may be given at less than two months' notice if the parties agree (**R.115(1)**, second sentence). In appeal **T1772/06** the period was only 6 weeks. In a case relating to the right to inspect a file prior to publication of the application, a 20-day advance notice was regarded sufficient to allow the parties to prepare themselves properly. In this case the board regarded the urgency of the case more important than the lack of agreement of all parties. (**J14/91** r.2)

An applicant may file submissions in response to the summons to bring the application closer to grant, which could lead to oral proceedings being cancelled. Such submissions can be discussed with the first examiner in an informal consultation (**Art.116:2**). (C-IV,8)

2 **Date of oral proceedings and postponement**
The practice for fixing and postponing the date of oral proceedings before departments of first instance is published in Not. EPO, OJ 2009, 68. The more restrictive practice of the boards of appeal is published in Not. Vice-Pres., Spec. Ed. 3 of OJ 2007, 115.

The EPO fixes a single date for oral proceedings without prior consultation with a party. However, in first instance ex-parte proceedings a party may be contacted by the examining division. The date may be any working day on which the relevant EPO office is open (E-III,6). The EPO will subsequently despatch the summons for oral proceedings according to **R.126**, both before the departments of first instance and before the boards of appeal, which informs the party of this date.

Another date will be fixed only if

- the party concerned files a request as soon as possible after the grounds preventing him from attending the oral proceedings have arisen, and
- the request advances serious reasons, sufficiently substantiated in a written statement, which justify the fixing of a new date.

A statement why another representative cannot substitute the representative prevented from attending the oral proceedings, as required before 2009, need no longer be filed.

Any other parties to the proceedings should be consulted about their availability.

A board of appeal or the Enlarged Board of Appeal will only exceptionally allow a change of date (Art.15(2) RPBoA; Art.14(3) Rules of Proc. EBoA). They will not contact a party to fix a date and still require a substitution statement where applicable (see e.g. **T1080/99** r.2.6).

Acceptable reasons for postponement are ones beyond the control of the party, e.g.

- previously notified summons to oral proceedings of the same party in other proceedings before the EPO or a national court for the same day, for the preceding or following day, or for the two preceding or following days where the other oral proceedings take place at a distant location
- serious illness
- death within the family
- marriage of a person whose attendance in oral proceedings is relevant
- military service or other obligatory civic duties
- business trips firmly booked before notification of the summons
- holidays firmly booked before notification of the summons; where holidays have been scheduled but not yet booked, the reason preventing rescheduling, such as school holidays, must be stated.

The reasons only apply to participants whose presence is essential. A more strict approach may be applied in opposition proceedings to prevent a series of postponements. (E-III,7)

The boards of appeal and the Enlarged Board of Appeal do not regard the following reasons as acceptable: other proceedings on the one or two preceding or following days, business trips, and holidays only scheduled.

Not acceptable reasons are excessive work pressure; a summons to oral proceedings before the EPO or a national court notified after the summons in the relevant proceedings; and need to travel during the weekend. Departments of first instance will try when requested to enable parties to travel on the same day.

The illness of a represented proprietor is not sufficient reason for adjournment of oral proceedings, even if the proprietor were to take part in the oral proceedings. Illness of an unrepresented party, a representative or an important witness is a good reason to request a change of the date of the oral proceedings. (**T275/89**)

R. 115(2) If a party duly summoned to oral proceedings before the European Patent Office does not appear as summoned, the proceedings may continue without that party.

1 **Absence at oral proceedings**

If the party was not duly summoned, the oral proceedings must be postponed. If a duly summoned party files a request for postponement with proper reasoning that the need for postponement was not his error, a new date must be fixed. If the need for postponement is due to carelessness of a party, the proceedings may still be postponed, but a decision on the costs will have to be taken. (E-III,8.3.3.1)

A notice of a party in grant proceedings that he will not attend oral proceedings is taken by the EPO as a request to take a decision on the file as it is.

If a duly summoned party fails to attend oral proceedings without notifying the EPO in advance, an apportionment of costs in favour of another attending party may be justified (**T930/92** hn.II, **T212/07** r.6).

A decision against a party who has been duly summoned but who fails to appear at oral proceedings may not be based on facts put forward for the first time during those oral proceedings. The late submission of new facts is worse procedural practice than non-attendance at oral proceedings; hence, the basic right of **Art.113(1)** is not forfeited by non-attendance. If the EPO decides not to disregard these facts but to examine them under **Art.114(1)**, the absent party must be given an opportunity to comment in accordance with **Art.113(1)**. The party who submitted the new facts is in principle responsible for any additional costs caused by a delay which is the result of the late submission. Evidence submitted for the first time during oral proceedings but notified previously, and which merely supports previous assertions of the party who submits them, may be used to support the reasons for the decision insofar as the relevant facts were already known to the other parties. New arguments not changing the grounds of the decision do not require an opportunity to comment by a non-attending party, since arguments do not constitute grounds or evidence in the sense of **Art.113(1)**. (**G4/92**, following **T484/90**, distinguishing **T574/89**)

A decision in oral proceedings may be based on a ground, e.g. extension under **Art.123(3)**, put forward for the first time during the oral proceedings, at least if the stage reached in the case was such that the absent proprietor could have expected the ground to be discussed (**T341/92** hn.I). Similarly, adding a clarifying restriction to a claim and removing formal deficiencies will not take an absent opponent by surprise, in interference of **Art.113(1)**, because he had to expect that the patentee would try to overcome any objections (**T202/92** r.6).

A party notifying the EPO in response to a proposal for a date for oral proceedings that it will 'take no further part in the proceedings' voluntarily surrenders its rights under **Art.113(1)** and a decision in oral proceedings may be based on any facts, grounds or evidence (**T892/94** r.2.5). During oral proceedings where the proprietor has decided to be absent the EPO does not have an opportunity to make any final amendment, however small, to make the patent maintainable; since the patentee's consent is required under **Art.113(2)**, the EPO can only revoke the patent if such a final amendment is necessary (**T986/00** hn).

Examining and opposition divisions are not bound by decision **T986/00** and may continue proceedings in writing if a party is absent at oral proceedings. A party desiring to rely on continuation in writing should enquire with the division whether it follows the decision. The EPO recommends divisions to follow the decision in view of the considerable increase in number of oral proceedings where applicants do not attend (OJ 2008, 471).

R. 116 Preparation of oral proceedings

Implementation of **Art.116**
EPC 1973: **R.71a**

1 **General**
Implementation of **Art.114(2)** and **Art.116.** See also E-III,5 and 6.
R.116 aims at preparing the ground for oral proceedings such that a decision can be reached closing the proceedings. In general, the EPO states its opinion when issuing the summons, thereby providing the parties an opportunity to present their comments required by **Art.113(1).** Written submissions from a party must reach the EPO and the other parties in time for them to be able to comment on their substance at the oral proceedings. Documents handed in during or just before oral proceedings do not fulfil this requirement and often lead instead to complaints from the other party that he has been taken off guard and is not prepared to discuss new points raised. Therefore, **R.116** sets a deadline for filing written submissions providing new facts or evidence (**R.116(1)**) or providing new requests in the form of amendments (**R.116(2)**). (OJ 1995, 418, 419; **T755/96**, r.2-4)

R. 116(1) When issuing the summons, the European Patent Office shall draw attention to the points which in its opinion need to be discussed for the purposes of the decision to be taken. At the same time a final date for making written submissions in preparation for the oral proceedings shall be fixed. Rule 132 shall not apply. New facts and evidence presented after that date need not be considered, unless admitted on the grounds that the subject of the proceedings has changed.

Implementation of Art.114(2)
R.132 Extension of period on request

1 **Opinion of EPO and opportunity to file submissions**
Together with the summons the EPO communicates points to be discussed in the oral proceedings. It also sets a final date for written submissions to be taken into account.
The provision implements the EPO's discretion under **Art.114(2)** to accept or refuse late filed new facts and evidence. It thus supplements the line already developed by the Boards of Appeal to deal with abuses of the procedure, i.e. to refuse to consider facts or evidence put forward late without good reason. **R.116** should not be construed as an invitation to file new evidence or facts departing from the legal and factual framework of the case prior to the hearing (**T39/93** hn.I). The EPO will first consider the relevance of the late filed facts or evidence or the allowability of the late filed amendments on a prima facie basis. If not relevant or allowable, the submissions will not be admitted. Before admitting the submissions, the EPO will next consider procedural expediency (does it cause a prolonged adjournment of the proceedings), the possibility of abuse of the procedure (e.g. has the party already had sufficient opportunity to address the issues, is there a proliferation of auxiliary requests) and the question whether the parties can reasonably be expected to familiarise themselves in the time available with the new facts, evidence or amendments. (E-III,8.6; H-II,2.7)

New facts and evidence may be filed late if the subject of the proceedings has changed (**R.116(1)**, last sentence). Examples of a change in the subject of the proceedings, which allow late filing of facts and evidence, are the bringing forward of new material by the other party in his own preparatory papers or the filing of amendments by the proprietor which have the result that a new document becomes relevant, or the introduction of a pertinent new document by the examining division during oral proceedings (**T951/97** hn). Documents may acquire relevance through an amendment of claims, making such documents admissible (**T366/11** r.3.5.6; E-III,8.6).

If a party considers that his submission overcomes the objections of the EPO and makes oral proceedings pointless, he should not wait for a response but telephone the EPO about cancellation of the oral proceedings (see e.g. **T1183/02**; E-III,7.2).

A computer-generated slideshow presentation may facilitate the understanding of a submission. It is in essence the presentation of written material and may contain such a quantity of information that parties must be provided with copies before the oral proceedings under **R.116(1)** (**T1122/01** r.2; **T1110/03** r.3, followed by **T555/06** r.1; E-III,8.5.1.1). A projection screen should be available in most meeting rooms; however, the EPO does not provide a computer or projector (E-III,8.5.1).

2 **Period for filing submissions**

Normally the EPO sets the final date for submissions two months before the date of the oral proceedings (D-VI,3.2). Although this period is an office period, it cannot be extended on request under **R.132** (**R.116(1)**, third sentence).

The provision does not exclude the application of the extension of **R.134** to the period for filing submissions. Hence, if the final date falls on a Sunday, the submission may still be filed on the following Monday (**T1366/07** r.1).

3 **Opinion of EPO in second instance**

R.116(1) does not apply to the boards of appeal and is regarded as an example of the 'unless otherwise provided' in **R.100(1)**. Hence, a board is not obliged to communicate in its summons the points to be discussed during the oral proceedings (Art.15(1) RPBoA is non-obligatory). (**G6/95**)

However, if the board does issue a communication, the parties must comply with **R.116** and make their submissions before the date fixed in the communication (**T97/94** hn.I).

R. 116(2) If the applicant or patent proprietor has been notified of the grounds prejudicing the grant or maintenance of the patent, he may be invited to submit, by the date specified in paragraph 1, second sentence, documents which meet the requirements of the Convention. Paragraph 1, third and fourth sentences, shall apply mutatis mutandis.

1 **Invitation to submit amendments**

This paragraph, like the previous one, is also designed to speed up the procedure and to prevent parties being unfairly confronted with new requests in oral proceedings. If the applicant or proprietor has been informed beforehand that refusal or revocation is likely (and why), then he can reasonably be expected to react if the EPO gives him adequate time to do so. The discretionary power to refuse new requests for amendment filed after the specified date is governed by **Art.123**, **R.137(3)** and **R.80** and in the exercise of this power the EPO must balance the applicant's interest in obtaining a proper patent protection and the EPO's interest in concluding the procedure by the issue of a decision (**G7/93** r.2.2 and 2.5; **T755/96** r.4.2).

New requests filed in response to a summons in first instance proceedings will normally be discussed at the oral proceedings (C-IV,8).

A refusal must be adequately reasoned in conformity with **R.111(2)** and should comprise the balancing of interests; a mere ground that it was filed too late is not adequate (**T755/96** r.5).

R. 117 Decision on taking of evidence

Where the European Patent Office considers it necessary to hear a party, witness or expert, or to carry out an inspection, it shall take a decision to this end, setting out the investigation which it intends to carry out, relevant facts to be proved and the date, time and place of the investigation. If the hearing of a witness or expert is requested by a party, the decision shall specify the period within which the requester must make known the name and address of any witness or expert concerned.

Implementation of **Art.117(2)**
EPC 1973: **R.72(1)**

1 **Period for making witnesses known**
The period is between two and four months according to **R.132** (E-IV,1.4).

R. 118 Summons to give evidence before the European Patent Office

Implementation of **Art.117(2)**
EPC 1973: **R.72(2)**

R. 118(1) A summons to give evidence before the European Patent Office shall be issued to the parties, witnesses or experts concerned.

R. 118(2) At least two months' notice of a summons issued to a party, witness or expert to testify shall be given, unless they agree to a shorter period. The summons shall contain:
(a) an extract from the decision under Rule 117, indicating the date, time and place of the investigation ordered and stating the facts in respect of which parties, witnesses or experts are to be heard;
(b) the names of the parties and particulars of the rights which the witnesses or experts may invoke under Rule 122, paragraphs 2 to 4;
(c) an indication that the party, witness or expert may request to be heard by a competent court of his country of residence under Rule 120, and an invitation to inform the European Patent Office, within a period to be specified, whether he is prepared to appear before it.

R.117 Taking of evidence by the EPO
R.120 Hearing by a competent national court
R.122(2)-(4) Reimbursement of witnesses or experts

R. 119 Examination of evidence before the European Patent Office

Implementation of **Art.117(2)**
EPC 1973: **Art.117(2)** + **R.72(3)** + (4)

R. 119(1) The Examining Division, Opposition Division or Board of Appeal may commission one of its members to examine the evidence adduced.

R. 119(2) Before a party, witness or expert may be heard, he shall be informed that the European Patent Office may request the competent court in the country of residence of the person concerned to re-examine his testimony under oath or in an equally binding form.

1 **Request for re-examination under oath**
The option to request a national court to hear a witness under oath is an instrument to put pressure on the person to be heard to speak the truth. See **R.120(2)**.

R. 119(3) The parties may attend an investigation and may put relevant questions to the testifying party, witness or expert.

R. 120 Hearing by a competent national court

Implementation of **Art.117(2)**
EPC 1973: **Art.117(4)**, (5) + (6)

R. 120(1) A party, witness or expert who is summoned before the European Patent Office may request the latter to allow him to be heard by a competent court in his country of residence. If this is requested, or if no reply is received within the period specified in the summons, the European Patent Office may, in accordance with Article 131, paragraph 2, request the competent court to hear the person concerned.

Art.131(2) Administrative and legal co-operation
The countries are restricted to contracting states.

R. 120(2) If a party, witness or expert has been heard by the European Patent Office, the latter may, if it considers it advisable for the testimony to be given under oath or in an equally binding form, issue a request under Article 131, paragraph 2, to the competent court in the country of residence of the person concerned to re-examine his testimony under such conditions.

Art.131(2) Administrative and legal co-operation

1 **Taking of evidence by national court**
The purpose of this provision is to obtain a new taking of the evidence and a statement under oath, on which possible penal sanctions can be based.

The EPO cannot take hearings under oath, as it does not have the power to enforce legal sanctions in the case of perjury. However, it can put pressure on a witness to tell the truth by threatening application of **R.120(2)**. The national court will cooperate because of **Art.131(2)**.

R. 120(3) When the European Patent Office requests a competent court to take evidence, it may request the court to take the evidence under oath or in an equally binding form and to permit a member of the department concerned to attend the hearing and question the party, witness or expert, either through the intermediary of the court or directly.

R. 121 Commissioning of experts

Implementation of Art.117(2)
EPC 1973: R.73

R. 121(1) The European Patent Office shall decide in what form the opinion of an expert whom it appoints shall be submitted.

R. 121(2) The terms of reference of the expert shall include:
(a) a precise description of his task;
(b) the period specified for the submission of his opinion;
(c) the names of the parties to the proceedings;
(d) particulars of the rights which he may invoke under Rule 122, paragraphs 2 to 4.

R.122(2) Expenses for travel and subsistence of witnesses or experts
R.122(3) Compensation for loss of earnings of witnesses and fees for experts
R.122(4) Payment of cost by EPO

R. 121(3) A copy of any written opinion shall be submitted to the parties.

R. 121(4) The parties may object to an expert. The department of the European Patent Office concerned shall decide on the objection.

R. 122 Costs of taking of evidence

Implementation of Art.117(2)
EPC 1973: R.74

R. 122(1) The taking of evidence by the European Patent Office may be made conditional upon deposit with it, by the party requesting the evidence to be taken, of an amount to be fixed by reference to an estimate of the costs.

1 **Deposit of estimate of cost**
The estimate of the cost is based on salary scales of the EPO.

R. 122(2) Witnesses or experts who are summoned by and appear before the European Patent Office shall be entitled to appropriate reimbursement of expenses for travel and subsistence. An advance for these expenses may be granted to them. This shall also apply to persons who appear before the European Patent Office without being summoned by it and are heard as witnesses or experts.

1 **Reimbursement of expenses**
An overview of compensation and fees payable to witnesses and experts is published in OJ 1983, 100.

As a rule, the party requesting evidence meets the costs of the witness or expert. However, in opposition proceedings the EPO may fix a different apportionment for reasons of equity. The EPO may make the taking of evidence conditional upon deposit with the EPO by the party who requested the evidence of an advance for reimbursement of expenses of witnesses or experts. (E-IV,1.9).

Persons not being summoned are only reimbursed if a party or the EPO requests taking their evidence, and the competent department decides to grant the request (E-IV,1.6.2). There is of course no reimbursement if the inventor or another employee accompanying the representative is allowed to give a clarification of facts, without being heard as witness.

R. 122(3) Witnesses entitled to reimbursement under paragraph 2 shall also be entitled to appropriate compensation for loss of earnings, and experts to fees for their work. These payments shall be made to the witnesses and experts after they have fulfilled their duties or tasks.

R. 122(4) The Administrative Council shall lay down the details implementing paragraphs 2 and 3. Any amounts due under these provisions shall be paid by the European Patent Office.

R. 123 Conservation of evidence

Implementation of **Art.117(2)**
EPC 1973: **R.75**

1 **General**
Implementation of **Art.117**.

The provision is a precautionary measure taken before the start of a procedure or earlier than requested in a procedure, and stemming from the probatio ad perpetuam rei memoriam. It aims at conserving evidence of facts liable to affect a decision which may later be difficult or impossible to submit, e.g. evidence from a witness about to emigrate or evidence of public prior use in the form of perishable matter.

The procedure involves (E-IV,2.2):
- filing a request according to **R.123(2)**;
- payment of the fee for conservation of evidence (**Rfees2(1)17**);
- indication of facts which are important for a decision probably to be taken later;
- reasons why the taking of evidence will be difficult or impossible at the later point of time.

R. 123(1) On request, the European Patent Office may, without delay, take measures to conserve evidence of facts liable to affect a decision which it may be called upon to take with regard to a European patent application or a European patent, where there is reason to fear that it might subsequently become more difficult or even impossible to take evidence. The date on which the measures are to be taken shall be communicated to the applicant for or proprietor of the patent in sufficient time to allow him to attend. He may ask relevant questions.

1 **Date for taking evidence**
There is no at least two months' notice of a summons as for the normal taking of evidence under R.118(2), because of the urgency of the case.

R. 123(2) The request shall contain:
(a) particulars of the requester as provided in Rule 41, paragraph 2(c);
(b) sufficient identification of the European patent application or European patent in question;
(c) an indication of the facts in respect of which evidence is to be taken;
(d) particulars of the means of giving or obtaining evidence;
(e) a statement establishing a prima facie case for fearing that it might subsequently become more difficult or impossible to take evidence.

R.41(2)(c) Particulars of applicant

R. 123(3) The request shall not be deemed to have been filed until the prescribed fee has been paid.

Rfees2(1)17 Fee for conservation of evidence

R. 123(4) The decision on the request and any resulting taking of evidence shall be incumbent upon the department of the European Patent Office which would have to take the decision liable to be affected by the facts to be established. The provisions with regard to the taking of evidence in proceedings before the European Patent Office shall apply.

1 **Competence of EPO departments**
Up to the decision to grant the examining division is competent, then the opposition division, thereafter the board of appeal (E-IV,2.3). After a refusal of the examining division the board of appeal should be competent.

R. 124 Minutes of oral proceedings and of taking of evidence

Implementation of Art.117(2)
EPC 1973: R.76

R. 124(1) Minutes of oral proceedings and of the taking of evidence shall be drawn up, containing the essentials of the oral proceedings or of the taking of evidence, the relevant statements made by the parties, the testimony of the parties, witnesses or experts and the result of any inspection.

1 **Drawing up of the minutes**
See E-III,10 for the procedure relating to the drawing up of the minutes and R.4(6) for the language of the minutes. The EPO may record taking of evidence by a dictaphone to assist in drawing up the minutes (E-IV,1.7). A typed out version of the evidence will be provided to the parties.

Only EPO employees are allowed to use any kind of sound recording device in the hearing room at oral proceedings (Not. Vice-Pres., OJ 1986, 63 and Spec. Ed. 3 of OJ 2007, 117). A verbatim record of the proceedings can only be obtained by using a shorthand writer. The same fear for recording deters the EPO from using video conferencing in opposition and in proceedings before a BoA. As a general rule for first instance oral proceedings, parties may use laptops, provided they do not disturb participants and are not used for sound recording (E-III,8.2.1). Use of portable computers is allowed in second instance oral proceedings with the same warning against disturbance and recording (OJ 2014 A21).

The minutes of oral proceedings in first instance proceedings should record arguments of parties relevant for the decision, any new requests of parties, comments of the division relevant for the decision, and an indication of the decision. (E-III,10.3)

The minutes of oral proceedings in appeal should record the requests of the parties on which a decision of the board is required, such as allowability of the appeal, and statements which have an impact on the definition of the subject-matter, such as a statement of surrender of subject-matter. Arguments of parties should not be recorded, as being not essential nor relevant. (T263/05 hn.IV)

R. 124(2) The minutes of the testimony of a witness, expert or party shall be read out, submitted to him, so that he may examine them or, where they are recorded by technical means, played back to him, unless he waives this right. It shall be noted in the minutes that this formality has been carried out and that the person who gave the testimony approved the minutes. If his approval is not given, his objections shall be noted. It is not necessary to play back the minutes or to obtain approval of them if the testimony has been recorded verbatim and directly using technical means.

1 **Minutes of taking of evidence**

According to current practice, the evidence of the person testifying is as a rule summarised section by section by the legal member and dictated in this form onto a dictaphone. The person being examined has the opportunity to raise objections immediately to the dictated text, so that it can be corrected at once.

The first sentence of **R.124(2)**, gives the person the right to have the whole of the testimony played back to him afterwards, unless he waives this right. Normally the person waives this right.

In order to enhance the authenticity of the minutes and to simplify and accelerate the taking of evidence, it could in certain cases make sense to produce the minutes verbatim using technical means instead of summarising the evidence. The requirements in **R.124(2)** of playing back the recording and obtaining approval would be impractical in this case. Therefore, the fourth sentence of **R.124(2)** rules that in the case of verbatim recording no playback or approval is necessary. (Spec. Ed. 5 of OJ 2007)

R. 124(3) The minutes shall be authenticated by the employee responsible for drawing them up and by the employee who conducted the oral proceedings or taking of evidence, either by their signature or by any other appropriate means.

Amended by decision of the Administrative Council of 15.10.2014, which entered into force on 01.04.2015. (OJ 2015 A17, A36 §4)

R. 124(4) The parties shall be provided with a copy of the minutes.

Chapter IV *Notifications*

R. 125 General provisions

Implementation of **Art.119**
EPC 1973: **R.77, R.82**

R. 125(1) The European Patent Office shall, as a matter of course, notify those concerned of decisions and summonses, and of any notice or other communication from which a time limit is reckoned, or of which those concerned must be notified under the Convention, or of which notification has been ordered by the President of the European Patent Office. Any notification to be made shall take the form of the original document, a copy thereof certified by or bearing the seal of the European Patent Office, a computer print-out bearing such seal or an electronic document containing such seal or otherwise certified. Copies of documents emanating from the parties themselves shall not require such certification.

Amended by decision of the Administrative Council of 15.10.2014, which entered into force on 01.04.2015. (OJ 2015 A17, A36 §2, 5)

1 **Documents to be notified**
Notification of a document is the act whereby the EPO makes the document available to a party. The possible ways in which a document can be notified are set out in **R.125(2)**.

The EPO will notify any communication from which a period is reckoned or which must be notified under the EPC or by order of the President. The EPO will not formally notify other communications.

R. 125(2) Notification shall be made:
(a) by postal services in accordance with Rule 126;
(b) by means of electronic communication in accordance with Rule 127;
(c) by delivery on the premises of the European Patent Office in accordance with Rule 128; or
(d) by public notice in accordance with Rule 129.

Amended by decision of the Administrative Council of 15.10.2014, which entered into force on 01.04.2015. (OJ 2015 A17, A36 §2, 5)
R.126 Notification by postal service
R.127 Notification by means of electronic communication
R.128 Notification by delivery by hand
R.129 Public notification

R. 125(3) Notification through the central industrial property office of a Contracting State shall be made in accordance with the law applicable to that office in national proceedings.

R. 125(4) Where a document has reached the addressee, if the European Patent Office is unable to prove that it has been duly notified, or if provisions relating to its notification have not been observed, the document shall be deemed to have been notified on the date established by the European Patent Office as the date of receipt.

1 **Irregular notification**
The EPO has to prove that a party failed to meet a period. Therefore, it has to establish the date of notification of the document that triggered the non-observed period. The advice of delivery of a registered letter (**R.126**) or the automatic log of an electronic communication (**R.127**) may be used as evidence. Where the notification of a document is irregular, the date of receipt established by the EPO will be regarded as the date of notification (**R.125(4)**). See **R.126(2)** for establishing the date of notification of registered letters.

If the EPO cannot establish the date of notification, e.g. because the advice of delivery is erroneous or lost, the date at which the addressee had certainly received the letter may be taken as the date of notification. This can be the date given by the addressee or, if not provided, the date of the letter of response. (E-II,2.6; see e.g. **J9/99**)

R. 126 Notification by postal services

Amended by decision of the Administrative Council of 15.10.2014, which entered into force on 01.04.2015. The amendment replaced 'post' by 'postal services', which removes the monopoly of the traditional postal authorities and allows the EPO to choose the most suitable and low cost postal service provider for notifying its documents (OJ 2015 A17, A36 §1; CA/47/14).
Implementation of **Art.119**
EPC 1973: **R.78**

1 **General**
The EPO notifies documents usually by postal service (E-II,2.3). See **R.127** for other means of delivery. The postal services used by the EPO may be the traditional postal authorities, commonly called 'the post', a courier service or any other service the EPO regards suitable (CA/47/14 §11, 16). Note, that the 'postal service' is the means of transmission and the 'postal service provider' is the operator of the service.

Communications from the EPO will be made to the address of the party or, if the party is represented, to the address of the representative (**R.130(1)**). The addresses are as given on the Request for Grant Form or the notice of opposition. A not-represented applicant having his residence or place of business in a contracting state may indicate in the Request for Grant Form an address for correspondence different from the address used in publications and the Register (e.g. a firm's patent department versus its head office). (Announcement by the President, OJ 2014 A99)

R. 126(1) Decisions incurring a period for appeal or a petition for review, summonses and other such documents as determined by the President of the European Patent Office shall be notified by registered letter with advice of delivery or equivalent. All other notifications by postal services shall be by registered letter.

1 **Registered letter with or without advice of delivery**
Decisions incurring a period for appeal (**Art.108**) or for a petition for review (**Art.112a(4)**), summonses (**R.115(1)**; **R.118(1)**) and other such documents as determined by the President are notified by registered letter with advice of delivery or equivalent (**R.126(1)**). All other notifications by post, such as non-appealable decisions and communications under **Art.94(3)**, are sent by registered letter without advice of delivery. The President has not yet decided to notify other documents with advice of delivery.

The standard advice of delivery used for some notifications was intended to allow the EPO to establish whether the parties have kept the time limits. However, the post does often not return advices of delivery to the EPO or returns them without being completed at the receiving end. To improve the establishment of the date of receipt, the EPO encloses an acknowledgment of receipt form with all communications sent by registered mail with advice of delivery. The addressee should fill in the form and return it immediately to the EPO by EPO Online Services, fax or post. (OJ 2010, 377)

The acknowledgement of receipt is only used if the advice of delivery presents difficulties. The date of returning the acknowledgement to the EPO is not relevant; only relevant is the date of receipt of the letter. (**T1553/13** r.7)

R. 126(2) Where notification is effected in accordance with paragraph 1, the letter shall be deemed to be delivered to the addressee on the tenth day following its handover to the postal service provider, unless it has failed to reach the addressee or has reached him at a later date; in the event of any dispute, it shall be incumbent on the European Patent Office to establish that the letter has reached its destination or to establish the date on which the letter was delivered to the addressee, as the case may be.

1 **Ten-day rule for notification**

The ten-day fiction in this rule establishes a fictitious day of receipt of a letter despatched by the EPO. According to the receipt theory (see **Art.119:2**), a period based on the notification of a letter starts on the day following the date of the addressee's receipt of the letter (**R.131(2)**). The fiction relieves the EPO from establishing the actual date of receipt of each letter; instead it uses the fictitious date for determining the start of the period.

According to **R.126(2)**, the fiction applies only to registered letters, with or without advice of delivery or equivalent, and delivered within the ten-day period. The 'equivalent' covers evidence of receipt other than the advice of delivery common for a postal authority.

The date stamped on the document to be notified is the date the EPO handed over the document to the postal service provider. The fictitious date of delivery, being regarded as the date of notification, is the date of handover plus ten days. This also applies if the fictitious date of delivery is a day on which the EPO is closed (see e.g. **T314/01** r.1). In that case the ten-day period is not extended to the next working day according to **R.134(1)**, because the handover date is not a period within which procedural steps are to be carried out before the EPO, as is implicitly required for the application of **R.134(1)**. For example, an EPO communication under **R.58** date stamped on 07.05.2008 and setting a two-month period for response is deemed delivered on 17.05.2008 (**R.126(2)**), which is a Saturday; the two-month period is triggered by the presumed delivery and expires on 17.07.2008 (**R.131(4)**).

Note that the correct formula 'ten days plus two months' for the expiry of a two-month period is not always equal to the inexact formula 'two months plus ten days', sometimes applied in administrations where the ten days is used as a safety margin after expiry of the normal period (see e.g. **T2056/08**).

2 **Delivery on or after the tenth day**

If a registered letter is received on or after the 10th day of the date printed on the document, the fiction does not apply and the date of notification is the actual date of delivery. In the event of a dispute, the burden is on the EPO to prove the date of delivery (**R.126(2)**).

If a registered letter fails to reach the addressee, no notification has taken place. However, if the EPO considers that the letter was delivered, it has to prove that the letter reached its destination (**R.126(2)**). See **R.125(4)** for irregular notification.

When a party receives a belated delivered communication or becomes aware of a communication that has failed to reach him, he should respond to the EPO explaining that notification was not made within the ten days and as a consequence he could not act as he would have wished in the proceedings. If the evidence satisfies the EPO, it will remedy any adverse procedural effects caused by the transmission and delivery problems in an appropriate manner. (OJ 2015 A62 §6)

R. 126(3) Notification in accordance with paragraph 1 shall be deemed to have been effected even if acceptance of the letter has been refused.

1 **Acceptance of letter**
A letter is regarded as received even if acceptance is refused (**R.126(3)**). National postal law governs who is competent to refuse a letter, e.g. an adult belonging to the family (**R.126(4)**).

R. 126(4) To the extent that notification by postal services is not covered by paragraphs 1 to 3, the law of the State in which the notification is made shall apply.

R. 127 Notification by means of electronic communication

Amended by decision of the Administrative Council of 15.10.2014, which entered into force on 01.04.2015. (OJ 2015 A17, A36 §3, 5)
Implementation of **Art.119**
EPC 1973: **R.77(2)(d)**

R. 127(1) Notification may be effected by means of electronic communication as determined by the President of the European Patent Office and under the conditions laid down by him.

1 **Online notification**
R.127 provides details of electronic notification of documents sent by the EPO to a party. Note, that a reverse communication, i.e. by a party to the EPO, may also be made using electronic communication under **R.2(1)**.

The EPO has started phasing in electronic communication on 01.09.2012 (Dec. Pres. OJ 2012, 486). In an initial phase a large number of pre-grant communications will be notified electronically to professional representatives that have informed the EPO that they wish to take part in the initial phase. The documents include decisions, summonses, notices and communications mentioned in a published list. (Dec. Pres. OJ 2015 A28 Art.2, 9(2)).

Electronic notification requires activation of a mailbox on a secure EPO server. The electronic document sent to the mailbox contains a link to a document in an electronic dossier of the EPO. No paper copies will be sent in parallel. The MyFiles service can be used for organising the representatives' files (OJ 2012, 22 §1).

The notification of an electronic document is governed by **R.127(2)**.

R. 127(2) Where notification is effected by means of electronic communication, the electronic document shall be deemed to be delivered to the addressee on the tenth day following its transmission, unless it has failed to reach its destination or has reached its destination at a later date; in the event of any dispute, it shall be incumbent on the European Patent Office to establish that the electronic document has reached its destination or to establish the date on which it reached its destination, as the case may be.

1 **Ten-day rule for notification of an electronic document**

The ten-day rule establishes a fictitious date where an electronic document transmitted by the EPO is delivered at a recipient, also called the date of notification. Any period triggered by the notification of the document under **R.131(2)** is triggered by this fictitious date. Relevant dates for the notification are the date of the document, i.e. the date printed on the document, the date of transmission by the EPO and the date of actual receipt, i.e. the date the document became available for the recipient. The date of transmission is the date indicated on the document, provided that the addressee can access it in the mailbox by that date (E-II,2.4).

The notification of an electronic document is governed by two legal fictions. The first one is laid down in **R.127(2)**, according to which the notification of an electronic document is deemed to have been effected on the tenth day after transmission of the document to the mailbox of the recipient. This legal fiction does not apply when the document failed to reach its destination or has reached its destination at a later date (**R.127(2)**). The second legal fiction is established by the Decision of the President (OJ 2015 A28 Art.9(4)), stating that when the document is available in the mailbox on the date of the document, the transmission is deemed to have occurred on the date of the document; hence, the tenth day should still be calculated from the date of the document in the case of a transmission on a day before the date of the document.

These two legal fictions have the following consequences for the notification of an electronically communicated document.

- When the document has become available on or before the date of the document, both legal fictions apply and the date of the document triggers the ten day period. Hence, the document is deemed notified on the tenth day following the date of the document (OJ 2015 A36 §3.3.1-2).
- When the document is not yet available in the mailbox on the date of the document, the second legal fiction does not apply and the date on which the document actually became available will be the date of transmission. If the EPO disputes the date of transmission according to the recipient, it has to establish the date on which the communication reached its destination (**R.127(2)**; OJ 2015 A36 §3.3.3). The document will be deemed notified on the tenth day following the date it actually became available.
- When the document is not yet available in the mailbox on the tenth day following the date of the document, both the first legal fiction, i.e. the ten-day rule, and the second legal fiction do not apply. The notification of the document will be the date the document actually became available. If the EPO disputes the date of transmission according to the recipient, it has to establish the date on which the communication reached its destination (**R.127(2)**).
- When the document fails to reach its destination, both legal fictions do not apply. The recipient will receive a notice of loss of rights, in response to which he may argue under **R.112(2)** that he never received the document. In such a case the EPO has to establish that the electronic document has reached its destination (**R.127(2)**).

R.127(2) is similar to the ten-day rule of **R.126(2)** for notification of registered letters, with the exception of the flexible character of the date of transmission. Since an electronic communication is not delivered to a physical person but to a destination, such as a mailbox or portal, the phrase 'delivered to the addressee' in **R.126(2)** is replaced by 'reach its destination' (CA/47/14).

R. 128 Notification by delivery by hand

Notification may be effected on the premises of the European Patent Office by delivery by hand of the document to the addressee, who shall on delivery acknowledge its receipt. Notification shall be deemed to have been effected even if the addressee refuses to accept the document or to acknowledge receipt thereof.

Implementation of **Art.119**
EPC 1973: **R.79**

1 **Delivery by hand**
Delivery by hand is sometimes used to avoid postal delays. This method of notification is restricted to the premises of the EPO according to **R.128** and happens mainly during oral proceedings.

R. 129 Public notification

Implementation of **Art.119**
EPC 1973: **R.80**

R. 129(1) If the address of the addressee cannot be established, or if notification in accordance with Rule 126, paragraph 1, has proved to be impossible even after a second attempt, notification shall be effected by public notice.

R.126(1) Notification by registered letter with advice of delivery

1 **Public notification**
Public notification is a last resort to notify a party; it is mainly theoretical; normally it is not assumed that the party will read it.

R. 129(2) The President of the European Patent Office shall determine how the public notice is to be given and the beginning of the period of one month on expiry of which the document shall be deemed to have been notified.

1 **Method of public notification**
The EPO will give notice under **R.129** by publication in the European Patent Bulletin. The document will be deemed to have been notified one month after the date of publication in the Bulletin. (Dec. Pres., Spec. Ed. 3 of OJ 2007, 127)

R. 130 Notification to representatives

Implementation of **Art.119**

EPC 1973: **R.81**

1 **General**
The provisions of the EPC state that communications, e.g. containing information or an invitation, must be sent to the applicant, proprietor or opponent. **R.130** is a lex specialis for these provisions: if a representative has been appointed, the communications must be sent to the representative and not to the party himself. As most parties are represented in proceedings before the EPO, the EPO will normally send the communications to the representatives following **R.130**.

R. 130(1) If a representative has been appointed, notifications shall be addressed to him.

1 **Notification to representative**
The rule of mandatory notification (**R.130(1)**: 'shall') applies to professional representatives (**Art.134(1)** and (8)) only. Hence, if the applicant acts through an employee (**Art.133(3)**), notification is effected at the address of the applicant, and not that of the employee.

Since **R.130(1)** mentions 'appointed', the EPO should notify the representative as from his appointment, not from receipt of any authorisation under **R.152(1)**.

If, contrary to **R.130(1)**, the EPO sends a communication to a party instead of to the duly appointed representative, the notification is not effective; the communication is regarded as notified only on the date the communication is received by the representative (**T703/92**). In this case the 10-day rule of **R.126(2)** is probably not applicable to the notification to the representative because of **R.125(4)**.

R.130(1) implies that in the case a party has not appointed a representative, notifications will be addressed to the party.

R. 130(2) If several representatives have been appointed for a single party, notification to any one of them shall be sufficient.

R. 130(3) If several parties have a common representative, notification to the common representative shall be sufficient.

1 **Notification to common representative**
In general the EPO sends one document (**Art.119**) to the common representative appointed according to **R.41(3)** or **R.151** (E-II,2.5); the other parties do not receive a document and are kept out of the proceedings if the common representative does not notify them.

Chapter V *Time limits*

R. 131 Calculation of periods

Implementation of **Art.120**
EPC 1973: **R.83**

1 **General**
The EPC distinguishes two classes of periods. The first class contains the periods of a legally indicated length fixed for carrying out a particular procedural act, the second class contains periods within which a party need not perform an act before the EPO and internal periods of the EPO (see **Art.120:3** for examples).

Failing other provisions for calculating periods, the EPO uses the calculation of **R.131** for all periods in the EPC, including 'negative periods', such as the pre-payment period of **R.51(1)** for advance payment of a renewal fee. There is no unanimity about the method for calculating the term of a patent (see **Art.63(1):1**).

A period is triggered by an event as defined in **R.131(2)**. The expiry of the period is defined by **R.131(3), (4), (5)** and **(2)** for periods laid down in terms of full years, months, weeks or days, respectively. The expiry of a period is the last day on which an act to be performed within the period can still be validly performed.

R. 131(1) Periods shall be laid down in terms of full years, months, weeks or days.

R. 131(2) Computation shall start on the day following the day on which the relevant event occurred, the event being either a procedural step or the expiry of another period. Where the procedural step is a notification, the relevant event shall be the receipt of the document notified, unless otherwise provided.

1 **Computation of periods**
R.131(2) governs the triggering of a period and its computation. It also defines the calculation of periods expressed as a certain number of days.

2 **Triggering of period by a procedural step**
According to **R.131(2)**, first sentence, a period is triggered by a relevant event. The meaning of 'relevant event' is clear from the German and French text of the provision: the event on the basis of which the start of the period is fixed.

The relevant event may be a procedural step. The procedural step may be taken by the applicant. For example, the filing of an application triggers the one-month period of **R.38(1)** for payment of the filing and search fee, and the removal of the cause of non-compliance triggers the two-month period of **R.136(1)** for filing the application for re-establishment.

In most cases the procedural step is taken by the EPO. For example, the publication of the search report triggers the six-month period of **R.70(1)** for filing the request for examination, the notification of the communication of **Art.94(3)** triggers an office period for filing observations.

R.131(2), second sentence, states that in the case of notification the relevant event is the receipt of the document notified (receipt theory, see **Art.119:2**). This applies to letters not sent by registered mail (**R.126(1)**), e.g. faxes not confirmed by letter, and to delivery by hand under **R.128**. The EPC provides otherwise in two cases. The first case is notification through the central industrial property office of a contracting state, where national provisions apply (**R.125(3)**). The second and most common case is notification by registered letter under **R.126(1)** or by means of electronic communication under **R.127(1)**, where the notification on the date of actual delivery is replaced by a fictitious notification on the tenth day following the date of posting (**R.126(2)**) or on the tenth day following its transmission (**R.127(2)**), respectively. If the letter is received after the tenth day, the relevant event is the actual receipt of the letter (**R.126(2)**).

Where the Rules specify a period to be observed following an invitation or communication from the EPO, the period always starts with the notification of such communication, since all decisions, notices and communications have to be notified to the parties (**Art.119**, **R.126**). Therefore, the provisions concerned do not expressly refer to the requirement of notification (see e.g. **R.55, 56, 58**).

3 **Triggering of a period by expiry of another period**

The relevant event in **R.131(2)** triggering a period may also be the expiry of another period. The two linked periods result in a so-called aggregate or composite period.

When the principles of aggregate periods under EPC 1973 are applied to EPC 2000, the EPC 2000 has probably four aggregate periods: 1) the one-year period for filing a request for re-establishment of **R.136(1)** triggered by the expiry of the unobserved period, 2) the two-month period for requesting re-establishment in the priority period and for filing a petition for review of **R.136(1)** triggered by the expiry of the unobserved period, 3) the six-month additional period for paying renewal fees with surcharge for a Euro-PCT application in a special case of **R.159(1)(g)** and triggered by the expiry of the 31-month period of **R.159(1)** and 4) the two-month grace period for payment of the extension fee triggered by the expiry of the basic period for paying the designation fee (see to **Art.79(2):2.3**). The aggregate character of these periods has not yet been confirmed by the EPO. The EPO tries to reduce the number of aggregate periods in the EPC because its calculation is liable to mistakes.

The expiry of an aggregate period is calculated as follows: the expiry of the first period is calculated according to **R.131** and **R.134**, i.e. including extensions due to non-working days of the EPO and reductions due to missing days at the end of a month; from that expiry the next period is calculated, again taking into account the extensions due to closure of the EPO and reductions due to missing days at the end of a month (the best explanation of the calculation can be found in Legal Advice **L5/93** rev. OJ1993, 229, cancelled by Dec. Pres. OJ2012, 446; other sources are **J1/89** hn.II and A-X,5.2.4). See for examples of aggregate period calculations **R.51(3):3** and **R.159(1)(g)**. Note that the above calculation is not applied to the six-month additional period in **R.51(2)** for payment of renewal fees (**J4/91** r.3.3).

4 **Computation of periods**
The computation of a period starts on the day following the day on which the relevant event occurred (**R.131(2)**, first sentence). The expiry of the period is determined by **R.131(3)-(5)**, depending on whether the period is a certain number of years, months or weeks. For example, the computation of a period of one week triggered by a relevant event on 1 June starts on 2 June according to **R.131(2)** and the period expires on 8 June according to **R.131(5)**. The duration of the period from 2 June to and including 8 June is seven days, which is equal to the one week. The start of the period is in particular relevant for the determination of the patent year in which the mention of the grant is published (see **Art.86(1):1**).

The start of the computation of a period on the day following the day on which the relevant event occurred, as stated in **R.131(2)**, first sentence, does not mean that a day is added for the computation of periods expressed in weeks, months or years (**J14/86** hn.II). Instead, a difference should be made between the day on which the relevant event occurred, which day is used for calculating the expiry of periods expressed in weeks, months and years, and the next day on which the periods starts to run, i.e. the day on which the computation of the period starts.

5 **Period expressed in days**
When a period is expressed as a certain number of days, computation shall start on the day following the day on which the relevant event occurred, and the period shall expire on the day on which the last day of the count has been reached (based on **R.131(2)**). For example, the computation of a period of seven days triggered by an event on a Monday starts on the following day, Tuesday, as the first day and expires on the next Monday as the seventh day.

R. 131(3) When a period is expressed as one year or a certain number of years, it shall expire in the relevant subsequent year in the month having the same name and on the day having the same number as the month and the day on which the said event occurred; if the relevant subsequent month has no day with the same number, the period shall expire on the last day of that month.

1 **Period expressed in years**
The last part of the provision takes account of leap-days. Examples of periods expressed in years can be found in **Art.63(1)** (term of the patent), **R.136(1)** (re-establishment), **Art.174** (denunciation of the convention) and **R.147(4)** (keeping of files). Note that the priority period in **Art.87(1)** is not expressed in terms of one year but 12 months.

R. 131(4) When a period is expressed as one month or a certain number of months, it shall expire in the relevant subsequent month on the day which has the same number as the day on which the said event occurred; if the relevant subsequent month has no day with the same number, the period shall expire on the last day of that month.

1 **Period expressed in months**
A deviation from this rule following **J4/91** hn.I occurs in the pre-payment period of **R.51(1)** and the six-month additional period of **R.51(2)** for renewal fees.

R. 131(5) When a period is expressed as one week or a certain number of weeks, it shall expire in the relevant subsequent week on the day having the same name as the day on which the said event occurred.

1 **Period expressed in weeks**
An example of a period expressed in weeks is the period of five weeks in the decision of the President under **R.67(1)** determining the date of completion of the technical preparations for publication.

R. 132 Periods specified by the European Patent Office

Implementation of **Art.120**
EPC 1973: **R.84**

R. 132(1) Where the Convention or these Implementing Regulations refer to "a period to be specified", this period shall be specified by the European Patent Office.

R. 132(2) Unless otherwise provided, a period specified by the European Patent Office shall be neither less than two months nor more than four months; in certain circumstances it may be up to six months. In special cases, the period may be extended upon request, presented before the expiry of such period.

1 **Duration of periods**
The Convention specifies periods or time limits to be specified by the EPO, the so-called office periods or office time limits. They have the procedural advantage that an applicant may request extension of the period under **R.132(2)**.

The Guidelines (E-VIII,1.2) give general directives for determining the duration of the periods to be set by the EPO in the interest of a uniform period calculation. The duration of the period is often based on the amount of work to be performed.

R.132(2) specifies a duration of 2 to 4 months for an office period. A two-month period is generally used for correcting formal or small deficiencies, for example the subsequent filing under **R.83** of documents referred to by a party. The upper limit of 4 months in **R.132(2)** is generally used for communications from examining or opposition divisions under **Art.94(3)** containing substantive objections to the application or patent. The 6-month period for special circumstances may be used for exceptionally complicated cases. It is also used for indicating whether to proceed with the application after receipt of the search report in the event that the request for examination has been filed before receipt of the search report (**R.70(2)**; E-VIII,1.2).

The 'unless otherwise provided' in **R.132(2)** allows that a provision in the EPC permits the EPO to set the duration of an office period shorter than the minimum duration of two months in **R.132(2)**. Since the amendment of **R.64(1)** of 01.04.2010 deleted the period to be specified between 2 to 6 weeks, the EPC has no such provisions anymore.

2 **Request for extension of a period**
In special cases, an office period may be extended on request (**R.132(2)**, second sentence). The request must be filed before expiry of the period (E-VIII,1.6).

Extension is only possible for a period in which a party must take an action before the EPO. Other periods, e.g. the 10 days of the 10-day rule of **R.126(2)**, cannot be extended. An office period may be excluded explicitly from extension under **R.132**.

The extension of a period does not result in an aggregate period but in a unitary period. For example: the date of notification of a communication stipulating a two-month period within which a deficiency is to be rectified is 30 December. The expiry date is 28 February. If the period is extended with one month, the unitary three-month period expires 30 March, and not as aggregate period of 2+1 month on 28 March. (see Legal Advice **L5/93** rev. point III, OJ1993, 229; cancelled by Dec. Pres. OJ2012, 446)

A request for extension removes an application from the PACE programme (**Art.94(1):5**).

3 Extension of periods in specific procedural stages

The possibilities to extend a period depends on the procedure before the EPO.

Periods set by the EPO in the procedure up to grant may be extended on request. A request for extension, even if filed without reasons, is normally allowed if the total period does not exceed six months, in spite of the 'in special cases' in **R.132(2)**. A short period can normally be extended by two months. A request for extension to a total period of more than six months may only be granted if the subject-matter of the application or patent is exceptionally complicated. Such a request must be reasoned, referring to exceptional circumstances such as illness or extensive biological research, but not to foreseeable or avoidable circumstances such as high workload (this is normal) or leave. (OJ 1989, 180-181; E-VIII,1.6)

A request for extension of a period in opposition proceedings will only be granted in exceptional, duly substantiated cases. (E-VIII,1.6)

Extension of a period set by a board of appeal requires a reasoned request (RPBoA12(5)). Since boards of appeals want to have their cases complete as soon as possible, it is recommended to submit responses rather near the start of a period than near the expiry.

4 Decision on request for extension

A decision by the examining division rejecting a request filed in due time for an extension of for example a period set for filing observations to a communication under **Art.94(3)** to more than six months or for a second extension cannot be appealed, because such a decision does not terminate proceedings (**Art.106(2)**). The decision will normally be notified after expiry of the non-extended period. The ensuing loss of rights under **Art.94(4)** will be notified under **R.112(1)** and can be overcome only by filing a request for further processing under **Art.121** and **R.135**, paying the fee for further processing and filing a response to the communication.

If the party considers the rejection unjust, he should at the same time file a secondary request for reimbursement of the fee for further processing. The two requests must be filed within two months from the notification of the loss of rights. The secondary request will be decided on in connection with the final decision granting the patent or refusing the application. The decision on the secondary request may be appealed together with the final decision (**Art.106(2)**) when the final decision on the application is adverse, or separately when the final decision is not adverse. The latter separate appeal does not make much sense because the appeal fee is much higher than the amount to be reimbursed. If there is no final decision, e.g. because of withdrawal of the application, the department of first instance may decide on the rejection itself in response to the request for reimbursement, the decision on which may again be appealed. (**J37/89**)

R. 133 Late receipt of documents

Implementation of **Art.120**
EPC 1973: **R.84a**

1 **General**
R.133 is modelled on **R.82.1** PCT and provides a remedy for all periods to be observed before the EPO or national offices (see **R.133(2)**), including the priority period, and missed due to a delay in the mail delivery. It supplements the remedies for failed time limits (further processing, re-establishment) and the extension and legal fiction in the case of disruption of mail delivery (**R.134(2)** and **R.134(5)**).

The application of **R.133** must be requested for each individual case; it provides a legal fiction of valid filing for a late received document. The provision cannot be used for documents lost in the post. **R.133** is one of the instances where the EPO uses the despatch theory instead of the receipt theory (see also **Art.119:2**). (OJ 1999, 301 §22-32)

In the case where **R.133** does not provide a remedy, even applying **R.134**, recourse may be had to remedies such as further processing or re-establishment.

2 **Late receipt of payments**
R.133 does not apply to fee payments, for which **Rfees7(3)** (bank transfers) and **ADA 5.1**(debit orders) are leges speciales (OJ 1999, 301 §25). Hence, documents and payments have different fail-safe provisions with five and ten day periods, respectively. If, for example, the act of payment and filing a written request for re-establishment must be completed at the latest on 12.02.2018, a letter containing the request must be posted at the latest on 07.02.2018 for **R.133** to be applicable and a bank transfer must be effectedat the latest on 02.02.2018 for **Rfees7(3)** to be applicable.

R. 133(1) A document received late at the European Patent Office shall be deemed to have been received in due time if it was delivered to a recognised postal service provider in due time before expiry of the period in accordance with the conditions laid down by the President of the European Patent Office, unless the document was received later than three months after expiry of the period.

Amended by decision of the Administrative Council of 15.10.2014, which entered into force on 01.04.2015. (OJ 2015 A17, A36 §1)

1 **Document received late and deemed delivered in time**
A document sent to the EPO is deemed to have been delivered in due time if it was delivered to a recognised postal service provider in due time before expiry of the relevant period (**R.133(1)** and Dec. Pres. 2015 A29).

The longer time for the actual delivery is not an extension of the period in the sense of **R.134** but a legal fiction concerning observance of the period to file a particular document, similar to the fiction of **Rfees7(3)** for late receipt of a particular fee. Despite this legal fiction that the time limit has been observed, the filing date of the document remains the day on which it was actually received (E-VIII,1.7). This is in particular relevant for the priority period, where the date of filing of the priority-claiming application triggers several periods.

A document is deemed to have been received by the EPO in due time, only if the following conditions are fulfilled (Dec. Pres. OJ 2015 A29; E-VIII,1.7):

- The document is despatched at least five days before the expiry of the relevant period. Note, that the 'at least' is intended by the EPO (E-VIII,1.7) but not included in the Decision of the President.

  The five days are calendar days, not working days. Where the relevant period is extended under **R.134(1)** or (2), the expiry of the extended period must be used for the calculation of the last day for the application of **R.133**.
- The document is sent by a recognised postal service provider mentioned in the Decision of the President. The recognised postal service providers include the postal authority of a country, commonly called 'the post'. The Decision also mentions several courier service providers.
- The document must be sent as registered letter or equivalent. The 'equivalent' covers evidence of receipt other than the advice of delivery common for a postal authority.
- The document must be sent by airmail if posted outside Europe. For the purpose of **R.133**, 'Europe' covers all countries of the CEPT, which comprises all EPC contracting states and a few extra states (see E-VIII,1.7 for a list).

At the request of the EPO, confirmation of the registration by the post office or of receipt by the delivery service provider must be supplied as evidence that the document was despatched in due time.

The remedy of **R.133(1)** is, unlike **R.82.1(b)** PCT, not applicable to documents received by the EPO later than three months after expiry of the time limit (**R.133(1)**). A loss of rights due to mail received later or lost should be remedied by further processing, re-establishment or a remedy for interruption in the delivery of the mail under **R.134(2)** or **R.134(5)**, whichever is applicable.

2 **Example of late receipt in case of priority claim**

As an example, a first patent application was filed on 17.11.2017. A subsequent European patent application was posted by registered letter in Sweden on 12.11.2018, i.e. seven days before expiry of the priority year on 19.11.2018 (17.11 is a Saturday), and received at the EPO on 26.11.2018. According to **R.133(1)** the subsequent application will be deemed to have been filed within the priority year and may validly claim the priority of the first application. Periods that run from the filing date (not the priority date) of the application will be calculated from the actual filing date and not from the expiry of the priority year (see E-VIII,1.7). Hence, the one-month period for payment of the filing fee and search fee (**R.38(1)**) expires on 02.01.2019 (26.12.2018 until and including 01.01.2019 are non-working days).

R. 133(2) Paragraph 1 shall apply mutatis mutandis to any period where transactions are carried out with the competent authority in accordance with Article 75, paragraphs 1(b) or 2(b).

Art.75(1)(b) Voluntary filing of a European patent application with a national authority

Art.75(2)(b) Compulsory filing of a European patent application with a national authority

R. 134 Extension of periods

Implementation of **Art.120**
EPC 1973: **R.85**

1 **General**

R.134 deals with automatic extension of periods in which a party has to complete an act before the EPO, both convention periods and office periods. Whereas an extension of a period under **R.132** must be requested by a party for an individual case and for a particular period, an extension under **R.134** occurs usually by operation of law for all parties.

Under **R.134**, periods to be observed before the EPO are extended on account of an obstacle to receive documents. The obstacle may be an inability to receive documents lying within the responsibility of the EPO, such as closure of an EPO filing office because of non-working days or defective means of communication in an EPO office (**R.134(1)**). The obstacle may also be external to the EPO, for example general dislocation of mail (**R.134(2)**). The EPO publishes the duration of general dislocations (**R.134(4)**). The extensions of **R.134(1)** and (2) also apply to periods to be observed before national patent offices, i.e. to the priority period within which a European application can be filed with a national office (**R.134(3)**).

The extension of a period leads to a longer period within which the required act may be validly completed. The extension does not lead to a legal fiction in the sense of **R.133**, where the act carried out late is deemed to have been completed in due time.

Whereas **R.134(2)** relates to delay in delivery due to a general dislocation of mail in a contracting state, **R.134(5)** relates to delay due to local interruption of communication in any state. **R.134(5)** does not fit in the system of **R.134**, because it does not give rise to an extension of a period (see title of rule) but to a legal fiction of the period being deemed to have been observed. The provision is in fact similar to **R.133** but restricted to a dislocation due to exceptional occurrences.

Although the extension of a period under **R.134** is in general automatic and does not require a request, a party should inform the EPO of any relevant event under **R.134(1)**, last sentence, and **R.134(2)**, so that the event may be investigated further. If the EPO agrees, the relevant dates will be published to inform all parties (**R.134(4)**). The application of the legal fiction of **R.134(5)** must always be requested.

Where a late receipt cannot be remedied by the extension of a period under **R.134(2)**, (3) or (5), a party may resort to other remedies, such as the legal fiction of timely receipt under **R.133**, possibly combined with an extension under **R.134**, further processing under **Art.121**, re-establishment under **Art.122** or a grace period such as the 6-month period for late payment of a renewal fee under **R.51(2)**.

Obstacles to receive documents are in particular relevant for filings that have a deadline other than expiry of a period. In such cases the extensions under **R.134** do not apply. Examples of such filings are filing a divisional application on the last day of pendency of the parent application and filing a first application on the day the invention is being published. If for example CMS is not available in such a case, the applicant should switch to another means of electronic filing or to the more dependable filing by fax.

R. 134(1) If a period expires on a day on which one of the filing offices of the European Patent Office under Rule 35, paragraph 1, is not open for receipt of documents or on which, for reasons other than those referred to in paragraph 2, mail is not delivered there, the period shall extend to the first day thereafter on which all the filing offices are open for receipt of documents and on which mail is delivered. The first sentence shall apply mutatis mutandis if documents filed by one of the means of electronic communication permitted by the President of the European Patent Office under Rule 2, paragraph 1, cannot be received.

Amended by decision of the Administrative Council of 15.10.2014, which entered into force on 01.04.2015. (OJ 2015 A17; A36 §5)
R.2(1) Filing of and formal requirements for documents
R.35(1) EPO filing offices for filing patent applications
R.134(2) Reasons for dislocation of mail not within responsibility EPO

1 **EPO not open or unable to receive documents**

R.134(1) sets out if and how the EPO will extend a period if on the day of expiry of the period a means of filing with an EPO filing office is not available.

R.134(1), first sentence, governs the situation where a period expires on a day on which at least one of the filing offices of the EPO in Munich, The Hague and Berlin is not open for receipt of documents, or on which mail cannot be delivered there. This rule is generally used in respect of those days on which a filing office is closed, i.e. non-working days, including all Saturdays and Sundays. The non-working days are regularly published in the OJ (see OJ 2018 A81 for closure days in 2019) and on the EPO website. The offices are closed from Christmas Eve till and including New Year's Day (OJ 2018 A51 for 2018, OJ 2018 A81 for 2019). Note, that a national holiday in either Germany or the Netherlands causes an extension of periods for filing also with a filing office in the other country where there is no holiday.

The 'reasons other than those referred to in paragraph 2' in the provision relate to exceptional internal obstacles to receiving documents, such as a natural disaster or strike that affects the functioning of the EPO.

2 **EPO unable to receive documents by fax or electronic communication**

The second sentence to **R.134(1)** states that the provision applies mutatis mutandis in situations where the EPO, due to reasons laying within the responsibility of the Office, would not be able to receive documents filed by a technical means permitted by **R.2(1)** (Spec. Ed. 5 of OJ 2007 p.200). The technical means are fax and electronic communication. An outage of the EPO fax server will cause an extension of periods; see e.g. OJ 2009, 479. If a means of electronic communication, i.e. OLF, CMS or Web-Form Filing (see R.2(1):7), is unavailable for reasons attributable to the EPO, an extension under **R.134(1), second sentence, may be available.**

An outage not attributable to the EPO will not cause an extension under **R.134(1)**. A party affected by such an outage may have recourse to **R.134(5)** or any other remedy.

The EPO tries to avoid unavailability of electronic communication due to maintenance of their electronic systems by scheduling maintenance for weekends; if maintenance is expected to cause unavailability, the EPO will announce the outage on the EPO **website** (search for 'online filing outages') several days in advance. Unavailability for other reasons, such as a malfunction, is in general also published on the website. A user in doubt about proper transmission of a document should contact EPO Customer services. (OJ 2018 A25 §7)

A party relying on an extension due to an outage is strongly recommended to use the publication as proof that the outage was attributable to the EPO. If, exceptionally, the outage was not published, a party must provide other evidence that the failure was due to the EPO and he should request further processing or re-establishment on an auxiliary basis. (Not. EPO OJ 2018 A25 §7)

2.1 GENERAL EXTENSION DUE TO OUTAGE OF ELECTRONIC COMMUNICATION

If an outage of one of the means of electronic communication on a certain day lasts four hours or more, there will be a general extension; i.e. any period expiring on that day will be extended for any party. The four hours strikes a balance between the interest of the public in that any short outage will not give rise to a general extension and the interest of a party not having to wait unreasonably long for the means to be in operation again. As an example, a party in a contracting state two hours east from CET need not wait till past midnight local time for filing his document if an outage starts at 18 h CET, because the period will be extended and he can file the next day. (OJ 2018 A25 §4)

A party who files on a day to which a period was extended under **R.134(1)**, second sentence, because of an outage of four hours or more is advised to 1) request the EPO to extend the period under R.134(1) and 2) provide proof that the outage was attributable to the EPO.

2.2 INDIVIDUAL EXTENSION DUE TO OUTAGE OF ELECTRONIC COMMUNICATION

If an outage of one of the means of electronic communication lasts less than four hours, there will not be a general extension but merely an individual extension applying only to an affected party that has filed a request. The party has to carry out the above steps 1) and 2), and 3) show that the outage made it impossible for him to file in due time. An outage from 20 till 22 h is less convincing than from 23 till 24 h that the party could not have completed the act in due time. Since the burden of proving receipt lies with the party alleging submission in time, the request must be duly substantiated. (EPO internal practice, based on OJ 2018 A25 §7)

3 Duration of extension

If a period expires on a day where at least one means of filing with one of the EPO filing offices is not available, the period will normally be extended under **R.134(1)** to the first day thereafter where all means of filing are again available for all filing offices. (**R.134(1)**). Any day on which at least one of the filing offices in Munich, The Hague or Berlin is closed causes an extension of the periods for all offices. Hence, a period expiring on Friday, 27 April, King's day in the Netherlands, will be extended to Monday, 30 April for all filing offices, both in the Netherlands and in Germany.

The extension under **R.134(1)** does not only apply to periods involving filing of a document but also to periods involving a payment (**J1/81** hn.II; A-X,6.1). When an EPO office is closed on the day a period for payment expires but the bank is open, the period will be extended, in spite of the possibility to pay within the non-extended period (**J1/81**). In the opposite case, i.e. the EPO is open but the bank is closed, e.g. because of a national holiday, the period is not extended. In such a case another method of payment should be used, e.g. debit order or credit card, asking someone in another country to make the payment, or applying a legal remedy, such as further processing or re-establishment, where appropriate. See **R.51(1):2** for extension of periods relating to renewal fees.

A non-working day of at least one filing office causes an extension of all periods expiring on that day, irrespective of the means of filing used by the party. Hence, even if electronic communication is available during the weekend, periods will be extended till the next working day on which all filing offices are open (implied by the mention of 'working days' in the two examples in OJ 2018 A25).

If on a working day one of the means of electronic communication is unavailable for receiving documents, a period expiring on this day will be extended to the first working day on which all means of electronic communication are available (OJ 2018 A25) and all filing offices are open (see previous paragraph). Hence, there will be an extension if CMS is not available, even though OLF and web-form filing are available. An extension due to an unavailable means of electronic communication should also give rise to an extension for other means of communication, such as filing by hand, post or fax (consequence of **J1/81** r.6, 7).

R. 134(2) If a period expires on a day on which there is a general dislocation in the delivery or transmission of mail in a Contracting State, the period shall extend to the first day following the end of the interval of dislocation for parties which are resident in the State concerned or have appointed representatives with a place of business in that State. Where the State concerned is the State in which the European Patent Office is located, this provision shall apply to all parties and their representatives. This paragraph shall apply mutatis mutandis to the period referred to in Rule 37, paragraph 2.

R.37(2) Forwarding of European patent applications

1 **Dislocation of mail**

Whereas **R.134(1)** concerns internal obstacles to the receipt of documents, **R.134(2)** relates to external dislocations of mail delivery or transmission. In this context, mail transmission covers the filing of documents using the technical means of communication permitted by the President of the EPO. (Spec. Ed. 5 of OJ 2007)

There is a general dislocation if the public in general is affected by it, i.e. also in the case of a local postal strike, but not in the case of a strike in a factory. In other words: 'general' is not restricted to 'nation-wide' (**J3/90** r.10). Whether there is a 'general dislocation' is to be decided by the facts and any credible information, especially from national patent offices, not only by a notice of the President. In case of doubt, the EPO will enquire of its own motion (**Art.114(1)**) whether or not a dislocation qualifies as a general dislocation within the meaning of **R.134(2)** (**J11/88** applied mutatis mutandis).

Individual cases where mail is delayed do not give rise to extension of the period under **R.134(2)** (**J4/87**). However, if the requirements of **R.133** have been met, the delay in an individual case may be excused.

The general dislocation must occur in an EPC contracting state, according to **R.134(2)**. The legislator took the view that only for the contracting states could the EPO be sure of obtaining the information necessary to enable the President to announce a general interruption or dislocation. Hence, it was decided not to extend **R.134(2)** to postal interruptions outside those states and to introduce a paragraph 5 and placing the burden of proof on the party. (**J13/05** r.3.2)

The extension is applicable to parties whose residence or place of business is in the contracting state concerned or who have appointed representatives with a place of business in that state (**R.134(2)**). The second sentence of **R.134(2)** is generally interpreted to refer to 'a state in which a filing office of the EPO is located'. It has the effect that a general dislocation in the Netherlands or Germany causes an extension of the periods applicable to all parties, because any mail or payment may be sent to either Munich, The Hague or Berlin, irrespective of the type of proceedings. Note, that the EPO office in Vienna is not a filing office.

2 **Extension on account of general interruption of mail**
The duration of a dislocation in postal services in a contracting state and the resulting extension of periods are published in the OJ. The EPO publishes the date of commencement and end of any dislocation (**R.134(4)**). The extension occurs automatically by operation of law, without a request from a party.

For example, a general dislocation of mail in the United Kingdom from 04.10.2007 to 02.11.2007 resulted in periods expiring in this interval being extended to Monday, 05.11.2007 for parties having their domicile or principal place of business in the United Kingdom or who have appointed representatives having their place of business in the United Kingdom (OJ 2007, 670).

According to the last sentence of **R.134(2)**, the fourteen month period within which a national office must forward a European application filed with it to the EPO under **R.37(2)** is also extended in the case of a general dislocation of mail.

The extension of the period is effective not only for delays in filing caused directly by the delayed mail service, but for all delays, even nonobservance of the period, e.g. a reply to a communication filed late by fax from a state affected by the general dislocation.

R. 134(3) Paragraphs 1 and 2 shall apply mutatis mutandis where acts are performed with the competent authority in accordance with Article 75, paragraphs 1(b) or 2(b).

Art.75(1)(b) Voluntary filing of a European patent application with a national authority
Art.75(2)(b) Compulsory filing of a European patent application with a national authority

1 **Extension on account of closed national office**
Periods under the EPC to be observed before a national office will be extended similar to periods to be observed before the EPO (**R.134(3)**). A party requiring an extension under this provision because of a failed electronic filing, must provide evidence that his filing failed because an electronic filing means of the national office was down.

The only act under the EPC to be performed before a national office within a period is the filing of a priority claiming European application within the priority period of twelve months. If the priority period expires on a day the national office is closed or the mail is dislocated, the priority year will be extended to the first day the national office can again receive mail. Thus, the application claiming priority can be filed with the national office on that first working day without losing the priority claim.

An extension of the priority period in a contracting state other than Germany or The Netherlands does not extend the priority period before the EPO. Hence, a European application for which the unavailed priority period expired on 14.07.2017 (Quatorze Juillet, Friday) can be filed at the latest on 17.07.2017 with the French national office but not with an EPO filing office.

This provision does not apply to periods within which other documents must be filed, because a national office does not give such documents a date of receipt but only forwards them to the EPO as a courtesy service.

R. 134(4) The date of commencement and the end of any dislocation under paragraph 2 shall be published by the European Patent Office.

1 **Publication of dislocation**
The extension of periods under **R.134(1)** to (3) occurs automatically by operation of law if the requirements are fulfilled. For reasons of clarity and in line with the current practice of the Office **R.134(4)** expressly provides that the EPO publishes a notice informing on the commencement and the end of the dislocation under **R.134(2)**. (Spec. Ed. 5 of OJ 2007)

R. 134(5) Without prejudice to paragraphs 1 to 4, a party concerned may produce evidence that on any of the ten days preceding the day of expiry of a period the delivery or transmission of mail was dislocated due to an exceptional occurrence such as a natural disaster, war, civil disorder, a general breakdown in any of the means of electronic communication permitted by the President of the European Patent Office under Rule 2, paragraph 1, or other like reasons affecting the locality where the party or his representative resides or has his place of business. If the evidence produced satisfies the European Patent Office, a document received late shall be deemed to have been received in due time, provided that the mailing or the transmission was effected at the latest on the fifth day after the end of the dislocation.

Amended by decision of the Administrative Council of 15.10.2014, which entered into force on 01.04.2015. (OJ 2015 A17, A36 §5)
R.2(1) Filing of and formal requirements for documents

1 **Fiction of timely receipt in case of interruption of mail**
Whereas **R.134(2)** covers only general dislocations in the delivery of mail inside EPC contracting states, **R.134(5)** has a broader applicability and covers dislocations of mail of a smaller scale inside and outside EPC contracting states due to an exceptional occurrence. Paragraph 5 was created to cover the 9/11 terror attacks.

A document received late will be deemed to have been received in due time under **R.134(5)** if all of the following requirements are met:

- The delivery or transmission of mail was dislocated. Since **R.134(5)** supplements **R.134(2)**, the dislocation must similarly be 'general', in the sense that more than one person using the mail service has been or could have been affected, even if the dislocation was merely minor or geographically limited (**J13/05** r.3.2). The decision held that loss of a mail bag was not a general dislocation. **R.133** should be used for individual dislocations.
- The dislocation was due to an exceptional occurrence. Examples of such occurrences are a natural disaster, war, civil disorder, a general breakdown in any of the means of electronic communication permitted by the President under **R.2(1)**, or other like reasons.

- The occurrence must have affected the locality where the party or his representative resides or has his place of business (**R.134(5)**); i.e. the locality of despatch, not the locality of receipt. Hence, the provision does not apply to a local dislocation in Munich affecting mail sent from Cologne to the EPO (J13/05 r.3.2). Occurrences affecting the locality of receipt should be dealt with under **R.134(1), (2)** or **R.133**.
- The dislocation must have existed on any of the ten days preceding the expiry of the period (**R.134(5)** first sentence).
- The mail must have been sent at the latest on the fifth day after the end of the dislocation (**R.134(5)** second sentence).
- The party must provide satisfactory evidence of all of the above facts.

If the EPO knows the circumstances of the dislocation and has published them, the party using **R.134(5)** need only submit proof that he sent the document in time; the EPO will assume compliance with the other requirements (OJ 2015 A61 §2).

In contrast with **R.134(2)**, the period is not extended under **R.134(5)** but the document received late is deemed received in due time. Moreover, this legal fiction is not applied automatically but requires the filing of a reasoned request.

See Not. of EPO OJ 2018 A82 for the application of **R.134(5)** to applicants and representatives who have their place of business or domicile in the USA, the Philippines, Hong Kong SAR, China, Indonesia and Japan and were affected by hurricanes and earthquake between 15 September and 1 October 2018.

Where the EPO has issued a loss of rights communication and a request for correction under **R.134(5)** is filed, the remedy of further processing or re-establishment where appropriate may be added as an auxiliary request.

Although the wording of the provision appears to imply that it is applicable to filing of documents only, the EPO applies it also to making payments in the case where the failure to observe a period for payment is the result of exceptional circumstances beyond the applicant's control. Examples of such circumstances are closure of banks and ban on cross-border payments. Evidence must be provided that on any of the ten days (l'un quelconque de dix jours) prior to expiry of the period payment could not be made and that the payment was ordered within five days after banks resumed business. (OJ 2015 A61)

Note, that the ten-day fail-safe provision of **Rfees7(3)** can also be used to remedy a late payment due to delay by the bank. Whereas **Rfees7(3)** may require payment of a 10% surcharge, use of **R.134(5)** is free of charge but requires the submission of more evidence. A correction of a payment under **R.134(5)** can be filed as a main request, a request under **Rfees7(3)** as a first auxiliary request, and, where appropriate, a request for further processing or re-establishment as a second auxiliary request.

R. 135 Further processing

R. 135(1) Further processing under Article 121, paragraph 1, shall be requested by payment of the prescribed fee within two months of the communication concerning either the failure to observe a time limit or a loss of rights. The omitted act shall be completed within the period for making the request.

Art.121(1) Further processing of an application
Implementation of: **Art.121(2)**
EPC 1973: **Art.121(2)**

1 **Fee for further processing**

R.135(1) requires that a fee be paid for further processing within two months from the notification of the communication concerning the failure to observe a time limit. The amount of the fee is given in **Rfees2(1)12** and depends on the nature of the omitted act and the period failed.

The fee for further processing for a failed payment is 50% of the late paid fee and a fixed amount for a failed filing of a document. If several acts have been omitted, the fee for further processing is the sum of the fees for each act. If for example a corrected sequence listing is not filed and the late furnishing fee is not paid within two months from invitation under **R.30(3)**, the fee for further processing is the fixed fee for late submitting the corrected listing plus 50% of the late furnishing fee. As an exception, the fee for further processing for all acts required under **R.71(3)** is only the fixed fee. (E-VIII,2)

The Rfees contains a special provision where the omitted act concerns both a payment and a filing. On payment it is recommended to indicate clearly that the payment is for further processing, since the amount of the payment is not distinctive for further processing.

Since no request in writing is necessary, the request can be made simply by payment of the further processing fee, thereby facilitating further processing after failure to meet a time limit for payment of fees. No reasoning need be provided why the time limit was not observed.

Since payment of the further processing fee is the only act that marks a remedy as further processing, the omission of the payment will be regarded as omission of a request for further processing.

Where a request for automatic debiting has been filed, the further processing fee will be debited automatically when a response to a communication is filed late within the further processing period.

2 **Period for requesting further processing**

According to **R.135(1)** the request must be filed within two months of notification under **R.126(2)** of the communication concerning either the failure to observe a time limit or a loss of rights. It is not clear why the provision expressly refers to a communication concerning a loss of rights. Since a failure to observe a time limit is a necessary condition according to **Art.121(1)** for the application of further processing, the 'loss of rights' in **R.135(1)** is superfluous as further processing is not available for cases without failure to observe a time limit. The EPO may improve the wording of the provision in the next review of the Implementing Regulations.

For legal reasons the two-month time limit has been fixed so as to provide the same length of time for filing a request for further processing as for filing a notice of appeal under **Art.108** or a request for a decision following the noting of loss of rights under **R.112(2)**.

The date of notification of the communication of loss of rights is not a starting point for a period in which the request may be filed but simply a reference point for calculating the expiry of the two months. Hence, a request filed between expiry of the non-observed period and notification of the communication is permissible (Legal Advice **L13/82** OJ1982, 196 §3, 4; cancelled by Dec. Pres. OJ2012, 446).

Failure to meet the two-month time limit can be remedied using re-establishment (consequence of **R.136(3)**). Further processing of the two-month time limit is excluded by **Art.121(4)**, first sentence.

3 Completion of the omitted act

R.135(1) also requires that the omitted act that brought about the failure to observe the time limit and the loss of rights, must be completed within the two-month period of the request.

The request for further processing is inadmissible if the omitted act is not completed within the two-month period. If a communication under **Art.94(3)** has not been replied to in due time, a response must be submitted together with the request for further processing; a request for an extension of the already expired period is not a completion of the omitted act. If a request for extension, filed just before expiry of the period, is refused, further processing is an adequate remedy to obtain an extension of approximately three months (see **R.132(2):4**).

4 Procedure

The procedure of further processing is triggered by payment of the further processing fee following a loss of rights with or without a decision.

If the application is refused following failure to meet a period, e.g. not filing the designation of the inventor after an invitation under **R.60(1)**, the decision will be notified to the applicant. The applicant can request further processing within two months from the date of notification of the decision. Since the loss of rights results from a decision, it is in principle possible to file an appeal against the decision. However, an appeal should only be lodged if the legality of the decision is to be clarified. If the applicant considers his reply to be in due time, he may file an appeal and simultaneously an auxiliary request for further processing, which allows further processing in case the appeal is inadmissible or not allowable. If the decision to refuse is well-founded, an appeal only will be of no avail and the grant proceedings will not continue.

If the application is deemed to be withdrawn, the applicant will be notified according to **R.112(1)** of the loss of rights. Within two months of the date of notification he must request further processing. If the applicant regards the notice under **R.112(1)** erroneous, he must apply for a decision under **R.112(2)** simultaneously with the request for further processing. If the EPO agrees, it will set aside the **R.112(1)** communication and refund the fee for further processing. Had the applicant requested further processing only after notification of the decision under **R.112(2)**, he would have risked non-observance of the two-month period for requesting further processing, making the request inadmissible. In that case he could try and request re-establishment in the two-month period of **R.112(2)**. See also **R.112(2):1**.

After receipt of the request for further processing the competent department of the EPO takes a decision. If the decision is positive, the legal consequences of the refusal or withdrawal will be deemed not to have ensued (**Art.121(3)**) and the proceedings will continue. A negative decision, usually closing the proceedings, is appealable.

An example of the procedure for further processing. The unavailed period for paying the search fee under **R.38(1)** expires on 01.02.2018. The communication under **R.112(1)** concerning the failure to observe the period and the deemed withdrawal under **Art.78(2)** is dated 09.03.2018 and is deemed notified under **R.126(2)** on 19.03.2018. The two-month period for filing the request for further processing expires on 19.05.2018 (Saturday), extended to 22.05.2018 (21.05.2018 is Whit Monday) under **R.134(1)**. The applicant must pay the fee for further processing, equal to 50% of the search fee (**Rfees2(1)12**), and the search fee (**Rfees2(1)2**) at the latest on 22.05.2018. He may pay these fees as from 02.02.2018.

R. 135(2) Further processing shall be ruled out in respect of the periods referred to in Article 121, paragraph 4, and of the periods under Rule 6, paragraph 1, Rule 16, paragraph 1(a), Rule 31, paragraph 2, Rule 36, paragraph 2, Rule 40, paragraph 3, Rule 51, paragraphs 2 to 5, Rule 52, paragraphs 2 and 3, Rules 55, 56, 58, 59, 62a, 63,64, Rule 112, paragraph 2, and Rule 164, paragraphs 1 and 2.

Amended by decisions of the Administrative Council of 16.10.2013, which entered into force on 01.04.2014. The amendment deleted **R.36(1)(a)** and **(b)** from the provision. The amended provision applies to divisional applications filed on or after 01.04.2014. (OJ 2013, 501)

By decision of the Administrative Council of 16.10.2013, which entered into force on 01.11.2014, **R.164(1)** and **(2)** have been added to **R.135(2)** (OJ 2013, 503).

Art.121(4) Excluded periods
R.6(1) Period for filing translation of application
R.16(1)(a) Period for action for entitled applicant
R.31(2) Period for filing information on deposition of biological material
R.36(2) Period for filing translation of divisional
R.40(3) Period for filing copy and translation of previous application
R.51(2) Period for payment of renewal fee with additional fee
R.51(3) Period for payment of renewal fee for divisional
R.51(4) Period for payment of renewal fee in case of reestablishment of rights
R.51(5) Period for payment of renewal fee in case of petition for review
R.52(2) Period for filing declaration of priority
R.52(3) Period for correcting declaration of priority
R.55 Period for correcting deficiencies to obtain date of filing
R.56 Period for filing missing parts of description or drawings
R.58 Period for correcting deficiencies regarding formal requirements
R.59 Period for correcting priority claim
R.62a Period for indicating independent claims for search
R.63 Period for filing statement with subject-matter to be searched
R.64 Period for payment of further search fees
R.112(2) Period for applying for decision on loss of rights
R.164(1) Period for paying further search fees for non-unitary inventions
R.164(2) Period for paying search fees for non-searched inventions
Implementation of: **Art.121(4)**
EPC 1973: No corresponding provision

1 **Periods excluded from further processing**

Although further processing has been set up as the standard legal remedy in cases of failure to observe time limits in the grant procedure, several periods have been excluded from further processing for various reasons. The present list of exclusions is the result of bargaining in the Administrative Council without a clear philosophy. The list will be amended in the near future.

Art.121(4) excludes the priority period of **Art.87(1)**, the periods for filing an appeal in **Art.108**, the period for filing a petition for review under **Art.112a(4)** and the period for requesting further processing in **R.135(1)** and re-establishment in **R.136(1)**. The reasons for these exclusions have been set out in **Art.121(4):1**.

Several exclusions in **R.135(2)** are based on the ground that further processing should not be available if another adequate legal remedy has already been provided (MR/24/00 Art.121). The periods in **R.6(1)** for filing the translation of **Art.14(2)**, in **R.36(2)** for filing the translation of a divisional, and in **R.40(3)** for filing of a copy of the previously filed application to which reference is made and a translation thereof are excluded because these time limits may be remedied under **R.58, 55** and **58**, respectively (Special Edition no. 1, OJ 1/2003, p. 159).

The periods under **R.51(3)** relating to the payment of renewal fees for divisional applications are excluded from further processing on the same ground. If the four-months period in **R.51(3)** for the payment of renewal fees without a surcharge expires and the renewal fees have not been paid, the remedy is already provided for in **R.51(3)**, last sentence, namely the payment with surcharge within six months as of filing the divisional application. Similarly the four-month periods in **R.51(4)** and **(5)** are excluded. (CA/PL17/06)

Further processing should neither be applicable to periods that have a remedial character. Hence, the six-month period of **R.51(2)** for payment of renewal fees is a period of grace (see Art.5*bis* of the Paris Convention – period of grace for payment of fees) (Special Edition no. 1, OJ 1/2003, p. 159). The six-month period of **R.51(3)** is excluded like the period under **R.51(2)**, as clarified by the reference in **R.135(2)** to the whole paragraph 3 of **R.51**. Similarly the six-month periods in **R.51(4)** and **(5)** are excluded (CA/PL14/06). The exclusion of the periods in **R.55, 56, 58** and **59** is based in particular on the fact that the procedure under these Rules is a form of legal remedy (Special Edition no. 1, OJ 1/2003, p. 159).

Some periods are excluded because failure to observe them does not result in a communication of the EPO. Thus, the necessary procedural calculating point for further processing period is lacking. The three-month period under **R.16(1)(a)** for enforcement of rights under **Art.61** is excluded from further processing because it is not monitored by the EPO and no communication can be issued if it is missed. Similarly, if the two-month period under **R.112(2)**, which allows for an administrative review of any loss of rights resulting from the Convention, is missed, the loss of rights becomes final without any further decision or communication being issued by the EPO. As the procedure under **R.112** already has a remedial character, further processing also has to be ruled out on substantive grounds (Special Edition no. 1, OJ 1/2003, p. 159). The period for paying additional search fees when there is a lack of unity of invention provided for in **R.64** is excluded, because this preserves the legal situation of the EPC 1973 and avoids complex procedural problems in a case where the Office is not aware of any real need for further processing (CA/PL17/06). Similarly, the periods in **R.164(1)** and **(2)** are excluded.

A period may be excluded from further processing to avoid procrastinating the procedure. The periods under **R.31(2)** for providing information on the deposition of biological material are excluded from further processing, because non-compliance would cause the invention to be regarded as not disclosed under **R.31**. Legal certainty requires that the information is available in due time before publication of the application (CA/PL17/06). Also in view of the publication of the application, the periods for late declaration of priority under **R.52(2)** and for correcting it under **R.52(3)** do not permit further processing (Special Edition no. 1, OJ 1/2003, p. 159). The periods in **R.62a** and **R.63** for responding to an invitation from the search examiner have been excluded to allow the search report to be published together with the application. It should be noted that, even though a re-establishment case causes a considerably longer procedural delay than further processing, the average delay in the proceedings is less for re-establishment because re-establishment is used ten times less frequently than further processing.

The list of exclusions in **R.135(2)** could have included a few more periods that have a remedial character (e.g. second one-month period in **R.45(2)**; **R.163**) or where another legal remedy has been provided (e.g. first one-month period in **R.45(2)**).

R. 135(3) The department competent to decide on the omitted act shall decide on the request for further processing.

Implementation of: **Art.121(2)**
EPC 1973: **Art.121(3)**

1 **Department competent to decide**
If the competent department decides not to allow further processing, the applicant can appeal the decision (**Art.106(1)**), provided the department that took the decision is not a board of appeal. When in the meantime responsibility has been transferred to the next department, e.g. from the Receiving Section to the examining division, the Receiving Section remains competent.

R. 136 Re-establishment of rights

R. 136(1) Any request for re-establishment of rights under Article 122, paragraph 1, shall be filed in writing within two months of the removal of the cause of non-compliance with the period, but at the latest within one year of expiry of the unobserved time limit. However, a request for re-establishment of rights in respect of any of the periods specified in Article 87, paragraph 1, and in Article 112a, paragraph 4, shall be filed within two months of expiry of that period. The request for re-establishment of rights shall not be deemed to have been filed until the prescribed fee has been paid.

Art.87(1) Priority period
Art.112a(4) Period for filing petition for review
Art.122(1) Re-establishment of rights
Implementation of: **Art.122(2)**
EPC 1973: **Art.122(2)** and (3)

1 **Request for re-establishment**
R.136(1) lays down that a request for re-establishment must include the filing of a written request and payment of a fee. Paragraph 2 adds the requirement of completion of the omitted act. The period for carrying out the acts is specified in the provision.

The written request must be filed in a way complying with **R.50**. The request must state the grounds on which it is based, and set out the facts on which it relies (**R.136(2)**). **R.136(2):2** sets out the requirements for the omitted act.

R.136(1) defines two periods for filing the request for re-establishment, a general period and a special period for re-establishment in the priority period and the period for filing a petition for review.

2 **General period for requesting re-establishment**

The general period is two months from the removal of the cause of non-compliance with the period. Within this period the written request must be filed, the payment made and the omitted act completed.

Where a party misses several time limits expiring independently of one another and each resulting in a loss of rights, he must apply for re-establishment and pay the fee for re-establishment in respect of each unobserved time limit. It is irrelevant whether the requests are filed in the same letter or in different letters and whether they are based on the same or different grounds. (J26/95)

3 **Special periods for requesting re-establishment**

R.136(1) defines that the request for re-establishment of rights for the priority period under **Art.87(1)** and the two periods for filing a petition for review under **Art.112a(4)** must be filed within two months of expiry of those periods. This short period for filing the request for re-establishment in the priority period is the minimum period fixed by the PLT, chosen because of the urgent need for clarity in view of the valid claiming of priority. The same period is chosen for re-establishment in the period for filing the petition for review in view of the overriding need for legal certainty in this late procedural stage (CA/PL 17/06).

The EPO will regard the two-month period from expiry of the non-observed period as an aggregate period. The calculation of aggregate periods is set out in **R.131(2):3**. For example, a priority application is filed on 30.03.2017. The priority period expires on 30.03.2018 (Good Friday), extended under **R.134(1)** to 03.04.2018. The two-month period for filing the request for re-establishment and filing the priority claiming application expires on Sunday 03.06.2018, again extended under **R.134(1)** to 04.06.2018.

4 **Removal of the cause of non-compliance**

The two-month period of **R.136(1)** is triggered by the removal of the cause of non-compliance, i.e. by the event through which the party became aware why a loss of rights had ensued. The following items are pertinent to the establishment of removal of the cause of non-compliance: how is the loss of rights notified, who must be notified and when is it notified. No request for re-establishment is necessary if the EPO could have warned the party timely of the non-compliance. In that event the loss of rights must be remedied under good faith (see **Art.125:2**).

The principle of good faith requires the EPO to warn the requester of any impending loss of rights if such a warning can be expected in all good faith. A warning can be expected if the deficiency, e.g. not completing the omitted act together with the request for re-establishment, is readily identifiable for the EPO and the requester can still correct it within the time limit (**T14/89**; **J13/90** r.7). If a warning can be expected but is not issued to the applicant within the time limit to be observed, the EPO must set a period in which the applicant can correct the deficiency and perform the procedural act in time. (**J13/90**)

The cause of non-compliance is removed when the party concerned is made aware of the loss of rights. If the party is represented by a duly appointed professional representative, then a notification of the loss of rights to him removes the cause of non-compliance (**J27/90** hn1). This also applies where the professional representative is instructed via a national patent attorney (**J27/90** hn1). The date of notification is the date at which the representative sees the document, not the day a secretary sees it: the cause of non-compliance is only removed if the representative himself is aware of the facts, as he is responsible for the decision whether or not to request re-establishment (**T191/82**). An independent renewal fee payment agency does not take away the responsibility of the representative: the representative is the person to act on the notification according to **R.112(1)** (**J27/90** hn2).

In the absence of circumstances to the contrary, the receipt of the **R.112(1)** notice triggers the 2-month time limit of **R.136(1)**, as the notice ought to remove the cause of non-compliance (**J27/90** hn1). This is often the case, in particular where a time-limit is not observed through ignorance of it or inadvertence. The actual becoming aware of the notification cannot be replaced by a fiction, e.g. the fiction that the notification is deemed to have been made on the 10th day following despatch according to **R.126(2)**, where the failure to complete the act is purely due to previous unawareness that the act had not been completed (**T428/98** hn.I).

5 **One-year period**

Re-establishment is not anymore possible if the request for re-establishment has not been filed and the omitted act completed within one year from the expiry of the unobserved period according to **R.136(1)**, first sentence, and **R.136(2)**, in order to guarantee legal certainty for the public (**J35/03** r.6). After the one-year period has elapsed, a third person may safely assume that the application or patent will not be revived. The option to file the grounds and complete the omitted act after expiry of the one-year period as allowed by (**J6/90**) are probably not anymore possible under the EPC2000.

Exceptionally, a refused or (deemed) withdrawn application may yet give rise to protective rights after expiry of the one-year period, if a new application in the sense of **Art.61** is filed by an entitled applicant after expiry of the one-year period (**G3/92**).

The six-month period of grace under **R.51(2)** for payment of the renewal fee plus additional fee is not to be deducted from the one-year period, as was the case under the old law, **Art.122(2)**, fourth sentence, EPC 1973. Now the one-year period begins on expiry of the six-month period. Since a **R.112(1)** communication will be sent to the applicant within two months from the due date after not paying the renewal fee, re-establishment will in practice be invoked seldom and the de facto extension of the six-month period does not put third parties at an unreasonable disadvantage (Special edition 1, OJ 2003, page 159).

The similar nature and purpose of the four-month period in **R.51(3)** for payment of renewal fees for a divisional application warrant an equal treatment with respect to the one-year period. Hence, the one-year period for re-establishing in the four-month period should run from expiry of the four-month period.

The EPO will regard the one year period as an aggregate period, because it is triggered by the expiry of the unobserved period. See A-IV,1.4.3 for an example; **R.131(2):3** for the calculation).

The one-year period is not applicable for requesting re-establishment in the priority period and the period for filing a petition for review, as is clear from the wording of **R.136(1)**.

6 **Concurrence of re-establishment and R.112(2) decision**

The 2-month period to apply for a decision according to **R.112(2)** starts ten days after the despatch of the **R.112(1)** communication of loss of rights by the EPO (**R.126(2)**). If the party is of the opinion that the EPO made a mistake with the communication under **R.112(1)**, he must request an appealable decision under **R.112(2)** and, if further processing is not possible, at the same time apply for re-establishment and pay the fee for re-establishment as an auxiliary request. Both requests must be filed within the shorter of two months after notification of the **R.112(1)** communication and two months of the removal of the cause of non-compliance. The removal is normally the actual receipt of the **R.112(1)** communication. The EPO will assess the correctness of the communication. If it decides the communication was erroneous, the party is notified and the procedure is continued. The fee for re-establishment will be refunded because the request for re-establishment is in that case without grounds. If the EPO decides the communication was correct, it will state so in an appealable decision under **R.112(2)**. The request for re-establishment will be dealt with after the decision of **R.112(2)** has become final.

7 **Fee for re-establishment**
The fee for re-establishment is fixed in **Rfees2(1)13**.

Loss of rights due to a late payment of the fee for re-establishment can be appealed after a communication of loss of rights under **R.112(1)** and a decision under **R.112(2)**. Re-establishment is excluded by **Art.122(4)**. The fee is refunded if it has been paid late or if there is no failure to meet a time limit. Payment without a written request is not regarded as a valid request for re-establishment, even if the payment indicated 're-establishment fee' and mentioned the relevant application (**J19/90**).

R. 136(2) The request shall state the grounds on which it is based and shall set out the facts on which it relies. The omitted act shall be completed within the relevant period for filing the request according to paragraph 1.

Implementation of: **Art.122(2)**
EPC 1973: **Art.122(2), (3)**

1 **Grounds and facts**
The English and French text of **R.136(2)** require the grounds and facts to be filed within two months, whereas the German text requires additionally that the substantiation of the facts ('glaubhaft machen') is filed within the same time limit. The broadest text should be used to interpret the EPC, i.e. the English and French text in this case. Hence, the request for re-establishment must contain the grounds and facts (**R.136(2)**); the facts may be substantiated later by providing means by which those facts are supported, e.g. medical certificates, sworn statements and the like. (**T324/90**)

Filing facts only with the statement of grounds of appeal in an appeal against a decision rejecting a request for re-establishment is too late: the party had not complied with his burden of allegation and proof for re-establishment (**J18/98**).

A broad statement such as a claim that 96% of the mail is delivered on the next working day does in general not reflect what happens in individual cases (**T777/98** r.2.2.2.2). See **Art.117** (taking of evidence) for means to make the facts credible ('glaubhaft' in the German version of **R.136(2)**).

2 **Omitted act**
The completion of the omitted act implies that the act meets the requirements of the EPC for admissibility. As an example, if a statement of grounds of appeal, late filed as completion of an omitted act, is inadmissible for the purpose of **Art.108**, the request for re-establishment itself is inadmissible. (**T167/97** hn)

R. 136(3) Re-establishment of rights shall be ruled out in respect of any period for which further processing under Article 121 is available and in respect of the period for requesting re-establishment of rights.

Art.121 Further processing of the patent application
Implementation of: **Art.122(4)**
EPC 1973: **Art.122(5)**

1 **Periods excluded from re-establishment**
Paragraph 3 rules out the re-establishment of rights in respect of any periods for which further processing is available. Either further processing or re-establishment of rights may be requested if a specific time limit has been missed. During the grant procedure only further processing will normally be available; re-establishment of rights thus only comes into play where further processing is excluded with regard to a specific period. The limitation of the possibility of re-establishment of rights during the grant procedure will, however, be offset to some extent by the fact that re-establishment of rights with regard to the period for further processing will continue to be possible. (Special edition 1, OJ 2003, 159)

The exclusion of the period for requesting re-establishment from re-establishment in **R.136(3)** is a repetition of **Art.122(4)**, first sentence.

R. 136(4) The department competent to decide on the omitted act shall decide on the request for re-establishment of rights.

Implementation of: **Art.122(2)**
EPC 1973: **Art.122(4)**

1 **Department competent to decide**
The department competent to decide on the omitted act also decides on the request for re-establishment.

Where the re-establishment is in respect of an unobserved time limit for appeal when the conditions for granting interlocutory revision are fulfilled, the department that took the contested decision will consider the re-establishment only if it can grant re-establishment within the three-month period of **Art.109(2)**; in all other cases the board of appeal will decide on the request for re-establishment (see e.g. **T65/11**, where the conditions for granting were not fulfilled). (E-VIII, 3.3)

If the department of first instance rejects a request for re-establishment and, after an appeal has been lodged, does not apply interlocutory revision according to **Art.109**, the board of appeal decides on the allowability of the request for re-establishment (**J22/86**).

Chapter VI *Amendments and corrections*

R. 137 Amendment of the European patent application

Amended by decision of the Administrative Council of 25.03.2009, which entered into force on 01.04.2010. The amendment replaces paragraphs (2) to (4) by new paragraphs (2) to (5). Amended **R.137** applies to applications for which the search report or the supplementary search report is drawn up on or after 01.04.2010. (OJ 2009, 299)

If the search report was drawn up before 01.04.2010, the previous version of **R.137** applies during the prosecution. The previous version has fewer restrictions for filing voluntary amendments, no compulsory submission of a basis for amendments, and a less restricted **R.137(5)**. See the April 2009 version of the Guidelines.

Implementation of **Art.123(1)**

EPC 1973: **R.86**

1 **General**

The provision restricts the possibilities in time for the applicant to amend the application of his own volition, in order to speed up the procedures. The extent of the amendments in terms of substance is restricted by **Art.123(2)**, (3) and **R.137(5)**.

R.80 is the corollary to **R.137** for amendments of a patent during opposition proceedings.

R. 137(1) Before receiving the European search report, the applicant may not amend the description, claims or drawings of a European patent application unless otherwise provided.

1 **No amendments before receipt of search report**

The purpose of the amendment prohibition of **R.137(1)** is not to disrupt the search by changes in the application.

The 'otherwise provided' allows exceptions where the amendments may be filed before receipt of the search report. The major exceptions are:

- **R.56** late filing of missing drawings or missing parts of application
- **R.58** late filing of missing claims, correction of deficiencies noticed under **R.57**
- **R.139**, second sentence: correction of obvious errors in the patent application.

The amendments under **R.58** should not extend beyond remedy of the deficiencies indicated by the Receiving Section (**R.57**).

This prohibition does not affect the possibility to correct errors in documents other than the description, claims or drawings in the stated period: abstract (**R.47**), request for grant (**R.41**), designation of the inventor (**R.19**), priority claims (**R.52**), authorisations (**R.152**) (see **R.139**, first sentence).

R. 137(2) Together with any comments, corrections or amendments made in response to communications by the European Patent Office under Rule 70a, paragraph 1 or 2, or Rule 161, paragraph 1, the applicant may amend the description, claims and drawings of his own volition.

R.70a(1) invitation to respond within period for filing request for examination

R.70a(2) invitation to respond within period for confirming request for examination
R.161(1) invitation to respond to PCT written opinion or examination report

1 **Voluntary amendment of the application**
At the start of the substantive examination the applicant will have an opportunity to amend the application of his own volition, as provided by **Art.123(1)**. **R.137(2)** allows a voluntary amendment to be made together with the response to the communication issued by the EPO under **R.70a(1)**, (2) or **R.161(1)**.

Any further voluntary amendment will only be admitted after consent of the examining division (**R.137(3)**). The combination of **R.137(2)** and (3) has as result that the response to the stated communications is the only possibility for filing voluntary amendments that the Office must admit.

The EPO does not use the common interpretation of the word 'together' in **R.137(2)** as meaning that the voluntary amendment and the response must be provided in one submission to the EPO but as meaning that the voluntary amendment must be filed within the same period as the period for filing the response. Hence, a voluntary amendment may also be filed before or after the response.

R.137(2) mentions the following three opportunities for filing voluntary amendments:

- The communication under **R.70a(1)** gives an opportunity to comment on the search report and opinion within the period for filing the request for examination.
- The communication under **R.70a(2)** allows an applicant to comment on the search report and opinion where the request for examination has already been filed, or on the extended supplementary search report and opinion, within the period for indicating whether he wishes to proceed further with the application.
- The communication under **R.161(1)** invites the applicant of a Euro-PCT application to comment on the written opinion or the preliminary examination report drawn up by the EPO as ISA or IPEA.

A response to any of the three communications is mandatory if the opinion notes deficiencies in the application, in which case a voluntary amendment must be filed as part of the response. If the opinion is positive, a voluntary amendment may be filed as the only response within the stated period. (B-XI,8)

In cases where no **R.70a** or **R.161(1)** communication is sent, for example where the examination fee has been paid early and **R.70a** does not apply or the **R.161** communication has been waived, the applicant may file voluntary amendments together with his response to the first communication from the examining division (H-II,2.2; note that this possibility for filing voluntary amendments is not covered by **R.137(2)**). The EPO applies a broader interpretation than the Guidelines and allows filing of voluntary amendments in these cases at any time during the grant proceedings.

A fourth opportunity is provided with the **R.161(2)** communication, allowing the applicant to amend voluntarily the Euro-PCT application before start of the supplementary search and within six months from notification of the communication.

A fifth opportunity for voluntary amendment is the amendment of the application documents following a search on a Euro-PCT application under **R.164(2)(b)**. (OJ 2014 A70 §16)

The voluntary amendment may include comments, corrections and amendments of the application. When an amendment of the claims has been received before the termination of the technical preparation for the publication of the application, the amended claims are included in the publication (**R.68(4)**).

R. 137(3) No further amendment may be made without the consent of the Examining Division.

1 **Voluntary amendments after first response**
After the response to the communication mentioned in **R.137(2)**, no voluntary amendments may be made without the consent of the examining division (**R.137(3)**). As an exception, **R.164(2)** provides for a right to amend voluntarily the application (**R.164(2):2.4**).

The examining division will admit amendments to the extent that they correct deficiencies noted in a communication of the examining division; such amendments are mandatory. Voluntary amendments filed after said response are admitted only at the examiner's discretion. The discretion must strike a balance between the applicant's interest in obtaining a good patent and the EPO's interest of bringing the procedure swiftly to a close (H-II,2.3). See H-II,2.3.1 for examples of the exercise of discretion.

If a request for amendment is refused, the EPO must send the applicant the reasons for the refusal (**Art.113(1)**; E-X,2.11 (GL2017 E-X, 2.10); H-II,2.6; H-III,3.1.4).

The examining division has a discretion to allow voluntary amendments until the decision to grant is handed over to the EPO's internal postal service (C-V,6.1) or the decision is pronounced in oral proceedings (E-III,9) (**G7/93** hn.1, **G12/91**, H-II,2.6). Allowance of a request for amendment filed after the communication under **R.71(3)** will be exceptional (**G7/93** hn.2). However, such a request must be admitted if the **R.71(3)** communication is the first communication in the examination (C-V,4.4). See also **R.71(6):2.** During opposition proceedings the proprietor may also amend the patent, but he is restricted by **Art.123(3)**, **R.80** and **R.138**.

R. 137(4) When filing any amendments referred to in paragraphs 1 to 3, the applicant shall identify them and indicate the basis for them in the application as filed. If the Examining Division notes a failure to meet either requirement, it may request the correction of this deficiency within a period of one month.

1 **Identification and indication of basis of amendments**
When an applicant amends the description, claims or drawings, he must identify the amendments and indicate the basis for them in the application as filed (**R.137(4)**, first sentence). The purpose of the provision is to simplify for the EPO the assessment of the allowability of the amendments. The indication is particularly important for the EPO's assessment where a literal basis for the amendment is not present. The provision of the basis and compliance with **Art.123(2)** are assessed independently (H-III,2.1).

Amendments may be identified by submitting replacement pages using a 'track changes' tool of the text editor or copied pages with handwritten amendments. In both cases additionally clean copies of the pages must be provided. (H-III,2.2)

The basis of the amendments is preferably indicated by a list of amendments made and their basis in the originally filed documents, where necessary with a short explanation why **Art.123(2)** is complied with (H-III,2.2). The indication must be specific and should not contain statements such as 'see the description as filed'. An indication is sufficient if, on consulting those parts of the application indicated, it is not necessary to look further (H-III,2.1).

2 **Applicability of R.137(4)**

The requirement to indicate the basis applies to any amendment filed before grant of the patent. Hence, it applies to both voluntary and mandatory amendments, to a first set of claims filed after the date of filing, and to any earlier filed amendments during an international phase.

The **R.137(4)** communication will not be sent for amendments filed during oral proceedings or in response to the summons thereto. In these cases the basis must be provided during the oral proceedings. If not provided, the amendments may be rejected as inadmissible under **R.137(3)**. (H-III,2.1.3)

Since **R.137(4)** applies to applications only, it does not apply to granted patents and the requirement need not be complied with for amendments of patents during opposition proceedings and any appeal in opposition. However, compliance is recommended because of procedural efficiency.

Note that the requirement of **R.137(4)** does not apply to applications for which the search report has been drawn up before 01.04.2010 (transitional provision of the amendment, OJ 2009, 299 Art.2). As a consequence, the requirement need not be complied with for any amendment of such applications made during grant proceedings including any appeal. (H-III,2.1.4)

3 **Missing identification of amendments**

If the applicant files amendments without identifying them or indicating the basis of them, the examining division may request correction of this deficiency within a non-extendible period of one month from notifying the applicant (**R.137(4)**, second sentence). The 'may' in the provision allows the examiner to issue the request for correction at his own discretion. In some cases it may be more efficient for the examiner to identify the basis himself than to issue an invitation under **R.137(4)**.

If the applicant does not respond in time to the invitation, the application will be deemed withdrawn under **Art.94(4)**. A failed one-month period can be remedied using further processing (**Art.121**).

R. 137(5) Amended claims may not relate to unsearched subject-matter which does not combine with the originally claimed invention or group of inventions to form a single general inventive concept. Nor may they relate to subject-matter not searched in accordance with Rule 62a or Rule 63.

R.62a Plurality of independent claims
R.63 Incomplete search due to unsearchable subject-matter

1 **Switching to unsearched subject-matter**

The procedural system of the EPC requires that an invention which is to be examined for patentability must be an invention for which a search fee has been paid (**G2/92**). Hence, unsearched subject-matter will not be examined. This is implemented by **R.137(5)**, which prohibits amended claims to relate to unsearched subject-matter by imposing the requirement of unity of invention between the invention defined in the amended claims and the original claimed invention. Hence, an amendment is not admissible if it relates to subject matter that was not searched and that is not unitary with the originally claimed and searched invention. The assessment requires establishing first whether the subject-matter was searched or should have been searched and second whether a unity objection would have been raised if the amended claims had been present in the set of claims on file at the time of the search (H-II,6.2).

R.137(5) and **R.64(1)** have the following relation. **R.64(1)** allows an applicant to pay further search fees for further inventions of a non-unitary application if he wants to ensure that one of the further inventions could become the subject of the claims of the application. Subject-matter for which no further search fee has been paid cannot be pursued in that application and amended claims may not relate to such unsearched subject-matter.

R.137(5) is complementary to **R.64(1)** and applies the principle of examination of only a searched invention to the grant proceedings, ruling out amendments circumventing this principle. It stops an applicant from switching to unsearched non-unitary subject-matter, for instance by dropping the originally filed, searched claims and replacing them with claims on originally non-unitary, unsearched subject-matter extracted from the description. The interpretation of **R.137(5)** must balance the interest of the EPO in collecting search and examination fees and the right of the applicant to amend his application (**Art.123(1)**). Because of the fundamental character of this right, which pursuant to **Art.164(2)** must prevail over any rule, **R.137(5)** must be interpreted strictly. (OJ 1995, 409; **T708/00** r.5-7)

The following unity test developed in **T708/00** achieves the strict interpretation. A set of claims is constructed comprising the claims as originally filed and the claims after amendment. Only if the set is non-unitary, the amendment of the claims may be refused. Reference is made to **Art.82** and **R.44** for the definition of unity of invention. The claims of a refused amendment can only be pursued in a divisional application (H-II,6.2).

The restriction of **R.137(5)** does not apply to amendments filed on entry into the European phase of a Euro-PCT application under **R.159(1)(b)** and in response to a **R.161** communication (OJ 2014 A70 §13). The originally claimed invention of a Euro-PCT application for the purpose of **R.137(5)** is the invention searched in the international phase or the invention searched under **R.164** and subsequently prosecuted before the EPO.

The requirement of **R.137(5)**, second sentence, does not apply to applications for which the search report has been drawn up before 01.04.2010 (transitional provision of the amendment, OJ 2009, 299 Art.2). As a consequence, the requirement need not be complied with for any amendment of such applications made during the grant or opposition procedure including any appeal.

The following three sections show applications of **R.137(5)**. The last section is an example of an incorrect application of the provision.

2 **Adding feature from description**

An objection under **R.137(5)**, first sentence, may arise if a feature from the description is added to a claim which has an effect unrelated to the effect(s) of the originally claimed invention. The addition causes non-unity between the amended claim and the original claim if the added feature restored novelty over the prior art. (H-II,6.2)

An amendment of a claim by including a feature which makes a contribution to the effect of the unamended claim and which is not searched but is disclosed in the context of the application as filed will not make the claim non-unitary and is therefore not objectionable under **R.137(5)**, even if an additional search is necessary (H-II,6.2). However, such a feature must be disclosed in the context of the claimed invention; if it is only disclosed in the context of a different inventive concept, an objection under **R.137(5)** may be raised (H-II,6.2). An additional search may also have to be carried out after the examiner has been convinced that a non-unity opinion is incorrect (C-IV,7.2).

3 **Multiple independent claims**

Under **R.62a** an applicant must select the independent claims he wants to be searched if there are multiple independent claims in one category that do not comply with **R.43(2)**. The subject-matter of the not-selected independent claims and claims dependent on them will not be searched. Amended claims may not relate to such subject-matter (**R.137(5)**, second sentence).

A convincing argument showing that the independent claims do fall within an exception of **R.43(2)** may result in an additional search (C-IV,7.2).

4 **Unsearchable subject-matter**

If the EPO cannot carry out a meaningful search, it will invite the applicant to submit a statement under **R.63(1)** indicating the subject-matter to be searched. If the statement does not solve all deficiencies, the EPO may issue a declaration that no search could be carried out or draw up a partial search report (**R.63(2)**). Amended claims may not relate to subject-matter not covered by the partial search report (**R.137(5)**, second sentence).

Where the EPO has issued a declaration of no search under **R.63**, the applicant can amend his claims again before the examining division (C-IV,7,2(i)). Since no search has been carried out, any amendment will inevitably relate to unsearched subject-matter and violate **R.137(5)**. The requirement of compliance with **R.137(5)** in C-IV,7.2(1) appears to be inconsistent for this case.

A correction of deficiencies which rendered a meaningful search impossible under **R.63** by an amendment complying with **R.137(5)** or a convincing refutation of the non-searchability opinion may result in an additional search. (C-IV,7.2)

5 **Unclear expressions**

A feature in a claim preceded by an expression like 'preferably' or 'optionally' can be ignored when assessing the scope of the claim (**Art.84:1.4**). Sometimes an examiner also ignores such a feature in the search. An amendment during prosecution making the feature non-optional may then be objected to under **R.137(5)** as being unsearched subject-matter. However, an exclusion of a feature from search merely based on its optional character lacks legal basis (see B-III,3.5) and the objection under **R.137(5)** is not in line with the purpose of the provision as set out in **T274/03** r.5, 6 and H-II,6.2. (CIPA Journal Oct. 2016 p. 46)

R. 138 Different claims, description and drawings for different States

If the European Patent Office is informed of the existence of a prior right under Article 139, paragraph 2, the European patent application or European patent may, for such State or States, contain claims and, where appropriate, a description and drawings which are different from those for the other designated States.

Art.139(2) National prior right
Implementation of **Art.118**
EPC 1973: **R.87**

1 **Amendment on account of national prior rights**

National prior rights are not comprised in the state of the art as defined in **Art.54(2)** and (3). Hence, different texts for different states are not justified in view of the principle of unity of the application laid down in **Art.118.** However, **R.138** provides an exception to this principle by allowing different claims, description and drawings for different states where national prior rights exist so as to ensure that the patent is also viable in those contracting states where the national prior rights are effective.

It is not allowed to file an application with different claims for different states in view of different national prior rights. The Receiving Section is not competent to decide on the justification to file the different claims. Moreover, it is rather unlikely that the applicant knows of the existence of prior rights at the date of filing his application, as by that date these prior rights have not yet been published. The different claims may be filed for the first time during the examination procedure.

According to **R.138**, the EPO must be 'informed' of the existence of the national prior rights. This means it must first investigate and evaluate them, before an applicant may file an additional set of claims (**J21/82 r.6**). The additional set of claims must be filed before the decision of the examining division is handed over to the EPO internal post services to be taken into account in the procedure (**G12/91**). The EPO must establish sufficiency of reason for deviating from unity of application. The EPO does not require nor suggest the applicant to file such an additional set (H-III,4.5).

The examiner will check that the separate claims comply with **Art.123(2)** and meet the other requirements of the EPC (H-III,4.5).

The examining division and, if appropriate, the board of appeal are competent to assess the different claims, descriptions and drawings. (**J21/82**)

Claims fees (**R.45**) are calculated only for the set of claims having the highest number of claims (A-III,9). All sets must be translated into the two official EPO languages other than the language of the proceedings under **R.71(3)**.

A similar procedure is possible in opposition (D-I,3; H-III,4.4). It is not possible to have different texts in respect of extension states (H-III,4).

2 **Amendment on account of European prior rights**

R.138 does not allow different texts of the application where European prior rights exist. This different treatment of national and European prior rights is a consequence of the changes in the EPC 2000 (see **Art.54(3):3**).

The prior art for applications filed before the EPC 2000 entry into force (13.12.2007) includes European prior rights only for those contracting states that are commonly designated. Such an application may contain different claims, description and drawings for states where the European prior right is effective and for states where it is not effective (**R.87** EPC 1973).

The prior art for applications filed on or after the EPC 2000 entry into force includes European prior rights effective for all contracting states. Such an application may not contain different claims, description or drawings for the different contracting states in view of this prior right (**R.138** EPC 2000). See **Art.54(3):3.2** for details of the states where European prior rights are effective.

R. 139 Correction of errors in documents filed with the European Patent Office

Linguistic errors, errors of transcription and mistakes in any document filed with the European Patent Office may be corrected on request. However, if the request for such correction concerns the description, claims or drawings, the correction must be obvious in the sense that it is immediately evident that nothing else would have been intended than what is offered as the correction.

Implementation of: **Art.123(1)**
EPC 1973: **R.88**

1 **General**

R.139 allows a party to correct on request errors in documents filed with the EPO. An error exists in a document if the document does not express the true intention of the person on whose behalf it was filed (**J8/80** r.4; **J6/91** r.2.2). The correction restores the document to the form in which the party intended to file it. The request may be filed at any time during pending grant and opposition proceedings (**J42/92**; H-VI,2.1; see **R.80:2** for opposition).

The department handling the procedure is competent to decide on a request for correction. If the correction concerns the description, drawings or claims, and the request is filed in an early stage, the Receiving Section may decide to hand the request over to the examining division because of its technical character (**J4/85**). During the examination and opposition procedure the department itself is competent, not a formalities officer, because the President has not entrusted this duty to him (**J10/82**).

If upon termination of the technical preparations for publication of the application a decision is still pending on a request for correction of items which a third party might expect to be able to take at face value, so that their rights would be jeopardised by correction, a reference to the request must be mentioned on the front page (A-VI,1.3).

The EPC has unfortunately not defined the meaning of the term 'amendment' and its relation to 'correction'. Linguistically there are two possible relations between an amendment and a correction, both of which are incompatible with the wording of the provisions of the EPC: 1) an amendment encompasses a correction and 2) an amendment and a correction have no hierarchical relation. **R.3(2)** supports the former, **Art.123**, **R.58**, **R.71(6)**, the title of Chapter VI of Part VII of the Implementing Regulations, **R.137** and **R.139** support the latter. The first relation has as consequence that corrections under **R.139** are subject to the restrictions of **R.137**, which is not the way the EPO applies the rules. The second relation leaves **R.139**, second sentence without the limitation of **Art.123(1)**, so that a correction can be made at any time during proceedings, which is the current practice of the EPO.

G3/89 has made **R.139**, second sentence, an implementation of **Art.123(2)**, such that a correction under **R.139**, second sentence may not extend the subject-matter of the application and has thereby chosen for amendments to include corrections. The decision was based on the dependency of articles and rules due to their order in the EPC and the importance of extension of subject-matter in opposition and revocation proceedings, where it is irrelevant whether the extension results from a correction under **R.139** or an amendment under **R.137**.

2 Conditions for correction

The provision does not restrict the possibility for correction to certain persons; hence, any party and any third person may correct documents filed by itself or in its name. The most frequent users of **R.139** are applicants and, to a lesser degree, proprietors.

Since **R.139** does not contain an explicit limitation to specific procedural stages, a request for correction may be filed at any stage of grant and opposition proceedings. The proceedings must be pending, otherwise the EPO has no jurisdiction (**J42/92** r.4-6). Even the approval of the text to be granted under **R.71(3)** does not estop the applicant from correcting an error under **R.139** (**T200/89** r.2.2, H-II,2.6). During examination proceedings a request for correction will be considered when filed before the decision has been handed over the EPO's internal postal service for transmission to the applicant in written proceedings (date at the bottom of the decision to grant form 2006A), or has been pronounced in oral proceedings (**G12/91**; H-VI,2.1). As set out below the principle of legal certainty may restrict the time window for filing a request for correction.

Correction of an error is not a right of a party. The word 'may' in **R.139** indicates that allowance of a correction is at the discretion of the EPO (**J6/91** r.5.3). Case law has developed the criteria for exercise of discretion in balancing the interests of the parties and the interests of the public. The correction may not breach legal certainty by misleading the public by erroneous information. Hence, a correction is normally allowable if it does not breach legal certainty and complies with the requirements in **R.139**. The following sections first set out the conditions applicable to all types of corrections and next the additional conditions specific for corrections under **R.139**, first and second sentence.

2.1 LEGAL CERTAINTY

A **R.139** correction should not breach legal certainty. **T824/00** r.6 derives this from the fact that the provision for correcting errors in documents is framed in a rule rather than in an article, which is evidence that the discretionary power under **R.139** is a subordinate value that should not prevail in a serious conflict with other values, e.g. the principle of legal certainty (see also **J4/82**, r.2). This is substantiated by the provision of re-establishment in **Art.122**, which defines precise limited circumstances and conditions in which true party intention may exceptionally prevail over procedural certainty in relation to loss of rights resulting from non-observance of certain time limits - with specific exclusions listed in **Art.122(4)** and third party protection laid down in **Art.122(5)**.

Legal certainty requires that the EPO can rely on statements of a party in proceedings, thereby defining the procedural stage at which certainty prevails over party intention (**J10/87** r.10). Hence, a **R.139** correction of a statement must be requested before the statement is relied on in a formal juridical act (**T824/00** r.8). Examples of juridical acts are entry in the Register, publication in the Bulletin, posting of a decision. Re-establishment in the period before the juridical act is excluded, because this period is not a time limit in the sense of **Art.122(1)** (**J7/90** r.3).

Corrections affecting information to be published must be made before its publication in the Bulletin or entry in the Register, because third parties must be able to rely on the information provided by the EPO. As an exception, a correction after publication may be allowed if the correction was obvious for the public. Examples of corrections relating to withdrawal of a patent application, designation of contracting states and priority data are given below.

A request for correction must be made without undue delay after the error was discovered (**G1/12** r.37; **J16/08** r.13; H-VI,2.1).

A **R.139** correction may not breach the principle of procedural legal certainty. A request for correction of a document does not reverse the effect of a decision already taken on the basis of the uncorrected document (**J3/01**, r.7). A correction of a request in written proceedings filed after a decision based on the uncorrected request has been handed over to the EPO's internal postal service should not be allowed because of breach of legal procedural certainty (**T824/00**, hn.I; **J3/01** r.10). In oral proceedings a request for correction should be submitted before closing of the debate prior to the pronouncement of the decision (see notes prior to **R.111**).

Similarly, a **R.139** correction does not re-open a procedural phase already terminated or a time-limit already expired (**J3/01** r.7). In **J27/96** the applicant requested addition of an erroneously omitted designation of a contracting state after expiry of the grace period for payment of the designation fee, with the aim to be reinstated in the grace period for payment of the fee. The board refused the correction. Even if it is accepted that the correction by addition of a designation has retroactive effect in the sense that the corrected designation is deemed to have been made as from the filing date of the application, that does not mean that the applicant is reinstated in the procedural phase when designations have to be made and fees to be paid with the consequence that the whole procedure of that phase must be available to him again. Correction of a mistake is an isolated procedural measure and not a case of re-establishment into a defined procedural phase as a whole. **J21/84**, r.9 decided similarly.

2.2 TYPE OF DOCUMENT

R.139 restricts correction to documents filed with the EPO. This includes documents filed in appeal (**G1/12** r.35). A failed payment cannot be corrected using **R.139**, because a failure to pay is not an error in a document (**T152/85** r.2). Debit orders may neither be corrected pursuant to **R.139**, because they are governed by the Arrangement for Deposit Accounts, to which the EPC provisions are not applicable; moreover, it is alien to the factual character of a payment to feign by correction, after the event, payment in due time of fees not in fact paid (**T170/83** r.8, referred to in A-X,7.1.1; see also **Rfees6(1):3**).

The first sentence of **R.139** contains conditions for correction of errors in any document. The second sentence of **R.139** contains additional conditions for the correction of errors in a description, claims or drawings, viz. the correction must be obvious (see below for an extensive discussion). The provisions for the application itself (**R.139**, second sentence) are stricter than for other documents because of the prohibition of extension of the application under **Art.123(2)**. It is clear from the language of **R.139** that correction of errors in documents other than a description, claims or drawings need not be obvious in the sense defined in the second sentence of **R.139** (**J8/80**, r.3). Correction of such errors is usually allowed (H-VI,2.2).

2.3 NATURE OF ERROR

According to **R.139**, correction is restricted to three types of error: linguistic errors, errors of transcription and mistakes. A linguistic error is an error in the language, e.g. a missing article before a noun, transposed words, a garbled sentence (**T565/97**; **T658/94**; **T609/95**). An error of transcription is a typing error, e.g. an erroneous application number, incorrect priority data, transposed digits in a parameter value, omitted feature in a claim retyped for a request (**J3/91**; **J2/92**; **T712/91**). A mistake may be said to exist in a document if the document does not express the true intention of the person on whose behalf it was filed. No mistake exists where the document did express the true intention and a change of mind was the reason for requesting correction.

The mistake may be an incorrect statement or an omission (**J8/80**, r.4), e.g. wrong application documents filed, missing designation, omitted priority claim, erroneous withdrawal of designation of contracting state or of patent application, wrong applicant in request for grant form, erroneous request in opposition proceedings, incorrect name of compound, wrong value of parameter or wrong reference in description (**J21/92, J8/01, J11/89, J10/87, J4/97, J18/93, T824/00, T955/92, T581/91, T417/87**). The definitions of error of transcription and mistake overlap where they relate to incorrect statements.

3 **Corrections under R.139, first sentence**

Correction of errors in documents other than a description, claims and drawings is briefly called 'correction under **R.139**, first sentence', even though the first sentence equally applies to correction of the description, claims and drawings. An allowed correction restores the document to the form intended by the party and has retroactive effect (**T219/86** r.5).

Case law relating to correction of designation of states and priority declarations has established general principles for correction under **R.139**, first sentence, as summarised in **J6/91** r.2 and endorsed by **G1/12**, which should be applied in addition to the conditions set out in the above paragraph 2.

- The correction under **R.139** may not be used to implement a change of mind or subsequent development of plans. To avoid such abuse the EPO checks if a mistake was made, what the mistake was, and what the correction should be (**J8/80**). A mistake caused by mixing up affairs of several clients is in principle corrigible (**J8/80** r.8). However, correction of a declaration filed by a representative without consulting the party is not allowable; the party must inform his representative in time of any change of mind or development of plans (**T309/03** r.2.4).
- If the correction is not self-evident, the burden of proof is a heavy one, and lies on the party. A mere statement of intention not supported by evidence is almost certain to be insufficient. There should be no reasonable doubt on the true intention of the person on whose behalf the application was filed. (**J8/80**)
- When the error concerns items third persons might expect to be able to take at face value, so that their rights would be jeopardized by the correction of the priority claim, the correction must be made promptly and in time for inclusion in the publication of the application, or at least a warning (A-V,3; **J21/84**), excepting special circumstances.

The same general rules apply to Euro-PCT applications. In the international phase only obvious errors may be corrected (**R.91.1(a)** PCT, PCT §8.5). Normally such a correction must be authorised by an international authority; in the case of errors in the Request form (**R.4** PCT), the rectification is made by the receiving Office (**R.91.1(e)(i)** PCT). A refused request may be published together with the application (see PCT §8.5). In order to apply the more lenient EPO practice to corrections not accepted by the international authority, the request for correction must be made again before the EPO as designated Office (after entry in the regional phase). Since the publication of the PCT application takes the place of the European publication (**Art.29** PCT, **Art.93** & **Art.153(3)** EPC), the warning has been duly published. When a correction is requested for the first time in the regional phase before the EPO, it is not possible any more to include a warning in the publication of the patent application, which publication has already taken place in the international phase (**J6/91** r.2.4)

Most corrections under **R.139**, first sentence relate to data in the Request for Grant form. The rule provides a possibility for the applicant to correct any errors of his own volition. When the EPO notes any errors in the form, it will invite the applicant to correct them under **Art.90(4)**. In that case correction is compulsory, but the applicant need not provide proof that a mistake was made, what the mistake was, and what the correction should be; he only has to proof that the correction does not implement a change of mind.

3.1 CORRECTION AND ADDING OF PRIORITY DECLARATION

Correction under **R.139**, first sentence, of errors with respect to priority claims may be allowable. However, under lex specialis **R.52(2)** an applicant may add a priority claim and under **R.52(3)** correct an existing priority claim without the restrictions of **R.139**. This option is available until expiry of the sixteen / four month period defined in **R.52(2)** and (3). Correction after this period is governed by **R.139** (A-V,3), where different conditions exist for correction before and after publication of the application.

The conditions developed in case law for correction of priority data under **R.139** are summarized in **J6/91** r.3. A correction must meet all conditions of the above sections 2 and 3: the EPO must be satisfied that an error was made, what the error was and what the correction should be, the request must be filed promptly and sufficiently early for a warning to be included in the publication of the application.

Correction of a priority declaration without a warning in the publication has, exceptionally, been allowed where one or both of the following additional special circumstances existed:

1 the EPO was partly responsible for the fact that no warning was published (**J11/89**);
2 the interest of the public was not seriously affected, for example the mistake was obvious on the face of the published application, or the public was otherwise informed about the full scope of protection sought by the applicant. (**J6/91** r.3)

3.1.1 Correction of omitted priority claim

An omitted first and only priority claim can be corrected under **R.139** in those cases where conditions of the above paragraph 3.1 have been fulfilled, and the application can still be published 18 months after the corrected priority date. (**J3/82**)

The omission of a priority declaration will, in nearly every case, be an error, and, in general, the applicant need not provide special evidence such as affidavits to prove that a mistake has been made and that the request for correction was not due to a change of mind (**J9/91** r.5).

The correction of a missing priority claim without a warning in the published application has exceptionally been allowed where the mistake was apparent on the face of the published application, e.g. an unusual priority claim; a third party is not adversely affected and is expected to inspect the file to obtain the correct information (A-III,6.5.2). For examples of apparent discrepancies see **J6/91** r.5.5, **J3/91** r.4.3, **J2/92** r.5.2.2 and **J11/92**.

The addition of a priority to an already claimed priority of earlier date under **R.139** is allowed, provided that the request is made sufficiently early for a warning to be included in the publication of the application (**J4/82**). In **J7/94** the addition of a second priority of later date without warning in the publication of the application was refused, because the addition was relevant for the evaluation of the state of the art (**J14/82** and **J11/89** not followed). Note that addition of a priority claim within sixteen months from the earliest priority date is not governed by **R.139** but by **R.52(2)**.

Since **R.139** has no express provisions protecting third parties comparable to the provisions of **Art.122(5)**, the solution of any problem regarding third party rights must be left to the national courts applying **Art.122(5)** mutatis mutandis (**J12/80** and **J10/87**).

3.1.2 *Correction of date, state and file number in priority declaration*

An error in the indication of the date and/or state of the previous filing in the Request for Grant form may be corrected under **R.139** in those cases where the conditions of the above paragraph 3.1 have been fulfilled (**J14/82, J3/91** r.3; A-III,6.5.3).

An erroneous file number of a priority document may be corrected without the restrictions of paragraph 3.1 (**J3/91** r.5). If the applicant has not provided a file number, the EPO will invite him under **R.59.** (A-III,6.5.3)

3.2 CORRECTION OF WITHDRAWAL OF A PATENT APPLICATION

A retraction of the withdrawal of an application as a whole may be allowable under **R.139** if, according to **J10/87**:

- the EPO has not officially notified the public of the withdrawal, e.g. in the Register or by a document in the online file, at the time the retraction of the withdrawal is applied for (see **J10/08** as an example);
- the erroneous withdrawal is due to an excusable oversight;
- there is no substantial delay of the proceedings;
- the EPO is satisfied that the interests of third parties who may possibly have taken notice of the withdrawal by inspection of the file are adequately protected.

Publication of the withdrawal in the Register (**J4/97** r.6; **J25/03** r.9) and in the Bulletin (**J15/86** hn.III) both amount to an official notification of the public, preventing retraction of the withdrawal. A withdrawal that could only be noticed by inspection of the file is treated differently from a withdrawal which was officially published (see the last item of the above list), because legal certainty for third parties is of greater importance after official publication by the EPO than after availability in the file (**J10/87** r.10).

3.3 CORRECTION OF OTHER ERRORS UNDER R.139, FIRST SENTENCE

A request for retraction of a withdrawal of a designation of a contracting state may be allowable if the wrong information has not yet been officially published, the error is excusable, the correction does not cause too much delay in the procedure and third persons are sufficiently protected (**J10/87**).

The EPC contains legi speciali for the correction of errors in a translation of a patent application in **Art.14(2)** and for correction of the designation of an inventor in **R.21.**

An error in the indication of the applicant is correctable (**J7/80**). A correction substituting the name of the applicant is allowable under **R.139,** first sentence, provided there is sufficient evidence to support the request for correction (**J18/93** hn).

The identity of an opponent or appellant may be corrected under **R.139,** first sentence, provided the requirements of the above section 3 have been complied with. The correction has retrospective effect, and the correct identity will be regarded as provided within the 9-month opposition period or the 2-month appeal period (**G1/12** r.37). See also **R.77(1):1.3** and **R.101(2):1.**

The correction of errors in the designation of the inventor is dealt with in **R.57:7. R.140** governs the correction of errors in decisions.

4 Correction under R.139, second sentence

The second sentence of **R.139** governs the correction of an error in a description, claims or drawings, i.e. the parts of the application or patent relating to the disclosure. Such a correction must comply with requirements of both **R.139**, first sentence and second sentence. The former restricts the type of correction that can be made and demands that a request be filed. The latter requires that the correction must be obvious in the sense that it is immediately evident that nothing else would have been intended than what is offered as the correction. The requirement of obviousness has been interpreted by the Enlarged Board of Appeal as follows (**G3/89** and **G11/91**, confirming **T401/88**, overruling **J19/80**, **J4/85** hn1, 2 and **T200/89** r.2.1).

The obviousness implies that the error in the application or patent must be obvious such that a skilled person is in no doubt that this information is not correct. If it is doubtful whether any information at all is incorrect, then a correction is ruled out. The same applies if incorrect information only becomes apparent in the light of the proposed correction. (**G3/89** r.5)

The correction of the error must be obvious in that it is immediately evident for a skilled person that nothing else would have been intended than what is offered as the correction. The whole disclosure must allow a skilled person - using the common general knowledge on the date of filing - directly and unequivocally to ascertain the precise content of the information the person making the request actually meant to give, instead of the incorrect particulars, on the date of filing or when making an amendment under **Art.123**. If there is any doubt that nothing else would have been intended than what is offered as the correction, a correction cannot be made. (**G3/89** r.6)

The above content of the information must be derived from the application as originally filed and any document used for proving the common general knowledge on the date of filing. The prohibition of extension under **Art.123(2)** does not allow to use other documents, such as the abstract and priority documents, for the correction, even if they were filed together with the patent application. (**G3/89** r.7)

The application as originally filed includes any late-filed missing parts of the description and missing drawings filed according to **R.56**, regardless of whether this resulted in a change of the date of filing. However, claims filed after the date of filing in response to an invitation according to **R.58** cannot be used in assessing the allowability of a request for correction. (A-V,3)

Where the application is filed in electronic form and the application documents are also available to the EPO in an admissible format on the date of filing (Spec. Ed. 3 of OJ 2007, 17 Art.3), the latter documents may also be used to determine the allowability of the request for correction (A-V,3).

The corrected information merely expresses what a skilled person would already derive from the application, and therefore does not change the contents as filed. Thus, the correction cannot be said to have a retroactive effect. Since such a correction is of a declaratory nature only, it does not infringe the prohibition of extension under **Art.123(2)** either. (**G3/89** r.4)

4.1 CORRECTION OF SPECIFIC ERRORS UNDER R.139, SECOND SENTENCE

A non-obvious error in the description or claims resulting from an erroneous calculation cannot be corrected under **R.139**. A correction of such an error is allowable under **Art.123(2)** EPC if the amendment is clearly implied by the disclosure of the application as filed. If more than one arithmetical possibility of correction can be envisaged, the correction chosen must be the one which the application as a whole clearly implies. (**T13/83**)

An applicant may not replace under **R.139** the complete documents forming a patent application, that is the description, claims and drawings, by other documents he had intended to file with the request for grant. Such a replacement constitutes an extension of the contents of the application, violating **Art.123(2)** to which **R.139** is bound. (**G2/95**, following **J21/85**, overturning **T726/93**)

If there is no proof of what the applicant intended to file as figure, the missing figure must be added under **R.56. R.56** is not a lex specialis of **R.139**: a correction of the figures is not restricted to the application of **R.56**, but may also be made by applying **R.139**.

More examples of errors are given in the above paragraph 2.3 and in H-VI,2.3.

R. 140 Correction of errors in decisions

In decisions of the European Patent Office, only linguistic errors, errors of transcription and obvious mistakes may be corrected.

Implementation of **Art.123(1)** and **Art.97(1)**
EPC 1973: **R.89**

1 **Procedure for correction**

The purpose of **R.140** is to correct an obvious clerical mistake in a decision where the decision does not express the manifest intention of the deciding body (**G8/95** r.3.2). The EPO makes the correction in the form of a decision, either of its own motion or on a reasoned request (H-VI,5; see e.g. **T150/89**). The request can be filed at any time, because **R.140** sets no time limit (**G1/10** r.15).

The competence for the correction lies with the body which has given the decision. Hence, the examining division has to decide on a request to correct errors in the decision to grant. (**G8/95** r.3.4)

A decision refusing a request for correction is appealable (see e.g. **T850/95b** and **T1093/05**). The reasons for the decision must have been sent to the requester previously to comply with **Art.113(1)** (H-VI,5).

The correction of the decision under **R.140** has a retrospective effect; hence, cancellation of the incorrect decision and issue of a new one is unnecessary and inappropriate; moreover, a body cannot cancel a decision it has issued. The body will issue a further decision giving the ground of correction or refusing the correction. (**T212/88** r.1)

2 **Errors in decisions**

According to **R.140**, the correction may relate only to linguistic errors, errors of transcription and obvious mistakes. For reasons of legal certainty of third parties the error must be obvious, i.e. it must be clear not only that the deciding body did not intend to decide as appears from the decision, but also in what form it did intend to decide. The intended decision can usually be derived from the file of the case. (**T1093/05** r.7)

It should be noted that a correction of a decision under **R.140** is a remedy directed only against the form in which a decision is expressed, whereas an appeal against a decision under **Art.106** is directed against the substance of the decision (**T1093/05** r.10). An error in the substance of the decision or in a procedural principle cannot be corrected under **R.140** (**G1/97** r.2(c)). If the decision to be corrected has been given in first instance, a correction in substance can be requested in an appeal according to **Art.106**, in as far as the decision does not meet the request of the appellant (**Art.107**).

The correction may relate to allegedly incorrect reasons for a decision, both in first and second instance (see e.g. **T867/96**) or a mistake in signing the decision (**T212/88** r.1). The correction may concern a priority claim which the EPO erroneously omitted from the granted patent (e.g. case EP1800984).

In **T965/98** the board allowed a correction under **R.139** of an obvious error in claims submitted during oral proceedings, the request for correction being filed during the preparation of the written reasons. The decision of the board given during the oral proceedings was amended under **R.140** to take into account the correction.

3 Errors relating to grant

The published specification of the patent is normally the first complete expression of the decision to grant the proprietor receives. The decision itself merely consist of an electronically generated form which refers to the documents indicated in the communication pursuant to **R.71(3)** stating that a patent is granted based on those documents (**T1093/05** r.2). The published specification allows him to check whether the specification actually corresponds to the text of the application in the **R.71(3)** communication which he approved.

The text of the specification may diverge in two ways from the intended specification: the decision to grant is not correct and the published specification consequently diverges or the decision to grant is correct and the published specification diverges from the decision.

Correction of bibliographic data is possible; requests for such correction are dealt with by the formalities officers (H-VI,3.2).

3.1 CORRECTION OF THE GRANTED PATENT

Art.98 attaches no legal consequences to the publication of the specification, thus the text of the published specification has no binding character.

The description, claims and drawings of a European patent cannot be corrected using **R.140** (**G1/10** r.3, 5). A request to this effect is inadmissible (**G1/10** hn.1). This applies after grant of the patent, in opposition proceedings and in limitation proceedings (**G1/10** r.13). The prohibition increases legal certainty of third parties and avoids adverse effects of correction, such as delaying opposition proceedings, change of scope of a patent in opposition without the possibility of appeal for an opponent, change of scope after 9 months from grant without the option of filing an opposition by a third party affected by the new scope (**G1/10** r.7). (H-VI,3)

An applicant has ample opportunity to correct mistakes, such as misspelled or incorrect words, under **R.139** in documents he has filed, including the opportunity under **R.71(6)** in the final stage of examination. The applicant alone is responsible for any errors remaining in the patent after the decision to grant, whether the error was made by him or by the examining division. **R.140** cannot be used to tidy up the patent after grant. (**G1/10** r.9-11).

If the text of the decision to grant does not correspond to the text approved by the applicant, e.g. because the examining division changed a claim after approval or disregarded amendments filed by the proprietor without giving him an opportunity to comment, it violates **Art.113(2)** and can only be corrected by filing an appeal. If the examining division agrees, it will allow interlocutory revision and it may reimburse the appeal fee. (**G1/10** r.12; see also **G8/95** r.3.1; **T1093/05** r.10-12)

An obvious mistake in a patent will not adversely affect opponents or others, because they should read the patent as if corrected and an actual correction should not be necessary (**G1/10** r.8). A proprietor can correct any perceived error in the patent as an amendment under **Art.123** during opposition or limitation proceedings according to the EBoA (**G1/10** r.13). However, tidying up a patent is not permissible in a limitation procedure according to the Guidelines (D-X,4.3).

Exceptionally, formatting or editing errors having occurred during the preparation of the text intended for grant but neither marked in said text nor indicated in the communication under **R.71(3)** may be corrected by the EPO of its own motion or at the request of the patent proprietor, even after grant. Such correction does not influence the start of the opposition period. (H-VI,3.3)

Note, that **R.140** explicitly allows correction of obvious mistakes in decisions and, hence, in the patent, because, as confirmed by **G1/10** r.3, the text of the patent is an integral part of the decision. By prohibiting correction of a patent using **R.140**, **G1/10** appears to prohibit what the legislator has permitted.

G1/10 is limited to correction of the description, claims and drawings of a patent and does not relate to correction of other matter, e.g. the bibliographic data referred to in **R.71(3)** (**G1/10** r.3; H-VI,3.2). A request for correction of the other matter under **R.140** during opposition proceedings will be referred to the examining division for correction during pending opposition proceedings (H-VI,3.5).

3.2 CORRECTION OF THE PUBLISHED SPECIFICATION

If the decision to grant is correct but the published specification diverges from the decision, the applicant was granted what it had requested; however, an error has occurred in laying down the decision in the published specification.

Since **Art.98** attaches no legal consequences to the publication of the specification, the text of the specification has no binding character. It merely serves to facilitate access of the public to the content of the patent. Mistakes in the published specification of the patent deviating from the decision to grant have no effect on the content of the patent granted. Only the text the decision to grant refers to is relevant (**Art.97(1)** & **R.71a(1)**). This text, i.e. the description, claims and drawings, is in the language of the proceedings (**Art.70(1)**). (C-V,10; **J14/87** hn1)

If the published specification diverges from the text as granted (see **R.71a(1)**), it may be corrected at any time. Since the specification should reproduce the decision to grant, the EPO must correct such errors on request or of its own motion (**T150/89**). The errors must be obvious, e.g. linguistic errors, errors of transcription or obvious mistakes. An example of such an error is where parts of the specification have fallen away, such as claims about which there was no doubt on allowability. See EP 0 326 761 B1 for an example of a patent having an incorrect set of claims. If necessary, the EPO republishes the patent specification. (C-V,10; H-VI,4)

3.3 CORRECTION OF TRANSLATION OF CLAIMS

Since the text of the patent in the language of proceedings is the authentic text (**Art.70(1)**), the translations of the claims are for information only and do not form part of the decision to grant. Hence, they cannot be corrected under **R.140** (H-VI,3.4). Correction under **R.139** can only be requested during pending proceedings (**J42/92**).

An error in these translations has no legal effect. However, the proprietor should check the translations of the specification filed with the national offices of the designated contracting states under **Art.65(1)** for similar errors in view of the effect of **Art.70(3)**.

Amendment is possible when the patent is maintained in amended form (**R.82(2)**) and before a national authority (**Art.70(4)**). (H-VI,3.4)

Chapter VII *Information on prior art*

R. 141 Information on prior art

Amended by decision of the Administrative Council of 28.10.2009, which entered into force on 01.01.2011. Amended **R.141** applies to all European applications and international applications filed on or after 01.01.2011. (OJ 2009, 585)
Implementation of: **Art.124(1)**
EPC 1973: **Art.124(1)**

R. 141(1) An applicant claiming priority within the meaning of Article 87 shall file a copy of the results of any search carried out by the authority with which the previous application was filed together with the European patent application, in the case of a Euro-PCT application on entry into the European phase, or without delay after such results have been made available to him.

Art.87 Priority right

1 **Prior art information of priority application**
Any applicant claiming priority must file a copy of any search results of the priority application and prepared by or for the patent office with which the priority application was filed (**R.141(1)**). Where multiple priorities are claimed, the obligation applies to all priority applications. The priority application may be a patent application, a utility model or a utility certificate, as allowed by **Art.87**. If priority of an international application is claimed, the search result is the international search report.

The copy must be a copy of an official document issued by the patent office. A translation of documents not drawn up in an EPO language is not required. Copies of documents cited in the search results need not be provided. (Not. EPO OJ 2010, 410 §2.1)

The submission of the search results does not give entitlement to a reduction of the search fee, unless the conditions of **Rfees9** apply. An applicant who wants an EPO search unaffected by search results of a priority application, should file the search results after completion of the EPO search in response to the **R.70b** invitation. Where **R.141(2)** applies, the applicant should file two priority applications, one to be searched and the other only for claiming priority from.

2 **Procedure**
The copy of the search results must be filed together with the direct European application or on regional entry of a Euro-PCT application. If not available at the date of filing or the date of national entry, the applicant must supply the copy immediately after he has received the search results (**R.141(1)**). The EPO prefers to receive the copy before drawing up the European search report, although a more independent search can be expected if the copy is submitted after the EPO has drawn up its search report. The obligation to submit exists as long as the application is pending.

The applicant need not submit search results if they are available to the EPO. In that case the EPO will include a copy in the file (**R.141(2)**).

When the EPO notes at the start of the substantive examination that no copy of the search results has been filed and that the copy is not deemed to be filed under **R.141(2)**, it will send the applicant an invitation under **R.70b** to file within two months the copy or a statement that the copy is not available, e.g. where the search results are not yet available to the applicant or where no search has been carried out on the priority application.

If the applicant states in response to the **R.70b** invitation that the copy is not yet available, the EPO may invite the applicant again later on under **R.141(3)** to file it. Within two months the applicant should respond by providing the copy or statement.

The EPO will always issue a **R.70b** invitation for a divisional claiming priority if no copy or statement has been provided on filing the divisional. If all relevant search results have already been filed for the parent, the applicant need not respond to the invitation. If the applicant has filed a statement of non-availability for the parent, a new statement or a copy of the search results must be filed for the divisional. (OJ 2010, 410 §3.2)

If the applicant does not respond to the invitations in time, the application will be deemed withdrawn under **R.70b(2)** or **Art.124(2)**. Further processing is available as remedy.

R. 141(2) The copy referred to in paragraph 1 shall be deemed to be duly filed if it is available to the European Patent Office and to be included in the file of the European patent application under the conditions determined by the President of the European Patent Office.

1 **Prior art information available to EPO**

The applicant need not file a copy of the search results if a copy is available to the EPO and can automatically be included in its file (**R.141(2)**; OJ 2010, 410 §2.2; OJ 2013, 217, A-III,6.12).

The EPO will include a copy of the search report of a priority application if it has drawn up the search report itself. The search report may be a European search report, an international (type) search report or a search report made by the EPO on behalf of a national office on a national application. (Dec. Pres., OJ 2010, 600)

The EPO will also include a copy of the search results of a priority application if that application was filed in AT, DK, ES, GB, JP, KR, or US (Dec. Pres. OJ 2011, 62; 2012, 540, 2013, 216; 2015 A2, A3 and 2016 A18, A19).

Likewise, the EPO includes a copy of the search results of the priority application in the file of a divisional application if the results have already been included in the file of the parent application (OJ 2010, 410).

R. 141(3) Without prejudice to paragraphs 1 and 2, the European Patent Office may invite the applicant to provide, within a period of two months, information on prior art within the meaning of Article 124, paragraph 1.

1 **Other prior art information**

R.141(3), referring to **Art.124(1)**, allows the EPO to request the applicant to provide information on prior art relied upon in national or regional proceedings concerning similar applications for patents or utility models in respect of an invention to which the European patent application relates. This pertains in particular to applications whose priority is not being claimed. (C-III,6)

An invitation under **R.141(3)** will be issued only during substantive examination and only in individual cases, independent from the provision of prior art under **R.141(1)** and (2). The EPO may also use the invitation to request a copy of the search results of **R.141(1)** if they have not been provided in response to the **R.70b** invitation. (OJ 2010, 410 §2.3)

The sanction for not responding to the invitation is provided in **Art.124(2)**.

Chapter VIII *Interruption of proceedings*

R. 142 Interruption of proceedings

The Travaux Préparatoires EPC 1973 held the procedure in the event of death of an applicant or proprietor to be an implementation of **Art.125** on taking into account general principles of procedural law, which explains the position of **R.142** in the Implementing Regulations (Münchner Gemeinschaftskommentar Art. 120, Rdn. 163). Since the provision relates to periods, this book treats it as an implementation of **Art.120**.
EPC 1973: **R.90**

1 **General**
The EPO will interrupt proceedings in three specific cases set out in **R.142(1)**. The interruption provides a remedy for failed time limits due to medical and financial hardship of the applicant and proprietor (**R.142(1)**(a) and (**b**)) and of their professional representative (**c**)). Note that the remedy does not apply to the opponent or his representative. See **R.84(2)** for the death or legal incapacity of an opponent.

The provision **R.142** can make non-observance of time limits to be regarded as not happened, similar to **Art.121** and **122**. **R.142** interrupts all periods, which start anew or continue to run after resumption of the proceedings.

In principle, the EPO applies **R.142** ex officio. However, in the case of **R.142(1)(a)**, last sentence, proceedings are interrupted on request only. (E-VII,1.1)

The interruption has legal effect from the date of the occurrence of the event. Where the interruption is requested, it is effective from the date of receipt of the request. Communications and decisions of the EPO notified during the interruption are regarded null and void and will be notified anew after resumption of the proceedings. (E-VII,1.3, 1.4)

The Legal Division is responsible for matters relating to the interruption and resumption of proceedings (**Art.20**).

R. 142(1) Proceedings before the European Patent Office shall be interrupted:

(a) in the event of the death or legal incapacity of the applicant for or proprietor of a European patent or of the person authorised by national law to act on his behalf. To the extent that the above events do not affect the authorisation of a representative appointed under Article 134, proceedings shall be interrupted only on application by such representative;

(b) in the event of the applicant for or proprietor of a patent, as a result of some action taken against his property, being prevented by legal reasons from continuing the proceedings;

(c) in the event of the death or legal incapacity of the representative of an applicant for or proprietor of a patent, or of his being prevented for legal reasons resulting from action taken against his property from continuing the proceedings.

Art.134 Representation before the European Patent Office

1 **Death of applicant or proprietor (R.142(1)(a))**
The legal incapacity of the applicant or proprietor to carry out legal transactions relating to his application or patent must be determined according to national law, since his interest in the application or patent is an interest in property (cf. **Art.74** and **2(2)**) (**J900/85** r.9, sometimes referred to as JXX/XX).

In general, the proceedings will be interrupted automatically and retroactively from the first day of the incapacity. Since **R.142(1)(a)** applies to applicants, proprietors and persons authorised by them under national law (e.g. a trustee), the proceedings will not be interrupted when an opponent or appellant, not being an applicant or proprietor, befalls one of the misfortunes mentioned in **R.142(1)**.

However, the proceedings will not be interrupted automatically if the unfortunate applicant or proprietor is represented and the authorisation of the representative is not affected (**R.142(1)(a)**, second sentence). For example, death of a party does not terminate an authorisation, unless provided to the contrary (**R.152(9)**). In such circumstances the representative must apply for interruption of the proceedings.

2 **Action against property of applicant or proprietor (R.142(1)b))**
E.g. bankruptcy. See e.g. **J7/83** and **J26/95**.

3 **Death of representative (R.142(1)(c))**
The test for legal incapacity of a representative laid down by the EPO is: was the representative concerned in a fit mental state to do the work required of him at the material time or did he lack the capacity to make rational decisions and to take necessary actions? (**J900/85** r.11, sometimes referred to as JXX/XX)

Only in the case of **R.142(1)(a)**, second sentence the proceedings will be interrupted on application. In all other cases, such as under (c), the interruption must be applied automatically by the EPO. The EPO must establish when the representative was legally incapacitated and specify the time limits which may have been interrupted. (**J902/87** r.2.6, sometimes referred to as JXX/87)

R. 142(2) When, in the cases referred to in paragraph 1(a) or (b), the European Patent Office has been informed of the identity of the person authorised to continue the proceedings, it shall notify such person and, where applicable, any third party, that the proceedings will be resumed as from a specified date.

R. 142(3) In the case referred to in paragraph 1(c), the proceedings shall be resumed when the European Patent Office has been informed of the appointment of a new representative of the applicant or when the Office has informed the other parties of the appointment of a new representative of the proprietor of the patent. If, three months after the beginning of the interruption of the proceedings, the European Patent Office has not been informed of the appointment of a new representative, it shall communicate to the applicant for or proprietor of the patent:

(a) where Article 133, paragraph 2, is applicable, that the European patent application will be deemed to be withdrawn or the European patent will be revoked if the information is not submitted within two months of this communication; or

(b) otherwise, that the proceedings will be resumed with the applicant for or proprietor of the patent as from the notification of this communication.

Art.133(2) Compulsory representation of non-EPC-state person

R. 142(4) Any periods, other than those for requesting examination and paying renewal fees, in force at the date of interruption of the proceedings, shall begin again as from the day on which the proceedings are resumed. If such date is less than two months before the end of the period within which the request for examination must be filed, such a request may be filed within two months of such date.

Implementation of**Art.94(1)**
EPC 1973: **R.90**

1 **Interruption of periods**
The purpose of **R.142(4)** is to specify how periods are to be calculated when the proceedings resume (J7/83 r.10). From the text of **R.142(1)**: 'proceedings .. shall be interrupted' it follows that all periods are interrupted (J7/83 r.8). On resumption of the proceedings, most periods begin again to run for their original duration.

As an exception, the period for filing the request for examination and the period for paying the renewal fees (**R.142(4)**, first sentence) are suspended (E-VII,1.4). On resumption of the proceedings, these periods are resumed for the non-elapsed portion, with a minimum of two months for the period for requesting examination as prescribed by **R.142(4)**, second sentence (J7/83 hn).

The due date for paying renewal fees (**Art.86(1)**) is not a period in the normal sense. The EPC does not prescribe a period for payment of the renewal fee, but simply states a date at which it must have been paid. Therefore, if the renewal fee falls due during the period of the interruption, **R.142(4)** must be interpreted as deferring the due date until the date the proceedings are resumed. In that case, the renewal fee can still validly be paid up to the day of the resumption (J902/87 hn.3; E-VII,1.5). The fee should preferably be paid some time in advance of the resumption for safety's sake. As is clear from **R.142(4)** and also from **R.14(4)**, the time left for paying the renewal fee will not be extended by 2 months as it is for the request for examination.

The six-month period for paying the renewal fee with additional fee (**R.51(2)**) is a period that will be suspended on the day of interruption and begins to run again for the remaining period on the date of resumption; the remaining period will not be extended to a minimum of two months as it is for the request for examination (E-VII,1.5). If the renewal fee becomes due on the day of resumption, the renewal fee with an additional fee can be paid during the following six months. (J902/87, a.o. r.3.12)

See **R.14(4):2** for an example how the periods are calculated in the case of a stay of proceedings.

Chapter IX *Information to the public*

R. 143 Entries in the European Patent Register

Implementation of: **Art.127**
EPC 1973: **R.92**

R. 143(1) The European Patent Register shall contain the following entries:

(a) number of the European patent application;
(b) date of filing of the application;
(c) title of the invention;
(d) classification symbols assigned to the application;
(e) the Contracting States designated;
(f) particulars of the applicant for or proprietor of the patent as provided in Rule 41, paragraph 2(c);
(g) family name, given names and address of the inventor designated by the applicant for or proprietor of the patent, unless he has waived his right to be mentioned under Rule 20, paragraph 1;
(h) particulars of the representative of the applicant for or proprietor of the patent as provided in Rule 41, paragraph 2(d); in the case of several representatives only the particulars of the representative first named, followed by the words "and others" and, in the case of an association referred to in Rule 152, paragraph 11, only the name and address of the association;
(i) priority data (date, State and file number of the previous application);
(j) in the event of a division of the application, the numbers of all the divisional applications;
(k) in the case of a divisional application or a new application under Article 61, paragraph 1(b), the information referred to in sub-paragraphs (a), (b) and (i) with regard to the earlier application;
(l) date of publication of the application and, where appropriate, date of the separate publication of the European search report;
(m) date of filing of the request for examination;
(n) date on which the application is refused, withdrawn or deemed to be withdrawn;
(o) date of publication of the mention of the grant of the European patent;
(p) date of lapse of the European patent in a Contracting State during the opposition period and, where appropriate, pending a final decision on opposition;
(q) date of filing opposition;
(r) date and purport of the decision on opposition;
(s) dates of stay and resumption of proceedings in the cases referred to in Rules 14 and 78;
(t) dates of interruption and resumption of proceedings in the case referred to in Rule 142;
(u) date of re-establishment of rights where an entry has been made under sub-paragraphs (n) or (r);
(v) the filing of a request for conversion under Article 135, paragraph 3;

(w) **rights and transfer of such rights relating to an application or a European patent where these Implementing Regulations provide that they shall be recorded;**
(x) **date and purport of the decision on the request for limitation or revocation of the European patent;**
(y) **date and purport of the decision of the Enlarged Board of Appeal on the petition for review.**

Art.61(1)(b) European patent applications non-entitled
Art.135(3) Further processing
R.14 Stay of proceedings
R.20(1) Publication of the mention of the inventor
R.41(2)(c) Particulars of applicant
R.41(2)(d) Particulars of representative
R.78 Procedure where the proprietor of the patent is not entitled
R.142 Interruption of proceedings
R.152(11) Authorisation of an association

1 **Additional entries in the Register**
The contracting states communicate the date of lapse also after the opposition period or a final decision in opposition to inform the EPO that no further renewal fee payments under **Art.39(1)** need be expected. The data is entered in a special section of the Register under **R.143(1)(p)**, even if no opposition is pending. Some contracting states take long to inform the EPO. Up to date information can be obtained from the national patent offices.

The date of re-establishment of rights is only entered under **R.143(1)(u)** if there has been an actual loss of rights which has been entered in the Register.

Whether an appeal has been lodged cannot be derived from the Register but it can from the file (see **R.145** and **R.146**) and the Online Register (see notes below).

The Register mentions the payment of renewal fees (important for **R.14(4)**).

2 **Inspection of the Register**
The inspection of the Register follows most of the provisions in **R.145** (Procedures for the inspection of files) and **R.146** (Communication of information contained in the files). The Register can be inspected without stated reason and can be carried out in one of the following ways (A-XI,4):

- Inspection of the online European Patent Register can be carried out free of charge on the website 'https://register.epo.org'. The online register includes the data of the Register of European Patents (**R.143**).
- A register monitoring tool Register Alert is available on the website, providing e-mail alerts whenever a change occurs in the Register relating to a self-selected EP or Euro-PCT application (OJ 2012, 22 §3). The service is available nearly 24 hours a day, 7 days a week.
- The MyFiles tool allows users to organise their favourite files in folders and permits secure file inspection for accessing their files prior to publication. (OJ 2006, 535; 2007, 142; 2012, 22 §1)
- Telephone request for information (see **Ante Art.127**).

R. 143(2) The President of the European Patent Office may decide that entries other than those referred to in paragraph 1 shall be made in the European Patent Register.

1 **Additional entries in the Register**

The following additional entries are made in the Register (Dec. Pres., OJ 2014 A86):

1 'No opposition filed' after expiry of the opposition period without a notice of opposition having been filed;
2 'Patent specification corrected on (date)' in the event of correction of errors;
3 Date of despatch of supplementary European Search report;
4 Date of despatch of first examination communication;
5 Date of receipt of request for re-establishment of rights;
6 Refusal of request for re-establishment of rights;
7 Opponent's name, address and country of residence or principal place of business;
8 Name and business address of the opponent's representative;
9 New documents coming to light after the European search report has been drawn up; this does not include documents introduced in opposition proceedings, for which reference should be made to the file;
10 For international applications for which the EPO acts as designated Office:
   a) the international filing number;
   b) the international publication number;
   c) the international publication date;
11 Date of request for limitation or revocation of the European patent;
12 Requester's name, address and country of residence or principal place of business;
13 Date of petition for review by the Enlarged board of Appeal;
14 Petitioner's name, address and country of residence or principal place of business;
15 File number of the petition for review;
16 Date of refusal, withdrawal or deemed withdrawal of divisional application, if this gives rise to the latter's non-publication.
17 Date of despatch of examining division's first communication in the sense of **R.36(1)** as valid till 01.04.2014, where this communication was issued before 01.04.2014.
18 Date of despatch examining division's communication with search results under **R.164(2)** annexed.

R. 144 Parts of the file excluded from inspection

The parts of the file excluded from inspection under Article 128, paragraph 4, shall be:

(a) the documents relating to the exclusion of or objections to members of the Boards of Appeal or of the Enlarged Board of Appeal;

(b) draft decisions and notices, and all other documents, used for the preparation of decisions and notices, which are not communicated to the parties;

(c) the designation of the inventor, if he has waived his right to be mentioned under Rule 20, paragraph 1;

(d) any other document excluded from inspection by the President of the European Patent Office on the ground that such inspection would not serve the purpose of informing the public about the European patent application or the European patent.

Art.128(4) Inspection of files

R.20(1) Waiver of right to be mentioned as inventor
Implementation of: **Art.128(4)**
EPC 1973: **R.93**

1 **Exclusion from inspection under (a) and (d)**
The exclusion from inspection of documents relating to exclusion of members of boards of appeal and of the Enlarged Board of Appeal under **Art.24** should apply also to exclusion of members of departments of first instance.

By decision of the President the following documents are also excluded from file inspection under **R.144(d)**: medical certificates, documents relating to the issue of priority documents, file-inspection proceedings or the communication of information from the files, requests for exclusion from inspection and requests for accelerated search and accelerated examination under the PACE programme (Dec. Pres., Spec. Ed. 3 of OJ 2007, 125 Art.1(1)). Immoral statements in a filed patent application according to **R.48(1)(a)** are not published but are available in the file for inspection.

2 **Exclusion from inspection on request**
Documents other than those referred to in Art.1(1) of the above decision of the President may be excluded from inspection at the reasoned request of a party if their inspection would be prejudicial to the legitimate personal or economic interests of a natural or legal person (Art.1(2) of Dec. Pres). The EPO may also exclude such other documents of its own motion if their inspection would be prima facie prejudicial to the interest of a person other than a party. If the request is rejected in a decision, the documents will be open for inspection as soon as the decision becomes final. (Dec. Pres., Spec. Ed. 3 of OJ 2007, 125 Art.1(2); D-II,4.3)

A request for exclusion of a document will be rejected if the document is filed to prove inventive step, of which the public must be informed (**T516/89**).

Exceptionally and on a substantiated request documents filed as evidence may remain unconsidered in the proceedings, not put into the file and returned to the filing party. Such an exception exists if the interest of the party in having them returned unconsidered clearly prevail over the interests of the other party and the public interest. This may be the case if the documents were filed in breach of a confidentiality agreement and if they did not belong to the state of the art but were third-party statements filed against an opposition, and if the other parties involved agreed with the request. (**T760/89**)

A party may request the EPO to exclude an otherwise public non-patent document from file inspection for reasons of copyright. The EPO will usually grant the request and make only the cover page of the document available via file inspection, allowing the public to retrieve the entire document from another source. Such a document is not considered excluded from file inspection and can be used as evidence. (D-II,4.3; not in GL 2017)

In **T811/90** the EPO did not inform the proprietor of withdrawal of the opposition and its forthcoming decision to maintain the patent as granted. The board decided that amendments to the patent filed by the unaware proprietor should not be open for inspection and, since the amendments did not fall under **R.144**, they should be returned to the proprietor.

R. 145 Procedures for the inspection of files

Implementation of: **Art.128(4)**
EPC 1973: **R.94**

1 **General**
Files of European patent applications and patents can be inspected under **Art.128** on the website of the EPO and from copies of the files. The files of international applications for which the EPO acts as a designated or elected Office can also be inspected. The means of inspection are governed by **R.145(1)**, the method of inspection by **R.145(2)**. An overview of the procedure is given in the Notice of the EPO published in OJ 2006, 535.

The EPC has no provisions for the inspection of the Register. However, the inspection of the Register follows basically the same rules as the inspection of the files, and most methods of inspection are also free of charge. Online inspection of the Register can be made from the same website as online inspection of files (see **R.145(1):1**). See also **R.143(1):2** and **R.146**.

R. 145(1) Inspection of the files of European patent applications and patents shall either be of the original document, or of copies thereof, or of technical means of storage if the files are stored in this way.

1 **Means of file inspection**
The files of direct-European and Euro-PCT applications and patents are progressively being created, maintained and processed in electronic form using the Phoenix file system (Dec. Pres., Spec. Ed. 3 of OJ 2007, 121).

The means of inspecting the files is laid down in the Decision of the President, published in Spec. Ed. 3 of OJ 2007, 123.

The primary means of inspection is online through Register on the EPO website (https://register.epo.org). The online facility is available 24 hours a day, 7 days a week. Files not yet in electronic form will as a rule be made available online within ten working days from entry of the relevant number in the online search engine, provided they have not been destroyed under **R.147**. Non-scannable files will be made available in their original form or as filed. (Dec. Pres., Spec. Ed. 3 of OJ 2007, 123 Art.1)

The publication server at the EPO website 'https://data.epo.org/publication-server' provides free access to European patent applications and patents downloadable in SGML/XML and PDF formats. The site gives also direct access to the register entries of the selected patent document (OJ 2005, 126 §I.1). The server is available 24 hours a day, 7 days a week.

On request the EPO will furnish copies of file documents on paper or, if more than 100 pages, on electronic storage media (OJ 2006, 535 §2.1). The EPO will provide certified paper copies of priority documents, (see **R.53(1)** and **R.54**) or any other document on file, on request and for a fee (A-XI,2.2).

R. 145(2) The President of the European Patent Office shall determine all file-inspection arrangements, including the circumstances in which an administrative fee is payable.

1 **Request for inspection**
Online inspection of the files on the EPO website can be made without request and is free of charge (Schedule of fees pursuant to **Rfees3(1)**; Dec. Pres., Spec. Ed. 3 of OJ 2007, 123 Art.1(1); see also **R.143(1):1**).

Inspection of paper files is discouraged (OJ 2006, 535 §1.3); the EPO will make files available by furnishing copies on request and subject to payment of a fee (**R.145(2)**). A request form for inspection is available on the EPO website (A-XI,2.2). The request for inspection itself is excluded from public inspection (see **R.144:1**). The fee is fixed under **Rfees3(1)**, i.e. the amount is determined by the President and is published in the OJ (OJ 2006, 535 §2.1). A duly paid fee is not refunded. Parties and their representatives may inspect free of charge the files of proceedings in which they are involved. However, copies must be paid for (**Rfees3(1)**).

Inspection of the files of non-published applications under **Art.128(1),(2)** or (3) requires the filing of a request, grounds and proof. An applicant can inspect the file of his own application prior to its publication online through MyFiles, a secure portal on the EPO website (OJ 2012, 22 §1).

R. 146 Communication of information contained in the files

Subject to the restrictions laid down in Article 128, paragraphs 1 to 4, and in Rule 144, the European Patent Office may, upon request, communicate information concerning any file relating to a European patent application or European patent, subject to the payment of an administrative fee. However, the European Patent Office may refer to the option of file inspection where it deems this to be appropriate in view of the quantity of information to be supplied.

Art.128(1) No inspection before publication
Art.128(2) Early inspection with approval of applicant
Art.128(3) Inspection of parent from publication divisional
Art.128(4) Inspection after publication
R.144 Parts of the file excluded from inspection
Implementation of: **Art.128(4)**
EPC 1973: **R.95**

1 **General**

The provision is intended for simple questions not requiring too much effort on the part of the EPO, such as whether the application has been refused during the examination procedure or whether an opposition has been filed. Many of these questions can be answered by inspection of the Patent Register. The amount of the fee is fixed under **Rfees3(1)**.

R. 147 Constitution, maintenance and preservation of files

Amended by decision of the Administrative Council of 14.10.2015 and entering into force on 01.11.2016 (OJ 2015 A83; 2016 A90).
Implementation of: **Art.128(4)**
EPC 1973: **R.95a**

R. 147(1) The European Patent Office shall constitute, maintain and preserve files relating to all European patent applications and patents in electronic form.

R. 147(2) The President of the European Patent Office shall determine all necessary technical and administrative arrangements relating to the management of electronic files according to paragraph 1.

1 **Form of files**

The electronic files of European patent applications and international applications for which the EPO acts under the PCT are created, maintained and processed in an electronic file system, Phoenix (Dec. Pres., Spec. Ed. 3 of OJ 2007, 121).

R. 147(3) Documents incorporated in an electronic file shall be considered to be originals. The initial paper version of such documents shall only be destroyed after expiry of at least five years. This preservation period starts at the end of the year in which the document was incorporated in the electronic file.

1 **Electronic files and paper documents**
The reliability and accessibility of electronic storage have made the electronic files of the EPO the primary storage of documents; the electronically stored documents are considered to be originals (**R.147(3)**, first sentence). Documents filed on paper are scanned as images upon receipt, checked on quality and stored in the electronic file. In 2014 93% of the applications were filed electronically.

The paper documents are stored in boxes, not in files. Files in the EPC are electronic files. Hence, the preservation periods for files in **R.147(4)** and (5) relate to electronic files. **R.147(3)**, second and third sentence lay down a preservation period for paper documents. They are kept till five years from the end of the year in which the document was scanned and stored in the file. The five-year period provides legal certainty in that possible discrepancies between the paper document and the document in the file, which is regarded to be the original, will be noticed and the document can be re-scanned if the quality of the initial scan was inferior. The five-year keeping period allows the EPO to clear out their storage of paper documents. (CA71/15e)

The five-year period does not apply to record copies of PCT applications filed with the EPO on paper and kept by the EPO on behalf of the International Bureau (OJ 2016 A90 §5).

R. 147(4) Any files shall be preserved for at least five years from the end of the year in which:
(a) the application is refused or withdrawn or is deemed to be withdrawn;
(b) the patent is revoked by the European Patent Office; or
(c) the patent or the corresponding protection under Article 63, paragraph 2, lapses in the last of the designated States.

Art.63(2) Extended term of the European patent

1 **Keeping of files**
The files in the electronic file system of the EPO, Phoenix, are stored during the entire period of paragraph 4 and 5 (Spec. Ed. 3 of OJ 2007, 121 Art.2), i.e. at least five years after the application or patent ceases to exist.

The five-year period will be extended when the term of the patent is extended under **Art.63(2)**, e.g. on account of war or as compensation for lengthy authorisation procedure, such as for pharmaceuticals.

Electronic files relating to a case in which appeal or opposition proceedings have taken place will not be destroyed before 25 years after the date of filing (OJ 1990, 365).

The patent often lapses because of non-payment of renewal fees. As these fees are paid before the year in respect of which they are paid, the patent lapses about one year after the last payment of the renewal fee, dependent on national law. For example, if the last renewal fee is paid in 2018, the patent lapses in 2019, and the electronic file can be inspected at least up to 31.12.2024.

The entries in the Register relating to applications and patents that have been destroyed will not be affected. However, the fact that the files have been destroyed will not be recorded. A request for inspection of a file (**Art.128**) after it has been destroyed will be met with the response that the period for keeping the files has expired and it has therefore been destroyed. Any fees received in respect of the inspection (**R.145(2)**) will be refunded. (OJ 1990, 365)

R. 147(5) Without prejudice to paragraph 4, files relating to applications which have given rise to divisional applications under Article 76 or new applications under Article 61, paragraph 1(b), shall be preserved for at least the same period as the files relating to any one of these last applications. The same shall apply to files relating to any resulting European patents.

Art.61(1)(b) Application filed by non-entitled person

1 **Keeping of files of earlier applications**

The file of the parent application is retained at least as long as the divisional application exists, in order to allow file inspection to check the origin of the divisional application and assess a possible extension of subject-matter (**R.147(5)**).

Chapter X *Legal and administrative co-operation*

R. 148 Communications between the European Patent Office and the authorities of the Contracting States

Implementation of **Art.131**
EPC 1973: **R.97**

R. 148(1) Communications between the European Patent Office and the central industrial property offices of the Contracting States which arise out of the application of this Convention shall be effected directly between these authorities. Communications between the European Patent Office and the courts or other authorities of the Contracting States may be effected through the intermediary of the said central industrial property offices.

R. 148(2) Expenditure in respect of communications under paragraph 1 shall be borne by the authority making the communications, which shall be exempt from fees.

R. 149 Inspection of files by or via courts or authorities of the Contracting States

Implementation of **Art.131**
EPC 1973: **R.98**

R. 149(1) Inspection of the files of European patent applications or of European patents by courts or authorities of the Contracting States shall be of the original documents or of copies thereof; Rule 145 shall not apply.

R.145 Procedures for the inspection of files

R. 149(2) Courts or Public Prosecutors' offices of the Contracting States may, in the course of their proceedings, communicate to third parties files or copies thereof transmitted to them by the European Patent Office. Such communications shall be effected in accordance with Article 128 and shall not be subject to any fee.

Art.128 Inspection of files

R. 149(3) The European Patent Office shall, when transmitting the files, draw attention to the restrictions which may, under Article 128, paragraphs 1 and 4, apply to file inspection by third parties.

Art.128(1) No inspection before publication
Art.128(4) Inspection after publication

R. 150 Procedure for letters rogatory

Implementation of: **Art.131(2)**
EPC 1973: **R.99**

The provision indicates how requests from the EPO, e.g. for taking of evidence before a national court under Art.117, are transmitted to the national courts.

R. 150(1) Each Contracting State shall designate a central authority to receive letters rogatory issued by the European Patent Office and to transmit them to the court or authority competent to execute them.

R. 150(2) The European Patent Office shall draw up letters rogatory in the language of the competent court or authority or shall attach to such letters rogatory a translation into that language.

R. 150(3) Subject to paragraphs 5 and 6, the competent court or authority shall apply national law as to the procedures to be followed in executing such requests and, in particular, as to the appropriate measures of compulsion.

R. 150(4) If the court or authority to which the letters rogatory are transmitted is not competent to execute them, the letters rogatory shall be sent forthwith to the central authority referred to in paragraph 1. That authority shall transmit the letters rogatory either to the competent court or authority in that State, or to the European Patent Office where no court or authority is competent in that State.

R. 150(5) The European Patent Office shall be informed of the time when, and the place where, the enquiry or other legal measure is to take place and shall inform the parties, witnesses and experts concerned.

R. 150(6) If so requested by the European Patent Office, the competent court or authority shall permit the attendance of members of the department concerned and allow them to question any person giving evidence either directly or through the competent court or authority.

R. 150(7) The execution of letters rogatory shall not give rise to any reimbursement of fees or costs of any nature. Nevertheless, the State in which letters rogatory are executed has the right to require the Organisation to reimburse any fees paid to experts or interpreters and the costs arising from the procedure under paragraph 6.

R. 150(8) If the law applied by the competent court or authority obliges the parties to secure evidence and the competent court or authority is not able itself to execute the letters rogatory, that court or authority may, with the consent of the European Patent Office, appoint a suitable person to do so. When seeking such consent, the competent court or authority shall indicate the approximate costs which would result from this procedure. If the European Patent Office gives its consent, the Organisation shall reimburse any costs incurred; otherwise, the Organisation shall not be liable for such costs.

Chapter XI Representation

R. 151 Appointment of a common representative

Implementation of: Art.133(4)

EPC 1973: **R.100**

1 **General**
The provision must be interpreted in the light of the necessity for the EPO to have one person to address during proceedings. For **R.151** to apply, each party or his duly authorised representative has signed the document (request for grant, notice of opposition, etc.) giving rise to his participation (A-VIII,1.3) and the parties have not appointed a common representative themselves.

A communication sent by the EPO to the common representative is sufficient (**R.130(3)**); the other parties may not receive any communication from the EPO. The EPO assumes that all joint members are aware of a communication sent only to the common representative (**T1908/09** r.3.1). An opposition or appeal must be filed by the common representative mentioning all joint members (**Art.99(1)**:1.1, 1.5; **Art.107**:1, respectively).

R. 151(1) If there is more than one applicant and the request for grant of a European patent does not name a common representative, the applicant first named in the request shall be deemed to be the common representative. However, if one of the applicants is obliged to appoint a professional representative, this representative shall be deemed to be the common representative, unless the applicant first named has appointed a professional representative. The same shall apply to third parties acting in common in filing a notice of opposition or intervention and to joint proprietors of a European patent.

1 **Appointment of common representative by EPO**
If there is more than one applicant, the Request for Grant form should preferably contain the appointment of a common representative (**R.41(3)**) to ensure unity of procedure as required under **Art.118**. The appointment of a common representative in the form is not compulsory. If there is more than one applicant and no common representative is appointed, the EPO applies **R.151(1)** to assign a common representative, because the EPO needs one address for correspondence. The same applies to joint proprietors and to parties acting in common in filing a notice of opposition or intervention (**R.151(1)**, last sentence and A-VIII,1.3), filing a request for limitation or revocation (**R.92** and **R.41(3)**) and petition proceedings (**R18/09** r.6).

R.151(1) is formulated in a knotty way and case law on its interpretation is scarce (see e.g. **T755/09** r.5, 6; **T1908/09** r.3.1). A possible interpretation is:

1 Is there more than one applicant?
   a) No, then the EPO communicates with the applicant or his representative.
   b) Yes, then
2 Has an applicant or representative been appointed as common representative in the Request for Grant form (**R.41(3)**)?
   a) Yes, then the appointed applicant or representative is the common representative.
   b) No, then
3 Is one of the applicants obliged to be represented and has appointed a representative (**Art.133(2)**)?
   a) No, then the first-named applicant or his representative is the deemed common representative.
   b) Yes, then
4 Is the first-named applicant represented?
   a) Yes, then the representative of the first-named applicant is the deemed common representative.

b) No, then the representative of the first-named applicant obliged to be represented is the deemed common representative.

Although **R.151(1)** does not mention the 'first-named' in the above point 4b, it has been inserted to cover all possible cases of multiple applicants. The insertion is plausible on account of the application of the rule in the first sentence of **R.151(1)**: 'the first-named applicant not obliged to be represented is considered to be the common representative' to the case where multiple applicants are obliged to be represented (Singer Art.133, rdn.42).

The above rule has the following undesirable consequence. If an application has two applicants who need not be represented and only the second-named applicant has appointed a representative, the rule appoints the first-named, not-represented applicant as the common representative, whereas the EPO prefers as common representative the representative of the second-named represented applicant.

2 **Acts by parties acting in common**

Parties acting in common, either applicants, proprietors or opponents, can only act through the common representative. If one of these parties, not being the common representative, carries out a procedural act, the EPO will not admit the act. E.g. an opponent not being the common representative who files a submission is regarded as a non-entitled person and the submission is treated as an act for which a signature is missing; the EPO will request a rectification under **R.50(3)** by having the common representative sign the submission.

R. 151(2) If the European patent application is transferred to more than one person, and such persons have not appointed a common representative, paragraph 1 shall apply mutatis mutandis. If such application is not possible, the European Patent Office shall invite such persons to appoint a common representative within a period to be specified. If this invitation is not complied with, the European Patent Office shall appoint the common representative.

1 **Appointment of common representative after transfer**

The appointment of a deemed common representative by the EPO according to **R.151(1)** applies equally to the transfer of the application, patent or opposition during grant, opposition or appeal proceedings to more than one person who have not appointed a common representative. The application of **R.151(1)** may be not be possible, if, e.g., heirs of an applicant cannot agree on the representation. In such cases **R.151(2)** obliges the EPO to request the new applicants to appoint a common representative within two months; otherwise, the EPO will appoint the common representative itself.

R.151(2) does not cover all possibilities that can arise after a transfer, such as where the assets of the first named applicant are inherited by one person obliged to be represented but who has not appointed a representative. The EPO covers these cases by not limiting the application of the last two sentences of **R.151(2)** to the situation of the first sentence, i.e. to a transfer to more than one person, but extending it to all cases where the appointment of a common representative after a transfer is not provided for in the EPC (J35/92).

R. 152 Authorisations

Implementation of: **Art.134(1)**
EPC 1973: **R.101**

1 **General**

A representative acting before the EPO must file a signed authorisation only in the cases set down by the President (**R.152(1)**; A-VIII,1.5). On the one hand, the EPO will relieve itself of the administrative burden of authorisations, as abuse is rare. On the other hand, the representatives in private practice often want an authorisation of their client in order to be able to recover their costs from the client. The decision of the President on authorisation (Dec. Pres., Spec. Ed. 3 of OJ 2007, 128) is a compromise, which requires filing of an authorisation only in cases where the status of the representative is not clear.

An authorisation on behalf of more than one applicant must be signed by all applicants (A-VIII,3.4).

See **Art.133:2** for details of authorisation.

R. 152(1) The President of the European Patent Office shall determine the cases in which a signed authorisation shall be filed by representatives acting before the European Patent Office.

1 **Compulsory filing of authorisation**

The President has determined the cases where an authorisation is to be filed (Dec. Pres., Spec. Ed. 3, L.1. of OJ 2007, 128). When in such a case the representative does not file the authorisation of his own motion, the EPO will invite him to do so within a period of at least two months (**R.132(2)**).

A professional representative whose name appears on the list of the EPO and who identifies himself as such will be required to file a signed authorisation in the circumstances set out in paragraphs (1) to (4) below. An original authorisation and one copy must be filed (Dec. Pres.; **T267/08** r. 5). Any individual authorisation submitted is placed on file even if it has not been requested. The EPO does not check authorisations on deficiencies. The issue of authorisation will in general be raised during the examination of formalities under **R.57(h)**. The procedure for correction is set out in **R.57:9**.

The EPO requires filing of an authorisation, preferably on the special EPO form, in the following cases:

1 If the EPO is informed of a change of representative involving professional representatives who are not members of the same association and the EPO is not notified that the previous representative's authorisation has terminated, then, in view of **R.152(6)**, the new representative must file, together with his appointment, an individual authorisation or a reference to a general authorisation already on file. If he does not, he will be requested to do so within a period to be specified by the EPO. If the EPO is informed before the end of this period that the previous representative's authorisation has terminated, the request may be disregarded. The EPO sends the previous representative a copy of the individual authorisation or notifies him of the number of the general authorisation and the name of the new representative, and informs him that the subsequent proceedings will be conducted with the new representative. (Dec. Pres., Spec. Ed. 3 of OJ 2007, 128 Art.1(2))

Note, that a withdrawal from representation does not automatically terminate an automatic debit order. Termination requires a separate revocation of the automatic debit order to be filed with the withdrawal. The EPO does not require an authorisation if a representative other than the appointed one and not being a member of the same association or law firm performs a procedural act on behalf of a party, provided that it is apparent from the file that he is acting at the request of that party. (A-VIII,1.5; not in GL 2017)

2 The EPO also requires an authorisation if the circumstances of a specific case necessitate this, particularly in case of doubt as to the professional representative's entitlement to act. (Dec. Pres., Spec. Ed. 3 of OJ 2007, 128 Art.1(3))

3 **R.152(1)** makes an exception to the general obligation to file an authorisation only for professional representatives. Hence, the legal practitioner of **Art.134(8)** and the employee of **Art.133(3)**, if they are not professional representatives, must file a signed authorisation or a reference to a general authorisation under **R.152(4)** already on file. If not filed together with the appointment, the EPO will request the practitioner or the employee, respectively, to file an authorisation within a period to be specified by it. (Dec. Pres., Spec. Ed. 3 of OJ 2007, 128 Art.2, 3)

4 In Euro-PCT proceedings a person representing a client in the capacity of legal practitioner or employee is required to file an authorisation only if he has not already filed an authorisation expressly covering proceedings established by the EPC with the EPO as receiving Office (A-VIII,1.5).

2 **Authorisation for divisional application**
A representative acting for a parent application is not automatically authorised to act for a divisional application. He will be validly authorised if a general authorisation covers divisionals, the authorisation for the parent application expressly states coverage of divisionals, or a separate authorisation covers the divisional.

R. 152(2) Where a representative fails to file such an authorisation, the European Patent Office shall invite him to do so within a period to be specified. The authorisation may cover one or more European patent applications or European patents and shall be filed in the corresponding number of copies.

R. 152(3) Where the requirements of Article 133, paragraph 2, have not been satisfied, the same period shall be specified for the appointment of a representative and the filing of the authorisation.

Art.133(2) Compulsory representation

1 **Authorisation of applicant from a non-contracting state**
Where the applicant has neither residence nor place of business in a contracting state and has not appointed a representative according to **Art.133(2)**, the request for appointment and authorisation will be sent to him. An office period of normally two months will be specified for filing both the appointment and the authorisation. The period may be extended according to **R.132**. The authorisation can also be filed by the applicant, even if he is obliged to be represented under **Art.133(2)**, because fulfilling the requirement to be represented is not itself a procedural step within the meaning of **Art.133(2)** (A-VIII,1.5). When the authorisation is not filed in due time, the sanction of **R.152(6)** follows.

R. 152(4) A general authorisation may be filed enabling a representative to act in respect of all the patent transactions of a party. A single copy shall suffice.

1 **General authorisation**
A party can file a general authorisation enabling a representative to represent that party in all its patent matters. It is recommended to use the special form for this purpose (OJ 2007, 27). The EPO will assign a number to the general authorisation; which number can e.g. be entered in the Request for Grant form on filing a patent application.

The representative need not file a separate authorisation for each case anymore but can simply quote the registration number of the general authorisation. A general authorisation may also enable an association of representatives in the sense of **R.152(11)**. Note, that legal practitioners are not covered by an authorisation of an association (see **R.152(11):1**). The Legal Division has authority to register general authorisations and to examine whether the persons mentioned in the authorisation are entitled under the EPC to represent the authorising party (**J9/99** r.1.5).

Even when a general authorisation is filed or referred to in a specific case, a representative has still to be appointed (**J17/98** hnI).

A general authorisation is also valid for acting before the EPO as designated or elected Office according to the PCT, but not automatically for acting before the EPO as receiving office, ISA or IPEA. The authorisation must expressly give permission to act in the international phase.

R. 152(5) The President of the European Patent Office may determine the form and content of:
(a) an authorisation relating to the representation of persons under Article 133, paragraph 2;
(b) a general authorisation.

Art.133(2) Compulsory representation
(a) This has not yet been done
(b) EPO Form 1004 (**R.152(4)**).

R. 152(6) If a required authorisation is not filed in due time, any procedural steps taken by the representative, other than the filing of a European patent application, shall be deemed not to have been taken, without prejudice to any other legal consequences provided for by this Convention.

1 **Effect of not filing an authorisation**
The office period of **R.152(2)** for filing the authorisation can be extended (**R.132**). Failure to observe the period can be redressed by further processing. The EPO informs the party of the nullity of his procedural steps (A-VIII,1.7).

The phrase 'without prejudice' in the provision means that other legal consequences may follow the consequence set out in **R.152(6)**. For example, when a representative files an opposition for a party and, upon request of the board of appeal, fails to provide a signed original authorisation and copy in due time, the EPO will consider the opposition void and reimburse the opposition and appeal fees (**T1700/11** r.9-10).

2 **Invalid authorisation**
When the EPO is informed that a representative has acted before the EPO on behalf of a party without being instructed to do so and without filing a valid authorisation, it will consider the proceedings null and void and reimburse all fees paid to the EPO (**J12/88**).

R. 152(7) Paragraphs 2 and 4 shall apply to the withdrawal of an authorisation.

R. 152(8) A representative shall be deemed to be authorised until the termination of his authorisation has been communicated to the European Patent Office.

1 **Communication of termination to EPO**
Sending a termination of an authorisation by a party to a representative is not effective before the EPO. The termination becomes effective before the EPO only on the date the EPO receives the termination. (**R4/15** r.3)

R. 152(9) Unless it expressly provides otherwise, an authorisation shall not terminate vis-à-vis the European Patent Office upon the death of the person who gave it.

R. 152(10) If a party appoints several representatives, they may act either jointly or singly, notwithstanding any provisions to the contrary in the communication of their appointment or in the authorisation.

R. 152(11) The authorisation of an association of representatives shall be deemed to be an authorisation of any representative who can provide evidence that he practises within that association.

1 **Authorisation of an association**
The provision allows a party to authorize several representatives as an association instead of singly. The authorisation of an association is deemed to be an authorisation of any representative practising within that association; each individual member of the association is entitled to act before the EPO, not the association itself. An advantage is that changes in the composition of the association only require a single registration with the EPO instead of separately for each file the firm is handling. The EPO keeps an internal list of representatives that have provided evidence that they practise within a given association. (**J8/10** r.5, 7)

The authorisation covers only professional representatives. Legal practitioners of an association are excluded from authorisation through an association, to avoid that a legal practitioner would be regarded authorised under **R.152(11)**, whereas he would not be under **R.152(1)** if he has not filed an authorisation (**J8/10** r.11; see **Art.134(8):1**). The association includes private practices and patent departments of companies (**J16/96** r.4 and Dec. Pres. OJ 2013, 500).

2 **Registration and appointment of an association**
An association of representatives must be registered with the Legal Division to enable its use in appointments and authorisations. The use of form 52304 is recommended. The Legal Division informs the applicant of the registration number of the association. (OJ 2013, 535 section I)

The association is appointed by entering its name and registration number in the same box of the Request for Grant form. The address in the form, which the EPO will use for notifying communications, may be different from the registered address. Documents submitted to the EPO can be signed by any member of the association; in addition to the signature, the name of the member and of the association and its registration number must be provided. (OJ 2013, 535 section I)

The association may be cited in authorisations. If the authorisation is a general authorisation, the appointment can also cite the registration number of the association issued by the Legal Division (see **Art.133:2.2**).

A general authorisation permits appointment of a group of representatives without mentioning them individually (**Art.133:2.1**), similar to a registered association. However, the general authorisation is linked to a specific party, whereas the association is independent of parties.

R. 153 Attorney-client evidentiary privilege

Amended by decision of the Administrative Council of 21.10.2008, which entered into force on 01.04.2009. The amendment added the word 'client' as clarification to the title. (OJ 2008, 513)
Implementation of: **Art.134a(1)**
EPC 1973: No corresponding provision

1 **General**
Art.134a(1)(d) bestows competence on the Administrative Council to adopt provisions governing the obligation of confidentiality of professional representatives and the privilege from disclosure in proceedings before the EPO in respect of communications between a professional representative and his client or any other person.

The obligation of confidentiality binding professional representatives is provided for by Article 2 of the Regulation on discipline for professional representatives. As some legal systems distinguish between this obligation of confidentiality and an evidentiary privilege protecting the confidentiality of attorney-client communications, **R.153** entrenches such an evidentiary privilege for communications between professional representatives and their clients which are subject to the representative's professional obligation of confidentiality. **R.153(1)** draws its language from the definition of the evidentiary privilege in US law as cited from Wigmore's Evidence in the Bristol- Myers Squibb v. Rhone Poulenc Rorer case (Southern District of New York, 19 April 1999).

It is clear that the word 'client' in **R.153(1)** encompasses any person for whom the representative may be acting, whether an individual or a corporation, the representative's employer, the associated or subsidiary company of the employer, etc.

The reference to Article 2 of the Regulation on discipline has been added to align the provision more closely with the US requirement that such communications should be of a confidential nature. The wording of the provision makes clear that only such communications subject to the representatives' obligation of secrecy are covered by the evidentiary privilege.

Article 2 of the Regulation on discipline reads:

'Professional secrecy. A professional representative shall be bound not to disclose information accepted by him in confidence in the exercise of his duties, unless he is released from this obligation.' (Spec. Ed. 1 of OJ 2003)

2 **Extent of privilege**
National law of most EPC contracting states does not contain a provision on privilege. The provision in the disciplinary rules of the epi do not confer the equivalent of a privilege laid down in law. As a first step towards protecting correspondence between representatives and parties for US discovery the Administrative Council has made use of its power under **Art.134a(1)(d)** to include **R.153** on attorney evidentiary privilege. It is not certain whether US courts will accept a provision in international law for the privilege; they may require a basis in national law. EPC contracting states are therefore strongly advised to include the privilege in their national civil laws.

In US discovery procedures parties are obliged to grant other parties inspection of all documents in their possession relating to the case in suit. Only documents covered by attorney client privilege are excepted from inspection. US case law on which documents are covered by the privilege is not consistent.

A US court will probably invoke the privilege of **R.153** if the document is a communication between a European representative and a party relating to an advice sought by the client, which is kept confidential and relates to proceedings before the EPO. The privilege will probably not cover communications that do not relate to an advice, do not relate to proceedings before the EPO, or are not kept confidential. As a consequence, an opinion on infringement of a European patent will not be covered by the privilege in a US court, because it does not relate to proceedings before the EPO. Note, however, that the privilege under **R.153** is broader and does cover infringement opinions.

R. 153(1) Where advice is sought from a professional representative in his capacity as such, all communications between the professional representative and his client or any other person, relating to that purpose and falling under Article 2 of the Regulation on discipline for professional representatives, are permanently privileged from disclosure in proceedings before the European Patent Office, unless such privilege is expressly waived by the client.

1 **Privilege from disclosure**

The wording of the provision makes clear that the privilege from disclosure covers only correspondence between representatives and clients. Employees acting for their employer under **Art.133(3)** are not covered by the privilege. It is not yet clear whether a representative as employee, e.g. a representative in a patent department of a company, is protected by the privilege.

The privilege covers all communications between a representative and his client in proceedings before the EPO, unless the privilege is waived by the client (**R.153(1)**). It does not relate to national proceedings, such as infringement proceedings. The protection of correspondence in these proceedings must be dealt with on a national level.

R. 153(2) Such privilege from disclosure shall apply, in particular, to any communication or document relating to:

(a) the assessment of the patentability of an invention;

(b) the preparation or prosecution of a European patent application;

(c) any opinion relating to the validity, scope of protection or infringement of a European patent or a European patent application.

1 **Documents covered by privilege**

The list of documents in **R.153(2)** that are covered by the privilege is non-exhaustive ('in particular').

R. 154 Amendment of the list of professional representatives

Implementation of: **Art.134(1)**
EPC 1973: **R.102**

1 **The list of professional representatives**
A person appearing on the list of professional representatives must pay an annual subscription to the Institute of Professional Representatives (epi), established under **Art.134a(1)(a)**. See **ADA.8** for the possibility to pay the subscription by debiting a deposit account of the EPO by direct debiting mandate.

R. 154(1) The entry of a professional representative shall be deleted from the list of professional representatives if he so requests or if, despite a reminder, he fails to pay the applicable annual subscription to the Institute within five months from either:
(a) 1 January for members on the list at that date; or
(b) the date of entry for members entered on the list after 1 January of the year for which the subscription is due.

Amended by decision of the Administrative Council of 28.06.2018, which will enter into force on 1.01.2019. (OJ 2018 A57)

1 **Deletion of entry because of non-payment of subscription**
A representative must pay the annual subscription for a certain year to the epi before 1 June of that year or, if he was entered on the list after 1 January, five months from the date of entry. He will receive a reminder before expiry of the period.

If not paid within five months, the Legal Division will send the representative an **Art.113** communication with the intention to remove his name from the list and an invitation to comment. Next, the EPO takes the appealable decision and removes his name from the list. Payment of the subscription before the period for filing an appeal has expired will close the procedure for removal and the representative will remain on the list.

The above procedure usually allows the deletion of the representative before the end of the year, so that epi would not be obliged to send him an invoice for the next year. (CA/46/18)

R. 154(2) Without prejudice to any disciplinary measures taken under Article 134a, paragraph 1(c), the entry of a professional representative may be deleted ex officio only:
(a) in the event of his death or legal incapacity;
(b) where he is no longer a national of one of the Contracting States, unless he was granted an exemption under Article 134, paragraph 7(a);
(c) where he no longer has his place of business or employment within one of the Contracting States.

Art.134(7)(a) National of a contracting state
Art.134a(1)(c) Disciplinary power of epi
'without prejudice' = 'without detriment (to existing right or claim)'

R. 154(3) Any person entered on the list of professional representatives under Article 134, paragraphs (2) or (3), whose entry has been deleted shall, upon request, be re-entered on that list if the conditions for deletion no longer exist.

Art.134(2) Entry on the list by passing eqe
Art.134(3) Entry on the list as grandfather

PART VIII IMPLEMENTING REGULATIONS TO PART VIII OF THE CONVENTION

R. 155 Filing and transmission of the request for conversion

Implementation of: **Art.135(1)**
EPC 1973: **Art.135(2)**, **Art.136(1)** + (2)

R. 155(1) The request for conversion referred to in Article 135, paragraph 1(a) or (b), shall be filed within three months of the withdrawal of the European patent application, or of the communication that the application is deemed to be withdrawn, or of the decision refusing the application or revoking the European patent. The effect of the European patent application under Article 66 shall lapse if the request is not filed in due time.

Art.135(1)(a) Conversion if application deemed withdrawn under Art.77(3)
Art.135(1)(b) Conversion in other cases provided by national law
Art.66 Equivalence of European filing with national filing

1 **Period for requesting conversion**
Since the request in the case of **Art.135(1)(a)** must be filed with a national office according to **Art.135(2)**, national law must be applied for calculating the three-month period. If the national office has not forwarded the application in due time under **Art.77**, a remedy under national law should be sought.

In the case of **Art.135(1)(b)** the request must be submitted to the EPO according to **Art.135(3)**. Hence, the rules of the EPC and not the national rules for determining periods apply, because the three-month period must be kept before the EPO (**Art.120**). If the period is not observed, further processing according to **Art.121** and **R.135** is possible.

R.155(3) contains a 20-month period from the filing or priority date running in parallel with the three-month period of **R.155(1)**. Hence, if the request has not been filed within the shorter of the 20-month period and the three-month period, the effect of **Art.66** lapses, i.e. the converted application does not retain the priority and filing date of the European application. (A-IV,6)

R. 155(2) When transmitting the request for conversion to the central industrial property offices of the Contracting States specified in the request, the central industrial property office concerned or the European Patent Office shall attach to the request a copy of the file relating to the European patent application or European patent.

R. 155(3) Article 135, paragraph 4, shall apply if the request for conversion referred to in Article 135, paragraphs 1(a) and (2), is not transmitted before the expiry of a period of twenty months from the date of filing or, if priority has been claimed, the date of priority.

Amended by decision of the Administrative Council of 21.10.2008, which entered into force on 01.04.2009. The amendment replaced the word 'or' after '1(a)' by 'and'. (OJ 2008, 513)
Art.135(1)(a) Conversion if application deemed withdrawn under Art77(3)
Art.135(2) Filing of the request for conversion of par 1(a)
Art.135(4) Effect of late-filed request

R. 156 Information to the public in the event of conversion

Implementation of: **Art.135(1)**
EPC 1973: **R.103**

1 **General**
The rule realizes the right of the public to know the origin of the national application that originated from the conversion of a European application.

R. 156(1) The documents accompanying the request for conversion under Rule 155, paragraph 2, shall be made available to the public by the central industrial property office under the same conditions and to the same extent as documents relating to national proceedings.

R.155(2) Transmission of request for conversion to national office

1 **Obligation to publish documents**
The documents related to the conversion are open for public inspection according to **R.156(1)** and national law, not according to **Art.128**.

R. 156(2) The printed specification of the national patent resulting from the conversion of a European patent application shall mention that application.

PART IX IMPLEMENTING REGULATIONS TO PART X OF THE CONVENTION

R. 157 The European Patent Office as a receiving Office

Implementation of: **Art.151**
EPC 1973: **Art.151(1)**, **Art.152(2)**, **R.104** + **Art.152(3)**

R. 157(1) The European Patent Office shall be competent to act as a receiving Office within the meaning of the PCT if the applicant is a resident or national of a Contracting State to this Convention and to the PCT. Without prejudice to paragraph 3, if the applicant chooses the European Patent Office as a receiving Office, the international application shall be filed directly with the European Patent Office. Article 75, paragraph 2, shall apply mutatis mutandis.

Art.75(2) Requirement for compulsory filing at national office of contracting state
R.157(3) Time limit for forwarding an international application by contracting state

1 **EPO as receiving Office**
The requirements for filing an international application with the EPO as PCT receiving Office are set out in Not. EPO OJ 2014 A33.

R.157(1) sets out the competence of the EPO acting as a rO under the PCT. The EPO is a competent receiving Office for residents and nationals of an EPC contracting state. Under **R.19.1** PCT, all contracting states except Liechtenstein and Belgium allow its residents and nationals to file an international application with its national office, the EPO or the International Bureau as rO, at the choice of the applicant (see PCT Applicant's Guide, International Phase (AG-IP), Annex B1 and PCT §2.3). The competent rO for Belgian residents and nationals is the EPO or the IB (OJ 2018 A17). An international application of a Belgian resident or national which may be of interest for national security must still be filed with the Belgium national office (see e.g. **Art.151**, second sentence).

The provision also states that an international application must be filed directly with the EPO if the latter has been chosen as a rO.

The reference to **R.157(3)** and **Art.75(2)** in **R.157(1)** provides an exception to the obligation to file directly with the EPO. **Art.75(2)** EPC prescribes that under national law, an international patent application may have to be filed nationally first, e.g. for reasons of national security. The effect of national security restrictions when the EPO acts as rO is dealt with in PCT §2.3.2. The national office will transmit the international application to the EPO as rO before the time limit prescribed in **R.157(3)** and the EPO will accord the date of receipt by the national office as the date of filing of the application (A-II,4.1.5(i)). An international application filed with a national office for transmittal to the EPO as rO but not complying with the national provisions mentioned in **Art.75(2)**, e.g. because the application turns out not to be prejudicial to national security, will be accorded the date of receipt with the national office as the date of filing.

The permitted methods of filing an international application with the EPO are governed by provisions of the PCT, decisions of the President and the Guidelines (see E-IX,1; Euro-PCT Guide §49; and Not. EPO OJ 2014 A33). The EPO as rO accepts international applications filed electronically using EPO Online Filing (OLF) Software, EPO CMS Online Filing, or EPO Web-Form Filing (OJ 2018 A45), or using PCT-SAFE software or ePCT-Filing (Dec. Pres. OJ 2014 A107). Applications must be filed in one copy (OJ 2006 p.439) and filing by fax requires confirmation (OJ 2007 se3 A3 Art.7).

2 **Filing date requirements**

The EPO will respond differently when an applicant files a European patent application to when an applicant files an international application.

If the applicant files a direct European patent application, a date of filing is accorded when the requirements of **R.40(1)** EPC are met (see also **Art.80** EPC). Hence, no claims are required and the EPO allows filing of a European patent application by reference to a previously filed application.

If the applicant files an international application with the EPO as receiving Office, the filing date requirements are governed by **Art.11** and **R.20** PCT. If the EPO acts as rO, it will follow the PCT requirements for according the international filing date; this implies that the application must contain at least one claim. The PCT does not allow the filing of an international application by reference to a previously filed application. Also, if an applicant subsequently wishes to file missing parts of the description or missing drawings, he must realize that the requirements under the EPC (**R.56** EPC) differ from those under the PCT (**R.20.5** and **R.20.6** PCT).

3 **Acknowledgment of receipt**

Upon receipt of an international application filed by hand, post or fax, the EPO automatically generates an acknowledgement of receipt and issues it by post within four working days. The acknowledgement will by issued directly by fax or directly by post on request and payment of a fee. The applicant should not include an acknowledgement form in the application documents. The acknowledgement lists the various documents filed (PCT request, description, etc.) but does not verify the number of sheets of the documents, in accordance with the requirements under **R.35(2)**. (Not. EPO OJ 2010 p.642 §4-8, 14-17)

When an international application is received on-line, an acknowledgement will be issued electronically within the submission session (see **R.2(1):7**).

R. 157(2) Where the European Patent Office acts as a receiving Office under the PCT, the international application shall be filed in English, French or German. The President of the European Patent Office may determine that the international application and any related item shall be filed in more than one copy.

1 **Language and number of copies**

R.157(2) implements the language provision **R.12.1** PCT and states that the languages of the international application accepted by the EPO as rO are English, French and German. **Art.14(2)** is not applicable when filing an international application with the EPO, because PCT provisions prevail over EPC provisions according to **Art.150(2)**. Hence, an international application in Swedish filed with the EPO as rO does not comply with **Art.11(1)(ii)** PCT; hence, the remedy of **R.19.4** PCT will be carried out, making the IB the rO instead (see PCT §2.3.3). See PCT §2.3.2 for the EPO as rO. **R.157(2)** explicitly mentions the three languages, English, French and German, rather than referring to the languages of **Art.14(1)**, because **Art.14(1)** does not apply when filing an international application with the EPO.

An international application must be filed in one copy. The EPO has not used the possibility of **R.157(2)**, second sentence to require more copies. (Dec. Pres. OJ 2006 p.439).

R. 157(3) If an international application is filed with an authority of a Contracting State for transmittal to the European Patent Office as the receiving Office, the Contracting State shall ensure that the application reaches the European Patent Office not later than two weeks before the end of the thirteenth month from filing or, if priority is claimed, from the date of priority.

1 **Transmittal of international application to EPO as rO**

R.157(3) EPC requires that the national office of an EPC contracting state must ensure that an international application filed with it under **R.157(1)**, last sentence (national security), has been received by the EPO two weeks before the end of the 13th month from filing or, where appropriate, the priority date. There is no sanction for non-compliance under the EPC. See PCT §2.3.2 for the effect of national security provisions on the operation of the EPO as rO.

If an international application is filed through a national office as an intermediary and does not reach the International Bureau (IB) in the prescribed period, it will be considered withdrawn (**Art.12(3)** PCT). The period is 3 months (**R.22.3** PCT) after the IB has notified the applicant that it has not received the record copy of the application within 14 months of the priority date (**R.22.1(c)** PCT) or that the record copy has not been received after the applicant has become active (**R.22.1(g)** PCT). The notification of the applicant allows him to take action, thereby lessening the harshness of the 14-month period. See also PCT §2.3.2.

R. 157(4) The transmittal fee for the international application shall be paid within one month of filing the application.

1 **Transmittal fee**

The amount of the transmittal fee levied by the EPO under **R.14.1** PCT for transmitting copies of the international application to other PCT authorities and for performing its tasks as rO is fixed in **Rfees2(1)18** (see also PCT §2.8.2). The transmittal fee must be paid within one month of filing the application (**R.157(4)**).

R. 158 The European Patent Office as an International Searching Authority or International Preliminary Examining Authority

Implementation of: **Art.152**
EPC 1973: **R.105**

R. 158(1) In the case of Article 17, paragraph 3(a) PCT, an additional international search fee shall be paid for each further invention for which an international search is to be carried out.

Art.17(3)(a) PCT Non-unity found during the search

1 **International search fee**
There is no specific basis in the Articles or Rules of the EPC for payment of the search fee in respect of an international search (**R.16.1** PCT) when the EPO acts as ISA. However, this fee is referred to in **Rfees2(1)2**, which directly refers to the corresponding **R.16.1** PCT. Note that **R.158(1)** only refers to *additional* international search fees, which become relevant upon a lack of unity finding.

Note also that there are some slight discrepancies between the terms used in the EPC and the PCT relating to international search. The term 'international search fee' used in **R.158(1)** EPC does not exist in the PCT; **R.16.1** PCT refers to the 'search fee'. This is in contrast to the wording of **Rfees2(1)2** which more closely matches the term in the PCT. Moreover, the 'additional international search fee' in **R.158(1)** EPC should be the 'additional fee' according to **R.40.1** PCT. **R.40.2(a)** PCT allows the ISA to determine the amount of the 'additional fee', the EPO having chosen the 'additional fee' to be equal to the 'search fee'.

The non-unity procedure before the ISA is given in PCT §4.3 and the procedure when the EPO is ISA in PCT §4.8.

During a supplementary international search, the EPO as SISA can raise a non-unity objection according to **R.45bis.6** PCT, in which case the PCT procedure is followed, see PCT §4.9.1 (OJ 2010 p.316 §7).

R. 158(2) In the case of Article 34, paragraph 3(a) PCT, an additional fee for international preliminary examination shall be paid for each further invention for which the international preliminary examination is to be carried out.

Art.34(3)(a) PCT Non-unity found during the examination

1 **International preliminary examination fee**
There is no specific basis in the Articles or Rules of the EPC for payment of the preliminary examination fee (**R.58.1** PCT) when the EPO acts as IPEA. However, this fee is referred to in **Rfees2(1)19**, which directly refers to the corresponding **R.58** PCT. Note that **R.158(2)** only refers to *additional* international preliminary examination fees, which become relevant upon a lack of unity finding during international preliminary examination.

Note also that there are some slight discrepancies between the terms used in the EPC and the PCT relating to international preliminary examination. The term 'fee for international preliminary examination' used in **R.158(2)** EPC is referred to as the 'preliminary examination fee' in **R.58** PCT. This is in contrast to the wording of **Rfees2(1)19** which more closely matches the term in the PCT.

The non-unity procedure before the IPEA is given in PCT §6.3.3 and the procedure when the EPO is the ISA in PCT §6.6.4.

R. 158(3) Where an additional fee has been paid under protest, the European Patent Office shall examine the protest in accordance with Rule 40.2(c) to (e) or Rule 68.3(c) to (e) PCT, subject to payment of the prescribed protest fee. Further details concerning the procedure shall be determined by the President of the European Patent Office.

R.40.2(c) PCT Non-unity procedure before ISA
R.68.3(c) PCT Non-unity procedure before IPEA

1 **Protest procedure**
The EPO, acting as ISA or IPEA, applies a protest procedure in accordance with **R.40.2** and **R.68.3** PCT, where an applicant, invited to pay additional international search or preliminary examination fees, wishes to do so 'under protest'. Review panels are responsible for examination of protests, each review panel being made up of three examiners (OJ 2015 A59). See OJ 2010 p.322 §5-7 for details of the protest procedure and protest fee payable upon filing the protest (see **R.40.1(iii)** / **R.68.2(v)** PCT; **Rfees2(1)21**). See also PCT §4.3.2; 4.8; 6.3.3; 6.6.4.

2 **Non-unity opinion and review procedure**
The non-unity procedures as presently applied before the ISA and IPEA are set out in PCT §4.3 and §6.3.3 and the procedures when the EPO is the ISA or IPEA in PCT §4.8 and §6.6 respectively. For non-unity during supplementary international search see PCT §4.9.1 (OJ 2010 p.316 §7 and p.322 §11-12).

R. 159 The European Patent Office as a designated or elected Office – Requirements for entry into the European phase

Implementation of: **Art.153**
EPC 1973: **R.107, Art.153(2)**

1 **Entry into the European phase**
An international application which has been accorded an international filing date and designates the EPO is equivalent to a regular European application and is referred to as a Euro-PCT application (**Art.153(2)**). The EPO may only process such an application after expiry of the 31-month period of **R.159(1)** (Art.23(1) PCT) or upon receipt of an express request at an earlier date (Art.23(2) PCT). Hence, a Euro-PCT application is a regular, pending European application as from its international filing date, but burdened with a temporal processing prohibition. The EPO may only process the application once the prohibition has been lifted (**G1/09** r.3.2.5; see also **J18/09**).

In view of the above, the phrase 'entry into the European phase' does not mean that the international application becomes a European application only on entry. In fact, the international application has been a European patent application since the international filing date. The title of **R.159** might suggest that the 'entry' means 'start of processing the application'. However, the EPO has already started processing when assessing compliance with **R.159**, even when these requirements have not been fulfilled. The 'entry into the European phase' should probably be regarded as meaning the 'start of prosecution of the application by the EPO'.

The EPO may not require compliance of the form and content of the application to requirements of the EPC different from or additional to those of the PCT (**Art.27(1)** PCT). However, it may require acts to be carried out similar to those due for a direct European patent application, such as payment of fees and filing a request for examination, including acts for which the period has expired during the international phase. The EPO may not require that the applicant carries out these acts before the expiry of the 31-month period, because of the processing prohibition of **Art.23(1)** PCT. The possibility for a later execution is provided by **Art.150(2)** and implemented in **R.159(1)**: all periods for acts under the EPC that would have expired in the international phase are extended to the expiry of the period for entry into the European phase. Paragraphs **(d)**, **(f)** and **(g)** of **R.159(1)** and **R.162** define the periods for requesting examination and paying the designation fee, renewal fees and claims fees as the longer of the period for entry into the European phase and the corresponding period for a direct European patent application.

2 Procedure for entry into the European phase

The procedure for entry into the regional phase before the EPO is set out in **R.159** - **R.162** and PCT §7.2 and §7.4. See also the Euro-PCT Guide.

Prior to expiry of the period for entering the regional phase before the EPO, the EPO sends the applicant of an international application an invitation (EPO Form 1201) to carry out the acts of **R.159** in due time as required for valid entry into the European phase. Informing the applicant is not regarded as 'processing' the application, therefore it does not violate the processing prohibition of Art.23(1) PCT.

Since the EPO is aware of its designation or election from the notification by the IB under **Art.20(1)(a)** and **R.47.1(a)** or **R.76.5** PCT and has received a copy of the international application from the IB under **Art.20(1)**, it will start processing the international application automatically upon expiry of the 31-month period without request from the applicant (R.49.1(a-bis) PCT; E-IX, 2.1.2). As a consequence, when an international application designates the EPO and the applicant decides not to prosecute the application before the EPO, the EPO will send a loss of rights communication under **R.160(2)** and **R.112(1)**, even if the applicant has not carried out any act for national entry into the European phase. Since the EPO has not been informed of the appointment of a representative, it will send the communication to the applicant, not to an agent that may have acted in the international phase. See **R.160** for remedies.

Applicants are recommended to use 'Form 1200 for entry into the European phase' for the acts to be performed under **R.159(1)** and other required acts. Use of Form 1200 is not mandatory. Form 1200 contains a pre-printed 'written request for examination'. If, upon entry into the European regional phase, the applicant does not use Form 1200 and only pays the fee for examination, the Euro-PCT application is deemed to be withdrawn because the 'written request for examination' was not filed. See in particular the Notes attached to the form.

At expiry of the 31-month period, the EPO will start processing the application automatically, even if the applicant takes no action at all before the EPO as designated or elected office. The EPO will first assess whether the applicant has completed the acts required under **R.159(1)** and any additional acts before the expiry. If not complied with, the European application will be deemed withdrawn under **R.160(1)**. If complied with, the EPO will start processing the application by carrying out the supplementary European search (if applicable) and the substantive examination.

3 **Early entry into the European phase**

The EPO is prohibited from starting the processing of an international application before expiry of the 31 month period from priority of **R.159(1)** (Art.23(1); Art.40(1) PCT). However, an applicant may wish the EPO to start earlier, for example to have the patent granted early or to correct in the regional phase before the EPO an error that has occurred in the international phase using the review and excuse procedure (see PCT §7.6). The EPO will start processing early if the prohibition is lifted by an express request of the applicant (Art.23(2); Art.40(2) PCT). The procedure is set out in Not. EPO OJ 2013 p.156 and E-IX,2.8. The filing of a divisional application is only possible after entry into the regional phase before the EPO (E-IX,2.4.1).

A request for early processing may be filed with the EPO at any time before expiry of the 31-month period. The request does not require a specific wording, but the applicant must clearly express that he wishes the processing of his application before the EPO as designated/elected Office to commence early under Art.23(2) PCT or Art.40(2) PCT. The request can be made by ticking a box in EPO Form 1200 (OJ 2017 A74). Automatic debiting can be used for payments to be made (OJ 2017 sp5 p.7, point 2).

For the request to be effective the applicant must comply with the requirements stipulated in **R.159(1)** as if the 31-month period expired on the date the applicant requests early processing. Note, that these so-called necessary requirements to make a request effective have no basis in the EPC. The following requirements must be complied with to make a request effective:

- payment of the filing fee (including any additional fee if the application comprises more than 35 pages),
- filing of a translation (if a translation is required under **Art.153(4)**),
- specification of the application documents, and
- payment of the search fee (where a supplementary European search report has to be drawn up under **Art.153(7)**).

It depends on the date on which early processing is requested which other requirements stipulated in **R.159(1)** must be complied with, since the (regular) periods for paying the designation fee (**R.39(1)**) and the renewal fee (**R.51(1)**) and for filing the request for examination and paying the examination fee (**R.70(1)**) may not have expired on the date the request for early processing is filed. (Not. EPO OJ 2013 p.156; E-IX,2.8)

If on the date the request for early processing is filed all necessary requirements for entry into the European phase are complied with, the request is effective and the Euro-PCT application will as from that date be processed in the same way as a normal Euro-PCT application which has entered the European phase without a request for early processing having been filed. On that date the international phase is regarded terminated in respect of the EPO as designated/elected Office. The EPO will issue the **R.161/162** communication directly after it has established that the request is effective. (OJ 2013 p.156 §10)

If a necessary requirement is not fulfilled when filing the request for early processing, the request will become effective only when this requirement is complied with. Fulfilment of a further requirement of **R.159(1)** for which the period has not yet expired when filing the request, e.g. payment of the designation fee or a renewal fee or filing the request for examination, does not affect the request becoming effective. Such further requirements must be complied with before expiry of the appropriate period, even if such a period expires before the end of the 31-month period. Since by filing an effective request for early processing the processing ban is lifted, as from that date it is no longer possible to delay acts till expiry of the 31-month period. (OJ 2013 p.156 §10, 18-22)

Note, that filing the certificate of exhibition (**R.159(1)(h)**) is not a necessary requirement (OJ 2013 p.156 §13). However, if an applicant wants to exclude a disclosure at an international exhibition from the prior art, he must take care that the certificate is filed at the latest the day the request becomes effective.

If an applicant desires early processing of his application and the IB has not yet sent the international application to the EPO under Art.20(1) PCT by that time, the applicant may but does not have to file a request with the IB to do so; if needed, the EPO will take care of this itself (R.44bis.2(b) and R.47.4 PCT; Not. EPO OJ 2013 p.156 §17). If the applicant wants to accelerate proceedings, he should file the application himself.

4 **Accelerated prosecution of a Euro-PCT application**

The prosecution of a Euro-PCT application may be accelerated on request both in the international phase and national or regional phase (OJ 2015 A94). The international phase can be shortened by early entry into the national phase by an express request (OJ 2015 A94) as set out in the previous section. The request can be made on Form 1200 (OJ 2017 A74). An early entry does not automatically lead to accelerated processing in the European phase; this requires a separate request (OJ 2015 A93 §13). If the **R.70(1)** period for requesting examination has not yet expired when entering the European phase early, the prosecution can be accelerated by filing the request for examination together with the request for early entry (OJ 2013 p.156 §15). The procedure in the regional phase may be shortened by waiving the **R.161** and **162** communication and filing a PACE request (see **R.161(1):3, R.161(2):2** and E-VIII,4.2).

R. 159(1) In respect of an international application under Article 153, the applicant shall perform the following acts within thirty-one months from the date of filing of the application or, if priority has been claimed, from the priority date:

(a) supply, where applicable, the translation of the international application required under Article 153, paragraph 4;

(b) specify the application documents, as originally filed or as amended, on which the European grant procedure is to be based;

(c) pay the filing fee provided for in Article 78, paragraph 2;

(d) pay the designation fee if the period under Rule 39 has expired earlier;

(e) pay the search fee, where a supplementary European search report has to be drawn up;

(f) file the request for examination provided for in Article 94, if the period under Rule 70, paragraph 1, has expired earlier;

(g) pay the renewal fee in respect of the third year provided for in Article 86, paragraph 1, if the fee has fallen due earlier under Rule 51, paragraph 1;

(h) file, where applicable, the certificate of exhibition referred to in Article 55, paragraph 2, and Rule 25.

Amended by decision of the Administrative Council of 21.10.2008, which entered into force on 01.04.2009 (OJ 2008 p.513).

Art.55(2) Formalities for non-prejudicial disclosure at an exhibition
Art.78(2) Payment of filing fee
Art.86(1) Renewal fees
Art.94 Examination of the European patent application
Art.153 The European Patent Office as designated Office or elected Office

Art.153(4) Translation of international application published in a non-EPO language
R.25 Certificate of exhibition
R.39 Designation fee
R.51(1) Payment of renewal fee on last day of month containing anniversary
R.70(1) 6-months from publication search report for payment examination fee

1 Acts for entry into the European phase

1.1 ACTS MENTIONED IN R.159(1)

R.159(1) lists the acts an applicant must perform on entry of his international application into the European regional phase. The period fixed in the provision is 31 months from the date of filing of the international application or, if it claims priority, from the earliest priority date. The EPO has made use of the option given under **Art.22(3)** [**Art.39(1)(b)**] PCT to fix a period for entry longer than the 30-month period of **Art.22(1)** [**Art.39(1)(a)**] PCT. Since the period is an EPC period (because the duration is fixed in **R.159(1)** EPC), it must be calculated using **R.131(4)** EPC and not **R.80.2** PCT.

The acts of specifying the documents for the European procedure under **R.159(1)(b)** payment of the filing fee under (**c**) must be carried out within the 31-month period. In some cases the normal periods for payment of the designation fee (**d**) and the renewal fee in respect of the third patent year (**g**) and filing of the request for examination expire later than the 31-month period. These acts may then be completed after expiry of the 31-month period. The filing of the translation (**a**) and the certificate of exhibition (**h**) and payment of a search fee in relation to a supplementary European search (**e**) are necessary in certain cases only. The specific conditions for each of the acts mentioned in **R.159(1)** are given in the notes below, including the consequences of not performing the act in due time and any available remedies.

1.2 ADDITIONAL ACTS FOR ENTRY INTO THE EUROPEAN PHASE

In addition to the acts mentioned in **R.159(1)**, the applicant may be required to or voluntary carry out additional acts, depending on the facts of the case. Details of the additional acts are given in the provisions referred to and in the notes below.

- pay the claims fees of **R.162(1)** within the period of **R.162(2)** if the international application, taking into account any amendment under **R.161**, has more than fifteen claims;
- provide upon invitation data concerning the inventor if not submitted in the international phase (**R.163(1)**);
- where priority is claimed, furnish upon invitation the number and copy of the priority application if not yet submitted (**R.163(2)**);
- where applicable, file upon invitation a sequence listing in the correct format if not yet submitted (**R.163(3)**);
- if not yet submitted, furnish upon invitation the applicant's address, nationality and state of residence or principal place of business (**R.163(4)**);
- appoint upon invitation a representative if the applicant does not have a residence or place of business within the territory of an EPC contracting state (**Art.133(2)**; **R.163(5)**);
- have a search carried out on claims not searched by the (S)ISA under **R.164**;
- file the certificate of exhibition in the exceptional case of **Art.55(2)**;
- provide any search results for a priority application under **R.141(1), possibly after** an invitation under **R.141(3)**.

See Not. EPO OJ 2010 p.498 §5-13 for the requirements the international application must comply with for validly referring to a deposited biological sample under **R.31** and OJ 2013 p.542 §III.1-3 for sequence listings.

1.3 FAILURE TO CARRY OUT ACTS IN TIME

If the applicant has not performed all acts of **R.159(1)** within the 31-month period, the EPO will communicate to the applicant the fact that the application has been deemed withdrawn (**R.160(2)** and **R.112(1)**). The EPO issues a loss of rights communication pursuant to **R.112(1)** which indicates that the Euro-PCT application is deemed to be withdrawn (**R.160(2)**) and also indicates the missing items. The applicant may use further processing according to **Art.121** and **R.135**. The two-month period for requesting further processing starts with the notification of the communication of loss of rights. The Euro-PCT application will be deemed withdrawn if not remedied in due time (**R.160(1)**).

Note that not all the acts of **R.159(1)** are mentioned in **R.160(1)**, which means that if, for example a renewal fee is not paid (**J1/08**) or if a certificate of an international exhibition is not filed upon entry into the EP regional phase, no communication of deemed withdrawal under **R.160(2)** will be issued.

Failure to carry out any of the above 'additional acts' results in a different response from the EPO depending on which act was missed. See for example **R.162(2)** for missed claims fees, **R.163(6)** for a number of formal requirements mentioned in **R.163**, and **R.30(3)** for a missing sequence listing.

The 31-month deadline for completing the acts may be deferred by abandoning a priority claim. An abandonment in the international phase must be made within 30 months from the priority date (R.90bis.3(a) PCT). The EPO will probably not process an abandonment filed with it before expiry of the 31 month period because of the processing prohibition of Art.23(1) PCT. An abandonment received after expiry of the 31 months will not affect the deadline (A-III,6.11).

2 Translation (R.159(1)(a))

2.1 FILING TRANSLATION

Where the language of the international application as published in the international phase is not German, English or French, the applicant must furnish a translation in one of these languages upon entry into the regional phase as required by **Art.153(4)**. The language of the translation becomes the language of the proceedings before the EPO.

If the international application is published in English, French or German, the applicant has 'chosen' the language of the proceedings. The applicant cannot then file a translation in one of the other official languages of the EPO (**G4/08** hn.1). Any translation which is nevertheless filed will be ignored.

Art.14(2) allows correction of a translation of direct European applications filed in a language other than English, German or French. The provision also applies by analogy to Euro-PCT applications, because Euro-PCT applications are equivalent to regular European applications (**Art.153(2)**). Hence, an English translation filed on entry into the European phase may be brought into conformity with an original Japanese PCT application throughout proceedings before the EPO. (**T1483/10** r.2.2; A-VII,7)

When the European phase is entered at the end of the PCT Chapter I stage (no Demand filed), the content of the translation must be the description, claims (if amended, both as originally filed and as amended, if the applicant wishes the amendments to form the basis for the proceedings, together with any statement under **Art.19** PCT), any text matter in the drawings, the abstract and any request for rectification of obvious mistakes under **R.91.1(d)** PCT. When entered at the end of the Chapter II stage, the content of the translation must be the description, claims, any text matter of the drawings as amended upon filing the Demand (**Art.34(2)(b)** and **R.66.1(b)** PCT) or later during international preliminary examination (**R.66.4** PCT) (if any of those parts has been amended, both as originally filed and as amended by the annexes to the international preliminary examination report (see **R.70.11** and **R.70.16** PCT) and claims amended under **Art.19** PCT, if the applicant wished these amendments to form the basis for the proceedings, together with any statement under **Art.19** PCT), the abstract, any request for rectification as referred to in **R.91.1(d)** PCT and any annexes to the international preliminary examination report. The translation(s) may be filed in a single copy. (see AG-NP-EP and Euro-PCT Guide §509-521)

2.2 EFFECT OF LATE FILING

If the translation of the application has not been filed within 31 months of the priority date (**R.157(2)**, **R.159(1)(a)** EPC), the application is deemed to be withdrawn (**Art.24(1)(iii)** [**Art.39(2)**] PCT, **R.160(1)** and **R.112(1)** EPC). One remedy is further processing, which can be achieved by paying the further processing fee and completing the omitted act, i.e. filing the translation, within two months of notification (**Art.121**, **R.135** and **Rfees2(1)12**). Another remedy, if applicable, is to ask within 2 months of notification for a decision under **R.112(2)** EPC and prove that the translation was filed in due time. If it can be proven that the translation was filed in time, contrary to the finding of the EPO, a request for a decision under **R.112(2)** can be filed.

Reinstatement (i.e. re-establishment) of rights can be requested as remedy for not filing a translation of the international application; a reference to **R.49.6(d)(i)** PCT has been explicitly added to the entry for re-establishment of rights in **Rfees2(1)13** (OJ 2007 p.692, III; **R.49.6** PCT). This leads to the rather strange situation that the applicant may request re-establishment in the period for filing the translation. The PCT overrules here **R.136(3)** EPC, which excludes re-establishment in periods for which further processing is available (**Art.150(2)** EPC, last sentence).

According to **R.49.6** PCT, reinstatement is only possible 'after failure to perform the acts referred to in **Art.22** PCT', i.e. for filing the translation and paying the national fee (i.e. the filing fee). Hence, reinstatement is not available for late paying of, for example, the designation fee or the examination fee. The acts which can be remedied pursuant to **R.49.6** PCT are the same as those for creating a prior-right effect (**Art.54(3)** EPC) of a Euro-PCT application under **R.165** EPC (**Art.153(5)** EPC).

Re-establishment is probably useful only if the applicant has not met the two-month period for requesting further processing, otherwise it is strongly recommended to use the remedy of further processing. However, if the applicant has missed requesting further processing for excusable reasons and entry of the international application before the EPO is still desired, re-establishment in the period of further processing may be requested while proving all due care.

3 **Amendment and basis for the grant procedure (R.159(1)(b))**

The grant procedure before the EPO as designated Office is normally based on the application documents as published by the IB, including any claims amended under **Art.19** PCT. The grant procedure before the EPO as elected Office is usually based on the documents on which the international preliminary examination report is based, including any annexes (**Art.34** PCT).

R.159(1)(b) implements **Art.28** PCT and allows the filing of amendments of the application on entry as basis for the grant procedure. **Art.28** PCT allows an applicant to amend the international application to comply with specific requirements regarding patentability or multiple dependencies of claims of national or regional offices (see **R.6.4(a)** PCT). Whereas multiple dependencies are usually removed for national entry in for example the US and KR, they should be maintained in EP to have as many fallback positions as possible.

The possibility of voluntary amendment on entry under **R.159(1)(b)** is a lex specialis alongside **R.137(2)**. Note that amendments on entry are made after receipt of the search report mentioned in **R.137(1)**, because the international search report has taken the place of the European search report (**Art.157(1)**). The Euro-PCT applicant has therefore more time for voluntary amendment than the direct European applicant (**J6/96**).

Amendments to the description, claims or figures can be filed as replacement pages. The complete set of claims should be replaced, not individual claims. Where the international application is published in a non-EPO language, the amendments must be filed in an EPO language, preferably the EPO language into which the international application is translated. (OJ 2009 p.338)

The applicant may indicate that any of the application documents are to be replaced for the grant procedure by amendments filed under **Art.19** PCT, **Art.34** PCT and/or filed for the first time on entry. Shortly after entry into the European phase, the EPO will give the applicant an additional opportunity to amend the application under **R.161**.

Since **R.160(1)** does not refer to **R.159(1)(b)**, there is no sanction on not specifying the documents on which the grant procedure is to be based.

4 **Filing fee (R.159(1)(c))**

4.1 PAYMENT OF FILING FEE

Upon entry into the regional phase a filing fee must be paid, which is equal to the filing fee of **Art.78(2)**, the amount of which is fixed in **Rfees2(1)1.**

On entering the European regional phase, a page fee must be paid as part of the filing fee for any international application containing over 35 pages (**Rfees2(1)1a**). The page fee is calculated as set out in (**Rfees2(1):4.1.**

There is no language reduction of the filing fee under **R.6(3)**, because **R.6(3)** refers only to the filing of an European patent application and because the application as received by the EPO at the start of the regional phase is always in English, French or German. Note, that the page fee is based on the international application as published, regardless of the language of publication (Euro-PCT Guide §538).

Deletion of **R.106** EPC 1973 has led to loss of the link between the 'national fee' referred to in **Art.22(1)** PCT and the 'filing fee' referred to in **R.159(1)(c)** EPC 2000. However, the 'filing fee' of **R.159(1)(c)** EPC is to be regarded as the 'national fee' of **Art.22(1)** PCT. (Euro-PCT Guide §534)

4.2 FAILURE TO PAY AND REMEDY

If the filing fee, including any page fee, is not paid within 31 months (**Art.78(2), R.159(1)(c)**), the Euro-PCT application is deemed to be withdrawn (**R.160(1)** and **R.112(1)**). Moreover, the application will not have a prior right effect (**Art.153(5), R.165**). A first remedy is to request further processing, pay the further processing fee (50% of the filing fee) and complete the omitted act, i.e. pay the filing fee, within two months of the notification (**Art.121, R.135, Rfees2(1)1** and **Rfees2(1)12**). A second remedy, applicable if the EPO has made a mistake, is to ask for a decision under **R.112(2)** and prove that the payment was made in time.

As discussed in section **2.2** above, under **R.49.6** PCT, the applicant may also request re-establishment (**Art.122, R.136**) for payment of the filing fee (which is equal to the national fee of **Art.22** PCT), despite further processing (**Art.121, R.135**) being available (**Rfees2(1)13**; OJ 2007 p.692, III).

5 Designation fee (R.159(1)(d))

5.1 DESIGNATION FEE

A flat designation fee covering all EPC contracting states must be paid on entering the regional phase (Art.79; A-III,11.2.5). Since all PCT contracting states are designated in the international application and all EPC contracting states are PCT contracting states, all EPC contracting states are designated upon entering the European regional phase, provided these states acceded to the EPC on or before the international filing date. The applicant may expressly withdraw the designation of one or more contracting states at any time up to grant of the patent. If any designations are withdrawn upon European phase entry, payment of the designation fee does not re-activate the withdrawn designations (A-III,11.2.4). The amount of the designation fee is fixed in **Rfees2(1)3**.

For most international applications the designation fee must be paid within 31 months from the date of filing or, where applicable, the priority date (**R.159(1)**). In the exceptional circumstance that the international search report is published after 25 months from the date of filing or priority and the period of **R.39(1)** therefore expires later than the 31 months, **R.159(1)(d)** does not apply and the designation fee may be paid up to the expiry of the six-month period of **R.39(1)**. This may also occur upon early entry into the European phase (OJ 2013 p.156 §10, 18, 19). See **AAD.3.2(c)** for the automatic debiting of the designation fee.

5.2 FAILURE TO PAY AND REMEDY

If the designation fee is not paid in due time (**R.159(1)(d)**), the Euro-PCT application is deemed withdrawn (**R.160(1)**) at expiry of the normal period of **R.159(1)(d)** (**G4/98** hn.II applied mutatis mutandis, A-III,11.2.3). The EPO will send a communication notifying the loss of rights under **R.160(2)** and **R.112(1)** if within the period of **R.159(1)(d)** the applicant did not pay the designation fee. (A-III,11.2.5).

The remedy after failure to pay the designation fee in due time is further processing, which can be achieved by paying the further processing fee (50% of the designation fee) and completing the omitted act, i.e. paying the designation fee, within two months of the notification (**Art.121, R.135, Rfees2(1)3** and **Rfees2(1)12**). No request in writing for further processing need be filed. Alternatively, if the applicant regards the payment as having been made in due time, the applicant can ask within 2 months of notification for a decision under **R.112(2)** and provide proof of timely payment.

5.3 DESIGNATION OF EXTENSION STATES

Extension fees for extension states (see A-III,12 and **Art.169:3**) designated in an international application must be paid within the same period as the designation fee (A-III,12.2).

If an extension fee is not paid within the applicable period, the request for extension is withdrawn. If the designation fee is paid such that the application is not deemed withdrawn under **R.39(2)** and one or more extension fees have not been paid, then no communication under **R.112(1)** will be issued notifying the applicant of the loss of rights. In this case, further processing under **Art.121, R.135** will not be possible in respect of extensions deemed withdrawn. However, if one or more extensions are deemed withdrawn due to non-payment of the extension fees and the application is deemed withdrawn due to non-payment of the designation fee, then a communication under **R.160(2)** and **R.112(1)** will be issued notifying the applicant of the loss of rights with respect to both the withdrawn application *and* the withdrawn extensions in question (provided the applicant has not actively withdrawn all designations and has not waived the right to receive a **R.112(1)** communication for the designations). In this case, further processing under **Art.121, R.135** is possible for both the deemed withdrawn application and deemed withdrawn extensions, with the further processing fee of **Rfees2(1)12** applying mutatis mutandis for extension fees. Re-establishment of rights according to **Art.122, R.136** is not possible for payment of extension fees. (A-III,12.2)

A grace period is available of 2 months from expiry of the period in which the designation fee is to be paid or 2 months from notification of the communication of loss of rights due to an omitted payment of the designation fee. Payments within the grace period attract a 50% surcharge. (A-III,12.2; OJ 2009 p.603)

5.4 VALIDATION OF NON-CONTRACTING STATE

A validation fee for a non-contracting state can be paid on entry into the European phase. The procedure for validation is similar to that for designation of extension states in the preceding section. See A-III,12.2, and **Art.79(2):2.2.**

6 Search fee for the supplementary European search (R.159(1)(e))

6.1 PAYMENT OF SUPPLEMENTARY EUROPEAN SEARCH FEE

In principle, a supplementary European search report is drawn up in respect of any Euro-PCT application (**Art.153(7)**). A search fee must be paid where a supplementary search report has to be drawn up (**R.159(1)(e)**). The amount of the search fee for the European supplementary search is set in **Rfees2(1)2.** No supplementary European search report will be drawn up and no search fee need be paid on entry for international applications for which the EPO as ISA has drawn up an (supplementary) international search report (**Art.153(7):3**). See **Art.153(7):4** for the cases for which a reduced search fee applies.

If a supplementary European search report is drawn up, the EPO will send an invitation under **R.70(2)** after issuing said search report, thereby inviting the applicant to indicate whether he wants to proceed further with the application, unless the right to this invitation has been waived by the applicant. See **R.164(1):2** for details of the procedure of the supplementary search report.

See **Rfees9** for a possible refund of the search fee in respect of the supplementary European search.

6.2 FAILURE TO PAY AND REMEDY

Any search fee must be paid within 31 months from filing or, where applicable, priority (**R.159(1)(e)**). If a due search fee is not paid within the 31 month period, the Euro-PCT application is deemed to be withdrawn (**R.160(1)**). One remedy is further processing, which can be achieved by paying the further processing fee (50% of the search fee) and completing the omitted act, i.e. paying the search fee, within two months from notification of the communication (**R.160(2)**; **R.112(1)**) informing the applicant of the deemed withdrawal (**Art.121, R.135, Rfees2(1)2** and **Rfees2(1)12**). No request in writing for further processing need be filed; acts in relation to fees can be carried out electronically. In the event that the EPO has made an error, the situation may be remedied by asking for a decision under **R.112(2)** and proving that the search fees were paid on time.

7 Request for examination (R.159(1)(f))

7.1 PAYMENT OF EXAMINATION FEE

The request for examination of the international application under the EPC is based on **Art.94** EPC, and includes a written request and payment of an examination fee (**Art.94(1)**, **R.70(1)**). The written request is contained (pre-printed) in the form for Entry into the European phase (EPO form 1200).

The amount of the examination fee is fixed in **Rfees2(1)6**. The examination fee may be reduced by 30% under **R.6(3)** EPC and **Rfees14(1)** for entitled persons using an admissible language for the written request for examination (see **R.6(3):2** EPC), if the written request for examination is filed in an admissible non-EPO language (A-X,9.2.3).

In addition, the examination fee may be reduced by 75% under **Rfees14(2)** if the EPO acted as IPEA in the international phase. If both reductions apply, the total reduction in the examination fee is 82.5% (A-X,9.3.2).

The amount of the examination fee is dependent on which international authorities acted as ISA, SISA and/or IPEA. If the EPO acted as ISA or SISA in the international phase, then the EPO does not draw up a supplementary European search report, whereas if the EPO did not act as ISA or SISA in the international phase, then the EPO will draw up a supplementary European search report (**Art.153(7)**). If a supplementary European search report is drawn up, the applicant has a 6-month period from a communication under **R.70(2)** and **R.70a(2)** to state whether he wants to continue with the prosecution of the Euro-PCT application and, if so, to correct any deficiencies in the opinion accompanying the supplementary European search report; failure to respond will result in the application being deemed withdrawn (OJ 2009 p.533 §5.1.5).

The examination fee must normally be paid within 31 months from the date of filing or, where applicable, priority (**R.159(1)**). In the exceptional circumstance that the international search report (which takes the place of the European search report (**Art.153(6)**)) is published after 25 months from the date of filing or priority and the period of **R.70(1)** will expire later than the 31 months, **R.159(1)(f)** does not apply and the request for examination may be filed up to the expiry of the six month period of **R.70(1)**. This may also occur upon early entry into the European phase (OJ 2013 p.156 §10, 18, 19). The period for payment of the examination fee is independent of whether or not a supplementary European search report will be drawn up.

The above periods are not affected by a possible supplementary European search report drawn up by the EPO or by the publication of the translation of an international application earlier published in a language other than an official EPO language (**Art.153(4)**). If a supplementary European search report has to be drawn up, the applicant will receive the communication of **R.70(2)** (E-IX,2.5.3), inviting him to indicate whether to proceed with the application.

See **R.159:4** for acceleration of prosecution before the EPO, and **Rfees-11**for refund of the examination fee.

7.2 FAILURE TO PAY OR FILE REQUEST AND REMEDY

If the examination fee is not paid in due time, the Euro-PCT application is deemed to be withdrawn (**R.160(1)**). One remedy is further processing, which can be achieved by paying the further processing fee (50% of the examination fee) and completing the omitted act, i.e. paying the examination fee, within two months of the notification of the communication (**R.160(2)** and **R.112(1)**) informing the applicant of the deemed withdrawal (**Art.121, R.135, Rfees2(1)6** and **Rfees2(1)12**). No request in writing for further processing need be filed; acts in relation to fees can be carried out electronically. In the event that the EPO has made an error, the applicant may remedy the situation by asking for a decision under **R.112(2)** and proving that the examination fee was paid on time.

In the case where no form 1200 is used on entry into the EP phase and the written request for examination has not been filed, the loss of rights can be remedied using further processing by filing the written request for examination and paying the fixed further processing fee of **Rfees2(1)12.** Note, that in the case where none of the acts of **R.159(1)** have been completed, i.e. no steps have been taken to enter the EP phase, further processing can also be used as remedy.

8 Renewal fees (R.159(1)(g))

8.1 PAYMENT OF RENEWAL FEES

The amount of the renewal fees is fixed in **Rfees2(1)4.** The renewal fee for the third year can be validly paid until the later of the due date according to **R.51(1)** and the expiry of the 31-month period (**R.159(1)(g)**). This is a consequence of the fact that the PCT provisions prevail over the EPC provisions (**Art.150(2)** EPC, last sentence and **Art.23, Art.40** PCT).

8.2 FAILURE TO PAY AND REMEDY

If the renewal fee is not paid in due time, the EPO informs the applicant as a courtesy that the renewal fee has not been paid and indicates that a six-month additional period applies in which he may still pay the renewal fee with a 50% additional fee (A-X,5.2.4; **R.51(2)**; **Rfees2(1)5**). The six-month period is triggered by the due date according to **R.51(1)** or the expiry of the 31-month period, depending on the case (**R.159(1)(g)**; see section 8.3 and 8.4 below).

If not paid at expiry of the 6-month additional period, the Euro-PCT application is deemed to be withdrawn (**R.51(2)** last sentence).

The failure to pay cannot be remedied by further processing because the period of **R.51(2)** is excluded in **R.135(2)**. However, because of this exclusion, re-establishment is possible under **Art.122** and **R.136**, provided all due care can be proven. In the event that the EPO has made an error, the applicant may remedy the situation by asking for a decision under **R.112(2)** and proving that the renewal fee was paid in due time.

Note, that non-payment of renewal fees is not mentioned in **R.160(1)** as a ground for deemed withdrawal of a Euro-PCT application.

8.3 DUE DATE BEFORE EXPIRY OF THE 31-MONTH PERIOD

There are two different cases for calculation of the last day on which the renewal fee can validly be paid. The first case is where the due date falls before the expiry of the 31-month period. This happens when the application does not claim priority or was filed within approximately 7 months from the priority date. The date of expiry of the 31-month period becomes the deferred due date according to **R.159(1)(g)**. This date also forms the basis for calculating the additional aggregate 6-month period of **R.51(2)** (**J1/89** r.4 and A-X,5.2.4). Any extension under **R.134** should be applied to both the expiry of the 31-month period and of the 6-month additional period. An example of an aggregate period calculation:

11.01.2016	priority date, relevant event for start of 31-month period;
09.05.2016	international filing date, relevant event for renewal fee;
31.05.2018	due date renewal fee in respect of the 3rd year;
11.08.2018	(Saturday) expiry of 31-month period;
13.08.2018	(Monday) expiry of 31-month period, extended under **R.134(1)**; deferred due date;
13.02.2019	expiry of 6-month period of **R.51(2)**.

Note, that the deviating calculation of **J4/91** for the additional period (see **R.51(2):1**) and the comparable calculation of periods for renewal fees for divisional applications according to **R.51(3)** are not applicable in this situation. Since the deferred due date is the expiry of a period, the calculation of aggregate periods must be used (see **R.131(2):3**).

8.4 DUE DATE AFTER EXPIRY OF THE 31-MONTH PERIOD

The second case is where the due date falls after the expiry of the 31-month period. This happens when the application is filed after about seven months from the priority date. In the second case the due date is the last day of a month according to **R.51(1)** and the calculation of the 6-month period follows the rules for a direct European application as given in **R.51(3):1**. Because the due date is not the expiry of a period which can be extended under **R.134** (**J4/91** r.3.2), the due date does not shift to the first working day if it falls on a non-working day. Only the payment of the renewal fee may validly be deferred to the next working day. The 6-month additional period runs from the due date, irrespective of whether or not the due date is a non-working day, to the last day of the sixth month (**J4/91**, de ultimo ad ultimo). If that day is a non-working day, **R.134** should be applied.

An example of a calculation:

13.12.2015	priority date, relevant event for start of 31-month period;
12.12.2016	international filing date, relevant event for renewal fee;
13.07.2018	expiry of the 31-month period;
31.12.2018	(New Year's Eve) due date renewal fee in respect of the 3rd year;
02.01.2019	last day for valid payment without additional fee (**R.134(1)**);
30.06.2019	(Sunday) expiry of 6-month period (**R.51(2)**);
01.07.2019	(Monday) last day for valid payment with additional fee (**R.134(1)**).

Beware, the 31-month period runs from the priority date, whereas the third year for the renewal fee is calculated from the international filing date!

Since the renewal fee in respect of the third year may be paid up to six months before the due date, the applicant may include the renewal fee in the payments made on entry also in the second case (see **R.51(1):1**).

9 **Certificate of exhibition (R.159(1)(h))**
A disclosure at an international exhibition may be removed from the prior art of a direct European application, when on filing of the application a statement about the display at the exhibition is made (**Art.55(2)**) and within four months from filing a certificate providing facts about the exhibition is submitted (**R.25**).

For a Euro-PCT application **R.159(1)(h)** requires that only the certificate be filed within the 31-month period of **R.159(1)**. The applicant will be notified of any defects in the certificate (A-IV 3.2).

An applicant may anticipate any EPO requirement by including a declaration on non-prejudicial disclosures under R.4.17(v) PCT when filing the international application. If done so, and no certificate was filed on entry into the European phase, the EPO will notice the omission and send the applicant a loss of rights communication under **R.112(1)**, which allows further processing as remedy.

If the applicant did not include the declaration in the PCT filing, the EPO will not notice a missing certificate and will not issue a loss of rights communication. In such a case further processing is not available because **R.135(1)** is not applicable where no loss of rights communication is issued. Re-establishment may be possible.

If the certificate has not been filed, there is no application of **Art.55(2)**.

R. 159(2) The Examining Division shall be competent to take decisions of the European Patent Office under Article 25, paragraph 2(a) PCT.

Art.25(2)(a) PCT Review procedure

1 **Review and excuse procedure**
The EPO may decide, in accordance with the review and excuse procedure of **Art.25** PCT, to allow an international application deemed to be withdrawn, or not accorded a filing date, to proceed as a European application. The examining division is competent to take decisions in relation to such applications, and the Receiving Section transfers copies of any documents received from the IB under the circumstances of **Art.25(1)(a)** PCT to the Examining Division. Where it is decided that the application can proceed as a European application, search and examination are carried out as for other applications, although the application may be accorded the date it was originally filed with the PCT rO and may claim the priority date, if any, of the international application (E-IX,2.9). See also PCT §7.6, in particular §7.6.3.

R. 160 Consequences of non-fulfilment of certain requirements

Amended by decision of the Administrative Council of 21.10.2008, which entered into force on 01.04.2009. (OJ 2008 p.513)
Implementation of: **Art.153**
EPC 1973: **R.108**

R. 160(1) If either the translation of the international application or the request for examination is not filed in due time, or if the filing fee, the search fee or the designation fee is not paid in due time, the European patent application shall be deemed to be withdrawn.

1 **Effect of non-compliance**

After expiry of the 31-month period of **R.159(1)**, the EPO automatically starts the processing of all international applications which designate the EPO, including those applications for which the applicant does not have the intention to obtain a patent under the EPC, for instance because of prejudicial prior art mentioned in the (supplementary) international search report. The EPO can only close the files of the latter applications after it has communicated the loss of rights to the applicant. Under **R.160(2)** if the EPO notes that the Euro-PCT application is deemed to be withdrawn, it shall communicate this to the applicant.

The notification of loss of rights triggers the two-month period for requesting further processing (**Art.121; R.135**) in which the applicant may remedy the loss of rights. If the applicant does not respond to the notification in due time, the loss of rights becomes final without the applicant being informed. **R.160(2)** specifically states that the applicant may also ask for a decision under **R.112(2)** if the applicant deems that the EPO has made a mistake. (E-IX,2.1.3)

R. 160(2) If the European Patent Office notes that the application is deemed to be withdrawn under paragraph 1, it shall communicate this to the applicant. Rule 112, paragraph 2, shall apply mutatis mutandis.

R.112(2) Review of opinion regarding loss of rights

1 **Procedure for correction**

If a Euro-PCT application is deemed withdrawn according to **R.160(1)**, the first sentence of **R.160(2)** requires the EPO to communicate the loss of rights to the applicant. This may occur because within 31 months from the date of filing or, if priority has been claimed, from the priority date:

- a required translation has not been filed (**R.159(1)(a)**),
- the filing fee has not been paid (**R.159(1)(c)**),
- the designation fee has not been paid (**R.159(1)(d)**),
- a required search fee in respect of the supplementary European search has not been paid (**R.159(1)(e)**, or
- the request for examination has not been filed (**R.159(1)(f)**).

The standard remedy is further processing. However, the applicant may, within two months from the notification, request the EPO to review its opinion on the loss of rights under **R.112(2)**, if he can prove that the periods were actually met (**R.160(2)**, second sentence). See **R.112(2):1** for the procedure. Any loss of rights ensues upon expiry of the normal period (E-IX,2.1.3; **G4/98**).

Not all acts of **R.159(1)** are mentioned in **R.160(1)**; this means that if, for example a renewal fee is not paid or if the certificate of an international exhibition is not filed upon entry into the EP regional phase, no communication of deemed withdrawal under **R.160(2)** will be issued.

2 **Further processing and re-establishment**
The normal period of **R.159(1)** for payment of the designation fee or search fee for the supplementary European search and for filing the request for examination is excluded from re-establishment because further processing is available as a remedy (**Art.121, Art.122, R.136(3)**). As discussed in **R.159(1):2.2**, since the EPO has withdrawn its reservation filed under **R.49.6** PCT, the applicant may, in principle, request re-establishment (**Art.122, R.136**) for payment of the filing fee and filing of the translation, despite further processing (**Art.121, R.135**) being available.

R. 161 Amendment of the application

Amended by decision of the Administrative Council of 26.10.2010 which entered into force on 01.05.2011 (OJ 2010 p.634; see also OJ 2009 p.582).
Implementation of: **Art.153**
EPC 1973: **R.109**

1 **Communication issued after entry into European phase**
Shortly after entry into the European phase the EPO despatches a communication under **R.161**, which can have several forms. If the EPO was (S)ISA, it will issue a communication under **R.161(1)** and will not carry out a supplementary European search. There are two types of the **R.161(1)** communication: either the communication includes an invitation to correct deficiencies or the communication does not include such an invitation. Only in the first case is a response mandatory. The invitation is not included if the EPO did not note any deficiencies in the international phase or if the applicant has already filed a response dealing with the deficiencies. If the EPO was not (S)ISA, it will issue a communication under **R.161(2)**, providing an opportunity to amend voluntarily the application, and, subsequently, it will carry out a supplementary European search.

Both types of **R.161(1)** communication and the **R.161(2)** communication also give the applicant the opportunity to make voluntary amendments. Hence, the applicant's right to amend voluntarily the application before the EPO as designated or elected Office, based on **Art.28(1), R.52.1** PCT and **Art.41(1), R.78.1** PCT, is implemented by **R.137(2)** when the EPO has acted as (S)ISA, and by **R.161(2)** when the EPO has not acted as (S)ISA.

R. 161(1) If the European Patent Office has acted as the International Searching Authority and, where a demand under Article 31 PCT was filed, also as the International Preliminary Examining Authority for a Euro-PCT application, it shall give the applicant the opportunity to comment on the written opinion of the International Searching Authority or the International Preliminary Examination Report and, where appropriate, invite him to correct any deficiencies noted in the written opinion or in the International Preliminary Examination Report and to amend the description, claims and drawings within a period of six months from the respective communication. If the European Patent Office has drawn up a supplementary international search report, an invitation in accordance with the first sentence shall be issued in respect of the explanations given in accordance with Rule 45*bis*.7(e) PCT. If the applicant does not comply with or comment on an invitation in accordance with the first or second sentence, the application shall be deemed to be withdrawn.

Art.31 PCT Demand for international preliminary examination

R.45bis.7(e) PCT Explanations in supplementary international search report

1 **Response to written opinion drafted by EPO as (S)ISA or IPEA**
R.161(1) applies to Euro-PCT applications where the EPO has acted as ISA, SISA, or both as ISA and IPEA. The **R.161(1)** communication always gives the applicant an opportunity to comment on the results of the examination by the EPO in the international phase.

The communication includes 'where appropriate' an invitation to correct any deficiencies in the application and to amend the application. The invitation is 'appropriate' if deficiencies are noted in the written opinion prepared by the EPO as ISA, in the explanations that are part of the supplementary international search report prepared by the EPO as SISA or in the IPER prepared by the EPO as IPEA. (OJ 2010 p.316; PCT §4.9.1; E-IX,3.2)

Where the communication contains an invitation to correct deficiencies, filing a response is mandatory and the application is deemed to be withdrawn if no response filed in due time. The mandatory response can be a correction of the deficiencies or a comment on the invitation, i.e. a substantive rebuttal of the alleged deficiencies.

The communication does not include an invitation to correct deficiencies if the EPO did not note any deficiencies and the written opinion or, where applicable, the IPER prepared by the EPO was positive (E-IX,3.3.2). The invitation is neither included if a response is already on file in the form of new amendments and/or comments filed upon entry of the regional phase before the EPO under **R.159(1)(b)**. The invitation is also omitted if amended claims were filed under **Art.19** PCT or **Art.34** PCT, provided that the EPO did not already consider the amendments as IPEA and these claims are maintained upon entry of the EP phase (OJ 2009 p.533 §5.2.3; E-IX,3.3.1). Filing a response is voluntary in the case of a **R.161(1)** communication without invitation.

Under **R.137(2)** the applicant may file amendments of his own volition within the **R.161(1)** period. These voluntary amendments may be filed during the entire period, as a separate letter or together with a mandatory response.

2 **Period for filing response**
The **R.161(1)** communication is sent to the applicant shortly after expiry of the 31-month period for entry into the European phase, typically after about two months. The period for filing a response is six months of notification of the communication (**R.161(1)**, first sentence).

If the applicant does not file the mandatory response in due time, the application is deemed withdrawn (**R.161(1)**, last sentence). Further processing under **Art.121** and **R.135** is available. Admission of any voluntary amendment filed after expiry of the period is at the discretion of the examining division (**R.137(3)**).

3 **Acceleration of processing**
The EPO will not start examining the Euro-PCT application upon receipt of the response under **R.161(1)**, but wait till expiry of the six-month period, because the applicant may file voluntary amendments during the entire period, either together with the mandatory response or by separate letter (see **R.137(2):1**). If an applicant does not want the EPO to wait till expiry of the six-month period, he may waive the remainder of the period. He can send the waiver together with or after the filing of the response. (OJ 2015 A94 §5)

The applicant can accelerate processing of the application by waiving his right to the **R.161(1)** communication, either in the Form 1200 or by separate letter. The EPO will not issue the **R.161** communication and start processing the application immediately only if the applicant has filed a waiver and, additionally, has complied with all requirements of **R.161** and **162** (OJ 2015 A94 §4). The requirements are payment of any claims fees and filing a mandatory response where required. If not complied with, the waiver will not be valid, a communication under **R.161(1)** will be issued and processing will start in principle only after expiry of the six-month period, even if a PACE request has been filed (E-IX,3.2). Note, that claims fees cannot be paid using automatic debiting if the communication has been waived, because the six-month period of **R.162(2)** will not be triggered (see **AAD.6.1(d)**); payment should be made on entry by other means (OJ 2017 sp5 Annex A2 page 53 point 3(d)). If the **R.161(1)** communication is waived, voluntary amendments may be filed at any time during the grant procedure (see **R.137(2):1**).

The examination can be further accelerated by filing a PACE request. The requirements for such a request are set out in **Art.94(1):5**. The request can be filed at any time during the European phase if the EPO was (S)ISA, for example together with the Form 1200 or with the response to the **R.161(1)** communication (OJ 2015 A93 §13). The applicant can enquire about the status of the file as set out in **Art.94(1):6**.

R. 161(2) Where the European Patent Office draws up a supplementary European search report on a Euro-PCT application, the application may be amended once within a period of six months from a communication informing the applicant accordingly. The application as amended shall serve as the basis for the supplementary European search.

1 **Amendment of application for which EPO did not act as ISA or SISA**
A **R.161(2)** communication is issued for Euro-PCT applications for which the EPO will draw up a supplementary search report under **Art.153(7)**. This is the case where the EPO did not act as ISA or SISA (Dec. AC OJ 2009 p.594); hence also if the EPO was IPEA but another office was ISA (**Art.152:3**). The **R.161(2)** communication gives the applicant the opportunity to file voluntary amendments within a period of six months. The applicant may also comment on the written opinion or IPER but he is not required to. The provision of such an opportunity for amendment on entry into the regional phase is required by the PCT. The application as amended will serve as the basis for the subsequent supplementary European search (**R.161(2)**, last sentence). Any comments submitted will be taken into account. (E-IX,3.1)

Any voluntary comments and amendments must be filed within six months of the **R.161(2)** invitation. Failure to meet the period can probably not be remedied using further processing, because no communication of failure to observe the period as required by **R.135(1)** will be issued. After receipt of the supplementary European search report, an applicant will have a second opportunity to file a voluntary amendment within the period of **R.70a(2)**. (H-II,2.2; C-II,3.1)

2 **Acceleration of processing**
The EPO will only start the supplementary search after expiry of the six-month period of **R.161(2)**, even if the applicant replies earlier the communication under **R.161(2)**.

If an applicant does not wish to use the entire six-month period, he can request an immediate start of the search in reply to the **R.161(2)** communication, thereby waiving the remaining part of the period. The request may be filed together with amendments. (OJ 2015 A94 §5)

The applicant can accelerate the start of the search by waiving the **R.161(2)** communication, either in the Form 1200 for entry into the European phase or by separate letter. A valid waiver requires payment of any claims fees under **R.162(1)** upon entry into the European phase. If the waiver is valid, no **R.161(2)** communication is issued (OJ 2015 A94, §4). See also **R.161(1):3**.

The EPO always accelerates the supplementary search; no PACE request for accelerated search is needed. The EPO strives to issue the supplementary search report within six months from expiry of the six-month period of **R.161(2)**, or, if the **R.161(2)** communication has been waived, from entry into the European phase (OJ 2015 A93 §6, 9, 10(iii)).

If the supplementary search report of PCT application has not been issued within six months from expiry of the period under **R.161(2)** and the applicant files an enquiry about the status of the file using Form 1012 (see **Art.94(1):6**), the EPO will issue the search report within one month from receipt of the enquiry. If the supplementary search report of an application filed before 01.06.2014 and claiming priority has not been issued yet and the applicant files an enquiry using Form 1012, the EPO will issue the search report within six months from receipt of the enquiry. (OJ 2016 A66 §6; E-VII,7)

The prosecution can be accelerated further by waiving the **R.70(2)** communication normally issued after completion of the supplementary search (OJ 2015 A94 §1).

A PACE request for accelerated examination can be filed once the examining division is responsible for the application (OJ 2015 A93 §12). The request can be filed at the earliest together with the confirmation required under **R.70(2)** or, if the **R.70(2)** communication is waived, together with the response to the first **Art.94(3)** communication (OJ 2015 A93 §12 and **R.70a(2):1**). The formal requirements for the request are set out in **Art.94(1):5**.

The grant can also be accelerated as set out in **Art.97(1):2**.

R. 162 Claims incurring fees

Implementation of: **Art.153**
EPC 1973: **R.110**

1 General

This rule provides the legal basis for levying claims fees for an international application in the European phase and is structured according to **R.45**. The claims fees are based on the number of claims present upon entry into the European phase (**R.162(1)**), or, if amended in response to the **R.161** communication, on the number of claims in the response. In the latter case, any claims fees overpaid in the period of **R.159(1)** are refunded (**R.162(3)**) or any underpaid claims fees are charged. (OJ 1999 p.660, 696)

Claims fees are payable for claims 16 and above (**Rfees2(1)15**). Applicants are advised to keep the number of claims to a maximum of fifteen if at all possible, or reduce the number of claims after European regional phase entry to a reasonable number using **R.161**, to avoid payment of the excess claims fees (see **R.45(1):2**).

R. 162(1) If the application documents on which the European grant procedure is to be based comprise more than fifteen claims, claims fees shall be paid for the sixteenth and each subsequent claim as laid down in the Rules relating to Fees within the period under Rule 159, paragraph 1.

Amended by decision of the Administrative Council of 06.03.2008 which entered into force on 01.04.2008 (OJ 2008 p.124).
R.159(1) Requirements for entry into the European phase

1 **Amount and period**
The amount of the claims fee is fixed in **Rfees2(1)15**. Claims fee are due only for those claims on which the grant procedure is to be based. In principle, the claims fees must be paid in the 31-month period of **R.159(1)** from the date of filing or, where applicable, date of priority.

R. 162(2) If the claims fees are not paid in due time, they may still be paid within the period under Rule 161, paragraph 1 or paragraph 2, as the case may be. If within this period amended claims are filed, the claims fees due shall be computed on the basis of such amended claims and shall be paid within this period.

Amended by decision of the Administrative Council of 14.12.2016 which entered into force on 01.01.2017. The amended rule applies to Euro-PCT applications for which the R.161/162 communication has not been issued on 01.01.2017. (OJ 2016 A102, A103)

The amendment is a response to **J11/12** and clarifies the unchanged practice of the office.
R.161(1) Invitation to respond to written opinion where EPO was ISA
R.161(2) Invitation to amend application where EPO was not ISA

1 **Effect of non-payment and further processing**
If the claims fees are not paid within the 31-month period they may still be paid within the six-month period of **R.161**, without a surcharge being payable (**R.162(2)**; E-IX,2.1.3).

The applicant may file amended claims in response to the **R.161** communication. The claims fees due shall be computed on the basis of such amended claims and shall be paid within this period.

If not paid by expiry of the **R.161** period, the excess claims are deemed abandoned (**R.162(4)**). The loss of rights may be remedied using further processing (**Art.121, R.135**), with the further processing fee being 50% of the unpaid claims fees. In the event the EPO has made an error, the applicant may ask, within 2 months after notification of the loss of rights, for a decision under **R.112(2)** and prove that the claims fees were timely paid.

2 **Special cases**
When automatic debiting is used, the claims fees are deemed paid on the last day of the six-month period of **R.162(2)** (**AAD.6.1(e)**). Where the communication under **R.161** and **162** is waived, any claims fees cannot be paid by automatic debiting and must be paid by another means of payment (sp5 OJ 2017 Annex A2 page 53 point 3(d)).

If a mandatory response to the **R.161(1)** communication is not filed in the six-month period, the EPO will inform the applicant that the application is deemed withdrawn. The applicant may respond by requesting further processing and filing amended claims in the two-month period for further processing. Since the amended claims will form the basis for the grant procedure, any claims fees must, according to **R.162**, be paid for the amended set of claims. A further processing fee has to be paid for both the late filing and the late payment (**Rfees2(1)12**). Any claims fees the EPO may already have debited using automatic debiting at expiry of the six-month period will be refunded and any claims fees due plus the further processing fee(s) will be debited on the last day of the further processing period (**AAD.6.1(h)**).

If a voluntary response to the **R.161** communication is not filed within the six-month period, the EPO will not send a loss-of-rights communication. The response is voluntary if the EPO was ISA and the IPER was positive, amendments were filed on entry into the EP phase, or the EPO was not ISA. If in such a case claims fees are due and are not paid within the six-month period, the EPO will send a loss-of-rights communication informing the applicant of the abandonment of the excess claims. In response he can pay the claims fees or leave the excess claims abandoned. However, he probably has also the possibility to file amended claims in the further processing period, e.g. with a smaller number of claims, and pay any claims fees for the amended claims; a further processing fee has to be paid for both the late filing and the late payment. A reason why the EPO should allow this possibility is the similarity of the case with payment of the designation fee and the extension fee. These two payments are two acts to be completed in the same period. The EPO does not send a loss of rights communication if an extension fee has not been paid in due time. However, the extension fee can be paid in the further processing period if this period was triggered by an unpaid designation fee (**Art.79(2):2.3**).

R. 162(3) Any claims fees paid within the period under paragraph 1 and in excess of those due under paragraph 2, second sentence, shall be refunded.

1 **Automatic refund**

If a European patent attorney is asked, for example by a US patent attorney, at the last minute to enter the regional phase before the EPO for a US applicant with an international application comprising a large set of claims, the European patent attorney can enter the European regional phase with the large set of claims. There is no immediate sanction if the claims fees on the large set of claims are not paid. The number of claims can then be reduced in response to the **R.161** communication and any claims fees for the reduced set paid.

However, if the excess claims fees were paid on entry and the European patent attorney later, under **R.161**, reduces the number of claims to a 'reasonable' number, the excess claims fees will be automatically refunded, under **R.162(3)**.

R. 162(4) Where a claims fee is not paid in due time, the claim concerned shall be deemed to be abandoned.

1 **Forced abandonment**

The EPO applies the same rule for reinstatement of a claim deemed abandoned after non-payment of the claims fee for direct European applications and Euro-PCT applications. Features of a claim deemed to have been abandoned pursuant to **R.162(4)** and which are not otherwise to be found in the description or drawings cannot subsequently be reintroduced into the application and, in particular, into the claims (A-III,9 and E-IX,2.1.3). See also **R.45(3):1.**

Further processing can be used to remedy non-payment of claims fees, because **R.162** is not excluded in **R.135(2)**.

R. 163 Examination of certain formal requirements by the European Patent Office

Implementation of: **Art.153**
EPC 1973: **R.111**

R. 163(1) Where the designation of the inventor under Rule 19, paragraph 1, has not yet been made within the period under Rule 159, paragraph 1, the European Patent Office shall invite the applicant to make the designation within two months.

R.19(1) Designation of the inventor
R.159(1) 31-month period for entry into European phase

1 **Invitation to submit data of inventor**

The period in **R.159(1)** is the 31-month period from the date of filing or, where applicable, priority.

R.163(1) uses the possibility offered by the PCT to file the data concerning the inventor later if national law allows that they be furnished at a time later than that of filing of a national application (**Art.4(1)(v)**, (4), **Art.22(1)** second sentence, (3), **Art.39(1)(b)** PCT).

If the data are not furnished upon entry into the European phase, the EPO invites the applicant to make the designation of inventor within two months of the notification of the invitation (**R.163(1)**). If not provided in due time, the Euro-PCT application will be refused (**R.163(6)**; E-IX,2.3.4). The loss of rights may be remedied with further processing (**Art.121, R.135**): within two months of notification of the communication, file the inventor's designation, and pay the fee (**Rfees2(1)12**). In the event the EPO has made an error, the applicant may ask, within two months of notification of the loss of rights, for a decision under **R.112(2)** EPC and prove that the data were filed in due time.

R. 163(2) Where the priority of an earlier application is claimed and the file number of the previous application or the copy thereof provided for in Rule 52, paragraph 1, and Rule 53 have not yet been submitted within the period under Rule 159, paragraph 1, the European Patent Office shall invite the applicant to furnish that number or copy within two months. Rule 53, paragraph 2, shall apply.

Amended by decision of the Administrative Council of 21.10.2008, which entered into force on 01.04.2009. (OJ 2008 p.513)
R.52(1) Declaration of priority
R.53 Priority documents
R.159(1) 31-month period for entry into European phase

1 **Invitation to submit data and copy of earlier application**
Applicants often sumbit copies of priority documents during the international phase, which the IB transmits to the EPO as designated Office (**R.17.2(a)** PCT). In the exceptional case that the EPO does not have the file number and/or copy of the priority document by expiry of the 31-month period of **R.159(1)**, it will invite the applicant to furnish them within a two-month period (**R.163(2)**). However, in the following two cases it will not request a copy of the document:

Firstly, according to the last sentence of **R.163(2)**, **R.53(2)** shall apply; accordingly, no copy will be requested under **R.163(2)** if the EPO can retrieve a copy from its own files, from participating patent offices through DAS, or from the CN, JP, KR or US patent offices through electronic exchange (OJ 2018 A78). See also **R.53(2):1**.

Secondly, the EPO as designated Office (dO) may not ask the applicant to furnish a copy, under **R.17.2(a)** PCT, second sentence (which prevails over **R.163(2)** under **Art.150(2)**) if the applicant has, in the international phase, submitted the priority document to the IB or the rO (**R.17.1(a)** PCT) or, when the rO has issued the priority document, asked the rO to transmit it to the IB (**R.17.1(b)** PCT), or has requested the IB to retrieve the priority document from a digital library if available (**R.17.1(b-bis)** PCT; PCT §2.10). In such a case the EPO as dO requests the IB to transmit the priority document to the EPO (**R.17.2(a)** PCT, first sentence). If, despite the applicant complying with **R.17.1(a)**, **R.17.1(b)** or **R.17.1(b-bis)** PCT, the IB does not transmit a copy of the priority document to the EPO as dO, the EPO may nevertheless proceed with substantive examination of the application. However, no European patent may be granted until such time as a copy of the priority document is on file. See also E-IX,2.3.5 and F-VI,2.1.

If the file number or the copy is not filed in due time, the right of priority is lost for the application under **R.163(6)**. Further processing under **Art.121** and **R.135** is available.

2 **Translation of priority document**
The EPO will only request a translation of a priority application not in an official EPO language if the validity of the priority claim is relevant for the assessment of the patentability of the invention concerned (**R.53(3)** EPC; **R.51bis.1(e)(i)** PCT).

R. 163(3) Where, at the expiry of the period under Rule 159, paragraph 1, a sequence listing complying with the standard provided for in the Administrative Instructions under the PCT is not available to the European Patent Office, the applicant shall be invited to file a sequence listing complying with the rules laid down by the President of the European Patent Office within two months. Rule 30, paragraphs 2 and 3, shall apply mutatis mutandis.

R.30(2) Late filed sequence listing not part of description
R.30(3) Invitation to file amended sequence listing
R.159(1) 31-month period for entry into the European phase

1 **Invitation to submit sequence listing**
The rule is based on **R.5.2(a)** and **R.13ter.3** PCT.

The EPO invites the applicant, where appropriate, to furnish the prescribed sequence listing in electronic form according to WIPO Standard ST.25, paragraph 39 ff. if not yet done so on expiry of the period for entry into the European phase. A late-furnished sequence listing will not form part of the description (**R.30(2)**). The late furnishing is subject to payment of a late furnishing fee (**R.30(3)**; **Rfees2(1)14a**). If the applicant does not furnish the prescribed sequence listing and pay the fee when invited to do so, the application will be refused in accordance with **R.30(3)**. Note that, as an exception, the sanction of non-compliance is not in **R.163(6)**, but in **R.30(3)**. A refusal under **R.30(3)** can be remedied using further processing (see **R.30(3):1**). (E-IX,2.4.2; OJ 2011 p.372; OJ 2013 p.542)

R. 163(4) Where, at the expiry of the period under Rule 159, paragraph 1, the address, the nationality or the State in which his residence or principal place of business is located is missing in respect of any applicant, the European Patent Office shall invite the applicant to furnish these indications within two months.

R.159(1) 31-month period for entry into European phase

1 **Invitation to furnish nationality or state of residence**

R.4.5(a) PCT requires the name, address and nationality/residence of all applicants to be furnished to the rO. However, if these indications are not furnished for all applicants, this can be overlooked by the rO under **R.26.2bis(b)** PCT (see PCT §2.2.3). In the national phase, any designated Office may ask for the missing indications to be furnished under **R.51bis.1(a)(vii)** PCT; the EPO has made use of this option in **R.163(4)** EPC.

If the address, nationality or state of residence of any applicant is missing at expiry of the period for entry into the European phase, the EPO invites the applicant to furnish these indications within two months of notification of the invitation (**R.163(4)**).

Failure to rectify this deficiency in due time, leads to refusal of the application according to **R.163(6)**. The applicant will be notified of this decision according to **R.126(1)**. Failure to file the indications in due time may be remedied by further processing (**Art.121**; **R.135**). (E-IX,2.3.1; **R.4.5(a)(ii)** and **(iii)** PCT; **R.51bis.1(a)(vii)** PCT; **R.26.2bis(b)** PCT)

2 **Signatures**

If an international application is not signed by all applicants in the international phase as required by **R.4.15** PCT, this can be overlooked by a rO under **R.26.2bis(a)** PCT. In the national phase, any designated office may ask for missing signature(s) under **R.51bis.1(a)(vi)** PCT; the EPO has not implemented this possibility. (see PCT §2.2.3)

R. 163(5) Where, at the expiry of the period under Rule 159, paragraph 1, the requirements of Article 133, paragraph 2, have not been satisfied, the European Patent Office shall invite the applicant to appoint a professional representative within two months.

Art.133(2) Compulsory representation
R.159(1) 31-month period for entry into European phase

1 **Invitation to appoint professional representative**
Art.27(7) PCT allows a designated Office to apply national law for representation after the processing of the international application before that Office has started. The EPO as designated Office applies **Art.133(2)** EPC via **Art.150(2)** EPC according to E-IX,2.3.1. The EPO starts processing the international application immediately after expiry of the 31-month period. Hence, an applicant who must be represented under **Art.133(2)** may himself carry out any act before the expiry, such as the acts of **R.159**. After the expiry, subsequent acts must be carried out or validated by a professional representative entitled to practise before the EPO under **Art.134(1)**. (See Euro-PCT Guide, §466-472)

If representation is required and no representative has been appointed by expiry of the 31-month period, the EPO will invite the applicant to appoint a representative within 2 months (**R.163(5)**; **Art.133(2)**; see also, A-III,16.2(i), applicable to Euro-PCT applications by the reference from E-IX,2.3.1 to A-III,2 to A-III,16). The sanction for non-compliance is refusal of the application under **R.163(6)**. Further processing under **Art.121** and **R.135** is available. (E-IX,2.3.1)

An agent appointed for the international phase will not be automatically regarded as agent for the national phase. Hence, a professional representative appointed for the international phase must be re-appointed for the European phase on regional entry, unless he was also explicitly appointed for the European phase before the EPO acting as rO. (Euro-PCT Guide §114)

R. 163(6) If the deficiencies noted under paragraphs 1, 4 or 5 are not corrected in due time, the European patent application shall be refused. If the deficiency noted under paragraph 2 is not corrected in due time, the right of priority shall be lost for the application.

1 **Sanctions on not correcting deficiencies**
If any of the periods in **R.163(1)**, **(2)**, **(4)**, **or (5)** is missed, further processing may be used as a remedy as **R.163** is not excluded from further processing under **Art.121(4)** or **R.135(2)**. See E-IX,2.3.4 for **R.163(1)**, E-IX,2.4.2 for **R.163(3)** referring to **R.30(3)** where **R.30(3)** is not excluded, and E-IX,2.3.1 for **R.163(4)** and **(5)**. Further processing should, mutatis mutandis, be possible in the case of **R.163(2)**, although it is not specifically mentioned in E-IX,2.3.5. Note that the sanction for not complying with **R.163(3)** is not in **R.163(6)**, but in **R.30(3)**.

R. 164 Unity of invention and further searches

Amended by decision of the Administrative Council of 16.10.2013 which entered into force on 01.11.2014 (OJ 2013 p.503). See EPO document CA/91/13 and OJ 2014 A70 for explanatory remarks. The amendment broadens the possibility to have the EPO as designated or elected office search one or more inventions not searched in the international phase.
Implementation of: **Art.153**
EPC 1973: **R.112**

1 **General**

Under **R.164** an applicant of a Euro-PCT application may on entry into the European phase and upon payment of a search fee obtain a search of any invention that was not searched by the EPO in the international phase. Such an invention may be a non-unitary invention claimed in the PCT application as filed and not searched in the international phase or an invention added to the claims on entry into the European phase.

There are two different procedures for the search, depending on the ISA that searched the application. **R.164(1)** provides for a procedure where the EPO did not act as ISA or SISA and in which a supplementary European search must be carried out. **R.164(2)** applies to the situation where the EPO acted as ISA or SISA and a supplementary European search is dispensed with under **Art.153(7)**. The provisions in **R.164(3)** and **(4)** clarify aspects of the procedure under **R.164(2)**, whereas **R.164(5)** provides for a refund of any search fee paid after an unjustified non-unity objection under **R.164(1)** or **(2)** in line with **R.64(2)** EPC.

If after the **R.164** procedure more than one invention has been searched by the EPO, the EPO will invite the applicant to select the invention to be prosecuted and restrict the application to this invention.

R.164 ensures that applicants of Euro-direct and Euro-PCT applications, irrespective of whether the EPO was (S)ISA or not, have equal rights regarding prosecution before the EPO, especially in the case of non-unity (OJ 2014 A70 §4). However, rights are not equal in that an applicant of a Euro-PCT application has two opportunities to have multiple inventions searched (in the international phase and in the European phase) and an applicant of a Euro-direct application has only one opportunity (see OJ 2007 se5 (EN) p.256). There is also difference in treatment between applicants of an international application where the EPO was ISA and where the EPO was not ISA regarding refund of the examination fee (see **R.164(4):3**).

2 **Basis of search**

The applicant has two opportunities to amend his Euro-PCT application voluntarily before the search under **R.164**. He may amend it on entry when specifying the application documents on which the grant procedure is to be based under **R.159(1)(b)** (see **R.159(1):3**) and in response to the **R.161** communication, issued shortly after entry (see **R.161(1):1**). The claims as pending at expiry of the response period for the **R.161** communication are the basis of any searches under **R.164**.

The amendments may not extend the subject-matter of the application as filed (**Art.123(2)**). However, both amendments are not restricted by the requirement of **R.137(5)** (OJ 2014 A70 §13); hence, the amended claims need not combine with the originally claimed invention(s) to form a single general inventive concept. Note, that this exception has no basis in the EPC.

The application on which the prosecution is to be based may be the application as filed or amended in the international phase, amended on entry or in response to the **R.161** communication. The amendments may add subject-matter from the description to the claims. The application may claim unsearched inventions, e.g. inventions for which no search fee was paid after a non-unity objection by the ISA. Note, that the EPO as SISA searches only the invention first mentioned in the claims; no search fee can be paid for other claimed inventions, which the SISA will therefore not search.

R. 164(1) If the European Patent Office considers that the application documents which are to serve as the basis for the supplementary European search do not comply with the requirement of unity of invention, it shall:

(a) draw up a partial supplementary search report on those parts of the application which relate to the invention, or the group of inventions within the meaning of Article 82, first mentioned in the claims;

(b) inform the applicant that, for the supplementary European search report to cover the other inventions, a further search fee must be paid, in respect of each invention involved, within a period of two months; and

(c) draw up the supplementary European search report for the parts of the application relating to inventions in respect of which search fees have been paid.

Art.82 Unity of invention

Applicable to any application for which the supplementary European search report under **Art.153(7)** has not been drawn up at 01.11.2014 (note a different wording in OJ 2014 A70 §23).

1 **Further searches where the EPO was not (S)ISA**

R.164(1) applies to Euro-PCT applications for which the EPO did not act as ISA or as SISA and will draw up a supplementary search report. It provides that an applicant of a Euro-PCT application in the European phase, where the EPO opines that the application lacks unity of invention, is entitled to have further searches performed upon payment of further search fees. Furthermore, the applicant is entitled to select, from among all inventions in the application documents which were searched by the EPO, the invention to be prosecuted in the European grant procedure.

The provision follows, where possible, the wording of **R.64** (non-unity). Accordingly, **R.62a** (plurality of independent claims) and **63** (no meaningful search possible) apply in the same way as to any supplementary search. (OJ 2014 A70 §7)

2 **Procedure**

2.1 ENTRY INTO THE EUROPEAN PHASE

When the EPO has not acted as ISA or SISA, the EPO will draw up a supplementary search report under **Art.153(7)**. The search fee for the supplementary search (**Rfees2(1)2**) must be paid under **R.159(1)(e)** within 31 months from filing or priority. The search fee will be reduced when the (S)ISA was one of the authorities mentioned in OJ 2011 p.616 and OJ 2012 p.584 (**Art.153(7)**).

The request for examination, which includes payment of the examination fee, must be filed within 6 months from the publication of the PCT search report (**R.70(1)** & **Art.153(6)**). If the 6 month period expires before 31 months from filing or priority, which is usually the case, the request must be filed within 31 months from filing or priority (**R.159(1)(f)**).

Shortly after entry, the EPO despatches the **R.161(2)** communication, giving the applicant a six-month period to amend the application. A response to the communication is not mandatory; the applicant may of course file arguments or amendments in which he takes the written opinion of the ISA other than the EPO into account. The opportunity for amendment may be used to reduce the number of claims, because the number of claims pending at expiry of the six-month period determines the claims fees to be paid (**R.162(2)**).

2.2 SUPPLEMENTARY SEARCH

After expiry of the 6-month period of **R.161(2)**, a search division will carry out a supplementary search under **Art.153(7)** based on the claims of the Euro-PCT application, possibly amended under **R.159(1)(b)** or **R.161(2)** (F-V,13.2).

The search examiner will assess the unity of the pending set of claims and, if found to be unitary, the procedure under **R.164(1)** will not be applied and he will carry out the supplementary search. When completed, the supplementary search report together with the search opinion will be transmitted to the applicant.

See **R.164(4):2** for the competence of the search division for the searches under **R.164(1)**.

2.3 SEARCH OF NON-UNITARY INVENTIONS

If the search division considers that the claims lack unity, the search division will draw up a partial supplementary search report on the invention first mentioned in the claims (**R.164(1)(a)**). The report states the unity objection and gives a specification of the separate inventions. The report does not include a search opinion (OJ 2014 A70 §8). The partial search report will be sent to the applicant together with an invitation to pay a further search fee for each non-unitary invention (**R.164(1)(b)**).

If an application has a plurality of independent claims in a claim category, the EPO will usually send first a request to indicate the independent claims to be searched under **R.62a(1)** followed by the invitation to pay further search fees. (B-VIII,4.5)

If no meaningful search can be carried out, the EPO will usually send first a request to indicate the subject-matter to be searched under **R.63(1)** followed by the invitation to pay further search fees. (B-VIII,3.4; C-III,3.1.3)

The fee reduction mentioned in the above section **2.1** does not apply to the further search fees (A-X,9.3.1). It should be noted that the further search fee in the European phase is lower than the additional fee for a further search in the international phase (see **Rfees2(1)2**).

Any further search fee must be paid within 2 months (**R.164(1)(b)**). The period is excluded from further processing (**R.135(2)**), but re-establishment is available. If no further search fees are paid, the applicant is taken to have elected the first searched invention for prosecution (C-III,3.1.1). The further search fees will be debited automatically where an automatic debit order is on file; if the applicant does not want this, he must inform the EPO before expiry of the 2-month period (OJ 2017 sp5 Annex 2 page 49 Point 3(b)).

If further search fees have been paid, the search division will draw up a supplementary search report relating to each invention for which a search fee has been paid (**R.164(1)(c)**). The supplementary search report together with a search opinion will be sent to the applicant; the search opinion contains the reasoning behind the lack of unity (B-XI,5). See **R.164(5)** for a refund of search fees.

2.4 END OF SEARCH PROCEDURE

At the end of the search procedure the EPO invites the applicant to respond to the search opinion if any objections to grant are noted (**R.70a(2)**) and to indicate whether he wants to proceed with the application in view of the results of the search (**R.70(2)**; **R.70a(2)**). The response must be filed within 6 months (E-IX,2.5.3). After receipt of the indication to proceed, the responsibility for the application transfers from the search division to the examining division (**R.10(3)**) and the substantive examination under **Art.94** begins.

At the beginning of the examination the applicant is invited to restrict the application to a single invention searched by the EPO for prosecution if not yet done so in response to the search opinion (**G2/92**; C-III,3.1.2; H-II,7.4.2). Note, that the invitation is not mentioned in the law. If the application is not properly restricted to a searched invention, the application may be refused under **R.164(1)** in line with **G2/92** (H-II,7.2).

A divisional application may be filed for any invention not pursued in the application. If the EPO has already drawn up a search report for such an invention, the search fee paid for the divisional may be refunded under **Rfees9(2)**.

If no indication to proceed is filed within 6 months, the application is deemed withdrawn (**R.70(3)**). See **R.70(2):2** for remedies. Since the examining division has not yet assumed responsibility, the examination fee paid under **R.159(1)(f)** is refunded in full (**Rfees11(a)**; A-VI,2.2).

2.5 EXAMPLE

As an example, an ISA different from the EPO opines that inventions A and B claimed in a Euro-PCT application are non-unitary. The applicant does not pay a further search fee and the ISA searches only invention A first mentioned in the claims. On entry into the European phase, the applicant specifies inventions B, A and C for prosecution, where C has been taken from the description. No amendment is made under **R.161(2)**. The partial supplementary search report relates to invention B, raises a non-unity objection to inventions B, A and C, and invites the applicant to pay further search fees for inventions A and C. The applicant pays a further search fee for invention C. The supplementary search report will now cover inventions B and C. The applicant selects invention C for prosecution to grant and deletes inventions A and B. Inventions A and B can only be pursued in divisionals.

R. 164(2) If the supplementary European search report is dispensed with and the Examining Division considers that in the application documents which are to serve as the basis for examination an invention, or a group of inventions within the meaning of Article 82, is claimed which was not searched by the European Patent Office in its capacity as International Searching Authority or Authority specified for supplementary international search, the Examining Division shall:

(a) inform the applicant that a search will be performed in respect of any such invention for which a search fee is paid within a period of two months;

(b) issue the results of any search performed in accordance with paragraph (a) together with:
- **a communication under Article 94, paragraph 3, and Rule 71, paragraphs 1 and 2, in which it shall give the applicant the opportunity to comment on these results and to amend the description, claims and drawings, or**
- **a communication under Rule 71, paragraph 3, and**

(c) where appropriate, in the communication issued under paragraph (b), invite the applicant to limit the application to one invention, or group of inventions within the meaning of Article 82, for which a search report was drawn up by the European Patent Office in its capacity either as International Searching Authority or as Authority specified for supplementary international search, or for which a search was performed in accordance with the procedure under paragraph (a).

Art.82 Unity of invention
Art.94(3) Examination of the European patent application
R.71(1),(2) Invitation to correct deficiencies
R.71(3) Invitation to approve text to be granted
Applicable to any application for which the first communication under **Art.94(3)** and **R.71(1)** and (2) or, as the case may be, **R.71(3)** has not been drawn up at 01.11.2014 (note a different wording in OJ 2014 A70 §24).

1 **Further searches where the EPO was (S)ISA**

R.164(2) applies to Euro-PCT applications for which the EPO acted as ISA or as SISA. It provides that an applicant of a Euro-PCT application in the European phase, where the EPO opines that the application includes a claimed invention that is not searched by the EPO as (S)ISA, is entitled to have this invention searched upon payment of a search fee. Furthermore, the applicant is entitled to select, from among all inventions in the application documents which were searched by the EPO, the invention to be prosecuted in the European grant procedure.

The focus in **R.164(2)** is on whether examination is requested for a non-searched invention, not on whether the application documents to be assessed by the examining division comply with the requirement of unity of invention (C-III,2.3).

2 **Procedure**

2.1 ENTRY INTO THE EUROPEAN PHASE

When the EPO has acted as ISA or SISA, the EPO will not draw up a supplementary search report under **Art.153(7)** and no search fee need be paid under **R.159(1)(e)** on entry into the European phase.

The request for examination, which includes payment of the examination fee, must be filed within 6 months from the publication of the PCT search report (**R.70(1)** & **Art.153(6)**). If the 6 month period expires before 31 months from filing or priority, which is usually the case, the request must be filed within 31 months from filing or priority (**R.159(1)(f)**).

Shortly after entry into the European phase the EPO issues a **R.161(1)** communication, giving a 6-month period for response. The application of **R.161(1)** is independent of the procedure in **R.164(2)**. If an invention for which a negative written opinion or IPER was drawn up is specified for prosecution, the communication will invite to applicant to respond to the deficiencies noted in the written opinion or IPER. A response to a negative opinion is mandatory, even if the applicant wants to prosecute another invention than the one on which the written opinion or IPER is based. He may respond by deleting the invention or addressing the deficiencies. (CA/91/13)

In response to the **R.161(1)** communication voluntary amendments may be filed. The opportunity for amendment may be used to reduce the number of claims, because the number of claims pending at expiry of the six-month period determines the claims fees to be paid (**R.162(2)**).

2.2 START OF EXAMINATION

After expiry of the six-month period for response to the **R.161(1)** communication, the examining division starts the substantive examination. See **R.164(4):1** for the competence of the examining division for the searches under **R.164(2)**.

As a first step the examiner will assess under **R.164(2)** whether the application documents claim any invention that was not searched by the EPO acting as ISA or SISA (see AG-IP §8.045 for non-unity before SISA).

Neither **R.164(2)**, nor the Guidelines, nor OJ 2014 A70 §13 explain when the EPO as designated or elected office considers an invention not to have been searched by the EPO as (S)ISA. In practice, the EPO applies a test similar to the test used for **R.137(5)**: an invention is considered as not searched by the EPO as (S)ISA if the invention lacks unity with each of the one or more searched inventions; if the invention is unitary with at least one searched invention, the invention is considered to have been searched.

If there are no unsearched inventions, the procedure under **R.164(2)** will not be carried out and the examiner will continue the examination procedure by issuing an **Art.94(3)** or a **R.71(3)** communication.

2.3 ADDITIONAL SEARCHES

If the examining division considers that the application claims one or more unsearched inventions, it will issue an invitation under **R.164(2)(a)** to pay a search fee for each unsearched invention. The communication may also invite the applicant to restrict the scope of the search under **R.62a(1)** (multiple independent claims) and / or **R.63(1)** (unsearchable claims) (C-III,3.1.3).

It should be noted that the further search fee in the European phase is lower than the additional fee for a further search in the international phase (see **Rfees2(1)2**). See **R.164(5)** for a refund of search fees.

Any search fee must be paid within 2 months (**R.164(2)(a)**). The period is excluded from further processing (**R.135(2)**), but re-establishment is available. The search fees will be debited automatically where an automatic debit order is on file; if the applicant does not want this, he must inform the EPO before expiry of the 2-month period (sp5 OJ 2017 page 49 point 3(b)).

If no search fee is paid, the procedure under **R.164(2)** ends at expiry of the 2-month period and the prosecution continues with a communication under **Art.94(3)** or **R.71(3)** (C-III,3.1.1), based on the first invention searched by the EPO in the international phase, and requesting the applicant to delete non-searched inventions from the claims.

If a search fee is paid, the examining division will search the corresponding invention. This search is neither a European search (see **R.164(4)**) nor a supplementary search, which latter term is reserved for searches under **Art.153(7)**. Rather, it is a 'search incident during substantive examination'.

If the claims are not sufficiently clear to identify a non-searched invention, the examining division will issue an **Art.94(3)** communication setting out the objection under **Art.84**. If after clarification claims relate to unsearched subject-matter, no invitation to pay a search fee under **R.164(2)** will be issued anymore and the claims can only be prosecuted in a divisional. (C-III,2.3)

If the invention to be searched has a plurality of independent claims in a claim category, the EPO will send first a request to indicate the independent claims to be searched under **R.62a(1)** before starting the search. (B-VIII,4.5)

If no meaningful search can be carried out on an invention to be searched, the EPO will send first a request to indicate the subject-matter to be searched under **R.63(1)** before starting the search. (B-VIII,3.4)

2.4 COMMUNICATION OF SEARCH RESULTS

The search results of each invention for which a search fee has been paid are communicated to the applicant in an annex to an **Art.94(3)** communication or a **R.71(3)** communication (**R.164(2)(b)**). The communication will also give the findings of the examining division (OJ 2014 A70 §16). The **Art.94(3)** communication invites the applicant to comment on the search report and the findings and to amend the application of his own volition within a set period (OJ 2014 A70 §16). The amendments at this stage are subject to the requirements of **R.137(5)**, first sentence (C-III,2.3; 3.1.3). The communication will also request the applicant to select a single invention for prosecution to grant from the inventions searched by the EPO both in the international and in the European phase (**R.164(2)(c)**). Other inventions in the application, searched and unsearched, can be pursued in a divisional.

The transmission of the **Art.94(3)** or **R.71(3)** communication to the applicant terminates the **R.164(2)** procedure.

If the applicant does not want to pursue the application anymore in view of the search results, he can refrain from responding to the communication, resulting in the application being deemed withdrawn. The examination fee will not be refunded, because the examining division assumed responsibility already on payment of the examination fee when entering the European phase (see **Rfees11**).

2.5 EXAMPLE

As an example, the EPO as ISA opines that inventions A and B claimed in a Euro-PCT application are non-unitary. The applicant does not pay a further search fee and only invention A first mentioned in the claims is searched. On entry into the European phase, the applicant specifies inventions B, A and C for prosecution, where C has been taken from the description. No amendments are filed in response to the **R.161(1)** communication. The examining division invites the applicant to pay search fees for inventions B and C. The applicant pays a search fee for invention C. The **Art.94(3)** communication includes the search results for invention C, the findings of the examining division for invention A and C, and a request to limit the application to a single invention. The applicant selects invention C and deletes inventions A and B from the claims. Inventions A and B can only be pursued in divisionals.

R. 164(3) In the procedure under paragraph 2(a), Rules 62a and 63 shall apply mutatis mutandis.

R.62a Plurality of independent claims
R.63
Unsearchable subject-matter
Valid as of 01.11.2014.

1 **Provisions applicable during search**

R.164(3) states explicitly for reasons of clarity that **R.62a** (plurality of independent claims) and **R.63** (unsearchable subject-matter) apply mutatis mutandis to the procedure under **R.164(2)(a)** (CA/91/13 §29).

The procedure in C-III,2.3 not to carry out the **R.164(2)** procedure if the claims are not sufficiently clear to identify a non-searched invention could be regarded as conflicting with **R.164(3)**, which obliges the EPO to carry out the **R.62a** procedure in case of unclarity during the **R.164(2)** procedure.

R. 164(4) Rule 62 and Rule 70, paragraph 2, shall not apply to the results of any search performed in accordance with paragraph 2.

R.62 Extended European search report
R.70(2) Confirmation of early filed request for examination

1 **Competence of the examining division for R.164(2) searches**

R.164(2) states that the examining division is responsible for the searches under this provision. This is emphasised in **R.164(4)** for reasons of clarity, by stressing that the results of a search under **R.164(2)** will not be issued as an extended search report under **R.62**, i.e. as a search report and an opinion. The results will instead be set out in an annex to an **Art.94(3)** communication. **R.164(4)** also states that no invitation under **R.70(2)** to indicate whether the applicant wishes to proceed further will be issued. Hence, if the applicant does not pursue the searched application after the **R.164(2)** search, the examination fee paid under **R.159(1)(f)** will not be refunded.

The competence of the examining division for the searches is in line with **R.159(1)(f)** for filing the request for examination. The provision refers to the period of 6 months from publication of the European search report in **R.70(1)**, where the term 'European search report' is interpreted as 'international search report' pursuant to **Art.153(6)**. The examining division will become responsible for the application from the time of filing the request for examination under **R.10(2)**, which is usually on entry into the European phase, when the examination fee has been paid. **R.70(2)** does not apply, because the request for examination was filed *after* transmission of the international search report to the applicant; note, that the 'European search report' in **R.70(2)** has also been interpreted as the 'international search report' (CA/91/13 §30), consistent with the interpretation of **R.70(1)**.

2 **Competence of the search division for R.164(1) searches**

J8/83 held that an applicant of a Euro-PCT application is entitled to the same rights as the applicant of a Euro-direct application, in particular regarding a refund of the examination fee if the application is withdrawn before substantive examination begins. To allow a refund, the decision equates the European search report in **R.70(2)** with the supplementary European search report. Since the request for examination under **R.159(1)(f)** is filed before the supplementary European search report has been transmitted to the applicant, the applicant will receive an invitation under **R.70(2)** to indicate whether he wants to proceed further with the application. If he does not send a positive response to the invitation, the application will be deemed withdrawn before the examining division has assumed responsibility for the application under **R.10(3)**. Hence, the examination fee will be refunded under **Rfees11**.

The search division is competent till a positive response to the **R.70(2)** invitation is received, and it is therefore responsible for the supplementary search and any further searches under **R.164(1)** (**R.10(3)**; F-V,13.2).

Note, that **Art.153(6)** equates the European search report with the international search report, whether or not the EPO acted as ISA. Hence, there are two European search reports for a Euro-PCT application for which the EPO did not act as (S)ISA.

R.159(1)(f) for filing the request for examination refers to the period of six months from publication of the European search report in **R.70(1)**. When **R.70(2)**, relating to the same European search report as **R.70(1)**, is interpreted to relate to the supplementary European search report, **R.70(1)** should also relate to the supplementary European search report for reason of consistency. However, the supplementary European search report is not published and can therefore not be used to define the period for paying the examination fee. Therefore the term 'European search report' in **R.70(1)** and (2) has been given different meanings: in **R.70(1)** it relates to the international search report following **Art.153(6)**, in **R.70(2)** it relates to the supplementary European search report following **J8/83**.

3 **Different treatment of applicants**

The competences set out in the previous two sections cause a difference in treatment of an applicant using the EPO as ISA and an applicant using another office as ISA. Suppose international applications I and II each claim the same two non-unitary inventions A and B; application I is searched by the USPTO as ISA, application II by the EPO as ISA. Both ISAs search only invention A. On entry into the European phase both applications claim A and B. For application I the EPO searches invention A as supplementary search and invention B upon payment of a further search fee under **R.164(1)**. For application II the EPO searches invention B upon payment of a search fee under **R.164(2)**. Both applicants are no longer interested in prosecuting the application in view of the search results and withdraw the application.

The examination fee will be refunded for application I. The examination fee will not be refunded for application II, even though the substantive examination has not yet begun. The actual search carried out under **R.164(2)** is identical to the search carried out under **R.164(1)** by the same examiner. The only difference is that the examiner acts as substantive examiner under the former and as search examiner under the latter provision. In these circumstances both applicants should be treated equally and the examination fee for applicant II should also be refunded. Although the facts are similar to those of **J8/83**, a similar decision is unlikely to be issued, because **R.164(4)** expressly rules out the application of **R.70(2)** in the procedure of **R.164(2)**.

R. 164(5) Any fee paid under paragraphs 1 or 2 shall be refunded if the applicant requests a refund and the Examining Division finds that the communication under paragraphs 1(b) or 2(a) was not justified.

1 **Refund of further search fee**

The applicant may request a refund of search fees if he regards the non-unity opinion (partly) unjustified under **R.164(1)** or (2). The examining division will refund the fees as under **R.64(2)** if it concurs with the applicant. A lack of sufficient justification of the non-unity opinion is also a ground for refund. (CA/91/13 §32; C-III,3.3)

A request filed during the search procedure under **R.164(1)** will only be dealt with after start of the examination, because only an examining division is competent to decide on the opinion. A request filed during the search procedure of **R.164(2)** can be dealt with immediately, because the examining division handles the search procedure (A-X,10.2.2). See **R.64(2):1** and C-IIi,3.3 for the refund procedure.

A search fee paid under **R.164** may be refunded if the search can be based on an earlier search according to **Rfees9(2)**. Accordingly, a search under **R.164** may give rise to a refund of a search fee paid for a later application, e.g. a divisional. (OJ 2014 A70 §22)

R. 165 The Euros-PCT application as conflicting application under Article 54, paragraph 3

A Euro-PCT application shall be considered as comprised in the state of the art under Article 54, paragraph 3, if in addition to the conditions laid down in Article 153, paragraph 3 or 4, the filing fee under Rule 159, paragraph 1(c) has been paid.

Art.54(3) European prior right
Art.153(3) Publication of Euro-PCT application
Art.153(4) Language of Euro-PCT application

R.159(1)(c) Filing fee for Euro-PCT application
Implementation of: **Art.153(5)**
EPC 1973: Art.158(1),(2)

1 **General**

This provision explicitly states that once the publication and language requirements of **Art.153(3)** and (4) have been satisfied and the filing fee has been paid for the Euro-PCT application, the application is considered to form part of the state of the art according to **Art.54(3)**. (OJ 2007 se5 (EN) p.256)

2 **Remedies**

As discussed in **R.159(1):2.2**, the EPO has withdrawn its previous reservation filed under **R.49.6** PCT. An applicant may therefore, in principle, request re-establishment (**Art.122**, **R.136**) for filing of the translation and payment of the filing fee, despite further processing (**Art.121**, **R.135**) being available. If such a request is granted, this could satisfy the publication/language requirements of **Art.153(3)** and (4) and hence create a prior right under **R.165**. (G-IV,5.2)

3 **Prior rights under EPC 1973**

In addition to the entry requirements specified in **R.165**, a prior right under the EPC1973 requires payment of the designation fee(s) in order to establish the 'commonly designated states' in accordance with **Art.54(4)** EPC1973.

Protocol on the Interpretation of Article 69

of 5 October 1973

as revised by the Act revising the EPC of 29 November 2000

1 **Introduction**

The revised text of the Protocol adopted by the Administrative Council in its decision of 28.06.2001 (Spec. Ed. 4 of OJ 2001, p. 55) has become an integral part of the Revision Act of 29.11.2000 under Art.3(2), second sentence of that act.

The Protocol on Interpretation of **Art.69** is an integral part of the Convention by the reference to it in **Art.164(1)**. It is intended to provide guidance on how **Art.69** should be applied with respect to determining the scope of protection of the granted European patent. The Protocol under EPC 1973 included only the current Art.1 Protocol; Art.2 Protocol was added by the revisions of EPC 2000.

The object of the Protocol is to avoid too much emphasis on the literal wording of the claims when considered in isolation from the remainder of the text of the patent in which they appear; and also to avoid too much emphasis upon the general inventive concept disclosed in the text of the patent as compared to the relevant prior art, without sufficient regard also to the wording of the claims as a means of definition. (**G2/88** r.4 third paragraph)

This is intended to form a 'middle way' between the former extremes of adopting a purely literal approach to the claims, and adopting a broader approach which uses the claims merely as guidelines. However, as infringement is determined on a country-by-country basis, different countries have maintained somewhat divergent approaches to determining the combination of fair protection and legal certainty mandated by Art.1 Protocol.

Art. 1 General principles

Article 69 should not be interpreted as meaning that the extent of the protection conferred by a European patent is to be understood as that defined by the strict, literal meaning of the wording used in the claims, the description and drawings being employed only for the purpose of resolving an ambiguity found in the claims. Nor should it be taken to mean that the claims serve only as a guideline and that the actual protection conferred may extend to what, from a consideration of the description and drawings by a person skilled in the art, the patent proprietor has contemplated. On the contrary, it is to be interpreted as defining a position between these extremes which combines a fair protection for the patent proprietor with a reasonable degree of legal certainty for third parties.

Art. 2 Equivalents

For the purpose of determining the extent of protection conferred by a European patent, due account shall be taken of any element which is equivalent to an element specified in the claims.

1 **Revision of the Protocol**

The provisions governing the extent of protection conferred by a European patent, i.e. **Art.69** and the Protocol on its interpretation, have turned out not to achieve, to the extent desired, the goal of ensuring as uniform an application and interpretation as possible. In particular, this is the case regarding the treatment of so-called equivalents and the importance of prior statements made by the applicant for or proprietor of a patent in the application or in the specification or during prosecution before the EPO or in proceedings concerning the validity of the patent.

The Diplomatic Conference revising the EPC discussed the incorporation of an explicit reference to equivalents into the Protocol, mainly to force UK courts to take equivalents into account, and the adoption of provisions on the use of the file history of the patent in determining the scope of protection, similar to the US. Several courts regard it as undesirable that a scope including equivalents increases with time when more equivalents are being developed over time.

There was no agreement on including provisions on the use of the file history (Dipl. Conf. document MR/24/00), nor on including an explicit definition of 'equivalents'; the intention being (as noted by the German delegation) to allow national courts sufficient latitude to apply the provisions to complex cases.(Spec. Ed. 4 of OJ 2007, Art.69)

2 **Transitional provision**

The revised Protocol on the Interpretation of **Art.69** is applicable to European patents already granted at the time of EPC 2000 entry into force and to European patents granted on European patent applications pending at, or filed on or after that time. (Spec. Ed. 4 of OJ 2007)

Although the Special Edition does not mention the 'or filed on or after', this must be included in view of **Art.7(1)**, first sentence of the Revision Act.

3 **Equivalents**

No definition of 'equivalents' is given in the Protocol or the EPC. The basic proposal by the WIPO from 1991 for the 'Treaty supplementing the Paris Convention as far as patents are concerned' extends the protection of a claim to cover not only all the elements as expressed in the claim but also equivalents. In **Art.21(2)(b)** it defines equivalents as:

An element ('the equivalent element') shall generally be considered as being equivalent to an element as expressed in a claim if, at the time of any alleged infringement, either of the following conditions is fulfilled in regard to the invention as claimed:

1 the equivalent element performs substantially the same function in substantially the same way and produces substantially the same result as the element as expressed in the claim, or

2 it is obvious to a person skilled in the art that the same result as that achieved by means of the element as expressed in the claim can be achieved by means of the equivalent element.

A similar definition was given in **T697/92**, using an equivalent in the assessment of inventive step. The interpretation of equivalents in the contracting states has not yet been harmonized (see for example Singer Art.69, rdn.7).

Use of the term 'elements' in Art.2 Protocol conforms with the terminology of the PLT, and was considered during the Diplomatic Conference to be more precise than the proposed alternative 'means', as well as being more applicable to fields such as chemistry.

Protocol on Jurisdiction and the Recognition of Decisions in respect of the Right to the Grant of a European Patent

(PROTOCOL ON RECOGNITION)

of 5 October 1973

1 **Protocol on Recognition**
The Protocol on Recognition serves to realize the material claims of **Art.61** on the European patent. It governs the competence of the national courts and the recognition of their decisions. The Protocol applies only to European patent applications (Art.1(1) Prot. on Rec.), not to granted patents. The Protocol is an integral part of the EPC according to **Art.164(1)**.

Chapter I *Jurisdiction*

Art. 1

Art. 1(1) The courts of the Contracting States shall, in accordance with Articles 2 to 6, have jurisdiction to decide claims, against the applicant, to the right to the grant of a European patent in respect of one or more of the Contracting States designated in the European Patent application.

Art. 1(2) For the purposes of this Protocol, the term "courts" shall include authorities which, under the national law of a Contracting State, have jurisdiction to decide the claims referred to in paragraph 1. Any Contracting State shall notify the European Patent Office of the identity of any authority on which such a jurisdiction is conferred, and the European Patent Office shall inform the other Contracting States accordingly.

1 **Authority having jurisdiction on entitlement**
At present the second sentence of **Art.1(2)** applies only for the patent office in Great Britain.

Art. 1(3) For the purposes of this Protocol, the term "Contracting State" refers to a Contracting State which has not excluded application of this Protocol pursuant to Article 167 of the Convention.

1 **Reservations**
The reservations under **Art.167** have ended on 07.10.1992, apart from the rights still in force for applications filed before this date (see **Art.167:1**).
Since **Art.167** has been deleted in the EPC 2000, Art.1(3) Prot. Rec. should also have been deleted.

Art. 2

Subject to Articles 4 and 5, if an applicant for a European patent has his residence or principal place of business within one of the Contracting States, proceedings shall be brought against him in the courts of that Contracting State.

Art. 3

Subject to Articles 4 and 5, if an applicant for a European patent has his residence or principal place of business outside the Contracting States, and if the party claiming the right to the grant of the European patent has his residence or principal place of business within one of the Contracting States, the courts of the latter State shall have exclusive jurisdiction.

Art. 4

Subject to Article 5, if the subject-matter of a European patent application is the invention of an employee, the courts of the Contracting State, if any, whose law determines the right to the European patent pursuant to Article 60, paragraph 1, second sentence, of the Convention, shall have exclusive jurisdiction over proceedings between the employee and the employer.

Art. 5

Art. 5(1) If the parties to a dispute concerning the right to the grant of a European patent have concluded an agreement, either in writing or verbally with written confirmation, to the effect that a court or the courts of a particular Contracting State shall decide on such a dispute, the court or courts of that State shall have exclusive jurisdiction.

Art. 5(2) However, if the parties are an employee and his employer, paragraph 1 shall only apply in so far as the national law governing the contract of employment allows the agreement in question.

Art. 6

In cases where neither Articles 2 to 4 nor Article 5, paragraph 1, apply, the courts of the Federal Republic of Germany shall have exclusive jurisdiction.

1 **Jurisdiction**

The following points summarize the provisions in Art.2 to 6:

1 If there is an agreement between parties, the court in a contracting state both parties have agreed to is competent, provided national labour law allows the agreement (Art.5(1)).

If there is no agreement or a not-allowed agreement or if the court is not in a contracting state, then

2 If the patent application relates to an employee invention, the courts of that contracting state are exclusively competent whose law determines the right to the patent under **Art.60(1)** (Art.4). According to **Art.60(1)** it is the contracting state in which the employee is mainly employed; if that state cannot be determined, it is the state in which the employer has the place of business to which the employee is attached.

If it is not an employer-employee case, then

3 If the applicant lives or works within a contracting state, a court in that contracting state is competent (Art.2).

4 If the applicant lives or works outside the contracting states and the claiming party lives or works within a contracting state, the courts of the latter contracting state are competent (Art.3).

5 If none of the previous cases applies, e.g. the applicant and the claiming party both live and work outside the contracting states, the courts in Germany are competent (Art.6).

Art. 7

The courts of Contracting States before which claims referred to in Article 1 are brought shall of their own motion decide whether or not they have jurisdiction pursuant to Articles 2 to 6.

Art. 8

Art. 8(1) In the event of proceedings based on the same claim and between the same parties being brought before courts of different Contracting States, the court to which a later application is made shall of its own motion decline jurisdiction in favour of the court to which an earlier application was made.

1 **Priority in the case of several courts**
A third party can start proceedings in different states, or different parties living in different states can each start proceedings in their own state. This provision gives the priority between the several courts.

Art. 8(2) In the event of the jurisdiction of the court to which an earlier application is made being challenged, the court to which a later application is made shall stay the proceedings until the other court takes a final decision.

Chapter II *Recognition*

Art. 9

Art. 9(1) Subject to the provisions of Article 11, paragraph 2, final decisions given in any Contracting State on the right to the grant of a European patent in respect of one or more of the Contracting States designated in the European patent application shall be recognised without requiring special procedure in the other Contracting States.

Art. 9(2) The jurisdiction of the court whose decision is to be recognised and the validity of such decision may not be reviewed.

Art. 10

Article 9, paragraph 1, shall not be applicable where:

(a) an applicant for a European patent who has not contested a claim proves that the document initiating the proceedings was not notified to him regularly and sufficiently early for him to defend himself; or

(b) an applicant proves that the decision is incompatible with another decision given in a Contracting State in proceedings between the same parties which were started before those in which the decision to be recognised was given.

Art. 11

Art. 11(1) In relations between any Contracting States the provisions of this Protocol shall prevail over any conflicting provisions of other agreements on jurisdiction or the recognition of judgments.

Art. 11(2) This Protocol shall not affect the implementation of any agreement between a Contracting State and a State which is not bound by the Protocol.

Rules relating to Fees

of 20 October 1977

as adopted by decision of the Administrative Council of

the European Patent Organisation of 7 December 2006

and last amended by decision of the Administrative Council of

the European Patent Organisation of 13 December 2017

Rfees 1 General

The following shall be levied in accordance with the provisions contained in these Rules:

(a) fees due to be paid to the European Patent Office (hereinafter referred to as the Office) as provided for in the Convention and in the Implementing Regulations and the fees and expenses which the President of the Office lays down pursuant to Article 3, paragraph 1;

(b) fees and expenses pursuant to the Patent Cooperation Treaty (hereinafter referred to as the PCT), the amounts of which may be fixed by the Office.

1 **References to Rules relating to Fees**
The Rules relating to Fees (Rfees) fix the amount of the fees and how they must be paid. The obligation to pay and the period for payment are laid down in the Convention. **Art.51** EPC provides the relation between the Rfees and the Convention. The Rfees are set by the Administrative Council (**Art.33(2)(d)**). A consolidated text of the Rfees is given in OJ 2018 sp2 p.1. A provision of the Rfees is called 'Article', not 'Rule'; i.e. **Rfees1** as used herein indicates Article 1 of the Rfees.

Rfees 2 Fees provided for in the Convention and in the Implementing Regulations

Rfees2(1) The fees due to be paid to the Office under Article 1, unless otherwise provided in paragraph 2, shall be as follows:

		EUR
1.	Filing fee (Article 78, paragraph 2) where	
	- the European patent application or, in the case of an international application, the form for entry into the European phase (EPO Form 1200) is filed online	120
	- the European patent application or, in the case of an international application, the form for entry into the European phase (EPO Form 1200) is not filed online	210
1a.	Additional fee for a European patent application comprising more than 35 pages (not counting pages forming part of a sequence listing) (Rule 38, paragraph 2)	plus EUR 15 for the 36th and each subsequent page
1b.	Additional fee in the case of a divisional application filed in respect of any earlier application which is itself a divisional application (Rule 38, paragraph 4)	
	- fee for a divisional application of second generation	210
	- fee for a divisional application of third generation	425
	- fee for a divisional application of fourth generation	635
	- fee for a divisional application of fifth or any subsequent generation	850
2.	Search fee in respect of	

	- a European or supplementary European search on an application filed on or after 1 July 2005 (Article 78, paragraph 2, Rule 62, Rule 64, paragraph 1, Article 153, paragraph 7, Rule 164, paragraphs 1 and 2)	1300
	- a European or supplementary European search on an application filed before 1 July 2005 (Article 78, paragraph 2, Rule 64, paragraph 1, Article 153, paragraph 7)	885
	- an international search (Rule 16.1 PCT and Rule 158, paragraph 1)	1775
	- a supplementary international search (Rule 45*bis*.3(a) PCT)	1775
3.	Designation fee for one or more Contracting States (Article 79, paragraph 2) in respect of an application filed on or after 1 April 2009	585
4.	Renewal fees for the European patent application (Article 86, paragraph 1), calculated in each case from the date of filing of the application	
	- for the 3rd year	470
	- for the 4th year	585
	- for the 5th year	820
	- for the 6th year	1050
	- for the 7th year	1165
	- for the 8th year	1280
	- for the 9th year	1395
	- for the 10th and each subsequent year	1575
5.	Additional fee for belated payment of a renewal fee for the European patent application (Rule 51, paragraph 2)	50% of the belated renewal fee
6.	Examination fee (Article 94, paragraph 1) in respect of	
	- an application filed before 1 July 2005	1825
	- an application filed on or after 1 July 2005	1635
	- an international application filed on or after 1 July 2005 for which no supplementary European search report is drawn up (Article 153, paragraph 7)	1825
7.	Fee for grant, including fee for publication of the European patent specification (Rule 71, paragraph 3), in respect of an application filed on or after 1 April 2009	925
8.	Fee for publishing a new specification of the European patent (Rule 82, paragraph 2, Rule 95, paragraph 3)	75
9.	Surcharge for late performance of the acts required to maintain the European patent in amended form (Rule 82, paragraph 3, Rule 95, paragraph 3)	120
10.	Opposition fee (Article 99, paragraph 1, Article 105, paragraph 2)	785
10a.	Limitation or revocation fee (Article 105a, paragraph 1)	
	- request for limitation	1165
	- request for revocation	525
11.	Fee for appeal (Article 108) for an appeal filed	-

	- by a natural person or an entity referred to in Rule 6, paragraphs 4 and 5	1880
	- by any other entity	2255
11a.	Fee for petition for review (Article 112a, paragraph 4)	2910
12.	Fee for further processing (Rule 135, paragraph 1)	
	- in the event of late payment of a fee	50% of the relevant fee
	- in the event of late performance of the acts required under Rule 71, paragraph 3	255
	- other cases	255
13.	Fee for re-establishment of rights / fee for requesting restoration / fee for reinstatement of rights (Rule 136, paragraph 1, Rule 26*bis*.3(d) PCT, Rule 49*ter*.2(d) PCT, Rule 49.6(d)(i) PCT)	640
14.	Conversion fee (Article 135, paragraph 3, and Article 140)	75
14a.	Fee for late furnishing of a sequence listing (Rule 30, paragraph 3)	230
15.	Claims fee (Rule 45, paragraph 1, Rule 71, paragraph 4, and Rule 162, paragraph 1) in respect of an application filed on or after 1 April 2009	
	- for the 16th and each subsequent claim up to the limit of 50	235
	- for the 51st and each subsequent claim	585
16.	Fee for the awarding of costs (Rule 88, paragraph 3)	75
17.	Fee for the conservation of evidence (Rule 123, paragraph 3)	75
18.	Transmittal fee for an international application (Rule 157, paragraph 4)	130
19.	Fee for the preliminary examination of an international application (Rule 58 PCT and Rule 158, paragraph 2)	1830
20.	Fee for a technical opinion (Article 25)	3900
21.	Protest fee (Rule 158, paragraph 3, Rules 40.2(e) and 68.3(e) PCT)	875
22.	Review fee (Rule 45bis.6c PCT)	875

Rfees2(1) was amended by decision of the Administrative Council of 13.12.2017, entering into force on 01.04.2018 (OJ 2018 A4).

In departure from the decision, the amendments of **Rfees2(1)1, 7, 18, Rfees2(2)7** and the insertion of **Rfees2(3)** have not yet entered into force, because the novel DOCX filing method to which the provisions relate is not yet available. The provisions in the law text above are as given in OJ 2018 sp2. The EPO will announce when DOCX filing will become available and the EPO will proceed in accordance with the amended provisions (OJ 2018 A28).

1 **Publication of fees**

Each issue of the OJ publishes the fees guidance currently in force or a reference to the latest issue in which it is reproduced. Current fee rates are included in the 'Schedule of fees, costs and prices' on the EPO website. The schedule of fees is published in OJ 2018, sp2. The text of **Rfees2(1)1, 7, 18** and **Rfees2(2)7** in the publication are not yet according to the decision of the Administrative Council of 13.12.2017 (OJ 2018 A4) but as published in OJ 2018 sp2. The Schedule of fees includes the Rfees, the PCT fees fixed by WIPO, and a table with miscellaneous fees. The level of the administrative fees is given in OJ 2014 A13 (not in OJ 2018 sp2).

A guidance for payment is given in OJ 2018 A32 and contains notices concerning fees, payments, refunds, reductions, and time limits for both European and international applications.

See **Rfees9** to **12** for refund of fees and **Rfees14** for reduction of fees.

2 Amendment of fee rates

The amount of the fees is normally increased each two years, as a compromise between regularly compensating for inflation and reducing the administrative effort of the fee changes. The EPO refrained from an overall fee increase in 2018 (OJ 2018 A4).

If within six months of a fee increase the old amount of the fee is paid, the fee will be regarded validly paid if the deficit is paid within two months of an invitation from the EPO. (OJ 2018 A4 Art.3(5))

3 Filing fee (Rfees2(1)1)

To encourage online filing of the European patent application and the form for entry into the European phase, the filing fee for online filing is lower than for filing not online, e.g. by paper or fax. The reduced fee applies also to filing by data carrier.

4 Page fee (Rfees2(1)1a and Rfees2(2)7)

4.1 AMOUNT OF PAGE FEE

The term 'additional fee under R.38(2)' is replaced by 'page fee' in this book for reasons of clarity.

A page fee for excess pages will be payable on filing (OJ 2008 p.10). The amount of the page fee defined in **R.38(2)** is fixed in **Rfees2(1)1a.** For a direct European application, the page fee must be paid within a month from filing the first set of claims or the copy of a previously filed application under **R.40(3)**, whichever period expires last (**R.38(3)**). For a Euro-PCT application the page fee must be paid on entry into the European phase (**R.159(1)(c)**). The sanction on non-payment is given in **R.38(3):1.**

The calculation of the number of pages for the page fee under **Rfees2(1)1a** is set out in the Not. EPO, OJ 2009 p. 118, section 3.2; see also A-III,13.2 and summary below.

4.2 NUMBER OF PAGES OF APPLICATION

4.2.1 *Direct European applications*

For direct European applications, the calculation of the page fee is based on the number of pages of the description, claims, any drawings and one page for the abstract, in the language of filing. The pages of the Request for Grant form do not count. The language reduction applies to the page fee if the conditions of **R.6(3)** are met. (A-III,13.2; A-X,9.2.2)

Pages with sequence listings are exempted from the page fee according to **Rfees2(1)1a**, because examiners do not read but only search them. However, a sequence listing not filed in the standardised representation required by **R.30(1)** will be subject to the page fee (OJ 2013 p.542 §I.1.6). It is recommended to replace such a sequence listing by filing a correct sequence listing under **R.30(3)** before expiry of the period for calculating the page fee to avoid the pages of the deficient listing being included in the calculation.

Where an application is filed without claims, the first set of claims filed after the date of filing will be included in the page count.

In the case of filing by reference under **R.40(1)(c)**, the number of pages of the certified copy will be used, excluding the pages for the certification and bibliographic data.

The page fee for an application filed with claims must be paid within one month of filing (**R.38(3)**). Since this month expires before the deadline for correcting formal deficiencies of the application under **R.57(i)** and **R.58**, the number of pages can only be determined on the documents as filed. In contrast, according to A-III,13.2, second paragraph, if there are formal deficiencies in the application, such as margins, line spacing and font size not complying with **R.49(5)** and (8), the EPO will use the number of pages after they have been corrected. However, there is no legal basis for requesting payment of the page fee after the one-month period of **R.38(3)**.

4.2.2 *Euro-PCT applications*

Since the page fee for a Euro-PCT application is payable on entry into the European phase, the calculation of the number of pages is made on the documents available on entry. Hence, amendments filed on entry are included in the calculation and those filed in response to the **R.161** communication or later are not. Amendments that increase the number of pages should therefore preferably be filed after entry. Similarly, an amendment in response to the **R.161** communication reducing the number of pages will not result in a refund of an already paid page fee.

The basis for the calculation is the international application as published, one page with the abstract, and any amendments under Art.19 PCT and Art.34 PCT that are maintained in the regional phase. Any page with bibliographic data and the Form 1200 are disregarded for the calculation. (OJ 2009 p.338)

Any amendments under Art.34 PCT or filed upon entry on which the European grant procedure is to be based (**R.159(1)(b)**) will be taken into account, provided they are available to the EPO by the date of payment of the page fee and on condition that this date is within the 31-month period of **R.159(1)**.

Replacement pages identified at the latest by the date of payment and preferably in the Form 1200 are taken into account by subtracting the replaced pages and adding the replacement pages, allowing the applicant to reduce the page fee. Without such identification, any new pages available on the date of payment will be included in the calculation.

See OJ 2009 p.340 for the calculation where the international application has not been published in an official EPO language.

4.2.3 *Issues affecting number of pages*

Pages of amendments, e.g. under **R.56** or **R.161**, filed after the date of payment of the page fee are not taken into account in the calculation. Consequently, an amendment reducing the number of pages and filed after the date of payment will not result in a refund.

The amount of the fee for further processing is calculated on the basis of the number of pages on file on expiry of the relevant period for which the page fee has not been paid.

5 Divisional fee (Rfees2(1)1b)

An additional fee must be paid for a divisional filed in respect of any earlier application which is itself a divisional (**R.38(4)**). The amount of the fee depends on the generation of the divisional. The generation of a divisional is equal to the number of divisionals in the sequence from the root application up to and including the divisional being filed. Hence, a first generation divisional is a divisional filed in respect of an earlier application that is not a divisional, i.e. in respect of a root application. (OJ 2014 A22; A-IV,1.1.2, 1.4.1.1)

Since the divisional fee is part of the filing fee according to **R.38(4)**, the language reduction is applicable if the conditions of **R.6(3)** are met (A-IV,1.4.1.1).

6 Search fee (Rfees2(1)2)

The amount of the search fee for a search on a direct European application and for a supplementary search on a Euro-PCT application is equal.

The search fee covers about 30% of the actual cost of a search. The other part is covered by renewal fees. See **Rfees9** for a refund of the search fee for a European search when the EPO can make use of an earlier search and OJ 2017 A95 for details about a refund of the search fee for an international search when the EPO as ISA can make use of an earlier search. Reduction of the supplementary search fee and cases where no supplementary search fee is due are dealt with in **Art.153(7)**.

An overview of the amount of the search fee for European and international searches is given in OJ 2018 A26. The search fees for applications filed before 01.07.2005 are lower than for applications filed on or after that date, because no search opinion needed be drafted for the former.

7 Designation fee (Rfees2(1)3)

An applicant of an application filed before 01.04.2009 or an international application entering the European phase before that date must pay a designation fee for each contracting state where he desires protection. The amount is fixed in **Rfees2(2)3** and **3a**.

A flat designation fee as set out in **Rfees2(1)3** is payable for applications filed on or after 01.04.2009 and international applications entering the regional phase on or after that date (OJ 2008 p.10). The period for payment and sanctions have not changed (see **Art.79(2):1**; **R.17(3)**; **R.36(4)**; **R.39** and **R.159(1)(d)**). (OJ 2008 p.10)

8 Examination fee (Rfees2(1)6)

8.1 AMOUNT OF EXAMINATION FEE

For European patent applications filed before 01.07.2005, the examination fee is higher, because for such applications the European search report is drawn up without a search opinion (see **R.62(1)**). The examination fee is also higher for Euro-PCT applications for which no supplementary European search report is drawn up, even if the application is filed on or after 01.07.2005. No supplementary European search report is drawn up if the EPO was ISA or SISA (OJ 2018 A26 §3(a)).

The higher examination fee is due for such a Euro-PCT application, because the written opinion prepared by the EPO as ISA is not of the same quality as the search opinion drawn up by the EPO as designated/elected office (CA/138/04 §16).

An overview of the amount of the examination fee is given in OJ 2018 A26.

8.2 REDUCTION AND REFUND OF EXAMINATION FEE

The examination fee for an international application is reduced under **Rfees14(2)** when the EPO has drawn up an international preliminary examination report.

Refund of the examination fee is governed by **Rfees11**.

9 **Fee for grant and publishing (Rfees2(1)7)**

The fee for grant and publishing of **Rfees2(1)7** applies to applications filed on or after 01.04.2009 and for international applications entering the European phase on or after that date. For applications filed or entered before 01.04.2009 the fee for grant and printing is fixed in **Rfees2(2)7**, the amount of the fee depending on the number of pages of the patent to be granted. Before 01.04.2009 no page fee was due on filing or entry; instead the page fee was levied at grant.

10 **Fee for publishing (Rfees2(1)8)**

The fee for publishing of a new specification amended in opposition or limitation proceedings is a flat fee, independent of the number of pages of the granted application.

11 **Appeal fee (Rfees2(1)11)**

Amended by decision of the Administrative Council of 13.12.2017 (OJ 2018 A4) and applicable to appeals filed on or after 01.04.2018.

The appeal fee will be gradually increased between 2017 and 2023 to increase the cost coverage of the BoA.

The appeal fee is reduced for natural persons and for the entities referred to in **R.6(4)** and (5) (see OJ 2018 A5 §6-8 for definitions). There are no restrictions on language and residence, because **Rfees2(1)11** refers only to the natural person and entity in **R.6(4)** and not to the entire provision; hence, the restrictions of **R.6(3)** and **Art.14(4)** to which **R.6(4)** refers do not apply.

Appellants wishing to benefit from the reduced appeal fee must file a declaration showing their entitlement, preferably using EPO Form 1011bis (Not. EPO OJ 2018 A5). An incorrect or missing declaration may cause termination of the appeal procedure (Not. EPO OJ 2018 A5 §9-11; **T1553/13** r.4; **Rfees8**).

By way of the reduction, the appeal fee rate is kept constant for SME's, universities and natural persons (approximately 5% of the appellants) so that their access to the appeal system is not impeded. (CA/43/16 Rev. 1 §60; CA/102/17 §70-80)

12 **Fee for further processing (Rfees2(1)12)**

The fee for further processing is a fixed amount in cases of a general failure to observe a time limit or a loss of rights but, in the event of belated payment of a fee, the fee for further processing amounts to 50% of the belatedly paid fee. In most cases in which further processing is requested, the applicant has not supplied a procedural document or paid a fee in due time.

In some cases, both those acts may be required, meaning that the fee for further processing would have to be paid twice. The most notable instance of such a case of accumulated requirements is that of the formal requirements to be met for the grant of a European patent under **R.71(3)**. Since the acts required by **R.71(3)** have the same legal basis, further processing in the case of belated payment of the fee for grant and publishing and filing the translation of the claims require one flat-rate fee as stated in the second indent of **Rfees2(1)12** (E-VIII,2). Since E-VIII,2 does not mention the claims fees under **R.71(4)**, they are not covered by the flat-rate fee and late payment requires an additional further processing fee.

13 **Fee for re-establishment (Rfees2(1)13)**

The relatively high fee for re-establishment reflects the exceptional nature of re-establishment compared to further processing.

The re-establishment of the priority right applies to Euro-direct applications but, in some cases, also to PCT applications entering the European regional phase under R.49*ter*.2 PCT. A request for the re-establishment of rights may also be made for an international application under R.26*bis*.3 PCT for which the EPO is the receiving Office.

14 **Claims fees (Rfees2(1)15)**
Claims fees are payable on filing of the application (**R.45**) or entry into the European phase (**R.162**) and, if the number of claims at grant is larger than at filing, also at grant for the added claims (**R.71(4)**). They are due for the 16th claim and up.

The amount of the claims fees for applications filed before 01.04.2009 and international applications that entered the European phase before that date is fixed in **Rfees2(2)15**.

For applications filed on or after 01.04.2009 and international applications that entered the European phase on or after that date, claims fees are payable under **Rfees2(1)15** for claims 16 to 50 and at an increased rate for claim 51 and up. (OJ 2008 p.10)

See **R.45(1):2** for ways of reducing claims fees.

15 **Protest fee (Rfees2(1)21)**
Rfees2(1)21 relates to the amount of the protest fee for non-unity in the international search (R.40.2.e PCT) and in the international preliminary examination (R.68.3(c) PCT).

16 **Reduction of PCT fees**
The search fee for an international search under **Rfees2(1)2** and the fee for the preliminary examination of an international application under **Rfees2(1)19** will be reduced if each applicant is a natural person who is a national and resident of a state which is not party to the EPC and which is a low-income or lower-middle-income economy. A table listing these states is available on the EPO website. If one of the applicants is a national or a resident of an EPC state, the reduction does not apply (OJ 2017 A115 Annex D.II(4); Euro-PCT Guide §215). The international filing fee and the handling fees may also be reduced (Euro-PCT Guide §183 and §352).

Rfees2(2) For European patent applications filed before 1 April 2009 and international applications which entered the regional phase before that date, the amount of the fees specified in Article 2, item 3, item 3a, item 7 and item 15 of the Rules relating to Fees as in force until 31 March 2009 shall be as follows:

3.	Designation fee for each contracting state designated (Article 79, paragraph 2), designation fees being deemed paid for all contracting states upon payment of seven times the amount of this fee	100
3a.	Joint designation fee for the Swiss Confederation and the Principality of Liechtenstein	100
7.	Fee for grant, including fee for printing the European patent specification (Rule 71, paragraph 3), where the application documents to be printed comprise:	
7.1	not more than 35 pages	925

7.2	more than 35 pages	plus EUR 15 for the 36th and each subsequent page
15.	Claims fee for the sixteenth and each subsequent claim (Rule 45, paragraph 1, Rule 71, paragraph 4, and Rule 162, paragraph 1)	235

Inserted by decision of the Administrative Council of 28.10.2009 which entered into force on 01.04.2010 (OJ 2009 p.587).

1 **Fees for applications filed or entered the European phase before 1 April 2009**
Rfees2(2) provides several fees for direct European applications filed before 1 April 2009 and international applications that entered the European phase before 1 April 2009. In particular, the designation fee payable depends on the number of designated states, the fee for grant includes a page fee, and the claims fees have no higher amount as from claim 51. The amounts of these fees are regularly increased together with the fees in **Rfees2(1)**. See **Rfees2(1)** for notes to the fees of **Rfees2(2)**. (OJ 2009 p.587)

Rfees 3 Fees, expenses and prices laid down by the President of the Office

Rfees3(1) The President of the Office shall lay down the amount of the administrative fees provided for in the Implementing Regulations and, where appropriate, the amount of the fees and expenses for any services rendered by the Office other than those specified in Article 2.

1 **Administrative fees and fees for services**
The amount of the administrative fees under **Rfees3(1)** has been laid down in Dec. Pres. OJ 2014 A13 and OJ 2016 A4. The amounts currently in force are published in OJ 2016 sp2 p.19 (however not in OJ 2018 sp2) and in the Interactive schedule of fees on the EPO website. Examples of administrative fees are the fees for registering a transfer (**R.22(2)**), inspection of paper files (**R.145(2)**) and issuing certified copies of priority documents (**R.54**). An example of a fee for a service is the fee for an international-type search of a national patent application (OJ 2016 A4).

The extension fee for extension states (**Art.169:3**) is not an administrative fee under **Rfees3** but is fixed in the Extension Agreement between an extension state and the EPO. The amount of the extension fee is EUR 102 for all extension states (see e.g. OJ 2018 sp2 p.22). Similarly, the validation fee for a validation state is neither an administrative fee under **Rfees3**; see **Art.169:6** for details. The different amounts of the validation fee for the respective validation states are given in OJ 2018 sp2 p.22.

Rfees3(2) He shall also lay down the prices of the publications referred to in Articles 93, 98, 103 and 129 of the Convention.

Art.93 application
Art.98 specification
Art.103 new specification after opposition
Art.129 OJ and the Patent Bulletin

1 **Price list for publications**
Patent applications and specifications are published on the Publication Server and can be downloaded free of charge. Paper copies can still be ordered on the EPO website (EPO Patent Information – Price list). Payment of these prices is not regulated by the Rfees (**Rfees1**).

Rfees3(3) The amounts of the fees provided for in Article 2 and of the fees and expenses laid down in accordance with paragraph 1 shall be published in the Official Journal and on the website of the European Patent Office.

1 **Publication of Schedule of fees**
Fees under **Rfees2** are published in OJ 2018 sp2 and Administrative Fees under **Rfees3(1)** in OJ 2016 sp2 p.19. Both are published in the Interactive schedule of fees on the EPO website.

The EPO grants a 20% discount on orders of more than 50 units of a single, listed paper excluding copies of patent documents (OJ 1995 p.372).

Rfees 4 Due date for fees

1 **Due date of a fee**
The term 'due date of a fee payment' has a special meaning in the EPC, namely the first day on which the payment can be validly made. The last day of valid payment is the day of expiry of the period pertaining to the fee. The due date is the date at which a legal ground comes into existence which forms the basis of the payment and causes the fee to become indebted.

Note, that, in contrast with the Guidelines, 'the due date of payment' in common English is the last date of valid payment. **R.71a(3)** and probably **AAD.5.1** (see also several places in the Notes to the AAD (OJ 2017 sp5 Annex A2)) use 'due' in the common English meaning.

2 **Prepayment of a fee**
A payment made before the due date is not valid and will be refunded to avoid payers escaping an increase of fees by early paying. There are four exceptions to this principle:

- The renewal fee in respect of the third year may be validly paid up to six months before it falls due; all other renewal fees may be validly paid up to three months before they fall due (**R.51(1)**; A-X,5.2.4).
- The fees paid voluntarily in response to a first **R.71(3)** communication can be credited to the fees payable for a second **R.71(3)** communication according to **R.71a(5)**. (A-X,5.1.1)
- The due date for the designation fee is the publication of the search report. If the designation fee is paid before the due date, e.g. even as early as on filing of the application, the EPO will retain the payment; the payment will only be considered valid as from the due date (A-X,5.2.2).
- A payment made shortly before the due date may not be refunded by the EPO but regarded as a payment taking effect on the due date (A-X,5.1.1).

Rfees4(1) Fees in respect of which the due date is not specified in the provisions of the Convention or of the PCT or of the Implementing Regulations thereto shall be due on the date of receipt of the request for the service incurring the fee concerned.

1 **Due date of specific fees**
Examples of the due date for some fees in order of procedure (A-X,5.2):
1 The filing fee and search fee are due on the day the application is filed.
2 The designation fee is due on publication of the search report, not on the filing date. See **Rfees4:1** for payment before the due date.
3 The examination fee is due when the written request for examination is filed. Since the request is contained in the Request for Grant form, the fee is due on the date of filing if the form is used on filing.
4 Any claims fees are due upon the filing of the first set of claims, which may be the date of filing or which may occur later.
5 The fee for grant and publishing falls due on notification of the communication of **R.71(3)**. Under **R.71(4)**, the same applies for the claims fees, unless they were already paid earlier under **R.45** or **R.162**.
6 Renewal fees fall due on the last day of the month containing the anniversary of the date of filing. See **Rfees4:1** for payment before the due date.
7 The opposition fee and appeal fee are due on the date of receipt of the notice of opposition and appeal, respectively (**T778/00** r.2.2). Similarly, the fees for limitation, revocation and petition for review are due on the date the request or petition is filed (A-X,5.2.6).
8 If a request incurs payment of a fee and no due date is specified, the fee is due on the date of receipt of the request (A-X,5.1.1).

Rfees4(2) The President of the Office may decide not to make services within the meaning of paragraph 1 dependent upon the advance payment of the corresponding fee.

Rfees 5 Payment of fees

Rfees5(1) The fees due to the Office shall be paid in euro by payment or transfer to a bank account held by the Office.

Amended by decision of the Administrative Council of 25.10.2007, which entered into force on 01.04.2008 and applies to payments made from that date. (OJ 2007, 533)

1 **Payment to EPO bank account**
All payments to the EPO must be made in euro, the currency of the contracting states that are member of the European Monetary Union (EMU, see the list of states in **Art.169:1.1**), without charge to the payee and directly to the EPO bank account. See OJ 2017 A100 for requirements for bank transfers and OJ 2016 sp2 p.32 for the details of the EPO bank account.

It is recommended to make separate bank transfers for each application, providing the application number and fee codes as payment reference. If the data does not fit in the payment reference field, the missing data is preferably provided by completing the "fee payment" tab on the Online Filing or CMS web page. (OJ 2017 A100 §3)

The term “payment to a bank account” in **Rfees5(1)**, as an alternative to “transfer to a bank account”, refers to effecting payment by depositing cash at the counter of a bank. See for instance **J7/81**.

Rfees5(2) The President of the Office may allow other methods of paying fees than those set out in paragraph 1.

1 **Other methods of payment**

The President has allowed the following methods of paying fees other than payment and transfer to the EPO bank account: debiting a deposit account held with the EPO, either using a debit order or automatic debiting (OJ 2017 sp5), and payment by credit card (OJ 2017 A72). See OJ 2018 A32 for a summary.

Publications and legal texts can only be ordered and paid online (Dec. Pres. OJ 2013, 90 and Not. EPO OJ 2013, 91).

The methods of payment in **Rfees5(1)** and **(2)** are exhaustive. Other methods of payment are not allowed; any payment made by such a method will be regarded as not received (**R2/09** r.2.3). For example, a payment by cheque will not be accepted (OJ 2007, 626). Note, that the EPO itself still uses cheques to make refunds if the person to whom the refund is to be made does not have a deposit account (A-X,10.3)

2 **Deposit account**

The Arrangement for Deposit Accounts (ADA) has been established by decision of the President. The version valid as of 01.12.2017 has been published in consolidated form in OJ 2017 sp5 p.11.

The ADA is an administrative regulation falling outside the EPC. Therefore, the provisions of the EPC, in particular **Art.14** for languages, **R.2** for filing methods and **R.139**, first sentence, for corrections do not apply.

A person may open a deposit account under **ADA.2**, a euro account held by the EPO in the name of the person. The holder of the account can make payments into the account to maintain sufficient funds commensurate with his payments of fees (**ADA.3**). Payment of a fee may be effected by filing a debit order with the EPO, whereby the EPO avails itself of a certain amount already with the EPO for a clearly specified purpose (**ADA.5**). Fees can also be paid by authorizing the EPO to debit upcoming fees by filing an automatic debit order (**ADA.7**). Access to the deposit account requires an EPO smart card.

The online user guide "Online Fee Payment" describes the operation of the payment system and provides a range of other payment facilities. A Fee Payment plan showing the amount of fees to be paid under the automatic debiting scheme within a period up to 40 days can be used to avoid shortfall of the account. A software tool enables offline preparation of batch debit orders.

The main advantage of payment through a deposit account is that payment can be made by filing online a simple debit order, possibly together with other documents, or by automatic debiting. In the latter case the EPO takes care of timely debiting the account.

2.1 DEBITING THE ACCOUNT

A debit order for paying one or more fees can only be filed online via a secure portal on the EPO website using one of the three accepted means prescribed by **ADA.5.1.2.** Debit orders filed in any other way, e.g. on paper, by fax or via web-form filing, or using a different format such as a PDF attachment, are invalid and will not be carried out (**ADA.5.1.3**; sp5 OJ 2017 page 4 point 1.1). See section 2.1.2 below for an exception.

If a payment period expires on a day on which one of the accepted means of filing debit orders is not available at the EPO, the payment period is extended to the first day on which all means are available again. A period may also be extended under **R.134(5)** in case of a general unavailability of electronic communications services or other like reasons. (**ADA.5.5**)

If a breakdown occurs at the payer's end, another payment method should be used, such as bank transfer or credit card (OJ 2017 sp5 p.4, point 1.2).

The day of receipt of the debit order will be regarded as the date on which the payment is made, provided the account contains sufficient funds; debit orders may specify a payment date later than the date of submission (**ADA.5.4.1**). A debit order may be revoked as a whole or in part, provided the notice of revocation is filed before midnight of the day the debit order is received (**ADA.6**).

The Online Fee Payment system allows submission of batch debit orders relating to multiple applications or patents and includes a validation of the debits orders. Debit orders in a batch which relate to the payment of renewal fees for "definitely closed" applications or granted patents will be automatically rejected. The same applies to debit orders in a batch which relate to fees for transfer of rights for "definitely closed" applications. An application is definitively closed if the loss of rights or the refusal has become final. The rejection relieves the EPO of the burden to refund such payments. (**ADA.5.3**; OJ 2017 A44, A45)

2.1.1 *Deficient debit order*

The software for filing of debit order prescribed in **ADA.5.1.2** ensures that the debit orders include all information necessary for automatic processing, such as the application number, amount, and fee code. A debit order, like any other form of payment cannot be corrected; a payment is a matter of fact and not a procedural declaration that can be corrected under **R.139** (**T170/83** r.8; A-X,7.1.1). However, account holders may notify any errors to the EPO; the EPO checks the information and makes any corrections necessary, retroactively to the original decisive payment date (**ADA.4.2**). Moreover, the EPO may overlook small amounts lacking (**Rfees8**).

A debit order is carried out notwithstanding incorrect information given in it, provided the intention of the person giving the order is clear (**T152/82**; A-X,4.2.3). Similarly, an evidently incorrect purpose is not prejudicial if the intended purpose can be established without difficulty from the remaining information; the inadvertent use of the payment by the EPO for a purpose different from the evidently intended purpose has no effect on the intended purpose (**J16/84**; A-X,7.1.2).

2.1.2 *Debit order via national authority*

The fees for a European patent application filed with a national authority under **Art.75(1)(b)** can be paid by a debit order submitted online with the EPO according to **ADA.5.1**. (**ADA.5.6.1**; **A-II,1.6**)

If a European application is filed on paper with a national authority, the fees may be paid also on paper using the Form 1020 debit order included with the application. The debit order will be regarded as filed in due time, even if received after expiry of the period for payment, provided that evidence is provided that the debit order was filed with the national authority together with the application and that the account contained sufficient funds on the date on which the period expired. (**ADA.5.6.1**; **5.6.2**)

2.1.3 *Shortfall of the account*

The account holder must ensure that sufficient funds are available in the account. The EPO will process debit orders in the following order of priority in case there are insufficient funds in the account to cover all indicated fees: first automatic debit orders before any other debit orders; next debit orders per application in ascending order of publication number; and finally the fees for each application in ascending order of fee code, as long as the funds allow (**ADA.5.2**). The EPO informs the account holder of the shortfall by fax or email (**ADA.5.2.4; AAD.7**; OJ 2015 sp3, Annex B 3.6 and 3.7).

After the deposit account is duly replenished, the payment is considered to have been made on the date of replenishment, not on the date of receipt of the debit order or the decisive payment date in case of automatic debiting (**ADA.5.2.4; AAD.8**). The date of replenishment is the date the payment was actually entered in the EPO bank account (**Rfees7(1)**). A replenishment is considered to have been made in due time if the payment was effected not later than ten days before expiry of the relevant period for payment (ten-day fail-safe provision **ADA.4.1; A-X,6.2.2**). The option of **Rfees7(3)** to pay with 10% surcharge within the ten days is not available for replenishment payments (**ADA.4.1**). Hence, a shortfall will cause these debit orders to be processed usually after expiry of the relevant period for payment and remedies for late paid fees may have to be applied

Further processing under **Art.121** and **R.135** is available for most late paid fees; the fee for further processing is usually 50% of the late paid fee (**Rfees2(1)12**). Some late paid fees, such as appeal fee, opposition fee, renewal fee plus additional fee, renewal fee for divisional, further search fees, and any fee paid in the further-processing period require re-establishment under **Art.122** and **R.136** as remedy; the fee for re-establishment (**Rfees2(1)13**) must be paid and all due care proved (**Art.122(1):4**). There is no remedy for fees paid late for re-establishment (**Art.122(4)**).

A shortfall can be avoided by checking the Fee Payment plan regularly (see the above section 2) and replenishing the account accordingly. For example, check twice weekly the total amount of the fees due for the next 20 days and replenish the account to the total amount, correcting for incidental extra payments. The EPO debits the account within two to three working days after the decisive payment date of a fee that must be debited automatically or on the date of receipt of the debit order for any other fee (**ADA.5.2.2**). Sometimes the debiting may take up to a few weeks because of high workload; such belated debits are included in the Fee Payment plan.

2.2 ANNUAL SUBSCRIPTIONS EPI

A professional representative can pay the annual subscription to the Institute of Professional Representatives before the European Patent Office (*epi*) by direct debiting of a deposit account held by the EPO on the basis of an agreement between the EPO and the *epi* (OJ 2017 sp5 p.83 Annex B.1 and B2). The representative must thereto file a direct debiting mandate signed by the account holder with the *epi*, not with the EPO. The *epi* will transmit the debit orders to the EPO, upon which the EPO debits the accounts and pays the sum to the *epi*. (**ADA.8**)

3 Automatic debiting

An applicant or proprietor may file an automatic debit order according to the Arrangements for the Automatic Debiting procedure (AAD). The version of AAD valid as of 01.11.2017 has been published in consolidated form in OJ 2017 sp5 p.22 Annex A1 and explanations in Annex A2.

An automatic debit order authorises the EPO to debit a deposit account for all fees due for an application or patent automatically on the expiry date of the fee. An automatic debit order must be filed and revoked online (**AAD.1** and **12**).

Applicants and proprietors can use the automatic debiting in all procedures for European patent applications and patents, and for PCT applications in the international phase where the EPO is receiving Office, ISA or IPEA and for PCT applications before the EPO as designated or elected office. Note, that an automatic debit order filed for the international phase is not applicable in the regional EP phase; a separate automatic debit order must be filed for both proceedings (**AAD.2**). An opponent cannot pay the opposition fee using automatic debiting; further excluded fees are listed in **AAD.4**.

The automatic debit order must be filed online via a secure portal on the EPO website (**AAD.1.2**). The online Request for Grant form and the form for entry into the European phase include a section with a drop-down menu where automatic debiting can be selected (OJ 2017 sp5 p.72 Annex 2, notes to point 5). The procedure for filing the automatic debit order during pending proceedings is governed by **AAD.10**.

AAD.3 specifies the fees that are covered by the automatic debiting and **AAD.4** the fees that are not. The date of payment under automatic debiting, i.e. the decisive payment date, is usually the last day of the period for paying a fee (**AAD.6.1(a)**). The fee for further processing is paid on the last day of the period for requesting further processing where the omitted act was a payment, and on the date of completion of the omitted act where the omitted act was the non-performance of a procedural act other than payment of a fee (**AAD.6.1(h)**). The fee for re-establishment, for limitation or revocation, for appeal and for petition for review is paid on the date of receipt of the request (**AAD.6.1(i)**).

Under the automatic debiting procedure all fees becoming due during the procedure will be paid automatically. Hence, the further search fees for all non-unitary inventions are automatically debited (Annex A2, notes to point 3); similarly, all claims fees are automatically debited (**AAD.3.2(d)**). If the applicant does not want to pay one or more of these fees, he must actively revoke the automatic debit order to stop all payments or inform the EPO that one or more fees are not to be paid (**AAD.12**). If a fee is paid by another means of payment and is received at least four days before the decisive payment date, the EPO will not carry out the automatic debit order in respect of that fee (**AAD.11**). Payment by another means can also be used to avoid a fee increase by paying early (Annex A2 notes to point 11)).

The procedure automatic debiting in case of shortfall is set out in **AAD.7-8**.

4 Credit card

As from 01.12.2017 it is possible to pay by credit card in euros. The date of payment is the date in Central European Time on which the transaction is approved, which date is indicated in the confirmation made available to the payer. A transaction failed before it is approved is considered not to have been made, even if the failure was not attributable to the payer. If a failure causes the payment to have been made after expiry of the period for payment, the period will still be considered to have been observed on condition that evidence is provided to the EPO that the payer received a confirmation of approval within the period. (Dec. Pres. OJ 2017 A72)

Credit card payments can be made online using either Mastercard or Visa. The EPO will bear any transaction charges. Any refund will not be made into the credit card account but will be paid into a deposit account with the EPO or, if not available, by cheque (A-X,10.3). (OJ 2017 A73)

Rfees 6 Particulars concerning payments

Rfees6(1) Every payment must indicate the name of the person making the payment and must contain the necessary particulars to enable the Office to establish immediately the purpose of the payment.

1 **Person making the payment**
Since the Rules relating to Fees use the general term 'the person making the payment' instead of 'the party' as in the EPC, a payment can be made by any person; it is not restricted to parties or their representatives (A-X,1). No representative is required for applicants who must be represented under **Art.133(2)** (Legal Advice **L6/91** rev. §1, OJ 1991 p.573; cancelled by Dec. Pres OJ 2012 p.446). However, any communication relating to the payment must be made by the party concerned or his representative. Any refund of a payment is made to the party or his representative, provided the latter is authorized to receive payments (A-X,10.4).

2 **Particulars of payment**
For the efficient processing of payments made by bank transfer, the payer must give the application number, the fee code(s) and the amount for each fee code, preferably in the payment-reference field of the (electronic) bank transfer (OJ 2017 A100). See **Rfees6(2)** for unclear or incomplete payment details.

3 **Correction of payment**
An omitted payment cannot be corrected under **R.139**, because an omitted payment is not covered by **R.139**, first sentence (**J21/84** r.7,8; **T170/83** r.8, last paragraph). A debit order for a deposit account can neither be corrected (however, see **Rfees5(2):2.1.1**).

Rfees6(2) If the purpose of the payment cannot immediately be established, the Office shall require the person making the payment to notify it in writing of this purpose within such period as it may specify. If he does not comply with this request in due time the payment shall be considered not to have been made.

1 **Purpose of payment**
When the purpose of the payment is obviously wrong, the error is not prejudicial if the EPO can derive the intended purpose from the remaining information (**J16/84**).

If the intended purpose can still not be established, the EPO must ask the payer (**Rfees6(2)**). If the EPO requests the payer to specify the purpose of a payment and the payer responds in due time, the payment and the original payment date remain valid (A-X,7.1.2).

If the payer does not reply to the request, the payment is considered not to have been made (**Rfees6(2)**, last sentence).

The inadvertent use by the EPO of a payment for a different purpose from that evidently intended by the payer has no effect on the purpose intended by the payer. (**J16/84**)

Rfees 7 Date to be considered as the date on which payment is made

1 **Date of payment**
Rfees7 governs which date the EPO considers as the date on which a payment has been made. **Rfees7(1)** gives the general rule for payments into and transfers to the EPO bank account. Rule for other methods of payment are given by the President (**Rfees7(2)**). **Rfees7(3)** sets out the conditions under which a late payment may be regarded as having been made in due time; **Rfees7(4)** gives the corresponding procedure.

Rfees7(1) The date on which any payment shall be considered to have been made to the Office shall be the date on which the amount of the payment or of the transfer is actually entered in a bank account held by the Office.

Amended by decision of the Administrative Council of 25.10.2007 (OJ 2007 p.533).

1 **Applicability of Rfees7(1)**
Rfees7(1) applies not only to payments of fees but also to payments serving to replenish a deposit account (**ADA.4.1**).

2 **Date of payment for payments into the EPO bank account**
The date of payment is the date the amount paid is actually entered into the EPO account. The amount is not 'actually entered' on the value date of the bank transfer but on the date on which the bank statement is issued that shows the amount (OJ 1997, 217, point 7). In general, the two dates will be the same for daily issued statements, but the date of the bank statement has the advantage over the value date that the former cannot retroactively be changed by the payer. **Rfees7(3)** contains provisions for an effective date earlier than the actual date of payment. This is allowed by the word 'considered' in **Rfees7(1)**, creating the possibility for a fictitious day of payment.

When a payment has still to be made on the last possible day, one should request the bank to make an urgent transfer on the same day. A deposit of the money with the bank where the EPO has its account is generally of no avail, because the money is often not entered into the account until the next day. It is safer to file a debit order online with EPO, or, in the absence of a deposit account with the EPO, ask a colleague to debit his account.

See **Rfees7(2):1** for the date of payment where another method of payment than payment into the EPO bank account is used.

Rfees7(2) Where the President of the Office allows, in accordance with the provisions of Article 5, paragraph 2, other methods of paying fees than those set out in Article 5, paragraph 1, he shall also lay down the date on which such payments shall be considered to have been made.

1 **Date of payment for debit order and automatic debiting**
The date of receipt by the EPO of a debit order is considered as the date of payment, provided the account has sufficient funds (**ADA.5.4.1**). Under the automatic debiting procedure fees are in general debited from the deposit account on the last day of the relevant period (**AAD.6.1(a)**). See **Rfees5(2):2.1.3** for the date of payment in case of shortfall of the account.

2 **Date of payment for credit card payment**
A payment by credit card is deemed to have been made on the date on which the transaction is approved. This date is indicated in the transaction confirmation made available to the payer (Dec. Pres. OJ 2017 A72, Art.3). Where, due to a failure in the transaction process, payment of a fee is not considered to have been made until after the expiry of the period, it shall be considered that this period has been observed if evidence is provided to the EPO that, within this period, the payer has received a confirmation that the transaction was approved (OJ 2017 A72, Art.4(2)).

Rfees7(3) Where, under the provisions of paragraphs 1 and 2, payment of a fee is not considered to have been made until after the expiry of the period in which it should have been made, it shall be considered that this period has been observed if evidence is provided to the Office that the person who made the payment
(a) fulfilled one of the following conditions in a Contracting State within the period within which the payment should have been made:
(i) he effected the payment through a banking establishment;
(ii) he duly gave an order to a banking establishment to transfer the amount of the payment; and
(b) paid a surcharge of 10% on the relevant fee or fees, but not exceeding EUR 150; no surcharge is payable if a condition according to sub-paragraph (a) has been fulfilled not later than ten days before the expiry of the period for payment.

Amended by decision of the Administrative Council of 25.10.2007 (OJ 2007 p.533).

1 **Ten-day fail-safe provision**
Rfees7(3) is called the 'ten-day fail-safe provision'. It creates the fiction of payment within a period where the actual payment is made after expiry of the period. All delays in the banking system will be at the risk of the EPO.

The ten-day fail-safe provision applies only to payments that have duly been initiated within the period for payment, i.e. in the way prescribed by **Rfees7(3)(a)**: effecting the payment through a bank or giving an order to a bank to transfer the payment. In addition, the payment must be initiated within a contracting state according to **Rfees7(3)(a)**. Hence, the arrangement does not apply to payments from outside the contracting states. Such payers should appoint a professional representative as soon as possible and effect payment through him.

Rfees7(3) distinguishes two cases where the payment is initiated before expiry of the period for payment but the payment is entered into the EPO account after the expiry. When the payment was duly initiated not later than ten days before expiry of the period for payment, the payment will be deemed to have been made in due time; no surcharge is payable (**Rfees7(3)(b)**). When the payment was duly initiated less than ten days before expiry of the period but before the expiry, the payment will only be deemed to have been made if a surcharge of 10% is paid. The ten-day fail-safe provision can also be used for payments replenishing a deposit account (**ADA.4.1**).

The extension of periods under **R.134** does not apply to the 10-day period, because the last day of that period does not end a period within which a procedural step must be taken. A change of fees between the day of initiating the payment and the day of actual payment under the 10-day rule necessitates the payment of the new fee, as the key date for the increase in fees is the date of actual payment and not the fictitious date of payment (J18/85).

The ten-day fail-safe provision must be applied for determining whether the normal period for payment was complied with or the payment was made in a further processing period following the normal period (A-X,6.2.4).

Since a payer in general arranges his payments to be effected in due time, there is no reason to pay the 10% surcharge of **Rfees7(3)(b)** in advance. **Rfees7(4)** provides for payment of the surcharge in arrears.

The term 'banking establishment' in **Rfees7(3)(a)** covers the banking services of post offices of contracting states for payment or transfer to a bank account held by the EPO.

See **R.134(5):1** for another remedy for a late payment caused by delay in the banking system.

Rfees7(4) The Office may request the person who made the payment to produce evidence as to the date on which a condition according to paragraph 3(a) was fulfilled and, where required, pay the surcharge referred to in paragraph 3(b), within a period to be specified by it. If he fails to comply with this request or if the evidence is insufficient, or if the required surcharge is not paid in due time, the period for payment shall be considered not to have been observed.

1 **Provision of evidence and payment of surcharge**

If a payment enters into the EPO bank account after expiry of the period for payment, the EPO will send a loss of rights communication to the applicant under **R.112(1)**. If the applicant claims that the payment was duly initiated according to **Rfees7(3)**, for direct payments to the EPO or **ADA.4.1, 5.1** and **5.5** or **5.6.2** for payment through a debit account, he must apply for a decision under **R.112(2)** and submit the requisite evidence for the claim. (A-X,6.2.6)

If the EPO accepts the evidence and the payment was initiated within the ten-day period, it will request the applicant to pay the 10% surcharge within a period to be specified (see e.g. J20/00 r.6). If the evidence is insufficient or the surcharge is not paid, the period for payment will be regarded as not observed. (**Rfees7(4)**)

Rfees 8 Insufficiency of the amount paid

A time limit for payment shall in principle be deemed to have been observed only if the full amount of the fee has been paid in due time. If the fee is not paid in full, the amount which has been paid shall be refunded after the period for payment has expired. The Office may, however, in so far as this is possible within the time remaining before the end of the period, give the person making the payment the opportunity to pay the amount lacking. It may also, where this is considered justified, overlook any small amounts lacking without prejudice to the rights of the person making the payment.

Amended by decision of the Administrative Council of 09.12.2008. (OJ 2009 p.7)

1 **Insufficient payment**

A period for payment is considered to have been observed only if the full amount due has been paid before expiry of the period (**Rfees8**, first sentence. If the amount paid is insufficient, the EPO can respond in one of the following three ways.

- The EPO may give the payer an opportunity to pay the amount lacking, provided there is sufficient time remaining till expiry of the period (**Rfees8**, third sentence).
- If there is not sufficient time, the EPO will refund the amount paid after expiry of the period (**Rfees8**, second sentence).
- If the amount lacking is small, the EPO may overlook the insufficient payment (**Rfees8**, last sentence). Although the small amount overlooked does not result in failing a period, it must still be paid to the EPO. The EPO will invite the payer, usually after expiry of the period, to pay the amount lacking. The EPO may apply **Rfees8**, last sentence, irrespective of whether another remedy is available, such as further processing (**Art.121**), re-establishment of rights (**Art.122**) or some other remedy.

Apart from overlooking a small amount lacking under **Rfees8**, last sentence, the EPC has also the remedy of further processing for an insufficient payment (**Art.121**). Each remedy has its own conditions: **Rfees8** requires a small amount and **Art.121(1)** payment of a further processing fee. The payer may choose between the two remedies where both can be applied. Where the further processing fee is a percentage of the late-paid fee, the fee is the full fee and not the deficit. (**J11/85, J27/92**)

Rfees8 prevents loss of rights where an inadvertent error has led to a slight underpayment. It is not intended as a remedy for a party who has deliberately paid a reduced fee without being entitled to it (**T905/90** r.10).

If a payment is entered in the EPO bank account within a period of 6 months after the date of increase of the rates but the old amount is paid, the payment will be regarded as valid if the payer pays the deficit within two months after a request by the EPO (OJ 2016 A3 Art.4(2)). The deficit must also be paid if the payment is entered in the EPO bank account on or after the date of the fee increase but the payer arranged the payment before the date of the increase; **Rfees7(3)** does not change this (**J18/85**).

2 **Smallness of underpayment**

The purpose of **Rfees8** is to remedy underpayment by a small amount. The smallness of the amount must be assessed on purely arithmetical grounds in relation to the full amount. The provision is not intended as a remedy when a reduced fee has been paid without entitlement. (**T905/90** r.10)

Underpayments in the order 10% or less were considered to be a small amount, 25% as not a small amount in **J11/85** (r.3). 20% of the opposition fee was considered to be a small amount (**T290/90** r.4b); 20% was considered as a small amount for a party misinformed by the EPO (**J27/92**). However, this case law is highly fact specific. Where several fees are paid together, the assessment of the small amount must be made in respect of the total amount (**J11/85** r.6).

Rfees 9 Refund of search fees

1 **Refund of fees, general**

A fee payment lacking a legal basis must be refunded. A legal basis is lacking if the payment relates to proceedings that are not pending, e.g. it relates to an application already deemed to be withdrawn. A legal basis is also lacking if the payment is made before the due date. If e.g. the payment is made before or on the due date and if no later than that date the legal basis ceases to exist (e.g. because the application is deemed to be withdrawn or is withdrawn), the amount paid is to be refunded. (A-X,10.1.1, listing two exceptions)

A payment made shortly before the due date may possibly not be returned by the EPO and be regarded as valid payment on the due date (A-X,5.1.1).

Fees which have not been validly paid must be refunded, e.g. filing, search or examination fee paid late without the further processing fee. (A-XI,10.1.2)

An excess payment by an insignificant amount will not be refunded, unless the payer requests so (**Rfees12**).

Refunds are made to the party concerned. If the representative is authorised to receive payments, refunds will be made to him. A refund will in general not be made to a third party who paid the fee. (A-X,10.4). A refund is made by crediting the deposit account of the payee; otherwise by cheque (A-X,10.3; OJ 2017 A73)

Fees paid on or after the due date are refunded only if there is a particular reason for a refund (A-X,10.2):

- The filing fee, any page fee and any divisional fee is refunded fully if the application is not dealt with as a European application (**Art.90(2)**) or if the national office does not forward the application filed with it to the EPO in due time (**R.37(2)**).
- The search fee is refunded fully if the application is not dealt with as a European patent application (**Art.90(2)**), if a national office does not forward the application filed with it to the EPO (**R.37(2)**), or if the application is withdrawn, refused or deemed to be withdrawn at a time the EPO has not yet begun to draw up the search report (**Rfees9(1)**). The search fee is refunded fully or in part if the EPO can make use of an earlier search as specified in **Rfees9(2)**. See PCT §2.8.6 for refund of the international search fee when the ISA can use an earlier search.
- An additional search fee paid in response to a non-unity communication of the search division will be refunded on request if the examining division finds no justification for charging the additional fee (**R.64(2)**).
- The designation fee may be refunded in the exceptional cases set out in **R.39(3):1**.
- Claims fees will be refunded if the application filed with a national office is deemed to be withdrawn pursuant to **R.37(2)** and if the number of claims of a Euro-PCT application is reduced after national entry into the European phase (**R.162(3)**). There is no refund if the number of claims at grant is smaller than on filing or on entry into the European phase.
- The examination fee will be refunded as specified in **Rfees11** if the examination is not carried out. Where the EPO has drawn up an international preliminary examination report under Chapter II PCT, the European examination fee will not be refunded but reduced (**Rfees14(2)**).
- The fee for grant and publishing is refunded if the application is withdrawn before notification of the decision to grant (**R.71a(6)**; see e.g. **J15/86** F&S IV).

- A renewal fee is refunded if the application is not anymore pending on the due date (see **Art.86(1):6**).
- All fees are refunded if no date of filing is accorded (A-II,4.1.4).
- Validly paid extension fees are not refunded (Art.3(3) Extension Ordinance).
- An opposition fee is refunded if the notice of opposition is deemed not filed (see **Art.101(1):1**).
- An appeal fee is reimbursed if the notice of appeal is deemed not filed (see **Art.108:5**) and in the case of a substantial procedural violation or early withdrawal under **R.103**.
- An excess payment is refunded where the full amount of a fee has been paid and the applicant is entitled to a reduction under **Rfees14**.

Rfees9(1) The search fee paid for a European or supplementary European search shall be fully refunded if the European patent application is withdrawn or refused or deemed to be withdrawn at a time when the Office has not yet begun to draw up the search report.

1 **Refund of search fee for non-pending application**

According to **Rfees9(1)** the search fee will be fully refunded if the application is withdrawn, refused or deemed to be withdrawn before the start of the search (Not. EPO, OJ 2009, 99).

The drawing up of the search report begins on the date the examiner carries out the first search task, i.e. triggering a pre-search algorithm generating a list of documents to be inspected. This date is recorded in the public part of the file. For applications not yet published, this information can be accessed using the MyFiles service; the EPO will also provide the applicant with the relevant information upon request. (A-X,10.2.1)

Rfees9(2) Where the European search report is based on an earlier search report prepared by the Office on an application whose priority is claimed or an earlier application within the meaning of Article 76 of the Convention or of Rule 17 of the Convention, the Office shall refund to the applicant, in accordance with a decision of its President, an amount which shall depend on the type of earlier search and the extent to which the Office benefits from the earlier search report when carrying out the subsequent search.

Art.76 divisional application
R.17 new application filed by an entitled person

1 **Conditions for refund of search fee**

The search fee for a European search report or supplementary European search report will be refunded (Dec. Pres., OJ 2017 A94) if the search report can be based on an earlier search report prepared by the EPO for:

- an application whose priority is claimed, or
- an earlier application within the meaning of **Art.76** (parent application of the present divisional application), or
- an original application within the meaning of **R.17** (i.e. the present application is a new application under **Art.61**).

The earlier search report must have been prepared by the EPO (**J8/81**). That is the case e.g. for a (supplementary) European search report (**Art.92**; **R.164(1)**), for a (supplementary) international search report drawn up by the EPO as (S)ISA (**Art.15 PCT**), for a search made by EPO on behalf of a national office on a national application (see OJ 2017 A94 for the relevant Contracting States), and for an international-type search carried out by the EPO (Art.15(5)

PCT); and likely also for search results under **R.164(2)**. An international-type search can be carried out by the EPO for a national application filed in an EPC Contracting State if the law of that state provides for an international-type search (OJ 1999 p.300). This is the case for CH, DK, FI, IS, NL, NO, and SE (PCT Applicant's Guide, Section B1). See OJ 2017 A94 for further details.

The search fees that can be refunded are the European search fee (**Art.78(2)**), the further search fee (**R.64(1)**) and the fee for the supplementary European search (**Art.153(7)**), and likely also the search fees under **R.164(1)** and **R.164(2)**.

2 **Amount of the refund**

The amount of the refund is either a full refund or a partial refund of the search fee, depending on the extent to which the EPO can base its search report on the earlier search. The full refund is between 70% and 100% and the partial refund between 17.5% and 25%, depending on the type of earlier search (Dec. Pres. OJ 2017 A94).

The EPO informs the applicant of the amount of the refund together with the search report and will make the refund. In the event of disagreement, the applicant may request an appealable decision to be issued by the Receiving Section or examining division (A-X,10.2.1).

3 **Criteria for applicable refund rate**

The criteria for determining the applicable refund level are given in OJ 2009 p.99. A full refund of the search fee applies where the search report can be completely based on the earlier search (i.e. no search needs to be carried out). This is the case, in particular, where the claims of the earlier and later application are identical or where the claims of the later application are limited by deleting alternative features from an independent claim or by moving a limiting feature from a dependent claim to the independent claim it refers to in the earlier application.

A partial refund applies where the search report can be based partly on the earlier search. This applies, in particular, where the claims of the later application are a further generalisation of the invention searched in the earlier application, or the claims are limited by a feature not disclosed in the earlier application but relating to the same invention as the searched earlier application.

No refund will be made where the subject-matter of the claims represent an invention different from that searched in the earlier application, or the conditions in the first section above have not been met, for example the priority of the earlier application is not claimed.

Rfees 10 Refund of the fee for a technical opinion

An amount of 75% of the fee for a technical opinion under Article 25 of the Convention shall be refunded if the request for a technical opinion is withdrawn at a time when the Office has not yet begun to draw up the technical opinion.

Rfees 11 Refund of examination fee

The examination fee provided for in Article 94, paragraph 1, of the Convention shall be refunded:

(a) in full if the European patent application is withdrawn, refused or deemed to be withdrawn before substantive examination has begun;

(b) at a rate of 50% if the European patent application is withdrawn after substantive examination has begun and
- **before expiry of the time limit for replying to the first invitation under Article 94, paragraph 3, of the Convention issued by the Examining Division proper or,**
- **if no such invitation has been issued by the Examining Division, before the date of the communication under Rule 71, paragraph 3, of the Convention.**

Amended by decision of the Administrative Council of 29.06.2016, which entered into force on 01.07.2016. Amended Rfees11(a) applies to applications withdrawn, refused or deemed to be withdrawn on or after 01.06.2016. Amended Rfees11(b) applies to applications for which substantive examination starts on or after 01.11.2016. (OJ 2016 A48)
Art.94(1) request for examination
Art.94(3) invitation to file observations
R.71(3) communication of text to be granted

1 **Refund of the examination fee**

The EPO will refund the examination fee at a rate depending on the moment in time when the grant procedure terminates, either due to refusal by the EPO, being deemed withdrawn or active withdrawal by the applicant. A reason for the refund is that an applicant should not have to pay for a service the EPO does not deliver. Moreover, the refund provides an incentive for the applicant to withdraw an application they are no longer interested in pursuing; this frees examiner capacity which can be deployed to reduce the EPO's backlog in examination.

The withdrawal of an application can be made conditional on the (partial) refund of the examination fee. (OJ 1988 p.354; E-VIII,7.3)

The implementation of **Rfees11** has been set out in OJ 2016 A49.

2 **Full refund**

If the procedure terminates before substantive examination has begun, the entire examination fee will be refunded (**Rfees11(a)**). The termination may be a withdrawal, refusal or deemed to be withdrawn.

The substantive examination begins on the date the examiner carries out his first task, i.e. identifying the European prior rights that where not yet available when the search was carried out. The date is recorded in Form 2095 in the public part of the file to ensure it is verifiable. For applications not yet published, the date will be visible only at the request of the applicant or his representative or by inspecting the file using the MyFiles service. (Not. EPO OJ 2013 p.153)

The EPO will inform the applicant at least two months before the start of the examination about the intended date of the start. The intended date does not bind the EPO; the examination may start later.

An applicant unsure whether substantive examination has begun and wanting to withdraw only if he receives the 100% refund may make the withdrawal contingent upon the refund (A-VI,2.5; conditional withdrawal).

3 **Partial refund**

If the application is actively withdrawn after the start of the examination but before expiry of the period for response to the first substantive communication of the examining division, 50% of the examination fee will be refunded (**Rfees11(b)**). There is no refund if the procedure terminates after this expiry. The termination must be an active withdrawal. A timely refusal or a deemed withdrawal does not give rise to a refund under **Rfees11(b)**. A withdrawal causes a clear end of the procedure without the possibility of reinstating the procedure through common remedies such as further processing.

For most files the withdrawal must be submitted before the expiry of the period for responding to the first **Art.94(3)** communication. If the period for response is extended upon request under **R.132(2)**, it should be possible to submit the withdrawal until expiry of the extended period. If the first **Art.94(3)** communication is a summons for oral proceedings, the withdrawal can be made up to the last date for submitting written submissions set therein under **R.116** according to EPO practice.

A few communications that are not issued under **Art.94(3)**, e.g. under **R.137(4)** or **R.56(3)**, are nevertheless taken into account under **Rfees11(b)** and a few communications that are issued under **Art.94(3)**, e.g. issued by formalities officers or under **R.164(2)(a)**, are not taken into account. The provision endeavours to cover these deviating cases by the wording 'issued by the examining division proper', where the word 'proper' is not defined. The word intends to exclude communications sent by formalities officers working on behalf of the examining division. The deviating cases can only be found in the Notice in OJ 2016 A49, which, however, has no legal force.

In cases where the first communication of the examining division is a **R.71(3)** communication, the withdrawal must be submitted at the latest on the day before the date of the communication for a 50% refund (A-VI,2.5). Note, that an applicant has no advance information when the communication will be sent.

Rfees 12 Refund of insignificant amounts

Where too large a sum is paid to cover a fee, the excess shall not be refunded if the amount is insignificant and the party concerned has not expressly requested a refund. The President of the Office shall determine what constitutes an insignificant amount.

1 **Insignificant amount**

An insignificant amount is 15 Euro or less (OJ 2018 A37). Hence, an overpayment of more than 15 Euro is refunded without request, an overpayment of 15 Euro or less is refunded only on request. The request must be made before expiry of the period of **Rfees13(2)**. (A-X,10.1.3)

Rfees 13 Termination of financial obligations

Amended by decision of the Administrative Council of 15.10.2007, which entered into force on 13.12.2007 (OJ 2007 p.533).

1 **General**

The provision takes care of the extinction of financial claims that have become out-of-date. It avoids the situation that parties will experience difficulties in providing evidence when rights are not executed for a long time.

The provision is not very relevant anymore because reminders for payment and refunds are processed by computer and will nearly always be carried out well before expiry of the periods mentioned in the provision.

Rfees13(1) Rights of the Organisation to the payment of a fee to the European Patent Office shall be extinguished after four years from the end of the calendar year in which the fee was due.

1 **Right of Organisation to payment**

Rfees1 defines what fees are: fees to be paid to the EPO and provided for in the Articles and Rules, and fees fixed by the President for special services.

The EPO is not entitled to most of these fees; a party is free to pay them. If a party does not pay, certain intended acts will not become effective, e.g. the request for examination (**Art.94(1)**), the opposition (**Art.99(1)**), the appeal (**Art.108**). In other cases the application will be regarded as withdrawn, e.g. when the filing fee or the search fee is not paid in time (**Art.78(2)**).

In a few cases the EPO has a right to a payment, e.g. for subscriptions to patent information databases.

Rfees13(2) Rights against the Organisation for the refunding by the European Patent Office of fees or sums of money paid in excess of a fee shall be extinguished after four years from the end of the calendar year in which the right arose.

1 **Right of party to refund**

Examples of rights of parties to a refund of a fee are refund of renewal fees paid twice by different payers or refund of the fee for further processing or re-establishment when the remedies were requested on an auxiliary basis and the main request was granted. Other examples are full or partial refund of a search fee under **Rfees9**, and reimbursement of an appeal fee according to **R.103(1)**.

Rfees13(3) The period laid down in paragraphs 1 and 2 shall be interrupted in the case covered by paragraph 1 by a request for payment of the fee and in the case covered by paragraph 2 by a reasoned claim in writing. On interruption it shall begin again immediately and shall end at the latest six years after the end of the year in which it originally began, unless, in the meantime, judicial proceedings to enforce the right have begun; in this case the period shall end at the earliest one year after the judgment enters into force.

Rfees13(4) The President of the European Patent Office may waive action for the enforced recovery of any sum due if the sum to be recovered is minimal or if such recovery is too uncertain.

1 **Sum due**

A sum is due if the EPO has rendered a service or has delivered goods to be paid afterwards, such as for example the delivery of publications ordered (**Rfees3(2)**).

Rfees 14 Reduction of fees

1 **General**

Where a fee is reduced - in contrast to cases of fee refunds - the reduced rate may be paid instead of the full fee. The factual conditions for a reduction of the fee must be met on or before the day the period for payment expires. (A-X,9.1)

If there is doubt about entitlement to a reduction of a fee, the full fee should be paid as a precaution. When the reduced fee is applicable, the EPO will refund the excess payment. When the reduced fee has been paid without entitlement, the amount lacking is, in general, not a small amount in the sense of **Rfees8**, and the payment will be deemed not to have been made. (T905/90 r.6, 10)

See **Art.153(7)** for reduction of the supplementary European search fee.

2 **Reduction of PCT fees**

The search fee in respect of an international search under **Rfees2(1)2** and the fee for the international preliminary examination of an international application under **Rfees2(1)19** will be reduced in favour of nationals of certain states not party to the EPC, if each applicant is a natural person who is a national and resident of such state (see OJ 2008 p.521, Euro-PCT Guide §215).

Rfees14(1) The reduction laid down in Rule 6, paragraph 3, of the Convention shall be 30% of the filing fee or examination fee.

Amended by decision of the Administrative Council of 13.12.2013, which entered into force on 01.04.2014. The amendment increases the rate of fee reduction. The amended provision applies to European patent applications filed on or after 01.04.2014 and to international applications entering the European phase on or after that date. (OJ 2014 A4)
R.6(3) use of an admissible non-EPO language

Rfees14(2) Where the European Patent Office has drawn up an international preliminary examination report, the examination fee shall be reduced by 75%. If the report was established on certain parts of the international application in accordance with Article 34, paragraph 3(c), PCT, the fee shall not be reduced if subject-matter not covered by the report is to be examined.

Art.34(3)(c) International preliminary examination report in the case of non-unity

Amended by decision of the Administrative Council of 13.12.2017, which entered into force on 01.04.2018 (OJ 2018 A4). The amendment increases the reduction as an incentive for applicants to use the EPO's services as IPEA and applies to payments made on or after 01.04.2018 (OJ 2018 A4, Art.3(3)).

1 **Reduction of examination fee for Euro-PCT application**

Rfees14(2) provides for a reduction in the amount of the examination fee where the EPO has already drawn up an international preliminary examination report (IPER). If the IPER of a non-unitary application covers only certain parts of the international application, the reduction will only apply if the examination is on subject-matter completely covered by the IPER (**Rfees14(2)**, second sentence).

Where both reductions of **Rfees14**(1) and (2) apply, the full fee is first reduced by 75% and the resulting amount by 30%, i.e. a total reduction of 82.5%. (Euro-PCT Guide §608)

Rfees 15 Entry into force

These Rules shall enter into force on 20 October 1977.

DONE at Munich, 20 October 1977 for the Administrative Council.
The Chairman

Notes to the

Patent Cooperation Treaty

of 19 June 1970,

amended on 28 September 1979

and modified on 3 February 1984 and 3 October 2001

(as in force from 1 April 2002)

and

Regulations under the PCT

as in force from 1 July 2018

Contents of notes to the PCT

1 Introduction

1.1 HISTORY

In the late nineteen fifties several member states of the European Economic Community started negotiations on the unification of patent law in Europe. The internationalisation of industry and commerce with their cross-border connections had increased the demand for patent protection in more than one state. The unification sought to reduce the laboriousness and ever-increasing complexity of international patent protection within Europe. In 1965 the work on the European patent system came to a standstill for political reasons. Thereupon the government of the USA encouraged the World Intellectual Property Organisation (WIPO) in Geneva, a specialized agency of the United Nations, to take up the task of simplifying patent protection on a world-wide scale. The differences between the patent laws in the world precluded a unified patent system from dealing with grant and maintenance of patents. Therefore, a world-wide system was developed for filing of patent applications, including the drawing up of a search report and, optionally, a non-binding examination report. The system aims at reducing the number of national applications to be filed with their different requirements regarding form and procedure, allowing the applicant to secure his rights for all desired states initially with a single application and procedure. Subsequent to the international procedure, the international application falls apart in a series of national patent applications for each state where protection is desired. Each state will subject the international application to a grant procedure according to the same national law of the state that governs national applications.

After a relatively short period of preparatory work, the Patent Cooperation Treaty, shortly PCT, was signed by twenty states on 19.06.1970 at the end of a diplomatic conference in Washington DC. Until 31.12.1970, the last day the Treaty was open for signature (Art.67(2)), fifteen more states signed the Treaty. The PCT entered into force according to Art.63 on 24.01.1978 and the first international patent application could be filed on 01.06.1978.

The PCT is an open treaty to which any state member of the Paris Convention may become party (Art.62(1)). At present (November 2018), the PCT is in force for 152 of the 177 member states of the Paris Convention. The list of PCT contracting states is regularly published by WIPO and each year in the fourth issue of the EPO OJ.

1.2 TREATY AND REGULATIONS

The Patent Cooperation Treaty has essentially the following aims:

- to simplify and render more economical the obtaining of protection of inventions in several countries,
- to improve access by the public to patent information, and
- to assist the economic development of developing countries by improving the national patent systems and facilitate access to modern technology. (Preamble of the Treaty)

The contracting states of the PCT constitute a Union for cooperation in the filing, searching and examination of applications for the protection of inventions (Art.1). The Union also renders special technical services, such as publication of patent applications (Art.50) and technical assistance for contracting states in developing their patent systems (Art.51).

1.2.1 *Provisions of the PCT*

The Treaty comprises 69 Articles and 118 Rules (Art.58). The provisions prescribe the procedures and requirements in great detail. Since the PCT has no instance for appeal to interpret, further develop and fill up holes in the provisions, the PCT Rules should cover all situations that might occur and are therefore very detailed. Moreover, the provisions have become rather complicated because of the numerous exceptions that the PCT had to permit in view of national peculiarities, in particular those of one of the contracting states.

The PCT Articles and Rules are supplemented by procedures outlined in the PCT Applicant's Guide, International Phase and National Phase parts, abbreviated below as AG-IP and AG-NP respectively, available on the WIPO website at www.wipo.int/pct. The PCT Applicant's Guide gives also general information about each of the contracting (this part of the website is frequently updated).

A summary of the procedures laid down in the PCT is given below in §1.3. A detailed account is given in §2 and following paragraphs; the items in the paragraphs follow, in general, the order of the Articles of the PCT.

1.2.2 *Definitions*

The PCT uses a series of terms that have a special meaning within its Articles and Rules. The following definitions affect the interpretation of many provisions or can cause confusion.

- An 'application' means an application for the protection of an invention in the form of a patent, inventor's certificate, utility certificate, utility model, patent or certificate of addition, inventor's certificate of addition, or utility certificate of addition (Art.2(i), see also Art.43).
- an 'international application' means an application filed under the PCT (Art.2(vii)). All references to applications in the following chapters of this Part are to international applications; the adjective 'international' is only added where otherwise confusion could arise.
- A 'regional application' means an application for a 'regional patent', i.e. a patent granted by a national or intergovernmental authority having the power to grant patents effective in more than one state (Art.2(iv), (v)).
- The 'priority date' of an international application claiming priority is the filing date of the earliest application whose priority is claimed (Art.2(xi)(a),(b)). Where the international application does not contain a priority claim, the 'priority date' is the international filing date of the application in the sense of Art.11(1) (Art.2(xi)(c)).
- A 'national Office' is a government authority of a contracting state entrusted with the granting of patents or an intergovernmental authority which several states have entrusted with the granting of patents (Art.2(xii)). Where a distinction between an intergovernmental and governmental authority is desired, the intergovernmental authority is called 'regional Office'.
- The 'request' is a part of the international application containing a petition that the international application be processed according to the PCT, the designation of states in which protection is desired, and bibliographic data (Art.4(1)).
- An 'agent' means a person having the right to practise before the national or regional office where the international application is being processed and who may be appointed by the applicant to represent him before that office acting under the PCT (R.2.2 and R.90.1). An 'agent' is a 'professional representative' in EPC terminology.

- A 'common representative' is an applicant representing all applicants where there are two or more applicants. A 'common agent' is an agent representing all applicants. (R.2.2*bis* and R.90.2).

1.2.3 *Organisation*

The PCT is administered by the WIPO, a specialised agency of the United Nations. The Assembly, formed by one delegate of each contracting state, maintains and develops the Union of contracting states and the implementation of the Treaty (Art.53(1),(2)). The International Bureau (IB) of WIPO carries out the administrative tasks concerning the PCT (Art.55(1)). The Assembly has established an Executive Committee, which has as its most important task the preparation of Assembly meetings (Art.54). The budget of the Union is financed mainly from fees and charges for services rendered by the IB (Art.57).

The tasks under the PCT, in particular the handling of the international patent applications, are not carried out by a single international patent office but by national and regional patent offices (Art.2(xii)). When carrying out tasks under the PCT, the national offices are bound by the provisions of the PCT and may apply national law only where the PCT permits so. An office may act under the PCT as a receiving Office (rO), designated Office, elected Office, International Searching Authority (ISA) (including ISA competent to carry out supplementary international searches (SISA)) or International Preliminary Examining Authority (IPEA) (see Art.2(xiii)-(xv), Art.16, Art.32, R.45*bis*). The IB coordinates the tasks of the offices and international authorities. The IB also carries out specific tasks under the PCT, such as the distribution of documents over the International Authorities (e.g. Art.20) and the publication of the international patent applications (Art.21). It can also act as rO (R.19.1(a)(iii)).

1.3 SUMMARY OF PROCEDURE

The procedure from the filing of an international application to the grant of one or more national patents can be divided into an international phase and a national phase. The international phase is governed by the PCT, whereas the national phase is governed by national law.

The international phase starts automatically on filing of an international application with a receiving Office (rO) and consists of three main steps. The first step is the processing of the application by the rO, which includes the accordance of an international filing date followed by a check on formal requirements and payments (Art.3-14). The second step is the establishment of an international search report by an ISA together with a written opinion of the ISA (Art.15-18). The search report and written opinion of the ISA give the applicant a first impression of his chances for obtaining a patent on his invention. After receiving the international search report, the applicant may amend the claims before the International Bureau (IB) (Art.19). He may also decide to withdraw the application (R.90*bis*.1), possibly in view of prejudicial prior art mentioned in the search report, before the much more expensive national phase begins. In the third step the IB publishes the international application and the search report (Art.21). The applicant has the option to request a supplementary international search (R.45*bis*) at an International Searching Authority competent to carry out Supplementary International Search (SISA) (other than the ISA that carried out the main international search) with the aim of finding prior art which was not found during the main international search (e.g. because of language limitations). By the end of the international phase, the IB makes the application and search report(s) available to the designated Offices, i.e. the national or regional offices where the applicant desires to obtain patent protection

(Art.20, 22-30). The international phase ends at the expiry of 30 months from the priority date (extended to 31 months in respect of some national/regional offices, including the EPO), and to start national prosecution, the international application must enter the national phase before each of the designated Offices.

The applicant has the option to have an international preliminary examination carried out by filing a so-called demand (Art.31). In the demand, the applicant requests an International Preliminary Examining Authority (IPEA) to draw up an 'International Preliminary Report on Patentability (Chapter II)' according to the provisions in Chapter II of the PCT (Art.31-42, R.70). The Report provides a preliminary and non-binding opinion on the novelty, presence of inventive step and industrial applicability of the invention (Art.33(1)). It gives the applicant a second impression of the patentability of the invention, on which he may decide whether or not to enter the national phase. The IB makes the Report available to the the national and regional offices (Art.36-42).

The provisions concerning international preliminary examination are set out in Chapter II PCT, which also contains the provisions about the entry into the national/regional phase for those international applications for wich a demand is filed. Until 2002, the period for entry into the national phase was longer in Chapter II than in Chapter I. Chapter II was therefore regarded asa second stage of the international phase which extended beyond the first stage under Chapter I. As a matter of terminology, the national/regional offices are called are 'designated Ofices' under Chapter I and 'elected offices' under Chapter II.

If no demand is filed, the IB converts the written opinion of the ISA into an 'International Preliminary Report on Patentability (Chapter I of the PCT)' (IPRP Ch.I) (R.44*bis*.1(b)). Note that the term 'International Preliminary Report on Patentability (Chapter II of the PCT)' (IPRP Ch.II) is used by WIPO and the regulations, Art.34 uses 'International Preliminary Examination Report (IPER)' instead. In R.70.15(b), the 'IPER' is re-defined as the IPRP Ch.II.

After the international phase, the international application splits up in national/regional applications by entering the national/regional phase for one or more designated Offices (called electeded Office under Chapter II), generally within a period of 30 months from the priority date. In the national/regional phase, the designated Office at issue may carry out formal and substantive examination, including a supplementeray search.

The applicant may decide to enter the national/regional phase early before a designated (or elected) office, before expiry of the period. In such a case, the application can be simultaneously in the international phase for some designated or elected states and in the national phase for other states. Any action taken in respect of the application still in the international phase has no effect on the proceedings of the application already in the national phase. (Art.23(2); Art.40(2))

1.4 ADVANTAGES

Use of the PCT has the following advantages:

- The applicant needs to file only one application complying with only a single set of requirements and in one language to obtain an application with the effect of a national or regional application for several states. Without the PCT he would have to file the application for each state or region. The PCT has rather strict formal requirements for the international application, e.g. for the drawings. However, once they are complied with, any designated Office must accept the application and may not impose additional requirements (Art.27(1)). The reverse is that, if deficiencies are not remedied in due time, the international application will be considered withdrawn for all designated states (Art.14), terminating the existence of the international application. The applicant then has to apply for a review procedure before each designated Office with a similar remedy for each state (Art.25).

- The final decision whether or not to seek to obtain a patent in a state can be taken at a relatively late moment in the procedure, i.e. near the end of the international phase. If the PCT route were not used, the decision should be taken within twelve months from the priority date. Now, the decision can be taken within 30 months from the priority date. At that time, the applicant already has the international search report and the international preliminary report on patentability, giving him a good assessment of the value of his application and his chances of obtaining a patent. The longer time available for making the decision also places the applicant in a better position to assess the technical and economic value of his application and to choose the states where protection is desirable. The international search report together with the international preliminary examination provides for a stronger patent also in countries with a registration system or with less-trained patent office personnel.
- A further advantage of the PCT route is that the initial costs are relatively low. The late entry into the national phase defers the costs of national entry. The costs of national entry are relatively high because of the fees to be paid to each national and regional office and the translations of the application to be made. The fees to be paid to the national offices are in general equal to the fees when filing directly with a national office, not using the PCT route. Some states have rebates for fees of applications arriving via the PCT route.

1.5 PATENT PROSECUTION HIGHWAY PILOT PROGRAMME

Several patent offices have signed bilateral agreements to promote work-sharing between the offices and permit accelerated prosecution of applications in the national phase. The cooperation is known as the Patent Prosecution Highway (PPH). The principles of PPH are set out on the web page www.jpo.go.jp/ppph-portal/aboutpph.htm. Information about PPH relating to PCT applications is given on www.wipo.int/pct/en/filing/pct_pph.html.

The EPO participates in the IP5 PPH pilot programme, sharing examination results between the patent offices of CN, EP, JP, KR and US. See for more information **Art.94(3):7.**

1.6 RELATION BETWEEN THE PCT AND THE EPC

The relationship between the PCT and the EPC is based on the Preamble of the EPC and on Art.150(1) EPC, which state that the EPC is a regional patent treaty within the meaning of Art.45(1) PCT. Hence, an international application may designate or elect a state party to both the PCT and the EPC, indicating that the application is for the grant of a regional, i.e. European, patent for that state (Art.45(1) PCT and Art.153 EPC). The provisions of the PCT treat a national and regional application and patent in the same way, which is evident from Art.2(iii)-(vi) PCT. Likewise, a national Office and a regional Office are equivalent (Art.2(xii) PCT), as is also clear from the frequent use of 'in or for a state' in many PCT provisions.

The provisions for the operation of the EPO under the PCT and the transition to the regional phase can be found in Art.150-153 EPC and corresponding regulations R.157-165 EPC. The EPO can perform any task under the PCT as a rO, designated Office and elected Office. The EPO may also act as International Searching Authority (ISA), International Searching Authority competent to carry out Supplementary International Search (SISA) and International Preliminary Examining Authority (IPEA), based on an agreement between the European Patent Organisation and the IB of the WIPO according to Art.16(3)(b) and Art.32(3) PCT (OJ 2017 A115, with a revised Annex A in OJ 2018 A24 and revised Annex D in OJ 2018 A35). In the international proceedings the provisions of the PCT apply, supplemented by the provisions of the EPC; in case of conflict, the provisions of the PCT prevail (Art.150(2) EPC).

All contracting states of the EPC are party to the PCT.

For information concerning the relationship between the EPO and the PCT see the EPO publication Euro-PCT Guide, describing the operation of the EPO as rO, ISA, SISA, IPEA, designated Office and elected Office.

2 Filing an international application

An international application is an application filed under the PCT (Art.2(vii)). The international application must contain a request, a description, one or more claims, zero or more drawings and an abstract (Art.3(2); §2.1; §2.11). The application must be filed in a prescribed language, i.e. a language accepted by the rO (Art.3(4)(i); R.12.1; §2.4). The physical requirements the international application must comply with are given in R.3 - R.11 (Art.3(4)(ii)), which are similar to the EPC requirements. Many deviations from the form requirements are allowed for certain states in so far as the laws of that state allow them (see e.g. R.6.3(c); R.6.4; R.11.5). The international application must also comply with the requirement of unity of invention (Art.3(4)(iii); R.13; §4.3) and is subject to the payment of fees (Art.3(4)(iv); R.14-16; §2.8). The invention described in the international application must be an enabling disclosure (Art.5). If the form and contents of an international application comply with the requirements of the PCT, the application may not be rejected in a national procedure because of different national requirements (Art.27(1)).

The permitted methods of filing an international application are determined by each rO and are set out in AG-IP, Annex C.

The IB and several rOs accept electronic filing, using the web-based ePCT or PCT-SAFE, using software installed on a local computer (see www.wipo.int/pct-safe/en and Practical Advice in PCT Newsletter 05/2014). The EPO as rO accepts PCT-SAFE as method of filing (R.2 EPC; OJ 2018 A45; A-II,1.3). The EPO also allows the filing of PCT applications and other documents by OLF, CMS and Web-form filing (OJ 2018 A45; OJ 2018 A46) and by the web-based ePCT-Filing (OJ 2014 A107; OJ 2016 A78).

When an international application is filed electronically, it may be converted by a rO from a pre-conversion format in which it was drafted (for example in a character coded format such as Microsoft Word™), to a format accepted for electronic filing (for example XML or PDF format). Errors may occur during such conversion, so rOs are allowed to specify whether they will accept international applications in such pre-conversion formats and if so, specify their accepted pre-conversion formats. In the international phase, the applicant may request correction of the international application to that of the pre-conversion format (see Sections 706 and 710 of the Admin. Instr.).

The EPO accepts documents in pre-conversion formats; the EPO acting as rO under the PCT follows a practice similar to that followed in the EP direct procedure.

The international application may not contain any matter contrary to morality or public order, or disparaging statements or irrelevant matter (Art.21(6), R.9). The physical requirements of the international application, such as number of copies, paper and print quality, margins, numbering, drawings, are provided in R.11. Each rO may determine the number of copies of the international application to be filed (R.11(1)(a), (b), see AG-IP Annex C for each rO). The EPO as rO requires one copy of the international application (R.157(2) EPC; Euro-PCT Guide §64). The rO checks whether the international application complies with the physical requirements (Art.14(1)(a)(v)). The rO allows correction of deficiencies (§3.2.1). If not duly corrected, the application will be considered withdrawn (Art.14(1)(b); R.29.1; §3.4).

Obvious mistakes in an international application may be rectified (R.91.1(a); §8.5).

Correspondence between the applicant and international authorities, other than the international application itself, is governed by R.92. Any letter from the applicant to the IB must be in English, French or the language of publication (R.92.2(d); §8.1.1)

The requirements for the different elements of the international application are described in the following paragraphs.

2.1 REQUEST

The request must contain a petition (Art.4(1)(i), R.4.1(a)(i)), to the effect that the international application shall be processed according to the PCT, preferably worded according to R.4.2. The request must contain data of the applicant, agent and inventor and the title of the invention (Art.4(1)(i)-(iv), R.4.1). Filing of the request constitutes designation of all contracting states bound by the PCT on the international filing date (R.4.9(a)). An example of a completely filled-in request form may be downloaded from the WIPO website.

The request must be made on a special printed form (PCT/RO/101) or presented as a computer print-out (R.3.1; AG-IP §5.015). Copies of the printed form are available free of charge from the rO or IB (R.3.2); editable versions of the request can be downloaded from the PCT website (www.wipo.int/pct). The request must contain a checklist indicating the content of the application documents (R.3.3 PCT, see also R.157(2) EPC). The request may contain declarations as required by national law of designated Offices and allowed under Art.27. Correction or addition of these declarations is possible (R.26*ter*; AG-IP §6.045-6.050).

The language of the request must be both a language accepted by the rO and a language of publication (R.12.1(c)). See §2.4 below. The requirements for the other items of the request are set out in the following paragraphs.

2.2 APPLICANT

Any resident or national of a PCT contracting state may file an international application (Art.9(1); R.18.1). The PCT is a closed system for applicants, whereas the EPC is an open system that allows anyone to file a European application, independent of nationality and residence (Art.58 EPC). The restriction to PCT members in Art.9 was intended to act as an incentive for states to accede to the PCT.

The Assembly has decided that the capacity of the applicant is not relevant for Art.9(1). Hence, a trustee or legal representative will be regarded as the applicant and not the person on whose behalf they are acting.

In principle, the applicant's name, address, nationality and residence must be indicated in the request according to Art.4(1)(iii) and R.4.1(a)(i), (ii), and (iii) in the form prescribed by R.4.4 and R.4.5. The state of nationality and the state of residence must be provided (R.4.5(b),(c)) to allow the rO to assess entitlement to file in the sense of Art.9(1). The request should be signed by the applicant (R.4.15).

National law determines whether a designated Office may request the applicant to furnish evidence of his entitlement to apply for a patent (R.4.17(ii); R.51*bis*.1(a)(ii)). R.51*bis*.2 governs the situations when entitlement evidence it is not required.

Amended versions of R.4.15 and R.51*bis* entered into force on 01.01.2013 reflecting the changes of the US patent law: there is no longer a requirement that an inventor must be named as applicant solely for the purpose of the US designation for international applications filed on or after 16.09.2012. Note that US national law still requires submission of a US inventor's oath or declaration. (PCT Newsletter 09/2012 and 10/2012)

2.2.1 *Residence and nationality*

The question of residency and nationality of the applicant is determined by national law and will be decided by the rO (R.18.1(a)). In any case, possession of economic activity or legal entity in a state is considered as residency or nationality, respectively (R.18.1(b)). Where the international application is filed with the IB as rO, the IB will ask the national Office of the state concerned to decide the question of nationality or residency (R.18.1(c)). The applicant may submit arguments relating to the question of residency and nationality (R.18.1(c); AG-IP §5.023).

2.2.2 *Applicants from non-PCT contracting states*

A person who is not a resident or national of a PCT contracting state, e.g. a resident and national of Argentina, may not file an international application (Art.9(1) with Art.62(1)). Note, that a Taiwanese applicant may only file an international application if he indicates China as country of nationality and residence, because Taiwan is not a PCT contracting state and WIPO, being an agency of the United Nations, considers that TW is part of CN.

A person who is both resident and national of a state party to the Paris Convention but not party to the PCT is also not allowed to file an international application (Art.9(1)). The Assembly has not used its power under Art.9(2) to allow such a person to file international applications. However, a contracting state may give notice under Art.62(3) that the PCT is applicable to the territory of a state, for the external relations of which it is responsible. In this way, the UK has declared the PCT applicable to the Isle of Man (AG-IP Annex C (GB)).

Since the residence and nationality of the applicant need only be complied with at the time of filing the international application, later changes will not affect the validity of the application itself.

An applicant, not being a national or resident of a contracting state, may still file an international application by making an entitled person, e.g. an agent in a contracting state, the second applicant (candidates for the EQE are recommended not to advise taking such action). After filing of the international application with a rO competent for the entitled person, the entitled person resigns as applicant, transfers his right to the first applicant and notifies the IB accordingly under R.92*bis*.1. Since the entitlement to file is not affected by changes after accordance of the international filing date, the filing of the international application is valid in the sense of Art.9(1) (AG-IP §11.019, see also §2.2.5 below). The entitled person is preferably made applicant under R.4.5(d) for a contracting state where no protection is desired, to avoid any negative consequences if the transfer to the original applicant is not carried out in time.

The same procedure can be used for filing an international application with a more convenient rO. For example, an Australian applicant who desires the EPO to act as ISA for an international application in a field which the applicant regards the EPO is particularly competent to search, but where the EPO does not act as ISA where the Australian Patent Office was rO (see §4.8), may appoint a UK agent who can temporarily act as second applicant for a state in which no protection is desired, thereby allowing filing in the UK and forcing the EPO to act as ISA (it is not recommended to use such a route for changing ISA in the EQE).

2.2.3 *Several applicants*

An international application may have several applicants (Art.9(3)). At least one of them must be a resident or national of a PCT contracting state (R.18.3). Likewise, the rO must be a competent rO for at least one of the applicants (R.19.2).

Neither R.4.5(a)(i) name, (ii) address, (iii) nationality and residence) nor R.4.15 (signature) make a reference to R.26.2*bis*(b) or R.26.2*bis*(a). This means that in the case of several applicants, all the indications under R.4.5 and all the signatures under R.4.15 must be provided for all applicants. However, according to R.26.2*bis*(a) and (b), upon performing the formalities examination, the rO might see that some of these indications/signatures are missing, but need not issue a communication that the indications/signatures are missing (cf. the wording of 'For the purposes of Art.14(1)(a)(i) ...' and 'For the purposes of Art.14(1)(a)(ii) ...' in R.26.2*bis*(a) and (b)). It is therefore an error if such indications/signatures are not provided as the requirements of R.4.5 or R.4.15 (which allow no exception) have not been met. However, according to AG-IP §5.032 and §5.088, the rO will not invite the applicant to provide missing indications and signatures if the indications and signature of at least one entitled applicant have been provided. Note that if an applicant files a notice of withdrawal, the IB will ask for all the signatures (R.90*bis*.5). In addition, the national Offices may ask for the missing indications (R.51*bis*.1(a)(vi) and (vii)). The EPO will typically not ask for missing signatures after entry into the regional phase before the EPO but will ask for any missing indications of address and nationality/residence (R.163(4) EPC).

The request may indicate different applicants for different designated states (R.4.5(d)). The PCT has no provisions for the residency and the nationality of an applicant for a designated state, in contrast with the residency or nationality for filing an international application (Art.9(1)). Hence, in an international application filed by a first applicant entitled to file according to Art.9(1) and by a second applicant who is not entitled, the second applicant may be the sole applicant for a designated state.

Where different types of protection are available for a state, the applicant(s) for these different types of protection must be the same, because the designation of a state by an applicant is unitary. Similarly, where a state is designated both for a national and a regional patent, the applicant(s) for both designations must be the same. (AG-IP §5.022)

Where the request does not indicate a common agent or common representative, the first-named applicant entitled according to R.19.1 to file an international application with the rO is considered to be the deemed common representative and will receive all notifications (R.90.2(b), see also §8.3.3). A deemed common representative has limited powers in relation to withdrawals (R.90*bis*; see §8.3.4).

2.2.4 *Deficient indication of applicant*

If the request does not contain the indications of the applicant (or of at least one applicant where there are several applicants) in the form prescribed by R.4.4 and R.4.5 (Art.14(1)(a)(ii)), the rO will invite the applicant as soon as possible to correct the deficiency under Art.14(1)(b) within an period of two months from the date of the invitation (R.26.1; see §3.2.1 for the procedure). Failure to correct the deficiency will result in the application being considered withdrawn and the rO will so declare (Art.14(1)(b); R.29.1). See §2.2.3 for deficiencies in the case of several applicants.

If the indications of nationality and residence do not support the applicant's entitlement to file, there is a prima facie defect under Art.11(1)(i), and no international filing date will be accorded. The rO will invite the applicant under Art.11(2)(a) to correct the deficiency (R.20.3-7). If the applicant can provide satisfactory proof that he was entitled to file on the date the rO received the international application and proposes a correction of his residence or nationality, the rO will consider the invitation to correct the defect under Art.11(1)(i) as an invitation to correct a defect under Art.14(1)(a)(ii) and R.4.5. The rO will subsequently correct the deficiency, which will no longer prevent the accordance of the actual date of receipt of the international application as the international filing date. (AG-IP §6.036)

2.2.5 *Change in indication of applicant*

Any changes in the person, name, residence, nationality or address of the applicant should be communicated in writing to the rO or the IB (AG-IP §11.020). The IB will, on the request of the applicant or the rO, record the changes (R.92*bis*.1(a)(i)) free of charge (AG-IP §11.018). The IB notifies all interested Offices and Authorities. The IB records the change if it receives the request within 30 months (see also §7.2) from the priority date (R.92*bis*.1(b)). Requests made shortly before expiry of the 30 month period should preferably be sent to the IB (AG-IP §11.020). Note, that the extended period for entering the national phase under Art.22(3) and Art.39(1)(b) is not applicable here, because of the specific period of 30 months stated in R.92*bis*.1(b). A change recorded after the international application has already entered the national phase is not effective. (AG-IP §11.020)

The change may also relate to a change in the person of applicant. The PCT does not contain any restrictions to the nationality and residence of the new applicant. The change does not affect the entitlement to file the international application, which is determined by the applicant indicated in the request at the time of filing of the international application. However, the nationality and residence of the new applicant may affect the right to file a demand (AG-IP §11.019; see also §6.1.1.1).

If the applicant or his agent requests a change in the person of the applicant, no assignment or other documentary proof of the change need be filed. However, a designated Office may request under Art.27(2)(ii) that the assignment is submitted in the national phase (see e.g. AG-NP §4.031).

The assignment or other proof must be filed if a request to assign the application to a new applicant is made by a person not yet named in the request and the request is not accompanied by the written consent of the applicant of record (AG-IP §11.021). If the agent of record requests a change in the person of the applicant, a power of attorney appointing the agent and signed by the new applicant must be furnished at the same time, if the agent is to represent the new applicant (AG-IP §11.022).

In the case of the death of the applicant during the international phase, the successor in title must request a change of applicant under R.92*bis*.1, indicating the reason for the change (AG-IP §11.023).

2.2.6 *Entitlement disputes*

The PCT has no provisions relating to entitlement disputes. Since the PCT does not provide regulations for international applications made by persons not having the right to file those applications, steps to transfer the applications over to the rightful persons may only be taken before national/regional offices. Such disputes fall within the competence of one or more national/regional courts. If such a court were to take a decision to change applicants whilst the application is still in the international phase, the applicant may be forced to ask the IB to record the change effective for at least the designated state in which the decision was taken. The effect of the decision on other designated states depends on international treaties between the states for recognition of national decisions.

More commonly, a decision will be taken after the international application has entered the national phase and any change in applicant should be registered under national law. The EPO as a designated or elected Office will apply Art.61 and R.14 EPC to give effect to the decision of a national court. If, during the international phase, the entire international application or the designation of the EPO has been withdrawn, the entitled applicant may probably not use Art.61(1)(b) EPC to file a new European patent application, because the international application designating the EPO will only be treated as a European application if any translation under Art.153(4) has been published and the filing fee is paid (Art.153(5) EPC).

A dispute between different applicants of an international application also falls within the competence of one or more national/regional courts. During the settlement of the dispute, the common representative or common agent remains in control of the proceedings of the international application (R.90.3(c)). However, a deemed common representative or his agent cannot withdraw the application or a designation without the signature of the other applicants (R.90*bis*.5). (see §8.3.4)

2.3 RECEIVING OFFICE

The applicant must file the international application with a competent receiving Office (rO) (Art.10). The applicant may choose between the rO of or acting for the state of which he is a resident (R.19.1(a)(i)) or a national (R.19.1(a)(ii)) and the IB (R.19.1(a)(iii)). If there are two or more applicants, the rO must be competent for at least one of the applicants (R.19.2(i)).

In general, a state has appointed one rO, which is often its national Office. In addition to or instead of that, a state can appoint an intergovernmental organisation such as the EPO acting as rO for that state (R.19.1(b)). Each EPC contracting state gives its residents and nationals in principle the choice to file their international applications with its national Office, the EPO or the IB. More than 20% of all PCT applications from the EPC contracting states have the EPO as rO. An advantage of filing with the national Office as rO instead of the EPO as rO is that a national language other than the official EPO languages (R.157(2) EPC) can be used; note that this advantage only applies if the ISA searches in that national language (e.g. Sweden, Finland, Spain; or the EPO searching in Dutch if the international application is filed at the national Office of NL (OJ 2018 A24). A further advantage can be obtained if the applicant files at the national Office and claims priority from a national patent application, because the request form contains a box where the applicant can request the rO to transmit a certified copy of the priority document to the IB (R.17.1(b)).

The competent rO(s) for each PCT contracting state and its address and telephone and fax numbers are given in AG-IP Annex B1. The Annex also indicates for each contracting state whether a resident of that state as applicant has a choice of rO, or that he must file his international application with the national Office of that state as rO for reasons of national security as allowed by Art.27(8) and limiting the choice of R.19.1. Where national security requires so, the national Office will not treat the international application as such and will not transmit the record copy to the IB (R.22.1). The IB as rO does not check compliance with national security provisions. (AG-IP §6.010 and Practical Advice in PCT Newsletter 06/2014)

All rOs accept filing of an international application by deposition and by mail (AG-IP §6.003). Many rOs accept filing by fax under R.92.4, often subject to confirmation within 14 days (R.92.4(d); AG-IP §11.069). Failure to duly confirm may result in the international application being considered withdrawn (R.92.4(g)(i)), but not in a loss of the filing date. See AG-IP Annex B1 and B2 for the provisions of each rO and also §8.1.2. Each rO may determine the number of copies of the international application to be filed (R.11.1, see AG-IP Annex C for each rO).

The PCT allows filing of an international application in electronic form or by electronic means (R.89*bis*). For the EPO as rO see OJ 2018 A45. A national Office may allow an applicant to accompany his international application filed on paper by a copy in electronic form (R.89*ter*.1). Filing by e-mail is not allowed (PCT Newsletter 12/2001). The international fee may be reduced if the request is prepared using the PCT-SAFE software (Schedule of Fees 4; AG-IP §5.189).

2.3.1 *IB as rO*

Applicants of all PCT contracting states also have the option of filing the international application with the IB as rO (R.19.1(a)(iii)). If there are two or more applicants, at least one applicant must be a resident or national of a contracting state (R.19.2(ii)). The IB accepts any language (AG-IP Annex C(IB)), including languages of non-PCT states. Hence, a Burman living in Australia may file in Burmese with the IB as rO. The IB also accepts filing by fax, requiring confirmation within 14 days from filing, and electronic filing (AG-IP Annex B2(IB) and R.92.4(d)).

2.3.2 *EPO as rO*

The EPO may act as a rO within the meaning of the PCT if the applicant is a resident or a national of a contracting state to the PCT and the EPC (Art.151 EPC; R.157(1) EPC; OJ 2014 A33).

The EPO as rO is regarded as a national Office acting for the EPC contracting states according to R.19.1(b) PCT, where the 'national Office' is construed as referring to an intergovernmental authority in the sense of Art.2(xii) PCT.

If the applicant chooses the EPO as rO for his international application, he must file it directly with the EPO (Art.151 EPC, R.157(1)), i.e. with the EPO filing Office in Munich, The Hague or Berlin (see Art.75(1):1; R.35(1) EPC; Euro-PCT Guide §60). The applicant may not of his own volition file his international application with a national Office acting as a mailbox for the EPO as rO under Art.75(1)(b) EPC and R.35(1) EPC. Since Art.151 EPC and R. 157(1) EPC declare Art.75(2) EPC, relating to national security provisions, to be applicable to international applications (as allowed by Art.27(8) PCT), the applicant is obliged to file his international application with a national Office where the national law so prescribes for reasons of national security (see AG-IP Annex B1 for the provisions of each EPC contracting state). Most states allow a resident to file an international application directly with the

EPO if the application claims the priority of an earlier application filed in that state. See R.157(3)-(4) EPC and notes thereto for the transmission of the international application by the national Office to the EPO as rO.

A direct filing with the EPO according to Art.151 EPC enables the EPO acting as rO to send the international application quickly to the IB and the competent ISA (Art.12; R.21; R.22 PCT) after the accordance of an international filing date and the formalities examination, without incurring delay through processing by a national office (Art.11 and R.20 PCT).

Fax transmittal of the application to the EPO under R.92.4(a) PCT is allowed; a confirmation copy is to be filed simultaneously (OJ 2007 se3, A.3 Art.2; Euro-PCT Guide §69).

The international application must be filed in one copy only (R.157(2) EPC; Euro-PCT Guide §64). Alternatively, it may be filed in electronic form (OJ 2018 A45 Art.2(1)).

2.3.3 *Non-competent rO*

A national Office may not be competent under R.19.1 PCT to act as rO for an international application it has received on account of the residence or nationality of the applicant. Also, a national Office need not treat an international application as such if it is in a language not accepted by the Office under R.12.1(a). In both cases the national Office will be considered to have acted on behalf of the IB and forward the international application to the IB, which will deem to have received the international application as rO on the date the national Office received the international application (R.19.4(a), (b)). The national Office may make the transmittal subject to payment of a fee, for its own benefit, equal to the transmittal fee of that Office (R.14, see AG-IP Annex C for the amount of the transmittal fee levied by each rO). The AG-IP does not indicate whether a rO levies the transmittal fee under R.19.4, the time limit and the sanction on non-compliance (probably no filing date following Art.11(1)(ii) and R.12.1). Fees paid to a non-competent national Office will be refunded: except any transmittal fee that may be levied by a non-competent national office (AG-IP §6.034). The transmittal fee (for the benefit of the rO), the international filing fee (for the benefit of the IB) and the search fee (for the benefit of the ISA) payable under R.14 should be paid to the rO. The periods for paying these fees start running on the date of actual receipt of the international application by the IB (R.19.4(c)).

An applicant can make use of a further applicant entitled to file at a rO in a different time zone in order to extend the time available for filing an application without receiving a later filing date by utilizing the time difference between states. From a state in the Middle-European time zone, one hour may be gained by filing by fax with the national Office of Great Britain (the UK Intellectual Property Office), or six hours by filing directly with the national Office of the USA (the United States Patent and Trademark Office).

2.4 LANGUAGE

2.4.1 *Languages accepted by rO*

The international application must be filed in a prescribed language (Art.3(4)(i)). The rO determines the prescribed language(s) (R.12.1(a)). Each rO accepts at least one language which is both a language accepted by the competent ISA and a language of publication (R.12.1(b)). When using this language, an applicant need neither provide a translation for the search nor for the publication.

AG-IP Annex C indicates the accepted language(s) for each rO. It also indicates the competent ISA(s). Annex D gives the languages accepted by each ISA. The languages of publication are currently Arabic, Chinese, English, French, German, Japanese, Korean, Portuguese, Russian and Spanish (R.48.3(a)). Half of all international applications are filed in English. The IB as rO accepts any language (AG-IP Annex C(IB)). Most rOs also accept international applications in one of the official languages of the state.

All elements of the international application are normally in the same language. However, for the accordance of an international filing date, it is sufficient that the description and the claims are in a language accepted by the rO (Art.11(1)(ii), R.20.1(c), AG-IP §5.013). The request must be filed in a language which is both a language accepted by the rO and a language of publication (R.12.1(c)). Hence, the languages of the request and the description may be different, e.g. a request in English and a description in Dutch.

The ISA or the rO may require a translation of the international application for search and publication (see §2.4.3). The SISA receives any translation filed under R.12.3. or 12.4 from the IB (R.45*bis*.4(e)(iv)). If the international application is filed in a language which is not accepted by the SISA and any translations filed under R.12.3 or 12.4 are not accepted either, the applicant must furnish a translation of the international application into a language accepted by the SISA (R.45*bis*.1(c)(i)).

2.4.1.1 Languages accepted by EPO as rO

The EPO as rO accepts only French, German and English as languages of the international application (R.157(2) EPC). It does not accept official languages of other EPC contracting states admissible under Art.14(2) EPC, because the PCT shall be applied in accordance with only Art.150-153 EPC and the corresponding Rules, unless otherwise provided in the PCT. As an example, an international application in Swedish filed with the EPO as rO will be transmitted to the IB under R.19.4(a)(ii), which will then become rO.

2.4.1.2 Languages accepted by National Office of EPC contracting state as rO

All rOs of the EPC contracting states have specified the EPO as competent ISA (Art.152 EPC). The EPO as ISA accepts English, French and German (and Dutch if the international application is filed in Dutch with the national Office of NL (OJ 2018 A24, EPO – WIPO Agreement Annex A(ii)). The rO of any EPC contracting state will accept at least one of the languages English, French and German. The Finnish and Swedish patent offices and the Nordic Patent Institute acting as ISA have special language provisions for rOs of the Nordic contracting states (see AG-IP Annex C and D).

Note that the acceptable official languages of the rO of an EPC contracting state need not be the same as the official languages admissible under Art.14(4) EPC; e.g. the Swiss rO accepts English, German and French, whereas under Art.14(4) EPC German, French and Italian are admissible. The rO of the following EPC contracting states do not accept international applications filed in the or one of the official languages of that state: Ireland (Irish), Switzerland (Italian), Portugal and Greece.

2.4.2 *Incorrect language*

If a national Office as rO does not accept the language of the international application, it will transmit the international application to the IB under R.19.4. The IB will act as rO and will regard as date of receipt the date on which the national Office received the international application. The IB as rO accepts any language (see §2.3.3).

2.4.3 *Translations*

The PCT distinguishes the following cases where the applicant must provide a translation of the international application in the international phase: the language of filing is not a language accepted by the ISA or SISA, the language of the ISA is not a language of publication. (see AG-IP §6.013-6.020).

2.4.3.1 Language not accepted by ISA

Where the language of the international application is not accepted by the ISA that is to carry out the search, the applicant must furnish to the rO a translation within one month of receipt of the international application by the rO (R.12.3(a)). The rO may accept a later furnishing of the translation subject to payment of a late furnishing fee equal to 25% of the international filing fee (R.12.3(e)).

The translation must be in a language which is all of the following: a language accepted by the ISA, a language of publication and a language accepted by the rO under R.12.1(a). If the international application is filed in a language of publication, the latter condition is not required and the language of the translation need not be a language accepted by the rO under R.12.3(a).

The above translation requirement does not apply to the request and any sequence listing (R.12.3(b)).

If the translation has not yet been provided by the time the rO notifies the applicant of the international filing date under R.20.2(c), the rO will invite the applicant to furnish the translation within one month from the date of receipt of the international application (R.12.3(c)(i)). The translation may also be furnished within the later of one month from the date of the invitation and two months from said date of receipt, subject to the payment of a late furnishing fee (R.12.3(c)(ii) and R.12.3(e)). If the applicant does not furnish the translation and possible payment on the invitation, the international application will be considered withdrawn and the rO will so declare (R.12.3(d)). A translation and payment received before the rO makes the declaration and before the expiry of 15 months from the priority date will be considered as received in time (R.12.3(d)).

2.4.3.2 Language accepted by ISA but not a language of publication

Some ISAs are able to search applications in a language other than a language of publication. As an example, the EPO as ISA also accepts international applications in Dutch if the rO is the Netherlands Patent Office (OJ 2017 A115, Annex A(ii); OJ 2018 A24), because historically many examiners in the Hague branch of the EPO are familiar with the language (OJ 1979 p.137).

In the case that the language of the search is not a language of publication, the applicant must file with the rO, within 14 months from the priority date, a translation of the application in a language of publication acceptable to the rO (R.12.4(a)). If not complied with, even after an invitation similar to the one in the previous paragraph (R.12.4(c)-(e)), the application will be considered withdrawn (R.12.4(d)). If the applicant files a supplementary international search request and the international application was filed in a language which is not accepted by the SISA, the applicant must furnish a translation of the international application into a language accepted by the SISA (R.45*bis*.1(c)(i)). However, if the applicant has filed a translation under R.12.3. or R.12.4 and the translation can be used as the basis of the supplementary international search, the IB will transmit the translation to the SISA (R.45*bis*.4(e)(iv)).

2.4.3.3 Parts of the international application in a different language

Where the abstract or any text matter of the drawings is filed in a language different from the language of the description and the claims, the rO will invite the applicant to furnish a translation into the language in which the application is to be published (Art.3(4)(i); R.26.3*ter*(a)). The rO will not issue an invitation to furnish a translation in cases where a translation of the international application is already required for the purpose of the international search or where the abstract and text matter is in the language in which the application is to be published (R.26.3*ter*(a)). The procedure for the correction is set out in §3.2.1 below.

Where the request is not in a language which is both a language accepted by the rO and a language of publication (R.12.1(c)), the rO will invite the applicant to file a translation in a publication language (R.26.3*ter*(c); see §3.2.1 for the procedure).

2.4.3.4 International application not in an official language of a contracting state

Some contracting states that accept international filings in languages other than the official language of that state may require, for reasons of national security (Art.27(8)), that an international application filed by a national or resident be accompanied by a translation into the official language. See e.g. AG-IP Annex C(IT, GR).

2.4.4 *Incorrect translation*

An incorrect translation of an international application may give rise to a scope of a patent granted on an international application that exceeds the scope of the international application in its original language. In such a case the contracting state concerned may retroactively limit the scope of the patent (Art.46).

2.5 AGENT

Each rO may apply national law to require the applicant to be represented by an agent (Art.27(7) and R.51*bis*.1(b)). AG-IP Annex C indicates for each rO whether the applicant must be represented by an agent. Some rOs do not require an agent, e.g. GB, IB and US. Most rOs do not require an agent for applicants resident in the state concerned, e.g. DE, EP, FR and JP. If the applicant is represented, the request must indicate so and provide the data of the agent (Art.4(1)(iii); R.4.7).

Each national Office must give the applicant an opportunity to correct non-compliance with the representation requirement where the applicant has not yet done so before expiry of the international phase (R.51*bis*.3(b)). The PCT does not have a sanction for non-compliance. Hence, a rO will probably apply the sanction provided in its national law on non-compliance with the representation requirement. Additional information about agents is given in §2.7 and §8.3.

2.5.1 *EPO*

The EPO as rO does not require the appointment of an agent if the applicant has a residence or principal place of business in one of the EPC contracting states. However, the EPO does require the appointment of an agent if the applicant has neither residence nor a place of business in one of those states. (Art.133(2) EPC via Art.27(7) PCT, AG-IP Annex C(EP))

In principle, a national of one of the EPC contracting states having his residence outside those states may only initiate the processing and file an international application with the EPO as rO without an agent (Art.27(7) PCT in combination with Art.133(2) EPC). In practice, the EPO also accepts all further acts of such a national before the rO. In addition, a national patent attorney (not being a European patent attorney) can act in the international phase before the EPO if the international application is filed at the national office (Art.49; R.83).

The use of the wording 'other person' in Art.49 PCT is the legal basis for representation by an employee of an applicant resident in an EPC contracting state (cf. Art.133(3) EPC).

2.6 INVENTOR

The name and address of the inventor(s) can be given in the request. Annex B1 and B2 of AG-IP indicates for each contracting state whether the information of the inventor must be given in the request when the state is designated (Art.4(1)(v); Art.4(4); R.4.1(a)(iv); R.4.6(a)) or may be supplied later in separate notices to each designated Office (R.4.1(c)(i), see e.g. R.163(1) EPC).

The EPC allows the information to be given on entry into the European phase (R.163(1) EPC). When, in contrast, the information is provided on filing of the PCT application, any statement containing the origin of the right of the applicant to the patent as required under R.19(1) EPC is not required (E-IX,2.3.4).

The request PCT/IB/101 allows the applicant also to be marked as 'inventor' (Box No.II). An inventor can be marked as 'inventor only' or as 'applicant and inventor' or as 'applicant only' (Box No.III). (AG-IP §5.035)

R.4.6(c) allows indication in the request of different inventors for different states where the national laws of the designated states are not the same in this respect (AG-IP §5.038-5.039).

National law determines whether a designated Office may request the applicant to furnish evidence of the identity of the inventor (R.4.17(i); R.51*bis*.1(a)(i); R.51*bis*.2(i) or a declaration or oath of inventorship (R.4.17(iv); R.51*bis*.1(a)(iv); R.51*bis*.2(iv)).

2.6.1 *Changes concerning the inventor*

Changes in the person, name or address of the inventor will, on request of the rO or the applicant, be recorded by the IB (R.92*bis*.1(a)(ii)) free of charge (AG-IP §11.018). See the first section of §2.2.5 for the time limits for filing any such request. The PCT has no provision similar to R.21(1) EPC that an inventor must give his consent to be removed from the international application; such a request need only be signed by the applicant as a normal letter under R.92.1 (AG-IP §11.018). If the inventor dies before the international application is filed, the request must indicate that he is deceased (AG-IP §11.025). If the inventor dies during the international phase, nothing need be done (AG-IP §11.026).

2.7 SIGNATURE

The request must be signed by the applicant, or, if there is more than one applicant, by all of them (R.4.15). An agent may sign the request on behalf of the applicant, provided he is duly appointed as set out in §8.3.2 (R.90.3). Where the rO requires an appointment of an agent and it is erroneous or missing, the signature is treated as missing until the power of attorney is submitted (AG-IP §5.089). Where an international application is filed with a rO that has waived the requirement of filing a separate power of attorney, e.g. the EPO (see PCT §8.3.2), the application may be signed by an agent and no signature of an applicant is required subsequently. Note that R.90*bis*.5 is not subject to 'waiver', so a notice of withdrawal must be signed by all applicants or a duly appointed agent.

The name of the person signing must be clearly indicated next to the signature (AG-IP §5.090). The signature is understood to mean a seal where the national law applied by the rO requires use of a seal instead of a signature (R.2.3).

2.7.1 *Missing signature*

Absence of a signature is regarded as a defect under Art.14(1)(a)(i) and R.26.2*bis*(a) for an international application with a single applicant. In the case of an international application with a single applicant whose signature is missing, the rO will invite the applicant to supply the signature following the procedure of R.26 (see §3.2.1). If not provided, the international application will be considered withdrawn (Art.14(1)(b); R.29).

When there are several applicants, one signature is sufficient for the rO (R.26.2*bis*(a)). Any missing second or further signature is not regarded as a defect under Art.14 and can be provided in the national phase (R.51*bis*.1(a)(vi)) (see notes to §2.2.3 for more details).

2.8 FEES

The international application is subject to the payment of fees (Art.3(4)(iv)). At filing of the international application three fees become due: the transmittal fee, the international filing fee (including a sheet fee if the international application has more than 30 sheets, see Schedule of Fees 1) and the search fee (see §2.8.2-4). Subsequently, if a request for supplementary international search is filed, a supplementary search handling fee and a supplementary search fee become due (see §4.2.4). If a demand for international preliminary examination is filed, a handling fee and a preliminary examination fee become due (see §6.1.2). Note, that the PCT currently has no provision for claims fees, although proposals were discussed in the PCT Working Group. Where national law requires claims fees, they will become due only on entry into the national phase (see §7.2.3).

The amount of the fees is fixed either in Swiss currency in the Schedule of Fees, annexed to the PCT (R.96), or in local currency by the national law of an Office. See e.g. OJ 2018 A35 for the international fees levied by the EPO; the equivalent amounts in euros of these fees are regularly updated (see AG-IP Annex C(EP) for the current amounts).

2.8.1 *Method of payment*

Payment of any fee must be made directly to the Office specified in the PCT to collect the particular fee, as indicated in the following paragraphs. The payment must be made in the currency or one of the currencies prescribed by that Office (see R.15.2(b)-(d); R.16.1(b)-(e); R.57.2(b)-(d); R.58.1(c)). The PCT has no provisions for dealing with the question of whether a payment is made on time; the time limits for payment are not harmonized. Therefore, payments in the international phase of the PCT follow the national law of the Office to be paid.

Hence, payments to the EPO as rO, ISA and IPEA should follow the provisions set out in the Rules relating to Fees (see Rfees1(b)) and the Arrangement for Deposit Accounts, the most important of which are: date of payment (Rfees7(1)), the 10-day fail-safe provision (Rfees7(3)), however, not applicable to payments from outside an EPC contracting state), payment by debit order (ADA.5.1). The automatic debiting procedure is available both in the international phase and in the regional phase before the EPO (AAD.2.1(b) and (e); see Rfees5(2):3). The amounts of the fees fixed by WIPO when paid to the EPO in euros are published in OJ 2017 A102.

All payments to the IB can be made by debiting a deposit account established with the WIPO (AG-IP Annex C(IB)).

2.8.2 Transmittal fee

Almost every rO requires that the applicant pay a transmittal fee to it for its own benefit, as payment for checking the international application and transmittal of a copy of the international application to the IB and ISA (R.14.1(a)). The amount is fixed by each rO (R.14.1(b)), and indicated in Annex C of AG-IP. The requirement to pay a transmittal fee to the EPO as rO is given in R.157(4) EPC; the amount is fixed in Rfees2(1)18.

The transmittal fee must be paid within one month from the date of receipt of the international application, i.e. not from the international filing date. The amount payable is the amount applicable on the date of receipt, i.e. not one month from the date of receipt. Hence, a shift of the international filing date, e.g. due to a later submission of a missing part or element (R.20.3), does not change the period for payment of the fee, which still runs from the original receipt date. (R.14.1(c))

2.8.3 International Filing fee

The applicant must pay an international filing fee to the rO for the benefit of the IB (R.15.1), for services provided by the IB including publication of the international application and communication with the applicant and various designated or elected Offices, the ISA, the SISA and the IPEA. The international filing fee consists of a fixed amount and an additional amount for each sheet of the application in excess of thirty (Schedule of Fees 1).

Since the international filing fee must be paid before the formalities check of Art.14(1)(a) and any resulting correction (see §3.2.1), the basis for calculating the number of pages for the additional amount is the documents as filed. The IB as rO accepts applications having pages with small print, which reduces the additional amount.

Schedule of Fees 4 and 5 and AG-IP Annex C indicate possible reductions of the fee for each rO when filing in electronic form (up to 300 CHF reduction) and for applicants from developing countries (90% reduction).

The international filing fee must be paid to the rO within one month from the date of receipt of the international application, i.e. not from the international filing date (R.15.3).

2.8.4 Search fee

All ISAs require that the applicant pay a search fee for its own benefit for carrying out the international search and establishing the international search report (R.16.1(a)) and the written opinion (R.43*bis*), the search fee being collected by the rO (R.16.1(b)).

The amount of the search fee is fixed by each ISA (inferable from R.16.1(b)), and indicated in Annex D of AG-IP). The right of the EPO as ISA to levy a search fee is not directly provided for in the EPC, but only indirectly via Art.51(1) EPC and Rfees2(1)2 referring to R.16.1 PCT and fixing the amount of the fee, or via Art.152 EPC and the WIPO - European Patent Organisation Agreement (OJ 2017 A115, Annex D-I). The search fee for carrying out the international search should cover the actual cost of the search, and is therefore higher than the search fee for European searches, the cost of which is partly paid for by other fees. Note that the basis for the search fee in respect of an international search performed by the EPO is not in R.158 EPC.

The search fee for carrying out the international search must be paid within one month from the date of receipt of the international application (R.16.1(f), referring to R.15.3)

2.8.5 *Non-payment and remedy*

If the applicant has not paid the (full amount of the) transmittal fee, the international filing fee and the search fee within one month from the date of receipt of the international application (R.14.1(c); R.15.3; R.16.1(f)), the rO will invite him to pay the amount due within a period of one month from the date of the invitation (R.16*bis*.1(a)). A rO may take a payment in response to an invitation subject to a late payment fee for its own benefit (R.16*bis*.2(a), see AG-IP Annex C for each rO). The EPO imposes a late payment fee (Dec. of Pres. OJ 1992 p.383; Euro-PCT Guide §189).

Any payment received by the rO after the period of one month from the date of receipt of the international application but before sending of an invitation is considered to have been received before expiry of that period (R.16*bis*.1(d)). Any payment received by the rO after the period of one month from the invitation but before making the declaration under Art.14(3) is considered to have been received before expiry of that period (R.16*bis*.1(e)).

If the applicant does not pay the amount due, including where applicable the late payment fee, within one month from the invitation, the international application is considered withdrawn under Art.14(3)(a) and R.16*bis*.1(c), whereupon the rO will so declare and proceed as provided in R.29 (see §3.2.1 below) (R.16*bis*.1(c)(i), (ii)).

2.8.6 *Refunds*

The international filing fee and the search fee are refunded where the international application is not treated as such for reasons of national security (see §2.3 above; R.15.4(iii) and R.16.2(iii)) or where the rO is not competent (see §2.3.3 above; AG-IP §6.035).

The PCT has no provision for the refund of the transmittal fee (see AG-IP §5.197).

The international filing fee and the search fee will be refunded according to R.15.4 and R.16.2 if no international filing date is accorded, or the international application is not treated as such because of national security prescriptions (see §2.3 above). The international filing fee is also refunded if the international application is withdrawn or considered withdrawn before the transmittal of the record copy to the IB (R.15.4(ii)). The search fee is also refunded if the international application is withdrawn or considered withdrawn before the transmittal of the search copy to the ISA (R.16.2(ii)). Non-establishment of an international search report does not give entitlement to a refund of the search fee, because this case is not mentioned in R.16.2.

All ISAs except JP are more lenient than required under R.16.2(ii), in that they refund the entire search fee if the international application is withdrawn or considered withdrawn under Art.14(1), (3) or (4) after the transmittal of the search copy but before the start of the international search (AG-IP Annex D).

An ISA must make a partial refund of the search fee if the search can be based on an earlier search of an earlier application the priority of which is claimed (R.16.3) or on an international-type search or other search to which reference is made in the request (R.41.1; R.4.12). Most ISAs provide for such a partial refund; the conditions are set out in AG-IP Annex D.

2.8.6.1 EPO refunds

The EPO as ISA refunds the entire search fee under the conditions of R.16.2 PCT and, in particular, when the international application is withdrawn or considered withdrawn before the start of the international search (Agreement European Patent Organisation - WIPO, OJ 2017 A115, Annex D-II(2), OJ 2017 A95).

The search fee will be refunded wholly or partially under R.16.3 and R.41 PCT if the EPO can base its international search report on an earlier search already made by the EPO on an application whose priority is claimed for the international application. The refund rate varies depending on the extent to which the EPO benefits from the earlier search; the criteria for the refund rate are the same as those for refund of a European search fee (see notes to Rfees9(2)). Note that a valid priority claim is necessary for such refunds. The refund levels for different types of earlier search are set out in the Dec. of Pres. of the EPO as published in OJ 2017 A95 and vary between 100% and 70% when the EPO makes full use of the earlier search and between 25% and 17.5% when the EPO only makes partial use of the earlier search; the refund level is based upon several factors including the date of the earlier search, the type of the earlier search, and also whether the earlier search included a written opinion. The criteria determining whether a refund is given on a full or partial basis are laid out in the Not. of Pres. of the EPO as published in the OJ 2009 p.99. An earlier search may be one of several different types including a European search on a European patent application, an international search on an international application, an international-type search or a search on a national application made by the EPO on behalf of a national office. (OJ 2017 A95)

An up-to-date overview of the conditions for refund and amount of refund of the search fee can be found on AG-IP Annex D(EP).

2.9 DESIGNATION OF CONTRACTING STATES

All contracting states bound by the PCT on the international filing date are designated automatically for an international application (Art.4(1)(ii) and R.4.9(a)(i)), including all kinds of protection (R.4.9(a)(ii)) as well as both national and regional patent protection (R.4.9(a)(iii)). Since in 2004 payment of designation fees has been abolished, Art.4(2) has become meaningless in terms of specific payment of designation fees (R.27.1(b)). The request may indicate different applicants for different states (R.4.5(d), see also §2.2.3). Under R.4.9(b), states may be (irrevocably) excluded from the designation because of self-designation problems (AG-IP §5.053; see §2.9.3). Withdrawal of a designation is possible prior to expiry of 30 months from the priority date (R.90*bis*.2(a)).

An international application accorded a filing date will have the effect of a regular national application in the designated state with a filing date equal to the international filing date (Art.11(3)).

2.9.1 *Special designations*

National law of a contracting state may provide that the designation of that state for the grant of a national patent in the request will be treated as an indication of the wish to obtain a regional patent for that state (Art.4(1)(ii); Art.45(2)). AG-IP Annex B1 indicates for each contracting state the competent designated Office, which will be a regional Office if national law provides so, using Art.45(2).

2.9.1.1 Disintegrated states

The effect of an international application filed during a certain period starting at the disintegration of a contracting state will be extended to its successor states if they become PCT contracting states. The IB will publish information on the extension. (R.32; AG-IP §11.089-11.093)

2.9.1.2 National and regional designations under the EPC

The EPO will act as designated or elected Office for those EPC contracting states for which the PCT is in force and which are designated in the international application (Art.153(1)(a) EPC). All EPC contracting states are PCT contracting states.

The following EPC contracting states have made use of Art.45(2) PCT to close the national route, because they prefer the well-examined European patents above their own less-examined, or un-examined registered patents: Belgium, Cyprus, France, Greece, Ireland, Italy, Latvia, Lithuania, Malta, Monaco, the Netherlands and Slovenia (situation November 2018 (AG-IP Annex B1; Euro-PCT Guide §122). Hence, an indication of the applicant to obtain a national patent in such a state is interpreted as the wish to obtain a European patent for that state (Art.4(1)(ii) PCT). (AG-IP §5.052)

2.9.1.3 Extensions under the EPC

The effects of a European patent may be extended to a state having an extension agreement with the EPO. The extension is governed by national law, which effectively makes use of the EPO for the grant of national patents (see notes to Art.169 EPC). The extension system may also be used for international applications. Thereto, an international application filed must designate both the EPO and the state having an extension agreement. The states having an extension agreement are listed in the notes to Art.169 EPC (see also AG-IP §5.054 and Annex B2(EP)). The applicable procedures are set out in OJ 1997 p.538.

2.9.1.4 Designation of the US

The US has made a reservation under Art.64(4) regarding the prior art effect of the international application; it has prior art effect from the earlier of the international publication date and the entry into the national phase before the US national Office (AG-NP, US.22-23). Since 16.09.2012 it is no longer required that a US application be filed by the inventor as applicant. Hence, an inventor for an international application designating the US need no longer be applicant for the US. However, the inventor must still sign an oath/declaration for the US that he is an original inventor and has authorised the filing of the application.

Some applicants often file in parallel a US application and an international application that does not enter the national phase in the US. This strategy allows the US application to be adapted to the US style of drafting and takes care that the files of the international application do not become part of any litigation relating to the US patent.

2.9.2 *Kind of protection*

A designation of a contracting state is treated as an indication of the wish to obtain a patent in the state, unless otherwise indicated (Art.4(3)). The PCT permits an applicant to apply for any kind of protection of inventions (Art.2(i), Art.3(1)). Kinds of protection other than patents are a utility model, a petty patent or a continuation-in-part (Art.43). A state permitting such other kinds of protection may also allow that the international application is for the grant of two different kinds of protection in respect of that state (Art.44). Annex B1 of AG-IP indicates for each contracting state the kinds of protection available via the national and regional route. For example: DE national: patent and utility model, DE regional: patent; FR only regional patent; JP: patent and utility model; US: patent. (AG-IP §5.055 and 5.056) A table with the types of protection available via the PCT in contracting states can be found on the PCT website: www.wipo.int/pct.

The international application is for the grant of every kind of protection available by way of the designation of each state (R.4.9(a)(ii)). The specification of the kind of protection desired in a state is deferred until entry into the national phase of the state.

If the kind of protection sought is a title of addition, such as a patent of addition, or a continuation-in-part, the applicant must indicate this for the designated state and indicate in the request the parent patent or parent application (R.4.11(a)(i) and (ii)).

Any state in which the grant of a utility model is sought may apply national law instead of the PCT provisions in respect of the claims and unity of invention, provided the applicant is given at least two months after entering the national phase to adapt his application accordingly (R.6.5, R.13.5).

2.9.3 *Exceptions to the all-inclusive designation system*

An applicant may exclude a contracting state from the all-inclusive designation if the designation of such a state has the effect that an earlier national application having effect in that state and the priority of which has been claimed will be deemed withdrawn (R.4.9(b)). At present (November 2018), only reservations from Germany, Japan, and South Korea remain applicable. The designation of Germany for the purposes of obtaining a European patent is not considered a self-designation and is thus not affected (Euro-PCT Guide §121). (AG-IP §5.053)

2.9.4 *Withdrawal of a designation*

The applicant may withdraw any designation prior to 30 months from the priority date (R.90*bis*.2(a); see also §7.2). Note, that the rule prohibits withdrawal after 30 months, even where the international phase extends to e.g. 31 months. Where a state is designated both nationally and regionally, the withdrawal of the designation of that state is taken to mean the withdrawal of the national designation only, unless otherwise indicated (R.90*bis*.2(b)). A withdrawal of all designations is treated as the withdrawal of the international application (R.90*bis*.2(c)). Withdrawal is free of charge (AG-IP §11.050). Note that withdrawal under R.90*bis*.2 is a different act compared to exclusion as allowed for certain states under R.4.9(b) (see §2.9.3).

The withdrawal can be effected by sending a notice signed by all applicants (or common agent or duly appointed common representative) for the designation concerned to the IB, or, if a demand is filed, to the IPEA (R.90*bis*.2(d); R.90*bis*.5). The designation will not be published if the notice of its withdrawal has reached the IB before the technical preparations for the international publication have been completed (R.90*bis*.2(e)). The technical preparations are generally completed by the 15th day prior to the date of publication (AG-IP §9.013). The last moment for submitting changes to be taken into account for publication is midnight (CET) at the end of Tuesday, 16 days before publication when that falls on a Thursday (PCT Newsletter 06/2014). The scheduled publication date is available in ePCT.

2.10 PRIORITY CLAIM

An international application may claim priority from one or more earlier applications filed in or for any country party to the Paris Convention (Art.8(1)) or in or for any Member of the World Trade Organization that is not party to the Paris Convention (R.4.10(a); see AG-IP §5.057, 5.060). The priority period is 12 months (Paris Convention Art.4C(1); R.2.4(a)). Under R.26*bis*.3 restoration of the right to priority, under certain conditions, is allowed if the international filing date is later than the date on which the priority period expired but within two months from that date (see §2.10.4).

The PCT applies the priority rules of the Stockholm Act of the Paris Convention (Art.8(2)(a)). Since the Paris Convention relates to external priority only, the PCT has added a provision that allows internal priority, i.e. the international application claiming the priority of an earlier application filed in or for a state may contain the designation of that state (Art.8(2)(b)). The effect of the internal priority in that state is governed by national law (Art.8(2)(b)). The EPC also allows internal priority (Art.87(1) EPC).

Since the international application has in each designated state the effect of a regular national application (Art.11(3),(4)), it may be used as a basis for a priority claim in a later application. A valid priority claim has the effects provided by Article 4 of the Paris Convention (Art.8(2)(a)), in particular the effect that the filing date of the earlier application is regarded as the filing date of the priority claiming application (see Art.2(xi)(a) and (b)).

The priority claim is important for the PCT procedure because it establishes the priority date for computing time limits under the PCT (Art.2(xi)). The validity of the priority claim is not determined during the international phase, although the matter is taken into consideration for establishing the international preliminary report on patentability. (AG-IP §5.060)

2.10.1 Requirements for claiming priority

A priority claim should be made in the request on filing, although a priority claim may be added after filing under certain conditions (see §2.10.2; R.4.1(b)(i); R.4.10(a); R.26*bis*.1(a)). The claim to the priority of an earlier application must indicate the filing date of the earlier application, its number, the country in which it was filed for an earlier national application, the regional Office for an earlier regional application, or the rO for an earlier international application (R.4.10(a)(i)-(v)). National law determines whether a designated Office may request the applicant to furnish evidence of his entitlement to claim the priority (R.4.17(iii); R.51*bis*.1(a)(iii); R.51*bis*.2(iii)).

A mistake in a priority claim may also be corrected if the correction does not change the (earliest) priority date (R.91.1(g)(iv)); such corrections can be submitted up to 26 months from the priority date (R.91.2; AG-IP 11.037).

The applicant must submit a certified copy of the earlier application to the rO or IB within 16 months of the priority date (R.17.1(a)). The copy will be regarded as received in time if received by the IB before the date of the international publication (R.17.1(a)). Where the priority document was filed with the rO of the international application, the applicant may, instead of submitting the document, request the rO either in the request form (R.4.1(c)(ii)) or by separate letter, to transmit the document to the IB (R.17.1(b)). Such a request must be filed within 16 months from the priority date and may be subject by the rO to the payment of a fee (R.17.1(b)). Both the EPO and the US national Office as rO require under R.17.(1)(b) a fee for the transmittal of the priority document to the IB at the applicant's request (AG-IP Annex C(EP, US)).

Alternatively, if the priority document is available electronically to the IB from a digital library, the applicant may request the IB to retrieve (free of charge) the priority document from the digital library (R.17.1(b-*bis*); Practical Advice in PCT Newsletter 12/2010; Dec. Pres. OJ 2018 A78); this request may be filed up to international publication. Many patent offices, including the EPO participate in DAS, the WIPO Digital Access Service for priority documents for making priority documents available electronically.

If the applicant complies with R.17.1(a), (b) or (b-*bis*), such that a certified copy of the earlier application is timely received by the IB, no designated Office may ask the applicant to submit a further copy (R.17.2(a); AG-IP §5.070; E-IX,2.3.5; F-VI,2.1).

The EPO furnishes a certified copy of a European application on request upon payment of an administrative fee (R.54 EPC; Rfees3(1)). For the US, the applicant must send a letter allowing the USPTO to 'release' the priority document to the IB or use DAS. Note, that the national Offices of certain states do not always furnish certified copies in time, making excuse procedures necessary before each designated Office. Upon entry of the European phase, the EPO includes priority documents in the file of Euro-PCT applications upon request using DAS free of charge; alternatively,it includes Chinese, Japanese, Korean, and US priority documents automatically into the files of such applications if DAS can not be used or is not requested, also free of charge (A-II, 5.4.3; Dec. Pres. OJ 2018 A78).

If the priority document or the request is not filed in due time, any designated Office may disregard the priority claim, provided it gives the applicant an opportunity to furnish the priority document (R.17.1(c)). If the priority document is not filed during the international phase, the EPO as designated Office invites the applicant to furnish it upon entry into the regional phase (R.163(2) EPC), failure of which will result in the loss of the priority claim under R.163(6) EPC.

The IB will forward copies of the priority document to each designated Office at the request of that Office (R.17.2(a)). It is one of the PCT's procedural and financial advantages that the applicant need only file a single priority document and does not have to provide certified copies for each designated state.

2.10.2 *Correction or addition of a priority claim*

The applicant may correct any item of a priority claim or add a missing priority claim of his own volition by submitting a notice to the rO or IB (R.26*bis*.1(a)). Adding a priority claim to an international application filed without a priority claim is also possible (R.26*bis*.1(a)).

The notice may be filed within a period of 16 months from the priority date or 16 months from the priority date as changed by the correction, whichever expires first (R.26*bis*.1(a)). Nevertheless, the notice may be filed at least up to four months from the international filing date (R.26*bis*.1(a)). The four month period is relevant for applications where the uncorrected priority date is more than 12 months before the filing date. The effect of the periods is that any correction or added priority claim can be included in the publication of the international application. The correction of the priority claim is free of charge (AG-IP §6.053). Where the correction changes the priority date, any period computed from the priority date and not already expired will be recomputed from the changed priority date (R.26*bis*.1(c)).

A priority claim may be added to an international application in conjunction with a request for restoration of priority (see §2.10.4; Practical Advice in PCT Newsletter 02/2010). Any such priority claim will remain in the application and serve as the basis for calculating periods during the international phase whether the request for restoration of priority is granted or not. (R.26*bis*.2(c)(iii) and Practical Advice in PCT Newsletter 09/2011)

For Euro-PCT applications, correction of a priority claim is possible even after the publication date, provided the interests of third parties are not adversely affected, which is the case when the mistake is apparent on the face of the published application (see notes to R.52(3) EPC; J2/92). A priority claim can be added later on (until 26 months from the priority date) under R.91.1(g)(iv) as a 'rectification of an obvious mistake' but only if the added priority claim does not change the original priority date (AG-IP 11.037).

The validity of a priority claim is not substantively checked in the international phase (this follows from the definition of the priority date in Art.2(xi) which defines the priority date 'for the purpose of computing time limits'. However, if the rO or, if the rO fails to do so, the IB, finds that the international application has an international filing date which is later than the expiry of the priority period and a request for restoration of priority under R.26*bis*.3 has not been submitted, that the priority claim does not comply with the requirements of R.4.10, or that any indication in the priority claim is inconsistent with the priority document, the office will invite the applicant to correct the deficiencies within the same period of R.26*bis*.1(a) for voluntary correction. If the international filing date is within two months of the expiry of the priority period, the office will notify the applicant that restoration of priority may be possible (R.26*bis*.2(a)). Examples of non-compliance with the requirements of R.4.10 include: the priority document not being filed in a country party to the Paris Convention or member of the World Trade Organisation, the priority claim being made after the 12-month priority period, and the required details of the date and country or Office of filing not having been provided (Art.8(2)(a), referring to the Paris Convention, in particular Art.4A(1) and 4C(1), 4D(1),(4); AG-IP §5.060). Failure to submit a correction results in the claim being considered not to have been made, i.e. void, for the purpose of the PCT procedures and the rO or IB so declares (R.26*bis*.2(b)). If the rO or IB receive a request for correction of a priority claim before the priority claim has been declared void and within one month of the R.26*bis*.1(a) period, the request will be considered as timely received (R.26*bis*.2(b)). The IB will publish information on a priority claim being considered void together with the application (free of charge) (R.26*bis*.2(d)). If an applicant attempts to correct or add a priority claim after the R.26*bis*.1 period has expired, the IB may publish information concerning the matter if the applicant requests so and pays a special fee (R.26*bis*.2(e)). The priority claim will not be considered void only because the number of the earlier application is missing, because an indication in the priority claim is not the same as the corresponding indication in the priority document, or because the international application has an international filing date outside, but within two months of, the priority period (R.4.10(a)(ii); R.26*bis*.2(c) (i-iii); Paris Convention Art.4D(5)).

An applicant may provide proof before a designated or elected Office that the determination of a priority claim being considered void by the rO or IB was erroneous; if satisfied, the Office must rectify the error if such an error is rectifiable under national law had it been made by the designated Office itself and treat the application as if the priority claim had not been considered void (R.82*ter*.1(a)).

2.10.3 *Withdrawal of a priority claim*

The applicant may withdraw any priority claim of an international application within the international phase before expiry of 30 months from the priority date (R.90*bis*.3(a) and (b); see §8.4 below). The withdrawal is free of charge (AG-IP §11.056). The withdrawal becomes effective at receipt of a notice addressed by the applicant or agent, at his option, to the IB, the rO, or the IPEA if a demand is filed (R.90*bis*.3(c)). Where the withdrawal changes the priority date, any period computed from the priority date and not already expired will be recomputed from the changed priority date (R.90*bis*.3(d)). The notice must be signed by all applicants or by a duly-appointed agent or common representative (R.90*bis*.5). If the notice is received by the IB after the completion of the technical preparations for publication, the international publication will still be published on the date as computed from the original priority date (R.90*bis*.3(e)).

2.10.4 Restoration of the right of priority

The priority provisions in the PCT allow restoration of a priority claim in an international application, even if the international application is filed after expiry of the priority period (R.26*bis*.2-3; R.49*ter*; AG-IP §5.062-5.066). The provisions align the PCT with Art.13 of the PLT. A request may be filed at the rO (R.26*bis*.3) during the international phase, or at a designated Office during the national phase (R.49*ter*.2). The PCT provisions given below apply to the rO, many of which are mirrored in R.49*ter*.2 for designated Offices.

The following conditions must be satisfied if a request for restoration of priority is to succeed:

- a request for restoration of priority must be filed within two months from expiry of the priority period (R.26*bis*.3(b)(i), 3(e))
- the request must state the reasons for failing to file the international application within the priority period (R.26*bis*.3(b)(ii)), preferably accompanied by a supporting declaration or other evidence (R.26*bis*.3(b)(iii)), and if required, within a period reasonable under the circumstances (R.26*bis*.3(f))
- the request must satisfy one of the criteria (see below) for restoration applied by the office
- payment of a fee, if required and as fixed by the office, within a period of two months, with an additional extension of up to 2 months at the option of the office (R.26*bis*.3(d))
- the priority claim in question must have been made at the time of filing the international application or added within two months of expiry of the priority period (R.26*bis*.3(c); R.26*bis*.1(a))

  See Practical Advice in PCT Newsletter 02/2010 for advice on how to add a priority claim not falling within the 12-month priority period and requesting restoration of priority.

Note that a priority claim will not be considered void only because the international application has an international filing date outside, but within two months of, the priority period. This means that if a rO (for whatever reason) does not accept the restoration of a priority claim (which request for restoration must be later than the date on which the 12-month priority period expired but within 2 months from that date), the calculation of time limits in the international phase will nevertheless be carried out as though the priority claim is valid. This occurs because a designated or elected Office might subsequently allow the restoration (under R.49*ter*.2) and then the national phase entry would still have been performed correctly with respect to the 'too early' priority date. (R.26*bis*.2(c)(iii); Practical Advice in PCT Newsletter 09/2011) (see also §2.10.2 above)

The request for restoration has to be filed with the designated Office within one month from expiry of the period for entering the national phase under Art.22 or, if a request for early processing has been filed, one month from receipt of the request by the designated Office (R.49*ter*.2(b)(i)). Before the EPO as designated Office, the one-month period is excluded from re-establishment (J13/16).

An office has a choice of applying two different criteria when deciding whether to restore the right of priority to an international application and may apply one, the other or both (R.26*bis*.3(a)). The criteria are that the failure occurred in spite of *due care* required by the circumstances having been taken (R.26*bis*.3(a)(i)), or that the failure was *unintentional* (R.26*bis*.3(a)(ii)), the latter tending to be the less stringent criterion. For the *unintentional* criterion, a statement indicating that the failure to comply with the priority period was not intentional should generally be sufficient, although a rO may require that the statement is submitted in the form of a declaration. For the due care criterion, the rO may require a declaration and/or supporting evidence. (PCT rO Guidelines, §166G; Practical Advice in PCT Newsletter 09/2011)

A rO may not refuse a request for restoration of priority without giving the applicant the opportunity to make observations on the intended refusal within a period which is reasonable under the circumstances (R.26*bis*.3(g), R.49*ter*.2(e)). Restoration of priority granted by a rO based on the due care criterion will in general be binding on all designated Offices (R.49*ter*.1(a)). Restoration of priority granted by a rO based on the unintentional criterion is only effective in designated Offices which apply that criterion (R.49*ter*.1(b)). Nevertheless, a designated Office may review a restoration of priority granted by a rO in certain limited circumstances (R.49*ter*.1(c-d)), similarly with a refusal to grant a restoration of priority by a rO (R.49*ter*.1(f)). If an applicant filing an international application has missed the 12-month priority period, but has a choice of rOs (e.g. GB, EP, IB) in which the application may be filed, the applicant should consider whether the national offices in territories in which entering the national phase is of interest will recognise a restoration of priority made by each of the available rOs (Practical Advice in PCT Newsletter 09/2011).

Offices were given the opportunity to declare that the restoration of the right of priority provisions are incompatible with their national law (R.26*bis*.3(j); R.49*ter*.1(g); R.49*ter*.2(h)). Such declarations of incompatibility have the potential to affect the time limit for national phase entry and the assessment of novelty and inventive step during the national phase, so some offices are now in the process of amending their national law in order that they can withdraw their declarations. See the document 'PCT Reservations, Declarations, Notifications and Incompatibilities' document published on the PCT website for details of any such declarations (www.wipo.int/pct). If a rO has made a declaration of incompatibility under R.26*bis*.3(j) that it does not accept requests for restoration of priority, the applicant can request that the rO forwards the international application to the IB (R.19.4(a)(iii)) as rO; the IB has made no declaration of incompatibility under R.26*bis*.3(j) and allows requests to be based on both criteria, the applicant can then request the IB as rO to restore the right of priority (Practical Advice in PCT Newsletter 09/2011).

2.11 DESCRIPTION, CLAIMS, DRAWINGS, ABSTRACT

An international application must contain a description, one or more claims, one or more drawings (where required) and an abstract (Art.3(2)). The requirements that each of these parts must comply with are set out in the following paragraphs (§2.11.1-5). The incorporation by reference provisions in the PCT allow, in certain circumstances, inclusion of accidentally omitted description, drawings and claims pages that are contained in a priority document, without affecting the international filing date (see §3.1.4 below).

Obvious mistakes in the international application may be rectified by following the procedure of R.91 (see §8.5 below). See Art.14(1)(a)(v), (b) and §3.2.1 for the correction of non-compliance with the physical requirements as set out in R.11.

Changes other than the correction of obvious mistakes are considered amendments (R.66.5). The claims may be amended after receipt of the ISR or if a demand is filed (Art.19 and 34). The description and drawings may be amended only if a demand is filed. Each designated and elected Office permits such amendments in the national phase (Art.28(1) and Art.41; see also §8.6). Since the possibilities for correction of defects are different for the different parts of the international application, they will be dealt with separately in the following paragraphs.

2.11.1 *Title*

An international application must contain a title (Art.4(1)(iv)). The title must be stated in the request (R.4.1(a)(ii)) and at the beginning of the description (R.5.1(a)), and must be short (preferably from two to seven words in English) and precise (R.4.3).

A missing title is regarded as a defect (Art.14(1)(a)(iii)). The rO will invite the applicant to furnish the title, failure of which results in the international application being considered withdrawn (Art.14(1)(b), see §3.2.1 for the procedure). The rO notifies the ISA of a missing title; the ISA will proceed with the international search, but stops if it is notified that the application is considered withdrawn (R.37.1). The ISA will establish a title itself if the title is missing and it has not received a notification that the rO has invited the applicant to correct the defect, or if the title is too long or not precise (R.37.2). The international search report states either the approval by the ISA of the title or the title as established by the ISA (R.44.2).

2.11.2 *Description*

The description must disclose the invention in a manner sufficiently clear and complete for the invention to be carried out by a person skilled in the art (Art.5). The parts of the description and their order are prescribed by R.5.1.

The international application must contain a description in order to be accorded an international filing date (Art.11(1)(iii)(d)). See §3.1.2 and §3.1.4 for the procedure to correct a missing description. The physical requirements, numbering of pages and lines, presentation of formulae and tables are set out in R.11.

Where the international application discloses a nucleotide or amino acid sequence, the application documents must be accompanied by a sequence listing in electronic form (see R.3.3(a)(ii); R.5.2; AG-IP §5.099-5.104, Euro-PCT Guide §159). Applicants are advised to file sequence listings in the preferred WIPO Standard ST.25 text-readable format because no page fees are levied for sequence listings filed in such a format. Full page fees are payable for sequence listings filed in image format or on paper. Mixed mode filings containing a description in paper format and a sequence listing in either both paper and electronic format on a physical medium, or else only in electronic form on a physical medium are no longer allowed. (PCT Newsletter 06/2009)

When a sequence listing is not provided together with the application documents, the ISA may invite the applicant to provide the sequence listing in electronic form (R.13*ter*.1(a)) on payment of a late furnishing fee (R.13*ter*.1(c)). The EPO levies this fee (OJ 2011 p.372; E-IX,2.4.2). No designated Office may request another sequence listing than the one complying with the PCT requirements (R.13*ter*.3). An international application may refer to biological material and/or to its deposit with a depositary institution, for which reference is made to R.13*bis* and AG-IP §11.075-11.088.

2.11.3 *Claims*

The claim or claims must define the matter for which protection is sought, and must be clear, concise and fully supported by the description (Art.6). The claim drafting rules in R.6, relating to numbering, dependencies, two-part form, references to the description, reference signs, are not mandatory. However, when drafted along these rules, claims must be accepted by all designated Offices. In the national phase the designated Office may require adaptation of the claims to national law. Where an ISA under its national law does not allow multiple dependent claims to serve as a basis for another multiple claim, it need not establish a search report (R.6.4(a); Art.17(2)(a)(ii), (b)). Compliance with the requirement of unity of invention (Art.3(4)(iii)) is checked by the ISA (Art.17(3)(a)).

The international application must contain at least one claim in order for an international filing date to be accorded (Art.11(1)(iii)(e)). See §3.1.2 and §3.1.4 for the procedure to correct the omission of the claims. The claims must commence on a new sheet (R.11.4(a)) and be numbered consecutively (R.6.1(b)).

2.11.4 *Drawings*

An international application may contain drawings (Art.3(2)). However, drawings are required when they are necessary for understanding of the invention (Art.7(1)). A designated Office may require that the applicant files drawings not necessary for understanding the invention but for its illustration (Art.7(2), R.7.2). Particular physical requirements for drawings are given in R.11.10, R.11.11 and R.11.13; see also AG-IP §5.128-5.163. Drawings may not contain text matter, except a single word or words when absolutely indispensable (R.11.11). Non-compliance with the requirements can be corrected under Art.14(1) (see §3.2.1). Obvious mistakes may also be corrected (see §8.5).

Black and white photographs admitting direct reproduction are accepted where a drawing does not render what is to be shown (AG-IP §5.159). If the international application containing a photograph is filed by fax, and the photograph is not transmitted properly, the photograph will be considered a missing drawing, the correction of which will result in redating of the international application (see AG-IP §11.070). In general, no transmission loss is incurred in electronic filing. Colour drawings or photographs are not admissible and, if not replaced on request by black and white drawings or photographs, will be reproduced in black and white in publications. In 2017 proposals were being discussed to permit colour drawings.

The rO will invite the applicant to furnish a missing drawing, i.e. a drawing referred to in the international application but not included in it, within the applicable period under R.20.7 (Art.14(2); R.20.5(a)). The period is not extendable (AG-IP §6.037). If the drawing is duly filed, the international filing date will be the date on which the drawing is received by the rO (Art.14(2)), or the incorporation by reference provisions may be employed to maintain the original international filing date (see §3.1.4). The international filing date may also be maintained but any reference to the missing drawings will be considered non-existent (Art.14(2)). Note, that redating may cause loss of priority.

All rOs accept an international application containing provisional drawings, provided the provisional drawings are replaced by drawings complying with the requirements of R.11 within the period set in R.26.2 for the correction of defects under Art.14(1)(b).

2.11.5 *Abstract*

An international application must contain an abstract (Art.3(2)). The abstract merely serves the purpose of technical information and cannot be taken into account for any other purpose, particularly not for the interpretation of the scope of protection (Art.3(3)). The requirements the abstract must comply with are set out in R.8 and R.11; amongst others it must be concise (preferably 50 to 150 words) (R.8.1(b)). See §3.2.1 for the correction of non-compliance with the physical requirements as set out in R.8 and R.11.

The request must indicate the figure to accompany the abstract (R.3.3(a)(iii)). If the applicant does not specify the number of the figure or specifies the number of a figure that is inappropriate according to the ISA, the ISA determines the number of the figure to accompany the abstract when published (R.8.2(a)). If no figure is deemed useful by the ISA, the abstract will be published without a figure (R.8.2(b)).

A missing abstract is regarded as a defect (Art.14(1)(a)(iv)). The rO will invite the applicant to furnish the abstract, failure of which results in the international application being considered withdrawn (Art.14(1)(b), see §3.2.1 for the procedure). The rO notifies the ISA of a missing abstract; the ISA will proceed with the international search, but stops if it is notified that the application is considered withdrawn (R.38.1). If the ISA has not received a notification that the rO has invited the applicant to correct the defect, and the abstract is missing or the abstract does not comply with R.8, the ISA will establish the abstract itself (R.38.2). An obvious mistake in the abstract may not be corrected using R.91, but the applicant may within one month from the date of mailing of the ISR submit comments on and/or propose modifications to the abstract established by the ISA (R.91.1(g)(ii); R.38.3). The international search report states either the approval by the ISA of the abstract or the abstract as established by the ISA (R.44.2).

3 Procedure before the rO

The rO performs the following procedural steps upon receipt of an international application:

1 a check of the requirements for according an international filing date, and, if required, a correction procedure (Art.11 and R.20);
2 a check of the requirements as to fees, language, form and content and, if required, a correction procedure (Art.14 and R.26); and
3 transmittal of copies of the international application (Art.12 and R.22).

3.1 ACCORDANCE OF INTERNATIONAL FILING DATE

3.1.1 *Requirements*

A receiving Office will accord as the international filing date the date of receipt of the international application, provided the receiving Office has found that, at the time of receipt (Art.11(1)):

i) the applicant is allowed to file an international application with the rO (Art.10, R.19; see §2.3);
ii) the application is in a language prescribed by the rO (Art.3(4)(i), R.12.1; see §2.4);
iii) the application contains at least the following elements:
   a) an indication that it is intended as an international application (R.4.2; see §2.1);
   b) the designation of at least one contracting state (R.4.9; see §2.9);
   c) the name of the applicant (R.4.5; see §2.2);
   d) a part which on the face of it appears to be a description (Art.3(2); see §2.11.2);
   e) a part which on the face of it appears to be a claim or claims (Art.3(2); see §2.11.3).

Ad (i) Although Art.11(1)(i) implies that no international filing date will be accorded if the applicant is not allowed to file an international application with a rO because of residence or nationality, R.19.4 provides that a filing date will still be accorded. In such a case the rO will forward the international application to the IB, which becomes rO without loss of filing date, provided the fee under R.19.4, if applicable, is paid (see §2.3.3). If a person who is not a resident or national of a PCT contracting state, e.g. a resident and national of Argentina, files an international application, no international filing date will be accorded (Art.11(1)(i); Art.9(1) with Art.62(1)) (see §2.2.2).

Ad (ii) An international application filed in a language not accepted by the rO will still be accorded a filing date, because the rO will forward the international application under R.19.4 to the IB that becomes the rO accepting all languages (see §2.3.1).

Ad (iii)b If a request is filed, all states are designated automatically for international applications (R.4.9(a)(i)) (see §2.9).

Ad (iii)c For the accordance of an international filing date it is sufficient that the name of the applicant is indicated in a way which allows his identity to be established (R.20.1(b)). For the accordance of an international filing date, the PCT does not provide for 'allowing the applicant to be contacted' (Art.5(1)(ii) (Patent Law Treaty) PLT). The following defects do not affect the filing date: non-payment of fees, missing signature, title or abstract, or non-compliance with the physical requirements of R.11.

Ad (iii)e For the accordance of an international filing date the PCT requires the presence at least one claim (Art.11(iii)(e)). This is contrary to the provisions of Art.5(1)(iii) PLT that for the accordance of a 'filing date' the filing of a description should be sufficient. In addition, the PCT has no provision for filing an international application by 'reference to a previously filed application replacing the description and any drawings' (cf. Art.5(7) PLT).

Note, that the date the receiving Office receives the international application counts as the international filing date and not the date the application is despatched (Art.11(1); see also §8.2.1).

3.1.2 *Application not treated as an international application*

If the international application does not comply with the above requirements, the rO will not accord an international filing date and will invite the applicant to file the required corrections (Art.11(2)(a) and R.20.3) within the applicable period of 2 months under R.20.7. The period is not extendable (AG-IP §6.037). If the application is not corrected in time, the rO notifies the applicant that his application will not be treated as an international application and notifies the IB accordingly (R.20.4(i),(ii)) and forwards a copy of the application to the IB (R.20.4(iv)). If the applicant considers the finding of the rO incorrect, he may apply for a review under Art.25 before each designated Office (see §7.6).

National security prescriptions may also require a rO not to treat an international application as such (Art.27(8)).

If the rO later discovers, or on the basis of the applicant's reply realises, that it has erred in sending the above invitation, it will continue the proceedings with an appropriate filing date (R.20.3(c); R.82*ter*.1).

3.1.3 *Filing of missing parts or missing elements*

Provisions of the PCT enable the inclusion ('incorporation by reference') of (accidentally) omitted elements or parts that are contained in the priority document without affecting the international filing date (R.20.5, 20.6; AG-IP §6.024-6.031). Late furnishing of an element or part of the description, claims or drawings which is or appears to be missing, may affect the international filing date. An 'element' may be the entire description or all of the claims, and a part may be part of the description, part of the claims, or part or all of the drawings pages. R.20.6 allows an applicant to file an international application without description and claims, merely claiming the priority of an earlier application and incorporating its elements by reference; this amounts to the 'filing by reference' of Art.5(7) PLT.

An applicant may wish to use the incorporation by reference procedure if he receives an invitation from the rO to correct a defect under Art.11(1) (R.20.3). The applicant may be asked to furnish a correction under Art.11(2) and R.20.3, in which case the international filing date is changed to the date on which the missing item is subsequently furnished (R.20.3(b)). Alternatively, the applicant may confirm (R.20.6(a)) that the missing element or part is incorporated by reference and is completely contained in the priority document, in which case, if accepted by the rO, the international filing date remains unchanged. Elements or parts should be filed in the language of the international application as filed, and additionally in the language of the translation if such has been filed (R.12.1*bis*).

The requirements for incorporation by reference are as follows:

1 the priority document must contain the element or part which is sought to be incorporated (R.20.6(b));
2 the PCT request must contain a conditional statement of incorporation by reference, although a reference to the priority document in the description is also sufficient (R.4.18; AG-IP §6.028); the requirement of R.4.18 is automatically met because such a statement is included in Form PCT/RO/101 or if the PCT-SAFE software is used (AG-IP §6.028).
3 the incorporation by reference (R.20.6-7) must be timely confirmed by written notice to the rO and accompanied by:
   a) sheet(s) containing the element or part as contained in the priority document (R.20.6(a)(i)),
   b) a copy of the priority document if not already furnished (R.20.6(a)(ii)),
   c) if required, a translation of the priority document into the language of filing of the international application (R.20.6(a)(iii)), and
   d) an indication as to where the part in question is located in the priority document (R.20.6(a)(iv)).
4 the priority claim must have been present at the initial filing date (R.4.18; AG-IP §6.027-028).

The period for confirming an incorporation by reference is 2 months from the date of an invitation sent by the rO (R.20.7(a)(i)), or in the case of no invitation being sent, 2 months from the date on which the elements referred to in Art.11(1)(iii) are received by the rO, i.e. 2 months from the initial filing date (R.20.7(a)(ii)).

R.20.8 allows for a rO or a designated Office to declare that several of the incorporation by reference provisions are incompatible with its national or regional law. If an office informs the IB of such, then the provisions shall not apply with respect to that office. See the 'PCT Reservations, Declarations, Notifications and Incompatibilities' document published on the PCT website for details of any such declarations (www.wipo.int/pct).

Designated and elected Offices have a limited power to review a decision made by a rO concerning the incorporation by reference (R.82*ter*.1(b-d); AG-IP §6.012). Note, that rOs have diverging interpretations of incorporation by reference; see Practical Advice in PCT Newsletter 07/2015.

3.1.3.1 Adding priority claim under the EPC

Contrary to what is prescribed in Art.5(6)(b) PLT, the EPC allows adding priority claims for filing any missing parts of the description and missing drawings after the date of filing (R.52(2) EPC; R.56(3) EPC; A-II,5.4.1). For the accordance of a date of filing under the EPC, claims are not required, hence R.56 EPC does not address the filing of missing claims (in line with Art.5(6)(b) and R.2(4) PLT). In the PCT, however, the accordance of an international filing date requires claims to be filed, thus R.20 PCT allows filing of any missing claims or filing the entire element of the claims. In the PCT, priority claim(s) must have been present at the filing date; so, adding such priority claims under R.26*bis*.1(a) would not be sufficient (R.4.18; AG-IP §6.027; §6.028).

3.1.4 *International filing date*

If the requirements were fulfilled on the day of receipt of the international application, the international filing date will be the date on which the international application was received by the rO (Art.11(1)). Where the sheets of the international application are not received on the same day, the date of receipt will be the date all of the requirements of Art.11(1) are fulfilled (R.20.5(b), (c)), or incorporated by reference (R.20.5(d) and R.20.6). If the international application has been duly corrected as stated in §3.1.2, the international filing date will be the date of receipt of the required correction (Art.11(2)(b)). The rO will stamp a copy of the international application, which becomes the record copy (R.20.2(b)), and which is considered the true copy of the international application for the purposes of the international procedure (Art.12(2)). The rO notifies the applicant and the IB of the filing date (R.20.2(c)), in practice within two months from filing.

Payment of fees is not required for the accordance of an international filing date (AG-IP §6.009).

Correction of a missing drawing (Art.14(2)) may result in the accordance of an international filing date later than the date of receipt of the international application (see §2.11.4).

If an international filing date has been accorded and the rO discovers within 4 months from filing that any of the items (i) to (iii) of Art.11(1) was not complied with, the application will be considered withdrawn (Art.14(4); R.30.1), and the applicant and the IB will be notified (R.29.1(ii)). If the IB or ISA discovers such non-compliance, they will draw the rO's attention to it (R.29.3). The applicant must be notified before the declaration under Art.14(4) is made and be given an opportunity to comment within a period of 2 months from the notification (R.29.4(a)) and/or confirm that a missing item is incorporated by reference (R.29.4(b); R.20.6(a); R.4.18). Note, that in this case the international application keeps its international filing date and priority may be claimed from it (AG-IP §6.012).

An applicant may prove in the national phase before a designated or elected Office that the international filing date is incorrect due to an error made by the rO or IB; if satisfied, the Office must rectify the error if such an error is rectifiable under national law had it been made by the Office itself and treat the application as though the error had not been made (R.82*ter*.1(a)).

3.1.5 *Effect*

An international application which is accorded a filing date will have the effect of a regular national application in each designated state (Art.11(3)) and will be equivalent to a regular national application within the meaning of the Paris Convention (Art.11(4)). The designated Offices are forbidden to start processing the application of their own motion within 30 months from the priority date (Art.23(1), Art.40(1), see also §7.2).

3.2 FORMALITIES CHECK

3.2.1 *Defects in the international application*

The rO checks the international application on the following defects (Art.14(1)(a)):

1 no signature (R.4.15; R.26.2*bis*(a); R.51*bis*.1(a)(vi); see §2.7.1);
2 missing indications concerning the applicant (R.4.4; R.4.5; R.26.2*bis*(b), R.51*bis*.1(a)(vii), see §2.2);
3 no title (R.4.3; R.37; see §2.11.1);
4 no abstract (R.8; R.38; see §2.11.5);

5 non-compliance of the international application and, where applicable, its translation with the physical requirements (R.11) to the extent that compliance therewith is necessary for a reasonably uniform international publication and a satisfactory reproduction (R.26.3(a), (b) and R.26.3*bis*).

Although Art.14(2) refers to missing drawings, this requirement is checked under R.20 implementing the requirements for accordance of the international filing date (Art.11(1)). The rO also checks whether the abstract, any text matter of the drawings or the request is in an accepted language (R.26.3*ter*(a); R.26.3*ter*(c); R.12.1; see §2.4.3.3).

In the case of a single applicant, if the rO finds any of these defects, it invites the applicant, preferably within one month from receipt of the international application (R.26.1), to correct them (Art.14(1)(b)), accompanied by observations if the applicant so wishes (R.26.1) following the procedure of R.26. In the case of multiple applicants, the rO will not send an invitation if certain signatures are missing (R.26.*bis*(a); AG-IP §5.088; see §2.2.3).

Corrections in the request may be stated in a letter, but corrections in all other parts of the international application must be in the form of one or more replacement sheets accompanied by a letter drawing attention to the differences between the replaced and replacement sheets (R.26.4). The correction is free of charge (AG-IP §6.053).

A correction must be furnished to the rO (R.26.4) within two months from the date of the invitation to correct (R.26.2). The correction must be in the language in which the international application is filed, unless the correction is in a furnished translation in which case the correction must be in the language of the translation (R.12.2(c)). The rO may extend the period ex officio or at the applicant's request and free of charge at any time before a decision is taken (R.26.2; AG-IP §6.037, and 6.053). Each rO may adopt its own procedure. The EPO is relatively strict, whereas the IB is very lenient. In practice, the IB as rO sends several reminders at one month intervals after the invitation and extends the period ex officio till after receipt of the correction, so that the correction can be considered as having been received timely. The correction must be presented as set out in R.26.4. The rO takes a decision under R.26.5. Failure to furnish the required correction in time results in the international application being considered withdrawn (Art.14(1)(b)). The effect of the deemed withdrawal is set out in §3.4.

If the IB notes any defects referred to in Art.14(1)(a)(i), (ii) or (v), it will bring this to the attention of the rO (R.28.1(a)). Subsequently, the rO will carry out the correction procedure according to R.26 unless the rO disagrees with the IB on the correction (R.28.1(b)).

3.2.2 *Unpaid fees*

If the rO finds that the prescribed fees have not been paid (or not enough fees have been paid) within the prescribed periods, the applicant is invited to pay any missing fees including a late payment fee (R.16*bis*.1, .2) If the fees are still not paid, the international application will be considered withdrawn (Art.14(3)(a)). The fees as prescribed by R.27.1(a) are: the transmittal fee (R.14; see §2.8.2), the international filing fee (R.15.1; see §2.8.3), the search fee (R.16; see §2.8.4) and, where required, the late payment fee (R.16*bis*.2; see §2.8.5). The period for correction of a missing or underpaid fee under R.16*bis* is not extendable (AG-IP §6.037). Any payment received by the rO before that Office sends the invitation under R.16*bis*.1(a) is considered to have been received before the expiration of the time limit under Rule 14.1(c), 15.3 or 16.1(f), as the case may be. In addition, any payment received by the rO before that Office issues a declaration that the international application is considered withdrawn (Art.14(3)) is considered to have been received before the expiration of the time limit in R.16*bis*.1(a).

3.3 COPIES

When the rO has accorded the international application a filing date and national security prescriptions do not thwart such action, the rO will transmit one copy of the application ('record copy') to the IB (Art.12(1); R.22.1(a)). The record copy is considered to be the authentic text of the international application ('true copy'; Art.12(2)). Where the applicant has made a translation for the ISA or for publication (see §2.4.3), the rO will also transmit this translation to the IB (R.22.1(h)). See §5.5 for the procedure.

The rO will keep one copy ('home copy') (Art.12(1)). At the latest on the same day as it sends the record copy to the IB, the rO will send a copy of the international application ('search copy') to the ISA, or, where the ISA requires a translation of the international application (§2.4.3.1), a copy of the request and the translation (considered to be the 'search copy') (Art.12(1); R.23.1(a), (b)). However, if no search fee has been paid yet, the search copy will only be transmitted immediately after payment (R.23.1). The ISA notifies the IB, rO and applicant of the receipt of the search copy (R.25.1).

Any designated Office may ask the IB to forward a copy of the international application prior to transmission of the search report under Art.20 (Art.13(1); R.31.1); the applicant may also send a copy to a designated Office or ask the IB to do so (Art.13(2); R.31.2).

The applicant may request the rO to furnish him a certified copy of the international application subject to payment of a fee (R.21.2).

3.4 APPLICATION CONSIDERED WITHDRAWN

If the rO declares, that an international application is considered withdrawn (Art.14(1)(b), (3), (4)), it will notify the applicant and the IB of such (R.29.1(ii)).

The effect of the international application being withdrawn or being considered withdrawn is that the international application ceases in any designated state to have the effect of a regular national application as provided in Art.11(3), with the same consequences as the withdrawal of a national application in that state (Art.24(1)). This effect applies to the following cases (Art.24(1)(i)-(iii)):

(i) Voluntary withdrawal of the international application or a designation of a state (R.90*bis*.1, 2).

(ii)(a) The international application is considered withdrawn if:
- The record copy is not received by the IB in time (Art.12(3)).
- Defects in the international application are not corrected (Art.14(1)(b)).
- The transmittal fee, the international filing fee, the search fee or, where required, the late payment fee is not paid (Art.14(3)(a), R.27.1).
- After accordance of the filing date the rO notices defects under Art.11(1)(i)-(iii) (Art.14(4)).

(ii)(b) The designation of a state can no longer be considered withdrawn under the all-inclusive designation system (Art.14(3)(b)).

(iii) The applicant fails to perform the acts necessary to enter the national phase in time (Art.22).

The decision of the rO to consider the application withdrawn cannot, in principle, be appealed, because the PCT does not provide for any appeal during the international phase. However, some rOs do reconsider their decisions on petition, and some national courts or appeal boards have accepted appeals against decisions taken by national Offices acting as rO. The reconsideration reduces the consequences a single error in the international phase might have, i.e. the loss of the application for all designated states, in particular those states whose national law does not provide remedies as mentioned in Art.48(2) for excusal of delay in meeting a time limit. A favourable decision will be accepted by the national Office acting as designated Office if it also acted as the rO, but other national Offices need not accept the favourable decision (AG-IP §6.054).

If the EPC provides a remedy for a similar case, the EPO will allow further processing or re-establishment of rights, as the case may be; the examining division is competent (R.159(2) EPC) for decisions under PCT Art.25(2)(a).

The PCT provides a relief by allowing a (considered) withdrawn international application to enter the national phase before each designated Office and apply national law to remedy the loss of rights. Thereto, Art.24(2) provides the necessary connection between the loss of rights in the international phase and the remedy available under national law. The so-called review and excuse procedure to be carried out before each designated Office is set out in §7.6.

4 International search

4.1 ISA

Each international application will be the subject of an international search during the international phase (Art.15(1)). The search is carried out by an International Searching Authority (ISA), whose task includes the preparation of the international search report (Art.16(1)). There are several ISAs operating under the PCT. Any national Office or intergovernmental organisation satisfying the requirements relating to manpower and documentation, can be appointed as ISA by the Assembly on conclusion of an Agreement between such Office or organization and the IB (Art.16(3)(a)-(c), R.36). A list of all national/regional offices that act as ISA or IPEA (including the Agreements between the offices and the IB of WIPO) can be found on www.wipo.int/pct. The KR office acting as ISA also searches JP documents which may be useful in detecting prior art. As well as the EPO, European ISAs also include the national offices of AT, ES, FI, SE and the Nordic Patent Institute (XN). (AG-IP Annex D)

4.1.1 Competent ISA

Each rO (except the IB according to R.35.3(c)) has specified which ISA or ISAs are competent for the searching of international applications filed with the rO (Art.16(2), R.35.1, R.35.2). The choice of ISA by the rO is often based on the presumed quality of the searches of the ISA. AG-IP Annex C indicates the ISA(s) competent for each rO. Normally, if the rO is also ISA, that ISA will perform the international search. If a rO specifies that various ISAs are competent (R.35.2(a)), the applicant must indicate his choice of ISA in the request (R.4.1(b)(iv); R.4.14*bis*).

The EPO as rO has specified only the EPO as ISA. The rOs of all EPC contracting states have specified the EPO as ISA; additionally, the rOs of several countries have specified an additional ISA (see AG-IP Annex C).

As from 01.01.2015 the EPO will act as an ISA for international applications containing business method claims filed with the USPTO or IB as rO; however, it will only issue a search report for claims including technical subject matter. (OJ 2014 A117)

Where the IB is the rO (R.19.1(a)(iii)), the competent ISA is the ISA which would have been competent had the application been filed at the rO which is the national office of or acting for a contracting state of which the applicant is a national or resident (R.35.3(a)). Where two or more ISAs are competent, the choice is left to the applicant (R.35.3(b)) and can be indicated in the Request (R.4.14*bis*).

See §2.4.3.1 for when the language of the international application is not acceptable to the ISA.

4.2 SEARCH

4.2.1 *Prior art documents*

The purpose of the international search is to discover relevant prior art by consulting at least the documentation specified in R.34 (Art.15(4)). Prior art is everything available to the public anywhere in the world by means of written disclosure prior to the international filing date (R.33.1(a)). The prior art taken into account during the international preliminary examination must be publicly available before the international filing date or, where a priority has been validly claimed, before the priority date (R.64.1(a)). Note that if the IPEA considers the priority claim to be invalid, prior art published up to the international filing date will be taken into account during international preliminary examination (R.64.1(b)).

The international search report will separately mention any disclosures made prior to the filing date in a different form, such as an oral disclosure, use or exhibition, when a written disclosure refers to it (R.33.1(b)). Prior rights with respect to the international filing date (not the priority date) of the international application will also be specially mentioned in the search report (R.33.1(c)). The search will be made in the technical field of the invention to which the international application relates and in neighbouring fields (R.33.2).

The value as prior art of a public disclosure by the applicant before the priority date may depend on the national law of the designated Offices (see Art.27(5), second sentence). The US has a one-year grace period for such disclosures by the inventor. The EPC does not have a general grace period, but only a 6-month grace period for disclosure due to evident abuse or for display at an international exhibition (Art.55(1) EPC).

4.2.2 *Not searchable matter*

The ISA need not extend its search to subject-matter of the international application relating to scientific or mathematical theories, plant or animal varieties or essentially biological processes other than microbiological processes and their products, schemes, rules or methods of doing business, methods for treatment of the human or animal body as well as diagnostic methods, mere presentation of information, and computer programs to the extent that the ISA is not equipped to search prior art concerning such subject matter (Art.17(2)(a)(i); R.39.1(i)-(vi)). The Agreement between the ISA and the IB under Art.16(3)(b) may state the subject-matter not required to be searched. The EPO as ISA will search claims if the subject-matter thereof would be searched under the EPC(Art.17(2)(a)(i); R.39.1(i)-(vi); Art.16(3)(b);OJ 2017 A115, Annex C). (see §4.8)

The ISA need not carry out a search if the description, claims and drawings fail to comply with the requirements to such an extent that a meaningful search cannot be carried out (Art.17(2)(a)(ii)).

If no search has been carried out, the ISA will draw up a declaration stating so and transmit it to the IB and the applicant (Art.17(2)(a); R.44.1). A search fee will not be refunded if no ISR has been established. The entry in the national phase is not affected by such a declaration (Art.22(2), see §4.3.3). If only certain claims relate to not-searched subject-matter, this will be indicated in the international search report, whereas for the other claims the results of the search will be stated (Art.17(2)(b)). If the national law of the national Office acting as ISA does not allow a multiple dependent claim to refer to another multiple dependent claim, such a dependency may result in unsearched claims and, consequently, an indication under Art.17(2)(b) in the international search report (R.6.4(a)).

Issuance of a declaration by the ISA stating that no international search will be carried out, leads to loss of the search fees with little chance for the applicant to argue his case against the declaration. In addition, the claims may not be amended after receiving the declaration (this follows from the wording of Art.19(1)). The IPEA is under no obligation to carry out international preliminary examination for unsearched claims, so filing a demand does not give any guarantee that the IPEA will agree to search and examine such claims (R.66.1(e)). See §6.6.5 for the policy of the EPO in such situations when acting as IPEA.

4.2.3 *Earlier search*

The applicant can request that the ISA take into account the results of an earlier search when carrying out its international search, which may be an international, international-type or national search, carried out by the same or a different ISA or a national office (R.4.12). In order that an earlier search is taken into account, the applicant should indicate so in the request form and specify the office concerned and the application in respect of which the earlier search was carried out (R.4.12(i)). The applicant should also indicate that the international application is the same as, or substantially the same as, the application (or a translation thereof) in respect of which the earlier search was carried out (R.4.12(ii)).

When an applicant requests that an ISA take into account an earlier search, the applicant should submit a copy of the earlier search to the rO (R.12*bis*.1(a)), which the rO will send to the ISA (R.23bis.1). The ISA may request that the applicant submit, within a reasonable period, a copy of the earlier application, the earlier search results (or acceptable translations thereof), and any documents cited therein (R.12*bis*.1(b)). If the applicant stated in the request form that the international application is the same as, or substantially the same as, the application (or a translation thereof) in respect of which the earlier search was carried out, then no copy of the earlier application is required (R.12*bis*.1(e)). Certain exceptions exist where no earlier search results need be submitted, for example if the earlier search was carried out by the same office which is acting as rO, then the applicant can request that the rO transmit the earlier search results to the ISA, where the rO may request a fee for such (R.12*bis*.1(c)). Other exceptions where no earlier search results need be submitted include if the ISA carried out the earlier search (R.12*bis*.1(d)), or if the earlier search results are already available to the ISA in an acceptable form and manner, such as from a digital library or priority document (R.12*bis*.1(f)).

Where an applicant has requested that earlier search results be taken into account, and has supplied any related documentation to the ISA upon request, if the earlier search was carried out by the same ISA, the ISA shall take the results of that search into account, to the extent possible, in carrying out the international search (R.41.1(i)). If the earlier search was carried out by a different ISA, the ISA may take the results of that search into account in carrying out the international search. Where the ISA uses the results of the earlier search, it must refund the search fee to the extent commensurate with the use and as fixed in the Agreement between the ISA and the IB under Art.16(3)(b) (R.16.3). Information on any refunds regarding use of earlier searches for each ISA is published in the PCT Applicant's Guide, Annex D.

An international-type search is a search similar to an international search carried out by an ISA on a national application filed with the national Office of or acting for a contracting state (Art.15(5)(a)). The competent ISA is the one that would have been competent if the national application were an international application filed with the same national Office as rO (Art.15(5)(c)).

The EPO as ISA will only (partly) refund the search fee if it can base the international search report on an earlier search made by the EPO on an application whose priority is claimed for the international application (OJ 2009 p.99; OJ 2014 A30; AG-IP Annex D(EP); A-X,10.2.3; see §2.8.6.1 for more details).

4.3 NON-UNITY

The search fee is intended to cover the expenses of the search of a single invention. Hence, an application must comply with the requirement of unity of invention (Art.3(4)(iii); R.13). Note, that the PCT has no provisions for filing divisional applications (see AG-IP §10.073). Divisional applications can only be filed in the national phase where national law permits so. Under the EPC, only a pending European patent application may be divided (R.36(1) EPC; A-IV,1.1.1). An international application is deemed to be a pending European application when the EPO actually acts as designated or elected Office (Art.153(2) EPC), i.e. when the requirements of R.159(1)(a) and (c) have been complied with on expiry of the 31-month period (J18/09; E-IX,2.4.1) or, if a request for early processing has been filed, the acts under R.159(1) EPC set out in E-IX,2.8 have been completed (E-IX,2.4.1).

The need for filing a divisional application with the EPO has been reduced strongly by R.164, allowing an applicant to continue prosecution before the EPO with claims that are non-unitary with the claims searched in the international phase.

4.3.1 *Unity requirement*

An international application complies with the requirement of unity of invention if the claims relate to a single invention or to a group of inventions so linked as to form a single general inventive concept (R.13.1). The requirement of unity for a group of inventions in R.13.2 PCT is verbally identical to the EPC requirement in R.44(1) EPC. The requirement for unity of a utility model may be determined by national law (R.13.5). AG-IP §5.115-5.123 explain the requirement for different categories of claims, the Markush formulation and intermediate and final products.

Any designated Office must accept an international application which complies with the PCT requirement of unity of invention (Art.27(1), Art.2(x)). As a consequence, the US national Office as designated Office may not apply its deviating rules for unity of invention in the national phase to an international application. However, a divisional, continuation or continuation-in-part based on the international application is subject to national rules for unity of invention.

4.3.2 *Non-unity procedure*

If the ISA finds that the application does not comply with the requirement of unity of invention, it will invite the applicant to pay one or more additional fees (Art.17(3)(a); R.40). The invitation must specify the reasons why the international application is considered not to comply with the requirement of unity of invention (R.40.1(i)) and indicate the amount to be paid (R.40.1(ii)). The number of additional fees to be paid depends on the number of further inventions. The amount of the additional fee is determined by the ISA (R.40.2(a)) and is payable directly to the ISA (R.40.2(b)), see AG-IP Annex D. The period for payment is one month from the date of the invitation (R.40.1(ii)).

If the applicant does not agree with the non-unity opinion of the ISA, he can have the opinion reviewed by paying the additional fee(s) under protest within the above period of R.40.1(ii) PCT. If not at least one additional fee is paid, the opinion will not be reviewed.

The protest must be supported by a reasoned statement why the requirement of unity is complied with or why the amount of additional fees is excessive (R.40.2(c)). The ISA may require that the applicant pay a protest fee for the examination of the protest (R.40.2(e)). The protest fee must be paid within one month from the date of the invitation (R.40.1(iii)). If the protest fee is not paid, the protest is considered not to have been made (R.40.2(e)). The amount of the protest fee levied by each ISA is stated in AG-IP Annex D.

The protest will be examined by a review body (R.40.2(c)). The body will order total or partial reimbursement of the additional fees to the extent that it finds the protest justified (R.40.2(c)). Where it finds that the protest was entirely justified, the protest fee will also be refunded (R.40.2(e)). The payment of the additional fees for a further search and/or a partial search will be indicated in the international search report (R.43.7). On request of the applicant, the text of the protest and the decision will be notified to the designated Offices together with the international search report (R.40.2(c)). This protest procedure is one of the two cases of 'appeal' possible in the international phase under PCT (see §6.3.3 for the second case).

For the EPO acting as ISA see §4.8.

4.3.3 *Effect on national phase*

Non-payment of the additional fee has the result that certain claims will not be searched (Art.17(3)(a)). It does not have any influence on the validity of the application, the processing of which continues in respect of all claims (AG-IP §7.021). Nevertheless, a designated state may consider unsearched parts as withdrawn, unless the applicant pays a special fee to the national office of that state (Art.17(3)(b)).

Upon entry into the regional phase before the EPO as designated or elected Office, the EPO reviews the non-unity finding and, if upheld, will invite the applicant to pay further search fees for claimed inventions not searched by the (S)ISA (R.164 EPC).

4.4 INTERNATIONAL SEARCH REPORT AND WRITTEN OPINION

The ISA establishes the international search report within the prescribed period (see §4.5) in the form as prescribed by R.43 (Art.18(1)). Timely rectifications of obvious mistakes (see §8.5) will be taken into account by the ISA (R.91.1; R.43.6*bis*). The report relates to the invention first mentioned in the claims and to those inventions for which additional fees have been paid (Art.17(3)(a)). The international search report may not contain opinions or explanations (R.43.9). The international search report is sent to the applicant and the IB (R.44.1). The IB will publish the search report (Art.21(3)) in the language in which the application is to be published (Art.21(4); R.48.3).

However, if a translation has been made for the purposes of the international search, the ISA may publish it in that language and if an application is to be published in the language of a translation which is not accepted by the ISA, then the search report may be published in a language which is both a language accepted by the ISA and a language of publication (R.43.4). If the application is not published in English, the international search report, or the declaration that no meaningful search could be made, is translated into English (Art.18(3), R.45.1). See §4.5 for periods.

The ISA applies an enhanced international search system in which it establishes a written opinion at the same time as it establishes the international search report (R.43*bis*.1(a)). The written opinion states whether the invention appears to be novel, to involve an inventive step and to be industrially applicable and whether the application complies with requirements of the PCT checked by the ISA (R.43*bis*.1(a)). The international search report and the written opinion give the applicant a good impression of the patentability of the invention, on which he may decide whether or not to continue the procedure. Even when no meaningful search could be made under Art.17(2)(a), a written opinion is established (R.43*bis*.1(a)), merely explaining why no opinion on patentability can be given.

The written opinion of the ISA is sent to the applicant and the IB together with the international search report (R.44.1). If no demand is filed, the IB converts the written opinion into an 'International Preliminary Report on Patentability (Chapter I of the PCT)' (IPRP Ch.I) (R.44*bis*.1(a)). The content of the IPRP Ch.I is identical to the written opinion of the ISA except for replacement of the front page. When a demand for international preliminary examination is filed, the written opinion of the ISA will be the first written opinion of the IPEA (R.66.1*bis*(a)), except where an IPEA decides differently under R.66.1*bis*(b)-(d) (only the EPO as IPEA does this - see list of PCT Reservations, Declarations, Notifications and Incompatibilities on the PCT web site: www.wipo.int/pct). The written opinion and report will not be accessible to third parties before expiry of 30 months from the priority date (R.44*ter*.1(a)). In contrast to the international search report, the written opinion is not published. On 01.07.2014, Rule 44*ter* was deleted and R.94.1(b) amended: the written opinion for international applications filed on or after that date will be publicly available from the date of international publication.

4.5 PROCEDURE BEFORE ISA

The ISA will start carrying out its tasks after receipt of the search copy from the rO (Art.12(1); R.23; §3.3). It will check the title and abstract of the international application (R.37; R.38; see §2.11.1 and 2.11.5), the result of which will be stated in the international search report (R.44.2). The international search report will normally be ready three months from receipt of the search copy by the ISA or, if that is later, nine months from the priority date (Art.18(1), R.42.1). There is no sanction if the international search report is established later than the prescribed time limit. Where the international search report or the declaration under Art.17(2)(a) are not in English, the IB will make a translation into English (R.45.1; AG-IP §9.017).

If the international search report is not available at the time of completion of the technical preparations for publication, the front page of the A2 publication will indicate such, and also that the international search report will be published separately as an A3 publication (R.48.2(g); AG-IP §9.015).

As soon as the ISA has established the international search report, it will transmit it or the declaration that no search could be made (Art.17(2)(a)) to the applicant and to the IB for the international publication (Art.18(2); R.44.1). The applicant will also be informed of the time limit for filing amended claims under Art.19. The ISA will, on request, send copies of the documents cited in the international search report to the applicant or a designated Office (Art.20(3); R.44.3).

The written opinion will be ready at the same time as the search report (R.43*bis*.1(a) and R.44.1). The ISA sends a copy to the applicant and the IB together with the search report or the declaration (R.44.1). When no demand is filed, the IB prepares the IPRP Ch.I based on the written opinion (R.44*bis*.1(a)) and transmits a copy to the applicant (R.44*bis*.1(c)). The IB transmits the report to the designated states, where required in English translation, after expiry of 30 months from the priority date (R.44*bis*.2, 3).

The applicant may file informal comments on the written opinion to the IB, which will become public when the file is made accessible. The purpose of the comments can be to rebut the opinion in the event that no international preliminary examination is requested. There is no express provision in the PCT for filing these comments. Informal comments are forwarded by the IB to designated offices together with the IPRP (AG-IP §7.030, 7.031)

4.6 AMENDMENT OF CLAIMS

After receipt of the international search report the applicant has one opportunity to amend his claims in view of the search report (Art.19(1)). Other parts of the international application may not be amended in this stage of the procedure. Amendments are not allowed where the ISA has declared under Art.17(2)(a) that no search report has been established (this follows from the wording of Art.19(1); AG-IP §9.004). The amendments may not go beyond the disclosure of the application as filed (Art.19(2)). The latter requirement is not enforceable in the international phase (AG-IP §9.009, 11.047). A designated Office may disregard extension of subject-matter in the national phase (Art.19(3)).

The amendment must be filed in the language in which the international application will be published (R.46.3) and must comprise replacement sheets for the entire set of claims as originally filed (R.46.5(a)) and an accompanying letter indicating the differences between the claims as filed and those as amended (R.46.5(b)(i)), which claims have been cancelled (R.46.5(b)(ii)), and the basis for the amendments in the application as filed (R.46.5(b)(iii)). If any claims are cancelled, no renumbering of the remaining claims is required. However, where the applicant does renumber claims, they must be renumbered consecutively. (AG-IP §9.005)

The amendments, possibly together with a brief statement (not exceeding 500 words) explaining the amendment (Art.19(1); R.46.4), must be filed directly with the IB (R.46.2) within two months of transmittal of the international search report by the ISA to the IB and the applicant, or 16 months from the priority date, whichever expires later (R.46.1). Amendments received before completion of the technical preparations for the publication of the application are considered received in time (R.46.1 and §5.3). If amendments are filed later than the demand, the applicant should preferably file a copy of the amendments, any statement under Art.19 and the letter explaining the differences and basis for the amendments (R.46.5(b)) with the IPEA (see R.62.2). Where the demand is filed later than the amendments, copies of the amendments and letter explaining the differences and basis for such amendments in the application as filed are preferably submitted together with the demand (R.53.9(a)(i)). See §5.1 below for the publication of the amendments.

4.6.1 *Effect of amendment*

An amendment of the claims under Art.19 will be published together with the international application (R.48.2(f)), if received in time, and may therefore be useful for better defining the scope of the claims in view of provisional protection in the designated states (Art.29; see §5.4). The publication also allows the applicant to effect the amendments with a single notification for all designated Offices. When the period of R.46.1 expires after completion of the technical preparation for publication and an amendment is filed after the completion, the amendment will be published later, separate from the application. Where a demand is filed, the applicant will have another opportunity to amend the claims (as well as the description and drawings) under Art.34(2)(b), making an amendment under Art.19 mainly useful for the purpose of provisional protection. The amendments under Art.19 may be superseded by later amendments (see §6.4). In the national/regional phase, the applicant is not bound by any amendments made in the international phase.

4.7 REPRESENTATION

An applicant need not be represented by an agent before the ISA, because Art.27(7) allows the application of national law as far as it relates to any requirement that the applicant be represented only before rOs and designated Offices. However, an applicant may be represented before the ISA by an agent.

An agent having the right to practise before the national Office with which the international application was filed, is also entitled to practise before the ISA in respect of that application (Art.49; R.90.1(a)). The ISA may require proof of the right to practise (R.83.1), which it may demand from the national Office before which the agent allegedly has the right to practise (R.83.2).

The agent may appoint a sub-agent to represent the applicant specifically before the ISA, provided the person appointed as sub-agent has the right to practise before the national Office which acts as ISA (R.90.1(d)(ii)). The applicant himself may appoint an agent to represent him specifically before the ISA, provided the person appointed as agent has the right to practise before the national Office which acts as ISA (R.90.1(b)). See also §8.3 below.

4.8 EPO AS ISA

The functioning of the EPO as ISA is governed by the Agreement between the European Patent Organisation and the IB of the WIPO (OJ 2017 A115 and OJ 2018 A24)

The EPO may act as ISA for applicants who are residents or nationals of an EPC contracting state for which the PCT has entered into force (Art.152 EPC). The competence of the EPO to act as ISA is based on the Agreement and Art.16(3)(b). The EPO will act as ISA for all international applications filed with the rO of any EPC contracting state, since the PCT is in force for all EPC contracting states. The EPO also acts as ISA for some fifty other rOs, including JP and US, as allowed by Art.152 EPC. The procedure before the EPO as ISA is described in Euro-PCT Guide Ch.C.

The Agreement provides in Art.4 which subject-matter is excluded from search and in Annex C which subject-matter is not-excluded. The EPO as ISA strictly adheres to R.39.1(iii) PCT and will not search claims relating to no more than methods of doing business. In such cases a declaration will be issued that no international search report will be established pursuant to Art.17(2). Under R.66.1(e) and 67.1(iii), the EPO acting as IPEA need not examine such claims (see §6.6.4). Where the claims include technical means, an international search report will be established. Where the technical means are so conventional that they were widely available and no documentary evidence is considered required because of their notoriety, the search report will state so and will not cite a document. (Not. EPO, OJ 2007 p.592)

An applicant of a priority application searched by the EPO may comment on objections raised in the search opinion and explain amendments in the application documents and submit them in a so-called PCT Direct letter when filing the priority claiming PCT application with the receiving Office. All receiving Offices will take the comments into account when carrying out the international search. The letter will add value to the search report and the written opinion of the ISA. It is particularly useful when using PPH (**Art.94(3):7**), which requires at least one allowable claim. The search fee will be refunded if the EPO as ISA can base its search on the earlier search report (see section 2.8.6.1 above). See OJ 2017 A21 for formal details of PCT Direct letters.

A search examiner may seek informal clarification on issues such as clarity or support of the claims by contacting the applicant informally by telephone and/or fax in cases where issuance of a full international search report is in doubt. If clarification cannot be provided over the telephone, an applicant may be given 2 weeks to respond to a written fax request. (OJ 2011 p.327; EPO PCT GL B,VIII-3.3)

Where the ISA finds that a sequence listing does not comply with the standard form, making the search more difficult, it will invite the applicant under R.13*ter*.1 to furnish it subsequently. The EPO as ISA subjects the furnishing to a late furnishing fee (OJ 2010 p.328; OJ 2011 p.376).

The EPO as ISA may carry out an international-type search according to Art.15(5)(a, b) on a national patent application if the application is filed with the patent authority of an EPC contracting state and the national law of that state provides for an international-type search. The EPO currently has working agreements for international-type searches with the national offices of several EPC contracting states. (see AG-IP Annex B1; OJ 1999 p.300; OJ 2017 A115, Art.8; B-II,4.5).

The EPO has fixed the amount of the search fee that may be levied by an ISA under R.16.1(a) PCT in Rfees 2(2) (see §2.8.4).

The EPO acting as ISA follows the protest procedure according to R.40.2(c)-(e) (R.158(3) EPC; see §4.3.2). Further details of the procedure may be determined by the President of the EPO (R.158(3) EPC). (OJ 2015 A59; OJ 2010 p.322)

In its decisions W4/87 and W3/93, the EPO as ISA allowed re-establishment under Art.122 EPC for a late paid protest fee pursuant to Art.48(2) PCT, even though the re-establishment should have effect only for the EPO as designated state and not for other designated states. See also §3.4 and §8.2.3.

The payment of the requested additional fees is a necessary requirement for filing a protest (R.40.2(c); W10/88). The invitation to pay additional search fees must be sufficiently substantiated by the ISA (R.40.1(i)); listing groups of claims will only suffice in clear-cut cases (W11/89, W16/91).

In procedures before the EPO as ISA, an attorney, patent agent or any other person (e.g an employee of an applicant) having the right to practise before the rO with which the international application was filed, is entitled to practise (Art.49 PCT). The applicant may appoint a European professional representative to represent him before the EPO acting as ISA (R.90.1(b) PCT).

4.9 SUPPLEMENTARY INTERNATIONAL SEARCH

Under PCT Chapter I, the applicant has the option of requesting that one or more supplementary international searches are carried out by International Searching Authorities that have stated their preparedness to carry out supplementary international searches (SISAs) in addition to the main PCT search. The aim of supplementary international searches is to provide a more comprehensive view of relevant prior art during the international phase. Applicants can thus reduce the likelihood of new prior art being found in the national phase, for example prior art published in languages in which the ISA is not competent to search, or prior art in areas which other authorities have particular specialisations. (Art.17(1); R.45*bis*; AG-IP §8.001-8.053).

As an alternative, an applicant may request that a PCT application is searched under the Collaborative Search & Examination (CS&E) pilot project. In this pilot, examiners of all IP5 patent offices (CN, EP, JP, KR and US) contribute to the ISR (OJ 2018 A47).

A request for a supplementary international search must be filed at the IB within 22 months of the (earliest) priority date and the appropriate handling and supplementary search fees paid where required; both fees should be paid to the IB (R.45*bis*.1(a); R.45*bis*.2(a); R.45*bis*.3(a); Schedule of Fees 2).

Copies of the supplementary international search report are transmitted to both the applicant and the IB (R.45*bis*.5(a), R.45*bis*.7(a), R.45*bis*.8(a)). The supplementary international search report may contain 'explanations' relating to the prospects for patentability in view of the citations and scope of the supplementary international search (R.45*bis*.7(e); AG-IP §8.049). Some SISAs (e.g. EPO, see §4.9.1) treat 'explanations' similarly to a 'written opinion of the ISA'. (OJ 2010 p.316)

Note that only a few authorities (AT, EP, FI, RU, SE and XN) currently offer supplementary international search services. The EPO has offered supplementary international search services since 01.07.2010 (OJ 2010 p.316; see §4.9.1 below). Other authorities are still considering whether they will offer supplementary international search services in the future. Demand from applicants for supplementary international searches has been very low; in 2016 only 47 supplementary international searches were requested (the EPO receiving about 94% of these requests) on 233,000 filed international applications.

4.9.1 *EPO as SISA*

The EPO has offered supplementary international search services since 01.07.2010. The fee for a supplementary international search is the same as for an international search and should be paid together with the handling fee for the supplementary search to the IB, not the EPO. If the international application was not filed in English, French, or German or a translation into any of these languages has not been filed previously, a translation into one of these languages should be filed along with the supplementary international search request. Only 3 requests for supplementary international search were received by the EPO in 2010, 7 in 2011 and 20 in 2012.

The EPO will draw up a supplementary international search report of similar scope as an international search report, including 'explanations' on the prospects for patentability under R.45*bis*.7(e) which are of equal value to a Written Opinion drawn up by the EPO as ISA (OJ 2010 p.316 item 6). Upon entering the European regional phase, the EPO will not draw up a supplementary European search report for Euro-PCT applications for which it has already carried out a supplementary international search. For a Euro-PCT application which contained negative 'explanations' issued by the EPO in relation to a supplementary international search report, such explanations must be dealt with in a substantive response to the R.161 EPC communication issued by the EPO shortly after entering the European regional phase. (R.161 EPC; E-VIII 3)

In the case of a lack of unity finding, the EPO will only carry out a supplementary international search for a single invention, i.e. the one first mentioned in the claims, or the invention specified by the applicant in the SIS request; further supplementary international search fees will not be accepted for further inventions. If an international application containing multiple inventions (for the first of which the EPO has carried out a supplementary international search) subsequently enters the European regional phase, the applicant may opt to have any of the further inventions searched by the EPO as dO/eO and the applicant may select the claims of any searched invention for examination.

Further inventions may be pursued in divisional applications. (R.164 EPC; E-VIII 2.4.1 and 4.2; Euro-PCT Guide §292-294)

5 International publication

5.1 CONTENTS OF THE INTERNATIONAL PUBLICATION

The IB publishes the application (Art.21(1)) in the form governed by the Admin. Instr. (R.48.1). The publication is only in electronic form (AG-IP §9.015). The international publication contains:

- a front page with bibliographic data, the abstract and the accompanying figure (R.48.2(a)(i), (b), (d));
- the description, claims and drawings, if any (R.48.2(a)(ii)-(iv));
- if available the international search report or the declaration under Art.17(2)(a) that no meaningful search could be made (Art.21(3), R.48.2(a)(v), R.48.2(c));
- any amended claims filed in response to Art.19(1) (R.48.2(f);
- any statement explaining amendments to the claims under Art.19(1) (R.48.2(a)(vi));
- any not-granted request for the correction of an obvious mistake referred to in R.91.3(d) (R.48.2(a)(vii));
- data relating to any deposited biological material furnished under R.13*bis* separately from the description (R.48.2(a)(viii));
- any information concerning a priority claim considered not to have been made under R.26*bis*.2(b-d) (R.48.2(a)(ix));
- any declaration under R.4.17 relating to identity of inventor, inventorship, applicant's entitlement or non-prejudicial disclosures (R.48.2(a)(x));
- any information concerning a request under R.26*bis*.3 for restoration of the right of priority, including the decision of the rO on such a request and information as to the criterion for restoration upon which the decision was based (R.48.2(a)(xi)).

The applicant may request the IB to omit matter irrelevant for the invention or which should be kept secret from the publication (R.48.2(l) and (n)). This matter will neither be accessible in the files of the international offices (R.94.1(d)).

If the international search report is not yet available at the time of completion of the technical preparations for the publication, e.g. due to a request for early publication under Art.21(2)(b), the publication will state so and also that the international search report will be published separately (R.48.2(g); AG-IP §9.015). Where amended claims have been filed, these are included in the publication (R.48.2(f); see §4.6). If, at the time of completion of the technical preparations, the period for amending the claims under Art.19 has not yet expired, the publication will state so, and also that any later filed amendments will be published (R.48.2(h)).

Expressions or drawings in the international application which, in the opinion of the IB, are contrary to morality or public order or disparaging may be omitted from the publication (Art.21(6), R.9).

The application is published in the language as filed if that language is a language of publication, i.e. Arabic, Chinese, English, French, German, Japanese, Korean, Portuguese, Russian or Spanish (R.48.3(a)). If the international application was filed in a language other than a language of publication, the applicant will have furnished a translation into a language of publication to the rO under R.12.3 (see §2.4.3.1) or R.12.4 (see §2.4.3.2), and the application will be published in the form of that translation (R.48.3(b)). If the application is not published in English, the title, abstract and search report are published at the same time also in English (R.48.3(c)). English is the most frequently used language of publication; in 2015 51% of the international applications were published in English; 19% in Japanese, 10% in Chinese, 8% in German, 5% in Korean, and 7% in other languages (PCT Statistics 2015).

The publication, including the bibliographic data, is available in electronic form on the WIPO and EPO websites and in paper form when ordered from the IB (Art.55(4), AG-IP §9.021). The Gazette does not publish any more information on published international applications as is possible under R.86.1(i)). The Gazette is available in electronic form on the Internet (R.86.2(c) and Section 407 of the Admin. Instr.).

5.2 PUBLICATION DATE

The international application is published promptly after the expiration of 18 months from the priority date (Art.21(2)(a)) by making the application available on the internet. The date of publication is, in general, on the first Thursday after said expiry (AG-IP §9.013) and is not affected by holidays (see also the November issue of the PCT Newsletter of each year).

The application may be published before the expiry of the 18th month on request of the applicant (Art.21(2)(b) or Art.64(3)(c)(i)), provided a publication fee is paid to the IB if the international search report is not yet available and has to be published separately (R.48.4).

A withdrawal under R.90*bis* of the international application, a designation or a priority claim, received after the technical preparations have been completed, will be published in the Gazette (R.48.6(a), (c)).

5.3 PREVENTING PUBLICATION

There will be no international publication if the international application is withdrawn or is considered withdrawn at least one day before the technical preparations for publication have been completed (Art.21(5); R.90*bis*.1(c); AG-IP § 9.014 and 11.049). Even if a rO declares that an international application has been withdrawn, publication of the international application will only be prevented if the notification of withdrawal transmitted by the rO reaches the IB before technical preparations are complete (R.29.1(v)). Withdrawal may be made conditional on the international application not being published. (AG-IP §11.049)

An applicant should not rely on a deemed withdrawal by not paying fees if he wants to avoid publication of the application. Some rOs are known not to have followed up on lack of payment by declaring the application to be considered withdrawn, causing the application still to be published. It is best practice to avoid publication by active withdrawal as set out in §8.4. (Practical Advice in PCT Newsletter 10/2014)

The technical preparations for publication are completed by the 15th day prior to the date of publication (AG-IP §9.014). If the date is critical, it is recommended to contact the IB for the exact day of publication. If, for example, the application is to be published on Thursday 18.04.2013, then the technical preparations are completed on Wednesday 03.04.2013, so that any withdrawal or amendment should be received by the IB at the latest on Tuesday 02.04.2013.

The international application will not be published if only states have been designated which do not require the publication of the application (Art.64(3)). As only the US has given a declaration to this effect, this possibility is of minor importance. (AG-IP §9.012(iv))

5.4 POSTPONEMENT OF PUBLICATION

Publication may be postponed if the applicant withdraws the (earliest) priority claim in due time (see §2.10.3), which withdrawal may be made conditional on non-publication (R.90*bis*.3(a); AG-IP §11.049), or the rO declares the priority claim as considered not to have been made under R26*bis*.2(b) after failure to correct a priority declaration. It is possible to request earlier publication under Art.21(2)(b) (see §5.2); a request for later publication is not admissible.

5.5 PROVISIONAL PROTECTION AND PRIOR RIGHT EFFECT

The effects of the publication of the international application on protection of any rights of the applicant in a designated state are the same as those which the national law of that state provides for the compulsory national publication of unexamined national applications as such (Art.29(1)). The rights may relate to provisional protection in a designated state or to a prior right effect of the international application. However, a designated state may make the protection of the applicant's rights effective only after the publication, or making available in a different form, of a translation in a language of the state if the international application is published in a different language (Art.29(2)). The protection may also be made dependent on the expiration of 18 months from the priority date (Art.29(3)) and on receipt of a copy of the published application by the designated Office (Art.29(4)). AG-IP Annex B1 and B2 give the requirements of each designated Office for provisional protection.

Only a person authorised by the applicant can obtain from the IB copies of any document in its file at any time (R.94.1(a)). The IB will also furnish said copies, except those relating to international preliminary examination (Art.38), to any person but not before the international publication (R.94.1(b)). The IB will charge the costs of the service to the requester (R.94.1(a)).

5.5.1 *EPO*

The publication of an international application for which the EPO is a designated Office will take the place of the publication of a European patent application under Art.93 EPC (Art.29(1) PCT; Art.153(3) EPC). However, where the international application is published in a language other than English, French or German, the publication will only be regarded as equivalent, if a translation in English, French or German is supplied to the EPO, which the EPO will subsequently publish (Art.29(2)(i) PCT; Art.153(4) EPC).

An international application will only have the prior right effect of Art.54(3) EPC if the application is supplied to the EPO in English, French or German, the filing fee of R.159(1)(c) EPC is paid to the EPO as designated Office, and the EPO publishes the application (Art.153(5) EPC; R.165 EPC). If for example an international application is in Japanese and the applicant only requires a prior right effect in Europe, the applicant must furnish a translation in English, French of German to the EPO and pay the filing fee (R.159(1)(c) EPC; R.165 EPC; G-IV, 5.2). Given that the EPO typically takes a few months for such publications and the EPO has not guaranteed it will publish a withdrawn application, if the applicant decides to withdraw the European application after having paid the filing fee to avoid payment of further fees, there may be no publication after the withdrawal and the applicant would not achieve his goal.

The provisional protection in accordance with Art.67(1), (2) EPC in the designated EPC contracting states will be effective from the date of the international publication for those international applications published in English, French or German and for which the EPO is a designated Office (indirect consequence of Art.153(4) EPC). The provisional protection will be effective from the date of the above-mentioned publication of the translation by the EPO, if the international publication was not in English, French or German (Art.153(4); Euro-PCT Guide §672). The provisional protection is subject to the national requirements of the designated states regarding translations of claims in a national language (Art.153(4) EPC, referring to Art.67(3) EPC, see NatLaw table III for the national requirements).

See also the notes to Art.153 EPC and R.159(1) EPC.

5.6 PROCEDURE BEFORE IB

5.6.1 *Receipt of record copy*

The IB is made aware of the filing of an international application by the notification by the rO of its filing date and number (R.20.2(c)). The IB will then monitor the receipt of the record copy. If the IB has not received the record copy within 13 months from the priority date, it reminds the rO that it should transmit the record copy to the IB promptly (R.22.1(b)). If the record copy has still not been received by the expiration of 14 months from the priority date, the IB notifies the applicant and the rO accordingly (R.22.1(c)). In such a case the applicant may request the rO to furnish him a certified copy free of charge, and send it on to the IB (R.22.1(d),(e)). The international application is regarded withdrawn if the IB has not received the record copy within 3 months from the notification of the applicant under R.22.1(c) or (g) (Art.12(3); R.22.3). The IB will notify the applicant, rO and ISA if it has received the record copy after expiration of the 3 month period (R.24.2(c)).

The IB will notify the applicant, rO and ISA of the receipt of the record copy (R.24.2(a)).

5.6.2 *Communication of international application*

As a next step, the IB publishes the international application (Art.21, R.48).

The IB communicates a copy of the international application, the international search report, any claim amendments under Art.19 and a notification of the fact and date of receipt of the record copy and of any priority document to each designated Office upon their request and at the time specified by that Office (Art.20(1)(a); R.47.1(a), (a-*bis*), (b)). Under R.44*bis*, the IB converts the written opinion of the ISA into the IPRP (Chapter I); this report is also communicated to the designated Offices but not before expiration of 30 months from the priority date (R.44*bis*.2). The IB effects the communication by making the documents available in a digital library (R.47.1(a) and R.93*bis*.1).

The international application as communicated is in the language in which it is published (R.47.3(a)). If this language is different from the language of filing, a designated Office may request the IB to furnish a copy in the language of filing (R.47.3(b)). Each designated Office that requires so, will receive the international search report in the English translation of R.47.1(d). Any late amendment of the claims under Art.19 not included in the communication will be sent promptly to the designated Offices by the IB, whereupon the IB notifies the applicant accordingly (R.47.1(b)).

Under Art.13, any designated Office may ask the IB to transmit a copy of an international application prior to the communication under Art.20 (R.31.1(a)). At present (situation November 2018), no Office has asked for such early transmitted copies (AG-IP §9.029).

An applicant may, at any time, transmit, or ask the IB to transmit, a copy of the international application to any designated Office (Art.13(2)), subject to payment of a fee (R.31.1(b), for the amount see AG-IP Annex B2(IB)). The designated Office may use the copy for national processing, provided the applicant has expressly requested the Office to commence the national processing early under Art.23(2) or Art.40(2). Where the applicant requests a designated Office to commence national processing before the communication of the international application under Art.20, the IB will promptly send it to the Office upon request of the applicant or the Office (R.47.4).

Promptly after expiration of 28 months from the priority date, the IB sends a notice to the applicant indicating the designated Offices to which the communication has been effected and those which have not requested the communication (R.47.1(c); R.49.1(a-*bis*)). On receiving the notice, the applicant knows that he does not have to send a copy of the international application to any of the designated Offices indicated on the notice as having been sent the communication (AG-IP §9.028).

5.6.3 *End of Chapter I stage*

The publication and communication to the designated Offices forms the last part of in the international phase where an international authority is active, unless a demand for international preliminary examination has been filed (§6 below). Entry into the national phase before the designated Offices must be made in due time (§7).

5.6.4 *Third party observations*

It is possible for third parties to submit to the IB observations referring to prior art which they believe to be relevant to the question as to whether the invention claimed in an international application is novel and/or involves an inventive step. Third party observations can be made at any time from the date of publication of the international application until the expiration of 28 months from the priority date, provided that the application is not withdrawn or considered withdrawn. No fee is payable for the use of this service. (AG-IP 11.109-11.110)

All observations must be submitted through ePCT public services, either directly or through a link on the bibliographical data tab of the published international application. The use of the system requires a standard WIPO user account. Each observation must include at least one citation that refers to a document published before the international filing date, or a patent document having a priority date before the international filing date, together with a brief explanation of how each document is considered to be relevant to the questions of novelty and/or inventive step of the claimed invention. Observations should be submitted in a language of publication; copies of prior art documents may be in any language. (AG-IP 11.111, 11.113; Practical Advice in PCT Newsletter 07-08/2012)

Although the third party is required to identify himself to the IB when logging in to the WIPO user account, the party can indicate, when submitting an observation, that he would like the observation to be published anonymously, in which case the IB will not reveal any details about the third party to the public, the applicant, any International Authority or any designated Office. (AG-IP 11.112)

The applicant is permitted to respond to observations by third parties (although he/she is not required to do so) until 30 months from the priority date, either through the ePCT system, using the private services option, or by sending a letter to the IB. The applicant's response will also be promptly made available to International Authorities and for public inspection. (AG-IP 11.114)

Each observation will be reviewed by the IB to determine whether it is an observation on the questions of novelty and/or inventive step. If approved, the observation will promptly be notified to the applicant and any International Authorities which have not yet issued their report, as well as being made available to the public via PATENTSCOPE. The observations will also be transmitted to the designated Offices after the expiration of 30 months from the priority date. However, the designated Offices are not obliged to take them into account during national processing. (AG-IP 11.116-11.117)

There is no express provision in the PCT for filing third party observations. Information on the service can be found in Admin. Instr. Part 8.

6 International preliminary examination

The applicant may request that his international application be subject to an international preliminary examination (Art.31(1)) to formulate a non-binding opinion on whether the claimed invention appears to be novel, to involve an inventive step, and to be industrially applicable (Art.33(1)-(4)).

The international preliminary examination is governed by the provisions of Chapter II of the PCT, giving this phase the name 'Chapter II stage'. The examination is carried out by an International Preliminary Examining Authority (IPEA) (Art.32(1); R.59). Filing of a demand constitutes election of all designated states. The results of the international preliminary examination will be used in the national phase before the offices of all elected states, such offices being known as 'elected Offices' (R.53.7).

The results may subsequently speed up examination of the international application and the granting of a patent before an elected Office. A PCT contracting state may declare that it is not bound by the provisions of Chapter II (Art.64(1)). No state has done so and all PCT contracting states are bound by Chapter II.

The report drawn up by the IPEA is called the International Preliminary Examination Report in the PCT Articles, but has been renamed in the PCT Rules as the 'International Preliminary Report on Patentability (Chapter II of the PCT)' (IPRP Ch.II) (Art.35(1); R.70.15(b)). The renaming was carried out for aligning with the 'International Preliminary Report on Patentability (Chapter I of the PCT)' being the Written Opinion of the ISA in the situation where the applicant does not file a demand (R.44*bis*.1(b)).

Before 2002 the period for entry into the national phase was shorter if no demand was filed (20 months without demand, 30 months with demand). Demands were often filed merely to extend the period for entry into the national phase. In particular, the number of international preliminary examination reports has steadily decreased from approx. 81,000 in 2001 to approx. 15,000 in 2012 and has remained stable at that level.

6.1 DEMAND

The applicant must indicate his wish to subject his international application to international preliminary examination by filing a request, called a 'demand' (Art.31(1), R.53). An applicant who is a resident or national of a PCT contracting state may file a demand (Art.31(2)(a)). No use has been made of the provision of Art.31(2)(b) allowing exceptions to the residence/nationality requirement of Art.31(2)(a). The formal requirements for the demand are laid out in R.53 (see also AG-IP §10.012-10.034). The filing of a demand constitutes election of all contracting states which are designated and are bound by Chapter II (R.53.7; see §6.1.4). The demand may contain a statement concerning amendments (R.53.9; see §6.4). The demand is subject to the payment of fees (Art.31(5); see §6.1.2).

6.1.1 *Requirements*

Copies of printed demand forms are available free of charge from the rO, the IPEA (R.53.1(b)), and the WIPO website. The EPO permits electronic filing of the demand using the EPO Online Filing software, CMS and Web-Form Filing (OJ 2018 A45) and ePCT (OJ 2016 A78).

6.1.1.2 Applicant

A demand can only be filed validly by an applicant who is a resident or national of a contracting state bound by Chapter II (Art.31(2)(a); see also R.54.2 and R.54.3).

For a demand filed by several applicants, the name, address, nationality and residence of each applicant must be given (R.53.4), but it is sufficient if the address, nationality and residence are provided for one of the applicants who has the right to file a demand (R.60.1(a-*bis*)). A demand filed by several applicants should be signed by all applicants (R.53.8), but it is sufficient if the signature of only one of the applicants is provided (R.60.1(a-*ter*)).

6.1.1.3 Language

The demand must be filed in the language of the international application, or in the language of publication if the international application has been filed in a language other than the language in which it was published (R.55.1). Where the competent IPEA does not accept either of these languages, the applicant must file both the demand and a translation of the international application, including any elements or parts incorporated by reference (R.20.6(b)), in a language which is both a language accepted by the IPEA and a language of publication (R.55.2(a); R.55.2(a-*bis*)). If a translation of the international application in a publication language acceptable to the IPEA was transmitted to the ISA as search copy and the IPEA and ISA are part of the same Office, the applicant need not furnish a copy of the translation: the IPEA will use the search copy (R.55.2(b)). If the IPEA does not have a copy of the international application in an accepted language either from the applicant or the ISA, it will invite the applicant to furnish a translation within an extendable period of at least one month from the invitation (R.55.2(c)). Failure to supply the translation will result in the demand being considered not to have been submitted and the IPEA will so declare (R.55.2(d)).

6.1.1.4 Competent Authority

The demand must be filed separately from the application (Art.31(3)) with the competent IPEA (Art.31(6)(a), see §6.1.3). The competent IPEA(s) is determined by the rO (see AG-IP, Annex D). A demand filed with the rO, ISA, IB or a non-competent IPEA will be date-marked upon receipt (R.59.3(a),(b)) and forwarded to the IB, which in turn forwards it to the competent IPEA (R.59.3(a),(c)(i)). An office or Authority may forward a demand directly to the competent IPEA instead of to the IB (R.59.3(f)). The applicant will be notified of the transmittal to the competent IPEA (R.59.3(c)(i)). The IPEA will regard the date marked on the demand as the date of receipt (R.59.3(e)). Where two or more IPEAs are competent, the IB will invite the applicant to indicate the IPEA; if no indication is furnished in time, the demand will be considered not to have been submitted (R.59.3(c)(ii), (d)).

The demand may be filed with the IB using ePCT. The demand will be transmitted to the competent IPEA under R.59.3. (see Practical Advice in PCT Newsletter 01/2014)

6.1.1.5 Time limit for filing demand

The demand must be filed within the later of three months from transmittal to the applicant of the international search report, or the declaration of non-establishment of an ISR under Art.17(2)(a), and the written opinion of the ISA, or 22 months from the priority date (R.54*bis*.1(a)). A later filed demand will be regarded as not submitted (R.54*bis*.1(b)).

The time limit for filing a demand is not affected by the applicant filing a request for a supplementary international search (R.45*bis*). This means that the preparation of an IPRP Ch.II can evolve in parallel to a supplementary international search. Where the applicant files both a request for supplementary international search and a demand for international preliminary examination, and the IPEA and the SISA are not the same Authority, the IB will, promptly upon receipt of the supplementary international search report, transmit a copy of the supplementary international search report to the IPEA (AG-IP §8.052).

6.1.2 *Handling fee and preliminary examination fee*

The demand is subject to payment of fees (Art.31(5)). The applicant must pay for each demand a handling fee, which is an administrative fee for the benefit of the IB and collected by the competent IPEA (R.57.1). The amount of the handling fee is fixed in item 3 of the Schedule of Fees (R.57.2(a); R.96.1). The 'handling fee' should not be confused with the 'supplementary search handling fee' payable when the applicant files a supplementary international search request (R.45*bis*.2; see §4.9).

An IPEA may require payment of a preliminary examination fee for its own benefit for carrying out the examination (R.58.1(a)). The fee is payable directly to the competent IPEA (R.58.1(c)). The amount of the fee is fixed by each IPEA, as stated in AG-IP Annex E.

The handling fee may be reduced by 90% for applicants from developing countries (see Schedule of Fees 5; AG-IP Annex E). The EPO as IPEA provides a 75% reduction of the preliminary examination fee for nationals/residents of a state listed as a low-income or lower-middle-income economy by the World Bank (OJ 2008 p.521).

6.1.2.1 Time limit for payment of fees

The handling fee must be paid within one month from the date on which the demand was submitted or 22 months from the priority date, whichever expires later (R.57.3(a)). Where the demand was filed with a non-competent Office and transmitted to the competent IPEA under R.59.3 (see §6.1.1.3), the fees must be paid within one month from the date of receipt of the demand by the competent IPEA, or 22 months from the priority date, whichever expires later (R.57.3(b)). The preliminary examination fee must be paid within the same period (R.58.1(b)). The amounts payable are the amounts applicable on the date of payment (R.57.3(d)).

6.1.2.2 Failure to pay fees

If the handling fee or preliminary examination fee is not duly paid within the period of R.57.3, the IPEA invites the applicant to pay within one month from the date of the invitation (R.58*bis*.1(a)). An IPEA may charge a late payment fee, to be paid within the same period (R.58*bis*.1(a)). The EPO as IPEA levies such a late payment fee (OJ 1998 p.282; Euro-PCT Guide §355). A payment received before the IPEA sends the invitation is regarded as received within the period of R.57.3 (R.58.1(c)).

The amount of the late payment fee is 50% of the amount of the unpaid fees, with the proviso that it will be at least equal to the amount of the handling fee and not more than twice the amount of the handling fee (R.58*bis*.2).

Where the applicant has not paid the amount due, including any late payment fee, in full in due time, the IPEA will consider the demand as not having been submitted (R.58*bis*.1(b)). A payment received by the IPEA before it considers the demand as not having been submitted will be regarded as having been received within the one month period from invitation (R.58*bis*.1(d)).

When the demand is regarded as not having been submitted, there will be no valid elections and no IPRP Ch.II will be drawn up (see also §7.2).

6.1.2.3 Refund

The handling fee will be refunded if the demand is withdrawn before the IPEA has sent the demand to the IB, or if the demand is regarded as not having been submitted (R.57.4). An IPEA may refund the preliminary examination fee if the demand is considered not to have been submitted (R.58.3, see AG-IP Annex E for the conditions and the amount of refund for each IPEA).

6.1.3 Competent IPEA

The preliminary examination is carried out by the International Preliminary Examination Authority (IPEA) (Art.32(1)). Any national Office or intergovernmental organisation satisfying the requirements relating to manpower and documentation, can be appointed as IPEA by the Assembly upon conclusion of an Agreement between such Office or organization and the IB (Art.32(3), R.63). See AG-IP Annex E for the IPEAs, e.g. EP, JP, US.

Each rO has specified the IPEA or IPEAs that are competent to carry out the preliminary examination of an international application filed with it (Art.32(2); R.59.1(a)). The choice of the IPEA by the rO is often based on the presumed quality of the examinations of the IPEA or its language capabilities. Where the IB is the rO, the competent IPEA is the one which would have been competent had the application been filed with the rO which is the national office of, or acting for, a contracting state of which the applicant is a national or resident (R.59.1(b)). Where two or more IPEAs are competent, the choice is left to the applicant (R.59.1(a); see also §6.1.1.3). AG-IP Annex C gives the competent IPEAs for each rO, and Annex E states the languages accepted by each IPEA.

6.1.4 *Elections*

A demand constitutes the election of all contracting states (R.53.7). Hence, all states are elected automatically. Exclusions are not possible, but withdrawal of an election is possible (R.90*bis*.4).

If there are two or more applicants, possibly having designated different states (R.4.5(d)), the demand should indicate each applicant for each elected state (R.53.4 juncto R.4.5(a), R.60.1(a-*bis*)). Each of these applicants, their agents, or the common representative should sign the demand according to R.53.8 and R.90.3. However, if the signature(s) of one or more of the applicants is missing, the IPEA will not invite the applicants to furnish the missing signature(s), provided that at least one of the applicants has signed the demand (R.60.1(a-*ter*); AG-IP §10.031)

6.1.4.1 Withdrawal of the demand or an election

An applicant may withdraw the demand or any or all elections (Art.37(1)). If all elections are withdrawn, the demand is considered withdrawn (Art.37(2)) and the processing of the application by the IPEA is discontinued (R.90*bis*.6(c)). The notice of withdrawal must be filed with the IB (Art.37(3)(a); R.90*bis*.4(b)), which will notify the IPEA and the elected Offices concerned (Art.37(3)(b)). If the withdrawal is filed with the IPEA, the IPEA will datemark the withdrawal and forward it to the IB, which will consider the date marked as the date of receipt (R.90*bis*.4(c)). See §8.4 for the signature required on the withdrawal. The withdrawal must be made within 30 months from the priority date (R.90*bis*.4(a)). The withdrawal is free of charge (AG-IP §11.060). See §6.1.2.3 for refund of fees.

Withdrawal of the election of a state will be regarded as withdrawal of the international application for that state, unless the withdrawal is effected before expiry of the period of Art.22, according to Art.37(4). Since the period of Art.22 is also 30 months for most contracting states, the withdrawal of an election for a state will not have the effect of withdrawal of the application for that state.

6.1.5 *Defective demand*

If the demand does not contain the prescribed particulars, or is not in the prescribed language or form (Art.31(3); R.53; R.55.1), the IPEA will invite the applicant to correct the defects within an extendable period of at least one month from the date of the invitation (R.60.1(a)). When the defects are duly corrected, the demand or notice will be considered as received on the actual filing date (R.60.1(b)). If the defects are not duly corrected, the demand or notice will be considered as not having been submitted, and the IPEA will so declare (R.60.1(c)). A common defect is that the demand does not indicate all applicants for the elected states as required by R.53.4 juncto R.4.5(d) (see also R.60.1(a-*bis*)).

6.2 PRELIMINARY EXAMINATION AND REPORT

The objective of the preliminary examination is to formulate a preliminary, non-binding opinion on whether the invention is novel, contains an inventive step, and is industrially applicable (Art.33(1)). The definitions used for novelty, inventive step and industrial applicability (Art.33(2)-(4), R.64, and R.65) are almost identical to those of the EPC. These definitions are acceptable to all PCT states. A contracting state may in its national examination apply additional or different conditions for patentability (Art.33(5)). The major differences with the EPC are that the PCT does not recognize oral disclosures as prior art (R.64.2) and does not examine prior rights (R.64.3).

The international preliminary examination is based on the international application including any amendments as set out in §6.4. If the claims, description or drawings have been amended but the replacement sheets were not accompanied by a letter indicating the basis for the amendments (R.46.5(b)(iii)), international preliminary examination may proceed as if the amendments had not been made (R.70.2(c-*bis*)). Claims relating to inventions for which no international search report has been established need not be examined (R.66.1(e)). The examination need not extend to claims relating to an invention that does not form unity with the main invention and for which no examination fee or additional fee has been paid (Art.34(3)(c), R.68.2). Timely rectifications of obvious mistakes (see §8.5) will be taken into account by the IPEA (R.91.1; R.66.1(d-*bis*); R.66.4*bis*)).

As of 01.07.2014, the IPEA will conduct a top-up search to discover prior art which has been published or has become available to the IPEA for search after the date on which the international search report was established (R.66.1*ter*).The IPRP (Ch.II) will indicate the date on which the top-up search was made or state that no top-up search was made (R.70.2(f)).

The examiner may exclude the following subject-matter from the examination: unsearched subject-matter (Art.17(2)(a), R.39.1, see §4.2.2, R.66.1(e)), subject-matter in fields excluded from patentability (Art.34(4)(a)(i); R.67.1, similar to R.39.1), subject-matter for which no meaningful examination can be carried out because it is not supported by the description or because it is unclear (Art.34(4)(a)(ii)), unnecessary independent claims (Art.6 juncto Art.34(4)(a)(ii)). The exclusion will be mentioned in the opinion (Art.34(2)(c); R.66.2(a)(i) and (vi)) and, if not remedied, also in the report (Art.35(3); R.70.2(d); R.70.12(iii)).

The international preliminary report on patentability (IPRP Ch.II) (referred to as an international preliminary examination report in the PCT Articles - see §6) states whether the claims appear to satisfy the criteria of novelty, inventive step and industrial applicability, but does not contain any statements whether or not the claimed invention is or seems patentable according to national law (Art.35(2)). The report cites the documents believed to support the conclusions, possibly with explanations (Art.35(2)). The report will also indicate unsearchable subject-matter (Art.35(3)). Replacement sheets containing amendments and corrections of obvious mistakes which have been taken into account, and also those that have not been taken into account, in the international application will be annexed to the report (Art.36(1); R.70.2(e); R.70.16). The report is drawn up in the language in which the international application is published, or, where the examination is carried out on a translation furnished under R.55.2 (§6.1.1.2), in the language of the translation (R.70.17). Form requirements for the report are given in R.70.

According to Art.38, the IPRP Ch.II remains confidential in the international phase. However, the report may become publicly available through the elected offices (see §8.7), because R.94.3 provides that if national law applicable to an elected Office allows access by third parties to the file of a national application, then that Office may allow access to any documents relating to an international application (AG-IP §10.080; AG-IP §11.072-11.074; see §8.7). For the particular case of the EPO, see §8.7, A-XI,2.1(v) and E-IX,2.10.

6.3 PROCEDURE BEFORE IPEA

6.3.1 *Procedure*

On receipt of the demand, the IPEA notifies the IB and the applicant of this fact and the date of receipt (R.61.1(a),(b)). Subsequently, the IB notifies the elected Offices and the applicant of the elections (Art.31(7), R.61.2, 3), and publishes information about the demand and elections in the Gazette (R.61.4). The IB forwards a copy of any Art.19 amendments, statement under Art.19, and letter explaining the differences and basis for the amendments (R.46.5(b)) to the IPEA unless the IPEA indicates that is has already received such copies (R.62.1(ii)). The IB will also forward a copy of the written opinion of the ISA, and if required an English translation (R.62*bis*.1), except where the IPEA and the ISA are the same Authority (R.62.1(i)).

The IPEA starts the examination when it is in possession of the demand, the international search report or a declaration under Art.17(2)(a), and the written opinion of the ISA (Art.34(1), R.69.1(a)(iii)), and, if applicable, amendments to the application submitted by the applicant (R.69.1(d),(e); Art.19; R.62; see §6.4), the necessary fees have been paid (see §6.1.2.2; R.69.1(a)(ii)), and any defects in the demand have been corrected (AG-IP §10.051; see also §6.1.5), provided that, the period of R.54*bis*.1(a) has not expired (unless the applicant expressly requests an earlier start) (R.69.1(a)). R.69.1(a) will be amended with effect of 01.07.2019; under the amended rule the examination starts immediately unless the applicant expressly requests otherwise.

The IPEA may request the IB to furnish a copy of the priority application (R.66.7(a)). Where the priority application is not in a language accepted by the IPEA, the IPEA may request the applicant to furnish a translation (R.66.7(b)). Where the applicant has not submitted a copy of the priority application under R.17.1 or has not furnished its translation, the international preliminary examination report may be drawn up as if no priority had been claimed (R.66.7).

The written opinion established by the ISA will, in general, be regarded as the first written opinion of the IPEA (R.66.1*bis*(a)). If the applicant does not file amendments and/or arguments upon filing the demand, the IPEA immediately proceeds to issuing the IPRP Ch.II. The EPO is the only ISA which does not accept written opinions prepared by other ISAs (R.66.1*bis*(b)).

The EPO as IPEA will conduct a top-up search (see §6.2), unless it regards such a search as not useful. The EPO will focus on documents that may become relevant as Art.54(3) prior art after entry into the EP phase and prior art cited in national proceedings for the same application. The top-up search will be carried out only for inventions in the application for which the examination fee or an additional fee has been paid. If relevant prior art is found, even if only giving rise to objections under Art.54(3), the EPO as IPEA will issue a second written opinion or conduct a telephone consultation. If no relevant prior art is found and the applicant does not file a substantive response to the first written opinion of the IPEA, the EPO will not send a second written opinion but will directly issue the IPER. (OJ 2014 A57)

According to Art.34(2)(c) the applicant is entitled to receive at least one written opinion from the IPEA. As the written opinion of the ISA is regarded as the first written opinion of the IPEA (R.66.1*bis*(a)), the IPEA is, in principle, not obliged to issue a 'second' written opinion (R.66.2). Only few IPEAs issue a second written opinion; the EPO acting as IPEA issues such a second written opinion under certain conditions (see §6.6.3).

If the IPEA issues a written opinion pursuant to R.66.2, the reasons for the opinion must be fully stated (R.66.2(b)) and contain an invitation to the applicant to submit a written reply together, where appropriate, with amendments (R.66.2(c)) within an extendable period of between 1 and 3 months, set by the IPEA (R.66.2(d)). The period for submitting a reply will usually be two months, which may be extended if requested by the applicant before expiration of the period (R.66.2(d),(e)). The applicant may respond to a written opinion with a written reply containing arguments and/or amendments addressing the comments in the written opinion (R.66.3). Such amendments of the claims, description and any drawings, to which the applicant has the right to make according to Art.34(2)(b), should be made as set out in §6.4. The IPEA may issue an additional written opinion and the applicant then has an additional opportunity to furnish arguments or amendments (R.66.4), although in practice such cases are rare.

Amendments, arguments and requests for rectification of obvious mistakes need not be taken into account by the IPEA if received after the IPEA has begun to draw up a written opinion of the IPEA or the IPRP Ch.II (R.66.4*bis*; AG-IP §10.068). The applicant may communicate in writing and orally with the IPEA, for example through a telephone interview with the examiner (Art.34(2)(a), (d); R.66.3; R.66.6; AG-IP §10.067).

6.3.2 *Termination of the procedure*

The examination will be discontinued if the demand or all elections are withdrawn (R.90*bis*.4 and 6(c)).

The international preliminary examination report will be ready by (R.69.2):

i) 28 months from the priority date, or
ii) 6 months from the start of the examination under R.69.1, or
iii) 6 months from the date of receipt by the IPEA of the translation of the application under R.69.2 (see §6.1.1.2),

whichever of the three periods expires latest (there is no sanction if the report is established later). Under normal circumstances, the applicant receives the report at the latest two months before national processing at the elected Offices may start (AG-IP, §10.074).

The IPEA transmits the international preliminary report on patentability (Ch.II) with its annexes to the applicant and the IB (Art.36(1); R.71.1). An elected Office may require that the IPRP Ch.II is translated into English if not drawn up in a language accepted by it (Art.36(2)(a); R.72.1(a)). The IB will prepare the translation of the report (Art.36(2)(b)). Subsequently, the IB transmits the IPRP Ch.II, together with the translation as prescribed, and its annexes, in the original language to each elected Office (Art.36(3)(a)); R.73). The communication will be effected after 30 months from the priority date (R.73.2).

Where an elected Office requires a translation of the annexes, the applicant must prepare the translation and transmit it to the elected Office (Art.36(2)(b); (3)(b), R.74).

6.3.3 *Non-unity*

If the IPEA considers that the international application does not comply with the requirement of unity of invention, it may examine the entire application and note the non-unity, invite the applicant to restrict the claims according to a proposed restriction, or invite the applicant to pay additional fees for the examination of the further inventions (Art.34(3)(a); R.68). See §4.3.1 for the requirement of unity before the ISA. Where the IPEA decides not to send the invitation, it will examine all claims and indicate in any written opinion and in the IPRP Ch.II that it considers that the requirement of unity is not complied with and state the reasons therefor (R.68.1).

When the IPEA invites the applicant to restrict the claims or to pay additional fees for examination of the further inventions, the applicant must respond within a period of one month from the date of the invitation (R.68.2(iii)). Each IPEA determines the amount of the additional fee (R.68.3(a)), which is the same as the amount of the examination fee for the majority of IPEAs (see AG-IP Annex E). The examination will be extended to the claims for which the additional fees are paid, and the report will indicate that the additional fees have been paid.

The IPEA need not carry out international preliminary examination for inventions which were not searched by the ISA (R.66.1(e)).

Where the claims are not restricted at all, or insufficiently, or the additional fees are not paid, the IPEA will establish an IPRP Ch.II on the main invention, i.e. the invention first mentioned in the claims (Art.34(3)(c); R.68.4; R.68.5). Where the applicant restricts the claims, or where the IPEA examines only the main invention, the claims that were not chosen or examined may be considered withdrawn by a state unless a special fee is paid by the applicant to the national Office of that state (Art.34(3)(b), (c)).

The additional fee(s) may be paid under protest (R.68.3(c)). The ensuing protest procedure as set out in R.68.3(c)-(e) is similar to the non-unity procedure during the international search (see §4.3.2). The amount of the protest fee for each IPEA is stated in AG-IP Annex E. The protest procedure is the second case of 'appeal' possible in the international phase of the PCT.

See §6.6 for special provisions relating to non-unity before the EPO as IPEA.

6.4 AMENDMENTS

6.4.1 *Amendment of the application*

The international preliminary examination is based on the international application as filed including any amendments as indicated in the demand (R.66.1).

6.4.1.1 Amendment under Art.19

After receipt of the international search report, the applicant has the possibility to amend only the claims of the international application under Art.19, as described in §4.6. The demand must indicate whether an amendment under Art.19 is to be taken into account for the international preliminary examination or considered reversed by an amendment under Art.34 (R.53.9(a), R.66.1(c)).

When making amendments under Art.19, the applicant must submit replacement sheet(s) containing a complete set of claims. accompanied by a letter indicating the differences between the claims as filed and those as amended and the basis for the amendments in the application as filed (R.53.9(a)(i); R.46.5(b)(i)-(iii); AG-IP §9.005).

An amendment under Art.19 filed after the demand will only be taken into account if received before the IPEA begins to draw up its report (R.66.1(d); R.66.4*bis*). An IPEA will not start international preliminary examination before expiry of the applicable period of R.54*bis*.1, unless expressly requested to do so by the applicant (R.69.1(a)).

6.4.1.2 Amendment under Art.34

If a demand is filed, i.e. before the IPEA, the applicant has, under Art.34, a second opportunity to amend the claims and a first opportunity to amend the description and any drawings. The amendment, i.e. any change other than the rectification of obvious mistakes (R.66.5), may not go beyond the disclosure in the international application as filed (Art.34(2)(b); R.70.2(c)). Non-compliance will be reported (AG-IP §11.047). Amendments concerning the description or drawings should be presented in the form of individual replacement pages for any pages containing amendments and an accompanying letter indicating the differences between the replaced and replacement sheets, the basis for the amended sheets in the application as filed, and preferably the reasons for the amendments (R.66.8(a); AG-IP §10.071). Where the only amendment is the deletion of an entire sheet, a letter explaining the reasons for the amendment suffices (R.66.8(b)). If any amendments are made to the claims, replacement pages for the entire set of claims as originally filed or previously amended should be submitted (R.46.5(a)), along with a letter indicating the differences between the claims as filed and those as amended (R.46.5(b)(i)), which claims have been cancelled (R.46.5(b)(ii)), and the basis for the amendments in the application as filed (R.46.5(b)(iii)) (R.68.8(c)). If any claims are cancelled, no renumbering of the remaining claims is required. If the claims, description or drawings are amended but the basis for the amendments is not furnished, the IPRP Ch.II may be established as if the amendments had not been made (R.70.2(c-*bis*)).

The amendments must be in the language of publication (R.55.3(a)), but, where the international application is translated under R.55.2 into a language accepted by the IPEA, the amendments and letter (R.46.5(b); R.66.8) explaining the differences and basis for the amendments must be in that language (R.55.3(b)). If the amendments or letter are filed in a language other than the required language, the IPEA will ask for a translation in the required language, if practicable in view of the time pressure (R.55.3(c)). If the translation of the amendments is not duly supplied, the amendments will not be taken into account for the purpose of the international preliminary examination and if the translation of the letter is not duly supplied, the amendments need not be taken into account for the purpose of the international preliminary examination (R.55.3(d)).

The filing of amendments is free of charge (AG-IP §10.071). In order to be taken into account, amendments should be filed at the time of filing of the demand, or at least before the IPRP Ch.II is established (Art.34(2)(b); R.66.1(b), (d)). Amendments received later need not be taken into account (R.66.4*bis*).

If the applicant intends to file amendments, but is not in a position to submit them together with the demand, that intention should preferably be mentioned in a letter filed with the demand (AG-IP §10.028). In such situations, current practice of the EPO acting as IPEA is to, shortly after the demand is filed, invite the applicant to file the amendments within a period of 1 month.

6.4.2 Basis for international preliminary examination

The applicant may indicate in the demand on which text the IPEA should start the examination (see check box on the demand form). For the description and the drawings, an applicant may choose between the form in which they were originally filed or as amended under Art.34. He may choose between the claims as originally filed, as amended under Art.19 or as amended under Art.34. The applicant may indicate that any amendments made to the claims under Art.19 are to be considered reversed (R.53.9(a)(ii)).

6.5 REPRESENTATION

An applicant need not be represented by an agent before the IPEA, because Art.27(7) limits the application of national law as far as it relates to any requirement that the applicant be represented before rOs and designated Offices. However, an applicant may be represented before the IPEA by an agent.

An agent having the right to practise before the competent national Office with which the international application was filed, is also entitled to practise before the IPEA in respect of that application (Art.49, R.90.1(a)). Hence, an agent appointed for the Chapter I stage, may also act before the IPEA. The IPEA may require proof of the right to practise (R.83.1), which it may demand from the national Office before which the agent allegedly has the right to practise (R.83.2).

The agent may appoint a sub-agent to represent the applicant specifically before the IPEA, provided the person appointed as sub-agent has the right to practise before the national Office which acts as IPEA (R.90.1(d)(ii)). The applicant himself may appoint an agent to represent him specifically before the IPEA, provided the person appointed as agent has the right to practise before the national Office which acts as IPEA (R.90.1(c); see also §8.3).

6.6 EPO AS IPEA

6.6.1 Competence

The EPO will act as IPEA for applicants who are residents or nationals of an EPC contracting state bound by Chapter II (Art.152 EPC). The competence of the EPO to act as IPEA is based on the Agreement between the European Patent Organisation and the IB of the WIPO under Art.32(3) PCT (OJ 2017 A115; see above §4.8). The EPO will only act as IPEA for ISAs located in EPC contracting states in order to avoid the additional workload caused by the examination of international applications without an international search report made by the EPO or a closely co-operating office (OJ 2017 A115, Art.3(2), Annex A). Where the Spanish national Office has acted as ISA, the EPO as IPEA may require a translation of the international application into an official EPO language to be filed together with the demand (R.55.2(a)). An international application filed in Sweden can also be examined by the EPO on request, provided the application is in English.

The international preliminary examination by the EPO as IPEA is normally carried out by one examiner. See Euro-PCT Guide Ch.D.II for an overview of the procedural steps to be taken before the EPO as IPEA. Any correspondence of the EPO is in English, French or German, depending on the language in which the international application is filed or translated (Agreement between EPO and WIPO, Annex F, OJ 2017 A115).

6.6.2 Fees

The EPO has fixed the amount of the examination fee that may be levied by an IPEA under R.58.1(a) PCT in Rfees2(1)19 (see §6.1.2). Note that the EPC has no provision for the payment of the preliminary examination fee but only for the payment of additional examination fees in the case of non-unity in R.158(2) EPC. The EPO levies a late payment fee pursuant to R.58*bis*.2 PCT (OJ 1998 p.282; Euro-PCT Guide §355).

6.6.3 *Examination procedure*

The written opinion prepared by the EPO as ISA will be considered by the EPO as the first written opinion for the purposes of international preliminary examination (R.66.1*bis*(a)). The EPO has made use of R.66.1*bis*(b) so will not use a written opinion prepared by another ISA as the first written opinion for its international preliminary examination (see list of PCT Reservations, Declarations, Notifications and Incompatibilities on www.wipo.int/pct).

If the EPO has acted as ISA, the EPO as IPEA will consider the written opinion of the ISA as the first written opinion for the purposes of international preliminary examination (R.66.1*bis*). However, the written opinion of the ISA will not be reissued as a first written opinion of the EPO as IPEA. The EPO makes use of the option under R.66.2 to issue a written opinion of the IPEA. Before issuing a 'negative' IPRP Ch.II, the EPO as IPEA will, as a rule, issue a second written opinion thereby giving the applicant a further opportunity to file further amendments and/or arguments to overcome any objections raised in this written opinion. The procedure may be different and a second written opinion may not necessarily be issued if a request for consultation by telephone is filed by the applicant. (OJ 2011 p.532; R.66.4; Euro-PCT Guide §376)

The EPO will assess the allowability of amendments for international applications in the same way as for European applications under Art.123(2) (Euro-PCT Guide, §364).

A request for a telephone consultation before the EPO, preferably filed together with the demand, will usually be granted. The EPO intends to allow applicants an additional round of amendment/argumentation either via a second written opinion or a telephone consultation, not both. Therefore, if a telephone consultation is requested before issuance of a second written opinion, then a second written opinion will not be issued and the applicant can respond to written minutes of the telephone consultation. If a telephone consultation is requested after issuance of a second written opinion, but before the IPRP is established, then the applicant will not be allowed to respond to the minutes of the telephone consultation, unless agreed upon during the telephone consultation. (R.66.6; OJ 2011 p.532, §5; Euro-PCT Guide §389-392).

6.6.4 *Non-unity procedure*

In the case of a non-unity finding by the IPEA, there are two possible ways to proceed.

The first possibility is that the IPEA will examine the entire application, but will indicate the alleged lack of unity in its written opinion and the IPRP (Art.34(3)(a); R.68.1).

The second possibility is that the IPEA will invite the applicant to restrict the claims or to pay an additional fee for each further invention (Art.34(3)(a); R.68.2). The additional fee for the EPO is equal to the preliminary examination fee (R.68.3(a); R.158(2) EPC; Rfees2(1)19).

The additional fee may be paid under protest (R.68.3(c) PCT), resulting in an internal review, similar to the non-unity procedure during the international search (R.68(c)-(e); R.158(3) EPC; see also §4.8 above). The protest fee payable to the EPO as IPEA under R.68.3(e) is fixed in Rfees2(1)21. Protests are examined in accordance with R.68.3(c-e) (see §4.3.2 and §6.3.3). Further details of the protest procedure may be determined by the President of the EPO (R.158(3) EPC). (OJ 2010 p.320; OJ 2010 p. 322)

6.6.5 *Not searched subject-matter procedure*

If a demand is filed, the EPO acting as IPEA need not conduct international preliminary examination on unsearched claims (R.66.1(e); C-III,3; F-V,13.1), see §4.8.

In the case of a declaration of non-establishment of an ISR by the ISA (see §4.2.2), the claims will not have been searched by the ISA. If a demand is filed, the IPEA need not conduct international preliminary examination on such unsearched claims (R.66.1(e)) and it is unclear how an applicant may proceed, if at all, in order to pursue examination of such claims in the international phase. The current policy of the EPO when acting as IPEA in such situations appears to be *normally* not to carry out international preliminary examination on subject matter which has not been searched. This is the case even if the claims are amended following receipt of the international search report or during any Chapter II procedure.

6.6.6 *Representation*

In procedures before the EPO as IPEA an attorney, patent agent or any other person having the right to practise before the rO with which the international application was filed, is entitled to practise (Art.49). The applicant may appoint a European patent attorney to represent him specifically before the EPO acting as IPEA (R.90.1(b), (c)).

7 Entry into the national phase

The international phase of the application is followed by the national phase, in which the international application is processed under national law before each designated Office in order to grant a patent for the invention. The entry into the national phase requires the applicant to carry out certain acts before each designated Office, which acts are governed by the provisions of both the PCT and national law. The following paragraphs outline the PCT provisions and indicate where national law may prescribe the procedure. The procedure for entry into the regional phase before the EPO as a designated or elected Office is set out in §7.4.

The requirements for entering the national phase before a designated Office and an elected Office are similar. Where in the following the same requirement is applicable before both Offices, the reference to the PCT first mentions the provision applicable to the designated Office, followed by the provision applicable to the elected Office between square brackets, e.g. Art.22 [Art.39]. If not stated to the contrary, 'designated Office' should be read in the following paragraphs as 'designated or elected Office'.

7.1 START OF NATIONAL PHASE

The PCT sets a time limit for entry into the national phase before a designated Office. The applicant may enter the national phase at any time before the expiry of the period, either voluntarily or involuntary. The latter case arises where the processing of the international application has been interrupted prematurely, e.g. because the application is considered withdrawn, in which case the applicant must enter the national phase early by using the special review and excuse procedure as described in §7.6 in order to safeguard his rights. A national Office may not process an international application before the expiration of the period for entry into the national phase (the processing prohibition of Art.23(1), [Art.40(1)]), except when an applicant expressly requests a national Office to start processing his application early (Art.23(2) [Art.40(2)]).

Where an applicant voluntarily withdraws the designation of a contracting state under R.90*bis*.2 before the expiration of the period for entry into the national phase, that Office is no longer a designated Office (Art.24(1)(i), (ii)). See §6.1.4.1 for the effect of the withdrawal of an election.

The national phase before a designated or elected Office must be entered before the expiry of 30 months from the priority date (Art.22(1) [Art.39(1)(a)]). National law may fix a period expiring later than the 30 months (Art.22(3); R.50 [Art.39(1)(b); R.77]). Several states, including the EPO, have extended the period to 31 months from the priority date or even up to 42 months for Canada (for each designated state, see AG-NP).

A number of national Offices do not yet apply the 30-month period for entering the national phase under Chapter I (i.e. without demand) as fixed in PCT Art.22(1); at present (November 2018), only 2 States: Luxembourg (LU), 20 months and Tanzania (TZ), 21 months. Note, however, that an applicant can use the EPO for LUand the ARIPO for TZ, which regional offices both apply a period of 31 months; furthermore the period is 30 months for LU and 31 months for TZ under Chapter II, i.e. if a demand is filed (Art.39(1)(a)).

A list of periods applicable for each designated/elected Office for entering the national phase under Chapters I and II of the PCT is available at: www.wipo.int/pct.

7.2 ACTS FOR ENTRY INTO NATIONAL PHASE

Entry into the national phase before an Office of or acting for a state requires the applicant to carry out the acts set out in Art.22 [Art.39(1)] if not already completed and any acts required by national law. Shortly before the end of the international phase, the IB notifies the applicant of the designated and elected states (R.47.1(c) [R.61.3]), which should act as a reminder of the acts to be carried out for entering the national phase. The acts to be carried out by the applicant are described in the following sections. See AG-IP §5.099-5.104 for the furnishing of sequence listings. Some designated Offices, e.g. the EPO, remind the applicant before the expiry of the period for entering the national phase. (see AG-NP §3.003)

Failure to comply with the requirements of Art.22 [Art.39(1)] in due time will cause the international application no longer to have the effect of a regular national application with the same consequences as the withdrawal of a national application in that state (Art.24(1)(iii) [Art.39(2)]). The designated Office may invite the applicant to remedy the failure using any available national provisions (Art.24(2) [Art.39(3)]); see e.g. R.160 EPC.

7.2.1 *Start of national phase processing*

The national phase before a designated Office may start with or without an explicit request. Some Offices, e.g. the EPO, regard the notification of its designation or election by the IB under R.47.1 [R.61.2] and the receipt of a copy of the international application sent by the IB under Art.20(1) as sufficient basis to start the national phase immediately after expiry of the period of Art.22 [Art.39(1)] without a request by the applicant.

7.2.2 *Form for national phase entry*

Most Offices provide a special form (free of charge) for entry into the national phase before that Office. Offices that do not start the national phase automatically may include in the form an opportunity to request a start of processing. The form typically includes a check list for the acts to be performed and its use is recommended, but never compulsory (R.49.4 [R.76.5]). The EPO provides Form 1200, the use of which is not obligatory.

7.2.3 *Kinds of protection*

The request form of international applications indicates by default that all kinds of protection available are desired (R.4.9(a)(ii)). Upon entry into the national phase, the applicant must indicate for each designated state which kind(s) of protection he desires if this is different from a patent (R.49*bis*.1(a), (b) [R.76.5]). This indication is also required for protection in the form of a continuation or continuation-in-part of an earlier application (R.49*bis*.1(d) [R.76.5]). If, upon filing an international application, an applicant intends to make an indication under R.49*bis*.1(a), the request must indicate such upon filing the application (R.4.11).

7.2.4 *Copy of the international application*

According to Art.20(1)(a), a copy of the international application is communicated to each designated Office by the IB (R.47.1(a)) promptly after the expiration of 28 months from the priority date (AG-IP §9.028). Any amendments of the claims under Art.19 and the brief statement (Art.19(1); R.46.4) explaining the amendments are regarded as part of the international application for the purpose of Art.22 (R.49.3) and are also transmitted to each designated Office together with the international application under Art.20(2). The IB also transmits the search report with any prescribed translations together with the international application to each designated Office (Art.20(1)(b); see §5.5.2). For international applications in respect of which no demand has been filed, the IB will additionally communicate to the designated offices the IPRP Ch.I, which has the same contents as the written opinion established by the ISA (R.44*bis*.1(a)).

Where an international preliminary examination has been carried out, the IB transmits the IPRP Ch.II, together with any translation as prescribed, with its annexes in the original language, to each elected Office (Art.36(3)(a)). The annexes include replacement sheets showing corrections and amendments under Art.19 and/or Art.34 and any letters (R.46.5(b); R.66.8(a),(b)) explaining such (R.70.16). Amendments under Art.19 considered reversed by amendments under Art.34 are not annexed unless the IPEA considers that the relevant amendment goes beyond the disclosure of the international application as filed (R.70.16).

According to Art.22(1) [Art.39(1)(a)], the applicant must furnish a copy of the international application, unless already provided by the IB (Art.20; R.47.1(a)), within the period for entering the national phase. Under normal circumstances, no designated Office requires a copy of the international application to be submitted by the applicant (AG-NP, §4.027). Most states require the IB to communicate the international application under Art.20; R.47.1(a). When this communication has not, or could not yet have, taken place, the Office of a state has two options. The first option, applied by the Offices of a few states (e.g. US), is to request the applicant to provide a copy only if he has not been notified by the IB under R.47.1(c) that the copy was transmitted to the designated Offices (see §5.5.2). This happens often when entering the national phase early. The second option, applied by most Offices (including the EPO), is to use the exception to Art.22(1) [Art.39(1)(a)] as provided in R.49.1(a-*bis*) [R.76.5] and never request the applicant to furnish a copy of the international application; instead the IB will provide the copy (R.93*bis*.1(a)). The Offices of some states (e.g. DK, FI, JP, NO, SE) request the applicant to provide a copy of the international application only where it was filed in the official language of that state.

7.2.5 Translation of the international application

A designated or elected Office may require a translation of the international application if the language in which it was filed or published is not a language accepted by the Office (Art.22(1); AG-NP §4.008; R.49.2 [R.76.5]). AG-NP indicates the accepted languages for each designated or elected Office. Where more than one language is accepted, the applicant may choose the language of the translation (R.49.2 [R.76.5]). The translation must be furnished as prescribed by R.49.2 [R.76.5] within the period for entering the national phase (Art.22(1) [Art.39(1)(a)]).

The translation must contain the description, the claims, any text matter in the drawings and the abstract (R.49.5(a) [R.76.5]; AG-NP §4.014)). If the claims are amended under Art.19, a designated or elected Office may also require a translation of both the claims as filed and as amended (for the complete set of claims) and the request (R.49.5(a), (b) [R.76.5]). The statement explaining amendments under Art.19 should also be translated; any Office may disregard the statement if not translated (R.49.3; R.49.5(c) [R.76.5]). Where an IPRP Ch.II has been established, a translation of an amendment under Art.19 will only be required if that amendment is annexed to the report (R.76.5(iv)).

An elected Office may require the applicant to translate any replacement sheet annexed to the report and transmit it to the elected Office (R.74.1).

The content of the translation as required by each designated Office is indicated in the AG-NP. The physical requirements for the translation are stated in R.49.5 [R.76.5]). National law may determine the number of copies to be furnished of any translation (R.51*bis*.1(c), [R.76.5]) and the certification or verification of the translations (R.51*bis*.1(d), 2(b) [R.76.5]). All designated Offices allow correction of translation errors (AG-NP §6.002). Where a translation error has caused the scope of a granted patent to exceed the scope of the international application in its original language, the Office concerned may retroactively limit the scope of the patent (Art.46).

7.2.6 Payment of fees

The applicant must pay any national fee to each designated Office within the period for entering the national phase (Art.22(1); R.49.1(a)(ii) [Art.39(1)(a); R.76.5]). The national fee comprises in general several fees, the number of which being commensurate to the size of the Office. The amount of the national fee and any reductions are indicated in AG-NP for each designated Office.

7.2.7 Naming of inventor

Where national law requires the indication of the name and address of the inventor(s), but allows them to be furnished after the filing of the international application, the applicant must furnish the data upon entering the national phase (Art.22(1) [Art.39(1)(a) + AG-NP §5.001]). See AG-NP §4.001(iv) and 4.030-4.031.

7.2.8 Priority Documents

A certified copy of the priority document must be filed in the international phase with the rO or the IB for each valid priority claim (see §2.10.1). The IB will forward copies of the priority document to each designated Office at its request; a designated Office may not require an applicant who has duly filed a copy of the priority document in the international phase to furnish such a copy (R.17.2(a)).

A designated Office may only request the applicant to furnish a translation of the priority document after expiration of the period of Art.22 (R.17.2(a)) [Art.39(1) (R.76.4)]. See AG-NP for the requirement of each designated Office to translate the priority document. Such a translation may be requested only where the validity of the priority claim is relevant for the patentability of the invention (R.51*bis*.1(e)(i)), or where the international filing data has been accorded on the basis of an incorporation by reference (R.51*bis*.1(e)(ii)).

7.2.9 *Amendment and correction before the designated Office*

Any designated Office must give the applicant at least one opportunity to amend the description, claims and drawings in accordance with national law and within a period set by the national office (Art.28(1), (3) [Art.41(1), (3)]). The period is at least one month after entry into the national phase; for a designated Office it may be later, dependent on the time of transmittal of the international application under Art.20 by the IB (R.52) and, for an elected Office it may be later, dependent on the time of transmittal of the international preliminary report on patentability under Art.36 (R.78). The national law of a designated or elected state may provide more extended periods for amendment (R.52.1(b) [R.78.1(b)]).

The amendments may be different for the various designated Offices, but may not go beyond the disclosure in the international application as filed, unless the national law of the designated state permits them to go beyond the said disclosure (Art.28(2) [Art.41(2)]). The correction of an obvious mistake according to R.91 may be presented as an amendment under Art.28 [Art.41], even if the authorisation of rectification has been refused during the international phase and the applicant has made a request for publication of the request for correction under R.91.3(d) (AG-NP §6.014-6.017).

7.2.10 *Representation*

Once processing of an international application has started in a designated Office, the Office may apply national law for any requirement that the applicant be represented by an agent having the right to represent applicants before the Office and/or that the applicant have an address in the designated state for receiving notifications (Art.27(7); R.51*bis*.1(b) [R.76.5]). Since a national office cannot start processing before expiry of the period for national entry (Art.23(1)), acts carried out before any designated Office before the expiry do not require an agent. (see e.g. Euro-PCT Guide §466)

7.3 PROCEDURE BEFORE THE DESIGNATED OR ELECTED OFFICE

Each designated and elected Office, not being a registration office and for which the examination is split into search and substantive examination stages, will start the processing of the application with a search. If the international search report is deemed sufficient, there will be no further search. If the report is deemed insufficient, there will be a supplementary search. Subsequently, the designated Office will fully examine the application, which may result in the grant of a patent. The designated Office will also use the IPRP Ch.I as prepared by the ISA. An elected Office will examine the application using the IPRP Ch.II as prepared by the IPEA as a basis, thereby reducing the cost and duration of the examination. An elected Office may not require that the applicant furnish papers connected with the examination of the same international application in any other elected Office (Art.42).

7.4 EPO AS DESIGNATED OR ELECTED OFFICE

The EPO will act as a designated Office within the meaning of Art.2(xiii) PCT for those states for which both the EPC and the PCT is in force and which have been validly designated in the international application for a European patent (Art.153(1)(a) EPC; Preamble to the EPC). The EPO will act as an elected Office within the meaning of Art.2(xiv) PCT if the applicant has elected any of the said states which are bound by Chapter II (Art.153(1)(b) EPC). All EPC contracting states are PCT contracting states and all PCT contracting states are bound by PCT Chapter II.

An international application for which the EPO is a designated or elected Office and which has been accorded an international date of filing, is equivalent to a regular European application and is called a Euro-PCT application (Art.11(4) PCT; Art.153(2) EPC). A Euro-PCT application will be treated as a European prior right if the requirements for publication in Art.153(3) and (4) have been complied with and the filing fee has been paid (Art.153(5) and R.165 EPC). A translation must also be filed if the Euro-PCT application is not (published in the international phase) in English, French or German. The procedure and requirements to which the EPO as designated or elected Office subjects the international application are governed by the EPC, except where the PCT provides otherwise (Art.150(2) EPC; Art.27 PCT).

7.4.1 *Entry into the regional phase before the* EPO

A review of important procedural steps before the EPO as designated Office and as elected Office is given in Euro-PCT Guide Ch.E.

The EPC has made use of the facility of Art.22(3) [Art.39(1)(b)] and has fixed in R.159(1) EPC the period for entering the regional phase before the EPO to 31 months from priority, both where Art.22 applies (i.e. the EPO acts as designated office) and where Art.39(1)(a) applies (i.e. the EPO has been validly elected). The 31-month period is an EPC period and should therefore be calculated according to R.131(4) EPC.

The applicant must perform the following acts to enter the regional phase before the EPO, preferably using the Form 1200 for entry into the regional phase provided by the EPO (see notes to R.159 EPC):

1 supply, where applicable, a translation of the international application (R.159(1)(a) EPC);
2 indicate the documents to be used for the grant procedure (R.159(1)(b) EPC);
3 pay the filing fee including, where applicable, the additional fee if the international application comprises more than 35 pages (R.159(1)(c); Rfees2(1)1a);
4 pay the designation fee if the period of R.39 EPC has already expired (R.159(1)(d) EPC);
5 pay the search fee in respect of the supplementary European search if required (R.159(1)(e) EPC);
6 pay, where applicable, the claims fees (R.162(1) EPC);
7 file the request for examination if the period of R.70(1) EPC has already expired (R.159(1)(f) EPC);
8 pay any renewal fee already fallen due (R.159(1)(g) EPC);
9 file, where applicable, the certificate of exhibition (R.159(1)(h) EPC);
10 provide the data concerning the inventor, if not yet submitted (R.163(1) EPC);
11 where priority is claimed, furnish the number and copy of the priority application, if not yet submitted (R.163(2) EPC);
12 where applicable, file a sequence listing conforming to the prescribed standard, if not yet submitted (R.163(3) EPC);

13 provide indications of address, nationality or residence of principal place of business of applicant, if not already provided (R.163(4) EPC);
14 appoint a professional representative if required under Art.133(2) (R.163(5) EPC);

If the requirements of items 1, 3, 4, 5 or 7 in the above list are not performed in due time (within 31 months), the Euro-PCT application is deemed to be withdrawn (R.160(1) EPC). If the requirements of items 10, 13 or 14 in the above list are not corrected in due time, the European patent application will be refused. If the deficiency of item 11 in the above list is not corrected in due time, the right of priority will be lost for the European patent application. (R.163(6); see notes to R.163(6) for possible remedies).

The EPO is prohibited from starting the processing of an international application before expiry of the 31-month period unless expressly requested to do so by the applicant (Art.23(1) and (2); Art.40(1) and (2) PCT). A request for early processing may be filed with the EPO at any time before expiry of the 31-month period. For the request to be effective the applicant must comply with the requirements stipulated in Rule 159(1) EPC as if the 31-month time limit expired on the date the applicant requests early processing. This means that (at least) items 1, 2, 3, and 5 of the above list must be complied with. It depends on the date on which early processing is requested which further requirements of Rule 159(1) EPC must be complied with, since the (regular) periods for paying the designation fee (R.39(1) EPC), the renewal fee (R.51(1) EPC) and for filing the request for examination and paying the examination fee (R.70(1) EPC) may not have expired on the date the request for early processing is filed. See Not. EPO, OJ 2013 p.156, E-IX,2.8 and R.159:3 EPC.

Entry into the European phase may be carried out in writing and by using the epoline software for electronic filing. The EPO provides a Form 1200, the use of which is recommended but not obligatory. (R.49.4 PCT; R.2 EPC; OJ 2018 A45)

The EPO has not waived the communication of the international application from the IB to the EPO under Art.20(1)(a), R.47.1. Therefore, the IB will communicate a copy of the international application to the EPO as designated or elected Office. The applicant need not furnish the copy mentioned in Art.22(1) (R.49.1(a-*bis*), [R.76.5], E-IX,2.7).

The EPO has made use of the facility of Art.27(7), R.51*bis*.1(b) PCT. Hence, if not already complied with upon entry into the regional phase before the EPO, the EPO will invite applicants having residence and principal place of business outside the territory of an EPC contracting state to appoint a representative entitled to practise before the EPO (Art.133(2) EPC via Art.150(2) EPC; R.163(5) EPC).

Where the EPO has acted as ISA, the search examiner will subsequently also be the primary examiner of the examining division in the regional phase before the EPO. Hence, a positive IPRP often causes the European patent to be granted before you can say 'Jack Robinson' (AG-IP §10.083).

The EPO withdrew all but one (R.66.1*bis*(b)) of its reservations under the PCT when the EPC 2000 entered into force (13.12.2007), including the reservation under PCT R.49.6. The latter withdrawal leads to a somewhat strange situation in that reinstatement (= re-establishment) of rights may be requested for payment of the filing fee and filing of a translation of the international application (Rfees2(1)13 referring to PCT R.49.6(d)(i)). This does not concord with R.136(3) EPC where re-establishment for this act for European regional phase entry is ruled out because further processing for this act is available (R.160(2) EPC). This is an example in the sense of Art.150(2) EPC, last sentence, that the provisions of the PCT (R.49.6) prevail over those of the EPC (R.136(3)).

7.5 LOSS OF EFFECT IN DESIGNATED STATE

The acts to be performed upon entering the national phase before a designated Office are specified in Art.22(1) [Art.39(1)(a)] and relate to the payment of fees and the furnishing of a translation of the international application, if prescribed by the designated Office. In exceptional cases, the name and address of the inventor must be furnished if not yet provided, and a copy of the international application must be furnished. All other acts to be carried out upon entry into the national phase may be performed within a period after entry into the national phase.

If an applicant does not perform the acts required for entry into the national phase before a designated Office in due time, the international application will lose the effect of a national application in respect of that Office (Art.24(1)(iii) [Art.39(2)]). Non-performance of the required acts will terminate the procedure before that Office. The termination will not affect the procedure before other designated Offices before which the national phase has been entered correctly. A designated Office may not reject an international application on the grounds of non-compliance with the requirements of the PCT without first giving the applicant an opportunity to correct the application to the extent and according to the procedure provided by national law (Art.26). The correction possibilities for the different acts upon entering the regional phase before the EPO are set out in the notes to R.159 to R.163 EPC.

Where an entry into the national phase before a designated Office has failed because the international application or the designation is deemed withdrawn in the international phase (Art.24(1)(ii)), the applicant may ask that Office to maintain the effect of the international application and to excuse the delay (Art.24(1)(iii) and Art.24(2)). The review and excuse procedure is set out in §7.6.

7.6 REVIEW AND EXCUSE PROCEDURE

The international phase of an international application may be terminated if the international application is regarded as withdrawn, is refused or has not entered the national phase in due time. The international authorities lose their competence to continue processing of the application and the procedures in Art.22 and Art.39 for entry into the national phase of a 'pending' international application are no longer applicable. There are no means of redress or appeal in the international phase, on the one hand because there is no time for it in the tight PCT schedule, and on the other hand because the different states could not agree on one system for it (J20/89, J15/91).

However, the PCT contains provisions that a loss of rights incurred by the applicant in the international phase may be remedied in the national phase before each of the designated Offices in which the applicant wishes his rights to be maintained. The remedy is available for both an erroneous determination, i.e. where the loss of rights was not justified under the provisions of the PCT, and a correct determination, for example a loss of rights due to a failed period. To avail himself of the remedy, the applicant must terminate the international phase early by entering the national phase before the desired Offices immediately after the loss of rights has occurred. The Offices will review whether the decision causing the loss of rights was justified or apply a remedy applicable under its national law. The early national entry deprives the applicant of his right to postpone payment of the national fees and filing of the translation until 30 months from priority.

7.6.1 *Erroneous determinations*

The first type of negative determinations of an international Office are erroneous determinations of the rO or the IB, refusing the application or regarding the application as withdrawn. The applicant may remedy the loss of rights by entering the national phase before the designated Office according to Art.25(1) and (2) within 2 months from despatch of the notification of loss of rights (R.51.1). The designated Office reviews the negative determination and, if the determination is due to an error or omission of the rO or the IB, the designated Office will treat the international application as if the error or omission had not occurred.

The following cases are liable to a review:

- The rO does not accord an international filing date, because the international application does not meet the requirements of Art.11(1), and the applicant has not duly corrected them after an invitation to do so (Art.11(2)(a), R.20.4). The negative decision with reasons is sent to the applicant and the IB (R.20.4(i-ii)).
- The rO considers the international application withdrawn because certain defects have been found in the application (Art.14(1)(a)) and the applicant has not duly corrected them after an invitation (Art.14(1)(b)), or because certain fees (Art.3(4)(iv) and Art.4(2)) have not been paid in time (Art.14(3)), or because it has discovered that an international filing date has been accorded in spite of non-compliance with one of the requirements of Art.11(1) (Art.14(4); R.27.1; R.29.1).
- The IB considers the application withdrawn because it has not received the record copy of the application in time (Art.12(3); R.22.3, R.24.2(c)). R.22 gives the applicant the opportunity to send a copy of the application to the IB in the case the rO is slow in transmitting such; this makes the IB considering the application withdrawn a mainly theoretical issue.

7.6.2 *Correct determinations*

The second type of negative determinations are correct determinations of an international Office, refusing the application or regarding the application as withdrawn. These determinations are often due to an error of the applicant, such as failure to meet a PCT time limit. A designated Office may remedy such losses under Art.24(2), and, where the loss relates to not-observed time limits, Art.48(2)(a) even obliges a designated Office to excuse any delay in meeting a time limit for reasons admitted under its national law in the same or comparable situations. R.82*bis*.1 mentions time limits fixed in the PCT and fixed by an Office as liable to excusal. In particular, R.82*bis*.2 mentions 'further processing' and 'restitutio in integrum' (i.e. re-establishment of rights) as means of excuse under national law. EP and US have such national means of redress, JP has none.

R.49.6 obliges all states to apply on request reinstatement of rights for failure to meet the time limit of Art.22 and Art.39 (also see Art.3(1)(b)(i) PLT). Several states, including CA, CN, DE, IN and KR, have declared that R.49.6 is at present (November 2018) incompatible with their national law.

Although Art.24(2) is a basis for carrying out the obligation stemming from Art.48(2)(a), it does not contain provisions on how to enter the national phase. A generally accepted solution is to regard Art.24(2) as a sub-category of Art.25(2), which sub-category relates to a negative determination which is not the result of an error or omission of an international Office. The procedural requirements for the second case are now the same as for the first case of the review: entry into the national phase under Art.25(1) and (2) within the time limit of R.51.

7.6.3 Procedure before national Office

To remedy a loss of rights which occurred in the international phase, the applicant must enter the national or regional phase for each designated Office before which he wishes to continue prosecution of the application. Thereto, the applicant must request the IB to send copies of the documents in the file which are necessary for reviewing the determination, to any one of the designated Offices named by the applicant (Art.25(1)(a)). The requests must be filed within 2 months of the date of the negative determination (Art.25(1)(c) and R.51.1), i.e. not the date of the receipt of the determination (see R.80.6) (note, no 10 days according to R.126(2) EPC are given if entry is sought before the EPO). Within the same 2 months (R.51.3) the applicant must enter the national or regional phase by paying the national fee (Art.25(2)(a)) and providing a translation as prescribed. The applicant must request the designated Office to review the negative determination (AG-NP, §6.026). If the applicant wants the designated Office to start processing his application immediately after a positive decision on the remedy and not wait until expiry of 30 months from priority, he must make an express request according to Art.23(2) [Art.40(2)] to the national Offices.

The review of a correct determination of a failure to meet a PCT time limit will in general result in a decision confirming the loss of rights. Nevertheless, the designated Office must, according to Art.48(2)(a), excuse the delay in meeting a time limit for reasons admitted under its national law. A designated Office may excuse the delay for other reasons (Art.48(2)(b)). In such cases, the applicant should request the designated Office not only to review the determination but also to excuse the delay (AG-NP, §6.026).

7.6.4 Decision by the EPO as designated Office on an erroneous determination

If the examining division of the EPO decides that the loss of rights was not justified under the PCT and was due to an error or omission of the rO or the IB, it must treat the application as if the error or omission had not occurred (Art.25(2)(a)). The application will be regarded as a valid European application for the states for which the EPO acts as designated Office. If the examining division (R.159(2) EPC) decides that the contested determination was correct, the application will remain ineffective. Such a decision can be appealed according to Art.106(1) EPC. (Euro-PCT Guide §654)

7.6.5 Decision by the EPO as designated Office on a correct determination

The EPO is bound by the equal treatment command of Art.48(2)(a) to excuse failures under the PCT in a way similar to failures under the EPC. The EPO will therefore excuse delays incurred in the international phase if a corresponding delay in respect of a European patent application can be remedied, e.g. using further processing or re-establishment under Article 24(2). If the EPO excuses the delay, it will deal with the international application as a valid Euro-PCT application. If the EPO does not accept the remedy, the applicant may appeal the decision. (Euro-PCT Guide §654)

Further processing under Art.121 EPC should be available to remdy a failure to meet the 2-month period of R.51.1 PCT (and other non-excluded periods set in the PCT), instead of the unreliable re-establishment of rights provisions (Art.122 EPC). Therefore, if a failed period has been fixed in the PCT or by an international Office (R.82*bis*.1(i, ii)), the applicant should request further processing before the EPO (Art.121 EPC) to retract the legal consequences of the failure. He must file with the EPO the request under Article 24(2), pay the fee for further processing and complete the omitted act within two months from the date of the communication informing the applicant of the withdrawal of the international application. The start of the two-month period is determined by R.80.6 PCT and the end may be extended according to R.134 EPC, but there are no 10 days according to R.126(2) EPC.

The periods for filing the request under Art.121; R.135(1) EPC and R.51.1 PCT are amenable to an excuse under Art.48(2)(a) PCT using re-establishment of rights. If an applicant only actually becomes aware of the withdrawal after expiry of the two-month period, he must then apply for re-establishment of rights within the R.136 EPC period. Art.48(2)(a) PCT excludes restitutio in cases similar to the ones excluded for re-establishment in Art.122(4) and R.136(3) EPC.

8 General procedural matters

8.1 CORRESPONDENCE

8.1.1 Formal requirements for correspondence

Any paper submitted by the applicant in the international phase other than the international application itself must be in the form of a letter or a paper accompanied by a letter identifying the international application (R.92.1(a)). The letter must be signed by the applicant (R.92.1(a)). The applicant will be informed of any non-compliance and will be invited to remedy the omission within a period between 10 days and one month from invitation (R.92.1(b)). If remedied in time, the omission will be disregarded; otherwise the applicant will be informed that the paper will be disregarded (R.92.1(b)).

Any letter or document, except demands (R.55.1) and amendments (R.55.3) sent by the applicant to the ISA or IPEA, must be in the same language as the international application (R.92.2(a)). However, where a translation of the international application has been made for the ISA or IPEA, the language of the translation must be used (R.92.2(a)). The ISA and IPEA may authorise the use of other languages (R.92.2(b)).

Any letter to the IB must be in English, French or any language of publication permitted by the Administrative Instructions (R.92.2(d)) and any letter from the IB is in English or French, (R.92.2(e)). Any letter to or from the EPO acting as rO, ISA or IPEA must be in English, French or German (R.92.2(b), OJ 2010 p.304 Art.7 and Annex D).

When the EPO acts in its capacity under the PCT, the applicant must perform all procedural acts with the EPO; he cannot perform them with a national office of a contracting state. As an exception, an international application may be filed with a national office if prior authorisation on national-security grounds is required (Art.151; Art.75(2) EPC; OJ 2013 p.18 §5).

The PCT request and demand forms include a field which allows applicants to indicate an e-mail address for the main applicant and/or agent. The applicant may authorise an office to send advance copies of any invitation or notification by email. Without authorisation, the e-mail address can only be used for rapid informal communications. E-mail communications do not replace paper notifications and paper copies of invitations or notifications remain the legal copies, including for the purposes of dating documents as per R.80.6. No response to any such e-mails is permitted and signed submissions should still be submitted by mail, fax or on-line. The advance notification service is a precursor to a new system being developed by WIPO which will allow PCT applicants to log-in to a secure file inspection system and access details of their international application.

The e-mail communication is an additional service to the applicant, which will, in effect, serve as an advance warning of any possible action to be taken, and can help to reduce the effects of delays in the dispatching and delivery of the paper notification to the recipient. It may also give the applicant extra time in view of the fact that the time limit given for responding to an invitation is calculated from the date of mailing of the paper version of the communication. (see Practical Advice in PCT Newsletter 07-08/2010)

8.1.2 Means of filing correspondence

Any document or letter from an international Office the despatch of which triggers a period, is sent by air mail or surface mail where surface mail reaches its destination within two days or where air mail is not available (R.92.3). Irregularities in the mail are dealt with in §8.2.2.

AG-IP Annex B states for each contracting state whether its national Office accepts the filing of documents by fax and the kind of documents that may be so transmitted (R.92.4(a)). An Office may require a fax to be confirmed in writing within 14 days (R.92.4(d), AG-IP Annex B). The EPO as rO requires such confirmation for applications and, only upon invitation, for other documents (OJ 2007 se3 A.3; Euro-PCT Guide §71). If not received, the national office may invite the applicant to file the confirmation within a reasonable time limit (R.92.4(e)(ii)), failing which, the office will declare an international patent application as considered withdrawn (R.92.4(g)(i)), or the other documents as not received (R.92.4(g)(ii)). The reasonable time limit set by the EPO is one month (AG-IP Annex B2(EP)). It is recommended to confirm documents making up an international application and replacement sheets immediately upon the transmittal of a fax. If a document is filed with the IB by fax, WIPO strongly recommends that the relevant team of WIPO is contacted by phone or email before or immediately after sending the fax (PCT Newsletter No. 12/2017).

The EPO permits under R.89bis.2 to file further documents relating to an international application in electronic form, for which the EPO Online Filing software can be used (OJ 2014 A50).

8.1.3 ePCT

ePCT is a WIPO online service that provides secure electronic access to the files of international applications filed under the PCT as maintained by the IB. Using the ePCT system, online requests can be submitted for different actions such as, e.g. withdrawal of the international application, and the most up-to-date bibliographic data and documents contained in the international application can be submitted and consulted, including those that have not yet been published. Certain documents that are not publicly available in PATENTSCOPE after publication (e.g. Chapter II related documents) are available via ePCT.

ePCT *public services* are available to all WIPO online account holders and do not require the use of a digital certificate. The functionality currently available is the online upload of electronic documents (with subsequent online viewing) and submission of third party observations with regard to novelty and inventive step.

ePCT *private services* enable account holders to access international applications filed as of 1 January 2009, which are owned or managed by them. In addition to the most up-to-date bibliographic data, almost all of the documents held by the International Bureau in relation to your international application can be viewed, including documents which have not yet been fully processed. This includes documents issued and received by the rO of the IB and the documents issued and received by other rOs and International Authorities to the extent that a copy is sent to the IB.

To access the ePCT public services, a WIPO online user account must be created via the WIPO Accounts service. If access to the ePCT private services is desired, a digital certificate need be uploaded for authentication purposes.

8.2 TIME LIMITS

8.2.1 Calculation

The calculation of time limits under the PCT is similar to that of the EPC (Art.47, R.79, R.80 PCT). Time limits in the PCT have to be calculated using the Rules of the PCT. This means that if the EPO acts as rO, ISA or IPEA and sends out a communication or invitation to correct, R.80 PCT has to be used to calculate any time limit for responding to the communication, not R.131 EPC. The PCT uses 'time limit' in the sense of 'expiry of a period'.

See R.80.1, 2 and 3 for the calculation of periods expressed in years, months and days, respectively. The PCT uses the local dates: the starting date of a period is the date which prevails in the locality where and at the time when the relevant event occurred (R.80.4(a)); the expiry date of a period is the date prevailing in the locality in which the document must be filed or the fee paid (R.80.4(b)).

Where the expiry of a period for submitting a document or making a payment to an Office falls on a day on which the Office is closed or ordinary mail is not delivered in the locality of the Office, the period will be extended to the next day where the Office is open and mail is delivered (R.80.5). The non-working days are published periodically in the PCT Gazette and PCT Newsletter. An Office may extend a period at any time before a decision is taken; see e.g. R.26.2. An Office will accept many acts performed by an applicant after expiry of a period but before issuing an invitation to perform as yet or take a decision; see e.g. R.16*bis*.1(d). If an Office or organisation is situated in more than one locality, then if a period is extended for one Office under R.80.5, the period also extends for the other Offices (R.80.5(iii)). This could occur for example if the EPO filing office in Rijswijk is closed on a certain day such as 5 May (Liberation Day in NL), in which case the period is also extended with respect to the EPO filing office in Munich, even if the Munich office itself is open on 5 May (see e.g. OJ 2014 A9 §5).

The PCT uses the despatch theory for communications from an Office to an applicant: a period starts on the day of the date stamp of a document or letter emanating from an Office, not on the date of receipt by the applicant (R.80.6). If an applicant proves before the Office that he received the document or letter more than seven days after the date it bears, the period will be treated as expiring later by the number of days which the document or letter was received later than the seven days (R.80.6). Note that the extra days should be added at the end of the period, not before the period is calculated. See §4.8 for an exception to the 7-day rule by the EPO as ISA (OJ 2012 p.10).

The PCT uses the receipt theory for communications from an applicant to an Office: a time limit is regarded as being met if the applicant's communication has been received by the Office within the time limit.

8.2.2 Mail irregularities

If any time limit fixed in the PCT is not met because of interruption in the mail service or unavoidable loss or delay in the mail, it must be deemed to be met if the requirements of R.82 are complied with (Art.48(1)). The party must provide evidence that the letter was sent by registered air mail at least five days prior to the expiration of the period (R.82.1(a)). If no air mail is available or where surface mail normally reaches its destination within two days, registered surface mail is also allowed (R.82.1(a)). Where the evidence of the mailing is satisfactory, the delay in arrival will be excused, or, if the letter was lost in the mail, substitution by a new copy will be permitted, provided the party proves that the substitute is identical with the original (R.82.1(b)). The evidence and, where applicable, the substitute letter, must be submitted within one month after the discovery of the delay or loss, but at least within six months after the expiration of the failed period (R.82.1(c)).

AG-IP Annex B indicates for each contracting state whether its national Office will apply the above excuse procedure for postal service providers other than postal authorities of the state, such as courier delivery (R.82.1(d), (e)). The EPO accepts postal service and courier delivery by recognized providers. Compare R.133 EPC for the practice under the EPC. The delivery service providers accepted by the EPO as international authority under R.82.1 PCT are the same as the ones when the EPO acts under R.133 EPC (see AG Annex B2 (EP) and OJ 2015 A29; E-IX,1.7).

If a party can prove that a time limit was not met due to a general failure of electronic communications services in the area where the party resides, war, revolution, civil disorder, strike, natural calamity or similar reason in his residency, the delay or loss will be excused for any mail (including surface mail and unregistered mail) (R.82*quater*.1). R.82*quater* allows the relevant Office to excuse a delay in meeting any time limit in the PCT regulations in case of force majeure. See OJ 2015 A61 §4 and A62 §3 for examples. However, R.82*quater* does not apply to the priority period or the period for entry into the national phase as these are set in the Paris Convention and PCT Articles respectively. Note that R.82*quater* PCT is modelled on R.134(5) EPC. The EPO allows application of R.82*quater* to correct a late payment caused by a delay in the banking system (OJ 2015 A61 §4).

8.2.3 *Excuse of delay in meeting time limit*

Failure to meet a time limit can, in principle, not be remedied in the international phase. However, the PCT allows the application of remedies permitted under the national law of a contracting state, but only with effect for that state (Art.48(2)). Possible national remedies are further processing, restitutio in integrum (or re-establishment), extension of the periods (R.82*bis*.2). Such remedies can only be obtained by entering the national phase before the national Office of the state and carrying out the review and excuse procedure as set out in §7.6.

Some Offices acting as rO, ISA or IPEA may allow the application of national remedies in the international phase to excuse failure to meet a time limit, thereby extending the effect of the national remedy to all designated or elected states (see also AG-IP §6.054). Although this practice goes against Art.48(2), it is used to mitigate the effect of the failure before Offices that do not have suitable national remedies, such as JP (for EPO practice see W4/87 r.7 and W3/93).

Under R.82*quater* an international office must excuse a delay in meeting a period if the applicant provides satisfactory evidence that the delay was due to war, revolution, civil disorder, strike, natural calamity, a general unavailability of electronic communications services or other like reason in the locality of his residence, business or stay. He must have taken the action as soon as possible after the event and provide the evidence to the international office within six months of the expiration of the period.

8.3 REPRESENTATION

A rO or, once the processing in the national phase has started, a designated Office, may apply national law as far as it relates to any requirement that the applicant be represented by an agent (Art.27(7); R.51*bis*.1(b)). Some rOs do not require appointment of an agent (e.g. GB, IB, US), some require appointment only for applicants not having a residence within the territory of the contracting state (e.g. DE, EP, FR, JP) (AG-IP Annex C). Similar rules apply to compulsory representation before the designated Offices (AG-NP).

8.3.1 *Entitlement*

An attorney, patent agent or other person, having the right to practise before the national Office with which the international application was filed, is entitled to practise before the IB, ISA and IPEA (Art.49; R.90.1(a)). If the international application was filed with the IB, an agent who has the right to practise before the national Office of, or acting for, the contracting state of which the applicant is a resident or national may practise before the IB as rO in respect of that international application (R.83.1*bis*(a)). In that case, he may also practise before the competent ISA and IPEA (R.83.1*bis*(b)). The right to practise before a national Office is governed by national law.

An agent appointed for the international phase will not automatically be regarded as an agent by a national Office during the national phase, so other agents may have to be appointed for the purposes of the national phase before each of the various designated Offices (R.90.1; AG-IP §11.001).

An agent entitled to practise before the national Office with which the application will be filed is entitled to practise before the rO, the IB, the ISA and the IPEA in the international phase (R.90.1(a)). An agent may also be appointed specifically to practise before the ISA or IPEA, provided he has the right to practise before the national Office which acts as ISA or IPEA (R.90.1(b), (c)). An agent may also be appointed specifically to practise before the authority specified for supplementary search, provided he has the right to practise before the national Office specified for supplementary search (R.90.1(b-*bis*)).

If there are two or more applicants and the international application is filed with the IB as rO, an agent must have the right to practise before the national Office of, or acting for, the contracting state of which at least one of the applicants is resident or national (R.83.1*bis*(a)). For example, a Swedish and Dutch applicant of one international application may choose a Swedish, Dutch or European patent attorney to act before the IB.

The IB, ISA and IPEA may require proof of the right to practise before the national Office (R.83.1). That national Office submits, on request, to the IB, ISA or IPEA conclusive evidence of the right (R.83.2).

8.3.2 *Appointment*

An applicant may effect the appointment of an agent in several ways. He may enter the name and address of the agent in the request or in the demand or in a separate power of attorney and sign the request, demand or power of attorney (R.90.4(a), (b)). The separate power of attorney (authorisation), signed by the applicant, authorises the agent to represent the applicant in relation to a specific international application. An agent can also be appointed by a general power of attorney, allowing the agent to represent the applicant in relation to any international application filed by that applicant. In that case the request, demand or a separate notice must refer to the power of attorney (R.90.5). Any changes in an indication of the agent after the filing of the application can be recorded with the IB under R.92*bis*.1(a)(ii).

An international authority may waive the requirement to submit a separate or general power of attorney (R.90.4(d); R.90.5(c)). The EPO acting as RO, ISA, IPEA or SISA has waived the requirement that a separate or general power of attorney be attached to the request, demand or separate notice; however, it may require the filing of the power of attorney if there is doubt as to the agent's entitlement to act (OJ 2010 p.335). The situation is similar with the US and the IB, the latter however only in its capacity as rO. In such cases the simplified EPO system under R.152 EPC for European applications can be used in the international phase. The waiver does not apply to any notice of withdrawal (R.90.4(e), R.90.5(a), (d)). An up-to-date list of waivers can be found on the PCT website: www.wipo.int/pct.

An agent may appoint a sub-agent to represent the applicant as agent before all competent international Offices or before one or more specific competent international Offices, unless otherwise indicated in the appointment of the agent (R.90.1(d)).

The appointment of an agent is considered nonexistent if the signature of the applicant is missing or if the name and address of the agent do not comply with R.4.4 (R.90.4(c)). The applicant will be invited to correct the defect under Art.14(1)(b) and R.26. The rO may extend the period for correction (R.26.2).

The power to act according to the PCT procedure can be excluded from an authorisation. Therefore, when filing a general authorisation at the EPO, it is recommended always to include the power to represent also in PCT proceedings. If an authorised representative is appointed by marking the appropriate box no. IV of the PCT request form signed by the applicant, no separate authorisation need be filed (R.90.4(a)), but the authorisation is only valid in the international phase. A separate or general authorisation can empower a representative to act in both the international and national phase.

8.3.3 *Common agent and Common representative*

Where there are two or more applicants, they may appoint a common agent or a common representative (i.e. one of the applicants, R.2.2*bis*) to act for all applicants. The appointment of the common agent is effected by each applicant signing, at his choice, the request, demand or separate power of attorney (R.90.4). It is possible to appoint more than one agent representing the same applicant or applicants (consequence of R.90.3(b)).

If no common agent is appointed, one of the applicants allowed to file an international application according to Art.9 and R.19.1 may be appointed as common representative by the other applicants (R.90.2(a)). If no common representative or common agent has been appointed, the first named applicant allowed to file an international application with the rO will be considered to be the (deemed) common representative of all the applicants (R.90.2(b)).

8.3.4 *Acts by agent or representative*

An act by an agent has the effect of an act by the applicant (R.90.3(a)). If there are two or more agents representing the same applicant or applicants, an act by one of those agents has the effect of an act by the said applicant or applicants (R.90.3(b)). An act by a common representative or his agent has the effect of an act by all applicants (R.90.3(c)). However, the deemed common representative has limited powers in relation to withdrawals (R.90*bis*.5; see §8.4). Note that according to R.2.1, the term 'applicant' can also mean 'agent or other representative of the applicant', which allows an agent to 'act' even where a provision only specifies the 'applicant'.

8.3.5 *Revocation and renunciation*

An appointment of an agent or common representative may be revoked by the applicants who made the appointment or by their successors in title (R.90.6(a)). The applicant may also revoke the appointment of a sub-agent (R.90.6). The appointment of an agent under R.90.1(a) or a common representative causes the revocation of any earlier appointment of an agent under that Rule or a common representative, unless otherwise indicated (R.90.6(b), (c)).

An agent or common representative may renounce his appointment by a notification signed by him (R.90.6(d)).

A revocation or renunciation must be submitted to the rO or IB. However, where the power of attorney relates to an appointment for a specific Office, the revocation or renunciation must be submitted to that Office (R.90.6(e)).

8.3.6 *Representation before the EPO as designated or elected Office*

Applicants not having their residence or principal place of business in an EPC contracting state must be represented by a professional representative before the EPO as designated or elected Office (R.163(5) EPC). However, until expiry of the 31-month period for entry into the European phase, applicants not having their residence or principal place of business in an EPC contracting state may carry out the steps required to initiate the procedure before the EPO as a designated or elected Office themselves. Payments to the EPO may be made by anybody. (Art.27(7); Art.133(2) EPC; Art.150(2) EPC, R.159(1) EPC; E-IX,2.3.1; Euro-PCT Guide §468)

8.4 WITHDRAWALS

During the international phase the applicant may withdraw the application, designations, priority claims, the supplementary search request, the demand or elections before the expiration of 30 months from the priority date (Art.37; R.90*bis*.1(a), 2(a), 3(a), 3*bis*(a), 4(a); see also §7.2). Note, that the extended period of 31 months for entering the national phase under Art.22(3) and Art.39(1)(b) is not applicable here, because R.90*bis*.2(a), 3(a), 4(a) specifically mention only 30 months. Withdrawals after expiry of the international phase must be made before the designated or elected Offices, the effect of which being governed by national law. See §5.3 for the effect of the withdrawal on the publication of the application.

The withdrawal of an application, designation or priority claim must by submitted to the IB, rO or, where Art.39(1) applies, the IPEA (R.90*bis*.1(b), 2(d), 3(c)). In contrast, the withdrawal of the demand or an election must be submitted to the IB (R.90*bis*.4(b)). If submitted to the IPEA instead, the IPEA will transmit it to the IB, which will consider it to have been received on the date of receipt by the IPEA (R.90*bis*.4(c)). The withdrawal of a request for supplementary search should be submitted to the SISA or to the IB (R.90*bis*.3*bis*(b)).

Any notice of withdrawal must be signed by the applicant (R.90*bis*.5) or his agent (R.2.1). Where there are several applicants and no common agent or common representative has been appointed, the 'considered' or 'deemed' common representative (see §8.3.3) may not sign a notice of withdrawal; the notice requires the signature of all applicants (R.90*bis*.5). Where an agent has been appointed by a separate or general power of attorney and has not yet submitted it, he should do so before or simultaneously with a notice of withdrawal. If an agent does not submit the general power of attorney, the respective authority will ask for it; the act of withdrawal only being deemed complete when received by the respective authority (R.90.4(e) and 5(d)). When the designation of the US is to be withdrawn, the signatures of the inventors that are indicated as applicants for the US in the request form are required for the withdrawal.

See for the withdrawal of designations §2.9.6, a priority claim §2.10.3 and the demand or an election §6.1.4.3. All withdrawals are free of charge (AG-IP §11.048).

8.5 OBVIOUS MISTAKES

An applicant may in general request that obvious mistakes in an international application or any other paper submitted by him be rectified (R.91.1.(a), AG-IP §11.033-11.044). A mistake will only be rectified if duly authorised by the competent Authority (R.91.1(b)). The competent Authority will authorise a rectification if it is obvious to the competent Authority that something else was intended than what appears in the document concerned and that nothing else could have been intended than the proposed rectification (R.91.1(c)). Omission of entire elements or sheets of the international application are not rectifiable under R.91.1(g)(i) (although such an omission may e.g. be rectifiable under R.20 or R.82 PCT), nor are mistakes in the abstract under R.91.1(g)(ii) (although a mistake in the abstract may be corrected using R.38.3). A mistake in an Article 19 amendment is not rectifiable unless under certain circumstances before the IPEA (R.91.1(g)(iii), R.91.1(b)(iii)). Rectification may be made of the applicant's own volition or on request of an authority that discovered the error (R.91.1(h)). The rectification is effected free of charge (AG-IP §11.033).

A mistake in a priority claim may be rectified using R.91 as long as the 'rectification' does not change the earliest priority date (R.91.1(g)(iv)). Note that such a 'rectification' is possible within 26 months from the priority date, whereas a 'correction' is only possible until around 16 months from the priority date under R.26*bis*.1.

The relevant competent Authority is as follows:

- the rO if the mistake is in the request (R.91.1(b)(i)),
- the ISA if the mistake is in the description, claims or drawings or in a correction thereof, unless the IPEA is competent (R.91.1(b)(ii)),
- the IPEA if the mistake is in the description, claims or drawings or in a correction thereof, or in an Art.19 or 34 amendment, where a demand for international preliminary examination has been made and not withdrawn before examination has started (R.91.1(b)(iii), R.69.1), or
- the relevant Office, Authority or Bureau (rO, ISA, IPEA or IB) if the mistake is in a document not referred to above that is submitted to that office, Authority or Bureau (R.91.1(b)(iv)).

The applicant must submit his request for rectification to the competent Authority (AG-IP §11.039) in the language in which the international application is filed (R.12.2). The rectification must be submitted to the competent Authority within 26 months of the priority date (R.91.2). The rectification must be filed in the language of the international application as filed, and additionally in the language of the translation if such has been filed (R.12.1*bis*). The request for rectification should specify the mistake to be rectified and the proposed rectification, and a brief explanation at the option of the applicant.

If authorisation of a request for rectification is received by or given by the IB after technical preparations for international publication are complete, a statement reflecting the rectification and rectified sheets, or the replacement sheets, request for rectification and the specification front page will be published (R.48.2(i)).

If an obvious mistake is rectified it shall be effective as from the international filing date if the mistake was in the international application as filed (R.91.3(c)(i)), and if in a document other than the international application as filed, from the date on which the document was submitted (R.91.3(c)(ii)).

If the authorisation is refused, the applicant may request the IB in writing within two months of the refusal to publish the refused request along with reasons for the refusal, subject to the payment of a special fee (R.91.3(d), see AG-IP Annex B2(IB) for the fee). A designated Office need not take a rectification into account if processing or examination of the international application has begun prior to it being notified of the rectification authorisation (R.91.3(e)), and may disregard a rectification if it would have refused authorisation had it been the competent Authority (R.91.3(f)).

8.6 AMENDMENTS

The international search will be carried out on the unamended international application, since the first opportunity to amend the claims of the international application is only after the applicant has received the international search report (Art.19(1)). However, before the search, any formal errors in the international application may already have been corrected under Art.11(2) and Art.14(1)(b), or any obvious mistakes rectified under R.91 (see §8.5).

The applicant has one opportunity to amend the claims of the international application under Art.19(1) in response to the international search report (see §4.6). The applicant may file a brief statement (500 words maximum) explaining the claim amendments (Art.19(1), R.46.4). In addition, a letter accompanying the replacement sheets must be filed explaining the differences between the replaced sheets and the replacement sheets (R.46.5; AG-IP §9.005). Amendments to the claims under Art.19 are not allowed where the ISA has declared, under Art.17(2)(a), that no international search report will be established (AG-IP §296). In addition, shortly after filing the international application, claims may be added if they are completely contained in a claimed priority application (R.20.5; R.20.6; see §3.1.3).

If a demand is filed, the applicant may amend the description, claims and drawings under Art.34(2)(b). Claim amendments under Art.34(2)(b) may be in addition to or instead of the amendments under Art.19(1). If filed in time, the examination will be carried out on the amended international application. See §6.4.1.2.

After entering the national phase, the applicant has a possibility to amend the international application under Art.28 and 41 before each designated or elected Office. Such an amendment opportunity is implemented before the EPO under R.161 EPC. (see §7.2.9)

8.7 ACCESS TO FILES

The availability of documents from the file of an international application is dependent upon the international filing date, the stage the international application is at, and the office which keeps the application on file (Art.38; IB: R.94.1, IPEA: R.94.2, elected Office: R.94.3).

Prior to international publication of an application, the international application is confidential in relation to third parties (Art.30(1)(a)), and the IB and the IPEA may only furnish copies of documents in their files to the applicant or a person authorised by the applicant (Art.30(2)(a), R.94.1(a), R.94.2), subject to payment of the cost of the service (R.94.1(a)). Copies of documents may also be furnished to judicial authorities (Art.30(2)(c), AG-IP §11.072).

Once international publication of an application by the IB under Art.21 has taken place, the content of the international application becomes public. See §5.1 for the contents of the international publication (Art.21, R.48). Copies of the publication of the international application may be obtained in electronic form from the websites of the EPO and in paper form by ordering from the IB (AG-IP §9.021, Art.50). Upon request by any person, the IB will furnish copies of priority documents, provided the international application was not withdrawn, or the relevant priority claim was not withdrawn or considered not to have been made prior to international publication (R.17.2(c)).

Once international publication has taken place, the IB will furnish at the request of *any* person, copies of any document in its file, with the exception of documents relating to international preliminary examination or the written opinion prepared by the ISA (R.94.1(b)). The furnishing of any document is subject to reimbursement of the cost of the service (R.94.1(b)). On 01.07.2014, Rule 44*ter* was deleted and R.94.1(b) amended: the written opinion for international applications filed on or after that date will be publicly available from the date of international publication.

The file of the international preliminary examination kept by the IPEA is, in principle, confidential, unless access is requested or authorised by the applicant (Art.38(1)). However, once an international preliminary report on patentability has been established, the IPEA will allow access to an elected Office (Art.38(1), R.94.2).

After the international preliminary examination report has been established, the IB communicates the report and any annexes to the elected Offices (Art.36(3)(a); R.73.2). The report in the files of an elected Office may be available for public inspection. An elected Office may also request the IB on behalf of a third party to provide a copy of the report (R.94.1(c); AG-IP §9.027).

After publication of the international application, any third party may access the file of the elected Office, provided national law permits so, and inspect the international preliminary report on patentability and its annexes if on file at the elected office (R.94.3, AG-IP §10.080, §11.074). Additionally, in respect of international applications filed on or after 01.07.1998, any person may inspect *any* documents relating to an international application contained in the file of the elected Office (R.94.3), including *any* documents relating to the international preliminary examination, e.g. the correspondence between the applicant and the IPEA. The inspection may be allowed to the same extent as provided by the national law applicable to the elected Office for access to the file of a national application and only after publication of the international application (R.94.3).

The EPO makes documents relating to PCT applications held by it in its capacity of rO or (S)ISA available for inspection free of charge through the European Patent Register, i.e. through online file inspection (Dec. Pres. OJ 2018 A14, Art. 1). Access is provided to third parties after the publication of the international application. Documents excluded under R.48.2(l) or R.94.1(d) or (e) or under Rule 144 EPC are not accessible.

In its capacity as a designated Office, the EPO allows access to its files and may communicate information from its files relating to international applications once international publication has taken place. In its capacity as an elected Office, the EPO allows access to its files (including the entire PCT Chapter II file) and may communicate information from its files relating to international applications once international publication has taken place and, as far as the PCT Chapter II file is concerned, the IPRP has been completed. (E-IX,2.10)

The rO, ISA including the SISA and IPEA keep the records of international applications for at least 10 years from the international filing date (R.93.1, 3). The IB keeps the file, including the record copy for at least 30 years from the date of receipt of the record copy under Art.12(1) and the basic records, theoretically, indefinitely (R.93.2).

8.8 SUNDRY PROVISIONS

8.8.1 *Revision of the Treaty*

The Treaty may be revised by a special conference of contracting states (Art.60(1)). Such conferences are rare because of the large number of contracting states and the fact that WIPO must pay the expenses of the delegates. The Assembly (see §1.2.3) itself may amend certain Articles (Art.61(2)(a)). The Assembly may also amend the Regulations of the Treaty (Art.58(2)(a)). The amendment of some Rules requires unanimous consent (Art.58(3)(a)(i); R.88.1).

Time limits in the Articles of the PCT may be modified outside any revision under Art.60 by a unanimous decision of the contracting states (Art.47(2); R.81).

8.8.2 *Reservations*

The PCT allows contracting states to make certain specific reservations, thereby modifying the international procedure to encompass national peculiarities (Art.64). Several of the more important reservations are given below.

A contracting state may declare not to be bound by Chapter II (Art.64(1)(a)). To date, all PCT contracting states are bound by Chapter II.

A contracting state may declare that, as far as it is concerned, international publication is not required (Art.64(3)(a), (b)). To date, only the US has declared thus, so this is only effective if the US is the only designated State (and the appropriate declaration is made by the applicant) (Art.64(3)(b)).

A contracting state may declare that the filing date for another state of an international application designating that first state is not equated to an actual filing date in that state for prior art purposes (Art.64(4)(a)). To date only the US has declared so.

An up-to-date list of all 'PCT Reservations, Declarations, Notifications and Incompatibilities' can be found on the PCT website: www.wipo.int/pct.

8.8.3 *Licensing indications*

Applicants interested in licensing the inventions contained in their international applications can request the IB to make this information available on the PATENTSCOPE website. Applicants should use a special form (PCT/IB/382 available in all publication languages) or send a letter indicating that the claimed invention is available for licensing. At the same time, they will also be able to include further licensing terms. No fee is payable for the use of this service. (AG-IP 11.102, 11.105)

Licensing indications may be submitted at any time from the filing of the international application until the expiration of the 30-month time period. The indications will be visible in the bibliographic data relating to the particular application but will not be part of the published international application itself. (AG-IP 11.103, 11.106)

There is no express provision in the PCT for indicating licensing indications.

The Vienna Convention on the Law of Treaties

1 **Vienna Convention**
The convention entered into force in 1980. An abstract has been published in OJ 4/1984 p.192-197. The EPO has declared these rules applicable to the interpretation of the EPC (G1, 5, 6/83). Not all contracting states of the EPC are party to the Vienna Convention (issue 4 of the OJ). Below some articles relevant for the interpretation of the EPC are reproduced.

Art. 4 Non-retroactivity of the present Convention

Without prejudice to the application of any rules set forth in the present Convention to which treaties would be subject under international law independently of the Convention, the Convention applies only to treaties which are concluded by States after the entry into force of the present Convention with regard to such States.

Art. 25 Provisional application

Art. 25(1) A treaty or a part of a treaty is applied provisionally pending its entry into force if:
(a) the treaty itself so provides; or
(b) the negotiating States have in some other manner so agreed.

Art. 25(2) Unless the treaty otherwise provides or the negotiating States have otherwise agreed, the provisional application of a treaty or a part of a treaty with respect to a State shall be terminated if that State notifies the other States between which the treaty is being applied provisionally of its intention not to become a party to the treaty.

Art. 31 General rule of interpretation

Art. 31(1) A treaty shall be interpreted in good faith in accordance with the ordinary meaning to be given to the terms of the treaty in their context and in the light of its object and purpose.

Art. 31(2) The context for the purpose of the interpretation of a treaty shall comprise, in addition to the text, including its preamble and annexes:
(a) any agreement relating to the treaty which was made between all the parties in connection with the conclusion of the treaty;
(b) any instrument which was made by one or more parties in connection with the conclusion of the treaty and accepted by the other parties as an instrument related to the treaty.

Art. 31(3) There shall be taken into account, together with the context:
(a) any subsequent agreement between the parties regarding the interpretation or the application of its provisions;
(b) any subsequent practice in the application of the treaty which establishes the agreement of the parties regarding its interpretation;
(c) any relevant rules of international law applicable in the relations between the parties.

Art. 31(4) A special meaning shall be given to a term if it is established that the parties so intended.

Art. 32 Supplementary means of interpretation

Recourse may be had to supplementary means of interpretation, including the preparatory work of the treaty and the circumstances of its conclusion, in order to confirm the meaning resulting from the application of article 31, or to determine the meaning when the interpretation according to article 31:
(a) leaves the meaning ambiguous or obscure; or
(b) leads to a result which is manifestly absurd or unreasonable.

Art. 33 Interpretation of treaties authenticated in two or more languages

Art. 33(1) When a treaty has been authenticated in two or more languages, the text is equally authoritative in each language, unless the treaty provides or the parties agree that, in case of divergence, a particular text shall prevail.

Art. 33(2) A version of the treaty in a language other than one of those in which the text was authenticated shall be considered an authentic text only if the treaty so provides or the parties so agree.

Art. 33(3) The terms of the treaty are presumed to have the same meaning in each authentic text.

Art. 33(4) Except where a particular text prevails, in accordance with paragraph 1, when a comparison of the authentic texts discloses a difference of meaning which the application of articles 31 and 32 does not remove, the meaning which best reconciles the texts, having regard to the object and purpose of the treaty, shall be adopted.

Examples of the agreements under Art.31.2(a) are the Protocols of the EPC.

The provision for several languages in Art.33 can be found in Art.177 of the EPC.

Paris Convention

1 **Paris Convention**
The official English text of the law (revised at Stockholm and as amended on 2 October 1979) is given only for the articles relevant for patents, i.e. Art. 2, 3, 4, 4bis, 4ter, 4^{quater}, 5, 5bis, 5ter, 5^{quater}, $5^{\text{quinquies}}$, 11, 19 and 22.

Art. 2 National Treatment

According to paragraph 1 a country of the Union must grant nationals of other countries of the Union the same protection of industrial property that it grants its own nationals. In addition the provisions prescribed by the Convention must be granted. The National Treatment rule applies to all advantages that national laws grant to nationals. So, no discrimination and no reciprocity.

Paragraph 2 provides that no requirements as to residence or establishment in the country where protection is claimed may be imposed for enjoyment of industrial property rights.

The last paragraph provides an exception for judicial procedures.

Art. 2(1) Nationals of any country of the Union shall, as regards the protection of industrial property, enjoy in all the other countries of the Union the advantages that their respective laws now grant, or may hereafter grant, to nationals; all without prejudice to the rights specially provided for by this Convention. Consequently, they shall have the same protection as the latter, and the same legal remedy against any infringement of their rights, provided that the conditions and formalities imposed upon nationals are complied with.

Art. 2(2) However, no requirement as to domicile or establishment in the country where protection is claimed may be imposed upon nationals of countries of the Union for the enjoyment of any industrial property rights.

Art. 2(3) The provisions of the laws of each of the countries of the Union relating to judicial and administrative procedure and to jurisdiction, and to the designation of an address for service or the appointment of an agent, which may be required by the laws on industrial property are expressly reserved.

Art. 3 Same treatment of persons

Nationals of countries outside the Union who are domiciled or who have real and effective industrial or commercial establishments in the territory of one of the countries of the Union shall be treated in the same manner as nationals of the countries of the Union.

The provision extends the National Treatment rule to nationals of non-member countries, provided they are domiciled or have a 'real and effective' industrial or commercial establishment in such a country.

Art. 4 A to I. Patents, Utility Models, Industrial Designs, Marks, Inventors' Certificates: Right of Priority - G. Patents: Division of the Application

Art. 4A(1) Any person who has duly filed an application for a patent, or for the registration of a utility model, or of an industrial design, or of a trademark, in one of the countries of the Union, or his successor in title, shall enjoy, for the purpose of filing in the other countries, a right of priority during the periods hereinafter fixed.

Art. 4A(2) Any filing that is equivalent to a regular national filing under the domestic legislation of any country of the Union or under bilateral or multilateral treaties concluded between countries of the Union shall be recognized as giving rise to the right of priority.

Art. 4A(3) By a regular national filing is meant any filing that is adequate to establish the date on which the application was filed in the country concerned, whatever may be the subsequent fate of the application.

Art. 4B Consequently, any subsequent filing in any of the other countries of the Union before the expiration of the periods referred to above shall not be invalidated by reason of any acts accomplished in the interval, in particular, another filing, the publication or exploitation of the invention, the putting on sale of copies of the design, or the use of the mark, and such acts cannot give rise to any third-party right or any right of personal possession. Rights acquired by third parties before the date of the first application that serves as the basis for the right of priority are reserved in accordance with the domestic legislation of each country of the Union.

Art. 4C(1) The periods of priority referred to above shall be twelve months for patents and utility models, and six months for industrial designs and trademarks.

Art. 4C(2) These periods shall start from the date of filing of the first application; the day of filing shall not be included in the period.

Art. 4C(3) If the last day of the period is an official holiday, or a day when the Office is not open for the filing of applications in the country where protection is claimed, the period shall be extended until the first following working day.

Art. 4C(4) A subsequent application concerning the same subject as a previous first application within the meaning of paragraph (2), above, filed in the same country of the Union, shall be considered as the first application, of which the filing date shall be the starting point of the period of priority, if, at the time of filing the subsequent application, the said previous application has been withdrawn, abandoned, or refused, without having been laid open to public inspection and without leaving any rights outstanding, and if it has not yet served as a basis for claiming a right of priority. The previous application may not thereafter serve as a basis for claiming a right of priority.

Art. 4D(1) Any person desiring to take advantage of the priority of a previous filing shall be required to make a declaration indicating the date of such filing and the country in which it was made. Each country shall determine the latest date on which such declaration must be made.

Art. 4D(2) These particulars shall be mentioned in the publications issued by the competent authority, and in particular in the patents and the specifications relating thereto.

Art. 4D(3) The countries of the Union may require any person making a declaration of priority to produce a copy of the application (description, drawings, etc.) previously filed. The copy, certified as correct by the authority which received such application, shall not require any authentication, and may in any case be filed, without fee, at any time within three months of the filing of the subsequent application. They may require it to be accompanied by a certificate from the same authority showing the date of filing, and by a translation.

Art. 4D(4) No other formalities may be required for the declaration of priority at the time of filing the application. Each country of the Union shall determine the consequences of failure to comply with the formalities prescribed by this Article, but such consequences shall in no case go beyond the loss of the right of priority.

Art. 4D(5) Subsequently, further proof may be required. Any person who avails himself of the priority of a previous application shall be required to specify the number of that application; this number shall be published as provided for by paragraph (2), above.

Art. 4E(1) Where an industrial design is filed in a country by virtue of a right of priority based on the filing of a utility model, the period of priority shall be the same as that fixed for industrial designs.

Art. 4E(2) Furthermore, it is permissible to file a utility model in a country by virtue of a right of priority based on the filing of a patent application, and vice versa.

Art. 4F No country of the Union may refuse a priority or a patent application on the ground that the applicant claims multiple priorities, even if they originate in different countries, or on the ground that an application claiming one or more priorities contains one or more elements that were not included in the application or applications whose priority is claimed, provided that, in both cases, there is unity of invention within the meaning of the law of the country. With respect to the elements not included in the application or applications whose priority is claimed, the filing of the subsequent application shall give rise to a right of priority under ordinary conditions.

Art. 4G(1) If the examination reveals that an application for a patent contains more than one invention, the applicant may divide the application into a certain number of divisional applications and preserve as the date of each the date of the initial application and the benefit of the right of priority, if any.

Art. 4G(2) The applicant may also, on his own initiative, divide a patent application and preserve as the date of each divisional application the date of the initial application and the benefit of the right of priority, if any. Each country of the Union shall have the right to determine the conditions under which such division shall be authorized.

Art. 4H Priority may not be refused on the ground that certain elements of the invention for which priority is claimed do not appear among the claims formulated in the application in the country of origin, provided that the application documents as a whole specifically disclose such elements.

Art. 4I(1) Applications for inventors' certificates filed in a country in which applicants have the right to apply at their own option either for a patent or for an inventor's certificate shall give rise to the right of priority provided for by this Article, under the same conditions and with the same effects as applications for patents.

Art. 4I(2) In a country in which applicants have the right to apply at their own option either for a patent or for an inventor's certificate, an applicant for an inventor's certificate shall, in accordance with the provisions of this Article relating to patent applications, enjoy a right of priority based on an application for a patent, a utility model, or an inventor's certificate.

See Art.87 EPC, 88 EPC, 89 EPC

Art. 4bis Patents: Independence of Patents Obtained for the Same Invention in Different Countries

Art. 4bis(1) Patents applied for in the various countries of the Union by nationals of countries of the Union shall be independent of patents obtained for the same invention in other countries, whether members of the Union or not.

Art. 4bis(2) The foregoing provision is to be understood in an unrestricted sense, in particular, in the sense that patents applied for during the period of priority are independent both as regards the grounds for nullity and forfeiture, and as regards their normal duration.

Art. 4bis(3) The provision shall apply to all patents existing at the time when it comes into effect.

Art. 4bis(4) Similarly, it shall apply, in the case of the accession of new countries, to patents in existence on either side at the time of accession.

Art. 4bis(5) Patents obtained with the benefit of priority shall, in the various countries of the Union, have a duration equal to that which they would have, had they been applied for or granted without the benefit of priority.

Art. 4ter Patents: Mention of the inventor in the patent

The inventor shall have the right to be mentioned as such in the patent.

Art. 4quater Patents: Patentability in case of restrictions of sale by law

The grant of a patent shall not be refused and a patent shall not be invalidated on the ground that the sale of the patented product or of a product obtained by means of a patented process is subject to restrictions or limitations resulting from the domestic law.

Art. 5 A. Patents: Importation of Articles; Failure to Work or Insufficient Working; Compulsory Licenses. - B. Industrial Designs: Failure to Work; Importation of Articles. - C. Marks: Failure to Use; Different Forms; Use by Co-proprietors. - D. Patents, Utility Models, Marks, Industrial Designs: Marking

Art. 5A(1) Importation by the patentee into the country where the patent has been granted of articles manufactured in any of the countries of the Union shall not entail forfeiture of the patent.

Art. 5A(2) Each country of the Union shall have the right to take legislative measures providing for the grant of compulsory licenses to prevent the abuses which might result from the exercise of the exclusive rights conferred by the patent, for example, failure to work.

Art. 5A(3) Forfeiture of the patent shall not be provided for except in cases where the grant of compulsory licenses would not have been sufficient to prevent the said abuses. No proceedings for the forfeiture or revocation of a patent may be instituted before the expiration of two years from the grant of the first compulsory license.

Art. 5A(4) A compulsory license may not be applied for on the ground of failure to work or insufficient working before the expiration of a period of four years from the date of filing of the patent application or three years from the date of the grant of the patent, whichever period expires last; it shall be refused if the patentee justifies his inaction by legitimate reasons. Such a compulsory license shall be non-exclusive and shall not be transferable, even in the form of the grant of a sub-license, except with that part of the enterprise or goodwill which exploits such license.

Art. 5A(5) The foregoing provisions shall be applicable, mutatis mutandis, to utility models.

Art. 5B The protection of industrial designs shall not, under any circumstance, be subject to any forfeiture, either by reason of failure to work or by reason of the importation of articles corresponding to those which are protected.

Art. 5C(1) If, in any country, use of the registered mark is compulsory, the registration may be cancelled only after a reasonable period, and then only if the person concerned does not justify his inaction.

Art. 5C(2) Use of a trademark by the proprietor in a form differing in elements which do not alter the distinctive character of the mark in the form in which it was registered in one of the countries of the Union shall not entail invalidation of the registration and shall not diminish the protection granted to the mark.

Art. 5C(3) Concurrent use of the same mark on identical or similar goods by industrial or commercial establishments considered as co-proprietors of the mark according to the provisions of the domestic law of the country where protection is claimed shall not prevent registration or diminish in any way the protection granted to the said mark in any country of the Union, provided that such use does not result in misleading the public and is not contrary to the public interest.

Art. 5D No indication or mention of the patent, of the utility model, of the registration of the trademark, or of the deposit of the industrial design, shall be required upon the goods as a condition of recognition of the right to protection.

Art. 5bis All Industrial Property Rights: Period of grace for payment of maintenance fees for the Maintenance of Rights; Patents: Restoration

Art. 5bis(1) A period of grace of not less than six months shall be allowed for the payment of the fees prescribed for the maintenance of industrial property rights, subject, if the domestic legislation so provides, to the payment of a surcharge.

Art. 5bis(2) The countries of the Union shall have the right to provide for the restoration of patents which have lapsed by reason of non-payment of fees.

Art. 5ter Patents: Patented Devices Forming Part of Vessels, Aircraft, or Land Vehicles

In any country of the Union the following shall not be considered as infringements of the rights of a patentee:

1. **the use on board vessels of other countries of the Union of devices forming the subject of his patent in the body of the vessel, in the machinery, tackle, gear and other accessories, when such vessels temporarily or accidentally enter the waters of the said country, provided that such devices are used there exclusively for the needs of the vessel;**
2. **the use of devices forming the subject of the patent in the construction or operation of aircraft or land vehicles of other countries of the Union, or of accessories of such aircraft or land vehicles, when those aircraft or land vehicles temporarily or accidentally enter the said country.**

Art. 5quater Patents: Importation of Products Manufactured by a Process Patented in the Importing Country

When a product is imported into a country of the Union where there exists a patent protecting a process of manufacture of the said product, the patentee shall have all the rights, with regard to the imported product, that are accorded to him by the legislation of the country of importation, on the basis of the process patent, with respect to products manufactured in that country.

Art. 5quinquies Industrial Designs

Industrial designs shall be protected in all the countries of the Union.

Art. 11 Temporary protection at certain International Exhibitions

Art. 11(1) The countries of the Union shall, in conformity with their domestic legislation, grant temporary protection to patentable inventions, utility models, industrial designs, and trademarks, in respect of goods exhibited at official or officially recognized international exhibitions held in the territory of any of them.

Art. 11(2) Such temporary protection shall not extend the periods provided by Article 4. If, later, the right of priority is invoked, the authorities of any country may provide that the period shall start from the date of introduction of the goods into the exhibition.

Art. 11(3) Each country may require, as proof of the identity of the article exhibited and of the date of its introduction, such documentary evidence as it considers necessary.

Art. 19 Special agreements

It is understood that the countries of the Union reserve the right to make separately between themselves special agreements for the protection of industrial property, in so far as these agreements do not contravene the provisions of this Convention.

Art. 22 Consequences of ratification or accession

Subject to the possibilities of exceptions provided for in Articles 20(1)(b) and 28(2), ratification or accession shall automatically entail acceptance of all the clauses and admission to all the advantages of this Act.

Cross-reference index

EPC 1973 - EPC 2000

The list compares the provisions of the EPC 1973 with thematically corresponding provisions of the EPC 2000. The list is an amended version of the list published in Special edition 1 of OJ 2007, p. 210.

EPC 1973	EPC 2000	EPC 1973	EPC 2000
-	Art. 4a	Art. 106(3)	Art. 106(2)
Art. 16 (elmts)	R. 10	Art. 106(4), (5)	Art. 106(3); R. 97
Art. 18(1)	R. 10	Art. 110(2), (3)	R. 100(2), (3)
Art. 52(4)	Art. 53(c)	-	Art. 112a
Art. 54(4)	-	Art. 115(1) (elmts)	R. 114(1)
Art. 54(5)	Art. 54(4)	Art. 115(2)	R. 114(2)
-	Art. 54(5)	Art. 117(2)	R. 119(1)
Art. 61(1) (elmts)	R. 16	Art. 117(3)	R. 118
Art. 77 (elmts)	R. 37	Art. 117(4) - (6)	R. 120
Art. 78(2) (elmts)	R. 38	Art. 121(1) (elmts)	Art. 121(3)
Art. 79(2) (elmts)	R. 39(1)	Art. 121(2), (3)	R. 135(1), (3)
Art. 79(3) (elmts)	R. 39(3), (4)	-	Art. 121(2), (4)
Art. 80 (elmts)	R. 40	Art. 122(2) - (4)	R. 136(1), (2), (4)
Art. 88(1) (elmts)	R. 53(1), (3)	Art. 122(5)	Art. 122(4);
Art. 90(1)(a)	Art. 90(1)		R. 136(3)
Art. 90(1)(b)	R. 57(e)	Art. 126	Rfees13(1), (2), (3)
Art. 90(1)(c)	R. 57(a)	Art. 134(3) - (7)	Art. 134(4) - (8)
Art. 90(2)	Art. 90(2), (4)	Art. 134(8)	Art. 134a(1)
Art. 90(3)	Art. 78(2);	-	Art. 134a(2)
	Art. 14(2)	Art. 135(2)	Art. 135(4);
Art. 91(1)	Art. 90(3); R. 57		R. 155(1)
Art. 91(2)	Art. 90(4)	Art. 136(1)	Art. 135(3);
Art. 91(3)	Art. 90(5)		R. 155(2)
Art. 91(4)	R. 39(2)	Art. 136(2)	Art. 135(2), (4);
Art. 91(5)	Art. 90(5); R. 60		R. 155(3)
Art. 91(6)	R. 56	-	Art. 138(3)
Art. 92(2)	R. 65	-	Art. 149a
Art. 93(1)	Art. 93(1), (2)	Art. 150(3)	Art. 153(2)
Art. 93(2)	R. 68(1)	Art. 150(4)	Art. 150(2)
Art. 94(2)	Art. 94(1); R. 70(1)	Art. 151(1) (elmts)	R. 157
Art. 94(3)	Art. 94(2)	Art. 151(2), (3)	-
Art. 95	-	Art. 152(1) - (3)	R. 157(1), (3), (4)
Art. 96(1)	R. 70(2)	Art. 153(2)	R. 159(2)
Art. 96(2)	Art. 94(3)	Art. 154(1), (2)	Art. 152
Art.96(3)	Art.94(4); R. 70(3)	Art. 154(3)	R. 158(3)
Art. 97(1), (2)	Art. 97(2), (1)	Art. 155(1), (2)	Art. 152
Art. 97(3)	R. 71(7)	Art. 155(3)	R. 158(3)
Art. 97(4), (5)	-	Art. 156	Art. 153(1)
Art. 99(3)	R. 75	Art. 157(1) - (3)	Art. 153(6), (7)
Art. 99(4), (5)	Art. 99(3), (4)	Art. 158(1), (2)	Art. 153(3), (5)
Art. 101(2)	Art. 101(1)	Art. 158(3)	Art. 153(4)
Art. 102(1), (2)	Art. 101(2)	Art. 159 - 162	-
Art. 102(3)	Art. 101(3)(a)	Art. 163(1) - (4), (6)	Art. 134(3), (4), (7)
-	Art. 101(3)(b)	Art. 163(5), (7)	-
Art. 102(4), (5)	R. 82(2), (3)	Art. 167	-
Art. 104(2) (elmts)	R. 88(1), (3)	-	R. 1
Art. 105 (elmts)	R. 89	-	R. 2
-	Art. 105a-c	R. 1	R. 3
Art. 106(2)	R. 98	R. 2	R. 4

EPC 1973	EPC 2000	EPC 1973	EPC 2000
R. 4 (elmts)	R. 36(2)	R. 39	R. 55
R. 5	R. 5	R. 40	R. 57
R. 6	R. 6	R. 41(1)	R. 58
R. 7	R. 7	R. 41(2), (3)	-
R. 8	R. 8	-	R. 59
-	R. 10	R. 42	R. 60
R. 9	R. 11	R. 43	R. 56
R. 10	R. 12	R. 44	R. 61
R. 11	R. 13	R. 44a	R. 62
R. 12	R. 9	R. 45	R. 63
R. 13(1) - (5)	R. 14	R. 46	R. 64
R. 13(4)	R. 78(1)	-	R. 65
R. 14	R. 15	R. 47	R. 66
-	R. 16	R. 48	R. 67
R. 15(1), (2)	R. 17	R. 49	R. 68
R. 15(3)	-	R. 50	R. 69
R. 16(1), (2)	R. 18	R. 51(1)	R. 70(2)
R. 16(3)	R. 78(2)	R. 51(2) - (11)	R. 71, 71a
R. 17	R. 19	R. 52	R. 72
R. 18	R. 20	R. 53	R. 73
R. 19	R. 21	R. 54	R. 74
R. 20	R. 22	-	R. 75
R. 21	R. 23	R. 55	R. 76
R. 22	R. 24	R. 56	R. 77
R. 23	R. 25	-	R. 78
R. 23a	-	R. 57	R. 79
R. 23b	R. 26	R. 57a	R. 80
R. 23c	R. 27	R. 58(1) - (3)	R. 81
R. 23d	R. 28	R. 58(4) - (8)	R. 82
R. 23e	R. 29	R. 59	R. 83
R. 24	R. 35	R. 60	R. 84
R. 25	R. 36	R. 61	R. 85
R. 26	R. 41	R. 61a	R. 86
R. 27	R. 42	R. 62	R. 87
R. 27a(1), (4)	R. 30	R. 62a	R. 87
R. 27a(2), (3)	-	R. 63	R. 88
R. 28(1), (2)	R. 31	-	R. 89 - 98
R. 28(4), (5)	R. 32	R. 64	R. 99
R. 28(3), (6) - (9)	R. 33	R. 65	R. 101
R. 28a	R. 34	R. 66(1)	R. 100(1)
R. 29	R. 43	R. 66(2)	R. 102
R. 30	R. 44	R. 67	R. 103
R. 31	R. 45	-	R. 104 - 110
R. 32	R. 46	R. 68	R. 111
R. 33	R. 47	R. 69	R. 112
R. 34	R. 48	R. 70	R. 113
R. 35	R. 49	-	R. 114
R. 36(1) - (3)	R. 50	R. 71	R. 115
R. 36(4)	-	R. 71a	R. 116
R. 36(5)	R. 2(1)	R. 72(1)	R. 117
R. 37	R. 51	R. 72(2)	R. 118
R. 38(1), (2), (6)	R. 52	R. 72(3), (4)	R. 119
R. 38(3) - (5)	R. 53	-	R. 120
R. 38a	R. 54	R. 73	R. 121

EPC 1973	EPC 2000
R. 74	R. 122
R. 75	R. 123
R. 76	R. 124
R. 77	R. 125
R. 78	R. 126
-	R. 127
R. 79	R. 128
R. 80	R. 129
R. 81	R. 130
R. 82	R. 125(4)
R. 83	R. 131
R. 84	R. 132
R. 84a	R. 133
R. 85	R. 134
R. 85a	-
R. 85b	-
-	R. 135
-	R. 136
R. 86	R. 137
R. 87	R. 138
R. 88	R. 139
R. 89	R. 140
R. 90	R. 142
R. 91	Rfees13(4)
R. 92	R. 143
R. 93	R. 144
R. 94	R. 145
R. 95	R. 146
R. 95a	R. 147
R. 96	-
R. 97	R. 148
R. 98	R. 149
R. 99	R. 150
R. 100	R. 151
R. 101	R. 152
-	R. 153
R. 102	R. 154
-	R. 155
R. 103	R. 156
R. 104	R. 157
R. 105	R. 158
R. 106	-
R. 107	R. 159
R. 108	R. 160
R. 109	R. 161
R. 110	R. 162
R. 111	R. 163
R. 112	R. 164
-	R. 165

Case Law Table

The table gives the number of the decisions and references to the sections of the book.

A reference without a colon refers to the text of the law. A reference with a colon refers to the text of the notes to the law. Hence, Art.90(3) refers to Article 90(3) EPC, R.46(1):2 refers to note 2 of Rule 46(1) EPC. 'P' refers to the Preamble of the EPC and 'Ante' before a reference refers to the section preceding that reference.

Where two decisions have the same reference, they are distinguished in this book by suffix 'a' and 'b'; see e.g. G1/05. References are given down to the level of sub-sections of the notes; hence, the reference to decision G1/95 actually cited in R.76(2):4.3.3 is shown in the table as R.76(2):4.3.

Decisions of the Enlarged Board of Appeal

G1/83	Art.54(5):2.3, 112(3):4
G5/83	P:2.2, 2.3; Art.52(1):1, 53:3, 54(4):2, (5):2.3, 112(3):4, 125:1.2
G6/83	Art.54(5):2.3, 112(3):4
G1/84	Art.99(1):1.1, 1.3, 112(3):1, 4, 177(1):1; R.77(1):1.2
G1/86	P:2.2; Art.108:3, 122(1):1, 2, 125:1.2; R.101(1):2
G1/88	Art.107:2, 164(2):2; R.82(1):1, 2, 3, (2):1
G2/88	Art.52(1):1, (2):2, 54(1):7.1, 7.2, (2):3.6, 84:1.3, 123(3):2; Ante Art.1:1
G4/88	Art.99(1):1.4
G5/88	Art.5(3):1, 10:1, (2):1, 125:2, 2.1
G6/88	Art.54(1):7.2; R.43(2):1
G7/88	Art.10:1
G8/88	Art.10:1
G3/89	Art.123(2):1.2; R.56:2, 139:1, 4
G1/90	Art.101(1):6; R.82(3):1, 112(1):2, 3
G2/90	Art.21:1, (3):1.2, (4):1; R.11(3):1
G1/91	Art.82:3, 101(3):1; R.86:1
G2/91	Art.107:3.1, 108:1
G3/91	Art.112(3):4
G4/91	Art.105(1):1.1, 1.2; R.93(1):1
G5/91	Art.19(2):1, 24:2, (2):1, 106(1):1, (2):1, 2, 125:1
G6/91	Art.14(2):1, (4):1, 94(1):3; R.6(3):1, 3.1, 3.3
G7/91	Art.110:9; R.84(2):1
G8/91	Art.110:9, 114(1):3
G9/91	Art.99(1):1.3, 101(3):1, 110:5, 111(1):1, 114(1):1, 3; R.76(2):4.1, 4.2, 4.3
G10/91	Art.99(1):1.3, 101(1):5, (2):1, 110:5, 111(1):1, 114(1):3; R.76(2):4.3, 81(1):1
G11/91	R.56:2, 139:4
G12/91	Art.101(1):6, 105(1):1.2, 110:7; R.10:1, 36(1):3.1, 71a(2):1, 79(1):1, 80:1; Ante R.111:1.2, 1.3, 1.4; R.137(3):1, 138:1, 139:2
G1/92	Art.54(1):1, (2):3.6
G2/92	Art.82:3; R.63(3):1, 64(1):3, 4, 137(5):1, 164(1):2.4
G3/92	Art.60(1):2, (3):1, 61(1):3, (2):1; R.136(1):5
G4/92	R.115(2):1
G5/92	Art.112(3):4
G6/92	Art.112(3):4
G9/92	Art.107:3.2, 111(1):1, 114(1):1; R.99(1):3
G10/92	R.71a(2):1
G1/93	Art.69(2):1, 123(2):1, 1.2, 2.1, 2.4, (3):3, 125:2.1
G2/93	R.31(2):1, 2
G3/93	Art.88(4):3, 112(1):1
G4/93	Art.107:3.2; R.99(1):3
G5/93	Art.112(3):1
G7/93	R.71(6):2, 71a(2):1, 116(2):1, 137(3):1
G8/93	Art.110:9; R.84(2):1
G9/93	Art.99(1):1.3, 105a:1, 112(3):1, 4, 125:2.1, 177(1):1
G10/93	Art.97(2):1, 107:3.2, 110:5, 114(1):3
G1/94	Art.105:1, (1):1.3; R.79(4):1
G2/94	Art.134(1):2, 2.1, 2.3
G1/95	R.76(2):4.3
G2/95	R.40(2):2, 139:4.1
G3/95	Art.53:2.1, 112(1):3
G4/95	Art.117:1, 134(1):2, 2.2

G6/95	Art.23(4):1; R.100(1):1, 116(1):3
G7/95	R.76(2):4.3
G8/95	Art.21(3):1.1, 2; R.140:1, 3.1
G1/97	Art.21:1, 111(1):3, 112(3):4, 112a:1, 127:1; R.140:2
G2/97	Art.125:2.2; R.112(1):3
G3/97	Art.99(1):1.1, 1.2, 1.4, 134:1; R.76(2):5
G4/97	Art.99(1):1.2
G1/98	Art.53:2.1, 64(2):1, 2, 118:1
G2/98	Art.87(1):5, 88(2):1, 2, (3):1, (4):1, 2, 123(2):1.2, 2.1, 2.3, 2.4, (3):3, 139(3):5
G3/98	Art.55(1):1, 112(1):3; R.38(1):1
G4/98	Art.76:2, (1):6, (2):1, 79(2):1.2, 86(1):4, 87(3):1, 90(5):2, 94(2):1, 112(1):3, 121(2):2, 122(2):2; R.17(3):1, 36(1):3.1, (3):1, (4):1, 159(1):5.2, 160(2):1
G1/99	Art.107:2, 3.2, 114(1):1; R.76(2):4.3, 80:3, 99(1):3
G2/99	Art.112(1):2
G3/99	Art.99(1):1.1, 1.5, 2.3, 107:1, 112(1):2
G1/02	Art.16:1; R.11(3):1, 112(2):1
G2/02	Art.87(5):1
G3/02	Art.87(5):1
G1/03	Art.53:3.2, 83:1, 3.1, 115:2, 123(2):1.2, 2.4, (3):3
G2/03	Art.53:3.2, 84:1.7, 123(2):2.4
G3/03	Art.109:1, 112(1):3; R.103(3):1
G4/03	Art.105(1):1.3, 112(1):2
G1/04	Art.53:3, 3.1, 3.4, 84:1.2, 112(1):1, 3
G2/04	Art.99(1):1.4, 107:1, 108:2, 112(1):1, 133:2.2; R.99(1):1, 101(2):1
G3/04	Art.105(1):1.1, 1.3, (2):1
G1/05a	Art.24(1):1, 2, (2):1, (3):1, 106(2):1
G1/05b	Art.76:2, 123(2):2.1
G1/06	Art.76:2, (1):1, 2, 6, 7, 8, 9, 10, 123(2):1.2, 2.1, 139(3):3, 5; R.36(1):1, 2
G2/06	Art.53:1.1, 1.2; Ante R.26:1; R.28(1):2
G3/06	Art.76(1):10
G1/07	Art.53:3.2, 3.4
G2/07	Art.33(1):4, 52(1):1, 53:2.2, 111(2):1.2; R.26(5):1
G1/08	Art.53:2.2
G2/08a	Art.24:2, (3):1
G2/08b	Art.53:3.5, 54(4):2, (5):1, 2, 2.1, 2.2, 2.3, 112(3):1, 4
G3/08a	Art.24(3):1
G3/08b	Art.52(2):5, 112(1):1, 3
G4/08	Art.129:2; R.3(1):2, 159(1):2.1
G1/09	Art.90(5):2, 106(1):2; R.36(1):3, 3.1, 159:1
G1/10	R.80:2, 140:1, 3.1
G2/10	Art.54(1):6.2, 61(1):3, 76(1):7, 8, 84:3, 88(4):2, 123(2):1, 1.2, 2.4, 139(3):5
G1/11	Art.21(3):1, 1.2
G1/12	R.22(3):1, 77(2):1, 101(1):1.2, (2):1, 139:2.1, 2.2, 3, 3.3
G2/12	Art.53:2.1, 64(2):1, 112(3):4; R.28(2):1
G1/13	Art.107:1
G2/13	Art.112(3):4; R.28(2):1
G1/14	Art.108:4
G2/14	Art.108:4
G3/14	Art.84:1, 100:2, 101(3):1; R.80:1
G1/15	Art.88(2):2
G1/16	Art.123(2):2.4
G1/18	Art.108:4, 112(3):3

Decisions on petitions for review

R1/08	Art.112a(2):1; R.106:1
R2/08	Art.112a(2):1; R.76(2):4.3, 106:1
R3/08	Art.112a(5):1; R.106:1
R4/08	R.106:1
R5/08	Art.112a(1):1, (4):1; R.107(2):1, 109(3):1
R7/08	Art.112(1):1, 112a(2):2
R10/08	Art.110:7, 112a(2):2
R2/09	Rfees5(2):1
R7/09	Art.112a(2):1; R.100(3):1
R18/09	R.151(1):1
R19/12	Art.24(3):1, 112(1):3; R.12a:1
R4/15	Art.108:4; R.152(8):1

R1/08	Art.112a(2):1; R.106:1
R2/08	Art.112a(2):1; R.76(2):4.3, 106:1
R3/08	Art.112a(5):1; R.106:1
R4/08	R.106:1
R5/08	Art.112a(1):1, (4):1; R.107(2):1, 109(3):1
R7/08	Art.112(1):1, 112a(2):2

Decisions of the Legal Board of Appeal

J17/12	R.14(1):1
J23/13	R.36(1):3.1
J12/14	R.56:1, (1):1
J13/16	R.136(3):1

Decisions of the technical boards of appeal

T1/80	Art.56:6.2, 110:6, 114(2):3, 123(2):3
T4/80	Art.54(1):6.3, 84:1.7, 123(2):2.4
T2/81	Art.94(3):2
T5/81	Art.56:2, 6.2, 97(2):1
T7/81	R.99(1):2, (2):1
T9/81	Art.54(4):2, (5):4, 177(1):1
T11/81	Art.56:3.2, 3.5, 5.3
T12/81	Art.54(1):1, 5, 6.1, (2):4.2
T15/81	Art.56:2, 8.3
T18/81	Art.56:5.4
T19/81	Art.56:5.4
T20/81	Art.56:3.6, 6.2
T21/81	Art.56:7.4
T24/81	Art.56:3.1, 6.2, 7, 7.1
T26/81	R.42(1):2
T32/81	Art.56:3.2; R.99(1):2
T9/82	Art.56:3.5
T10/82	Art.99(1):1.2
T11/82	Art.123(2):3; R.42(1):1
T13/82	R.101(1):1.3, 103(1):3
T22/82	Art.56:8.4
T32/82	Art.84:1.1, 113(2):1
T36/82	Art.56:4.2
T37/82	Art.123(2):3
T39/82	Art.56:4.3
T41/82	Art.108:1, 5; R.103(1):1
T52/82	Art.123(2):2.2
T65/82	Art.56:8.4
T69/82	Art.56:7.2
T79/82	Art.56:7.1
T84/82	Art.94(3):1, 5
T85/82	Art.57:2
T94/82	Art.84:1.5, 4
T107/82	Art.54(2):1, 56:3.1
T109/82	Art.56:7.1, 8.3
T110/82	Art.82:1
T113/82	Art.56:6.3
T119/82	Art.56:4.3, 5.4, 8.4
T128/82	P:2.2; Art.54(4):2
T130/82	Art.108:4
T146/82	Art.61(1):3; R.14(3):1
T150/82	Art.64(2):1, 2, 84:1.8; R.43(6):1
T152/82	Rfees5(2):2.1
T162/82	Art.23(3):1, 94(3):5
T172/82	Art.123(2):2.1
T181/82	Art.54(1):5, 56:6.3, 7, 7.4, 112(1):1
T184/82	Art.56:6.2, 123(2):3
T191/82	R.136(1):4
T192/82	Art.56:7.4
T2/83	Art.56:4.1, 4.2, 5.2, 8.3
T6/83	Art.52(2):5
T13/83	Art.123(2):2.2; R.139:4.1
T14/83	Art.83:2.1, 3
T16/83	Art.52(2):7
T20/83	Art.56:7.4
T21/83	Art.54(1):1
T36/83	Art.53:3.3, 54(4):2, 57:3
T49/83	Art.53:2.1
T61/83	Art.53:3.4
T69/83	Art.56:7.4
T81/83	Art.122(1):4
T84/83	Art.117(1):2
T91/83	Art.56:7.2
T104/83	Art.56:5.4
T144/83	Art.53:3, 3.1, 3.3, 57:1, 3
T148/83	Art.56:5.4
T164/83	Art.56:6.3
T169/83	Art.54(2):3.2, 69(1):1, 88(4):1
T170/83	Art.14(4):6, 104(1):1; R.139:2.2; Rfees5(2):2.1, 6(1):3
T173/83	Art.55(1):2
T177/83	Art.54(1):4
T188/83	Art.54(1):6, 84:1.7
T204/83	Art.54(2):3.2
T206/83	Art.54(2):4.3, 56:3.6, 5.4, 83:2.1, 88:3, (4):2
T208/83	Art.53:3.4
T219/83	Art.101(1):6, 114(1):2, (2):3
T220/83	Art.108:6; R.101(1):1.3
T6/84	Art.83:2.1, 2.2
T13/84	Art.123(2):3
T38/84	Art.56:7.2
T41/84	Art.56:7.1
T42/84	Art.106(1):1; R.103(1):3, 111(2):1
T51/84	Art.52(2):1
T73/84	Art.101(2):2, (3):1; R.75:1
T81/84	Art.53:3.3
T89/84	Art.110:2; R.101(1):1.2, 2
T106/84	Art.56:7.1, 7.3
T122/84	Art.114(1):3; R.76(2):4.3, 4.4
T142/84	Art.56:4.3; R.76(2):4.4

T145/84	Art.56:7.1
T153/84	R.103(1):3
T156/84	Art.114(2):2, 115:4; R.76(2):4.4
T163/84	Art.56:8.4
T167/84	Art.54(1):4, (3):1
T170/84	R.43(1):1
T171/84	Art.54(2):4.5, 56:3.6, 83:2.1, 2.2, 3
T176/84	Art.56:3.2, 3.3, 3.5, 6.2
T194/84	Art.76(1):9
T195/84	Art.56:2, 3.2, 3.4
T198/84	Art.54(1):5, 6.2
T199/84	Art.56:4.2
T208/84	Art.52(2):5
T237/84	R.43(7):1
T258/84	R.76(2):4.4
T270/84	Art.56:7.2
T271/84	Art.56:7.1; R.76(2):4.4
T273/84	Art.111(1):2, 114(2):1; R.76(2):4.4
T289/84	Art.54(1):5.2
T17/85	Art.54(1):6.3
T25/85	Art.99(1):1.1; R.76(2):2.1, 2.2, 77(2):1, 101(1):1.2
T26/85	Art.54(1):6.3, (2):4.3, 4.4
T61/85	Art.123(2):2.1
T66/85	Art.123(2):2.1
T68/85	Art.84:1.6
T98/85	Art.123(3):2
T99/85	Art.100:2
T115/85	Art.52(2):5
T116/85	Art.53:3, 3.1, 3.4
T123/85	Art.107:2, 3.2; R.80:3
T124/85	Art.56:2
T127/85	Art.84:4, 100:2; R.80:1
T133/85	Art.84:1.2, 123(2):3
T149/85	Art.14(4):3, 99(1):2.2, 3
T152/85	R.139:2.2
T153/85	Art.54(1):2, 3, 108:6, 110:6
T155/85	Art.56:4.3
T162/85	Art.82:3, 100:2
T163/85	Art.52(2):1, 8
T165/85	Art.56:7.1
T181/85	Art.56:7
T194/85	Art.123(3):2
T213/85	Art.108:6
T219/85	Art.83:3
T220/85	Art.100:2
T222/85	Art.101(1):2; R.76(2):4.3, 4.4, 4.5, 77:4, 111(2):2
T226/85	Art.83:3, 84:3.2
T229/85	Art.56:6.2, 7.3
T231/85	Art.54(1):7.2
T244/85	Art.106(2):2
T247/85	R.82(1):3
T248/85	Art.54(1):4, 64(2):1, 2
T253/85	Art.111(1):2
T260/85	Art.84:3.3, 123(2):1.1, 2.1
T262/85	Art.114(2):3
T291/85	Art.54(1):2
T292/85	Art.53:2.3, 84:4.1, 123(2):2.4
T294/85	Art.114(2):3
T7/86	Art.56:5.2
T17/86	Art.123(2):2.3
T19/86	Art.53:3.3, 54(5):2.1
T23/86	Art.100:2
T30/86	Art.54(1):7.1
T38/86	Art.52(2):5, 7
T48/86	Art.56:5.4
T63/86	Art.110:6, 111(1):2
T114/86	Art.54(1):5
T117/86	Art.104(1):1, 108:1
T132/86	Art.56:4.2
T162/86	Art.53:2.3
T194/86	Art.54(2):3.6
T197/86	Art.56:7.4
T219/86	Art.99(1):1.2; R.76(2):2.2, 139:3
T234/86	R.76(2):4.4, 4.5, 103(1):3
T237/86	Art.101(2):2, 107:2; R.75:1
T246/86	Art.76(1):8, 85:1, 123(2):1.1
T263/86	Art.56:4.2
T281/86	Art.53:2.3
T290/86	Art.53:3.2, 3.3, 54(5):2.1, 2.2, 57:3
T300/86	Art.54(2):2.4
T313/86	Art.123(2):2.4
T317/86	R.76(2):3, 77(1):1.3, (2):1
T335/86	Art.56:7.2
T349/86	Art.99(1):1.4
T355/86	Art.99(1):1.4
T378/86	Art.123(3):2
T385/86	Art.53:3, 3.1, 3.4
T389/86	Art.56:8.1, 108:3
T390/86	R.82(1):3, 111(1):1
T398/86	R.103(1):3
T406/86	Art.54(2):3.6, 114(2):1; R.80:4, 111(2):1
T416/86	Art.123(2):2.1, 2.2
T9/87	Art.114(1):3; R.76(2):4.2, 4.3
T19/87	Art.116(1):1
T28/87	Art.56:3.5; R.42(1):1
T51/87	Art.56:3.6
T56/87	Art.54(2):3.2, 56:3.1
T59/87	Art.54(1):7.2
T77/87	Art.54(2):4.5, 83:3, 85:1
T81/87	Art.88(4):2
T105/87	Art.110:5
T124/87	Art.54(1):5, 6.3, 114(2):1
T128/87	Art.99(1):2.3, 125:2.2
T133/87	Art.111(1):2

T37/96	Art.54(2):3.1
T161/96	Art.125:2.2
T165/96	Art.54(2):2.3, 3.1
T233/96	Art.54(5):2.1
T234/96	Art.56:3.5
T239/96	Art.107:3.3
T349/96	Art.56:3.5
T394/96	Ante R.111:1.4
T541/96	Art.83:3
T596/96	Art.123(2):2.4
T626/96	Art.56:7.2
T674/96	R.80:1
T755/96	R.111(2):1, 116:1, (2):1
T789/96	Art.53:3.5
T823/96	Art.123(2):1.2
T867/96	R.140:2
T986/96	Art.56:3.2
T990/96	Art.54(2):4.1
T1028/96	Art.24(1):1, (4):1
T1/97	R.101(2):1
T56/97	Art.54(5):2.1
T167/97	R.136(2):2
T223/97	R.80:1
T227/97	R.31(2):2
T276/97	Art.76(1):9
T291/97	Art.55(1):2
T298/97	Art.99(1):1.4, 107:1, 133(3):1; R.101(2):1
T323/97	Art.123(2):2.4
T517/97	Art.105(1):1.3, (2):1; R.36(1):3.1
T565/97	R.139:2.3
T584/97	Art.54(5):2.1
T598/97	Art.115:3
T631/97	R.64(1):3
T633/97	R.76(2):4.4
T775/97	Art.53:3.3, 3.5
T904/97	Art.76(1):10
T951/97	R.116(1):1
T967/97	Art.56:4.5
T1129/97	Art.84:1
T1149/97	Art.123(3):1
T1165/97	Art.57:1
T1173/97	Art.52(2):5
T1177/97	Art.52(2):5
T1194/97	Art.52(2):8, 84:1.9
T1212/97	Art.54(2):3.3
T4/98	Art.54(5):2.1
T26/98	Art.56:3.2
T91/98	Art.56:4.1
T97/98	R.101(2):1
T164/98	Art.56:3.2
T201/98	Art.94(3):5
T226/98	Art.107:3.2
T257/98	Art.56:5.2
T266/98	Art.107:3.2
T414/98	Art.56:5.2
T428/98	Art.122(1):4; R.136(1):4
T480/98	Art.84:1.4
T587/98	Art.76(1):7, 139(3):3, 5
T621/98	Art.134(1):2
T656/98	Art.107:1; R.22:1, (3):1
T685/98	Art.94(4):1
T728/98	Art.84:1, 1.3
T777/98	Art.122(1):4; R.136(2):1
T814/98	R.101(2):1
T862/98	Art.116(1):1
T893/98	Art.56:3.6
T965/98	R.140:2
T1020/98	Art.84:1, 2
T1043/98	Art.56:3.5
T35/99	Art.53:3.2
T485/99	Art.54(5):2.1
T525/99	Art.84:1.5
T711/99	Art.99(1):1.4
T744/99	Art.88(4):2
T964/99	Art.53:3.4
T965/99	Art.53:3.4
T998/99	Art.87(1):5, 112(1):1
T1019/99	Art.56:6.2
T1050/99	Art.123(2):2.4
T1080/99	Art.54(2):4.5; R.115(1):2
T9/00	Art.99(1):1.1, 1.4
T52/00	Art.104(1):1
T74/00	Art.99(1):1.4
T278/00	R.111(2):1
T398/00	Art.54(2):3.2, 123(2):1.2
T555/00	Art.76(1):10
T641/00	Art.56:6.3, 8.2
T643/00	Art52:9.2
T708/00	Art.92:4; R.64(1):3, 137(5):1
T778/00	Art.108:5; Rfees4(1):1
T824/00	Art.122:1; R.139:2.1, 2.3
T986/00	R.115(2):1
T1102/00	Art.123(2):2.4
T1173/00	Art.83:2.2
T15/01	Art.87(1):5, 107:1, 110:2, 112(1):1, 3; R.22(3):1, 101(2):1
T56/01	R.43(2):2
T131/01	R.76(2):4.3
T178/01	R.11(3):1
T314/01	R.126(2):1
T500/01	Art.84:1
T694/01	Art.105:1, (1):1, 111(1):3, (2):1.2
T836/01	Art.54(5):2.2
T866/01	Art.53:1.1, 1.2
T991/01	Art.54(2):2.1
T1056/01	Art.87(4):3
T1122/01	R.116(1):1
T1158/01	Art.76(1):10, 114(1):3
T1212/01	Art.56:7.2

T21/02	Art.109:1
T50/02	Art.54(2):2.4, 3.1
T125/02	Art.53:3.4
T210/02	Art.56:6.2
T333/02	Art.54(1):2
T482/02	Art.99(1):1.1, 106(2):1, 2
T511/02	Art.54(2):2.2
T619/02	Art.52(1):1, (2):1, 3, 4, 7, 57:2
T663/02	Art.53:3.2
T684/02	Art.54(1):7.2, 101(1):6
T713/02	Ante Art.90:1; R.111(2):2
T720/02	Art.76(1):10
T797/02	Art.76(1):10
T885/02	Art.23(3):1
T890/02	Art.56:3.6
T900/02	R.103(1):2
T914/02	Art.52:5
T966/02	Art.99(1):1.1, 101(1):2
T988/02	Art.84:1
T1170/02	Art.54(1):6.2, 123(2):1.2
T1183/02	R.116(1):1
T1197/02	Art.53:3.4
T39/03	Art.76(1):10
T90/03	Art.76(1):10
T152/03	Art.54(2):2.4
T172/03	Art.54(2):1, 56:2, 3.1, 8.2
T175/03	Art.123(3):3
T190/03	Art.116(4):2
T254/03	Art.108:2
T258/03	Art.52(2):1, 7
T267/03	Art.54(2):2.2
T274/03	R.137(5):5
T307/03	Art.116:3, 139(3):3, 4, 5
T309/03	R.139:3
T315/03	P:4.1; Art.9(2):1, 21:1, 53:1.1, 1.2, 2.1, 2.2, 116(1):1; Ante R.26:1; R.26(1):1, (3):1, 28(1):1, 3, 103(1):2
T330/03	Art.53:3.4
T383/03	Art.53:3.1, 3.2
T394/03	Art.64(2):2
T423/03	Art.76(1):8
T424/03	Art.52(2):5
T504/03	Art.53:3.4
T525/03	R.43(2):2
T606/03	Art.53:1.2; R.28(1):3
T748/03	Art.52(1):1
T928/03	Art52:9.2
T956/03	Art.107:1
T1002/03	Art.94(3):5
T1012/03	Art.116:1
T1020/03	Art.53:3, 54(5):2.1, 2.2
T1110/03	Art.54(2):2.2; R.116(1):1
T1165/03	Art.99(1):1.1
T1172/03	Art.53:3.2, 3.3
T23/04	Art.107:3.2
T35/04	Art.56:5.2
T56/04	Art.84:1
T70/04	Art.110:6
T125/04	Art52:9.2
T143/04	Art.53:3.4
T154/04	Art.52(2):1, 5, 56:8.2, 112(1):1
T328/04	R.31(2):1
T347/04	R.103(1):2
T376/04	Art.110:5; R.76(2):4.3
T386/04	Art.107:2
T388/04	Art.52(2):7, (3):1
T470/04	Art.110:6
T474/04	Art.117(1):2
T659/04	Art.52(2):8
T735/04	Art.115:2
T738/04	Art.117:1
T861/04	Art.54(2):2.2
T868/04	Art.123(2):2.4
T887/04	Art.105(1):1
T936/04	Art.139(3):3
T937/04	Art.104(1):1
T986/04	Art.110:5
T1060/04	Art.110:6
T1064/04	R.71(6):2
T1178/04	Art.99(1):1.4, 107:1, 3.2, 134(1):2
T1181/04	Art.106(1):1; R.71(3):5.4
T1242/04	R.63(1):1, (2):2
T1255/04	R.71(3):3.3, (6):1, 6, 103(1):2
T1273/04	Art.110:6
T1329/04	R.29(3):1
T1341/04	Art.107:3.2
T5/05	Art.87(1):4.3, 5, (4):2
T142/05	Art.123(3):1
T263/05	Art.101(1):6, (3):1; R.43(2):1, 80:1, 86:1, 124(1):1
T340/05	Art.110:9
T380/05	Art.83:3.1
T452/05	Art.105(1):1
T470/05	Art.123(2):2.3
T490/05	Art.104(1):1
T515/05	Art.101(2):1, 111(1):2
T537/05	Art.107:2
T591/05	Art.106(1):2, 107:2
T642/05	Art.108:6
T688/05	Art.52(2):7
T704/05	Art.109(2):1
T743/05	Art.108:3
T788/05	Art.87(1):4.1, 8, 139(3):4
T795/05	Art.123(2):2.4
T798/05	R.76(2):4.3
T898/05	R.29(3):1
T927/05	Art.133:1
T1093/05	Art.97(1):5; R.140:1, 2, 3, 3.1
T1213/05	Art.53:1.1, 1.2
T1227/05	Art.56:8.2

Decisions on PCT protests

Decisions of the Disciplinary Board of Appeal

Index to the AEPC

A reference without a colon refers to the text of the law. A reference with a colon refers to the text of the notes to the law. Hence, Art.90(3) refers to Article 90(3) EPC, R.46(1):2 refers to note 2 of Rule 46(1) EPC. 'P' refers to the Preamble of the EPC and 'Ante' before a reference refers to the paragraph preceding that reference. 'R.31(2),:3' refers to R.31(2) and to R.31(2):3; 'Art.108, :6' refers to Art.108 and Art.108:6.